*Political Development
and Social Change*

POLITICAL DEVELOPMENT AND SOCIAL CHANGE

SECOND EDITION

Jason L. Finkle
UNIVERSITY OF MICHIGAN

Richard W. Gable
UNIVERSITY OF CALIFORNIA, DAVIS

JOHN WILEY & SONS, INC.
New York · London · Sydney · Toronto

Library of Congress Catalogue Card Number: 72-149769

ISBN O-471-25890-3 (cloth)
ISBN O-471-25891-1 (paper)

Printed in the United States of America.

10 9 8 7 6 5 4 3 2 1

For Lisa and Cyrel

Preface

Continuity and change describe the relationship of the present edition of this volume to the first edition published in 1966. Like the statesmen of the developing nations, we have not sought change merely for the sake of change. We have attempted to preserve the ideas, theories, and concepts that seemed to be most useful in analyzing political development and social change. In the process of selection and arrangement, we have reevaluated some of our earlier judgments—judgments that, in some cases, appear less impressive now than when originally made.

As in the first edition, we have provided a conceptual framework for understanding and analyzing the contemporary process of political development and its relationship to other societal transformations. The unifying theme of the book is the relationship of political development to social change. Our objective is to bring some degree of order to the plethora of terms and concepts, approaches and theories, and constructs and models that abound in a burgeoning field of intellectual investigation.

We think that our decision to treat the problems of political development in combination with social change is justified on both theoretical and empirical grounds. The multiple and interrelated transformations in all of the systems by which man organizes his life and society constitute the general process of modernization. However, an attempt to account for so great a range of phenomena involves the risk of accounting for nothing in a satisfactory way. To avert this pitfall, we focused on the elements of the social system that impinge more or less directly on the polity—the social changes most likely to be consequential for political development as well as those most affected by changes in the polity.

The emerging countries are engaged in the task of political development and nation-building, and their success in this undertaking is largely dependent on the rate, direction, and quality of social change that they can effect. Thus, at least until the developing nations have achieved an ability to generate and absorb persistent transformation and have attained the stability, legitimacy, and unity that is concomitant with nationhood, there will remain compelling reasons for political scientists to examine modernization with an acute sensitivity to the multiplicity of interconnected factors involved in social change. As political scientists ourselves, we have brought together a wide range of ideas, approaches, and empirical research, which has resulted in a volume that might be classified as comparative political sociology rather than orthodox political science.

We are uncomfortably aware that many of the outstanding contributions to the scholarly literature on modernization and development have been omitted. These omissions are not the result of an oversight, but are the result of agonizing choices that had to be made because of space limitations. We decided to reproduce, in most cases, entire articles complete with footnotes, and we adopted the following guidelines for selecting the articles: (1) whenever possible, we chose articles that contained a strong theoretical orientation combined with empirical research; (2) we chose the shorter article when confronted with two articles of approximately equal quality; (3) with a few notable exceptions, we attempted to select a recent article on a subject, particularly when the newer article incorporated or alluded to ideas and findings contained in earlier research efforts; (4) we avoided articles with a single-country focus, and included such articles only when they introduced concepts and methodologies that were applicable to developing nations generally; (5) although it was not a prime consideration, we selected articles with illustrations and analyses from widely varied areas and countries; and (6) we included a small group of articles whose intellectual content seemed so overwhelmingly attractive or provocative that we simply could not omit them, notwithstanding any or all of our guidelines.

The nature of the changes we have introduced in this new edition reflect our values as well as the new state of the discipline:

1. We have relinquished the dichotomous classification of societies as traditional or modern. Even the most industrialized nations have many "traditional" characteristics, while preindustrial societies possess many of the traits usually imputed to "modernity." Although the language employed in this volume does not always correspond to this judgment, we feel that all societies are transitional and that more can be learned by starting from this assumption than by casually utilizing traditional-modernity classifications.

2. There is less formal emphasis on the systems approach as a mode of inquiry. In part, this deemphasis grows out of our recognition that the systems approach has been accepted largely by political scientists, and there is less need to call attention to it as an analytical tool for studying developing nations.

3. The present edition contains more empirical and quantitative research. Although there are many reasons for this change, the most important one is that the profession has grown to the point where more significant research is available which combines theory and empiricism.

4. More material has been introduced that employs historical analysis, especially analysis of political development in earlier periods of Western society. In the search for understanding how political development takes

place, scholars have reexamined the Western experience looking for patterns and sequences relevant to the latter-day developing nations.

5. More anthropologically based research is contained in the present volume. This reflects the growing interest of anthropologists in political questions as well as the ability of political scientists to utilize anthropological concepts and findings in political research.

6. A new section has been added dealing with political instability, violence, and revolution. In addition to the obvious reasons for including material on these subjects, we feel that the discipline has been excessively concerned with order and stability. We find that instability and revolution may be closely associated with particular aspects of change and development and, in some cases, may be the impetus to political development.

We think that one criterion of a "developed" society is the ability of its members voluntarily to cooperate with one another. By this standard, we found the academic community to be highly developed. Our contributors were gracious collaborators even when, in a few cases, we performed cruel surgery on their writings for the purpose of conciseness.

JASON L. FINKLE
RICHARD W. GABLE

Acknowledgments

For considered judgments and suggestions of ways to improve our first edition, we are indebted to Frank M. Andrews, Samuel H. Barnes, Roger W. Benjamin, Alexander J. Groth, Alberto Guerreiro-Ramos, Leslie L. Howard, Samuel P. Huntington, Warren F. Ilchman, John H. Kautsky, Donald S. Rothchild, Peter Savage, Edgar L. Shor, Ruth S. Simmons, Fred R. von der Mehden, and James W. White. Also we thank Susan Morris, Elizabeth Owens, and Judith Rice for special assistance in varied aspects of the preparation of this volume.

J. L. F.
R. W. G.

Contents

Political Development
and Social Change

PART I

TRANSITIONAL SOCIETIES

AND POLITICAL DEVELOPMENT

INTRODUCTION

Political development in the newly independent or less industrialized countries is a cause as well as a consequence of other types of social change. To understand how and why political development occurs, it seems necessary to view the polity within a conceptual framework capable of accounting for significant changes elsewhere in the social system. We begin, then, with the assumption that the political system is functionally related to nonpolitical elements of the social system and that the attempt to understand this relationship and its properties constitutes a meaningful approach to the study of political development.

While any social system, preindustrial as well as industrial, can be better understood from this perspective, there are persuasive reasons for employing this approach in analyzing the processes of change occurring today in the transitional societies of Asia, Africa, and Latin America. Without desiring to engage in a discourse on the merits of a "multidisciplinary approach," our judgment is that the developing nations at this time do not possess institutions sufficiently autonomous and differentiated from one another to warrant the perpetuation of conventional disciplinary purity in the social sciences. The formidable boundaries separating the traditional academic disciplines must be crossed if there is to be progress in this field. Economists have sought to answer questions about entrepreneurship and managerial skills by utilizing the theories and methods of psychology; political scientists have invaded the preserve of anthropology and sociology to explain authority relationships; psychologists have borrowed from the fields of economics and political science to deepen their analyses. In short, social scientists concerned with the processes of modernization in the developing nations are increasingly likely to utilize multidisciplinary skills to examine the dynamics of development and change.

To give a brief example, in carrying out research on an advanced industrial society like the United States, a choice may be made whether to take cognizance of family structure in the study of economic and political behavior; but in investigating developing societies it is *mandatory* to be alert systematically to kinship patterns. The phenomena being observed in developing societies, and particularly the process of political development, require that a wider array of methodologies and investigative techniques be marshalled within an analytical framework capable of relating political variables to a full range of social and other variables. Although those things we call political and those things we call social may be treated as distinct at the analytical level, the distinction breaks down at the empirical level where the points of articulation between them are frequent, numerous, and intense.

A final justification for dealing with political development in a context of social change should be stressed. Despite the energy and talent currently being brought to bear on the problems of political development, social scientists are profoundly aware of gaps and uncertainties in their analysis of this process. Even though there are deficiencies in our understanding of industrial societies, the problem is one of achieving a deeper understanding of those variables already identified as relevant to these interests. The student of political development, on the other hand, is at this stage of history engaged in a search for those variables that are relevant to political development. The difference is between knowing more about something and trying to identify what it is you should know more about. Therefore, to approach political development within the framework of social change creates a higher level of sensitivity to a broader range of possible variables and to their interrelationships.

A word of caution should be voiced as we begin. The points of articulation between politics and society are not, of course, uncharted in our studies of industrial societies. It would be erroneous, nevertheless, to assume that our understanding of the interaction between political and social variables in an industrial society is easily transferrable to preindustrial societies. Furthermore, our knowledge of political development in the industrialized nations unfortunately lags behind our ability to explain other aspects of Western political systems.

The three articles in Chapter 1 explore the process of change in those societies which we refer to as "transitional." The characteristics of the more than one hundred nations designated as developing, or modernizing, are so varied and diverse that it would be impossible to describe even a few of the better known countries. Each has its own history and culture. The changes that they are experiencing differ greatly. Therefore, social scientists construct models to understand the major outlines of transitional societies and formulate theory to analyze the processes of change.

Any model or abstraction tends to blur some of the significant details of reality, yet they are analytical tools of great utility and no better substitute has been devised. However, the constructs must be constantly refined to improve their accuracy and utility, and one must be constantly aware of the danger of regarding typologies, models, and "ideal types" as actual descriptions of reality.

In the first article, Gideon Sjoberg suggests that the folk typology, as formulated by Robert Redfield,[1] however useful, most nearly corresponds to "primitive" society and is inadequate for understanding and interpreting the more complex developing societies in Asia, Europe, and Latin America. Redfield's classic formulation for understanding "folk society" was based upon empirical research in Mexico and the theoretical insights of Maine, Tönnies, and Durkheim, as well as those of Redfield himself. Although the concept of folk society should not be discarded, its indiscriminate application to communities in all nonindustrialized areas has given rise to serious misinterpretations of transitional societies. Therefore, Sjoberg designs a model of "feudal" society, not in its historical sense, but as a construct more suitable to the complex social systems that are not yet industrial but no longer qualified as folk societies. Sjoberg's presentation represents an important effort to refine and improve a widely used model.

Gusfield goes beyond Sjoberg to criticize the very concept of dichotomous models, at least insofar as these constructs are used as polar opposites in a linear theory of social change. More specifically, he argues that such concepts as "tradition" and "modernity" mislead us greatly in our efforts to understand concrete situations. For example, it is an oversimplification and a distortion to view traditional societies as static, normatively consistent, or structurally homogeneous. Modernization and development do not necessarily imply the replacement of the old by the new; nor should we assume that what passes for "tradition" and "modernity" are mutually exclusive systems, always in conflict. The desire to be modern and the desire to preserve tradition may operate concurrently as significant movements in the new nations and developing economies. In fact, these twin desires have in some instances reinforced one another, in the sense that tradition and modernity may form the bases of ideologies and movements in which polar opposites may be converted to aspirations, while traditional forms may supply support for (as well as against) the process of change. Thus, while tradition may be stretched and modified, a unified and nationalized society may make great use of the traditional in its search for a consensual base to political authority and economic development.

The utility of structural functional analysis for understanding social change and modernization is ably demonstrated by Neil J. Smelser, who sees economic development as involving fundamental alterations in the social structure. These social changes, in turn, influence the rate and quality of economic development. While Smelser is undoubtedly sensitive to the empirical world in his theoretical analysis, he stresses that he is primarily concerned with presenting an "ideal type" construct, in the sense the term was employed by Max Weber.

The three key concepts Smelser discusses are differentiation, integration, and the discontinuities between differentiation and integration. An apprecia-

---

[1] "The Folk Society," *American Journal of Sociology*, **52**: 293–308, January, 1947.

tion of the meaning of these concepts is fundamental to an understanding of the stresses and strains of social development. When the family system is no longer capable of satisfying the needs of economic production and new structural forms emerge to engage in production, adjustment between the old and new structures becomes necessary. While these adjustments are generally recognized as inevitable concomitants of economic development, they in turn produce new problems concerning the relationship of these differentiated structures to one another. Government, particularly in industrial societies, is likely to play a prominent role as the integrative mechanism, but it is by no means the only social unit to perform the function. The appearance of numerous differentiated structures in a society experiencing modernization does not mean that integrative mechanisms capable of resolving relationships between these structures will emerge. Thus, social change in developing societies, even under the best of circumstances, is likely to be uneven, discontinuous, and characterized by acute disturbances.

The complex character of the development process itself is reflected in the lack of consensus on the parameters and ingredients of political development and its linkage to social change. A graphic way to highlight the complexity of the problem is to conceive of a community—for example, a village in India —as a social system with economic and political subsystems. External and internal inputs into this village social system have often yielded higher standards of living, better educational facilities, a higher rate of literacy, and countless other increments in the quantitative indicators associated with social and economic modernization.

Yet numerous reports emanating from community development projects in India indicate that the kinds of transformation generally associated with political development have not occurred. Community development assistance has often been administered through traditional elites—caste and class leaders—and has had the consequence of reinforcing their hold on village political life despite the introduction of new and higher standards of living and qualitative improvements in the way of life. In many cases there has been no greater equality, no increase in political participation, no expansion in the capacity of the political system to resolve its own village problems, and no greater differentiation in political roles. Thus, social change was not accompanied by political development, thereby suggesting that social and economic development may have lasting effects on the community without corresponding change in the political system. This example does not tell us what political development is, but it does imply that sociodemographic and structural indices of modernization may not be able, either separately or together, to tell us what we desire to know about political development.

The second chapter in this Part deals with the nature of the political system and the meaning of political development. The diverse attempts to provide definitions of political development are described by Lucian W. Pye. He does not presume to reconcile these differences, but he does seek to illuminate the semantic confusion which he feels impedes the purposes and understanding of those concerned with political development. Pye finds three meaningful themes which prominently recur in the literature on political development: (1) a general spirit or attitude toward equality, (2) an increase in the capacity and capabilities of the political system *per se*, and (3) increased differentiation, specialization, and integration of structures, with all that is implied in these concepts. He concludes by suggesting that the "problems of political development revolve around the relationships between the political culture, the authoritative structures, and the general political process."

The article by Gabriel A. Almond and G. Bingham Powell, Jr., provides an overview to their developmental approach to political systems. In compact form and logical order, the principal concepts and terms used in their analysis are introduced and defined, *viz.* political system, structure, and culture. The political system is described as consisting of interacting roles, structures, and subsystems, and of underlying psychological propensities which affect these interactions. Such a process is viewed as involving inputs from the environment or from within the political system itself, the conversion of these inputs within the system, and production of outputs into the environment. This discussion of flows of inputs and outputs leads to a consideration of the functions of political systems. The long-time concern of Almond is to adapt systems theory in a developmental direction. Political development is, therefore, presented in terms of the interrelations of three kinds of political functions: capabilities, conversion functions, and system maintenance and adaptation functions.

Chapter 1

Transitional Societies and the Process of Change

FOLK AND "FEUDAL" SOCIETIES

Gideon Sjoberg

Until the past decade sociologists in the United States directed only a small portion of their efforts toward a comparative study of society. As a result, the distinctions between folk and feudal orders and the differential effects of the process of industrialization and urbanization on the two kinds of society have been little perceived. This oversight is, of course, understandable in the light of American history; only incipient forms of "feudalism" have been evidenced in this country. Attention therefore was not turned toward feudalism, even on the world scene. Recent political changes, however, have placed the United States in a position of world leadership; reform programs are being carried out in many "backward" countries. Through failure to interpret correctly the functionings of other societies, a number of these plans have been naïvely conceived. At the same time, sociologists and anthropologists are becoming increasingly concerned with the comparative study of sociocultural systems; a critical evaluation, therefore, of present-day perspectives is requisite.

The primary purpose of this paper is to formulate a typology of the feudal social system in contradistinction to that of the folk order. Then, through an analysis of the differential effects on folk and feudal societies of social change resulting from the industrial-urban process, justification is offered for their separation. Although other sets of typologies are logically possible, the study should contribute toward the development of a comparative sociology.

It is not suggested here that the concept "folk society" should be discarded. Actually it serves many useful purposes. Yet its indiscriminate application to communities in all nonindustrialized areas has given rise to serious misinterpretations of existing conditions. Although no one society need correspond exactly to the constructed type, the value of the "model" for understanding and interpreting social action is enhanced if it does not diverge too widely from reality.

Redfield,[1] employing the ideal-type method, has provided us with one of the most careful and logically consistent formulations of the folk order. This is a small, isolated, nonliterate, and homogeneous society with a strong sense of solidarity.

SOURCE. Gideon Sjoberg, "Folk and 'Feudal' Societies," *American Journal of Sociology*, **58**, 231–239, November 1952. Reprinted by permission of The University of Chicago Press. Copyright 1952 by The University of Chicago Press.

[1] Robert Redfield, "The Folk Society," *American Journal of Sociology*, **52** (1947), 293–308; see also Alvin Boskoff, "Structure, Function, and Folk Society," *American Sociological Review*, **14** (1949), 749–758.

The primary group ties—those of kinship in particular—are of crucial importance to its effective functioning. Furthermore, a minimum of division of labor is present, from which it can be deduced that stratification in terms of social classes is unknown. Finally, the value orientation is sacred, and the actions of the members tend toward strict conformance to the norms of the folk.

The so-called "primitive" societies most nearly correspond to this folk typology; some isolated tribal communities fit the constructed type rather well. On the other hand, the concept is much less meaningful for interpreting complex societies in Asia, Europe, and even Latin America. Although a few writers[2] have recognized certain distinctions between "folk and peasant" and "nonliterate and literate" societies, no systematic presentation of these differences and their implications for social change seems to be extant.

The Feudal Society

Both feudal and folk societies are static and have sacred-value orientations; consequently, the action patterns of their members are clearly defined. But the feudal society is far more heterogeneous and complex than is the folk order. Their essential differences can best be stated in terms of the respective social structures. The feudal order is characterized by rigid class or caste-like stratification and complex state, educational, and economic institutions—all of which necessitate an extensive division of labor. Furthermore, it has a relatively large population and an extended territorial base.

It should be noted before proceeding, however, that the concept "feudalism" has been used in several ways. Historians conventionally have taken as their criteria certain restricted institutional patterns of

medieval Europe, especially the lord-vassal relationship.[3] Although this structural arrangement may have existed at times in other societies also,[4] the application of the concept in this manner is too limited for sociological analysis. The formulations of Boeke, Weber, and Rüstow,[5] although quite incomplete, more nearly fulfil our requirements. The more inclusive meaning given herein to the concept "feudalism" avoids the pitfalls of historicism and the resultant emphasis on uniqueness.

The structural arrangement of the feudal society is outlined below. In order to demonstrate a degree of empirical plausibility for this typology, brief references are made to social situations which correspond rather closely to its criteria.[6]

Typically, feudalism is predicated on a large peasant population. These individuals live in small village settlements and gain their livelihood primarily from intensive cultivation of the soil through the use of a

[2] See, e.g., A. L. Kroeber, *Anthropology* (rev. ed.; New York: Harcourt, Brace & Co., 1948), p. 284, and Robert Bierstedt, "The Limitations of Anthropological Methods in Sociology," *American Journal of Sociology*, **54** (1948), 22–30.

[3] F. L. Ganshof, *Qu'est-ce que la Féodalité?* (2nd ed., Neuchâtel: Éditions de la Baconnière, 1947); Otto Hintze, "Wesen und Verbreitung des Feudalismus," *Sitzungsberichte der Preussischen Akademie der Wissenschaften, philosophisch-historische Klasse* (1929), pp. 321–347; Carl Stephenson, *Mediaeval Feudalism* (Ithaca: Cornell University Press, 1942).

[4] Ch'i Ssu-ho, "A Comparison between Chinese and European Feudal Institutions," *Yenching Journal of Social Studies*, **4** (1948), 1–13.

[5] J. H. Boeke, *The Interests of the Voiceless Far East* (Leiden: Universitaire Pers Leiden, 1948), pp. 1–8; Max Weber, *Wirtschaft und Gesellschaft* (Tübingen: J. C. B. Mohr, 1925), 3, Part 2, 724 ff.; Alexander Rüstow, *Ortsbestimmung der Gegenwart: Eine universalgeschichtliche Kulturkritik*. I: *Ursprung der Herrschaft* (Erlenbach-Zürich: Eugen Rentsch Verlag, 1950).

[6] In constructing any typology, a mass of descriptive material is essential. Many sociologists fail to recognize that Weber, the popularizer of the ideal-type method, relied heavily upon a great accumulation of historical materials for his typologies. The author has avoided constructing types about merely one historical situation; special study was made of China, Japan, India, and France, and surveys of other areas were read to check the generalizations offered.

simple technology. Scattered about the countryside, they form the backbone of the feudal system. But the peasant villages, significantly, are not isolated from one another. Field studies which have focused strictly upon the local community have often lost sight of the total sociocultural setting.

Unlike the members of a folk order, the peasants provide sufficient surplus food to sustain a limited number of population concentrations—the focal points of the feudal society. Towns spring up as political, religious, and trading centers, and although only a small portion of the total populace inhabit these communities, their social significance extends far beyond mere numbers. That these towns are quite unlike industrial cities is obvious: feudal towns do not exhibit the social disorganization and individualization commonly associated with present-day industrial-urban centers.[7] However, it must not be inferred that life in the feudal town is not distinct from that in the feudal village. These towns, moreover, are linked to one another. But inasmuch as transportation and communication still are relatively undeveloped, the contacts between the various communities are not comparable to those in industrial-urban societies.

Within the towns reside many of the elite, particularly its most important members. The ruling stratum is at the very least composed of a governmental bureaucracy and a priestly and/or scholar group. In addition, a nobility, a landlord group, and militarists or warriors, among others, may be present in various combinations. The unique cultural-historical development of a given social order determines the exact com-

position of the elite; it varies not only among societies but from time to time within a society.

But the significant feature of the stratification pattern is its bifurcation—a small minority supported by and "exploiting" a large subservient populace which passively accepts its role. The traditional Chinese society evidenced this most strikingly. To be sure, hierarchical gradations occur in both the upper stratum and the masses, but these are slight when compared to the basic cleavage within the society as a whole. The upper class is differentiated in terms of its monopoly of power and authority, the "correct" kinship groupings, and the highly valued achievements. Particularly important in this context are institutionalized differences in personal attributes. Distinctive dress, speech, and manners render the elite easily recognizable at all times.[8] And inasmuch as an individual's status within the elite or the masses is ascribed, social mobility is minimized.

A closer examination of the ruling minority is essential. As noted, political functionaries are one of the constituent elements. For in a feudal society a complex and highly institutionalized state system extends its control directly or indirectly over the masses. Among other forms, this state system may be a monarchy or possibly a theocracy such as existed in medieval Europe. Aside from exerting legal control, the political functionaries exact some kind of tribute from the peasantry. This serves to perpetuate the elite and support such groups as an army, which protects the society from external aggression. Political functionaries are recruited from the upper class and thus reflect an inherently conservative tradition which is gauged to preserve the status quo.

Scholars and priests are another integral

[7] See, e.g., Morton H. Fried, "Some Preliminary Considerations of Larger Units in Chinese Social Organization," *Transactions of the New York Academy of Sciences*, Ser. 2, **11** (1949), 121–126; Roger Le Tourneau, *Fès: Avant le Protectorat* (Casablanca: Société Marocaine de Librairie et d'Édition, 1949). The latter study, which has received no formal recognition by sociologists in this country, is a most detailed description of a feudal city.

[8] An illuminating discussion of personal attributes in a feudal order may be found in Cornelius Osgood, *The Koreans and Their Culture* (New York; Ronald Press Co., 1951), Ch. 8. This discusses the city of Seoul at the end of the nineteenth century.

element of the elite. Usually they merge into one group, for the educational and religious institutions are characteristically identical. In addition, some of these individuals may be political bureaucrats. The scholar's prime qualification is his knowledge of the sacred writings and traditions of the past; these govern the actions of the present. Memorization and understanding of the ancient thought-ways are preconditions for his assumption of a role in the highly institutionalized educational system. Scholarship is notable for its compiling and preserving qualities and not for any degree of originality. This aspect of the typology is empirically attested by the characteristics of such groups as the Chinese literati, the Indian Brahmins, and the medieval European clergy.

The scholar-priests perform an important function as official carriers of the classical written tradition which provides the social system with a sophisticated and elaborate justification for its existence and continued survival. Inconsistencies (present in all societies) are explained away. Through the sacred writings a continuity is achieved and the past more easily retained. This is not possible among the folk, whose history is perpetuated solely by oral transmission. The ideology of the sacred writings, by standardizing the action patterns of the elite, also establishes solidarity over a broad geographic area. As a result, the homogeneity of the upper class is typically greater than that of the masses.[9] Finally, the scholar-priests' existence as members of the elite brings about a striking divergence of their religious actions from those of the masses, who comprehend little of the philosophical basis of the religion they practice.

Landlords often constitute part of the elite class—for example, in China and in medieval Europe. But the landlord fac-

tion per se is not an essential component of feudalism as conceived herein. At times the political bureaucrats assume functions similar to those of the landlords; this occurred in India before the arrival of the British. The strength of the landlord stems from his direct control over the peasantry and concomitantly over the surplus food supply. Finally, other special groups may comprise the elite; for example, in Japan prior to the Meiji Restoration the topmost position of prestige and power was commanded by the military, or *samurai*, but some of these also doubled as governmental leaders.

Economically and politically the elite class dominates the mass populace. The latter supply the ruling minority with food, goods, and services but receive little in return. The trading relations of the city, therefore, are not with the countryside but with other towns, sometimes in quite distant regions. The relationship between the upper stratum and the masses is not entirely one-sided, however. Guidance is offered in the "moral" or religious sphere—the elite's ideal patterns are those emulated by the masses. Protection from outside attack and conquest is also the responsibility of the upper stratum. But more concrete functions may be performed—for example, the Chinese bureaucrats had an important duty in water control, chiefly for purposes of irrigation.

The peasants are not the only components of the masses. Characteristic of a feudal economic system is handicraft manufacturing based on a household economy. This requires skilled artisans. Most typically they reside in the towns, although some may be village-dwellers, where commonly they are also part-time farmers. The characteristic organizational units of artisans in the towns are guilds, each of which embraces a different occupational grouping: potters, weavers, metal workers, and carpenters, among others.

Not only do the guilds maintain a monopolistic control over recruitment through the apprenticeship system, but they also establish the norms of work. Furthermore, the actions of the members

[9] On this point see E. Shouby, "The Influence of the Arabic Language on the Psychology of the Arabs," *Middle East Journal*, **5** (1951), 284–302, and Gerald F. Winfield, *China: The Land and the People* (New York: William Sloane Associates, Inc., 1948), p. 184.

are prescribed down to the family level; in time of crisis the guild functions as a welfare agency. The artisans are instrumental in providing the elite with the luxury goods and services for the "conspicuous consumption" which clearly differentiates the latter from the disadvantaged members in the society.

Finally, another group within the feudal order must be considered. Typically, a small minority (or minorities) reside in the feudal society but occupy a marginal position, not being fully integrated into the social system. These persons are ranked even lower than peasants and artisans. Feudal orders often have scorned the merchant: he usually has too much contact with foreigners and is therefore a transmitter of "dangerous" ideas. Other outsiders have been slaves, the "untouchables" of India and the Eta class of Japan. These groups provide special goods and perform those services considered degrading by members of the morally valued occupations. In this way, they are functionally important to the entire society, particularly the elite.

To recapitulate: folk and feudal societies are similar in that both are relatively static and possess a sacred-value orientation. As such, the action patterns of their members are predictable, for there exists a minimum of internal conflict and disorder. In their structural arrangements, however, they differ perceptibly.

Implications for Social Change

What are the implications of separating folk and feudal societies for sociological in-terpretation? A clearer understanding of contemporary social change follows from treating these as distinct social systems.

That industrial urbanization is bringing about change in the sociocultural organization of many societies is obvious.[10] But the resistance of the feudalistic structure to this process has been equally significant. Recent evidence for this is overwhelming: only a few exemplary cases are presented here. Authorities on China have often commented on how the elite in that country during the twentieth century has held firmly to the Confucianist ideology, the feudalistic governmental structure, the traditional family system, and even the feudal economic organization, although the forces making for change have been formidable.[11] (That the present Chinese regime will eradicate the feudalistic past is most doubtful.) And the tenacity of feudalism in Europe has only recently come to public consciousness. France is a case in point, although other countries (e.g., Germany and Italy) might also be cited. Despite the fact that France has experienced industrial urbanization for over a century, many feudalistic institutions have survived: a kind of handicraft system is still an important element in the economy, the pro-monarchical group continues to reassert itself in one form or another, and the feudalistic church and family systems are still in evidence.[12] All this has fostered the schisms and conflicts so typical of France since the Revolution.

Even the material coming to light on Russia reveals that the Soviets, though

---

[10] The industrial-urban process is not the only factor which has induced change in "backward" areas. The state system per se, including colonial government, could be considered. Yet, to deal primarily with industrialization and urbanization is not unreasonable, even though these are being carried forward by the state. It is the industrial factor which makes the present-day state so potent.

[11] See, e.g., Marion J. Levy, Jr., and Shih Kuoheng, *The Rise of the Modern Chinese Business Class* (New York: Institute of Pacific Relations, 1949), pp. 8–17, 34 ff.; John King Fairbank, *The United States and China* (Cam-bridge: Harvard University Press, 1948), pp. 240 ff.; *Far Eastern Culture and Society* ("Princeton University Bicentennial Conferences," Ser. 2, Conference 7) (Princeton: Princeton University Press, 1946), p. 21.

[12] For two excellent discussions of this subject see: Edward Mead Earle (ed.), *Modern France* (Princeton: Princeton University Press, 1951), esp. John E. Sawyer, "Strains in the Social Structure of Modern France," Ch. 17; Donald C. McKay, *The United States and France* (Cambridge: Harvard University Press, 1951), Chs. 7 and 8.

using forceful persuasion, have found it difficult to subdue at least one of the feudalistic subsystems within their borders —a Moslem group in Central Asia. The persistence of the Moslem religion, with its month of fasting (Ramadan), and the latent power of the old aristocracy have served as stumbling blocks to the efficient industrialization of this regime.[13] (As a matter of fact, the Soviet power complex is itself a reincarnation, loosely speaking, of the feudal regime which existed prior to the 1917 revolution.) Evidence for the survival of feudalistic patterns in the Middle East and India[14] is also readily obtainable.

On the other hand, the rapid disintegration and, at times, loss of cultural identity of folk, or "primitive," societies is common knowledge. Examples can be found in the Americas and in Australia, Africa, and various parts of Asia. Specifically, India comes to mind. There the feudal order has maintained itself, whereas the tribal units, much to the concern of many anthropologists and government officials, are being "detribalized."[15]

[13] Mark Alexander, "Tensions in Soviet Central Asia," *The Twentieth Century*, **150** (1951), 192–200.

[14] See, e.g., Lewis V. Thomas and Richard N. Frye, *The United States and Turkey and Iran* (Cambridge: Harvard University Press, 1951); Halford L. Hoskins, "Point Four with Reference to the Middle East," *Annals of the American Academy of Political and Social Science*, **268** (1950), 85–95; J. A. Curran, Jr., *Militant Hinduism in Indian Politics: A Study of the R.S.S.* (New York: Institute of Pacific Relations, 1951); Radhakamad Mukerjee *et al.*, *Inter-Caste Tensions: A Survey under the Auspices of UNESCO* (Lucknow, India: Lucknow University Press, 1951); Kingsley Davis, *The Population of India and Pakistan* (Princeton: Princeton University Press, 1951), *passim*.

[15] D. N. Majumdar, *Races and Cultures of India* (2nd rev. ed.; Lucknow, India: Universal Publishers, Ltd., 1950), pp. 97, 179, 187; J. H. Hutton, "Primitive Tribes" in L. S. S. O'Malley (ed.), *Modern India and the West* (London: Oxford University Press, 1941), pp. 415–444; and various issues of the *Eastern Anthropologist*, published in Lucknow, India, esp. Vol. **3**, September 1949.

The question now arises: How is the feudalistic social structure able to survive in the face of industrial urbanization? For one thing, the elite strives to retain its traditional advantages at all cost. The elite is assumed to have "everything to lose and nothing to gain" from social change. The following discussion points to some of the conditions which make this resistance possible.

The upper stratum's ability to ward off the consequences of industrial urbanization first arises from its command of technical intelligence. To insure the continuance of the society, positions in the complex governmental and educational institutions must be staffed; the alternative is chaos. A modicum of order must be maintained by all ruling groups if they are to preserve their positions of power (this is true even of revolutionary elements). Reliance upon the feudal functionaries who possess the necessary knowledge to sustain a degree of efficient organization is therefore mandatory. As a result, feudal political or educational bureaucrats, because of this strategic location, are able to veto (either formally or informally) any proposed radical change.[16]

The survival of the elite, particularly within governmental and educational and/ or religious institutions, is greatly enhanced by the prevailing language patterns. The speech of the upper class markedly differs from that of the folk. But more important is the nature of the written language—the medium by which officialdom conducts its affairs. It may be a completely different one from that spoken by the masses—for example, Latin in medieval Europe—or, as

[16] An interesting situation has evolved in the case of colonial rule. Inasmuch as members of the elite have commanded the important governmental and educational posts, their contact with the foreign rulers has been far more extensive than that of the masses. The upper-class individuals, especially those who are able to accommodate somewhat, gain access to the implements of the foreigner's power—education, technological knowledge, etc. Actually, this reinforces their status and increases their possibilities for survival; this in turn aids in the preservation of feudal traits.

in the case of the Chinese and Japanese scripts, most difficult to master. In any event, knowledge of the literary language requires much leisure—the prerogative of the elite. Few of the folk are able to gain access to the sacred knowledge possessed by the political and intellectual leaders; thus, criticism or rejection of the elite's moral ideals is quite unlikely. Through this monopoly of the written language the elite seals itself off from the masses. And these written languages have a remarkable survival quality. Latin is a striking example. In addition, the Arabic literary language and the Chinese and Japanese scripts display an inflexibility which assures their continued usage for some time to come, despite the various attempts at reform.[17]

The written tradition, especially as embodied in the sacred literature, is the product of the privileged group. As such, it prescribes the ideal action patterns in family, religious, and interpersonal situations. Many of these rules are carried over into the urban-industrial society through enacted legislation. For example, many of the law norms which are applied to the contemporary industrial-urban communities of India stem from the sacred writings of the Hindus and thus perpetuate the ideal norms not of the lower castes but of the Brahmins.[18] This pattern has no correlate in folk orders. Among the folk, once the oral traditions are lost, they can never be recovered.

Although it is difficult to express the following in strictly objective terms, research reveals that the superiority-inferiority structure is tenacious. Possibly one reason for this is the rationalization it receives in the religious writings. Yet, whatever the explanation, empirical materials lend credence to the "toughness" of this structural nexus in a society. In Japan after World War II, lower-class individuals when asked by pollsters for their opinions would refer the interviewer to upper-class leaders who would speak for them.[19] Employer-employee relations in feudal countries now undergoing industrialization also reflect the continuance of earlier traditions. In southeast Asia, China, and Japan, the employer-laborer relationship exhibits a direct correspondence to the elite-mass system of feudalism.[20] And the prestige of the European nobility has died slowly, even in a country as democratic as England.

Up to this point, only resistance to the industrial-urban complex has been examined. An objection could be raised: Did not the elite in Japan actually instigate the industrialization of the nation? The rebuttal to such an argument is that industrial urbanization was only partially accepted. Many of the value orientations and structural arrangements which ordinarily are correlated with it were summarily rejected. The feudalistic ruling group who retained control of the governmental bureaucracy impeded the "modernization" of women's role in society and the development of a small-family system. Consequently, an overpopulation problem was fostered which may ultimately threaten the whole industrial-urban structure. Furthermore, the state was able to perpetuate many feudal traditions by maintaining rigid control over the educational system and by keeping the workers in a position of subservience.[21]

[17] Shouby, *op. cit.*; John De Francis, *Nationalism and Language Reform in China* (Princeton: Princeton University Press, 1950).
[18] Benjamin Lindsay, "Law," in O'Malley, *op. cit.*, pp. 107–137; Dinshah Fardunji Mulla, *Principles of Hindu Law* (10th ed.; Calcutta: Eastern Law House, Ltd., 1946). Ch. 2.

[19] Frederick S. Hulse, "Some Effects of the War upon Japanese Society," *Far Eastern Quarterly*, 7 (1947), 37.
[20] See, e.g., Bruno Lasker, *Human Bondage in Southeast Asia* (Chapel Hill: University of North Carolina Press, 1950), *passim*; John Campbell Pelzel, "Social Stratification in Japanese Urban Economic Life" (unpublished Ph.D. dissertation, Harvard University, Department of Social Relations, 1950); Shih Kuo-heng, *China Enters the Machine Age* (ed. and trans. Hsiao-tung Fei and Francis L. K. Hsu) (Cambridge: Harvard University Press, 1944), pp. 116 ff.
[21] Some works discussing the persistence of feudalism in Japan and its effects are: Nobutaka Ike, *The Beginnings of Political Democracy in Japan* (Baltimore: Johns Hopkins Press, 1950), Parts III and IV; Hugh Borton (ed.); *Japan*

Recent happenings in a number of folk orders testify to the significance of an elite class. The ability of "primitive" societies to adjust to, or frequently combat, industrial urbanization and the kind of social organization which ordinarily accompanies it is dependent upon the development of an elite which is sufficiently trained to comprehend the implications of what is transpiring. This is strikingly evident in Negro Africa. In the Belgian Congo the government contributed toward the formation of an educated *noire élite*; only then did formal resistance to "modernization" arise.[22] And the incipient opposition of the natives in South Africa and in British West Africa[23] is being led by the educated among them. Only these are able to utilize such mediums as books, newspapers, and the radio—and thus publicize the "evils" of the prevailing social change. In other words, the growth of an institutional apparatus, one not found among the folk, is essential if this society is to preserve its identity. Interestingly enough, anthropologists may place themselves in a position of a "neo-elite" when studying "primitive" peoples. For only after the folk customs have been recorded is it possible for governments to make adjustments in their policies to prevent the disappearance of those groups which lack an educated and political elite.[24]

Among the masses in the feudal order the artisans or craftsmen constitute a group which has a vested interest in keeping the situation stabilized. Although in some countries their resistance has not been noticeably effective, nevertheless the artisans play a role in checking the diffusion of the industrial-urban complex. For if and when it occurs, it does so at the expense of this group. Should a society desire to maintain a minimum of order, the artisans must not be destroyed too rapidly. Furthermore, they are at times active in repelling the intrusion of the new type of economic system.[25]

Second, modern feudal societies are typically overpopulated. In contrast, folk societies are by nature small and are not faced with this problem. Kingsley Davis[26] has offered what is perhaps the most plausible set of explanations showing how overpopulation acts as a deterrent to industrial-urban expansion. Overpopulation, for one thing, focuses economic effort on consumption goods rather than on heavy industry, discounting future for present advantage. The situation of low capitalization is apparent first in agriculture, where land becomes increasingly scarce and expensive. Moreover, a high ratio of farm population to agricultural resources results in the production of food crops for sustenance rather than export crops for investment surplus. As a result of overpopulation, labor is immediately cheaper than machinery, which discourages the rationalization of industry. Finally, rapid population growth implies a high fertility and a somewhat lower, though still high, death rate. This creates an unusually heavy burden of young dependents.

One of the most crucial problems now

[*footnote 21 continued*
(Ithaca: Cornell University Press, 1950), esp. Chs. 7 and 12; Warren S. Thompson, "Future Adjustments of Population to Resources in Japan," in *Modernization Programs in Relation to Human Resources and Population Problems* (New York: Milbank Memorial Fund, 1950), pp. 142–153.

[22] See recent issues of the journal *La Voix du Congolais*, particularly Vol. **6** (1950).
[23] Ellen Hellmann (ed.), *Handbook on Race Relations in South Africa* (Cape Town: Oxford University Press, 1949), Ch. 20; also see various issues of the journal *Race Relations* (published in Johannesburg, South Africa), esp. Vol. **16**, No. 3 (1949), and Vernon McKay, "Nationalism in British West Africa," *Foreign Policy Reports*, **24** (1948), 2–11.
[24] This is apparent in the United States government-sponsored surveys of nonliterate peoples of Oceania after World War II, as well as in studies of American Indians during the last fifty years.
[25] Levy and Shih Kuo-heng, *op. cit.*, p. 35; R. G. Kakade, *A Socio-Economic Survey of Weaving Communities in Sholapur* (Poona: Gokhale Institute of Politics and Economics, 1947), *passim*.
[26] Davis, *op. cit.*, pp. 218–219.

faced by many countries, especially those in Asia, is how to combat the great inertia inherent in overpopulation. This is further complicated by the resistance of the feudal elite, who impede the process of industrial urbanization sufficiently to facilitate a progressive increase in the population.

An ideal typology has been constructed in contradistinction to that of the folk. One essential of the former is the two-class system—a small elite supported by a large peasant population. Even more significant are the existent and highly developed state and educational and/or religious institutions—through dominant positions in these structures the elite class controls the society. The feudal manufacturing system is much more elaborate than that within the folk order: for example, handicraft workers are present. All this implies an extensive division of labor. Although both feudal and folk societies have a sacred-value orientation and exhibit a minimum of internal change, their social structures are markedly divergent. An understanding of the effects of the industrial-urbanization process in many areas of the world is possible only if these two typologies are separated; too often the distinctions have not been emphasized.

Other implications stem from the foregoing discussion; only a few are mentioned here. First, many sociologists and anthropologists have given undue emphasis to the local community, especially when this is a mere segment of the larger sociocultural setting. Community-bound research stresses the family unit and neglects the study of governmental and educational institutions, through which the family necessarily must work in order to achieve its power and influence. From this it follows that, methodologically, the lumping-together of folk and feudal societies is often not justified. Doubts might legitimately be expressed concerning the validity of such a technique as the "cross-cultural survey" when generalizations are attempted beyond the area of family or kinship system.

Finally, more attention needs to be devoted to the effects of industrial urbanization upon feudalistic societies. Few problems are of greater significance. In Asia, particularly, conflicts of great magnitude have been evidenced as the industrial-urban complex has spread into that region. Europe has been experiencing a similar fate for many decades.

Obviously, despite the resistance of the feudal structure, the industrialization and urbanization process has been moving forward. However, instead of encompassing the whole society (which is now almost the case in the United States), in the feudal order the industrial-urbanized society will in all probability be superimposed upon the existing structure, with the latter remaining to some degree intact. Bifurcation within the society would therefore still persist, although in quite different form and with quite different effects. This possibility has found empirical expression in such countries as France and Italy, where enclaves of peasants still perpetuate the feudal organization. Overpopulation combined with the resistance to change inherent among the elite have contributed to this situation. A similar co-existence of two societies was deliberately planned by the Netherlands government in its rule over the Netherlands East Indies. The Dutch envisaged a "plural" economy, which also meant a bifurcated social structure.[27] Industrial urbanization has thus led to a modification rather than a destruction of feudal societies (folk orders, in contrast, seem to be disappearing). Though any attempt at generalization is fraught with difficulties, such an adjustment in feudal countries is not unlikely for a long time to come. But whatever the outcome, the imposition of the industrial-urban society upon an already highly developed social organization such as that found in feudalism will unquestionably be accompanied by disorganization, severe strains, and conflict.

[27] J. S. Furnivall, *Netherlands India* (Cambridge: Cambridge University Press, 1939), esp. pp. 446 ff.

TRADITION AND MODERNITY: MISPLACED POLARITES IN THE STUDY OF SOCIAL CHANGE[1]

Joseph R. Gusfield

While riding the Kodama express from Tokyo to Kyoto several years ago, I saw what might be taken as a symbolic expression of transitional development. The Japanese passenger in the seat across from mine had made himself comfortable during his nap by unlacing his shoes and pulling his socks partly off. Half in and half out of both shoes and socks, he seemed to make a partial commitment to the Western world which his clothing implied. One could only wonder about his future direction either back into his shoes and socks or out of them and into sandals and bare feet.

This particular example has been chosen because it accentuates the idea of change in contemporary new nations and economically growing societies as one which entails a linear movement from a traditional past

toward a modernized future.[2] A significant assumption in this model of change is that existing institutions and values, the content of tradition, are impediments to changes and are obstacles to modernization. It is with this assumption that our paper is concerned. We wish to call attention to the manifold variations in the relation between traditional forms and new institutions and values, variations whose possibilities are either denied or hidden by the polarity of the traditional-modern model of social change. We want, further, to explore the uses of tradition and modernity as explicit ideologies operating in the context of politics in new nations. Our materials are largely drawn from modern India,

[2] There is a wide literature analyzing concepts of tradition and modernity or development. Leading efforts to conceptualize these societal types are W. W. Rostow, *The Stages of Economic Growth* (Cambridge: Cambridge University Press, 1960); Gabriel Almond and James Coleman, *The Politics of Developing Areas* (Princeton, N.J.: Princeton University Press, 1960), chap. i; Daniel Lerner, *The Passing of Traditional Society* (Glencoe, Ill.: Free Press, 1958), chaps. ii, iii.

SOURCE: Joseph R. Gusfield, "Tradition and Modernity: Misplaced Polarities in the Study of Social Change," *American Journal of Sociology*, **72,** 351–62, January, 1967.

[1] Presented at the annual meeting of the American Sociological Association, Chicago, September 2, 1965.

although we shall refer to other Asian and African countries as well.

The concepts of economic development and of economic modernization have now been generalized to many areas of national life by social scientists. There is now a discussion of communication development, educational development, and, most widely used, of political development.[3] While these are sometimes used to relate specific institutions to economic growth and development as possible correlative influences or effects, they are also utilized as independent concepts. Some writers have viewed political modernization as implying the necessary framework within which nationhood can be achieved and operate. Others have seen certain institutions and political values as inherently valuable and legitimate perspectives toward change.[4]

At the same time that the concept of development has become generalized, a large number of specific studies of new

nations (many to be discussed here) have made us aware of the wide variety of outcomes and possibilities for change and continuity. These have led to a more critical appreciation of the many possible interrelations between new and old aspects of social, economic, and political life. The view that tradition and innovation are necessarily in conflict has begun to seem overly abstract and unreal.

In the study of economic growth we have come to be aware that Weber's conception of traditional versus rational economic behavior is a great distortion of the realities of many concrete situations. In the study of political alternatives and possibilities we have become sensitive to the reifying effect of unilinear theories. They make Anglo-American political forms either inevitable or necessarily superior outcomes of political processes in new nations. Functional theories of political and economic development now seem less viable.[5] An emphasis on what Shils calls the issue of consensus at the macrosociological level leads to a concern for how pre-existing values and structures can provide bases for identification with and commitment to larger social frameworks than those of segmental groups and primordial loyalties.[6] Here traditional symbols and leadership forms can be vital parts of the value bases supporting modernizing frameworks.

In exploring the concepts of tradition and modernity we shall discuss the assumptions of conflict between them. These assumptions are inconsistent with recent studies which will reveal a wide range of possible alternatives and show that "tradition" is a more specific and ambiguous phenomenon than usually realized.

[3] See the various volumes published by Princeton University Press under the series title "Studies in Political Development." Also see A. F. K. Organski, *The Stages of Political Development* (New York: Alfred A. Knopf, Inc., 1965).

[4] We can distinguish several different uses of the concept "political development." Sometimes it is used as functional to economic development. Here the writer seeks to determine the political conditions essential to support effective economic change. For one example, see Wilfred Malenbaum, "Economic Factors and Political Development," *Annals*, CCCLVIII (March, 1965), 41–51; in the same volume, Lucien Pye uses the concept as independent of economic forms but gives it a substantive content (see Pye, "The Concept of Political Development," *Annals*, CCCLVIII [March, 1965]). Shils gives the concept of "modernity" a meaning closer to that of a goal toward which political elites aspire. This makes concern for a given state of society a perspective rather than an empirical theory and is thus closer to the use we make of it in the last section of this paper. "Our central concern will be with the vicissitudes of the aspiration toward the establishment of a political society" (Edward Shils, "On the Comparative Study of the New States," in C. Geertz [ed.], *Old Societies and New States* [New York: Free Press, 1963], pp. 1–26, at p. 6).

[5] Moore has suggested that we now know that a variety of political forms are capable of both congruence and conflict with economic development (Wilbert Moore, *Social Change* [Englewood Cliffs, N.J.: Prentice-Hall, Inc., 1963], p. 112).

[6] This is a major problem discussed in Clifford Geertz (ed.), *op. cit.* See especially papers by Shills, Geertz, D. Apter, and M. Marriott.

Fallacies in the Assumptions of the Traditional-Modern Polarity

In assuming that new economic and political processes face an unchanging and uniform body of institutional procedures and cultural values, the linear theory of change greatly distorts the history and variety of civilizations. In this section we will examine seven assumptions of this theory and indicate the difficulties in its use.

Fallacy I: Developing Societies Have Been Static Societies

It is fallacious to assume that a traditional society has always existed in its present form or that the recent past represents an unchanged situation. What is seen today and labeled as the "traditional society" is often itself a product of change. The conquests of foreign powers and the growth of social and cultural movements deeply influenced the character of family life, religious belief and practice, and social structure in India over many centuries.[7] Islamic civilization provided vital alternatives to caste and to political groupings. The impact of British culture and institutions has been immense.[8] Even India's caste system has by no means been a fixed and invariant system.[9]

The conception of India as a non-industrial and agricultural society, only now opened to industrialism, also needs revision. The decline of native Indian industries in the late eighteenth and early nineteenth centuries was a consequence of the protection of British textile manufacturers, then spearheading the Industrial Revolution in England. The shift of both rural and urban artisians to the land was an important ingredient in the buildup of an agricultural surplus population. Even the system of land tenure in existence just before independence was the product of fairly recent changes.[10] To speak of the traditional feudal structure of India is to confuse recent history with past history. Tradition has been open to change before its present encounters with the West and with purposeful, planned change.

Fallacy 2: Traditional Culture Is a Consistent Body of Norms and Values

In elaborating the distinction and interaction between the "great tradition" of urban centers and the "little tradition" of village communities, anthropologists have called our attention to the diversity and the existence of alternatives in what has been supposed to be a uniform body of rules and values. We must avoid accepting the written and intellectualized versions of a culture as only the literate form of a common set of beliefs and behavior patterns.

[7] For a critical analysis and refinement of those views of India based on Hindu scriptures, as where those of Max Weber, see M. N. Srinivas, *Caste in Modern India* (Bombay: Asia Publishing House, 1962), especially Introduction and chaps. i and xii. A similar point is made in Harold Gould, "The West's Real Debt to the East," *Quest* (January–March, 1962), pp. 31–39.

[8] Percival Spears, India (Ann Arbor: University of Michigan Press, 1960); Charles Heimsath, *Indian Nationalism and Hindu Social Reform* (Princeton, N.J.: Princeton University Press, 1964), chap. i; Srinivas, *op. cit.*, chap. v; Gould, *op. cit.*

[9] Srinivas, *op. cit.*; Bernard Cohn, "Power, Land and Social Relations in 19th Century Banaras" (Paper presented at meeting of the American Asian Studies Society, Washington, D.C., 1964).

[10] R. C. Dutt, *Economic History of India* (London: Routledge & Kegan Paul, 1908), pp. 32, 261; S. Bhattacharya, *East India Company and the Economy of Bengal* (London: Luzac, 1954), pp. 158–59; Vikas Misra, *Hinduism and Economic Growth* (London: Oxford University Press, 1962), chap. iii; Milton Singer, "Changing Craft Traditions in India," in W. Moore and A. Feldman (eds.), *Labor Commitment and Social Change in Development Areas* (New York: SSRC, 1960), pp. 258–76; Neil Smelser, *Social Change in the Industrial Revolution* (Chicago: University of Chicago Press, 1959), pp. 109–16; Robert Frykenburg, "Traditional Processes of Power: Land Control in Andrha" (Paper presented to the meeting of the Association for Asian Studies Society, Washington, D.C., 1964); Daniel Thorner, *The Agrarian Prospect in India* (Delhi: University Press, 1956).

The distinction between "popular" religion and the religion of the literati elite has long been a recognition of this difficulty in characterizing the "religion" of a society.[11]

Even within the literate forms of a tradition, inconsistency and opposition are marked; the Sermon on the Mount and *The Wealth of Nations* are both part of Western culture. Catholicism and Protestantism are Christian religions, and even within the single Church of Peter, diverse monastic orders have expressed a catholicity of values. Hindu philosophical and religious teaching is consistent with a number of diverse orientations to life. The doctrine of the four *ashramas*, for example, conceives of the good life as one in which men pursue different values at different stages in the life cycle.[12]

The importance of this diversity is that it provides legitimizing principles for a wide set of alternative forms of behavior. This point has been rather convincingly made in the recent discussion of economic development and cultural values in India.[13] Neither the behavior of popular religion nor teachings of the scriptures are devoid of moral bases for materialistic motivations or for disciplined and rational pursuit of wealth. Everyone need not be a *sadhu* (holy man) at all times.

Fallacy 3: Traditional Society Is a Homogeneous Social Structure

Like other societies, Indian society has institutionalized different styles of life in different groups, both within and without the caste system. Such divisions of labor make it possible for specific communal and status groups to be the bearers of traditions which differ from the dominant streams yet enable valued social functions to be performed. While Weber referred to "the Protestant ethic," the specific sects who carried the ethic were by no means typical of all Protestant groups.[14] The role of foreign and pariah peoples has often been commented upon as a source of economic growth, innovation, and entrepreneurial behavior.[15] The Jews in Europe, the Muslims in West Africa, the Chinese in Indonesia, and the East Indians in East Africa are examples of groups whose marginality has rendered them able to engage in the impersonality of market behavior and to remain aloof from the status consumption demands of the indigenous population. In India, the Parsees and the Jains have been potent carriers of economic innovation and the development of large-scale industrial production.

Generalizations about the anti-economic character of the Hindu traditions lose sight of the provision for specific groups which are ethically capable of carrying a logic of economic growth and change. Within the caste system of Hinduism, the untouchables have been able to perform tabooed occupations necessary to the economy. Other castes have developed traditions of

[11] In a study of religious behavior among low-caste sweepers, Pauline Kolenda has recently presented a vivid picture of the differences in the Hinduism of higher and of lower social levels ("Religious Anxiety and Hindu Fate," *Journal of Asian Studies*, XXIII [June, 1964], 71–82).

[12] For a description of the doctrine of Ashramas, see K. M. Sen, *Hinduism* (London: Penguin Books, 1961), Chap. iii.

[13] Milton Singer, "Cultural Values in India's Economic Development," *Annals*, CCCV (May, 1956), 81–91. See the clash of viewpoints among Goheen, Singer, and Srinivas in the discussion of "India's Cultural Values and Economic Development," *Economic Development and Cultural Change*, VIII (October, 1958), 1–13. Vikas Misra (*op. cit.*), similarly to Singer and Srinivas, does not see the cultural elements of Hinduism as an impediment to economic growth.

[14] For an account of the atypicality of Quaker economic rationality among American colonials, see F. B. Tolles, *Meeting House and Counting House*; *The Quaker Merchants of Colonial Philadelphia, 1682–1763* (Chapel Hill: University of North Carolina Press, 1948).

[15] Sheldon Stryker, "Social Structure and Prejudice," *Social Problems*, VI (1959), 340–54; Bert Hoselitz, "Main Concepts in the Analysis of the Social Implications of Technical Change," in Hoselitz and Moore, *Industrialization and Society* (New York: UNESCO, 1963), pp. 11–29, especially pp. 24–28.

business and commerce which, although dishonored in Hindu "tradition," are permissible and even obligatory for the Marwari, the Chettiar, and the Baniya. It is their very legitimation within existing structure that permits their acceptance and implementation of innovating economic behavior.

Fallacy 4: Old Traditions Are Displaced by New Changes

The capacity of old and new cultures and structures to exist without conflict and even with mutual adaptations is a frequent phenomenon of social change; the old is not necessarily *replaced* by the new. The acceptance of a new product, a new religion, a new mode of decision-making does not necessarily lead to the disappearance of the older form. New forms may only increase the range of alternatives. Both magic and medicine can exist side by side, used alternatively by the same people.

The syncretism of inconsistent elements has long been noted in the acceptance of religious usages and beliefs. Paganism and Catholicism have often achieved a mutual tolerance into a new form of ritualism drawn from each in Spanish-speaking countries.[16] The "great tradition" of the urban world in India has by no means pushed aside the "little tradition" of the village as they made contact. Interaction has led to a fusion and mutual penetration.[17] We have become increasingly aware that the outcome of modernizing processes and tra-

ditional forms is often an admixture in which each derives a degree of support from the other, rather than a clash of opposites.

Fallacy 5: Traditional and Modern Forms Are Always in Conflict

The abstraction of a "traditional society" as a type separate from a specific historical and cultural setting ignores the diversity of content in specific traditions which influence the acceptance, rejection, or fusion of modernist forms. Japan is unlike the Western societies in the ways in which "feudalism" and industrial development have been fused to promote economic growth.[18] Commitment to emperor and to family, a collectivistic orientation, and a high degree of vertical immobility have been factors supporting social and economic change in the Japanese context while they appear to have been factors producing resistance in the individualistic culture of the West. In this context the hardened commitment of labor to a specific employer operated to promote economic growth while the same process appeared an impediment in the West.[19]

Traditional structures can supply skills, and traditional values can supply sources of legitimation which are capable of being utilized in pursuit of new goals and with new processes. In one Indonesian town, Geertz found the sources of economic ex-

---

[16] For one account of such syncretism, see Robert Redfield, *The Folk Culture of Yucatan* (Chicago: University of Chicago Press, 1941), chap. ix.

[17] "While elements of the great tradition have become parts of local festivals, they do not appear to have entered village festival custom 'at the expense of' much that is or was the little tradition. Instead we see evidence of accretion in a transmutation form without apparent replacement and without rationalization of the accumulated and transformed elements" (McKim Marriott, "Little Communities in an Indigenous Civilization," in M. Marriott [ed.] *Village India* [Chicago: University of Chicago Press, 1955], p. 196).

[18] For some analyses of this phenomenon in Japan, see Reinhard Bendix, *Nation-Building and Citizenship* (New York: John Wiley & Sons, 1965), chap. vi; Robert Scalapino, "Ideology and Modernization: The Japanese Case," in D. Apter (ed.), *Ideology and Discontent* (New York: Free Press, 1964), pp. 93–127; Everett Hagen, *On the Theory of Social Change* (Homewood, Ill.: Dorsey Press, 1962), chap. xiv.

[19] For a description and analysis of labor commitment in Japan, see James Abegglen, *The Japanese Factor* (Glencoe, Ill.: Free Press, 1958); Solomon B. Levine, *Industrial Relations in Post-war Japan* (Urbana: University of Illinois Press, 1958), chap. ii. Richard Lambert describes a similar process operating in western India but sees it as a possible impediment to economic growth (Lambert, *Workers, Factories and Social Change in India* [Princeton, N.J.: Princeton University Press, 1963], especially chap. iii and pp. 214–21).

pansion largely among the *prijaji*, the Muslim group representing new forces in religion as well as in business. In another town, the source of economic innovation and business expansion was in the traditional nobility. The *prijaji* could build on, but were also hampered by, the characteristics of the bazaar modes of trading and the closed social networks of a pariah group. The traditional nobility, however, was well equipped to form a business class through the wide social networks and the strength of their authority, which rested on a traditional base.[20]

Anthropologists have made the same point in connection with problems of selective culture change. One traditional culture may possess values more clearly congruent with modernization than another; another may cling more tenaciously to its old ways than another. Ottenberg's study of tribes in West Africa found them able to accept and utilize the British culture in Nigeria to a much greater extent than was true of the other major Nigerian tribes. The Ibo's system of voluntary associations, coupled with their values of individualism and achievement, adapted them well to the kinds of opportunities and demands which British colonialism brought. In contrast, the Masai in East Africa are a notorious case of resistance to culture change, fiercely upholding existing ways with very little accommodation.[21]

Fallacy 6: Tradition and Modernity Are Mutually Exclusive Systems

A given institution or cultural system contains several aspects or dimensions.

Each dimension does not function in the same way in response to new influences on a society. Tradition and modernity are frequently mutually reinforcing, rather than systems in conflict.

Earlier theories of economic growth viewed extended family systems and caste structure as impediments to economic growth.[22] We now recognize, however, that such relations are complex and can vary from one context to another. Caste as an unalloyed impediment to economic growth has been much exaggerated through failing to balance its role in the division of labor and in caste mobility (one dimension) against its tendencies toward status demands as limitations on desire to accumulate capital (a second dimension).[23] Efforts on the part of castes to become mobile, to attempt improvements in their material as well as their ritual position are by no means new to Indian life. The expanded scope of regional castes, the development of caste associations, and the importance of castes in politics are not impediments to economic growth.[24] They enable credit facility, occupational sponsorship and training, and political influence to be made available on a basis of segmental, traditional loyalties. This brings an element of trust and obligation into an economic context where suspicion and distrust are otherwise frequently the rule between persons

---

[20] Clifford Geertz, "Social Change and Economic Modernization in Two Indonesian Towns," in Hagen, *op. cit.*, chap. xvi.

[21] Simon Ottenberg, "Ibo Receptivity to Change," in M. Herskovits and W. Bascom, *Continuity and Change in African Culture* (Chicago: University of Chicago Press, 1959), pp. 130–43; Harold Schneider, "Pakot Resistance to Change," *ibid.*, pp. 144–67. Also see the description and analysis of labor commitment in East Africa in A. Elkin and L. Fallers, "The Mobility of Labor," in W. Moore and A. Feldman, *op. cit.*, pp. 238–54.

[22] For a generalized statement of this view, stressing an open system of social mobility as a prequisite for economic growth, see Kingsley Davis, "The role of Class Mobility in Economic Development," *Population Review*, VI (July, 1962), 67–73.

[23] This is a major conclusion of V. Misra, *op. cit.*

[24] Caste associations and caste loyalties appear to be important sources of social support in urban India and are growing in size and number (*see* Srinivas, *op. cit.*; M. Weiner, *The Politics of Scarcity* (Bombay: Asia Publishing House, 1962), chap. iii; Bernard Cohn, "Changing Traditions of a Low Caste," *Journal of American Folklore*, LXXI (July-September, 1958), 413–21; Lloyd and Suzanne Rudolph, "The Political Role of India's Caste Associations," *Pacific Affairs*, XXXIII (March, 1960), 5–22.

unconnected by other ties than the "purely" economic.

Studies of the impact of industrialization on family life in preindustrial and primitive societies similarly indicate the compatibility of extended family forms with industrialism.[25] In the context of Indian economic growth, the large extended families of the Tatas, Birlas, and Dalmias are among the most striking instances of major industrial organizations growing out of and supported by traditional family units. Berna's study of entrepreneurship in Madras provides additional information, among small businesses, of the extended family as a major source of savings and capital accumulation.[26]

The role of traditional values in the form of segmental loyalties and principles of legitimate authority are of great importance in understanding the possibilities for the occurrence of unified and stable polities at a national level. The contemporary Indian political process utilizes caste, village, and religious community as basic segmental groups through which the individual and the family are drawn into modern political institutions. Primary ties of kinship and clan are in process of fusion to centralized structures of national, participative politics.[27]

The "stuff" of much modern politics in India is itself drawn from the pre-existing struggles between caste, religion, region, and economic groupings. We have become aware that much of what appears to be ideological and economic conflict in Indian politics is actuated and bolstered by struggles for social and ecnomomic position among the various caste groups.[28]

The setting of traditional and pre-existing conflicts in the context of new institutions is crucial to understanding Indian educational change. Critics of Indian education often point to the intensive desire for humanistic curriculums among both educators and students, contrasting this with the presumed necessities of technical and agricultural skills in economic development. They fail to see that the politics of egalitarianism revolves around the quest for status in traditional terms. Groups that have not been part of the educational structure in the past now utilize it to gain status increases as well as jobs. This is of great importance in a nation attempting to draw formerly isolated groups into a national identity.[29]

Fallacy 7: Modernizing Processes Weaken Traditions

This discussion of Indian education suggests that new institutions and values may, and often do, fuse and interpenetrate the old. In his influential paper on caste mobility, M. N. Srinivas has shown that, while higher social levels appear to be "westernizing" their life styles, when lower and mid-

[25] William Goode, "Industralization and Family Change," in B. Hoselitz and W. Moore, *op. cit.*, chap. xii; Jean Comhaire, "Economic Change and the Extended Family," *Annals*, CCCV (May, 1956), 45–52; Manning Nash, *Machine Age Mays* (Glencoe, Ill.: Free Press, 1958).

[26] James Berna, "Patterns of Entrepreneurship in South India," *Economic Development and Cultural Change*, VII (April, 1959), 343–62.

[27] This is a dominant theme in contemporary discussion of Indian politics (Joseph Gusfield, "Political Community and Group Interests in Modern India," *Pacific Affairs*, XXXVI [Summer, 1965], 123–41, and the literature cited there).

[28] "The 'revolution of rising expectations' is in reality an explosion of social competition . . . not aimed at American, British or Russian living standards, but are demands by one group for improvement . . . vis-à-vis another group within India" (Weiner, *op. cit.*, p. 71).

[29] The social composition of university students in India shows a very high preponderance of high castes in the student bodies, although leveling processes are at work. This situation, and its significance is described in my forthcoming "Equality and Education in India," in Joseph Fisher [ed.], *Social Science and the Comparative Study of Educational Systems* (Scranton, Pa: International Textbook Publishers, 1967). For a general analysis of Indian higher education, see Allen Grimshaw, "National Goals, Planned Social Change and Higher Education: The Indian Case," in R. Feldmesser and B. Z. Sobel, *Education and Socal Change* (New York: John Wiley & Sons, in press).

dle levels seek mobility they do so by becoming more devotedly Hinduistic, following more Brahminical styles, and otherwise Sanskritizing their behavior.[30] The fluidity introduced by political competition under independence and democracy becomes harnessed to a more traditional orientation.

The technological consequences of increased transportation, communication, literacy, and horizontal mobility, in furthering the spread of ideas, also intensifies the spread and influence of the "great tradition" into more and more communities and across various social levels.[31] Pilgrimages to distant shrines become easier and enable the conception of a unified, national religion to take firmer root. Caste groups can now be formed on regional and even national lines, buttressed by associational life and written journals. The spread of community development and of educational facilities brings in its wake new, semiurban personnel who carry the Sanskritic traditions fully as much, if not more so, than they do the westernizing influences.[32] The communities of the "little tradition" are, in fact, more open to such traditional winds of change than to wholly new movements. The holy men and the wandering players who carry religious messages and dramas drawn from the Hindu great traditions are more likely to effect attention than the movies.[33]

Tradition, Ideology, and Nationhood

Tradition is not something waiting out

there, always over one's shoulder. It is rather plucked, created, and shaped to present needs and aspirations in a given historical situation. Men refer to aspects of the past as tradition in grounding their present actions in some legitimating principle. In this fashion, tradition becomes an ideology, a program of action in which it functions as a goal or as a justificatory base. The concern for tradition as an explicit policy is not an automatic response to change but is itself a movement capable of analysis.

In similar fashion, to be "modern" appears in many new nations as an aspiration toward which certain groups seek to move the society. "Modern" becomes a perceived state of things functioning as a criterion against which to judge specific actions and a program of actions to guide policy. In Scalapino's apt phrase, intellectuals in new nations utilize "teleological insight"—the assumed ability to read the future of their own society by projecting it in accordance with the experience and trends of "advanced" nations.[34] Such insight operates as a crucial determinant in developing goals, but it too is a creation of choice among possibilities, not a fixed and self-evident set of propositions.

The desire to be modern and the desire to preserve tradition operate as significant movements in the new nations and developing economies. It is our basic point here that these desires, functioning as ideologies, are not always in conflict; that the quest for modernity depends upon and often finds support in the ideological upsurge of traditionalism. In this process, tradition may be changed, stretched, and modified, but a unified and nationalized society makes great use of the traditional in its search for a consensual base to political authority and economic development.

Traditional and National Unification

Writing about African intellectuals in the formerly French colonies, Immanuel Wallerstein remarks that these parts of

[30] "Sanskritization and Westernization," in Srinivas, *op. cit.*

[31] McKim Marriott, "Changing Channels of Cultural Transmission in Indian Civilization," in L. P. Vidyarthi (ed.), *Aspects of Religion in Indian Society* (Meerut: Kedar Nath Ram Nath, 1961), pp. 13–25.

[32] The schoolteacher, in these decades of expanding primary education, is a source of Sanskritic as well as Western influences. See David Mandelbaum's account in "The World and the World View of the Koda," in M. Marriott (ed.), *Village India*, pp. 223–54, especially pp. 239ff.

[33] John Gumperz, "Religion as a Form of Communication in North India," *Journal of Asian Studies*, XXIII (June, 1964), 89–98.

[34] Scalapino, *op. cit.*, p. 106.

Africa are the chief centers for the ideological development of "Negritude"—the preservation and development of a uniquely indigenous African culture.[35] Here, where the intellectuals were trained in the French language and where they fully accepted the French culture, it is necessary to identify and discover a national cultural tradition and to self-consciously aid its development. In a similar fashion, an Indian colleague of mine once remarked that "Indians are obsessed with Indianness."

Many observers have noted the phenomenon of the revival of indigenous tradition as a phase of nationalistic and independence movements, especially where intellectuals had come to look to some other country as a basic source of new values.[36] Such reactions have set in among Russian intellectuals against France in the nineteenth century, among the Indonesians against the Dutch, among the Japanese against Europe; and against the British among the Indians both during and after the struggle for independence. The Indian intellectuals, westernized and European in cultural orientation, underwent a renaissance of traditional Hinduism as one aspect of the struggle against colonial dominion.[37] Despite their general commitment to modernization (often against the British post-Sepoy rebellion policy of maintaining native custom), a recrudescence of Indian national identity was partially fostered by explicit adoption of customs and styles which were both

traditional and closer to popular behavior. It was this ideology which Gandhi gave to the movement, even as he sought the abolition of many features of that tradition.

The issue of the nationalist movement is not abated in its victory. For the new elites of newly independent nations, the issue is not so much that of overcoming tradition but of finding ways of synthesizing and blending tradition and modernity. While it is now possible for the urbanized and intellectual elite to wear Saville Row and avoid the clothes of Chowri Bazaar without being a traitor, the issues of personal integrity and of political functions still remain.

Those who depict the elites in India as cut off from roots in an indigenous civilization ignore the ways in which Hinduism and Indian family life exert strong pulls as continuing aspects of Indian life, even where highly westernized. Almost always the Indian intellectual speaks a regional language as his mother tongue, is steeped in classic Sanskrit literature, and is deeply tied to an extended family. Parental arrangement is still the very dominant mode of marital selection, and he is often married to a highly traditional wife.[38]

Independence, even within the westernized circles, has given continuing support to a movement toward the recapturing of Hindu folklore and the furtherance of tradition as a source of national unity in a common culture. What Indian book or journal does not have its section that links modern thought or institutions to analogues in Hindu scripture? How often is the romanticization of the village and the rejection of the city not found among vigorous exponents of political democracy and economic change? This ideological construction of Indian tradition is offered as a "great tradition," and this Indian populism is found among intellectual and urbanized

[35] Immanuel Wallerstein, *Africa—the Politics of Independence* (New York: Vintage Books, 1961), pp. 75–76.

[36] *Ibid.*, chap. vii; John Kautsky, *Political Change in Underdeveloped Areas* (New York: John Wiley & Sons, 1962), pp. 53–54; Heimsath, *op. cit.*, chap. xii; Mary Mattosian, "Ideologies of Delay Industralization," *Economic Development and Cultural Change* (April, 1958), pp. 217–28.

[37] This "revivalist" stream was only one of the major themes in Indian nationalism, but it had a great impact throughout the movement (Heimsath, *op. cit.*; A. R. Desai, *Social Background of Indian Nationalism* [Bombay: Popular Book Depot, 1959], chaps, xiii, xviii).

[38] Shils has made this point in his study of Indian intellectuals (Edward Shils, *The Intellectual between Tradition and Modernity* [The Hague: Mouton & Co., 1961], especially pp. 60–67).

elites as it is in the provincial and peasant villages.

Nationalism is deeply committed to both horns of the dilemma of tradition and modernity. The effort to define a national heritage in the form of a set of continuing traditions is also a way of coping with the wide gap that separates elite and mass, city and village, region and region in the Indian context. It is a complement to the modernizing processes which are involved in the aspiration toward a unified nation. A common culture that cuts across the segmental and primordial loyalties is a basis for national identity and consensus. Without it, the modernization based on nationhood lacks a foundation for legitimating central authority.

In describing these movements we are not referring to efforts to pit tradition against modernity. This is certainly to be discovered in populist and aristocratic movements which call for the rejection of economic growth and the resistance or abolition of imported institutions and values. In India this can be seen in the xenophobic and militant Hinduism which characterized the RSS and still is a potent political force in the Hindu Mahasabha and, to a lesser degree, in the Jan Sangh party.[39] This appeal to an undisturbed society avoids the dilemma fully as much as does the ideology based on a linear theory of change.

The synthesis of tradition and modernity is evident in Gandhian influence. Was Gandhi a traditionalist or a modernizer? Asking the question poses the immense difficulty in separating the various streams in reform and social change blowing over the Indian subcontinent. Certainly his genius

lay in uniting disparities, in utilizing the traditional authority of the holy man for social reforms and for political union. His leadership of the independence movement gave India a common experience which has been one of the crucial legacies of the independence movement to its present national existence and to the authority of the Congress Party.

The Gandhianism of the neo-Gandhians, such as Vinoba Bhave and Jayaprakash Narayan, represents an important ideological development in the search for political institutions which will cope with the problems of nationhood within indigenous cultural forms.[40] But Gandhian Socialism represents only one form in which this drive toward a synthesis is manifest. The recent movement toward the development of local autonomy and participation in India rests both on the growing political power of village communities and the ideological force which has recreated a tradition of Indian village democracy. In the various proposals for a system of Panchayati Raj (movement toward greater local power in economic decisions at the village level), Indian government and politics are wrestling with the problem of creating a consensus for developmental policies which will have the legitimating support in tradition, even if the tradition is newly discovered.[41]

The Mediating Elites

Elsewhere we have analyzed the growing political power of new, less westernized,

[39] See Richard Lambert, "Hindu Communal Groups in Indian Politics," in R. Park and I. Tinker (eds.), *Leadership and Political Institutions in India* (Madras: Oxford University Press, 1960), pp. 211–24. Even the Swatantra Party, a movement led by an antitraditionalist set of ideologies, its anti-Congress character has drawn to it strong forces of antimodernism (see Howard Erdman, "India's Swatantra Party," *Pacific Affairs* [Winter, 1963–64], pp. 394–410).

[40] This quest for an indigenous form of political democracy is marked in Narayan's writings, as well as in conversation (see Jaya Prakash Narayan, *The Dual Revolution* [Tanjore: Sarvodaya Prachuralaya, 1959] *Swaraj for the People* [Varanasi: Ahkhib Bharat Sarva Seva Sangh, 1961]).

[41] See the analysis of the Panchayats in my paper on Indian political community, cited above (n. 27); and in Reinhard Bendix, "Public Authority in a Developing Political Community: The Case of India," *Archives Europeennes de Sociologie*, IV (1963), 39–85, especially 61 ff.

and more localistic political elites and sub-elites in India.[42] Such people, with sources of power in state and region, mediate between the westernized elites and the mass of the Indian society in ways which bring a greater degree of traditional commitments and styles, of caste and other primordial ties, into the political and cultural arena.

The very process of political egalitarianism and modernization contains the seeds of new ideologies of tradition. Literacy in India not only stimulates a common cultural content but has also led to ideologies of regionalism, extolling the virtues of regional languages and cultures.[43] While such movements impede the development of an all-India cultural consensus, they are neither antimodern nor specifically anti-India. They do, however, presage the decline of that form of national elite that has been associated with colonial cultural influences. India appears to be approaching and entering a phase in which modernization will be directed and implemented by persons whose loyalties and ideologies are considerably more traditionalized than has been true in the past decades.

The Ambiguities of Modernity

Just as "tradition" is renewed, created, and discovered, so too "modernity" as a goal toward which men aspire appears in some specific historical guise. The post-colonial elites owed much to the cultures of the colonial powers in India. Through travel, through language and literature, through colonial educational institutions, they had absorbed a picture of modernity as it was practiced in one country at one time. It is not a random selection that led the Indian elites to conceive of politics in the British mode or led Nehru's political

pronouncements and judgments of the 1950's to echo the liberalism of Harold Laski in the 1920's.

But being modern is far more ambiguous than being British. The disappearance of the postcolonial elites carries with it an increase in the range of alternatives ideologically open to the new, more traditionalized political groups. The possible routes to economic wealth and political nationhood are considerable, as we have shown in the earlier section of this paper. As countries come onto the scene of self-conscious aspiration toward the modern, they are presented with more and more successful models of the process. England, Germany, the United States, Japan, the Soviet Union are highly diverse in political institutions and histories. In the sense of having achieved high standards of living and egalitarian societies, they are all reasonably "developed."

The Cultural Framework of Modernity

We cannot easily separate modernity and tradition from some *specific* tradition and some *specific* modernity, some version which functions ideologically as a directive. The modern comes to the traditional society as a particular culture with its own traditions. In this respect it has been impossible to divorce modernization from some process of westernization. McKim Marriott has made this point most vividly in analyzing the reasons for villagers' rejection of Western and westernized doctors. The role of the doctor, as a technical expert, grants him authority in modern culture but not in the Indian village where technical and commercial skills have a low approval. Efficiency and thrift, those two great Western virtues, are not such in the eyes of the peasant in Utter Pradesh.[44]

---

[42] Gusfield, "Political Community and Group Interests in Modern India," *op. cit.*

[43] Witness the rise of self-conscious rediscovery of Hindi literary tradition. The linguistic and cultural renaissances in many parts of India are post-independence phenomena (see Selig Harrison, *India: The Most Dangerous Decade* (Princeton, N.J.: Princeton University Press, 1960).

[44] "It is important to note that a distinction can be made between 'Western' and 'scientific' medicine. Westerners conceive of a Western medicine as a system of curing based on 'rational' techniques and 'scientific' concepts of cause and effect. But this characteristic . . . only partly determines the total range of

The social scientist's designation of specific institutional forms as modern may also function as ideology and as aspiration, specifying what it is in a particular culture which is emulative. The concept of political development is far more difficult and culture-bound than is that of economic development. Even with the latter, we clearly recognize a diversity of institutional routes to industrialization and higher incomes. To label, apart from a specific context, either a capitalistic, socialistic, or communistic approach to economic growth as antithetical to economic growth would certainly seem fallacious to the economist. Similarly, the industrialized and egalitarian societies of the West have by no means demonstrated either a uniform or an unchanging form of polity. The Soviet Union, France, Germany, and the United States (and we might well include Japan) are hardly a single form of political structure, and each of these has in turn undergone many changes during its history. They are

---

practices involved in treatment and cure. Treatment is bedded in a social as well as a scientific matrix, and many practices of the Western doctor are based on cultural values and ideas of personal relationships that are peculiar to Western society" (McKim Marriott, "Western Medicine in a Village of Northern India," in S. N. Eisenstadt [ed.], *Comparative Social Problems* [New York: Free Press, 1964], pp. 47–60, at p. 59).

all national polities, to be sure, and all ones in which the population is mobilized, to a degree, to political participation and loyalty. These facts, however, state problems in a wider fashion, without specific institutional directives.

To conclude, the all too common practice of pitting tradition and modernity against each other as paired opposites tends to overlook the mixtures and blends which reality displays. Above all, it becomes an ideology of antitraditionalism, denying the necessary and usable ways in which the past serves as support, especially in the sphere of values and political legitimation, to the present and the future. We need a perspective toward change which does not deny the specific and contextual character of events.

I do not know much about the total style of life of that passenger on the Kodama express. To think of him as fixed on a continuum between tradition and modernity (as well as between Kyoto and Tokyo) hides the immense variations and possibilities, the capacity for blending opposites, which human beings and nations possess. In the concepts of the traditional and the modern, we are certainly wrestling with a feature of social change. We need to recognize that there is a variety of events on the wrestling program and that the outcomes, unlike many wrestling matches, are quite in doubt.

MECHANISMS OF CHANGE
AND ADJUSTMENT TO CHANGE[1]

Neil J. Smelser

Introduction

A thorough analysis of the social changes accompanying economic development would require an ambitious theoretical scheme and a vast quantity of comparative data. Because I lack both necessities—and the space to use them if I possessed them— I shall restrict this exploratory statement in two ways. (1) Methodologically, I shall deal only with ideal-type constructs, in Weber's sense; I shall not discuss any individual cases of development, or the comparative applicability of particular historical generalizations. (2) Substantively, I shall consider only modifications of the social structure; I shall not deal with factor-allocation, savings and investment, inflation, balance of payments, foreign aid, size of population, and rate of population change—even though these variables naturally affect, and are affected by, structural changes. These omissions call for brief comment.

Max Weber defined an ideal-type construct as a

one-sided accentuation ... by the synthesis of a great many diffuse, discrete, more or less present and occasionally absent *concrete individual* phenomena,

which are arranged ... into a unified *analytical* construct. In its conceptual purity, this mental construct cannot be found anywhere in reality.[2]

The analyst utilizes such ideal constructs to unravel and explain a variety of actual historical situations. Weber mentions explicitly two kinds of ideal-type constructs— first, "historically unique configurations," such as "rational bourgeois capitalism," "medieval Christianity," etc.; and second, statements concerning historical evolution, such as the Marxist laws of capitalist development.[3] While the second type presupposes some version of the first, I shall concentrate on the dynamic constructs.

"Economic development" generally refers to the "growth of output per head of population."[4] For purposes of analyzing the relationships between economic growth and the social structure, it is possible to isolate the effects of several interrelated technical, economic, and ecological processes that frequently accompany development. These may be listed as follows: (1) In the realm of technology, the change *from* simple and traditionalized techniques *toward* the application of scientific knowledge. (2) In agriculture, the evolution *from* subsistence farming *toward* commercial production of agricultural goods. This means specialization in cash crops, purchase of non-agricultural products in

SOURCE. Neil J. Smelser, "Mechanisms of Change and Adjustment to Change," in Bert F. Hoselitz and Wilbert E. Moore, eds., *Industrialization and Society* (The Hague: UNESCO and Mouton, 1963), pp. 32–54.

the market, and often agricultural wage-labor. (3) In industry, the transition *from* the use of human and animal power *toward* industrialization proper, or "men aggregated at power-driven machines, working for monetary return with the products of the manufacturing process entering into a market based on a network of exchange relations."[5] (4) In ecological arrangements, the movement *from* the farm and village *toward* urban centers. These several processes often, but not necessarily, occur simultaneously. Certain technological improvements—e.g., the use of improved seeds—can be introduced without automatically and instantaneously causing organizational changes;[6] agriculture may be commercialized without any concomitant industrialization, as in many colonial countries;[7] industrialization may occur in villages;[8] and cities may proliferate even where there is no significant industrialization.[9] Furthermore, the specific social consequences of technological advance, commercialized agriculture, the factory, and the city, respectively, are not in any sense reducible to each other.[10]

Despite such differences, all four processes tend to affect the social structure in similar ways. All give rise to the following ideal-type structural changes, which have ramifications throughout society: (1) Structural differentiation, or the establishment of more specialized and more autonomous social units. I shall discuss the occurrence of this process in the different spheres of economy, family, religion, and stratification. (2) Integration, which changes its character as the old social order is made obsolete by the process of differentiation. The state, the law, political groupings, and other associations are particularly salient in this integration. (3) Social disturbances—mass hysteria, outbursts of violence, religious and political movements, etc.—which reflect the uneven advances of differentiation and integration, respectively.

Obviously, the implications of technological advance, agricultural reorganiza-

tion, industrialization, and urbanization differ from society to society, as do the resulting structural realignments. Some of the sources of variation in these ideal patterns of pressure and change are described in the next paragraphs.

1. Variations in premodern conditions. Is the society's value system congenial or antagonistic to industrial values? How well integrated is the society? How "backward" is it? What is its level of wealth? How is the wealth distributed? Is the country "young and empty" or "old and crowded"? Is the country politically dependent, newly independent, or completely autonomous? Such pre-existing factors shape the impact of the forces of economic development.[11]

2. Variations in the impetus to change. Do pressures to modernize come from the internal implications of a value system, from a wish for national security and prestige, from a desire for material prosperity, or from a combination of these? Is political coercion used to form a labor force? Or are the pressures economic, as in the case of population pressure on the land or that of loss of handicraft markets to cheap imported products? Or do economic and political pressures combine, as, for example, when a tax is levied on peasants that is payable only in money? Or are the pressures social, as they are when there is a desire to escape burdensome aspects of the old order? Factors like these influence the adjustment to modernization greatly.[12]

3. Variations in the path toward modernization. Does the sequence begin with light consumer industries? Or is there an attempt to introduce heavy, capital-intensive industries first? What is the role of government in shaping the pattern of investment? What is the rate of accumulation of technological knowledge and skills? What is the general tempo of industrialization? These questions indicate elements which affect the nature of structural change and the degree of discomfort created by this change.[13]

4. Variations in the advanced stages of modernization. What is the emergent distribution of industries in developed economies? What are the emergent relations between state and economy, religion and economy, state and religion, etc.? While all advanced industrialized societies have their "industrialization" in common, uniquely national differences remain. For instance, "social class" has a different social significance in the United States than in the United Kingdom, even though both are highly developed countries.

5. Variations in the content and timing of dramatic events during modernization. What is the import of wars, revolutions, rapid migrations, natural catastrophes, etc., for the course of economic and social development?

These sources of variation render it virtually impossible to establish hard and fast empirical generalizations concerning the evolution of social structures during economic and social development.[14] Therefore, my purpose here is not to search for such generalizations, but rather to outline certain ideal-type directions of structural change that modernization involves. On the basis of these ideal types, we may classify, describe, and analyze varying national experiences. Factors like those indicated above determine, in part, a nation's distinctive response to the universal aspects of modernization; but this in no way detracts from their universality. While I shall base my remarks on the vast literature of economic development, I can in no sense attempt an exhaustive comparative study.

Structural Differentiation in Periods of Development

The concept of structural differentiation can be employed to analyze what is frequently termed the "marked break in established patterns of social and economic life" in periods of development.[15] Simply defined, "differentiation" is the evolution from a multifunctional role structure to several more specialized structures. In illustration, we may cite here three typical examples. During a society's transition from domestic to factory industry, the division of labor increases, and the economic activities previously lodged in the family move to the firm. As a formal educational system emerges, the training functions previously performed by the family and church are established in a more specialized unit, the school.[16] The modern political party has a more complex structure than do tribal factions, and the former is less likely to be fettered with kinship loyalties, competition for religious leadership, etc.

Formally defined, then, structural differentiation is a process whereby

> *one* social role or organization . . . differentiates into *two or more* roles or organizations which function more effectively in the new historical circumstances. The new social units are structurally distinct from each other, but taken together are functionally equivalent to the original unit.[17]

Differentiation concerns only changes in role structure. It must not be confused with two closely related concepts. The first of these involves the cause or motivation for entering the differentiated role. Someone may be motivated to engage in wage-labor, for instance, by a desire for economic improvement, by political coercion, or indeed by a wish to fulfil traditional obligations (e.g., to use wages to supply a dowry). These "reasons" should be kept conceptually distinct from differentiation itself. The other related concept concerns the integration of differentiated roles. For example, as differentiated wage-labor begins to emerge, there also appear legal norms, labor exchanges, trade unions, and so on, that regulate—with varying degrees of success—the relations between labor and management. Such readjustments, even though they sometimes produce a new social unit, should be considered separately from role specialization in other functions.

Let us now inquire into the process of differentiation in several different social realms.

DIFFERENTIATION OF ECONOMIC ACTIVITIES

In underdeveloped countries, production typically is located in kinship units. Subsistence farming predominates; other industry is supplementary but still attached to kin and village. In some cases, occupational position is determined largely by an extended group, such as the caste.[18]

Similarly, exchange and consumption are deeply embedded in family and village. In subsistence agriculture, there is a limited amount of independent exchange outside the family; thus production and consumption occur in the same social context. Exchange systems proper are still lodged in kinship and community (e.g., reciprocal exchange), and stratification systems (e.g., redistribution according to caste membership), and in political systems (e.g., taxes, tributes, payments in kind, forced labor).[19] Under these conditions, market systems are underdeveloped, and the independent power of money to command the movement of goods and services is minimal.

As the economy develops, several kinds of economic activity are removed fom this family-community complex. In agriculture, the introduction of money crops marks a differentiation between the social contexts of production and of consumption. Agricultural wage-labor sometimes undermines the family production unit. In industry, several levels of differentiation can be identified. Household industry, the simplest form, parallels subsistence agriculture in that it supplies "the worker's own needs, unconnected with trade." "Handicraft production" splits production and consumption, though frequently consumption takes place in the local community. "Cottage industry," on the other hand, often involves a differentiation between consumption and community, since production is "for the market, for an unknown consumer, sold to a wholesaler who accumulates a stock."[20] Finally, manufacturing and factory systems segregate the worker from his capital and not rarely from his family.

Simultaneously, similar differentiations emerge in the exchange system. Goods and services, previously exchanged on a non-economic basis, are pulled progressively more into the market. Money now commands the movement of increasingly more goods and services; it thus begins to supplant—and sometimes undermine—the religious, political, familial, or caste sanctions which had hitherto governed economic activity.[21] This is the setting for the institutionalization of relatively autonomous economic systems that exhibit a greater emphasis on values like "universalism," "functional specificity," and "rationality."[22]

Empirically, underdeveloped economies may be classified according to the respective distances they have moved along this line of differentiation. Migratory labor, for instance, may be a kind of compromise between full membership in a wage-labor force and attachment to an old community life. Cottage industry introduces extended markets but retains the family-production fusion. The employment of families in factories maintains a version of family production. The expenditure of wages on traditional items, like dowries, also manifests the half-entry into the more differentiated industrial-urban structure.[23] The causes of such partial differentiation may lie in resistance on the part of the populace to give up traditional modes, in the economics of demand for handmade products, in systems of racial discrimination against native labor, or elsewhere.[24] In any case, the concept of structural differentiation provides a yardstick for discerning the distance that the economic structure has evolved toward modernization.

DIFFERENTIATION OF FAMILY ACTIVITIES

One consequence of the removal of economic activities from the kinship nexus is the family's loss of some of its previous functions, and its thereby becoming a more specialized agency. As the family ceases to be an economic unit of production, one or more members leave the household to seek employment in the labor market. The family's activities become more concentrated on emotional gratification and socialization. While many halfway houses, such as family hiring and migratory systems, persist, the trend is toward the segregation of family functions from economic functions.[25]

Several related processes accompany the differentiation of the family from its other involvements. (1) Apprenticeship within the family declines. (2) Pressures develop against nepotism in the recruitment of labor and management. These pressures often are based on the demands of economic rationality. The intervention frequently persists, however—especially at the managerial levels—and in some cases (e.g., Japan), family ties continue to be a major basis for labor recruitment. (3) The direct control of elders and collateral kinsmen over the nuclear family weakens. This marks, in structural terms, the differentiation of the nuclear family from the extended family. (4) An aspect of this loss of control is the growth of personal choice, love, and related criteria as the foundation for courtship and marriage. Structurally, this is the differentiation of courtship from extended kinship. (5) One result of this complex of processes is the changing status of women, who generally become less subordinated economically, politically, and socially to their husbands than they had been under earlier conditions.[26]

In such ways, structural differentiation undermines the old modes of integration in society. The controls of extended family and village begin to dissolve in the enlarged, complicated social setting which differentiation creates. Thereupon, new integrative problems are posed. We shall inquire presently into some of the lines of integration.

DIFFERENTIATION OF RELIGIOUS SYSTEMS

Because of Max Weber's monumental thesis linking ascetic Protestantism and capitalism,[27] a disproportionate amount of attention has been devoted to the initiating role that *formal* religious values play in economic development. Although much excellent work has been done in this area,[28] insufficient emphasis has been given to the important role of secular nationalism in the industrial takeoff.

With the world organized as it is, nationalism is a *sine qua non* of industrialization, because it provides people with an overriding, easily acquired, secular motivation for making painful changes. National strength or prestige becomes the supreme goal, industrialization the chief means. The costs, inconveniences, sacrifices, and loss of traditional values can be justified in terms of this transcending, collective ambition. The new collective entity, the nation-state, that sponsors and grows from this aspiration is equal to the exigencies of industrial complexity; it draws directly the allegiance of every citizen, organizing the population as one community; it controls the passage of persons, goods, and news across the borders; it regulates economic and social life in detail. To the degree that the obstacles to industrialization are strong, nationalism must be intense to overcome them.[29]

In fact, nationalism seems in many cases to be the very instrument designed to smash the traditional religious systems—those like, e.g., the classical Chinese or Indian—which Weber himself found to be less permissive than Protestantism for economic modernization.

On the other hand, nationalism, like many traditionalistic religious systems, may hinder economic advancement by "reaffirmation of traditionally honored ways of acting and thinking,"[30] by fostering anticolonial attitudes after they are no longer relevant,[31] and, more indirectly, by encouraging passive expectations of "ready-made prosperity."[32] We can distinguish among these contrasting forces of "stimulus" and "drag" that such value systems bring to economic development by using the logic of differentiation in the following way.

In the early phases of modernization, many traditional attachments must be modified to permit more differentiated institutional structures to be set up. Because the existing commitments and methods of integration are deeply rooted in the organization of traditional society, a very generalized and powerful commitment is required to pry individuals from these attachments. The values of ascetic and this-worldly religious beliefs, xenophobic national aspirations, and political ideologies (like, e.g., socialism), provide such a lever. Sometimes these diverse types of values combine into a single system of legitimacy. In any case, all three have an "ultimacy" of commitment, in whose name a wide range of sacrifices can be demanded and procured.

The very success of these value systems, however, breeds the conditions for their own weakening. In a perceptive statement, Weber notes that, at the beginning of the twentieth century, when the capitalistic system was already highly developed, it no longer needed the impetus of ascetic Protestantism.[33] By virtue of its conquest of much of Western society, capitalism had solidly established an institutional base and a secular value system of its own—economic rationality. Its secular economic values had no further need for the "ultimate" justification they had required during the newer, unsteadier days of economic revolution.

Such lines of differentiation constitute the secularization of religious values. In the same process, other institutional spheres—economic, political, scientific, etc. —become more nearly established on their own. The values governing these spheres are no longer sanctioned directly by religious beliefs, but by an autonomous rationality. In so far as this replaces religious sanctions, secularization occurs in these spheres.

Similarly, nationalistic and related value systems undergo a process of secularization as differentiation proceeds. As a society moves increasingly toward more complex social organization, the encompassing demands of nationalistic commitment give way to more autonomous systems of rationality. For instance, the Soviet Union, as its social structure grows more differentiated, is apparently introducing more "independent" market mechanisms, "freer" social scientific investigation in some spheres, and so on.[34] Moreover, these measures are not directly sanctioned by nationalistic or communistic values. Finally, it seems reasonable to make the historical generalization that, in the early stages of a nation's development, nationalism is heady, muscular, and aggressive; as the society evolves to an advanced state, however, nationalism tends to settle into a more remote and complacent condition, rising to fury only in times of national crisis.

Hence there is a paradoxical element in the role of religious or nationalistic belief systems. In so far as they encourage the breakup of old patterns, they may stimulate economic modernization. In so far as they resist their own subsequent secularization, however, these same value systems may become an impediment to economic advance and structural change.

DIFFERENTIATION OF SYSTEMS OF STRATIFICATION

In analyzing systems of stratification, we concentrate on two kinds of issues.

1. Are ascribed qualities subject to ranking? Ascription focuses primarily on those aspects of the human condition that touch the biological and physical world— kinship, age, sex, race or ethnicity, and territorial location. To what extent is status determined by birth in a certain tribe? in a certain family? in a certain ethnic group? in a certain place—a region of the country or "the wrong side of the tracks"? Some ascription exists in all societies, since the infant in the nuclear

family always and everywhere begins with the status of his parents.[35] The degree to which this ascribed ranking extends beyond the family varies from society to society. In our own ideology, we minimize the ascriptive elements of class and ethnic membership; but in practice these matter greatly, especially for Negroes.

2. The degree to which all positions in society (occupational, political, religious, etc.) are consequences of status ascribed from birth. For example, the American egalitarian ideology places a premium on the maximum separation of these positions from ascribed categories; but in fact, family membership, minority-group membership, etc., impinge on the ultimate "placing" of persons. In many non-industrialized societies, the link between ascription and position is much closer. Criteria like these reveal the degree of openness, or social mobility, in a system.

Under conditions of economic modernization, structural differentiation increases along both dimensions discussed.

Other evaluative standards intrude on ascribed memberships. For instance, McKim Marriott has noted that, in the village of Paril in India,

Personal wealth, influence, and mortality have surpassed the traditional caste-and-order alignment of kind groups as the effective bases of ranking. Since such new bases of ranking can no longer be clearly tied to any inclusive system of large solidary groupings, judgments must be made according to the characteristics of individual or family units. This individualization of judgments leads to greater dissensus [*sic*].[36]

Of course, castes, ethnic groups, and traditional religious groupings do not necessarily decline in importance *in every respect* during periods of modernization. As political interest groups or reference groups for diffuse loyalty, they may become even more significant.[37] As the sole bases of ranking, however, ascriptive

standards become more differentiated from economic, political, and other standards.[38]

Individual mobility through the occupational hierarchies increases. This is indicative of the differentiation of the adult's functional position from his point of origin. In addition, individual mobility is frequently substituted for collective mobility. Individuals, and no longer whole castes or tribes, compete for higher standing in society. The phenomenon of growing individual mobility seems to be one of the universal consequences of industrialization. After assembling extensive empirical data on patterns of mobility in industrialized nations, Lipset and Bendix conclude that "the overall pattern of [individual] social mobility appears to be much the same in the industrial societies of various Western countries."[39] Patterns of class symbolization and class ideology may, however, continue to be different in industrialized countries.

One of Emile Durkheim's remarkable insights concerned the role of integrative mechanisms during periods of growing social heterogeneity. Attacking the utilitarian view that the division of labor would flourish best without regulation, Durkheim demonstrates that one concomitant of a growing division of labor is an *increase* in mechanisms for coordinating and solidifying the interaction among individuals whose interests are becoming progressively more diversified.[40] Durkheim locates this integration largely in the legal structure; however, similar kinds of integrative forces can be discerned elsewhere in society.

Differentiation, therefore, is not by itself sufficient for modernization. Development proceeds as a contrapuntal interplay between differentiation (which is divisive of established society) and integration (which unites differentiated structures on a new basis). Paradoxically, however, the course of integration itself produces more *differentiated* structures—e.g., trade unions, associations, political parties, and a mushrooming state apparatus. Let us illustrate this complex process of integration in several institutional spheres.

ECONOMY AND FAMILY

Under a simple kind of economic organization, like subsistence agriculture or household industry, there is little differentiation between economic roles and family roles. All reside in the kinship structure. The *integration* of these diverse but unspecialized activities also rests in the local family and community structures, and in the religious traditions which fortify both.

When differentiation has begun, the social setting for production is separated from that for consumption; and the productive roles of family members are isolated geographically, temporally, and structurally from their distinctively familial roles. This differentiation immediately creates integrative problems. How is information about employment opportunities to be conveyed to working people? How are the interests of families to be protected from market fluctuation? Whereas such integrative exigencies had been faced by kinsmen, neighbors, and local largesse in premodern settings, modernization creates dozens of institutions and organizations designed to deal with the new integrative problems—labor recruitment agencies and exchanges, labor unions, government regulation of labor allocation, welfare and relief arrangements, cooperative societies, savings institutions.[41] All these involve agencies which specialize in integration.

COMMUNITY

When industrialization occurs only in villages, or when villages are built around paternalistic industrial enterprises,[42] many ties of community and kinship can be maintained under the industrial conditions. Urbanization, however, frequently creates more anonymity. As a result, in expanding cities there often emerge voluntary associations—churches and chapels, unions, schools, halls, athletic clubs, bars, shops, mutual-aid groups, etc. Sometimes the

growth of these integrative groupings is retarded because of the movement of migratory workers,[43] who "come to the city for their differentiation" and "return to the village for their integration." In cities themselves, the original criterion for associating may have been the common tribe, caste, or village; this criterion sometimes persists or is gradually replaced by more "functional" groupings based on economic or political interest.[44]

POLITICAL STRUCTURE

In a typical premodern setting, political integration is closely fused with kinship position, tribal membership, control of the land, or control of the unknown. Political forms include chieftains, kings, councils of elders, strong landlords, powerful magicians and oracles, etc.

As social systems grow more complex, political systems are modified accordingly. Fortes and Evans-Pritchard have specified three types of native African political systems. These, listed in terms of their respective degrees of differentiation from kinship lineages, are as follows: (1) small societies in which the largest political unit embraces only those united by kinship—thus political authority is conterminous with kinship relations, (2) societies in which the political framework is the integrative core for a number of kinship lineages, and (3) societies with a more formal administrative organization. Such systems move toward greater differentiation as the society's population grows and economic and cultural heterogeneity increases.[45] In colonial and recently-freed African societies, political systems have evolved much further; parties, congresses, pressure groups, and even "parliamentary" systems have emerged.[46] In describing the Indian village, Marriott speaks of the "wider integration of local groups with outside groups."[47] Sometimes such wider political integration is, like community integration, based on extension and modification of an old integrative principle. Harrison has argued that modern developments in India have changed the significance of caste from the "traditional village extension of the joint family" to "regional alliances of kindred local units." This modification has led to the formation of "new caste lobbies" which constitute some of the strongest and most explosive political forces in modern India.[48] We shall mention some of the possible political consequences of this persistence of old integrative forms later.

We have indicated the ways in which differentiation in society impinges on the integrative sphere. The resulting integrative structures attempt, with more or less success, to coordinate and solidify the social structure which the forces of differentiation threaten to fragment. In many cases, the integrative associations and parties are extremely unstable: labor unions turn into political or nationalistic parties, religious sects become political clubs, football clubs become religious sects, and so on.[49] This fluidity indicates the urgent need for reintegration during rapid, irregular, and disruptive processes of differentiation. The initial response is a trial-and-error type of reaching for many kinds of integration at once.

We have outlined some structural consequences of technological advance, agricultural commercialization, urbanization, and industrialization. We have analyzed these consequences in terms of differentiation and integration. The structural changes are not, one must remember, a simple function of industrialization alone. Some of the most far-reaching structural changes have occurred in countries where industrialization has hardly begun. For instance, colonialism or related forms of economic dominance create not only an extensive differentiation of cash products and wage-labor, but also a vulnerability to world price fluctuations in commodities.[50] Hence many of the structural changes already described, and the consequent social disturbances to be described presently, are characteristics of societies which are still technically pre-industrial.

Discontinuities in Differentiation and Integration: Social Disturbances

The structural changes associated with modernization are disruptive to the social order for the following reasons:

1. Differentiation demands the creation of new activities, norms, rewards, and sanctions—money, political position, prestige based on occupation, etc. These often conflict with old modes of social action, which are frequently dominated by traditional religious, tribal, and kinship systems. Traditional standards are among the most intransigent obstacles to modernization; and when they are threatened, serious dissatisfaction and opposition to the threatening agents arise.

2. Structural change is, above all, *uneven* during periods of modernization. In colonial societies, for instance, the European powers frequently revolutionized the economic, political, and educational frameworks; but they simultaneously encouraged or imposed a conservatism in traditional religious, class, and family systems.

The basic problem in these [colonial] societies was the expectation that the native population would accept certain broad, modern institutional settings . . . and would perform within them various roles—especially economic and administrative roles—while at the same time, they were denied some of the basic rewards inherent in these settings . . . they were expected to act on the basis of a motivational system derived from a different social structure which the colonial powers and indigenous rulers tried to maintain.[51]

In a society undergoing post-colonial modernization, similar discontinuities appear. Within the economy itself, rapid industrialization—no matter how coordinated—bites unevenly into the established social and economic structures.[52] And throughout the society, the differentiation occasioned by agricultural, industrial, and urban changes always proceeds in a see-saw relationship with integration: the two forces continuously breed lags and bottlenecks. The faster the tempo of modernization is, the more severe the discontinuities. This unevenness creates *anomie* in the classical sense, for it generates disharmony between life experiences and the normative framework which regulates them.[53]

3. Dissatisfactions arising from conflict with traditional ways and those arising from *anomie* sometimes aggravate each other upon coming into contact. *Anomie* may be partially relieved by new integrative devices, like unions, associations, clubs, and government regulations. However, such innovations are often opposed by traditional vested interests because they compete with the older undifferentiated systems of solidarity.[54] The result is a three-way tug-of-war among the forces of tradition, the forces of differentiation, and the new forces of integration.[55] Under these conditions, virtually unlimited potentialities for group conflict are created.[56]

Three classic responses to these discontinuities are anxiety, hostility, and fanatasy. If and when these responses become collective, they crystallize into a variety of social movements—peaceful agitation, political violence, millenarianism, nationalism, revolution, underground subversion, etc.[57] There is plausible—though not entirely convincing—evidence that the people most readily drawn into such movements are those suffering most severely under the displacements created by structural change. For example:

> [Nationalism appeared] as a permanent force in Southeast Asia at the moment when the peasants were forced to give up subsistence farming for the cultivation of cash crops or when (as in highly colonized Java) subsistence farming ceased to yield a subsistence. The introduction of a money economy and the withering away of the village as the unit of life accompanied this development and finally established the period of economic dependence.[58]

Other theoretical and empirical data suggest that social movements appeal most to those who have been dislodged from old social ties by differentiation without also being integrated into the new social order.[59]

Many belief systems associated with these movements envision the grand, almost instantaneous integration of society. Frequently, the beliefs are highly emotional and unconcerned with realistic policies. In nationalistic movements in colonial societies, for instance, "the political symbols were intended to develop new, ultimate, common values and basic loyalties, rather than relate to current policy issues within the colonial society."[60] Furthermore, belief systems of this kind reflect the ambivalence that results from the conflict between traditionalism and modernization. Nationalists alternate between xenophobia and xenophilia; they predict that they will simultaneously "outmodernize" the West in the future and "restore" the true values of the ancient civilization; they argue both for egalitarian and for hierarchical principles of social organization at the same time.[61] Nationalism and related ideologies unite these contradictory tendencies in the society under one large symbol. If these ideologies are successful, they are then often used as a means to modernize the society and thus to erase those kinds of social discontinuity that caused the initial nationalistic outburst.

Naturally, early modernization does not inevitably produce violent nationalism or other social movements. Furthermore, when such movements do arise, they take many different forms. Below are listed the five factors which seem most decisive in the genesis and molding of social disturbances.

1. The scope and intensity of the social dislocation created by structural changes. "The greater the tempo of these changes . . . the greater the problems of acute malintegration the society has to face."[62]

2. The structural complexity of the

society at the time when modernization begins. In the least developed societies, where "the language of politics is at the same time the language of religion," protest movements more or less immediately take on a religious cast. In Africa, for instance, utopian religious movements apparently have relatively greater appeal in the less developed regions; whereas the more secular types of political protest, like trade union movements and party agitations, have tended to cluster in the more developed areas.[63] The secularization of protest increases, of course, as modernization and differentiation advance.

3. The access that disturbed groups have to channels that influence social policy. If dislocated groups have access to those responsible for introducing reforms, agitation is usually relatively peaceful and orderly. If this avenue is blocked—because of either the isolation of the groups or the intransigence of the ruling authorities—demands for reform tend to take more violent, utopian, and bizarre forms. This is the reason that fantasy and unorganized violence are likely to cluster among the disinherited, the colonized, and the socially isolated migrants.[64]

4. The overlap of interests and lines of cleavage. In many colonial societies, the social order broke more or less imperfectly into three groupings: (*a*) the Western representatives, who controlled economic and political administration, and who were frequently allied with large local land-owners; (*b*) a large native population who —when drawn into the colonial economy— entered it as tenant farmers, wage-laborers, etc.; (*c*) a group of foreigners—Chinese, Indians, Syrians, Goans, Lebanese, etc.— who fitted between the first two groups as traders, moneylenders, merchants, creditors, etc. This view is oversimplified, of course; but several colonial societies approximated this arrangement.[65] The important structural feature of such an arrangement is that economic, political, and racial-ethic memberships *coincide* with each other. Thus, *any* kind of conflict is likely to assume racial overtones and to arouse the more diffuse loyalties and prejudices of the warring parties. Many colonial outbursts did, in fact, follow racial lines.[66] In so far as such "earthquake faults" persist after independence has been attained, these societies will probably be plagued by similar outbursts.[67] If, on the other hand, the different lines of cleavage in the society crisscross, the society is more nearly able to insulate and manage specific economic and political grievances peacefully.[68]

5. The kind and amount of foreign infiltration and intervention on behalf of protest groups.

Structural Bases for the Role of Government

Many have argued, on economic grounds, for the presence of a strong, centralized government in rapidly modernizing societies. Governmental planning and activity are required, for example, to direct saving and investment, to regulate incentives, to encourage entrepreneurship, to control trade and prices, etc.[69] To their arguments, I should like to add several considerations that emerge from the analysis of structural change during periods of rapid development.

1. Undifferentiated institutional structures frequently constitute the primary social barriers to modernization. Individuals refuse to work for wages because of traditional kinship, village, tribal, and other ties. Invariably, a certain amount of political pressure must be applied to loosen these ties. The need for this pressure increases, of course, in proportion to the rate of modernization desired.

2. The process of differentiation itself creates conditions demanding a larger, more formal type of political administration. Thus, another argument in favor of the importance of strong government during rapid and uneven modernization is based on the necessity to accommodate the growing cultural, economic, and social heterogeneity, and to control the political

repercussions of the constantly shifting distribution of power accompanying extensive social reorganization.

3. The probability that periods of early modernization will erupt into explosive outbursts creates delicate political problems for the leaders of developing nations. We shall conclude this essay on the major social forces of modernization by suggesting the kinds of government that are likely to be most effective in such troubled areas. First, political leaders can increase their effectiveness by openly and vigorously committing themselves to utopian and xenophobic nationalism. This commitment is a powerful instrument for attaining three of their most important ends. (*a*) They can enhance their own claim to legitimacy by endowing themselves with the mission of creating the nation-state. (*b*) They can procure otherwise unobtainable sacrifices from a populace which may be committed to modernization in the abstract, but which resists making concrete breaks with traditional ways. (*c*) They can use their claim to legitimacy to repress protests and to prevent generalized symbols, such as communism, from spreading to all sorts of particular grievances. However, these political leaders should not take their claim to legitimacy too literally. They should not rely on their nationalistic commitment as being strong enough to enable them to ignore or smother grievances completely. They should "play politics," in the usual sense, with aggrieved groups, thus giving these groups access to responsible political agencies, and thereby reducing the conditions that favor counterclaims to legitimacy. One key to political stability seems to be, therefore, the practice of flexible politics behind the façade of an inflexible commitment to a national mission.

Conclusion

I have attempted to sketch, in ideal-type terms, the ways in which economic and social development are related to the social structure. I have organized the discussion around three major categories: differentiation, which characterizes a social structure that is moving toward greater complexity; integration, which in certain respects balances the divisive character of differentiation; and social disturbances, which result from the discontinuities between differentiation and integration.

Four qualifications must be added to this analysis. (1) I have not tried to account for the determinants of economic development itself. In fact, the discussion of differentiation, integration, and social disturbances has presupposed a certain attempt to develop economically. However, these three forces condition the *course* of that development once it has started. (2) For purposes of exposition, I have presented the three major categories in the order restated above. However, this ordering must not be inferred to mean that any one of the forces assumes causal precedence in social change. Rather, they form an interactive system. Disturbances, for instance, may arise from discontinuities created by structural differentiation; but these very disturbances may shape the course of future processes of differentiation. Likewise, integrative developments may be set in motion by differentiation; but they, in their turn, may initiate new lines of differentiation. (3) Even though the forces of differentiation, integration, and disturbances are closely linked empirically, we should not "close" the "system" composed of the relationship among the three forces. Differentiation may arise from sources other than economic development; the necessity for integration may emerge from conditions other than differentiation; and the sources of social disturbances are not exhausted by the discontinuities between differentiation and integration. The "all-at-once" character of the transition from less differentiated to more differentiated societies should not be exaggerated. Empirically, the process evolves gradually and influences the social structure selectively. This essay has emphasized various halfway arrangements and compromises in order to illustrate this gradualness and irregularity.

NOTES

[1] I am grateful to Professors William Petersen, Herbert Blumer, Reinhard Bendix, and Kingsley Davis of the University of California, Berkeley, for critical comments on an earlier version of this essay.

[2] Max Weber, *The Methodology of the Social Sciences* (Glencoe, Ill., 1949), pp. 90, 93.

[3] *Ibid.*, pp. 93, 101–103.

[4] W. A. Lewis, *The Theory of Economic Growth* (Homewood, Ill., 1955), p. 1.

[5] M. Nash, "Some Notes on Village Industrialization in South and East Asia," *Economic Development and Cultural Change*, 3, 271.

[6] W. H. Becket, for instance, distinguishes between "technical improvement" and "organizational improvement" in agriculture. See "The Development of Peasant Agriculture," in P. Ruopp (ed.), *Approaches to Community Development* (The Hague, 1953), pp. 138–143. For an analysis of the interplay between technological advance and productive reorganization during the Tokugawa period in Japan, see H. Rosovsky, "Japanese Economic Development and the Western Model" (mimeographed), pp. 7–17.

[7] For example, J. H. Boeke, *The Structure of the Netherlands Indian Economy* (New York, 1942), pp. 76–89.

[8] Nash, *op. cit.*; T. Herman, "The Role of Cottage and Small-Scale Industries in Asian Economic Development," *Economic Development and Cultural Change*, 4, 356–370; H. G. Aubrey, "Small Industry in Economic Development," in L. W. Shannon (ed.), *Underdeveloped Areas* (New York, 1957), pp. 215–225.

[9] T. Hodgkin, *Nationalism in Colonial Africa* (New York, 1957), Ch. 2.

[10] B. F. Hoselitz, "The City, the Factory, and Economic Growth," *American Economic Review*, 45, 166–184; K. Davis and H. H. Golden, "Urbanization and the Development of Pre-Industrial Areas," *Economic Development and Cultural Change*, 3, 6–26; Nash, *op. cit.*, p. 277.

[11] S. Kuznets, "Problems in Comparisons of Economic Trends," in S. Kuznets, W. E. Moore, and J. J. Spengler (eds.), *Economic Growth: Brazil, India, Japan* (Durham, N.C., 1955), pp. 14–19; Kuznets, "International Differences in Income Levels: Some Reflections on Their Causes," *Economic Development and Cultural Change*, 2, 22–23; A. Gerschenkron, "Economic Backwardness in Historical Perspective," and R. Linton, "Cultural and Personality Factors Affecting Economic Growth," both in B. Hoselitz (ed.), *The Progress of Underdeveloped Areas* (Chicago, 1952), pp. 3–29, 80 ff.; H. G. J. Aitken (ed.), *The State and Economic Growth* (New York, 1959).

[12] E. Staley, *The Future of Underdeveloped Areas* (New York, 1954), pp. 21–22; W. W. Rostow, *The Stages of Economic Growth: A Non-Communist Manifesto* (Cambridge, 1960), pp. 26–35; W. E. Moore, *Industrialization and Labor* (Ithaca and New York, 1951), Chs. 1–4, Hoselitz, "The City, the Factory," pp. 177–179.

[13] United Nations, Department of Economic and Social Affairs, *Processes and Problems of Industrialization in Underdeveloped Countries* (New York, 1955), Ch. 1; C. P. Kindleberger, *Economic Development* (New York, 1958), pp. 184–185, 315–316; N. S. Buchanan and H. S. Ellis, *Approaches to Economic Development* (New York, 1955), pp. 275 ff.; Kuznets, "International Differences," pp. 21–22.

[14] For instance, Blumer has questioned the generalization that "early industrialization, by nature, alienates and disaffects workers, makes them radical, and propels them to protest behavior." He even concludes that "industrialization . . . is neutral and indifferent to what follows in its wake" (H. Blumer, "Early Industrialization and the Laboring Class," *The Sociological Quarterly*, 1, 9). If one searches for specific generalizations like those Blumer has rejected, of course, he will inevitably be disappointed. One must not conclude, however, that the establishment of ideal-type constructs about the consequences of industrialization, and their use in interpreting national experiences are fruitless.

[15] Kuznets, "International Differences," p. 23.

[16] N. J. Smelser, *Social Change in the Industrial Revolution* (Chicago, 1959), Chs. 9–11.

[17] *Ibid.*, p. 2.

[18] Boeke, *op. cit.*, pp. 8–9, 32–34; E. E. Hagen, "The Process of Economic Development," *Economic Development and Cultural Change*, 5, 195; B. K. Maden, "The Economics of the Indian Village and Its Implications in Social Structure," *International Social Science Bulletin*, 3, 813–821; D. F. Dowd, "Two-thirds of the World," in Shannon, *op. cit.*, pp. 14 ff. For qualifications on the degree to which caste dominates occupation in India, see K. Davis, *The Population of India and Pakistan* (Princeton, N.I., 1951), pp. 163 ff.

[19] K. Polanyi, C. M. Arensberg, and H. W.

Pearson (eds.), *Trade and Market in the Early Empires* (Glencoe, Ill., 1957); N. J. Smelser, "A Comparative View of Exchange Systems," *Economic Development and Cultural Change*, **7**, 173–182; Boeke, *op. cit.*, pp. 36–39; M. R. Solomon, "The Structure of the Market in Underdeveloped Economies," in Shannon, *op. cit.*, pp. 131 ff.

[20] These "levels," which represent points on the continuum from structural fusion to structural differentiation, are taken from Boeke, *op. cit.*, p. 90.

[21] F. G. Bailey, *Caste and the Economic Frontier* (Manchester, 1957), pp. 4–5.

[22] M. J. Levy, Jr., "Some Sources of the Vulnerability of the Structures of Relatively Non-Industrialized Societies to Those of Highly Industrialized Societies," in Hoselitz, *The Progress of Underdeveloped Areas*, pp. 116–125. The pattern variables of T. Parsons are also relevant (discussed in *The Social System* [Glencoe, Ill., 1951], pp. 58–67). For applications of the pattern variables to economic development, see G. A. Theodorson, "Acceptance of Industrialization and Its Attendant Consequences for the Social Patterns of Non-Western Societies," *American Sociological Review*, **18**, 477–484; and B. F. Hoselitz, "Social Structure and Economic Growth," *Economia Internazionale*, **6**, 52–77.

[23] Examples of these compromises may be found in Moore, *op. cit.*, pp. 29–34; *idem.*, "The Migration of Native Laborers in South Africa," in Shannon, *op. cit.*, pp. 79 ff.; A. I. Richards (ed.), *Economic Development and Tribal Change* (Cambridge, n.d.), Ch. 5; C. A. Myers, *Labor Problems in the Industrialization of India* (Cambridge, Mass., 1958), pp. 52, 175; S. Rottenberg, "Income and Leisure in an Underdeveloped Economy," in Shannon, *op. cit.*, pp. 150–151; Aubrey, "Small Industry in Economic Development," in Shannon, *op. cit.*, pp. 215 ff.; A. Doucy, "The Unsettled Attitude of Negro Workers in the Belgian Congo," *International Social Science Bulletin*, **6**, 442–451; G. Balandier, "Social Changes and Social Problems in Negro Africa," in C. W. Stillman (ed.), *Africa in the Modern World* (Chicago, 1955), pp. 60–61; Smelser, *Social Change*, Ch. 9; Herman, *op. cit.*, pp. 357–358.

[24] Noneconomic barriers are discussed at length in Moore, *Industrialization and Labor*, Chs. 2–4. On the persistence of handicrafts, see A. L. Minkes, "A Note on Handicrafts in Underdeveloped Areas," *Economic Development and Cultural Change*, **1**, 156–158; Herman, *op. cit.*, pp. 362–365; T. Uyeda, *The Small Industries of Japan* (Shanghai, 1938), pp. 84–112.

[25] For case studies, see M. J. Levy, Jr., *The Family Revolution in Modern China* (Cambridge, Mass., 1949), and Smelser, *Social Change*.

[26] Kindleberger, *op. cit.*, pp. 59 ff.; Moore, *Industrialization and Labor*, pp. 29–34, 71–75; E. F. Frazier, "The Impact of Colonialism on African Social Forms and Personality," in Stillman, *op. cit.*, pp. 76–83; UNESCO, *Social Implications of Industrialization and Urbanization South of the Sahara* (Geneva, 1956), pp. 108–109, 115–117, 187, 216–220, 369–372, and 616 ff.; K. El Daghestani, "The Evolution of the Moslem Family in the Middle Eastern Countries," *International Social Science Bulletin*, **6**, 442–451; B. J. Siegel, "Social Structure and Economic Change in Brazil," and S. J. Stein, "The Brazilian Cotton Textile Industry, 1850–1950," both in Kuznets, *et al.*, *Economic Growth*, pp. 388 ff., 433–438; W. Elkan, *An African Labour Force* (Kampala, Uganda, 1956), Ch. 5; Myers, *op. cit.*, p. 177; Linton, *op. cit.*, pp. 83–84; H. Belshaw, "Some Social Aspects of Economic Development in Underdeveloped Areas," in Shannon, *op. cit.*, pp. 88 ff., 191 ff.; G. St. J. Orde Browne, *The African Labourer* (London, 1933), pp. 100–105.

[27] Weber's relevant works include *The Protestant Ethic and the Spirit of Capitalism* (London, 1948); *The Religion of China* (Glencoe, Ill., 1951); and *The Religion of India* (Glencoe, Ill., 1958). For secondary treatments, see T. Parsons, *The Structure of Social Action* (New York, 1937), Chs. 14–15; and R. Bendix, *Max Weber* (New York, 1959), Parts I and II.

[28] R. N. Bellah, *Tokugawa Religion* (Glencoe, Ill., 1957); C. Geertz, *The Social Context of Economic Change* (Cambridge, Mass., 1956).

[29] K. Davis, "Social and Demographic Aspects of Economic Development in India," in Kuznets *et al.*, *Economic Growth*, p. 294; Gerschenkron, *op. cit.*, pp. 22–25; Rostow, *op. cit.*, pp. 26–29.

[30] B. F. Hoselitz, "Non-Economic Barriers to Economic Development," *Economic Development and Cultural Change*, **1**, 9.

[31] Cf., for example, the Indonesian expulsion of needed Dutch teachers and engineers. It has been maintained that the upsurge of regionalism in India has led to a deterioration of English as a linguistic medium for education in Indian universities. See S. E. Harrison, *India: The Most Dangerous Decades* (Princeton, N.J., 1960), pp. 60–95.

[32] J. van der Kroef, "Economic Developments in Indonesia: Some Social and Cultural Impediments," *Economic Development and Cultural Change*, **4**, 116–133.

[33] *The Protestant Ethic and the Spirit of Capitalism*, pp. 181–182.

[34] E. Crankshaw, "Big Business in Russia," *Atlantic*, **202**, 35–41. For discussion of the balance among political and other elements in Soviet society, see R. A. Bauer, A. Inkeles, and C. Kluckhohn, *How the Soviet System Works* (Cambridge, Mass., 1957), Part II.

[35] K. Davis, *Human Society* (New York, 1957), Ch. 14, T. Parsons, "An Analytical Approach to the Theory of Social Stratification," *Essays in Sociological Theory* (rev. ed.; Glencoe, Ill., 1954), Ch. 4.

[36] Marriott, "Social Change in an Indian Village," *Economic Development and Cultural Change*, **1**, 153; UNESCO, *op. cit.*, p. 152; J. S. Coleman, *Nigeria: Background to Nationalism* (Berkeley and Los Angeles, 1958), pp. 70–73.

[37] In some cases, these ascriptive pegs become the basis for political groupings long after the society has begun to modernize. See E. H. Jacoby, *Agrarian Unrest in Southeast Asia* (New York, 1949), pp. 27–28, 50, 76, 91–93, 123–125, and 248; Coleman, *op. cit.*, pp. 332–367. Harrison has argued that the present significance of caste in India is "if anything, stronger than before," but that this significance appears as competitiveness in the new political arena of the country (Harrison, *op. cit.*, Ch. 4; also Davis, *Population of India*; p. 171). William Petersen has suggested that, in the advanced society of Holland, a process of "pillarization" has occurred, in which semi-ascribed religious groups have become the major focus of political and social competition ("Dutch Society vs. Mass Society," University of California Public Lectire, May 9, 1960).

[38] For a study of the cross-cultural similarity in the ranking of industrial occupations in developed countries, see A. Inkeles and P. H. Rossi, "National Comparisons of Occupational Prestige," *American Journal of Sociology*, **61**, 329–339.

[39] S. M. Lipset and R. Bendix, *Social Mobility in Industrial Society* (Berkeley and Los Angeles, 1959), pp. 13 ff. Of course, the transition from collective to individual mobility is not instantaneous. See Marriott, *op. cit.*, p. 153; and Davis, "Social and Demographic Aspects," pp. 308–313.

[40] E. Durkheim, *The Division of Labor in Society* (Glencoe, Ill., 1949), Chs. 3–8. A recent formulation of the relationship between differentiation and integration may be found in R. F. Bales, *Interaction Process Analysis* (Cambridge, Mass., 1950).

[41] Smelser, *Social Change*, Chs. 12–13; T. Parsons and N. Smelser, *Economy and Society* (Glencoe, Ill., 1956), Ch. 3; also Nash, *op. cit.*, p. 275; A. Mehta, "The Mediating Role of the Trade Union in Underdeveloped Countries," *Economic Development and Cultural Change*, **6**, 20–23.

[42] Smelser, *Social Change*, pp. 99–108; Myers, *op. cit.*, pp. 52–54; Stein, *op. cit.*, pp. 433 ff.

[43] Orde Browne, *op. cit.*, pp. 112–116; Doucy, *op. cit.*, pp. 446–450; Elkan, *op. cit.*, Chs. 2–3.

[44] UNESCO, *op. cit.*, pp. 84–85, 105, 120–121, 128–130, 220–221, 373–377, and 469–473; D. Forde, "The Social Impact of Industrialization and Urban Conditions in Africa South of the Sahara," *International Social Science Bulletin*, **7**, 119–121; Hodgkin, *op. cit.*, pp. 85 ff.; Hoselitz, "The City, the Factory," p. 183; Coleman, *op. cit.*, pp. 73–80; Harrison, *op. cit.*, pp. 330–332.

[45] M. Fortes and E. E. Evans-Pritchard (eds.), *African Political Systems* (London, 1940), pp. 1–25.

[46] D. Apter, *The Gold Coast in Transition* (Princeton, 1956); Hodgkin, *op. cit.*, pp. 115–139; G. A. Almond and J. S. Coleman, *The Politics of Developing Areas* (Princeton, 1960).

[47] Marriott, *op. cit.*, p. 152.

[48] Harrison, *op. cit.*, pp. 100 ff.

[49] Hodgkin, *op. cit.*, pp. 85 ff.

[50] Jacoby, *op. cit.*, Ch. 1; R. Emerson, L. A. Mills, and V. Thompson, *Government and Nationalism in Southeast Asia* (New York, 1942), pp. 135–136; S. A. Mosk, *Industrial Revolution in Mexico* (Berkeley and Los Angeles, 1950), pp. 3–17.

[51] S. N. Eisenstadt, "Sociological Aspects of Political Development in Underdeveloped Countries," *Economic Development and Cultural Change*, **5**, 298.

[52] P. T. Bauer and B. S. Yamey, *The Economics of Underdeveloped Countries* (Chicago, 1957), p. 64.

[53] E. Durkheim, *Suicide* (Glencoe, Ill., 1951), Book II, Ch. 5.

[54] Davis, "Social and Demographic Aspects," pp. 296 ff.

[55] E.g., M. A. Jaspan, "A Sociological Case Study: Community Hostility to Imposed Social Change in South Africa," in Ruopp, *op. cit.*, pp. 97–120.

[56] E.g., the conflict between migratory workers and full-time resident workers; see Elkan, *op. cit.*, pp. 23–24.

[57] For theoretical discussions of this relationship between strain and disturbance, see T. Parsons, R. F. Bales, *et al.*, *Family, Socialization, and Interaction Process* (Glencoe, Ill., 1955), Chs. 2, 4; Smelser, *Social Change*, Chs. 2, 9–10.

[58] Jacoby, *op. cit.*, p. 246.

[59] Emerson, *et al.*, *op. cit.*, pp. 25–29; Eisenstadt, *op. cit.*, pp. 294–298; W. Kornhauser, *The Politics of Mass Society* (Glencoe, Ill., 1959), Parts II and III; S. M. Lipset, *Political Man* (Garden City, N.Y., 1960), Ch. 2; M. Watnick, "The Appeal of Communism to the Underdeveloped Peoples," in Hoselitz, *Progress of Underdeveloped Areas*, pp. 152–172.

[60] Eisenstadt, *op. cit.*, p. 294.

[61] M. Matossian, "Ideologies of Delayed Industrialization," *Economic Development and Cultural Change*, **6**, 217–228.

[62] Eisenstadt, *loc. cit.*, J. S. Coleman, "Nationalism in Tropical Africa," in Shannon, *op. cit.*, pp. 42 ff.; Hodgkin, *op. cit.*, p. 56.

[63] Hodgkin, *op. cit.*, pp. 95–150; Coleman, "Nationalism in Tropical Africa," pp. 38 ff.

[64] B. Barber, "Acculturation and Messianic Movements," *American Sociological Review*, **6**, 663–669; H. R. Niebuhr, *The Social Sources of Denominationalism* (New York, 1929); J. B. Holt, "Holiness Religion: Cultural Shock and Social Reorganization," *American Sociological Review*, **5**, 740–747; B. G. M. Sundkler, *Bantu Prophets in South Africa* (London, 1948); P. Worsley, *The Trumpet Shall Sound* (London, 1957).

[65] Emerson *et al.*, *op. cit.*, pp. 136–140; Hodgkin, *op. cit.*, pp. 60–75; C. Robequain, *The Economic Development of French Indo-China* (London, 1944), pp. 79–88; J. S. Furnivall, *Colonial Policy and Practice* (Cambridge, 1948), pp. 116–123; F. Machlup, "Three Economic Systems Clash in Burma," *Review of Economic Studies*, **3**, 140–146.

[66] Emerson *et al.*, *op. cit.*, pp. 141–143; Jacoby, *op. cit.*, Ch. 8.

[67] J. M. van der Kroef, "Minority Problems in Indonesia," *Far Eastern Survey*, **24**, 129–133, 165–171; Harrison, *op. cit.*, Chs. 3–6.

[68] Lipset, *Political Man*, Ch. 3.

[69] J. J. Spengler, "Social Structure, the State, and Economic Growth," in Kuznets *et al.*, *Economic Growth*, pp. 370–379.

Chapter 2

The Meaning of Political Development

THE CONCEPT OF POLITICAL DEVELOPMENT

Lucian W. Pye

. . . Western social science was peculiarly unprepared for providing ready intellectual guidance on the problems of political and social development. Indeed, the very stress of contemporary social science that knowledge must be well grounded in empirical investigation caused many social scientists to feel excessively ill-equipped to pass judgments on the prospects of development in strange and unknown societies; thus, paradoxically, men who considered themselves realists above all else often felt it appropriate to drift along with the almost euphorically optimistic view of the possibilities for rapid development in the new state which were so common a few seasons ago. Since many of the guiding considerations which had given a sense of direction and discipline to the social sciences were directly challenged by the emergence of the problems of development, there was an understandable degree of confusion in the field's reactions. Although by now much of this confusion has subsided and there is a general acceptance of the importance of understanding the nature of political development, there is still

SOURCE. Excerpted from Lucian W. Pye, "The Concept of Political Development," *The Annals of the American Academy of Political and Social Science*, **358**, 1–13, March 1965; using only pp. 4–13.

considerable ambiguity and imprecision in the use of the term "political development."

Diversity of Definitions

It may therefore be helpful to elaborate some of the confusing meanings which are frequently associated with the expression political development. Our purpose in doing so is not to establish or reject any particular definitions, but rather to illuminate a situation of semantic confusion which cannot but impede the development of theory and becloud the purposes of public policy.

Political Development as the Political Prerequisite of Economic Development. When attention was first fixed on the problem of economic growth and the need to transform stagnant economies into dynamic ones with self-sustaining growth, the economists were quick to point out that political and social conditions could play a decisive role in impeding or facilitating advance in per capita income, and thus it was appropriate to conceive of political development as the state of the polity which might facilitate economic growth.

Operationally, however, such a view of political development tends to be essentially negative, because it is easier to be precise about the ways in which performance of a political system may impede or prevent economic development than about how it can facilitate economic growth. This is true because, historically, economic growth has taken place within a variety of political systems and with quite different ranges of public policies.

This leads to the more serious objection that such a concept of political development does not focus on a common set of theoretical considerations, for in some cases it would mean no more than whether a government is following intelligent and economically rational policies while in other situations it would involve far more fundamental considerations about the basic organization of the polity and the entire performance of the society. The problems of political development would thus vary entirely according to the particular economic problems.

Another fundamental difficulty with such a view of political development has become increasingly apparent during the last decade as the prospects for rapid economic development have become exceedingly dim in many of the poor countries. Economies manifestly change far more slowly than political arrangement, and in large numbers of countries substantial economic growth—to say nothing of industrial development—is not likely in our generation although there may still be substantial political change, much of which might, according to other concepts, seem to deserve the label of political development.

Finally there is the objection that in most underdeveloped countries people clearly are concerned with far more than just material advancement, and are anxious about political development quite independently of its effects on the rate of economic growth. Therefore to link political development solely to economic events would be to ignore much that is of dramatic importance in the developing countries.

Political Development as the Poli-tics Typical of Industrial Societies. A second common concept of political development, which is also closely tied to economic considerations, involves an abstract view of the typical kind of politics basic to already industrialized and economically highly advanced societies. The assumption is that industrial life produces a more-or-less common and generic type of political life which any society can seek to approximate whether it is in fact industrialized or not. In this view the industrial societies, whether democratic or not, set certain standards of political behavior and performance which constitute the state of political development and which represent the appropriate goals of development for all other systems.

The specific qualities of political development thus become certain patterns of presumably "rational" and "responsible" governmental behavior: an avoidance of reckless actions which threaten the vested interests of significant segments of the society, some sense of limitations to the sovereignty of politics, an appreciation of the values of orderly administrative and legal procedures, an acknowledgment that politics is rightfully a mechanism for solving problems and not an end in itself, a stress on welfare programs, and finally an acceptance of some form of mass participation.

Political Development as Political Modernization. The view that political development is the typical or idealized politics of industrial societies merges easily with the view that political development is synonymous with political modernization. The advanced industrial nations are the fashion makers and pace setters in most phases of social and economic life, and it is understandable that many people expect the same to be true in the political sphere. It is, however, precisely the too easy acceptance of this view that agitates the defenders of cultural relativism who question the propriety of identifying industrial, that is, Western, practices as the contemporary and universal standards for all political systems.

Granting this objection, particularly when significance becomes attached to mere fad and fashion, it is still possible to discern in the movement of world history the emergence of certain conventions and even social norms which have increasingly been diffused throughout the world and which people generally feel should be recognized by any self-respecting government. Many of these standards do trace back to the emergence of industrial society and the rise of science and technology, but most of them have by now a dynamic of their own. Mass participation, for example, reflects the sociological realities of industrialized life, but it also has been taken to be an absolute right in the spirit of current world views. Other ideals, such as the demand for universalistic laws, respect for merit rather than birth, and generalized concepts of justice and citizenship, seem now to hold a place above any particular culture and thus reasonably belong to some universal standards of modern political life.

The question immediately arises as to what constitutes form and what is substance in this view of political development. Is the test of development the capacity of a country to equip itself with such modern cultural artifacts as political parties, civil and rational administrations, and legislative bodies? If so, then the matter of ethnocentrism may be of great relevance, for most of these institutions do have a peculiarly Western character. If, on the other hand, importance is attached only to the performance of certain substantive functions, then another difficulty arises in that all political systems have, historically, in one fashion or another, performed the essential functions expected of these modern *and* Western institutions. Thus, what is to distinguish between what is more and what is less "developed"? Clearly the problem of

political development—when thought of as being simply political "modernization"—runs into the difficulty of differentiating between what is "Western" and what is "modern." Some additional criteria seem to be necessary if such a distinction is to be made.

Political Development as the Operations of a Nation-State. To some degree these objections are met by the view that political development consists of the organization of political life and the performance of political functions in accordance with the standards expected of a modern nation-state. In this point of view there is an assumption that, historically, there have been many types of political systems and that all communities have had their form of politics, but that with the emergence of the modern nation-state a specific set of requirements about politics came into existence. Thus, if a society is to perform as a modern state, its political institutions and practices must adjust to these requirements of state performance. The politics of historic empires, of tribe and ethnic community, or of colony must give way to the politics necessary to produce an effective nation-state which can operate successfully in a system of other nation-states.

Political development thus becomes the process by which communities that are nation-states only in form and by international courtesy become nation-states in reality. Specifically, this involves the development of a capacity to maintain certain kinds of public order, to mobilize resources for a specific range of collective enterprises, and to make and uphold effectively types of international commitments. The test of political development would thus involve, first, the establishment of a particular set of public institutions which constitute the necessary infrastructure of a nation-state, and, second, the controlled expression in political life of the phenomenon of nationalism. That is to say, political development is the politics of nationalism within the context of state institutions.

It is important to stress that from this point of view nationalism is only a necessary but far from sufficient condition to ensure political development. Development entails the translation of diffuse and unorganized sentiments of nationalism into a spirit of citizenship and, equally, the creation of state institutions which can translate into policy and programs the aspirations of nationalism and citizenship. In brief, political development is nation-building.

Political Development as Administrative and Legal Development. If we divide nation-building into institution-building and citizenship development we have two very common concepts of political development. Indeed, the concept of political development as organization-building has a long history, and it underlies the philosophy of much of the more enlightened colonial practices.

Historically, when the Western nations came in contact with the societies of the rest of the world, one of the principal sources of tension was the discovery that such societies did not share the same Western concepts about law and the nature of public authority in the adjudication of private disputes. Wherever the European went one of his first revealing queries was: "Who is in charge here?" According to the logic of the European mind, every territory should fall under some sovereignty, and all people in the same geographic location should have a common loyalty and the same legal obligations. Also, in these early clashes of culture the European response was to search for legal redress, and the absence of a recognizable legal order made life uncomfortable for these early Europeans. The Western mind, in groping for a *modus vivendi* to carry out day-to-day relations with what appeared to be exotic and bizarre cultures, naturally turned to the law as a means for achieving order and predictability; and in doing so it estab-

lished the notion that political development rested upon the existence of an orderly legal process.

In time, however, it was discovered that the smooth operation of an explicit and formalized legal system depended upon the existence of an orderly administrative system. The realization of law and order thus called for bureaucratic structures and the development of public administration, and throughout the colonial period the concept of development was closely associated with the introduction of rationalized institutions of administration. And certainly one of the principal heritages of the colonial era for the area of nation-building was that it left behind, in varying degrees, administrative structures which have become the important elements in the infrastructures of now independent nation-states. Indeed, it is now common to evaluate the relative successes of various colonial governments according to the extent to which they succeeded in leaving behind workable administrative systems.

Today the tradition continues, as most newly independent countries consider the strengthening of bureaucracies to be a first task in political development. Much of foreign aid and technical assistance which is conceived to be a value for political development centers on programs in public administrations. Yet recent history, like the longer history of colonialism, has demonstrated that political development involves much more than the building of the authoritative structures of government. More important, when such development moves conspicuously ahead of other aspects of social and political development, it may create imbalances in the system which become in time impediments to nation-building in the full sense. Unquestionably the strengthening of public administration is central in any program of nation-building; the point is only that political development must also cover the nonauthoritative institutions of a polity.

Political Development as Mass Mobilization and Participation. Another aspect of political development involves primarily the role of the citizenry and new standards of loyalty and involvement. Quite understandably, in some former colonial countries the dominant view of what constitutes political development is a form of political awakening whereby former subjects become active and committed citizens. In some countries this view is carried to such an extreme that the effective and mass demonstrational aspect of popular politics becomes an end in itself, and leaders and citizens feel that they are advancing national development by the intensity and frequency of demonstrations of mass political passion. Conversely, some countries which are making orderly and effective progress may, nevertheless, be dissatisfied, for they feel that their more demonstrative neighbors are experiencing greater "development."

According to most views, political development does entail some degree of expanded popular participation, but it is important to distinguish among the conditions of such expansion. Historically, in the West this dimension of political development was closely associated with the widening of suffrage and the induction of new elements of the population into the political process. This process of mass participation meant a diffusion of decision-making, and participation brought some influence on choice and decision. In some of the new states, however, mass participation has not been coupled with an electoral process, but has been essentially a new form of mass response to elite manipulation. It should be recognized that even such limited participation has a role to play in nation-building, for it represents a means of creating new loyalties and a new feeling of national identity.

Thus, although the process of mass participation is a legitimate part of political development it is also fraught with the dangers of either sterile emotionalism or corrupting demagoguery, both of which can sap the strength of a society. The problem, of course, is the classic issue of balancing popular sentiments with public order: that is, the fundamental problem of democracy.

Political Development as the Building of Democracy. This brings us to the view that political development is or should be synonymous with the establishment of democratic institutions and practices. Certainly implicit in many people's view is the assumption that the only form of political development worthy of the name is the building of democracies. Indeed, there are those who would make explicit this connection and suggest that development can only have meaning in terms of some form of ideology, whether democracy, communism, or totalitarianism. According to this view, development only has meaning in terms of the strengthening of some set of values, and to try to pretend that this is not the case is self-deceiving.

As refreshing as it is to find examples of forthright and explicit identification of democracy with development, there is substantial resistance within the social sciences to such an approach. In part this is no doubt the result of a common aspiration within the social sciences to become a value-free science. Even when it is recognized that in an extreme form this aspiration is naive, there is still a sense of propriety which dictates that the categories of social science analysis should reflect reality rather than values.

Also, as a practical matter in the conduct of foreign aid policies Americans have for interesting and revealing reasons believed, probably quite falsely, that it would be easier for us in our relations with underdeveloped countries to talk about "development" rather than "democracy." In this brief survey of attitudes and views we cannot go any deeper into the complex ambiguities which surround the view that development is close to, but not really the same as, democracy. We must instead proceed with our analysis and note that there are those who are equally forthright in asserting that development is fundamentally different from democracy, and that the very attempt to introduce democracy can be a positive liability to development.

Political Development as Stability and Orderly Change. Many of those who feel that democracy is inconsistent with rapid development conceive of development almost entirely in economic or social order terms. The political component of such a view usually centers on the concept of political stability based on a capacity for purposeful and orderly change. Stability that is merely stagnation and an arbitrary support of the status quo is clearly not development, except when its alternative is manifestly a worse state of affairs. Stability is, however, legitimately linked with the concept of development in that any form of economic and social advancement does generally depend upon an environment in which uncertainty has been reduced and planning based on reasonably safe predictions is possible.

This view of development can be restricted mainly to the political sphere because a society in which the political process is capable of rationally and purposefully controlling and directing social change rather than merely responding to it is clearly more "developed" than one in which the political process is the hapless victim of social and economic "forces" that willy-nilly control the destiny of the people. Thus, in the same fashion, as it has been argued that in modern societies man controls nature for his purpose, while in traditional societies man sought mainly to adapt to nature's dictates, we can conceive of political development as depending upon a capacity either to control social change or to be controlled by it. And, of course, the starting point in controlling social forces is the capacity to maintain order.

The problem with this view of development is that it leaves unanswered how much order is necessary or desirable and for what purposes change should be directed. There is also the question of whether the coupling of stability and change is not something which can only occur in the dreams of a middle class, or at least in societies that are far better off than most of the currently underdeveloped ones. Finally, on the scale of priorities there is the feeling that the maintenance of order, however desirable and even essential, stands second to getting things done, and thus development calls for a somewhat more positive view of action.

Political Development as Mobilization and Power. The recognition that political systems should meet some test of performance and be of some utility to society leads us to the concept of political development as the capabilities of a system. When it is argued that democracy may reduce the efficiency of a system there is an implied assumption that it is possible to measure political efficiency; and in turn the notion of efficiency suggests theoretical or idealized models against which reality can be tested.

This point of view leads to the concept that political systems can be evaluated in terms of the level or degree of absolute power which the system is able to mobilize. Some systems which may or may not be stable seem to operate with a very low margin of power, and the authoritative decision makers are close to being impotent in their capacity to initiate and consummate policy objectives. In other societies such decision makers have at their command substantial power, and the society can therefore achieve a wider range of common goals. States naturally differ according to their inherent resource base, but the measure of development is the degree to which they are able to maximize and realize the full potential of their given resources.

It should be noted that this does not necessarily lead to a crude authoritarian view of development as simply the capacity of a government to claim resources from the society. The capacity to mobilize and allocate resources is usually crucially affected by the popular support which the regime commands, and this is why democratic systems can often mobilize resources more efficiently than repressive authoritarian ones. Indeed, in practical terms the problem of achieving greater political development in many societies may involve primarily the realization of greater popular favor —not because of any absolute value of democracy but because only with such support can the system realize a higher degree of mobilization of power.

When political development is conceived of in terms of mobilization and an increase in the absolute level of power in the society, it becomes possible to distinguish both a purpose for development and also a range of characteristics associated with development. Many of these characteristics, in turn, can be measured, and hence it is possible to construct indices of development. Items in such indices might include: prevalence and penetration. of the mass media measured in terms of newspaper circulation and distribution of radios, the tax basis of the society, the proportion of population in government and their distribution in various categories of activities, and the proportion of resources allocated to education, defense, and social welfare.

Political Development as One Aspect of a Multidimensional Process of Social Change. The obvious need for theoretical assumptions to guide the selection of the items that should appear in any index for measuring development leads us to the view that political development is somehow intimately associated with other aspects of social and economic change. This is true because any item which may be relevant in explaining the power potential of a country must also reflect the state of the economy and the social order. The argument can be advanced that it is unnecessary and inappropriate to try to isolate political development too completely from other

forms of development. Although to a limited extent the political sphere may be autonomous from the rest of society, for sustained political development to take place it can only be within the context of a multidimensional process of social change in which no segment for dimension of the society can long lag behind.

According to this point of view, all forms of development are related, development is much the same as modernization, and it takes place within a historical context in which influences from outside the society impinge on the processes of social change just as change in the different aspects of a society—the economy, the polity and social order— all impinge on each other.

The Development Syndrome

There are other possible interpretations of political development—for example, the view common in many former colonies that development means a sense of national self-respect and dignity in international affairs, or the view more common in advanced societies that political development should refer to a postnationalism era when the nation-state will no longer be the basic unit of political life. It would also be possible to distinguish other variations on the theme which we have just presented. For our purposes we have gone far enough to point out, first, the degree of confusion that exists with the term political development and, second, the extent to which behind this confusion there does seem to be a certain more solid basis of agreement. Without trying to assert any particular philosophical orientation or theoretical framework, it may be useful to scan the various definitions or points of view which we have just reviewed in order to isolate those characteristics of political development which seem to be most widely held and most fundamental in general thinking about the problems of development.[1]

[1] The themes basic to the concept of political development which follow reflect the work of

The first broadly shared characteristic which we would note is a general spirit or attitude toward equality. In most views on the subject political development does involve mass participation and popular involvement in political activities. Participation may be either democratic or a form of totalitarian mobilization, but the key consideration is that subjects should become active citizens and at least the pretenses of popular rule are necessary.

Equality also means that laws should be of a universalistic nature, applicable to all and more or less impersonal in their operations. Finally, equality means that recruitment to political office should reflect achievement standards of performance and not the ascriptive considerations of a traditional social system.

A second major theme which we find in most concepts of political development deals with the capacity of a political system. In a sense capacity is related to the outputs of a political system and the extent to which the political system can affect the rest of the society and economy. Capacity is also closely associated to governmental performance and the conditions which affect such performance. More specifically, capacity entails first of all the sheer magnitude, scope and scale of political and governmental performance. Developed systems are presumed to be able to do a lot more and touch upon a far wider variety of social life than less developed systems can. Secondly, capacity means effectiveness and efficiency in the execution of public policy. Developed systems presumably not only do more than others but perform faster and with much greater thoroughness. Finally, capacity is related to ration-

ality in administration and a secular orientation toward policy.

A third theme which runs through much of the discussion of political development is that of differentiation and specialization. This is particularly true in the analysis of institutions and structures. Thus, this aspect of development involves first of all the differentiation and specialization of structures. Offices and agencies tend to have their distinct and limited functions, and there is an equivalent of a division of labor within the realm of government. With differentiation there is also, of course, increased functional specificity of the various political roles within the system. And, finally, differentiation also involves the integration of complex structures and processes. That is, differentiation is not fragmentation and the isolation of the different parts of the political system but specialization based on an ultimate sense of integration.

In recognizing these three dimensions of equality, capacity, and differentiation as lying at the heart of the development process, we do not mean to suggest that they necessarily fit easily together. On the contrary, historically, the tendency has usually been that there are acute tensions between the demands for equality, the requirements for capacity, and the processes of greater differentiation. Pressure for greater equality can challenge the capacity of the system, and differentiation can reduce equality by stressing the importance of quality and specialized knowledge.

Indeed, it may, in fact, be possible to distinguish different patterns of development according to the sequential order in which different societies have dealt with the different aspects of the development syndrome. In this sense development is clearly not unilinear, nor is it governed by sharp and distinct stages, but rather by a range of problems that may arise separately or concurrently. In seeking to pattern these different courses of development and to analyze the dif-

[*footnote 1 continued*
the Committee on Comparative Politics of the Social Science Research Council and will be developed in much greater detail in a forthcoming volume, *The Political System and Political Development*, to be published in the series, "Studies in Political Development," by the Princeton University Press.

ferent types of problems, it is useful to note that the problems of equality are generally related to the political culture and sentiments about legitmacy and commitment to the system; the problems of capacity are generally related to the performance of the authoritative structures of government, and the questions of differentiation touch mainly on the performance of the nonauthoritative structures and the general political process in the society at large. This suggests that in the last analysis the problems of political development revolve around the relationships between the political culture, the authoritative structures, and the general political process.

A DEVELOPMENTAL APPROACH TO POLITICAL SYSTEMS: AN OVERVIEW

Gabriel A. Almond and G. Bingham Powell, Jr.

The Political System

The term "political system" has become increasingly common in the titles of texts and monographs in the field of comparative politics. The older texts used such terms as "government," "nation," or "state" to describe what we call a political system. Something more is involved here than mere style of nomenclature. This new terminology reflects a new way of looking at political phenomena. It includes some new names for old things, and some new terms to refer to activities and processes which were not formerly recognized as being parts or aspects of politics.

The older terms—state, government, nation—are limited by legal and institutional meanings. They direct attention to a particular set of institutions usually found in modern Western societies. If one accepts the idea that the study of such institutions is the proper and sole concern of political science, many problems are thereby avoided, including the thorny question of limiting the subject matter of the discipline. However, the costs of such a decision are

very high. The role played by formal governmental institutions such as legislatures and courts in different societies varies greatly; in many societies, particularly in those outside the Western world, their role may not be so important as that of other institutions and processes. In all societies the role of formal governmental institutions is shaped and limited by informal groups, political attitudes, and a multitude of interpersonal relationships. If political science is to be effective in dealing with political phenomena in all kinds of societies, regardless of culture, degree of modernization, and size, we need a more comprehensive framework of analysis.

The concept of "political system" has acquired wide currency because it directs attention to the entire scope of political activities within a society, regardless of where in the society such activities may be located. What is the political system? How do we define its boundaries? What gives the political system its special identity? Many political scientists have dealt with these questions; while the precise language of their definitions varies considerably, there is some consensus. Common to most of these definitions is the association of the political system with the use of legitimate physical coercion in societies. Easton speaks of *authoritative allocation of values;*

SOURCE: Excerpted from Gabriel A. Almond and G. Bingham Powell, Jr., *Comparative Politics: A Developmental Approach* (Boston: Little, Brown and Company, 1966), Chap. II, using only pp. 16–30, 34–41.

Lasswell and Kaplan, of *severe deprivations;* Dahl, of *power, rule, and authority.*[1] All these definitions imply legitimate, heavy sanctions; the rightful power to punish, to enforce, to compel. We agree with Max Weber[2] that legitimate force is the thread that runs through the action of the political system, giving it its special quality and importance, and its coherence as a system. The political authorities, and only they, have some generally accepted right to utilize coercion and command obedience based upon it. (Force is "legitimate" where this belief in the justifiable nature of its use exists.) The inputs which enter the political system are all in some way related to legitimate physical compulsion, whether these are demands for war or for recreational facilities. The outputs of the political system are also all in some way related to legitimate physical compulsion, however remote the relationship may be. Thus, public recreation facilities are usually supported by taxation, and any violation of the regulations governing their use is a legal offense. When we speak of the political system, we include all the interactions which affect the use or threat of use of legitimate physical coercion. The political system includes not only governmental institutions such as legislatures, courts, and administrative agencies, but *all structures in their political aspects.* Among these are traditional structures such as kinship ties and caste groupings; and anomic phenomena such as assassinations, riots, and demonstrations; as well as formal organizations like parties, interest groups, and media of communication.

We are not, then, saying that the political system is concerned solely with force, violence, or compulsion; rather, that its relation to coercion is its distinctive quality. Political elites are usually concerned with goals such as national expansion or security, social welfare, the aggrandizement of their power over other groups, increased popular participation in politics, and the like; but their concern with these values as politicians is related to compulsory actions such as law making and law enforcement, foreign and defense policy, and taxation. The political system is not the only system that makes rules and enforces them, but its rules and enforcements go all the way to compelling obedience or performance.

There are societies in which the accepted power to use physical compulsion is widely diffused, shared by family, by clan, by religious bodies, or other kinds of groups, or taken up privately, as in the feud or the duel. But we consider even these as political systems of a particular kind, and still comparable with those polities in which there is something approaching a monopoly of legitimate physical coercion.

If what we have said above defines the "political" half of our concept, what do we mean by "system"? A system implies the interdependence of parts, and a boundary of some kind between it and its environment. By "interdependence" we mean that when the properties of one component in a system change, all the other components and the system as a whole are affected. Thus, if the rings of an automobile erode, the car "burns oil"; the functioning of other aspects of the system deteriorates, and the power of the car declines. Or, as another example, there are points in the growth of organisms when some change in the endocrine system affects the over-all pattern of growth, the functioning of all the parts, and the general behavior of the organism. In political systems the emergence of mass parties, or of media of mass

[1] David Easton, *The Political System* (New York: Alfred A. Knopf, Inc., 1953), pp. 130 ff., and his *A Framework for Political Analysis* (Englewood Cliffs: Prentice-Hall, Inc., 1965), pp. 50 ff.; Harold D. Lasswell and Abraham Kaplan, *Power and Society* (New Haven: Yale University Press, 1950); Robert A. Dahl, *Modern Political Analysis* (Englewood Cliffs: Prentice-Hall, Inc., 1963), pp. 5 ff.

[2] See Max Weber, "Politics as a Vocation," in his *From Max Weber: Essays in Sociology,* ed. Hans H. Gerth and C. Wright Mills (New York: Oxford University Press, 1946), pp. 77–78.

communication, changes the performance of all the other structures of the system and affects the general capabilities of the system in its domestic and foreign environments. In other words, when one variable in a system changes in magnitude or in quality, the others are subjected to strains and are transformed; the system changes its pattern of performance, or the unruly component is disciplined by regulatory mechanisms.

A second aspect of the concept of "system" is the notion of boundary. A system starts somewhere and stops somewhere. In considering an organism or an automobile, it is relatively easy to locate its boundary and to specify the interactions between it and its environment. The gas goes into the tank, the motor converts it into revolutions of the crankshaft and the driving wheels, and the car moves on the highway. In dealing with social systems, of which political systems are a class, the problem of boundary is not that easy. Social systems are made up not of individuals, but of roles. A family, for example, consists of the roles of mother and father, husband and wife, sibling and sibling. The family is only one set of interacting roles for its members, who also may have roles outside the family in schools, business firms, and churches. In the same sense a political system is made up of the interacting roles of nationals, subjects, voters, as the case may be, with legislators, bureaucrats, and judges. The same individuals who perform roles in the political system perform roles in other social systems such as the economy, the religious community, the family, and voluntary associations. As individuals expose themselves to political communication, form interest groups, vote, or pay taxes, they shift from nonpolitical to political roles. One might say that on election day as citizens leave their farms, plants, and offices to go to the polling places, they are crossing the boundary from the economy to the polity.

Another example of a shift in the bound-ary of the political system might occur when inflation reduces the real income of certain groups in the population. When such a change in the economic situation of particular groups gets converted into demands for public policy or for changes in political personnel, there is an interaction between the economy and the polity. Certain psychic states resulting from changes in the economic situation are converted into demands on the political system. Demands are made on trade-union or other pressure-group leaders to lobby for particular actions by the legislature or by executive agencies. Somewhere in this process a boundary is crossed from one system to another—from the economic system to the political system.

The boundaries of political systems are subject to relatively large fluctuations. During wartime the boundaries become greatly extended as large numbers of men are recruited into military service, as business firms are subjected to regulations, and as internal security measures are taken. In an election the boundaries again are greatly extended as voters become politicians for a day. With the return to more normal conditions, the boundaries of the political system contract.

The problem of boundaries takes on special significance because systems theory usually divides interaction processes into three phases—input, conversion, output. Any set of interacting parts—any system—which is affected by factors in its environment may be viewed in this fashion. The inputs and outputs, which involve the political system with other social systems, are transactions between the system and its environment; the conversion processes are internal to the political system. When we talk about the sources of inputs, their number, content, and intensity, and how they enter the political system, and of the number and content of outputs and how they leave the political system and affect other social systems, we shall in effect be talking about the boundaries of the political system.

Structure and Culture

The terms "structure" and "culture" are also of central importance in our analytical scheme. By "structure" we mean the observable activities which make up the political system. To refer to these activities as having a structure simply implies that there is a certain regularity to them. Thus, in a court one can speak of the interactions between the judge, the jury, the prosecuting and defense attorneys, witnesses, the defendant, and the plaintiff. This example should make clear that when we speak of political activity, we are not referring to the total activities of the individual who may be involved in it, but just to that part of his activities which is involved in the political process. Judges, lawyers, witnesses, defendants, and plaintiffs are all men who have a variety of other spheres of activity. That particular part of the activity of individuals which is involved in political processes we refer to as the role. The units which make up all social systems, including political systems, are *roles*. The individual members of a society usually perform roles in a variety of social systems other than the political system—for example, in families, business firms, churches, social clubs.

One of the basic units of political systems, then, is the political role. We refer to particular sets of roles which are related to one another as *structures*. Thus, judgeship is a role; a court is a structure of roles. The reason we use the terms "role" and "structure" rather than "office" and "institution" is that we wish to emphasize the actual behavior of the individuals who are involved in politics, and the actual performance of the particular institution with which we may be concerned. Both "office" and "institution" may refer to formal rules, such as those presumed to govern the behavior of judges and juries, or to some ideal mode of behavior toward which we might wish them to aspire. "Role" and "structure" refer to the observable behavior of individuals. Legal rules and ideal norms

may affect that behavior, but they rarely describe it fully.

Beginning with the concept of role as one of the basic units of a political system, we may speak of a subsystem (for example, a legislative body) as consisting of related and interacting roles; and of the political system as a set of interacting subsystems (for example, legislatures, electorates, pressure groups, and courts).

We need to introduce two other concepts before we leave this discussion of role and structure. If this book is to have a developmental emphasis, we have to deal with those processes which maintain or change political systems over time. The incumbents of political roles are superseded or die. New sets of political roles are established, and old ones may be abolished or may atrophy. Every political system is continually involved in *recruiting* individuals into political roles. We speak, then, of the *recruitment function*, which must be performed in all political systems if its roles are to be manned and if its structures are to function. A principal aspect of the development or transformation of the political system is what we call *role differentiation*, or *structural differentiation*. By "differentiation" we refer to the processes whereby roles change and become more specialized or more autonomous or whereby new types of roles are established or new structures and subsystems emerge or are created. When we speak of role differentiation and structural differentiation, we refer not only to the development of new types of roles and the transformation of older ones; we refer also to changes which may take place in the relationship between roles, between structures, or between subsystems. Thus, for example, courts were established as separate structures long before they acquired independence or autonomy from the other structures of the political system. In speaking of the *developmental aspect* of role and structure then, we are interested not only in the emergence of new types of roles or the atrophy of old ones, but also in the changing patterns of interaction among roles, structures, and subsystems.

There is another principal dimension which runs throughout this book, the concept of political culture. We all know that there is more to a man than what shows on the surface. In the same sense, there is more to a political system than may be clearly manifested over a given period of time. For example, Italy under Fascism appeared to be a quite formidable and powerful political system. It repressed opposition, held massive and impressive parades, and defeated the Ethiopians. But then it had great difficulty coping with the Greeks, and it began to collapse in Africa when whole army divisions retreated and surrendered without much of a fight. A simple obesrvational study of Italian politics during this period would not have helped us predict the capacity of the Italian political system to carry out its policies. Had we known more of the mood and the attitude of the Italian population, more of the morale and the commitment of its soldiers, more of the resoluteness of its officers and of the capacity for policymaking of its political elites, we might have been able to predict the viability of this political system when confronted with unusual pressure and opposition.

In studying any political system, therefore, we need to know its underlying propensities as well as its actual performance over a given period of time. We refer to these propensities, or this psychological dimension of the political system, as the *political culture*. It consists of attitudes, beliefs, values, and skills which are current in an entire population, as well as those special propensities and patterns which may be found within separate parts of that population. Thus, regional groups or ethnic groups or social classes which make up the population of a political system may have special propensities or tendencies. We refer to these special propensities located in particular groups as *subcultures*. Similarly, there may be traditions and attitudes current in the different roles, structures, and subsystems of the political system. Thus, French military officers or bureaucratic officials may have a special culture which differentiates them from French politicians, for example.

Thus, the analysis of the political system must consist not only of observation of the actual patterns of behavior and interaction over a period of time, but also of those subjective propensities located in the political system as a whole and in its various parts. As we learn about the *structure* and *culture* of a political system, our capacity to characterize its properties, and to predict and explain its performance, is improved.

We need also to speak of two concepts that are related to political culture. The propensities, atitudes, beliefs, and values to which we have referred are the consequence of *political socialization*. This is the process whereby political attitudes and values are inculcated as children become adults and as adults are recruited into ro¹es. Finally, we need a concept to deal with the developmental aspect of political culture, a concept comparable to that of differentiation in the dimension of political structure. The term commonly used here is *secularization*. Secularization is the process whereby men become increasingly rational, analytical, and empirical in their political action. We may illustrate this concept by comparing a political leader in a modern democracy with a political leader in a traditional or primitive African political system. A modern democratic political leader when running for office, for instance, will gather substantial amounts of information about the constituency which he hopes will elect him and the issues of public policy with which that constituency may be concerned. He has to make estimates of the distribution and intensity of demands of one kind or another; he needs to use creative imagination in order to identify a possible combination of demands which may lead to his receiving a majority of the votes in his constituency. A village chief in a tribal society operates largely with a given set of goals and a given set of means of attaining those goals which have grown up and been hallowed by custom. The secularization of culture is the processes whereby traditional orientations and attitudes give way to more dynamic decision-making processes involving the gathering of information, the evaluation of information, the laying out of alternative courses of action, the selection of a course of action among these possible courses, and the means whereby one tests whether or not a given course of action is producing the consequences which were intended.

When we use the developmental concepts "structural differentiation" and "cultural secularization," we do not imply that there is any inevitable trend in these directions in the development of political systems.[3] If we examine the histories of political systems, it becomes quite clear that regressions, or reversals, occur commonly in the development of political systems. Thus, the Roman Empire reached a very high level of structural differentiation and cultural secularization, and then fell apart into a large number of less differentiated and less secularized political systems. Whatever the direction may be in a given period of time and in a given political system, we may still speak of development in terms of the degree of differentiation and secularization.

Inputs and Outputs

We have described the political system as consisting of interacting roles, structures, and subsystems, and of underlying psychological propensities which affect these interactions. Such a process may be viewed as consisting of inputs from the environment or from within the political system itself, the conversion of these inputs within the system, and the production of outputs into

the environment. Outputs may produce changes in the environment, which in turn may affect the political system (feedback).

David Easton, the first political scientist to analyze politics in explicit system terms, distinguishes two types of inputs into the political system: *demands* and *supports*.[4] Demands may be subclassified in many ways. The following classification illustrates the range and the variety of demands made upon the political system: (1) demands for allocations of goods and services, such as demands for wage and hour laws, educational opportunities, recreational facilities, roads, and transportation; (2) demands for the regulation of behavior, such as provisions for public safety, controls over markets, and rules pertaining to marriage, health, and sanitation; (3) demands for participation in the political system—for the right to vote, to hold office, to petition government bodies and officials, and to organize political associations; (4) demands for communication and information, such as demands for the affirmation of norms, the communication of policy intent from policy elites, or the display of majesty and power of the political system in periods of threat or on ceremonial occasions. A political system may face these sorts of demands in many combinations, forms, and degrees of intensity.

A second type of input is supports.

> Inputs of demands are not enough to keep a political system operating. They are only the raw material out of which finished products called decisions are manufactured. Energy in the form of actions or orientations promoting and resisting a political system, the demands arising in it, and the decisions issuing from it must also be put into the system to keep it running.[5]

[3] See S. P. Huntington, "Political Development and Political Decay," *World Politics*, April, 1965.

[4] David Easton, "An Approach to the Analysis of Political Systems," *World Politics*, April, 1957, pp. 383–408. For a full elaboration of Easton's approach, see his *A Systems Analysis of Political Life* (New York: John Wiley & Sons, Inc., 1965).

[5] Easton, *World Politics, op. cit.*, p. 390.

Examples of support classifications are: (1) material supports, such as the payment of taxes or other levies, and the provision of services such as labor on public works or military service; (2) obedience to law and regulations; (3) participatory supports, such as voting, political discussion, and other forms of political activity; (4) attention paid to governmental communication, and the manifestation of deference or respect to public authority, symbols, and ceremonials. If the political system and the elites acting in its roles are to process demands effectively, supports must be received from other social systems and from individuals acting in the political system. Generally speaking, demands affect the policies or goals of the system, while supports such as goods and services, obedience, and deference, provide the resources which enable a political system to extract, regulate, and distribute—in other words, to carry out its goals.

We do not wish to leave the impression, of course, that inputs necessarily come only from the society of which the political system is a part. It is typical of political systems that inputs are generated internally by political elites—kings, presidents, ministers, legislators, and judges. Similarly, inputs may come from the international system in the form of threats, invasions, controls, and assistance from foreign political systems. The flow of inputs and outputs includes transactions between the political system and the components of its domestic and foreign environments, and inputs may come from any one of these three sources—the domestic society, the political elites, and the international environment.

On the output side of the process we may speak of four classes of transactions initiated by the political system. These usually correspond closely to the supports we have listed; they may or may not be responsive to demands, depending on the kind of political system which is involved. These are: (1) extractions, which may take the form of tribute, booty, taxes, or personal services; (2) regulations of behavior, which may take a variety of forms and affect the whole gamut of human behavior and relations; (3) allocations or distribution of goods and services, opportunities, honors, statuses, and the life; (4) symbolic outputs, including affirmations of values, displays of political symbols, statements of policies and intents.

The Functional Aspects of Political Systems

This discussion of flows of inputs and outputs leads logically to a consideration of the *functions* of political systems. We have already suggested that *functionalism* is an old theme in political theory. In its modern form, the stress on functionalism is derived from anthropological and sociological theory. The chief social theorists associated with functionalism are the anthropologists Malinowski and Radcliffe-Brown and the sociologists Parsons, Merton, and Marion Levy.[6] Although these men differ substantially in their concepts of system and function, essentially they have said that the ability to explain and predict in the social sciences is enhanced when we think of social structures and institutions as performing functions in systems. By comparing the performance of structures and the regulatory role of political culture as they fulfill common functions in all systems, we may analyze systems which appear very different from one another.

The functioning of any system may be

[6] Bronislaw Malinowski, *Magic, Science and Religion and Other Essays* (Garden City: Doubleday & Company, Inc., 1954); A. R. Radcliffe-Brown, *Structure and Function in Primitive Society* (New York: The Free Press of Glencoe, 1957); Talcott Parsons, *Essays in Sociological Theory Pure and Applied* (New York: The Free Press of Glencoe, 1959) and *The Social System* (New York: The Free Press of Glencoe, 1951); Talcott Parsons and Edward Shils (eds.), *Toward a General Theory of Action* (Cambridge: Harvard University Press, 1951); Robert K. Merton, *Social Theory and Social Structure* (New York: The Free Press of Glencoe, 1957); Marion Levy, *The Structure of Society* (Princeton: Princeton University Press, 1952).

viewed on different levels. One level of functioning is the system's *capabilities*, that is, the way it performs as a unit in its environment. Animals move while plants do not. Some machines process data; others produce power. An economy produces and distributes physical goods and services. Families produce children and socialize them into adult roles and disciplines. At this level we are focusing on the behavior of the system as a unit in its relations to other social systems and to the environment.

When we speak of the capabilities of a political system, we are looking for an orderly way to describe its over-all performance in its environment. The categories of capability which we use grow directly out of our analysis of types of inputs and outputs. Some political systems are primarily *regulative* and *extractive* in character. Totaliarian systems suppress demands coming from their societies and are unresponsive to demands coming from the international environment. At the same time, they regulate and coerce behavior in their societies, and seek to draw maximum resources from their populations. Communist totalitarianism differs from fascist totalitarianism in having a strong *distributive* capability as well. This means that the political system itself actively shifts resources from some groups in the population to other groups. In democracies outputs of regulation, extraction, and distribution are more affected by inputs of demands from groups in the society. Thus we may speak of democracies as having a higher *responsive* capability. These concepts of *regulative*, *extractive*, *distributive*, and *responsive* capability are simply ways of talking about the flows of activity into and out of the political system. They tell us how a system is performing in its environment, how it is shaping this environment, and how it is being shaped by it.

The second level of functioning is internal to the system. Here we refer to *conversion processes*. Physiological examples would be the digestion of foods, the elimination of waste, the circulation of the blood, and the transmission of impulses through the nervous system. The conversion processes, or functions, are the ways systems transform inputs into outputs. In the political system this involves the ways in which demands and supports are transformed into authoritative decisions and are implemented. Obviously the capabilities and the conversion processes of a system are related. In order for an animal to be able to move, hunt, and dig, energy must be created in the organism, and the use of the energy must be controlled and directed.

The conversion processes of one political system may be analyzed and compared with those of other systems according to a sixfold functional scheme. We need to look at the ways in which (1) demands are formulated (interest articulation); (2) demands are combined in the form of alternative courses of action (interest aggregation); (3) authoritative rules are formulated (rule making); (4) these rules are applied and enforced (rule application); (5) these applications of rules are adjudicated in individual cases (rule adjudication); and (6) these various activities are communicated both within the political system, and between the political system and its environment (communication).

Finally, we shall speak of *system maintenance and adaptation functions*. For an automobile to perform efficienctly on the road, parts must be lubricated, repaired, and replaced. New parts may perform stiffly; they must be broken in. In a political system the incumbents of the various roles (diplomats, military officers, tax officials) must be recruited to these roles and learn how to perform in them. New roles are created and new personnel "broken in." These functions (in machines, maintenance and replacement of parts; in political systems, *socialization* and *recruitment* of people) were discussed earlier in this chapter. They do not directly enter into the conversion processes of the system, but they affect the internal efficiency and propensities of the system, and hence condition its performance.

. . .

The Development of Political Systems

The events which lead to political development come from the international environment, from the domestic society, or from political elites within the political system itself. A political system may be threatened by a rival nation, or be invaded by it. In confronting this challenge it may find that it needs more resources and more effective ways of organizing and deploying its resources—a standing army, for example, or an officialdom to collect taxes. It may have to adapt itself structurally, that is, develop new roles, if it is to survive. If the international threat continues over a long period of time, it may have to adapt itself culturally, inculcating attitudes of militance and acquiring the skills and values associated with warfare.

The challenge may come from internal change in the society of which the political system is a part. Thriving commerce and manufactures may create a middle class which demands that it be heard in the making and implementation of public policy. The political elites themselves may confront the political system with a challenge as they seek to increase the resources available to them for the purpose of constructing impressive buildings or monuments, or for creating a military force capable of conquering neighboring political systems.

The impulses for political development consequently involve some significant change in the magnitude and content of the flow of inputs into the political system. *Development* results when the existing structure and culture of the political system is unable to cope with the problem or challenge which confronts it without further structural differentiation and cultural secularization. It should also be pointed out that a decline in the magnitude or a significant change in the content of the flow of inputs may result in "development" in the negative or regressive sense. The capabilities of the political system may decline or be overloaded; roles and structures may atrophy; the culture may regress to a more traditional pattern of orientation. History is full of cases of the decline of empires and their breakup into less differentiated and less secularized components.[7] Transitional and developed societies also may exhibit the collapse of differentiated modern structures and the dominance of irrational appeals and attitudes when the strains become too great.

We need some way of talking about these challenges which may lead to political development, these changes in the magnitude and content of the flow of inputs which put the existing culture and structure under strain. As a beginning we may suggest four types of problems for or challenges to a political system. The first of these is the problem of penetration and integration; we refer to this as the problem of *state building*. The second type of system-development problem is that of loyalty and commitment, which we refer to as *nation building*. The third problem is that of *participation*, the pressure from groups in the society for having a part in the decision making of the system. And the fourth is the problem of *distribution*, or welfare, the pressure from the domestic society to employ the coercive power of the political system to redistribute income, wealth, opportunity, and honor.

The problem of state building may arise out of a threat to the survival of the political system from the international environment. It may also arise out of a threat to the political system from the society in the form of revolutionary pressure challenging the stability or the survival of the political system. Or, it may result from the development among the political elite of new goals, such

[7] Samuel P. Huntington, "Political Development and Political Decay," *World Politics*, April, 1965; S. N. Eisenstadt, *The Political Systems of Empires* (New York: The Free Press of Glencoe, 1962).

as national expansion or the creation of an extravagant court life. State building occurs when the political elite creates new structures and organizations designed to "penetrate" the society in order to regulate behavior in it and draw a larger volume of resources from it. State building is commonly associated with significant increases in the regulative and extractive capabilities of the political system, with the development of a centralized and penetrative bureaucracy related to the increase in these capabilities, and with the development of attitudes of obedience and compliance in the population which are associated with the emergence of such a bureaucracy.

While it is an oversimplification to put it this way, we might view the problem of state building and its successful confrontation by a political system as essentially a structural problem. That is to say, what is involved is primarily a matter of the differentiation of new roles, structures, and subsystems which penetrate the countryside. Nation building, on the other hand, emphasizes the cultural aspects of political development. It refers to the process whereby people transfer their commitment and loyalty from smaller tribes, villages, or petty principalities to the larger central political system. While these two processes of state and nation building are related, it is important to view them separately. There are many cases in which centralized and penetrative bureaucracies have been created, while a homogeneous pattern of loyalty and commitment to the central political institutions has never emerged. The Austro-Hungarian Empire and even modern Italy represent cases in point. In fact, there are examples, particularly among the great empires such as Imperial Rome, in which the elite never sought to create a common national culture of loyalty and commitment, but were content to develop a centralized and penetrative bureaucracy, while at the same time permitting culturally distinct component units to survive and retain some autonomy.

The problem, or challenge, of participation commonly has to do with rapid increases in the volume and intensity of demands for a share in the decision making of the political system by various groups and strata in the domestic society. Such increases in demands for participation are usually associated with, or have the consequence of producing, some form of political infrastructure—political groups, cliques, and factions, and representative legislative assemblies. Demands for participation may also challenge a political system to develop political competence and the attitudes associated with it among groups in the society, and responsive attitudes and bargaining skills among the elite.

Finally, the problem of distribution, or welfare, occurs when there is a rapid increase in the volume and intensity of demands that the political system control or affect the distribution of resources or values (for example, opportunity) among different elements of the population. A positive response to such a challenge by the political elite may produce fundamental changes in bureaucratic organization, and in the political attitudes of both the political elite and the general population.

We have listed these problems of system development in the sequence in which they have occurred in the emergence of the political systems of Western Europe. By and large, state and nation building occurred before the nations of Western Europe had to confront the problems of participation and welfare. But our purpose is to develop an analytical scheme which will enable us to explain the characteristics of any political system. In our efforts to account for the peculiar patterns of performance of political systems, we must examine the ways in which they have encountered these system-development problems in the past or are encountering them in the present. Relating system challenges to system responses is the way to explanation and prediction in the field of political development. In the broader sense, it opens up for us the whole of man's history of experimentation and innovation in politics as a source for the creation of a useful theory of political change. If we can relate the structural and cultural characteristics of political systems to the ways in which they have confronted and coped with these common system-development problems, we have taken the first steps in the direction of a theory of political growth which, for example, can help us explain why French and British politics differ in particular ways. Such a theory may also be helpful to people who are concerned with the question of how to influence political development—our own governmental officials and the elites of the new nations.

. . . The way in which a political system responds to the four types of challenges, or problems, has to be described in terms of the three functional levels to which we have already referred. Thus, the confrontation of a system-development problem may be related to the changing patterns of political-system capabilities—*i.e.*, growth or decline in *regulative, extractive, distributive, symbolic*, and *responsive* capabilities. The manner in which a system responds to these problems must also be described in terms of the consequences for the performance of the conversion functions of the political system. Thus, when we say that Britain was confronted with the challenge of participation in the course of the eighteenth and nineteenth centuries, we must describe her response to this challenge in terms of what happened to the conversion functions and to interest groups, political parties, media of communication, Parliament, and Cabinet which performed these conversion functions. Finally, the response of the political system to a challenge must also be described in terms of the system-adaptation processes of role differentiation and secularization.

If a political system centralizes and nationalizes—in other words, if it successfully confronts the challenges of state and nation building—how is this reflected in the development of new political roles and structures and in its recruitment processes to these roles and structures; and how does it create the attitudes and propensities appropriate to the new pattern of operations of the political system? As we examine the interaction between challenges to the system and the cultural and structural and performance responses to these challenges, we may begin to develop a theory which will tell us how a particular pattern of challenge-and-response at a certain stage in the development of a political system affects and conditions the future capacity of that system to respond to other challenges and problems. A good illustration of this is the experience of Prussia and Germany with the problem of state building. The degree of bureaucratization, centralization, and militarization which entered into the response of the Prussian elite in the eighteenth century is said to have created a cultural and structural pattern which prevented the German political system from responding effectively in the nineteenth and twentieth centuries to demands for increased participation. In general this kind of analysis will direct our attention to the question of how the solution to one problem affects the capacity of the system to solve other problems of development.

There are at least five major factors which must be considered in the analysis of political development. First, there is no doubt that the stability of a system is heavily dependent upon the types of problems it faces. Much of the stability and success of the gradual development of the political systems of the United States and of Great Britain may be attributed to their relative isolation during long periods of their formative history. In comparing the British experience with the Italian and German, one can hardly avoid noting how in the latter cases the systems were subjected to many diverse and intense pressures simultaneously. Demands for unification, participation, and welfare appeared suddenly. The effect was cumulative and reinforcing. It is generally recognized that a major problem in the new nations today is the cumulative revolutions they must face. People demand participation, national unity, economic betterment, law and order—simultaneously and immediately.

A second factor is the resources the system can draw upon under various circumstances. Support as well as demand can fluctuate, and may descend to critical levels. For example, the French Fourth Republic collapsed in 1958. Although a cumulation of demands, from the Algerians, the army, and various internal groups, was the immediate cause, the Republic fell so quickly and so easily because few people bothered to try to save it. The rate of tax evasion and of general civil disobedience, as well as popular statements and the findings of opinion polls, had long hinted at the low support level; the change in the system was no surprise to most observers.

Developments in other social systems constitute a third factor which may affect political development. The extent to which the political system is loaded or overloaded will vary with the capabilities of other social systems in the domestic society and the international system. When an economy develops new capabilities—new systems of production and distribution—the loading of the political system with demands for welfare may be significantly reduced, thereby affecting political development. Or a religious system may develop regulative capabilities, reducing the flow of innovative demands on the political system. Or the international political system may develop a regulative or distributive capability which reduces the pressure on the domestic political systems. A case in point is the international military or technical assistance units of the United Nations, which may reduce the pressure for the development of extractive and regulative capabilities in some of the new nations. Thus, the existence or the development of capabilities in other social systems may affect the magnitude of the challenges confronting political

systems, keep the flow at an incremental and low-intensity level, and, perhaps, help avoid some of the disruptive consequences of cumulative pressures. On the other hand, a breakdown in family, religious, or economic systems may create discontent, disorder, and new demands which load and perhaps overload the polity.

A fourth factor to consider is the functioning pattern of the system itself. Some kinds of political systems can withstand demand and support fluctuations better than others. In general terms we may note that a system with a developed and differentiated bureaucracy can accommodate demands for new regulations and services much more readily than can a less differentiated system. Law and order can be maintained much more easily if an organized army or police force is available. And a system geared to a high level of responsiveness to inputs from many sources can cope with demands from new groups and with loss of support from some old ones. Some systems are geared for change and adaptation; others are not.

A final factor is the response of the political elites to political-system challenges. Such responses cannot be predicted, at least not entirely, from the system's cultural patterns. In a given system some sorts of responses may lead to accommodation of new demands without changes of the political system or with a minor level of such change, while other responses may lead to disaster. Elites may misjudge the seriousness and intensity of input fluctuations, and either radically modify the system or fail to respond until it is too late. The arguments about how important such responses are have long occupied the attention of historians. What sort of responses by Louis XV and Louis XVI could have averted the French Revolution? At what point had the demands become so intense that no response would have resulted in peaceful accommodation?

Political change is one of the most pervasive and fundamental concerns of our analysis. We shall return to it, by different routes, in every chapter. The world of politics has never waited for the observer to finish his quiet contemplation. In the present century political development seems to be proceeding at an ever-accelerating rate, overwhelming our comparative "snapshots" by making them obsolete before we finish our books and articles. It is increasingly obvious that the study of politics must be a dynamic system-and-process analysis, and not a static and structural one.

PART II

INDIVIDUALS AND IDEAS
IN DEVELOPING POLITIES

INTRODUCTION

Part I introduced the reader to some of the distinctive properties of transitional societies and set forth a conceptual framework for understanding how political development is related to social change. Our interest is in political development, a process closely related to other dimensions of social change but occupying a uniquely central position in it. As aptly phrased by Karl von Vorys, "It is a process which includes social and economic changes, but whose focus is the development of the governmental capacity to direct the course and the rate of social and economic change."[1] Political development, then, depends upon, is associated with, and, most important, may regulate, control, and order other kinds of social change when a society chooses to modernize. Therefore, it is essential for us to understand some of the many social changes which occur when a society modernizes and how these changes relate to political development.

A significant distinction between styles of life in traditional society and modern society is how the individual relates to his environment. In both the actual and the cognitive sense, man in traditional society is dominated by the vicissitudes of nature and feels that he has little control over his environment. He lacks confidence and a sense of power in his ability to manipulate either his physical or social environment, an attitude reinforced by experience. He is likely to be born in a village with an ascribed status that determines his occupation, expectations, and relations with other people. His physical and mental horizon are limited. He will spend his life in or near the village of his birth and, in many instances, he will never travel more than a day's distance from his home. His mental outlook is equally constricted as he remains isolated from new ideas, new technology, and the influences of modernity that may exist but a few hundred miles from his village. The forces of nature which constantly harass him appear overwhelming. Drought,

[1] "Toward a Concept of Political Development," *Annals of the American Academy of Political and Social Science*, **358**, 19, March 1965.

floods, pests, and crop disease are unceasing threats to his farm. Disease, famine, and accidents punish him and his family. With his limited powers these forces are beyond his control and his helplessness breeds a sense of impotence; he finds it dangerous to experiment in the face of all these odds.

This sense of impotence and of danger in the environment induces him to rely on other people for decisions—the elders of the family, village leaders, landlords, and others in positions of authority. In turn, he expects the same submissiveness and dependence from those beneath him as he gives to his superiors. Thus, as a parent, elder, or village leader he may be authoritarian. Impotence, dependence, and anxiety at experimenting are bred into each successive generation. This style of life inhibits the formation of a creative or innovative personality so that life goes on the same generation after generation. The social and political structure remains hierarchical, if not authoritarian, methods of production continue unchanged or are modified only slightly, and the level of income and standard of living remain constant.[2]

Traditional man experiences life in communities. A community has a common cultural configuration which knits people together. There is a single set of stable, habitual preferences and priorities in men's behavior, thoughts, and feelings. As a result of learned habits, common memories, operating preferences, symbols, events in history, and personal associations, a people become used to certain food, clothes, taxes, and marriage ceremonies; they have similar ideas about good and bad, what is beautiful and ugly, or what is familiar and strange; and they bring up their children expecting them to behave in similar ways. Karl W. Deutsch defines community as a "collection of living individuals in whose minds and memories the habits and channels of culture are carried."[3]

In a community, habits and preferences are transmitted by a system of communications. Indeed, the "processes of communication are the basis of the coherence of societies, cultures, and even of the personalities of individuals."[4] Thus, a community consists of people who communicate with one another. People are better able to communicate when they have a common language— a condition which is defined as one of assimilation.

In contrast to modern society where communications, technology, mobility, and patterns of interdependence have resulted in what may be called a national community, traditional society finds each village and tribe constituting a small community isolated from other small communities. The people within each village are assimilated but other villages in the same national territory—in many cases in nearby villages—may have significantly different cultural characteristics, including dissimilar language. Deutsch defines a nationality as "an alignment of large numbers of individuals from the middle

---

[2] See Everett E. Hagen, "A Framework for Analyzing Economic and Political Change," in Robert E. Asher, ed., *Development of Emerging Countries: An Agenda for Research*, The Brookings Institution, Washington, D.C., 1962, pp. 12–15.

[3] *Nationalism and Social Communication: An Inquiry into the Foundations of Nationality*, John Wiley & Sons, Inc., New York, 1953, p. 63.

[4] *Ibid.*, p. 61.

and lower classes linked to regional centers and leading social groups by channels of social communication and economic intercourse, both indirectly from link to link and directly with the center."[5] Thus, to the extent that being a member of a nation consists of the ability to communicate effectively on a wide range of subjects with members of one large group, the cohesiveness and semi-isolation of villages in traditional society constitute impediments to the emergence of a nation.

The convulsive impact of modernization on traditional and transitional society is merely suggested by the quantitative and structural indicators employed by social scientists to describe this transformation. Patterns of child rearing begin to change; new personality types challenge and replace the dominant position of traditional personalities; marginal men, creative and innovative personalities appear with greater frequency and assume increasingly major roles in the transitional process. Changes in residence and occupation occur as people move from farm to flat, from field to factory. New social opportunities appear as status and prestige are no longer ascribed. Patterns of group affiliation and conceptions of personal indentity undergo change. Daniel Lerner has spoken of these changes in terms of mobility: "Physical mobility released man from his native soil; social mobility freed man from his native status; psychic mobility liberated man from his native self."[6]

The learning of many new habits and unlearning of many old ones is an excruciatingly slow process that may extend over decades or generations. However, some changes in the process of modernization today may be rapid. Urbanization may occur quickly as masses of people decide to move to the city, even though jobs may not be immediately available. The skills and processes of science and technology may be introduced in a relatively short period of time. New, modern transportation and communications systems may be installed relatively quickly and markets may expand rather rapidly. The concentration of people in cities and new work situations force people into new contacts. Economic, social, and technological developments make mass media of communications possible and permit a lightning-like exchange of ideas. The barriers between the little communities begin to fall and regional, and eventually national, communities emerge. Under these circumstances people experience, in Deutsch's term, "social mobilization."[7] This is a process in which "major clusters of old social, economic and psychological commitments are eroded or broken and people become available for new patterns of socialization and behavior." Old habits are uprooted and mobilized persons, participating in intensive communications, are inducted into some relatively stable new patterns of group membership, organization, and commitment.

A mobilized population is a political public and nationalism is an inevi-

---

[5] *Ibid.*, p. 75.
[6] *The Human Meaning of the Social Sciences*, Meridian Books, Inc., New York, 1959, p. 18.
[7] See below, Chap. 12.

table consequence of a nationally mobilized community. In the developing nations, nationalism itself often becomes the dominant ideological commitment, in turn leading to a higher degree of mobilization. All these changes have a cumulative impact and are reflected in individual and group political behavior—apathy, insularity, and the hold of the "past" are replaced by political organizations and attitudes more appropriate to the difficulties of coping with modernity. In short, these changes are the makings of "mass politics."

In this part of the book we focus on some of the basic psychological and social changes in developing polities which appear to move men toward modernity. The following part will concentrate on economic changes and other transformations related to economic development that have consequences for political development. Over a long period of time, psychological changes occur in the personality makeup of individuals. New ideas emerge that motivate people to action and influence the course of development. As ideas are communicated between larger and larger groups of people, social mobilization is achieved. How, and by whom, are these changes initiated and promoted? How, and by whom, are they resisted and obstructed?

The search for "first causes" of development started in the more limited field of economic development. Economists sought to explain how development begins. When economic theories of growth and development did not provide complete and satisfactory answers, they began to explore for causes in social, administrative, and political institutions, as did other social scientists. This search produced a spate of literature on social and cultural obstacles to development and the identification of social, political, and other preconditions for economic development. In pushing the exploration ever more deeply, economic historians and sociologists identified a range of beliefs, attitudes, and values which they believed permitted or encouraged the generation of enterprise and entrepreneurship. Max Weber's exposition of the "Protestant ethic hypothesis" was a classic statement of the influence of attitudes and values, and it continues to exert an impressive influence on many authors searching for the causes of economic growth.

The inevitable next step was to push the search into the foundations of human behavior and motivation. Psychologists and psychologically-oriented social scientists are now exploring the dependence of entrepreneurship and economic development on the mergence of innovative personalities or the presence of achievement motivation in individuals.

Everett E. Hagen, an economist, provocatively employs the insights of sociology and psychology to construct a theory of social change which attempts to explain how economic growth begins.[8] He inquires into the forces which disrupt the great stability of traditional society and cause groups to emerge which abandon traditional ways and turn their energies to the tasks of modernization. What influences some groups to alter sub-

[8] Everett E. Hagen, *On the Theory of Social Change*, Dorsey Press, Homewood, Illinois, 1962, Ch. 4.

stantially their needs, values, and cognitions? His answer is formulated in the concept of "withdrawal of status respect." Hagen finds that the innovational and creative personality is a deviant individual who belongs to a rejected group. He is a member of some social group which perceives that its purposes and values in life are not rightfully acknowledged by other groups in society whose respect and esteem they value.

Albert O. Hirschman has elsewhere questioned whether the relationship between deviance and the emergence of able and vigorous entrepreneurs is reliable. He asks, "aren't there some deviants, for example, homosexuals or ex-convicts, who have not shown particularly strong entrepreneurial inclinations? Must social scientists perhaps entertain the Toynbee-type hypothesis of 'optimum deviancy,' with all the attendant difficulties of defining the optimal point?"[9] Furthermore, Hirschman suggests that Hagen's deviants may well make for economic development, but development in turn creates an *esprit de corps* among its principal agents and welds them into an identifiable group, with a personality and perhaps an ideology of its own. Thus, looking back it may appear as though the separateness of the group was a cause of development when, in actual fact, it was its result.[10]

In an article summarizing his imaginative and significant study, *The Achieving Society*,[11] David C. McClelland discusses the conditions and personality traits which lead particular individuals and groups in society to become entrepreneurs—to exploit opportunities, to take advantage of favorable trade conditions, and, in general, to shape their own destinies. Explanation is found in changes which occur in the minds of men: a personality characteristic becomes more prevalent in individuals which McClelland designates as a "need for Achievement." Where a high need for Achievement is found, economic development is likely to follow.[12] He does

[9] "Comments on 'A Framework for Analyzing Economic and Political Change,'" In Asher, *op. cit.*, p. 39.

[10] *Ibid.*, pp. 39–40; see also, Hirschman, "The Search for the Primum Mobile," *The Strategy of Economic Development* (New Haven: Yale University Press, 1958), pp. 1–7.

[11] D. Van Nostrand Company, Inc., Princeton, New Jersey, 1961.

[12] Cf. Alex Inkeles, "Making Men Modern: On the Causes and Consequences of Individual Change in Six Developing Countries," *American Journal of Sociology*, **75**, 208–225, September, 1969; "The Modernization of Man," in Myron Weiner (ed.), *Modernization: The Dynamics of Growth* (New York: Basic Books, Inc., 1966), Chap. X. To McCelland, personality is the independent variable and the social structure, or that part of it which is the economy, is the dependent variable. Changes occur in the mind of men with the result that economic development is likely to follow. For Inkeles, the reverse is true. Inkeles finds that, to a striking degree, the same syndrome of attitudes, values, and ways of acting defines the modern man in each of the six countries he studied. The characteristics of modern man include: a disposition to accept new ideas and try new methods; a readiness to express opinions; a time sense that makes men more interested in the present and future than the past; a better sense of punctuality; a greater concern for planning, organization, and efficiency; a tendency to see the world as calculable; a faith in science and technology; and a belief in distributive justice. Admittedly, these characteristics embrace more than the need for Achievement, but modern man, as Inkeles describes him, clearly is achievement-oriented. Inkeles finds that elements of the social structure change individuals. Education is the most powerful factor in making men modern, but occupational experience in largescale organizations, and especially in factory work, makes a significant contribution to creating modern attitudes and teaching individuals to act like modern men.

not merely argue that the achieving society possesses large numbers of individuals with a high need for Achievement. McClelland contends, based on systematic empirical investigations along historical lines, that the presence of individuals with a high need for Achievement is *antecedent* to entrepreneurship and economic growth. He also sees need Achievement to be the link between the Protestant ethic and the rise of capitalism.

The critical questions, then, are: What produces the need for Achievement and how can the need for Achievement be stimulated? The need for Achievement is seen as resulting from child rearing practices and early socialization. The answer to the second question may be somewhat incomplete and tentative, but some psychologists feel that beginnings to an answer are emerging. Recently, McClelland and David G. Winters reported on experimental efforts in developing nations as well as in the United States to change motivation so that individuals could express their entrepreneurial personalities and thereby contribute to economic growth.[13] They concluded that it is practicable to run need for Achievement training courses for businessmen and to compare their yields, at least roughly, in terms of an activity level score. There is encouraging evidence that need for Achievement courses may actually increase the subsequent activity levels of the businessmen who take them.

In explaining the origins of development, both Hagen and McClelland concentrate on psychological changes occurring within the individual. At another level, however, ideology may be a force which is equally important in the multiple dimensions of the modernization process. The next chapter deals with ideology as a force which continues to have enormous effect on the behavior of men and nations, a force which some observers view as critical to the unity, growth, and performance of developing societies.

In an article which explores both political and economic consequences of ideology, Harry G. Johnson makes a strong case that, although there are substantive differences among new nations with respect to the ideology of economic policy, there are also important similarities which permit their being discussed collectively. These similarities result from common influences that affect all developing countries. Johnson insightfully identifies and analyzes three influences: (1) political nationalism, which has its counterpart in economic nationalism; (2) the economic ideas and experiences inherited from the interwar period (especially the 1930's) which have provided a common body of interpretation, thought, and policy prescription, a sort of international language of economic development; and (3) the dual role of the advanced countries as advisers and sources of foreign aid. The consequences of this ideology for the economic policies of the developing nations include policies of economic autarky, concentration on industrialization at the expense of agricultural development, a preference for economic planning

---

[13] *Motivating Economic Achievement* (New York: The Free Press, 1969). See, especially, Chap. II.

and for public control of industry, and hostility to large foreign enterprises operating in their countries.

The nationalist elites who make use of ideology are termed "assaulted" individuals by Matossian because they are caught between the pressures of traditionalism and modernization. The West may be resented, but the intellectuals who construct the ideology are partly Westernized. Their desire is to resolve the conflict resulting from exposure to the West and to create a sense of identity for themselves as individuals and for the nation as a whole. They search for their true selves and endeavor to create a national character.

The ideologies these elites formulate and embrace also attempt to reduce the ambiguity between the newness of the West and the oldness of the indigenous culture. The past is turned to many uses, both negative and positive. It may be employed as an escape, or it may be used to sanction innovation and national self-strengthening.

From the analysis of Matossian it becomes clear why the intelligentsia of developing nations may be sincerely attached to contradictory premises. Their ideologies provide criticism and comfort, stand for class equality and exhort the masses to follow orders and accept unequal rewards, and condemn the peasant for his backwardness while praising him for being a *real* representative of his culture. In these tensions is the hint of an explanation why "all-people's" parties are so common in the developing nations during the initial phases of educating the masses for democracy, a topic to which we will return in Part VI.

The article by Malenbaum and Stolper flatly questions the usefulness of political-economic ideology in providing answers to the difficult problems of economic development. The authors are not concerned with the symbolic and nation-building utility of ideology, but confine their analysis to the question of whether economic growth is dependent on any particular ideology. Is there a distinct ideological route that best serves the cause of economic progress? The authors compare the economic ideologies and rates of economic growth of India and Communist China and of West Germany and East Germany, and conclude, on the basis of their investigation, that economic progress is not determined by the ideology to which a nation adheres except to the extent that that ideology happens to coincide with conditions and needs of the nation. The Communist formula did not contain the essential ingredient for more rapid progress in East Germany as contrasted with West Germany, but democracy in a free society did not provide an assurance of rapid economic achievement in India as contrasted with Communist China.

Robert N. Bellah, in the last article of this chapter, distinguishes between religion and ideology and identifies the role of each in the process of modernization. In traditional societies religion is a prescriptive value system containing relatively specific norms which govern social, political, and economic life. In modern society, religious values lay down the basic principles of ethical conduct, but the religious system does not attempt to regulate the details of concrete behavior. It is ideology rather than religion which governs economic, political, and social life, thereby permitting behavioral flexibility.

When Turkey and Japan modernized, "new religions" were introduced to permit greater flexibility rather than scrapping the existing religions. Islam was replaced by Kemalism in Turkey in such a way that it had the legitimacy of religious symbols. In Japan an ideological movement—essentially political in nature, with the objective of modernizing Japan after the Meiji Restoration—was given an openly religious coloration. The central value of loyalty to the emperor was used to legitimize the immense changes that were being made in all spheres of social life and to justify abandoning many of the sacred prescriptions of the traditional orders.

Both cases neatly convey the functional utility of ideology in modernization. However, in both countries the traditional religion has not disappeared —the differentiation between religion and ideology remains to be completed. Traditional religion persists in political life.

Chapter 3

Personality and Entrepreneurship

HOW ECONOMIC GROWTH BEGINS:
A THEORY OF SOCIAL CHANGE

Everett E. Hagen

This paper proposes a theory of how a "traditional" society becomes one in which continuing technical progress (hence continuing rise in per-capita production and income) is occurring. I shall define a traditional state of society in the following section. The hypotheses which I present to explain the change from this state to one of continuing technological progress may be relevant also to the analysis of other types of social change.

The theory does not suggest some one key factor as causing social change independently of other forces. Rather, it presents a general model of society, and deals with interrelationships among elements of the physical environment, social structure, personality, and culture. This does not imply a thesis that almost anything may cause something, so that one must remain eclectic and confused. Rather, certain factors seem of especial importance in initiating change, but their influence can be understood only by tracing inter-

relationships through the society. It is implied that general system analysis is a fruitful path to advance in societal theory. Since presented in brief compass, the model is necessarily presented rather starkly here.[1]

The purely economic theories of barriers which explain the absence of growth seem inadequate. The assumption that the income of entire populations is too low to make saving easy; that markets in low-income countries are too small to induce investment; that costly lumps of expenditure for transport facilities, power plants, etc., which low-income countries cannot provide, are a requisite to growth—these and related theories are internally consistent but seem without great relevance to reality. Empirical study of low-income societies demonstrates that the supposed conditions and requirements do not in fact exist or are not of great importance.

Neither are the differences among nations with respect to growth explained by differences in the degree of contact with the West. Contact with the technical knowledge of the West is a requisite for growth,

SOURCE. Everett E. Hagen, "How Economic Growth Begins: A Theory of Social Change," *Journal of Social Issues*, **19**, 20–34, January 1963. This manuscript is derived in part from and in a few paragraphs is identical with an article in *Development Research Digest*, Vol. **1**, No. 3, January 1963 (prepared by the National Planning Association, Washington, D.C.).

[1] The model is presented at greater length in E. E. Hagen, *On The Theory of Social Change* (Homewood, Illinois: Dorsey Press, 1962). This paper is in essence an abstract of various chapters of that book.

but forces quite independent of the degree of contact determine whether a nation uses that knowledge. The most spectacular example of this fact is that among the four great Asian nations, Indonesia and India had the most contact with the West during the period 1600–1900, China had an intermediate amount, and Japan the least. Moreover, Indonesia and India experienced the most Western investment, China an intermediate amount, and Japan none whatever until her economic growth was already well under way. Yet among the four countries Japan began to develop first, and has developed rapidly; Indonesia is the laggard; and if China solves her agricultural problem here growth will probably be faster than that of India.

These facts suggest some hypotheses which a theory of growth should not emphasize. Certain other facts give more positive indications of the elements with which a plausible theory must deal.

Economic growth has everywhere occurred interwoven with political and social change. Lipset and Coleman have demonstrated the correlation between economic change and the transition from authoritarian to "competitive" politics in Asia, Africa, and Latin America, and the same relationship is found in every country elsewhere that has entered upon economic growth.[2] The timing is such that it is clear that the economic growth does not occur first and cause the political-social change. Rather, the two are mutually dependent. Whatever the forces for change may be, they impinge on every aspect of human behavior. A theory of the transition to economic growth which does not simultaneously explain political change, or explains it merely as a consequence of the economic change, is thus suspect.

One last consideration will serve to lead up to the exposition of the model. It is this: the concept is rather widely held in the West that the present low-income societies can advance technically simply by imitating the technical methods already developed in the West. That concept is ethnocentric and incorrect. Mere imitation is impossible. A productive enterprise or process in the West depends for its efficiency on its position in a technical complex of facilities for supplies, services, transportation, and communication, and on a complex of economic, legal, and other social institutions. The management methods which work well within the plant and in its relationships to other units, depend on a complex of attitudes toward interpersonal relationships which are not closely paralleled by attitudes elsewhere. When the process is lifted out of its complex, to adapt it so that it will function in an underdeveloped economy requires technical and especially social and cultural creativity of a high order.

Requirements for the transition to economic growth, then, are (1) fairly widespread creativity—problem-solving ability, and a tendency to use it—and (2) attitudes toward manual-technical labor and the physical world such that the creative energies are channeled into innovation in the technology of production rather than in the technology of art, war, philosophy, politics, or other fields. I believe that exploration of these facets of the process of economic growth is a useful approach to a theory of social change.

What is in point is not widespread genius but a high degree of creativity in a few individuals and a moderately high level in a larger number. I shall suggest reasons to believe that the traditional state of a society is associated with a rather low level of creativity among the members of the society. Further, the persons in tradi-

---

[2] S. Lipset, "Some Social Requisites of Democracy: Economic Development and Political Legitimacy," *American Political Science Review*, Vol. 53 (March 1959); G. A. Almond, J. S. Coleman *et al.*, *The Politics of the Developing Areas* (Princeton: University Press, 1960). Adapting their method slightly, I used it in "A Framework for Analyzing Economic and Political Change," in R. Asher and others, *Development of the Emerging Countries: An Agenda for Research* (Washington, D.C.: Brookings Institution, 1962).

tional society who are in position to innovate are the elite—perhaps the lower elite, but certainly not the peasants and urban menials. It is well known that being concerned with tools, machinery, and in general physical processes seems demeaning to the elite and is repugnant to them. It seems to me that a theory of economic growth must give considerable attention to the forces which change those two aspects of personality.

The Stability of Traditional Society

When I refer to a traditional society I have in mind a traditional agricultural society, for while there have also been traditional hunting and fishing societies and traditional pastoral societies,[3] they can hardly accumulate many artifacts and hence continuing technical progress is hardly possible in them. A traditional agricultural society is of course one in which things are done in traditional ways, but two other characteristics which have been typical of the world's traditional societies and turn out to be essential qualities of the type are also worthy of note here.

First, the social structure is hierarchical and authoritarian in all of its aspects— economic, political, religious. The existence of an authoritarian hierarchy does not refer merely to a large mass who were submissive and to a small class who rule. Rather, every individual in a traditional hierarchy except perhaps for one or a few at the very apex is submissive to authoritarian decisions above him, and in turn exercises authority on persons below him. And this is true even of the lowliest peasant, who as he grows older and becomes a husband, a father, and an elder in his village, becomes increasingly an authority in some aspects of his social relations.

Secondly, one's status in the society is, with little qualification, inherited. One

---

[3] Industrial societies will probably also become traditional in time, which is to say that technical progress will come to an end, at least for a time.

does not earn it; one is born to it. The families of the politically dominating groups, who usually also are economically powerful landed groups, provide the officers of the armed forces and the professional classes as well as the political leaders. Lesser elites also perpetuate their status, though with somewhat greater mobility.

These characteristics of the society as well as its techniques of production are traditional and change very slowly. While the model of a completely unchanging traditional society is a construct, an ideal type, it is sufficiently relevant to reality to be useful. From the beginning of agriculture in the world until say 1600 the traditional state of society persisted everywhere except that occasionally, here and there, was a bursting out of the traditional mode for a few hundred years, then a lapse back into it, sometimes at the original technical level, sometimes at a higher one. The present-day transition to economic growth is such a bursting out. We must ask, Why has the traditional state of society been so persistent? and then, Why have the bursts of change occurred? Or at least, Why have the modern bursts of change occurred?

One condition sometimes suggested as an answer to the first question is that the instruments of power were in the hands of the elite. The traditional authoritarian hierarchical state persisted, it is suggested, because the elite kept the simple folk in subjection by force. This explanation seems inadequate. It is possible for a small group to keep an unwilling ninety-seven per cent of a society in subjection by force for a decade or two, or perhaps for a generation or two, though if the subjection persists even this long one must ask whether it really was entirely unpleasing. But that the masses were kept in subjection primarily by force for many centuries seems improbable. The authoritarian hierarchical traditional social structure must have persisted because submitting to authority above one, as well as exercising authority, was satisfying, and secondly because the conditions of life recreated personalities, generation after generation, in which it continued to be so.

CREATIVE AND UNCREATIVE PERSONALITY

To suggest probable reasons why authoritarian social structure was satisfying, let me digress to discuss certain aspects of personality.

Many elite individuals in traditional societies are prevented from using their energies effectively in economic development by their repugnance to being concerned with the grubby material aspects of life. The repugnance includes being concerned with the details of running a business effectively, as well as performing manual-technical labor—"getting their hands dirty." Often the repugnance is largely unconscious; the individuals concerned often deny it, because it does not occur to them that any middle- or upper-class person anywhere would have any more favorable attitude toward engaging in such activity than they have. Why does this attitude exist?

It is deep rooted. I would explain it as follows. Every person in any society who holds or gains privileged position in life must justify it to himself, in order to be comfortable. If he has gained it by his abilities, justification is easy. The person who gains it by the accident of birth is forced to feel that it is due him because he is essentially superior to the simple folk. Typically, the elite individual in traditional societies feels that his innate superiority consists in being more refined than the simple folk. One evidence of his greater refinement is that he does not like the grubby attention to the material details of life which is one of their distinguishing characteristics. However this attitude may have developed historically, once it exists the elite child acquires it from infancy on by perceiving the words, the attitudes, the tone of voice of his elders. By the time he is six or eight years old, it is deeply bred into his personality.

This attitude alone would not contribute to the lack of innovation in social and political fields. Presence of a low level of creativity, however, would help to explain absence of innovation in these fields as well as in techniques of production.

The explanation of a low level of creativity and justification for the assertion that it exists are more complex.

One component of creativity is intelligence, and intelligence is in part due to biological characteristics. However, although individuals differ greatly in inherited intellectual capacity, the best evidence suggests no reason to assume any appreciable average difference in this respect between the individuals of traditional societies and those of other societies. There are varying degrees of innate intelligence in both. Persons in traditional societies are not less creative because they are less intelligent.

A more relevant component is certain attitudes. In formal psychological terms, I would suggest as characteristics central to creativity high need (for) achievement, high need autonomy, high need order (though this needs further definition), and a sense of the phenomena about one as forming a system which is conceptually comprehensible, rather than merely being arbitrary external bundles.

A person who has high need achievement feels a sense of increased pleasure (or quite possibly a lessening of chronic anxiety, which is the same thing) when he faces a problem or notes a new and irregular phenomenon in a field of interest to him; by the pleasure he anticipates in using his capacities he is drawn to use his energies to understand and master the situation. A person with high need autonomy takes for granted that when he has explored a situation in an area of interest to him, his evaluation of it is satisfactory. He does not think he "knows it all"; he seeks ideas; but when he has thus gained a perspective he assumes that his discriminations and evaluations are good; he feels no anxiety about whether the judgments of other persons differ from his.

He does not rebel against the conventional view for the sake of rebelling, but neither does he accept it because it is generally accepted. In Rogers' phrase, the "locus of evaluative judgment is within him."[4]

A person with high need autonomy and also high need order, in the sense in which I use that phrase here, tolerates disorder without discomfort, because sensing that the world is an orderly place, he knows that within the disorder there is complex and satisfying order, and he is willing to tolerate the disorder, and in fact even enjoys it somewhat, until the greater order shall suggest itself to him. Such a person is alert to phenomena which contradict his previous assumptions about the scheme of things, for he assumes that he will be able to perceive the order implicit in them and thus gain an enlarged understanding of the world. In Poincaré's terms, he has a "capacity to be surprised"; in Rogers', "openness to experience."[5]

These characteristics are not fully independent of each other. In technical jargon, they may not be orthogonal. This categorization of personality therefore does not quite go to the roots of things. But it will do for my present purpose.

This personality complex may be contrasted with one which for the moment I shall term merely uncreative. It includes low need achievement and need autonomy, high need dependence, high need submission-dominance, and a sense of the world as consisting of arbitrary forces.

If an individual does not trust his own capacity to analyze problems, then when he faces a problem, anxiety rises in him. He anticipates failure, and avoids problems. He will find comfort in the consensus of a group (not on a majority decision opposed by a minority, for this involves a clash of judgment and the necessity of choosing

between the two judgments). He will find it comfortable to rely on authority for guidance—the authority of older men or of the appropriate person in the hierarchy of authority and status which is always found in a traditional society. He will enjoy having a position of authority himself; one reason for this is that if he must make a decision, he can give it the sanction of his authority; persons below him, if they in turn find it comfortable to rely on authority, will not question his decision, and he does not need to feel anxiety lest analysis of it would prove it to have been wrong. It is right because a person with the proper authority made it.

A person with such needs will avoid noting phenomena that do not meet his preconceptions, for their existence presents a problem. In any event, since he senses the world as consisting mainly of arbitrary forces, an unexpected phenomenon provides no clue to him. It is simply a possible source of failure or danger.

I shall suggest below that the experiences in infancy and childhood which give a person this perception of the world inculcate rage and need aggression in him, but also fear of his own need aggression, and therefore anxiety in any situation within his group in which power relationships are not clearly defined and conflict leading to aggressiveness might occur. Hence he likes a clearly defined structure of hierarchical authority, in which it is obviously proper for him to submit to someone above him or give orders to persons below him, without clash of judgment. In addition, his need aggression also causes him to feel pleasure in dominating those below him—his children, his juniors, his social inferiors.

Thus there are dual reasons why the authoritarian hierarchy is satisfying. It is appropriate to give this personality type not merely the negative label "uncreative" but also the positive one "authoritarian."[6]

[4] H. H. Anderson, ed., *Creativity and Its Cultivation* (New York: Harper & Bros., 1959), p. 76.
[5] Poincaré's phrase is quoted by Erich Fromm in H. H. Anderson, *op. cit.*, p. 48; Rogers' is at *ibid.*, p. 75.

[6] It is not congruent in all respects with the one portrayed by Adorno and associates in *The Authoritarian Personality*.

While it is evident that these two personality types exist, to this point it is purely an assumption that authoritarian personality is typical in traditional societies. One reason for thinking that this is true is that this hypothesis explains many things about traditional societies which otherwise are puzzling. It explains, for example, why many persons in traditional societies not only follow traditional methods, but seem to cling almost compulsively to them, even though to an outsider trial of a new method seems so clearly to their advantage. It explains why the method of decision of local problems in so many traditional societies is by consensus of the village elders, through a long process of finding a least-common-denominator solution on which all can agree, rather than by majority vote. It explains, too, why authoritarian social and political systems have persisted in such societies for such long periods.

That a hypothesis explains a number of phenomena which are otherwise puzzling is strong reason for accepting it. However, there is also more direct reason for believing that authoritarian personality is unusually prevalent in traditional societies. This reason lies in the existence of some evidence that childhood environment and childhood training in traditional societies are of the kind which tend to produce such personality.

Perhaps the factor which is most important in determining whether childhood environment will be such as to cause the formation of creative personality or such as to cause the formation of authoritarian personality is the opinions of the parents concerning the nature of infants and children. Suppose that the parents take for granted that infants are organisms which, while delicate and in need of protection for a time, have great potentials; organisms which as they unfold will develop capacity for understanding and managing life. A mother who regards this as an axiomatic fact of life will if she is sensible take precautions to keep her child's explorations of the world around him from causing harm or alarm to him, but she will let him explore his world and will watch with interest and pleasure as his muscular capacities develop, his range of activity expands, and he accomplishes in endless succession the hundreds of new achievements which occur during infancy and childhood.

His repeated use of his new physiological capacities, as they unfold, is from his viewpoint problem solving—intensely interesting problem solving. Assume that it is successful because his mother has taken safeguards so that he will not fall out of his crib, cut himself, break the glassware, fall down stairs, etc., and because his mother offers advice and restraint when necessary. Assume, however, that his venturings do not meet repeated restraint, because his mother trusts his developing capacities and does not check his every step. Then he will repeatedly feel joy at his own successful problem solving and pleasure in his mother's pleasure. There will be deeply built into him the pattern that initiative is rewarded, that his judgment is adequate, that solving problems is fun.

If his mother wants him to be self-reliant, presses him to do things as soon as his capacities have developed, usually refuses to let him lapse into babyhood after he has gained capacities, and shows displeasure when he does not do things for himself, then the stimulus of her displeasure when he does not show initiative will be combined with that of her pleasure when he does so. I have mentioned only his mother. During the first year or more of his life, her attitude is the most important one in his life; after that the attitude of his father (and so that of his siblings) toward his behavior will also be important.

Suppose, alternatively, that the child's parents have as a part of their personalities the judgment that children are fragile organisms without much innate potential capacity to understand or manage the world. Then during the first two years or so of life the mother is apt to treat the child over-solicitously, and to shield him somewhat anxiously from harm. In doing so, unintentionally she also keeps the child from using his unfolding initiative. The use of initiative comes to alarm him, because it alarms her. Then, after these first few years of life, when the parents think the child is old enough to be trained, parents with the view that children are without much potential inner capacity train the child by a continual stream of commands and instructions concerning what is good to do and not good to do, the proper relationships to them and to others, and in general how he should live. Exercise of initiative on his part frequently brings alarm and displeasure and hence causes him anxiety. He can avoid anxiety only by passively obeying the instructions of these powerful persons so important in his life. The instructions will often seem arbitrary to him, and the repeated frustration of his initiative will create anger in him. He will repress it, but this does not mean that it disappears.

The practices and attitudes of older siblings and playmates who have been brought up under the same influences will provide models which in various ways will reinforce the same lesson.

The impact of these parental attitudes on the child may be reinforced by certain related attitudes of the parents. The existence of any child restricts the freedom of his parents, and interferes with their relations to each other. Moreover, the child exerts a will independent of theirs, and they are not always sure that they can control him. If the parents, especially the mother, are relaxed confident people, they will not be disturbed by these problems. Suppose, however, that they are somewhat anxious persons who feel that they themselves do not understand the world (as they are apt to feel if their own childhood was like that which I have just described). Then their child may repeatedly make them anxious, and unconsciously they

may hate him for causing them anxiety and also interfering with their freedom. The child is sure to sense their hostility; it will both make him more afraid to venture and increase his pleasure in venting his frustration by controlling someone below him later in life.

Exposure to the one or the other of these parental attitudes will have an impact on the child through infancy and childhood, but for brevity I shall mention specifically only the most conspicuous manifestation, that during the "period of infantile genitality," which usually occupies about the fourth and fifth years of life. At this age a boy knows that he is a male, like his father, and that he will become big, like his father, and he begins to wonder whether he can successfully rival his father. Specifically, he becomes a rival of his father for his mother's attentions. If his father and mother are perceptive and understanding persons, they will accept him into their fellowship and let him gain an adequate degree of the feminine attention he needs. However, without anxiety or arbitrariness, they will teach him that he can postpone his demands when the circumstances require it, and need not feel anxiety at the postponement. He will learn, as before, that one's initiative must be judicious, and he will also reinforce powerfully the earlier lesson that the exercise of his initiative is safe and brings pleasure.

If the father is weak and the mother is not arbitrary and somewhat rejecting, the son may gain his mother's attentions not because his parents understand his needs and meet them but because his father gives up at the boy's aggressive persistence. In this case too the son will learn that initiative is successful, though he will learn it with overtones of anxiety.

Suppose, however, that the parents doubt their own ability to manage problems, and, having no faith in the capacities of children, regard the boy's initiative as a danger rather than a valuable attribute. Then they will be disturbed by the boy's emerging rivalry with his father during the period of infantile sexuality, will resent the boy's encroachment, and will "put the boy in his place." The experience will reinforce the anxiety and alarm that the boy felt earlier at the exercise of initiative. It will also reinforce the anger that the boy felt earlier at his parents' arbitrary restrictions, and since he cannot vent his anger at his parents, there is apt to build up in him an unformed desire to exercise arbitrary authority himself, and lord it over someone under him, later in life—just as the college freshman humiliated by hazing at the hands of sophomores often waits his turn to vent his humiliation on the new freshmen the next year.

The impact of the one or other type of parental personality on girls during this period is not quite parallel to that on boys, because of the different sexual role which girls have already learned. The differences will not be discussed here.

In these ways, creative or authoritarian personality is formed. There are many other aspects to the process, and many other aspects of authoritarian and creative personalities, which cannot be discussed here:[7] This brief discussion will, I hope, give the general flavor of both the personality types and the process which forms them.

I think that the reader may already have realized that the parental attitudes which lend to create authoritarian personality in the children are themselves components of authoritarian personality in the parents. That is, persons in whom authoritarian personality was created by the circumstances of their childhoods are apt to have such a view of life that they will in turn create an environment which will cause authoritarian personalities to appear in their children. The type, like most other personality types, tends to be self-perpetuating.

[7] For example, models are important in personality formation, and it is of interest to ask where the son of a weak father obtains models of successful behavior. There are several possibilities. This and other complexities must be passed over here.

It is of great importance, then, that the scattered evidence which is available suggests that precisely the sort of childhood environment and training sketched above as conducive to the emergence of authoritarian personality is the sort prevalent in traditional societies. Fairly intensive sketches of childhood environment in Burma by Hazel Histon[8] and in Java by Hildred Geertz,[9] and more fragmentary sketches relating to many Latin societies, indicate that in all of these cases childhood environment is precisely of this type. These sketches refer primarily to the simple folk, but there is some empirical evidence to suggest that they are true of personality and childhood environment among the elite as well.

And there is even more convincing evidence that various of the conspicuous characteristics of authoritarian personality are present in many traditional societies in Latin America and Asia. Though our knowledge concerning African countries is more limited, they are probably present in those countries as well. Hence it seems likely that a low level of creativity is also characteristic of such societies.

Presumably this personality type developed initially because the every day phenomena of the physical world were bewildering to unscientific man. Convinced of his inability to fathom the world, man began to protect his children jealously when they were infants and then train them minutely in the way in which they should behave to be safe. And so authoritarian personality appeared and perpetuated itself. Repugnance to concerning oneself with the humble material matters of life and with manual-technical labor also appeared among the elite, in the way

[8] "Family Patterns and Paranoidal Personality Structure in Boston and Burma" (Ph.D. dissertation, Radcliffe College, April 1959).
[9] *The Javanese Family* (New York: Free Press of Glencoe, Inc., 1955) and "The Vocabulary of Emotion: A study of Javanese Socialization Processes," *Psychiatry*, **22**, (August 1959), 225–37.

sketched earlier in this essay, and tended to perpetuate itself.

Social Change

How, then, did social change ever occur? and technological progress and economic development ever begin?

Study of a number of countries in which there has occurred a transition from a traditional state to continuing economic development suggests that an important factor initiating change was some historical shift which caused some group or groups of the lesser elite, who previously had had a respected and valued place in the social hierarchy, to feel that they no longer were respected and valued. This derogation in some societies consisted of explicit indication of contempt for the functions or position of the lesser elite, in others of behavior by a new higher elite which seemed immoral, unmanly, or irreligious to the groups below them, and thus indicated contempt for the moral standards of the lesser elite.

I shall omit the example of England, which is complex and difficult to mention briefly, and shall refer briefly to highlights of three other examples. In the 1650's the Tsar of Russia and Patriarch of Moscow, to attain diplomatic ends by adopting Greek practices, ordered certain changes in the ritual of the Orthodox church which the faithful felt to be heretical and to endanger their souls. There followed conflict and persecution, in waves of varying severity, even down to 1900. The Old Believers, who were the victims of this withdrawal of respect for their status in the society, were prominent in economic development in Russia in the nineteenth century. Concerning the twentieth I have no information.

In Japan the feudal group known as the Tokugawa, who gained national power in 1600, imposed a peace which deprived the samurai of their traditional function; imposed rigid distinctions among social classes which had the effect of relegating the so-called wealthy peasants, descen-

dants of the lesser elite, to the rank of peasant; and to some extent demeaned other feudal groups, the so-called outer clans. It was the lesser samurai and wealthy peasants, apparently especially of the outer clans, who were the innovators in Japan's industrial revolution.

In Colombia, in the 1530's the Spanish settled on a high plateau around Bogotá and in the valleys around Cali and Medellín. Through historical developments I shall not sketch, during the next two centuries the settlers of the other two areas came to look down on those in Antioquia, the valley around Medellín. The social friction continues to the present; and the Antioqueños have been the leaders in economic innovation out of all proportion to their numbers in the population.

I shall call such events "withdrawal of status respect" from the group no longer accorded its old place. It is important to note that the situation is one in which a group of the elite once had full status respect and later lost it. What are the results? Let me speculate concerning them.

I suggest that among the adults of the first generation so affected, the reaction is anger and anxiety. Their children, however, seeing that their parents' role in life causes anxiety, do not find it a fully satisfying model. Alternative roles are in general not open to them, and so they respond by repressing somewhat within themselves their parents' values—by ceasing to have *any* role values with the same clarity and intensity their parents did. The process, I suggest, is cumulative in successive generations, and in the second or third or fourth generation there appears pronounced "normlessness," shiftlessness, anomie, or, in Merton's term, retreatism. It can be observed, for example, in Negroes of the southern United States, American Indians on any reservation, first and second generation immigrants, and colonial subjects.[10]

[10] In groups who are not of the lower elite, but instead are of the "simple folk," the later reaction may be not creative innovation but violent social revolt. For lack of space, that

Historical records suggest that it also characterized the Antioqueños, the samurai, and the Old Believers.

There is reason to suspect that retreatism affects men more than women because of the differences between the normal social roles of the sexes. After several generations, then, there will appear men who are retreatist and weak, but women who are less so. The women will probably feel some pity for their children's lot in life, and will cherish them tenderly. But, reacting to the ineffectiveness of their husbands, the women will have an intense desire that their sons shall be more effective, and will respond with delight to each achievement in infancy and boyhood. During the period of infantile sexuality, the boy will win in the rivalry with his father, both because his initiative pleases his mother and because his father is weak.

Obviously not all home environments in some generation of a group of the lesser elite from whom status respect has been withdrawn will be like this, but it is plausible to believe that some such environment will appear occasionally, or even fairly often. Some combinations and intensities of such maternal attitudes, combined with weakness in the father, provide an almost ideal environment for the formation of an anxious driving type of creativity.

Where a considerable degree of creativity is inculcated, but the anxiety is great, a variant type of individual may appear, one who gives himself security by being traditional and authoritarian in most aspects of his behavior, and then dares to be bold and creative in some other aspect. Henry Ford was such a person, as was J. Pierpont Morgan. And this type has been important in economic development in Japan, the Soviet Union, and Germany.

Thus, I suggest, there gradually emerges a group of individuals, creative, alienated from traditional values, driven by a

[*footnote 10 continued*
branch of the theory cannot be expounded here.

gnawing burning drive to prove themselves (to themselves, as well as to their fellows), seeking for an area in which to do so, preferably an area in which they can gain power, and preferably also one in which in some symbolic way they can vent their rage at the elites who have caused their troubles. Moreover, their (perhaps unconscious) rage at the group disparaging them will cause them to turn against some of the values of the group disparaging them. The fact that the disparaging group, in the cases cited above, was traditional, is one of the reasons why the disparaged group rejected traditional values and turned to innovation.

What they turn to will be determined in part by the models they find during their childhood somewhere in their history or their folklore or the tales their elders tell them of the life around them, and in part by the objective opportunities of the world around them. In the modern world, to few socially rebellious groups of traditional societies will any other road to power, recognition, and proof to oneself of one's ability seem as inviting as economic prowess, and creative individuals in most such groups will become economic innovators. In the cases of England, Japan, and Colombia, which I have examined in some detail, such groups have provided a disproportionate share of the leaders in the transition to economic growth.

A word is in point concerning the complexity of the situation in colonial societies. Here there has been rather harsh withdrawal of status respect, but by invading groups from the West who became colonial conquerors. These groups have not traditional but "modern" values toward manual-technical work. The tendency of disparaged groups to reject the values of the disparaging group may cause them to reject engaging their energies in the occupations of the conquerors. Thus even though they desire to gain symbols of economic power, an additional emotional block is put in the way of the indigenous elite becoming effective industrialists. This fact may explain some of the ambivalence and erratic behavior sometimes manifested.

The theory of some of whose central points have been sketched so briefly above proceeds in broad sweeps, and of course is subject to a corresponding margin of error. It seems plausible to me because it is internally consistent and because it explains many aspects of social, political, and economic behavior in low-income countries for which no other very logical explanation seems available.

If it is correct it does not follow that economic growth will succeed only where certain rather special historical conditions have existed. For the forces of modern history have caused social tensions among the social classes of low-income societies themselves, by virtue of which some degree of withdrawal of status respect has existed among the indigenous social classes of almost all of them, and what values various groups are alienated from or drawn to is confused and uncertain. However, innovational personality is clearly appearing, in varying degree. The drive for security, self-reassurance, and power will surely lead many innovational individuals to technological innovation, though frequently within social forms differing from those of the West.

THE ACHIEVEMENT MOTIVE IN ECONOMIC GROWTH[1]

David C. McClelland

From the beginning of recorded history, men have been fascinated by the fact that civilizations rise and fall. Culture growth, as Kroeber has demonstrated, is episodic, and sometimes occurs in quite different fields.[2] For example, the people living in the Italian peninsula at the time of ancient Rome produced a great civilization of law, politics, and military conquest; and at another time, during the Renaissance, the inhabitants of Italy produced a great civilization of art, music, letters, and science. What can account for such cultural

SOURCE. David C. McClelland, "The Achievement Motive in Economic Growth," in Bert F. Hoselitz and Wilbert E. Moore, eds., *Industrialization and Society* (The Hague: UNESCO and Mouton, 1963, pp. 74–96.

[1] This paper is a summary of the author's book. *The Achieving Society*, published by Van Nostrand Co. in Princeton, N.J., in the fall of 1961.
[2] A. L. Kroeber, *Configurations of Culture Growth* (Berkeley, California, 1944).

flowerings? In our time we have theorists like Huntington, who stresses the importance of climate, or Toynbee, who also feels the right amount of challenge from the environment is crucial though he conceives of the environment as including its psychic effects. Others, like Kroeber, have difficulty imagining any general explanation; they perforce must accept the notion that a particular culture happens to hit on a particularly happy mode of self-expression, which it then pursues until it becomes overspecialized and sterile.

My concern is not with all culture growth, but with economic growth. Some wealth or leisure may be essential to development in other fields—the arts, politics, science, or war—but we need not insist on it. However, the question of why some countries develop rapidly in the economic sphere at certain times and not at others is in itself of great interest, whatever its relation to other types of culture growth. Usually, rapid economic growth has been explained in terms of "external" factors—favorable opportunities for trade, unusual natural resources, or conquests that have opened up new markets or produced internal political stability. But I am interested in the *internal* factors—in the values and motives men have that lead them to exploit opportunities, to take advantage of favorable trade conditions; in short, to shape their own destiny.

This interest is not surprising; I am a psychologist—and, furthermore, a psychologist whose primary research interest is in human motivation, in the *reasons* that people behave as they do. Of course, all people have always, to a certain extent, been interested in human motivation. The difference between their interest and the twentieth-century psychologist's interest is that the latter tries to define his subject matter very precisely and, like all scientists, to measure it. How can human motives be identified, or even measured? Psychologists' favorite techniques for conducting research in this area have always been the interview and the questionnaire. If you want to know what a man's motives are, ask him. Of course, you need not ask him directly; but perhaps, if you talk to him long enough in an interview, or ask him enough in a questionnaire, you can infer what his motives are—more or less the same way that, from a number of clues, a detective would infer who had committed a crime.

Whatever else one thinks of Freud and the other psychoanalysts, they performed one extremely important service for psychology: once and for all, they persuaded us, rightly or wrongly, that what people said about their motives was not a reliable basis for determining what those motives really were. In his analyses of the psychopathology of everyday life and of dreams and neurotic symptoms, Freud demonstrated repeatedly that the "obvious" motives—the motives that the people themselves thought they had or that a reasonable observer would attribute to them—were not, in fact, the real motives

for their often strange behavior. By the same token, Freud also showed the way to a better method of learning what people's motives were. He analyzed dreams and free associations: in short, fantasy or imaginative behavior. Stripped of its air of mystery and the occult, psychoanalysis has taught us that one can learn a great deal about people's motives through observing the things about which they are spontaneously concerned in their dreams and waking fantasies. About ten or twelve years ago, the research group in America with which I was connected decided to take this insight quite seriously and to see what we could learn about human motivation by coding objectively what people spontaneously thought about in their waking fantasies.[3] Our method was to collect such free fantasy, in the form of brief stories written about pictures, and to count the frequency with which certain themes appeared—rather as a medical technician counts the frequency with which red or white corpuscles appear in a blood sample. We were able to demonstrate that the frequency with which certain "inner concerns" appeared in these fantasies varied systematically as a function of specific experimental conditions by which we aroused or induced motivational states in the subjects. Eventually, we were able to isolate several of these inner concerns, or motives, which, if present in great frequency in the fantasies of a particular person, enabled us to know something about how he would behave in many other areas of life.

Chief among these motives was what we termed "the need for Achievement" (*n* Achievement)—a desire to do well, not so much for the sake of social recognition or prestige, but to attain an inner feeling of personal accomplishment. This motive is my particular concern in this paper. Our early laboratory studies showed that people "high" in *n* Achievement tend to work harder at certain tasks; to learn

[3] J. W. Atkinson (ed.), *Motives in Fantasy, Action, and Society* (Princeton, N.J., 1958).

faster; to do their best work when it counts for the record, and not when special incentives, like money prizes, are introduced; to choose experts over friends as working partners; etc. Obviously, we cannot here review the many, many studies in this area. About five years ago, we became especially interested in the problem of what would happen in a society if a large number of people with a high need for achievement should happen to be present in it at a particular time. In other words, we became interested in a social-psychological question: What effect would a concentration of people with high n Achievement have on a society?

It might be relevant to describe how we began wondering about this. I had always been greatly impressed by the very perceptive analysis of the connection between Protestantism and the spirit of capitalism made by the great German sociologist, Max Weber.[4] He argues that the distinguishing characteristic of Protestant business entrepreneurs and of workers, particularly from the pietistic sects, was not that they had in any sense invented the institutions of capitalism or good craftsmanship, but that they went about their jobs with a new perfectionist spirit. The Calvinistic doctrine of predestination had forced them to rationalize every aspect of their lives and to strive hard for perfection in the positions in this world to which they had been assigned by God. As I read Weber's description of the behavior of these people, I concluded that they must certainly have had a high level of n Achievement. Perhaps the new spirit of capitalism Weber describes was none other than a high need for achievement— if so, then n Achievement has been responsible, in part, for the extraordinary economic development of the West. Another factor served to confirm this hypothesis. A careful study by Winterbottom had shown that boys with high n Achieve-

ment usually came from families in which the mothers stressed early self-reliance and mastery.[5] The boys whose mothers did *not* encourage their early self-reliance, or did not set such high standards of excellence, tended to develop lower need for achievement. Obviously, one of the key characteristics of the Protestant Reformation was its emphasis on self-reliance. Luther stressed the "priesthood of all believers" and translated the Bible so that every man could have direct access to God and religious thought. Calvin accentuated a rationalized perfection in this life for everyone. Certainly, the character of the Reformation seems to have set the stage, historically, for parents to encourage their children to attain earlier self-reliance and achievement. If the parents did in fact do so, they very possibly unintentionally produced the higher level of n Achievement in their children that was, in turn, responsible for the new spirit of capitalism.

This was the hypothesis that initiated our research. It was, of course, only a promising idea; much work was necessary to determine its validity. Very early in our studies, we decided that the events Weber discusses were probably only a special case of a much more general phenomenon —that it was n Achievement as such that was connected with economic development, and that the Protestant Reformation was connected only indirectly in the extent to which it had influenced the average n Achievement level of its adherents. If this assumption is correct, then a high average level of n Achievement should be equally associated with economic development in ancient Greece, in modern Japan, or in a preliterate tribe being studied by anthropologists in the South Pacific. In other words, in its most general form, the hypothesis attempts to isolate one of the key factors in the economic development, at least, of all civilizations. What evidence do

[4] Max Weber, *The Protestant Ethic and the Spirit of Capitalism*, trans. Talcott Parsons (New York, 1930).

[5] M. R. Winterbottom, "The Relation of Need for Achievement to Learning and Experiences in Independence and Mastery," in Atkinson, *op. cit.*, pp. 453–478.

we have that this extremely broad generalization will obtain? By now, a great deal has been collected—far more than I can summarize here; but I shall try to give a few key examples of the different types of evidence.

First, we have made historical studies. To do so, we had to find a way to obtain a measure of *n* Achievement level during time periods other than our own, whose individuals can no longer be tested. We have done this—instead of coding the brief stories written by an individual for a test, we code imaginative literary documents: poetry, drama, funeral orations, letters written by sea captains, epics, etc. Ancient Greece, which we studied first, supplies a good illustration. We are able to find literary documents written during three different historical periods and dealing with similar themes: the period of economic growth, 900 B.C.–475 B.C. (largely Homer and Hesiod); the period of climax, 475 B.C.–362 B.C.; and the period of decline, 362 B.C.–100 B.C. Thus, Hesiod wrote on farm and estate management in the early period;

Xenophon, in the middle period; and Aristotle, in the late period. We have defined the period of "climax" in economic, rather than in cultural, terms, because it would be presumptuous to claim, for example, that Aristotle in any sense represented a "decline" from Plato or Thales. The measure of economic growth was computed from information supplied by Heichelheim in his *Wirtschaftsgeschichte des Altertums.*[6] Heichelheim records in detail the locations throughout Europe where the remains of Greek vases from different centuries have been found. Of course, these vases were the principal instrument of Greek foreign trade, since they were the containers for olive oil and wine, which were the most important Greek exports. Knowing where the vase fragments have been found, we could compute the trade area of Athenian Greece for different time periods. We purposely omitted any consideration of the later

[6] F. Heichelheim, *Wirtschaftsgeschichte des Altertums* (Leiden, 1938).

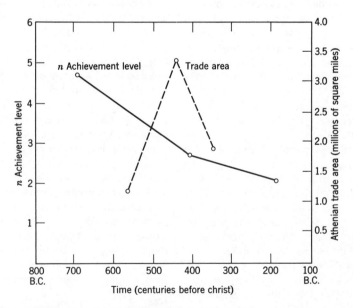

Figure 1. Average *n* Achievement level plotted at midpoints of periods of growth, climax, and decline of Athenian civilization as reflected in the extent of her trade area (measured for the sixth, fifth, and fourth centuries B.C. only).

expansion of Hellenistic Greece, because this represents another civilization; our concern was Athenian Greece.

When all the documents had been coded, they demonstrated—as predicted—that the level of *n* Achievement was highest during the period of growth prior to the climax of economic development in Athenian Greece. (See Figure 1.) In other words, the maximum *n* Achievement level preceded the maximum economic level by at least a century. Furthermore, that high level had fallen off by the time of maximum prosperity, thus foreshadowing subsequent economic decline. A similar methodology was applied, with the same results, to the economic development of Spain in the sixteenth century[7] and to two waves of economic development in the history of England (one in the late sixteenth century and the other at the beginning of the industrial revolution, around 1800).[8] The *n* Achievement level in English history (as determined on the basis of dramas, sea captains' letters, and street ballads) rose, between 1400 and 1800, *twice*, a generation or two before waves of accelerated economic growth (incidentally, at times of Protestant revival). This point is significant because it shows that there is no "necessary" steady decline in a civilization's entrepreneurial energy from its earlier to its later periods. In the Spanish and English cases, as in the Greek, high levels of *n* Achievement preceded economic decline. Unfortunately, space limitations preclude more detailed discussion of these studies here.

We also tested the hypothesis by applying it to preliterate cultures of the sort that anthropologists investigate. At Yale University, an organized effort has been made to collect everything that is known about all the primitive tribes that have been studied and to classify the information systematically for comparative purposes. We utilized this cross-cultural file to obtain the two measures that we needed to test our general hypothesis. For over fifty of these cultures, collections of folk tales existed that Child and others had coded.[9] just as we coded literary documents and individual imaginative stories, for *n* Achievement and other motives. These folk tales have the character of fantasy that we believe to be so essential for getting at "inner concerns." In the meantime, we were searching for a method of classifying the economic development of these cultures, so that we could determine whether those evincing high *n* Achievement in their folk tales had developed further than those showing lower *n* Achievement. The respective modes of gaining a livelihood were naturally very different in these cultures, since they came from every continent in the world and every type of physical habitat; yet we had to find a measure for comparing them. We finally thought of trying to estimate the number of full-time "business entrepreneurs" there were among the adults in each culture. We defined "entrepreneur" as "anyone who exercises control over the means of production and produces more than he can consume in order to sell it for individual or household income." Thus an entrepreneur was anyone who derived at least 75 per cent of his income from such exchange or market practices. The entrepreneurs were mostly traders, independent artisans, or operators of small firms like stores, inns, etc. Nineteen cultures were classified as high in *n* Achievement on the basis of their folk tales; 74 per cent of them contained some entrepreneurs. On the other hand, only 35 per cent of the twenty cultures that were classified as low in *n* Achievement con-

[7] J. B. Cortés, "The Achievement Motive in the Spanish Economy between the Thirteenth and the Eighteenth Centuries," *Economic Development and Cultural Change*, **9** (1960), 144–163.

[8] N. M. Bradburn and D. E. Berlew, "Need for Achievement and English Economic Growth," *Economic Development and Cultural Change*, 1961.

[9] I. L. Child, T. Storm, and J. Veroff, "Achievement Themes in Folk Tales Related to Socialization Practices," in Atkinson, *op. cit.*, pp. 479–492.

tained any entrepreneurs (as we defined it) at all. The difference is highly significant statistically (Chi-square $= 5.97$, $p < .02$). Hence data about primitive tribes seem to confirm the hypothesis that high n Achievement leads to a more advanced type of economic activity.

But what about modern nations? Can we estimate their level of n Achievement and relate it to their economic development? The question is obviously one of the greatest importance, but the technical problems of getting measures of our two variables proved to be really formidable. What type of literary document could we use that would be equally representative of the motivational levels of people in India, Japan, Portugal, Germany, the United States, and Italy? We had discovered in our historical studies that certain types of literature usually contain much more achievement imagery than others. This is not too serious as long as we are dealing with time changes within a given culture; but it is very serious if we want to compare two cultures, each of which may express its achievement motivation in a different literary form. At last, we decided to use children's stories, for several reasons. They exist in standard form in every modern nation, since all modern nations are involved in teaching their children to read and use brief stories for this purpose. Furthermore, the stories are imaginative; and, if selected from those used in the earliest grades, they are not often influenced by temporary political events. (We were most impressed by this when reading the stories that every Russian child reads. In general, they cannot be distinguished, in style and content, from the stories read in all the countries of the West.)

We collected children's readers for the second, third, and fourth grades from every country where they could be found for two time periods, which were roughly centered around 1925 and around 1950. We got some thirteen hundred stories, which were all translated into English. In all, we had twenty-one stories from each of twenty-three countries about 1925, and the same number from each of thirty-nine countries about 1950. Code was used on proper names, so that our scorers would not know the national origins of the stories. The tales were then mixed together, and coded for n Achievement (and certain other motives and values that I shall mention only briefly).

The next task was to find a measure of economic development. Again, the problem was to insure comparability. Some countries have much greater natural resources; some have developed industrially sooner than others; some concentrate in one area of production and some in another. Economists consider national income figures in per-capita terms to be the best measure available; but they are difficult to obtain for all countries, and it is hard to translate them into equal purchasing power. Ultimately, we came to rely chiefly on the measure of electricity produced: the units of measurement are the same all over the world; the figures are available from the 1920's on; and electricity is the *form* of energy (regardless of how it is produced) that is essential to modern economic development. In fact, electricity produced per capita correlates with estimates of income per capita in the 1950's around .90 anyway. To equate for differences in natural resources, such as the amount of water power available, etc., we studied *gains* in kilowatt hours produced per capita between 1925 and 1950. The level of electrical production in 1925 is, as one would expect, highly correlated with the size of the gain between then and 1950. So it was necessary to resort to a regression analysis; that is, to calculate, from the average regression of gain on level for all countries, how much gain a particular country should have shown between 1925 and 1950. The actual gain could then be compared with the expected gain, and the country could be classified as gaining more or less rapidly than would have been expected on the basis of its 1925 performance. The procedure is directly comparable to what we do when we predict, on the basis of some measure of I.Q., what grades a child can be expected to get in school, and then classify him as an "under-" or "over-achiever."

The correlation between the *n* Achievement level in the children's readers in 1925 and the growth in electrical output between 1925 and 1950, as compared with expectation, is a quite substantial .53, which is highly significant statistically. It could hardly have arisen by chance. Furthermore, the correlation is also substantial with a measure of gain over the expected in per-capita income, equated for purchasing power by Colin Clark. To check this result more definitively with the sample of forty countries for which we had reader estimates of *n* Achievement levels in 1950, we computed the equation for gains in electrical output in 1952–1958 as a function of level in 1952. It turned out to be remarkably linear when translated into logarithmic units, as is so often the case with simple growth functions. Table 1 (next page) presents the performance of each of the countries, as compared with predictions from initial level in 1952, in standard score units and classified by high and low *n* Achievement in 1950. Once again we found that *n* Achievement levels predicted significantly (r = .43) the countries which would perform more or less rapidly than expected in terms of the average for all countries. The finding is more striking than the earlier one, because many Communist and underdeveloped countries are included in the sample. Apparently, *n* Achievement is a precursor of economic growth—and not only in the Western style of capitalism based on the small entrepreneur, but also in economies controlled and fostered largely by the state.

For those who believe in economic determinism, it is especially interesting that *n* Achievement level in 1950 is *not* correlated either with *previous* economic growth between 1925 and 1950, or with the level of prosperity in 1950. This strongly suggests that *n* Achievement is a *causative* factor—a change in the minds of men which produces economic growth rather than being produced by it. In a century dominated by economic determinism, in both Communist and Western thought, it is startling to find concrete evidence for psychological determinism, for psychological developments as preceding and presumably causing economic changes.

The many interesting results which our study of children's stories yielded have succeeded in convincing me that we chose the right material to analyze. Apparently, adults unconsciously flavor their stories for young children with the attitudes, the aspirations, the values, and the motives that they hold to be most important.

I want to mention briefly two other findings, one concerned with economic development, the other with totalitarianism. When the more and less rapidly developing economies are compared on all the other variables for which we scored the children's stories, one fact stands out. In stories from those countries which had developed more rapidly in both the earlier and later periods, there was a discernible tendency to emphasize, in 1925 and in 1950, what David Riesman has called "other-directedness"—namely, reliance on the opinion of particular others, rather than on tradition, for guidance in social behavior.[10] *Public opinion* had, in these countries, become a major source of guidance for the individual. Those countries which had developed the mass media further and faster—the press, the radio, the public-address system—were also the ones who were developing more rapidly economically. I think that "other-directedness" helped these countries to develop more rapidly because public opinion is basically more flexible than institutionalized moral or social traditions. Authorities can utilize it to inform people widely about the need for new ways of doing things. However, traditional institutionalized

[10] David Riesman, with the assistance of Nathan Glazer and Reuel Denney, *The Lonely Crowd* (New Haven, Conn., 1950).

TABLE 1.   *Rate of growth in Electrical Output (1952–1958) and National n Achievement Levels in 1950*

Deviation from Expected Growth Rate[a] in Standard Score Units

National n Achievement levels (1950)[b]	Above Expectation			
High n Achievement				
3.62 Turkey	+1.38			
2.71 India[c]	+1.12			
2.38 Australia	+ .42			
2.32 Israel	+1.18			
2.33 Spain	+ 0.1			
2.29 Pakistan[d]	+2.75			
2.29 Greece	+1.18	3.38	Argentina	− .56
2.29 Canada	+ .08	2.71	Lebanon	− .67
2.24 Bulgaria	+1.37	2.38	France	− .24
2.24 U.S.A.	+ .47	2.33	U. So. Africa	− .06
2.14 West Germany	+ .53	2.29	Ireland	− .41
2.10 U.S.S.R.	+1.61	2.14	Tunisia	−1.87
2.10 Portugal	+ .76	2.10	Syria	− .25
Low n Achievement				
1.95 Iraq	+ .29	2.05	New Zealand	− .29
1.86 Austria	+ .38	1.86	Uruguay	− .75
1.67 U.K.	+ .17	1.81	Hungary	− .62
1.57 Mexico	+ .12	1.71	Norway	− .77
.86 Poland	+1.26	1.62	Sweden	− .64
		1.52	Finland	− .08
		1.48	Netherlands	− .15
		1.33	Italy	− .57
		1.29	Japan	− .04
		1.20	Switzerland[e]	−1.92
		1.19	Chile	−1.81
Correlation of n Achievement		1.05	Denmark	− .89
level (1950) × deviations from ex-		.57	Algeria	− .83
pected growth rate = .43, p < .01		.43	Belgium	−1.65

Header columns: "National n Achievement levels (1950)[b]", "Above Expectation", "Below Expectation"

[a] The estimates are computed from the monthly average electrical production figures, in millions of Kwh, for 1952 and 1958, from United Nations, *Monthly Bulletin of Statistics* (January 1960), and *World Energy Supplies*, 1951–1954 and 1955–1958 (Statistical Papers, Series J).

The correlation between log level 1952 and log gain 1952–58 is .976. The regression equation based on these thirty-nine countries, plus four others from the same climatic zone on which data are available (China-Taiwan, Czechoslovakia, Roumania, Yugoslavia), is: log gain (1952–58) = .9229 log level (1952) + .0480.

Standard scores are deviations from mean gain predicted by the regression formula (M = − .01831) divided by the standard deviation of the deviations from mean predicted gain (SD = .159).

[b] Based on twenty-one children's stories from second-, third-, and fourth-grade readers in each country.

[c] Based on six Hindi, seven Telegu, and eight Tamil stories.

[d] Based on twelve Urdu and eleven Bengali stories.

[e] Based on twenty-one German Swiss stories, mean = .91; twenty-one French Swiss stories, mean = 1.71; over-all mean obtained by weighting German mean double to give approximately proportionate representation to the two main ethnic population groups.

values may insist that people go on behaving in ways that are no longer adaptive to a changed social and economic order.

The other finding is not directly relevant to economic development, but it perhaps involves the means of achieving it. Quite unexpectedly, we discovered that every major dictatorial regime which came to power between the 1920's and 1950's (with the possible exception of Portugal's) was foreshadowed by a particular motive pattern in its stories for children: namely, a low need for affiliation (little interest in friendly relationships with people) and a high need for power (great concern over controlling and influencing other people).

The German readers showed this pattern before Hitler; the Japanese readers, before Tojo; the Argentine readers, before Peron; the Spanish readers, before Franco; the South African readers, before the present authoritarian government in South Africa; etc. On the other hand, very few countries which did not have dictatorships manifested this particular motive combination. The difference was highly significant statistically, since there was only one exception in the first instance and very few in the second. Apparently, we stumbled on a psychological index of ruthlessness—i.e., the need to influence other people (*n* Power), unchecked by sufficient concern for their welfare (*n* Affiliation). It is interesting, and a little disturbing, to discover that the German readers of today still evince this particular combination of motives, just as they did in 1925. Let us hope that this is one case where a social science generalization will not be confirmed by the appearance of a totalitarian regime in Germany in the next ten years.

To return to our main theme—let us discuss the precise ways that higher *n* Achievement leads to more rapid economic development, and why it should lead to economic development rather than, for example, to military or artistic development. We must consider in more detail the mechanism by which the concentration of a particular type of human motive in a population leads to a complex social phenomenon like economic growth. The link between the two social phenomena is, obviously, the business entrepreneur. I am not using the term "entrepreneur" in the sense of "capitalist": in fact, I should like to divorce "entrepreneur" entirely from any connotations of ownership. An entrepreneur is someone who exercises control over production that is not just for his personal consumption. According to my definition, for example, an executive in a steel production unit in Russia is an entrepreneur.

It was Joseph Schumpeter who drew the attention of economists to the importance that the activity of these entrepreneurs had in creating industrialization in the West. Their vigorous endeavors put together firms and created productive units where there had been none before. In the beginning, at least, the entrepreneurs often collected material resources, organized a production unit to combine the resources into a new product, and sold the product. Until recently, nearly all economists—including not only Marx, but also Western classical economists—assumed that these men were moved primarily by the "profit motive." We are all familiar with the Marxian argument that they were so driven by their desire for profits that they exploited the workingman and ultimately forced him to revolt. Recently, economic historians have been studying the actual lives of such entrepreneurs and finding—certainly to the surprise of some of the investigators—that many of them seemingly were not interested in making money as such. In psychological terms, at least, Marx's picture is slightly out of focus. Had these entrepreneurs been above all interested in money, many more of them would have quit working as soon as they had made all the money that they could possibly use. They would not have continued to risk their money in further entrepreneurial ventures. Many of them, in fact, came from pietistic sects, like the

Quakers in England, that prohibited the enjoyment of wealth in any of the ways cultivated so successfully by some members of the European nobility. However, the entrepreneurs often seemed consciously to be greatly concerned with expanding their businesses, with getting a greater share of the market, with "conquering brute nature," or even with altruistic schemes for bettering the lot of mankind or bringing about the kingdom of God on earth more rapidly. Such desires have frequently enough been labeled as hypocritical. However, if we assume that these men were really motivated by a desire for achievement rather than by a desire for money as such, the label no longer fits. This assumption also simplifies further matters considerably. It provides an explanation for the fact that these entrepreneurs were interested in money without wanting it for its own sake, namely, that money served as a ready quantitative index of how well they were doing—e.g., of how much they had achieved by their efforts over the past year. The need to achieve can never be satisfied by money; but estimates of profitability in money terms can supply direct knowledge of how well one is doing one's job.

The brief consideration of the lives of business entrepreneurs of the past suggested that their chief motive may well have been a high *n* Achievement. What evidence have we found in support of this? We made two approaches to the problem. First, we attempted to determine whether individuals with high *n* Achievement behave like entrepreneurs; and second, we investigated to learn whether actual entrepreneurs, particularly the more successful ones, in a number of countries, have higher *n* Achievement than do other people of roughly the same status. Of course, we had to establish what we meant by "behave like entrepreneurs"—what precisely distinguishes the way an entrepreneur behaves from the way other people behave?

The adequate answers to these questions would entail a long discussion of the sociology of occupations, involving the distinction originally made by Max Weber between capitalists and bureaucrats. Since this cannot be done here, a very brief report on our extensive investigations in this area will have to suffice. First, one of the defining characteristics of an entrepreneur is *taking risks* and/or innovating. A person who adds up a column of figures is not an entrepreneur—however carefully, efficiently, or correctly he adds them. He is simply following established rules. However, a man who decides to add a new line to his business *is* an entrepreneur, in that he cannot know in advance whether his decision will be correct. Nevertheless, he does not feel that he is in the position of a gambler who places some money on the turn of a card. Knowledge, judgment, and skill enter into his decision-making; and, if his choice is justified by future developments, he can certainly feel a sense of personal achievement from having made a successful move.

Therefore, if people with high *n* Achievement are to behave in an entrepreneurial way, they must seek out and perform in situations in which there is some moderate risk of failure—a risk which can, presumably, be reduced by increased effort or skill. They should not work harder than other people at routine tasks, or perform functions which they are certain to do well simply by doing what everyone accepts as the correct traditional thing to do. On the other hand, they should avoid gambling situations, because, even if they win, they can receive no sense of personal achievement, since it was not skill but luck that produced the results. (And, of course, most of the time they would lose, which would be highly unpleasant to them.) The data on this point are very clear cut. We have repeatedly found, for example, that boys with high *n* Achievement choose to play games of skill that incorporate a moderate risk of failure. Figure 2 represents one study. The game was adapted from one used by the psychologist Kurt Lewin. Each child was given a rope ring and told that he could stand at any distance that he

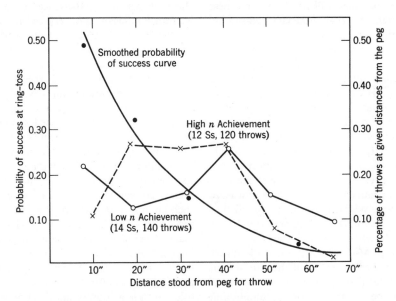

Figure 2. Percentage of throws made by five-year-olds with high and low "doodle" *n* Achievement at different distances from the peg and smoothed curve of probability of success at those distances. 26 *S*s, 10 throws each. Plotted at midpoints of intervals of 11 inches beginning with closest distance stood (4 in. to 14 in., 5 in. to 15 in., etc.).

preferred from the peg, to try to throw the ring over the peg. The children with high *n* Achievement usually stood at middle distances from the peg, where the chances of success or failure were moderate. However, the children with low *n* Achievement evinced no particular preference for any position. They more frequently stood at extremes of distance—either very close to the peg, where they were sure to throw the ring over it, or very far away, where they were almost certain not to. They thus manifested behavior like that of many people in underdeveloped countries who, while they act very traditionally economically, at the same time love to indulge in lotteries—risking a little to make a great deal on a very long shot. In neither of the two last examples do the actors concentrate on the realistic *calculated* risk, as do the subjects with high *n* Achievement.

We have recently concluded a somewhat analogous study, which indicated that boys with high *n* Achievement tend to perform better and to work harder under conditions of moderate risk—boys not only in the United States, but also in Japan, Brazil, and India. In each of these countries, the boys with high *n* Achievement did not invariably perform a laboratory task better than the boys with low *n* Achievement. They did better only under conditions involving some degree of competition, some risk of doing worse than others or of not getting a sense of personal achievement. There was still another group of boys in the sample from each country. These boys were identified by their optimistic attitude toward life in general, as manifested in their answers to a questionnaire. The members of these groups always had more success than the others, no matter what the competitive or risk situation was. I like to think of these boys as the conscientious ones, who will do their work cheerfully and efficiently under any kind of incentive conditions. They may form the backbone of the civil service, because they can tolerate routine; but they will not be the business entrepreneurs, because the latter constantly seek situations in which they can obtain a sense of personal achievement from having overcome risks or difficulties.

Another quality that the entrepreneur seeks in his work is that his job be a kind that ordinarily provides him with accurate knowledge of the results of his decisions. As a rule, growth in sales, in output, or in profit margins tells him very precisely whether he has made the correct choice under uncertainty or not. Thus, the concern for profit enters in—profit is a measure of success. We have repeatedly found that boys with a high n Achievement work more efficiently when they know how well they are doing. Also, they will not work harder for money rewards; but if they are asked, they state that greater money rewards should be awarded for accomplishing more difficult things in games of skill. In the ring-toss game, subjects were asked how much money they thought should be awarded for successful throws from different distances. Subjects with high n Achievement and those with low n Achievement agreed substantially about the amounts for throws made close to the peg. However, as the distance from the peg increased, the amounts awarded for successful throws by the subjects with high n Achievement rose more rapidly than did the rewards by those with low n Achievement. Here, as elsewhere, individuals with high n Achievement behaved as they must if they are to be the successful entrepreneurs in society. They believed that greater achievement should be recognized by quantitatively larger reward.

We are now investigating to learn whether business executives do, in fact, have higher n Achievement. Our analysis of this question is not yet finished; but Figure 3 indicates what, on the whole, we shall probably find. Four conclusions can be drawn from it. (1) Entrepreneurs ("junior executives") have higher n Achievement than do a comparable group of nonentrepreneurs ("adjusters"), whose chief job was quasijudicial (tax claim and insurance adjusters). A very careful study in the General Electric Company has confirmed this finding: on the average, production managers have higher n Achievement than do staff specialists of comparable education and pay. (2) The more successful junior executives have higher n Achievement than the less successful ones. (3) Turkish executives have a lower *average* level of n Achievement than American executives. This finding supports the general impression that the "entrepreneurial spirit" is in short supply in such countries. (4) Nevertheless, the more successful Turkish executives have a higher level of n Achievement than do the less successful ones. This confirms our prediction that n Achievement equips people peculiarly for the business executive role—even in a country like Turkey, where business traditions are quite different from those of the West.

There are two successful, and one unsuccessful, methods by which the business community recruits people with the "entrepreneurial spirit"—with high n Achievement. The unsuccessful way is easiest to describe and is still characteristic of many underdeveloped countries. In a study of the occupational likes and dislikes of boys in Japan, Brazil, Germany, India, and the United States, we found that (as Atkinson had predicted on theoretical grounds) the boys with high n Achievement usually aspire toward the occupation of highest prestige *which they have a reasonable chance to enter and to succeed.*[11] For example, their ambitions will be centered on the professions, which are the highest prestige occupations in most countries—*if* the boys themselves are from the upper class and thus have the opportunity and backing to enter the professions. In other words, when the business leadership of a country is largely recruited from the élite (as it is in many countries, because only the élite

[11] J. W. Atkinson, "Motivational Determinants of Risk-Taking Behavior," *Psychological Review,* **64** (1957), 359–372.

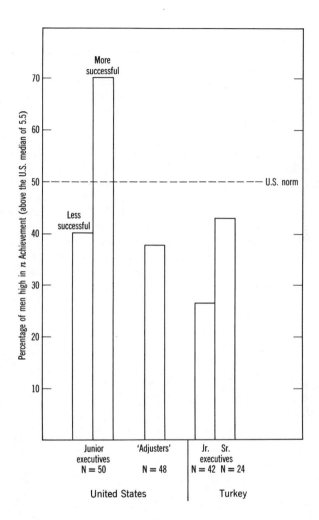

Figure 3. Percentages of different types of executives high in *n* Achievement in the United States and Turkey (after data supplied by N. M. Bradburn).

has access to capital and to government), it will *not* tend to attract those with high *n* Achievement who are not from the upper class.

Developments in many of the Western democracies were quite different. In the most rapidly advancing countries, business leadership was drawn, at least in the early stages, largely from the middle classes.

A business career was the highest prestige occupation to which a middle-class boy with high *n* Achievement could aspire—especially if he were a member of a disliked minority group, like the Protestants in France or the Jews in many countries, to whom other channels of upward mobility were closed. Thus a constant "natural" flow of entrepreneurial talent from the middle classes provided economic leadership of a high quality.

The other successful method of recruiting entrepreneurial talent is the one that has been adopted, for example, in the U.S.S.R. There, the central government took a severe, achievement-oriented, "pass-or-fail" attitude toward its plant managers, so that only the "fittest" survived. We believe that those "fittest" were the ones with the highest n Achievement, although we have no supporting evidence as yet. In the free enterprise system, the recruiting method may be compared to a garden in which all plants are allowed to grow until some crowd the others out. In the Soviet system, it is comparable to a garden in which plants that have not reached a specified height by a certain time are weeded out. In many underdeveloped countries, it is comparable to a garden where only certain plants are permitted to live in the first place, so that the gardener has to take them whatever size they attain.

Of course, no country represents a pure type; but perhaps the analogy, oversimplified though it is, helps to illustrate my point.

What produces high n Achievement? Why do some societies produce a large number of people with this motive, while other societies produce so many fewer? We conducted long series of researches into this question. I can present only a few here.

One very important finding is essentially a negative one: n Achievement cannot be hereditary. Popular psychology has long maintained that some races are more energetic than others. Our data clearly contradict this in connection with n Achievement. The changes in n Achievement level within a given population are too rapid to be attributed to heredity. For example, the correlation between respective n Achievement levels in the 1925 and 1950 samples of readers is substantially zero. Many of the countries that were high in

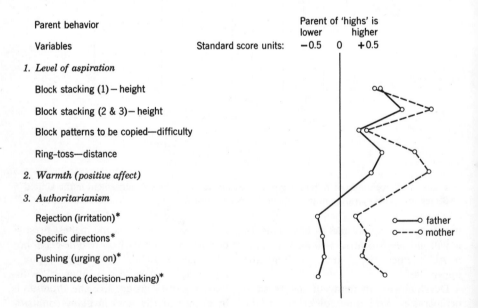

Figure 4. Mean differences in the behavior of parents of sons with low and high n Achievement working in task situations (after Rosen and D'Andrade). The asterisk indicates parents of "highs" predicted to be lower, permitting more independence.

n Achievement at one or both times may be low or moderate in *n* Achievement now, and vice versa. Germany was low in 1925 and is high now; and certainly the hereditary makeup of the German nation has not changed in a generation.

However, there is substantiating evidence that *n* Achievement is a motive which a child can acquire quite early in life, say, by the age of eight or ten, as a result of the way his parents have brought him up. Winterbottom's study of the importance of early self-reliance and achievement training has been supplemented by a much more detailed inquiry by Rosen and D'Andrade.[12] They actually entered the homes of boys with high and low *n* Achievement and observed how the boys were treated by their parents while they were engaged in various kinds of work, e.g., stacking blocks blindfolded. The principal results are summarized in Figure 4, which indicates the differences between the parents of the "high *n* Achievement boys" and the parents of boys with low *n* Achievement. In general, the mothers and the fathers of the first group set higher levels of aspiration in a number of tasks for their sons. They were also much warmer, showing positive emotion in reacting to their sons' performances. In the area of authority or dominance, the data are quite interesting. The mothers of the "highs" were more domineering than the mothers of the "lows," but the *fathers* of the "highs" were significantly *less* domineering than the fathers of the "lows." In other words, the fathers of the "highs" set high standards and are warmly interested in their sons' performances, but they do not directly interfere. This gives the boys the chance to develop initiative and self-reliance.

What factors cause parents to behave in this way? Their behavior certainly is involved with their values and, possibly, ultimately with their religion or their general world view. At present, we cannot be sure that Protestant parents are more likely to behave this way than Catholic parents—there are too many subgroup variations within each religious portion of the community: the Lutheran father is probably as likely to be authoritarian as the Catholic father. However, there does seem to be one crucial variable discernible: the extent to which the religion of the family emphasizes individual, as contrasted with ritual, contact with God. The preliterate tribes that we studied in which the religion was the kind that stressed the individual contact had higher *n* Achievement; and in general, mystical sects in which this kind of religious self-reliance dominates have had higher *n* Achievement.

The extent to which the authoritarian father is away from the home while the boy is growing up may prove to be another crucial variable. If so, then one incidental consequence of prolonged wars may be an increase in *n* Achievement, because the fathers are away too much to interfere with their sons' development of it. And in Turkey, Bradburn found that those boys tended to have higher *n* Achievement who had left home early or whose fathers had died before they were eighteen.[13] Slavery was another factor which played an important role in the past. It probably lowered *n* Achievement—in the slaves, for whom obedience and responsibility, but not achievement, were obvious virtues; and in the slaveowners, because household slaves were often disposed to spoil the owner's children as a means for improving their own positions. This is both a plausible and a probable reason for the drop in *n* Achievement level in ancient Greece that occurred at about the time the middleclass entrepreneur was first able to afford, and obtain by conquest, as many as two slaves for each child. The idea also clarifies the slow economic development of the South in the United States by attributing

[12] B. C. Rosen and R. G. D'Andrade, "The Psychosocial Origins of Achievement Motivation," *Sociometry*, 22 (1959), 185–218.

[13] N. M. Bradburn, "The Managerial Role in Turkey" (unpublished Ph.D. dissertation, Harvard University, 1960).

its dilatoriness to a lack of n Achievement in its élite; and it also indicates why lower-class American Negroes, who are closest to the slave tradition, possess very low n Achievement.[14]

I have outlined our research findings. Do they indicate ways of accelerating economic development? Increasing the level of n Achievement in a country suggests itself as an obvious first possibility. If n Achievement is so important, so specifically adapted to the business role, then it certainly should be raised in level, so that more young men have an "entrepreneurial drive." The difficulty in this excellent plan is that our studies of how n Achievement originates indicate that the family is the key formative influence; and it is very hard to change on a really large scale. To be sure, major historical events like wars have taken authoritarian fathers out of the home; and religious reform movements have sometimes converted the parents to a new achievement-oriented ideology. However, such matters are not ordinarily within the policy-making province of the agencies charged with speeding economic development.

Such agencies can, perhaps, effect the general acceptance of an achievement-oriented ideology as an absolute *sine qua non* of economic development. Furthermore, this ideology should be diffused not only in business and governmental circles, but throughout the nation, and in ways that will influence the thinking of all parents as they bring up their children. As Rosen and D'Andrade found, parents must, above all, set high standards for their children. The campaign to spread achievement-oriented ideology, if possible, could also incorporate an attack on the extreme authoritarianism in fathers that impedes or prevents the development of self-reliance in their sons. This is, however, a more delicate point, and attacking this, in many countries, would be to threaten

values at the very center of social life. I believe that a more indirect approach would be more successful. One approach would be to take the boys out of the home and to camps. A more significant method would be to promote the rights of women, both legally and socially—one of the ways to undermine the absolute dominance of the male is to strengthen the rights of the female! Another reason for concentrating particularly on women is that they play the leading role in rearing the next generation. Yet, while men in underdeveloped countries come in contact with new achievement-oriented values and standards through their work, women may be left almost untouched by such influences. But if the sons are to have high n Achievement, the mothers must first be reached.

It may seem strange that a paper on economic development should discuss the importance of feminism and the way children are reared; but this is precisely where a psychological analysis leads. If the motives of men are the agents that influence the speed with which the economic machine operates, then the speed can be increased only through affécting the factors that create the motives. Furthermore—to state this point less theoretically—I cannot think of evinced substantial, rapid long-term economic development where women have not been somewhat freed from their traditional setting of "Kinder, Küche und Kirche" and allowed to play a more powerful role in society, specifically as part of the working force. This generalization applies not only to the Western democracies like the United States, Sweden, or England, but also to the U.S.S.R., Japan, and now China.

In the present state of our knowledge, we can conceive of trying to raise n Achievement levels only in the next generation—although new research findings may soon indicate n Achievement in adults can be increased. Most economic planners, while accepting the long-range desirability of raising n Achievement in future generations, want to know what

[14] B. C. Rosen, "Race, Ethnicity, and Achievement Syndrome," *American Sociological Review*, **24** (1959), 47–60.

can be done during the next five or ten years. This immediacy inevitably focuses attention on the process or processes by which executives or entrepreneurs are selected. Foreigners with proved entrepreneurial drive can be hired, but at best this is a temporary and unsatisfactory solution. In most underdeveloped countries where government is playing a leading role in promoting economic development, it is clearly necessary for the government to adopt rigid achievement-oriented standards of performance like those in the U.S.S.R.[15] A government manager or, for that matter, a private entrepreneur, should have to produce "or else." Production targets must be set, as they are in most economic plans; and individuals must be held responsible for achieving them, even at the plant level. The philosophy should be one of "no excuses accepted." It is common for government officials or economic theorists in underdeveloped countries to be weighed down by all the difficulties which face the economy and render its rapid development difficult or impossible. They note that there is too rapid population growth, too little capital, too few technically competent people, etc. Such obstacles to growth are prevalent, and in many cases they are immensely hard to overcome; but talking about them can provide merely a comfortable rationalization for mediocre performance. It is difficult to fire an administrator, no matter how poor his performance, if so many objective reasons exist for his doing badly. Even worse, such rationalization permits, in the private sector, the continued employment of incompetent family members as executives. If these private firms were afraid of being penalized for poor performance, they might be impelled to find more able professional managers a little more quickly. I am not an expert in this field, and the mechanisms I am suggesting may be far from appropriate. Still, they may serve to illustrate

my main point: if a country short in entrepreneurial talent wants to advance rapidly, it must find ways and means of insuring that only the most competent retain positions of responsibility. One of the obvious methods of doing so is to judge people in terms of their *performance* —and not according to their family or political connections, their skill in explaining why their unit failed to produce as expected, or their conscientiousness in following the rules. I would suggest the use of psychological tests as a means of selecting people with high *n* Achievement; but, to be perfectly frank, I think this approach is at present somewhat impractical on a large enough scale in most underdeveloped countries.

Finally, there is another approach which I think is promising for recruiting and developing more competent business leadership. It is the one called, in some circles, the "professionalization of management." Harbison and Myers have recently completed a world-wide survey of the efforts made to develop professional schools of high-level management. They have concluded that, in most countries, progress in this direction is slow.[16] Professional management is important for three reasons. (1) It may endow a business career with higher prestige (as a kind of profession), so that business will attract more of the young men with high *n* Achievement from the élite groups in backward countries. (2) It stresses *performance* criteria of excellence in the management area—i.e., what a man can do and not what he is. (3) Advanced management schools can themselves be so achievement-oriented in their instruction that they are able to raise the *n* Achievement of those who attend them.

Applied toward explaining historical events, the results of our researches clearly shift attention away from external factors and to man—in particular, to his motives and values. That about which he thinks and

[15] David Granick, *The Red Executive* (New York, 1960).

[16] Frederick Harbison and Charles A. Myers, *Management in the Industrial World* (New York, 1959).

dreams determines what will happen. The emphasis is quite different from the Darwinian or Marxist view of man as a creature who *adapts* to his environment. It is even different from the Freudian view of civilization as the sublimation of man's primitive urges. Civilization, at least in its economic aspects, in neither adaptation nor sublimation; it is a positive creation by a people made dynamic by a high level of n Achievement. Nor can we agree with Toynbee, who recognizes the importance of psychological factors as "the very forces which actually decide the issue when an encounter takes place," when he states that these factors "inherently are impossible to weigh and measure, and therefore to estimate scientifically in advance."[17] It is a measure of the pace at which the behavioral sciences are developing that even within Toynbee's lifetime we can demonstrate that he was mistaken. The psychological factor responsible for a civilization's rising to a challenge is so far from being "inherently impossible to weigh and measure" that it has been weighed and measured and scientifically estimated in advance; and, so far as we can now tell, this factor is the achievement motive.

[17] Arnold J. Toynbee, *A Study of History* (abridgment by D. C. Somervill; Vol. 1, New York, 1947).

Chapter 4

Ideology and Nationalism

THE IDEOLOGY OF ECONOMIC POLICY IN THE NEW STATES

Harry G. Johnson

Any discussion of this subject necessarily demands a high degree of abstraction and involves a great deal of generalization which may not closely fit the facts about any particular new state. Each new state obviously has its own historical background in which both the general ideology and the particular policies of the colonizing nation (whether European or American) have had a formative influence on the development of its general and economic ideology. And each new state has its own particular economic structure and corresponding economic problems toward which its economic policy and ideology are necessarily oriented. Thus there are, as one might expect, substantive differences among new nations with respect to the ideology of economic policy.

There are, to begin with, wide differences in attitudes toward the issue of free enterprise versus state control of economic activity. For example, contrast the Republic of the Philippines, which has been strongly influenced by the United States ideology on economic affairs, or Malaya, which has

been strongly influenced by British ideas, with Indonesia, where the colonial background was Dutch. On a lesser scale, there is a difference between Pakistan and India with respect to the question of state ownership. State ownership is insisted on strongly in Indian ideology, whereas Pakistan has been much more tolerant of free enterprise. This obviously cannot be explained by differences in colonial background, and it is difficult to explain by referring to differences in the dominant religions; rather, the explanation seems to lie in the different inheritances of the two from the British. In particular, the Indians inherited British socialism and most of the Indian civil service, whereas the Pakistanis inherited the traditions of the British army, while they did not inherit an effective civil service to develop into a centralized and centralizing elite after Partition. The shortage of talented administrators in Pakistan has influenced attitudes there toward the management of the economy. The Pakistan Industrial Development Board, for example, has started new industries with the deliberate objective of getting them into private hands quickly so as to economize on the administrative talent available.

A second area of difference concerns the importance attached to agriculture and the

SOURCE: Harry G. Johnson, "The Ideology of Economic Policy in the New States," in Harry G. Johnson (ed.), *Economic Nationalism in Old and New States* (Chicago: University of Chicago Press, 1967), pp. 124–41.

101

emphasis given to the need for land reform; these differences reflect differences in population pressure on the land and also differences in systems of land tenure which in part come from indigenous cultural origins, in part from the practices of colonial powers. There are also differences between countries depending on whether their agriculture is primarily a subsistence type of agriculture—producing, say, for local markets as well as for the people who live on the land—or whether it is an agriculture which produces predominantly for export and so is an important source of foreign exchange. Related differences concern the relative importance of plantation and peasant agriculture in export trade. The land reform problem is probably most bitter in Latin America—which can hardly be described as a collection of new states, but which in many ways manifests similar problems.

Third, there are differences in the prevailing attitudes toward foreign investment and foreign enterprises, ranging from great suspicion coupled with the desire to appropriate or confiscate foreign enterprises, at the one extreme, to positive policies of encouraging foreign enterprise, at the other. These differences obviously depend on the nature of the development problem, on the strength of the need for massive applications of capital and specialized technology, and also on the past colonial history of the country in question.

Finally, of course, there are always special factors at work in particular new states. For example, in Pakistan, a religious state, the question of the ethics of interest charges has been a perennially important issue, since Islam forbids the taking of *riba* (usury). Contractual interest payments prevail there as elsewhere, but there is a strong minority group that believes that the religious principle should be legally enforced. To do so, of course, would be fatal to national economic organization. Again, as a populous nation of continental proportions, India is prone to develop imperialist ambitions not possible for the majority of smaller new nations.

Despite these significant differences, there are substantial similarities among the ideologies of economic policy in the new states—at least, sufficiently so for it to be useful to discuss them collectively. These similarities can be traced to a number of common factors which work to a greater or lesser degree in all of these nations. This paper will discuss their contributions to the ideology of economic policy in the new states.

Three of these common influences or factors are especially significant; in fact, they overlap and influence each other to a large extent. These influences are: (1) political nationalism, which has its counterpart in economic nationalism; (2) ideas on economic development formed by the economic and intellectual history of the interwar period (especially the 1930's) that are part of a world "milieu of ideas" which has been diffused and disseminated among the new nations, providing a common body of interpretation, thought, and policy prescription, a sort of international language of economic development; and (3) the relations between the developing countries and the advanced countries, which focus on questions of development assistance and which in turn impart certain common formative influences.

Political and Economic Nationalism

Almost by definition, nationalism is a driving force in the new states. It is the motivation for their formation, the key to their politics, and also, an objective of their development, in the sense that the cultivation of feelings of nationalism and of attachment to the nation is essential to the formative processes of, and a means for the integration of, the nation and the differentiation of it from other nations. Our concern here is with the implications of nationalism for the ideology of economic policy rather than with the problems of social and political integration. The essential point, looking at the matter from a psychological point of view, is that nationalism is concerned with establishing the self-respect of members of the nation in comparison with members of other nations and with creating a distinctive national identity. National identity is a very complex concept which involves both comparability of achievement with other nations and differentiation of the nation from other nations—both imitation and separation. Moreover, because there is a basic self-doubt involved in any serious concern about identity, nationalism involves hostility toward other nations and a tendency to adopt a double standard of morality with respect to them. The notion of the double standard of morality cannot be explored in detail here, but it colors every aspect of the attitudes of new nations toward the advanced countries with which they trade and from which they receive aid.

From the point of view of its effects on political and economic behavior, nationalism attaches value to having property owned by nationals and having economic functions performed by nationals. Further, nationalism attaches particular value to property and functions which are considered important to the identity and the power of the nation. In general terms, this imparts a strong tendency for economic policy to have, as a major objective, the creation of an economy similar to those of nations that are regarded as powerful, and to have that national economy controlled by nationals.

This objective has two major aspects. In the first place, where the national economy lacks productive facilities that are considered important to the power of powerful nations, national policy attempts by all available means to create such facilities. But it is not just a question of creating facilities; it is also a question of creating facilities *under national control*. This in turn tends to mean a preference for public ownership as a means of insuring control, hostility to investment by foreign enter-

prises, and a desire to prevent, control, or restrict and regulate such foreign investment. Both these preferences involve self-contradictions to some extent, at least from the viewpoint of the economist interested in economic efficiency. The preference for public ownership and control creates the problem of selection and utilization of managerial talent; hostility to foreign investment imposes obstacles to obtaining capital, enterprise, and technology of the best kind for developing the country's resources.

Second, where the facilities exist but are not controlled by nationals, there is a tendency to attempt to take over control of them. This may involve confiscation, nationalization, or seriously restrictive government regulations. This tendency applies not merely to productive enterprises but also to other kinds of positions of control, such as administrative jobs in the government and positions in the military services.

Nationalism, therefore, involves an ideological preference in economic policy for a number of goals. One of them, obviously, is as much self-sufficiency as is possible. Another is public ownership and public enterprise in key economic sectors and, where public ownership and public enterprise are impracticable, extensive public regulation and control of private enterprise. A third is to ensure as far as possible domestic participation in or control of the ownership of foreign enterprises and of their management. All of this involves discrimination in favor of nationals in general, but it also involves discrimination in favor of certain kinds of nationals—that is, the discrimination is not homogeneous. Discrimination is applied particularly in favor of those who are part of the government organization itself or who can be attached to and controlled by it. This may involve discrimination within the nation as well as against foreign nationals, inasmuch as the routes by which people may enter the governmental structure may be barred to significant groups within the country itself.

This discrimination involves relying on nationality rather than on economic efficiency, competence, or productive performance in the selection of personnel. This in turn involves conflicts between the avowed determination to encourage economic development and the growth of the nation and the national economy, and the effectiveness of the means used to pursue these objectives. A great many of the problems and disappointments of economic development policy in practice can only be understood in terms of the mismatching of means and stated ends—perhaps one might put the point the other way around: that the stated ends are not the real ends but a cover for the real ends, which are concerned with ownership and control rather than development per se.

The foregoing remarks relate to the general character of the influence of nationalism on the ideology of economic policy in new states. But nationalism also contributes some specific biases to that economic policy. The most important of these is the insistence on industrialization coupled with a relative neglect of agriculture and indeed a frequently deliberate exploitation of agriculture in order to finance industrialization. This is so typical that, as Peter Bauer has remarked, the difference between an advanced country and a backward country is that an advanced country overpays its farmers and a backward country underpays its farmers. (Of course, in both cases, what is involved is exploitation of the majority by a minority, since the farmers are few in advanced countries and many in underdeveloped countries.)

This objective of policy is in large part directed at achieving a "modern-looking" nation-state. To the new nations, the power of the established leading nations is evident in their industrial productiveness; it is not so apparent that their economic efficiency is also manifested in the efficiency of their agriculture, which is productive enough to enable them to be nearly self-sufficient in foodstuffs—and, in the case of the United States, to produce an agricultural export surplus—while employing only a small fraction of their populations in agriculture. In part also, the emphasis on industrialization is a consequence of the view prevalent in most cultures that agriculture is a backward way of life, and of the tendency of those engaged in it to earn disfavor by resisting the forces of national integration.

Much of the insistence on industrialization in new states is, however, connected indirectly with the role of the nation as a military unit. Industry is desired as the foundation of military power. In this respect the development of industry and science has brought a major change in the economic prerequisites of military power and success. In the past, the capacity to wage successful war depended on having a sufficient agricultural surplus to support forces in the field; while weaponry could be fabricated by rural handicraft skills (this was a potent reason why major military campaigns started in the late summer, after the harvest was assured—a custom still observed in the two major wars of this century). Now, the capacity to wage war depends on the presence of efficient industrial capacity, both to produce the weaponry and, more important, to provide a reservoir of skills capable of maintaining and operating it. It is true that international competition in the provision of armaments is reasonably efficient, so that a nation could rely on production of an agricultural surplus for the world market to finance its military needs, but this involves sufficient uncertainty and lack of control over supplies to be unattractive.

Insistence on industrialization is not only general; it also concentrates on certain specific industries regarded as of crucial importance to nationhood. The selection of these industries for special favor is motivated more by casual observation of developed countries and by a rather naïve mythology of economic history than by rational analysis of the logic of industrial organization or of comparative advantage.

In the ambitious less developed countries, the establishment of a domestic steel industry is regarded as the sine qua non of economic development. In those countries that have laid the basis for modern industry, such as India and the Latin-American countries, the automotive industry has come to assume the role of demonstrator of industrial competence. Neither industry suggests itself to rational economic analysis as especially likely to speed growth through feedback and linkage effects, and both are notoriously vulnerable to fluctuations in demand and production.

The second bias in economic policy in new states attributable to nationalism is the preference for economic planning. This bias involves some complex psychological motivations. One element is imitation of what was for long believed to be the essence of the superiority of the Russians over their capitalist competitors, in a mythology cultivated by the social and economic critics of free enterprise in the capitalist countries. Another is the appeal of the promise of surpassing the performance of the leading capitalist nations and at the same time establishing moral superiority over them by adopting the policies recommended by their own social critics. Still another is the possibility of using the controls associated with planning to secure nationalist objectives otherwise difficult to implement.

A third specific bias in economic policy is indiscriminate hostility to the large international corporations. These tend to be regarded as agencies of the colonialism and imperialism of the advanced countries in which they make their headquarters and as a threat to national independence and identity; they are identified with the economic power of their parent countries. This attitude is partly justified and partly not. The large international corporations are political entities serving their own interests; but precisely for that reason, their operations are not likely to be dominated by the national interests of their country of origin—on the contrary, they frequently conflict with those interests. Paradoxically enough, it is frequently found that both the parent country and the country in which the corporations have subsidiary operations regard these operations as inimical to their respective national interests: both in England in the 1920's and in the United States in the 1960's complaints have been voiced that, by investing abroad, national corporations were depriving nationals of employment opportunities and aggravating the country's balance-of-payments problem.

Prevailing Concepts of the Development Problem

The second major common force which has shaped the ideology of economic policy in the new states is the general climate of ideas on economic development prevailing in policy-making circles, national and international, in the modern world. These ideas were formed in the interwar period and carried down into the period since World War II, during which the new nations have emerged into independence. They have three major sources in interwar experience.

One was the peace settlement after World War I, which established the equivalent of contemporary new nations in Europe as a result of the application of the principle of national self-determination and the consequent breakup of the Austro-Hungarian Empire. The main contribution of these events was to lend a strongly nationalistic tone to discussions of economic policy and development problems in these countries, discussions which, moreover, derived most of their ideas from observation of German economic policy, the reading of German writings, and the experience of academic studies in Germany by various leading participants. These ideas were disseminated in the Anglo-Saxon literature of economic development with the voluntary or enforced migration of Central European intellectuals in the 1930's, particularly to the United Kingdom but also to the United States. While fundamentally concerned with policies for developing the Balkan states on the

German model, the central concepts were presented as universals and later proved equally congenial to the psychological attitudes of the new nations in their relations with the developed countries and in their conception of their development problems. Influential economists in this group include Mandelbaum, Kaldor, Rosenstein-Rodan, and Balogh. Balogh's intellectual history and writings are particularly interesting in this respect: a fairly simple conceptual framework, translating into economic language the power politics of the 1930's relationship between Hungary and Germany, is turned successively to the war and postwar relationship of the United Kingdom (and Europe in general) to the United States, then (briefly) to the rivalry between Britain and Germany in postwar Europe, and subsequently to the relationship between the less developed and the advanced countries.

This infiltration of ideas from Central Europe into the Anglo-Saxon tradition did a great deal to implant the habit of thinking in nationalist rather than cosmopolitan terms in the Western economic tradition and to establish the fictional concept of the nation as an economic entity endowed with consistent objectives and a consensus in favor of realizing them by national economic policy. More concretely, this group of economists was largely responsible for the strong emphasis on the need for industrialization, and the potency of protectionist policies as means of achieving it, that constitutes the prevalent strand in the contemporary "conventional wisdom" of the theory of economic development policy. In effect, in spite of the dominance in the mainstream of economic thought of the liberal and cosmopolitan ideas of the English classical economists, the nationalist and interventionist ideas of the German economist Friedrich List have been transmitted indirectly through Germany's Central European emulators to become the dominant ideas of Anglo-Saxon economics on questions relating to the promotion of economic development in the new nations.

The second important source of contemporary ideas on the problem of economic development was a legacy of the great depression that began in 1929, coinciding with generally good harvests in the cereal-exporting countries. The depression had a catastrophic effect in reducing the money prices of primary products, which fell much farther than those of manufactured goods—and the more backward regions of the world from which the new nations have since been created depended on their earnings from exports of primary products not only to finance their purchases of manufactured goods but also to service the debts they had incurred for overhead investments designed predominantly to increase their capacity to export primary products. Underlying this adverse experience lay the fact that, in manufacturing production generally, a major element of cost—wages—is contracted in money terms and changes only slowly, so that a reduction of demand is met by unemployment rather than price reduction; whereas in primary production prices are competitively determined and contractions of demand reduce the incomes of the producers rather than the volume of output—in fact, output of agricultural products may even expand as cultivators seek to offset lower prices by a larger volume of production. Further, the inelasticity of demand for primary products in response to reductions in their prices aggravated the loss of income to producers; and the problems of the backward primary-producing regions were exacerbated by the universal resort of the advanced manufacturing countries to agricultural protectionism, designed to improve the incomes of their domestic producers and achieving this effect at the expense of producers in the primary-producing countries. The effect of these events was traumatic, in the sense that it convinced most observers concerned with development, both in the primary-producing regions and outside, that dependence on the export of primary products inevitably meant both slow and unstable economic growth, a fate from which the only escape lay in policies of deliberate industrialization. This view still has a modicum of justification, inasmuch as the advanced, industrial countries still pursue policies of agricultural protectionism, in forms which concentrate the burden of adjustment to world market disturbance on producers in the less developed countries, and have in fact been intensifiying these policies in the postwar period. But basically it is a view founded on a particularly disastrous historical experience which is extremely unlikely to be repeated.

The third source of contemporary ideas on the development problem was changes in intellectual perspective which occurred in Europe during the depression years of the 1930's in response to the depression and contemporary interpretations of it. Two in particular were important: the rise of political socialism, and the Keynesian revolution in economics.

One relevant aspect of the socialist thinking of the time was its emphasis on the apparent success of Communist five-year planning in Russia in achieving economic growth and full employment, in sharp contrast to the economic collapse and resultant misery in the capitalist countries. With this went the notion that the success of Russian planning lay in its concentration on investment in heavy industry rather than the production of consumer goods. (In the light of hindsight, this concentration appears to have been the result of Stalin's nationalism and of doubtful economic benefit; and planning oriented toward heavy industry appears to score its success by avoiding the difficult allocation problems entailed in securing for consumers a rising standard of living in an environment of free choice among abundant quantities and varieties of goods.) The contrast between capitalist reality and a largely mythological Russian alternative did much to implant among the intellectuals a belief in the necessity and effi-

cacy of centralized planning centered on the accelerated growth of heavy industry. On the other hand, among non-Communist or Fabian socialists, the drastic breakdown of capitalism fostered the view that all that barred the achievement of the just and equitably prosperous society was the inherent defectiveness of the capitalist system itself—that all that was required to achieve enough output to provide plenty for all was the introduction of intelligent socialist management of the economy, to be implemented by widespread nationalization of industry and the adoption of sweeping policies of income redistribution. Nationalization appeared to be all that was required to liberate productive potentialities from the chains of capitalism; once this had been accomplished, distribution rather than production appeared as the pressing problem of socio-economic policy. The socialist emphasis of the 1930's on centralized economic planning, nationalization of industry, and redistribution-of-income policies, to the neglect of policies of promoting economic efficiency, has continued to exercise a strong influence on contemporary ideas on the priorities of policy in the new nations.

The Keynesian revolution in economics —which in the minds of many of Keynes' followers, though not of Keynes himself, was inextricably intertwined with the socialist ideas just described—conveyed the same general message: that the failure of the system to perform satisfactorily was due to mismanagement, and could be remedied by the application of scientific intelligence. Keynes himself, who was a liberal, looked to the intelligent use of general fiscal and monetary policies to provide the remedy; his more socialist followers looked rather to planning, income-redistribution policies, and social ownership or control of industry. But both assumed implicitly that production and economic growth would look after themselves if only the system were properly managed.

Subsequent thinking on the development

problem was not only influenced in a general way by these fundamental presuppositions of the Keynesian system of thought, but was influenced in detail by Keynes' implicit assumptions about the structure of the economy about which he was theorizing and by the short-run nature of his analysis. Specifically, Keynes was essentially theorizing about an advanced economy in which both modern machinery and the skilled labor required to man it were present in adequate supply but were idled by a deficiency of aggregate demand for output. In this situation, attention naturally focused on the existence and plight of the unemployed labor, and the appropriate policy prescription was to raise aggregate demand sufficiently to draw this labor back into employment in manning the capital equipment it was trained to operate. The theory indicated that this could be accomplished by using expansionary fiscal and monetary policy to stimulate investment in new capital equipment, and thus through the investment-consumption multiplier relationship to stimulate consumption expenditure as well. In the short-run context of the theory, however, investment was regarded simply as a kind of demand for final output that did not simultaneously satisfy consumption, not as a means of providing additional productive capacity for the economy as a whole.

From this conceptual apparatus for analyzing the short-run employment problem in an advanced economy, contemporary development theory carried over two key concepts that have proved in the light of experience to have relatively little empirical foundation and to be dangerously misleading guides to development policy. First, the assumption of the existence of mass unemployment or "disguised unemployment" (employment in lower-grade jobs than those for which the workers were qualified) of skilled workers, valid for recession conditions in a capitalist economy, was accepted as valid for the normal condition of the less developed economies, which were assumed to be characterized by armies of disguised unemployment concealed in the subsistence agricultural sector of the economy. This assumption distracted attention from the problem of training the labor force in modern industrial skills that is an essential part of the process of initiating self-sustaining economic development. Second, Keynesian theory threw major emphasis on the level of fixed capital investment as the determinant of the level of income and employment; while this was a short-run theory, it was easily converted (by Harrod and Domar) into a long-run growth theory by introducing the effect of investment on the stock of capital. The resulting growth model, which made the rate of growth depend on the proportion of income saved and the incremental effect of investment on productive capacity, became the basic conceptual framework for development theory and policy. The consequence was to emphasize the strategic role of fixed capital investment in development, again to the neglect of the importance of the accumulation of labor skills and also of managerial and marketing skills. This emphasis was reinforced by what was believed to be the source of strength of Russian economic planning: its concentration on investment in heavy industry.

The fundamental theme of this set of ideas about the development problem that emerged from the experience of the 1930's and its intellectual interpretation was that the defects of the capitalist system were the root cause of economic backwardness, not the backwardness of people and their cultures in relation to the requirements of modern industrial society. Development, it was believed, was readily accessible to any country if it would only throw off the shackles of the private enterprise system, adopt economic planning, accumulate capital, and invest it to industrialize itself and eliminate its dependence on primary production. These ideas began to be propagated and applied with the emergence of the new nations in the late 1940's and

1950's; they were reinforced by the presentation by various imaginative scholars of theories of development (partaking of the character of myths) that either supported or could be interpreted as supporting the notion that a self-sustaining growth process could be initiated by a brief sharp national effort. These theories included Rostow's "take-off" hypothesis, according to which, once the preconditions for growth have been established, the transition to a self-generating growth process occurs in a historically brief take-off phase; Myrdal's notion of "circular cumulative causation," according to which growth once initiated feeds on itself; and the theory of Leibenstein and other writers concerned with population pressure as an obstacle to development that a "critical minimum effort" would be both necessary and sufficient to overcome the demographic barrier to growth of income per head.

This set of ideas is evidently congenial to political and economic nationalism. It makes backwardness and stagnation the consequence of the capitalist system as practiced by the advanced countries, and development a condition that can be achieved without fundamental social and economic change, and in a relatively short period of time. Further, it makes it appear possible for development to be achieved along with the implementation of social, cultural, and equalitarian restrictions on the freedom of competition and the practice of widespread intervention in the processes and consequences of industrialization. It suggests that one can have one's cake and eat it too—that there exists some mysterious source of untapped economic energy, which, if liberated, can provide both for development and for the liberal fulfillment of other social goals.

Needless to say, these appearances are grossly misleading. The transformation of a traditional agricultural society into a modern industrial society necessitates fundamental changes in cultural values and social structure, involving the depersonaliza-tion of economic relationships, the inculcation of a general concern for efficiency, and the willingness to accept and indeed strive for change. The results of trying to achieve economic development without basic social and cultural changes and consistently with the maintenance of pre-industrial social and cultural objectives were, inevitably, widespread economic waste and a general tendency for development programs to produce disappointing results and in particular to fail to establish the hoped-for self-sustaining process of growth at an adequate rate. This experience has gradually been changing contemporary notions about the development problem, toward increased emphasis on programs for the training and education of the labor force as compared with material investment programs, recognition of the virtues of competition as contrasted with centralized administration in countries short of administrative talent, and interest in production of specialized industrial products for the world market as compared with self-sufficient industrialization. But the prevailing concepts of development theory are still basically protectionist, autarkist, and centralist. In particular, the new interest in expansion of international trade as a means of promoting development, manifested at the 1964 United Nations Conference on Trade and Development, represents an attempt to extend protectionist philosophy and methods beyond the limitations of the domestic market of the nation-state rather than a conversion of development theorists and policy-makers to a more free-trading philosophy.

Policies and Attitudes of the Advanced Countries Toward the New Nations

The policies and attitudes of the advanced countries toward the new nations became an important formative influence on the latter in consequence of the cold war and its results in inducing the advanced countries to provide development assistance on a growing scale to the new nations as a means of strengthening the independence or enlisting the support of these nations. This influence has tended to support and reinforce the ideology of economic policy resulting from the two sets of forces previously discussed. The developed countries have formed certain ideas as to what a new nation should aim at and how it should behave, and the new nations, as a means of securing the benefits associated with the favor of the advanced countries, have tended to cast themselves in the expected mold.

In the first place, at least until recently, the advanced countries have placed considerable emphasis on autarky and on the pursuit of autarkic policies. The most important of the advanced countries concerned have been, as a result both of economic geography and of economic policy, themselves autarkic and have envisaged the problems and the desirable policies of the less developed new states in the same terms. The United States and Russia are by nature continental economies and naturally virtually self-sufficient, apart from any additional tendency in this direction imparted by economic policies of protectionism and autarky. While France and England are more heavily committed to international trade by geography, their policies and, above all, their ideals of proper economic policy, stress the objective of self-sufficiency as a result of their recent historical experiences.

The bent of the aid-giving countries toward expecting autarkic policies on the part of the new, less developed nations was strongly reinforced by the fact that, at least in the early stages of the evolution of development assistance policy, India was the new nation that commanded the most attention. Like the two largest of the advanced countries, India is a continental economy, naturally equipped for self-sufficient economic development. Moreover, many experts in the field of development economics have derived their main experience of development problems from a brief field trip to India at governmental expense and automatically think of India as the type-case of underdevelopment. This habit is also ingrained in the Indian economists themselves, who typically arrive at international conferences armed with papers that begin and are loaded with the phrase "an underdeveloped country like India" (it is next to impossible to find another underdeveloped country like India, unless one considers mainland China, and the pairing of the two is for political reasons unlikely to occur even to the most unworldly of social scientists). In short, India, the one new country about which it is possible to think in American or Russian terms, happens to have been the first of such countries to attract a major development assistance effort from the advanced countries, and the basis on which they formulated their views of the development problem.

Finally, in this connection, for obvious psychological and political reasons, the officials of the advanced countries responsible for dealing with the less developed countries tend to think in terms of planning within a national framework. Government inevitably thinks in terms of national units and also in terms of planning, regardless of whether the country it governs is nominally free enterprise, socialist, or Communist; and, confronted with the obligation to do something about the problems of another country, it automatically conceives these problems in the same terms. It is one of the paradoxes of contemporary history that, in spite of the mythology of United States adherence to free enterprise and abhorrence of socialist planning, United States government officials have probably done as much as indigenous political processes to implant the concepts of economic planning in foreign countries—first through the Marshall Plan and then through the Foreign Aid Program. In this activity they have been supported by the development of the basic technology of organizing economic information, national income accounts, and input-output tables—tools whose usefulness lies mainly in providing the prerequisites of economic planning.

This consideration introduces a second aspect of the influence of the advanced countries on the new nations: the emphasis of the former on the need for economic planning by the latter. This emphasis is associated with the autarkic approach of the advanced to the problems of the less developed countries; more important, it is associated with the notion that aid should be proportioned to the development efforts put forth by the less developed countries on their own behalf. The most readily understandable and evaluable measure of the seriousness of development purpose of a less developed country is its national development plan; without the existence of such a plan, carefully designed to be properly ambitious, a developed aid-giving country cannot be sure either that its aid is deserved and merited, or that it will serve the desired catalytic function in promoting economic development. (The practice of working up ambitious development plans dependent on vast sums of foreign aid for their success, and then using these plans as an argument to the developed countries for them to provide the required aid, is sometimes referred to as the Indian rope trick, because it is an effective means by which the Indian planners rope the developed countries into providing external assistance for Indian economic development.) Consequently, new nations desirous of aid are under strong pressure to practice economic planning—as a means of extracting economic aid, if nothing else. These observations apply with particular force to bilateral aid; but the international institutions concerned with channeling multilateral development funds are equally insistent on the presentation of national development plans to validate claims on the limited total of funds they have at their disposal.

A third aspect of the influence of the attitudes of the developed countries on those of the less developed concerns the question of industrialization versus agricultural development. It is natural for the representatives of the advanced countries, especially the United States and Russia, to consider industrial capability as the measure of national competence; industry is the field of economic activity in which these two countries compete and in which the other advanced countries seek to emulate them. Furthermore, the emphasis on industrial as against agricultural development is consistent with certain ideological or empirical characteristics of the two protagonists in the world power struggle. Marxist theory has consistently underemphasized the role of improvements in agriculture in the process of increasing productivity and income per head, so that the Russian model of economic development is almost entirely concerned with investment in industrial production. The United States, on the other hand, has been only too successful in increasing agricultural productivity, and as a result has been burdened by the production of surpluses of agricultural products—surpluses which it has been convenient to dispose of under the guise of helping to feed the poor countries of the world. This has implicitly meant favoring the industrialization of regions of the world that would absorb United States agricultural surpluses, rather than encouraging these regions to render themselves independent of United States surplus disposal policies by developing their own production of agricultural products. Finally, the discrimination of developed countries in favor of industrial rather than agricultural development of the less developed countries has been fostered by the general bias of urban-reared governmental personnel against the rural style of life and by the fact that (except for large irrigation projects) agricultural development does not permit the erection of large visible living monuments to the efficacy of governmental development assistance, whereas new factories or industries provide an unlimited opportunity for this kind of monument building.

The only major area of development

policy that offers scope for a major conflict of interest between the developed aid-
giving countries and the aid-receiving new
nations concerns the role of the large international corporations in economic development; and this is a source of conflict only
between the private enterprise aid-givers
and the new nations. Even in this context,
the potentialities of conflict are weakened
by the consequences of the intellectual developments of the 1930's, which generated
widespread public distrust in the capitalist
countries of the economic power of big
business, a distrust particularly ingrained
in those who chose to become public servants. Thus, though the conflict may be
severe at the level of expressed national
ideologies, it has been far less so at the
operating level of relations between the
officials of the developed and of the less
developed countries, since the former officials tend to share the hostility to the international corporations evidenced by the

latter, though for economic and social
rather than nationalistic reasons.

Summary

This paper has been concerned with three
of the main sources of the prevailing ideology of economic policy in new states:
their own political and economic nationalism; the heritage of ideas from the interwar
period concerning the nature of the development problem; and the influence of the
advanced countries as advisers and sources
of foreign aid. These three sources converge in establishing certain major elements
of the ideology of economic policy in the
new nations. In particular, they interweave
in support of: policies of economic autarky; concentration on industrialization
at the expense of agricultural development;
a preference for economic planning and for
public control of industry; and hostility to
operations in the country by large foreign
enterprises.

IDEOLOGIES OF DELAYED INDUSTRIALIZATION

Mary Matossian

History and value are worlds apart, but men are drawn to both, with an emotional commitment to the first and an intellectual commitment to the second; they need to ask the two incompatible questions, and they yearn to be able to answer "Mine" and "True." [1]

J. R. LEVENSON

It is difficult to discern, at first glance, any important common characteristics in ideologies such as Gandhism and Marxism-Leninism, Kemalism, and Shintoism. If they have anything in common, it seems to be a strong infusion of self-contradiction. But on second glance the diverse characteristics and geographic origins of these ideologies fade into the background. In their very self-contradictions one may detect recurrent patterns.

SOURCE. Mary Matossian, "Ideologies of Delayed Industrialization: Some Tensions and Ambiguities," *Economic Development and Cultural Change*, 6, 217–228, April 1958. Reprinted by permission of The University of Chicago Press. Copyright 1958 by The University of Chicago Press.

[1] J. R. Levenson, " 'History' and 'Value': Tensions of Intellectual Choice in Modern China," *Studies in Chinese Thought*, Arthur Wright, ed., Chicago, 1953, p. 150.

The recurrent patterns can, I think, be accounted for by the similarity of context in which these ideologies have emerged. This context is the industrially backward country which has the following characteristics: (1) it has been in contact with the industrial West for at least fifty years; (2) in it there has emerged a native intelligentsia composed of individuals with at least some Western education; and (3) large-scale industrialization is currently being contemplated or has been in progress for no more than twenty-five years. The ideologies which have emerged in such conditions would include Marxism-Leninism, Shintoism, Italian Fascism, Kemalism, Ghandism, the current Egyptian Philosophy of the Revolution, Sun Yat-sen's Three Principles of the People, the Indonesian Pantjasila, and many others. [2]

Industrially backward countries have two common problems; the destruction of traditional institutions and values, sometimes even before the impact of industralism is felt; and the challenge of the

[2] Perhaps Nazism should be included, even though it emerged on the German scene about sixty years after industrialization began. In any case, Nazism has many characteristics of ideologies of delayed industrialization.

modern West.[3] The "assaulted" individual must reorient himself in at least three directions: (1) in his relationship to the West, (2) in his relationship to his people's past, and (3) in his relationship to the masses of his own people. It is the "assaulted" intellectual, and his relationship to the uneducated masses, which will be considered here in particular: for although everyone has ideas and wishes, only intellectuals devise ideologies.

Ideology may be defined as a pattern of ideas which simultaneously provides for its adherents: (1) a self-definition, (2) a description of the current situation, its background, and what is likely to follow, and (3) various imperatives which are "deduced" from the foregoing. In ideology there is a strong tendency to merge fact and value, to superimpose upon "things as they are" the things that are desired.[4] Sjahrir, the Indonesian socialist, said that the weaker the intellect, the greater the element of wish in the formulation of a man's thought. He has held that the element of wish is strongest among "backward" persons.[5] Perhaps it would be more accurate to say that the intellectual in an industrially backward country cleaves to contradictory propositions because of the situation in which he finds himself. His experience and his present problems tend to direct his reasoning into certain channels. His ego needs protection which science and logic cannot provide. This seems to be true of all men to some extent. If the intellectual is to lead the masses of an industrially backward country in the undertaking of great endeavors, he must provide them with incitement balanced by comfort, with self-criticism balanced by self-justification.

To seek a "morphology" and "natural history" of ideologies of delayed industrialization seems premature, given the present state of Western knowledge. The following analysis is not intended to provide neat answers to big questions, but to indicate some areas where further probing might be productive.

The impact of the modern industrial West is the initial challenge in the industrially backward country. The various ways in which the West has disrupted traditional societies are beyond the scope of this analysis. The point to note here is that irreversible processes are set in motion. The contemporary scene is littered with fallen idols, desecrated by unsanctioned violence, an uncomfortable place in which to live. Thus, all ideologies of delayed industrialization are essentially revolutionary—in Mannheim's usage, utopian.[6] They direct activity toward changing a social order which is already changing. Even the superficially conservative ideologies turn out to be pseudo-conservative in the sense that they advocate a change in the status quo. Pseudo-conservative or radical, these ideologies advocate the

---

[3] These are the two important situational factors with which Rupert Emerson accounts for Asian nationalism. See "Paradoxes of Asian Nationalism," *Far Eastern Quarterly* **13** (February 1954), pp. 131–142.

John K. Fairbank has pointed out that as contact with the West increases, the response increases but is less discernible because Western culture has been incorporated in indigenous culture. He says, " 'Westernization' gives way to 'modernization,' the demand for defense is followed by the demand for reform, and by the time when a reform accelerates into a revolution, the entire society has become involved in a process of change which is too cataclysmic and far-reaching, too autonomous, to be called any longer a mere 'response.' " See "China's Response to the West: Problems and Suggestions," *Journal of World History*, **3**, pp. 404–405.

[4] In a moment of unusual insight Gamal Abdul Nasser wrote: "Our souls are the vessels in which everything we are is contained; and everything we are, everything placed in this vessel, must take their shape, even truth. I try as much as humanly possible to prevent my soul from altering the shape of truth very much, but how far can I succeed? That is the question." *Egypt's Liberation: The Philosophy of the Revolution*, Washington, D.C., 1955, p. 29.

[5] Soetan Sjahrir, *Out of Exile*, New York, 1949, pp. 89–90.

[6] See Karl Mannheim, *Ideology and Utopia*, London, 1936.

manipulation of the disagreeable Present. In this sense, *Les extremes se touchent*.[7]

The first problem of the "assaulted" intellectual is to assume a satisfactory posture *vis-à-vis* the West. The position taken is frequently ambiguous, embracing the polar extremes of xenophobia and xenophilia. The intellectual may resent the West, but since he is already at least partly Westernized, to reject the West completely would be to deny part of himself.

The intellectual is appalled by discrepancies between the standard of living and "culture" of his own country, and those of modern Western nations.[8] He feels that something must be done, and done fast. He is a man on the defensive, searching for new defensive weapons. As Gamal Abdul Nasser wrote to a friend in 1935:

> Allah said, "Oppose them with whatever forces you can muster!" But what are these forces we are supposed to have in readiness for them?[9]

Another characteristic of the "assaulted" intellectual is his uneasy attitude toward himself and his own kind—the intelligentsia and middle classes. Often he scorns his kind (and by implication, himself) as "pseudo," "mongrel," neither truly native nor truly Western. In order to find self-respect, he goes in search of his "true self"; he tries to "discover India"; he revisits the West. For example, Gandhi wrote in 1908:

> You, English, who have come to India are not good specimens of the English nation, nor can we, almost half-Anglicized Indians, be considered as good specimens of the real Indian nation...[10]

Speaking of the lack of good Indonesian literature, Sjahrir wrote in 1934:

> In reality, our cultural level is still too low for a real renaissance. There is no thought, no form, no sound, and what is worse, there is not yet enough earnestness and integrity among us. There is still only unsavory counterfeit, which is published with great fuss, but which still has little merit.[11]

Nehru, while in prison in 1944, recalled:

> The present for me, and for many others like me, was an odd mixture of medievalism, appalling poverty and misery and a somewhat superficial modernism of the middle classes. I was not an admirer of my own class or kind, and yet inevitably I looked to it for leadership in the struggle for India's salvation; that middle class felt caged and circumscribed and wanted to grow and develop itself.[12]

Nehru leans toward xenophilia, but his close associate Gandhi took an emphatic xenophobic posture. He asserted that Indians, to be successful in dealing with the British, must "consciously believe that Indian civilization is the best and that the European is a nine days' wonder." Of course, Indian civilization has some defects, he admits, such as child marriage and religious prostitution. But, "the tendency of Indian civilization is to elevate the moral being, that of the

---

[7] See Samuel P. Huntington, "Conservatism as an Ideology," *American Political Science Review*, **51**, p. 460. Levenson (*loc. cit.*, p. 149), holds that the very existence of traditionalism belies its ultimate doctrine.

[8] The usage of the word "culture" depends on the extent to which the ideologist is Westernized. It may mean ideals, values, or simply habits. Sun Yat-sen, a trained physician, deplored such Chinese habits as spitting, letting gas loudly, and never brushing the teeth, as "uncultured." He said that foreigners "can see that we are very much lacking in personal culture. Every word and act of a Chinese shows absence of refinement: one contact with the Chinese people is enough to reveal this." *San Min Chu I*, Shanghai, 1927, pp. 135–138.

[9] Nasser, *op. cit.*, p. 27. See also Jawaharlal Nehru, *The Discovery of India*, London, 1946, p. 34.

[10] Mohandas K. Gandhi, *Hind Swaraj*, Ahmedabad, 1946, p. 73.

[11] Soetan Sjahrir, *op. cit.*, p. 5.

[12] Nehru, *op. cit.*, p. 36.

Western civilization is to propagate immorality."[13]

The "assaulted" intellectual works hard to make invidious comparisons between his own nation and the West. He may simply claim that his people are superior, as did Gandhi: "We consider our civilization to be far superior to yours."[14] Or he may hold that his ancestors had already rejected Western culture as inferior.[15] But these assertions can elicit conviction only among a few and for a short while. More often the intellectual says, "We are equal to Westerners", or "You are *no better* than I am." Around this theme lies a wealth of propositions: (1) "In the past you were no better (or worse) than we are now."[16] (2) "We once had your good qualities, but we were corrupted by alien oppressors."[17] (3) "We have high spiritual qualities despite our poverty, but you are soulless materialists."[18] (4) "Everything

[13] Gandhi, *op. cit.*, pp. 45–46 and 74.

[14] *Ibid.*, p. 72.

[15] *Ibid.*, p. 46, and Levenson, *loc cit.*, p. 158.

[16] For example, see Sun Yat-sen, *op. cit.*, p. 140. This is a common assertion of Arab ideologists. Of course, there is truth in it, but how does it serve to solve the problem at hand, except to bolster the ego of the "assaulted"?

[17] Levenson, *loc. cit.*, p. 167, reports that the Chinese used the Manchus as their scapegoat. The Arabs blame the later Ottoman sultans, and the Russians blame the Mongols. There is some truth in these assertions—but it remains to be seen why the native subject peoples failed to get rid of their "alien oppressors."

[18] For example, "European superiority to China is not in political philosophy, but altogether in the field of material civilization." Sun Yat-sen, *op. cit.*, p. 98. See Herman Finer, *Mussolini's Italy*, New York, 1935, p. 170 for the Fascist case. See Masaki Kosaka, "Modern Japanese Thought," *Journal of World History*, 3, p. 610, for the Japanese case. The Indonesian socialist, Sjahrir, however, rejects the notion:

"Here there has been no spiritual or cultural life, and no intellectual progress for centuries... Most of us search unconsciously for a synthesis that will leave us internally tranquil. We want to have both Western science and Eastern philosophy, the Eastern 'spirit' in the culture. But what is this Eastern spirit? It is, they say, the sense of the higher, of spirituality, of the eternal and religious, as opposed to the

worthwhile in your tradition is present or incipient in ours."[19] The slogan, "trade, not aid," when used metaphorically is another variation on this theme. The nationalist claims to seek a blend of the "best" in East and West. But why must both East and West inspire the new culture? Behind this there is perhaps the implicit wish to see the "East" a genuine partner, an equal, of the West.[20]

The foregoing postures *vis-à-vis* the

materialism of the West. I have heard this countless times, but it has never convinced me." *Op. cit.*, pp. 66–67.

[19] See Levenson, *loc. cit.*, pp. 160–161, for a Chinese case; or Mohammed Naguib, *op. cit.*, p. 134: "There is nothing in the Koran that calls for theocratic government; on the contrary, the Prophet was in favor of parliamentary rule."

[20] Levenson, *loc. cit.*, p. 174. The "assaulted" intellectual is sometimes comforted by the thought that Westerners have borrowed some element from his own culture. K. M. Panikkar, in *Asia and Western Dominance*, London, 1953, devotes two chapters to the subject of the impact of Asia on the West. However, the element that Westerners borrow may be one which the native intellectual has already rejected as "backward." For example, Americans in Arab countries who adopt the bedouin headdress on occasion are a source of amusement or irritation to the educated city Arab. He looks down on the bedouin, and he does not want the American to identify Arabs with bedouins. Speaking of such British adventurers as Doughty, Lawrence, and Glubb, an Egyptian intellectual remarked: "We're sick to death of Britishers who can recite the Koran." (As quoted by Roland Pucetti, "Three British Bedouins," *Middle East Forum*, 33, p. 34.)

Sjahrir thinks that Westerners who are seeking "Light from Asia" are wasting their time. He says: "I know only too well what the Eastern attributes, so admired by the Westerner, really are. I know that those attributes are molded and nourished only by the hierarchical relationship of a feudal society—a society in which a small group possess all the material and intellectual wealth, and the vast majority live in squalor, and are made acquiescent by religion and philosophy in place of sufficient food.

"That longing of Westerners for the East, in effect, amounts to the same thing as longing for the lost land of the Middle Ages, and the greater goodness and universality that presumably characterized it." *Op. cit.*, p. 160.

West may be comforting to the intellectual, but they will not stimulate action unless certain imperatives are "deduced" from them. For example, "We must purge our national culture of alien corruptions and realize our true character which has been lying dormant within us." But doses of self-criticism are equally important incentives to action, because they make it impossible to relax in complacency. In 1931, Joseph Stalin, leader of one of the most spectacular cultural transformations in human history, told Soviet industrial managers,

> One feature of the history of old Russia was the continual beatings she suffered for falling behind, for her backwardness. She was beaten by the Mongol khans. She was beaten by the Turkish beys. She was beaten by the Swedish feudal lords. She was beaten by the Polish and Lithuanian gentry. She was beaten by the Japanese barons. All beat her—for her backwardness: for military backwardness, for cultural backwardness, for political backwardness, for industrial backwardness, for agricultural backwardness. She was beaten because to do so was profitable and could be done with impunity. . . .
>
> That is why we must no longer lag behind. . . . We are fifty or a hundred years behind the advanced countries. We must make good this distance in ten years. Either we do it, or they crush us.[21]

Another man who administered blunt criticism was Mustafa Kemal Ataturk, who told the Turkish Grand National Assembly in 1920,

> We have accepted the principle that we do not, and will not, give up our national independence. Although we always respect this basic condition, when we take into consideration the level of prosperity of the country, the wealth of the nation, and the general mental

level, and when we compare it with the progress of the world in general, we must admit that we are not a little, but very backward.[22]

Ataturk praised the Turkish nation, however, for high moral qualities and great past achievements. Although he was probably a xenophile by conviction, he succeeded to a remarkable degree in overcoming the xenophobia of his people by means of his ideological rhetoric. When it was suggested that to borrow from the West "all that Turkey needs" might conflict with the national ideal, Ataturk retorted that the national principle itself had become *internationally* accepted; and also,

> Countries are many, but civilization is one and for the progress of a nation it is necessary to participate in this one civilization.[23]

Ataturk justified the importation of specific alien inventions, such as terms from non-Turkish languages, with the assertion that the so-called import was actually indigenous: according to the Sun Language Theory, Turkish was the mother of all the languages of the world, so that "borrowed" words were actually prodigal sons come home.[24] This technique of encouraging an import by calling it indigenous was complemented by the technique of eradicating the indigenous by calling it imported. For example, Ataturk pointed out that the fez was a headgear imported from Europe a hundred years before.

When the intellectual in an industrially backward country surveys modern Western civilization, he is confronted with five hundred years of scientific, artistic, social, economic, political, and religious developments. He sees a flood of heterogeneous Western cultural elements, from jazz to steel mills, pouring into his country. Then,

[21] J. S. Stalin, *Problems of Leninism*, Moscow, 1947, p. 356.

[22] Mustafa Kemal Ataturk, *Atatürk'ün Söylev ve Demeçleri*, I, Istanbul, 1945, p. 29.

[23] Ataturk, *op. cit.*, 3, Ankara, 1954, pp. 67–68 and 87.

[24] Uriel Heyd, *Language Reform in Modern Turkey*, Jerusalem, 1954, pp. 33–34.

fearing that he will be "swamped" by the deluge, and lose his own identity, he tries to control cultural imports. In order to do this, he must find a standard to determine exactly what should be borrowed. The standard used by the nationalist is that the element to be imported should be in "conformity" with his own national culture and should serve to strengthen his nation. This formula is very elastic, and can be used to justify the borrowing or rejection of practically anything. But the Marxist-Leninist holds that the element to be imported should be one that is "progressive" in terms of the Marxist-Leninist pattern of social evolution. According to this pattern, the "bourgeois" West is decaying; it is the "toilers" of both East and West who ride the wave of the future.[25] Imperialism is the highest and the last stage of capitalism. However, Western industrialism and science are the great hope for the non-Western peoples; and the Soviet Union is represented as a model of rapid industrialization and scientific development. If the industrially backward nation borrows from the West only what is most "progressive," it can skip a part, or a stage, of the long and difficult social development of the West. Then, as the West decays, the former backward nations will surpass the best that the West has ever achieved.

The tension between archaism and futurism is another ambiguity in ideologies of delayed industrialization. It is closely related to the xenophobia–xenophilia tension, because the West is "the new" and the native culture is "the old" at the onset of contact.

Archaism is an attempt to resurrect a supposed "golden age," or some part of it. This "golden age" is usually not in the disagreeable recent past, but in a more

[25] Marxism-Leninism is of course not the only ideology that contains this proposition. Western ideologists who talk of "the Decline of the West" and "the Awakening of the East" have contributed to, and reinforced, such sentiments.

remote period, and it can only be recovered by historical research and interpretation. For example, Mussolini gloried in imperial Rome and the medieval "corporate state"; the Slavophiles glorified the peasant *mir* and the indigenous Christian Orthodox practices in Russia; the Shintoists revived an ancient mythology that defied the Emperor; Sun Yat-sen and Chiang Kai-shek exhorted the Chinese to revive Confucian ethics; Gandhi urged that India return to the age of "Rama Raj"; and Ataturk exulted in the barbaric virtues of the Osmanli nomads. According to Gandhi,

> It was not that we did not know how to invent machinery, but our forefathers knew that, if we set our hearts after such things, we would become slaves and lose our moral fibre. They, therefore, after due deliberation, decided that we should only do what we could with our hands and feet. They further reasoned that large cities were a snare and a useless encumbrance and that people would not be happy in them, that there would be gangs of thieves and robbers, prostitution and vice flourishing in them, and that poor men would be robbed by rich men. They were, therefore, satisfied with small villages.[26]

[26] *Hind Swaraj*, p. 46. Gandhi's archaism went to incredible lengths. In the same work (pp. 42–43) he indicted Western medicine:
"I have indulged in vice, I contract a disease, a doctor cures me, the odds are that I shall repeat the vice. Had the doctor not intervened, nature would have done its work and I would have acquired mastery over myself, would have been freed from vice and would have been happy.
"Hospitals are institutions for propagating sin. Men take less care of their bodies and immorality increases."
These opinions might be dismissed as unimportant since they were expressed so early in Gandhi's career. However, in a preface to a new edition of *Hind Swaraj* which Gandhi wrote in 1938, he said:
"The booklet is a severe condemnation of 'modern civilization.' It was written in 1908. My conviction is deeper today than ever. I feel that, if India will discard 'modern civilization,' she can only gain by doing so." p. 11.

According to Mussolini,

> Rome is our point of departure and of reference; it is our symbol, or if you like, it is our Myth. We dream of a Roman Italy, that is to say wise and strong, disciplined and imperial. Much of that which was the immortal spirit of Rome resurges in Fascism.[27]

According to Sun Yat-sen,

> So, coming to the root of the matter, if we want to restore our race's standing, besides uniting all into a great national-body, we must first recover our ancient morality—then, and only then can we plan how to attain again to the national position we once held.[28]

But Nehru condemns archaism:

> We have to come to grips with the present, this life, this world, this nature which surrounds us with its infinite variety. Some Hindus talk of going back to the Vedas; some Moslems dream of an Islamic theocracy. Idle fancies, for there is no going back, there is no turning back even if this was thought desirable. There is only one-way traffic in Time.[29]

Archaism may slip into a futuristic ideology, such as Marxism, and create an ambiguity. Adam Ulam has suggested that Marxism has its greatest appeal for semiproletarianized or uprooted peasants who are nostalgic for the "good old days" when their actions were governed by nature, the village elders, the family patriarch, and the religious authorities— instead of the less congenial factory boss and the state. To the uprooted peasant Marxism offers a comforting strain of archaism: that is, it envisions a utopia in which state and factory, as coercive institutions, have "withered away."[30]

Whenever a resurrection of the past is contemplated, the question arises, "What part of the past?" or "Which age was our golden age, and why?" Sometimes the age selected is an imperial age, when the people in question enjoyed their greatest authority over others. Sometimes a period of "pristine simplicity" is admired. But new imperial conquests are incompatible with the weak political and economic position of industrially backward countries, and a return to the "simple life" is incompatible with industrialization. In such cases archaism is not a solution to the problem at hand, but an escape from it.

However, there are more constructive uses of the past. The intellectual may discover that in the remote past his people possessed the very virtues which are supposed to make a modern nation great. For example, the Kemalists glorify their ancestors as brave, tolerant, realistic, generous, peaceful, and respectful of women; in short, "spiritual" exemplars of the well-bred Western European gentleman. These "genuine" Turks were temporarily "corrupted" by Arab-Persian-Byzantine culture, but they are now due to take their rightful place among "civilized" nations.[31] The manifest content of such an ideological position may be archaistic, but its latent content is futuristic.

The Communists also use the past in this way. But they have characteristic standards for determining what elements of the past are desirable. The Chinese Communists have cultivated peasant literature and art because they are "progressive," being products of a "progressive" class; whereas gentry culture is rejected as "feudal."[32] In the Soviet Union the pre-revolutionary leaders most cherished by the Communist regime are those it considers "progressive" for their time (such as Peter the Great), whereas "reactionaries" (such as Dostoyevsky, until recently) have been under a cloud.

---

[27] As quoted by Finer, *op. cit.*, p. 191.
[28] Sun Yat-sen, *op. cit.*, pp. 125–126.
[29] Nehru, *op. cit.*, p. 447.
[30] Adam Ulam, "The Historical Role of Marxism and the Soviet System," *World Politics*, **8**, pp. 20–45.

[31] See Halide Edib Adivar, *Turkey Faces West*, New Haven, 1930, pp. 1–9.
[32] Levenson, *loc. cit.*, p. 184.

Nationalists, when selecting elements from their past, ask, "What will tend to strengthen the nation?" But tradition has lost its natural charm, and traditionalism is something the nationalist must "work at." He uses the shared traditions of his people as raw material with which to build national morale; but tradition is a means, existing only for the sake of national strength, and not as an axiomatic, self-justified good.[33] For example, Sun Yat-sen said in 1924:

Our position now is extremely perilous; if we do not earnestly promote nationalism and weld together our four hundred millions into a strong nation, we face a tragedy—the loss of our country and the destruction of our race. To ward off this danger, we must espouse nationalism and employ the national spirit to save the country.[34]

There are other uses of the past besides escapism, the sanctioning of innovations, the glorification of "progressive" individuals and groups, and national self-strengthening. The past may be used to eradicate what the intellectual feels to be undesirable in the present and for the future. By publicizing the results of historical research, showing that a supposedly indigenous cultural element (like the fez) is of foreign origin, he may thereby stigmatize it. He may use other grounds to stigmatize the Ottoman and Chinese literary languages; they are the languages of reactionary and oppressive ruling classes who have cared only for their own welfare, rather than the welfare of the people.

The concern of both nationalists and Communists for vernacular languages and peasant arts is closely related to a third problem of the "assaulted" intellectual: his relationship with the uneducated masses. Some intellectuals have a sentimental, patronizing, or contemptuous

attitude toward the masses.[35] Sun Yat-sen said:

The Ming veterans spread the idea of nationalism through the lower classes; but, on account of their childish understanding, the lower classes did not know how to take advantage of the ideas, but were, on the contrary, made tools of by others.[36]

Mohammed Naguib of Egypt wrote in 1955:

Given the deplorable conditions in Egyptian villages, however, the distinction between compulsion and cooperation is irrelevant. The average *fellah* has fallen too low to be able to help himself without a great deal of compulsory assistance from the government.[37]

Other intellectuals, like Nehru, wonder if the peasants are the "true" Indians, while they (the intellectuals) are only "pseudos." The Russian Narodniki went "back to the people" to learn from them and to teach them; and so have Turkish intellectuals in our own century. Undeniably, many intellectuals have felt sincere compassion for the sufferings of the peasants and sincere respect for the folk arts. But it is unlikely that the attitude of an intellectual toward the uneducated masses in an industrially backward country (or in any country) is free from ambiguity: he looks up to "the people" and down on "the masses."

However he may feel about the majority of his compatriots, the intellectual must face the practical problems of industrializa-

---

[33] Levenson, *loc. cit.*, pp. 172–173. See also Emerson, *loc. cit.*, pp. 136–142.
[34] Sun Yat-sen, *op. cit.*, p. 12.

[35] See the statement of an Arab, al-Kawakebi, in Hazim Z. Nuseibeh's *The Ideas of Arab Nationalism*, Ithaca, 1956, p. 132. See also D. P. Mukerji, "The Intellectual in India," *Confluence*, **4**, p. 446, and James Mysberg, "The Indonesian Elite," *Far Eastern Survey*, **26**, p. 39.
[36] Sun Yat-sen, *op. cit.*, pp. 61–62.
[37] Naguib, *op. cit.*, p. 149.

tion and modernization. The intellectual knows that a government which really *represents* the thinking of the uneducated masses will not attack these problems boldly and comprehensively. The peasant may long for riches, but he is not eager to give up his traditional ways. To attain its ends, the intelligentsia must arouse the masses to strenuous effort, or, as Alexander Gerschenkron puts it, give them an emotional "New Deal."[38]

The intelligentsia must provide just the right amount of criticism, and just the right amount of comfort necessary to make the masses follow its lead into the "battle" of industrialization. That is why ideologies of delayed industrialization condemn the peasant for his backwardness, and then praise him for being a *real* representative of the indigenous culture. Such ideologies may stand for class equality and simultaneously exhort the masses to follow orders and to accept unequal rewards, both as individuals and as occupational groups. This does not mean that "assaulted" intellectuals are necessarily cynical and manipulative; they may be sincerely attached to contradictory premises.

In most cases, when an ideology of delayed industrialization emerges, the traditional rulers (king, sultan, tsar, etc.) have been overthrown, or are on the verge of being overthrown. But when traditional rulers remain in power, as in Japan, they are supported by new social groups and assume new social functions. They must now mobilize the masses to meet the challenge of the modern industrial West. Whether there has been a massive social revolution or a "circulation of elites," the cultural revolution is inevitable.

Rupert Emerson has suggested that if reform and revolution in industrially backward countries are led by Westernized intellectuals drawn from various social strata rather than by traditional elites, the prevalent ideology tends to include a stronger egalitarian element. The intelligentsia, having no solid power base of its own, is especially in need of mass support. This is particularly true, he believes, in areas which have been longest under Western domination, such as India, where the traditional native elite lost most of its power and indoctrination in Western political values went deep. But in countries like Japan, where the traditional elite took command of social and economic reform, the prevalent ideology tends to put a premium on hierarchical values: loyalty, obedience, respect.[39] This theory may be useful in explaining differences between developments in India and Japan, but its applicability elsewhere is dubious. It is important here to distinguish between symbolic values, which may be egalitarian, and their accompanying operational values, which may be hierarchical. It is also important to define "equality": is it legal, economic, spiritual, or does it refer to the possession of a common culture?

The tension between egalitarian and hierarchical values is sometimes resolved theoretically by the doctrine of "tutelage." According to this doctrine democracy must be introduced into a country in two stages. In the first stage, a single, "all-people's" party of the most "enlightened" and "progressive" elements of the nation takes over the government and acts as a faculty for educating the masses in democratic ways. At some time in the indefinite future the masses will be ready for direct self-government and the "all-people's" party will "wither away." This doctrine, with various modifications, has appeared in Turkey, India, and China; but when the doctrine has been applied, it has led to a variety of unexpected results.

In order to understand an ideology it is important to determine what problems its

---

[38] Alexander Gerschenkron, "Economic Backwardness in Historical Perspective," in *The Progress of Underdeveloped Areas*, Bert Hoselitz, ed., Chicago, 1952, pp. 22–25.

[39] Emerson, *loc. cit.*, p. 140.

initiators are trying to solve. In the case of intellectuals in industrially backward countries, the three main problems are: (1) What is to be borrowed from the West? (2) What is to be retained from the nation's past? (3) What characteristics, habits, and products of the masses are to be encouraged. It is remarkable that intellectuals in widely separate parts of the world have reacted similarly to these problems.

POLITICAL IDEOLOGY AND ECONOMIC PROGRESS: THE BASIC QUESTION

Wilfred Malenbaum and Wolfgang Stolper

In the underdeveloped countries—where live most of the world's people—the hope for economic progress now flames with great intensity. The new international capital facilities of the postwar period, the new programs for sharing modern science and technology, the new interest of wealthy lands in progress in the poor countries— all these present the latter with an opportunity to be rid of the poverty and squalor of their material existence. Their eyes naturally turn to the more developed countries for capital and technical knowledge, and for ideas.

The United States and the democratic nations of the West took the postwar initiative in international programs of financial and technical assistance. These countries were confident that their own vigorous progress, under the stimulus of market demand in a free society, would provide a helpful model for expanded rates of economic growth in the poorer nations. Since 1953, however, Russia and its satel-

lites have also played an active role; they now provide a wide range of development assistance to poorer nations— including important politically uncommitted nations like India. Russia's economic history offers a different model, with programed progress in a totalitarian society. Moreover, the Communist lands, focusing attention on their own rates of economic expansion, proclaim their intention to overtake the nations of the West and thus provide unequivocal evidence to the world of how outmoded are capitalist economic systems.

Since the aspirations of the people in the poor countries as well as the urgings of popular leaders require that these nations pay heed to whatever methods and procedures promise to increase their rate of economic advance, the present competition between democratic and Communist models has inevitably given economic programs for accelerating a nation's growth a significant political dimension. Ideological alternatives are thrust upon the less-developed nations. Even where the ways of totalitarianism are repugnant to leaders and to traditions—as is certainly true in many such lands—domestic political pressures demand an open mind, perhaps an open door.

Leaders in the new and underdeveloped countries are bound to ask: Are totalitarian regimes more adept at initiating a process of

SOURCE. Wilfred Malenbaum and Wolfgang Stolper, "Political Ideology and Economic Progress," *World Politics*, 12, 413–421, April 1960. This article was written while both authors were staff members of the Center for International Studies, M.I.T. The present form of the paper reflects the major editorial contribution of Richard W. Hatch of the Center. But the authors alone are responsible for the views presented.

continuous economic growth than democratic governments? If the methods of communism do in fact promise a surer or less expensive route to economic well-being, some of these nations, deeply committed as they are to a free society, may also ask: How much more economic progress in five or ten years, say, for how much less freedom? The relevance of these questions is clear. These nations need material progress; they are confronted with alternative roads differentiated on ideological grounds.

These questions may raise no problem for the Soviet policy maker. He has been given a doctrinaire identification of means and ends. Unwittingly, perhaps, the policy maker in the West accepts a similar pattern of thought. Preoccupied with the importance of "democratic means," he tends to identify the ends—progress—with his means—the market economy, the private sector, individual freedom of choice. It is necessary therefore to pose the more basic question: To achieve economic progress, must there be a choice of ideologically distinct routes?

Comparative Performance

History now provides the material for some judgment on the role of ideology in economic progress under today's conditions. In each of two pairs of comparable lands—India and China, West Germany and East Germany—there is available reasonably documented experience of some ten years of effort to achieve more rapid rates of economic growth from essentially the same starting points. India and West Germany chose paths under democracy; in both lands, government places a high premium upon private property and individual privilege. In East Germany and in China, on the other hand, the methods used can be traced directly to the totalitarian experience of the Soviet Union; in the development effort, as in other aspects of the social order, individual rights are completely subordinated to those of the state.

In 1950 both India and China had per-capita incomes of about $50—lower than in any other large nation. The two countries initiated their development operations at about the same time and from the same type of economic structure. In both, at least 80 per cent of the working force was in agriculture and small-scale enterprise. If anything, India gave promise of greater progress in view of its advantages in basic resources per man, in transport facilities and modern industry, and in training and leadership attributes. Thus, India apparently had greater scope for using its surface water potential and for exploiting the intensive margins of agricultural cultivation. With the same relative efforts, therefore, larger returns could be anticipated in India than in China. So, at any rate, did it seem in the pre-Plan period.[1]

Yet by 1959 per capita gross national product in India was only some 12–15 per cent above its 1950 level, while in China it had expanded to about double the earlier figure. Almost half (45 per cent) of this difference in performance can be associated with the proportionately greater investment made in China; the remaining difference measures the extent to which each additional unit of capital in China was associated with larger flows of current income.

With an initial gross investment ratio just below 10 per cent, absolute real investment in China had increased by 1958 to five times the 1950 level; in India it about doubled. Foreign aid did not explain this difference: indeed, China's investment was more nearly financed from its current output than was India's. Communist methods made possible a relatively large (40 per cent) feedback of new output into China's domestic investment. But India's voluntary per-

[1] For an analysis of the comparative pre-Plan status and subsequent performance of the two countries, see Wilfred Malenbaum, "India and China: Development Contrasts," *Journal of Political Economy*, **64** (February 1956), 1–24; and *idem*, "India and China: Contrasts in Development Performance," *American Economic Review*, **49** (June 1959), 284–309.

formance in this respect was impressive also. During favorable harvest years, marginal savings rates in India may well have exceeded those in China.

The Chinese put more effort into expanding physical output as against services; a larger proportion of new capital was allocated to agriculture and small industry; the degree of utilization of resources, and especially of labor, was increased significantly. Over the whole period, government played a much larger role in economic life in China than in India. And of course, compared with India's, China's producers and consumers had limited freedom of choice—in techniques of production, in final goods for consumption. Greater regimentation in China was accompanied by considerable flexibility on the part of government. In response to actual developments in the economy, relative emphasis was shifted away from the initial concentration on heavy industry, for example. By and large, China's economic progress has been steady. In India, government adheres to models of growth which are permissive; comparatively few restraints are imposed on individuals whose usual ways of life did not in the past generate economic expansion. There have been impressive spurts of industrial output in India's essentially private modern industry sector, as well as some record crops in years with favorable monsoons. The total performance has been less even; the degree of plan fulfillment has not increased steadily, for example.

In prewar years, East and West Germany constituted an historical, cultural, and economic whole. Their labor and other factor endowments were quite similar; their industrial and agricultural establishments were comparably modern and efficient. While actual output per man showed a slight margin for the western half of the country, there was probably little difference in the productive potential of the two parts. The west did have a real advantage in its soft coal resources and in the lower cost of water transport and

water power facilities. In order to escape the effects of Allied bombings in the west during the war, industry in the east was favored. Later, while the Marshall Plan was pumping funds into West Germany, Russian reparations and levies were exacting a heavy toll—perhaps one-fourth of industrial production—from current output in East Germany. While Allied troops were basically fed from outside, the Russian occupation lived off the land. Still Russian demands did serve to stimulate output, particularly in coal and potash, in synthetic rubber and gasoline. There is some evidence that East Germany was getting on its feet more rapidly in the years to 1948. Although it still had a significantly lower product per person than West Germany (some 40 per cent lower) in 1950, an objective appraisal suggested that, as of that date, output potential over the next decade, say, could be more rapid than in the west.[2]

West Germany expanded its gross national product about 10 per cent more than did East Germany between 1950 and 1958. In the light of the different roles of the occupying authorities, it is not surprising that West Germany was able to maintain both higher investment and higher consumption levels. More surprising is the fact that the output gain associated with each unit of investment was also greater in the west, despite the opportunities

[2] For an analysis of the comparative status and performance of the two countries, see Wolfgang Stolper, *The Structure of the East German Economy*, to be published by Harvard University Press. Preliminary results have appeared in Wolfgang Stolper, "The Labor Force and Industrial Development in Soviet Germany," *Quarterly Journal of Economics*, **71** (November 1957), 518–545; and *idem*, "The National Product of East Germany," *Kyklos*, **12** (April 12, 1959), 131–166. A German translation of the *Kyklos* article has appeared in *Konjunkturpolitik*, (West) Berlin, 1959, No. 6, together with two extremely interesting critical discussions by Werner Gebauer, "Eine neue Berechnung des mitteldeutschen Sozialprodukts," *ibid.*, pp. 344–353, and by Bruno Cleitze, "Niveauentwicklung und Strukturwandlung des Sozialprodukts Mitteldeutschlands," *ibid.*, pp. 374–382.

which under-utilized facilities offered East Germany in 1950.

In contrast to West Germany, East Germany focused on heavy industry and self-sufficiency. There was a relative neglect of agriculture and consumer-goods output generally. Emphasis on heavy industries, especially from an uneconomic raw materials base, was costly for an area renowned for its skilled labor and the quality of its machinery output (optics, electrical goods, and fine mechanical products). The rigid system of controls imposed by East German authorities encountered heavy resistance, especially in farm areas. Major difficulties arose in meshing the complex components of a modern industrial system. All this stands in great contrast to a West Germany which gave ready scope to its entrepreneurs by maintaining a predominantly free market. The effects of these alternative approaches are most apparent in foreign trade—of basic importance in both countries. With competitive prices and market incentives, West Germany expanded its international role along the lines of its comparative advantage. Controlled prices, allocation schemes borrowed from Russia, and the inefficient bilateralism of a trade in which three-fourths of the total was dominated by Russia and the satellites meant that East Germany could not realize its industrial capabilities.

The advocates of neither democratic nor Communist methods can find in the experiences of India and China, of West and East Germany, evidence of a systematic relationship between ideology and the rate of economic progress. Leaders in the underdeveloped lands—and policy-makers in the wealthier nations—cannot expect dogma to bring the growth they seek. Do the two sets of case histories permit a consistent explanation?

Underlying Factors

By focusing on the technical determinants of economic growth, some light can be thrown upon the apparent paradox.

Let us think of the rate of growth as the product of the rates at which output per unit of capital changes and the capital stock itself expands. By committing itself to the achievement of more rapid economic expansion, a government commits itself to change the nation's savings (or investment) ratios and its capital-output ratios—usually both. There are alternative courses of action to these ends. And it is with respect to the methods, more than to the ends, that a government's action reflects its adherence to democracy or to communism. Totalitarian regimes can squeeze consumption, or can limit the increases in consumption in ways unacceptable to a government dependent on the ballot box. Thus, at some time in East Germany or China, rationing has been carried to extreme levels; family life has been communalized; a large part of crop production has been procured from the peasantry under pressure at low prices for resale at high prices. While such measures permit larger allocation to investment, it may be noted that under Communist control they also permitted large appropriations to the Soviet Union, as in the case of East Germany. On the other hand, in West Germany, where there was a clear opportunity for gain by the investor, voluntary savings increased rapidly. Even in a poor nation like India, consumption habits did permit very large voluntary savings in years when there was rapid growth in income for the mass of the people.

The capital-output ratios depend upon the economic wisdom in new investment allocation as well as the vigor with which the nation's human resources are applied to already existing capital. We know well that, in free societies, individual motivations have resulted in efficient over-all performance, in large returns per unit of capital. On the other hand, the right of freedom of economic choice scarcely assures such results everywhere. Russia and China provide concrete evidence that the much larger range of centralized economic decisions necessary to achieve progress in a controlled system can be made with effective results. However, this has not always been true either; indeed, involuntary transfers of savings have been known to generate apathy and even active noncooperation on the part of the population.

The needed changes in the savings ratios and in input-output relationships can certainly be visualized with democratic as well as Communist methods. These basic parameters have not only economic but psychological and sociological dimensions. Both Communist and democratic regimes will find the new measures more effective if they take cognizance of existing relationships in the society. This is particularly true for democratic nations, which depend much more upon voluntary cooperation and hence upon the existing pattern of motivational forces in the society. Success by Communist methods places upon government the requirement for more action and more perseverance in assuring its fulfillment; success under democracy requires action based on greater insight into the structure of the society and the economy.

These observations can be illustrated in the two sets of countries. Both East and West Germany had relatively modern, efficient, and complex industrial and agricultural organizations. The profit incentive—even modified in some measure by restraints of a government seeking social-welfare objectives—was of tremendous importance for economic performance. The situation in India and China was completely different. Their economies were market-oriented to only a limited degree. Custom and tradition were of pervasive importance in economic activity—especially in rural areas, where most of the population, workers, and even output are centered. Attainment of specific objectives required carefully planned governmental programs much more than reliance upon the price and profit mechanism.

The very different economic circumstances prevailing in the two sets of coun-

tries place very different sets of requirements upon governments seeking more rapid economic progress—whether by democratic or by Communist methods. West Germany's faith in the free market made obvious sense; the government's recognition of the need for change permitted it to superimpose a broad and flexible system of fiscal controls, as well as capital allocations, wherever these were necessary to make the nation's resource endowments best serve its economic needs. In this free society, state control increased; about half of all investments were directly or indirectly affected by government.

In contrast, East German planners slavishly copied the Russian model, a pattern prepared for substantially different resource endowments than prevailed in East Germany. Steel produced with Ukrainian iron ore and Polish coal was expensive. In Germany it was exceedingly difficult for government to acquire the know-how for establishing and administrating precise controls. Thus, it is hard to substitute, for example, for the consistent price system which competitive forces can mold. With the currency reforms in 1948, West Germany acquired such a system. In East Germany, it has yet to evolve. Ubiquitous government may long incur the costs of an inefficient combination of resources.

China's ties to a Russian model of rapid, large-scale industrialization did not impede early recognition of the emptiness of industrialization without agricultural advancement in a nation where most people will long remain rural; of the complementarities, rather than the competitiveness, of large industry and many types of small enterprises suitable to a heavy endowment of labor. Important deviations from Communist economic lore were soon made in the allocation of large percentages of investment resources to agriculture and the small-scale sector. A form of communal organization was created with continuous and strong guidance and controls to assure the change that the economy on its own could not generate.

The government of India's models of growth are largely derived from the patterns and relationships found in Western capitalist societies; neither the concepts, nor the values, of the multipliers relevant to a market-conscious economy in the throes of expansion are directly applicable in an institutionalized and static society. The major task of rural improvement and growth was placed upon a national community development and extension scheme. While this action recognized the need, especially in the initial years, of injecting into rural India a new force for change, government did not provide the programs with sustained, strong leadership. In modern industry, where the parallels between Western nations and India were greatest, borrowed doctrine was often in conflict with India's own formulation of the needs of a socialist state. India tries to allocate 50–60 per cent of all investment to the government sector while expecting the private sector to produce more than 90 per cent of total product. These contrasting ratios are not necessarily in conflict; but they do demand close scrutiny of day-to-day investment and production developments to assure that the drive to high levels of investment in the public sector does not impede continued performance and expansion in the private sector.

This examination of underlying factors permits an interesting conclusion. The two more successful nations—Communist China and democratic West Germany—operated on the same sets of technical determinants of growth as did India and East Germany. Their relative success was due to the degree to which they geared their development programs to the existing structure of their economies. Cold and objective appraisals were made of the stages necessary to achieve a state of continuing progress from inadequate starting points. Throughout, they demonstrated flexibility in selecting courses of action. Only those were finally adopted in which practice gave promise of the changes needed in savings rates and in technical input-output coefficients. In democratic India and Communist East Germany, on the other hand, governmental operations on these basic parameters have manifested much less objectivity and flexibility. Indeed, India, where growth under democracy demands a greater interplay of new and old relationships in the society, evidenced less of an experimental and flexible approach to its problem of expansion than did China.

Ideology and Economic Progress

Thus no simple ideologic-economic relationship exists. The West German performance means that the Communist formula does not contain the essential ingredient to more rapid progress; nor has democracy in a free society provided India with a guaranty of rapid economic achievement. Not only is economic progress not determined by the ideology to which a nation adheres; indeed, it can be most costly for a nation to adhere persistently to doctrines which counter indigenous economic and social relationships.

Whenever doctrine and policy are borrowed, whenever the results of foreign experience are applied, actual experience with them must be subjected to constant analysis. Only such study can indicate the changes needed to achieve effective results —whether these changes be in the knowledge or ideas imported, or in indigenous habits or relationships. It is not an ideology or an economic theory that will bring growth; it is more energetic and imaginative responses to the record as revealed by intensive study. This is especially true for democratic nations which rule out change by force; new programs must take root indigenously.

The growth record in the poorer nations over the past decade can scarcely give unmitigated satisfaction either to the leaders in the underdeveloped areas or to the policy-makers in the West. At the least, there is still room for great humility with respect to our know-how about the process of growth. The free market and private enterprise may work—as by and large they have under our conditions—but they may also have but limited relevance in the economic and social circumstances prevailing in the poorer lands. West Germany seems to have worked out a compromise between free enterprise and controls which serves its growth needs. There is undoubtedly some composite path which will provide the centralized direction and coordinated performance needed in India, consistent with its democratic aspirations. The specific actions to be taken can be deduced only from a full reading of the actual record of the decade. Dogma can give way to hypothesis, certainty to experimentation.

It is such a composite path—well within the extremes of permissiveness and compulsion—which nations seeking economic progress under democracy need to pursue. Given the limited growth achievements of these lands in the past decade, capital-exporting countries will inevitably provide greater assistance. It is high time that major research efforts—perhaps on a joint basis in each developing nation—be applied to discovering the actual bottlenecks which have been hindering that nation's economic expansion. A development program tailored to these specific tasks has a chance of both achieving material progress and nurturing democratic political ideals.

RELIGIOUS ASPECTS OF MODERNIZATION IN TURKEY AND JAPAN[1]

Robert N. Bellah

The process of modernization of the "backward" nations such as Turkey and Japan, which will be considered here, involves changes in the value system as well as economic, political, and social changes. In traditional societies the value system tends to be what Howard Becker calls

SOURCE. Robert N. Bellah, "Religious Aspects of Modernization in Turkey and Japan," *American Journal of Sociology*, **64**, 1–5, July 1958. Reprinted by permission of The University of Chicago Press. Copyright 1958 by The University of Chicago Press.

"prescriptive."[2] A prescriptive system is characterized by the comprehensiveness and specificity of its value commitments and by its consequent lack of flexibility. Motivation is frozen, so to speak, through commitment to a vast range of relatively specific norms governing almost every situation in life. Most of these specific norms, usually including those governing social institutions, are thoroughly integrated with a religious system which invokes ultimate sanctions for every infraction. Thus changes in economic or political institutions, not to speak of family and

[1] This paper is a fragment of a larger study of the relations between religion and politics in modern Asia and the tentative conclusions put forward here may be altered as a result of the larger study. I am indebted to Niyazi Berkes and Talcott Parsons for reading earlier versions of this paper.

[2] For a recent definition of "prescriptive" and "principial" see Howard Becker, "Current Sacred-secular Theory and Its Development," in Howard Becker and Alvin Boskoff (eds.), *Modern Sociological Theory in Continuity and Change* (New York: Dryden Press, 1957).

education, in traditional societies tend to have ultimate religious implications. Small changes will involve supernatural sanctions.

Yet such a society, when faced with grave dislocations consequent to Western contact, must make major changes in its institutional structure if it is to survive. What changes must be made in the organization of the value system so that these structural changes may go forward?

We may say that the value system of such a society must change from a prescriptive type to a "principial" type, to borrow again from Becker. Traditional societies, as we have said, tend to have a normative system, in which a comprehensive, but uncodified, set of relatively specific norms governs concrete behavior. But in a modern society an area of flexibility must be gained in economic, political, and social life in which specific norms may be determined in considerable part by short-term exigencies in the situation of action, or by functional requisites of the relevant social subsystems. Ultimate or religious values lay down the basic principles of social action; thus such a normative system is called "principial," but the religious system does not attempt to regulate economic, political, and social life in great detail, as in prescriptive societies. Looking at this process another way, we may say that there must be a differentiation between religion and ideology, between ultimate values and proposed ways in which these values may be put into effect. In traditional prescriptive societies there is no such discrimination. Difference of opinion on social policy is taken to imply difference as to religious commitment. The social innovator necessarily becomes a religious heretic. But in modern society there is a differentiation between the levels of religion and social ideology which makes possible greater flexibility at both levels.

How is the normative system in a traditional society to be changed from prescriptive to principial, and how is the differentiation of the religious and ideological levels

to be effected, especially in the face of the concerted effort of the old system to avoid any changes at all? I would assert that only a new religious initiative, only a new movement which claims religious ultimacy for itself, can successfully challenge the old value system and its religious base. The new movement, which arises from the necessity to make drastic social changes in the light of new conditions, is essentially ideological and political in nature. But, arising as it does in a society in which the ideological level is not yet recognized as having independent legitimacy, the new movement must take on a religious coloration in order to meet the old system on its own terms. Even when such a movement is successful in effecting major structural changes in the society and in freeing motivation formerly frozen in traditional patterns so that considerable flexibility in economic and political life is attained, the problems posed by its own partly religious origin and its relation to the traditional religious system may still be serious indeed.

Let us turn to the example of Turkey.[3]

Ottoman Turkey in the eighteenth century was a traditionalistic society with a prescriptive value system. Virtually all spheres of life were theoretically under the authority of the religious law, the Shari'ah. Indeed, the government was supposed to have an area of freedom within the law. But this freedom had become narrowly restricted. Precedents of governmental procedure were tacitly assimilated to the religious law.

Beginning with Selim III in the late eighteenth century, a series of reforming sultans and statesmen attempted to make major changes in Turkish society in an effort to cope with increasingly desperate internal and external conditions. While some changes were made, especially in areas remote from the central strongholds of the

---

[3] Throughout the discussion of Turkey I shall rely heavily on lectures and unpublished material of Niyazi Berkes, of the Islamic Institute at McGill University, who is undertaking a pioneering study of Turkish modernization.

religious law, the reforming party was unable to attain any ultimate legitimation in the eyes of the people, and, although Turkish society was shaken to its foundations, periods of reform alternated with periods of blind reaction in which reformers were executed or banished.

The last of these reactionary periods was that of the rule of the despotic Sultan Abdul Hamid II, who was overthrown in 1908 by a coup of young army officers whom we know as the "Young Turks." By this time it had become clear to leading intellectuals that more was needed than another interim of liberal reform. They saw that a basic change in the cultural foundation of Turkish society was demanded if the long-delayed changes in economic, political, and social structure were to be effected. Some felt that a modern purified Islam could provide the new cultural basis, but orthodox Islam was so deeply imbedded in the fabric of traditional society that the Islamic modernists found little response in the religious party. Others looked to Western liberal democracy as a satisfactory foundation. Those sensitive to the mind of the Turkish masses, however, pointed out that the Turkish people would never accept a value system so obviously "made abroad" and which could so easily be condemned by the conservatives with the stigma of unbelief.

It was Ziya Gökalp, a sociologist much influenced by Durkheim, who ardently championed Turkish nationalism as the only satisfactory cultural foundation for the new Turkey.[4] Gökalp found the referent for all symbols of ultimate value in society itself. His answer to the religious conservatives was that the true Islam was that of the Turkish folk, not of the effete religious hierarchy which was largely educated in the Arabic and Persian languages rather than the Turkish language. Here at last was an ideology to which the people could respond with emotion and which could challenge religious conservatism on its own grounds.

[4] A translation by Niyazi Berkes of selected writings of Ziya Gökalp is forthcoming.

But the course of world history did as much as Gökalp's eloquence to decide in favor of the nationalist alternative for Turkey. Not only did World War I shear Turkey of her empire, but the subsequent invasions of Anatolia threatened the very life of the nation itself. Mustafa Kemal, who led the ultimately successful effort of national resistance, partly chose and partly was impelled to make the nation the central symbol in his subsequent drive for modernization. As a result, the highest value and central symbol for the most articulate sections of the Turkish people became not Islam but Turkism, or nationalism, or Kemalism, or, simply, "the Revolution." Having a strong national and personal charismatic legitimacy, Mustafa Kemal, later known as "Ataturk," was able to create a far-reaching cultural revolution in which the place of religion in the society was fundamentally altered. We may note some of the landmarks in this revolution. In 1924 the office of caliph was abolished. In the same year all religious schools were closed or converted into secular schools. The most important change of all took place in 1926: the Muslim Civil Law was abandoned and the Swiss Civil Code adopted almost without change. Finally, in 1928, the phrase in the constitution stating that the religion of Turkey is Islam was deleted, and Turkey was declared a secular state.

That the Turks were deeply conscious of what they were doing is illustrated by the following quotation from Mahmud Essad, the minister of justice under whom the religious law was abandoned:

> The purpose of laws is not to maintain the old customs or beliefs which have their source in religion, but rather to assure the economic and social unity of the nation.

> When religion has sought to rule human societies, it has been the arbitrary instrument of sovereigns, despots, and strong men. In separating the temporal and the spiritual, modern civilization has saved the world from numerous calamities and has

given to religion an imperishable throne in the consciences of believers.[5]

This quotation illustrates well enough the transition from prescriptive to principial society and the differentiation of religion and ideology as two distinct levels. It is clear that the great advances of Turkish society in economic, political, and social life are based on this new cultural foundation. But implicit in Essad's words are some of the yet unsolved problems about that new cultural pattern.

For Essad and other Turkish reformers "the Revolution" was a criterion for everything, even for the place of religion in society, and thus, whether consciously or not, they gave the revolution an ultimate, a religious, significance. The six principles upon which the constitution is based—republicanism, nationalism, populism, étatism, secularism, and revolution—are taken as self-subsisting ultimates. Thus the religious implications of the political ideology remain relatively unchecked. These express themselves in party claims to ultimate legitimacy and in an inability on the part of the party in power to accept the validity of an opposition, which are not in accord with the flexibility appropriate in a modern principial society.

On the other hand, Islam in Turkey has not on the whole been able to redefine its own self-image and face the theological issues involved in becoming a religion primarily, in Essad's words, "enthroned in men's consciences." Nor has it been able to provide a deeper religious dimension of both legitimation and judgment of the six principles which are the basis of the new social life. It remains, on the whole, in a conservative frame of mind in which the ideological claims are considerable, thus still posing a threat, possibly a great one, to return the society to a less differentiated level of social organization. Considering the trend of the last forty years, however, we seem to be observing a differentiation

in the process of becoming, but it is too soon to say that it has been entirely accomplished.

Japan, while illustrating the same general processes as Turkey, does so with marked differences in important details.[6] Premodern Japan was a traditionalistic society with a prescriptive normative system closely integrated with a religious system composed of a peculiar Japanese amalgam of Shinto, Confucianism, and Buddhism. In the immediate premodern period, however, a conjuncture of the Confucian stress on loyalty and a revived interest in Shinto began to have explosive consequences. The actual rule at this time was in the hands of a military dictator, or Shogun, hereditary in the Tokugawa family. The emperor was relegated to purely ceremonial functions in the palace at Kyoto, But, as economic and social conditions deteriorated under Tokugawa rule, important elements in the population became alienated from the political status quo. They proved extremely receptive to the religious message of the revival Shintoists and legitimist Confucians, who insisted that the true sovereign was the emperor and that the Shogun was a usurper. According to their conception, the emperor is divine, descended from the sun-goddess, and his direct rule of the Japanese people could be expected to bring in a virtually messianic age.

This movement was already vigorous when Perry's ships moved into Tokyo Bay in 1853. The inability of the Tokugawa government to keep foreigners from desecrating the sacred soil of Japan added the last fuel to the flames of resentment, and, with the slogan "Revere the Emperor; expel the barbarians," a successful military coup overthrew the Tokugawa and restored the emperor to direct rule.

I would suggest that Japan was at this point, in 1868, virtually at the beginning of serious Western influence, in a position

---

[5] Quoted in Henry E. Allen, *The Turkish Transformation* (Chicago: University of Chicago Press, 1935), p. 34.

[6] For a more extensive treatment of the Japanese case, especially the premodern background see my *Tokugawa Religion* (Glencoe, Ill.: Free Press, 1957).

that Turkey reached only in the early 1920's under Mustafa Kemal. But she reached it in quite a different way. Unlike Turkey, one of the very foundations of the old traditional order in Japan, the divine emperor, provided the main leverage for the radical reorganization of that order. The young samurai who put through the Meiji Restoration used the central value of loyalty to the emperor to legitimize the immense changes they were making in all spheres of social life and to justify the abandoning of many apparently sacred prescriptions of the traditional order. No other sacredness could challenge the sacredness inherent in the emperor's person.

Here we see an ideological movement, essentially political in nature, whose aim was the strengthening and thus the modernizing of Japan, taking a much more openly religious coloration than was the case in Turkey. There was in the early Meiji period an attempt to make Shinto into the national religion and a determined effort to root out all rival religions. Christianity was sharply discouraged, but it was on Buddhism, the chief native religious tradition with little relation to the imperial claims to divinity, that the ax fell. The Buddhist church was disestablished, and all syncretism with Shinto prohibited. In the words of D. C. Holtom:

> Members of the royal family were debarred from continuing in Buddhist orders; Buddhist ceremonials in the imperial palace were prohibited; Buddhist temples all over the land were attacked and destroyed. A blind fury of misplaced patriotic zeal committed precious Buddhist writings, fine sculptures, bronzes, woodcarvings, and paintings to the flames, broke them in pieces, cast them away, or sold them for a pittance to whosoever would buy. Buddhist priests were prohibited from participating in Shinto ceremonies. They were subjected to beatings and threatened with military force. Monks and nuns in large numbers were obliged to take up secular callings.[7]

Grave foreign protests on the subject of Christianity plus serious unrest among the masses devoted to Buddhism forced the abandoning of the policy of religious persecution. Liberal elements within the country agitated for the complete separation of church and state, and the Meiji leaders were brought to understand that religious freedom was a principle of the modern society they were trying to establish. Consequently, the government included in the constitution of 1889 a clause guaranteeing freedom of religion. At the same time it continued its support of the state Shinto cult, whose main aim was the veneration of the emperor. It solved this seeming contradiction by declaring that state Shinto was not a religion but merely an expression of patriotism. Nevertheless, the existence of the national cult imposed a real limitation on the independence and effectiveness of the private religious bodies. Though in the 1920's there was a strong tendency to differentiate religion and ideology, in times of stress such as the late 1930's and early 1940's religion was completely subordinated to and fused with a monolithic ideology, an ideology which had demonic consequences both for Japan and for the rest of the world. The new, 1946, constitution, by disestablishing Shinto and deriving sovereignty from the people rather than from the sacred and inviolable emperor, theoretically completed the process of secularization.

But, in fact, serious religious problems remain. All religious groups with the exception of the Christians were compromised by their connection with the nationalistic orgy. In the absence of any really vigorous religious life, except for the popular faith-healing cults and the small Christian community, the religious impulses of the Japanese people find expression for

[7] D. C. Holtom, *Modern Japan and Shinto Nationalism* (Chicago: University of Chicago Press, 1947), p. 127.

the more radical in the symbol of socialism, for the conservatives in a longing for a new and more innocent version of state Shinto. Here, as in Turkey, the differentiation between religion and ideology remains to be completed.

Other examples of the processes we have been discussing come readily to mind. Communism is an example of a secular political ideology which successfully came to power in the prescriptive, religiously based societies of Russia and China. But Communism itself makes an ultimate religious claim, and here, as in the case of Japan, a secular ideology claiming religious ultimacy has embarked on courses of action which hinder, rather than further, the transition to modern principial society. It is perhaps safe to say that alongside the serious political and economic problems which Communism faces today is the perhaps even more serious cultural problem, the problem of the differentiation of the religious and ideological levels.

In conclusion, it seems worthwhile to stress that the process of secularization, which is in part what the transition from prescriptive to principial society is, does not mean that religion disappears. The function of religion in a principial society is different from that in a prescriptive society, but it is not necessarily less important. Moreover, in the very process of transition religion may reappear in many new guises. Perhaps what makes the situation so unclear is its very fluidity. Even in highly differentiated societies, such as our own, traditional religion, so deeply associated with the prescriptive past, is still in the process of finding its place in modern principial society.

PART III

THE CONCOMITANTS OF

POLITICAL DEVELOPMENT

INTRODUCTION

During the process of modernization the political system undergoes transformation, both in its structure and its functions. In this transformation the relations between the political system and society are both autonomous and interdependent. Political development is partly independent of economic, social, or other forms of change. But also, it influences and is influenced by social and economic developments including industrialization and urbanization. The political system in modernizing society comes to deal with an ever wider range of problems; it becomes, as was pointed out, the generalized problem solver for the entire society. For example, the political system comes to occupy a dominant role in economic development. However, since political development is a process by which a political system acquires an increased capacity to sustain successfully and continuously new types of goals and demands and the creation of new types of organization, political development may depend, in turn, upon basic changes in society and the economy.

In this part we are concerned with changes in the environment within which political development occurs, namely, economic development, social changes relative to economic development, industrialization, and urbanization. These concomitants of political development have sometimes been viewed as the preconditions of political development and at other times as the consequences of political development. Moreover, political development may take place relatively independently of these changes. At the same time it must be noted that these interrelationships are both positive and negative. That is, the relationship may be one of stimulation and inducement; it may also be one of hampering and preventing.

The analysis by W. W. Rostow is a provocative theoretical statement on the changes that occur prior to and at the time of "take-off" into economic development. His hypothesis, supported by historical data, is that economic development proceeds in several distinguishable stages: the preconditions for "take-off," the "take-off," and sustained economic progress.[1]

In brief, the sequence of economic development consists of a long period (up to a century or, conceivably, more) when the preconditions for take-off are established. The take-off is the brief interval of two or three decades during which the economy and the society of which it is a part transform themselves in such ways that economic development is, subsequently, more or less automatic. This is followed by a long period during which economic growth becomes relatively self-sustaining and regularized.

J. J. Spengler focuses his discussion precisely on the political preconditions of economic development and then shows their interrelations by extending his analysis to the political consequences of economic development. In other words, he identifies what he regards as the minimum political preconditions of economic development and proceeds to show the changes that take place in these preconditions as economic development moves ahead.

The *precondition approach* to economic development is viewed by Albert Hirschman as a "council of perfection." His sharp critique, although not included in this volume, is introduced below and should be considered when reading Rostow and Spengler. According to Hirschman, theories which postulate a specific precondition for development are empirically vulnerable as development has occurred somewhere without benefit of that prerequisite. Moreover, he argues, different theories neutralize one another. For instance, it seems difficult to insist at one and the same time that the general climate of opinion must be favorable to industrial progress and that a strategic factor of particular importance is the presence of minority groups or of individuals with deviant, i.e., socially disapproved, behavior. "One rather suspects that when economic opportunity arises it will be perceived and exploited primarily by native entrepreneurs or by deviant minorities, depending on whether or not the traditional values of the society are favorable to change."[2]

Continuing his discussion of the search for the *primum mobile*, Hirschman writes: "While we were at first discouraged by the long list of resources and circumstances whose presence has been shown to be needed for economic development, we now find that these resources and circumstances are not so scarce or so difficult to realize, *provided, however, that economic development itself first raises its head*. This is of course only a positive way of stating the well-known proposition that economic development is held back by a series of 'interlocking vicious circles.' Before it starts, economic development is hard to visualize, not only because so many different conditions must be fulfilled simultaneously but above all because of the vicious circles: generally the

---

[1] Subsequently, Rostow elaborated this analysis by adding the stage of traditional society before the preconditions stage and dividing the period of sustained economic progress into the drive to maturity and the age of high mass consumption. See "The Stages of Economic Growth," *The Economic History Review*, **12**, 1–16, August 1959. The older article appears here because of the more detailed treatment given to the precondition and the take-off stages, which are more crucial to an understanding of the process of modernization.

[2] Albert O. Hirschman, *The Strategy of Economic Development* (New Haven: Yale University Press, 1958), p. 4.

realization of these conditions depends in turn on economic development. But this means also that once development has started, the circle is likely to become an upward spiral as all the prerequisites and conditions for development are brought into being."[3]

Hirschman concludes that "This approach permits us to focus on a characteristic of the process of economic development that is fundamental for both analysis and strategy: development depends not so much on finding optimal combinations for given resources and factors of production as on calling forth and enlisting for development purposes resources and abilities that are hidden, scattered, or badly utilized."[4]

Spengler's discussion of the "political preconditions" also includes a consideration of when state intervention is indicated to achieve economic development. The need for government action and its shortcomings are examined. Alexander Eckstein in the following article suggests a potential correlation between individualism and economic development. "The extent to which this potential is translated into reality will depend upon the role played by individual choice and initiative in resource allocation, regardless of whether the choices and decisions are in fact arrived at primarily within the confines of the economic or political process."

Eckstein sees economic growth as a broadening of the range of alternatives open to society. In traditional society there is little scope for the exercise of choice, individual or social. In modern society there is a much greater scope for individual choice and decentralized decision-making in the economic sphere. This condition is an important aspect of individualism.

In summing up his discussion of the role of the state and the categories of state action in the process of economic development, Eckstein suggests that it may be useful to attempt to work with the concept of an "optimum level and pattern of state intervention." This optimum would have to be defined in relation to two broad sets of objectives: (1) striving for rising standards of living combined with an increase, and/or (2) preservation of the scope for the exercise of individual choice and initiative.

The relationship of the political system to economic growth is only one aspect of societal interdependence. Bert F. Hoselitz points out that economic development is a process which affects the entire social, political, and cultural fabric of a society. When the rapidly "explosive" take-off occurred, Hoselitz observes, social institutions had been created which allowed capital formation and made available a number of highly skilled and specialized services. The creation of these social institutions and the institutionalization of entrepreneurship (defined as "an innovating uncertainty-bearing activity") required the establishment of a social framework within which these developments could take place. Hoselitz, like Hagen in Chapter 3, sees such a social framework being crested as a result of the appearance of behavioral deviance, i.e., the emergence of cultural or social marginality, and the process of redefinition of societal objectives by an elite.

[3] *Ibid.*, p. 5.
[4] *Ibid.*

Manning Nash is also concerned with the relation of economic development to its antecedent and subsequent social and cultural changes, but he broadens his analysis to include more than social institutions. He feels that generalizations about the process of economic development in terms of pattern variables are not very useful because shifts in pattern variables are never specified in amount or degree. On the other hand, the more empirical literature presents no systematic or consistent interpretation of the way in which different social and cultural arrangements affect development.

Therefore, Nash proceeds to build an intermediate diagnostic scheme based on the proposition that economic development is a process of social and cultural change. Social and cultural change is viewed as a function of the alternatives generated by a given social system and, since different groups or individuals are differentially situated in the social structure, there exists in any society a variety of realistic impulses to change. Nash identifies three cultural features which may affect social decisions to undertake economic development: (1) the pattern of stratification in society and the amount of social mobility possible, (2) the system of social values which justify, explain, and define social position and the means of attaining it, and (3) the organization of the economic and political sybsystems for self-sustained development. These categories of analysis are used to compare and contrast the potential for development in Burma and Cambodia. In conclusion, a scheme is offered as a preliminary way of gauging the social and cultural factors which are most intimately associated with economic development so that a society's potential for economic development may be assessed.

Industrialization is not identical with or a necessary cause of modernization, even though it appears to be widely desired by developing nations. In the West, modernization did occur as a result of the twin processes of industrialization and commercialization, but in many non-Western areas modernization has been a result of commercialization and bureaucracy, rather than industrialization.[5] Some of the values appropriate to industrial countries have been spread by enterprising men, sometimes in the context of politics and trade, sometimes in the context of religion and education. Thus, modernization should be viewed as a separate and distinct process from industrialization—caused by it in the West but causing it in other areas.

Many developing nations are attempting to industrialize, sometimes too soon or too rapidly. The analysis by George A. Theodorson of the consequences of industrialization for the social patterns of non-Western nations is a vivid portrayal of the concomitants of political development. He argues that industrialization will lead to new societal patterns and "These patterns will resemble, in time, certain dominant patterns of western industrialized society, which *may not be rejected by any people who accept the machines of the West.*" These changes are presented within the framework of systems analysis, using Parsons' pattern variables, which were introduced in Part I.

[5] David E. Apter, *The Politics of Modernization* (Chicago: The University of Chicago Press, 1965), pp. 43–44.

The changes result in a creation of new roles, new facilities, and new rewards, and in recognition of previously unimportant resources and skills. As a result, new individuals are placed in positions of power. This new power structure challenges the old and creates one of the many pressures for political development. Like the "assaulted" individuals Matossian describes, these leaders are men of two cultures—they are emotionally tied to the old system, but at the same time they are anxious to reap the benefits of a system which promises to relieve some of their economic problems. If they endeavor to stop the inevitable social change which Theodorson insists will accompany industrialization, they will increase social disorganization. Less productivity and a serious delay in the achievement of the desired basic economic goals will result. On the other hand, if only those elements of the old culture are retained which do not conflict with the new human relationships that inevitably accompany a machine society, modernization may proceed without serious disruption. Devising such a strategy poses a real test of the social and political acumen of the new leaders.

Urbanization is sometimes, but not always, a consequence of industrialization. Shanti Tangri asserts that urbanization is neither a necessary nor sufficient condition for economic development. It can be a desirable condition for development, but under certain conditions it can be a factor which slows it down. Reminiscent of the sociologists of previous generations, he contends that the role of urbanization cannot be determined without estimating the costs or benefits of such urban phenomena as *anomie*, political and ideological ferment, and transformation of cultural and social values.

As discussed in Part II, there is an ideology of economic development which may dictate a number of costly investments in modern factories, transportation systems, and the attendant social institutions which the people today demand when industrialization and urbanization occur. India, for example, has tried to become a welfare state before creating the basic economy required to sustain it. The ideology of the elites and the political leaders of developing nations tends to outrun technological and economic capabilities.

As a result, economic and other frustrations soon ensue with serious political consequences. Urban unemployment is often high. From the swelling ranks of the colleges and universities emerge the intelligentsia, who provide the leadership for political action—often mob action. Physical densities, media communications, and other facilities in cities make political organization easier. Political action may substitute for traditional social patterns. The political party in India, for example, is described as an alternative social structure to the traditional family. The purposelessness of life in the city may be transformed into a cause. Fanaticism and an ethos of dedication are used to maintain political unity around charismatic leaders. The consequences are dangerous for democracy.

Tangri poses an alternative to leaders faced with these political problems. He urges a return to the village. Appropriate allocations and actions for the development of the countryside are necessary, supplemented by an ideological campaign. He feels that the village still has a romantic, emotional, political, or philosophical attraction for many. By exporting the problems of unemployment and poverty to cities, political instability is increased, but, Tangri maintains, there is a greater level of tolerance for these old and familiar problems in the village. Is this a strategy of despair, romantic idealism, or sound political advice for the leaders of the developing nations?

Samuel P. Huntington is also concerned about the political instability which may result from the growth of the city, but his focus is on the social, economic, and psychological divergences which occur between people living in rapidly changing cities and those remaining in more static rural settings. In a short, close-reasoned analysis, he describes why this gap between city and countryside is typically present in societies undergoing rapid social and economic change. He sees the city-country gap as "the primary source of political instability in such societies and a principal, if not the principal, obstacle to national integration."

Modernization changes the nature of the city and the balance between the city and the countryside. The urban elements begin to assert themselves and overthrow the ruling rural elite. Initially, the society is still rural but its politics become urban. As politics become more and more urban, it becomes less and less stable. At this point the effort to achieve political stability may lead to an alliance between some urban groups and the countryside. The inauguration of the rural masses into national politics, the "Green Uprising," usually involves the mobilization of the peasants for political combat.

The instability of the city is an almost inevitable characteristic of modernization. Rural instability, on the other hand, may be avoidable. Huntington concludes with an analysis of how revolution might be avoided and the city-country gap closed. The articles in Chapter 15, particularly the selection by Eric R. Wolf, explore in greater detail the issue raised by Huntington concerning the effects of rapid change and urban-rural gaps.

Chapter 5

Economic Development

THE TAKE-OFF INTO SELF-SUSTAINED GROWTH[1]

W. W. Rostow

The purpose of this article is to explore the following hypothesis: that the process of economic growth can usefully be regarded as centering on a relatively brief time interval of two or three decades when the economy and the society of which it is a part transform themselves in such ways that economic growth is, subsequently, more or less automatic. This decisive transformation is here called the take-off.[2]

The take-off is defined as the interval during which the rate of investment increases in such a way that real output per capita rises and this initial increase carries with it radical changes in production techniques and the disposition of income flows which perpetuate the new scale of investment and perpetuate thereby the rising trend in per-capita output. Initial

SOURCE. W. W. Rostow, "The Take-Off into Self-Sustained Growth," *The Economic Journal*, **66**, 25–48, March 1956.

[1] I wish to acknowledge with thanks the helpful criticisms of an earlier draft by G. Baldwin, F. Bator, K. Berrill, A. Enthoven, E. E. Hagen, C. P. Kindleberger, L. Lefeber, W. Malenbaum, E. S. Mason, and M. F. Millikan.
[2] This argument is a development from the line of thought presented in *The Process of Economic Growth* (New York, 1952), Ch. 4, especially pp. 102–105. The concept of three stages in the growth process centering on the take-off is defined and used for prescriptive purposes in *An American Policy in Asia* (New York, 1955), Ch. 7.

changes in method require that some group in the society have the will and the authority to install and diffuse new production techniques;[3] and a perpetuation of the growth process requires that such a leading group expand in authority and that the society as a whole respond to the impulses set up by the initial changes, including the potentialities for external economies. Initial changes in the scale and direction of finance flows are likely to imply a command over income flows by new groups or institutions; and a perpetuation of growth requires that a high proportion of the increment to real income during the take-off period be

[3] We shall set aside in this article the question of how new production techniques are generated from pure science and invention, a procedure which is legitimate, since we are examining the growth process in national (or regional) economies over relatively short periods. We shall largely set aside also the question of population pressure and the size and quality of the working force, again because of the short period under examination; although, evidently, even over short periods, the rate of population increase will help determine the level of investment required to yield rising output per capita (see below, p. 28, note 2). By and large, this article is concerned with capital formation at a particular stage of economic growth; and of the array of propensities defined in *The Process of Economic Growth* it deals only with the propensity to accept innovations and the propensity to seek material advance, the latter in relation to the supply of finance only.

returned to productive investment. The take-off requires, therefore, a society prepared to respond actively to new possibilities for productive enterprise; and it is likely to require political, social, and institutional changes which will both perpetuate an initial increase in the scale of investment and result in the regular acceptance and absorption of innovations.

In short, this article is an effort to clarify the economics of industrial revolution when an industrial revolution is conceived of narrowly with respect to time and broadly with respect to changes in production functions.

Three Stages in the Growth Process

The historian examining the story of a particular national economy is inevitably impressed by the long-period continuity of events. Like other forms of history, economic history is a seamless web. The cotton-textile developments in Britain of the 1780's and 1790's have a history stretching back for a half century at least; the United States of the 1840's and 1850's had been preparing itself for industrialization since the 1790's, at the latest; Russia's remarkable development during the two pre-1914 decades goes back to 1861 for its foundations, if not to the Napoleonic Wars or to Peter the Great; the remarkable economic spurt of Meiji Japan is incomprehensible outside the context of economic developments in the latter half of the Tokugawa era; and so on. It is wholly legitimate that the historian's influence should be to extend the story of the British industrial revolution back into the seventeenth century and forward far into the nineteenth century; and that Heckscher should embrace Sweden's transition in a chapter entitled, "The Great Transformation (1815–1914)."[4] From the perspective of the economic historian the isolation of a take-off period is, then, a distinctly arbitrary process. It is to be judged, like such other arbitrary exercises

[4] E. F. Heckscher, *An Economic History of Sweden*, Tr. G. Ohlin (Cambridge, Massachusetts, 1954), Ch. 6.

as the isolation of business cycles and secular trends, on whether it illuminates more of the economic process than it conceals; and it should be used, if accepted, as a way of giving a rough framework of order to the inordinately complicated biological problem of growth rather than as an exact model of reality.

There is difficulty in this set of conceptions for the statistical analyst of economic development as well as for the historian. At first sight the data mobilized, for example, by Clark, Kuznets, Buchanan and Ellis exhibit a continuum of degrees of development both within countries over time and as among countries at a given period of time, with no *prima facie* case for a clearly marked watershed in the growth process.[5] In part this statistical result arises from the fact that historical data on national product and its components are only rarely available for an economy until after it has passed into a stage of more or less regular growth; that is, after the take-off. In part it arises from the fact that, by and large, these authors are more concerned with different levels of per-capita output (or welfare)—and the structural characteristics that accompany them—than with the growth process itself. The data they mobilize do not come to grips with the inner determinants of growth. The question raised here is not how or why levels of output per capita have differed but rather how it has come about that particular economies have moved from stagnation—to slow, piece-meal advance— to a situation where growth was the normal economic condition. Our criterion

[5] Colin Clark, *The Conditions of Economic Progress* (London, 1951, second edition); Simon Kuznets, "International Differences in Capital Formation and Financing" (mimeographed; Conference on Capital Formation and Economic Growth, November 1953) (National Bureau of Economic Research, New York, 1953); Norman Buchanan and Howard Ellis, *Approaches to Economic Development* (Twentieth Century Fund, New York, 1955). See also the United Nations data presented as a frontispiece to H. F. Williamson and John A. Buttrick, *Economic Development* (New York, 1954).

here is not the absolute level of output per capita but its rate of change.

In this argument the sequence of economic development is taken to consist of three periods: a long period (up to a century, or conceivably, more) when the preconditions for take-off are established; the take-off itself, defined within two or three decades; and a long period when growth becomes normal and relatively automatic. These three divisions would, of course, not exclude the possibility of growth giving way to secular stagnation or decline in the long term. It would exclude from the concept of a growing economy, however, one which experiences a brief spurt of expansion which is not subsequently sustained; for example, the United States industrial boom of the War of 1812 or the ill-fated spurts of certain Latin American economies in the early stages of their modern history.

Take-offs have occurred in two quite different types of societies; and, therefore, the process of establishing preconditions for take-off has varied. In the first and most general case the achievement of preconditions for take-off required major change in political and social structure and, even, in effective cultural values. In the vocabulary of *The Process of Economic Growth*, important changes in the propensities preceded the take-off. In the second case take-off was delayed not by political, social, and cultural obstacles but by the high (and even expanding) levels of welfare that could be achieved by exploiting land and natural resources. In this second case take-off was initiated by a more narrowly economic process, as, for example, in the northern United States, Australia and, perhaps, Sweden. In the vocabulary of *The Process of Economic Growth*, the take-off was initiated primarily by a change in the yields; although subsequent growth brought with it changes in the propensities as well. As one would expect in the essentially biological field of economic growth, history offers mixed as well as pure cases.

In the first case the process of establishing preconditions for take-off might be generalized in impressionistic terms as follows:

We start with a reasonably stable and traditional society containing an economy mainly agricultural, using more or less unchanging production methods, saving and investing productively little more than is required to meet depreciation. Usually from outside the society, but sometimes out of its own dynamics, comes the idea that economic progress is possible; and this idea spreads within the established *élite* or, more usually, in some disadvantaged group whose lack of status does not prevent the exercise of some economic initiative. More often than not the economic motives for seeking economic progress converge with some non-economic motive, such as the desire for increased social power and prestige, national pride, political ambition and so on. Education, for some at least, broadens and changes to suit the needs of modern economic activity. New enterprising men come forward willing to mobilize savings and to take risks in pursuit of profit, notably in commerce. The commercial markets for agricultural products, domestic handicrafts, and consumption-goods imports widen. Institutions for mobilizing capital appear; or they expand from primitive levels in the scale, surety and time horizon for loans. Basic capital is expanded, notably in transport and communications, often to bring to market raw materials in which other nations have an economic interest, often financed by foreign capital. And, here and there, modern manufacturing enterprise appears, usually in substitution for imports.

Since public-health measures are enormously productive in their early stages of application and, as innovations go, meet relatively low resistance in most cultures, the death rate may fall and the population begin to rise, putting pressure on the food supply and the institutional structure of agriculture, creating thereby an economic depressant or stimulus (or both in turn), depending on the society's response.[6]

The rate of productive investment may rise up to 5 per cent of national income;[7] but this is unlikely to do much more than keep ahead of the population increase. And, in general, all this activity proceeds on a limited basis, within an economy and a society still mainly characterized by traditional low-productivity techniques and by old values and institutions which developed in conjunction with them. The rural proportion of the population is likely to stand at 75 per cent or over.

In the second case, of naturally wealthy nations, with a highly favorable balance between population and natural resources and with a population deriving by emigration from reasonably acquisitive cultures, the story of establishing the preconditions differs mainly in that there is no major problem of overcoming traditional values inappropriate to economic growth and the inert or resistant institutions which incorporate them; there is less difficulty in developing an *élite* effective in the investment process; and there is no population problem.[8] Technically, much the

same slow-moving process of change occurs at high (and, perhaps, even expanding) levels of per-capita output, and with an extensive growth of population and output still based on rich land and other natural resources. Take-off fails to occur mainly because the comparative advantage of exploiting productive land and other natural resources delays the time when self-reinforcing industrial growth can profitably get under way.[9]

The beginning of take-off can usually be traced to a particular sharp stimulus. The stimulus may take the form of a political revolution which affects directly the balance of social power and effective values, the character of economic institutions, the distribution of income, the pattern of investment outlays and the proportion of potential innovations actually applied; that is, it operates through the propensities. It may come about through a technological (including transport) innovation, which sets in motion a chain of secondary expansion in modern sectors and has powerful potential external economy effects which the society exploits. It may take the form of a newly

[6] Historically, disruptive population pressure has been generated in pretake-off societies not only by the easy spread of highly productive measures of public health but also by the easy acceptance of high-yield new crops, permitting a fragmentation of land holdings, earlier marriage and a rise in the birth rate; e.g., Ireland and China.

[7] The relation of the investment rate to growth depends, of course, on the rate of population rise. With stagnant population or slow rise a 5 per cent investment rate could yield substantial growth in real output per capita, as indeed it did in pre-1914 France. On the other hand, as noted on page 242 investment rates much higher than 5 per cent can persist in primitive economies which lack the preconditions for growth, based on capital imports, without initiating sustained growth. For some useful arithmetic on the scale and composition of capital requirements in a growing economy with a 1 per cent population increase see A. K. Cairncross, *Home and Foreign Investment* (Cambridge, 1953), Ch. 1.

[8] Even in these cases there have often been significant political and social restraints which

had to be reduced or eliminated before take-off could occur; for example, in Canada, the Argentine and the American South.

[9] Theoretically, such fortunate societies could continue to grow in per-capita output until diminishing returns damped down their progress. Theoretically, they might even go on as growing nonindustrial societies, absorbing agricultural innovations which successfully countered diminishing returns. Something like this process might describe, for example, the rich agricultural regions of the United States. But, in general, it seems to be the case that the conditions required to sustain a progressive increase in agricultural productivity will also lead on to self-reinforcing industrial growth. This result emerges not merely from the fact that many agricultural improvements are labor-saving, and that industrial employment can be stimulated by the availability of surplus labor and is required to draw it off; it also derives from the fact that the production and use of materials and devices which raise agricultural productivity in themselves stimulate the growth of a self-sustaining industrial sector.

favorable international environment, such as the opening of British and French markets to Swedish timber in the 1860's or a sharp relative rise in export prices and/or large new capital imports, as in the case of the United States from the late 1840's, Canada and Russia from the mid-1890's; but it may also come as a challenge posed by an unfavorable shift in the international environment, such as a sharp fall in terms of trade (or a wartime blockage of foreign trade) requiring the rapid development of manufactured import substitutes, as in the case of the Argentine and Australia in the 1930's and during the Second World War.[10] All these latter cases raise sharply the profitability of certain lines of enterprise and can be regarded as changes in the yields.

What is essential here, however, is not the form of stimulus but the fact that the prior development of the society and its economy result in a positive sustained, and self-reinforcing, response to it: the result is not a once-over change in production functions or in the volume of investment, but a higher proportion of potential innovations accepted in a more or less regular flow, and a higher rate of investment.

In short, the forces which have yielded marginal bursts of activity now expand and become quantitatively significant as rapid-moving trends. New industries expand at high rates, yielding profits which are substantially reinvested in new capacity; and their expansion induces a more general expansion of the modern sectors of the economy where a high rate of ploughback prevails. The institutions for mobilizing savings (including the fiscal and sometimes the capital-levy activities of govern-

ment) increase in scope and efficiency. New techniques spread in agriculture as well as in industry, as increasing numbers of persons are prepared to accept them and the deep changes they bring to ways of life. A new class of business-men (usually private, sometimes public servants) emerges and acquires control over the key decisions determining the use of savings. New possibilities for export develop and are exploited; new import requirements emerge. The economy exploits hitherto unused backlogs in technique and natural resources. Although there are a few notable exceptions, all this momentum historically attracted substantial foreign capital.

The use of aggregative national-income terms evidently reveals little of the process which is occurring. It is nevertheless useful to regard as a necessary but not sufficient condition for the take-off the fact that the proportion of net investment to national income (or net national product) rises from (say) 5 per cent to over 10 per cent, definitely outstripping the likely population pressure (since under the assumed take-off circumstances the capital–output ratio is low),[11] and yielding a distinct rise

[10] Historically, the imposition of tariffs has played an important role in take-offs, e.g., the American Tariffs of 1828 (cotton textiles) and 1841–42 (rail iron); the Russian tariffs of the 1890's, etc. Although these actions undoubtedly served to assist take-off in leading sectors, they usually reflected an energy and purpose among key entrepreneurial groups which would, in any case, probably have done the trick.

[11] The author is aware of the substantial ambiguities which overhang the concept of the capital–output ratio and, especially, of the dangers of applying an overall aggregate measure. But since the arithmetic of economic growth requires some such concept, implicitly or explicitly, we had better refine the tool rather than abandon it. In the early stages of economic development two contrary forces operate on the capital–output ratio. On the one hand there is a vast requirement of basic overhead capital in transport, power, education, etc. Here, due mainly to the long period over which such investment yields its return, the apparent (short-run) capital–output ratio is high. On the other hand, there are generally large unexploited backlogs of known techniques and available natural resources to be put to work; and these backlogs make for a low capital–output ratio. We can assume formally a low capital–output ratio for the take-off period because we are assuming that the preconditions have been created, including a good deal of social overhead capital. In fact, the aggregate marginal capital–output ratio is likely to be kept up during the take-off by the requirement

in real output per capita. Whether real consumption per capita rises depends on the pattern of income distribution and population pressure, as well as on the magnitude, character, and productivity of investment itself.

As indicated in Table 1, I believe it possible to identify at least tentatively such take-off periods for a number of countries which have passed into the stage of growth.

The third stage is, of course, the long, fluctuating story of sustained economic progress. Overall capital per head increases as the economy matures. The structure of the economy changes increasingly. The initial key industries, which sparked the take-off, decelerate as diminishing returns operate on the original set of industrial tricks and the original band of pioneering entrepreneurs give way to less single-minded industrial leaders in those sectors; but the average rate of growth is maintained by a succession of new, rapidly growing sectors, with a new set of pioneering leaders. The proportion of the population in rural pursuits declines. The economy finds its (changing) place in the international economy. The society makes such terms as it will with the requirements for maximizing modern and efficient production, balancing off, as it will, the new values against those retarding values which persist with deeper roots, or adapting the latter in such ways as to support rather than retard the growth process. This sociological calculus interweaves with basic resource endowments to determine the pace of deceleration.

It is with the problems and vicissitudes of such growing economies of the third stage (and especially with cyclical fluctuations and the threat of chronic unemployment) that the bulk of modern theoretical economics is concerned, including much

[*footnote 11 continued*
of continuing large outlays for overhead items which yield their return only over long periods. Nevertheless, a ratio of 3–1 or 3.5–1 on average seems realistic as a rough bench- mark until we have learned more about capital–output ratios on a sectoral basis.

recent work on the formal properties of growth models. The student of history and of contemporary underdeveloped areas[12] is more likely to be concerned with the economics of the first two stages; that is, the economics of the preconditions and the take-off. If we are to have a serious theory of economic growth or (more likely) some useful theories about economic growth, they must obviously seek to embrace these two early stages—and notably the economics of the take-off. The balance of this article is designed to mobilize tentatively and in a preliminary way what an economic historian can contribute to the economics of take-off.

The Take-off Defined and Isolated

There are several problems of choice involved in defining the take-off with precision. We might begin with one arbitrary

[12] A number of so-called underdeveloped areas may have, in fact, either passed through the take-off process or are in the midst of it, e.g., Mexico, Brazil, Turkey, the Argentine, and India. I would commend for consideration —certainly no more until the concept of take-off is disproved or verified—the dropping of the concept of "underdeveloped areas" and the substitution for it of a quadripartite distinction among economies: traditional; pre-take-off; take-off; and growing. Against the background of this set of distinctions we might then consider systematically two separable questions now often confused. First, the stage of growth, as among growing economies. It is legitimate to regard Mexico and the United States, Great Britain and Australia, France, and Japan, as growing economies, although they stand at very different points along their national growth curves, where the degree of progress might be measured by some kind of index of output (or capital) per head. Second, the foreseeable long-run potential of growing economies. Over the long pull, even after they are "fully developed," the per-capita output levels that different economies are likely to achieve will undoubtedly vary greatly, depending notably on resource endowments in relation to population. The arraying of levels of output per capita for different economies, now conventional, fails to distinguish these three elements; that is, the current rate of growth; the stage of growth; and the foreseeable horizon for growth.

TABLE 1.   *Some Tentative, Approximate Take-off Dates*

COUNTRY	TAKE-OFF	COUNTRY	TAKE-OFF
Great Britain . .	1783–1802	Russia . . .	1890–1914
France . . .	1830–1860	Canada . .	1896–1914
Belgium . . .	1833–1860	Argentine[c] . .	1935–
United States[a] .	1843–1860	Turkey[d] . .	1937–
Germany . .	1850–1873	India[e] . . .	1952–
Sweden . . .	1868–1890	China[e] . . .	1952–
Japan[b] . . .	1878–1900		

[a] The American take-off is here viewed as the upshot of two different periods of expansion: the first, that of the 1840's, marked by railway and manufacturing development, mainly confined to the East—this occurred while the West and South digested the extensive agricultural expansion of the previous decade; the second the great railway push into the Middle West during the 1850's marked by a heavy inflow of foreign capital. By the opening of the Civil War the American economy of North and West, with real momentum in its heavy-industry sector, is judged to have taken off.

[b] Lacking adequate data, there is some question about the timing of the Japanese take-off. Some part of the post-1868 period was certainly, by the present set of definitions, devoted to firming up the preconditions for take-off. By 1914 the Japanese economy had certainly taken off. The question is whether the period from about 1878 to the Sino-Japanese War in the mid-1890's is to be regarded as the completion of the preconditions or as take-off. On present evidence, I incline to the latter view.

[c] In one sense the Argentine economy began its take-off during the First World War. But by and large, down to the pit of the post-1929 depression, the growth of its modern sector, stimulated during the war, tended to slacken; and like a good part of the Western World, the Argentine sought during the 1920's to return to a pre-1914 normalcy. It was not until the mid-1930's that a sustained take-off was inaugurated, which by and large can now be judged to have been successful despite the structural vicissitudes of that economy.

[d] Against the background of industrialization measures inaugurated in the mid-1930's the Turkish economy has exhibited remarkable momentum in the past five years founded in the increase in agricultural income and productivity. It still remains to be seen whether these two surges, conducted under quite different national policies, will constitute a transition to self-sustaining growth, and whether Turkey can overcome its current structural problems.

[e] As noted in the text it is still too soon (for quite different reasons) to judge either the Indian or Chinese Communist take-off efforts successful.

definition and consider briefly the two major alternatives.

For the present purposes the take-off is defined as requiring all three of the following related conditions:

1. a rise in the rate of productive investment from (say) 5 per cent or less to over 10 per cent of national income (or net national product);

2. the development of one or more substantial manufacturing[13] sectors, with a high rate of growth;

[13] In this context "manufacturing" is taken to include the processing of agricultural products or raw materials by modern methods; e.g., timber in Sweden; meat in Australia; dairy products in Denmark. The dual requirement of a "manufacturing" sector is that its processes set in motion a chain of further modern sector

3. the existence or quick emergence of a political, social and institutional framework which exploits the impulses to expansion in the modern sector and the potential external economy effects of the take-off and gives to growth an on-going character.

The third condition implies a considerable capability to mobilize capital from domestic sources. Some take-offs have occurred with virtually no capital imports; e.g., Britain and Japan. Some take-offs have had a high component of foreign capital; e.g., the United States, Russia, and Canada. But some countries have imported large quantities of foreign capital for long periods, which undoubtedly contributed to creating the preconditions of take-off, without actually initiating take-off; e.g., the Argentine before 1914, Venezuela down to recent years, the Belgian Congo currently. In short, whatever the role of capital imports, the preconditions for take-off include an initial ability to mobilize domestic savings productively, as well as a structure which subsequently permits a high marginal rate of savings.

This definition is designed to isolate the early stage when industrialization takes hold rather than the later stage when industrialization becomes a more massive and statistically more impressive phenomenon. In Britain, for example, there is no doubt that it was between 1815 and 1850 that industrialization fully took hold. If the criterion chosen for take-off was the period of most rapid overall industrial growth, or the period when large-scale industry matured, all our take-off dates would have to be set forward; Britain, for example, to 1819–48; the United States to 1868–93; Sweden to 1890–1920; Japan to 1900–20; Russia to 1928–40. The earlier dating is chosen here because it is believed, on present (often inadequate) evidence, that the decisive transformations

[*footnote 13 continued*
requirements and that its expansion provides the potentiality of external economy effects.

(including a decisive shift in the investment rate) occur in the first industrial phases; and later industrial maturity can be directly traced back to foundations laid in these first phases.

This definition is also designed to rule out from the take-off the quite substantial economic progress which can occur in an economy before a truly self-reinforcing growth process gets under way. British economic expansion between (say) 1750 and 1783, Russian economic expansion between (say) 1861 and 1890, Canadian economic expansion between 1867 and the mid-1890's—such periods—for which there is an equivalent in the economic history of almost every growing economy— were marked by extremely important, even decisive, developments. The transport network expanded, and with it both internal and external commerce; new institutions for mobilizing savings were developed; a class of commercial and even industrial entrepreneurs began to emerge; industrial enterprise on a limited scale (or in limited sectors) grew. And yet, however essential these pretake-off periods were for later development, their scale and momentum were insufficient to transform the economy radically or, in some cases, to outstrip population growth and to yield an increase in per-capita output.

With a sense of the considerable violence done to economic history, I am here seeking to isolate a period when the scale of productive economic activity reaches a critical level and produces changes which lead to a massive and progressive structural transformation in economies and the societies of which they are a part, better viewed as changes in kind than merely in degree.

Evidence on Investment Rates in the Take-off

The case for the concept of take-off hinges, in part, on quantitative evidence on the scale and productivity of investment in relation to population growth. Here, as noted earlier, we face a difficult problem; investment data are not now available historically for early stages in economic history. Following is such case as there is for regarding the shift from a productive investment rate of about 5 per cent of NNP to 10 per cent or more as central to the process.[14]

A PRIMA FACIE CASE

If we take the aggregate marginal capital-output ratio for an economy in its early stage of economic development at 3.5-1 and if we assume, as is not abnormal, a population rise of 1-1.5 per cent per annum it is clear that something between 3.5 and 5.25 per cent of NNP must be regularly invested if NNP per capita is to be sustained. An increase of 2 per cent per annum in NNP per capita requires, under these assumptions, that something between 10.5 and 12.5 per cent of NNP be regularly invested. By definition and assumption, then, a transition from relatively stagnant to substantial, regular rise in NNP per capita, under typical population conditions, requires that the proportion of national product productively invested move from

[14] In his important article, "Economic Development with Unlimited Supplies of Labour," *Manchester School*, May 1954, W. Arthur Lewis indicates a similar spread as defining the transition to economic growth:

> The central problem in the theory of economic development is to understand the process by which a community which was previously saving and investing 4 or 5 per cent of its national income or less, converts itself into an economy where voluntary saving is running at about 12–15 per cent of national income or more. This is the central problem because the central fact of economic development is rapid capital accumulation (including knowledge and skills with capital). We cannot explain any "industrial" revolution (as the economic historians pretend to do) until we can explain why saving increased relatively to national income.

Presumably Mr. Lewis based this range on empirical observation of contemporary "under-developed" areas on which some data are presented below. As in footnote 7, page 236, it should be emphasized that the choice of investment proportions to symbolize the transition to growth hinges on the assumptions made about the rate of population increase.

somewhere in the vicinity of 5 per cent to something in the vicinity of 10 per cent.

THE SWEDISH CASE

In the appendix to his paper on international differences in capital formation, cited above, Kuznets gives gross and net capital formation figures in relation to gross and net national product for a substantial group of countries where reasonably good statistical data exist. Excepting Sweden, these data do not go back clearly to pretake-off stages.[15] The

[15] The Danish data are on the margin. They begin with the decade 1870–79, probably the first decade of take-off itself. They show net and gross domestic capital formation rates well over 10 per cent. In view of the sketch of the Danish economy presented in Kjeld Bjerke's "Preliminary Estimates of the Danish National Product from 1870–1950" (Preliminary paper mimeographed for 1953 Conference of the International Association for Research on Income and Wealth), pp. 32–34, it seems likely that further research would identify the years 1830–70 as a period when the preconditions were actively established, 1870–1900 as a period of take-off. This view is supported by scattered and highly approximate estimates of Danish National Wealth which exhibit a remarkable surge in capital formation between 1864 and 1884.

Estimates of National Wealth in Denmark

	1000 millions of kroner.	Source
1864	3.5	Falbe-Hansen, *Danmarks statistik*, 1885.
1884	6.5	Falbe-Hansen, *Danmarks statisik*, 1885.
1899	7.2	Tax-commission of 1903.
1909	10.0	Jens Warming, *Danmarks statistik*, 1913.
1927	24.0	Jens Warming, *Danmarks erhvervs- or samfundsliv*, 1930.
1939	28.8	Economic expert committee of 1943, *Økonomiske efterkigrsproblemer*, 1945.
1950	54.5	N. Banke, N. P. Jacobsen og Vedel-Petersen, *Danske erhvervsliv*, 1951.

(Furnished in correspondence by Einar Cohn

Swedish data begin in the decade 1861–70; and the Swedish take-off is to be dated from the latter years of the decade.

Kuznets' calculations for Sweden are shown in Table 2.

THE CANADIAN CASE

The data developed by O. J. Firestone[16] for Canada indicate a similar transition for net capital formation in its take-off (say, 1896–1914); but the gross investment proportion in the period from Confederation to the mid-nineties was higher than appears to have marked other periods when the preconditions were established, possibly due to investment in the railway net, abnormally large for a nation of Canada's population, and to relatively heavy foreign investment, even before the great capital import boom of the pre-1914 decade (Table 3).

THE PATTERN OF CONTEMPORARY EVIDENCE IN GENERAL[17]

In the years after 1945 the number of countries for which reasonably respectable national income (or product) data exist has grown; and with such data there have

[footnote 15 continued
and Kjeld Bjerke.) It should again be emphasized, however, that we are dealing with a hypothesis whose empirical foundations are still fragmentary.
[16] O. J. Firestone, Canada's Economic Development, 1867–1952, with Special Reference to Changes in the Country's National Product and National Wealth, paper prepared for the International Association for Research in Income and Wealth, 1953, to which Mr. Firestone has kindly furnished me certain revisions, shortly to be published. By 1900 Canada already had about 18,000 miles of railway line; but the territory served had been developed to a limited degree only. By 1900 Canada already had a net balance of foreign indebtedness over $1 billion. Although this figure was almost quadrupled in the next two decades, capital imports represented an important increment to domestic capital sources from the period of Confederation down to the pre-1914 Canadian boom, which begins in the mid-1890's.
[17] I am indebted to Mr. Everett Hagen for mobilizing the statistical data in this section, except where otherwise indicated.

developed some tolerable savings and investment estimates for countries at different stages of the growth process. Within the category of nations usually grouped as "underdeveloped" one can distinguish four types.[18]

1. *Pretake-off economies*, where the apparent savings and investment rates, including limited net capital imports, probably come to under 5 per cent of net national product. In general, data for such countries are not satisfactory, and one's judgment that capital formation is low must rest on fragmentary data and partially subjective judgment. Examples are Ethiopia, Kenya, Thailand, Cambodia, Afghanistan, and perhaps Indonesia.[19]

2. *Economies attempting take-off*, where the apparent savings and investment rates, including limited net capital imports, have risen over 5 per cent of net national product.[20] For example, Mexico (1950)

[18] The percentages given are of net capital formation to net domestic product. The latter is the product net of depreciation of the geographic area. It includes the value of output produced in the area, regardless of whether the income flows abroad. Since indirect business taxes are not deducted, it tends to be larger than national income; hence the percentages are lower than if national income was used as the denominator in computing them.
[19] The Office of Intelligence Research of the Department of State, Washington, D.C., gives the following estimated ratios of investment (presumably gross) to GNP in its Report No. 6672 of August 25, 1954, p. 3, based on latest data available to that point, for countries which would probably fall in the pretake-off category:

	Per cent		Per cent
Afghanistan	5	Pakistan	6
Ceylon	5	Indonesia	5

[20] The Department of State estimates (*ibid.*) for economies which are either attempting take-off or which have, perhaps, passed into a stage of regular growth include:

	Per cent		Per cent
The Argentine	13	Colombia	14
Brazil	14	Philippines	8
Chile	11	Venezuela	23

Venezuela has been for some time an "enclave

TABLE 2[a]

DECADE	DOMESTIC GCF GNP (%)	DOMESTIC NCF NNP (%)	DEPRECIATION TO DGCF (%)
1. 1861–70	5.8	3.5–	(42)
2. 1871–80	8.8	5.3	(42)
3. 1881–90	10.8	6.6	(42)
4. 1891–1900 . . .	13.7	8.1	43.9
5. 1901–10	18.0	11.6	40.0
6. 1911–20	20.2	13.5	38.3
7. 1921–30	19.0	11.4	45.2

[a] (Kuznets). Based on estimates in Eric Lindahl, Einan Dahlgren and Karin Kock, *National Income of Sweden, 1861–1930* (London: P. J. Kingston, 1937), Parts One and Two, particularly the details in Part Two.

These underlying totals of capital formation exclude changes in inventories.

While gross totals are directly from the volumes referred to above, depreciation for the first three decades was not given. We assumed that it formed 42 per cent of gross domestic capital formation.

TABLE 3. *Canada: Gross and Net Investment in Durable Physical Assets as Percentage of Gross and Net National Expenditure (for Selected Years)*

	GCF GNP	NCF NNP	CAPITAL CONSUMP-TION AS PERCENTAGE OF GROSS INVESTMENT
1870	15.0	7.1	56.2
1900	13.1	4.0	72.5
1920	16.6	10.6	41.3
1929	23.0	12.1	53.3
1952	16.8	9.3	49.7

(NCF/NDP 7.2 per cent; Chile (1950) NCF/NDP 9.5 per cent; Panama (1950) NCF/NDP 7.5 per cent; Philippines (1952) NCF/NDP 6.4 per cent; Puerto Rico economy," with a high investment rate concentrated in a modern export sector whose growth did not generate general economic momentum in the Venezuelan economy; but in the past few years Venezuela may have moved over into the category of economies experiencing an authentic take-off.

(1952) NCF (Private)/NDP 7.6 per cent; India (1953) NCF/NDP, perhaps about 7 per cent. Whether the take-off period will, in fact, be successful remains in most of these cases still to be seen.

3. *Growing economies*, where the apparent savings and investment rates, including limited net capital imports, have reached 10 per cent or over; for example, Colombia (1950) NCF/NDP, 16.3 per cent.

4. *Enclave economies* (1) cases where the apparent savings and investment rates, including substantial net capital imports, have reached 10 per cent or over, but the domestic preconditions for sustained growth have not been achieved. These economies, associated with major export industries, lack the third condition for take-off suggested above (p. 32). They include the Belgian Congo (1951) NCF/NDP 21.7 per cent; Southern Rhodesia (1950) GCF/GDP 45.5 per cent, (1952) GCF/GDP 45.4 per cent. (2) Cases where net capital exports are large. For example, Burma (1938) NCF/NDP, 7.1 per cent; net capital exports/NDP, 11.5 per cent; Nigeria (1950–51) NCF/NDP 5.1 per cent; net capital exports/NDP, 5.6 per cent.

THE CASES OF INDIA AND COMMUNIST CHINA

The two outstanding contemporary cases of economies attempting purposefully to take-off are India and Communist China, both operating under national plans. The Indian First Five Year Plan projects the growth process envisaged under assumptions similar to those in paragraph 1, page 241. The Indian Planning Commission estimated investment as 5 per cent of NNP in the initial year of the plan, 1950–51.[21] Using a 3/1 marginal capital–output ratio, they envisaged a marginal savings rate of 20 per cent for the First Five Year Plan, a 50 per cent rate thereafter, down to 1968–69, when the average proportion of income invested would level off at 20 per cent of NNP. As one would expect, the sectoral composition of this process is not fully worked out in the initial plan; but the Indian effort may well be remembered in economic history as the first take-off defined *ex ante* in national product terms.

We know less of the Chinese Communist First Five Year Plan than we do of the concurrent Indian effort, despite the

[21] Government of India, Planning Commission, *The First Five Year Plan*, 1952, Vol. 1, Ch. 1.

recent publication of production goals for some of the major sectors of the Chinese economy.[22] Roundly, it would appear that, from a (probably) negative investment rate in 1949, the Chinese Communist regime had succeeded by 1952 in achieving a gross rate of about 12 per cent; a net rate of about 7 per cent.

On arbitrary assumptions, which have a distinct upward bias, these figures can be projected forward for a decade yielding rates of about 20 per cent gross, 17 per cent net by 1962.

So far as the aggregates are concerned, what we can say is that the Indian planned figures fall well within the range of prima facie hypothesis and historical experience, if India in fact fulfils the full requirements for take-off, notably the achievement of industrial momentum. The Chinese Communist figures reflect accurately an attempt to force the pace of history, evident throughout Peking's domestic policy, whose viability is still to be demonstrated. In particular, Peking's agricultural policy may fail to produce the minimum structural balance required for a successful take-off, requiring radical revision of investment allocations and policy objectives at a later stage.

We have, evidently, much still to learn about the quantitative aspects of this problem; and, especially, much further quantitative research and imaginative manipulation of historical evidence will be required before the hypothesis tentatively advanced here can be regarded as proved or disproved. What we can say is that prima facie thought and a scattering of historical and contemporary evidence suggests that it is not unreasonable to consider the take-off as including as a necessary but not sufficient condition a quantitative transition in the proportion of income

[22] These comments are based on the work of Alexander Eckstein and the author in *The Prospects for Communist China* (New York and London, 1954), Part V, pp. 222 ff. The statistical calculations are the work of Mr. Eckstein.

productively invested of the kind indicated here.

The Inner Structure of the Take-off

Whatever the importance and virtue of viewing the take-off in aggregative terms—embracing national output, the proportion of output invested, and an aggregate marginal capital–output ratio—that approach tells us relatively little of what actually happens and of the causal processes at work in a take-off; nor is the investment-rate criterion conclusive.

Following the definition of take-off (pp. 238–240 above), we must consider not merely how a rise in the investment rate is brought about, from both supply and demand perspectives, but how rapidly growing manufacturing sectors emerged and imparted their primary and secondary growth impulses to the economy.

Perhaps the most important thing to be said about the behavior of these variables in historical cases of take-off is that they have assumed many different forms. There is no single pattern. The rate and productivity of investment can rise, and the consequences of this rise can be diffused into a self-reinforcing general growth process by many different technical and economic routes, under the ægis of many different political, social and cultural settings, driven along by a wide variety of human motivations.

The purpose of the following paragraphs is to suggest briefly, and by way of illustration only, certain elements of both uniformity and variety in the variables whose movement has determined the inner structure of the take-off.

THE SUPPLY OF LOANABLE FUNDS

By and large, the loanable funds required to finance the take-off have come from two types of sources: from shifts in the control over income flows, including income-distribution changes and capital imports;[23]

and from the plough-back of profits in rapidly expanding particular sectors.

The notion of economic development occurring as the result of income shifts from those who will spend (hoard[24] or lend) less productively to those who will spend (or lend) more productively is one of the oldest and most fundamental notions in economics. It is basic to the *Wealth of Nations*,[25] and it is applied by W. Arthur Lewis in his recent elaboration of the classical model.[26] Lewis builds his model in part on an expansion of the capitalist sector, with the bulk of additional savings arising from an enlarging pool of capitalist profits.

Historically, income shifts conducive to economic development have assumed many forms. In Meiji Japan and also in Czarist Russia the substitution of government bonds for the great landholders' claim on the flow of rent payments led to a highly Smithian redistribution of income into the hands of those with higher propensities to seek material advance and to accept innovations. In both cases the real value of the government bonds exchanged for land depreciated; and, in general, the feudal landlords emerged with a less attractive arrangement than had first appeared to be offered. Aside from the confiscation effect, two positive impulses arose from

horizons open up, rather than merely from a shift of income to groups with a higher (but static) propensity to save. He may well be right. This is, evidently, a matter for further investigation.

[23] Mr. Everett Hagen has pointed out that the increase in savings may well arise from a shift in the propensity to save, as new and exciting

[24] Hoarding can, of course, be helpful to the growth process by depressing consumption and freeing resources for investment if, in fact, nonhoarding persons or institutions acquire the resources and possess the will to expand productive investment. A direct transfer of income is, evidently, not required.

[25] See, especially, Smith's observations on the "perversion" of wealth by "prodigality"—that is, unproductive consumption expenditures—and on the virtues of "parsimony" which transfers income to those who will increase "the fund which is destined for the maintenance of productive hands." Routledge edition, London, 1890, pp. 259–260.

[26] *Op. cit.*, especially pp. 156–159.

land reform: the state itself used the flow of payments from peasants, now diverted from landlords' hands, for activity which encouraged economic development; and a certain number of the more enterprising former landlords directly invested in commerce and industry. In contemporary India and China we can observe quite different degrees of income transfer by this route. India is relying to only a very limited extent on the elimination of large incomes unproductively spent by large landlords; although this element figures in a small way in its program. Communist China has systematically transferred all nongovernmental pools of capital into the hands of the State, in a series of undisguised or barely disguised capital levies; and it is drawing heavily for capital resources on the mass of middle and poor peasants who remain.[27]

In addition to confiscatory and taxation devices, which can operate effectively when the State is spending more productively than the taxed individuals, inflation has been important to several take-offs. In Britain of the late 1790's, the United States of the 1850's, Japan of the 1870's there is no doubt that capital formation was aided by price inflation, which shifted resources away from consumption to profits.

The shift of income flows into more productive hands has, of course, been aided historically not only by government fiscal measures but also by banks and capital markets. Virtually without exception, the take-off periods have been marked by the extension of banking institutions which expanded the supply of working capital; and in most cases also by an expansion in the range of long-range financing done by a central, formally organized, capital market.

Although these familiar capital-supply functions of the State and private institutions have been important to the take-off, it is likely to prove the case, on close examination, that a necessary condition for take-off was the existence of one or more

[27] *Prospects for Communist China*, Part IV.

rapidly growing sectors whose entrepreneurs (private or public) ploughed back into new capacity a very high proportion of profits. Put another way, the demand side of the investment process, rather than the supply of loanable funds, may be the decisive element in the take-off, as opposed to the period of creating the preconditions, or of sustaining growth once it is under way. The distinction is, historically, sometimes difficult to make, notably when the State simultaneously acts both to mobilize supplies of finance and to undertake major entrepreneurial acts. There are, nevertheless, periods in economic history when quite substantial improvements in the machinery of capital supply do not, in themselves, initiate a take-off, but fall within the period when the preconditions are created: e.g., British banking developments in the century before 1783; Russian banking developments before 1890, etc.

One extremely important version of the plough-back process has taken place through foreign trade. Developing economies have created from their natural resources major export industries; and the rapid expansion in exports has been used to finance the import of capital equipment and to service the foreign debt during the take-off. United States, Russian, and Canadian grain fulfilled this function, Swedish timber and pulp, Japanese silk, etc. Currently Chinese exports to the Communist Bloc, wrung at great administrative and human cost from the agricultural sector, play this decisive role. It should be noted that the development of such export sectors has not in itself guaranteed accelerated capital formation. Enlarged foreign-exchange proceeds have been used in many familiar cases to finance hoards (as in the famous case of Indian bullion imports) or unproductive consumption outlays.

It should be noted that one possible mechanism for inducing a high rate of plough-back into productive investment is a rapid expansion in the effective demand for domestically manufactured consumers' goods, which would direct into the hands of vigorous entrepreneurs an increasing proportion of income flows under circumstances which would lead them to expand their own capacity and to increase their requirements for industrial raw materials, semi-manufactured products and manufactured compounds.

A final element in the supply of loanable funds is, of course, capital imports. Foreign capital has played a major role in the take-off stage of many economies: e.g., the United States, Russia, Sweden, Canada. The cases of Britain and Japan indicate, however, that it cannot be regarded as an essential condition. Foreign capital was notably useful when the construction of railways or other large overhead capital items with a long period of gestation, played an important role in the take-off. After all, whatever its strategic role, the proportion of investment required for growth which goes into industry is relatively small compared to that required for utilities, transport and the housing of enlarged urban populations. And foreign capital can be mightily useful in helping carry the burden of these overhead items either directly or indirectly.

What can we say, in general, then, about the supply of finance during the take-off period? First, as a precondition, it appears necessary that the community's surplus above the mass-consumption level does not flow into the hands of those who will sterilize it by hoarding, luxury consumption, or low-productivity investment outlays. Second, as a precondition, it appears necessary that institutions be developed which provide cheap and adequate working capital. Third, as a necessary condition, it appears that one or more sectors of the economy must grow rapidly, inducing a more general industrialization process; and that the entrepreneurs in such sectors plough back a substantial proportion of their profits in further productive investment, one possible and recurrent version of the plough-back process

being the investment of proceeds from a rapidly growing export sector.

The devices, confiscatory and fiscal, for ensuring the first and second preconditions have been historically various. And, as indicated below, the types of leading manufacturing sectors which have served to initiate the take-off have varied greatly. Finally, foreign capital flows have, in significant cases, proved extremely important to the take-off, notably when lumpy overhead capital construction of long gestation period was required; but take-offs have also occurred based almost wholly on domestic sources of finance.

THE SOURCES OF ENTREPRENEURSHIP

It is evident that the take-off requires the existence and the successful activity of some group in the society which accepts borrowers' risk, when such risk is so defined as to include the propensity to accept innovations. As noted above, the problem of entrepreneurship in the take-off has not been profound in a limited group of wealthy agricultural nations whose populations derived by emigration mainly from north-western Europe. There the problem of take-off was primarily economic; and when economic incentives for industrialization emerged commercial and banking groups moved over easily into industrial entrepreneurship. In many other countries, however, the development of adequate entrepreneurship was a more searching social process.

Under some human motivation or other, a group must come to perceive it to be both possible and good to undertake acts of capital investment; and, for their efforts to be tolerably successful, they must act with approximate rationality in selecting the directions toward which their enterprise is directed. They must not only produce growth but tolerably balanced growth. We cannot quite say that it is necessary for them to act as if they were trying to maximize profit; for the criteria for private profit maximization do not necessarily converge with the criteria for an optimum rate and pattern of growth in various sectors.[28] But in a growing economy, over periods longer than the business cycle, economic history is reasonably tolerant of deviations from rationality, in the sense that excess capacity is finally put to productive use. Leaving aside the question of ultimate human motivation, and assuming that the major overhead items are generated, if necessary, by some form of state initiative (including subsidy), we can say as a first approximation that some group must successfully emerge which behaves as if it were moved by the profit motive, in a dynamic economy with changing production functions; although risk being the slippery variable, it is under such assumptions Keynes' dictum should be borne in mind: "If human nature felt no temptation to take a chance, no satisfaction (profit apart) in constructing a factory, a railway, a mine or a farm, there might not be much investment merely as a result of cold calculation."[29]

In this connection it is increasingly conventional for economists to pay their respects to the Protestant ethic.[30] The historian should not be ungrateful for this light on the grey horizon of formal growth models. But the known cases of economic growth which theory must seek to explain take us beyond the orbit of Protestantism. In a world where Samurai, Parsees, Jews, North Italians, Turkish, Russian, and Chinese Civil Servants (as well as Huguenots, Scotsmen and British North-country-

men) have played the role of a leading *élite* in economic growth John Calvin should not be made to bear quite this weight. More fundamentally, allusion to a positive scale of religious or other values conducive to profit-maximizing activities is an insufficient sociological basis for this important phenomenon. What appears to be required for the emergence of such *élites* is not merely an appropriate value system but two further conditions: first, the new *élite* must feel itself denied the conventional routes to prestige and power by the traditional less acquisitive society of which it is a part; second, the traditional society must be sufficiently flexible (or weak) to permit its members to seek material advance (or political power) as a route upwards alternative to conformity.

Although an *élite* entrepreneurial class appears to be required for take-off, with significant power over aggregate income flows and industrial investment decisions, most take-offs have been preceded or accompanied by radical change in agricultural techniques and market organization. By and large the agricultural entrepreneur has been the individual land-owning farmer. A requirement for take-off is, therefore, a class of farmers willing and able to respond to the possibilities opened up for them by new techniques, landholding arrangements, transport facilities, and forms of market and credit organization. A small purposeful *élite* can go a long way in initiating economic growth; but, especially in agriculture (and to some extent in the industrial working force), a wider-based revolution in outlook must come about.[31]

[28] For a brief discussion of this point see the author's "Trends in the Allocation of Resources in Secular Growth," Ch. 15, *Economic Progress*, ed. Leon H. Dupriez, with the assistance of Douglas C. Hague (Louvain, 1955), pp. 378–379. For a more complete discussion see W. Fellner, "Individual Investment Projects in Growing Economics" (mimeographed), paper presented to the Center for International Studies Social Science Research Council Conference on Economic Growth, October 1954, Cambridge, Massachusetts.

[29] *General Theory*, p. 150.

[30] See, for example, N. Kaldor, "Economic Growth and Cyclical Fluctuations," *Economic Journal*, March 1954, p. 67.

[31] Like the population question, agriculture is mainly excluded from this analysis, which considers the take-off rather than the whole development process. Nevertheless, it should be noted that, as a matter of history, agricultural revolutions have generally preceded or accompanied the take-off. In theory we can envisage a take-off which did not require a radical improvement in agricultural productivity: if, for example, the growth and productivity of the industrial sector permitted a

Whatever further empirical research may reveal about the motives which have led men to undertake the constructive entrepreneurial acts of the take-off period, this much appears sure: these motives have varied greatly, from one society to another; and they have rarely, if ever, been motives of an unmixed material character.

LEADING SECTORS IN THE TAKE-OFF

The author has presented elsewhere the notion that the overall rate of growth of an economy must be regarded in the first instance as the consequence of differing growth rates in particular sectors of the economy, such sectoral growth rates being in part derived from certain overall demand parameters (e.g., population, consumers' income, tastes, etc.), in part from the primary and secondary effects of changing supply factors, when these are effectively exploited.[32]

On this view the sectors of an economy may be grouped in three categories:

1. *Primary growth sectors*, where possibilities for innovation or for the exploitation of newly profitable or hitherto unexplored resources yield a high growth rate and set in motion expansionary forces elsewhere in the economy.

2. *Supplementary growth sectors*, where rapid advance occurs in direct response to —or as a requirement of—advance in the primary growth sectors; e.g., coal, iron, and engineering in relation to railroads.

withering away of traditional agriculture and a substitution for it of imports. In fact, agricultural revolutions have been required to permit rapidly growing (and urbanizing) populations to be fed without exhausting foreign exchange resources in food imports or creating excessive hunger in the rural sector; and as noted at several points in this argument, agricultural revolutions have in fact played an essential and positive role, not merely by both releasing workers to the cities, and feeding them, but also by earning foreign exchange for general capital-formation purposes.

[32] *Process of Economic Growth*, Ch. 4, especially pp. 97–102; and, in greater detail, "Trends in the Allocation of Resources in Secular Growth," see page 248, footnote 28.

These sectors may have to be tracked many stages back into the economy, as the Leontief input–output models would suggest.

3. *Derived growth sectors*, where advance occurs in some fairly steady relation to the growth of total real income, population, industrial production or some other overall, modestly increasing parameter. Food output in relation to population, housing in relation to family formation are classic derived relations of this order.

Very roughly speaking, primary and supplementary growth sectors derive their high momentum essentially from the introduction and diffusion of changes in the cost–supply environment (in turn, of course, partially influenced by demand changes); while the derived-growth sectors are linked essentially to changes in demand (while subject also to continuing changes in production functions of a less dramatic character).

At any period of time it appears to be true even in a mature and growing economy that forward momentum is maintained as the result of rapid expansion in a limited number of primary sectors, whose expansion has significant external economy and other secondary effects. From this perspective the behavior of sectors during the take-off is merely a special version of the growth process in general; or, put another way, growth proceeds by repeating endlessly, in different patterns, with different leadings sectors, the experience of the take-off. Like the take-off, long-term growth requires that the society not only generate vast quantities of capital for depreciation and maintenance, for housing and for a balanced complement of utilities and other overheads, but also a sequence of highly productive primary sectors, growing rapidly, based on new production functions. Only thus has the aggregate marginal capital–output ratio been kept low.

Once again history is full of variety: a considerable array of sectors appears to have played this key role in the take-off process.

The development of a cotton-textile industry sufficient to meet domestic requirements has not generally imparted a sufficient impulse in itself to launch a self-sustaining growth process. The development of modern cotton-textile industries in substitution for imports has, more typically, marked the pretake-off period, as for example in India, China, and Mexico.

There is, however, the famous exception of Britain's industrial revolution. Baines' table on raw-cotton imports and his comment on it are worth quoting, covering as they do the original leading sector in the first take-off.[33]

Why did the development of a modern factory system in cotton textiles lead on in Britain to a self-sustaining growth process, whereas it failed to do so in other cases? Part of the answer lies in the fact that, by the late eighteenth century, the preconditions for take-off in Britain were very fully developed. Progress in textiles, coal, iron

[33] E. Baines, *History of the Cotton Manufacture* (London, 1835), p. 348.

and even steam power had been considerable through the eighteenth century; and the social and institutional environment was propitious. But two further technical elements helped determine the upshot. First, the British cotton-textile industry was large in relation to the total size of the economy. From its modern beginnings, but notably from the 1780's forward, a very high proportion of total cotton-textile output was directed abroad, reaching 60 per cent by the 1820's.[34] The evolution of this industry was a more massive fact, with wider secondary repercussions, than if it were simply supplying the domestic market. Industrial enterprise on this scale had secondary reactions on the development of urban areas, the demand for coal, iron and machinery, the demand for working capital and ultimately the demand for cheap transport, which powerfully stimu-

[34] The volume (official value) of British cotton goods exports rose from £355,060 in 1780 to £7,624,505 in 1802 (Baines, *op. cit.*, p. 350). See also the calculation of R. C. O. Matthews, *A Study in Trade Cycle History* (Cambridge, 1954), pp. 127–129.

TABLE 4. *Rate of Increase in the Import of Cotton-wool, in Periods of Ten Years From 1741–1831.*[a]

	PER CENT		PER CENT
1741–1751	81	1791–1801	67½
1751–1761	21½	1801–1811	39½
1761–1771	25½	1811–1821	93
1771–1781	75¾	1821–1831	85
1781–1791	319½		

[a] From 1697 to 1741, the increase was trifling: between 1741 and 1751 the manufacture, though still insignificant in extent, made a considerable spring: during the next twenty years, the increase was moderate: from 1771 to 1781, owing to the invention of the jenny and the water-frame, a rapid increase took place: in the ten years from 1781 to 1791, being those which immediately followed the invention of the mule and the expiration of Arkwrights's patent, the rate of advancement was prodigiously accelerated, being nearly 320 per cent: and from that time to the present, and especially since the close of the war, the increase, though considerably moderated, has been rapid and steady far beyond all precedent in any other manufacture.

lated industrial development in other directions.[35]

Second, a source of effective demand for rapid expansion in British cotton textiles was supplied, in the first instance, by the sharp reduction in real costs and prices which accompanied the technological developments in manufacture and the cheapening real cost of raw cotton induced by the cotton gin. In this Britain had an advantage not enjoyed by those who came later; for they merely substituted domestic for foreign-manufactured cotton textiles. The substitution undoubtedly had important secondary effects by introducing a modern industrial sector and releasing in net a pool of foreign exchange for other purposes; but there was no sharp fall in the real cost of acquiring cotton textiles and no equivalent lift in real income.

The introduction of the railroad has been historically the most powerful single initiator of take-offs.[36] It was decisive in the United States, Germany and Russia; it has played an extremely important part in the Swedish, Japanese, and other cases. The railroad has had three major kinds of impact on economic growth during the take-off period. First, it has lowered internal transport costs, brought new areas and products into commercial markets and, in general, performed the Smithian function of widening the market. Second, it has been a prerequisite in many cases to the development of a major new and rapidly enlarging export sector which, in turn, has served to generate capital for internal development; as, for example, the American railroads of the 1850's, the Russian and Canadian railways before 1914. Third, and perhaps most important for the take-off itself, the development of railways has led on to the development of modern coal, iron, and engineering industries. In many countries the growth of modern basic industrial sectors can be traced in the most direct way to the requirements for building and, especially, for maintaining substantial railway systems. When a society has developed deeper institutional, social and political prerequisites for take-off, the rapid growth of a railway system with these powerful triple effects has often served to lift it into self-sustaining growth. Where the prerequisites have not existed, however, very substantial railway building has failed to initiate a take-off, as, for example, in India, China, pre-1895 Canada, pre-1914 Argentine, etc.

It is clear that an enlargement and modernization of Armed Forces could play the role of a leading sector in take-off. It was a factor in the Russian, Japanese, and German take-offs; and it figures heavily in current Chinese Communist plans. But historically the role of modern armaments has been ancillary rather than central to the take-off.

Quite aside from their role in supplying foreign exchange for general capital-formation purposes, raw materials and foodstuffs can play the role of leading sectors in the take-off if they involve the application of modern processing techniques. The timber industry, built on the steam saw, fulfilled this function in the first phase of Sweden's take-off, to be followed shortly by the pulp industry. Similarly, the shift of Denmark to meat and dairy products, after 1873, appears to have reinforced the development of a manufacturing sector in the economy, as well as providing a major source of foreign exchange. And as Lockwood notes, even the export of Japanese silk thread had important secondary effects which developed modern production techniques.[37]

[35] If we are prepared to treat New England of the first half of the nineteenth century as a separable economy, its take-off into sustained growth can be allocated to the period, roughly, 1820–50 and, again, a disproportionately large cotton-textile industry based substantially on exports (that is, from New England to the rest of the United States) is the regional foundation for sustained growth.

[36] For a detailed analysis of the routes of impact of the railroad on economic development see Paul H. Cootner, *Transport Innovation and Economic Development: The Case of the U.S. Steam Railroads*, 1953, unpublished doctoral thesis, M.I.T.

[37] W. W. Lockwood, *The Economic Development of Japan* (Princeton, 1954), pp. 338–339.

To satisfy the demands of American weaving and hosiery mills for uniform, high-grade yarn, however, it was necessary to improve the quality of the product, from the silkworm egg on through to the bale of silk. In sericulture this meant the introduction of scientific methods of breeding and disease control; in reeling it stimulated the shift to large filatures equipped with machinery; in marketing it led to large-scale organization in the collection and sale of cocoons and raw silk ... it exerted steady pressure in favor of the application of science, machinery, and modern business enterprise.

The role of leading sector has been assumed, finally, by the accelerated development of domestic manufacture of consumption goods over a wide range in substitution for imports, as, for example, in Australia, the Argentine, and perhaps in contemporary Turkey.

What can we say, then, in general about these leading sectors? Historically, they have ranged from cotton textiles, through heavy-industry complexes based on railroads and military end products, to timber, pulp, dairy products, and finally a wide variety of consumers' goods. There is, clearly, no one sectoral sequence for take-off, no single sector which constitutes the magic key. There is no need for a growing society to recapitulate the structural sequence and pattern of Britain, the United States or Russia. Four basic factors must be present:

1. There must be enlarged effective demand for the product or products of sectors which yield a foundation for a rapid rate of growth in output. Historically this has been brought about initially by the transfer of income from consumption or hoarding to productive investment; by capital imports; by a sharp increase in the productivity of current investment inputs, yielding an increase in consumers' real income expended on domestic manu-

factures; or by a combination of these routes.

2. There must be an introduction into these sectors of new production functions as well as an expansion of capacity.

3. The society must be capable of generating capital initially required to detonate the take-off in these key sectors; and especially, there must be a high rate of plough-back by the (private or state) entrepreneurs controlling capacity and technique in these sectors and in the supplementary growth sectors they stimulated to expand.

4. Finally, the leading sector or sectors must be such that their expansion and technical transformation induce a chain of Leontief input–output requirements for increased capacity and the potentiality for new production functions in other sectors, to which the society, in fact, progressively responds.

Conclusion

This hypothesis is, then, a return to a rather old-fashioned way of looking at economic development. The take-off is defined as an industrial revolution, tied directly to radical changes in methods of production, having their decisive consequence over a relatively short period of time.

This view would not deny the role of longer, slower changes in the whole process of economic growth. On the contrary, take-off requires a massive set of preconditions going to the heart of a society's economic organization and its effective scale of values. Moreover, for the take-off to be successful, it must lead on progressively to sustained growth; and this implies further deep and often slow-moving changes in the economy and the society as a whole.

What this argument does assert is that the rapid growth of one or more new manufacturing sectors is a powerful and essential engine of economic transformation. Its power derives from the multiplicity of its forms of impact, when a society is prepared to respond positively to this impact. Growth in such sectors, with new production functions of high productivity, in itself tends to raise output per head; it places incomes in the hands of men who will not merely save a high proportion of an expanding income but who will plough it into highly productive investment; it sets up a chain of effective demand for other manufactured products; it sets up a requirement for enlarged urban areas, whose capital costs may be high, but whose population and market organization help to make industrialization an on-going process; and, finally, it opens up a range of external economy effects which, in the end, help to produce new leading sectors when the initial impulse of the take-off's leading sectors begins to wane.

We can observe in history and in the contemporary world important changes in production functions in non-manufacturing sectors which have powerful effects on whole societies. If natural resources are rich enough or the new agricultural tricks are productive enough such changes can even outstrip population growth and yield a rise in real output per head. Moreover, they may be a necessary prior condition for take-off or a necessary concomitant for take-off. Nothing in this analysis should be read as deprecating the importance of productivity changes in agriculture to the whole process of economic growth. But in the end take-off requires that a society find a way to apply effectively to its own peculiar resources what D. H. Robertson once called the tricks of manufacture; and continued growth requires that it so organize itself as to continue to apply them in an unending flow, of changing composition. Only thus, as we have all been correctly taught, can that old demon, diminishing returns, be held at bay.

ECONOMIC DEVELOPMENT: POLITICAL PRECONDITIONS AND POLITICAL CONSEQUENCES

J. J. Spengler

For good or ill, life under the conditions imposed by the modern industrial system ... is in the longrun incompatible with the prepossessions of mediaevalism.

THORSTEIN VEBLEN, IN "THE OPPORTUNITY OF JAPAN".

This paper has to do with the political preconditions and the political consequences of economic development. It relates principally to the underdeveloped world, a

SOURCE. J. J. Spengler, "Economic Development: Political Preconditions and Political Consequences," *Journal of Politics*, **22**, 387–416, August 1960; Using only pp. 387–389, 392–393, 395–416. This is a revised version of a paper prepared for the Social Science Research Council Committee on Comparative Politics.

term which embraces Asia (with the exception of Soviet Asia, Japan, and Israel), almost all of Africa, much of Latin America and portions of Southern and Eastern Europe. Around 1950, according to Shannon, 147 of the world's 195 political entities, embracing about 54 per cent of the world's landed area, were classifiable as underdeveloped. Within areas variously described as underdeveloped live between 60 and 75 per cent of the world's population.[1]

[1] See L. W. Shannon, *Underdeveloped Areas* (New York, 1957), pp. 6–12, 478–479. See also P. T. Bauer and B. S. Yamey, *The Economics of Underdeveloped Countries* (London, 1957), Ch. 1; N. S. Buchanan and H. S. Ellis, *Approaches To Economic Development* (New York, 1955), Ch. 1; G. M. Meier and R. R. Baldwin, *Economic Development* (New York, 1957), Ch. 1 and pp. 478–479; Eugene Staley, *The*

After passing in review some of the characteristics of the underdeveloped world and touching upon the determinants of economic development, I shall examine, in order, the growth-oriented role of government in general, the specific roles or functions of government affecting economic development, the minimum political preconditions of economic development, and the changes that take place in some of these preconditions as economic development proceeds.

Concomitants or Indicators of Underdevelopment

Of the concomitants or indicators of economic development, the cultural and the political are most significant for the present discussion, though the economic, the technological, and the demographic are most important from the immediately economic point of view. Here it is necessary only to note that, in the underdeveloped world, per-capita income, capital equipment, and capital formation are very low; inferior technologies predominate; enterprise is lacking; accessible natural resources are badly exploited; natality and (usually) natural increase are relatively high, in part because so much of the population is rural and agricultural; and the age composition of the population is unfavorable to productivity and the education of youth.[2]

Economic backwardness is associated with various cultural circumstances unfavorable to economic growth. Society is tradition-bound, stable and disposed to preserve stability. The family often is of the extended sort. Land may be communally owned and operated. Educational attainment, together with literacy, is low. Much economic activity may remain un-

monetized and free of the regulative influence of markets. The "middle class" is unimportant, and the socio-legal system in effect usually unduly restricts enterprise. The values stressed may not encourage economic development, and incentives favorable to work and enterprise may be weak. And so on. Of course, as a country progresses economically, its cultural environment becomes more favorable to economic progress, within limits. It is usually assumed, however, that the rapidity with which a nation's cultural environment becomes favorable to economic development may be increased through appropriate governmental action, particularly when there are at hand successful working models. It is also taken for granted that persistent economic growth is most likely to get under way *after* suitable institutional arrangements have been established in respect of law, family, education, motivation, reward systems, and the like.

Developed countries resemble each other more closely in economic than in political respects, since the prerequisites to economic development are more specific and exacting than those essential to political development and self-government. Underdeveloped countries resemble one another in some but not in all respects, in part because a given political condition may be favorable to economic development under some circumstances, but not under others. For example, while sometimes absolutist régimes have effectively promoted economic development (e.g., in the Soviet Union), at other times they have retarded it by establishing sanctions against deviant persons who might initiate development.[3] Similarly, parliamentary régimes

[footnote 1 continued
Future of Underdeveloped Countries (New York, 1954), Ch. 1.
[2] E.g., see Harvey Leibenstein, *Economic Backwardness and Economic Growth* (New York, 1957), Chs. 4–5; Benjamin Higgins, *Economic Development* (New York, 1959), Part I.

[3] See B. F. Hoselitz, "Noneconomic Factors in Economic Growth," *American Economic Review*, **47** (May 1957), 39; also Talcott Parsons, *Structure and Process in Modern Societies* (Glencoe, 1960), pp. 101–102, 106. In the eighteenth and early nineteenth centuries, states often indirectly fostered economic growth by allowing freedom of action to private individuals whose enterprise gave rise to economic development.

have sometimes fostered and sometimes retarded economic growth. Self-government, though typically a concomitant of economic development, has not always brought it about. The pseudo-biblical precept engraved on Premier K. Nkrumah's statue in Accra ("Seek ye first the political kingdom and all other things shall be added unto you") has yet to acquire the status of a political axiom. For while only nine negligibly populated non-self-governing political units out of a total of 106 units-so describable were economically developed around 1950, but 39 of the 89 self-governing political entities were so classifiable. Moreover, the 50 self-governing underdeveloped entities included 55 per cent of the world's population, whereas the 97 non-self-governing underdeveloped units included only 8 per cent.[4] Of the political characteristics common to all underdeveloped countries, the most important is a dearth of administrative personnel possessed of technical competence and other requisite attributes. . . .

Determinants of Economic Development

The determinants of economic development have been variously classified. One may, with Lewis, group them under three principal heads: (1) wide-ranging efforts to economize in the sense of minimizing input per unit of output, or of maximizing output per unit of input; (2) "the increase of knowledge and its application," particularly to production; (3) "increasing the amount of capital or other resources per head."[5] But such a grouping, even though

it allows adequate weight to the role of the entrepreneur, tends to understate the roles of cultural, political, and other non-economic factors. It may also overlook social-structural and related obstacles to the formation and the effective investment of capital. There is merit, therefore, in lists of determinants such as the one Rostow has proposed. He suggests that growth depends upon certain propensities which reflect a society's underlying value system and summarize its response to its environment: (1) the propensity to develop fundamental physical and social science; (2) "the propensity to apply science to economic ends"; (3) "the propensity to accept innovations"; (4) "the propensity to seek material advance"; (5) the propensity to consume, by which saving also is conditioned; (6) "the propensity to have children." The propensities are related, on the one hand, to the more immediate economic causes of economic growth, and, on the other, to determinants or circumstances underlying the propensities in question.[6]

Typological studies suggest that growth-favoring factors, being intercorrelated, tend to cluster even as do growth-retarding factors. Facilitation of a society's economic development therefore initially entails the introduction and the strengthening of enough favorable factors. In proportion as these variables are loosely instead of tightly interconnected, initial growth-favoring changes must be large if they are to be propagated through the system of inter-related variables and bring about new, intervariable equilibria that remain sufficiently unstable to make for continuing growth. . . .[7]

---

[4] Shannon, *op. cit.*, p. 27, also pp. 468ff.; *idem*, "Is Level of Development Related to Capacity for Self-Government?" *American Journal of Economics and Sociology*, **47** (July 1958), 367–381, and "A Re-examination of the Concept 'Capacity for Self-Government'," *Journal of Negro Education*, **26** (Spring 1957), 135–144. See also W. S. and E. S. Woytinsky, *World Commerce and Governments* (New York, 1955), pp. 563–567, 582–583, 586.

[5] William Arthur Lewis, *The Theory of Economic Growth* (London, 1955), p. 11.

[6] See Rostow, *The Process of Economic Growth* (New York, 1952), Chs. 1–3. For yet another list of factors which directly or indirectly affect economic development, see J. J. Spengler, "Economic Factors in the Development of Densely Populated Areas," *Proceedings of the American Philosophical Society*, **95** (1951), 21–24.

[7] See Parsons, *op. cit.*, Chs. 3–4, and *The Social System* (Glencoe, 1951), Ch. 5; Leibenstein,

The Role of Government in General

The role of government with reference to economic development may be described in various ways. It may, for example, be described simply as one of increasing the magnitude and the effectiveness of the immediate determinants of economic growth, or it may be analyzed in terms of function, or of economy-oriented tasks associated with government.

The rate of economic growth is dependent upon the functions performed in a society, upon the skill with which they are performed and upon the relative importance attached to some functions as compared with others. Through time each of these conditions may change. The total number of functions performed in a society may change, both because new ones are introduced and because the relative importance of old ones becomes negligible. These two types of change are most likely to be correlated immediately with changes in a people's individual and collective aspirations and objectives, though they may also be correlated with changes in methods of production. The skill with which functions are performed is affected by (among other things) the manner in which responsibility for their performance is distributed among the institutions that might assume such responsibility—some institutions are comparatively better suited than others to provide for the performance of particular functions. At any one time, however, the manner in which these functions are distributed may be quite stable and relatively unmodifiable. This is likely to be the case if much of the existing distribution has won the sanction of history and has acquired, therefore, the support of various groups. Under such circumstances it may be difficult to introduce a more efficient distribution. Witness the difficulties attendant upon introducing into Country B economic arrangements found effective in Country A when their introduction into B entails changes in arrangements which, even though making for inefficiency, enjoy widespread support in B.[8]

Functions or operations which are essentially economic in character have been variously distributed among institutions, in time and in space. Similarly, the manner in which these functions, together with the institutions responsible for them, have been coordinated in societies has differed from time to time and from country to country. We may turn to the theory of the firm for a partial analogy. Within limits, some functions or operations carried on by business firms require smaller inputs per unit of output as the total volume of output rises. Other functions are performed with maximum efficiency—i.e., input per unit of output is minimized—at relatively low levels of output. Accordingly, allowing for the extent to which particular functions are interrelated, some distributions of functions among firms are more efficient, from the standpoint of the economy as a whole, than are other distributions; and firms tend to vary greatly in size, with their magnitudes affected by the kinds of functions or operations performed. Furthermore, whereas the activities carried on within any firm will be coordinated by its management, the activities of all firms viewed as firms will be coordinated by a mechanism existing outside firms and providing indicators in the light of which they adjust their activities. This mechanism usually is the "market," or if not, a set of coordinating arrangements that functions in a manner analogous to that of the "market."

[footnote 7 continued
op. cit., Chs. 9, 12; W. E. Moore, "Problems of Timing, Balance and Priorities in Development Measures," *Economic Development and Cultural Change*, 2 (January 1954), 239–248; G. A. Theodorson, "Acceptance of Industrialization and Its Attendant Consequences for the Social Patterns of Non-western Societies," *American Sociological Review*, 18 (October 1953), 477–484.

[8] E.g., see James Baster, "Development and the Free Economy: Some Typical Dilemmas," *Kyklos*, 7 (Fasc. 1, 1954), 10–11.

It is commonly supposed that, in an economy which is competitive, or which behaves in accordance with rules suited to maximize efficiency when demand patterns are given, functions tend to become optimally distributed among firms and the activities of firms tend to be efficiently coordinated. In reality, of course, economic functions do not always get so appropriately distributed among firms, or among the institutions that might perform them; and this is particularly true of societies in which the economy is neither highly differentiated within itself, nor quite sharply differentiated from other subsystems or sets of specialized institutions. Accordingly, from the fact that, in space and time, economic functions have been variously distributed among institutions,[9] it is not to be inferred that the resulting distribution was necessarily the "best" attainable, or the one most favorable to economic development. It is only to be inferred that functions have been variously distributed and coordinated, and that the resulting distributions often were unfavorable to economic developments. It is also to be inferred that societies and economies have been relatively inflexible and resistant to economic change when economic functions have become intermixed with noneconomic functions in the same institutional context (e.g., in the family, in the village community or in essentially religious or political institutions). It is to be inferred, finally, that it is difficult to transfer, with little or no modification, to Country B from Country A, the particular cluster of economic (or of economic and noneconomic) functions that

[9] Concerning the manner in which various functions have been redistributed among institutions, or sets of interrelated institutions, see P. A. Sorokin, *Social and Cultural Dynamics* (New York, 1937), **3**, Part I, esp. Ch. 7. On the functions of the firm, see G. J. Stigler, "The Division of Labor Is Limited by the Extent of the Market," *Journal of Political Economy*, **59** (June 1951), 185–193; R. H. Coase, "The Nature of the Firm," *Economica*, **4** (November 1937), 386–405.

have gotten assembled and coordinated in A.

As has been noted, the economically oriented role of government varies in intensity over time. Why this is so has been dealt with by Talcott Parsons and N. J. Smelser. They note that a society tends to become differentiated into four analytically distinguishable subsystems (or social structures), each of which becomes specialized in the performance of one of the four primary functions (or sets of functions) whereon depends satisfaction of a society's "needs," and hence its continuity. The first, the economy, performs the adaptive function. It is primarily responsible for the production of income, of generalized facilities which may be put to an indefinite number of uses, and which support the performance of the other three functions. A second subsystem has to do with social control, with maintaining "solidarity," with so relating the prevalent cultural value-patterns to the motivational structures of individuals that "undue internal conflict" can be avoided and that society, as a totality, can continue to function. This subsystem focuses upon *inter*unit relationships, which integrate various social units and subsystems into a society. A third subsystem performs a somewhat similar function at the *intra*unit level; it institutionalizes and maintains values and behavior patterns in the face of change and copes with the tensions that originate in the strains to which the system is subject. This subsystem insures that individuals fulfill the roles assigned to them.

The fourth subsystem, or polity, has to do with the attainment of essentially collective goals, with the mobilization of wealth or output to accomplish a society's overall or system goals. It embodies a "generalized capacity to mobilize the resources of the society including wealth, 'political responsibility,' etc., to attain particular and more or less immediate collective goals of the system." Its function is carried out by government in that "political goals and values tend to have primacy over other in an organ of government."[10] The polity is concerned to maximize a society's capacity to realize collective goals. It may make capital (i.e., generalized purchasing power) available and encourage productive enterprise, subject to the condition that it retains the right to intervene and select the uses to which facilities are put.[11] The polity may also affect the economy indirectly through the medium of either of the integrating subsystems, each of which conditions the functioning of the economy. The polity's potential role is greatest in a modern society. In a relatively undifferentiated society, economic and noneconomic functions tend to be fused; in a modern totalitarian society, on the contrary, the economy is dominated by the polity.[12]

Because it is the function of the economy to supply output to the other subsystems, its behavior is not always and solely dominated by the satisfaction of individual wants.

> The goal of the economy is not simply the production of income for the utility of an aggregate of individuals. It is the maximization of production relative to the whole complex of institutionalized value-systems and functions of the society and its sub-systems. . . . Utility . . . is the *economic value* of physical, social or cultural objects in accord with their *significance as facilities* for solving the adaptive problems of social system.[13]

Accordingly, and because individual motivation is "conceived as a process of the internalization of social norms," neither economic nor social welfare is completely reducible to terms of individual welfare functions. This argument, insofar as it is valid, weakens that supporting consumer sovereignty, even as do arguments suggested by modern welfare economics.[14]

The significance of economic and political values varies. In Western societies, "economic values occupy a high position in the hierarchy [of values];" yet even here a significant part of the individual's "economic" motivation is independent of the rewards to be had.[15] It is to be inferred that, as societies undergo economic development, the relative importance of economic values increases, at least until they are weakened by growing affluence, and that the rationality of economic behavior—i.e., its adaptability as a means to given ends—increases. Even so, the importance of the role of the state (or governmental organs) tends to fluctuate considerably. When collective or system goals command little effective attention, the use to which resources are put will be determined largely within the economic subsystem where consumer desires play a major role. When, however, collective or system goals become ascendant, the demands of the polity upon the economy greatly increase, and much more of the available supply of economic facilities is directed to the satisfaction of these goals.[16] Econo-

---

[10] Parsons and Smelser, *Economy and Society* (Glencoe, 1956), pp. 48–49; also pp. 14ff. Non-governmental agencies frequently are affected with public interest, and governmental organs may be intermixed with private. See *ibid.*, pp. 60, 82–85.

[11] E.g., see *ibid.*, pp. 56–78, 98–99.

[12] *Ibid.*, pp. 79–83.

[13] *Ibid.*, p. 22; author's italics. The goal of the economy may be viewed as "defined strictly by socially structured goals." *Loc. cit.*

[14] *Ibid.*, p. 32. The argument supporting consumer freedom respecting the use of disposable income is weakened only slightly. For other criticisms of consumer freedom, see R. A. Dahl and C. E. Lindblom, *Politics, Economics, and Welfare* (New York, 1953), pp. 164ff., 394ff., 414–430; F. D. Holzman, "Consumer Sovereignty and the Rate of Economic Development," reprinted from *Economia Internazionale*, 11 (May 1958), 1–20. See also J. de V. Graaf, *Theoretical Welfare Economics* (Cambridge, 1957); J. E. Meade, *Trade and Welfare* (London, 1955).

[15] Parsons and Smelser, *op. cit.*, pp. 175–184. The system of rewards prevailing in society tends to encompass too much inequality in some ranges and too little in others.

[16] See B. F. Hoselitz's paper in Hugh G. J. Aitken (ed.), *The State and Economic Growth* (New York, 1959).

mic development itself is a system goal (or a set of system goals), especially in countries bent upon economic development. Since economic and noneconomic obstacles to economic development are numerous, it is widely held that economic development requires a great deal of governmental intervention and activity.

When is State Intervention Indicated?

The upsurge of interest in "forced" economic development and in the capacity of "welfare economics" to furnish policy-guiding norms has been accompanied by much questioning of the liberal democratic theory of the relationship of government to economic activity. This theory has held that, under free competition, optimal marginal equivalences tend to be approximated in the overwhelmingly predominant private sector, and that most, though not all, economically warrantable goals tend to be realized. It has also held that, when private enterprise is unable to achieve a specified goal, the state may intervene, either by assisting private enterprise or by itself undertaking to transform inputs into the desired output. It has generally been held that, so long as the social benefit supposedly consequent upon a course of action exceeds its cost (appropriately defined), the action should be undertaken. It should be undertaken under state auspices if private enterprisers are no longer able, at the relevant conduct-determining margin, to derive enough gross income from the undertaking to cover the costs entailed.[17] The state may intervene, either indirectly through recourse to penalties (e.g., taxes) and grants-in-aid (e.g., subsidies) designed to induce entrepreneurs to shunt resources into the sector

[17] The underlying problem has been treated extensively. E.g., see A. Lerner, *Economics of Control* (New York, 1944); W. J. Baumol, *Welfare Economics and the Theory of the State* (Cambridge, 1952); J. de V. Graaf, *Theoretical Welfare Economics*. I ignore the companion case in which social costs exceed social benefits even though private gain remains in excess of private cost at the relevant margin.

indicated for further expansion, or directly through recourse to governmental entrepreneurship or joint governmental participation with private enterprisers.

The liberal theory outlined has contemplated principally actions whose benefits are indiscriminate, in that recipients thereof cannot be made to pay sufficiently for the services benefitting them (e.g., the services of public-health or public-education facilities). At issue in any given situation, therefore, is whether the action in question is truly indiscriminate, whether it has significantly beneficial side effects for which the responsible entrepreneur is unable to obtain adequate remuneration from the beneficiaries of these effects.[18] Underlying the assessment of a contemplated action is the supposition that great weight must be given to consumer sovereignty and freedom of choice, and the inference that, with few exceptions, the changes sought are relatively small, and hence quite easy to evaluate in terms of current individual preferences.

Economic development, especially when "forced," is likely to require considerable sacrifice of consumer freedom and sovereignty, and to be accompanied by effects which, being large and only imperfectly foreseeable, are not unarbitrarily assessable. (1) Decision may consist in determining whether to undertake a heavy investment that is likely to produce a notable but not wholly anticipatable change in an economy's structure. If an economy is stagnant and requires transformation, the domestic market may offer little guidance; in fact, even in underdeveloped but developing countries the guidance to be had from the domestic market may be quite limited. Under the circumstances, it is unlikely that actual and prospective yields directly realizable from the investment in question would cause it to be undertaken by private entrepreneurs, even though careful judgment suggested that it should be undertaken; hence state intervention would be indicated. (2) Setting developmental pro-

[18] Bauer and Yamey, *op. cit.*, p. 164.

cesses in motion may call for considerable capital-intensive investment (even though analysis based on essentially static premises suggests that, in capital-short and labor-long economies, capital-intensive investment should not be emphasized). Such heavy initial investment, much of it capital-intensive, may be recommended on the ground that it breaks the fetters of the past; or that it opens up "new product horizons;"[19] or that it is highly conducive to economic growth in the long run, in that it checks population growth, stimulates investment in skills and physical assets and permits escape from a low-income subsistence equilibrium. In the event that enough private investment is not forthcoming to meet these various requirements, state intervention or support becomes necessary. (3) It may also be contended that, since the expansion of any particular kind of output depends upon the commensurate expansion of both the demand for it and the supply of those particular inputs from which it is made, growth in general presupposes a more or less parallel expansion of all the relevant sectors of an economy. Such balanced expansion is attainable, it is sometimes argued, only if the state intervenes.[20]

[19] See A. O. Hirschman, "Investment Policies and 'Dualism' in Underdeveloped Countries," *American Economic Review*, **47** (1957), 561–569. Hirschman is concerned also with the interregional spread of development.
[20] The issues raised in this paragraph are treated by Higgins, *op. cit.*, by A. O. Hirschman, *The Strategy of Economic Development* (New Haven, 1958); by Leibenstein, *op. cit.*; and by A. Gerschenkron in B. F. Hoselitz (ed.), *The Progress of Underdeveloped Areas* (Chicago, 1952), pp. 3–29. On balanced growth, see also R. Nurkse, *Problems of Capital Formation in Underdeveloped Countries* (New York, 1953), pp. 11ff.; Bauer and Yamey, *op. cit.*, pp. 247–250; M. Fleming, "External Economies and the Doctrine of Balanced Growth," *Economic Journal*, **65** (June 1955), 241–256. Leibenstein (*op. cit.*, Ch. 15) points out that urban-industrial investment is more conducive to the growth of per-capita productive power than is rural investment. The former gives rise to an environment more

Two sets of difficulties attend attempts to make state policies contribute to economic growth compatibly with the principles of "welfare economics," even though distributive effects are ignored. (1) Application of these principles is encumbered when an economy is imperfectly competitive and (therefore) a number of adjustments may be indicated; or when a large, future-oriented structural change is contemplated, for which adequate, nonarbitrary guidance is not to be found in the present.[21] (2) Even though welfare is defined in a sufficiently arbitrary manner to evade some difficulties of the latter sort, there remains the need to ascertain if a policy is performing up to expectations, and to respond appropriately. Agencies of the state tend to be less able than private entrepreneurs to determine whether undertakings are proceeding successfully, and they are commonly less disposed to make such determination. It is usually essential, therefore, to establish competent and informed independent bodies charged with the critical assessment of governmental undertakings affecting economic development.[22] Private entrepreneurs, being interested primarily in profits, continually assess ventures in terms of their actual or prospective profits, and tend to take suitable corrective action. There is not, in respect of many ventures undertaken by the state, so sensitive an indicator of per-

favorable to the development of an entrepreneurial class, of knowledge and new skills and techniques, of an essentially intellectual and innovational climate, and of fertility control. Leibenstein's argument is partly based upon the premise that the relevant variables are loosely connected, with the result that relatively heavy stimuli are required to modify the socio-economic and demographic equilibrium existing in underdeveloped countries.
[21] E.g., see J. E. Meade, *Trade and Welfare*, Chs. 4–8; J. de V. Graaf, *op. cit.*, Chs. 6, 12.
[22] See E. A. Shils, "The Intellectuals, Public Opinion, and Economic Development," *Economic Development and Cultural Change*, **6** (1951), 55–62; also my forthcoming essay, "Public Economic Policy in a Dynamic Society."

formance as a profits index. Furthermore, both politicians and civil servants, together with the interest groups they represent, may be reluctant to discover failure, let alone rectify it. For these and other reasons, one encounters fewer and less effective corrective mechanisms in the public sector than in the private. This lack may be accentuated, furthermore, if the rate at which the future is discounted in the public sector is too low and too much emphasis is placed upon the distant future and long-term policies (e.g., in the formulation of conservation policies). It may be accentuated also insofar as the positive and presumably beneficial effects of governmental ventures prove easier of observation than do the associated negative and presumably detrimental effects.

Specific Roles or Functions of Government

The state, of course, may contribute, positively or negatively, to economic development by pursuing courses which indirectly or directly affect economic growth. It may contribute indirectly through actions suited to strengthen the private sector, and directly by carrying on appropriate activities in the public sector. An economy is not always reducible, of course, to terms of a private sector and a public sector. The two sectors may overlap and become intermixed, inasmuch as many of the choices available lie on a continuum running from one extreme to the other.[23]

The negative actions of government include failure to maintain law and order; corruption in public administration, together with plundering of commercial and other enterprising classes; exploitation

[23] In this section, I draw heavily upon Lewis, *op. cit.*, Ch. 7. See also Parsons, *Structure and Process* . . . , Chs. 3–4; R. A. Dahl and C. E. Lindblom, *Politics, Economics and Welfare*, pp. 6–8; and, on the limitations to which governmental development efforts are subject, Bauer and Yamey, *op. cit.*, and Buchanan and Ellis, *op. cit.*,

of submerged classes, together with denial to them of access to superior occupations; abuse or exclusion of foreigners possessing requisite skills, enterprise, capital, new tastes, etc.; nonmaintenance of essential public services; failure to provide critical assistance and stimuli to economic sectors in which development may be triggered off; unduly restrictive regulation of economic activities; diversion of an excessive fraction of the community's surplus above consumption into unproductive forms of public capital; imposition of taxes which are arbitrary, uncertain and of a sort to blunt incentive; waste of resources in war; premature development of effective trade unions, together with "welfare-state" legislation; denial of adequate returns on private investments in public utilities, etc.; and diversion of resources from economic to uneconomic activities.

Economic activity can be carried on in the private sector, with some prospect of eventuating in continuing economic development only if certain functions are satisfactorily performed by the government. These include: (1) the maintenance of law and order and security against aggression; (2) sufficient support of education and public health; (3) adequate support of basic research, of the introduction of scientific findings from abroad and of the diffusion of applied scientific knowledge through agricultural extension and similar services; (4) provision, insofar as economically indicated and possible, of certain basic forms of overhead capital. Just as, through (2) and (3), the state may foster the development of a more effective labor force, so through (1) it may augment the capacity of the society to withstand the tensions that accompany economic development.

Satisfying the money requirements of economic development presupposes performance of at least two sets of functions: (5) control of the issue and supply of paper money and bank credit, through an effective central banking system and in a manner capable of preventing marked inflation; (6)

making provision, insofar as practicable and necessary, for action on the part of the central banking system and cognate agencies to prevent undue deflation. It does not seem advisable for an underdeveloped country to pursue monetary policies designed to maintain full employment. Its situation, together with the nature of its unemployment (much of it in agriculture and of long standing), differs from that encountered in developed countries; moreover, factor immobility is too great and bottlenecks are too many to permit such policies to work. (7) Provision needs to be made for the establishment, under public or public-private auspices, of financial institutions suited to assemble small savings (e.g., savings banks), to supply short-term and intermediate credit, to channel long-term capital from its sources to securities markets and to facilitate the inflow of foreign capital. (8) The government may contribute notably to the formation of attitudes favorable to economic development. (9) It may influence the uses to which resources are put (e.g., through conservation policies, zoning regulations, etc.), the manner in which industry is dispersed in space (so as to prevent excessive concentration, depressed areas, etc.), the degree of specialization (e.g., to prevent monoculture, etc.). (10) Should the government undertake to influence income distribution, it must proceed warily lest capital formation, the acquisition of skill, the suitable distribution of the labor force, etc., be checked. (11) The system of taxes employed should be so constituted as to diminish private capital formation and economic incentive very little. (12) to meet the many needs of a developing economy, a well-tested, stable, appropriately oriented, and explicit legal and administrative structure is required, together with effective administrative and judicial personnel. Among the needs that must be met are: provision for the establishment and operation of required types of business organization (e.g., partnership, private corporation, cooperative, public

and quasi-public corporations, trade union) and for the associated forms of decision-making power; rules facilitating the holding and the conveyance of property; guarantees of mobility and of freedom of entry on the part of labor and other factors of production into employments for which they are technically qualified; suitable definitions and regulations relating to contractual content, sanctions, limitations, etc.; rules insofar as required to avert retardation of growth by quasi-monopolistic and related arrangements; and so on. (13) A government may facilitate economic development by institutionalizing public as well as private initiative, since both are likely to be required, and by drawing on the relevant experience of countries which have achieved high levels of development.

More positive action may be undertaken by a government. It may undertake reform of the system of land tenure. It may attempt to step up capital formation and investment through facilitation of foreign loans, higher taxation and limited inflation, or through the use of unemployed and under-employed manpower to construct economic overhead capital (e.g., highways, railways). The success of such measures turns largely on whether resources are diverted from consumption or from the formation of private capital (which, frequently, is put to more productive use than public capital), and on whether increases in money-income restore to non-savers (e.g., wage-earners) what inflation and increased taxes have taken away from them. The state may draw up a plan to put resources to particular uses and attempt to implement it by giving to entrepreneurs acting in conformity therewith greater access to resources in short supply (e.g., capital, foreign exchange, skilled labor). It may attempt to affect the course of development directly, by setting up a development corporation to which it channels public revenue, by utilizing public revenue to finance the construction of economic and social overhead capital, by establishing specific agencies to perform entrepreneurial functions, and so on.

Minimal Political Conditions for Economic Development

While it is not possible always to distinguish sharply between political and economic factors, it is possible to identify a number of essentially political conditions,[24] most of which are prerequisite to economic development in the present-day underdeveloped world. The kind of society envisaged is noncommunist (in the contemporary empirical sense); it may be democratic in the American or British sense, or "dictatorial" in the Latin American sense. The minimal requirements may be grouped under four main heads: minimal public services; growth-supporting and growth-stimulating arrangements; personnel; and political instruments.

Minimal Public Services. If the state does not make provision for certain minimal services, not much economic activity can be carried on, and little impetus can be given to economic growth. It is, of course, a matter of judgment how large at the minimum the supply of any of these services must be. Here it is noted only that this minimum must be met and that as it is increased economic growth tends (within limits) to be stimulated, though not necessarily in proportion to the increase in services. Having already discussed these services, I shall merely list what the state needs to do:

1. Maintain law, order, and security.
2. Support education and public health.
3. Provide for the issue and suitably controlled supply of paper money and bank credit.
4. Provide for the creation of banks to assemble savings, to supply short-term and intermediate credit and to afford access to domestic and foreign long-term capital.

5. Provide as much of a legal and administrative structure as is required to permit various types of business organization to function, to maintain private and public property and to prevent excessive monopolization of important activities.

6. Treat foreign personnel and capital so that as much is attracted as is warranted by the desire to get economic development under way.

Growth-Supporting and Growth-Stimulating Arrangements. Only the last-mentioned of the services just enumerated actually gives impetus to economic development. Impetus is supplied by entrepreneurs, private or public, but it can be provided only if they have access to capital, to land and natural resources, and to technology that reduces input requirements and creates new goods. Accordingly, the state must pursue positive policies calculated to give support to entrepreneurs while minimizing the impact of policies that are unwelcome to enterprise.

1. Tax revenue needs to be raised through taxes that diminish very little both incentive to economic activity and propensity to form capital.
2. Governmental expenditure should, insofar as possible, assume forms essential or relatively conducive to economic growth.
3. Inasmuch as effective highly centralized planning under government auspices is quite out of the question in most, if not all, underdeveloped countries, reliance must be placed largely upon decentralized, private economic decision-making which provides entrepreneurs and others with ample incentive to uncover and test potential opportunities. Hence the state must support a climate of opinion in which entrepreneurial decisions can be made freely and effectively.
4. The state must support basic research, together with the adaptation and diffusion of applied technological knowledge.

[24] For analysis of political science research on such conditions, see Ralph Braibanti, "The Relevance of Political Science to the Analysis of Underdeveloped Areas," in Braibanti and J. J. Spengler (eds.), *Tradition, Values and Socio-Economic Development* (Durham, 1960).

5. The state must facilitate the provision of economic and social overhead capital where need for it is indicated, even though the prospective current return on such capital is insufficient to attract private investment.

6. It is desirable, on a number of grounds, among them national prestige, that something like a five-year plan be kept in effect, and that there be established a development corporation, perhaps to help administer such plan and perform various other functions now normally carried on by such corporations. It is desirable that such a plan be subject to revision from year to year as the relative importance of different objects of investment changes. Such a plan, together with changes in it, needs to be made in consultation with the private sector; for, since much of the investment undertaken should serve to increase the productivity of private facilities, or to assist newly developing private enterprise, it should be directed into channels where it gives greatest stimulus to long-run growth. Given such a plan, public capital expenditures are more likely to be made in light of their comparative capacity to stimulate economic growth, and if a public development corporation has been established, better direction tends to be given to expenditures included under (4) and (5). The existence of such a plan may even facilitate foreign borrowing. It is always essential, however, whether such a plan be in existence or not, that attention be directed to estimating whether public or private investment expenditure would be the more productive. It is essential also to recognize that the effectiveness with which a development corporation can function turns on its position in the governmental hierarchy and, therefore, varies as this position changes.

7. It is possible, given the arrangements described under (6), that the ever present tendency to inflation can be better kept under control. For then budgetary practice can be more nearly arranged to keep governmental income and outgo in balance, unless imbalance in the private sector indicates some need for an offsetting imbalance in the public sector.

8. It has already been noted that the effectiveness of governmental economic policy is much less subject to critical assessment and rectification than is private economic policy. Furthermore, in many underdeveloped countries there do not exist competent private agencies (e.g., universities, research bureaus) which are both free and able to evaluate governmental economic policies. Hence, governmental expenditure tends to be less conducive to development than it might be. It is essential, therefore, that such competent and free critical agencies be developed and that they have access to the information requisite for periodical assessments of governmental economic policies.[25]

Personnel. Under this head we consider personnel in the employ of agencies of the state. In any economy with both a public and a private sector, between which personnel are free to migrate, it is not possible to specify the number of employees in the public sector, or their quality, since migration may modify both number and quality. From the standpoint of a country's development, of course, migration of relatively skilled personnel from one sector to the other necessarily weakens the capacity of the personnel-losing sector to contribute to economic development. Respecting governmental personnel, at least two conditions may be laid down as essential to economic development.

1. *Quantity and quality of governmental personnel.* The available information indicates that, as yet, in all of the underdeveloped countries, the supply of suitable personnel available to fill governmental posts, particularly those having to do with economic development, is insufficient for getting economic growth under way. Furthermore, much of this personnel is short of technical knowledge, probity and

[25] On this problem see Shils, *op. cit.*, pp. 56–62.

other qualities essential to effective performance. The defects noted—in quantity and quality—are similar to those characteristics of personnel in the private sector. It is generally true that personnel improve in quality at about the same rate in both the public and the private sector, and it is probable that the degree of shortage of qualified personnel is no more pronounced in the public than in the private sector.[26] The shortage of qualified governmental personnel is particularly serious in many underdeveloped countries in which the government is being counted upon to perform much of the innovating and pioneering role largely performed by the private entrepreneur in the West.[27]

The stock of qualified personnel at the disposal of a government thus sets an upper limit to the developmental functions that it can undertake. While a government may draw personnel from the private sector in order to raise this limit, it does not follow that development will thereby be made greater. The outcome depends upon where the personnel in question could make the greater contribution to economic development, in the private or in the public sector. It is essential, therefore, that the stock of qualified personnel be increased in both the private and the public sector, through investment in appropriate education, and so on.

2. *Disposition of governmental personnel.* Because of the shortage of qualified personnel that can perform functions which the state may need but not undertake, it is particularly important that use of governmental personnel be carefully economized. Governmental personnel should be employed only in undertakings in which the input of personnel per unit of output is relatively low, with high priority being given to the performance of the "minimal public services" discussed above. Such personnel should not be engaged in the performance of tasks which non-governmental personnel can do quite (if not more) effectively, in part because *technically qualified* personnel tend to be more scarce in the public than in the private sector. For, under civil-service regulations, the attributes specified as being requisite in those who would perform given sets of tasks tend to be greater than is required in reality or in the private sector. For example, one may need to possess, if he would perform a set of tasks S efficiently, only attributes $abcd$; and yet he may be required by civil-service regulations to possess, at a minimum, attributes $abcdef$ to qualify for the occupational post to which responsibility for the performance of S is assigned. In this instance, attributes ef are nonessential; moreover, in the private sector, they tend to be treated as nonessential, with the result that in this sector under *ceteris paribus* conditions the potential supply of performers of S is relatively greater than in the public sector. It is largely because civil-service rules so frequently are inimical to the economical use of manpower, skilled and otherwise, that efforts have been made, though not with much success, to exempt public corporations and com-

[26] We may turn to several sources for indications of shortages of governmental personnel sufficiently qualified to fill the posts to which they are assigned. Each year, in its Annual Report, the Consultative Committee on the Colombo Plan discusses the shortage of technical personnel and the role of technical assistance under the plan in somewhat alleviating this shortage. Similarly, in the reports of Missions of the International Bank for Reconstruction and Development, the development-retarding effects of shortages of technical personnel, together with qualitative defects in the technical attainments of such personnel, are noted. See also J. J. Spengler, "Public Bureaucracy, Resource Structure, and Economic Development: A Note," *Kyklos*, **11** (Fasc. 4, 1958), 459–486; F. W. Riggs, "Public Administration: A Neglected Factor in Economic Development," *Annals of the American Academy of Political and Social Science*, **305** (May 1956), 70–80; P. Franck, "Economic Planners in Afghanistan," *Economic Development and Cultural Change*, **1** (February 1953), 323–340.

[27] On how this shortage retards development, see e.g., H. W. Singer, "Obstacles to Economic Development," *Social Research*, **20** (Spring 1953), 19–31; also Shils, *op. cit.*, pp. 55–56.

panies from the incidence of these rules.[28] Economical use of a nation's more skilled manpower virtually requires, therefore, that the bulk of the business of transforming inputs into outputs, be these indicated by the market or by agencies of the state, be confined to the private sector.[29]

Political Instruments. Under this head are considered the roles of two instruments, here labelled "political," namely, party structure and welfare state.

1. *Party structure.* As has been indicated, the economic and social costs of economic development are bound to be heavy; there is scope for much controversy regarding priorities; and there are many individuals whose situation will be affected adversely, at least for some time, by economic development. The resulting burden will vary with country, of course, being much greater in heavily populated, low-income countries (e.g., in Asia) than in those where population pressure is less marked and the capacity to increase per-capita income is greater (e.g., in much of Latin America and parts of Africa). In many of these countries (especially in those situated in Asia), economic development is much more likely to be realized, given one dominant political party (e.g., the Congress Party in India), or a pair of parties,[30]

each strongly committed to economic development, than given a multiplicity of parties (as in pre-1940 France).[31] Only a well-entrenched party, or a pair of parties strongly committed to economic development, is likely to be able to keep the ideology of development effectively alive, to impose the necessary costs of development on the population, and yet to remain in office long enough to get economic growth effectively under

calculated to appeal to a majority of the voters, and each will arrive at much the same estimate regarding the content of this position (again making allowance for certain differences in "party" appeal). This is the kind of situation found in the United States. If attitudes are not distributed fairly evenly along a continuum, or if there are more than two parties, the party (or parties) temporarily in power will not have a sufficiently strong and persisting mandate from the voters to carry out a development program. This line of argument is based upon H. Hotelling's "Stability in Competition," *Economic Journal,* **39** (March 1929), 41–57, esp. Part II.

[31] The above argument must make allowance for a country's stage of development and for its social structure at or near the time its growth is getting effectively under way. In nineteenth-century Germany and Japan, the social structure, together with cognate conditions, was favorable. Capital formation could continue at high levels and labor remained content with the share going to it. This seems to have been true also in Britain and France in that the trade-union movement was not strong at the time economic development was getting under way. In general, the underlying population did not resist bearing the costs of development, any more than did the post-1945 German population; hence the presence of two or more parties did not prove inimical to development. A similar situation is not so likely to be found in present-day underdeveloped countries. E.g., see Karl de Schweinitz, "Industrialization, Labor Controls, and Democracy," *Economic Development and Cultural Change,* **7** (July 1959), 385–404, and comments on this article by Robert Freedman, together with de Schweinitz's reply, in *ibid.,* **8** (January 1960), 192–198. Of course, union pressure may operate, in a quite imperfectly competitive society, to compel entrepreneurs to improve methods of production, etc. See A. Sturmthal, "Unions and Economic Development," *ibid.,* pp. 204–205.

[28] E.g., see A. H. Hanson, *Public Enterprise and Economic Development* (London, 1959), pp. 459–464.

[29] See *ibid.,* Ch. 15, also Chs. 5, 11–14; also Spengler, "Public Bureaucracy . . . ," *loc. cit.* The discussion above relates to mixed economies. Weaknesses inherent in bureaucratic undertakings in mixed economies are present also in centralized economies, but their output-depressing effects may be swamped by very high rates of capital formation. E.g., see Janos Kornai, *Overcentralization in Economic Administration* (London, 1959); also M. Polanyi, *The Logic of Liberty* (London, 1951), Chs. 8–10.

[30] Normally, in a two-party country with attitudes distributed rather regularly along a continuum, the platforms of the two parties will tend to be quite similar (given allowance for ambiguities), since each will take a position

way.[32] A dictatorship might find itself in a somewhat similar position, given that it sought to promote economic growth and had fairly widespread support.[33]

2. *Welfare state.* This term is used to denote a state which diverts a considerable fraction of the national income to the support of so-called welfare objectives (various forms of social security, highly subsidized housing) and which sanctions legislation (e.g., minimum-wage legislation) and institutions (e.g., a strong trade-union movement) which exercise heavy upward pressure on real wage rates. While it may be granted that some provision for state-administered social-welfare objectives is essential (particularly since the security-providing extended family and clan and village organizations will probably be undergoing dissolution), and while it may be admitted that some increase in real

wages is necessary (to sustain faith in the gradual advent of a better economic world), it is not compatible with capital formation and economic development for these two objectives to be given strong support. Nor need they be, inasmuch as a rising per-capita income is compatible with an increasing rate of capital formation so long as both output per head and the marginal propensity to save are rising. It may be concluded, therefore, that, for the present and for some years to come, no more than a quite limited welfare state is compatible with a high rate of economic growth in presently underdeveloped lands. For this reason a multiparty system is not compatible with economic growth; it is too likely to give in to ever present demands for "liberal" welfare-state provisions.

Economic Development and Changing Political Conditions

As economic development proceeds, growth-affecting political conditions and requirements change. Per-capita expenditure for education and health tends to increase significantly. Institutional provisions respecting "money" become more complex. There is greater emphasis upon preventing deflation; monetary policy is increasingly directed to narrowing economic fluctuations and fostering fuller employment; less attention is given to cushioning fluctuations in the prices of primary goods. Moreover, as an economy progresses, its banking system becomes more differentiated, and its ratio of paper to physical assets rises. The legal structure also becomes more complex and differentiated as does the public and the private organizational structure for which legal institutions must design appropriate rules.[34] Foreign economic relations tend to become subject to greater regulation, much of it restrictive, especially after external trade has begun to lag behind national income.

As an economy advances, it may toler-

[32] As was noted earlier, even when there is not initially a single party, the processes associated with carrying out a development program tend to channel power into the hands of a single party. See Brzezinski, *op. cit.*, pp. 62–64. The fact that economic development in the West was accomplished under predominantly private entrepreneurial leadership, democratic auspices, and the political leadership of two or more parties has little influence today in underdeveloped countries (see *ibid.*, pp. 58–59; Shils, *op. cit.*, pp. 55–56). Furthermore, the examples of Russia and China are at hand, and the Communist Party is now representing itself as the political instrument through which industrialization is to be achieved. See Kautsky, *op. cit.* Presumably, in countries where durable political parties have been lacking, development is likely to be retarded. If this be true, and if D. A. Rustow is correct in remarking the absence of durable political parties from a number of underdeveloped countries, lack of effective party organization may be a political deterrent to growth. See Rustow, "New Horizons for Comparative Politics," *World Politics*, 9 (July 1957), 541–542.

[33] The above analysis suggests that, if there are but two parties, a parliamentary system may be better suited to foster economic growth than a federal system of the sort found in the United States. Under the latter, power is more widely dispersed, with the result that, except in times of crisis, it is very difficult to focus attention, effort, and resources upon as costly an undertaking as economic development.

[34] E.g., see E. V. Rostow's account of the newly acquired rules of public law, in *Planning for Freedom* (New Haven, 1959).

ate larger amounts of growth-checking taxation and public expenditure, since the economic system itself becomes more autonomous and more able and willing to supply growth-capital. While emphasis upon governmental intervention and centralized economic planning may for a time increase as an economy progresses, it eventually tends to decline insofar as the need for economic and social overhead capital and for state aid to newly developing industries falls off. This outcome is quite likely. Such increase in emphasis upon the public sector may, for a time, make conditions worse in the private sector, though this is not a necessary outcome. Development corporations are not likely to be continued after an economy has become autonomous and characterized by self-sustaining growth. Budgetary policy becomes of greater importance as the economy progresses, particularly if, as some believe, the advent of "affluence" makes greater freedom increasingly necessary, together with the supply of "cultural" and "collective" goods and services, the production and/or distribution of which are not considered well suited to private enterprise. Economic progress is attended also by a great increase in the competence of private criticism of governmental economic policies, though not necessarily in its effectiveness.

While highly skilled personnel are always in short supply, governmental personnel tend to improve in quantity and quality as an economy improves, thereby permitting the government to undertake more of those economic tasks of which it is empirically capable, given adequacy of personnel. Rising income is associated with the increase of skilled personnel, income and personnel interacting through time to augment each other.

In general, as has been implied, economic development tends eventually to be accompanied by both political and economic decentralization. It is accompanied by decentralization of both legal norm-making power and use-determining, economic decision-making power, with both forms becoming more widely distributed in space and among households and/or corporate groups. The disposition of economic power in space and among groups and individuals tends to be rather closely associated with that of political power. Political decentralization entails the distribution of norm-making power among a plurality of groups or organs, together with the subjection of centralized norm-making to restraints imposed by dispersed, norm-affecting groups whose initially heterogeneous aspirations enter into such consensus as comes to underlie norms held valid for all members of a society.[35] Economic decentralization requires that the mechanisms employed to discover what final goods and services should be produced reflect an ever widening range of consumer preferences, be these mechanisms "free markets" in which price and effective economic demand rule, or political devices designed to register such non-economic indicators as votes. Such decentralization results because, as an economy becomes more consumer-oriented, centralized determination of what is to be produced becomes increasingly difficult.

Among the concomitants of decentralization are the decline of one-party rule and the rise of the welfare state. An effective one-party system, though often favorable to economic growth, appears to be incompatible with a complex economy in which consumer goods, together with a high level of education, have come to play a paramount role. Similarly, the welfare state, though initially incompatible with the effective development of economically retarded lands, eventually becomes a part of the set of arrangements whereby, in high-income economies, collective goods and services are supplied and expenditure is kept abreast of "full-employment" output in pacific times.

[35] See Hans Kelsen, "Centralization and Decentralization," in Harvard Tercentenary Conference, *Authority and the Individual* (Cambridge, 1937), pp. 210–239, esp. 212–213, 216–217, 223, 227–229; also 231–232 on struggles for local autonomy, and 233–234 on federalism as a form of decentralization.

INDIVIDUALISM AND THE ROLE OF THE STATE IN ECONOMIC GROWTH

Alexander Eckstein

I

Economic growth can be viewed as a broadening of the range of alternatives open to society. Clearly, technological and resource constraints are likely to be so compelling and overriding in primitive or underdeveloped economies as to leave comparatively little scope for the exercise of choice—either individual or social. On the other hand, the situation is quite different—at least in degree—at more advanced stages of economic development. At these stages, one of the principal manifestations of this broadening in the range of alternatives is precisely the greater opportunity to exercise choice over the form in which choices in the economy become institutionalized. This, in turn, requires a delineation of the spheres of public vs. private choice and a determination of the relative weight of each sphere.

One of the aspects of individualism, and possibly the one most relevant for our purposes, is the scope for individual choice and decentralized decision-making in the economic sphere. In a preponderantly free enterprise market economy the institutionalization of these ingredients of individualism is more or less automatically assured. This does not, however, mean that this system necessarily assures equal scope for the exercise of choice on the part of all individuals in the economic system, or that it provides a greater scope for individual

SOURCE. Alexander Eckstein, "Individualism and the Role of the State in Economic Growth," *Economic Development and Cultural Change*, **6**, 81–87, January 1958. Reprinted by permission of The University of Chicago Press. Copyright 1958 by The University of Chicago Press. Read at the January 1957 meeting of the American Council of Learned Societies, Panel II on Economic Growth and the Individual.

choice than an alternative system might. In contrast to preponderantly free enterprise market systems, in economies in which the public sector looms quite large, the scope for individual choice and decision making may be more a function of the political rather than the economic system. Thus the mechanism through which economic policy is formulated and the role of the ballot box in economic policy formulation become major conditioning factors.

In essence, what this suggests is that there is a potentially positive correlation between individualism and economic development. The extent to which this potential is translated into reality will depend upon the role played by individual choice and initiative in resource allocation, regardless of whether the choices and decisions are in fact arrived at primarily within the confines of the economic or political process. With this context in mind, let us attempt to spell out some of the factors and variables that are likely to condition the role the state may be expected or forced to play in the process of economic growth and its impact upon the position of the individual.

II

In analyzing the role of the state in the process of economic growth, the following elements may be considered as essential:

1. *The hierarchy of objectives, goals, and ends of economic development.* This necessarily involves an examination of both the qualitative and quantitative aspects, that is, the character, range, and variety of the ends sought as well as the level to be attained. The interplay of these dimensions of content, range, and level will be one of the principal factors defining the ambitiousness of the particular economic develop-

ment program. In respect to content, several broad categories of objectives or motivations may be cited, for instance, those revolving around nationalism and those related to a striving for rising standards of living. In a sense, these might be considered as ultimate ends which need to be, and are in fact, broken down into a series of derived and possibly more concrete goals. Thus, at the stage when these objectives are disaggregated and sorted out as to the ranges and levels involved, they inevitably tend to become competitive rather than complementary entities in the sense that under *ceteris paribus* assumptions, the wider the range, the lower will have to be the level, and vice versa.

2. *The time horizon in economic development.* This entails a definition of the rate at which the goals are to be attained. In a sense, it is but another aspect of the hierarchy of objects, since rapid or leisurely growth may be an explicitly stated end in and of itself.

3. *The means available* for attaining— at the desired rate—the content, range, and level of ends explicitly or implicitly formulated. Here one would have to consider such variables as resource and factor endowments and the state of the arts prevailing in the particular economy.

4. *The structure and character of institutions: social, economic, and political.* This is possibly the most complex of all the categories listed here. The considerations most relevant for our purposes revolve around the rigidity of the institutional framework, its capacity to generate, absorb, and adapt itself to economic change and to the disruptive forces of industrialization. This would mean investigating factors such as the prevailing value system, class structure, social mobility, contractual and legal arrangements, degree and character of urbanization, land tenure system, degree of commercialization and monetization, character and structure of state organization, structure of political power, etc. However, analysis of these variables is greatly complicated by virtue

of the fact that some of them are rather intangible, while their particular chemical max—that is, the nature of combinations and interaction between the different institutional factors—and the reaction produced may be quite unpredictable. In effect, it is much easier to provide *ex post facto* rationalizations or explanations as to why and in what ways certain types of institutional structure were more conducive to industrialization than others, than to assess *ex ante* the height and the tensile strength of institutional barriers and their resistance to economic development.

5. *The relative backwardness of the economy.* From an economic point of view, relative backwardness—and the emphasis should be on relative—involves certain advantages and disadvantages. The disadvantages lie principally in the field of foreign trade, while the so called "advantages of backwardness" may be found in the realm of technology. Thus industrially advanced countries enjoy certain competitive advantages in world markets, and particularly in the markets of the underdeveloped areas themselves. This in and of itself can under certain conditions become a major handicap in the industrialization of backward countries. On the other hand, as Professor Gerschenkron has pointed out, one of the essential ingredients of relative backwardness is a gap in the levels of technology used and applied. Therefore the backward country can reap large potential gains by importing advanced technology from abroad and thus, in effect, make a technological leap from comparatively primitive to highly advanced levels.

At this point another aspect of relative backwardness may be usefully introduced, namely the gap in material welfare or standards of living, and the gap in national power produced by differences in levels of industrialization. All three of these gaps— in consumption, technology, and power— could be viewed as different aspects of a "demonstration effect" through which the gulf between a potential and actual state is forcefully brought home. Characteristically, it is in this shape that the pressure for industrialization of backward countries is manifested. Once the disequilibrating and innovating forces of modernization, industrialization, and urbanization have been introduced on an appreciable scale,[1] one could say that, *ceteris paribus*, the greater the relative backwardness, the more acute will tend to be the "tension" arising from this chasm between the potential and the actual, and thus the greater will be the pressure for industrialization.

Given the five categories of elements and variables considered above, we are now in a position to state our hypothesis concerning the conditions under which the state will tend to play a greater or lesser role in the process of economic growth. On this basis then one could say that:

a. The greater the range of ends and the higher the level of attainment sought;

b. The shorter the time horizon within which the ends are to be attained, that is the more rapid the rate of economic growth desired;

c. The more unfavorable the factor and resource endowments;

d. The greater the institutional barriers to economic change and industrialization;

e. The more backward the economy in relative terms the greater will tend to be the urge, push, and pressure for massive state intervention and initiative in the process of industrialization, and at the same time, the greater will be the need for such intervention if a breakthrough, rather than a breakdown, is to be attained.

III

Assuming that the state is compelled to make a major commitment on behalf of industrialization, what types of measures may the state be expected to adopt and what effect may these have upon the position of the individual, or more specifically, upon the individual choice and decentralized decision-making in the economic sphere? From this point of view, a sharp distinction needs to be made between the elements and the degree of state power applied in the process of economic growth.

In analyzing the qualitative aspects of state intervention affecting the economic sphere, one could perhaps distinguish between five categories of action: provision of social overhead, provision of economic overhead, application of direct and indirect levers and controls, government operation of enterprises extending beyond the overhead sectors, and central planning.

Provision of social overhead might entail maintenance of law and order in the society, provision and enforcement of legal and contractual obligations, supply of educational, health, and social welfare facilities, assumption of military and defense functions, etc. In effect, these are categories of action which to the extent that they are provided at all, are usually furnished by public rather than private agencies.

Provision of economic overhead may involve the institution of central banking and of monetary and fiscal facilities, the development of a highway and railroad network and of other public utilities.

Application of direct or indirect levers and controls may be based on a wide variety of measures, such as introduction of tariffs, railroad rate discrimination, tax privileges and other types of subsidies, rationing of goods and of credit, price controls, etc.

Government operation of enterprises extending beyond the overhead sectors may range from management of some industries, or a few firms in different industries, to public ownership of all means of production.

Central planning may involve more or less total concentration of economic decision-making in the hands of a national planning board.

Admittedly, this fivefold classification is arbitrary, and the line of demarcation

---

[1] This scale effect is, of course, both crucial and indeterminate, in the sense that what will be the operationally significant range will inevitably vary from country to country, depending upon size, institutional framework, etc.

between the different categories is quite blurred. Yet, in terms of their effect upon the exercise of individual choice and initiative, they present qualitatively rather significant differences. Thus, most of the items in the first two categories belong to what, in industrializing societies at least, are usually considered as the minimal and essential functions of a state. In contrast, centralized and comprehensive planning combined with total government operation of the economy may be regarded as maximum functions. One of the key questions that needs to be posed in this context is which one, or which combination, of categories will the state use to promote economic development? Whichever means it uses, how massively, to what degree, and with what intensity will it apply its power to the provision of these different categories? Moreover, how will particular kinds and degrees of state intervention affect factor supply, particularly the supply of capital and entrepreneurship?

It may turn out that the more massively and rapidly the state provides what can be considered its minimum functions, the less may be the pressure or the need for it to provide the maximum functions. Therefore, the reliance upon maxima may in effect be a function of past and current failure to provide the minima. In these terms, then, one could say that a necessary precondition for the broadening of opportunities for the exercise of individual choice, individual initiative, and the growth of individual values in underdeveloped countries, launched on a development program, is a high degree and rapid application of state power for the supply of social and economic overhead, combined with partial controls and planning as circumstances may demand them.

Theoretically one could, of course, visualize a system in which amidst public ownership of the means of production, national planning, and resource allocation was—within wide limits—based upon the operation of free consumer choice and consumer autonomy. Realistically, however, it would be extremely difficult to build sufficient checks and balances into such a Lange-like model to prevent it from slipping into a totalitarian mold. On the other hand, this is much less true in the case of partial planning and partial government operation of enterprises, which in many situations is needed to reinforce the provision of social and economic overheads, if comprehensive government planning and management is to be avoided.

The failure of the state in the minimum fields tends to be more or less directly reflected in capital formation and the growth of entrepreneurship. Thus, in many traditional societies, accumulations of merchant and other forms of capital tend to be dissipated because of: (1) the absence of adequate and contractual arrangements to protect these holdings from the more or less arbitrary ravages of officialdom, and (2) the failure of the state to institute a social security system, so that old age assistance, poor relief, and similar functions must be privately assumed through the family and kinship system. At the same time, condition (1) tends to reinforce the economic risks of various types of business and industrial investments. Moreover, the same condition further encourages the flow of capital into land investment, which in an environment of acute population pressure and agrarian value orientation, represents one of the safest and most profitable forms of holding. However, from the standpoint of the economy, this is merely a transfer payment, ultimately representing a leakage of investment into consumption. In effect, then, this is a milieu in which the state—through sins of commission and omission—tends to undercut actual and potential sources of capital accumulation, while at the same time making its contribution to the narrowing of business opportunities. Under these conditions the scarcities of entrepreneurial and technical talent tend to be further intensified through the neglect of education facilities. Moreover, to the extent that some education is provided, its orientation is frequently inhospitable to the growth of scientific and technical knowledge.

Viewed in these terms, perhaps one of the most important contributions the pre-industrial European city made to the industrialization of the continent was that it provided a legally and more or less militarily protected haven for the accumulation and conservation of capital, and for its investment in fields that were eminently productive from a point of view of economic development.

Amidst such circumstances, the formidable barriers to modernization and industrialization are likely to be perpetuated, while economic, social, and political tensions mount under the impact of innovating influences ushered in—as a rule—through foreign contact. Unless some means are found for alleviating these tensions through a process of change and adaptation, the potentially explosive forces in society may be expected to burst forth, sweeping away the older order, capturing the state, and using it as a total and far-reaching instrument for mounting an industrial revolution.

On this basis, one could argue that if India, for instance, wishes to avoid a totalitarian path to industrialization, her current plans and efforts do not provide for enough, rather than for too much, state intervention. Thus the large gap in the financial resources available for the implementation of the Second Five Year Plan may be a symptom of the inability and the reluctance of the Indian state to mobilize the means adequate for the implementation of the ends sought. But, even more fundamentally, perhaps, the inadequacy of the government efforts to spread adult education—both basic and technical education—rapidly, may be an important factor in inhibiting the attainment of certain economic objectives, while at the same time it serves to reinforce the great gulf between the small elite and the rural masses—a factor representing marked potential dangers in the political realm.

To sum up this phase of my argument,

it may perhaps be useful to attempt to work with the concept of an "optimum level and pattern of state intervention" paralleling other optima—e.g. the optimum propensity to consume—incorporated in different types of economic and social science models. For our present purposes, this optimum would have to be defined in relation to two broad sets of objectives, i.e., striving for rising standards of living combined with an increase and/or preservation of the scope for the exercise of individual choice and initiative. The definition would also have to take account of the specific circumstances in each case, particularly in relation to the qualitative and quantitative aspects of state intervention, and to the variables listed in Section II above.

IV

We have discussed thus far the role the state may need to play in the process of economic growth without any reference to the character of the state and its capacity to perform the tasks required of it. Historically, however, particularly in the underdeveloped countries, the state—and the social structure on which it was based—was one of the very agencies hampering economic development. The same conditions that create the need for massive state intervention in one form or another, also tend to breed a type of state which is singularly unequipped to intervene effectively on behalf of economic development. That is economic backwardness is usually associated with political and other forms of backwardness.

Thus in China, for instance, the state has played a passive to actively negative role vis à vis the economy. The very concept of economic change and economic dynamism was alien to such a society with the nexus between economic growth and national power and/or welfare only very dimly understood, if perceived at all. The function of the economy was a largely static one, being charged with the primary task of supporting the ruling elite. Therefore, the state assumed very few responsibilities in the economy, beyond assuring that it would provide a stable, continuing, and adequate source of revenue for the imperial household and the gentry-bureaucracy.

The continuing failure of the traditional Chinese state to respond to the challenge of modernization, the institutional rigidities permeating the traditional social structure, the incapacity and unwillingness of the ruling classes to come to terms with change, their inability to understand the character of the innovating influences and to follow a policy of enlightened self-interest, have all served to retard the process of industrialization for so long that cumulative tensions of such explosive proportions were generated that they could no longer be contained, while at the same time perhaps nothing short of such an explosive force could have broken the shackles of the old order and swept away the barriers to economic growth. The violent eruption of the Chinese economy into what seems to bear the earmarks of an industrial revolution under totalitarian control can thus be viewed as an illustration of a resort to maximum solutions in the face of repeated and continued failure of the old state to perform and furnish the minimal functions referred to in the preceding section.

This course of development contrasts sharply with that experienced in Japan, where the breakdown of the old order accelerated by innovating influences produced a realignment of elites. The new elite, which bore some continuity with the old, then set out very deliberately to use the state as an instrument for modernization and industrialization. In doing this, the state from the outset paid major attention to developing rapidly the social and economic overhead sectors and to provide a general framework within which all types of enterprises, private and public, large and small, would grow. The state in effect conceived its role as initiator and promoter of the development process, leaving much of the execution to private enterprise.

While this is not intended to suggest that the Japanese experience can necessarily be duplicated in other countries, and in different circumstances, it is worthwhile to note that the state was able to perform this kind of a role amidst conditions which *ex ante* would have seemed exceptionally unfavorable. Not only were factor and resource endowments poor—in many respects poorer, perhaps not only absolutely but relatively, than those of some major underdeveloped areas today—but institutional barriers were formidable too.

However, an analysis of the conditions under which the state would or would not be *capable* of performing the functions required of it would be beyond the scope of this paper. Rather, I have tried to confine myself more specifically to a spelling out of the conditions under which and the ways in which the state may be *required* to assume a large role in initiating and promoting economic development without jeopardizing the growth of opportunities for the exercise of individual choice and initiative in the economic sphere.

Chapter 6

Social Aspects of Economic Development

ECONOMIC GROWTH AND DEVELOPMENT: NONECONOMIC FACTORS IN ECONOMIC DEVELOPMENT

Bert F. Hoselitz

An adequate treatment of the varied ways in which economic and noneconomic factors interact in a process of economic growth or development would require an entire book. In order to remain within the short space at my disposal, I shall therefore discuss a special problem and hope that this discussion will convey in a rough way the general flavor of the manner in which we might proceed with a consideration of noneconomic factors in economic development. I should like to select the question of the change which occurs in an economy as it leaves a state of relatively slow growth or stagnation and starts a process of rapid growth. This apparently discontinuous break with the past, which is usually associated with rapid industrialization, has often been described. Students of the different industrial revolutions have pointed to the rapid pace with which an economy broke out of a previous condition of relative immobility and attained within one or at most two generations a level of performance on which self-

sustained growth was possible. Much of this evidence has recently been collected in an interesting paper by W. W. Rostow on "The Take-off into Self-Sustained Growth" (*Economic Journal*, 1956). Apart from a detailed discussion of the take-off period, Rostow's essay also contains a discussion of three stages with the take-off as center. The first stage or period is one of preparation in which the preconditions of the take-off are established. This period may last a century or more. The second stage is the take-off itself, and the third period is the stage of self-sustained growth, when the further development of the economy occurs as a more or less normal and self-generating process.[1]

If we view the development process as following roughly such a tripartite schema,

[1] Rostow was, of course, not the first to have discovered the sudden incidence of industrial revolutions, nor to have stipulated a tripartite periodization. A similar scheme was presented by G. Célestine, "Dynamique des niveaux de production et de productivité," *Économie et Humanisme*, July–August 1952, pp. 60–67; and in one of my articles, "Algunos aspectos de las relaciones entre el cambio social y el desarollo económico," *De Economía*, July–August 1954, pp. 611–624. Further references to this process are cited in that article.

SOURCE. Bert F. Hoselitz, "Economic Growth and Development: Noneconomic Factors in Economic Development," *American Economic Review*, **47**, 28–41, May 1957.

we are confronted with the problem of how to account for this explosive change which has so aptly been called an industrial revolution. Its inception is, as has often been observed, rather striking and sudden, and it usually ends almost as suddenly as it began. It has been accompanied in most cases by a concomitant population "explosion" which has obscured somewhat the rapidity and suddenness of economic growth during the discontinuous take-off period if measured in terms of per-capita income. What is perhaps most important about the structural changes taking place during the take-off period is the adaptation of previously existing institutions for new ends, especially for capital formation. In fact, Rostow makes the difference in the rate of investment (i.e., the ratio of net capital formation to net national product) the criterion of whether an economy is in a pre-take-off stage or is entering the phase of industrial revolution. Now why should an economy suddenly be capable of saving and investing a larger proportion of its net income, especially if it has apparently been unable to alter the rate of net investment for a very long period previous to the take-off? The answer may be found if we ask whether or not general environmental conditions have been created in the pre-take-off phase which make an increase in net capital formation attractive and achievable.

These "environmental conditions" must be sought chiefly in noneconomic aspects of the society. In other words, apart from the build-up of economic overhead capital, such as a communications and transport system and investment in harbor facilities, some warehouses, and similar installations favoring especially foreign trade, most of the innovations introduced during the preparatory period are based upon changes in the institutional arrangements in the legal, educational, familial, or motivational orders. Once these new institutions have been created, they operate as "gifts from the past," contributing freely to the vigorous spurt of economic activity in the period of take-off. We may then consider

that from the point of view of providing an explanation of the process of economic growth, the main functions of the preparatory stage are the changes in the institutional order, especially in areas other than economic activity, which transform the society from one in which capital formation and the introduction of modern economic organization is difficult or impossible, to one in which the accumulation of capital and the introduction of new production processes appear as "natural" concomitants of general social progress.

Let us examine a few cases more in detail in order to see what role some noneconomic institutions have played in bringing about the explosive situation of an industrial revolution and in particular how they have affected the supply of productive factors. For although it has often been asserted that the chief bottleneck experienced by underdeveloped countries is the shortage of capital, there are other factors which are relatively scarce—above all, certain types of skilled labor (including the services of entrepreneurial personnel). For this reason there is special interest in institutional changes during the preparatory period which tend to affect the supply of capital or of such services as administrative and entrepreneurial activity and technical and scientific skills.

The need for capital on a relatively large scale requires the availability of institutions through which savings can be collected and channeled into projects employing productive capital. Hence a banking system or its equivalent in the form of a state agency collecting revenue and spending it on developmental projects is required. What is also required in a society in which investment decisions are made by private individuals is a legal institution, such as the corporation, which allows the combination of capitals of various individuals in order to support enterprises which, for technological reasons, can be undertaken economically only on a large scale. In Britain all these institutions were in existence at the time its industrial revolution began. It is granted that joint stock companies required a special charter for their formation, and up to the early nineteenth century such charters were granted only for overseas commercial enterprises or for large-scale transportation enterprises. But as capital requirements in industry increased, the corporate form of enterprise came to be more and more widely applied to industry also. By the third decade of the nineteenth century, corporate charters for industrial firms were not uncommon and within the next fifteen years they became the rule in all but small enterprises.

It is also true that bank credit did not play an overwhelming role in the early phases of the industrial revolution in Britain. In fact, in contrast to France and Germany, a relatively large amount of capital employed in the early cotton and iron industry was supplied by merchants and even landowners. But here again, as the requirements of capital supply grew in dimension, the banks began to play a more and more important role.

Institutions providing for the collective use of capital also had been established in other European countries long before they entered the take-off phase. In France, the Napoleonic codes provided for joint-stock companies of two kinds (*sociétés en actions* and *sociétés en commandite*), and both these types of corporate enterprise were adopted by other European countries. The German legal reform lagged behind that of France, but it is significant that a Prussian commercial code, embodying much of the French type of company legislation, was introduced at a very early stage in the industrial upsurge of Germany, whereas the general civil code did not become law until the turn of the twentieth century.

In Japan, because of the absence of traditions of corporate bodies similar to the medieval European company and because of the strong governmentally induced impetus to industrialization in its early phase, the supply of capital had to be channeled through institutions which differed from those of the West. Although Japan adopted in due course the institution of the Western corporation, the immediate post-restoration process of capital formation relied upon governmental capital creation and, more importantly, upon a change in the structure and hierarchy of Japanese society. In the new social order inaugurated with the Meiji restoration there developed an association of *samurai* and large-scale capitalist merchants and farmers. This association, which later also aided in the development of the monopolistic *zaibatsu*, had antecedents which reach far back into the pre-Meiji period. All through the nineteenth century, the economic basis of Tokugawa society had begun to crumble. Although political power remained officially in the hands of the *shogun*, it began slowly to pass into the hands of some of the more powerful clans; at the same time the economic basis of a predominantly agrarian quasi-feudal society had ceased to function. There were masses of impoverished *samurai* who, in order to make a livelihood, were forced into a life of business or farm administration. Moreover, there was a simultaneously rising class of merchants and large farmers and farmer-money-lenders, whose presence disturbed the officially imposed rough equality among the members of the nonnoble classes. The gradual acquisition of power by these elements and their association with disgruntled *samurai* was a phenomenon whose beginning must be looked for in the period when, on the surface, the rule of the *shogun* appeared unimpaired. But this association was an important factor leading to a reinterpretation on the part of Japan's political elite of the over-all systemic objectives of the society. Whereas before the Japanese government had been concerned only with power, it was not clearly recognized that within this concern the development of the economy was an important, and perhaps the most important, feature. In this way an institutional framework, supported by an ideology, was created which became an efficient and powerful support of capital formation.

It is within a framework of this kind that a comparative institutional analysis of patterns of capital formation in economic development might be undertaken. Given the social and political forces at play, one could appraise by means of such an analysis the role which might be played by development corporations and investment banks or fiscal bodies in the collection of savings and the channeling of these savings into productive investment. One could appraise in this latter case the alternative function of a policy of forced savings either by inflation or by taxation and could relate the potential efficacy of each of these alternative policies to existing social and political institutions.

At the same time, one would find that the lack of suitable institutions or the presence of institutions which may lead to dissipation of accumulated savings will tend to prevent a society from arriving at a stage in which a take-off is likely or even possible. For example, nineteenth-century China had a series of institutional arrangements which facilitated the accumulation of capital. One was the institution of licensed merchants, such as the *hong* merchants at Canton who were supported by the government in their monopolistic control of foreign trade; another was the institution of imperially licensed salt merchants who enjoyed regional monopolies in the production and sale of salt. There were other groups of privileged traders, and even a large number of not specially privileged ones, who achieved considerable success in the amassing of large fortunes. But within the Chinese system the merchants operated upon the sufferance and with the support of the bureaucracy, and thus any profits made in trade or industry had to be shared with officials. The officials invested their share in land or spent it on luxury consumption, with the result that large accumulations of liquid funds tended to become sporadically dissipated rather than channeled into productive investment.

Moreover, even in the few instances in which, with the aid and support of officials, capital was invested in productive enterprises, profits, instead of being reinvested, were distributed among a large number of claimants among the officialdom; the demands on trading, shipping, or industrial firms for the distribution of earnings among officials on all levels of the administrative scale were so strong that it was often difficult to maintain the initial capital intact. Thus the institutional tie-up between the merchant class and officialdom in China, superimposed upon the heavy tax system, contributed in Ch'ing China to the unavailability of capital accumulations of sufficient magnitude to form a foundation for rapid industrial development.

Let us now turn to the second problem of supply: the availability of skilled labor of various kinds, chiefly entrepreneurial services and the services of skilled administrators, engineers, scientists, and managerial personnel. These rather than manual skills are the types of labor normally in short supply in nonindustrialized countries, and it is the overcoming of bottlenecks in the supply of these kinds of services that a major developmental effort usually needs to be made. Since entrepreneurship and administrative talent on the one hand and scientific and engineering services on the other usually are associated with different institutions, it will be convenient to separate the discussion of the institutions within which these skills and inclinations to the pursuit of these occupations are fashioned. We shall first turn to the problem of the diffusion of science and technology.

As in the case of institutions designed to aid in the accumulation of capital, technological and scientific investigations had become institutionalized in Western Europe long before the countries which experienced a period of take-off actually entered the phase of industrialization on a rapid scale. For Britain this fact is well documented and has often been noted. The Royal Society was officially formed in

1662, although by 1645 there had been already in existence a small club of "divers worthy persons, inquisitive into natural philosophy, and particularly of what was called the New Philosophy, or Experimental Philosophy." Although its early extensive interest in technology was not fully maintained throughout the early eighteenth century,. it was revived by the middle of the century and strengthened by the establishment in 1754 of the Society for the Encouragement of Arts, Manufactures, and Commerce. It is superfluous to describe in this place the institutionalization of scientific and technical progress in Britain during the seventeenth and eighteenth centuries more specifically, since a perusal of Robert K. Merton's *Science, Technology and Society in Seventeenth Century England* (Bruges, 1938) and G. N. Clark's *Science and Social Welfare in the Age of Newton* (Oxford, 1937) will yield exhaustive descriptions of this process. By the onset of the industrial revolution, technological research was widespread and had spilled over from being practiced in the laboratories of "experimental philosophers" to being carried on also in workshops, mines, and manufactories. In France and also in Germany, academies similar to the Royal Society were established in imitation of this organization, soon after it had started to operate, and in France especially technological training was given a tremendous impetus by the foundation of the École Polytechnique in 1794. This school became the pet of Napoleon, and it was through its influence more than any other that by the beginning of the nineteenth century France was in the forefront of scientific achievement. By 1825, Justus Liebig, who had studied under Gay-Lussac in Paris and had there convinced himself of the superiority of the French method, introduced laboratory science into Germany, and from that time on experimental and applied research in mechanics, chemistry, metallurgy, and other fields became common in German universities and technological institutes.

Thus in the various European countries there existed firmly entrenched institutions for scientific and technological research and training well before the onset of rapid industrialization. Similarly in Japan there had been considerable interest in "Dutch studies" under the Tokugawa. Many Japanese were engaged in learning Dutch and by means of this language became acquainted with Western science and technology. Schools for Dutch studies were established, not only by the *shogun* himself, but also by some of the more important clans, notably the Saga in whose territory Nagasaki was located. These schools taught not only languages but also such subjects as Western mathematics, astronomy, geography, physics, and metallurgy. The result was that before Perry's arrival there had been founded a number of iron smelting plants and foundries built by native engineers on the Western model, and by 1853 the Saga foundry cast the first satisfactory iron gun. In the same year a reverberatory furnace was built by Japanese engineers of the Satsuma clan, and shortly thereafter two more furnaces and supporting fabricating works by the Satsuma clan and the Mito clan.[2] It would be false to exaggerate the influence of these institutions and technical attainments. They are symptoms rather than results of a change in institutional arrangements affecting scientific research and technological achievement in Japan. But the practice of Dutch studies and the adoption of Western techniques before the fall of the *shogunate* set a stage which made possible the rapid adoption of Western educational and research facilities in science and technology once the new order had set in.

Again the picture was different in nineteenth-century China. Rather than enter into a lengthy elaboration of the role of Western science and technology in Ch'ing China, I should like to cite a passage from

[2] Cf. Thomas C. Smith, *Political Change and Industrial Development in Japan: Government Enterprise, 1868–1880* (Stanford, 1955), pp. 4–7.

Hsiao-Tung Fei, who is an accurate and imaginative interpreter of Chinese "traditional" society. Fei says:

> In Chinese traditional society the intelligentsia have been a class without technical knowledge. They monopolized authority based on the wisdom of the past, spent time on literature, and tried to express themselves through art. Chinese literary language is very inapt to express scientific or technical knowledge. This indicates that, in the traditional scheme, the vested interests had no wish to improve production but thought only of privilege. Their main task was the perpetuation of established norms in order to set up a guide for conventional behavior. A man who sees the world only through human relations is inclined to be conservative, because in human relations the end is always mutual adjustment. And an adjusted equilibrium can only be founded on a stable and unchanging relation between man and nature. On the other hand, from the purely technical point of view, there are hardly any limits to man's control of nature. In emphasizing technical progress, one plunges into a struggle in which man's control over nature becomes ever changing, ever more efficient. Yet these technical changes may lead to conflict between man and man. The Chinese intelligentsia viewed the world humanistically. Lacking technical knowledge, they could not appreciate technical progress. And they saw no reason to wish to change man's relation to man.[3]

If we turn to institutions regulating the supply of entrepreneurial or managerial services, the picture is similar. But with reference to entrepreneurship in particular, there appears also to be involved not only an institutional but above all a motivational factor. Accumulation of capital and technical or scientific knowledge can be

[3] Hsiao-Tung Fei, *China's Gentry* (1953), p. 74.

explained by pointing to the institutions through which practices of behavior leading to investment or the acquisition of technical knowledge may be furthered. Entrepreneurship is a more evasive thing. It is not so much a particular set of institutions through which it is brought to bear, but its presence or absence; its vigor or debility depends rather upon a whole series of environmental conditions and appropriate personal motivations. It has been shown—in my opinion successfully—that entrepreneurship is associated with a personality pattern in which achievement motivation is strong. But the presence of strong achievement motivation in a group of individuals does not necessarily produce an abundance of entrepreneurs unless certain other general conditions of social structure and culture strongly favor achievement-oriented individuals to enter economic pursuits. High achievement motivation has also been found among military leaders and may be found among scholars, priests, and bureaucrats. It is not too difficult to show that in a society in which the acquisition of wealth is regarded as a good thing in itself, persons with the appropriate motivational disposition will tend to enter an entrepreneurial career. But what about societies in which the accumulation of wealth in itself is frowned upon, or where it is considered to be a worthy object only if performed under certain restrictive conditions? What about a society in which the warrior, the priest, or the government official is rated vastly above the merchant or the industrialist?

Thus when we discuss the factor of entrepreneurship we must go beyond the mere analysis of social institutions in a limited sense and must include in our purview the entire social fabric in which this type of social behavior becomes predominant. But if we put the question in this form, we are immediately confronted with the further question of whether the same type of social constellation which provides a fruitful field for the development and exercise of entrepreneurial activity does not simultaneously further institutions designed to facilitate capital formation and scientific and technical progress. I believe, on the basis of my reading of the social and economic history of those peoples which have shown the capacity for rapid economic advance and those which have so far failed in this capacity, that the overall social framework which favors entrepreneurship also favors scientific and technical progress and the development of institutions fostering the formation of capital.

In support of this proposition, one could show that the countries of Western Europe and Japan which have developed viable institutions for the accumulation of capital and its channeling in large lumps into productive investment and institutions enhancing the supply of persons capable of tackling the scientific and technological problems required for efficient production, also have developed vigorous entrepreneurial personalities, and that China, which in the nineteenth and early twentieth century has failed to produce these institutions, also has had a paucity of able entrepreneurs. The fact that Chinese emigrants in South Asia have, on the whole, succeeded in commerce and, at any rate, appear to have outdistanced in business acumen and entrepreneurial spirit members of their host peoples is rather a confirmation of this proposition. For I do not mean to argue that the Chinese have less inherent capacity for business leadership than other nations. The social fabric of imperial China was such that whenever potential motivations for entrepreneurial activity developed in aspiring young men, they were deflected into other career lines; and the men who in Western Europe or Japan would have taken on a business career tended to become officials or scholars in China. And once they had attained such positions their preoccupation was, as Professor Fei has argued, directed upon preservation of existing human relations rather than on innovations either in technology or in business enterprise.

Let me summarize the argument presented so far in a few sentences, in order to outline the conclusions at which we might arrive. Economic growth is a process which affects not only purely economic relations but the entire social, political, and cultural fabric of a society. The predominant problem of economic growth in our day is the overcoming of economic stagnation, which normally takes place through a process of industrialization. In most recorded cases in which industrialization took place and led to a level of self-sustaining growth, this phase of economic development was initiated by a rapidly "explosive" period which, in concordance with Rostow, we may call the take-off. The rapid structural and organizational changes affecting the productivity of a society which take place during the take-off phase are made possible because in a previous phase social institutions were created which allow the successful overcoming of supply bottlenecks, chiefly in the field of capital formation and the availability of a number of highly skilled and specialized services. The creation of these social institutions in turn, especially the "institutionalization" of entrepreneurship, i.e., an innovating uncertainty-bearing activity, requires the establishment of a social framework within which these new institutions can exist and expand. In the last resort, we may thus have to answer the question of how such a social framework develops or is brought about by conscious design.

The answer to this question must be based on a general theoretical understanding of the nature of social and cultural change and, so far as I am aware, no general theory of social change which is universally accepted by sociologists exists as yet. It is clearly impossible for a non-specialist to develop such a theory, but from the existing literature some general hints of what are some of the main points in this process of theorizing may be gleaned. Among these pieces of a theory of change, three concepts and their implications appear to be most significant for our problem. These are the appearance of behavioral deviance, the emergence of cultural or social marginality, and the process of redefinition of societal objectives by an elite. I have discussed these processes more extensively in another place and shall confine myself here, therefore, to presenting merely a sketch.[4]

Let us first turn to a brief consideration of social deviance. Although it may occur in many fields of social action, we are concerned here primarily with those forms of deviant behavior which are relevant for economic activity and organization. Now if the concept of deviance is to have operational meaning, it cannot be interpreted as signifying simply behavior which is new, but it must imply that this set of innovating acts is opposed in some way to existing social norms or approved forms of behavior. In other words, a deviant always engages in behavior which constitutes a breach of the existing order and which is either contrary to, or at least not positively weighted in, the hierarchy of existing social values. If we apply this concept to the behavior displayed by businessmen and merchants in the course of the economic development of Western Europe, we find that we can speak of genuine deviance in those periods and societies in which entrepreneurial behavior did not belong in the category of social actions which were considered as constituting the "good life." As late as the fifteenth century this was true of financial entrepreneurship, which was always tainted by the official opposition against usury. And later, when financial entrepreneurship became fully respectable, industrial entrepreneurship came to be regarded with some disdain because it dirtied one's hands. These sentiments toward business or financial activity as not

quite proper for a gentleman to carry on are familiar in many underdeveloped countries today. For this reason, deviant behavior is often exercised by persons who, in some sense, are marginal to society. In medieval Europe the earliest moneylenders were often foreigners. In Italy at the time of Gothic and Langobard rule, they were Syrians, Jews, and Byzantines. Later when Italians turned to financial entrepreneurship on a large scale, the Genoese and Pisans, Sienese and Florentines, who were all lumped together under the name of "Lombards," became the financial entrepreneurs north of the Alps.

The role of marginal individuals in various economic pursuits in many underdeveloped countries is eminently manifest today. One could cite the Chinese in various South Asian countries, the Indians in East Africa, and the widely scattered Lebanese who make their appearance as businessmen in West Africa, Latin America, and elsewhere in less advanced countries. We also should count a considerable number of American and other voluntary Western expatriates among this class of marginal individuals. Some who attempt to find an escape from their marginal position in the arts have tended to congregate on the Seine or the Arno, but those who find business more congenial are to be found all over Latin America and more recently also in many parts of Asia and Africa.

What is the mechanism which allows marginal individuals to perform the roles they apparently have so widely accepted? As Robert E. Park, the inventor of the concept and of the significance of social marginality, has stressed, marginal men are—precisely because of their ambiguous position from a cultural, ethnic, or social standpoint—very strongly motivated to make creative adjustments in situations of change, and, in the course of this adjustment process, to develop genuine innovations in social behavior. Although many of Park's very general propositions about marginality have been considerably re-

[4] Cf. my article "Sociological Approach to Economic Development," in Centro Nazionale di Prevenzione e Difesa Sociale, *Atti del Congresso Internazionale di Studio sul Problema delle Aree Arretrate* (Milan, 1955), pp. 755–778.

fined by subsequent researchers, the theory of social marginality has not advanced enough to supply sufficiently convincing evidence for the role it may play in the explanation of episodes of social deviance wherever they occur. Even if it is admitted that marginal individuals tend to make creative adjustments more often than to relapse into new or old orthodoxies, the record is not at all clear, and there are some students who warn us that marginal individuals are more prone than others to experience *anomie* and thus to become carriers of trends leading towards social disorganization rather than to innovations of a creative type.

In circumstances in which a certain amount of deviant behavior has been displayed, the establishment of a new social institution is invaluable. E. H. Carr, writing in a different context, expressed the opinion that "the ideal, once it is embodied in an institution, ceases to be an ideal and becomes the expression of a selfish interest, which must be destroyed in the name of a new ideal."[5] Carr here expresses succinctly the interaction between social deviance and the growth of institutions. Once a form of deviant behavior can find the shelter of an institution, it becomes routinized, it ceases to be deviant, and it tends to become an accepted mode of social action. But the institution in which it is "laid down" forms an advance post, so to speak, from which further deviance is possible. Thus the institutions which arose in Western Europe before the industrial revolution and in Japan before the Meiji restoration were already the end products of a process of social change; but they, in turn, made possible, by their very existence, further social and economic change.

Whether or not deviant social behavior will lead to new social institutions and the routinization of new forms of behavior depends upon a number of factors which we cannot discuss here in detail. However, it is clear that one of the most important

[5] Edward Hallet Carr, *The Twenty Years Crisis* (London, 1940), p. 92.

determinants of the relative success of deviance will be the system of sanctions which exist in a society. Such sanctions may be internalized, i.e., they may reside ultimately in the values and beliefs of people; or they may be external sanctions, i.e., they may be imposed by individuals in power, by the elite, against actual or would-be deviants. In imperial China, it appears that both types of sanctions were very strong. In pre-Meiji Japan, internal sanctions had broken down in some areas and the power of the *shogun* had decreased sufficiently so that many external sanctions were not adequate to prevent the formation of new institutions, or at least of their rudiments.

But it is clear from what has been said that the over-all strength and multiplicity of sanctions is an important determinant of the forms of deviance which are possible and successful, the kinds of persons (marginal or nonmarginal individuals) who may engage in deviant action, and the speed with which deviance will result in new social institutions. Moreover, we should remember that sanctions rest with a different force upon different individuals in a society and that often the position in the social scale which a person occupies determines the degree to which he is subject to internal or external sanctions. We may then distinguish two cases in which change is slow because sanctions against deviance are strong. One is the case of an authoritarian regime in which external sanctions are strong and in which deviant behavior is often reserved for outsiders or marginal persons. The autocratic empires of antiquity and the medieval period roughly conformed to this picture, although in all these instances the force of external sanctions was buttressed by a vigorous system of widely accepted social values which constituted supporting internal sanctions.

The other case—which is of greater importance for us—is the country in which internal sanctions against social change among the masses of the people are quite strong and in which the members of the elite wish to employ this for whatever societal objects they favor. As long as an elite is interested primarily in maintaining its own position of power and privilege, this may mean that the masses are degraded, that economic progress is slow, and that general poverty prevails. But in a few cases the members of the elite have reinterpreted the social objectives to lie in the direction of economic progress. This, I believe, was one of the main changes in Japan after the Meiji restoration, and it appears to be paramount in many underdeveloped countries of today.

In general, the outward aspects of social transformation occurring under the impact of deviance, as against one taking place through a reorientation of social objectives on the part of an existing elite, will vary. The second type of social change may be more "orderly"; rather than developing entirely new institutions, new meaning may be given to existing old ones; and whereas in the former process industrialization will be preceded normally by a substantial alteration in relations between social classes, this will not take place, or only to a smaller extent, in the second case. For example, the basic social relations in Japan have changed singularly little from the time it was a quasifeudal empire based primarily upon agriculture to the present when it is a predominantly industrial nation. Similarly, in some underdeveloped countries, where the development effort is spearheaded by the governmental elite, rigorous controls are often exercised to prevent social disorganization of various forms from setting in or taking on major proportions.

Since the development of new institutions by means of deviance has usually been outside the control and often even in opposition to the aims of the elite, it has been designated as an autonomous process.

It also has involved conflict, and in Marxian theory it was described as a dialectic process called forth by the intrinsic historical forces of the class struggle. The alterations of social institutions by the elite, on the other hand, may be designated as a process of induced or planned change and, depending upon the distribution of power within a society, may proceed at a controlled rate. Moreover, in a system of induced change, some influence may be exerted on the timing with which new social institutions are created or old ones imbued with new meanings. Thus the clear distinction between a preparatory period for a take-off which could be relatively easily identified for countries with autonomous patterns of social and economic change becomes blurred in a country with induced change. Nevertheless, it appears that even in conditions in which social and economic change is controlled very tightly, the function of new institutions to influence changes in social behavior must not be overlooked with impunity. This seems to indicate that ultimately a theoretical system may have to be evolved in which the interrelations between the various processes determining institutions embodying social change are elucidated. We have more precise knowledge on the manner in which deviance leads to the establishment of new social institutions than on the process of how this is attained by methods of induced social change, because the former can be studied on the example of the social and economic history of Western countries. There, numerous sources exist, and the process has been going on for centuries. It would be an important step forward in our understanding of the noneconomic aspects of economic development if we could develop more certain knowledge of these processes as they occur presently in situations of induced economic growth.

SOME SOCIAL AND CULTURAL ASPECTS OF ECONOMIC DEVELOPMENT

Manning Nash

The aim of this paper is to replace the omnibus category of an "undeveloped country or region" with a set of concepts which discriminates among the existing varieties. The diagnostic scheme is based on social and cultural features of low per-capita income populations. Three assumptions underlie the rationale of procedure:[1]

1. Long stagnant or slow-growing economies require structural change to develop rapidly, and structural change is a form of social and cultural transformation.

2. Undeveloped regions differ in their susceptibility and resistance to the process of social transformation from a state of relatively slow growth to a state of self-sustained growth.

3. A specification of social and cultural variables indicates differential strategies for different kinds of undeveloped societies.

To decide which social and cultural aspects of a society are relevant for the diagnosis of its particular condition of poverty requires steering between two

SOURCE. Manning Nash, "Some Social and Cultural Aspects of Economic Development," *Economic Development and Cultural Change*, 7: 137–150, January, 1959. Reprinted by permission of The University of Chicago Press. Copyright 1959 by The University of Chicago Press.

---

[1] I take as given the resource base, the physical environment, and other technical-economic factors. The two sets of data—techno-economic and socio-cultural—of course must always be combined in a single model, if sense is to be made of any case. The matter of relative vs. absolute growth, as well as ways of relating the techno-economic to the socio-cultural, is discussed by C. P. Kindleberger, *Process of Economic Development*, New York, 1958, Chs. 1–3.

poles of analysis. On the one hand is the anthropological empiricism of building up culture areas by the mapping or plotting of discrete cultural traits, complexes, or patterns; on the other is the *Ideal typenstellung* which divides the world into the polarities of "modern" versus "traditional." Both procedures yield analytically useful classifications. Certainly at one level of analysis, the anthropological contention that social life is some kind of organized whole and that no part of a people's life may be ignored in analysis is relevant for the study of social change. Similarly, the ideal type provides a few clear-cut themes by which the empirical diversity may be ordered and held in the mind, while the significant questions about interdependence of parts may be posed.

I seek to balance between empirical complexity and analytical simplification by developing a notion of the areas of social and cultural life most intimately related to and strategic for social change in the direction of increased wealth and income. My procedure is to describe a series of cultural patterns and social structures at a level of abstraction which permits their identification in more than one society or one culture. The notion or model I offer is diagnostic, i.e., it is a provision for organizing concepts which can discriminate between existing varieties of underdevelopment, but which is still close enough to reality to encompass a wide variety of data. The cultural and social features of relevance to this scheme are of two kinds: (1) those which current theory indicates are most pertinent and relevant for the understanding of social change, and (2) those commonly taken to be intimately connected with the structure and dynamics of the economic subsystem of a society. I shall use, illustratively, material from Burma and Cambodia, so that a categorization on the basis of the concepts can be inspected.

A relatively voluminous body of literature, both analytic and descriptive, is concerned with the relation of economic development to its antecedent and subsequent cultural change. There are statements that the general nature of the social transformation involved in economic development is contingent upon changes in social structure. These structural shifts are from functionally particular allocation of economic roles, functional diffuseness in carrying out such roles, ascription criteria in the attainment of the roles, to the polar opposite set, i.e., universalistic, specificity, achievement, and collectivity features. Levy has, for example, applied this schema to China and Japan and finds that variations in the development of the two nations are related to these variables.[2] Hoselitz has modified Levy's ideas and generalized about the process of economic growth in terms of these aspects of social structure.[3] But such a schema will not perform the task set in this paper, for as Hagen notes, shifts in the "pattern variables" are never specified in amount or degree and perhaps cannot be empirically stipulated.[4]

If we move from the most general statements, as exemplified above and manifested in various other general theories,[5] to the literature which takes a more empirical bent by listing factors of society and culture thought to be related to economic development, we find no systematic or consistent interpretation of the way in which different social and cultural arrangements affect development. Kindleberger makes a careful survey of a good part of the anthropological and sociological literature on the inhibiting or facilitating role in economic development of one or another social feature, but arrives at no determinate system of grading the variables.[6] Another attempt to survey some of the literature treating specific social and cultural factors in economic development is found in Shannon.[7] This work is a reflection of the vast amount of information, partial theory, and speculation which has grown up about the attempts to relate the technical-economic variables in economic growth to the social-cultural aspects of the process.

Drawing on this literature and asserting without further documentation the consensual areas of knowledge about the social and cultural factors involved in economic development, I shall build my intermediate diagnostic scheme.

Economic development is a discontinuous process which, following Rostow, Hoselitz, and others, has been divided into three stages. The central period is a stage of "take-off," the break with the relatively stagnant or slow-growing economic past. Prior to the "take-off" period is a time of building resources and skills, while subsequent to the take-off is a state of self-sustained growth.[8]

[2] Marion J. Levy, Jr., "Some Sources of the Vulnerability of the Structures of Relatively Non-Industrialized Societies to Those of Highly Industrialized Societies," in Bert F. Hoselitz, ed., *The Progress of Underdeveloped Areas*, Chicago, 1952, pp. 113–125; and "Contrasting Factors in the Modernization of China and Japan," in Simon Kuznets, W. E. Moore, and J. J. Spengler, eds., *Economic Growth: Brazil, India, Japan*, Durham, N.C., 1956, pp. 496–536.
[3] Bert F. Hoselitz, "Social Structure and Economic Growth," *Economia Internazionale*, **6**, 3 (August 1953), 52–72.
[4] Everett E. Hagen, "The Process of Economic Development," *Economic Development and Cultural Change*, **5**, 3 (April 1957), 193–215.

[5] W. A. Lewis, *The Theory of Economic Growth*, Homewood, Ill., 1955; and W. W. Rostow, *The Process of Economic Growth*, New York, 1952.
[6] Kindleberger, *op. cit., passim.*
[7] Lyle W. Shannon, *Underdeveloped Areas*, New York, 1957.
[8] W. W. Rostow, "The Take-Off into Self Sustained Growth," *Economic Journal*, **66**, 261 (March 1956), 25–48; and Bert F. Hoselitz, "Noneconomic Factors in Economic Development," *American Economic Review*, **47**, 2 (May 1957), 28–41.

It is generally conceded that the "take-off" is led by a particular segment of society, either an elite, as in Japan,[9] or a class blocked in social or economic mobility, as in the rise of the bourgeoisie in Western Europe. The success of the dissident social segment and elitist reorientation of goals is closely tied to the group's administrative abilities and to their skills in enlisting the energies and sentiments of a good part of the population in a program of development (or, less likely, their ability to distribute or allocate rewards and benefits which will serve as self-evident attractions for new economic activity). If we accept the widely held and frequently repeated generalization that economic development involves some industrialization and some use of new technology, then part of the process is dependent upon the relations of the developing region to the developed countries, in which the technology, industry, and skill for mechanization is to be found and from whom they must, at least initially, borrow heavily.

Taking the above as true, or at least as highly probable, it is possible to consider economic development as a process of social and cultural change. The process of economic development is analytically composed of three linked kinds of social action: (1) the choice to institute changes and to seek greater wealth and income; (2) the bringing together of the means and facilities to implement the choice; and (3) the organization of social and cultural life so that growth is a built-in feature of the social system. This conceptualization of the process defines the social and cultural features connected with development: what in a people's life is likely to lead to a choice for social change in the direction of development? How are human and nonhuman resources aggregated or developed? What mode of social integration is possible as an emergent for self-sustained growth?

Since social and cultural change is a function of the alternatives generated by a given social system, and different groups or individuals are differentially situated in the social structure, there exists in any society a variety of realistic impulses to change.[10] The first cultural feature to be considered in terms of a social decision to undertake development is the pattern of stratification. If the wealth, power, and prestige of a society is strongly polarized between two groups with relatively little mobility between them, it appears that social change on the structural level is unlikely and that new economic opportunities will not be a chief concern of the dominant group and hardly even a perception of the subordinate group. There is, of course, the instance of the dominant group of a society becoming the subordinate group in relations between societies, but the proposition still holds that if the width of the gap is great, the perception of new economic opportunity is not likely. To make this concrete, consider Burma.[11] In Burma, the elite is based in urban locales and characterized by an incipient class system on Western lines. This group is dominant over a rural peasantry of some 16 millions. But there are channels of social mobility between classes in the cities, and from countryside to town. Educational institutions, both religious and secular, offer means of moving up the hierarchy, and there exists a fairly defined mode of social mobility. Burma, then, is a society with some social mobility, incomplete polarization of wealth, power, and prestige, and therefore has the social environment to induce some group to seek social and cultural change. Cambodia,[12] as another example from the same

---

[9] W. W. Lockwood, *The Economic Development of Japan*, Princeton, 1954.

[10] Manning Nash, "The Multiple Society in Economic Development: Mexico and Guatemala," *American Anthropologist*, **59**, 5 (October 1957), 825–833.

[11] The information on Burma is taken from Frank N. Trager *et al.*, *Burma*, New Haven, 1956, 3 vols.

[12] The material on Cambodia comes from David J. Steinberg, *Cambodia: Its People, Its Society, Its Culture* (Country Survey Series), New Haven, 1957.

area, exhibits a pattern of stratification like Burma's but with the added complication of an inherited nobility, in some conflict with the urban segments seeking development. Burma's path on structural grounds should be easier than Cambodia's, though the resistance to change in Cambodia is not likely to be extreme.

Apart from the gradation of stratification, though intertwined with it, is the system of social values which justify, explain, and define social position and the means of attaining it. Value systems are hierarchies of related propositions tied directly to, but not determined by, the experiential world of the members of a society. Value hierarchies change over time in the relative importance of given values and in the emergence of new values and the loss or modification of old ones. The repetitiveness over time of patterns of social action is in part a condition for the stability of the value aspect of the social system. Since both Burma and Cambodia have been under foreign domination and both have recently won independence, we may expect, and in fact find, that given this value hierarchy, the elite is able to emphasize goals of economic development and to incorporate new aspirations. The indices of values conducive to development (here combined with the stratification aspect) are these:

1. Conflicting religious systems, philosophies, and world views in a society indicate the malleability of the value complex and the fact that experience may be variably determined.

2. If the prevailing distribution of wealth, power, and prestige is in some contradiction to the value pattern, then social change and new economic patterns are likely to find sanction among a sizeable segment.

Both Burma and Cambodia are Theravada Buddhist countries, and the overwhelming majority of the population is Buddhist. Buddhism's other-worldliness is not in conflict with success in this world, and the twelve-fold path has many roads which may lead to development. In addition to the religious ideology is the presence of Western beliefs in material progress, combined with socialist and nationalist ideologies resulting from the wars for independence. In Burma, there is a social group in the cities aiming to bring about an economically abundant "welfare state." In Cambodia, too, there exists the range of values which would permit accumulation of wealth. A French-trained civil service and middle class aspires to greater income and more industry. In both countries, then, there are "spearhead" groups for economic development. It must be remembered that the "spearhead" group confronts or is in relation to social segments only partially sharing its values or viewing the desirability of social change from the same perspective. Therefore, a further stipulation on the nature of social and normative cleavage is necessary to assess the potential for change and economic growth. A social segment whose conditions of mobility involve others in the society rising in the social scale (either by recruitment, as in the European experience, or by abolition of inherited obstacles to mobility, as India is doing, in part) stands a better chance of perceiving and acting upon new economic opportunity simply because the social risk is less. In this connection, a nationalist ideology, or drives to nationalist integration and incorporation of diverse cultural traditions, provides a potent impulse toward change and development as a course of action; however, it may inhibit the successful organization of growth.

In Burma, the elite group interested in development is in a position to symbolize the aspirations of the whole nation. The organization of the elite group, with its close ties between secular and religious offices, effectively communicates the nationalist, development ideology to the rural peasantry. Buddhism is the vehicle of symbolic identification between the mass of peasants and the development-oriented urban elite. In Cambodia, the elite group is less well organized, and the effective development and transmission of development ideologies is less.

In forging a national consciousness oriented toward development goals, Burma appears slightly more advanced than Cambodia. The economically powerful Chinese minorities are more closely integrated into the economic and administrative structure of Burma than they are in Cambodia. Efforts are being made (in the directions of expulsion and xenophobia) in Cambodia to lessen the dependence of the rural peasantry on the Chinese commercial segment, but so far, the native elite is not well enough organized, socially or ideologically, to modify the structure greatly. The social and cultural pluralism of Cambodian society is greater than that of Burman society, and the national identification of Cambodians is apparently less than in Burma. Consequently, the spatial spread of development drives is more restricted in Cambodia, as is the extent of the market.

It must be repeated that *no* particular cluster of stratification or value patterns is, per se, inhibiting to social change or economic development—all societies change over time, and most social changes have repercussions in the levels of living. What is here maintained is that societies need differing magnitudes of economic opportunity and social rewards before some members are willing or able to emphasize an aspect of their value system leading to development. Burma has a slight edge over Cambodia, though both societies would fall in the same general class.

Given the social decision to undertake social change and development, how can the segment which is the leading group get sufficient means to significantly alter the level of living? This is usually phrased as the problem of capital formation in underdeveloped areas. There are really three problems subsumed in the notion of capital formation: (1) amount of savings, (2) form of savings, and (3) channelling savings into productive investments. The amount of savings is firstly a function of the absolute level of wealth of a society, and secondly of the values and institutions of a culture in relation to patterns of consumption, time perspective, and agencies of accumulation. A poor country produces relatively little which is available for uses other than direct personal consumption: its time perspective of investment is likely to be short and the agencies of aggregation rudimentary. Small peasant farmers, if they make up the bulk of the economically active population, as they do in Burma and Cambodia, do not as individual family or economic units have a large enough level of wealth to permit significant savings. To the extent that a farming family is heavily weighted on the subsistence side of production, as against the exchange side, its savings, whatever the level, do not come in the form which is useful or available for reinvestment in technical progress.

Given the size, number, and kind of economic units operating in Burma and Cambodia, we must weight farm families on a subsistence-exchange ratio. Non-farm economic units must also be weighted by the attractions for them in investment in productive channels.[13]

It is plain that a great deal of saving does in fact go on in any society of national size. But the problem is that savings come in such relatively small doses that they do not usually provide the basis for important reinvestment which would significantly alter the share of the national product reinvested.

The desire to save—the so-called ethic of abstemious living, or puritanical expenditure pattern—is part of a society's value system. No group in the recorded cultures of man saves for the act of saving. Saving is a function of the ends-in-view of the receivers of income. In both Burma

---

[13] But see the ingenious use of such an index for a Nigerian community by Michael G. Smith, *The Economy of Hausa Communities of Zaria* (Colonial Research Studies No. 16), London, 1955, *passim*, but especially pp. 139 ff.

and Cambodia, farm familes are anchored in small communities. In these rural communities, income is subjected to communal claims in the form of forced loans, feasts, and status maintenance activities. These claims on production are more important, I believe, in reducing the savings available for non-consumption investment, than is the miscalled "extended family." The emphasis on the dilution of incentive to save because individuals are involved in wider networks of kinsmen than they are in our society is a product of armchair anthropology, rather than the result of research. For example, Belshaw indicates that extended families may be important in the initial aggregation of capital and also in the channelling of investment.[14] To put it as generally as possible, in view of the fragmentary empirical data, much of the rural farming section of Burma and Cambodia does not now accumulate capital because: (1) low absolute level of production; and consequently (2) low savings; and those savings made are (3) claimed by communal expenditure or status obligations; (4) so that capital form is of a kind not easily alienated from the economic unit, or oriented toward technical and economic progress.

In the nonrural, nonfarming sectors, rates of saving are higher, but the size of the economic units makes the absolute level of any given firm rather small, thereby inhibiting its ability to bear risk or to promote long-range investment. The agencies for accumulating capital—the joint stock company, the limited liability form of ownership, the stock and securities market, the central banking system—are not well developed or widespread in either Burma or Cambodia. Significant lumps of capital are hard to come by, relative to the amount of savings which the gross national product might indicate. The more developed are the

institutions for aggregating large amounts of capital, the closer is a society to the take-off period. Burma's development corporation, part of the national administrative apparatus, is more highly organized than Cambodia's and serves as a more efficient agency of planning and capital aggregation.

Obviously, the government of underdeveloped countries provides one of the chief agencies for the aggregation of capital and for the provision of the legal basis for the emergence of forms of organization capable of forming capital. The government has recourse to development corporations, banking systems, monetary control, taxation, and confiscation.

The abilities of governments to carry out any of the possible measures open to them depends, in large part, on the degree and kind of national integration. Therefore, the extent to which the territory under consideration is in fact welded into a society by a set of conventional understandings is crucial. The greater the social cleavages in terms of cultural definitions as to the ends to be sought, the more difficult it is for a government to perform the aggregating functions of capital formation, and the more difficult it is for a governing group to provide the legal and institutional basis for the private formation of capital.

In societies like Burma and Cambodia, the government has the problem of initiating and sustaining drives to national integration. The task is one of creating a national culture and forming a national society from a plurality of cultural traditions and semi-locally organized societies. The large Chinese and Indian minorities, the rural peasants, the hill tribes, and the urban elites occupy the same territory, but they do not form yet a single society. Burma is a better integrated national entity than is Cambodia, but still the ability to levy on the production of the peasantry is not well developed. Consequently, the government invests money in activities and organizations only tangentially related to economic development, but

[14] C. S. Belshaw, *In Search of Wealth*, Memoir No. 80 of the *American Anthropologist*, Menasha, Wis., 1955.

symbolically or politically important in developing a national consciousness. Investment by government in the means of coercion—armies, police, bureaucracies—in order to maintain power over cultural and social diversity, or to carry out programs of taxation or confiscation, is often a severe drain on limited resources. The closer ties in Burma between the religious agencies and development agencies, as compared to Cambodia, indicates greater possibilities for making palatable to the run of Burmans the sacrifices in immediate consumption for development ends.

The rate of savings, then, the form of savings, and whether or not it goes into productive channels is intimately tied to the social and cultural aspects of a nation, but there is no easy rule for the *ex ante* identification of the institutional locus for promoting or inhibiting savings, for their form, and for their allocation, to ends conducive to further growth. But to date, the urban elite of Burma appears to be in a better position vis-à-vis their cultural diversity than is that of Cambodia.

The third category of social action in economic development is the organization of economic activity for self-sustained growth. The relevant dimensions are of two kinds: (1) the development of persons and organizations who will either invent or adapt new technology and new economic organization; and (2) the spread of the market and the increase of scale of productive enterprise. In these two categories are a host of variables—from schools, books, research institutes, literacy, public health, managerial skills, and labor force commitment; to the provision of roads, uniform currency, weights, and measures, and the reduction of the use of fraud and coercion in business transactions.

The motivational order of self-sustained economic growth is not stressed here, since it is assumed that if levels of living are raised, there will be commitment to the higher level. What the organization of economic development means is the creation of the environment in which continu-

ally improved inputs, human and non-human, are applied to the productive process as a matter of course. The social structures and cultural patterns which foster this are extremely variable theoretically and probably empirically exhibit a wide range.

In Burma, there exists the tradition of learning, of literacy, and of scholarship. The government is stressing literacy oriented toward some of the literature of daily life and work, rather than the esoteric and religious materials which formerly made up the content of Burmese literacy. In Cambodia, the literacy rate is less and the tradition not as widespread. Emphasis on secular learning is something almost exclusively tied to the urban areas.

The government organization involved in providing this social organization of development must prevent the rise of internal monopoly which restricts the market size and creates a larger zone of technological indifference. The royal-client organization of the Cambodian government seems a less promising instrument for these tasks than does the rudimentary parliamentary system of Burma. The danger in both countries is one of bureaucratic commitment to the maintenance of non-economic but state-run or sponsored industry.

The argument has now come full circle—from the conditions under which development is likely to become a goal, to the circumstances which make it self-sustaining. I should like to restate the argument and provide a graphic profile of Burma and Cambodia. Several caveats must be entered, lest serious misunderstanding ensue. There is small probability of a theory of economic development and cultural change which can be stated at a level relevant for action. Given the nature of social causation as "cumulative," the particular constellation of social and cultural features in a given society is the relevant dimension of analysis, rather than the general order of social integration.

This scheme is a way of picking from the welter of social facts those most intimately associated with economic development and cultural change. It offers a first approximation to ordering social and cultural features in a manner consistent with interpreting the major sources of stability and lability in a society.

To assess a society's potential for economic development in terms of meaningful alternatives, these are the diagnostic social and cultural features:

1. *The Pattern of Social Stratification*

(*a*) The more extreme the polarization of wealth, power, and prestige between classes or social segments, the less likely is new economic opportunity to be perceived or acted upon.

(*b*) The more restricted the channels of social mobility between the top group and the segment just under it, the greater the possibility of the latter group seeking new means of mobility.

(*c*) The greater the gap between the legitimate sanctioned means of attaining wealth and the actual ways in which current holders of wealth have attained it, the greater likelihood of accepting structural change.

(*d*) The more frequent the recruitment of lower class members into upper class strata by merit or achievement, the larger the opportunity for seeking development.

2. *The Value System*

(*a*) The more there are competing ideologies and philosophies, the easier it is to win commitment to development.

(*b*) The greater the stress on nationalism, the more probable it is that development can be made one of the national goals.

(*c*) The greater the value agreement between different segments of the elite, the easier it is to transmit development values.

(*d*) The more varied the definition of the same general complex, from social segment to social segment, the less the social risk for an elite group in emphasizing the

manipulative or material gain aspects of the value complex conducive to development.

3. *The Economic Subsystem*

(*a*) The more economic units are weighted on the subsistence side of production and the more they are anchored in local, communal organizations, the more difficult it is for them to save or for savings to take a form useful for rapid development.

(*b*) The lower the level of absolute wealth, the shorter the time perspective of investment, the more difficult it is to secure capital for long-run projects.

(*c*) The more developed and varied the agencies of accumulation (joint stock companies, securities markets, central bank, etc.), the more likely that significant amounts of capital can be productively channelled.

(*d*) The less the market or segments of it are monopolized, the greater the possibility of new investment.

(*e*) The more the holders of wealth are actually involved in the business of production, the more likely they are to respond to new economic opportunities.

4. *The Political Subsystem*

(*a*) The greater the sovereignty of the government over its territory without the use of coercive instruments, the easier is a program of development.

(*b*) The more organized the group holding political power, the easier it is to embark on development programs.

(*c*) The greater the allegiance of persons in the territory to ideas of nation and central government, the more likely that development can be undertaken.

(*d*) The greater the width of recruitment into political office, the more likely that development can be organized.

(*e*) The less the ideological cleavage in the elite, the greater the possibility of bureaucratic or noneconomic goals (too great a cleavage results in civil war and, of course, no development).

These rubrics are offered as a preliminary way of gauging the social and cultural aspects relevant to economic development and cultural change. Charting or interpreting a given social system according to this scheme is a subtle, unstandardized, and as yet not very reliable operation. The difficulty of stating the range of alternatives to action in a social system is enormous: and this difficulty is increased, rather than lessened, because social scientists cannot assess alternatives without getting into complex action and application programs which involve value and political choices extraneous to research as it is now conceived. Lastly, the notion of "economic development" is not a self-justifying one, and the various social and cultural costs people are willing to pay for material improvement is an open question, since no one is able to specify what sacrifices are involved in one or another course.

The accompanying diagrams are a first approximation to making a cultural and social profile of a given society in terms of the variables enumerated above.[15] Burma and Cambodia, according to the

[15] See figures.

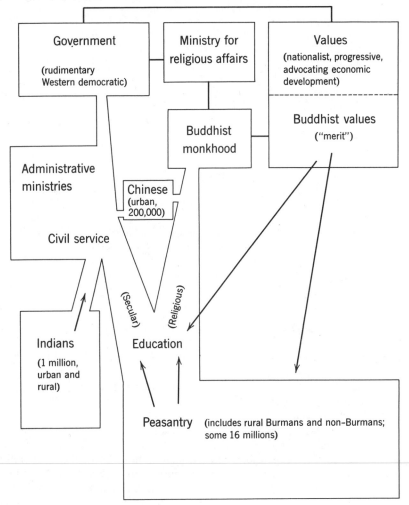

Figure 1. Generalized social profile of Burma.

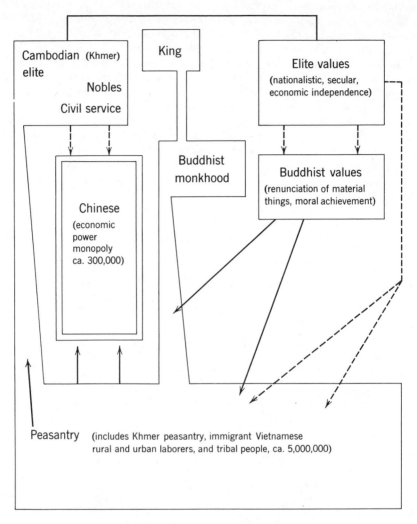

Figure 2. Generalized social profile of Cambodia.

profile, belong to the same "species" as far as economic development potential is concerned. Nonetheless, for reasons stated in the text, Burma's path appears to be less precarious than Cambodia's.

Whether or not this categorization is more than a function of theory and is worthy of the further expansion and elaboration it so obviously requires can only be resolved by empirical work, oriented to the end of examining and specifying alternatives generated by different societies and cultures. Such a research task is on the agenda of anthropology, and perhaps of history.

Appendix

Across the top of the diagrams, it is shown how the elites are divided into two organizations—the political and religious. Connected to these are their corresponding values. Emanating from the elite's structural blocks are the channels of mobility, which depict the hierarchical ladder connecting these sectors to the base of the population—the peasantry.

It should be noted that there is a wide difference between the social structure of the rural peasant communities and that of the urban populations. In both countries, the social organization of the rural villages is primarily based upon traditional age-sex and ascriptive statuses dependent upon kinship and residential criteria, while in the cities an incipient class structure is found which is similar to that found in Western societies. In both the rural and urban settings, however, educational achievement plays probably the most important role as the vehicle for mobility—the rural people beginning in the religious educational institutions and the urban workers in the secular institutions. Criteria of wealth are more important for urban-setting mobility. Thus, for simplicity, the diagrams depict the educational aspect of mobility into the political and religious spheres wherein reside the society's definitions of power and prestige.)

The integration into the social structure of the economically important minority populations in both nations is shown by their direct connections (or cleavages) with other segments and/or mobility among segments. Solid arrows from the value blocks[16] depict their effective trans-

[16] The idea of "value blocks" is a shorthand way of stressing the dominant canons of a complex world view.

mission to the peasantry, and broken arrows from the value blocks show that attempts are made to instill the more development-oriented values but are hindered by traditional ones.

Organizational contrasts in mobility via educational institutions are evident. The Burman pattern is more closely articulated than the Cambodian, indicating that Burman values are potentially in less conflict with rapid development. The more highly organized governmental agencies for economic development are found in Burma. The block for administration ministries and civil service has the possibility of being more task-oriented than the royal-client form of political organization obtaining in Cambodia. The economically important minority populations are incorporated into the administrative apparatus in Burma, while in Cambodia the economically powerful Chinese are isolated by strong social and cultural barriers from the rest of Cambodian society. The broken arrows from the Cambodian political elite to the Chinese signify that concerted efforts are being made to curtail the economic power of the Chinese, but to date the structure is not much modified. The solid arrows from the Cambodian peasantry to the Chinese minority show the real economic dependence of the peasantry on the Chinese for credit and commercial outlets.

Chapter 7

Industrialization and Urbanization

ACCEPTANCE OF INDUSTRIALIZATION AND ITS ATTENDANT CONSEQUENCES FOR THE SOCIAL PATTERNS OF NON-WESTERN SOCIETIES

George A. Theodorson

It is the main thesis of this paper that the industrialization of nonmachine societies will eventually lead to the development of new societal patterns.[1] These patterns will resemble, in time, certain dominant patterns of Western industrialized society, which *may not be rejected by any people who accept the machines of the West.*

The view that only very limited aspects of Western culture can be imported into the nonmachine societies while certain other "less desirable" aspects can be excluded is naive, unless it is based on an understanding of those aspects of culture which are independent of the industrial economic institution, and those which are inextricably tied up with it.

This discussion is pertinent today when many non-industrial societies are anxious to industrialize. A growing industrial plant is

SOURCE. George A. Theodorson, "Acceptance of Industrialization and Its Attendant Consequences for the Social Patterns of Non-Western Societies," *American Sociological Review*, **18**, 477–484, October 1953. Reprinted by permission of The American Sociological Association.

[1] The special case of the mechanization of agriculture will not be discussed here.

seen as security from economic want, economic imperialism, and military threats. In the short run national pride may encourage deliberate policies to perpetuate old customs and beliefs side by side with the new importations. Some of these short range compromises with the old social system may run against the long range interests of the national leaders.

Knowing what must accompany industrialization would save time, money, and effort, and prevent confusion. Any attempt by planners to stop an inevitable social change accompanying industrialization at the same time that industrialization is being encouraged, will increase disorganization and make it impossible for them to achieve their goals. On the other hand, knowledge of what need not change may be used to soften the impact of industrialization, appease vested interests to some extent, and intelligently blend the new with the old. This paper will contribute only indirectly to the solution of the latter problem.

The first half of the discussion will deal with the disorganizing effects of the change in social relationships engendered by the participation of members of a non-industrial society in activity oriented to modern machines. The second half of the paper will deal with the new patterns of social relationships which will develop in relation to the demands imposed by the machine.

Disintegration of Certain Aspects of the Old Order

"Every society is an organized entity. ... New technological practices are disruptive to such entities. . . ."[2] Thus social disorganization is a short range result of the decline of the old system.

One important change which will occur in a society with the introduction of industrialization will be the creation of new roles. These new roles are predominantly economic in nature—thus introducing an entirely new pattern of behavior into a society. Previously there had been no predominantly economic roles. Economic behavior was performed in roles which integrally combined other institutions with the economic. In non-industrialized and especially non-literate societies economic ". . . forms which we differentiate quite sharply are not only indistinguishable, but in many instances are so intimately linked with the non-economic institutions that we can only discern them at all by giving the closest attention to their economic role."[3]

This separation of the economic functions from a totally integrated system, would throw the entire system into a state of disequilibrium. All role behavior in an integrated system of human interaction tends to maintain and support other aspects of the system. The indigenous power structure is weakened through its loss of control over the economic sanctions. "Schapera describes the influence of money economy

upon the family system of the Kgatla, a Bantu people of Bechuanaland. Here . . . the marriage was arranged by the elders. But with urban employment the sons were released from economic dependence upon the fathers, they were given physical separation from the cultural system, and their marriages were perforce delayed. All three factors combined to make the youth act independently in seeking a marriage partner, to undermine the authority of the parental generation, and to lessen materially the unity of the family as system of interdependence."[4]

Another factor which further disrupts the old system is the decline of certain old roles, such as skilled craftsmen and magicians. This development would incur the opposition of those individuals whose positions are challenged. This was true in the case of the Kgatla cited above.[5]

It may be hypothesized that the conservatism encountered in the form of opposition to industrialization is to a considerable degree resistance on the part of those who expect to lose most from the changes, and not alone due to the resistance of deep seated values. This interpretation may be implied from Wilbert E. Moore's discussion of the problems involved in recruiting indigenous labor for the factory.[6] The fears of the threatened members of the non-industrialized society are based on sound fact, and are not simply an irrational reaction to change. Not only are their skills declining in importance, but new facilities have been created which give their possessors new sources of instrumental power. The people who have gained the new facilities (monetary gains for the factory workers)[7] become economically independent of the old order.

The creation of new facilities leads to the development of new rewards. The

---

[2] Walter R. Goldschmidt, "The Interrelations Between Cultural Factors and the Acquisition of New Technical Skills," in Bert F. Hoselitz (ed.), *The Progress of Underdeveloped Areas*, Chicago: The University of Chicago Press, 1952, p. 139.
[3] Melville J. Herskovits, *Economic Anthropology*, New York: Alfred A. Knopf, 1952, p. 155.

[4] Goldschmidt, *op. cit.*, pp. 140–141.
[5] *Ibid.*, p. 141.
[6] Wilbert E. Moore, *Industrialization and Labor*, Ithaca: Cornell University Press, 1951, Ch. 2.
[7] It is assumed that there is no question of the fact that the use of money accompanies industrialization.

facilities themselves as signs of instrumental power become rewards to some extent.[8] For example, in the United States money, which is in reality a facility for instrumental activity, has come to be regarded as a reward and a source of direct gratification. In the newly industrializing society the new facilities of the factory workers consist primarily of skills, tools, and money. These facilities, having become rewards, place prestige and higher social status in the hands of new individuals in the society. It is not that these factory workers are supplanting the old elite, but they are rising above agricultural and craftsmen classes to which they were previously inferior, assuming that the poorest and lowliest people are the ones first attracted to the factory.[9] An individual making a choice will always seek to optimize his gratifications. Apparently the persons receiving the least gratifications under the old system will be the first to be attracted to the new possibilities.

Thus far we have discussed those facilities which have been introduced into the society for the first time by industrialization. However, there are elements in the old social system which had not been important previously, such as certain skills and resources, which now become significant. These skills and resources become more important as new symbols of prestige, at the same time that older symbols in the society are losing their former prominence. Thus certain aspects of the old system are discouraged by the introduction of the industrial system, while other aspects become more important. The industrial system tends to respect people who work with their hands, while ". . . in all the unmechanized civilizations the trader and the mechanic rank far down in the social scale."[10] The industrial system values even

more highly certain other skills such as executive and scientific abilities, but these mental skills are quite different from those possessed by the old elite.

The creation of new roles, new facilities, and new rewards, and the prominence of previously unimportant resources and skills, all tend to place new individuals in positions of power. The new power structure challenges the old, and later tends to produce a new elite. Even the common factory workers may come to have more power and influence than certain previously higher classes who remained in agricultural pursuits. This gain of power and influence is even more pronounced in the case of the entrepreneurs, especially when they rise from within the society, and are not merely foreign investors and managers.

Even if the new elite merely consists of members of the old elite this does not affect the analysis. The fact that they are the same individuals makes no difference, for they will have to have new attitudes, behavior, expectations, and values, in order to perform their new roles successfully. Thus from the point of view of the social system there is an entirely new elite. On the other hand, if the new elite consists of individuals who have risen from below and who seek to incorporate themselves into the old elite, they necessarily will modify the old elite in the process. They must maintain role behavior and orientations, compatible with their positions in the industrial system, which will not be the same as the traditional orientations and expectations of the old elite. In either case the analysis holds and the power structure of the society is modified.

A further development which is disruptive of the old order stems from the fact that industrialization always leads to the production of large quantities of cheap goods. Even in a country where a low wage policy prevails, the people will have enough money to buy at least some of the products of industrialization. The mass production of large quantities of cheap goods will make

[8] Talcott Parsons, *The Social System*, Glencoe, Illinois: The Free Press, 1951, p. 513.
[9] Moore, *op. cit.*, p. 304.
[10] Ralph Linton, "Cultural and Personality Factors Affecting Economic Growth," in Hoselitz, *op. cit.*, p. 85.

available to them material products which they never before dreamed of possessing. This will be true not only of the factory workers but also of those who have remained in agriculture, for the growing cities will provide an opportunity to sell surplus produce at a profit. This is an incentive to produce more, and the new agricultural techniques and implements make possible the additional production. This will extend to every village within the circle of the new industrialization. Thus some degree of improvement of the common people's standard of living will occur. However, in countries where a small group wishes, and is able, to keep most of the benefits of industrialization to itself, this improvement will not be very great. Low wages, systems of land ownership, and systems of taxation may keep the majority of the people poor. This situation of only slight improvement for the majority cannot last forever because industrialization eventually provides a greatly improved standard of living for everyone. It may, however, last for some time, long enough to create an explosive situation in the short run.

When people have for centuries held a fatalistic attitude, bad conditions are accepted, and this helps to maintain the stability of the social system. "In a society in which people regularly expect to be hungry annually, and in which traditions and proverbs accustom them to expect such a period of privation, their whole attitude toward economic effort is affected. . . . Among the Bamba scarcity is within the ordinary run of experience, and accepted as such."[11] Some degree of amelioration may open their thinking to the possibilities of even greater improvements, and, ironically, lead to impatience and general dissatisfaction. Thus the people of the areas we are trying to protect from Communism may become more receptive to the seemingly quick and easy solutions offered by the Communists. There should be a sensitivity to the potential dangers of a slow process

[11] Herskovits, *op. cit.*, pp. 293–294, quoted from Audrey J. Richards.

of aid to "underdeveloped areas" by those in charge of these programs.

In the section above the causes of the disintegration of the old order have been discussed. There are, however, certain forces tending to delay this disintegration, thus prolonging the period of disorganization. Among the most important of these is the continued emotional dependence of the workers on the old community. This emotional dependence will cause them to conform to some degree to the normative patterns of the community. This brings them under the influence of the embattled conservative leadership. Thus the emotional dependence provokes modes of orientation which slow down the adjustment of the native factory worker to the new industrial element in his environment. It must be emphasized that the advent of industrialization introduces only instrumental activities, and does not constitute a total functioning social system. When the native recruit is unhappy and discontented in the new factory situation it is not simply that he is nostalgic for the traditional atmosphere of his youth. Although there is this longing for the old way of life, a much more important and more elusive point is that man gains most of his satisfactions and feelings of security from a well rounded and integrated pattern of interaction. This means that he needs an orderly life based on mutual patterns of expectations that cover all phases of his activities within and without the immediate factory situation. The old patterns of interaction and patterns of expectations are inadequate in a system which involves an entirely different economic orientation. Thus social relationships are disrupted. There is a great deal of insecurity, and the morale and efficiency of the factory worker are greatly reduced.

A new social system is needed in the industrial community, a system which would integrate the new economic system with those aspects of the old culture which can be adjusted to industrialization. It should provide reasonably integrated patterns of action and expectations covering all interaction among individuals, no matter how close or how distant. Where the native population has no such integrated system of expectations, the period of adjustment will be longer than where one exists.

An interesting problem is posed here for those who wish to increase the efficiency of native labor, hasten their adjustment to the nonvillage life in the growing factory areas, and to increase the number of workers who come and stay at their new factory positions. The above analysis would imply that some ambitious planner should try to encourage the development of new patterns of expectations in the various institutions of the newly developing social system. This would demand first of all some knowledge of the form the institutions will have to take so that no patterns of expectations will be introduced or encouraged that would later interfere with the projected goals of industrialization envisaged by the national leaders of the "underdeveloped" countries. It is not within the scope of this paper to suggest methods of hastening the development of new patterns of expectations, but the general direction of this development will be discussed in the following section.

So far, the discussion has been concerned with the decline of the old order through the creation of new roles, new facilities, new rewards, and new sources of prestige and power. The resultant general picture of social disorganization presented above is not likely to remain permanently. There is a tendency to restore a relative equilibrium in any ongoing process of interaction.[12] Further changes will develop which will provide the basis for this new integration.

Reorganization of the Social System

The reorganization of the society can be analyzed in terms of four of Talcott Parsons' five pattern variables.[13] The thesis

[12] Parsons, *op. cit.*, pp. 481–482.
[13] Briefly the four pattern variables may be defined as follows: (1) *Specificity*—concern with only one aspect of a person; *diffuseness*—concern with the total person. (2) *Particularism*

advanced here is that an increase in universalism, achievement, suppression of immediate emotional release (affective-neutrality), and specificity all accompany industrialization in the long run. The remainder of this paper will be concerned with the dynamics of this development.

Industrialization means the introduction of machinery, and many leaders of nonindustrial societies have expressed the view that machines, and *only* machines are what they want from the industrial world. This is certainly an oversimplification of what industrialization means. Because machines are very expensive they necessarily must be used economically. In the early stages of industrialization labor is far less scarce than machinery. This means that there is a strong constraint on the part of those related to the industrial process to adjust labor to the machines. It is very difficult to tolerate inefficient use of the machines, insofar as this can be avoided. The necessity of teaching and enforcing these modes of adjustment demands a certain type of social organization. This social organization centered about the need to adjust to the machines in the factory system engenders certain unique social relationships. The native's first major change in the patterning of his relations to others is experienced in the factory situation.

—orientation to a person on the basis of some special relationship to him based on membership in a certain collectivity (e.g. a kinship grouping); *universalism*—orientation based on the possession of a certain attribute or attributes (achieved or ascribed) regardless of the particular person who possesses it. (3) *Achievement*—emphasis on actual performances of an individual; *ascription*—emphasis on certain qualities of an individual, either given at birth or automatically conferred later, regardless of performances. (4) *Affectivity*—giving open expression to immediate desires either to do or not to do something (immediate emotional release); *affective-neutrality*—suppressing immediate desires for a long range interest (suppression of emotional release).

The pattern variable of self-orientation vs. collectivity-orientation is not included in this paper. For a fuller discussion of the pattern variables see: Parsons, *op. cit.*, pp. 58–67.

The Necessity to Adjust to Machinery and its Effects on Social Organization[14]

The first adjustment a man has to make to machines is the long hours he has to spend away from his home community. The extent to which he is away from his old ties determines the degree to which his relationship toward them will change. A long period of the day goes by in a new social situation without the supervision of the old normative system. Furthermore, his relationship to his family changes from the old pattern of responsibilities and expectations which depended on his being with them a good deal of the day. Spending less time in his home community also means that the close relationships formerly possible cannot be the same. Since the immediate family is in the end the most intimate and most psychologically satisfying human group, the worker, with less time, will choose to spend proportionately more of that time with his immediate family, and less time with his extended family[15] and the others in the community. Devoting more of his waking hours to machines, then, means less time with his family, less time with his home community, and proportionately more time with his close family than with his neighbors. Because his constant close relations with his neighbors decrease substantially, his relations to them change. His relations are less diffuse, because he has less time to know them thoroughly. They are less particularistic because there are fewer groups in which he and his neighbors are integrated. Because he is dealing with relatively unfamiliar people on a specific-universalistic basis, his relations with them will be less emotionally involved.

Secondly, because the machines are expensive and complicated the individuals working with them must be selected on the basis of achievement.[16] Thus, in the factory situation achievement becomes dominant over ascription. The ability to run the machines is a specific demand, and diffuse standards become irrelevant. Thus the pattern variable of specificity is further strengthened. Furthermore, it is difficult to combine particularism and achievement as a general pattern. A person's cousin may not be as qualified as someone unrelated to him. It is impossible in the long run for the extended family to comprise the factory unit because the criteria for the old status system of the family will not fit the criteria of the factory (physical strength, dexterity, and the like). Achievement-universalism will be fostered not only by the demand for efficient labor for the expensive machines, but also by the demands imposed on the factory unit by competition from domestic or foreign competitors. The Japanese attempt to integrate the new industrial system with the old familial organization shows unmistakable signs of disintegration.[17]

Third, while in the non-industrialized

[14] In terms of M. J. Levy Jr.'s conceptual scheme as developed in *The Structure of Society*, this is an analysis of the functional requisites of the industrial system and the structural requisites (particularly of relationship structures) that logically and necessarily follow therefrom. This paper will particularly emphasize the derivation of the structural requisites from the functional requisites. Marion J. Levy, Jr., *The Structure of Society*, Princeton: Princeton University Press, 1952.

[15] Some writers have noted the disintegrating effect of industrialization on the extended family. Ralph Linton comments, "Modernization of the unmechanized culture, . . . cannot fail to weaken or even destroy joint family patterns." From Linton, *op. cit.*, p. 84. Talcott Parsons expresses the same view on pages 178 and 510 of *The Social System*.

[16] "Advanced degrees of industrialization greatly accentuate the importance of differences in ability on the part of individuals. . . . Slight differences in skill may be reflected in enormous differences in output under such circumstances. . . . The difference in damage that can be done by the relatively less skilled in highly industrialized situations as opposed to relatively non-industrialized ones is also enormous." Marion J. Levy, "Some Sources of the Vulnerability of the Structures of Relatively Non-Industrialized Societies to Those of Highly Industrialized Societies," in Hoselitz, *op. cit.*, pp. 120–121.

[17] Moore, *op. cit.*, pp. 30–31.

societies discipline is self-imposed, that of the industrial operative is imposed from outside. This routine is imposed on the worker because he is no longer self-employed, because the great expense of the machinery and fuel demands constant operation, and because of the demands for coordination imposed by the greater division of labor. One of the most serious problems facing the new factory in the underdeveloped area is that of absenteeism and labor turnover due to the reluctance of the workers to accept the new factory discipline.[18] The worker must do his work regardless of his private desires of the moment. Gratification must be postponed.

This continuous attention demanded by the machine and the restrictions thus imposed on the worker, in turn, led to a new kind of relationship between him and his superiors, and between him and his fellow workers. Before the introduction of the machine the relation of the individual member of the working group to those who possessed authority was diffuse. In the factory situation the relation of the individual toward his superiors becomes very specific. The superiors are only interested in those aspects of the individual which are relevant to the efficient use of the machines. This is one of the important changes in the relations of the worker which initiates the process of separating the economic from the other institutions in the social system.

In the factory situation the relations of the individual worker to his equals can no longer be based on the diffuse relations which existed when each member of a working group knew every other member as a total individual because of constant contact. The laborers in the factory spend a good deal of their time there, and the main contact they have with the majority of their fellow workers is in this context. All they know of the majority of their fellow workers is their achievements, skills, and personalities as production workers. Evaluations and adjustments are in terms of the factory system. Thus specificity is

[18] Moore, *op. cit.*, Ch. 5.

necessarily dominant. In Japan the attempt to maintain diffuse relationships in the factory system was possible only in the short run.[19] Strains were produced in the Japanese attempt to adapt the machine to their premachine society. These strains eventually led to the breakdown of the system of diffuse factory relations, and to an adjustment more consistent with a machine society which demands the separation of the economic from the other institutions.

Since the economic system has become separated from the other systems, economic considerations become of prime importance in judging individuals and allocating roles within the economic system. With further specialization of the industrial system only one particular skill becomes relevant. Thus, in selecting an electrician, only that skill is significant, and literary and artistic talents, religious and political beliefs, and sociability are not considered. Since instrumental activity is the only kind of performance demanded by these roles, diffuse and particularistic considerations are of no relevance to the individual's ability to perform the role satisfactorily. Although this specificity is not always complete in all situations in an industrial economy, still it is the dominant pattern and the accepted value.

A fourth effect of industrialization is a further growth of specificity due to a new orientation to a larger community. Mass production produces a huge quantity of goods which must be sold to a large and far flung number of people. It would be impossible to know all these people thoroughly—which would be necessary if diffuse standards were to apply. The modern market by its nature demands specific orientations. At the same time the scope of political power grows with industrialization and the authorities of a large nation cannot possibly deal with all citizens on the basis of diffuse standards. In addition, the vastness of the new economic and political relationships are as disruptive of particularism as they are of diffuseness. Time considerations alone

[19] Moore, *op. cit.*, pp. 30–31.

demand a universalistic orientation in the large modern market or nation.

Another impetus to the specificity-universalistic complex is the impersonality of the modern factory. This impersonality is due to the large size of the modern productive enterprise and also to the need for large amounts of capital, which in turn leads to the corporate system with its absentee stockholder owners. In the factory the managers and workers are for the most part strangers to each other, and this is certainly true of the owners and workers, who often never meet. The only kind of standards which can be used for allocation of roles in such a situation must be specific and universalistic.

Since the economic system is very important and generally the dominant system in an industrial society, its values tend to dominate the other systems. Levy writes, ". . . it is impossible to confine these patterns rigidly to the economic aspect of action. . . . Highly universalistic relations in the economic aspects of action are functionally incompatible with highly particularistic ones in the political (i.e. allocation of power and responsibility) aspects of action. It is because of such functional interrelationships among different spheres and aspects of action that these clusters of patterns seem on the whole to appear widely diffused in social systems rather than narrowly confined."[20]

The kinship system is an exception to the above analysis for by its nature it is diffuse, emotional, particularistic, and predominantly ascriptive.[21]

Conclusion

There may well be strong attempts on the part of the leaders of some of the industrializing countries to integrate some of the old patterns of human relationships into the newly developing industrial society. It is the opinion of the writer that some of the leaders of these non-industrial societies are in a sense marginal men, or men of two cultural systems. They are emotionally tied to the old system, but at the same time they are anxious to reap the benefits of a system which promises to relieve some of their economic problems. This conscious attempt on the part of many non-industrialized countries to integrate the old culture with a complex technology quite foreign to them can be successful only insofar as the old cultural elements do not, in the long run, conflict with certain patterns of human relationships basic to a machine society. This integration could provide cultural continuity which would most certainly ease the transitional period, make it more productive, and hasten the process of industrialization. However, insofar as old cultural elements are preserved in the face of the demands of the new and promising factory system, there will be additional strains that will have to be overcome in the long run, such as less productivity, and a serious delay in the achievement of the desired basic economic goals. Another interesting question, not within the province of this paper, is the question of what kinds of intermediate adjustments could be made which would tend to support old social relationships, but in which provision is made for their slow dissolution. This writer thinks, however, that this approach would be unrealistic, despite its short run advantages.

While this paper has discussed some of the long run consequences of industrialization for underdeveloped areas, it does not imply that there cannot be any cultural continuity, or cultural forms which are peculiar to the society in question. A good deal of variation in industrialized societies is possible. There is no evidence, for example, that any of the following have to change: music, art, religious beliefs about the nonempirical world, and many folkways.

It must be reiterated that there is no implication that any non-industrial society must accept the pattern of development outlined in this paper. However, insofar as a society does accept the value of industrialization and seeks to bring it about, then the development discussed above is to be expected.

[20] Levy, *op. cit.*, pp. 122–123.
[21] Parsons, *op. cit.*, p. 186.

URBANIZATION, POLITICAL STABILITY, AND ECONOMIC GROWTH

Shanti Tangri

Sociologists and economists have in general tended to agree about the mutually beneficent influence of urbanization and economic development. The argument runs in terms of economies of population aggregation and value transformations conducive to economizing, enterprising, and innovative behavior. Generalizations in this field are based largely on the historical experience of Western developed economies.[1]

I have argued elsewhere that urbanization is neither a necessary nor a sufficient condition for economic growth.[2] Under certain conditions, however, and up to a point, it can be a desirable condition for growth, while under other conditions, or beyond a certain point, it can be a factor in slowing down growth. In contemporary India the process of urbanization, in both magnitude and nature, seems to be a factor retarding rather than accelerating growth.

Here I do not propose to review the

SOURCE. Shanti Tangri, "Urbanization, Political Stability, and Economic Growth," in Roy Turner, ed., *India's Urban Future* (Berkeley: University of California Press, 1962), pp. 192–212.

[1] For a brief (and unsympathetic) review of non-Weberian theories of the city see Don Martindale and Gertrude Neuwirth's Prefatory Remarks (pp. 9–62) in their translation of *The City*, by Max Weber (Glencoe, Ill.: Free Press, 1958). For a more limited and relevant discussion see William L. Kolb, "The Social Structure and Functions of Cities," *Economic Development and Cultural Change*, 3, 1 (October 1954), 30–46.

[2] "Patterns of Investment and Rates of Growth, with Special Reference to India" (Doctoral dissertation, University of California, Berkeley, 1960). For a historical criticism of the "industrialization through urbanization" thesis see Carl Bridenbaugh, *Cities in the Wilderness* (New York: Ronald Press, 1938), and *Cities in Revolt* (New York: Knopf, 1955).

highly important but well-discussed issues of social overhead capital, economies of scale for industrial plants and cities as a whole, external economies, consumer densities, pools of labor, skills, and knowledge, centers of communication and innovation, etc.[3] My contention is rather that we cannot determine the role of urbanization without estimating the economic costs or benefits of such urban phenomena as *anomie*, political and ideological ferment, and transformation of cultural and social values. For drawing policy conclusions we need also to know comparable costs and benefits associated with social change among rural populations. I have been unable to find comparative studies of this nature. Reviewing the literature on social and economic change leads me to believe, however, that the socioeconomic costs of tradition-oriented rural attitudes, though never measured, are usually assumed to be prohibitive enough to make growth extremely slow, if not impossible, while similar costs of urbanization are seldom considered to be high enough to prevent or retard change. Indeed, this is what the historical experience of Western societies seems to indicate.[4] That perhaps is not and will not be the case in India and some other underdeveloped countries. As the benefits of urbanization have been discussed extensively in the literature, I will discuss primarily the other side of the case. In this context a few words about the relative rural-urban potential for economic development are in order.

[3] See, for example, Eric Lampard, "The History of Cities in Economically Advanced Areas," *Economic Development and Cultural Change*, 3, 1 (October 1954), 81–136.
[4] *Ibid.*, p. 132.

The Rural-Urban Potential for Asset Formation

In the cities, the savings of entrepreneurial and managerial classes tend to be high, and those of middle and lower classes to be low or negative, because of low incomes and/or higher consumption standards and lower earner-dependent ratios in families. Thus, while the proportion invested out of industrial incomes tends to be relatively high, compared to investments out of agricultural income,[5] it is not clear how the total urban savings-income ratio compares on a per-capita basis with the rural savings-income ratio. Lack of empirical information precludes judgment on the relative rural-urban potential for asset formation out of internal savings.

However, the possibilities of asset creation without prior or concomitant savings are quite extensive and impressive in rural areas[6] and insignificant in urban areas. In the villages people often cooperate to help each other in building houses or fences, or in other acts requiring group effort; not so in the cities, where exchange of labor is monetized and thus involves problems of financing. Again, in the villages there are unused resources— such as common village lands, forests, tanks, wells, ponds, labor, and skills which can be used for asset creation given an appropriate program of mobilization. A villager repairs his own home more readily than a city dweller. Also there is a lesser expectation, on the part of an idle villager, as compared to an urbanite, of finding alternative sources of income, whether the relative expectations of the urbanite and villager are justified or not by the realities of job markets.[7] Thus, lower opportunity costs of the villager make it easier for him to donate his labor to his neighbor or to his community. Finally, many materials and assets which the villager has use for are not desired by the urbanite. The villager can dig up clay and lime and bring palm leaves from the outskirts of the village and husks from his fields, to thatch his roof or plaster his walls or add a room to his house. The urbanite will live in a crowded brick hovel rather than in a thatched mud house. He may not be able to afford a new brick house, but a mud house is not an asset in his eyes—and if it were, the municipal authorities would probably not tolerate, much less encourage, its construction.

The deepening, cleaning, and lining of village tanks and wells as sources of water supply for humans and animals and for irrigation and the construction of warehouses

---

[5] P. N. Rosenstein-Rodan thinks the former ratio is often as high as 35 per cent and the latter between 10 and 15 per cent. (This and other references to him are based on personal conversations and a seminar he gave at the Massachusetts Institute of Technology in the spring of 1959.) Wilfred Malenbaum derives the figure 10 per cent for the latter ratio from sample data on India; cf. *The Non-Monetized Sector of Rural India* (Cambridge, Mass.: Center for International Studies, M.I.T., 1956), p. 11. He thinks the figure may be a slight overestimate. Some economists think the figure is much lower. For an argument that most estimates of rural capital formation are downward biased see Basil S. Yamey and Peter T. Bauer, *Economics of Underdeveloped Countries* (Chicago: University of Chicago Press, 1957), pp. 16–31.

[6] Yamey and Bauer, *op. cit.* A detailed analysis of the rural-urban potential for capital formation in the underdeveloped countries is given in my "Patterns of Investment and Rates of Growth . . . "

[7] Whether people are pushed or pulled to towns, one can argue that economic opportunities in towns must be better than in villages, that potential migrants must believe them to be so, and that in the long run their perception must be validated by experience, otherwise the flow of population would cease or reverse itself. If this reasoning is correct, differentials in reality and perceptions of reality by villagers about relative opportunities become irrelevant for long-run population flows. This reasoning assumes that migration can be based on "irrational" considerations only in the short run. In fact, only a small minority of the migrants need realize their expectations in order for the myth to survive that opportunities in the city are greater than in the country—in other words, people's irrational behavior in regard to spatial mobility can persist even in the long run.

for storing agricultural produce—a vital step for stabilizing agricultural prices and increasing output, for preventing significant losses in food supplies, and for freeing the cultivator from the usurious controls of moneylenders—involve the use of local labor, materials, skills, and organization. Constructing schools, clinics, and community centers, digging ditches and canals and building roads, terracing, bunding, and hedging fields, planting suitable trees on fallow land, controling soil and wind erosion, and developing village ponds as sources of fish supplies: these also are dependent on similar uses of labor and skills.

In addition, the potentialities of increased agricultural output resulting from better practices and marketing, and the consolidation of holdings, net of expenses of innovation, seem impressive.[8] Addition of new facilities, such as brickkilns, multiplies this potential several times, brickmaking being one of the simplest and least expensive operations, ideally suited for local production, distribution, and use in most communities.[9]

In ten years of planned development India has not come anywhere near to exploiting this potential fully, and this in spite of the demonstration by Communist China of its powerful role in the initial phases of development.[10]

[8] See, for example, Albert Mayer, McKim Marriott, and Richard L. Park, *Pilot Project, India: The Story of Rural Development at Etawah, Uttar Pradesh* (Berkeley and Los Angeles: University of California Press, 1958), pp. 233–287.
[9] *Kurukshretra: A Symposium on Community Development in India, 1952–1955* (New Delhi: Community Projects Administration, 1955), pp. 298–308. The facts reported here are also cited in Mayer *et al.*, *Pilot Project, India*, pp. 272–278.
[10] Wilfred Malenbaum, "India and China: Contrasts in Development Performance," *American Economic Review*, **46**, 3 (June 1959), esp. pp. 305–307. See also Tillman Durdin, "Red China Plans Vast Irrigation," New York *Times*, November 3, 1958, and other similar reports in the *Times*.

The Cost of Theologies and Ideologies

Around the theory of indivisibilities, ably propounded by Professors Rosentein-Rodan, Nurkse, and others, has grown an almost mystical complex of belief with many variations.[11] Crudely put, it amounts to this: in underdeveloped countries you have got to have a "big push" if you want to generate self-sustaining growth (enough to outstrip population growth). The big push is then related to big projects and the most up-to-date technology.

All of these ideas have some validity. But political beliefs and historical associations have taken this discussion partly from the realm of theory and reality into that of dogma. Many Marxists are for this way of thinking because it fits the Russian model. Some ardent nationalists are for it because other theories seem to stress rural and agricultural development, a thing which the British rulers used to stress.

Rightly or wrongly, to many this British attitude was an indication of Britain's desire to keep India a nonindustrial, raw-material-supplying colony. To some, like Pandit Nehru, the big dams are "temples of a new faith" in India.[12] To others, steel mills are the crux of economic development. To yet others, steel mills and shipyards are the symbols of national power and autonomy. Psychological symbols and national power may legitimately compete with economic goals. Steel mills, unlike shipyards, are perhaps economically justified in India. The point, however, is this: if economic criteria indicate that a network of rural feeder roads is more productive for the economy than an airline, or fertilizer factories are more remunerative than steel mills, it needs to be explicitly stated that the choosing of steel mills and airlines involves the adop-

[11] For a brief review of these theories see Benjamin H. Higgins, *Economic Development, Principles, Problems and Policies* (New York: Norton, 1959), pp. 384–408.
[12] Takashi Oka, "Dam in India Looms as 'Temple of Faith'," *Christian Science Monitor*, January 28, 1958.

tion of other criteria. Indeed, the commitment of the bulk of the nation's resources to construction of dams and irrigation systems with long gestation periods is not easy to justify on economic grounds, when the urgent problems of food, shelter, and clothing can be solved much more quickly with simple technologies, less capital, and more labor.[13]

The example of big dams illustrates that gigantomania is not always biased toward urbanization. However, due to the correlations between economic development, industrialization, and urbanization which most people carry in their minds, it tends to favor urbanization and industrialization, particularly capital-using industrialization at the cost of labor-using, agricultural, and industrial development. It results in inefficient use of resources for the "short run" (which may extend to fifteen or twenty or more years) in exchange for added but more uncertainly anticipated benefits in the "long run." In an economy like that of India, when high interest rates of 40 or 50 per cent per annum,[14] reflecting the scarcity of capital (and not the artificially controlled low rates of interest, such as 3 or 4 per cent in the imperfect capital market), are used to discount the flow of future outputs, it is not at all clear that such long-run investments are always more productive, even in the long run, than a series of short-run, quick-maturing, and quickly depreciating investments.

I am not aware of any published information which attempts to justify long-run projects in India on such economic grounds. When people are so wedded to their theories that they apply them without even trying to test them, wasteful allocation of resources is likely to occur—and the theories take on the character of theologies. Thus, very often the zeal for setting up the most modern factories and transportation systems increases the real costs of industrialization and urbanization.

Another important reason for the increased expensiveness of urbanization in India is the modern and egalitarian ideology of public welfare. England in the eighteenth and nineteenth centuries could ignore the social costs of slums, unsanitary conditions, and fire hazards to a greater extent than can India in the twentieth century.

Because of bad sanitation, Josiah Strong believed, there were 156,660 "unnecessary" deaths in U.S. cities in 1890.[15] Today, public health measures are introduced first in the cities. The resulting population growth, with overcrowding of housing, schools, hospitals, and transport systems, and shortages of food and other necessities, is a well-known story. Thus are being built the pressures, the strains, and the tensions which may lead to political turmoil or to an authoritarian regime. And hence, as Rostow has stated, the responsibility of the "non-Communist literate elites in . . . transitional societies [to] ensure that the humane decision to save lives does not lead to an inhumane society."[16]

---

[13] If it is assumed that both the production of more consumers' goods and the labor-intensive mode of production for consumers' as well as capital goods will only stimulate population expansion and not raise per-capita incomes, and that population growth cannot be checked otherwise, then a "capital-intensive" investment program may be the only economically feasible program for development. Cf. Walter Galenson and Harvey Liebenstein, "Investment Criteria, Productivity and Economic Development," *Quarterly Journal of Economics, 69*, 3 (August 1955), 343–370. As I have argued elsewhere (see note 2), such a program is not politically feasible in a democracy. It amounts to controlling population growth by starving a section of the people (the unemployed) or spreading consumption goods more thinly over an expanding population, thus keeping general mortality rates high. Even in Communist Poland such a program was overthrown by the people, and only terror and purges enabled Stalin to carry it through in the Soviet Union.

[14] Rates of interest as high as 5 or 6 per cent per month have been reported to the author by several people in villages and traditional sections of old cities.

[15] *The Twentieth Century City* (New York: Baker and Taylor, 1898), p. 58.

[16] W. W. Rostow, *The Stages of Economic Growth: A Non-Communist Manifesto* (Cambridge: Cambridge University Press, 1960), p. 144.

This welfare philosophy is affecting villages also. Describing wastages of cement and steel in one Indian village, René Dumont wrote, "Even European villages do not yet possess all these amenities. India has tried to become a welfare state before creating the basic economy required to sustain it. Comfort has been given priority over production."[17] But this priority of comfort over production becomes operative first in the cities and then radiates out.

Most experts expect housing conditions to get worse in the urban areas of the underdeveloped areas in the coming decade or two.[18] This certainly appears to be the prospect in India.[19] As congestion and slums grow, the need to spend more on urban areas to provide for public health services and social amenities will also increase. The amenities are more expensive because of higher standards expected by urbanites. And if, in addition, a city has already exceeded the population mark of 400,000–500,000, which Rosenstein-Rodan considers optimal from the point of view of social overhead capital, per unit costs of social services may rise rapidly. The number of cities in excess of this size is likely to increase very rapidly in the coming decades in India, thus making urbanization an increasingly expensive process.

If many of the economic, social, and political troubles of the developed economies flow from the fact that ideology lags behind technology, the troubles of the underdeveloped areas become more acute because ideology outruns technology.

Economic Frustrations: Unemployment, Underemployment, and Misemployment

In spite of all the deficiencies in the available employment statistics,[20] it is evident that the trend of growing unemployment in India is not likely to reverse itself in the near future. Urban unemployment accounts for perhaps half of the total. In the larger cities, Malenbaum points out, of all the employed 51.8 per cent were literate and only 3 per cent had any college education, while of the unemployed 78.4 per cent were literate and 5.1 per cent had college education. Some 46 per cent of all the educated unemployed are concentrated in the four major cities of India.[21]

The interval between completion of education and first employment is often quite long. "Thus, while some 50 per cent of the illiterate unemployed have been out of work for at least a year, 75 per cent of the matriculates and intermediates are in this category."[22] Majumdar's study of a large sample of alumni of Lucknow University holding Master's degrees indicates that the more highly educated are unemployed longer. Of the unemployed in this sample, 44 per cent had been unemployed for over two years, 18 per cent for a year and a half, and 27 per cent for a year. A somewhat similar pattern emerges from a sample survey conducted by the Delhi Employment Exchange.[23]

[17] "Agricultural Defeat in India," *New Statesman and Nation*, **58**, 1501 (December 19, 1959), 871.
[18] See, for example, Burnham Kelley (ed.), *Housing and Economic Development* (Cambridge, Mass.: Massachusetts Institute of Technology, 1955).
[19] Pitambar Pant's confident optimism about the housing situation is based on minimal average-cost estimates for the Third and Fourth Plans, far below those actually achieved in the first two Plans.

[20] For a review of these see K. N. Raj, "Employment and Unemployment in the Indian Economy: Problems of Classification, Measurement and Policy," *Economic Development and Cultural Change*, **7**, 3, Part I (April 1959), 258–278.
[21] Wilfred Malenbaum, "Urban Unemployment in India," *Pacific Affairs*, **30**, 2 (June 1957), 138–150.
[22] *Ibid.*, p. 146.
[23] For the Lucknow sample see D. N. Majumdar, *Unemployment Among the University Educated: A Pilot Inquiry in India* (Cambridge, Mass.: Center for International Studies, Massachusetts Institute of Technology, 1957). For the Delhi survey see Motilal Gupta, "Problems of Unemployment in India" (Doctoral dissertation, Netherlands School of

Corresponding to underemployment and seasonal or disguised unemployment in the villages, there is considerable disguised unemployment and/or misemployment in the cities, as reflected in the rapid growth of the low-productivity service sector in which unskilled, uneducated workers, and especially the transients, seek means to subsist. Among the educated in the Majumdar sample, "about three-quarters of those who sought service in a firm and a substantial majority of those who sought service in government or sought a profession of their own failed to achieve it." Economic frustration can only be high in such situations. None of the 237 who answered Majumdar's question as to the factors responsible for difficulty in getting a job blamed it on their own shortcomings. While only about 12 per cent blamed it on bad luck, the rest blamed society in one way or another, to wit: "government," 48 per cent; "society," 13 per cent; "lack of proper and systematic training," 26 per cent—which usually meant lack of opportunities for these.

If the educated unemployed provide leadership, these transients, whom Hoselitz calls the *lumpen proletariat*, provide the raw material for mobs. Political parties, trade unions, business and religious groups, displaced landlords, and princes willing to provide ideological, financial, and organizational resources for making effective use of these two groups are not scarce in the cities.

Rapidly increasing enrollments in colleges and schools, and demographic and economic trends, are likely to swell the ranks of both of these groups in the coming decade. This *lumpen intelligentsia*, as Lewis Feuer calls it, with little skill, opportunity, or capital for entrepreneurship in economic activity, turns to political entrepreneurship where, with less capital, training, and skills, a man can manage to exist, if not get ahead. Moreover, opportunity costs in economic enterprise are higher than in political enterprise. Social values, historical associations, and ideological fashions make economic enterprise a less and political a more desired activity as a means to status and power.

Physical densities, communication, and other facilities make political organization relatively easier in cities. Groups with resources and tightly knit organizations, like the Communists or the Rashtriya Swayam-Sewak Sangh (R.S.S.) are at a relative advantage in such situations. Part of the success of Communists in Kerala and Bengal, two of the most densely populated areas in India, may be due to this reason.[24] The R.S.S. similarly is, by and large, an urban lower-middle-class movement. Psychological densities—intense interchange of ideas, rumors, and stimulations in crowded situations—are conducive to demagoguery and crowd formations. Speakers and audiences tend to stimulate each other into states of irresponsibility and frenzy in situations of crowding and anonymity which are more easily obtained in cities than in villages. Extremist groups with less scruples and more resources stand to gain from situations in which crowds can be turned into mobs.

Noneconomic Frustrations: Sex, Sports, Recreation, and the Arts

Education, urban environment, increasing interregional and international contacts, and foreign and native motion-pictures are either widening the gap between the old and new generations, or promoting a double standard of morality among many. Students and some illiterates watch Hollywood movies—the former partly and the latter mainly—for their sex appeal. And these very people often turn around to criticize American society, as depicted in these movies, as lewd, materialistic, and corrupt, while describing their frustrating cultural framework as spiritualistic and

[*footnote 23 continued*
Economics, Rotterdam, privately published, 1955), p. 43.

[24] Benjamin Higgins explains the success of the Communist party in the crowded sections of Indonesia partly on the same grounds.

pure. There is less segregation of the sexes in big cities, particularly among students. But economic insecurity and intellectual fashion, by preventing early marriages, are choking off the traditionally accepted avenues for sex gratification, while extramarital sex gratification is severely limited because of strong social mores, joint family living, overcrowded housing and the consequent lack of privacy, and relative immobility of most people (due to the lack of money, motorcars, "metros," and motels). Strong cultural sanctions also operate against prostitution among the educated middle classes. Sexual frustration in this group is, thus, quite high. In addition, there are neither sufficient opportunities to participate in sports nor to attend sports spectacles where, on weekends, like their American counterparts, they may work off their steam by yelling some team to victory. There are few opportunities for youth to develop and display its talents in the theater, literature, or other forms of creative life—the market for art being limited. Rowdy politics becomes a channel for youth's repressed exuberance. For many it is an inexpensive substitute activity, and for some an attractive avenue to social climbing and psychic satisfaction. The dictatorships of Russia, Nazi Germany, and Latin America have well demonstrated their understanding of the role of sports and stadia in politics. Even in an affluent democracy like America, one wonders to what extent the political apathy of college students may be attributable to the existence of vast opportunities for economic, artistic, romantic, and extracurricular satisfactions. In the contemporary Indian urban context, political apathy is conducive and activism is detrimental to political stability. Unless there is a change in the nature of this activism, or in economic trends, the politics of irresponsibility are likely to increase in the cities.

Sources and Patterns of Extremism

Cities either give birth to political and other leaders or draw them there. A major consequence of Western education has been the growth of nationalist and culturally revivalist, as well as socialist and Communist, ideologies.[25] A conservative-liberal coalition is in power in India, but liberalism has as yet not taken deep roots there. It is from the villages that the ruling Congress party derives its support. In the cities it has been losing steadily. Calcutta, though not quite typical of other cities, may yet turn out to be the model of political sickness likely to spread in other cities.

Revolutions, Brinton has remarked, leave behind both a uniting tradition and a memory of successful revolt.[26] The process of winning independence developed self-confidence in the common man and it trained cadres of politically active workers. Students participated more heavily than perhaps any other group in the revolutionary struggles. Theirs were the highest aspirations—theirs also the deepest disappointments—and theirs the strongest and most emotive reactions. Education, youth, and unemployment produce explosive mixtures.

A political party in India, Weiner has pointed out, is often an alternative social structure *vis-à-vis* the traditional family.[27] Some bolt from the discipline, frustration, and pettiness of the joint family wedded to the past to take sanctuary in the discipline, dedication, and intrigues of the political party devoted to the future. Purposelessness of life is transformed into a cause and an overriding loyalty that makes many young persons sacrifice health,

[25] For the Indian case see Bruce T. McCully, *English Education and the Origins of Indian Nationalism* (New York: Columbia University Press, 1940).
[26] Crane Brinton, *The Anatomy of Revolution* (New York: Vintage Books, 1957), pp. 262–264.
[27] Myron Weiner, *Party Politics in India: The Development of a Multi-Party System* (Princeton, N.J.: Princeton University Press, 1957), p. 8. He treats this theme at length in "Politics of Westernization in India" (Institute of East Asiatic Studies, University of California, Berkeley, April 1957). [Mimeographed.]

money, and other careers. The more demanding the discipline of a party, the greater the dedication of its members. Again, in India, dedication and self-sacrifice, per se, as Singer has noted, are time-honored traditions.[28] Thus, the same person will often respect and admire a liberal humanist like Nehru, a conservative reformer like Gandhi, a fascist like Subhash Bose, and a rightist revolutionist like Savarkar. This ethos of dedication, though quite useful for maintaining political unity around charismatic symbols like Nehru and Gandhi, is dangerous for democracy. Fanaticism can grow more easily and nondemocratic charismatic symbols can replace the present ones, in this psychological climate. The tradition has not lost ground in the cities. If anything, it has been intensified by two puritanic movements—Gandhism and Marxism. The saving grace of the villager is his belief in many gods—often warring gods. Through the centuries he has learned to pray to them and yet live without them. Divergences of professed and practiced faith do not generate serious anxieties. But the urbanite is a monotheist, and a true believer. His rationalism leads him to a passion for consistency, and in the context of limited knowledge, poor education, poverty and insecurity, and an atmosphere of superstition, this often leads to intolerance. Educated, urban middle classes provide most of the political leadership, including that of the Communist party.[29] The strongholds of Muslim fanaticism before the creation of Pakistan were in educational centers like Aligarh, Dacca, Lahore, Calcutta, Karachi, Peshawar, and Rawalpindi. Hindu conservatives and reactionaries have derived large numbers of their leaders and workers from Delhi, Nagpur, Poona,

Lahore, and Benares. The chances are that in India, if dictatorship comes, it will be of the Left. Left radicalism appeals more to the science worshiping mind of youth. It also offers a more complete and intellectually satisfying credo. It has international support as well as internationalist ideology. The first yields tremendous organizational advantages, while the second appeals to urban cosmopolitanism.

The ruling party has a reservoir of material resources in its business supporters, but it lacks youthful manpower. The socialists have manpower, but lack material resources. The rightists get their financial backing from feudal social classes which are on the way out. Only the Communists have access to both youthful manpower and finances in ample and increasing quantities. The budget of the Communist party in one state alone is reported to be larger than that of the Praja Socialist party for the entire country. Moreover, the Communist credo has "worked" elsewhere. Communist countries are developing rapidly. To the man in a hurry to change the world, communism seems the wave to ride.

Few young men seek political activity in the ranks of the party in power. To defend the *status quo* is not heroic, especially when there are unemployment, poverty, crime, waste, inequalities, and corruption all around. Besides, the party in power has a fairly well-established hierarchy with large numbers of older people, wherein social climbing is more difficult, while opposition groups have use for any man —trained or untrained. There is more room for expansion of the party machinery —hence more opportunities for status or power within the party structure, and, if one has faith enough in the rightness of one's cause, in society at a later date. Communists, in general, are in a better position to absorb newcomers. Well integrated, well financed, with a ready-made ideology tailored to all levels of comprehension, they have a well-designed program for action, so that each new entrant finds plenty

[28] Milton Singer, "Cultural Values in India's Economic Development," *The Annals of the American Academy of Political and Social Science*, **305** (May 1956), 81–91.
[29] Gene D. Overstreet, and Marshall Windmiller, *Communism in India* (Berkeley and Los Angeles: University of California Press, 1959), pp. 357–364.

to be busy with. The newcomers work like missionaries for a cause and a judgment day. Their internal and external supporters give finances in a big and religious way. Living in a democracy, they are free to organize and operate. When their irresponsible actions are repressed, they acquire a halo of martyrdom. This adds another dimension of romance and adventure to oppositional politics, which thrives in an atmosphere where jailgoing has acquired social prestige.

Whether urban educated youth goes Right or Left,[30] it is not likely to be the standard-bearer of liberal democracy if social and economic conditions continue to worsen. It is perhaps the lower middle class in the cities, unskilled and semi-educated, culturally conservative or confused, and politically adrift, whose politics are the most volatile. This floating population in the political arena makes it easier for opportunistic (as well as idealistic) politicians to resign from and reënter political parties, and to reshuffle political alliances with a staggering and confusing frequency. A kind of unrestrained *laissez-faire* politics prevails. Individuals as well as parties seek to maximize their political gain with little regard to rules and principles essential for the maintenance and growth of a responsible representative political system.[31]

Cities also reveal patterns of mutative extremism. After the death of S. P. Mukerji, the leader of the Rightist Jana Sangha, his parliamentary seat was captured by a Communist. Aligarh University, which was a hotbed of Rightist Muslim politics, became a center of Communist activity after the creation of Pakistan.[32] Egalitarian, populist, and welfare-state ideas are shared by most, if not all, political parties. Emotive issues, like language or corruption, unite radicals of the Right and the Left against all moderates. All kinds of opportunistic alliances between all kinds of political groups take place all the time, but the spiritual and psychological affinity of what Hoffer calls the "True Believers"[33] —the fanatics of all faiths, political and otherwise—makes the actual or potential union of Right and Left radicals more dangerous. As the power of the ruling party declines and as youth becomes increasingly disillusioned with the *status quo*, the liberals and moderates are likely to lose. It may be that the old administrative, religious, and cultural cities like Delhi, Banaras, and Ajmer will move to the Right and industrial-commercial cities like Calcutta, Madras, and Bombay to the Left. Where responsible and strong trade-

---

[30] For the view that the collapse of democracy would lead, initially, to the emergence of a Rightist or military rather than a Communist dictatorship in India see M. F. Millikan and W. W. Rostow, "Foreign Aid: Next Phase," *Foreign Affairs*, April 1958, pp. 418–436. For the opposite view see Taya Zinkin, "India and Military Dictatorship," *Pacific Affairs*, **30**, 1 (March 1959), 89–91.

[31] For a description of such politics see S. L. Polai (ed.), *National Politics and 1957 Elections in India* (New Delhi: Metropolitan Book Company, 1957), esp. pp. 12–15; also, Margaret W. Fisher and Joan V. Bondurant, *The Indian Experience with Democratic Elections* (Indian Press Digest, No. 3 [Berkeley: University of California, December, 1956]), pp. 69ff. For Pakistan see K. S. Newman, "Pakistan's Preventive Autocracy and Its Causes," *Pacific Affairs*, **32**, 1 (March 1959), 18–33.

[32] For the Calcutta by-election see Polai (ed.), *op. cit.*, p. 157. The social, historical, and political causes for this political mutation of Leftist into Rightist extremism, and vice versa, differ from situation to situation. For the Italian case see, for example, "Party-Ocracy versus Democracy: An Exchange Between Ignazio Silone and J. K. Galbraith," *Radical Humanist*, **22**, 45 (November 9, 1958), 527–528 and 531.

The psychological factors that make this mutation possible are, however, fairly constant. See Eric Hoffer, *The True Believer: Thoughts on the Nature of Mass Movements* (New York: Harper, 1951) and *The Passionate State of Mind* (New York: Harper, 1955), and Brinton, *op. cit.*, also, T. W. Adorno *et al.*, *The Authoritarian Personality* (New York: Harper, 1950), and A. H. Maslow, "The Authoritarian Character Structure," *Journal of Social Psychology*, **18**, 2nd half (November 1943), 401–411.

[33] In his book of that title, previously cited.

unions take root, as in Bombay, socialists rather than Communists may gain by this shift. But if unemployment and living conditions continue to worsen, the greatest gains will ultimately be for the extremists.

In such conditions even the villages are likely to go over to extremist politics—but perhaps with a time lag. The swastika may appeal to the peasant and the hammer and sickle to the intellectual, but their transmutation or alliance is not inconceivable—and if it comes it will, like plague and cholera, come from the cities.

Intellectuals and Slums

Growing slums, worsening sanitary conditions, lowering living standards, and unemployment concentrate misery visibly, not in inaccessible villages, but in areas which are the habitat of writers, social reformers, artists, poets, teachers, religious preachers, humane societies, dreamers, city planners, sociologists, journalists, and economists. They arouse the concern and the ire of these and other socially sensitive and articulate individuals and groups. Some of their protest—especially when it comes from professional groups—helps rectify some evils, such as graft, inefficiency, and waste. But, by and large, it merely adds to feelings of dissatisfaction with the *status quo*. Believing that they are bystanders, not participants, in processes of social change, many intellectuals become angry men—young and old. Their anger, in turn, leads only to callousness on the part of authorities, who dismiss their criticism as "destructive." A vicious circle of irresponsible and angry criticisms on both sides is thus initiated.

A society in a perpetual state of anger is not a stable society.

Transients and Anomie

Because of housing shortages, low incomes, transportation costs, and other factors, immigrants from rural areas are primarily males. In the four biggest cities, 60 per cent of the population is male as compared to 51.4 per cent for India as a whole.[34]

This ratio is even higher among working classes and migrants. Gambling, racing, dope peddling, prostitution, and cult religiosity tend to spread in rapidly growing cities. The result is a demoralized, unhealthy, pitiful mass which, unlike an industrial reserve army, Hoselitz asserts, is not easy to convert into a disciplined factory work-force.[35] It is true, as Knowles points out, that these people can be converted into an effective labor force if fed and trained properly.[36] But it is easier to turn them into a riotous mob; it needs less training and discipline, and the demand for this alternative is fairly high and frequent in the cities.

Opportunity costs of political rioting are very low for these marginal people. Crowded housing or, more commonly, lack of any housing whatsoever (one quarter of Bombay's population sleeps on the streets) makes physical access to them very easy. They are eager to talk about their troubles. Political workers find the uprooted urban "rice-roots" receptive to their ideas and leadership. The Communists often have the most convincing explanations for all the troubles of these unfortunates, even though at times, as among the refugees from Pakistan, the rightists manage to get a foothold.

There are no estimates of the total economic costs of social disorganization that arise in such contexts. Juvenile delinquency, drunkenness, murder, theft, and robbery involve increased costs, including those for police and justice administra-

[34] Malenbaum, "Urban Unemployment in India." The number of women per thousand men is as follows: Calcutta, 602; Bombay, 569; Ahmedabad, 764; Kanpur, 699. See also Bert F. Hoselitz, "The City, the Factory, and Economic Growth," *American Economic Review,* **45,** 2 (May 1955), 178–179.
[35] *Ibid.*
[36] William H. Knowles, "Discussion on 'Urbanization and Industrialization of the Labor Force in a Developing Economy,'" *American Economic Review,* **45,** 2 (May 1955), 188–190.

tions and for institutions for the detention, reform, and rehabilitation of convicts. Some sketchy information available for three rural-urban districts in Bombay State indicates that over-all crime rates and their economic costs are much higher in the cities.[37]

Besides, political demonstrations and rioting dislocate traffic, trade, and production and result in loss of property and sometimes even of life. No cost estimates for these are available. The greater frequency and magnitude of these in the cities suggests that these costs are higher there.

Workers and Entrepreneurs

Per-capita output and income are generally higher in cities than in villages. This is, however, largely a result of the higher per-capita investment and the associated modern technology in cities. Effects of urban environment, per se, as distinct from those of more investment or superior technology, on labor morale, productivity per man-hour, hours of work, quality of work, and mobility of the labor force need to be ascertained. It is not inconceivable that the proportion of time lost due to strikes (many for noneconomic reasons) increases while the pace of work slows down—at least in the very big cities where relatively more workers are unionized. Unions in India, being largely controlled by political workers from outside

their ranks, can and often do use labor for organizing strikes, protest marches, and demonstrations for furthering their political ends. Language riots in Bombay are a case in point.[38] Husain's study of industrial location in East Pakistan indicates that social disorganization is minimal and workers' morale is maximal where workers are not torn away from their rural habitat.[39] In this respect trade unions can play an important role in reducing rather than aggravating costs of urbanization. By providing a new sense of community and a web of social relationships and activities, they can integrate immigrants into new meaningful and satisfying life-patterns and help build their morale. The responsibility of the unions is high, because in Indian cities there are few secondary social organizations or religious institutions which can create a sense of belongingness corresponding to that provided by the growth of sects like Methodism and Presbyterianism during the Industrial Revolution in England.[40] There are no such significant movements for creating a new social mileu for immigrants in place of the one they left behind. The operation of caste panchayats in cities to some extent prevents the alienation of the worker from his traditional society. In the years to come, however, the strength of this institution is likely to diminish.[41] And to the extent it does

---

[37] See, for example, *Annual Police Administration Report of the State of Bombay, Including Railways for the Year 1957* (Bombay: Government of Bombay, Police Department, 1959), pp. 96–101, 160–171.

Several limitations of the data, as published, do not permit a more definite conclusion, or an exact statement of comparative costs. Available data for 1925 indicate that drunkenness is increasing and social maladjustment is more rife in industrial cities. See B. S. Haikerwal, *Economic and Social Aspects of Crime in India* (London: Allen & Unwin, 1934), p. 46. Haikerwal, however, is inconsistent about his feelings regarding the relative incidence of crime in cities and villages; see, e.g., pp. 12, 48.

[38] For the crucial role of unions in precipitating such disturbances in the autumn of 1956 see Marshall Windmiller, "The Politics of States Reorganization in India: The Case of Bombay," *Far Eastern Survey*, **25**, 9 (September 1956), 129–144.

[39] A. F. A. Husain, *Human and Social Impact of Technological Change in Pakistan* (Dacca: Oxford University Press, 1956). This study contradicts the contrary view expressed by Hoselitz, *op. cit.*, pp. 181–184.

[40] On the role of religion in both resisting and aiding social change, and that of Protestant sects in reintegrating communities disrupted by rapid industrialization and urbanization see W. Arthur Lewis, *The Theory of Economic Growth* (Homewood, Ill., Richard D. Irwin, Inc., 1955), pp. 101–107.

[41] The role of caste in economic development is the subject matter of much writing which is

not diminish, city society will merely duplicate village society on a large scale. Cities then become collections of villages. The argument for urbanization as a vehicle for value transformations conducive to industrialization then disappears.

Cities, by concentrating the labor force in relatively small areas, and by making possible the organization of labor, are creating conditions in which the clash of labor and entrepreneurial interests becomes more well-defined. Unions are already exercising an influence on governmental policies much greater than is warranted by the size of their membership. The consequent upward pressure on wages and consumption may not be a bar to increased investment, if such wage increases result in equal or larger productivity increases. The relation of wages to productivity in India, however, has not been empirically explored. Again, if entrepreneurial consumption can be kept in check, it will be somewhat easier to restrain workers' consumption. In practice, it has not been easy to restrain the consumption of either group.

Successful measures to keep both wages and profits—or strictly, the share of wages and profits that goes into consumption—from rising would necessitate greater regulation of both groups by government, entailing more political, economic, and social controls, more administrative personnel, and increased costs. It would also necessitate a greater capacity for public agencies to fulfill roles of entrepreneurship if private enterprise should become discouraged as a result of such measures. How far the new educated groups, pouring out of colleges and universities with largely

[*footnote 41 continued*
excellently reviewed by Morris David Morris in "Caste and the Evolution of the Industrial Workforce in India," *Proceedings of the American Philosophical Society*, **104**, 2 (April 1960), 124–133; also, see his "The Recruitment of an Industrial Labor Force in India, with British and American Comparisons," *Comparative Studies in Society and History*, **2**, 3 (April 1960), 305–328.

a nontechnical and half-baked education and with a tradition of averseness to economic enterprise and initiative, will make better managers, directors, and planners of enterprises under public rather than private control is yet an open question.

Exposure Effects: Sociological, Economic, and Political

Cities are being integrated into a growing network in and outside the country more rapidly than villages. With rapidly increasing contacts between different groups, tensions are mounting. Patterns of in-migration tend to heighten the tensions associated with regionalism in India.

Increased intergroup contacts are raising the levels of aspiration, without increasing levels of achievement. Consequently, the sense of *absolute deprivation* is increasing among urbanites. Closer contact with upper classes and their modes of living increases the sense of *relative deprivation*. At the same time, urban political and social ideologies are sensitizing the norms whereby people evaluate "social injustice," thus increasing the intensity of resentment and hostility. English commoners may derive satisfactions from the luxuries that their Queen enjoys—as Samuelson suggests[42]—but commoners in India are becoming averse to such "vicarious consumption" in proportion to the degree of their urbanization. Indian motion-pictures and literature, platforms of political parties and political speeches, and the sermons of preachers and social reformers often reflect as well as stimulate this emergent social ethos. The darshana-seeking villager loses his sense of awe and respect for political and other heroes and elites as he observes them from closer quarters and imbibes urban egalitarian ideas. As the erstwhile demigods look more human to him, their actions appear more inhuman.

[42] Paul A. Samuelson, "The Dilemmas of Housing," in Kelley (ed.), *Housing and Economic Development*, p. 35.

Both the numbers of malcontents and the intensity of discontent increase.

Patterns and levels of consumption also change as a result of exposure or demonstration effects. Lower expenditures on food within some income groups, and a substitution of refined-processed foods and sugar for more nutritious foods, have implications for the health and productivity of urbanites. But the changed pattern, particularly among middle- and upper-income groups, also involves more use of luxuries and foreign goods. Thus, there is the flow of scarce resources away from socially useful expenditure into the manufacturing of luxuries, and also a drain on foreign exchange. Levels of consumption also tend to rise, affecting the volume of internal savings available for capital formation.

Successful revolts in some countries raise the morale of revolutionists in others. The revolution of communications transmits knowledge as well as social unrest across oceans.

Slowing Down the Dynamo

W. Arthur Lewis has said,

Towns tend to be prominent in organizing most political movements, whether their aim is greater freedom or less, if only because government is usually done from cities to which the politically ambitious are attracted. . . . Town is the home of the mob, and mobs are as prone to sweep tyrants into power, who reduce the opportunities for economic freedom, as they are to take part in liberating movements. The town is also the home of monopolists—the traders' associations, the guilds, the workers' combinations—whose aim is to restrict opportunities and to keep out new men. The town takes the lead in movements for reducing the amount of work done, and for working sullenly or resentfully. . . . If therefore a case can be made for saying that towns lead out of stagnation into growth, as good a case can be made

for saying they lead out of growth into stagnation.[43]

In India, towns are not likely to lead into stagnation, but they can lead into slower economic growth and political instability, because of the diversion of resources from more to less productive investments. Urban populations have more access to, and influence on, political processes. As conditions worsen, towns are likely to demand and get progressively larger proportions of the national pie at the cost of the countryside.

As the international economy developed, disparities of income grew between the rich and the poor nations, in the past century or so. Now, as the Indian economy develops, disparities are likely to grow between the village and the city. But what worked politically in the nineteenth-century world of colonial powers is hardly likely to work in the egalitarian twentieth century. This trend can be reversed by appropriate allocations and actions for development of the countryside. There is little reason to believe that the rural exodus would continue if economic and social opportunities for advancement were expanding rapidly enough in the villages. In the Majumdar study, out of 327 respondents, 35 per cent were rural in origin. Of these, 35 per cent were willing to return to their villages after the completion of their studies. The other 65 per cent, who were unwilling to do so, were largely motivated by economic considerations. When the entire group of former students from rural areas was asked whether they were willing to return to villages if given a job similar to the one they held, 60 per cent said yes. Of the rest, 63 per cent again gave an economic reason for their answer— they expected chances for their economic advancement to be better in the cities.[44] If a majority of these highly educated (they all had Master's degrees), "westernized,"

[43] *Op. cit.*, pp. 150–151.
[44] Majumdar, *op. cit.*, pp. 33–34.

urbanized Indians of rural origin were willing to return to the villages, given proper opportunities there, it is not unreasonable to assume that unskilled and tradition-oriented migrants can be persuaded to return with as much, if not greater, ease under similar conditions. And it should certainly be easier for those who are still in the villages to keep on living there.

Economic measures for correcting the pace and nature of urbanization can be supplemented by an ideological campaign, especially, because the village still has a romantic, emotional, political, or philosophical attraction for many, even among the intelligentsia and other groups of urban origins. There is no reason to believe that many idealistic and educated men will not choose to work in villages if they are assured that it is not the end of the road for their careers.

Conclusion

There are more opportunities for making a person a participant in economic planning and development in rural than in urban areas. This, by itself, reduces political disaffection. Also, in villages there is a greater level of tolerance for the old and familiar problems of unemployment and poverty. By exporting these problems to cities, political instability is increased. There are many avenues for significant increases in agricultural and rural industrial output. There are greater opportunities for capital formation with the use of idle labor and other resources in villages. The levels and patterns of consumption unfavorable to economic growth can be prevented from emerging with less difficulty in rural than in urban areas.

Higher direct and indirect costs of social disorganization, welfare ideologies, and overhead capital in cities are reducing the flow of output obtainable from investment of available resources—some of which, like labor, are going to waste partly because of a pattern of development which is urban-oriented. If these trends continue,

political discontent will grow in the cities, and if public discontent fails to change governmental policies peacefully, streets may become the arbiters of political destiny. But the problem cannot be solved by expanding employment only or largely in urban areas. The employment elasticity or urbanization may be greater than one—every new job in the city is likely to attract more than one person from the country, thus worsening the problems and tensions in cities.

Increased sports, circuses, sex, spectacles, festivals, cultural shows, and demonstrations of military prowess can provide some substitute satisfactions and distractions to discontented youth. But the real effective solvent of tensions is rapidly expanding social and economic opportunity for advancement through orderly processes, in rural as well as in urban areas. The former have progressively lost their human and material capital to the latter. This flow can and needs to be reversed for the benefit of both. Communist China is doing it by coercive measures.[45] India has to do it by economic inducement and persuasion.

Meanwhile the great march of men from the backwoods to the metropolises continues at an ever accelerating pace. The new frontier—albeit a dangerous one—is not the wilderness with its promise of freedom, gold, or virgin lands, but the skyscraper with its promise of food and shelter.

Unlike the promise of the wilderness, the promise of this frontier may turn out to be an illusion. Like the countless who fell by the wayside or collapsed after reaching the streets of Calcutta in the Bengal famine of 1942, many more are likely to discover that escaping from the stagnation of the village does not necessarily mean salvation in the city slum.

Development patterns which cannot slow down this explosive and skewed

---

[45] Gordon Walker, "Old Chinese Socialism Tested," *Christian Science Monitor*, February 8, 1958.

growth of cities (big ones growing faster than the others) will involve a great wastage of human resources. "A social order is stable," Hoffer has said, "so long as it can give scope to talent and youth. Youth itself is a talent—a perishable talent."[46] This is one resource which if not utilized for development is likely to become political lava in a country where the social fabric of democracy is still very inflammable.

[46] *The Passionate State of Mind*, p. 20.

THE CITY-COUNTRY GAP: URBAN
BREAKTHROUGH AND GREEN UPRISING

Samuel P. Huntington

One crucial political result of modernization is the gap it produces between countryside and city. This gap is, indeed, a preeminent political characteristic of societies undergoing rapid social and economic change. It is the primary source of political instability in such societies and a principal, if not the principal, obstacle to national integration. Modernization is, in large part, measured by the growth of the city. The city becomes the locus of new economic activities, new social classes, new culture and education, which make it fundamentally different from the more tradition-bound countryside. At the same time modernization may also impose new demands on the countryside which intensify its hostility toward the city. The city dweller's feelings of intellectual superiority to and contempt for the backward peasant are matched by the country dweller's feelings of moral superiority to and yet envy of the city slicker. The city and the countryside become different nations, different ways of life.

Historically, the emigration of the peasant from village cottage to city slum was a decisive and irreversible change. In the later modernizing countries, however, the very process of modernization itself has made the move less decisive and has reduced the gap between city and countryside. The radio brings the language and the hopes of the city to the village; the bus brings the language and the beliefs of the village to the city. City cousins and country cousins are more often in contact with each other. The

modern infrastructure of modernization has thus narrowed the rural-urban gap, but it has not eliminated it. The differences are still fundamental. The standard of living in the city is often four or five times that of the countryside. Most of those in the city are literate; a substantial majority of those in the countryside are illiterate. The economic activities and opportunities in the city are almost infinitely more varied than those in the countryside. The culture of the city is open, modern, secular; that of the countryside remains closed, traditional, and religious. The difference between the city and the countryside is the difference between the most modern and the most traditional parts of society. A fundamental problem of politics in a modernizing society is the development of the means for bridging this gap and re-creating through political means the social unity which modernization has destroyed.

The expansion of political participation is reflected in the changing relationship between city and countryside and their changing patterns of political instability and stability. In a typical traditional phase, the countryside dominates the city both politically and socially, and in the countryside a small aristocratic group of landowners dominates a large passive peasant mass. Outside the village the level of political participation is low. It is limited to aristocrats, landowners, high bureaucratic officials, ecclesiastics, and high-ranking military officers. All these are drawn from the same small ruling elite, and the distinctions among the various roles and functions are still relatively primitive. Except in centralized bureaucratic empires, the city plays a minor or secondary role in most traditional

SOURCE: Excerpted from Samuel P. Huntington, *Political Order in Changing Societies* (New Haven: Yale University Press, 1968), using only pp. 72–78.

societies. It may well be the seat of government, but the government itself requires few professional officials and is dominated by the rural elite whose wealth and power is based upon their control of land. In such a society, the countryside is preeminent and both city and countryside are stable.

Modernization changes the nature of the city and the balance between city and countryside. Economic activities multiply in the city and lead to the emergence of new social groups and to the development of a new social consciousness by old social groups. New ideas and new techniques imported from outside the society make their appearance in the city. In many cases, particularly where the traditional bureaucracy is fairly well developed, the first groups within the traditional society to be exposed to modernity are the military and civilian bureaucrats. In due course, students, intellectuals, merchants, doctors, bankers, artisans, entrepreneurs, teachers, lawyers, and engineers emerge on the scene. These groups develop feelings of political efficacy and demand some form of participation in the political system. The urban middle class, in short, makes its appearance in politics and makes the city the source of unrest and opposition to the political and social system which is still dominated by the country.

Eventually the urban elements assert themselves and overthrow the ruling rural elite, thereby marking the end of the traditional political system. This urban breakthrough is usually accompanied by violence, and at this point the politics of the society becomes highly unstable. The city is still but a small growth in society as a whole, but the groups within the city are able to employ their superior skills, location, and concentration to dominate the politics of the society at the national level. In the absence of effective political institutions, politics becomes a city game fought out among the elements of the emerging urban middle class. The community is divided by a fundamental gap; the society is

still rural but its politics have become urban. The city is becoming the dominant source of political power, but the middle-class groups in the city are committed to opposition first to the rural elite which they have dislodged but then also to each other. The sources of instability in a modernizing society are seldom in its poorest or most backward areas; they are almost always in the most advanced sectors of the society. As politics becomes more and more urban, it becomes less and less stable.

At this point the re-creation of political stability requires an alliance between some urban groups and the masses of the population in the countryside. A crucial turning point in the expansion of political participation in a modernizing society is the inauguration of the rural masses into national poltics. This rural mobilization or "Green Uprising" is far more important politically for the later modernizing countries than it was for most early modernizers. In the latter, urbanization and industrialization usually reached high levels before the bulk of the rural population became available for political mobilization. The rural population was less important numerically when it became more involved politically. The one major exception was the United States. In eighteenth-century America, the war of independence, the norms of equality and democracy, the relatively high levels of literacy and education, and the relatively widespread distribution of land ownership (outside the south) combined to produce extensive agrarian political participation before the rise of the city. Somewhat similarly, in later modernizing countries the telescoping of modernization tends to spread political consciousness and the possibility of political action through the countryside at a time when urban development and industrialization are still at relatively low levels. In these countries, consequently, the key to political stability is the extent to which the rural masses are mobilized into politics within the existing political system rather than against the system.

The timing, the method, and the auspices of the Green Uprising thus decisively influence the subsequent political evolution of the society. The uprising may occur rapidly or it may occur slowly and proceed through several stages. It usually takes one of four forms. In a colonial society, the Green Uprising may occur under the auspices of the nationalist intellectuals who, as in India and Tunisia, mobilize the peasant groups into politics within the framework of the nationalist movement to support them in their struggles with the imperial power. Once independence is achieved, however, the problem for the nationalist leaders is to organize and sustain this rural participation and support. If the nationalist party fails to do this, some other group of urban leaders opposed to it or opposed to the political system of which it is a part may move to win the support of the peasants. In a competitive party system, the Green Uprising often takes the form of any segment of the urban elite developing an appeal to or making an alliance with the crucial rural voters and mobilizing them into politics so as to overwhelm at the polls and the more narrowly urban-based parties. The victories of Jefferson and Jackson over the Adamses had their twentieth-century counterparts in Turkey, Ceylon, Burma, Senegal, the Sudan, and other modernizing countries. Thirdly, the Green Uprising may take place, in part at least, under military leadership, if as in South Korea and perhaps Egypt a rural-oriented military junta comes to power and then attempts to develop a broad power base in the countryside to overwhelm and contain its urban opponents. Finally, if no group within the political system takes the lead in mobilizing the peasants into politics, some group of urban intellectuals may mobilize and organize them into politics against the political system. This results in revolution.

Each form of the Green Uprising involves the mobilization of the peasants for political combat. If there is no combat, there is no mobilization. The crucial differences involve the target of the uprising and the framework in which it occurs. In the nationalist case, the target is the imperial power and the mobilization takes place within the framework of a nationalist movement which replaces the imperial power as the source of legitimacy in the political system. In the competitive case, the target is the ruling party and the mobilization takes place within the framework of the political system but not within the framework of the ruling party. In the military case, the target is usually the former ruling oligarchy and the mobilization is part of the effort by the military leaders to construct a new political framework. In the revolutionary case, the target is the existing political system and its leadership and the mobilization takes place through an opposition political party whose leadership is dedicated to replacing the existing political system.

The instability of the city—the instability of coups, riots, and demonstrations—is, in some measure, an inescapable characteristic of modernization. The extent to which this instability manifests itself depends upon the effectiveness and the legitimacy of the political institutions of the society. Urban instability is thus minor but universal. Rural instability, on the other hand, is major but avoidable. If urban elites identified with the political system fail to lead the Green Uprising, the way is opened for an opposition group to come to power through revolution with the support of the peasants and to create a new institutional framework in the form of a single party to bridge the gap between country and city. If urban elites identified with the political system are, however, able to bring the peasants into politics on their side, they are able to surround and to contain the instability of the city. The rural strength of the regime enables it to survive the hostility of the city in the early phases of modernization. The price of rural support, however, is the modification or abandonment by the regime of many of its Western or modern values and practices. Thus, paradoxically, the Green

Table 1. *Political Modernization: Changes in Urban-Rural Power and Stability*

PHASE	CITY	COUNTRYSIDE	COMMENTS
1. Traditional Stability	Stable Subordinate	Stable Dominant	Rural elite rules; middle class absent; peasants dormant
2. Modernization Take-off	Unstable Subordinate	Stable Dominant	Urban middle class appears and begins struggle against rural elite
3. Urban Breakthrough	Unstable Dominant	Stable Subordinate	Urban middle class displaces rural elite; peasants still dormant
A4. Green Uprising: Containment	Unstable Subordinate	Stable Dominant	Peasant mobilization within system reestablishes stability and rural dominance
A5. Fundamentalist Reaction	Stable Dominant	Unstable Subordinate	Middle class grows and becomes more conservative; working class appears; shift of dominance to city produces rural fundamentalist reaction
B4. Green Uprising: Revolution	Unstable Subordinate	Unstable Dominant	Peasant mobilization against system overthrows old structures
B5. Modernizing Consolidation	Stable Dominant	Unstable Subordinate	Revolutionaries in power impose modernizing reforms on peasantry
6. Modern Stability	Stable Dominant	Stable Subordinate	Countryside accepts modern values and city rule

Uprising has either a highly traditionalizing impact on the political system or a profoundly revolutionary one.

If revolution is avoided, in due course the urban middle class changes significantly; it becomes more conservative as it becomes larger. The urban working class also begins to participate in politics, but it is usually either too weak to challenge the middle class or too conservative to want to do so. Thus, as urbanization proceeds, the city comes to play a more effective role in the politics of the country, and the city itself becomes more conservative. The political system and the government come to depend more upon the support of the city than upon that of the countryside. Indeed, it now becomes the turn of the countryside to react against the prospect of domination by the city. This reaction often takes the form of rural protest movements of a fundamentalist character, which vainly attempt to undermine the power of the city and to stop the spread of urban culture. When these opposition movements are stalemated or defeated, modernization, in its political

sense, has reached modernity. Both city and countryside again become stable, but the dominant power now rests with the former rather than with the latter. The society which was once unified by a rural traditional culture is now unified by a modern urban one.

Whether a society evolves through a more or a less revolutionary path thus depends upon the choices made by its leaders and their urban opponents after the city asserts its role in the political system. At this point either the leaders of the system mobilize the peasantry into politics as a stabilizing force to contain urban disorder or the opposition mobilizes them into politics as a revolutionary force to join in the violent destruction of the existing political and social order. A society is, in these terms, vulnerable to revolution only when the opposition of the middle class to the political system coincides with the opposition of the peasants. Once the middle class becomes conservative, rural rebellion is still possible, but revolution is not.

PART IV

THE "MODERNIZERS"

INTRODUCTION

In the discussion of individuals and ideas in Part II, we made frequent reference to the role played by elites in modernizing nations. Similarly, in Part III the discussion of the concomitants of political development pointed up some of the ways elites function to bring about social and economic development. The articles in this part focus specifically on certain significant groups of elites—the intellectuals, the military and the bureaucrats. These groups may be, and usually are, the modernizers in the processes of social transformation, but they also may be forces which lead the resistance to change. Therefore, when we title this Part "The 'Modernizers,' " we are stating a fact and expressing some doubt about the modernizing role played by these elites.

In the process of modernization, social relations change, old norms no longer obtain, the traditions of the past cease to provide guidance for decisions and actions, the old leaders may no longer have status, nor are they always able to wield the social and political power they once held, and sharp discrepancies may be created between those who represent modernity and the masses. These transformations are often stimulated, initiated, or guided by relatively small groups of people whom we have come to call "elites." Elites, according to Harold Lasswell, are those with the most power in a group or a society. They are able to get the most of what there is to get within the system where they wield power. A political elite is the top power group in a political system; they are people who are able to wield power so that they can achieve objectives.

The new elites usually include different individuals from those who constituted the traditional elites. They are the urbanized assaulted individuals; the educated from the universities, the military officers who are entering a middle class, and achievement-oriented bureaucrats who find the destiny of their newly independent nation thrust upon them. These elite also sometimes include in their numbers members of the old elites who are capable of assuming the new roles demanded by the systems-transforming process of modernization. If any of these groups are not in positions of power for the moment, they often are able to wield power in the opposition, which is a force that is assuming greater importance in many developing countries.

These elites must create new social and political institutions that will mobilize the nation, link all the people together into a national communications network, provide the symbols of national integration, and assure a tolerant, if not wholesome, environment for the entrepreneur. The unfortunate reality of many developing nations is that there may be a crippling shortage of professional modernizing politicians, skilled military leaders, risk-taking businessmen, and efficient administrators. Where do the social and political leaders who make modernization possible come from? How do the elites emerge—how are they recruited?

Lester G. Seligman addresses himself to these questions. He sees elite recruitment as both reflecting and affecting the social system. On one hand, it reflects the value system of society, the degree and the type of representativeness of the system, the basis of social stratification and its articulation with the political system, and the structure and change in political roles. On the other hand, elite recruitment patterns determine avenues for political participation and status, influence the kind of policies that will be enacted, accelerate or retard changes, affect the distribution of status and prestige, and influence the stability of the system. Furthermore, as an indicator of development and change, elite recruitment illuminates various changes in the social system: economic changes, as seen in the shifts from agriculture to industry and from rural to urban concentration; in the political system, as seen in new parties, associations, and interest groups; and in the level of politicization, as seen in the new kinds and increasing amounts of participation of the people.

Seligman's discussion of the legitimation of elites builds on a recognition of the dualistic character of transitional society, as identified by Sjoberg, Nash, and others of our preceding authors. In pointing to political parties as the principal agencies for selecting and representing political elites, Seligman provides a useful typology of political parties and anticipates the more extensive treatment in Chapter 14 on "Transitional Politics and Party Systems."

The intellectuals are a particularly important elite in the new states of Asia and Africa. Edward Shils, in a pioneering study of the role of elites, maintains that the "gestation, birth, and continuing life" of these states is in large measure the work of intellectuals. They have created the political life of the underdeveloped nations; they have been "its instigators, its leaders, and its executants." By contrast, in the past new states were founded by other groups for distinctly different reasons and using different techniques. In the West politics have never been a preserve of the intellectuals.

Shils characterizes what he means by "intellectuals," explains why intellectuals provide the ideas and political drive in developing countries, and sketches the political outlook of the intellectuals. Using India as his major example, he then outlines three stages in the politics of the intellectuals: constitutional liberalism, politicized nationalism, and assumption of power in a sovereign state ruled by indigenous elites. When the third stage is reached, a schism occurs among the intellectual-politicians—some are in and others are out. The "outs" attract other intellectuals and they become the voice of opposition, persisting in the same types of criticisms of government and the bureacracy as they made before independence during the period of politicized nationalism. The one new feature which characterized this opposition is disillusionment, which becomes a source of despondent inaction, on one hand, or a rigid form of activist extremism.

In any case, the intellectuals can be expected to play major roles in the political life of the new states for some time in the future. The emerging professional politician and the military elites may not originate among the intellectuals as much as they did, but the opposition parties, the civil service, and higher education will continue to call for intellectuals.

Although the military leaders may be among the intelligentsia by virtue of education and outlook, the importance of the military in political development does not result from the intellectual capacity of the officer corps but derives from the kinds of skills and resources available to most contemporary armies. Military establishments *everywhere* fare well in competing for resources. The emerging nations, irrespective of national income or resources, appear determined to maintain military establishments patterned after the armies of the wealthier and more industrialized nations. The impetus for such resource allocation may be fear of external aggression or internal insurgency, but it also reflects the psychological needs of newly independent people who may be overly conscious of the differences between themselves and the industrial nations. Modern armies have become a symbolic expression of a commitment to modernization and development. External assistance programs often have encouraged military expenditures but the developing nations have also shown a willingness to invest their own scarce resources in military organizations.

Do these military expenditures constitute nothing more than a means of providing for national defense, thereby draining national budgets that already lack sufficient funds for education, agricultural development, and industrial growth? Or can military expenditures also be justified because they contribute to national development? This question is being asked by serious students of the development process who, although they may feel uncertain about the precise way development takes place, have come to think that there is no single route to development and modernization and that one should not overlook the possibility that the military may stimulate or accelerate modernization. The conviction that the incentives, drives, and stimuli for development may originate in numerous and even unanticipated sectors of society and that diverse structures may play a prominent role in modernization has led to a growing interest in the military as a potential innovator in the development process.

Those who maintain that the military should not be treated as a "necessary evil" only to be used for purposes of national defense argue that there is historical justification for thinking of the military as a system capable of contributing to the development process. This argument is buttressed by citing the "developmental" contribution of the Army Corps of Engineers in the United States which built roads, cleared rivers, and assisted in the construction of railroads in the earlier stages of American development—and still performs some of these functions today. The Turkish and Israeli armies are examples of a military with a high sense of national dedication utilizing their men, machines, materials, and organizational skills in the cause of national development. Because the military is usually a prime beneficiary of internal resources and external aid, the anomalous result in many developing nations is that the military, "the managers of the instruments of violence," possesses more of the skills and resources needed for modernization than almost any other sector, and these skills are only distantly related to the command of violence.

Therefore, a full and realistic analysis of the role of the military must consider (1) the military as a socializing agent, (2) the military as a "modernizing" agent, and (3) the military as an active participant in the national political system. There is historical evidence that the military, under the right conditions, is an effective socializing agent. In Turkey, peasant youths acquired a sense of belonging to the Turkish nation and a feeling for the responsibilities of citizenship as a result of military service. The Israeli and Iranian armies have shown that they can be "modernizing" agents by teaching literacy to soldiers and by building and operating schools in the remote frontier villages. The armies of Latin America have been used to construct transportation arteries, and have even been active in various community development projects. However, the activities of building a road, constructing a hospital, teaching the unlettered to read and write, and even disseminating a spirit of citizenship do not add up to the ability to govern.

Furthermore, a professional army committed to modernization may be reluctantly "forced" to intervene in politics when social and political breakdowns occur. Lucian Pye acknowledges that there is validity to this explanation, but points out that it does not adequately account for interventionist behavior by the military. He stresses that the internal organization of the army and its authority relationships convey an overly simplified view that complex problems which baffle political and intellectual elites can be successfully resolved by the "right orders," and the right orders are a possession of the military. Pye's analysis is in general agreement with a penetrating study of the political interventionist military by Morris Janowitz, which concludes that the military intervenes in politics not simply in response to disruptions in the political and social system but, in part, as a consequence of the skill structures and organizational composition of the army in a transitional society. However, Janowitz asserts in that study, "Those organizational and professional qualities which make it possible for the military of a new nation to accumulate political power, and even to take over political power, are the same as those which limit its ability to rule effectively."[1]

In an attempt to identify the factors explaining varying incidence of military intervention between states, Robert D. Putnam reviews the literature in the field and singles out four broad categories: (1) aspects of socioeconomic development; (2) aspects of political development; (3) characteristics of the military establishment itself; and (4) foreign influences. Putnam finds no dearth of suggestions about factors presumed to be causally related to military intervention in politics. The problem, however, comparable to that in the entire field of political development and social change, is to subject this array of theoretical propositions to some kind of empirical testing. Although Putnam's efforts are confined to Latin America, his findings have significance for comparative politics and political development in general.

For each Latin American country Putnam constructs an index of military intervention over the last decade. This index is correlated with various statistical indicators of social mobilization and economic development and with certain other data. Understandably, the methodology is limited by the kinds of issues which can be tested quantitatively. Putnam concludes that social mobilization clearly increases the prospects for civilian rule and that traditions of militarism play an important role in accounting for contemporary military intervention. Neither foreign training missions nor foreign examples of successful intervention seem to have any impact. Other findings, Putnam feels, call for further inquiry. He specifically raises the question of why economic development seems to encourage, rather than inhibit, military involvement in politics. Attention should also be called to the fact that, while Putnam discerns a correlation between social mobilization and civilian rule, and while authors Nie, Powell, and Prewitt (in Chapter 12) find a correlation between social mobilization and political participation, Huntington, on the other hand, theorizes (in Chapter 14) that social mobilization leads to military rule.

Like Putnam, Perlmutter is concerned with the active and increasing role of the army in politics. Military intervention in politics in the form of coups and countercoups, both successful and unsuccessful, has been a recurrent theme not just in most Latin American republics, but also in five independent Arab states, in fourteen new African states, in several Southeast Asian polities, and in Pakistan in South Asia.

Perlmutter undertakes to classify and explain types of civil-military relations in developing polities. Although the Middle East and North Africa is the immediate area of his interest, he also makes reference to developments in Latin America, Southeast Asia, and the rest of Africa. Perlmutter begins by defining a modern praetorian state as "one in which the military tends to intervene and *potentially* could dominate the political system." A praetorian

[1] *The Military in the Political Development of New Nations: An Essay in Comparative Analysis* (Chicago: The University of Chicago Press, 1964), p. 1.

state may develop when civilian institutions lack legitimacy or are in a position to be dominated by the military. Conditions conducive to this type of state may exist even before the army has intervened in politics. In characterizing the praetorian army Perlmutter suggests, contrary to the finding of Putnam, that the political involvement of military officers may be abetted by foreign intervention—such as the counterinsurgency training and military aid of the United States in Latin America.

Perlmutter concludes that the praetorian army is not a positive force for achieving political development. The military has not been successful in creating effective political party systems and other institutional arrangements associated with political development. The success of Ataturk in Turkey is noteworthy as an exception to the more general failure of the military to establish self-sustaining political institutions. At best, military rule may be conducive to economic development by capitalizing on its greater familiarity with modern technology and organizational skills; but, even this process serves to further enhance military domination over political institutions and procedures.

The bureaucrats are the final group of "modernizers" to be considered. S. C. Dube notes that the bureaucracy "forms an important element of the modernizing elite in many of the economically less developed countries which have attained national independence during the last two decades." It should be understood that Dube writes out of a background in India where one of the most developed forms of colonial bureaucracy in the world evolved and where a well-prepared, highly skilled cadre of civil officers stood ready to take over the reins of administration. Non-British colonies did not have as well trained and organized bureaucracies, nor did other British colonies outside the subcontinent of India. The assertion that the bureaucracy in their respective countries was "the first large and organized group to enter the transitional phase between tradition and modernity . . . that they were among the pioneers who sought to break away from the traditionally affective and emotion-based communal society and to set in motion the forces that were to contribute towards the emergence of a different type of society—a society characterized by affective neutrality and based on rational ends-means calculations for individual goals" is probably an overstatement. However, his analysis of the major characteristics of bureaucracy in transitional societies and its problems in the context of the culture of politics, the emerging ethos, and the expanding sphere of state activity and new institutional arrangements has a sufficiently generalized quality to be of value in thinking about the role of bureaucracy in many developing societies. It should be noted that Dube uses some of the elements of systems analysis and certain of the pattern variables in his presentation.

Dube contends that as societies undergo the transformation toward modernity, "the supremacy of administration was replaced largely by the sovereignty of politics." In many countries "the bureaucracy was trained well enough to accept political direction, and only in a few exceptional cases did it try to gain the upper hand." At the same time he acknowledges that in several respects "the hard core of bureaucratic culture has been unyielding, and has offered great resistance to innovation."

Fred W. Riggs argues that bureaucratic interests can actually obstruct political development. His general thesis is that "premature or too rapid expansion of the bureaucracy when the political system lags behind tends to inhibit the development of effective politics. A corollary thesis holds that separate political institutions have a better chance to grow if bureaucratic institutions are relatively weak." In support of this proposition he discusses the relation of bureaucracy to the party system, the electorate, interest groups and the legislature. A controversial, and much debated, assertion of Riggs is that the merit system cuts at the root of one of the strongest props of a developing party system, namely spoils. When politics are deprived of spoils, party machines may lose much of their vigor. Political development, by implication, requires vigorous political parties. Therefore, an efficient, career bureaucracy may be able to resist the politician's attempts to assert effective control.

Thus, in considering the role of bureaucracy in the process of political development, we are confronted with one of the numerous dilemmas of modernization. An efficient bureaucracy is required for social and economic development. But a merit bureaucracy may impede the evolution of a functioning party system with the result that political development may be hindered.

Chapter 8

The Role of Elites

ELITE RECRUITMENT AND
POLITICAL DEVELOPMENT

Lester G. Seligman

In any political system, political roles must be defined, filled, and vacated. Elite recruitment refers to the process whereby such "staffing" takes place. "The political recruitment function takes up where the general political socialization function leaves off. It recruits members of the particular subcultures—religious communities, statuses, classes, ethnic communities and the like, and inducts them into the specialized roles of the political system."[1] For the actors themselves, recruitment embraces two processes: (1) the transformation from nonpolitical roles to eligibility for influential political roles, and (2) the assignment and selection of people for *specific* political roles. Recruitment includes both *eligibility* for elite status and *selection* or *assignment* to specific

SOURCE. Lester G. Seligman, "Elite Recruitment and Political Development," *Journal of Politics*, **26**, 612–626, August 1964.

[1] Almond, G. and Coleman, J., *The Politics of the Developing Areas* (Princeton), p. 31; Lasswell, H. D., Lerner, D., and Rothwell, E., *The Comparative Study of Elites* (Stanford, 1952); Apter, D., "Nationalism, Government and Economic Growth," *Economic Development and Cultural Change*, **7**, 2 (January 1959), 117–136.

elite positions.[2] Recruitment is therefore a central function of any political system, and the processes of recruitment are a good indicator of the values and distribution of political influence.

The elite recruitment pattern both reflects and affects the society. As a dependent variable it expresses the value system of the society and its degree of consistency and contradictions, the degree and the type of representativeness of the system, the basis of social stratification and its articulation with the political system, and the structure and change in political roles. As a factor which affects change, or as an independent variable, elite recruitment patterns determine avenues for political participation and status, influence the kind of policies that will be enacted, accelerate or retard changes, effect the distribution of status and prestige, and influence the stability of the system.

As an indicator of development and change, elite recruitment is useful because it illuminates several change components. It reflects economic changes in the shifts from

[2] Seligman, L., "Political Recruitment and Party Structure," *APSR*, **55**, 1 (March 1961), 77; "Recruitment in Politics," *PROD*, **1** (1958), 14–17.

agrarian emphasis to industry and from rural to urban concentration; shifts in the political infrastructure—the organizations, associations, and interest groups; and the level of politicization and the kind and degree of participation of the people. In this way, the various elements of development, which move at an uneven rate, can be apprehended and measured through the analysis of recruitment.

In the following pages several facets of elite recruitment will be discussed comparatively with reference to the new nations. They are as follows: (1) elite legitimation, (2) paths of power, (3) elite representativeness and (4) the relationship between elite recruitment and political change.

Whether a new state can maintain both stability and development hinges, to a large extent, on the integration of its political elites. They stand in the strategic center of development possibilities. Development requires the assimilation of new values, yet development will be self-defeating if it threatens the fabric of society itself or if it inculcates values and behavior incompatible with durable growth. Planned development demands the organization and rationalization of resource allocation consistent with goals of growth and higher levels of income. Development, therefore, disrupts traditional values of status, prestige, and income. [3]

Development entails an uneven distribution of its gains. Vested interests— occupational, religious, linguistic—may be dislocated and deprived, while newer groups receive new opportunities. Older stratifications are disrupted and new social escalators emerge. The balance of deprivation and advantage will be accepted by various elements only if the substantive justifications of the decisions are accepted. Acceptance will also depend upon whether those who gain *and* those who lose retain consensual political identifications. This may be accomplished not only through the products of policies but

through the processes as well. Thus, the management of the tensions depends on the degree to which there is agreement on decision-making methods. This agreement among decision-makers and acceptance of them will depend upon the *integration among the elites.* As Raymond Aron has stated: "The composition of the governing elite may be progressively altered, the relative importance of the various groups in the elite may be changed, but a society can only survive and prosper if there is true collaboration between those groups. In one way or another, there must be unity of opinion and action on essential points in the elite." [4]

The Legitimation of Elite Recruitment

The Central Values. In general, political elites are legitimated by their embodiment and/or evocation of sacred values of the system. In a new state, the goal of development is interwoven with the goals of nationalism. The political oligarchy which led the movement for independence heads the new state. Thus both nationalism and modernization are primary in the legitimation of the governing elites. There are also complementary goals: self-identifications, international prestige, cultural renaissance.

With the gaining of independence, formal democratization is introduced. A parliament, a judicial system, universal suffrage, an electoral system, and a progressive written constitution are introduced. These are, perhaps, among the easiest changes made. But the gaps in the social structure, the loose articulation of various parts of the society make effective democracy remote. The absence of a democratic tradition makes the new democratic constitution only a superficial graft. [5]

This formal democratization manifestly fulfills the goal of popular consent. But

---

[3] Lerner, Daniel, *The Passing of Traditional Society* (Glencoe: Free Press, 1958), pp. 46–50.

[4] [Italics mine] "Social Structure and Ruling Class," *Br. J. of Soc.* **1** (1950), 10; Nadel, S. F., "The Concept of Social Elites," *Int. Soc. Sci., Bull.* **7**, 3 (1956), p. 420.

[5] Chief H. O. Davis, "The New African Profile," *Foreign Affairs*, **40**, 2 (January, 1962), 293–302 for a perceptive report on this point.

it is also a means toward the solution of a more egregious problem—the weakening of the traditional pluralism and the creation through participation of common identification with the new state and its values. Among the new states, the government is the vehicle for the transition from the vested traditional pluralism to a pluralism more characteristic of modern societies.

Dualistic Legitimations. The nationalistic ideology attempts to cover the traditionalistic cleavages with a patina of solidarity. Citizenship in the new state is upheld as superordinate to the loyalties to tribal, regional, ethnic, linguistic groups. Nonetheless, legitimations remain dualistic. The groups and institutions of the traditional pluralism are deeply rooted and capable of great resistance. Traditional values cannot be totally rejected without threatening solidarity. Paradoxically, the new nationalism itself stimulates the older parochial loyalties. In some respects traditional groups become more sensitive about their identity and status, rather than less so.[6]

The new elite cadres also reflect this dualism. Though they are selected for their achievements in behalf of nationalism, they are products or "ejected groups" of traditional backgrounds.[7] They incorporate the old virtues of family background and respected status plus the newer one of education, skill, and heroic achievement in behalf of national liberation. The ruling are emancipated children of the traditional social structure. While rejecting the old, they cannot help but embody it.

In older democratic systems elites are legitimated by conflicting values. Despite the differentiation of the political sphere, there are ambivalent norms. There are dualistic expectations regarding the ethical norms that invest political roles and expectations of political effectiveness. Alongside legitimations based upon public consent, there are vestigial expectations derived from the mixed Western heritage (monarchy, aristocracy) about political leadership.

Charismatic Leadership as Legitimation. Charismatic leaders[8] are highly functional in the new states, because the Nehrus, Nassers, Sukarnos and Ben Gurions stand above the traditional cleavages in the society. As venerated leaders of a heroic past, they are symbols of the unified nation to all segments of the population. By inviting identification with themselves they foster a broader identification with the nation. These leaders are usually "heroes of renunciation," who gave up much of their lives for the sake of the cause and earned their right to power in this way. They epitomize in their lives the sacrifice and struggle against colonial rule. These leaders play other roles. They are the architects and spokesmen of the drive for economic development.[9] They are also the "central figures"[10] within the national movement that can balance the contending interests. They enjoy international prestige because they are respected in the political world of the West. This recognition nourishes the pride of the citizenry. Thus, charismatic leaders personify and integrate many conflicting needs within emerging nations.[11]

[6] Emerson, R., *From Empire to Nation* (Cambridge: Harvard, 1960), p. 329.
[7] The "marginality" explanation of new elites is stressed by E. Hagen, "A Framework for Analyzing Economic and Political Change" in R. E. Asher, ed., *Development of the Emerging Countries* (Washington: Brookings, 1962), pp. 23, 24, and B. Hoselitz, *Sociological Aspects of Economic Growth* (Glencoe: Free Press, 1960) especially Chapter 3.
[8] The ambiguity in Weber's definition of the concept of charisma has been perceptively criticized by Shils, Parsons, Friedrich, Blau, and others.
[9] Rustow, D., *Politics and Westernization in the Near East* (Princeton, 1956), p. 29. Kahin, G. McT., Pauker, Guy J., and Pye, Lucian W., "Comparative Politics in Non-Western Countries," *American Political Science Review*, 49 (1955), 1025.
[10] Seligman, L., "The Study of Political Leadership," *American Political Science Review*, 44 (1950), 904–915, reprinted in *Political Behavior*, ed. H. Eulau (Glencoe: Free Press, 1956), pp. 177–183.
[11] Emerson *op. cit.*, p. 281.

These strong personalities give strident voice to both the hated and loved symbols of the new nationalism. Nasser, Sekou Toure, or Ho Chi Minh invoke a militant anti colonialism almost constantly. Exaggerated national pride compensates for past humiliations and alleged humiliations. Not all charismatic figures fit this pattern. Some, like Houphouet-Boigny of the Ivory Coast, are more moderate and less flamboyant in their appeals. These latter seem more intent on affirmative elaboration of the national goals, rather than the attack on national scapegoats.

Charismatic leaders have not only a mass following, they also have an elite recruitment function. They draw around them a corps of younger "new intellectuals"[12] who serve as acolytes to the master, as catalysts, and shock troops in the march toward modernization. Linked to the charismatic leaders' multiple functions these circles of intellectuals, technicians, and managers also elaborate the ideology of leadership and translate it into action.

The Bases of Eligibility and Selection

Eligibility and the Dominant Values. The recruitment process itself reflects, and thereby reinforces, the dominant values. In highly traditional systems, like Yemen and Saudi Arabia, such ascriptive factors as kinship determine eligibility to rule, and family succession legitimates role selection. In sharp contrast are more modern democratic systems, where popular election is associated with wide eligibility for elite selection. It is the degree of exclusivity of recruitment eligibility which discriminates one political system from another. Systems that confer broad eligibility for elite status and roles tend to be democratic and modern. Those which restrict elite eligibility are more traditional and authoritarian.

There appears to be a high correlation between political prestige and the degree of exclusivity. While political positions enjoy high prestige in both systems, the prestige is higher in the newer states. In general, where political power is concentrated,[13] a political career enjoys high status and is much sought after. Political offices are prized for their prestige, emoluments, and power. The political sphere more exclusively embodies and expresses the sacred values of the society and thereby substitutes for the crumbling traditional values. Deference toward political leaders substitutes for the deference formerly shown tribal leaders and religious leaders and therefore fits the traditional hierarchical patterns.

Political roles enjoy lower prestige in the older democratic political systems. In older, Western systems politics is differentiated and somewhat distinct from religious and economic spheres. It must compete with business and the professions for prestige. There is also a relationship between prestige of political elite roles and the roles which involve the greatest knowledge and responsibility. If the skill involved is considerable, i.e., the exercise of political authority, then the position will be highly valued.

Representation. In Western systems, a basic criterion of eligibility is representativeness. Political careers are launched and impelled by some significant group that chooses a candidate as its agent, spokesman, or symbolic trustee. The group may be a geographic area, occupational group, an ethnic group or circle of party leaders. Representation is achieved by articulating a group interest. Political parties can be differentiated according to whether they are congruent with one type of group or represent a plurality of groups.[14] Parties always legitimate such representativeness.

In the new states as modernization and development take place, new differentia-

---

[12] Benda, Harry J., "Non-Western Intelligentsias as Political Elites," *Political Change in Underdeveloped Countries*, ed. J. H. Kautsky (New York: Wiley, 1962), p. 238 *passim.*

[13] Shils, E., "The Concentration of Charisma," *World Politics*, 11 (1958–59), 2.

[14] Duverger, M., *Political Parties* (New York: Wiley, 1954), Ch. 2.

tions in the society emerge—occupational groups, working-class organizations, professionals, managers, and so on. Society becomes more cross-hatched along functional lines.[15] These new interests seek self-protection through political representation.[16] They are attracted to the dominant party because the policies of this party favor modernization and development, and because this party is the government capable of granting and withholding the supports necessary for development.

A significant shift in legitimations takes place with modernizing advance. Elected and appointed officials become legitimated by their representation of specific groups. Leaders are chosen because they speak for occupational groups or specific geographic areas. This shift may be called a transfer by public officials in the focus of representation. The focus of representation[17] refers to the group of people represented. In other words, the scope of representation changes. Groups may be sectarian, single-interest groups. When the basis of group formation and cohesion may be a broad outlook or *Weltanschauung*, a sectarian group may become a political party. Proportional representation favors such sectarian groups becoming political parties.

Parties and Groups—A Typology

Political parties are the principal agencies for accomplishing the selection and representation of political elites. Parties may be classified on this basis: *Populist parties*, *Sectarian parties*, and *Pluralist parties*.

1. *Populist Parties*. These parties make claim to the broadest representation of the

[15] Weiner, M., *The Politics of Scarcity* (University of Chicago Press, 1962).
[16] The converse is not uncommon. A group in the political elites directly fosters the development of an economic interest group.
[17] Eulau, H., Wahlke, J., Buchanan, W., Ferguson, L., "The Role of the Representatives: Some Empirical Observations on the Theory of Edmund Burke," *American Political Science Review*, **53**, 3 (September 1959), 744–745.

people as a whole. They may be large or small in size, but they claim to total representation of the people. Such parties espouse an overriding nationalism, that is superordinate to any lesser identification such as class, region, or language.

2. *Sectarian Parties*. These parties are restricted in their representation. They make a specific appeal to a specific group, e.g., religious or ethnic or regional group. They do not aspire to mass membership. Sectarian parties are usually more concerned with maintaining their ideological purity than with winning votes.

3. *Pluralistic Parties*. These are the parties with large memberships, and aggregations of a variety of interests. These are the parties that Duverger calls mass parties. The membership embraces a variety of interests, unified by broadly defined ideology. The party tries to be inclusive rather than exclusive.

In most emerging states, one party, the party of national liberation, dominates the political scene. These are parties born of the nationalist movement, which aggregate a mixture of traditional and modernizing support. (Examples of these are the PRI in Mexico, the Congress Party in India, Mapai in Israel, CPP in Ghana).

In older democratic systems, the competition among political parties for electoral support makes necessary the cooptation of new leadership aspirants. Parties must attempt to represent new segments of the population if they are to maintain their competitive position. The competition for the support of the voters is regularly furthered by a "slate" that reflects a cross section of a highly differentiated population. Parties must also be representative, because expectations of governing effectiveness are associated with it.

Political Skill. Another basis of eligibility and selection is *skill*. In the new states, oratorical ability is a valued and necessary talent for a political leader, because the ability to arouse the public by direct methods is essential for political success. High value is placed upon rhetorical skill in evoking the sacred symbols of the past and present. Ranking after this ability, comes organizational capacity and education. In general, politicians are generalists and amateurs who approach political problems ideologically, rather than in a problem-solving way. In the new states, the recognition comes tardily that technicians and experts are necessary in the political elites. The usefulness of economists, public administrators and sociologists is disputed because they threaten to de-ideologize politics. The men with older scientific skills, e.g., chemistry, physics, pose less threat. The recruitment of the elites by the newer social technical skills is one of the cutting edges of change.

In Western states, politicians play a more differentiated role.[18] Political elites include many specialists in a variety of skills—entrepreneurship, bargaining, organization, propaganda, which are differentiated by their specificity and levels. They tend to resemble the structure of all occupations—callings, trades, professions, etc. They are professionalized, in the sense that the veterans are oriented more toward the techniques rather than goals.[19] Among politicians the mastery of these techniques creates a "community of skills" that transcends partisanship. Negotiating, bargaining, and administrative skills are highly valued. Politicians tend to be pragmatic rather than ideological, and oratory declines in importance.

Associated with skill are criteria about its exercise. In Western systems a public ethics exists which demands moral probity and efficiency among both politicians and administrators. In the new states, this ethics is lacking, both on the professional level and in public norms.

Selection. Selection, the process whereby those eligible for political roles are assigned

roles, takes several forms. Selection may be made by the ruling oligarchy of a party, or by units of the party. The former method results in choosing among deserving veterans on the basis of their loyalty and length of service. A kind of bureaucratic succession to political office occurs. Members anticipate nomination to the highest political positions only at the end of their political careers. The larger and more heterogeneous a party (pluralistic party) the more selection devolves to the component groups. Groups, conversely, will focus their efforts on the nomination and selection of candidates. A primary objective then becomes a party list representative of the constituent groups.

Career Paths and Mobility

In every society there are more or less definable grooves to political power.[20] In highly traditional societies, the route to power is through kinship succession. The politically "eligible" are the aristocrats, and then kinship or family preferments determine the pattern of elite roles. Age is a significant factor in assignment to positions. Seniority weighs heavily in determining level and status.

In modern Western societies, however, the legislative bodies have been the principal training ground for the political elite. Distinction must be drawn between the "pure" politician, who uses the political escalator exclusively, and politicians who enter politics by way of other occupational routes. The "pure" politician is often the party official, who earns his livelihood from political activity and moves into elective office. The mixed type usually enters politics from another occupation, or for whom politics is a part-time activity. To the extent to which political career paths are various, prestige and influence are diffused. An increase in the diversity of the paths to power is a mark of the pluralism of the system.

The rate and kind of political mobility

[18] Pye, L., "The Non-Western Political Process," *Journal of Politics*, **20** (August 1958), 468–486.
[19] Seligman, L., "The Professionalization of Political Elites" (mimeo).

[20] The determinateness of the routes themselves distinguishes one political system from another.

is a significant factor. "It can be shown that many events and developments of history were shaped, in part at least, by whether the actors involved were improving, declining, or remaining stationary in their social and political positions."[21] In general, in normal periods the rate of political ascent tends toward bureaucratic step-by-step escalation. Elite circulation then follows a more or less regular pattern of political attrition, where issues at the focus of attention prevent the entry of some and allow the entry of others.

This doesn't bar another pattern of more rapid entrepreneurial ascent. This is more characteristic during periods of crisis and/or rapid change when men of new skills, status, and personality are much in demand. Just as the rates of upward mobility are significant so are the rates of declining mobility and political mortality significant in elite behavior. From the casualties of the ambitious come the politically dissident. The spurned and defeated are fertile recruiting grounds for the disaffected. Political mobility is therefore an indicator of change and stability in a system.

Elite Representativeness

The security of an elite rests in large part on the degree of its representativeness. An elite must be both *symbolically* and *functionally* representative. Various segments of the society must have formal opportunity for decision-making and also appear to share in the prestige of political elite status. On the one hand, if the elite becomes too oligarchical it jeopardizes the broad public participation and support it needs to further development goals. On the other hand, if in its desire to be representative it becomes too diffuse, some of its effectiveness may be lost.

The maintenance of representation is difficult and critical. Change gives rise to new elements in the population that seek political recognition. A perennial problem

for any political elite is how much of new elements it will allow to enter, without threatening its status and power. How many newcomers can an elite accept without jeopardizing its prestige and influence? By the same token, how can "obsolete" elite members be retired, without threatening revolt and dissension? This is part and parcel of an ongoing problem in any political system, i.e., the relationship between internal mobility and stability.[22] This can be better understood by examining some of the dislocations created by an imbalance in representation.

A good index of the dysfunction of political representation is the political weight of those excluded and denied opportunities for elite positions and influential access. The following are some of the common pathologies in emerging nations.

1. *Opposition Elements are Denied Legitimate Participation.* Ruling oligarchies refuse to consult with them or give them recognition. Under extreme conditions members of the oppositions are openly suppressed or driven underground.

2. *Acute Generational Cleavages.* The younger elements, with high aspirations for status, are severely restricted in opportunities for appointive or elective public office. General differences are especially acute in countries undergoing change. Young intellectuals are among the most politically volatile elements.[23] Extremist groups—political sects violently rejecting both traditional and modernist values—are often the result.

3. *Excessive Selection by Particularistic Criteria,* i.e., people from the right families and backgrounds are overrepresented. The skilled elements, who wish their merit recognized, are restricted and their "merit" qualifications insufficiently recognized.

4. *Alienated Aspirants.* Societies under-

[21] Marsh, E., *The Mandarins* (Glencoe: Free Press, 1961), p. 11.

[22] Lipset, S. M., and Bendix, R., *Social Mobility in Industrial Society* (London: Heinemann, 1959), p. 3.

[23] Weiner, M., *Party Politics in India* (Princeton: Princeton University Press, 1960), p. 10; also Shils, E., "Intellectuals in the New States," *World Politics*, **12**, 3 (April 1960), 339, *passim*.

going rapid change unleash influences which break up traditional patterns before new associations with socially constructive functions are prepared to stand in their place. As a result, a category of displaced persons is created. These are individuals thrust out of old positions of former authority.

When the normal routes to political influence are blocked to such elements, as commonly occurs in overbureaucratized parties, then an anomic recruitment takes place.[24] Such groups may resort to violence or provocative acts in order to receive political recognition. They may form separate political cliques, cabals, or political parties. Under conditions of severe political repression they may become underground revolutionaries. The particular form of expression is affected by the styles of political activity in each culture.

Elite Integration

All the factors discussed hitherto are relevant to political elite integration: The legitimations of political elites, the way they enter, are selected and trained for elite roles, their representativeness, all affect the degree of harmony among the multiple elites. Whether political discussions can be made with deliberation and without schism can ultimately be related to factors in elite recruitment.

Intra-elite accommodations depend upon the kind of differences to be reconciled. Among emerging non-Western political systems, elite political differences tend to be ideological and intransigent.[25] Competition among elites is enacted in a concealed and secretive manner. Opposition tends to be extremist, extravagant, and conspiratorial. Rival elites view each other as subversive and mutually exclusive. Political parties view the acquisition of power as their permanent monopoly.

In older Western systems, the oppositions are included in decision-making in a variety of ways. Moreover, parties operate

on expectations of some alternations in power. The inclusion within a common framework of rules of the game and substantive values reduces differences to conflicts over issues. The interests to be reconciled are specific. Competition among rival elites is open, election contests and politics are open to public scrutiny. Even in systems hitherto notable for their cleavages, like France, there is a general commitment to common values.[26]

Consensus among elites is sustained by the necessity to bargain and compromise if each interest is to gain anything at all. The very multiplicity of interests (a feature of a modern pluralistic society) makes such balance a necessity. Reasonable harmony is maintained by the instrumental rather than affective character of political life. For many citizens and groups, there are "zones of indifference" about which involvement is low.[27] Elite integration is facilitated by the socialization of politicians, and the professionalization of politics.[28] Politicians derive from common cultural and social background. As politics is increasingly the preoccupation of a corps of skilled experts in administration, bargaining, propaganda, and technology, the amateur politician declines in importance. The Western politician increasingly associates with other professionals—scientists, experts, professional journalists, lobbyists, etc. The political milieu is a community of skill, governed by unwritten codes and characterized by devotion to techniques.

Elite consensus in Western systems is fostered by the overlap of affiliations of elite members.[29] Memberships in voluntary

[24] Apter, *op. cit.*, p. 117.
[25] Apter, *ibid.*; Chief H. O. Davis, *op. cit.*

[26] Williams, Philip, "Political Compromise in France and America," *American Scholar*, **26**, 3 (Summer 1957), 273–288.
[27] Berelson, B., Lazarfeld, P., and McPhee, W., *Voting* (Chicago, 1954), Ch. 14.
[28] Guttsman, W. L., "Changes in British Labor Leadership" in Marvick, D., *Political Decision Makers* (Glencoe: Free Press, 1960), p. 132.
[29] Janowitz, M., "Social Stratification and the Comparative Analysis of Elites," *Social Forces*, October 1956, p. 84.

associations of many types create a social affinity and common sharing of interests. Elites are neither monolithic nor insulated from each other. In the occupational, religious, and social spheres, elite members lead similar lives. Political roles are, therefore, a limited and restricted part of their lives.

POLITICAL DEVELOPMENT AND THE DILEMMAS OF ELITE RECRUITMENT

In new states, the modernizing elites are committed to achievement and performance and are legitimated by their success. At the same time, these elites can never be free of traditional legitimations—the utopian visions of the movement, the past of the people.[30] In this sense the elites must always face in two directions.[31]

Maintaining the balance between the impulse to change and the constraints of conservation is contingent on two factors: (1) rate of change and (2) methods of change. If the rate of change is too rapid, then serious splits with traditional values result.[32] Counter-modernization movements result—religious, linguistic groups rebel and demand a return to fundamentalism.[33] If the rate of change is too slow, then expectations generated by the independence movement cannot be fulfilled. Disillusionment is inevitable and new leaders may arise espousing rapid modernization through more drastic methods.

The tensions between the insistent demands of modernization and tradition result in the rise of a new movement and ideology, which may be called the New Nationalists. This ideology may come from the newer ranks of the governmental bureaucracies, and the new men of skill. Underlying their fresh perspective is a political generational cleavage. They are impatient with traditionalists who resist change.

Another dilemma revolves around the rate of change. With economic development come new social differentiations—chiefly occupational groups. These groups seek political representation as an expression of their social status.[34] Where modernization is too rapid high expectations are fostered by the mobility of these groups. This may impel them to become autonomous centers of power. On the other hand, if change is too slow, the traditional elements may be intransigent in their resistance to the new differentiations.[35]

A third dilemma rotates around the exclusiveness or inclusiveness of the political elites. An expansion of elite membership may diminish control and extend the range of conflict; an elite too restricted is denied its representativeness. In any event, elites must channel or coopt the new differentiations, allowing them representation. If individuals from new strata are not permitted entry into elite positions, then efforts at collective mobility may result. If such groups with their extreme antitraditional outlooks are too rapidly absorbed into power positions, much dissension may result.

What has been presented are categories and propositions that may be used for comparative assessments of elite recruitment in the context of political development. Many aspects of this subject have been omitted, which deserve mention.

First, the mechanisms of new elite emergence deserve fuller treatment. As a

---

[30] Duverger, *op. cit.*, pp. 425, 426, 427; Eckstein, H., *A Theory of Stable Democracy* (Princeton: Center of International Studies, 1961), pp. 16, 17.

[31] Rustow, D., "New Horizons for Comparative Politics," *World Politics*, **9**, 4 (July 1957), 533.

[32] Emerson, R., *op. cit.*, p. 329.

[33] Hoselitz, B. in *Tradition, Values and Socio-Economic Development*, ed. R. Braibanti and J. Spengler (Duke University Commonwealth Studies Center), 1961, pp. 90–113.

[34] Eisenstadt, S., "Sociological Aspects of Political Development in Underdeveloped Countries," in Lipset, M., and Smelser, N. J., *Sociology* (1961), pp. 608–622.

[35] Milikan, M., and Blackmer, D., *The Emerging Nations* (Boston: Little Brown, 1961), p. 19.

country undergoes change, in what sectors and under what stimuli are the budding aspirant elites likely to emerge? At what points are political opportunity and predispositions likely to converge? Questions of this type can be answered not by aggregate analyses but by smaller scale studies.

Second, in making comparative elite recruitment analysis the starting points must be made clearer. The term "traditional" covers a range of starting levels, that need greater precision if causal propositions are to be formulated. Finally, the concept of *elite* needs further refinement. Too often it is used to apply to an aggregate that on further examination is highly differentiated, segmentalized, and overlapping with other leadership groups.

THE INTELLECTUALS IN THE POLITICAL DEVELOPMENT OF THE NEW STATES

Edward Shils

The Political Significance of Intellectuals in Underdeveloped Countries

The gestation, birth, and continuing life of the new states of Asia and Africa, through all their vicissitudes, are in large measure the work of intellectuals. In no state-formations in all of human history have intellectuals played such a role as they have in these events of the present century.

In the past, new states were founded by military conquest, by the secession of ethnic groups led by traditional tribal and warrior chiefs, by the gradual extension of the power of the prince through intermarriage, agreement, and conquest, or by separation through military rebellion. In antiquity, the demand that subjects acknowledge the divinity of the Emperor was no more than a requirement that the legitimacy of the existing order be recognized.[1] The interests of dynasty and kinship group, the lure of majesty, considerations of power, aspirations for office, and calculations of economic advantage have been the components of political decisions and the grounds for pursuit of power in the state. It is only in modern times in the West that beliefs about man's nature, his past, and his place in the universe, and about the ethical and metaphysical rightness of particular forms of political order—the concerns of intellectuals—have played an important part in public life.

In the West in modern times, however, politics—particularly civil politics—have never been a preserve of the intellectuals. Well-established aristocrats and landed gentry with ample leisure have provided much of the personnel of politics, both oligarchical and democratic; clergymen and high ecclesiastical officials and, above all, businessmen—the former earlier, the

SOURCE. Edward Shils, "The Intellectuals in the Political Development of the New States," *World Politics*, **12**, 329–368, April 1960. This article is a revised version of a paper presented at a conference on political modernization held under the auspices of the Committee on Comparative Politics of the Social Science Research Council at Dobbs Ferry in June 1959.

of the specifically modern view that a political order must be based on articulately affirmed beliefs. It too, however, was more concerned with the protection of dynastic interests and the guarantee of public order. The substance of the religion was less important than its acceptance, and in this way it differed from the more intrinsically ideological orientation toward politics that is characteristic of the modern intellectual.

[1] The maxim of the Peace of Augsburg: *Cuius regio, eius religio,* was the beginning

latter more recently—have likewise added to the pool. Retired army officers, trade unionists and, of course, mere professional politicians of diverse occupational backgrounds have also been among the incumbents of or contenders for political office and the leaders in the agitation surrounding selection and decision. Intellectuals, too—professors and teachers, scientists, journalists, authors, etc.—have had a substantial share in all these activities. Radical, much more than conservative, politics have been their province, but there too they have had to share the territory with politicians and trade unionists who were not intellectuals. Modern revolutionary politics have been a domain very much reserved for intellectuals; even those who were not intellectuals by training or profession have been almost forced into becoming so by the ideological nature of modern revolutionary politics.

The prominence of intellectuals in the politics of the new states of Asia and Africa arises in part from the special affinity which exists between the modern intellectual orientation and the practice of revolutionary or unconstitutional politics, of politics which are uncivil in their nature. But even in the small space allotted to civil politics before the new states' acquisition of sovereignty and in its larger area since then, intellectuals have had a prominent position. They have not had to share their political role to the usual extent with the other participants in the building and ruling of states.

It was the intellectuals on whom, in the first instance, devolved the task of contending for their nations' right to exist, even to the extent of promulgating the very idea of the nation. The erosion of the conscience and self-confidence of the colonial powers was in considerable measure the product of agitational movements under intellectual leadership. The impregnation of their fellow-countrymen with some incipient sense of nationality and of national self-esteem was to a large extent the achievement of intellectuals,

both secular and religious. The intellectuals have created the political life of the underdeveloped countries; they have been its instigators, its leaders, and its executants. Until Gandhi's emergence at the end of the First World War, they were its main followers as well, but this changed when the nationalist movement began to arouse the sentiments of the mass of the population.

One of the reasons for the political preeminence of the intellectuals of the underdeveloped countries is a negative one. There was practically no one else. In so many of the colonial countries, the princely dynasties were in decay, their powers and their capacities withered, even before the foreigners appeared. Chiefs and princes squirmed under foreign rule; they intrigued and schemed, and at times even resorted to arms, but they organized no political movements and they espoused no ideology. They sought only, when they protested, to retain or regain their own prerogatives. There were no great noble families producing, in generation after generation, courtiers and ministers who with the emergence of modern forms of public politics moved over into that sphere as of right, as they did in Great Britain from the seventeenth to the nineteenth century. The traditional intellectuals, the custodians of sacred texts, usually—with a few great exceptions like al-Afghani—and no political concerns. They were interested in keeping their traditional culture alive, and this traditional culture had little political content other than to recommend leaving authority to those who already had it. They were ready to adapt themselves to any ruler, native or foreign, who left them alone to carry on their scriptural studies, their traditional teaching, and their observances.[2]

[2] The religious reform movements like the Brahmo Samaj, Arya Samaj, the Ramakrishna Mission, and the Muslim Brotherhood which contributed so much to national consciousness were primarily movements for the purification of religious life, and for the reform of social institutions. Their political significance was either indirect or an afterthought.

Moreover, there was generally no military force either to fight against the foreign ruler once he was established or to supply the educated personnel for a modern political movement.[3] There was no military officer class except for a few subalterns in the jealously guarded army of the foreign ruler. There were many professional soldiers, but they were noncommissioned officers and other ranks and had no political interest whatsoever. The movement instigated in 1881 by the Egyptian Colonel Ahmed Orabi Pasha[4] had no counterparts until the tremors and tribulations of independence began to be felt. There was no profession of politics which men entered early, usually from some other profession, and remained in until final and crushing defeat or the end of their lives. There were very few merchants and industrialists who out of civic and "material" interest took a part in politics on a full or part-time scale—although many of them contributed substantially to the financial support of the nationalist and even the revolutionary movements. Prudence and the narrowness of their concerns kept businessmen out of politics. The "foreignness" of many business enterprisers in underdeveloped countries has further diminished the significance of this class as a reservoir of political personnel. There was and there still is scarcely any endogenous trade union movement which produces its own leaders from within the laboring class, and there have been practically none of those self-educated workingmen who helped to give an intellectual tone to the European and American socialist and revolutionary movements in their early years. There was no citizenry, no reservoir of civility, to provide not only the audience and follow-

ing of politics but the personnel of middle and higher leadership. In short, if politics were to exist at all in underdeveloped countries under colonial rule, they had to be the politics of the intellectuals.

The intellectuals did not, however, enter into the political sphere merely because other sections of the population forswore or abdicated their responsibilities. They entered because they had a special calling from within, a positive impetus from without.

The Intellectual Class in Underdeveloped Countries

What Is an Intellectual? We deal here with the modern intellectuals of the new states—not with traditional intellectuals. Whom do we regard as modern intellectuals in the new states? The answer, in a first approximation, is: all persons with an *advanced modern education*[5] and the intellectual concerns and skills ordinarily associated with it. For a variety of reasons, the present definition of the intellectuals is a less selective or discriminating one

[3] The practitioners of the guerrilla warfare and terrorism which have been carried on in various parts of Asia and Africa against the European rulers have always included a significant admixture of intellectuals.

[4] It was, in any case, more of a protest against unsatisfactory service conditions than a political movement.

[5] This definition is ceasing to be adequate because the extension of opportunities for higher education is changing the composition and outlook of the group of persons who have availed themselves of these opportunities. Furthermore, the increase of those with an advanced technical or scientific and specialized education is creating a body of persons whose interests are narrower than their predecessors' in their own countries, and whose contact with the humanistic and political tradition of the hitherto prevailing higher education is becoming more attenuated. They themselves will not merely be different from the conventional political intellectuals of the colonial or recently colonial countries, but will also less frequently identify themselves as "intellectuals." This will make a considerable difference. In this respect, the underdeveloped countries will begin to approximate the more advanced countries.

This definition is not intended to deny the existence of a class of traditional intellectuals, largely religious in their concerns. Nor does it seek to obscure the influence of traditional intellectuals in political life (like the Muslim Brotherhood, the Darul Islam, etc.) or of traditional ideas on modern intellectuals.

than we would use to designate the intellectuals in the more advanced countries. This is in no way condescension toward the new states. It is only an acknowledgment of the smaller degree of internal differentiation which has until now prevailed within the educated class in the new states, and the greater disjunction which marks that class off from the other sections of the society. It is also a recognition of a means of identification employed in the new states by the intellectuals themselves and by others.

In the new states, and in colonies which are shortly to achieve independence, the intellectuals are those persons who have become modern not by immersing themselves in the ways of modern commerce or administration, but by being exposed to the set course of modern intellectual culture in a college or university. Passage through this course of study is the qualification for being regarded as an intellectual, just as the possession of the diploma is regarded as a qualification for practicing a profession which is the prerogative of the intellectual. The "diplomatization" of society to which Max Weber referred, although it exists on a smaller scale than in Germany or Great Britain because there are fewer posts available, is as impressive in underdeveloped countries as in the advanced ones. It is not, however, the diploma which makes the intellectual. It is his prolonged contact with modern culture[6] which does so. The diploma is only an emblem, however valuable, of a part of his outlook which he and others regard as vitally important. The possession of a *modern intellectual culture* is vital because it carries with it a partial transformation of the self and a changed relationship to the authority of the dead and the living.

The Occupational Structure of the Intellectuals. The professions of the intellectuals

in underdeveloped countries are civil service, journalism, law, teaching (particularly college and university, but also secondary-school teaching), and medicine. These are the professions in which intellectuals are to be found and which require either intellectual certification or intellectual skill. (There are other professions with similar qualifications of certification and skill, such as engineering and accounting, which have usually been regarded as marginal to the circle within which the intellectuals dwell.)

The occupational structure which intellectuals enter in the underdeveloped countries is notably different from that of the more advanced countries. The occupational distribution of the intellectuals in underdeveloped countries is a function of the level of economic development and of their having only recently been colonial territories. Because they were impoverished countries, they lacked a fully differentiated middle class. They lacked and still lack a stratum of authors who could live from the sale of their literary products.[7] They have only a very meager class of technical intellectuals (electrical engineers, technologists, industrial chemists, statisticians, accountants). They have lacked the higher levels of scientific and humanistic personnel, the physicists, biologists, geneticists, historians, and philosophers who carry on the intellectual work which is the specific manifestation of the modern intellectual outlook.[8]

---

[6] This does not mean that all intellectuals in underdeveloped countries who possess diplomas are intellectually equal, or that all intellectuals possess diplomas. There are a few who do not.

[7] By very rough methods I estimated that there might be as many as one hundred professional literary men in India who are able to maintain themselves by their writings. The Director of the *Sahitya Akademi* thinks that there are only about fifty. Think then of the size of this stratum in Ghana, Nigeria, Egypt, or the Sudan!

[8] India is a very partial exception. It is practically alone in its possession of a large corps of intellectuals, a fair number of whom work at a very high level. This is partly a function of the much longer period that modern intellectual life has existed in India. The British stayed longer in India and exercised greater influence there than any other European power did in its colonial territory, and as a result many more

They lacked nearly all of these latter professions under colonial conditions, and most of the underdeveloped countries still lack most of them today under conditions of independence. In the colonial era, they lacked them because poverty and the absence of a significant development of industry prevented the emergence of demand for technical intellectuals, because illiteracy prevented the emergence of a market for literary products, and because the higher levels of modern intellectual creation and enquiry received no indigenous impulse and were too costly for poor countries to maintain. As a result, persons trained in those subjects found little opportunity for employment in their own country, and few therefore attempted to acquire these skills.[9]

Under colonial conditions, the underdeveloped countries lacked the effective demand which permits a modern intellectual class, in its full variety, to come into existence. Persons who acquired intellectual qualifications had only a few markets for their skills. The higher civil service was by all odds the most attractive of these, but opportunities were restricted because it was small in size and the posts were mainly pre-empted by foreigners. (In India in the last decade of the British Raj, there were only about 1200 such posts in the Indian Civil Service and, of these, a little less than half were filled by Indians. In other countries, the number of posts was smaller and the proportion held by persons of indigenous origin was also much smaller.)

Journalism, as a result of generally widespread illiteracy, was a stunted growth and provided only a few opportunities, which were not at all remunerative. Journalism under colonial conditions was

[*footnote 8 continued*
modern intellectual institutions came into being.
[9] There are other important reasons, growing out of the culture of these countries, which precluded interest in these fields. We do not deal with them here since our interest lies primarily in the political sphere.

much more of an unprofitable political mission than a commercially attractive investment, and most of it was on rather minuscule scale.

The medical profession was kept small by the costliness of the course of study, the absence of an effective demand for medical services, and the pre-emption of much of the senior level of the medical service by the government and its consequent reservation for foreigners.

Teaching at its lower levels was unattractive to intellectuals because it involved living in villages away from the lights and interests of the larger towns, and because it was extremely unremunerative. Nor were there many opportunities in it. On the secondary and higher levels, opportunities were also meager. Of all the underdeveloped countries, only India had an extensive modern college and university system before 1920; after that date, the additions to the Indian system of higher education came very slowly until the eve of the Second World War and the chaos which accompanied it. Outside of India there were at most only a few thousand posts available in institutions of higher learning in all of colonial Asia and Africa, and some of these were reserved for Europeans (and Americans, in the two American colleges of the Middle East). Thus opportunities for teaching on the upper levels of an extremely lean educational system were few. Where the authorities sought to maintain a high standard, they were very particular about whom they chose to employ. (It should be added that political considerations, at this time of nationalistic, anti-colonialist effervescence, likewise restricted the chances of entry, since many able young men disqualified themselves by the high jinks of adolescent politics during their student days).

The Legal Profession. For these reasons, many of the intellectually gifted and interested who also had to gain their own livelihood entered the course of legal study and then the practice of the profession of the law. Entry to the legal profession was not restricted on ethnic grounds, the course of study was short and inexpensive and could be easily undertaken. There was, moreover, a considerable effective demand for legal services.

The colonial powers were concerned with order and justice and, in their various ways, had attempted to establish the rule of law in the colonial territories. The wealthy landowning classes and the newer wealthy merchants were frequently engaged in litigations in which huge sums were involved and the possibility of lawyers to earn handsome fees gave an éclat to the legal profession which only the higher civil service otherwise possessed.

Furthermore, in countries like India, Egypt, or Nigeria, for example, what else could a university or college graduate do with his qualifications if he did not wish to settle for a clerkship in the government or in a foreign commercial firm? The law schools were therefore able to attract throngs of students. Once the legal qualification had been obtained, the young lawyer went into the nether regions of the bar, where he had much time for other interests. The leisure time of the young lawyer was a fertile field in which much political activity grew.

This existence of a stratum of underemployed young lawyers was made possible by their kinship connections. The aspirants to the intellectual professions in the underdeveloped countries almost always came from the more prosperous sections of society. They were the sons of chiefs, noblemen, and landowners, of ministers and officials of territories in which indirect rule existed, and of civil servants and teachers in countries under direct rule. In some countries, they occasionally came from prosperous mercantile families, though seldom in large numbers.

These social origins, against the background of the diffuse obligations accepted by members of an extended kinship system, meant that even where the income gained from a profession was inadequate to maintain a man and his immediate family,

he could still continue to associate himself with the profession. The deficiencies in his earnings were made up by his kinsmen. Unlike teaching, the civil service, and most journalism, where membership in the profession is defined not merely by qualification and intermittent practice but by actual employment, a person need not earn a living by legal practice in order to be a lawyer. This is why the legal profession in nearly all the underdeveloped countries has been, before and since independence, crowded by a few very successful lawyers and a great number of very unsuccessful ones.

These are also some of the reasons why the legal profession supplied so many of the outstanding leaders of the nationalist movements during colonial times, and why the lawyer-intellectuals form such a vital part of the political elites of the new states.

Students. No consideration of the intellectual class in underdeveloped countries can disregard the university students. In advanced countries, students are not regarded as *ex officio* intellectuals; in underdeveloped countries, they are. Students in modern colleges and universities in underdeveloped countries have been treated as part of the intellectual class— or at least were before independence— and they have regarded themselves as such. Perhaps the mere commencement of an adult form of contact with modern intellectual traditions and the anticipation—however insecure—that acquisition of those traditions would qualify one for the *modern* intellectual professions conferred that status on university and college students and, derivatively, on secondary-school students.

The student enjoyed double favor in the eyes of his fellow-countryman. As one of the tiny minority gaining a modern education, he was becoming qualified for a respected, secure, and well-paid position close to the center of society, as a civil servant, teacher, or lawyer. As a bearer of the spirit of revolt against the foreign ruler, he gained the admiration and confidence of those of his seniors who were imbued with the national idea.

Formally, the student movements in the colonial countries began their careers only in the 1920's, but long before that the secondary schools, colleges, and universities had been a source of personnel for the more ebullient and aggressive nationalistic movements. Since the beginning of the present century, students have been in a state of turbulence. This turbulence flowed more and more into politics, until the students became vital foci of the national independence movements. The secondary schools, colleges, and universities attended by the students of underdeveloped countries became academies of national revolution. It was not the intention of the administrators and teachers that they should become such; rather, the contrary. Nonetheless they did, both in their own countries and in the metropolitan centers of London and Paris, where many of the most important architects of independence were trained, and where they found the intellectual resonance and moral support which sustained them in lean years.

The London School of Economics in particular has probably contributed much more to the excitation of nationalistic sentiment than any other educational institution in the world. At the School of Economics, the late Professor Harold Laski did more than any other single individual to hearten the colonial students and to make them feel that the great weight of liberal Western learning supported their political enthusiasm.

However, it was not only in the universities of London and Paris, but in shabby clubs and cafés, cheap hotels and restaurants, dingy rooming houses and the tiny cluttered offices of their nationalist organizations that the colonial students were educated in nationalism, acquired some degree of national consciousness, and came to feel how retrograde their own countries were and what they might be if only they became their own masters and modernized themselves. Personalities like Mr. Krishna Menon, Dr. Nkrumah, and Dr. Banda were themselves formed in these milieux, and in turn formed many of those who were to play an active part in the movement in their own countries.

The political propensities of the students have been, in part, products of adolescent rebelliousness. This has been especially pronounced in those who were brought up in a traditionally oppressive environment and were indulged with a spell of freedom from that environment—above all, freedom from the control of their elders and kinsmen. Once, however, the new tradition of rebellion was established among students, it became self-reproducing. Moreover, the vocational prospectlessness of their post-university situation has also stirred the restiveness of the students.

The Unemployed Intellectual. In most underdeveloped countries during the colonial period, the unemployed intellectual was always a worry to the foreign rulers and to constitutional politicians, and a grievance of the leaders of the independence movement. He still remains a problem in the underdeveloped countries which have had a higher educational system for some length of time and which are not rapidly expanding their governmental staffs. In Ghana or Nigeria, there is a shortage of intellectuals and all graduates can find posts; in Pakistan, which inherited only a very small part of the higher educational system of British India, the government has tried to restrict entrance to the universities, especially in "arts" subjects. In India and Egypt, however, despite rapid expansion of opportunities for the employment of intellectuals in government, there has been a more than proportionate expansion in the number of university graduates and the problem remains as acute as ever.

Yet the difficulty is not so much "intellectual unemployment" as under- and mal-employment. Most of the graduates, sooner or later, do find posts of one sort or another, but they are not posts which conform with expectations. They are ill-paid, unsatisfying in status and tenure, and leave their incumbents in the state of restlessness which they experienced as students.

The Political Outlook of the Intellectuals

Intense Politicization. The nature of the political movements which preceded independence and the indigenous traditions of the underdeveloped countries both forced political life into charismatic channels. Charismatic politics demand the utmost from their devotees.

When the intellectuals of the colonial countries were ready to engage in politics at all, they were willing to give everything to them. Politics became the be-all and end-all of their existence. Those who were not restrained by fear of the loss of their posts in government schools and colleges or by the material and psychological advantages of their jobs became highly politicized. Some of the intellectuals who graduated in the years of nationalistic fervor did not even attempt seriously to enter upon a professional career but went directly into agitational and conspiratorial politics. Their middle-class origins and the economy of the extended family system, together with the relatively few needs of charismatically sensitive intellectuals, helped to make possible this consecration to politics. For these reasons and because an autonomous intellectual life in the modern sense had scarcely taken root in any of the underdeveloped colonial countries, politics of a very intense sort had the intellectual field largely to itself.

The high degree of political involvement of the intellectual in underdeveloped countries is a complex phenomenon. It has a threefold root. The primary source is a deep preoccupation with authority. Even though he seeks and seems actually to break away from the authority of the powerful traditions in which he was brought up, the intellectual of underdeveloped countries, still more than his confrere in more advanced countries, retains the need for incorporation into some self-transcending, authoritative entity. Indeed, the greater his struggle for emancipation from the traditional collectivity, the greater his need for incorporation into a new, alternative collectivity. Intense politicization meets this need. The second source of political involvement is the scarcity of opportunities to acquire an even temporary sense of vocational achievement; there have been few counterattractions to the appeal of charismatic politics. Finally, there has been a deficient tradition of civility in the underdeveloped countries which affects the intellectuals as much as it does the non-intellectuals. Let us consider each of these aspects.

The intellectual everywhere is concerned with his relations to authority. In underdeveloped countries, where authorities have tended on the whole to be more unitary, and where alternative authorities, and the authority of alternative traditions, have not yet emerged because of the small size of the primordial community and its relatively low degree of internal differentiation, the preoccupation of the intellectual with authority is all the greater. It is difficult for him to escape from a sense of its presence and a feeling of dependence on it. Such continuous presence, and the unindulgent attitude of traditional indigenous authority, once childhood has passed, breed resentment and antipathy which are submerged but not dissolved in the obedience required for the continuance of daily existence in the primordial community.

The external air of submission hides a deeper and unceasing enmity. Distant authority which has force at its disposal, which is impersonal, as bureaucratic authority must be, and which is not suffused with any immediately apprehensible charisma, provides an easy target for this enmity.

When one shares in authority, when one "is" authority, as a leading politician of the ruling party or as a civil servant, the antagonism toward authority is curbed by the counterbalancing need to be absorbed into it. For an intellectual in an underdeveloped country, authority is usually something into which he must be absorbed or against which he must be in opposition. It is seldom something about which he can be neutral while he goes about his business. The very structure of the underdeveloped countries, both in their primordial and in their wider aspects, both during the colonial period and during independence, is such that one can never be indifferent about authority. It cannot be overlooked, one's "business" cannot be carried on without regard to it.

Distant authority carries with it none of the compensations and urgencies of immediately present and permeative authority. Distance does not make for indifference among the politicized, among those whose passions are strong and no longer bound down by the weight of primordiality and tradition. The distance of authority renders revolt against it psychologically more practicable. Distant authority is "alien" authority. Even when it is ethnically "identical" with those over whom it rules, this "alienation" exists in those societies which are used to being ruled by visible and proximate authorities. (When distant authority is also ethnically alien, whether it be of the same general racial and cultural stock or as alien in color, cultural tradition, provenience, and physical appearance as the colonial authorities were, the impulse to revolt is all the stronger.)

The revolt against authority cannot, however, be complete and unequivocal. The need, from which no human being can every wholly liberate himself, to be a member of an authoritative, transcendent collectivity remains. The individual, striving to emancipate himself from his primordial collectivity, must feel himself a part of some other more congenial, alternative collectivity. It must, moreover, be an authoritative one, a charismatically authoritative one. Where, in an underdeveloped society, with its relative churchlessness, its

still feeble professional and civil traditions, and in the face of persisting particularistic loyalties, both subjective and objective, can the modern intellectual find such an authoritative collectivity? It is really only the "nation" which is at hand, and that organized body which represents the "nation"—namely, the "party of national independence."

This is one reason why the intellectual immerses himself, at least for a time, in intense political activities; it is why he seeks a "cause," an encompassing ideal. It is also the reason for the oppositional character of the politics of the intellectuals who themselves do not share in the authority. The belief in the efficacy of political action and in the political sources of evil and the remedies of evil also finds some of its explanation here. This is why the relatively unpolitical intellectual, or the intellectual who is indirectly connected with political affairs, the more specialized intellectual who wishes to work within his own professional intellectual tradition and to exercise his influence in the public sphere over the longer run and beyond the immediate disputes of the parties, is regarded as not being a "genuine intellectual" and even as a traitor to the ideals which the intellectual is properly called to serve.

The intense politicization of the intellectual is accentuated by the provision, through politics, of opportunities for individual effectiveness and achievement. In a society where status is traditionally determined by such primordial qualities as kinship connection, age, sex, and rank order within the family, the possibility of achievement, of making a mark on events by one's own actions, is minimal. In the larger society of the underdeveloped countries, although the narrower primordial determinants of status are to some extent transcended, the possibilities of achievement remain small. The opportunities for the satisfactory employment of an educated person under conditions of colonial rule were meager as long as the most authoritative positions in the civil service and in commerce were reserved to foreigners. They remain small under conditions of sovereignty as long as the economy is backward and posts integral to the modern part of the economy are relatively few, and as long as opportunities for specifically intellectual employment or the sale of the products of creative intellectual work are restricted.

The educated person acquires some degree of emancipation from the predominantly primordial tradition of status-determination. The content of this modern education, and its dissolution of the hold of traditional cultural standards and the traditional patterns of life, arouse in him the need to determine his status and his self-esteem by his own achievements. Where can such a person make his mark in a society which gives him little room to do so?

The political movement with its demands and challenges is almost the only arena open to him. A political movement, unlike a business firm or a university or a government department, can absorb as many people as apply to it. It can give him tasks to perform and it can thereby offer him the possibility of seeing the effects of his actions. By shooting, demonstrating, marching, agitating, threatening and bullying, fighting, destroying, obstructing, helping to organize, running errands, distributing handbills, and canvassing, he can see some effects and can believe in the importance of his deeds in thwarting or coercing a distant impersonal bureaucratic authority, or in serving the will of the new charismatic authority to which he gives himself.

Especially during the period of late adolescence and youth, when the impulses of self-assertion and the striving for individuality and creativity are at their height, and before the traditional system of status has reasserted its empire over him, politics seem to be the only field in which he can act with some expectation of satisfying effectiveness.

Once independence has been attained, the need for effectiveness and achievement does not die away. Politics remain a major alternative to apathetic idiocy or regression into the acceptance of the traditional pattern of life. Politics will in fact remain a major alternative open to the intellectuals for achievement and for absorption into a wider, no longer primordial collectivity as long as the under-developed societies remain underdeveloped. Only when they have become more differentiated occupationally, and when they have developed a sufficiently large and self-esteeming corps of professional intellectuals, carrying on the specifically intellectual professions with their own corporate traditions and corporate forms of organization, will the passionate sentiment and energy flow into channels other than the political.

Nationalism. The nationalism of the intellectuals usually made its first appearance alone, free from the complications of socialist and populist ideas. Only in those underdeveloped countries where the nationalist movement has come more lately on the scene has it been involved in other ideological currents which are not necessarily integral to it.

The nationalism of the intellectuals of the underdeveloped countries emerged at a time when there was little sense of nationality among the peoples whose nationality the intellectuals were proclaiming. Its first impetus seems to have come from a deepening of the feeling of distance between ruler and ruled, arising from the spatial and ethnic remoteness of the foreign rulers, and the dissolution of the particularistic tie which holds ethnically homogeneous rulers and ruled together. The identification of oneself as a subject of an unloved (however feared and respected) ruler with others who shared that subjection was one phase of the process. The discovery of the glories of the past, of cultural traditions, was usually but not always an action, *ex post facto*, which legitimated the claims asserted on behalf of that newly imagined collectivity.[10]

[10] The stirrings of religious reform and the effort to rehabilitate the dignity of the tradi-

The assimilation of modern culture, which, historically, was a foreign culture, was an essential element in this process. The first generation of constitutional politicians in most underdeveloped countries were relatively highly "Westernized." The usual antagonism toward the older generation made the next, younger generation more antagonistic toward Western culture, and encouraged their rudimentary attachment to the indigenous traditional culture to come forward a little more in their minds. This provided a matrix for the idea of a deeper national culture and, therewith, of the nation which had only to be aroused to self-awareness. It was neither a simple attachment to their indigenous culture nor a concretely experienced love of their fellow-countrymen which made the intellectuals so fervently nationalistic. These would have presupposed a prior sense of affinity, which for many reasons was lacking and often still is. In fact, however, "fellow-countrymen" became so to the modern intellectuals primarily by virtue of their common differentiation from the foreign ruler. Fierce resentment against the powerful, fear-inspiring foreign ruler was probably a much more significant factor than either a sense of affinity or a conscious appreciation of the traditional culture.

The resentment of the modern intellectual grew from several seeds: one of the most important was the derogation implied in the barrier against entry into or advancement in the civil service. The other, closely related to this, was the feeling of injury from insults, experienced or heard about, explicit or implicit, which the foreign rulers and their businessmen fellow-nationals inflicted on the indigenous modern intellectuals. Lord Curzon's derogatory remarks about the educated Bengali in his famous Calcutta University Convocation Address were only among the more egregious of an infinite multitude of such slights, injuries, and denigrations. The belittlement extended into every sphere of life, cultural, intellectual, religious, economic, political, and personal. A sense of distress and of anticipated insult became part of the indigenous intellectuals' relationship with foreigners for a long time. Even now in independence, the alertness to insult and the readiness to perceive it persist. They were at their height in the early period of nationalism.

The situation was rendered all the more insufferable by the genuine and positive appreciation which the native intellectuals often felt for the foreign culture, and their feeling of the inferiority of their own in comparison with it. Nationalism of an extremely assertive sort was an effort to find self-respect, and to overcome the inferiority of the self in the face of the superiority of the culture and power of the foreign metropolis.

It was therefore logical that prior to independence the politics of the intellectuals, once the movement for constitutional reform had waned, should have been concerned with one end above all others: national independence. It was generally assumed by most politicized intellectuals that any other desiderata would be automatically realized with the attainment of that condition. The actual attainment of independence and of a condition in which the tasks of political life have become as demanding and as diversified as they must inevitably become in a polity where the state takes unto itself so many powers and aspires to so much, has not greatly altered the situation. Nationalism still remains one of the greatest of all motive forces;[11] it underlies many policies to which it is not really germane and serves as a touchstone of nearly every action and policy.

The socialistic and the populistic ele-

[11] Although it is by no means the chief reason, this nationalistic concentration is a significant factor in accounting for the poverty and uniformity of intellectual life of the underdeveloped countries.

ments in the politics of the intellectuals of underdeveloped countries are secondary to and derivative from their nationalistic preoccupations and aspirations. Economic policies have their legitimation in their capacity to raise the country on the scale of the nations of the world. The populace is transfigured in order to demonstrate the uniqueness of its "collective personality." The ancient culture is exhumed and renewed in order to demonstrate, especially to those who once denied it, the high value of the nation. Foreign policy is primarily a policy of "public relations" designed not, as in the advanced countries, to sustain the security of the state or enhance its power among other states, but to improve the reputation of the nation, to make others heed its voice, to make them pay attention to it and to respect it. The "world," the "imperialist world," remains very much on the minds of the intellectuals of the new states. It remains the audience and the jury of the accomplishments of the nation which the intellectuals have done so much to create.

Nonetheless, despite the pre-eminence of the nationalistic sensibility, it does not rest upon a *tabula rasa*, cleared of all other attachments. The intellectuals of underdeveloped countries are not as "uprooted," as "detribalized," as they themselves sometimes assert with so much melancholy, or as, with more spite, their foreign and domestic detractors often allege. They have remained attached in many ways to their traditional patterns of social life and culture. These deeper attachments include parochial attachments to their own tribes and ethnic and caste communities, and almost inevitably seek expression in public policies and in domestic political alignments. The presence of these attachments is a supplementary generator of nationalistic sentiment. It is against them, and in an effort to overcome them—within themselves and in their fellow-countrymen—that many intellectuals in underdeveloped countries commit themselves so fervently to intense nationalism.

By a similar process, the extensive use of a foreign language in daily intellectual life also feeds the force of nationalism. The intellectuals' very large amount of reading in French and English and their feeling of continued dependence on these cultures, their continuing and still necessary employment of French or English for their own cultural creations and even for political, administrative, and judicial purposes, and their awareness of the slow and painful course through which their nation must pass before its own language becomes adequate to the requirements of modern life cannot avoid touching their sensibilities. The constant reaffirmation of their nationalistic attachment is an effort to assuage this wound.

Socialism. The socialism of the intellectuals of the underdeveloped countries grows, fundamentally, from their feeling for charismatic authority, from their common humanity, and from the antichrematistic traditions of their indigenous culture. More immediately, it is a product of the conditions and substance of their education, and of their nationalistic sensibility.

The intellectuals of underdeveloped countries are, in general, devotees of authority, even though they may be inflamed against some particular authority. They regard the existing distribution of authority as the source of present economic and social inequities and they seek a new distribution of authority as the instrument to abolish them. Their critical view of the state as it exists at present in their own country is partly a manifestation of their distrust of impersonal authority and of their faith in a more charismatic alternative.[12] They do not believe in the capacities of businessmen to increase the well-being of the nation. They have little sympathy, conscious or unconscious, with the man who is engaged in the pursuit of wealth.

None of the great traditional cultures

[12] *Vide* the Gandhian socialists and the Bhoodan movement in India.

gives a high rank to the merchant; even when they revolt against the traditional culture, or slip away from it unwittingly, the intellectuals usually retain that part of it which allots no high place to the businessman. In their mind, the life of the businessman is unheroic; it is untouched by sacredness and they will have none of it. Intellectuals very seldom seek careers in private business; when necessity forces them into it, they are ill at ease and restless. The intellectual who works for a private business firm lays himself open to the charge of having deserted his calling, even though he has deserted it no more than a civil servant or a lawyer. The notion of an economic system ruled by the decisions of businessmen, out to make a profit for themselves, is repugnant to the intellectuals of underdeveloped countries—even more than it is in advanced countries, where the businessman does not fare very well either at the hands of the intellectuals.

As long as the intellectuals of underdeveloped countries pursued the paths of constitutional reform and confined their attention to administration and representation, these deeper dispositions whose source was the traditional indigenous culture did not enter into their politics. They accepted most of the existing regime. When, however, they began to direct their attention to the society and the nation, when they ceased being politically "superficial" and began to touch on politically "sacred" things, the socialist potentiality of their fundamental orientation became more manifest.

These inner developments within the intelligentsia of underdeveloped countries coincided with the upsurge of socialist thought among the European intellectuals. To these, the intelligentsia of the underdeveloped countries felt drawn. The attractive power of the metropolis was enhanced by the congeniality of intellectual socialism. From the 1920's to the 1940's, the example of the late Professor Harold Laski elicited and fortified the socialistic

disposition of many young intellectuals of the English-speaking underdeveloped countries; Jean-Paul Sartre has played a parallel role among the French-speaking intellectuals from 1945 onward.

The spread of socialistic ideas was aided by the large-scale migration of Asian and African intellectuals to Europe for further study and professional training. The great stream of Asians to European educational centers began in the 1890's; their intensive politicization, in the 1920's. The stream of the African students began in the 1920's and became much wider after 1945. From the end of the First World War and the Russian Revolution, the young Asians and Africans, impelled by events in the world and at home, found themselves in an atmosphere which gave the encouragement of a nearly universal assent to their socialist aspirations.

The association between socialism as a domestic policy and hostility toward an imperialistic foreign policy—a connection which is inherent in the postulates of socialist thought and its Leninist variant, although not all socialists have at all times shared it—made European, and especially British and French, socialism even more acceptable to the Asian and African students who came to the intellectual capitals of the European metropolis.

To these factors which made socialism appear such a bright ideal should be joined the nature of large-scale business enterprise in their own countries. In practically all instances, large-scale business enterprise in the underdeveloped countries was owned and controlled by foreign capitalists. Not just the Europeans, and latterly the Americans, owned large firms in Africa and Asia, but Chinese, Syrians, Lebanese, Parsees, Armenians, Greeks, and Italians, away from their own countries, showed exceptional enterprise. Encountering few indigenous competitors, they built up extensive organizations and ample fortunes in underdeveloped countries. The ethnic diversity and separateness of the peoples, even within large, centrally governed countries, often brought about a situation in which private businessmen who were of the same "nationality" as those in the midst of whom they lived and conducted their affairs, but who were of a different "community," were regarded as outsiders who had no moral claims on the loyalty of the intellectuals. Businessmen, by the nature of their calling, could never be part of the "people"; their ethnic distinctness was further justification for treating them as alien to the "people."

On the other side, a socialistic economic system conducted in accordance with principles which are of intellectual origin, guided by persons who are imbued with these "principles," seems to be the only conceivable alternative to a privately operated economy. The intellectuals who dare to differ from such obvious conclusions constitute a small fraction of the intellectual classes in most of the underdeveloped countries, both colonial and sovereign.

The socialism of the intellectuals of underdeveloped countries, it should also be stressed, is a product of their pained awareness of the poverty of their own countries. The heightening of national sensibility led perforce to the discovery of the "people." Agitational activities brought them into contact with the "people"; the vague doctrine of nationalism, even in its liberal form, brought the idea of the "people" into the consciousness of the intellectuals. Often, too, on return from a period of foreign study where they had encountered socialist ideas and experienced a heightened national consciousness, the sight of their impoverished fellow-countrymen had a traumatic force. Confrontation with the poverty of their country evoked anguish and desperation in many intellectuals. They have been humiliated by their sense of the backwardness of their country. They have learned how gradually the advancement of the Western countries has moved, and they have heard of the speedy progress of the Soviet Union from a backward country to the status of one

of the most powerful industrial nations in the world. What could be more harmonious with their present perceptions, their aspirations, and their background than to espouse a socialist solution to their unhappy problem? And if to this is added the fact that their countries have been held in subjection by capitalistic countries and the socialist countries proclaim their hostility to imperialism, the disposition toward socialism receives another impulsion.

Populism. The populism of intellectual politics in underdeveloped countries has a familial affinity to the populism of the intellectuals of more advanced countries during the past century and a half. It is a part of a universal process consequent on the emergence of an incipient and fragmentary world-wide intellectual community. It is a phenomenon of the tension between metropolis and province which arises from the trend toward that worldwide intellectual community.

The populism of the intellectuals is German in origin. It was a critique of the pretensions of a worldly, urban, and urbane authority. It was a critique of the feebleness of the petty elites of the system of *Kleinstaaterei*, alongside the grandeur of the Holy Roman Empire, and of the Germany which could emerge if the regime of the princelings could be abolished and all of Germany unified. It was a critique of the central institutional system, and particularly of the claims of the state, of the universities, and of the ecclesiastical authorities to embody what was essential in their society and of their insistence, on that basis, on their right to rule over it. It was a rejection of the urban bourgeoisie. It was a denial that the "nation" could be found in existing authoritative institutions and an assertion that the root of the future lay in the "folk."

In Russia, populism was a product of a similar situation, aggravated by resentment against a prevailing enchantment by the West, which was more pronounced than the Francophilia of the princely courts against which the first generations of romantic

German populism had been a reaction. In Russia, the intellectuals had carried on a passionate love affair with Western Europe and many had been disappointed and had even come to feel guilty for deserting their "own" for foreign idols. Alienated from their own authorities of state, church, and university, hostile to their own mercantile bourgeoisie, disillusioned with Western European socialism after its failures in the revolutions of 1848, it had nowhere to turn except to the "people," whom it glorified as a repository of wisdom and as the source of Russia's salvation.

American populism was not very different in its general origins. It, too, was the product of a reaction against the Anglophile intellectual elite of the Eastern seaboard and the political and industrial elites who ruled the country from the Eastern cities. In America, too, therefore, it was an effort to find a firm foundation for intellectuals who were alienated from the authorities of their society and from their xenophilic fellow-intellectuals. In America also it was a phase of the struggle of province against metropolis.

In the underdeveloped countries, the process has been essentially the same. Alienated from the indigenous authorities of their own traditional society—chiefs, sultans, princes, landlords, and priests—and from the rulers of their modern society—the foreign rulers and the "Westernized" constitutional politicians (and since independence, politicians of the governing party)—the intellectuals have had only the "people," the "African personality," the "Indian peasant," etc., as supports in the search for the salvation of their own souls and their own society.

The "people" are a model and a standard; contact with them is a good. Esteem and disesteem are meted out on the basis of "closeness to the people" or distance from them. It is a common worry of and an accusation against the intellectuals of the underdeveloped countries that they are "out of touch with the people," uprooted, *déraciné*, "brown" or "black" (as the case may be) "Englishmen" or "Frenchmen," etc. Many make the accusation against themselves, most make it against their fellow-intellectuals.

Factually it is usually quite untruthful. Most intellectuals in underdeveloped countries are not as "cut off" from their own culture as they and their detractors suggest. They live in the middle of it, their wives and mothers are its constant representatives in their midst, they retain close contact with their families, which are normally steeped in traditional beliefs and practices. The possession of a modern intellectual culture does remove them, to some extent, from the culture of their ancestors, but much of the latter remains and lives on in them.[13]

The experience to which the allegation of being "cut off" from the "people" refers is not to any serious extent a real result of the intellectuals' acceptance of the "foreign," modern culture. It rests rather on their own feeling of distance from the rest of their fellow-nationals, which is a product of the ethnic, tribal, kinship and caste particularism of these underdeveloped societies and of the consequent lack of a true sense of civil affinity with the rest of their fellow-countrymen. It is the resultant of the superimposition of a nationalistic ideology, which demands fellow-feeling, on a narrower particularism, inharmonious with it and psychologically contradictory to it. There is a genuine feeling of strain; all the burden of this strain is put upon the fact that they possess some elements of an exogenous culture.

The frequent reiteration of the charge testifies to an awareness of this tension, and the choice of the foreign culture as its focus is a manifestation of a desire to find

[13] Much of the intellectuals' self-accusation rests on the populistic assumption that the "people," not being distracted or corrupted by modern culture, are the bearers of the traditional culture in its fullness and its glory. This assumption is probably an error; the "people" are quite unlikely to be in more than fragmentary possession of the corpus of traditional culture.

a way out which will conform to the requirements of ideological nationalism. Because the intellectuals assert it and, to some extent, believe it, they often try to make amends for it by some form of nativism, which extols the traditional ways of the people and juxtaposes them with modern and thus "foreign" ways.

This nativistic reaction accentuates demagogic political tendencies, and fosters a race among contenders for the distinction of being more "for" the "people" or more "akin" to them. It accentuates prejudice against the educated and a hostility against the modern education which the intellectuals of the new states need if they are to perform intellectual functions in a productive way, and without which they would not be intellectuals and their countries would flounder and sink.

Nonetheless, despite this preoccupation with the "people," the populism of the intellectuals of underdeveloped countries does not necessarily bring with it either intimacy with the ordinary people, a concrete attachment to them, or even a democratic attitude. It is compatible with them but it does not require them. It is equally compatible with a dictatorial regime which treats the people as instruments to be employed in the transformation of the social and economic order, and their culture and outlook as a hindrance to progress.

Populism can be the legitimating principle of oligarchical regimes, as well as of democratic regimes and of all the intermediate types. The "people" constitute the prospective good to be served by government policy, and they serve as the emblem of the traditional culture which is thus glorified even while it is being eroded and its traditional custodians disregarded or disparaged.

Oppositionalism. The populism of the intellectual is a product of opposition to the authorities who rule at home and to the foreign culture which fascinates him and his fellow-intellectuals in his own country. It is one facet of an oppositional syndrome.

The origins of this inclination to oppose constituted authority seem, at first glance, easy to locate. Practically all politics in the colonial period, once the constitutional phase had passed, consisted and still consist of root and branch opposition. Whether they took the form of conspiracy, sabotage, riots, assassination, clandestine or open journalism, public meetings, boycotts, demonstrations and processions, civil disobedience or unco-operative participation in representative institutions, opposition and obstruction of the foreign ruler were the main aims. Where it was impossible to share in the responsible exercise of authority, opposition was in fact the only alternative.

The degree of alienation from the constituted authority varied but it was almost always deeper and more drastic than the opposition which exists in advanced pluralistic societies.[14] It was the opposition of politicians excluded or withdrawn from the constitutional order, who accepted neither the rules nor the ends of the prevailing system. It was, therefore, the opposition of politicians who refused in principle to consider the problems of the government as real tasks needing resolution. It was an opposition which was convinced by situation, temperament, and principle that it would never share authority with the foreign ruler. The only authority to which it aspired was complete and exclusive control of the entire machinery of state. Until that point was reached, its only policy was opposition.

The oppositional attitude of the intellectuals has another point of origin far removed from the political experience of a colonial situation. In most underdeveloped countries the traditional character of

[14] Its only parallel in the West is the conduct of the Irish members in the House of Commons in the latter part of the last century and of Communistic members of European parliaments when they were a small minority and did not seek a popular front. The "Irish members" had considerable resonance in India and their influence still survives, even where its origin has been forgotten.

the culture sustains diffuseness in the exercise of authority. Diffuse authority, omnicompetent in the tasks facing the society, at least according to legendary beliefs, derives its legitimacy in part from its comprehensive effectiveness. Even though the substantive actions performed by such diffuse traditional authorities are no longer respected by intellectuals, the older pattern of expectation persists. Specific, delimited, impersonal, constitutional authority gives the appearance of being a weak authority, an unloving one which possesses no inner relationship with the ruled. The diffuseness of a charismatic authority is desired, and the bureaucratic rule of the foreign power or of its sovereign indigenous successor arouses little enthusiasm or even willing acknowledgment of any deeper legitimacy. The intellectuals of underdeveloped countries, despite their immersion in modern culture and their overt acceptance of modern political principles, are at bottom averse to a relatively weak, self-limiting government, even when that government is their own, bound to them by common ethnic ties, a common culture, and comradeship in the struggle for independence.

This is one of the underlying grounds for the widespread disillusionment which overcomes so many intellectuals in underdeveloped countries after independence. It must be remembered that, whatever has happened since, practically every new state of the postwar world began as a modern constitutional regime of representative institutions and public liberties. They have all had to employ modern bureaucratic methods of administration, even when they lacked the requisite personnel. They have tried to operate the rule of law. They all began as remote impersonal machines, exercising authority without the diffuseness of charisma or tradition. Their equilibrium has depended on a great charismatic personality who, at the peak of the governmental mountain, offset the distaste for bureaucratic-legal rule.

Thus, the establishment of a tradition

of opposition in political life has, as has happened so often in almost every sphere of life in underdeveloped countries, coincided with a fundamental disposition resting on an indigenous cultural tradition.

It would be wrong perhaps to claim a universal validity for a generalization which could be drawn from Max Weber's criticism of Bismarck and the paralyzing influence which his autocracy in the Reichstag exerted on the opposition parties of that body. It was Max Weber's view that the irresponsible opposition which the Bismarckian regime and its Wilhelmine successor evoked would make the opposition parties incapable of responsible, efficient rule when they were given the opportunity to govern. He also asserted— and this is more important for our present discussion—that they would become incapable of conducting themselves as a responsible opposition, working within the rules of the parliamentary game. In certain of the underdeveloped countries, this generalization does not seem to be applicable. In India, for example, certain of the intellectual politicians, and above all the Prime Minister, have shown great adaptability in turning from a condition of complete and irreconcilable opposition to a responsible hard-headed exercise of authority, and some of the socialists and independents conduct their opposition in a most intelligent and responsible manner. The same obtains in varying degrees in Ghana and in Tunisia. Certain intellectual politicians have shown considerable capacity to rule, even though they have not been as democratic or liberal as they once aspired to be or as Mr. Nehru has succeeded in being. Not a few firebrands of the days of the independence movement have turned out to be responsible parliamentarians of the highest order.

Nonetheless, much truth remains in Max Weber's proposition. The intellectuals of the underdeveloped countries since they acquired independence, insofar as they are not in authority, do incline toward an anti-political, oppositional attitude.

They are disgruntled. The form of the constitution does not please them and they are reluctant to play the constitutional game. Many of them desire to obstruct the government or give up the game of politics altogether, retiring into a negative state of mind about all institutional politics or at least about any political regime which does not promise a "clean sweep" of the inherited order.

Incivility. Although the intellectuals of the underdeveloped countries have created the idea of the nation within their own countries, they have not been able to create a nation. They are themselves the victim of that condition, since nationalism does not necessarily become citizenship. Membership in a nation which is sovereign entails a sense of affinity with the other human beings who make up the nation. It entails a sense of "partness" in a whole, a sense of sharing a common substance. This feeling of being part of the whole is the basis of a sense of concern for its well-being, and a sense of responsibility to it and for it. It transcends ineluctable divisions, softening them and rendering them tolerable to civil order, regarding them as less significant than the underlying community of those who form the nation. In political life, these dispositions form the virtue of civility.

Civility has hitherto not been one of the major features of the politicized intelligentsia of the underdeveloped countries. An intense politicization is difficult to bring into harmony with civility. Intense politicization is accompanied by the conviction that only those who share one's principles and positions are wholly legitimate members of the polity and that those who do not share them are separated by a steep barrier. The governing party in many sovereign underdeveloped states, and those intellectuals who make it up or are associated with it, tend to believe that those who are in opposition are separated from them by fundamental and irreconcilable differences. They feel that they *are* the state and the nation, and that those

who do not go along with them are not just political rivals but *total* enemies. The sentiments of the opposition are, *mutatis mutandis*, scarcely different. These are the fruits of intense politicization.

The incivility of the politicized intellectuals has a history which precedes their birth. Traditional societies, based on kinship and hierarchy, are not civil societies. They do not know the phenomenon of citizenship, since rights and obligations are not functions of membership in a polity determined by territorial boundaries. The primordial qualities of traditional societies —kinship, age, sex, locality, etc.—are not qualities which define the citizen. In a pluralistic society they are not by any means incompatible with citizenship. In the more unitary, traditional society, they suffocate incipient civility.

The moral structure of the independence movement has enabled this uncivil tradition to persist. The independence movement conceived of itself as the embodiment of the nation, and after its victory it became and conceived of itself as identical with the state. Given the oppositional dispositions which come to the surface in parliamentary and journalistic circles not attached to the government party, there often appears to be a semblance of justification for the belief of an impatient and hypersensitive government that the opposition is subversive of the state and cannot be reconciled to it.

This does not imply that there are not civil intellectuals in every underdeveloped country, some of them in the government, some of them in opposition, and some in journalism, the universities, and the other liberal professions. They are, however, in a marked minority. The traditions by which they are sustained, although they do exist in some of the states, are frail.

Three Stages in the Politics of the Intellectuals in Underdeveloped Countries

THE FIRST STAGE

(a) *Constitutional Liberalism.* The first efflorescence of the modern intellectual in the underdeveloped countries occurred roughly between the years when India was recovering from the trauma of the Mutiny and its repression and the First World War. In the few countries where there was anything of a class with a modern education and a certain amount of political stirring, these were the years of constitutional liberalism, eloquently and courteously argued. This first stage came considerably later to Black Africa and lasted a shorter time than it did in British India and the Middle East. In Southeast Asia, too, the course of development was greatly telescoped. The backwardness of Southeast Asia and Black Africa in the construction of modern cultural and legal institutions, and the smaller numbers of persons who went abroad for higher studies, resulted in a much smaller intellectual class than in India, and a later, briefer, and feebler life of constitutional liberalism. Where the intellectual class scarcely existed, politics could only be embryonic.

This was the stage of the politics of lawyers and journalists. Their politics were the politics of *honoratiores*. They were well-educated men, many of whom had studied in the metropolitan countries; they had absorbed and appreciated something of the metropolitan culture and the liberal constitutional political outlook, which, in the circles in which they moved in the France and Great Britain of that period, appeared to be almost unchallenged.

They were not revolutionaries and they did not always aspire to independence, at least, not in the immediate future. One of their main grievances in this earliest phase was the restriction of the right of entry of their fellow-countrymen into the civil service which ruled their country on behalf of the foreign sovereign. They also desired that legislative institutions should be a little more representative of persons like themselves. These two concerns could be interpreted crudely as a manifestation of a narrow class interest, but they were actually broader and better than that.[15] There were serious grounds, in

[15] Nor were these their only interests. They

their own self-image, for their claim to share in the administration of the country and for a vote in the determination of the budget.

They had been brought up in a hierarchical tradition in which the landowning classes and the learned, in their own view and that of others, were the possessors of a "stake in the country." Insofar as it was a country, they felt it to be "theirs," and "theirs" almost exclusively. Many came from families which had in the past exercised great influence and which, in the countryside, still continued to do so. It was therefore part of their conception of the right order of things that they should share in the ruling of their own country, under a sovereign whom they were not in the main inclined to challenge in principle.

The liberal constitutional ideas which they acquired in the course of their mainly legal studies fitted in with their conceptions. Europe was boiling with democratic agitation—the labor and socialist movements were in process of formation. In the main, however, the very small trickle of Africans and the larger numbers of Asians who before the First World War went to the metropolis for advanced studies did not, on the whole, come into contact with these circles. They wanted a liberal governmental and legal order in the administration of which they could share.

Since they were largely lawyers, they developed the rhetorical skills and the proposed the liberalization of the legal system, greater equity in its administration, and certain liberal social reforms such as the improvement of the legal position of women, the provision of more ample educational facilities, etc.

Obviously, there was some element of "class" and "self-interest" in some of their demands, such as the insistence that imported foreign manufactures should not be allowed to enjoy any advantages over indigenously produced industrial goods. The interest of the whole society, the interest of a class and of an individual might all coincide on particular issues. This is probably the most that can be credited to the charge against the first generation made by the actors who came on the political stage a little later.

self-confidence in dealing with authority which are an indispensable part of the equipment of the modern politician.[16] The structure of legal practice also gave them the time and the resources to absent themselves from their professional activities. As the occasion demanded, they were able, while still continuing to practice their professions, to devote themselves to public agitation, to attend and address meetings, to write books, pamphlets, and articles for the press, to meet representatives of their rulers from time to time in order to argue their claims, and to participate in consultative and representative bodies.

Side by side with this form of lawyers' politics, a daily and periodical press struggled to come into existence, largely in the metropolitan language but also in the indigenous languages. The journalists were not professionals. They were often political lawyers who had either left their profession or practiced it alongside of journalism; there were also among them men who had been teachers, or who had aspired to join the government service, or had actually been in governmental employ. They were usually well-educated men, with the gravity of the Victorian and Continental bourgeois liberals whom they admired. All this gave dignity and decorum to the political life of that stage of political development.

As journalists, they were not following a career in the material sense of the word. They were not trying to become rich. They were not interested in being purveyors of news and diversion. They were not seeking a livelihood in journalism. Where they could not gain their livelihood from journalism or from their auxiliary professions, they unquestioningly relied on the support of their kinsmen and patrons. They were journalists because there was a small literate public which could be

reached and rendered coherent and articulate on behalf of the ideal of constitutional government in which the best-qualified of the ruled would have some hand.

These journalists and lawyer-politicians had few followers other than themselves, i.e., like-minded men in similar stations of life, such as liberal businessmen or princes, chiefs, and landowners. Leaders and followers together constituted no more than a small group. Only in India were the absolute numbers fairly large. In the Middle East they were fewer, and in the rest of Africa and in Southeast Asia their numbers were negligible. Nonetheless they created, by their activity, the foundations of a still surviving tradition of the modern intellectuals in politics.

They did not have the field to themselves, even at the time of their greatest pre-eminence. They were being challenged by a more aggressive group, less complaisant toward their Western rulers and toward Western culture. These new rivals claimed that constitutional tactics led nowhere. They were the forerunners of the political type which came to the center of the political arena in the second stage. During the first stage, however, there was also another trend of intellectual activity which profoundly affected subsequent political developments, though it was not in itself primarily political or even political at all.

(b) Moral Renewal. An impassioned effort of religious and moral self-renewal accompanied the development of political life of the underdeveloped countries during their colonial period. It was at first a feature of the countries which possessed conspicuous evidence of great indigenous achievements in the past—i.e., of the countries with a literary and architectural inheritance which in the midst of present degradation could remind contemporaries that their country had once been great. It was therefore also a characteristic of countries with an indigenous traditional intelligentsia made up of the custodians of sacred writings. Thus it was that in India

---

[16] It seems to me not accidental that even now the highest flights of Indo-Anglian prose have the rhetorical quality of high-grade lawyers addressing a court or a parliamentary body.

and in the Middle East, through much of the nineteenth century, protagonists of the traditional cultures, and particularly of the religions of Hinduism and Islam, sought to purify their inheritance, to restore it to its pristine greatness or to fuse it with modern elements. Both in India and in the Middle East, the aim was to reinstate the dignity of the traditional religious culture, and the society which was based on it, and thereby to establish its worth in the face of the encroachment of Western culture and religion.[17]

This movement to evoke a national self-consciousness, through the renewal of cultural traditions which had been allowed to decay, was not directly political. There was not much contact between the modern men who represented constitutional liberalism, and the energetic, pious traditionalists.[18] The two movements seemed to run almost independently of each other; there was no antagonism between them, often little mutual awareness.

The agents of moral renewal were not secular social reformers. They were not modern intellectuals in the sense of the word used here. They were men of the traditional culture who were sufficiently sensitive to the impact of modern culture to feel the need to reaffirm their own.[19] Their task was the cleansing of the cultural —and this meant largely religious— inheritance of their society from what they claimed were historically accidental accretions which had brought it into disrepute among modern men and allowed their country to sink in the world's esteem and in its own and, particularly, to appear enfeebled and unworthy in comparison with Western achievements. They claimed

[17] Movements to "re-establish" the glory of African civilization are a much later product.
[18] There were of course exceptions like al-Afghani, Mohammed Abdou, and M. G. Ranade.
[19] Their influence made itself felt, however, in both India and the Middle East, primarily among modern intellectuals. They exerted little effect on their fellow traditional intellectuals, who persisted in their torpor.

that what was essential in their religious traditions could—by restoration and cleansing or by syncretism—be reformulated in an idiom more appropriate to the modern situation, and that if this were done, it would recommend itself to their fellow-countrymen who were needlessly and even perniciously enamored of Western culture. They were not unqualifiedly fanatical enemies of Western culture. They claimed that much of what it had to offer—particularly science, technology, and forms of organization—were necessary for the improvement of their countries and the reestablishment of their greatness among the nations. They insisted, however, that their countrymen must not lose their own souls to the West. They must instead rediscover their own essential being by the acceptance of a new and purer version of their own cultural tradition.

The older generation of modern "Victorian" intellectuals did not pay much heed to these preachments, although they were not hostile. In the next stage of political development, this effort of moral rediscovery and self-renewal had very profound repercussions. When, in the second stage, constitutional liberalism seemed to disappear or to be confined in a very narrow space, the movement of moral and religious reform was taken up and developed into a passionate nationalism. Now, even where the religious element in the traditional culture is passed over, praise of the essence of the traditional culture has become a plank in the platform of every movement for independence and of every new state.

The Second Stage. From constitutional liberalism and religious-moral renewal, the intellectuals of the colonial countries passed to a fervently politicized nationalism. With this shift, there also occurred a shift in the mode of political action and its audience.

India was the first of all the underdeveloped colonial countries to execute this movement; it was the one in which the traditional indigenous culture was richest and most elaborate and in which that culture had developed most systematically and comprehensively. It was also the country where the foreign rulers had been longest established in a thoroughgoing way and where the contact of the indigenous intellectuals with a metropolitan Western culture had given birth to a longer and richer modern tradition than was possessed by any other country of Asia or Africa. It was the country with the largest and most differentiated modern intelligentsia. The first long phase of fascination with the West had already begun, in the India of the 1880's, to produce from within itself a reaction in favor of more purely Indian things.

This was also the time of growing strength in the socialist movement in Europe and of the growth of anarchism. Terrorism was in the ascendancy in Russia and Ireland. Tales of the Russian underground spread in Asia, together with the repute and glory of the deeds of the "Nihilists" in Russia, the Sinn Fein in Ireland, and the Carbonari in Italy. Massini, Stepnyak, and Kropotkin were names well known among the younger generation of Indian intellectuals. Yeats was becoming a figure of weight among the literary intelligentsia and along with this went a feeling for the Irish Renaissance and a belief in the possibilities of a comparable Indian Renaissance. The writings of these *rishis* became known in India, imported from England; some of them appeared in Bengali translations.

The new generation which came to the surface of public life around the turn of the century was no longer content with constitutional agitation, or with such limited goals as more places in the Indian Civil Service and more consultative and deliberative institutions in which Indians would be amply represented. Indian traditional culture was being revived through the Ramakrishna Mission and the Arya Samaj, and a new Indian self-consciousness took hold of young men who, while not deeming themselves religious, were possessed by a profound resonance toward traditional Indian symbols. The Maharashtrian and Bengali terrorists gave no thought to the kind of social or political order which they wished to see established. They wished only to have India free of foreign rule, free to be itself, in its own Indian way.

Parallel developments a third of a century later could be seen in areas as far apart as the Gold Coast and Egypt. A half-century later, they began to appear in East Africa. The same pattern was visible in more foreshortened form in Syria and Iraq. The proportions and the tone of the movements in these smaller countries, with much smaller intelligentsias, have been roughly what they were in India.

In these smaller countries, too, there was a tendency to regard the older generation of liberal constitutionalists and piecemeal reformers as excessively subservient to the foreign rulers and as excessively bemused by their foreign culture and their foreign forms of government. The later, populistic phase of intellectual politics, which in a variety of forms continues into the present, only intensified and made more complex and luminous an already established pattern. The generally socialistic orientation of the politics of the Asian and African intellectuals, which took form after the First World War and became preponderant after the Second World War, in a similar fashion only elaborated the inherent potentiality of intense nationalism.

The intensification of political concerns was the outgrowth of the earlier political interest, in fusion with the more acute sense of nationality which the heightened awareness of the traditional indigenous culture had helped to arouse. The politics of the "second generation" touched a very much deeper chord than that which the earlier generation had reached; it is a chord which still vibrates. The greater depth of the new political movement meant also that it was more passionate, more in the complete possession of politics.

The fundamental politicization of the intelligentsia of Asia and Africa led to the discrediting of the first liberal generation. The politics of cultured and urbane gentlemen, speaking French or English to perfection, interested in much else besides politics, was not for this generation.

The politics of the second generation received a further powerful impetus from its participation in a cosmopolitan movement, in which *foreign*, Western countries were involved. The intellectuals of the second generation, like those who preceded and those who have followed, were also held by their attachment to Western culture. The extremist nationalist movements in Asia and subsequently in Africa had a Western legitimation for their strivings. They drew inspiration and comfort from abroad, they felt that their actions were one with a mighty surge all over the world, a surge toward a new order of freedom, with possibilities unknown and unregarded.[20] This sense of being a part of the larger world infused into the politics of the second generation the permanently bedeviling tension between province and metropolis, and added, as it always does, the heat which arises from conflicting loyalties.

When the second generation was still in its youth in India, and only in conception in other Asian and African colonial countries, the Russian Revolution took place. Only a little while thereafter M. K. Gandhi established his ascendancy over the political scene in India.[21] These two events precipitated the populistic consciousness, which had been only latent in the exacerbated nationalism which had preceded them.

The early leaders of the second generation had been deferential to "ancient traditions," in contrast to the liberal, moderate, and progressive attitude of the earlier constitutional politicians, who had not given political significance to indigenous cultural traditions. The "people" had, however, not yet acquired the eminence which was later to be their due in the political outlook of the intellectuals. Now, under the guidance of Gandhi and an attenuated Leninism, they ascended to a central position.

Socialism was no further away than a step of the imagination. The preceding generation had been neither socialist nor anti-socialist. The issue had never arisen, as long as civil-service personnel policies, the extension of representative institutions, and criticism of the "drain" had been the main objects of political debate.[22] Politics now became "total politics" and its claims on those who gave themselves to it became all-embracing. Politics in colonial countries became a vocation, without becoming professionalized. Many came to live "for" politics, but few lived "from" politics in the way in which professional

[20] The role of exiles and expatriates living in the metropolitan centers of Great Britain, France, Germany, and Switzerland helped to maintain a continuous link between the revolutionary and radical tendencies in the metropolis and those in the underdeveloped countries. These exiles and expatriates provided a sort of training school for young Asians and Africans who had gone abroad to study, and they constituted a continuous representation of the interests of their countries before the public opinion of the ruling metropolis.

Like exiles and expatriates everywhere, they also were more "uprooted" than their countrymen who either stayed at home or returned home after a few years. This "uprootedness" did not, however, diminish the intensity of their politics. Rather, the contrary.

[21] And with it, he began his march toward ascendancy over the Western colonialist conscience. A skeptical attitude about the rightfulness of imperialism had already existed in the West for a long time, but it was Gandhi more than anyone else outside the European Socialist and the Communist movements who impressed it on the consciousness of the Western educated classes. As a result, a body of Western Allies was formed and its existence was a reassurance and a stimulus to the politicized intellectuals who continued to stand in need of a sustaining tie with modern "Western" culture.

[22] In Africa after the Second World War, nationalism, intense politics, socialism, and populism came into life almost simultaneously, as if they were inseparably involved with each other.

politicians live from it. The politics of the colonial intelligentsia became in a sense more profound; that is, they came into contact with the deeper layers of the intelligentsia's existence. The politics of the intellectuals became charismatic politics.

As one might expect from charismatic politics, a tremendous pull was exerted on the youth. Leadership still lay with the lawyers and a few who had once served the government as officials and clerks[23] or had been tempted sufficiently to prepare themselves to do so. A large and important part of the following, however, consisted of students—college and university students in countries with colleges and universities and high school students where these were absent. A great deal of the clamor and volatility of the politics of the second generation of the intellectuals came from the students.

The Third Stage. The third stage of intellectual politics sees the intellectuals in power in a sovereign state, ruled by an indigenous elite.

With this stage the intellectuals who have reaped the fruits of the struggle become dissociated from the intellectual class. A schism occurs in the corps of intellectual-politicians. One sector comes into power and takes to it like a fish to water. The exercise of authority—which is not identical with the efficient exercise of authority—seems to be almost as natural as breathing to those intellectuals who are in power. To an increasing extent, they see themselves as different from the intellectuals who do not share their power, and whom they chide as naggers, unreasonable critics, backsliders from the great national cause. The intellectuals in power feel themselves less continuous with the intellectual class than they did during the struggle

[23] Where there were few indigenous lawyers or others with higher education, leadership was exercised by clerks with secondary or elementary education. The educated, the *évolues*—intellectuals—have kept the lead, the highly educated when they have been available, the less well-educated where the former were lacking.

for independence. As the burdens and challenges of office preoccupy them, and as they spend so much of their time with party bosses and machine-men who have never been or who long since ceased to be intellectuals, their own image of themselves as intellectuals wanes and they become more sensitive to the anti-political dispositions of their old companions.

This drift toward schism is aggravated by the fact that the opposition becomes the magnet which draws the intellectuals. Although within the political elite, at the peak of government there are many who were once intellectuals by education, vocation, or disposition and who have now become hardened politicians, no longer paying any attention to things of intellectual interest. Those who remain intellectuals in vocation and disposition seem to find their natural habitat on the opposite benches. There—and in common rooms and cafés—gather the intellectuals who in their outlook, in their studies and their self-identification, remain intellectuals.

The transformation of the intellectuals in power discloses the duality of the oppositional mentality. The hatred of authority is often no more than a facet of the fascination and love that it evokes. When they come to power, intellectuals who have hated it quickly allow the identification with it, against which they struggled previously, to come into full bloom. They attach to themselves the regalia of authority and feel that they and the state are now identical. Whereas during the struggle for independence, they felt that they represented the nation and that all who disagreed with them were outside the national community and had allowed their souls to be possessed by the foreigner, now when they are in power, they regard themselves and the state as identical and all those who disagree with them as enemies of the state.[24]

[24] Mr. Nehru is something of an exception, although he too regards the opposition as an unavoidable pestilence, as an inconvenient

On the other side of the floor, where it is allowed to exist, the oppositional mentality retains all of its old forms. Bureaucratic administration is criticized as too remote and too impersonal. The government is charged with corruption; it is alleged to be "too distant" from the people, and to be the betrayer of the national idea. It is accused of damaging the reputation of the country in the world, or of turning the country over to a new form of foreign control.

The oppositional mentality of the third stage, however, possesses one feature which the second did not possess—i.e., disillusionment. Whereas the opposition of the second generation imagined an amorphously happy condition once their antagonists were removed, the oppositional mentality of the post-colonial period has no such utopian euphoria to assuage its present melancholy.

Oppositionalism, which was so involved in an intense politicization, tends among some of those who are out of power to shrivel into an anti-political passivity. It is not that politics no longer engages the attention. It still does, but among many intellectuals it has become a source of despondent inaction.

Among others, a quite substantial bloc, it flows into a more rigid form of activistic extremism. In some instances, this extremist alternative to passivity takes on a traditionalistic guise; in others, it assumes a Leninist visage. Both of these foster the intense and total rejection of the muddled, compromising, and often compromised, incumbent government, in the name of a higher ideal.

The Prospects of the Intellectuals in the Political Life of the New States

Practically every new state has begun its career with a commitment to a regime of

representative government and public liberties. Whatever might be the democratic and consultative elements in the indigenous tradition of government, the particular constitution which was actually chosen to give form to self-government is evidence of the role of intellectuals in the establishment of the new states. It was only through the influence of the intellectuals in contact with the modern political ideas which circulated in the larger world that this decision could have been made. This alone would be sufficient to testify to the still living inheritance of the notables who peopled the first stage of modern political life in the then colonial countries.

The fate of the new states, whether they persist and flourish as democracies, or whether they regress into more oligarchical forms of government, is as undeterminable as anything which lies in the future. As long, however, as they do not disintegrate into tribal and local territorial sovereignties, and as long as they at least aspire to be "modern," the intellectuals will go on playing a large role in the fulfillment of whatever possibilities fortune allots to their societies.

In most of the new states, the intellectuals still constitute a notable part of the ruling political elite, although their position is no longer as preponderant as when politics were a charismatic movement. Politics, as the new states were consolidated, became a profession and ceased to be a calling or a mission. The emerging professional politician, military or civilian in origin, is forced to be less of an intellectual in his outlook. The inevitability of the formation of a political machine has meant, and will continue even more to mean, that organizers with little intellectual disposition, interest, or sympathy will move into a more prominent position in the political elite. Back-benchers and party functionaries will include a very considerable proportion of place-holders, and the tasks they will have to perform will not be very attractive to intellectuals, living in the traditions of modern intellectuals.

[footnote 24 continued
part of the community which remains, notwithstanding, as much a part of the community as he himself is. At the other extreme is that other intellectual in politics, Dr Nkrumah, who regards any criticism or disagreement as *staatsfeindlich*.

Nonetheless, even on the government benches, if the regime continues to be more or less democratic there will remain some readiness of the professional party leaders to receive and sponsor intellectuals. The prestige of modern education will continue to be high and any political party and government will therefore wish to draw on its beneficiaries. Furthermore, the reservoir of persons available for political leadership will continue to be limited in the foreseeable future; this will force the party leaders to look in the intellectuals' direction, however reluctantly. At the same time, however, the oppositional tendencies of intellectuals and the hypersensitivity to criticism on the part of politicians of any sort—and of the politicians of new states in particular—will add to this reluctance.

Opposition parties, insofar as they are allowed to exist, will certainly draw on intellectuals for their critical ideas concerning the government and for leadership and following. Such parties are their natural home.

If the underdeveloped countries become completely oligarchical and are ruled by a military junta or a one-party state, the role of intellectuals in political life in the narrower sense will certainly decline. The diminution of public political life will tend to narrow the area permitted to intellectuals. Even then, single-party regimes are likely, because of their ideological nature, to find a place for some intellectuals within their leading circles.[25]

[25] The professional army officer in the new states is to a certain extent an intellectual since he, especially in the technical branches, is the recipient of a modern education. In fact, the intrusion of the military into politics in the Middle East, at least, may be partly attributed to their attachment to modern ideas about order, efficiency, and probity in government, ideas which are not part of the indigenous tradition of government and which come to them through their modern training. The military *coups d'états* which have occurred in many of the new states may be interpreted as, at least in part, revolutions of the technological intelligentsia, acting on behalf of modern ideas of efficiency and progress.

Regardless of the fate of democracy in underdeveloped countries, intellectuals will undoubtedly continue to be called upon for the civil service and for higher education. There will be increasing scope for intellectuals as the governments expand the range of their activities and as the demand grows for highly qualified persons for engineering, teaching, publicity and propaganda, health and social services, and research in social and natural sciences.

If the new states avoid the fate of the Latin American countries in the first century of their independence, and progress economically and socially, then indifferently of the political regime which rules them, the intellectual classes will become larger and more differentiated, and more fully incorporated into their own cultural institutional system in a variety of technological, administrative, educational, and therapeutic capacities.

This incorporation of the intellectuals into their own societies will depend to a large extent on the establishment of an equilibrium between the demand for and the supply of intellectuals. If there always is such a surplus of university and college graduates that their salaries are low and many of them have to take posts which they regard as unsuitable, the process of incorporation will be obstructed. Instead the oppositional mentality will go on reproducing itself. Where a public political life is permitted, there they will be a perpetual source of unsettledness.[26]

[26] This, in turn, would increase the demand for an ideological oligarchy, from outside the government, and would also impel the government itself to adopt oligarchical measures.

There is also the opposite danger of a disequilibrium in the relations between the intellectuals and the central institutional system arising from an excessive demand for intellectuals in technological and administrative roles. In countries which entered upon independence with an insufficient supply of qualified intellectuals and a very scanty complement of intellectual institutions, it is definitely possible to draw practically all of the best intellectuals into executive and technological roles, leaving too few for civil

Let us imagine that the economics of the new states develop toward greater productivity and that a measure of liberal political life survives the burdens under which the new states now labor. The intellectual classes will become more diversified than they are at present, as they find employment in applied science and technology, in governmental, industrial, and commercial administration, in scientific and scholarly research, and in the profession of letters. With this diversification, there will be less unity of sentiment, less sense of a common identity among them. The "intellectuals" will become only one part of the educated class and a situation which already exists in the advanced countries will emerge.

There will be more specialization, more philistinism, and a less general cultural sympathy in the new intelligentsia than in the old. The new intelligentsia will also be much less political in its outlook and more practical and professional. Each intellectual profession will, as it has long since done in the advanced countries, nurture its own traditions and ways of working. As in the past, these traditions will draw on the more differentiated and more elaborate intellectual traditions of the advanced countries. Creativity will come to be more appreciated and one necessary condition for its realization will thus be provided. The intellectuals of the underdeveloped countries will cease in the course of this process to be as dependent and provincial as they are now. They will become, as some already are, full citizens, with completely equal status, in the intellectual community of the world.

The opportunities for fruitful and satisfying employment of the skills of the intellectuals in the various spheres of civil and economic life and the establishment of absorbing and guiding traditions of an autonomous creativity in intellectual life proper will foster an attenuation of ideological dispositions. It can never eradicate them but it can reduce the commonness of their occurrence and mollify their asperity. Many with political interests will no longer feel the urgent obligation to participate directly in day-to-day political life. More of them will be content to play an equally vital but less immediate part in the formation of the life of their countries. They will concern themselves less than they do now with the issues of the here and now, and will deal with problems which are of longer-run significance, more remote from the immediate issues of party politics and of the prospects and favors of the incumbent political elite. The indirect influence on politics which comes from the cultivation of the matrix of opinion, and from the provision of the personnel and the institutional conditions of long-term development, will bring satisfaction to a larger proportion than it now does, and politicians will perhaps learn to appreciate the equal and perhaps even greater value to the community of this kind of activity on the part of intellectuals.

Their direct participation in politics will probably continue to have a radical bent. The traditions of the modern intellectual are too deeply rooted and the tendency is too intrinsic to the exercise of intellectual powers for this to be avoided—even if it were ever desirable. The radicalism of the intellectual's politics need not however be revolutionary or ideological; it can also work within the civil order. In the espousal of this standpoint at the center of political decision, in party councils, in parliaments and in cabinets, the intellectual will continue to have a unique and indispensable role, the abdication of which cannot be compensated by purely intellectual creativity or the efficient performance

[*footnote 26 continued*
and intellectual functions. The rapid growth of the public services and the general trend toward the governmental pre-emption of so many diverse functions might well result in too small a proportion of the intellectual classes being left free for independent creative work and for vital activity in that publicistic borderland between the intellectual and the political.

of executive, technological, and educational functions. In order, however, for this possibility to exist, the political society— the civil order itself—must first come into existence.

This brings us to one of the prototypical paradoxes of political development. For the intellectuals to inherit their true estate, they must live in a political society. But this civil order cannot be achieved unless the intellectuals, who would be among its greatest beneficiaries, help, against the greatest difficulties, to bring it about. Some of these difficulties reside within the intellectuals themselves, within the political and cultural traditions which enter into their constitution. The outcome then depends on whether those intellectuals who speak for civility in a modern society will by their talents, virtue, and good fortune be able to outweigh their own inhibitions, the dense incivility of their fellow-intellectuals, and the rocky obduracy of the traditional order.

Chapter 9

The Military

ARMIES IN THE PROCESS OF POLITICAL MODERNIZATION

Lucian W. Pye

Only a few years ago it was generally assumed that the future of the newly emergent states would be determined largely by the activities of their Westernized intellectuals, their socialistically inclined bureaucrats, their nationalist ruling parties, and possibly their menacing Communist parties. It occurred to few students of the underdeveloped regions that the military might become the critical group in shaping the course of nation-building. Now that the military has become the key decision-making element in at least eight of the Afro-Asian countries, we are confronted with the awkward fact that there has been almost no scholarly research on the role of the military in the political development of the new states.

An underlying assumption behind much of Western political thought is that political institutions are above all else the products of the dynamic forces peculiar to a particular society and thus reflect the distinctive values and the styles of action common to that society. It is acknowledged, of course, that once institutions are established they tend to become dynamic and hence in-

fluence the values and the expectations of the population. There is thus an assumption of a circularity of relationships or a state of equilibrium. The fundamental view, however, is still that the dynamics of the system lie within the society as a whole and that it is the institutions which must be responsive. Government institutions can display initiative, but fundamental change originates within the society.

When we turn to the newly emergent countries this model no longer seems appropriate. For in these societies the historical pattern has been the introduction of institutions from outside, with a minimum concession to the values and behavior of the people. These fundamentally authoritative structures have thus tended to be shaped according to foreign standards. Rather than responding to indigenous values they have often proved to be the dominant factor in stimulating further changes throughout the society.

These considerations suggest that it might be useful to organize our analysis of the political role of the army, first, with respect to the political implications of the army as a modern institution that has been somewhat artificially introduced into disorganized transitional societies: and second, with respect to the role that such an army

SOURCE. Lucian W. Pye, "Armies in the Process of Political Modernization," *Archives Europèennes de Sociologie*, **2**, 82–92, 1961. Reprinted by permission.

277

can play in shaping attitudes toward modernity in other spheres of society. By such an approach we may hope to locate some of the critical factors for explaining why it is that the military has been a vigorous champion of progress and development in some countries and a retarding influence in others. We may also hope to gain a basis for judging the probable effectiveness of armies in promoting national development and eventually democratic practices.

The Army as a Modern Organization

In large measure the story of the underdeveloped countries is one of countless efforts to create organizations by which resources can be effectively mobilized for achieving new objectives. This is the problem of establishing organizations that, as rationalized structures, are capable of relating means to ends. The history of much of the Western impact on traditional societies fits comfortably within this theme, for the businessman, planter, and miner, the colonial administrator, the missionary, and the educator each in his own way strives to fit modern organizations into tradition-bound societies. Similarly, the story of the nationalists and of the other Westernized leaders can be treated on essentially identical terms, for they too try to change the habits of their people by creating modern organizations.

Needless to say, there are not many bright spots in this history, and it is open to question as to who has been the more tragically heroic or comically futile: the Westerners struggling to establish their organizations in traditional societies, or the nationalist politician and the indigenous administrator endeavoring to create a semblance of order out of chaos. On balance the attempts to establish military organizations seem to have been noticeably the most successful.

It would be wrong to underestimate the patient care that has gone into developing and training colonial armies, and in the newly independent countries the military

have been treated relatively generously in the allocation of scarce resources. But in comparison to the efforts that have been expended in developing, say, civil administration and political parties, it still seems that modern armies are somewhat easier to create in transitional societies than most other forms of modern social structures. The significant fact for our consideration is that the armies created by colonial administration and by the newly emergent countries have been consistently among the most modernized institutions in their societies. Viewed historically, some of these armies have been distinguished: the Indian Army, the Malay Regiments, the Philippine Scouts, the Arab Legion, the Gurkha Regiments and the King's Own African Rifles, to mention only the more celebrated ones.

It would take us too far afield to explore the relative advantages military leaders have in seeking to establish armies in transitional societies. We need only note that there is a paradoxical relationship between ritualized and rationalized modes of behavior that may account for the ease with which people still close to a traditional order adapt themselves to military life. Viewed from one perspective, a military establishment comes as close as any human organization can to the ideal type for an industrialized and secularized enterprise. Yet from another point of view, the great stress on professionalism and the extremely explicit standards for individual behavior make the military appear to be a more sacred than secular institution. If discipline is needed to minimize random and unpredictable behavior, it is also consonant with all the demands that custom and ritual make in the most tradition-bound organization.

For these reasons, and for others related to the hierarchic nature of the organization, the division between traditional and rationally oriented behavior is not very great within armies.[1] Indeed, in

[1] It is significant that the most common weaknesses of civil bureaucracies in the new

any army there is always a struggle going on between tradition and reason. Historically, during periods of little change in the state of military technology the tendency has been for the non-rational characteristics to become dominant.[2] Given this inherent conflict in any military organization the question arises as to why the forces of custom and ritual do not readily dominate the armies of the newly emergent countries, and so cause them to oppose the forces of change. In societies where traditional habits of mind are still strong one might expect the military to be strongly conservative. Such was largely the case in the West during the pre-industrial period. By contrast, in most of the newly emergent countries armies have tended to emphasize a rational outlook and to champion responsible change and national development.

This state of affairs is largely explained by the extent to which the armies in these countries have been influenced by contemporary Western military technology. In particular nearly all of the new countries have taken the World War II type of army as their model.[3] In so doing they have undertaken to create a

countries—like exaggerating the importance of procedure to the point of ritualizing the routine, and the lack of initiative and of pragmatic and experimental outlook—are not as serious drawbacks to smooth functioning of military establishments. On the contrary, the very qualities that have hobbled civil administration in these countries have given strength and rigidity to their military establishments.

[2] The classic discussion of the spirit of militarism as contrasted with the rational military mind is Alfred Vagts, *A History of Militarism: Romance and Realities of a Profession* (New York, W. W. Norton, 1937).

[3] World War II was in itself a decisive event in the birth of many of these countries and, of course, the availability of large quantities of surplus equipment and arms made it realistic to aspire to a modernized army. American military aid has contributed to making the military the most modernized element not only in recipient countries, but also in neighboring countries which have felt the need to keep up with technological advances.

form of organization that is typical of and peculiar to the most highly industrialized civilization yet known. Indeed, modern armies are essentially industrial-type entities. Thus the armies of the new countries are instinct with the spirit of rapid technological development.

The fact that these new armies in pre-industrial societies are modelled after industrial-based organizations has many implications for their political roles. One of their characteristics is particularly significant: the specialization that modern armies demand in skills and functions is only distantly related to the command of violence. There has generally been a tremendous increase in the number of officers assigned to staff functions as contrasted with line commands. As the armies have striven to approximate their ideal models they have had to establish all manner of specialized organizations and departments that require skills that are either in short supply or non-existent in their societies. The Burmese army, for example, in addition to its engineer and signal corps has special sections on chemical warfare, psychological warfare, and even a historical and archeological section. All the new armies have attempted to introduce specialized training schools and advanced techniques of personnel management and procurement. Consequently, numbers of the more intelligent and ambitious officers have had to be trained in industrial skills more advanced than those common to the civilian economy.

The high proportion of officers assigned to staff functions means that large numbers of officers are forced to look outside their society for their models. The fact that army leaders, particularly the younger and more ambitious, generally come from those trained in staff positions means that they are extremely sensitive to the needs of modernization and technological advancement. This kind of sensitivity bears little relationship to the command of physical violence and tests of human endurance—in short, to the martial spirit as we customarily think of it. In consequence the officers often find that they are spiritually in tune with the intellectuals and students, and those other elements in society most anxious to become a part of the modern world. They may have little in common with the vast majority of the men they must command. In this respect the gap between the officer class and the troops, once largely a matter of social and economic class (as it still is to some degree), has now been widened by differences in the degree of acculturation to modern life.

It should be noted that these revolutionary changes in military life have significantly influenced the status of the military profession in different societies and hence have had an interesting effect on relative national power. Cultures that looked down on the military at an earlier stage of technology now accord high prestige to the same profession as it has raised its technology. For example, when armies depended entirely on human energy and animal power the Chinese placed the soldier near the bottom of the social hierarchy; with present levels of advanced military technology the soldier is now near the top of the social scale in both Communist and non-Communist China. The change has been more in the nature of the military profession than in basic Chinese cultural values. Conversely, peoples once considered "martial" may now show little interest in, or aptitude for, the new kind of soldiering.

Above all else, however, the revolution in military technology has caused the army leaders of the newly emergent countries to be extremely sensitive to the extent to which their countries are economically and technologically underdeveloped. Called upon to perform roles basic to advanced societies, the more politically conscious officers can hardly avoid being aware of the need for substantial changes in their own societies.

It might seem that those occupying positions in other modern-type organizations in underdeveloped societies would also feel much the same need for change. To whatever extent this may be so, three distinctive features of armies seem to make them somewhat more dynamic in demanding changes.

First of all, armies by nature are rival institutions in the sense that their ultimate function is the test of one against the other. All other organizations operate within the context of their own society; although their initial inspiration may have come from abroad, their primary focus is on internal developments. The civil bureaucracy, for example, can, and indeed has to, deal with its domestic problems with little regard for what other bureaucracies in other countries are doing. The soldier, however, is constantly called upon to look abroad and to compare his organization with foreign ones. He thus has a greater awareness of international standards and a greater sensitivity to weaknesses in his own society.

Second, armies for all their concern with rationality and becoming highly efficient machines are relatively immune to pragmatic tests of efficiency on a day-to-day basis. Armies are created for future contingencies, and in many underdeveloped countries these contingencies have never had to be faced. Even in countries where the army is forced to deal with internal security problems, such as Burma and Indonesia, the effects have been mainly to increase the resources available for building up the army according to the ideal model, with remarkably few concessions being made to practical needs. Other modernized organizations in underdeveloped societies have to cope with more immediate and day-to-day problems; hence they must constantly adjust themselves to local conditions. They cannot adhere as rigidly as armies can to their Western prototypes. Just as Western armies have often existed in a dream world of planning for types of wars that never occur, so armies of underdeveloped countries can devote themselves to becoming modernized and more "efficient" with little regard to immediate reality. Members of other modern-type organizations may desire to see social change in their society, but they are likely to be more conscious of the need to accommodate their ambitions to existing conditions.

Finally, armies always stand at some distance from their civilian societies and are even expected to have ways of their own, including attitudes and judgments, that are remote if not completely apart from those of civilian life. Thus again armies of the newly emergent countries can feel somewhat divorced from the realities of a transitional society and focus more on the standards common to the more industrialized world. In consequence they are often unaware of the difficulties inherent in modernizing other segments of their society. Within their tradition all problems can be overcome if the right orders are given.

Armies as Modernizing Agents

So much for the army as one of the more modernized of the authoritative agencies of government in transitional societies. When we consider it as a modernizing force for the whole of society, we move into a less clearly defined area where the number of relevant considerations becomes much greater and where we are likely to find greater differences from country to country. Indeed, we shall be able to deal only generally with the social and political aspects of military service and some of the more indirect influences of armies on civilian attitudes.

In all societies it is recognized that armies must make those who enter them into the image of the good soldier. The underdeveloped society adds a new dimension: the good soldier is also to some degree a modernized man. Thus it is that the armies in the newly emergent countries come to play key roles in the process by which traditional ways give way to more Westernized ideas and practices. The very fact that the recruit must break his ties and associations with civilian life and adjust

to the more impersonal world of the army tends to emphasize the fundamental nature of this process, which involves the movement out of the particularistic relationships of traditional life and into the more impersonal and universalistic relationships of an industrialized society.

Army training is thus consistent with the direction taken by the basic process of acculturation in traditional societies. Within the army, however, the rate of acculturation is greatly accelerated. This fact contributes to the tendency of army officers to underestimate the difficulties of changing the civilian society.

Probably the most significant feature of the acculturation process as it takes place under the auspices of the army is that it provides a relatively high degree of psychological security. The experience of breaking from the known and relatively sheltered world of tradition and moving into the more unknown modern world is generally an extremely traumatic one. In contrast to the villager who is caught up in the process of being urbanized, the young army recruit from the village has the more sheltered, the more gradual introduction into the modern world. It is hardly necessary to point out the disturbing fact that the urbanization process as it has taken place in most Asian, African, and Latin American societies has generally tended to produce a highly restless, insecure population. Those who have been forced off the land or attracted to the cities often find themselves in a psychologically threatening situation. These are the people who tend to turn to extremist politics and to look for some form of social and personal security in political movements that demand their total commitment. In contrast, those who are exposed to a more technologically advanced way of life in the army find that they must make major adjustments, but that these adjustments are all treated explicitly and openly. In the army one can see what is likely to happen in terms of one's training and one's future. This is not the case in the city.

It should also be noted that the acculturative process in the army often tends to be more thorough and of a broader scope than the urbanization process. In all the main Asian cities there are those who still follow many of the habits and practices of the village. They may live still within the orbit of their family and have only limited outside associations and contacts. These people have made some adjustment to the modern world, but they are likely to be faced with even more in the future, and thus they remain potential sources of political tension.

It should also be noted that the acculturative process in the army tends to be focused on acquiring technical skills that are of particular value for economic development. Just as the army represents an industrialized organization, so must those who have been trained within it learn skills and habits of mind which would be of value in other industrial organizations. In the West, armies have played a very important role in providing technical training and even direct services in the process of industrial development. The German army trained large numbers of non-commissioned officers who performed important functions as foremen in the German steel mills and in other industries. In the United States the Corps of Engineers, of course, played a central role in the whole development of the West; and after the Civil War army veterans provided considerable amounts of the skill and knowledge which, when combined with the influx of immigrants, provided a basis for much of our industrial development. In Latin America the Brazilian Army has played an important part in opening the interior, in promoting the natural sciences, and in protecting the Indian population. In Asia, too, we can see much the same story being enacted now. Before the war the compulsory training in the Japanese Army provided the whole society with increasing reservoirs of man power which contributed directly to the development of an industrial society. Army veterans in India have played an important role not only in lower-level industrial jobs, but also in managerial positions. In Malaya and the Philippines the army has been the main instrument for training people in operating and maintaining motor vehicles and other forms of machinery.

Politically the most significant feature of the process of acculturation within the army is that it usually provides some form of training in citizenship. Recruits with traditional backgrounds must learn about a new world in which they are identified with a larger political self. They learn that they stand in some definite relationship to a national community. In this sense the army experience tends to be a politicizing experience. Even if recruits are not given explicit training in political matters, they are likely to learn that events in their society are determined by human decisions and not just by chance and fate. Within the army the peasant may come to realize that much in life can be changed and that commands and wishes have consequences. Thus even aside from any formal training in patriotism the recruit is likely to achieve some awareness of the political dimensions of his society. It is therefore not surprising that in many of the newly emergent countries veterans have had appreciable political influence even after only limited military experience.

Armies in the newly emergent countries can thus provide a sense of citizenship and an appreciation of political action. In some cases this can lead to a more responsible nationalism. Indeed, the recruit may be impressed with the fact that he must make sacrifices to achieve the goals of nationalism and that the process of nation-building involves more than just the shouting of slogans. At the same time there is always the potential danger that the armies will become the center of hyper-nationalistic movements, as in the case of prewar Japan.

Because the army represents one of the most effective channels for upward social mobility, military-inspired nationalism often encompasses a host of personalized emotions and sentiments about civilian society. Invariably the men, and sometimes even the officers, come from extremely humble circumstances, and it is only within the army that they are first introduced to the possibility of systematically advancing themselves. In transitional societies, where people's station in life is still largely determined by birth, and by chance opportunities, powerful reactions usually follow from placing people in a position where they can recognize a definite and predictable relationship between effort and reward. The practice of giving advancement on merit can encourage people, first, to see the army as a just organization deserving of their loyalties, and then possibly, to demand that the same form of justice reign throughout their society.

Those who do move up to positions of greater respect and power through the army may often carry with them hostilities toward those with greater advantages and authority in civilian society. The tendency of the military to question whether the civilian elite achieved their station by merit adds another conflict to civil-military relations in most underdeveloped countries. More often than not the military show these feelings by seeking to make national loyalty and personal sacrifice the crucial test of national leadership.

The relationship between armies and civilian leaders varies, of course, according to the circumstances of historic development. Broadly speaking, however, it is helpful to distinguish three different general categories of such relationships.

There are first those patterns of development in which the military stand out because in a disrupted society they represent the only effectively organized element capable of competing for political power and formulating public policy. This situation is most likely to exist when the traditional political order, but not necessarily the traditional social order, has been violently disrupted and it becomes necessary to set up representative institutions before any of the other modern-type political organizations have been firmly established. The outstanding example of this pattern of development is modern China from the fall of the Manchu dynasty in 1911 to the victory of the Communists. Indeed, it is possible to think of this period as one dominated by a constant struggle to escape from the grim circumstances that obtained when only military organizations survived the fall of the traditional systems. Hence the military became the only effective political entity. Thereafter nothing could be done without them, and yet the military could do little without effective civilian institutions. Comparable situations seem to exist at present in some Middle Eastern countries where Western influence brought a commitment to republican institutions but left the army as the only effective modern political structure in the entire society.

A second category includes those countries where the military, while formally espousing the development of democracy, actually monopolizes the political arena and forces any emerging civilian elite to concentrate on economic and social activities. In many ways this arrangement is reminiscent of the Belgian variety of colonialism. At present, the most outstanding example of this form of rule is Thailand.

A third major category, which is probably the largest, consists of those countries in which the organization and structures essential to democratic government exist but have not been able to function effectively. The process of modernization has been retarded to such a point that the army, as the most modernized organization in the society, has assumed an administrative role and taken over control. In these cases there is a sense of failure in the country, and the military are viewed as possible saviors.[4]

---

[4] Johnson, John J., ed., *The Role of the Military in Underdeveloped Countries*, Princeton University Press, Princeton 1962.

TOWARD EXPLAINING MILITARY INTERVENTION IN LATIN AMERICAN POLITICS

Robert D. Putnam*

I. Introduction

Military intervention in politics is extremely common. Outside the North Atlantic area, the armed forces are more likely than not to be among the most important power contenders in any political system, and military regimes are at least as widespread as either totalitarian or democratic ones. It is surprising, therefore, that until recently this phenomenon has attracted little attention from students of politics. Though there has been some speculation about the causes of military intervention, our actual knowledge of the subject is meager indeed.

The preeminence of the mulitary in politics in Latin America has long been recognized, but, even in this case, as recently as 1960 George Blanksten could complain that "political studies of the Latin American armed services are sorely needed."[1] Aside from a few vague remarks about "Hispanic heritage" and "backwardness," virtually no empirically based explanations of Latin American militarism have been offered. Since Blanksten wrote, of course, Johnson and Lieuwen have undertaken excellent analyses of this topic, but both authors' works have been primarily historical studies of the development and extent of military intervention in various coun-

tries, rather than verified, general explications of the causes of this phenomenon.[2]

A study of the factors that account for the varying political role of the military in Latin America would thus be useful both for students of Latin American politics and for students of comparative politics generally. Latin America constitutes in many respects an ideal "laboratory" for analyzing militarism. The range of military involvement is great—from "pure" military regimes, such as Argentina's present regime, to "constitutional" military regimes, such as El Salvador's, to military "protectorates," such as Brazil's, to civil-military coalitions, such as Argentina's under Perón, to regimes in which the military is merely one among numerous important "power groups," such as Mexico's, to regimes in which the military is virtually nonpolitical, such as Costa Rica's. In this "laboratory," certain independent variables are held constant—colonial background, nature of the struggle for independence, length of independence, religious background, cultural authority patterns.[3] This means that we cannot examine the impact of these constants on the propensity for military intervention, but it does allow us to focus more clearly on other possible explanations. The purpose of this research note is to investigate in this Latin American "laboratory" some of the more important speculations

SOURCE: Robert D. Putman, "Toward Explaining Military Intervention in Latin American Politics," *World Politics*, 20:83–110, October, 1967.

* I should like to thank the following individuals for their help in the preparation of this research note: Hayward R. Alker, Jr., Karl W. Deutsch, Robert H. Dix, Richard Simeon, and Rosemary Putnam.

[1] "The Politics of Latin America," in Gabriel A. Almond and James S. Coleman, eds., *The Politics of the Developing Areas* (Princeton 1960), 502.

[2] John J. Johnson, *The Military and Society in Latin America* (Stanford 1964); Edwin Lieuwen, *Arms and Politics in Latin America* (New York 1961) and *Generals vs. Presidents* (New York 1964).

[3] Certain of these variables are, to be sure, not entirely constant throughout the area, but they are so nearly so as to warrant ignoring their effects.

about the sources of military involvement in politics.

II. Theoretical Propositions

A survey of the literature on military intervention in politics discloses four broad categories of factors suggested as causes of, or conditions for, intervention or abstention: (1) aspects of socioeconomic development; (2) aspects of political development; (3) characteristics of the military establishment itself; and (4) foreign influences. I shall here present and explicate the relevant hypotheses and shall refrain from setting out the broader theoretical perspectives of the various authors.[4] In particular, I shall limit my attention to propositions that answer the question, What accounts for the varying incidence of military intervention in politics? (There are many other interesting questions in this general area, concerning the political and ideological orientations of military regimes, the political, social, and economic consequences of military intervention, and so on, but these will be ignored here.)

One of the most common hypotheses links the propensity for military intervention with social and economic underdevelopment. Samuel Finer argues that *the propensity for military intervention is likely to decrease with increased social mobilization.*[5] The concept of social mobilization

refers to such developments as urbanization, the rise of mass education and mass communications, the development of a money economy, and increased mass participation in social and political activities and associations. Social mobilization increases the number of potential political actors and diffuses increased political resources to these actors. The assumption underlying this hypothesis is that these actors will be willing and able to sustain civilian political institutions.[6]

Finer and others have also argued that *economic development, especially industrialization, diminishes the propensity for military intervention,*[7] This effect of economic development stems partly from the increased socio-technical complexity that puts public administration beyond the skills of the armed forces, partly from the civilian opportunities for social mobility which economic development opens up, and partly from greater wealth, which allows and encourages stable, civilian government.[8] Germani and Silvert have articulated a hypothesis hinted at by others, namely, that *military intervention is inhibited by the rise of middle strata in the social structure,* since these middle strata have in especial measure both the motivation and the ability to create and sustain stable civilian political institutions.[9] These same authors also argue that *the likelihood*

---

[4] The following works were consulted in preparing this inventory of theoretical propositions: Robert J. Alexander, "The Army in Politics," in H. E. Davis, ed., *Government and Politics in Latin America* (New York 1958); Stanislaw Andrzejewski, *Military Organization and Society* (London 1954); Samuel E. Finer, *The Man on Horseback* (New York 1962); William F. Gutteridge, *Military Institutions and Power in the New States* (New York 1965); Samuel P. Huntington, *The Soldier and the State* (Cambridge, Mass., 1957); Morris Janowitz, *The Military in the Political Development of New Nations* (Chicago 1964); John J. Johnson, ed., *The Role of the Military in Underdeveloped Countries* (Princeton 1962); and the works cited in footnote 2.

[5] Pp. 87–88. The term "social mobilization" (which Finer himself does not use) was intro-

duced in this sense by Karl W. Deutsch in "Social Mobilization and Political Development," *American Political Science Review*, LV (September 1961), 493–514.

[6] Huntington's counterhypothesis linking social mobilization with *increased* military intervention is discussed later in this section.

[7] Finer, 113–15; Alexander, 158.

[8] Janowitz's attack on this proposition (pp. 18–20) is weakened by his failure to distinguish the military-civilian dimension from the democratic-authoritarian dimension and by his failure to recognize that a correlation can be important without being perfect.

[9] Gino Germani and Kalman Silvert, "Politics, Social Structure and Military Intervention in Latin America," *Archives Européennes de Sociologie*, II (Spring 1961), 62–81.

of military intervention is greater, the greater the cleavages and the less the consensus in a society. (This proposition is related to the proposition discussed below linking military intervention and political violence.)

A second set of variables, correlated with but distinct from those involving social mobilization and economic development, may be grouped under the heading "political development." The most obvious hypothesis, as stated by Finer, is that *"where public attachment to civilian institutions is strong, military intervention in politics will be weak. . . . Where public attachment to civilian institutions is weak or non-existent, military intervention in politics will find wide scope—both in manner and in substance."*[10] Though this proposition is important, it is also somewhat unsatisfying, for it fails to take our search for explanation very far from the phenomenon that we are trying to explain. A more interesting hypothesis, suggested by Finer, Johnson, and others, is that *the propensity for military intervention in politics decreases with increasing popular attention to and participation in politics.*[11] Another set of hypotheses relates military intervention to weaknesses in civilian political institutions: *military intervention decreases with increasing strength and effectiveness of political parties, of political interest groups, and of civilian governmental institutions.*[12] Huntington's theory of political development and decay stresses the importance of "the institutionalization of political organizations and procedures." "Political decay"—of which a notable symptom is military intervention—arises out of an imbalance between social mobilization and political institutionalization. Therefore, *the greater the social mobilization and the less the political institutionalization, the greater the likelihood of*

military intervention.[13] A final aspect of political development that is relevant here concerns the role of violence. Lieuwen and Needler have argued that *the tendency toward military intervention increases with increasing political violence.*[14] Obviously, the military have an important advantage in a political game where violence is trump, for that is their strong suit.

The third set of hypotheses concerns the way internal characteristics of a military establishment affect its predisposition to political intervention. *"Professionalization"* of the military is linked with decreased military intervention (Huntington) *and with increased military intervention* (Finer).[15] This apparent contradiction can perhaps be resolved if we consider a few of the possible components of "professionalization." Many students of civil-military relations have suggested that *military intervention decreases with the development within the military of a norm of civilian supremacy.*[16] As with the proposition linking military abstention with the legitimacy of civilian institutions, the proposed explanatory factor in this hypothesis is "too close" to the phenomenon to be explained. On the other hand, if the hypothesis is given a historical focus, it is rather more interesting. Thus, with respect to Latin American armies it is commonly asserted that military intervention is the prevailing norm because of the Hispanic heritage.[17] Similarly, it is argued that *the propensity for military intervention increases with the habituation of the military to intervention,* or more simply, that intervention breeds more intervention.[18]

The larger and more sophisticated the

---

[10] P. 21.

[11] Finer, 87; John J. Johnson, "The Latin-American Military as a Politically Competing Group in Transitional Society," in Johnson, ed., Role of the Military, 127.

[12] Finer, 21, 87–88, 115; Alexander, 157.

[13] Samuel P. Huntington, "Political Development and Political Decay," *World Politics,* XVII (April 1965), 386–430.

[14] Lieuwen, "Militarism and Politics in Latin America," in Johnson, ed., *Role of the Military,* 132–33; Martin C. Needler, *Latin American Politics in Perspective* (New York 1963), 76.

[15] Huntington, *The Soldier and the State,* 84; Finer, 24ff.

[16] For example, Finer, 32.

[17] For example, Alexander, 153.

[18] *Ibid.,* 154–55.

armed forces, the more likely that they will have the administrative and technical skills necessary for running a government and that the military will have a preponderance of armed power over civilians. Thus, some have argued that *the size and sophistication of the military establishment are positively related to the propensity for intervention in politics.*[19] Janowitz has discussed a variety of other internal characteristics of the military establishment which he sees as related to the propensity for political involvement, such as political ideology, social and political cohesion, and career and recruitment patterns. I shall not pursue these propositions here since I do not have the data necessary to test them.

Two final factors often adduced to explain military intervention, especially but not exclusively in the Latin American context, involve foreign influences. First, it is often alleged that *military training missions from foreign nations inculcate attitudes favorable or unfavorable to military intervention in politics.* Edelmann echoes many others in arguing that "the influence of German, Italian, and certain other military missions" has been among the "most important" causes of military intervention in Latin America,[20] while Johnson argues that the effect of U.S. missions is to transmit norms of civilian supremacy along with their tutelage in military techniques.[21] Second, it is often argued that by a kind of "demonstration effect" *military intervention in one country encourages intervention by the armed forces of other countries in their own political systems,* or more simply, that coups are contagious.[22]

III. Methodology

There is no dearth of suggestions about what factors are causally related to military intervention in politics. The problem is to subject this array of propositions to some kind of empirical testing. The primary method used here is correlational analysis. For each Latin American country an index is constructed representing the extent of military intervention in politics over the last decade. This is our "dependent variable." This index will be correlated with a variety of other data intended to represent or reflect some of the suggested independent variables. The strength of the empirical relationships will be summarized by the standard Pearsonian correlation coefficient r.[23]

This technique is a powerful one for testing hypotheses such as those outlined above, for it allows us to weigh and summarize all the relevant evidence. In particular, we can go beyond mere lists of illustrations and exceptions. This technique is, of course, not the only possible one—other complementary techniques are the case-study method and the comparative historical method. Nor is it without its limitations. First, the present analysis is "synchronic," rather than "diachronic"; that is, it compares information on military intervention and, for example, social mobilization at the present time in the various Latin American countries. With one important exception, we shall not compare data that would allow us to examine changes in the degree of intervention and mobilization in one country over time.

Second, as already suggested, we shall not examine all the factors that might be linked theoretically to military intervention. In particular, two classes of factors are beyond the scope of this investigation. First, we cannot examine propositions involving variables that are virtually constant throughout the Latin American area, such as religion, colonial background, length of independence, and the like. However, it is precisely these factors that could not possibly account for the wide variation

[19] Janowitz, 42.

[20] Alexander T. Edelmann, *Latin American Government and Politics* (Homewood 1965), 189.

[21] "The Latin American Military," in Johnson, *Role of the Military*, 129.

[22] Lieuwen, "Militarism and Politics," *ibid.*, 134.

[23] See Hubert M. Blalock, Jr., *Social Statistics* (New York 1960), 273ff.

among these countries in military intervention.[24] Second, a number of theoretically interesting and relevant variables must be ignored here because we lack the data necessary to test them. We lack direct information on the political allegiances of the populations, on the extent of social cleavage and consensus in the various countries, and on the internal characteristics and norms of the military, such as those discussed by Janowitz. For a few of these factors we can make some attempt to use indirect indicators, but these attempts must be especially tentative. On the other hand, the relative success or failure of attempts to explain military intervention with the factors for which data are available will give us some indication of how much variation is left to be explained by *other* factors.

Before proceeding further, the term "military intervention" must be more precisely defined. In doing so, I shall borrow Robert Gilmore's definition of militarism: "The military institution is concerned with the management and use of controlled violence in the service of the state according to terms laid down by the state. When the military institution veers from this role to participate in or to influence other, nonmilitary agencies and functions of the state, including its leadership, then militarism exists in greater or lesser degree."[25]

Obviously, the persuasiveness of this study depends on the validity of the index of military intervention used as the dependent variable. The heart of this index, which I shall call the "MI index," is a rating assigned to each country for each year of the decade 1956–1965, based on the extent of military intervention in the political life of that country for that year. This rating is

on a scale from zero to three, from least to most intervention. Thus, for the decade, a country's MI score could range between zero and thirty.

The ends of the scale are easiest to define. A rating of zero is given to a country in which the armed forces were essentially apolitical, their role restricted to that of a minor pressure group on strictly military matters. Latin American examples of this level of intervention during the period studied were Uruguay and Costa Rica, as well as Bolivia during the years just after the 1952 revolution. A country that was ruled directly by a military regime, either individual or collective, and in which civilian groups and institutions were reduced to supplicants or tools of the military, is rated three. Examples of this level of intervention were Paraguay and (after the coups of the early 1960's) Brazil, Ecuador, Guatemala, Honduras, and Bolivia. Ratings of one and two are assigned to levels of intervention falling between these two extremes. A rating of two is given when a country was ruled by a military-civilian coalition in which the civilian elements had some real influence, or by civilians subject to frequent demands from a powerful military establishment, or by a dictatorship (often of a personalistic variety) based on force of arms, but not solely responsible to the armed forces.[26] Examples of this level of intervention in Latin America during the last decade were Brazil and Argentina (except for periods of direct rule by military juntas), Venezuela after Pérez Jiménez, and Nicaragua (a "familistic" dictatorship in which the armed forces played an important, but not predominant, role). A rating of one is given when a country was ruled by essentially

[24] Obviously, this study can consider only the range of variation in the independent variables which occurs in Latin America. For example, levels of social mobilization above or below the level achieved in Latin America might have effects on militarism which could not be detected in this study.

[25] Robert L. Gilmore, *Caudillism and Militarism in Venezuela* (Athens, Ohio, 1964), 4–5.

[26] In this connection it may be helpful to note Gilmore's distinction between "militarism" (as defined above) and "caudillism": "Caudillism is a political process in which violence is an essential element. . . . [It] may be defined as the union of personalism and violence for the conquest of power" (pp. 5, 47). Caudillist regimes, such as Haiti's, are rated two.

civilian institutions, with civilian power groups preeminent, but with the armed forces still a significant political force in nonmilitary matters. Examples of this level of intervention were Mexico and Chile, and Colombia after Rajos Pinilla.

This rating method explicitly excludes from consideration certain political characteristics of related interest. I have not considered the degree of "democracy" in a country, apart from the extent of military intervention. Thus, for example, Castro's Cuba, despite its quasi-totalitarian character, is rated only one, since the available evidence suggests that the military play only a minor role in contemporary Cuban politics. Nor have I considered the ideological complexion of the military establishment; both the reactionary Paraguayan regime and the reformist regime in El Salvador are rated three.

In constructing the index I have used the literature on Latin American militarism, textbook accounts of Latin American politics, general histories of the period, and the *Annual Register* of political events. In cases of ambiguity, I have gone directly to monographic literature on specific countries. My sources are given in Appendix I, which also gives the actual year-by-year ratings for the various countries. Naturally, in a number of cases conclusive information on the precise political role of the military in a

given year was lacking. In such cases I followed whatever seemed to be the preponderance of evidence, and since such cases invariably involve a difference of only a few points in the final country score, the overall effect is marginal.

This description of the construction of the MI index is some warrant for its validity, but fortunately there is an independent check on its plausibility. After the ratings had been compiled, I discovered a rather detailed classification by Martin C. Needler of the "normal political role of the military" in each Latin American country. A comparison of his rankings with my ratings will not "prove" the accuracy of either, because both employ the "reputational" method. However, the strong concordance between the two assessments, shown in Table I, should increase our confidence in the MI index. With the exception of Needler's final category, the mean MI score for each category differs significantly from the others as it should. Moreover, the overlap in the range of MI scores between adjacent categories is, with the same single exception, one MI point at most. The only exception to this almost perfect concordance results from Needler's inclusion of Cuba and Nicaragua in the category of countries where the military are "in control," and, as I have argued above, the weight of the evidence suggests that this

Table I. A Comparison of Two Ratings of Military Intervention in Twenty Latin American Countries

NEEDLER'S RANKING ACCORDING TO "NORMAL POLITICAL ROLE OF MILITARY"	MEAN MI INDEX SCORES	RANGE OF MI INDEX SCORES
1. "None" ($N = 1$)	0.0	0
2. "Limited" ($N = 5$)	8.8	0–15
3. "Intervene" ($N = 5$)	21.8	20–23
4. "Veto Power" ($N = 5$)	24.4	22–28
5. "In Control" ($N = 4$)	23.2	16–30
(Category 5, excluding Cuba and Nicaragua)	(28.5)	(27–30)

SOURCE: Needler, *Latin American Politics in Perspective*, 156–57.

categorization of these two countries is misleading.[27] In sum, then, although there might be some disagreement about the exact rating for a given country, the MI score seems a farily good measure of the extent of military intervention in the politics of each Latin American nation.

The data on the independent variables for each country are of three general types. In the first place, certain standard statistics, such as extent of urbanization, measures of economic development, and literacy rates, have been gathered from a number of statistical handbooks. Second, some variables based on rankings by informed observers have been drawn from *A Cross-Polity Survey* by Banks and Textor.[28] Finally, information on several dichotomous characteristics, such as the incidence of German military training missions, has been compiled from standard treatments of Latin American politics. Sources for data on all these variables are given in Appendix II.

The data on the independent variables involve problems of reliability and validity. "Reliability" refers to the accuracy of the statistics in measuring whatever it is that they measure. How accurate, for example, are the data on per capita GNP? As is well known, statistical data from Latin America are often not of the highest quality, and the reader is referred to the sources listed in Appendix II for discussions of this problem in particular cases. It is important to understand that in general the effect of unreliability in measurement of variables is

[27] The fact that the differences in MI scores among Needler's third, fourth, and fifth categories are much less than the differences involving his first and second categories comports with one's intuitive notion of the "distance" between the levels of intervention indicated by the descriptions of his categories. Thus, for example, the difference between a military that habitually "intervenes" and one that has "veto power" is less than the difference between one that "intervenes" and one whose political role is "limited." Needler's ratings of individual countries are given in Appendix I.

[28] Arthur S. Banks and Robert B. Textor, *A Cross-Polity Survey* (Cambridge, Mass, 1963).

to *reduce* the obtained correlation coefficients slightly below the values that would be expected if there were no such measurement error.[29] "Validity" refers to the accuracy of the statistics in measuring the concepts in which we are interested. How well, for example, does per capita GNP or the proportion of the GNP derived from agriculture indicate "socio-technical complexity"? We cannot resolve these problems; we can only use appropriate caution in interpreting the results.[30]

IV. Results

SOCIOECONOMIC DEVELOPMENT

The correlations between the MI index and various statistical indicators of social mobilization and economic development are given in Table II. Five variables measure social mobilization: (1) percent of

[29] See George A. Ferguson, *Statistical Analysis in Psychology and Education* (New York 1959), 289. Given the probable error margins for the data used here, reliability coefficients in the range .8–.9 would be expected. This would mean, for example, that an obtained coefficient of .20 understates the actual correlation by about .02–.05 and that a coefficient of .60 understates the actual correlation by about .06–.15. For error estimates, see Bruce M. Russett and others, *World Handbook of Political and Social Indicators* (New Haven 1964). For a detailed analysis of GNP error and a calculation of an approximate reliability coefficient, see Hayward R. Alker, Jr., "The Comparison of Aggregate Political and Social Data . . . ," *Social Sciences Information*, v (September 1966), 1–18.

[30] For a few of the variables, data were not available for all twenty Latin American countries. In some cases, I have estimated the missing data and calculated coefficients including this "best guess" data. Unless these "guesses" are *wildly* off (and I do not believe that they are), the error introduced by including them is probably less than the error that would be introduced by ignoring the countries they represent. Precise data on Uruguay, for example, are often missing, yet it would be quite misleading to ignore the fact that this country fits many of our hypotheses remarkably well. Coefficients based on "best guess" data are indicated as such, and in all cases coefficients have also been presented without this "best guess" data.

Table II. *Military Intervention as a Function of Social Mobilization and Economic Development*

VARIABLE NUMBER	VARIABLE CONTENT	CORRELATION WITH MI INDEX
1	Percent of population in cities over 20,000	−.49
2	Percent of adults literate	−.47
3	Newspaper circulation per 1,000 population	−.57
4	University students 1,000 population	−.45
5	Radios per 1,000 population	−.44
6	Per capita GNP (1957)	−.30
7	Percent of GNP derived from agriculture	.26 (.18)
8	Percent of labor force in agriculture	.24
9	Percent of population in the primary sector	.39
10	Percent of labor force earning wages or salaries	−.42 (−.32)
11	Percent of labor force employed in industry	−.29
12	Percent of population in middle and upper [social] strata	−.48 (−.45)

SOURCES: See Appendix II. For Variables 7, 10, and 12, the correlation coefficients are based on data including "best guess" estimates for two or three countries for which precise data are not available. Coefficients in parentheses are based on data *not* including these estimates. See footnote 30.

population in cities over 20,000 (2) percent of adults literate, (3) newspaper circulation per 1,000 population, (4) university students per 1,000 population, and (5) radios per 1,000 population. As one might except, these variables are highly intercorrelated: the mean intercorrelation is .81. They are also fairly closely correlated in the expected direction with military intervention: the mean correlation is −.48.[31] To simplify sub-

sequent analysis, I have added together each country's (standardized) scores on these five indicators to form a single index of social mobilization, or "SM index." This index represents very accurately the factor common to these five indicators—all of the intercorrelations among the five components and all of their individual correlations with the MI index can be accounted for in terms of covariation with the SM index. This index itself correlates −.53 with the MI index. The conclusion must be that social mobilization is fairly strongly, and negatively, related to military inter-

[31] There is considerable debate about whether tests of statistical significance are appropriate in cases, like the present study, in which we have not a random sample from a larger universe but a complete universe, viz., all contemporary Latin American countries. Strictly speaking, significance testing is merely a way of checking inferences from a random sample to the universe from which that sample is drawn. On the other hand, Blalock and Gold have argued that significance tests may help us sift important from unimportant findings, even when there is no question of inferring to a larger universe. See Blalock, 270, and David Gold, "Some Problems in Generalizing Aggregate Associations," *American Behavioral Scientist*, VIII (December 1964), 16–18. Gold, however, adds the qualification that when one is dealing

with small *N*'s (as we are here), "judgments of importance that can be made reasonably from the *size* of associations should take precedence over tests of significance." Keeping in mind the problems associated with significance-testing in this situation, one may find the following figures helpful: assuming a one-tailed test and an *N* of 20, an $r \geq .38$ is significant at the .05 level; $r \geq .31$ is significant at the .10 level; and an $r \geq .23$ is significant at the .33 level. These significance levels are derived from the *World Handbook*, 262.

vention. More than one-quarter of the total variance in the MI index can be accounted for by covariation with social mobilization. (The square of a correlation coefficient, termed the "coefficient of determination," indicates what proportion of the variance in one variable is accounted for by covariation with the other. Here, for example, $-.53$ squared equals .28 or 28 percent.)[32]

Six of the variables are closely related to economic development: (1) per capita GNP, (2) percent of GNP derived from agriculture, (3) percent of the labor force in agriculture, (4) percent of the population in the primary sector, (5) percent of the labor force earning wages or salaries, and (6) percent of the labor force employed in industry. Again, these variables are highly intercorrelated: the average intercorrelation among them is .72. Each is moderately correlated with military intervention in the expected direction: the mean correlation of the six with the MI index is $-.32$.[33] As in the case of social mobilization, to make subsequent discussion simpler I have added together each country's (standardized) scores on these six indicators to form a single index of economic development, or "ED index." Like the SM index, the ED index represents very accurately the factor common to its six components. This ED index correlates $-.37$ with the MI index.

Before we can decide definitely on the relationship between economic development and military intervention, however, we must take into account their joint correlation with social mobilization. This procedure, in fact, produces a most remarkable result: if we remove the effect of social mobilization, economic development itself turns out to be *positively*, not negatively, correlated with military intervention! The pattern of simple, or zero-order, correla-

tions among these three variables is given in Figure 1. Since the ED index and the SM index are very highly intercorrelated, the partial correlation between economic development and military intervention, controlling for social mobilization, becomes $+.26$. The explanation of this finding is that the SM-MI and SM-ED correlations are so strong that they "mask" the real, positive ED-MI correlation.*

A more sophisticated procedure for analyzing this pattern of interrelations is provided by causal path analysis.[34] This technique allows us to calculate "causal weights," or "path coefficients," indicating the nature and importance of the causal relationships among a set of variables, provided (1) we are willing to posit some particular pattern of causal relations among

* Editor's footnote: Edward R. Tufte points out the problem of multicollinearity in this analysis. If two or more describing variables are highly intercorrelated, then it is difficult and perhaps impossible to assess their independent effects on the response variable. As correlation between two independent variables approaches unity, it becomes impossible to tell one variable from the other. Thus, it may be desirable to separate out the independent effects of economic development and social mobilization on a particular response variable such as military intervention in politics. Yet, the multicollinearity deadlock makes it impossible to assess reliably the independent effects of these two variables. See Tufte, "Improving Data Analysis in Political Science," *World Politics.* **21**, 653–4, July, 1969.

[34] The discussion that follows is not intended to be a complete presentation of the logic and methodology of causal path analysis. For introductions to this recently developed technique, see Hubert M. Blalock, Jr., *Causal Inferences in Nonexperimental Research* (Chapel Hill 1964); Raymond Boudon, "A Method of Linear Causal Analysis . . . ," *American Sociological Review,* xxx (June 1965), 365–74; and Otis Dudley Duncan, "Path Analysis: Sociological Examples," *American Journal of Sociology,* Lxxii (July 1966), 1–16. For a readable and comprehensive introduction of political scientists, see Hayward R. Alker, Jr., "Causal Inference in Political Analysis," in Joseph Bernd, ed,. *Mathematical Applications in Political Science,* 2nd Series (Dallas 1966).

[32] See Blalock, 295-99.
[33] In calculating this mean correlation and in compiling the ED index that follows, I have reversed the scoring for Variables 7-9, so that a large positive number always refers to a high level of development.

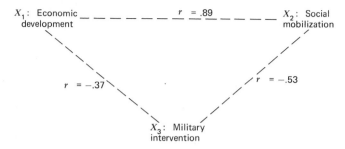

Figure 1.   Intercorrelations among economic development, social mobilization and military intervention.

the variables, and (2) we are willing to ignore (at least temporarily) the possible effects of variables not included in the set being considered. In our present case, the first of these conditions can be met by assuming that military intervention is a result, rather than a cause, of social mobilization and economic development. As a first approximation, this is probably true; later in this research note I shall explore this point further. (Path analysis does *not* require us to decide which way(s) the causal arrow joining development and mobilization should point.) If we can make the assumption implied in the second condition —that there is no fourth variable intruding —we can calculate from the correlation coefficients given in Figure 1 the causal weights, or path coefficients, given in Figure 2.[35] These weights imply that the direct effect of social mobilization on military intervention is strongly negative and that the direct effect of economic development on military intervention is moderately positive. Path analysis also allows us to estimate the proportion of the variance in a

dependent variable which remains unaccounted for by a system of independent variables.[36] Social mobilization and economic development together account for about thirty-three percent of the variance in the MI index, leaving sixty-seven percent yet to be explained.

The remaining hypothesis linking socioeconomic development and military intervention refers to the rise of the middle strata. Accurate information on the class structure of the Latin American countries is difficult to obtain, but Germani and Silvert present data on "the percentage of the population in middle and upper [social] strata."[37] The correlation of this variable with the MI index is $-.48$, supporting the notion that the rise of the middle strata is associated with a decline in military intervention. However, because this measure of class structure is almost perfectly correlated with the SM index ($r = .94$), it makes

[35] The equations for calculating the path coefficients (or p's) in this case are quite simple:

$$r_{21} = p_{21}$$
$$r_{32} = p_{32} + r_{21}p_{31}$$
$$r_{31} = p_{31} + r_{21}p_{32}.$$

This is a simple algebraic system of three equations and three unknowns. For the general equation of path analysis, see Duncan, 5.

[36] The equation for calculating the residual variance is quite simple:

$$p_{3u}^2 = 1 - p_{32}^2 - p_{31}^2 - 2p_{32}r_{12}p_{31}.$$

See Duncan, 6.

[37] R. Vekemans and J. L. Segundo present numerically identical data under the heading "Percent of population at intermediate and senior grades of employment," in "Essay on a Socio-economic Typology of the Latin American Countries," in E. de Vries and J. M. Echavarria, eds., *Social Aspects of Economic Development in Latin America*, Vol. 1 (Paris 1963).

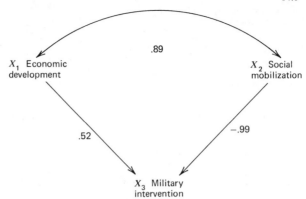

Figure 2.   Path coefficients for relationships among economic development, social mobilization and military intervention.

virtually no *independent* contribution toward explaining variance in levels of military intervention.

In sum, then, there seems to be good evidence that both social mobilization and economic development affect a country's propensity for military rule. Social mobilization definitely inhibits military intervention in politics, as predicted. The direct effect of economic development seems to be to encourage military intervention, although there is also a strong indirect effect linking economic development and military abstention, by way of social mobilization. The implications of this complicated pattern of findings can be brought out by several examples. Colombia and El Salvador are, in terms of the ED index, equally developed economically, but Columbian society is considerably more mobilized, as measured by the SM index. For the period under consideration, the Colombian military were much less involved in politics than were their Salvadoran counterparts. On the other hand, Venezuela and Costa Rica are about equally mobilized socially, but Venezuela is considerably more developed economically. As the preceding analysis would have predicted, Venezuelan politics in the period studied were much more subject to military intervention. Altogether the variables examined in this section account for about one-third of the total variance in the incidence of military intervention in Latin American politics.

POLITICAL DEVELOPMENT

Data on political development are much less readily available than data on socioeconomic variables. The correlations between military intervention and the political variables for which we can obtain data are given in Table III.

First, let us consider briefly the question of public commitment to civilian rule. Alexander Edelmann argues that among the most important influences counteracting military intervention in Latin America are "constitutional and legal restrictions imposed on members of the military regarding political activity. . . . Written not only on paper but also in the aspirations of liberty-loving citizens, they serve notice on the military of what their fellow countrymen expect."[38] If Edelmann is right that constitutional restrictions reflect popular norms and that these popular norms inhibit military intervention, then there should be a high correlation between constitutional restrictions and military abstention from politics. In fact, the correlation between military intervention and constitutional limits on military political activity is only −.18. The mean MI score for the fourteen

[38] Pp. 192–93.

Table III. Military Intervention as a Function of Political Development

VARIABLE NUMBER	VARIABLE CONTENT	CORRELATION WITH MI INDEX
13	Constitutional restrictions on the military	−.18
14	Percent of voting-age population voting	−.13
15	Interest articulation by parties	.04
16	Interest articulation by associations	−.19
17	Stability of party system	−.36
18	Interest aggregation by parties	−.63
19	$\log_{10}$ (10 × deaths from domestic group violence per million population)	.20
20	Weighted Eckstein "instability" index	−.08

SOURCES: See Appendix II.

nations that as of 1959 had some constitutional restrictions on political activity by the military is 17.4, while the mean MI score for the entire region is 18.4. The evidence clearly fails to confirm Edelmann's hypothesis. The explanation may be either that constitutions and popular aspirations are unrelated or that these aspirations do not affect military intervention.

A frequent hypothesis is that popular political participation inhibits military intervention. The best available indicator of such participation is the proportion of the adult population that votes in national elections.[39] Table III shows that the correlation between electoral turnout and military intervention, though in the predicted direction, is quite low. As a matter of fact, if we control for the level of social mobilization, the remaining partial correlation between turnout and military intervention is virtually zero.

[39] It is true that the accuracy of electoral turnout as an indicator of partipation is limited by variations in the social and institutional context of the act of voting. Voting does not have the same meaning in the U.S. and the USSR, in the Netherlands and Uganda. Restriction of our attention to the Latin American countries minimizes this problem. For a fuller discussion of the problem, see Germani and Silvert.

In assessing the hypotheses linking military intervention to the weakness of political parties and pressure groups—the political infrastructure—we are forced to rely almost exclusively on the judgments compiled for the *Cross-Polity Survey*. Four scales presented there are relevant: (1) extent of interest articulation by political parties, (2) extent of interest articulation by associations, (3) stability of the party system, and (4) extent of interest aggregation by political parties. The correlations of the two variables involving interest articulation are, in fact, negligible, viz., .04 for parties and −.19 for associations. Judging by these statistics, strong and articulate parties and pressure groups do not necessarily inhibit military intervention, nor do weak parties and pressure groups necessarily encourage intervention.[40] The stability of the party

[40] Edelmann argues that one particular sort of interest group is especially likely to inhibit military intervention: "The most serious threat of all to the power of the military is that posed by the labor unions . . ." (p. 194). Actually, the correlation between military intervention and the proportion of union members is −.07. Huntington argues that political decay varies directly with the extent of party fragmentation. The comparable *Cross-Polity Survey* variable is called "Party System: Quantitative"; this correlates .23 with the MI index; controlling for social mobilization reduces this to .16.

system is somewhat more strongly related to military intervention, and the extent of aggregation by political parties is quite strongly related, with coefficients of −.36 and −.63 respectively. These figures, especially the latter one, strongly suggest that in contemporary Latin America political parties and military regimes represent mutually exclusive mechanisms for reaching political decisions. On the other hand, these relationships are hardly surprising, because they approach being tautological. In any country where a military regime was in power most experts would be likely *ipso facto* to rate as insignificant the role of parties in aggregating interests and resolving political problems.

The final proposition to be considered in this section on political development links military intervention to the role of violence in politics. Two different indices of political violence in the Latin American countries are available. Harry Eckstein compiled from the *New York Times Index* an enumeration of violent events occurring in every country in the world in the period 1946–1959 and tallied these in ten categories ranging from civil wars to police roundups. I have computed for each Latin American country an index based on five of his categories, with "warfare" and "turmoil" weighted by a factor of four, "rioting" and "large-scale terrorism" weighted by two, and "small-scale terrorism" weighted by one.[41] (These were the only categories dealing with mass violence.) The other index of political violence is based on the variable "Deaths from Domestic Group Violence per Million Population, 1950–1962" presented in the *World Handbook of Political and Social Indicators*. To reduce the skewing effect caused by the great variance in this variable (from 2,900 for Cuba to 0.3 for Uruguay), I have used a logarithmic transformation to "squash" the distribution. (Given the nature of the dis-

tribution, the effect of this transformation is to raise the correlation coefficient obtained with the MI index.) The first index of political violence, based on Eckstein, is virtually unrelated to military intervention. The second index is slightly related in the expected direction, with $r = .20$, but this relationship disappears when controls are introduced for socioeconomic development.

Our conclusions about the hypotheses linking military abstention and political development must be cautious because of the limitations of the data available. With this qualification in mind, we can conclude that (apart from the trivial relationship between rule by the military and rule by political parties) there is very little evidence linking political development to military abstention in any straightforward way. Widespread participation in elections, strong parties and pressure groups, and freedom from political violence are neither necessary nor sufficient conditions for military abstention.

THE MILITARY ESTABLISHMENT

Several students of military intervention have stressed the importance of internal characteristics of the military establishment in determining the extent and nature of military intervention. Unfortunately, data are available for only a few, very gross, characteristics of the armed forces of the Latin American countries. Table IV shows the relationships between the MI index and these characteristics—military expenditures as a proportion of GNP, military personnel as a proportion of the adult population, and total military personnel.

The strong positive relationship between military intervention and military spending is hardly surprising and is probably the result of circular causation. Interestingly, militarism in the sense of intervention in politics does not seem to be linked to militarism in the sense of the proportion of men in arms. Still more interesting is the *negative* correlation between absolute size of the military establishment and extent of

[41] I have borrowed this weighting technique from Eldon Kenworthy, "Predicting Instability in Latin America" (unpublished).

Table IV. Military Intervention as a Function of Internal Characteristics of the Military

VARIABLE NUMBER	VARIABLE CONTENT	CORRELATION WITH MI INDEX
21	Defense spending as a percent of GNP	.55
22	Military personnel as a percent of adults	.07
23	Military personnel in thousands	− .24

SOURCES: See Appendix II.

military intervention. This finding directly contradicts the proposition relating intervention to the size and sophistication of the armed forces. The finding cannot be attributed to the spurious effects of either simple population size (for the correlation between population size and the MI index is virtually zero) or socioeconomic development. Possibly the negative correlation reflects an inhibiting effect of either greater "professionalism" or lower internal cohesion in larger military establishments. Of course, the relative weight of this variable in determining military intervention is not great, for it accounts at best for only about six percent of the total variance in the MI index.

FOREIGN INFLUENCES

One of the most common explanations of military intervention in Latin America is that German military training missions during the late nineteenth and early twentieth centuries "infected" Latin American officers with ideas of military involvement in politics. As it turns out, this is a good example of a proposition that has been "tested" by time rather than evidence. The correlations between the MI index and the incidence of German, French, Chilean, and U.S. missions are given in Table V.

The two most notable figures are the slight *negative* correlation between German influence and military intervention and the moderate *positive* correlation between Chilean missions and military intervention. The average MI score for the countries that had German missions is 15.2.[42] The average score for those that had French missions is 18.7, and for those with Chilean missions, 23.0. (It will be recalled that the mean score

[42] This negative finding is independent of the particular period during which the various missions were in residence. The mean MI score for only those countries that had German missions in the nineteenth century—generally the period referred to in this connection—is lower still: 13.6.

Table V. Military Intervention as a Function of Incidence of Foreign Military Training Missions

VARIABLE NUMBER	VARIABLE CONTENT	CORRELATION WITH MI INDEX
24	German military training missions	− .20
25	French military training missions	.03
26	Chilean military training missions	.36
27	U.S. Mutual Defense Assistance Agreements	.06

SOURCES: See Appendix II.

for the area as a whole is 18.4.) Neither the negative finding involving German missions nor the positive one involving Chilean missions can be attributed to spurious correlations with socioeconomic development. The explanation for the German finding seems to be simply that a plausible hypothesis has been repeatedly affirmed without adequate testing. Without more detailed information about the Chilean missions, that correlation will have to go unexplained.

The data on U.S. military missions refer to the twelve countries having Mutual Defense Assistance Agreements with the U.S. as of 1960 and are included only for general interest. The fact that the correlation of U.S. missions with military abstention is at present negligible need not imply that over a period of several decades such contacts will not affect the political orientations of the Latin American armed forces.

The other major foreign influence often alleged to affect military intervention is the "demonstration effect" of military coups in other countries. Historians of particular instances of military intervention have from time to time apparently uncovered some direct evidence of such influence, but the question to be considered here is to what extent this kind of "coup contagion" is a general phenomenon. The technique to be used is a familiar one in mathematical sociology.[43] I first listed all the successful military coups in Latin America from 1951 to 1965. The number of countries experiencing coups in each half-year period was then tallied.[44] Essentially, the technique consists

[43] See James S. Coleman, *Introduction to Mathematical Sociology* (Glencoe 1964), 288–311.
[44] Attempted but unsuccessful coups were ignored, partly for the conceptual reason that the definition of an "attempted coup" is problematic, partly for the practical reason that adequate information on attempted coups is lacking. The period of a half-year is chosen as representing about the optimum length of time during which contagion might be expected to operate. An analysis using one-year intervals produced results exactly comparable to those reported. I tallied countries rather than coups so as to exclude the effects of "contagion" within a single country.

of comparing the obtained distribution of coups with the distribution that would be expected if the incidence of coups were random across countries. If coups are contagious, we would expect more periods during which there were either *no* coups or *many* coups than we would expect if coups were distributed randomly throughout the fifteen-year span. Table VI compares the obtained distribution with the distribution that would be expected if the thirty-two coups of this period had been distributed randomly. (This random distribution is given by the formula called Poisson's distribution.) The evidence clearly disconfirms the contagion hypothesis. If anything, the data suggest that coups are slightly *more evenly* distributed (not less evenly, as the contagion hypothesis suggests) than chance alone would imply, although overall the differences are rather small.

Table VI. Number of Countries with Military Coups in Half-Year Periods, 1951-1965

NUMBER OF COUNTRIES	NUMBER OF PERIODS	
	OBTAINED DISTRIBUTION	RANDOM DISTRIBUTION
0	8	10.3
1	13	11.0
2	8	5.9
3 or more	1	2.8
	30	30.0

SOURCE: *The Annual Register* (London 1951–1966).

These findings conclusively disconfirm several widely repeated propositions about military intervention. Neither German military missions nor "coup contagion" can be blamed for military involvement in Latin American politics.

HISTORICAL TRENDS AND INFLUENCES

I have already described the construction of the MI index for the period 1956–1965.

Exactly the same procedures were used in compiling MI scores for the periods 1906–1915 and 1951–1955 (see Appendix I). Taken together these data allow us to examine the relative incidence of military intervention at selected periods over the last half-century. Table VII gives the relevant data. The average levels of interven-

Table VII. The Incidence of Military Intervention in Four Five-Year Periods

PERIOD	MEAN MI INDEX PER ANNUM
1906–1915	1.53
1951–1955	2.02
1956–1960	1.87
1961–1965	1.81

tion show that although the extent of intervention since 1950 has been somewhat higher than it was a half-century earlier, the general trend within the later period has been downward.[45] The intercorrelations among the scores for the most recent five-year periods, given in Figure 3, illustrate the not surprising fact that the extent of military intervention in the various countries tends to be quite constant, at least over this fifteen-year period.

Hypotheses linking military intervention or abstention to traditional norms in the military establishments imply that there will be a significant correlation between past and present levels of intervention. The simple

[45] The lower level of intervention in the earlier period probably reflects (1) the fact that after the turn of the century civilian government enjoyed a period of considerable success in Latin America and (2) my decision (see footnote 26) to distinguish "caudillism" from "military intervention."

correlation between the MI scores for the period 1956–1965 and the period exactly a half-century earlier is .47, thus moderately confirming this prediction. Perhaps, however, this correlation merely reflects the fact that the countries predisposed to military intervention by socioeconomic conditions in 1906–1915 were at the same relative level of socioeconomic development at mid-century. Perhaps, that is, continuities in socioeconomic development, rather than continuities in traditions of militarism, account for the association.

Precise information on earlier levels of socioeconomic development in all twenty Latin American countries is impossible to obtain. Fortunately, for one indicator of social mobilization—literacy—we can make some reasonable estimates. Among those seven countries for which 1910 literacy rates are available, these rates correlate almost perfectly ($r = .98$) with the 1950 literacy rates for inhabitants of sixty-five and over —the generation who were young adults in the earlier period. Relying on this fact, we can use the 1950 rates for those sixty-five and over—which can be closely estimated for all of the countries—as indicators of the levels of social mobilization a half-century ago.

Figure 4 displays the intercorrelations among our four variables: literacy in 1910 and 1960 and military intervention in 1906–1915 and 1956–1965. Of the several hundred possible causal models that might be used to fit this set of correlations, all but four can be eliminated as inconsistent with the pattern of correlations obtained or with the temporal ordering of the variables.[46]

[46] This elimination process follows the technique suggested by Herbert Simon and Hubert M. Blalock, Jr. See Blalock, *Causal Inferences*, 61–94 and *passim*.

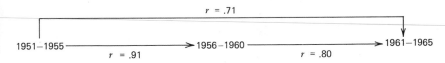

Figure 3.   Intercorrelations among MI indices for three recent five-year periods.

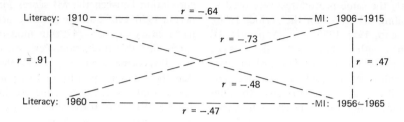

Figure 4.   Intercorrelations among literacy rates, 1910 and 1960 and military intervention scores, 1906-1915 and 1956-1965.

The four possible causal models are shown in Figure 5. If we assume that military intervention in 1906–1915 could not have significantly influenced literacy rates in 1910 (even though it might have influenced *later* literacy rates), we can eliminate Models A and B. If, in addition, we assume that 1910 literacy rates do not affect 1956–1965 military intervention directly, but only indirectly through their influence on 1960 literacy rates, we can also eliminate Model C.

Having decided on a particular causal model, we can apply the technique of causal path analysis to examine the interrelationships among social mobilization and military intervention for the two periods. The results of this analysis, given in Figure 6, show that both contemporary literacy rates and earlier levels of military intervention make independent contribu-

tions toward explaining present levels of military intervention. The figure also reveals that military intervention itself has a deleterious effect on subsequent levels of literacy. One implication of this pattern of findings is that part of the strong correlation earlier noted between social mobilization and (contemporary) military intervention can be traced to the impact of earlier military intervention on both contemporary levels of mobilization and contemporary levels of intervention.[47]

Another surprising fact revealed by this historical analysis is that levels of socioeconomic development were relatively much more important determinants of mili-

[47] Perhaps an analogous explanation would apply to the relationship between economic development and military intervention. We lack the data necessary to carry this analysis further.

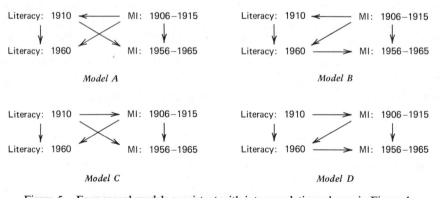

Figure 5.   Four casual models consistent with intercorrelations shown in Figure 4.

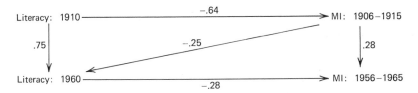

Figure 6. Path coefficients for relationships among literacy rates, 1910 and 1960; and military intervention, 1906-1915 and 1956-1965.

tary intervention a half-century ago than today. As shown in Figure 4, the correlation between 1910 literacy rates and 1906–1915 military intervention was $-.64$, while a half-century later the analogous correlation was $-.47$. In terms of variance explained, the impact of literacy on military intervention dropped from forty-one percent to twenty-two percent. We lack earlier data on the other indicators of social mobilization, but it is interesting and significant that the overall index of social mobilization for 1960 correlates $-.67$ with the 1906–1915 MI index, as compared to $-.53$ with the 1956–1965 MI index. Over the last fifty years in Latin America the political sphere has become more autonomous; that is, factors other than socioeconomic development have become relatively more important determinants of military intervention.[48]

V. Conclusions

The statistical analyses presented in this research note have answered some questions about military intervention. Social mobilization clearly increases the prospects for civilian rule. Traditions of militarism play an important role in accounting for contemporary military intervention. Neither foreign training missions nor foreign examples of successful intervention seem to have any impact.

But some of the findings call for further reflection and inquiry. How can we account

for the fact that the direct effect of economic development seems to be to encourage, rather than to inhibit, military involvement in politics? What are we to make of recent speculations linking political institutionalization and military abstention, in the light of the present negative findings?[49] What are the implications of the declining (although still important) strength of the relationship between military intervention and levels of socioeconomic development?

Overall, the independent variables we have examined here account for somewhat less than half of the total variance in contemporary military intervention.[50] One way of beginning the search for other significant factors is to examine so-called "deviant cases," that is, countries with MI scores considerably higher or lower than would be predicted on the basis of the variables examined here. Let me illustrate this technique.

Figure 7 displays a "scattergram" of the relationship between military intervention and social mobilization. Obviously, a few countries are widely out of line with the relationship characterizing the remaining countries. Argentina has a much higher MI

---

[48] Huntington argues that one aspect of political development is an increasing autonomy of politics from other social spheres. See "Political Development and Political Decay," 401–30.

[49] Huntington's theory of political development (*ibid.*) implies that social mobilization leads to military rule and that civilian rule depends on strong political institutions; neither of these propositions is confirmed by the present study. It would be worth further investigation to determine whether the propositions do apply to other underdeveloped areas.

[50] Among the other independent variables considered and rejected in the present study were (1) total population ($r = .02$), (2) racial composition ($r = .16$), and (3) rates of social change (for urbanization, $r = -.18$).

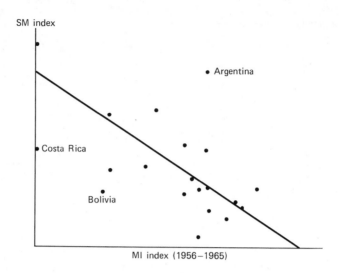

Figure 7. Scattergram of relationship between social mobilization and military intervention.

score than would be expected on the basis of its social development, while Bolivia and Costa Rica have MI scores much lower than would be expected. The effect of these deviant cases is to lower substantially the obtained correlation coefficients. If we remove Argentina from the analysis, the coefficient rises from −.53 to −.67, and if we remove Bolivia and Costa Rica as well, the coefficient rises to −.79. The proportion of variance explained has risen from twenty-eight percent to sixty-two percent. Similar analyses could be presented using the other independent variables discussed in this research note.

Let me be clear that the import of this discussion of deviant cases is *not* that these variables "really" explain the higher amounts of variance, for obviously we cannot "write off" countries like Argentina, Bolivia, and Costa Rica. Rather, this analysis focuses our attention on the countries

that are most anomalous when analyzed in terms of the variables considered here, as well as on the characteristics that might explain their deviance. In the case of Bolivia, the 1952 revolution drastically reduced (temporarily, at least) the role of the military to a level below that which might have been expected for a country at its level of socioeconomic development. From this perspective, the events of 1964–1965 in Bolivia might be interpreted as a "return to normalcy." The "Argentine paradox" is a familiar one to students of Latin America; the present study graphically reveals once again the extent of this paradox. The case of Argentina and, by contrast, the case of Costa Rica suggest the importance of pursuing the suggestions of Germani and Silvert that military intervention is related to the extent of cleavage or consensus in a society.

Appendix I. Year-by-Year Military Intervention Scores

	1906	1907	1908	1909	1910	1911	1912	1913	1914	1915	1951	1952	1953	1954	1955	1956	1957	1958	1959	1960	1961	1962	1963	1964	1965	MI INDEX 1906–15	MI INDEX 1956–65	NEEDLER'S RANKINGS*
Costa Rica	1	1	1	1	1	1	1	1	1	1	0	0	0	0	0	0	0	0	0	0	0	0	0	0	0	10	0	0
Uruguay	1	1	1	1	1	1	1	1	1	1	0	0	0	0	0	0	0	0	0	0	0	0	0	0	0	10	0	1
Bolivia	1	1	1	1	1	1	1	1	1	1	3	1	0	0	0	0	0	0	0	1	1	1	1	2	3	10	9	1
Chile	1	1	1	1	1	1	1	1	1	1	1	1	1	1	1	1	1	1	1	1	1	1	1	1	1	10	10	1
Mexico	2	2	2	2	2	1	1	2	2	2	1	1	1	1	1	1	1	1	1	1	1	1	1	1	1	18	10	1
Colombia	2	2	2	2	1	1	1	1	1	1	1	1	3	3	3	3	3	2	1	1	1	1	1	1	1	14	15	1
Cuba	1	1	1	1	1	1	1	1	1	1	2	3	3	3	3	3	3	3	1	1	1	1	1	1	1	10	16	4
Panama	0	0	0	0	0	0	0	0	0	0	2	2	2	2	2	2	2	2	2	2	2	2	2	2	2	0	20	2
Nicaragua	1	1	1	1	2	3	2	2	2	2	3	3	3	3	3	2	2	2	2	2	2	2	2	2	2	17	20	4
Peru	1	1	1	1	1	1	2	2	2	2	3	3	3	3	3	2	2	2	2	2	2	3	2	2	2	14	21	2
Brazil	1	1	1	2	2	2	2	2	2	1	2	2	2	3	3	2	2	2	2	2	2	2	2	3	3	16	22	2
Haiti	3	3	3	3	3	3	3	3	3	3	3	3	3	3	3	3	3	3	3	3	3	1	1	1	1	30	22	3
Ecuador	2	2	2	2	2	2	2	2	2	2	2	2	2	2	2	3	2	2	2	2	2	2	3	3	2	20	23	2
Honduras	2	2	2	2	2	2	2	2	2	2	2	2	2	2	2	2	3	3	2	2	2	2	3	2	2	20	23	2
Argentina	1	1	1	1	1	1	1	1	1	1	3	3	3	3	3	3	2	2	2	2	2	3	3	2	2	10	23	3
Venezuela	2	2	2	2	2	2	2	2	2	2	3	2	2	3	3	3	3	3	2	2	2	2	2	2	2	20	23	3
Guatemala	2	2	2	2	2	2	2	2	2	2	2	3	3	3	3	3	3	3	3	3	3	2	2	2	2	20	26	3
El Salvador	2	2	2	2	2	2	2	2	2	2	3	3	3	3	3	3	3	3	3	3	3	3	2	2	2	20	27	4
Dominican R.	2	2	2	2	2	2	2	2	2	3	3	2	2	2	3	3	3	3	3	3	3	2	2	3	3	21	28	3
Paraguay	2	2	2	2	2	2	1	1	1	1	2	2	2	2	3	3	3	3	3	3	3	3	3	3	3	16	30	4

* Martin C. Needler, *Latin American Politics in Perspective* (New York 1963), 156–57. Rankings of "Normal Political Role of Military": 0 = "None"; 1 = "Limited"; 2 = "Intervene"; 3 = "Veto Power"; 4 = "In Control."

SOURCES: *The Annual Register* (London 1951–1966); Frank Brandenburg, *The Making of Modern Mexico* (Englewood Cliffs 1964); H. E. Davis, ed., *Government and Politics in Latin America* (New York 1958); John E. Fagg, *Latin America: A General History* (New York 1963); Robert L. Gilmore, *Caudillism and Militarism in Venezuela* (Athens, Ohio, 1964); John J. Johnson, *The Military and Society in Latin America* (Stanford 1964); Edwin Lieuwen, *Arms and Politics in Latin America* (New York 1961) and *Generals vs. Presidents* (New York 1964); John Martz, *Central America* (Chapel Hill 1959); Dana G. Munro, *The Five Republics of Central America* (New York 1918) and *The Latin American Republics: A History*, 2nd ed. (New York 1950); Martin C. Needler, ed., *Political Systems of Latin America* (Princeton 1964); Franklin D. Parker, *The Central American Republics* (New York 1964); J. Fred Rippy, *Latin America: A Modern History* (Ann Arbor 1958); Robert E. Scott, *Mexican Government in Transition* (Urbana 1959); William S. Stokes, *Latin American Politics* (New York 1959); Theodore Wyckoff, "The Role of the Military in Latin American Politics," *Western Political Quarterly*, XIII (September 1960), 745–63.

Appendix II. Sources of Data for Independent Variables

VARIABLE NUMBER	VARIABLE CONTENT	SOURCE NUMBER AND PAGE
1	Percent of population in cities over 20,000	I, 228
2	Percent of adults literate (1960)	XI
3	Newspaper circulation per 1,000 population	II, 108
4	University students per 1,000 population	I, 228
5	Radios per 1,000 population	II, 118
6	Per capita GNP (1957)	II, 115
7	Percent of GNP derived from agriculture	II, 172; III, 70
8	Percent of labor force in agriculture	II, 177
9	Percent of population in the primary sector	IX, 64
10	Percent of labor force earning wages or salaries	III, 38
11	Percent of labor rorce employed in industry	X, 90
12	Percent of population in middle and upper [social] strata	IX, 64
13	Constitutional restrictions on political activity by military	VIII, 132
14	Percent of voting-age population voting	II, 84
15	Interest articulation by parties	V, 37
16	Interest articulation by associations	V, 33
17	Stability of party system	V, 43
18	Interest aggregation by parties	V, 38
19	Log_{10} (10 $\times$ deaths from domestic group violence per million population)	II, 99
20	Weighted Eckstein "instability" index	IV, Appendix I
21	Defense spending as a percent of GNP	II, 79
22	Military personnel as a percent of adult population	II, 77
23	Military personnel strength in thousands	III, 41
24	German military training missions	VI
25	French military training missions	VI
26	Chilean military training missions	VI
27	U.S. Mutual Defense Assistance Agreements	VII, 201
28	Percent of adults 65 and over literate (1950)	XII
29	Percent of adults literate (1910)	XIII

SOURCES: *I*. Gino Germani, "The Strategy of Fostering Social Mobility," in E. de Vries and J. M. Echavarria, eds., *Social Aspects of Economic Development in Latin America*, Vol. I (Paris 1963). *II*. Bruce M. Russett and others, *World Handbook of Political and Social Indicators* (New Haven 1964). *III*. Center of Latin American Studies, *Statistical Abstract of Latin America* (Los Angeles 1962). *IV*. Harry Eckstein, *Internal War: The Problem of Anticipation*, a report submitted to the Research Group in Psychology and the Social Sciences, Smithsonian Institution (Washington 1962). *V*. Arthur S. Banks and Robert B. Textor, *A Cross-Polity Survey* (Cambridge, Mass., 1963). *VI*. John J. Johnson, ed., *The Role of the Military in Underdeveloped Countries* (Princeton 1962), 108, 163; John J. Johnson, *The Military and Society in Latin America* (Stanford 1964), 69–71; William S. Stokes, *Latin American Politics* (New York 1959), 129–32. *VII*. Edwin Lieuwen, *Arms and Politics in Latin America* (New York 1961). *VIII*. Stokes, *Latin American Politics*. *IX*. Gino Germani and Kalman Silvert, "Politics, Social Structure and Military Intervention in Latin America," *Archives Européennes de Sociologie*, II (Spring 1961), 62–81. *X*. R. Vekemans and J. L. Segundo, "Essay on a Socio-economic Typology of the Latin American Countries," in de Vries and Echavarria. *XI*. United Nations, *Compendium of Social Statistics* (New York 1963. *XII. Ibid.*; United Nations, *Demographic Yearbook* (New York 1955, 1964); UNESCO, *World Illiteracy at Mid-Century* (Paris 1957). *XIII. ibid.*; UNESCO, *Progress of Literacy in Various Countries* (Paris 1953).

THE PRAETORIAN STATE AND THE PRAETORIAN ARMY: TOWARD A TAXONOMY OF CIVIL-MILITARY RELATIONS IN DEVELOPING POLITIES

Amos Perlmutter*

What was considered an unnatural and deviant phenomenon before 1945 has now become widespread: the active and increasing role of the army in politics. A government dominated by an army was considered "unnatural" not because it was a new phenomenon—it had been recognized by political philosophers from Machiavelli to Mosca—but because some social scientists refused to accept military rule as being as natural as civilian rule. This hesitation of social scientists to study the military has had a variety of causes, ranging from ignorance of historical and political facts to antagonism toward war and the military profession. As recently as the 1930's, military government was identified as the ultimate type of totalitarianism.[1]

Military political interventionism has recurred in the form of coups and counter-coups, both successful and unsuccessful, in most Latin American republics, in five independent Arab states, in fourteen new African states, in several Southeast Asian polities, and in Pakistan. These events confirm the historical and political fact that when civilian government is ineffective, the executive is unable to control the military. Many civil-military combinations are possible: the army can take over the government with or without the consent of civilian politicians, on their behalf or against them, in order to eliminate one civilian group and establish another, or to eliminate rivals in the military.

This article is an attempt to classify and explain types of civil-military relations in developing polities. We will examine, analyze, and compare various sets of propositions. Since the Middle East and North Africa is the immediate area of our interest, it will naturally receive a large share of our attention. Several of the propositions emerge from a close study of civil-military relations in the Middle East over a period of several years.

Extending our study beyond the Middle East, we have examined our propositions as they relate to Latin America, Africa, and Southeast Asia. The scope of this article cannot include a comprehensive examination of all the propositions.[2]

SOURCE: Amos Perlmutter, "The Preatorian State and the Praetorian Army: Toward a Taxonomy of Civil-Military Relations in Developing Polities," *Comparative Politics*, 1:382–404, April, 1969.

* The list of colleagues who have read various versions of this article is too long to include here. I am especially grateful to Professors S. M. Lipset, S. P. Huntington, J. C. Harsanyi, E. Nordlinger, and E. Rosenstein, and to M. D. Feld, I. North, and G. Orren for their great help in clarifying the concepts of this article.

[1] Harold D. Lasswell, "The Garrison State," *American Journal of Sociology*, XLVI [January 1941], 455–468.

[2] I am now engaged in relating the propositions to the cases of twelve states in depth (in four areas), comparing the states along the continuum of praetorianism. (The countries are Mexico, Argentina, Brazil, Turkey, Egypt, Syria, India, Burma, Indonesia, Tunisia, Ghana, and Nigeria.) The propositions are divided into five clusters: (1) the military and society—particularly the transformation from oligarchical to radical praetorianism; (2) milltary intervention—coups and patterns of miiitary intervention: (3) types of military roles, particularly along the continuum of arbitrator-ruler; (4) the military and modernization-development—whether military rule has

Toward a Definition of a Modern Praetorian State

In order to establish an analytical model, we must distinguish clearly between historical and modern praetorianism. An example of historical praetorianism would be the action of a small military contingent in the Imperial capital of Rome, who moved to preserve the legitimacy of the empire by defending the Senate against the encroachment of triumphant or rebellious military garrisons marching on the capital.

The influence of the Roman Praetorian Guard was based on three factors: the Guard's monopoly on local military power, the absence of definitive rules of succession, and the prestige of the Roman Senate. In other words, though there was no hard and fast rule as to how the *princeps* was to be chosen, the Senate's decree made him a legitimate ruler. The provincial armies would accept that decision. As the sole resident military force, the Praetorian Guards were able to impose their candidate upon the Senate. They were thus able to manipulate a widely subscribed *concept of legitimacy* and to attain a degree of political influence and power far beyond their actual numerical and military resources. When, however, the provincial armies stumbled upon the secret that emperors need not be made in Rome, the legitimizing powers of the Senate disappeared, and with them the strength of the Praetorians.[3]

Here is the link between historical and modern praetorianism. A modern praetori-an state is one in which the military tends to intervene and *potentially* could dominate the political system. The political processes of this state *favor* the development of the military as the core group and the growth of its expectations as a ruling class; its political leadership (as distinguished from bureaucratic, administrative, and managerial leadership) is chiefly recruited from the military, or from groups sympathetic, or at least not antagonistic, to the military. Constitutional changes are effected and sustained by the military, and the army frequently intervenes in the government. In a praetorian state, therefore, the military plays a dominant role in political structures and institutions.

Broadly speaking, a modern praetorian government may develop when civilian institutions lack legitimacy or are in a position to be dominated by the military.

Praetorianism has existed in all historical periods. In view of the general trend toward modernization, it may be said that various types of praetorianism probably represent certain stages of development.[4] At present, praetorianism often appears in states which are in the early and middle stages of modernization and political mobilization.[5] In underdeveloped states, the

---

brought about *more or less* stability than non-military rule; (5) the relationship between military organization and political skill. I have also begun quantitative analyses of qualitative data on military and modernization in five Middle Eastern countries. These analyses will be based on cross-national data (1950-1962) and on quantitative correlations between social, political, and economic indicators and the level and pace of military, economic, and political performances.

[3] I am grateful to my friend M. D. Feld of Harvard University for this analysis, which he has written especially for the benefit of this article.

[4] David C. Rapoport, "Praetorianism: Government Without Consensus" (unpub. Ph.D. diss., University of California, Berkeley, 1960), pp. 14–15, defines praetorianism as a constitutional form of "government without consent." Rapoport's thesis provides an outstanding theoretical discussion of praetorianism. Although the present essay closely follows Rapoport's definition of praetorianism, it emphasizes the descriptive aspects of the subject and foregoes discussions of constitutionalism, consensus, and authority, which are discussed at length in Rapoport's work.

[5] This essay has been directly influenced by the works of Professor Samuel P. Huntington, especially his seminal essay, "Political Development and Political Decay," *World Politics*, XVIII (April 1965), 386–430. For some time, we have carried on an intellectual dialogue which, I hope, has resulted in a more positive approach to a theory of civil-military relations in developing polities. Especially excellent is Huntington's most persuasive chapter, "Prae-

army is propelled into political action when civilian groups fail to legitimize themselves. The army's presence in civilian affairs indicates the existence of corruption that is not expected to disappear in the near future;[6] that material improvements and ideological perspectives do not match; that traditional institutions are unable to bring about material improvement; and that modernized elites are incapable of establishing political institutions and structures which will sustain the momentum of social mobilization and modernization. Moreover, modern institutions which could direct these changes are difficult to organize because of the traditional orientation of the people. In the ensuing disorganization, both economy and ideology suffer setbacks.[7]

The salient characteristic of modern military organizations in developing policies is their professionalism. The professionalism and institutionalization of the military entails the establishment of military colleges, specialized training, the formation of a unified professional group and of a national army. Praetorian conditions are connected with professional military establishments and structures, some of which are institutionalized ahead of concomitant political and socioeconomic structures—political parties, parliaments, a centralized administrative bureaucracy, national authority, middle classes, and a national ideology. Therefore, corporate professionalism is not a guarantee against praetorianism. In fact, in praetorian polities the military interventionists are the professional soldiers, the graduates of the military academies, whose life career is the army.

Praetorianism occurs when the civilian government comes to a standstill in its pursuit of nationalist and modernist goals (modernization, urbanization, order, unification, and so forth).

Thus, praetorianism is generally associated with the disintegration of an old order and the rise of a decapitated new one. Another distinction between modern and historical (i.e., patriarchal, patrimonial, and *caudillismo* types[8]) praetorianism is that, in

---

torianism and Political Decay," in *Political Order in Changing Societies* (New Haven, 1968), pp. 192–263. He argues there that the concept of praetorianism becomes a useful operational tool to explain the relationship between political development and modernization. In our view Huntington's analysis of the role of political decay in modernizing polities becomes most crucial in the case of praetorianism.

[6] Huntington's central thesis (the Gap hypothesis) is that political modernization breeds both political instability and praetorian political order. *Political Order*, pp. 32–39, 53–56. See Gino Germani and Kalman H. Silvert, "Politics, Social Structure and Military Intervention in Latin America," *Archives européennes de sociologie*, II, No. 1 (1961), 62–81.

[7] The most impressive analysis of breakdown in modernization is found in S. N. Eisenstadt's extensive studies (by the author's admission, mostly of a preliminary nature) of the relationship between traditionalism, modernization, and change. See especially his "Breakdowns of Modernization," *Economic Development and Cultural Change*, XII (July 1964), 345–367; "Political Modernization: Some Comparative Notes," *International Journal of Comparative Sociology*, V (March 1964), 3–24; *Modernization and Change* (Englewood Cliffs, 1966); and "Some Observations on the Dynamics of Tradition," Working Paper, Ballagio, July 1968.

[8] It is most interesting to observe that some of the historical types of preatorianism were also associated with the disintegration of legitimate authority. After patriarchal power had declined, patriarchal praetoriansim no longer exercised authority without restraint. The military took over, but only for a short period. In patrimonial (prebureaucratic) political systems, the military became a permanent establishment. Since the military was the most powerful and rational structure after the patrimonial system, it took over when patrimonial legitimacy disintegrated. In the *caudillismo* case, the union of personalism and violence seized the disintegrating patrimonial state apparatus. Under the guise of Republicanism (in Latin America) and Liberalism (in nineteenth-century Spain), the *caudillismo* became the driving force of the new nation. On personal patriarchal and patrimonial types of domination see Max Weber, *Economy and Society*, III, ed. G. Roth and K. C. Wittich (New York, 1968).

the latter, the authority relationship between the military establishment and political order was based on a traditional orientation. In modern praetorianism, authority relationships are based on a legal-rational orientation.

Conditions conducive to a praetorian state may exist even before the army has intervened in politics. However, as these conditions generate other, supporting conditions, which we will discuss later, the chances for military intervention increase.

Social Conditions Contributing to Praetorianism

LOW DEGREE OF SOCIAL COHESION

In a state with low social cohesion, personal desires and group aims frequently diverge; the formal structure of the state is not buttressed by an informal one; institutions do not develop readily or operate effectively; social control is ineffective; and channels for communication are few. These conditions indicate the lack of meaningful universal symbols that can bind the society together. The syndrome of disintegration of which these conditions are a part is typical in a state in which the traditional patterns of social cohesion have broken down and have not yet been replaced by new ones.[9]

A break in the syndrome of social and economic disorganization is made possible only by the action of a group separated from the society—a revolutionary group, a party, a bureaucracy, or the army. If the ruling civilian leaders lack political experience and symbols of authority, military personnel may be able to manipulate the symbols of their institution to rule and introduce some coherence by force. Although the level of articulateness and sophistication in most cases tends to be lower in military than in civilian leaders,

attributes such as impartiality and courage that may accrue to the military may also make the military leaders effective. They may be more able to communicate with the people at large because they can elicit a psychological response on the symbolic level. And they may be able to overcome the praetorian syndrome to the extent that they maintain some isolation from the divisions of the politically active population and blur the existing lines of cleavage.

THE EXISTENCE OF FRATRICIDAL CLASSES

In addition to the polarization between the wealthy few and the many poor in underdeveloped countries, a praetorian state may exhibit gradation and variation within these two groups as well as in the middle class (if it exists). The different and unequal groups within all three major social layers —the bottom, the middle, and the top— will therefore tend to conflict. The result is a lack of class consciousness.

The top group is usually divided between traditionalists and modernists. The latter includes landowners who have adopted modern technology. The top-layer division between traditionalists and modernists is paralleled by a bottom-layer division. For example, large foreign-owned industrial enterprises may employ an urban worker elite. Because of the benefits this elite receives from the system, it is little inclined to suffer the deprivations that political action designed to benefit its less privileged brethren may entail. Yet, it is precisely these elite workers, concentrated in large enterprises, rather than the hundreds of thousands of domestics, shopkeepers' apprentices, and others, who technically could be organized.[10]

Such "buying off" of the urban workers who have the greatest potential for being organized for revolutionary action was characteristic of prerevolutionary China. The phenomenon appears throughout the

[9] See Nadav Safran, *Egypt in Search of Political Community* (Cambridge, Mass., 1961), p. 2, for an analysis of the consequences of this lack of parallelism in the development of Egypt.

[10] See Jean and Simmone Lacouture, *Egypt in Transition* (New York, 1958), pp. 367–387, for a discussion of divisions of this type in the Egyptian working class.

underdeveloped world. The urban workers in the large enterprises may be quite well off, but the masses of unemployed, semi-employed, and agricultural workers may live in near subhuman conditions. With reference to the urban workers of Cuba, MacGaffey and Barnett write: "Permanently employed skilled and semi-skilled workers tended to develop a stake in the existing political and economic order. Even those not organized into unions had their interests carefully protected by labor laws. Although they themselves might be denied opportunities for upward social mobility, skilled workers and those at the foreman level were in a position to provide their sons with an education that would enable them to move ahead."[11]

Thus, not only does the underdeveloped society as a whole lack unifying orientations, but its various sectors tend to be further fragmented and incapable of mounting unified action even for the narrower benefits of a particular sector. This is not to argue that similar differences within classes were absent during the developmental process in Western Europe or North America. It merely emphasizes that such divisions are particularly acute in the underdeveloped countries, where social and economic development have been rapid and where many stages of development have occurred simultaneously.

SOCIAL POLARITY AND NONCONSOLIDATED MIDDLE CLASS

The absence of a strong, cohesive, and articulate middle class is another condition for the establishment of a praetorian government. This absence is manifested in the polarization of the class structure—the gap between the few rich and the many poor.

Cohesiveness is necessary for the development of political and ideological articulateness. Such articulateness, when combined with socioeconomic power, constitutes the foundation for the political in-

fluence of any class. A struggle for power among the different strata of the middle class—the class which historically has acted as the stabilizer of civilian government during modernization—creates conditions beneficial to praetorianism.

The middle classes in most praetorian states are small, weak, ineffective, divided, and politically impotent. In the Middle East, for example, according to Morroe Berger, the middle class in most states amounts to no more than 6 percent of the population, and at the most 10 percent. Berger emphasizes that the composition of this middle class differs from that of the West during its industrialization process. The Middle Easterners of this class are either bureaucrats or small self-employed businessmen. They are rarely employers.[12] Not only is this middle class small, but, since it occupies different types of economic positions, the economic interests of its members diverge. Furthermore, their political interests diverge. Middle-class parties in underdeveloped countries are thus extremely fragmented.

In Latin America (Argentina and Brazil, for instance) we see a large, growing, and more cohesive middle class (10 to 19 percent, 20 percent and more), yet these middle classes are precipitators of military intervention and praetorianism. There is no common denominator between the fratricidal middle classes of the Middle East and the large middle class in Argentina-Brazil except that in Latin America military interventionism assures the middle class of power if and when they fail to come to power by electoral means. In the Middle East the military does not intervene as a class or even as surrogate for the middle class. Preconditions for praetorianism obtain when social classes are *politically* impotent, or when one social class is at least potentially more powerful than the rest.

[11] Wyatt MacCaffey and Clifford R. Barnett, *Cuba* (New Haven, 1962), p. 144.

[12] Morroe Berger, "The Middle Class in the Arab World," in Walter Lacqueur, ed. *The Middle East in Transition* (New York, 1958), pp. 63–65.

One could look at the political expectations of middle classes in order to explain military intervention, but praetorianism does not depend solely on the structural weaknesses, fratricide, and political impotence of the middle class. When the middle class looks for political allies, the military class could become its most useful instrument. The chances for the opposite, however, are better.

RECRUITMENT AND MOBILIZATION OF RESOURCES

Low levels of recruitment for group social action and for mobilization of material resources are further conditions of praetorianism. A state in the transitional stage not only lacks commonly valued patterns of action but also lacks common symbols that contribute to mobilization for social and political action. The most encompassing organization in theory—the government— is supported by only a few divided groups of the inchoate larger social groups. The government thus has difficulty in obtaining support for its activities. Its programs are subverted, and development projects fail. This failure in human mobilization results from the disparate value orientations of groups and members of society.

Material resources, needed by the government as much as human resources, are also withheld from it. Industrialists disguise their profits to cheat on taxation, bureaucrats take bribes, peasants hoard. The withholding of resources may take many forms but the result is always the same—the developmental activities of the government are subverted.[13]

---

[13] For a discussion of the importance of resource accumulation and use by the political institutions, see S. N. Eisenstadt, *The Political Systems of Empires* (London, 1963), esp. Chs. 6, 7. For Eisenstadt, the promotion of " . . . free resources and . . . [the] freeing [of] resources from commitments to particularistic-ascriptive groups . . ." is one of the conditions for the creation and maintenance of autonomous political institutions. p. 119.

Political Conditions Contributing to Praetorianism

CENTER AND PERIPHERY[14]

On the whole, the roles of intellectuals, scholars, bureaucrats, merchants, colonial administrators, and modernizing elites have been centralized in developing polities. An affirmative attitude toward establishing authority "imposes the central value system of that society."[15] The whole movement of modernization has revolved around the authority of the center. The conflict between the center and the periphery has been overlooked by nationalist leaders and their modernizing elites, as it has been by colonial administrators. Modernizing groups have invested greater intellectual efforts, administrative craftsmanship, and wealth into the center. In the end, the neglected periphery retaliates. Several African military coups have occurred when the periphery has struck back against the center, while the center, subject to the onslaught of modernization, is itself torn asunder. The backlash is not wholly traditionalist; the clash is not necessarily between the center and the periphery, but between coalitions of traditionalists and modernizing elites, associated with the center and the periphery, who are manifestly exposed to one another.[16] Here the military organization becomes instrumental—and its characteristic as a mobilizing force is exposed. In cases where the military sides with the

---

[14] These ideas are borrowed from Edward Shils' seminal studies on ideology and civility. See "Primordial, Personal, Sacred and Civil Ties," *British Journal of Sociology*, VIII (June 1957) 130–146; "Ideology, Center and Periphery," in *The Logic of Personal Knowledge* (Glencoe, 1961), pp. 117–130. A parallel interpretation of the role of primordial forces in the process of political integration is given by Clifford Geertz, "The Integrative Revolution," in Clifford Geertz, ed. *Old Societies* and *New States* (Glencoe, 1963).

[15] Shils, "Ideology, Center and Periphery," p. 117.

[16] See Aristide R. Zolberg, *Creating Political Order* (Chicago, 1966).

periphery (the Alawi-Druze in Syria and the minorities in Nigeria since 1966), the center of authority is challenged by the periphery, which claims that the military is the center. The confrontation is even more bitter when the military organization really represents the center. The military then operates as a mobilizing force in the "gap" (Huntington) between social mobilization and political institutionalization—processes which, again, are attracted toward the center.

LOW LEVEL OF POLITICAL INSTITUTIONALIZATION AND LACK OF SUSTAINED SUPPORT FOR POLITICAL STRUCTURES

According to Samuel P. Huntington, "the strength of political organizations and procedures varies with their *scope of support* and their *level of institutionalization.*"[17] In praetorian states the level of support for political organizations—that is, the number and diversity of the members of such organizations—is low. Thus, the political parties tend to be fragmented, each supported by different social groups which in themselves are not cohesive. The labor movement is similarly fragmented: each category of worker belongs to a different union, and the unions are distrustful of one another. This phenomenon is a political manifestation of the lack of social cohesion discussed above.

The level of institutionalization—that is, the degree to which political organizations develop their own traditions and the extent to which these organizations act autonomously—is also low in praetorian states. Traditional political institutions, incapable of dealing with social and economic changes, have been eliminated and new institutions are not yet accepted as legitimate. Their legitimacy is often hampered by the degree to which they represent particular interests, because their values belong to a small group and are not the autonomous values of the institutions. Huntington notes

also the frequency of military intervention in states in which institutionalization has not taken place.[18]

Although a state may exhibit most social characteristics of praetorianism, its political institutions and procedures may have a relatively high degree of stability. If so, the political institutions themselves will be able to act upon the society, and army intervention in constitutional changes will be rare. Such a state is not praetorian, but it may become so. India is a nonpraetorian nation that fits this description. Again it must be emphasized that the presence of some praetorian conditions does not necessarily lead to army intervention. Conversely, army intervention may occur even though some praetorian conditions are missing.

WEAK AND INEFFECTIVE POLITICAL PARTIES

Weak and ineffective political parties manifest a low level of political institutionalization. This condition deserves special mention because strong parties have been most successful agents of comprehensive modernization and industrialization and of the resulting elimination of conditions that lead to praetorianism. Strong parties need not be totalitarian; they can include pluralistic groups, as do the *Partido Revolucionario Institucional* (PRI) of Mexico and India's Congress Party.

Few underdeveloped countries have strong parties of the pluralistic type. In Egypt, the Wafd party was captured by land-owing interests and lost the support of other politically articulate and more progressive forces. Similarly, in Peru, *Alianza Popular Revolucionaria de América* (Apra) has tended to lose its acceptance among the masses because it has increasingly represented the interests of the newly-arrived middle class. When such politically ineffective parties more and more represent particular interests, their leaders become less capable of promoting projects necessary

---

[17] Huntington, "Political Development," 394.

[18] Ibid.

for the economic growth and integration of their countries. Many underdeveloped countries do not have parties even of the low degree of effectiveness and strength of the Wafd and Apra.

FREQUENT CIVILIAN INTERVENTION IN THE MILITARY

Military intervention into civilian affairs is usually not precipitated by military groups. In most cases, civilians turn to the military for political support when civilian political structures and institutions fail, when factionalism develops, and when constitutional means for the conduct of political action are lacking. The civilians therefore begin to indoctrinate the military with their political ideologies. Several examples of this process can be found in the Middle East and Latin America.

In Turkey, the Committee for Union and Progress, founded by the Young Turks, brought about the revolution in 1908 which helped the Young Turk movement to power. More recently, the People's party, or at least affiliations among the officers, intervened indirectly in the Turkish coups of 1960–1961. Prime Minister Menderes, head of the Justice party, interfered in military affairs and meddled with military appointments. Elsewhere in the Middle East the politicization of the military was begun by extremist nationalist politicians. The Iraqi nationalists, led by the socialist Ahali group, perpetrated a series of coups and countercoups in Iraq between 1936 and 1940. Since its initial participation, the army has not withdrawn from the political scene: between 1940 and 1958 it contributed to the establishment and maintenance of a relatively stable government under the oppressive measures of Nuri al-Sa'id.

The Muslim Brotherhood and Young Egypt (Misr al Fatat)—nationalist and fascist movements—have collaborated with Egyptian army officers since the late 1930's.[19] The Ba'th party and the Arab

Socialist party, led by the latter's founder, the Syrian nationalist Akram Haurani, changed the Syrian army from an obscure colonial force into the most militant nationalist force in the country. Since that time, only two Syrian coups in more than twenty (successful and unsuccessful) were neither initiated nor sponsored by the new Arab Ba'th Socialist party that emerged from the union of the two original parties.

A similar pattern of politicization of military officers by civilian groups emerged in Latin America.[20] The politicization of the military in twentieth-century Latin America has been precipitated by middle-class parties. According to José Nun, a divided middle class has provoked military intervention (the military being the best organized institution of middle-class origin) to protect class interests when they have been threatened by a ruling oligarchy or by working-class organizations.

The factors mentioned in connection with civilian politicization of the military are general conditions for praetorianism.

---

[19] On Muslim Brotherhood-army relationships, see Richard P. Mitchell, "The Society of the Muslim Brothers" (unpub. Ph.D. diss., Princeton University, 1960), pp. 61–250; Ishak Musa Husaini, *The Moslem Brethren* (Beirut, 1956), pp. 125–130; Eleiz er Beeri, "On the History of the Free Officers," *The New East (Hamizrah Hehadash)*, XIII, No. 51 (1963), 247–268; Kamil Isma'il al-Sharif, *al-Ikhwan al-Muslimin Fi Harb-Filastin (The Muslim Brotherhood in the Palestine War)* (Cairo, 1951); J. and S. Lacouture, *Egypt*, pp. 131 ff. On relationships between Free Officers, Egypt, and the Axis, see Lukasz Hirszowicz, *The Third Reich and the Arab East* (London, 1966), pp. 229–249.

[20] José Nun, "A Latin American Phenomenon: The Middle Class Military Coup," in *Trends in Social Science Research in Latin American Studies: A Conference Report* (Berkeley, 1965); and Liisa North, *Civil-Military Relations in Argentina, Chile, and Peru* (Berkeley, 1966). For a related argument concerning the military and the "new" middle class in the Middle East, see Manfred Halpern, "Middle Eastern Armies and the New Middle Class," in John J. Johnson, ed. *The Role of the Military in Underdeveloped Countries* (Princeton, 1962), pp. 277–315.

Other factors—defeat in war,[21] death of a powerful army leader, foreign intervention, and conflicts among senior and junior officers—are secondary causes. If the primary conditions are absent, these secondary causes alone cannot bring about a praetorian state.

The Praetorian Army

The code of the professional army dictates that promotions be determined by ability, expertise, and education. In reality, such principles of professionalization are not well inculcated or observed. Character (i.e., class) or political leanings often overrule expertise in the selection and promotion of officers. In some cases, professional standards do not exist, either because the praetorian army does not have a professional tradition or because the tradition has deteriorated. For example, in Argentina at the end of the nineteenth century, "institutional formal norms were never sufficiently enforced for the maintenance of discipline. Personal relationships and political affiliations remained major factors in the preservation of cohesion within the army and its control by civilian governments."[22] In the Imperial German army, the emphasis on aristocracy and the distrust of the bourgeoisie made character take precedence over intellect as a criterion for officer selection.[23]

Today, army affairs have become intertwined with politics. In Argentina, for example, appointments and promotions still are made on the basis of the political affiliations of the officer rather than on his professional qualifications. The officer's career is insecure, and in order to advance in the military hierarchy, he must establish political alliances with key superiors.

Political activity is contrary to the professional ethics and standards of the modern military, and yet, even in praetorian states, the remnants of professionalism may survive to the extent that conflicts arise between political activity and formally adopted professional norms. Often, however, these conflicts merely deepen the political involvements of the officers by drawing a widening circle of political activists from the officer corps. The officer corps, therefore, tends to break into factions and cliques.

Army coups in Iraqi politics between 1936 and 1941 illustrate this tendency. They eliminated moderate political leadership and transformed the government into a military dictatorship although, by itself, no single group in the army was capable of sustaining army rule. The army's inability to sustain its rule resulted in the assassination of such key military leaders as Bakr Sidqi and Ja'far al-'Askari. The military coups in Iraq left the army divided. Although the army became the single deciding factor in the political life of Iraq between 1936 and 1941, it could not serve as an effective and stabilizing alternative to the regimes and cabinets that it had toppled. In fact, the army turned into a source of political instability as it sought to replace cabinets that were "corrupt" or "collaborating" with the British. Iraq inaugurated the first praetorian army in the Middle East since the Young Turk army intervention in 1908, and Iraq was looked upon by many Arab ideological groupings as the future Arab Prussia.[24] Curiously enough, the political failures of the Iraqi army did not discourage Middle Eastern praetorian armies, including the Iraqi army itself. Since the 1958 coup the Iraqi army has returned to its former practices, eliminating

---

[21] See Edward A. Shils and Morris Janowitz, "Cohesion and Disintegration in the Wehrmacht in World War II," *Public Opinion Quarterly*, XII (Summer 1948), 288–292. Shils and Janowitz demonstrated that the defeat and disintegration of the Wehrmacht were due to the collapse of primary-group cohesion.

[22] North, p. 17.

[23] R. Kitchen, *The German Officer Corps, 1890–1914* (Oxford, 1968), pp. 28–32.

[24] Majid Khadduri, *Independent Iraq: A Study in Iraqi Politics from 1932–1958*, 2d ed. (London, 1960), pp. 124–125.

civilian politicians from left to right as well as decimating its own ranks. Since 1958, the Iraqi army has propelled Iraq into a praetorian syndrome from which there seems to be little chance for return to civilian rule or stability.[25]

A decade after the army's political debacles in Iraq, the Syrian army chose a similar pattern, and it become notorious for mixing internal army rivalries with politics. There are many examples of ambitious Syrian army officers, especially the Ba'thist (steadily growing in strength among senior officers), who have eliminated their army rivals by allying with a Ba'th faction that these rivals oppose, or, especially since the left Ba'th party's rise to power in 1966, who have created a wedge between rival Ba'th factions to advance personal causes and have finally achieved a complete takeover of the Ba'th by the army, which represents the extreme wing of the Ba'th. This wing was overthrown in the 1969 coup, and the army, run by Alawi officers, has finally destroyed the Ba'th left wing. This, of course, does not preclude the reemergence of the left under the aegis of another officer.

Finally, the divisiveness and political involvement of the officers may be abetted by foreign intervention—such as the counterinsurgency training and military aid of the United States in Latin America[26] and Egypt's intervention in the internal rivalries of the Syrian, Iraqi, Yemeni, and Jordanian armies.

Two Types of Praetorian Armies

The two basic types of praetorian armies are the arbitrator-type and the ruler-type. The former tends to be more professionally oriented (with a greater emphasis on expertise) and has no independent political organization and little interest in manufacturing a political ideology. The latter has an independent political organization (an instrument for maintaining order) and, in most cases, a fairly coherent and elaborate political ideology.

The arbitrator-type army imposes a time limit on army rule and arranges to hand the government over to an "acceptable" civilian regime. The arbitrator-type army does not necessarily relinquish its political influence when it returns to the barracks; in fact, in many cases, it acts as guardian of civilian authority and political stability. Such is the essence of the Kemalist legacy in Turkey: the army serves as the guardian of the constitution.[27] The army of Brazil similarly defends the constitution.[28] A time limit was imposed by Generals Nagib of Egypt (1952–1954) and Abboud of the Sudan (1958–1963); it may yet be imposed by General Ayub Khan of Pakistan (since 1958) and possibly by the Burmese military group. It is essential that the arbitrator rule in cooperation with civilians ("non-corrupt") and that his source of political power not be in the barracks.

An arbitrator army may eventually become a ruler army, if the conditions for the return of a civilian regime are not fulfilled. It is even possible for a ruler army eventually to turn the reins of power over to a civilian regime, if the conditions for the return of civilian rule are fulfilled. Although the arbitrator army is committed to a time limit, the ruler army is not. The arbitrator army expects an eventual return to the barracks; the ruler army makes no such provision and, in most cases, does not even consider it.

When civilian political viewpoints are first diffused within an officer corps, ideological divisions tend to develop. Later, one political orientation may succeed in becom-

---

[25] Uriel Dann, *Iraq Under Qassem* (Jerusalem, 1969).

[26] See Irving Louis Horowitz, "The Military in Latin America," in Seymour Martin Lipset and Aldo Solari, eds. *Elites in Latin America* (London, 1966).

[27] The transformation of army rebels of 1960–1961 into permanent senators only reiterates the persistence of the Kemalist legacy in Turkey, at least as of 1967.

[28] Charles Simmons, "The Rise of the Brazilian Military Class, 1840–1890," *Mid-America*, XXXIX (October 1957), 227–238.

ing dominant. This orientation may or may not parallel that of some civilian group. Thus, given extreme conditions for praetorianism, the arbitrator will become the ruler.

The arbitrator-type tends to preserve military expertise; it is conservative and, on the whole, tends to maximize civilian power.[29] The ruler-type, although it does not abandon expertise, sometimes subordinates it to political considerations and may even support an already existing political ideology. It sacrifices professionalism to political expediency. In general, the ruler-type prefers to maximize an army ruler. It is imperative that he rule with the help of the army. A radical ruler dominates only with the help of the army and always at the expense of civilian rule and politicians.

Both types are ideologically committed, and here, too, the differences between them depend on their attitudes toward their role in politics and on the state of praetorian conditions in the respective polity. Since the ruler army usually has an independent political organization, it tends to manufacture an ideology to legitimize its rule. It identifies with a popular ideology manufactured elsewhere, or with symbols such as "nation," "progress," "modernization," and so forth.

Although the arbitrator army tends to be more conservative than the ruler army, we find ideologically motivated radicals and conservatives in each. Thus, the two types can be placed on a left-right continuum. The actions of either type are conditioned by three factors: (1) the internal structure of the army and the extent to which it has developed an identifiable political consciousness, organization, and autonomy; (2) interaction with civilian politicians and structures; and (3) the type of political order that the army desires to eliminate and the type of political order that it wishes to

establish or reject, if it has no alternative regime in mind).

Although the present analysis treats the civilian and military spheres of action analytically as independent variables in conflict and interaction, the military organization cannot be fully divorced from the civilian social context that determines civilian politics. Initially, the political commitments and ideological positions of the military in the praetorian state are sustained either by the civilian politicians who encourage the army to enter politics, or by the general, sociopolitical, civilian context. After a certain level of political involvement has been attained, officers can then influence positions taken by civilian politicians. This development has been true of the Ba'th party in Syria, which originally infiltrated the army to avoid losing its support and which now shares the same goals as the army. The more fully the army is immersed in politics, and the greater is its desire to change the sociopolitical context, the greater are the chances for political instability.

An army may display most characteristics of the ruler-type army—including a well-articulated ideology to which the officer corps adheres—*without* actually ruling. An example of this situation is the Peruvian army.[30] In such a case, the army presents a unified point of view and acts as the stabilizer of civilian governments that hold views similar to its own.

THE ARBITRATOR-TYPE OF PRAETORIAN ARMY

The arbitrator-type army has several distinguishing characteristics which we will now describe.

Acceptance of existing social order. In an underdeveloped country, acceptance of the existing order often implies antirevolutionary ideology. Thus, the arbitrator-type army may be the instrument of conservative and antiliberal forces as, for example, were the Ottoman army before the 1908

[29] Samuel P. Huntington, *The Soldier and the State: The Theory and Politics of Civil-Military Relations* (New York, 1964), pp. 80–81, 93–94.

[30] North, pp. 52–57.

coups and the Iraqi army in the 1920's.[31] The Argentine military establishment has displayed an arbitrating orientation since the fall of Juan Perón in 1955; it has been anti-leftist and, especially, anti-Castro.[32] Traditional Latin American *caudillismo* may also serve as an example because the *caudillos* usually do not attempt to change the social order.[33] On the other hand, the arbitrator-type army may ally itself with labor, as Perón did in Argentina. Huntington demonstrates patterns of civil-military alliances where the military allies with non-conservative forces.[34] On the basis of military interventionism in the Middle East, we propose that the radicalization of the society and the army eliminates the chances for an arbitrator-type and that a radical-army coalition brings a ruler-type to power (Egypt, 1952–1954). On the whole, a ruler-type implies structural reforms in society and formation of a new bureaucracy; in the case of arbitrators, there is little fundamental change in regime and society.

Willingness to return to the barracks after civilian disputes are settled. The officers of the arbitrator-type army are civilian-oriented. Even where the civilian groups are not organized enough to set up a government, and where officers occupy positions in the government, the officers obey the instructions of civilian political groups. They do not inject their own viewpoint. They desire to return to normality, which means that they accept the status quo. The arbitrator-type army returns to the barracks because its officers are aware that they lack the skills to govern and are content to avoid further political involvement.

An example of a return-to-the-barracks army is the Chilean military from 1924 to 1933. When officers participated in politics because civilian political groups had become disorganized, the participation was limited, and the professional norms of the military establishment were largely retained even during periods of fairly deep involvement.[35]

No independent political organization and no attempt to maximize army rule. This point can be illustrated by examples from Egypt, Iraq, and elsewhere.

General Nagib of Egypt (1952–1954), who was recruited by Nasser and the Society of Free Officers as early as 1951 to head the list of Free Officers in the elections for the administrative committee of the Officers' Club, had no political organization of his own.[36] He was not a charter member of the Free Officers, but he was chosen from among three candidates to become the titular head of the 1952 coup.[37] Lacking the support of a political organization of his own, Nagib was finally ousted in 1954 by the Free Officers' political organization, the Revolutionary Command Council (RCC), which was the executive committee of the Free Officers' first political party, the Liberation Rally.[38] Nagib had made efforts to maximize civilian participation in the RCC cabinet and had opposed the policy of Nasser and the RCC to legitimize the military dictatorship.

In Iraq, the officers responsible for the first coup d'état of October 29, 1936, led by General Bakr Sidqi, had no political organization of their own. After Bakr Sidqi's assassination they were left leaderless and divided. The coup was followed by a countercoup, and that one by several military coups, until a civilian government was finally established in 1941.[39]

Time limit for the rule of the army until an alternative and "acceptable" regime is estab-

---

[31] Khadduri, pp. 78–80.

[32] Kalman H Silvert, "The Costs of Anti-Nationalism: Argentina," in Kalman H. Silvert, ed. *Expectant Peoples* (New York, 1963), pp. 366–369.

[33] North, pp. 1–10.

[34] Huntington, *Political Order*, pp. 219–237.

[35] North, pp. 34–37.

[36] Lacouture, pp. 144–145.

[37] Eleizer Beeri, *The Officer Class in Politics and Society of the Arab East* (*Ha-Ktzuna ve-hashilton Ba-Olam ha-Aravi*) (Israel, 1966), pp. 78–80.

[38] Shimon Shamir, "Five Years of the Liberation Rally," *The New East* (*Hamizrah Hedadash*), VIII, No. 4 (1957), 274.

[39] Khadduri, pp. 76–80, 126 ff.

lished. The arbitrator-type army will return to the barracks if it is assured that corruption and other evils of the former regime have been eliminated. This type views prolonged army rule as detrimental to the professional integrity of the army. The arbitrator army encourages political groups which it considers capable of establishing order, preserving stability, and guaranteeing that the new government will not return to the practice of the old.

The existence of organized civilian groups has a bearing on the army's decision to surrender its rule. Where no such groups exist —that is, in a state of near anarchy—the arbitrator-type army may continue to govern despite its civilian orientation and its desire to return to its own affairs. In such a situation the arbitrator army continues to govern by default, because it is the only organized group in the state. Where organized civilian groups do exist, the military as a whole withdraws from the government, although at times a key military figure will continue as chief of state. Thus, in Chile, Ibañez, an officer, was chief of state in the late 1920's and early 1930's, but the military institution as a whole was not politically involved.[40]

Concern with professionalism. In an arbitrator-type army, the officer corps, or important sectors of it, is strongly opposed to political involvement because involvement may destroy the professional norms of the military institution. Professional norms are valued because they provide security and predictability for the officer's career. When we speak of professionalism here, we mean corporateness. We do not refer to the collective sense that arises from organic, professional unity and consciousness,[41] but rather to the "military mind" and Huntington's definition of the military ethic.[42] Professionalism here is related to the *political* attitude of the military. Unlike lawyers and physicians, soldiers depend upon the state for security. Because a change of regime may threaten its position, the military is usually extremely sensitive to political change. The civil service, likewise dependent on the state, is also politically sensitive; but it has little physical power—the element which places soldiers in office. The arbitrator-type tends to defend the existing regime, lest its professional integrity be violated. In fact, this type may intervene to protect the military against the threat posed by a disintegrating or unstable regime.

Tendency to operate from behind the scenes as a pressure group. Because of its fear of open involvement in politics, the arbitrator-type army tends to influence civilian governments to respond to popular demands, thereby making it unnecessary for the military to intervene openly. However, the refusal by the military to take open responsibility for its actions may increase instability. The arbitrator army constitutes "power divorced from responsibility";[43] moreover, since the arbitrator-type officer corps lacks cohesion, factionalism may result or existing factionalism may be aggravated. This factionalization may then lead to a pattern of coup and countercoup which makes little sense to an outside observer, because the frequent changes in government are not accompanied by changes in policies but reflect instead personal rivalries in the officer corps. Most of the unsuccessful coups in Syria have been of this type, and the number of opportunistic officers has increased since the collapse of the United Arab Republic in 1961. The Ba'th party, since coming to power in 1963, has become an avenue of advancement for ambitious officers.

Civilians usually are also involved in these personalistic cliques and attempt to use them for their own ends. Such entanglements may result in a vicious circle:

---

[40] North, pp. 34–37.
[41] Huntington, *The Soldier*, pp. 10–11.
[42] Ibid., Ch. 3, pp. 59–79.

[43] Dankwart A. Rustow, "The Military in Middle Eastern Society and Politics," in Sydney Nettleton Fisher, ed. *The Military in the Middle East* (Columbus, 1963), pp. 34–37.

civilian action tends to deepen military cliquishness, and vice versa, because the mixing of army and civilian motives blurs the separation of the army from the civilian sociopolitical context and results in the army's inability to change the political situation. This pattern has appeared in the Latin American sequences of coups d'état (*cuartelazos*).[44] More recently, it has manifested itself in Syria under the rule of the leftist Ba'th officers who have governed there since the coup of February 26, 1966.[45]

Low level of national consciousness. On the whole, this type of military has a low level of national consciousness and identification. The absence of such attitudes characterized Arab officers in the Ottoman army before the turn of the century, Circassian and Turkish officers in Muhammad 'Ali's army, the nineteenth-century Latin American *caudillo* type, Kurdish and Assyrian officers in the Iraqi army before 1936, Druze, 'Alawi, and Ismai'li officers in the Syrian army before independence in 1945, Bedouin officers in the Jordanian Arab Legion until 1956, and Druze officers in the Israeli army.

Fear of civilian retribution. Such a fear was apparent in General Gürsel's attitude during the 1960–1961 coup in Turkey.[46] The presence of organized civilian groups may produce fears in the military concerning the actions that civilian politicians might later take—such as the dismissal of officers, demotions, unprestigious appointments and assignments. Moreover, if an army has become unpopular because of repressive measures, and especially if the soldiers have

been recruited from the native population, doubts about the civilian population's willingness to follow its orders may cause the army to withdraw, fearing violent mass action as well as civilian political retribution.

THE RULER-TYPE OF PRAETORIAN ARMY

The ruler-type of praetorian army has characteristics that oppose those of the arbitrator-type.

The officer corps rejects the existing order and challenges its legitimacy. Throughout developing countries, traditional parliamentary politics and liberalism have become identified with status quo politics. The ruler type of praetorian army increasingly tends to abandon or convert existing institutions, ideologies, and procedures in favor of the newer institutions for modernization, and political mobilization that are proposed by theories of rapid growth. To nonconservative praetorians, these new theories are more suitable for altering traditional institutions than are the old and "corrupt" ideologies of traditional liberalism and parliamentarianism. But they also reject as corrupt those radical-revolutionary civilian regimes which favor rapid modernization under a one-party system. Thus, the ruler-type officers oppose both the political corruption of the traditional parliamentary liberal regimes and some of the modernizing authoritarian one-party systems. Their opposition does not mean that the officers are revolutionaries: rather, they tend to be reformers, and their sometimes self-proclaimed conversion to revolutionary causes is likely to be much more superficial than their conversion to anticonservatism.[47] Of all reformist groups in the state, the army tends to be least reformist. As a reformer it may be adamantly opposed to Communism or, as in contemporary Latin America, to Castro. In Peru, the military in general has opposed the local revolutionary party

[44] See George Blanksten, *Ecuador: Constitutions and Caudillos* (Berkeley and Los Angeles, 1951), pp. 51–54, for a discussion of this phenomenon. For Latin American cases of this type, see L. N. McAlister, "Civil-Military Relations in Latin America," *Journal of Inter-American Studies* (July 3, 1961), pp. 342–343.

[45] Amos Perlmutter, "From Opposition to Rule: The Syrian Army and the Ba'th Party," *Western Political Quarterly*, forthcoming.

[46] See Walter F. Weiker, *The Turkish Revolution 1960–1961* (Washington, 1963), for a complete discussion of this event.

[47] Huntington, *The Soldier*, pp. 93–94, discusses briefly the conservatism of the professional officer, albeit in non praetorian states.

(Apra), but this has not prevented reform orientation in the army.[48]

Thus, we can distinguish at least three subtypes of the ruler army that reject the existing order and challenge its legitimacy: (1) *the antitraditonalist radical reformer army*, represented by the regimes of 'Abd al-Karim Qasim in Iraq (1958–1963) and Juan Perón in Argentina (1945–1955); (2) *the antitraditionalist antiradical reformer army*, represented by the military regimes of Gamal Abdel Nasser in Egypt (since 1952), Houari Boumedienne in Algeria (since 1965), General Suharto in Indonesia (since 1965), the army junta in Ghana (since 1966), and the anti-Castro, anti-Communist military rulers in Latin America; and (3) *the antitraditionalist republican reformer army*, represented by Mustafa Kemal (Ataturk) of Turkey (1919–1923) and Ayub Khan of Pakistan (since 1958).

With these subtypes in mind, we can place the praetorian type on a left-right continuum linked to political order. The ruler army chooses the new political order as a reaction to that order which it has replaced. Therefore, the ideology of the praetorian army depends on the nature of the ideology it has rejected. Choice here is rather limited; it will depend on what means the army takes to transform society into "something else," most often into something initially unknown to the army. It took Nasser a decade to opt for Arab Socialism; in that period it was clearer to him what political system to destroy than what political system he ought to create.

Thus, Nasser is more leftist than the Wafd, just as Ayub Khan is more radical than the old Muslim League party. Boumedienne is to the right of Ben Bella, and Suharto is to the right of Sukarno. "Basic democracy" in Pakistan grew as an alternative to the regime it replaced. Although the Pakistani army, as an offshoot of the British Indian army, had kept aloof from politics,

the need for reform and modernization enhanced its propensity for institutional autonomy and made a temporary ruler of a professional and antitraditionalist reformer like Ayub Khan, who had been dedicated to military professionalism and maximizing civilian rule.[49] Ayub Khan, imbued with the British Civil Service tradition, chose to blend a very modified version of British democracy with the "military mind" and the political reality of Pakistan. The resulting mixture of traditional values and professionalism brought forth the concept of "basic democracy"—the ideology of the Pakistani army since 1958.[50]

Houari Boumedienne rejected the radicalism of Ben Bella's regime. However, he has not abandoned Arab Socialism, but has merely reduced its ideological intensity and commitments. In this process he has become an antiradical type of ruler. Although he has so far adopted no ideology of his own, by eliminating the Ben Bella legacy he has moved toward the modernization of Algeria without Ben-Bellist radicalism.

In Indonesia, the army since the 1965 Communist coup has been liquidating the old regime, whereas Sukarno's "guided democracy" had radicalized it. The political evolution of the Indonesian army[51] indicates that, even if it does not offer an alternative ideology, it may proceed along the lines of a modified guided democracy without the vehemence, the radicalism, and the messianism that marked the reign of President Sukarno.

The Ghanaian military junta has been acting as a temporary ruler since 1966. It has presided over the dissolution of Nkru-

[48] See Richard Patch, "The Peruvian Elections of 1962 and Their Annulment," *American Universities Field Staff Reports* (West Coast South America Series), IX (September 1962), 6.

[49] Huntington, *The Soldier*, pp. 83–85.

[50] For an analysis on parallel lines, emphasizing the role of the army as the bearer of explicit political norms and images, see Moshe Lissak, "Modernization and Role-Expansion of the Military in Developing Countries: A Comparative Analysis," *Comparative Studies in Society and History*, IX (April 1967), 249–255.

[51] Daniel S. Lev, "The Political Role of the Army in Indonesia," *Pacific Affairs*, XXVI (Winter 1963–1964), 349–364.

mah's radical-socialist and mobilization system. It also has decided in favor of modernization without radicalism and eventual return to the barracks.

No confidence in civilian rule and no expectation of returning to the barracks. This attitude may be a consequence of the development by an important sector of the officer corps of an independent political orientation opposed to the ruling civilian groups. Alternatively, civilian disorganization may have reached the point where progressive elements are unable to put their programs into effect. Ruler-type officers distrust politicians to the extent that they themselves feel it necessary to occupy formal positions in the governmental structure. Thus, by the time the ruler army intervenes, the civilians have already manifested their inability to control the situation. In Egypt, for example, officers blamed civilians for the Palestinian crisis and for the Cairo riots of January 1952, and they did not even trust those civilians—such as the more radical members of the Wafd or the Muslim Brotherhood—who held political philosophies similar to their own.

In the early 1950's, after a number of years of civil war, the Colombian army led by Rojas Pinilla lost confidence in civilian rule, took control of the government, and implemented a Perón-type developmental program. When this occurred, only part of the army shared Rojas Pinilla's orientations. Since that time, the army has shown an inclination to adopt developmental ideologies based on technological and evolutionary change. The army may again take over the government of Colombia; as yet it has no confidence in civilian rule.

Political organization and tendency to legitimize and maximize army rule. The ruler-type army considers itself the one elite group capable of governing; therefore, it usually tries to assure the indefinite continuation of army rule by capitalizing on the uncertainty of politics. Taking advantage of the lack of political and social cohesion, the ruler-type army establishes an independent organization and strengthens its rule in order to manipulate unruly, disorganized forces. In order to achieve stability, it must legitimize itself through the creation of its own political party or some type of corporate group and create an ideology to support its political organization.

In Egypt, the Society of Free Officers, led by Nasser, was officially established in 1949. Its origins date back to 1938–1939. After 1945, the group became active, especially in recruiting allies in the army. Nasser's was not the only political organization in the Egyptian army: the Muslim Brotherhood had organized an army cell led by Mahmud Labib and later by 'Abd al-Mun'im 'Abd al-Ra'uf, and Anwar al-Sadat, who joined Nasser in 1949, had previously headed an army political club of his own.[52]

As far back as the 1930's, Egyptian officers, imbued with the radical nationalist atmosphere of Egypt and inspired and guided by civilians, helped to establish independent political organizations, cells, and secret societies in the army. Most of these organizations were intended to maximize the political consciousness of the officers (this was especially true of Nasser's group, 1949–1952) and, especially, to recruit officers for nationalist political parties and movements. Once in office after the coup, they established a Revolutionary Command Council (RCC) which acted as the executive committee of the Free Officers but was actually the executive arm of the new government run by the army. Almost immediately, the Liberation Rally, the army-dominated party, was established.[53] These organizations illustrate Nasser's attempts to legitimize army rule and its nationalist ideology and to *eliminate* all civilian opposition to the army.

[52] For the most detailed description of Egypt's officer-politicians, see Lacouture, *Egypt*, pp. 125–129, and Beeri, *The Officer Class*, pp. 67–73; also, Anwar al-Sadat, *Revolt on the Nile* (London, 1957), p. 74. See also fn. 19.

[53] Shamir, "Five Years," 261–278.

In Syria, Adib Shishakly founded the Arab Liberation Movement in 1952 in order to legitimize the military dictatorship he had established in 1951.[54] Since the coups by Shishakly and Nasser, military coups in the Middle East have followed the precedent of establishing a Revolutionary Command Council to legitimize army rule and eliminate civilian and army opposition. The formation of an RCC does not guarantee the success of this type of army political organization, nor does it guarantee the legitimacy of army rule. However, it gives the army independence in political action and maneuverability where strong civilian organizations exist. Where they do not exist, the army's political party serves to preserve the military dictatorship.

Legitimization of the army as the guarantor of stability and progress does not necessarily imply permanent army rule. In Turkey, the Kemalist legacy serves as a watchdog to prevent the civilian regime from returning to corrupt practices. By civilianizing his regime through the army, Ataturk also legitimized the army's role in politics as the defender and protector of the constitution and of republican and honest civilian rule; in effect, he maximized civilian rule by legitimizing the army as its sole protector. On the other hand, Nasser gave a civilian role to army-created political parties and bureaucracies; this practice has maximized Egypt's modernization and army domination but does not guarantee civilian rule.

An army need not have an ideology or a political organization of its own in order to favor a ruler-type of praetorianism. In Iraq, when the army came to power after the 1958 revolution, like all other national organizations it participated in the struggle between the oligarchs and the new generation, and many military leaders were closely associated with ideological groups. Nevertheless, the army as a separate group never formulated its own set of ideals but merely carried out the programs of other civilian groups under army rule.[55]

It is interesting that, although the army and the Ba'th party in Syria share a common political ideology, they do not hold the same view of army rule. Whereas the Ba'th advocates parliamentary rule, the army prefers a ruler-type of praetorianism. The February 1966 coup indicates the trend toward such army rule: an army faction took over Ba'th's left wing, signifying further attrition of Ba'thist and civilian groups in Syria. In this case, the ideology of a civilian party served to legitimize the rule of the army.

The political consolidation of the Indonesian army occurred when many officers were absorbed into the national elite. They supported Sukarno's "guided democracy" to keep political parties out of power and to weaken the Indonesian Communist party. The army, then, participated in civic action and boosted economic development to compete with the Indonesian Communist party at the grass-roots level. The evolution of the army as a political organization in Indonesia strengthened its ruler-type position. When the Indonesian Communist party struck the army, the army struck back, and since 1965 it has been engaged in dissolving the old order and establishing the new order under army rule.[56]

Conviction that army rule is the only alternative to political disorder. This point, a corollary to the preceding three points, is seen clearly in Nasser's political philosophy. In his book *Philosophy of the Revolution*, Nasser argues that "only the army" can meet and solve the praetorian conditions

[54] Patrick Seale, *The Struggle for Syria* (London, 1965), pp. 124–131.

[55] Khadduri, "The Role of the Military in Iraqi Society," in Fisher, ed. *The Military*, p. 47.

[56] I am indebted to Daniel S. Lev for his help in my understanding of the Indonesian army. For most of the points made here on the Indonesian army, see Lev, "The Political Role," 360–364. For the interpretation of Lev's analysis, only I am responsible.

of Egypt and that the army plays the "role of vanguard" in the Egyptian revolution.[57]

This was also the attitude of some of the extreme radical nationalists in the Iraqi army during the late 1930's, among them Salah al-Din al-Sabbagh.[58] His antiforeign and anti-imperialist convictions led him to believe that the army was destined to relieve Iraq and Islam of the yoke of external and internal oppressors.

In 1951, two years after his coup d'état, Adib Shishakly of Syria (1949–1954), after meddling unsuccessfully with bitterly divided civilians, established a military dictatorship. Most army leaders in the Middle East now tend to espouse Shishakly's and Nasser's enterprises. If many still act as arbitrators, especially in Syria, it is more because of the effective opposition of civilian groups and army rivalry than because the army favors civilian rule.

The politicization of professionalism. Where the army has—or dominates—an independent political organization, however minimal, the ruler-type is common. We have seen that this pattern is widespread in the Middle East. In Latin America, the military neither acts as an autonomous group nor possesses an independent political organization; it acts, rather, as an agent of more powerful social classes or political groups, and here an arbitrator-type is more likely. Thus, in oligarchical praetorianism we often find the ruler-type, whereas in radical praetorianism the arbitrator-type prevails.[59] In the latter case, the military must act in alliance with stronger and better-deployed political groups. In the Middle East, fragmented and impotent social forces are challenged by military organizations, which seem to provide the elements for maintaining order. Thus the military organization becomes a surrogate political structure, at least for the purposes of maintaining an *ad hoc* order and suppressing violence.

When the ruler-type army is committed to political action, it is forced to break with traditional concepts of the professional soldier. Political considerations take precedence over internal organization and career security. When political objectives become paramount, career stability suffers. Politicization will, to some extent, destroy professional status and rank. A low-ranking military officer may, in certain political situations, be superior to an officer of higher rank who is not politically inclined. Such has been the case in the Syrian army since 1966. The politically-involved officer corps must have a set of norms different from those of the nonpolitical officer corps.

The Thai army, which is rooted in the traditional bureaucracy, challenges the thesis that army rulers' political involvement diminishes the professional integrity of the army. Since 1932, "army officers have led the ruling group, dominated the institutions of government, and set the style of Thai politics."[60] But the "style of Thai politics" is bureaucratic. Thus Thailand, whose politics and social structure are bureaucratic[61] and patterned on subordinate-superordinate lines,[62] mixes well with the professional norms of the officer class.

Operation in the open. The ruler-type army operates in the open because it wants to use the symbols attached to the military institutions to gain support for its programs and activities. As Lucian W. Pye points out, the military has both traditional and modern components, and organizationally it is a peculiar combination of the two.[63]

[57] Gamal Abdel Nasser, *Egypt's Liberation: The Philosophy of the Revolution* (Washington, 1955), pp. 32–33, 42–45.

[58] Khadduri, *Independent Iraq*, pp. 200–206. See Col. Salah al-Din al Sabbagh, *Fursan al Uruba fi al Iraq* (*The Knights of Arabhood in Iraq*) (Damascus, 1956), pp. 29–30.

[59] Huntington, *Political Order*, pp. 208–219.

[60] David A. Wilson, "The Military in Thai Politics," in Johnson, ed. *The Role*, p. 253.

[61] Fred W. Riggs, *Thailand: The Modernization of a Bureaucratic Polity* (Honolulu, 1966).

[62] Wilson, pp. 266–268.

[63] Lucian W. Pye, "Armies in the Process of Political Modernization," in Johnson, ed. *The Role*, p. 75.

The army, therefore, may be quite acceptable to a population for whom it represents a technologically advanced organization. For the traditionalists, the army symbolizes heroic leadership and honor, even though the officers in fact may be technologists and managers. Since the military operates in the open, it can use these symbolic representations, as well as other types of ideological appeals, to obtain popular support. In Pye's words, "The great stress placed on professionalism and the extremely explicit standards for individual behavior make the military appear to be a more sacred than secular institution."[64]

High level of national consciousness. In a praetorian country, the commitment to nationalism is more intense in the ruler-type army than in any other section of the population. Ideologically, nationalism is the most popular and most successful common denominator of praetorianism. It can be a rallying point for all civilians and militarists, a point of least rivalry, and a common factor for ideological consolidation. The praetorian ideology is not, however, limited to nationalism. In contrast to the arbitrator-type, whose ideological commitments are lower, the whole spectrum of radical political ideologies has at one time or another been supported by praetorians.

Little fear of civilian retribution. By the time ruler-type praetorianism develops, the army tends to exercise so much power that it does not need to fear civilians. In Egypt the emergence of the army as ruler took place after an extended period of disorganization, growing violence (especially in urban areas), and the manifest failure of civilians to maintain order—not to mention the failure of civilian leadership in constructive development programs. Furthermore, the civilians were incapable of defending Egypt against imperialist powers.

The Praetorian Army as Modernizer and Leader of Political Development

The military has failed in many efforts to establish effective and longlasting political

[64] Ibid.

parties or other sustaining political institutions and procedures. Despite his attempts to do so on three separate occasions, Nasser has yet to establish a lasting and viable party. In the states discussed here, we doubt the durability of army-created tutelary political structures—"basic democracy" and, especially, Arab Socialism—beyond the period of army domination and rule.

Tutelary political structures are no guarantee for relieving the praetorian syndrome, although they are established in the hope that political stability and progress may be achieved, at least in the long run. The praetorian armies lack confidence that civilian rule can achieve these goals. Therefore, some tutelary political structures established under military rule have weaknesses similar to those of the political structures they replace, and others are no more than a shadow of the military-dominated state. When a military dictatorship uses the army to determine the dictatorial apparatus, praetorianism merely entrenches itself further.

A military dictatorship may lead a successful modernization effort. In such cases the army, adopting technocratic and scientific orientations, may withdraw from attempts at leading political development. Concentration on technology and science lessens the threat to military dictatorship that might result from the formation of civilian organizations. It is for this reason, perhaps, that Nasser has not abandoned the "philosophy of the revolution" that provides a praetorian political philosophy in which army rule converges ideologically with economic and scientific modernization.[65]

The ruler-type army tends to prefer or-

[65] No penetrating and objective study yet exists concerning the army's role in the economic modernization of Egypt, where the army has demonstrated limitations in the management of large-scale economic and industrial enterprises. One article on that subject is James Heaphey's "Organization of Egypt: Inadequacies of a Non-political Model for Nation-building," *World Politics*, XVIII (January 1966), 177–193.

ganizational models to political institutions as a system of control. Whereas civilian ideologists search for political utopias, officers seek managerial models to conduct social reform and modernization. The politicized army acts as a bureaucracy. Modernization is clothed in organization. Nasserism, Arab Socialism, and the emerging ideological consolidation of the Peruvian army[66] are thus the ideologies of scientific and organizational models.

The only successful case of a militarily-established political party remains that of Ataturk, who did it by dissolving the military dictatorship and making the civilian cause primary. Turkey may be described as the country which most closely fits the model of a praetorian army that has altered the sociopolitical context and created civilian political organizations. The steps taken by the Turkish officers were inspired initially by civilian actions, but the officers soon became independent of civilian groups. In the Kemalist transformation, the Turkish officers (1) took the primary role in selecting a system of government for the country; (2) chose their allies from among civilian politicians and from the civil services; (3) became the source of revolutionary change, making an effort to transfer the state from praetorian to non-

[66] Ibid.; see also Patch, "Peruvian Elections," 6.

praetorian rule; (4) formed their own "civilian" political party; and (5) institutionalized the Kemalist tradition that the army in the barracks must serve as the protector of civilian rule.[67]

In the future, the example of Turkey must be more carefully examined. Most praetorian ruler-types have fulfilled the first three goals of the Kemalist transformation. But because of failures to satisfy the latter two, no praetorian ruler as yet has approximated the Kemalist achievement—stable, sustaining, and progressive civilian political order.

In the absence of evidence to the contrary, dedication to modernization and social change does not necessarily alter the political conditions of praetorianism. In fact, once civilian political groups and organizations have been eliminated, modernization could enhance the military domination over political institutions and procedures.

[67] On Ataturk's political program and accomplishments, see (in addition to Rustow, fn. 43, and Weiker, fn. 46) George Antonius, *The Arab Awakening* (New York, 1965); Rustow, "The Turkish Army and the Founding of the Republic," *World Politics*, XI (October 1958), 513–552; Kemal Karpat, *Turkey's Politics* (Princeton, 1959); and Daniel Lerner and Richard D. Robinson, "Swords and Ploughshares: The Turkish Army as a Modernizing Force," *World Politics*, XIII (October 1966), 19–44.

Chapter 10

The Bureaucracy

BUREAUCRACY AND NATION BUILDING IN TRANSITIONAL SOCIETIES

S. C. Dube

Bureaucracy forms an important element of the modernizing élite in many of the economically less developed countries which have attained national independence during the last two decades. Trained in the colonial tradition, this organized and articulate segment of the native society functioned as a bridge between the dependent indigenous people and the ruling power from the West. Although it had to work under the direction of the imperial power and had largely to carry out its policies, it was not without nationalist sentiments and aspirations. Held suspect during the days of the struggle for freedom, both by politically oriented fellow-countrymen and by the alien rulers, members of this class had, by and large, acquired a progressive orientation and the more sophisticated among them had definite ideas regarding the programmes of economic and social growth to be adopted by their country at the attainment of national independence. In many countries they were the only organized body of natives with considerable training and experience in administration; they naturally found themselves called upon to assume major re-

SOURCE. S. C. Dube, "Bureaucracy and Nation Building in Transitional Societies," *International Social Science Journal*, **16,** 229–236, 1964.

sponsibilities in the formulation and implementation of national plans for economic development and social change.

The general change in political climate, the assumption of power by the political élite, the changing alignments of power and pressure groups, and the emergence of new institutional and administrative patterns raised in their wake a series of complex problems for the bureaucracy. In consequence, it had to make some significant adjustments in its thought- and work-ways and to adapt itself to the new ethos. On the other hand, in many sensitive areas it found itself either openly resisting or accepting some of the new elements only theoretically. Thus, with or without the overt acceptance of the new patterns, it stood for continuity of some of the established norms. In meeting these intricate problems of adjustment and value-conflict, the character of bureaucracy in transitional societies is undergoing a rapid change. Since it occupies a pivotal position in these societies, and will possibly continue to do so in the foreseeable future, an understanding of the character and culture of bureaucracy is essential for those concerned with the programmes of economic growth and social change in the economically less developed countries.

Planning for economic growth is an extremely complicated business which involves highly specialized knowledge and developed manipulative skills; the implementation of these plans presupposes deep administrative insights and a keen evaluative perspective. In the context of the programmes of community development, it is common these days to emphasize the ideal of planning by the people, but the crucial fact that this stage must necessarily be preceded by the stages of planning for the people and planning with the people is not given sufficient emphasis. The acceptance of these three stages means successively diminishing functions for the bureaucracy in matters of local and regional planning and in developmental administration, but it is essential to bear in mind that the gap between the first and the third stage is very considerable and that the transition to the final stage depends largely upon the manner in which the process is initiated and the first two stages are carried out. Both these stages involve considerable direct participation by the bureaucracy; the second stage particularly—which requires the initiation of a process of withdrawal—has critical significance. Optimism, bordering on wishful thinking, cannot alone diminish the importance of bureaucracy; its role in the process of planning and developmental administration is bound to figure prominently for several decades, The problem of the integration of local, regional, and national plans demands knowledge and skills which perhaps only the bureaucracy possesses. Of course, as the process acquires greater complexity the technocrat is drawn into it more deeply, for without the utilization of his specialized knowledge planning for successive stages would become increasingly difficult. Nevertheless, much maligned and distrusted as it is, bureaucracy is not without a vital role to play in the process of planning for economic and social development. Modifications in its structure, values, and work-ways are necessary to adapt it to the idiom of the fast changing situation, but the fact remains that it cannot be done away with. An understanding of its character and the initiation of imaginative plans for changing its structure and values so as to make it a more effective instrument for development must therefore be considered an essential prerequisite to planned change in these countries.

Discriminatingly recruited on the basis of specified criteria and carefully trained according to established and time-tested plans, bureaucracies in most of the former colonies and dependencies became efficient instruments of administration. Although they were oriented more to functions of law and order and the collection of revenues, they were also entrusted from time to time with some nation-building responsibilities. In discharging their responsibilities they showed all the classical characteristics of bureaucracies: they were formally organized with unambiguous demarcation of roles and statuses and were articulated to clearly defined goals; they were efficient and equipped with the required knowledge; they were well-versed in formal rules of procedure and recognized their predominance; and finally they were trained to function in an impersonal manner under conditions of near anonymity.

In addition to the above, bureaucracies in these societies had certain special characteristics. In their respective countries they were perhaps the first large and organized group to enter the transitional phase between tradition and modernity—the twilight zone lying between societal types described variously in continua such as communal-associational, sacred-secular, status-contract, and *gemeinschaft-gesellschaft*. In other words, they were among the pioneers who sought to break away from the traditionally affective and emotion-based communal society and to set in motion the forces that were to contribute towards the emergence of a different type of society—a society characterized by affective neutrality and based on rational ends-means calculations for individual goals. As a distinct subcultural entity within the larger framework of their society, they were at least partly absolved from the traditional obligation of having to share communal attitudes, sentiments, and repressive authority, and were among the first to constitute a group characterized by specialized division of labour, by different but complementary interests and sentiments, and by restrictive authority. It is not suggested here that they could break away completely from tradition to adopt the ideals and values of modernity; in the critical areas of choice-making they had before them a wide zone of fluid values in which were present the elements of both tradition and modernity. The logic and rationale of selectivity in the process of choice-making has not been analysed in depth, but the fact that, gradually and in an increasing measure, bureaucracy adopted several elements of modernity is not without significance.

It might be useful to describe here some special features of these bureaucracies, as they emerged and crystallized during the colonial phase.

1. Bureaucracy constituted a special sub-cultural segment—the high prestige strata of the society. Entrance to it was theoretically not barred to any section of the community, although in actual practice only the traditionally privileged could provide the necessary general background and the expensive education required for success in the stiff tests prescribed for entry into its higher echelons. In limited numbers others also gained entrance into the relatively closed group of higher civil servants. Middle-level and lower positions in it attracted the less privileged. Bureaucracy had a class bias and it tended to have a stratification of its own; its upper crust functioned as a privileged class. On the whole it symbolized achievement rather than ascription. Over time, it came to have distinct vested interests, and was sensitive to all threats to its position and privilege which it guarded jealously against encroachment from any quarter.

2. It existed largely in the twilight zone of cultures. Partly traditional and partly modern, it could and did in fact choose from the elements of both. In several ways it was alienated from the masses and uprooted from the native cultural traditions; significant differences in styles of living and in modes of thought separated the two. The Western rulers, on the other hand, never conceded equality to it. In consequence, bureaucracy maintained dual identification and was characterized by a dual ambivalence.

3. Besides offering security of tenure and relatively higher emoluments, bureaucratic positions carried vast powers which made them additionally attractive and important. The powers vested in a minor functionary gave him prestige, perquisites and privileges far beyond those justified by his emoluments and position in the hierarchy. Formally the role and status of functionaries at different levels were defined, but in actual practice the system of expectation and obligation between them tended to be diffused rather than specific.

4. Within the framework of the over-all policy laid down by the imperial power, in day-to-day administration the bureaucratic machine enjoyed considerable freedom from interference. Thus there were few hindrances to its exercise of power, which was often authoritarian in tone and content. Bureaucracy had, in general, a paternalistic attitude to the masses. The masses, on their part, accepted the position and looked to the administration for a wide variety of small favours.

5. Administration was concerned mainly with collection of land revenue and with maintenance of law and order. The general administrator under these conditions enjoyed supremacy. Subject matter specialists of welfare and nation-building departments were relegated to secondary positions and functioned under the guidance and control of the generalist.

6. Bureaucracy was carefully trained in

formal administrative procedure and routine. Stereotypes in this sphere were well-developed and were scrupulously observed.

7. In the limited framework of its functions and set procedures bureaucracy found a self-contained system. It resented and resisted innovations.

8. Its attitude to the nationalist forces within was most ambivalent. Few within the bureaucracy were devoid of patriotic sentiments and aspirations, but only in rare exceptions could they openly side with the forces of nationalism. Requirements of their official position made them an instrument for the execution of imperialist policies. This naturally aroused in the nationalist leadership feelings of anger and distrust against them. This rejection by the leaders of the nationalist forces as well as by the politically-conscious masses was largely at the root of their ambivalent attitude towards the nationalist forces.

Bureaucracy welcomed the advent of independence as much as any other group in the former colonies and dependencies, but the first years of freedom were for it a period of great stress and strain. It had covertly resented Western domination, but in the first decade of independence it remained under the shadow of suspicion because of its former association and identification with the alien power. While its power and prestige were decreasing, its burdens and responsibilities were increasing. Attacked from several sides simultaneously and with mounting pressures, bureaucracy found itself in a difficult and uncomfortable position.

The more important areas in which it had to work for a redefinition and consequent readjustment of its position and responsibilities were (a) the culture of politics, (b) the emerging ethos, and (c) the expanding sphere of State activity and the new institutional arrangements.

The Culture of Politics

In the new order the supremacy of administration was replaced largely by the sovereignty of politics. Politics became the most important activity and the politician came to occupy a position of unquestionable supremacy in matters of decision making. Within the framework of this culture of politics, there was an unmistakable tendency towards the merging of political roles with personal and social roles; the expectations of the politician from his followers and administrative subordinates were diffused. Politics centred round individuals; informal factions or groups formed around key personalities were thus more meaningful units of political organization than the formal structure of political parties. Personal loyalty to politicians, under these conditions, played an important part in the process of political identification and decision-making. Administration under such leadership could not remain wholly impersonal. The political élite was nurtured more in the politics of agitation than in the politics of nation building, and as a hangover from the past it persisted in its agitational approach. Nucleated around individuals, political processes lacked organic unity; communication was not adequately articulated. In general, political parties represented some kind of a revolutionary world view and philosophy, and on larger international and national issues they stood for an unlimited Utopia. On specific issues, especially of a regional or local character, the position was significantly different; political opinion on them was often narrow, sectarian, and parochial. Thus political thinking regarding issues at different levels lacked cohesion and integration. The attitude of the political élite was characterized by ambivalence. They sought to work for modernization, without giving up their love for tradition; attempts to harmonize, synthesize, and integrate the elements of the two, even on a conceptual level, were neither systematic nor serious.

In many countries the bureaucracy was trained well enough to accept political direction, and only in a few exceptional cases did it try to gain the upper hand.

Adjustment and adaptation to this political culture, however, was not without problems and difficulties. The new order posed a definite threat to bureaucracy's structure, values, and interests. While its formal structure remained intact, the definition of roles and statuses within the hierarchy was disturbed by the emergence of the politician as the focal point of decision-making. The personal nature of political decision-making was another unsettling factor. It not only affected the internal status system of the bureaucracy, but also sometimes bypassed its special knowledge and sidetracked its procedural routine. In many specific contexts administration could not function in an impersonal manner. Interpersonal relations between the politician and the administrator tended to be uneasy. The politician recognized the value and importance of the bureaucracy, but he continued to have a definite antagonism towards it, to exhort and admonish it to change its ways, and to ridicule it for some of its modes of thought and action that were out of tune in the new order. Much of this criticism was valid, but the manner in which it was made was often irritating to the bureaucrats. Many members of the bureaucracy had silently admired the self-sacrificing patriots as heroes, but in close proximity they saw them without the halo that surrounded them during the days of the national struggle. Often, the gap between their profession and their practice particularly annoyed the perceptive members of the bureaucracy. The politician was himself adopting many of the ways which he criticized in the bureaucrat. Some members of the administration were all too willing to adapt, but their over-readiness to do so was viewed by the discerning administrator as a dangerous departure that could in the long run undermine the very character and role of the bureaucracy.

The Emerging Ethos

The emerging ethos also presented bureaucracy with a series of problems.

In the new setting it could not maintain its image of power, nor could it continue to exist as a high-prestige class enjoying exceptional privileges. A closer identification with the masses was called for; the paternalistic and authoritarian tone of administration had also inevitably to change. On a theoretical and emotional level the desirability of this basic change was conceded, but a system of rationalization was developed at the same time to justify the maintenance of the *status quo*. Today a great contradiction persists between emotional awareness of the desirable and willingness to accept it in practice.

The Expanding Sphere of State Activity and New Institutional Arrangements

The structure, values, and work-ways of the bureaucracy in almost all former colonies and dependencies were geared to law and order and to revenue administration for which it was efficiently trained. Administration for nation building necessitated a different approach involving a new value attitude orientation and a modified institutional set-up. It is in these spheres that the failures of the bureaucracy are perhaps the most pronounced.

By and large the bureaucracy resists innovations in its structural arrangement. It appears to have a firm faith in the superiority of the pyramidal structure of administration and in the infallibility of the generalist. Efforts to nuclearize the administration for nation building are resented, and there is great resentment if any attempt is made to dislodge the general administrator from his high pedestal. Concepts of inner-democratization, of administrative decentralization, and of delegation of authority and responsibility at best receive only lip service. Coordination becomes difficult because of faulty communication between the general administrator and the technical specialist. Effective utilization of the specialist is blocked by the accepted or assumed supremacy of the general administrator whose self-confidence borders almost on arrogance. The latter perhaps realizes that he is not trained for certain jobs, but he rarely concedes this publicly. Innovations have been made in these spheres, but the marks of bureaucratic resistance are still evident.

Subconsciously the bureaucrat still perhaps believes in the efficacy of the traditional approach to administration. New approaches are discussed and half-heartedly accepted, but only in rare cases do they receive a fair trial. Extension and community development approaches, for instance, have encountered considerable resistance from the bureaucracy. Indeed, many members of the administration would be glad to revert to type, and would willingly reverse the process that has gained partial acceptance for these approaches after years of experimentation and persuasion.

It is generally recognized that the cumbrous administrative routine, good in its time, today practically immobilizes developmental administration. Yet, all attempts to change the rules of procedure result invariably in the formulation of rules that are as complex as those they seek to replace, if not more so.

Efforts at deconcentration of power, such as the experiment of democratic decentralization for development in India, meet with even greater resistance. Doubtless the infant "grass roots democracy" is not without shortcomings, but its threats to the perpetuation of bureaucratic vested interests have alerted the administrator, whose approach to the experiment is extremely guarded, wooden, and unimaginative.

Attempts have been made at reorienting the bureaucracy to the new philosophy of administration, but they have often been viewed as mere short-lived fads and fancies. Indirectly the new approach has made some headway, but there is little evidence to suggest that its utility has been generally accepted.

In the tasks of nation building in transitional societies bureaucracy has a vital role to play. It consists, by and large, of people with progressive motivation, wide administrative experience, and a rich store of pooled knowledge. Far from being written off, it cannot be ignored. It must also be conceded that it has played an important part in the process of economic and social growth and has been willing to go part of the way at least to adjust to the new situation. It has functioned both as a model and as an instrument for modernization. But its effective utilization has been blocked by some of the paradoxes of the new political culture and by the inner contradictions within its own structure and ordering of values. In several respects the hard core of the bureaucratic culture has been unyielding, and has offered great resistance to innovation. The blame does not lie entirely at its own door, but at the same time the present state of uncertainty cannot be allowed to continue indefinitely. Lack of adequate understanding of its culture and values and of a balanced assessment of its past and future roles has been an important factor in the failure to utilize bureaucracy more effectively in programmes of economic growth and planned change.

BUREAUCRATS AND POLITICAL DEVELOPMENT: A PARADOXICAL VIEW[1]

Fred W. Riggs

Introduction

A phenomenon of the utmost significance in transitional societies is the lack of balance between political policy-making institutions and bureaucratic policy-implementing structures. The relative weakness of political organs means that the political function tends to be appropriated, in considerable measure, by bureaucrats. Intra-bureaucratic struggles become a primary form of politics. But when the political arena is shifted to bureaucracies—a shift marked by the growing power of military officers in conflict with civilian officials—the consequences are usually ominous for political stability, economic growth, administrative effectiveness, and democratic values. It seems important, therefore, to give serious attention to the relation between political and administrative development, to the question of how balanced growth takes place.

In this chapter, accordingly, I deal with the way in which bureaucratic interests affect political development; not how the declared political aims of officials impinge on politics, but how the existence and self-interest of bureaucratic institutions affect, directly or indirectly, the growth of political institutions. My theme will be the conditions under which non-bureaucratic power

centers capable of subjecting bureaucrats to political control flourish or decline. I recognize that there are other important respects in which political development can and does occur, but this paper will be limited to this particular aspect of the subject.

In Western countries it has become a habit to think of the bureaucracy as an instrumental apparatus for the execution of policies established through "political," non-bureaucratic institutions. There have, of course, been serious scholars, as well as emotional writers, who have stressed the difficulty of keeping bureaucrats under control or, as the administrative cliché has it, "on tap but not on top."[2]

One consequence of this conventional attitude is that relatively few scholars have devoted themselves to an analysis of the political role of bureaucrats, the part they play in politics or in political development. However, in my opinion bureaucrats probably always have some influence in politics—although the extent of such influence varies from precious little to a great deal. In the developing countries the extent of bureaucratic involvement in politics is exceptionally high. If this opinion is correct, then it is even more important in the study of the developing countries to consider the role of bureaucrats in politics than to examine this topic in the study of more advanced political systems.

In his major work on government,[3] Carl J. Friedrich suggests that constitutionalism can emerge only after a sub-

SOURCE. Excerpted from Fred W. Riggs, "Bureaucrats and Political Development: A Paradoxical View," in Joseph LaPalombara, ed., *Bureaucracy and Political Development* (Princeton: Princeton University Press, 1963), pp. 120–167; using only 120–135, 139–153.

---

[1] The author is grateful for many useful suggestions made by participants of the Social Science Research Council Conference on Bureaucracy and Political Development, and particularly for the help provided by Professors John T. Dorsey and Edward W. Weidner.

[2] As one example of a serious analysis of the problem of maintaining bureaucratic accountability see Charles S. Hyneman, *Bureaucracy in a Democracy*, New York, Harper, 1950.

[3] *Constitutional Government and Democracy*, rev. ed., Boston, Ginn, 1950, pp. 25–27, 57.

stantial development of the bureaucracy, for without a governmental apparatus to bring under control, the challenge would not be present to bring into being a system designed to impose limitations and rules upon those who exercise administrative authority. I believe the experience of the developing countries is consistent with Friedrich's observation, but it suggests a corollary, namely that the imposition of constitutional control over a bureaucracy is a difficult task, and the more powerful, relatively, the bureaucracy becomes, the more arduous the achievement.

It we make a quick survey of the transitional societies today, we will be impressed by the weakness of their extra-bureaucratic political institutions in contrast with the burgeoning growth of their bureaucracies. In every country a great expansion of governmental agencies and a proliferation of functions has taken place, especially in the new nations that were recently under colonial rule. By contrast, parliamentary bodies have, in the main, proved ineffectual and, even in the countries like India and the Philippines where they have been most vigorous, their role in basic decision making has been questioned.[4]

Elections have often been conducted

[4] For example, Norman Palmer, a careful observer of Indian politics, has written in connection with the operation of the constitutional and parliamentary system, "the main decisions are made to a large degree outside normal channels. This fact calls attention to the great influence of 'nonpolitical' forces in India, to the role of personalities and charismatic leadership. Most of the major policies are in fact determined within the Congress Party and not by the agencies of government; and within the Congress Party they are made by Jawaharlal Nehru and a handful of associates. . . . there is a kind of unreality about the operation of the governmental agencies in India, and any examination of their functioning soon leads to other sources of influence and power." "The Political Heritage of Modern India," in George McT. Kahin, *Major Governments of Asia*, Ithaca, Cornell University Press, 1958, pp. 294–295. This seems like an overstatement—but perhaps it is sufficiently true to support the position taken in this paper.

in such a way as to give but a poor reflection of the popular will; the courts have not generally shown themselves to be bulwarks of the rule of law; and chief executives have more often than not shown themselves to be arbitrary and authoritarian, relying on their charismatic leadership qualities or a party machine rather than on formal political institutions as the basis of power. Under these conditions it is not surprising that bureaucrats themselves have often had to play a crucial part in determining what would, or perhaps *would not*, be done.

In speaking of non-bureaucratic power I have in mind, of course, primarily those institutions through which, in democratic countries, public interests are articulated, aggregated, and communicated to policy makers, there to be translated into decisions which can and are to a large extent subsequently implemented.

However, I do not rule out of the concept those systems in which the representation of popular interests is highly defective, but in which, nevertheless, a non-bureaucratic political system exists which is able to impose its control upon the governmental apparatus. I have in mind those states—whether of the Fascist or Communist type—in which a political party under highly centralized guidance seizes power and uses its party machinery to impose discipline upon the governmental bureaucrats. Because of the close affinity of the party bureaucracy to the formal bureaucracy in such states, some students lump the two groups together as a single bureaucracy. In my opinion this obscures a fundamental political issue, and hence I shall use the term "bureaucracy" to refer only to the formal hierarchy of government officials, speaking of all other bureaucracies, whether of corporations, trade unions, churches, or political parties, as "non-bureaucratic" or as "non-governmental bureaucracies."

Development as Differentiation

The phenomenon of development involves a gradual separation of institutionally distinct spheres, the differentiation of separate structures for the wide variety of functions that must be performed in any society.

It is clear that in very traditional or simple societies such differentiation has taken place to an extremely limited extent. A single set of officials or authorities, as in feudalism, may exercise undifferentiated military, political, administrative, religious, and economic functions.

By contrast, a highly developed political system contains a large number of explicitly administrative structures, each specialized for specific purposes: agricultural, transport, regulatory, defense, budgetary, personnel, public relations, planning, etc. Moreover, a set of political structures—parties, elections, parliaments, chief executives, and cabinets—are designed to formulate the rules and pose the targets which the administrative structures then implement.

Undoubtedly the principle of the separation of politics and administration is as much a target for aspiration as a statement of actual conditions in a real government, like that of the United States; but the extent of realization of this separation is marked indeed if one compares it with what prevailed in any traditional or primitive folk society. Moreover, the separation of politics and administration is only one facet of a differentiated society, since both the political and administrative institutions are themselves differentiated from economic, religious, educational, and social structures of a distinct and separate character in the advanced Western societies.

The process of modernization in the developing countries is marked by the progressive creation of formally distinct social structures, adapted from Western models, to which differentiated political and administrative tasks are assigned. But in this process the older institutional base of a traditional society lingers on. Although eroded and embattled, it struggles to remain alive, to retain positions of influence.

We find, then, in the transitional society, a dualistic situation. Formally superimposed institutions patterned after Western models coexist with earlier, indigenous institutions of a traditional type in a complex pattern of heterogeneous overlapping. The new patterns thrive best at the center and in the higher levels of society; the older patterns persist most vigorously at the periphery, in the rural hinterlands and the lower levels of society; but the mixture is everywhere present and produces new forms characteristic of neither the Western nor the traditional institutional systems.[5]

The relative speed of change in the functional sectors of a transitional society also varies. Those sectors in which technology, the purely instrumental means, predominate are able to change more rapidly than those in which social and personal values are implicated. For this reason it was often in such spheres as military technology, agricultural crops, formal schooling in science, language, and Western learning that innovations were first made in non-Western countries.[6]

---

[5] Even the most developed societies retain admixtures of traditional elements and are therefore also to some extent "transitional." The differences are not absolute, but in degree and proportions.

[6] This proposition has been elaborately demonstrated with historical examples by Arnold J. Toynbee. By way of summary he writes, in *The World and the West*, New York, Oxford, 1953, p. 68: "When a travelling culture-ray is diffracted into its component strands—technology, religion, politics, art, and so on—by the resistance of a foreign body social upon which it has impinged, its technological strand is apt to penetrate faster and farther than its religious strand ... the penetrative power of a strand of cultural radiation is usually in inverse ratio to this strand's cultural value."

Harold Lasswell and Abraham Kaplan distinguish "techniques" from "technics." The former consist of those parts of a technology which belong to the social order, hedged about by sanctions, mores, values; the latter those which are free of such involvements. "Technicalization" refers to a transformation from technique to technic. (*Power and Society*,

In the governmental sphere, this principle means that development in public administration, bureaucratic change, takes place more readily than counterpart changes in politics: technics change more easily than techniques. The reasons are apparent. The initial demand for Western institutions in many non-Western countries was in the military sphere, for defense against an intrusive imperial power. To develop the means of defense, rulers employed foreign military advisers and sent students to European military academies. The costs of modern arms were high, and so in national finance, in taxation, especially in customs, and state monopolies like salt, in budgeting and accounting, transformations were carried out. Defense needs also created a demand for effective control over outlying areas of a traditional realm, and so led to a reorganization of territorial administration, the creation of a Ministry of Interior, recruitment of a career service of district officers, prefects, governors, and a central secretariat to control their operations.[7]

While this proliferation and expansion of bureaucratic machinery was taking place in most of the non-Western countries, no corresponding development of the non-bureaucratic political system occurred. In the independent countries, political leadership was still provided by traditional rulers—as in Siam, Iran, Ethiopia, Japan—

although in the Japanese case perhaps the greatest success was achieved in establishing new political institutions, a central legislature, political parties, and a cabinet system. This success is, of course, directly relevant to the phenomenal Japanese achievement of industrialization and the greater effectiveness of its governmental institutions as compared to those of other non-Western countries. Even here, however, bureaucratic elements, especially from the armed forces, tended to exercise disproportionate influence in the political structures, notably in the period leading to the Second World War.[8]

In the countries under colonial rule the proposition is even more patently true—at least until recently. Here the colonial administration itself created a bureaucratic apparatus not subject to political control within the dependent territory, so that administrative institutions proliferated while political structures remained embryonic and largely extra-legal, hence unable to relate themselves effectively to control over the bureaucracy. A striking exception was the Philippines under American administration where nationalist opposition groups were quickly given opportunities to share in the conduct of the government. In India, especially after the First World War and the Montagu-Chelmsford reforms, Indian participation in formal politics, notably in provincial government, laid a substantial foundation for the post-independence development of vigorous political institutions. Subsequently in other British dependencies legislative bodies and political parties were permitted, and they began to share in the formation of policy and control over administration. In a somewhat different way, the same has been true, perhaps, in some of the French-controlled territories. Ultimately this legislative ex-

[*footnote 6 continued*
New Haven, Yale University Press, 1950, p. 51.) In this terminology, the process of modernization has involved technicalization, and change has been more rapid in technics than in techniques.

[7] The general pattern of such transformations is discussed in my article, "Prismatic Society and Financial Administration," *Administrative Science Quarterly*, **5** (June 1960), espec. pp. 9–16. For a detailed case study of one such transformation, see Walter Vella, *The Impact of the West on Government in Thailand*, Berkeley, University of California Press, 1955. See also E. Herbert Norman, *Japan's Emergence as a Modern State*, New York, Institute of Pacific Relations, 1940. The sequence in areas under colonial rule has been different in important respects, but fundamentally similar.

[8] The extent to which postwar, extra-bureaucratic political development in Japan was influenced, directly or indirectly, by the Occupation, will long remain an interesting subject of study.

perience, plus the ordeal of revolutionary opposition, provided the ex-colonial countries with a stronger political foundation than the countries which never felt an imperial yoke.

In the contemporary era of large-scale technical assistance under international and bi-national programs, we see a continued infusion of external pressure and assistance in the expansion and proliferation of bureaucratic organs, with relatively little attention to the growth of strictly political institutions. The reasons are quite evident. Administration is regarded as a technical matter (technics) subject to foreign, "expert" advice, whereas politics is so closely linked with fundamental values and social mores (techniques) that aid would be construed as "intervention."[9]

Moreover, the demand for economic development and modernization impinges directly on agricultural, industrial, public health, and educational spheres in which external assistance is fed directly to segments of the bureaucracy, and only weakly mediated through central political institutions. The foreign experts and advisers, for their part, while competent to deal with technical matters in a variety of program fields, and even the related administrative questions, would scarcely claim any competence to assist in the establishment of new political institutions.

The question naturally arises: what is the relationship between this burgeoning of bureaucratic institutions and the course of political development? The relationship may be examined from two sides: the effect of political weakness on administrative effectiveness,[10] and the consequences of bureaucratic expansion for the political system. In this article

I shall limit myself to an examination of the latter set of relationships.

My general thesis is that premature or too rapid expansion of the bureaucracy when the political system lags behind tends to inhibit the development of effective politics.[11] A corollary thesis holds that separate political institutions have a better chance to grow if bureaucratic institutions are relatively weak.

Some historical evidence for this proposition is suggested by a comparison of the history of feudal societies with those in which traditional government had a more bureaucratic basis. An outstanding example of a traditional bureaucratic system was imperial China.[12] Here the elaborate complexity and pervasiveness

[9] Until the last few years it perhaps did not even occur to U.S. policy makers that political development should or could be a goal in overseas programs.

[10] In another paper, "Bureaucracy in Transitional Societies" (mimeo. 1959), I have argued that political weakness has led to administrative ineffectiveness in many of these countries.

[11] A perceptive public administration adviser shrewdly pointed to this problem in the following words: "Efficient administrative machines can be used to prevent as well as to promote development, and much of the effort that it takes to produce the appearance, if not the reality, of improvement in public administration can become, as it has in the Philippines, a means of concealing inability or unwillingness to undertake needed action on other fronts." Malcolm B. Parsons, "Performance Budgeting in the Philippines," *Public Administration Review*, **17**, 3 (Summer 1957), 173–179.

The view taken here is not, of course, that bureaucrats or bureaucracy are essentially evil monsters, and certainly the need for administrative services which can be performed only by public officials argues for an expansion and improvement, not curtailment, of bureaucracy. The argument is presented, however, that effective administration by bureaucrats is contingent upon the simultaneous growth of extra-bureaucratic institutions capable of maintaining effective control over officials, of keeping them responsible to the formal political authorities, and responsive to the public and clientele interests directly affected by their work. Ideally, such responsibility is to the whole population through democratic processes, but even under totalitarian conditions there must be responsiveness to a party control machine with an extra-bureaucratic power base.

[12] Karl A. Wittfogel, *Oriental Despotism*, New Haven, Yale University Press, 1957, is a comprehensive examination of the history and dynamics of bureaucratic systems.

of an ubiquitous bureaucracy may be related to a notable weakness of autonomous political structures. In modern times it was only on the wreck of the bureaucracy, in a period of war-lordism and administrative anarchy, that political parties were finally able to emerge and lay the basis for a powerful one-party structure capable of re-organizing and controlling the bureaucracy. In a sense, the war-lord period represented a feudalization of Chinese society.

Russian history is parallel to Chinese in this respect. The Czarist bureaucracy left little scope for autonomous politics and revolutionary movements could survive only abroad. The war-caused bureaucratic collapse cleared the ground for a short-lived fluorescence of free politics, followed by the triumph of a monocratic party.

In the West, autonomous political institutions developed best in countries with a feudal background, where bureaucratic power was weak and fragmented. This was notably true in England. For different reasons—its frontier character, for example—American bureaucracy was also relatively weak and fragmented. In France, despite a long feudal background, the absolute monarchy consolidated national power through a growing bureaucratic apparatus, and this course of development may be related to the continuingly precarious basis of French political life.

But such historical examples are merely suggestive. Rather than explore them in more detail, it may be more fruitful to investigate the inner workings of the political and bureaucratic systems in contemporary transitional societies to see whether or not we can discover some more specific reasons for the suggested relationships. I will examine, in turn, the relation of bureaucracy to party systems, the electorate, legislatures, courts, and executive leadership.

Bureaucracy and the Party System

Let us consider, first, the basis of recruitment to a bureaucracy and its relation to political development. It has become axiomatic in modern public administration that bureaucrats *ought* to be selected on the basis of universalistic achievement criteria, best expressed in an examination system; and that employment should be for a career. The pressure of international advisers and the demand for technically qualified personnel to staff the program-oriented services of modern government has meant the proliferation in all the developing countries of civil service and personnel systems rooted in the merit and career concepts. Indeed, so deeply engrained are these ideas that even to question their utility is to risk castigation as a heretic and subversive.

Yet the merit system cuts at the root of one of the strongest props of a nascent political party system, namely spoils. Once political parties are strongly established, once the public is widely mobilized for political action, prepared to give volunteer support, and to contribute financially from a broad base of party membership, it is possible to reduce or perhaps even eliminate spoils as an element of support for party activity.

Certainly, if American history can be taken as suggestive, the spoils system played an important part in galvanizing the parties into action. Even today, although national politics and the federal administration has been substantially purged of spoils, a strong residue of spoils appointments still remains. If local politics, on which our party machines rest, were to be deprived of spoils, they might well lose much of their vigor. Without for a moment denying the evils associated with the spoils system, one cannot escape noting the intimate relation between spoils and the growth of political parties.

It is, of course, no easy matter to organize spoils in such a way as to strengthen political parties. A natural tendency exists to use opportunities for patronage appointments and graft through public contracts to favor relatives and friends of individual politicians rather than to reward those who work for a party as an organization. But without official sanction for at least some degree of spoils in the bureaucracy, it is difficult to institutionalize procedures and rules for the use of spoils to reward bona fide party workers.[13]

A second relation of spoils to political growth ought to be considered. No doubt a career bureaucracy of specialists is administratively more capable than a transitory bureaucracy of spoilsmen. But, by the same token, the career bureaucracy can project greater political power on its own, resist more successfully the politician's attempts to assert effective control. What is lost in administrative efficiency through spoils may be gained in political development, especially if party patronage can also be used as a lever to gain control over administration.

The existence of a career bureaucracy without corresponding strength in the political institutions does not necessarily lead to administrative effectiveness—as I have argued elsewhere.[14] Without firm political guidance, bureaucrats have weak incentives to provide good service, whatever their formal, pre-entry training and professional qualifications. They tend to use their effective control to safeguard their expedient bureaucratic interests—tenure, seniority rights, fringe benefits, toleration of poor performance, the right to violate official norms—rather than to advance the achievement of program goals. Hence the career, merit bureaucracy in a developing country not only fails to accomplish the administrative goals set for it but also stands in the way of political growth.

Not, of course, that one would want to see a wholesale transformation in developing countries of their present career bureaucracies into spoils. However, it might be that, by judicious selection, a range of positions, a "schedule C," could be declared open for political appointment with a counterpart provision that they should be filled only by persons who meet requirements for service to a winning party.[15]

It is characteristic of a one-party state for the dominant group to eliminate all rivals. The loss for freedom is a gain for political and administrative development in the perverse sense that policy direction is sharpened and bureaucratic performance held to a higher level.

But in a polity shaped by bureaucratic dominance, opposition groups tend to be tolerated, and a ruling party takes shape as a coalition of diverse elements. The ruling coalition lacks coherence or unity—although it may well be the inheritor of a revolutionary tradition from an earlier period of common struggle against foreign rule. It would perhaps be too strong to say that the coalition is formed of elements congenial to the bureaucrats, but at least they are typically ambitious men attracted by the crumbs to be gathered off the tables of the elite, rather than by any hope of creating a better political or social order. In a sense they form a sodality of the gentry.[16] Because the distribution of crumbs—"pork," to use the American equivalent—can reach far corners, the coalition, with bureaucratic backing, can usually count on electoral success.

[13] Even the hope of contracts might open sources of finance to opposition parties which would otherwise be doomed to poverty and ineffectiveness.

[14] "Bureaucracy in Transitional Societies," *op. cit.*

[15] Moreover, the needs for technical competence in the twentieth century are undoubtedly greater than they were in the nineteenth. Hence any move to open the door for spoils appointments certainly ought to set minimum standards, and reserve key technical positions for non-partisan recruitment.

[16] The word "gentry" is here used in a technical sense to refer to a "ruling class" whose members base their power primarily on access to bureaucrats or bureaucratic status. Both an aristocracy and a gentry possess wealth (chiefly in land) and power, but an aristocracy's wealth is the source of its power, whereas a gentry's wealth is the fruit of its power. For a perceptive analysis of the most classical instance of a gentry see Chung-li Chang, *The Chinese Gentry*, Seattle, University of Washington Press, 1955.

Without the hope of spoils, and with minimal opportunities for penetrating the career services, the opposition parties can attract only the confirmed idealist, the bitterly disappointed, the fanatic, and the maladjusted: all predominantly drawn from the intelligentsia. Moreover, without real hope of an electoral victory and spoils, there is no strong incentive for these hostile fractions to coalesce, to form a unified opposition, nor is there much reason for them to be loyal to a system of government which offers them no hope of rewards. The hostile political fractions then become cults, sectarian, a total way of life, an absorbing preoccupation for the small minorities attracted to them. Addicted to violence and extremism, to poly-functionalism[17]—since they cater to the religious, social, and economic as well as the political interests of their members—they form cancerous growths in the body politic. They serve, also, as the breeding grounds of a one-party dictatorship since, with an appropriate spin of the wheel of fortune, one of them may someday find itself catapulted into power.[18]

In a working democracy the opposition parties help to keep the party in power politically alert and responsible to public demands. The hostile fractions in a bureaucratic polity, although labeled opposition parties, cannot really have this effect. Instead, they undermine the system, weaken the coherence of the ruling party, and strengthen the relative power of the bureaucracy which may be called on—through police or army—to suppress one or more of the fractions as they resort, in turn, to violence. (In pointing to the role that spoils played in the growth of the party system in the West, I do not mean to suggest that the same course should or will be followed elsewhere—but some functional equivalent must be found if effective party systems are to grow.)

Bureaucracy and the Electorate

It was one of the favorite theses of the colonial regime that political participation ought to begin at the local level. The administration of central government, it was said, ought to be left to the colonial bureaucracy; the development of village, communal, and municipal councils would provide ample opportunity for the political education of the indigenous population. After having mastered the techniques of democratic politics at this level, the population would be prepared to take over a major share in government at the provincial level, ultimately at the national. This theory was also propagated by Sun Yat Sen and the Kuomintang for Nationalist China, and has been tested in recent years in Taiwan.

Strangely enough, nationalist revolutionaries and the intelligentsia of the dependent countries never looked with favor on this thesis. They called it a delaying tactic of imperial rule, and sought to plunge immediately into national politics, bypassing the local level. The same tendency has persisted since independence in the new nations. The dominant elite, having gained control in the center, manipulate the bureaucracy as an instrument of control over local government,

[17] "Poly-functionalism" may be defined as a condition intermediate between being functionally "diffuse" and functionally "specific." In other words, it serves fewer ends than a traditional family, but many more than a Western-style "association." Elsewhere I have called such poly-functional groups "clects."

[18] Examples of such tightly knit minority "parties" or fractions are described in many works, but their characteristics are often attributed to racial, ethnic, religious, or other local and cultural features rather than to general functional relationships common to most of the "transitional" societies. See, for a good example, Myron Weiner, *Political Parties in India*, Princeton, Princeton University Press, 1957, especially pp. 223–264. Although Indian political development has been outstanding in comparison with most of the other new states, the inability of sectarian opposition parties to form a stable coalition or unified opposition is a major obstacle to further strengthening of democratic politics in India.

giving little more than lip service to the philosophy of decentralization and local autonomy. One suspects there must be some deep-seated dynamism that moves the ruling groups in a developing country—whether under colonial or native control—to strengthen central bureaucratic administration at the expense of local self-government.

Let us seek clues to this paradox by considering the changes taking place in these countries.

In the former, traditional situation, local affairs were, in fact, largely controlled by local leaders—gentry, notables, petty chiefs, or headmen—and even within the community, the affairs of sub-groupings came under caste, clan, family, and temple control.[19]

The new regimes in developing countries, whether ruled by foreign imperialists or a native intelligentsia, have sought major socio-economic transformations in their societies. In this effort, they uniformly met resistance from traditional leaders and groups at the local levels. Insofar as their modernizing goals were limited, they permitted local affairs to be run in the age-old fashion, but to the extent that they wished to extend the domain and speed of development, they had to seize administrative control and impose change. For a modernizing elite—whether native or foreign—the value of development always outweighs local autonomy.[20]

As, gradually, local populations became enmeshed in the transformation, some among them began to desire the products of the new order, and so the modernizing central leadership discovered new allies in the small community. It then seemed practical to urge local self-government, with the expectation that rural elites, when exercising local autonomy, would continue and finance the very policies desired by the central authorities—the extension of roads and bridges, building of schools, improved sanitation and health measures, more rational agricultural practices, further expansion of the market system. Interestingly, spokesmen of local interests came, in large measure, to accept these targets, but not their costs. Who would pay for change?

Although central governments always imposed some taxes on the rural population, most of the revenue of the new nations comes from the more productive sectors, located in the major urban areas, and from customs revenues imposed on international trade. Hence the cost of local improvements has been largely financed from the center. Indeed, only this ability to pay for modernization enabled national governments to extend the range of their control as far as they have. If the center had merely demanded change, requiring localities to finance their own development, it is doubtful if the modernization of rural hinterlands would have gone as far as it has—limited as that is.

Proposals for more local self-government, however, have met an impasse, for, while local leaders have been all too willing to manage local improvements, they have been unwilling to finance them. They want the central government to pay for

---

[19] For an explicit account of this system in village India, see Bernard S. Cohn, "Some Notes on Law and Change in North India," *Economic Development and Cultural Change*, **8** (October 1959), 79–93. An earlier characterization of the same situation in India is provided by Henry Maine in *Lectures on the Early History of Institutions*, London, J. Murray, 1893, p. 380. For an account of Chinese local control in the traditional system see Martin Yang, "Former Rural Control in China" (Unpublished manuscript, no date). Even Karl A. Wittfogel, who argues most strongly for the totally despotic character of the traditional bureaucratic system in China, refers to this characteristic local sphere of autonomy as a "beggars' democracy," *op. cit.* pp. 108–125. In feudalistic societies the extent of autonomy for local ruling groups was, of course, even more marked.

[20] The developmental patterns desired by the elite, of course, are typically one-sided—they serve their own economic, political, or national interests more than the interests of the local populations concerned.

development programs, but not to staff and control them. Naturally, no central regime is willing to turn over its funds for unsupervised use by local authorities. Every bureaucracy insists on maintaining some control over the use of its own money.

By contrast, in the "developed" countries, local self-government, to the extent that it is effective, rests on the ability and willingness of local communities to tax themselves for a substantial part of the services they want. When central funds *are* allocated for use by local authorities, they often involve matching of contributions and, necessarily, some central supervision. Even in developed countries, any programs which are fully financed from the center are typically run by field offices of central government rather than by autonomous local authorities, even where co-opted grass roots organizations participate in making and implementing policies. The measure of local autonomy in a country is certainly related to the ratio of locally financed and controlled programs to local programs which are centrally financed and controlled. In developed countries this ratio is large; in the developing ones, very low.

The weakness of local self-government in transitional societies means, of course, that the bulk of the citizenry are denied meaningful participation in modern-style politics. Of course, traditional forms of self-rule may persist. Even where local elections are held, they tend to be of limited significance. They may, of course, become the focus of great local excitement, and certainly they can have an impact on the local scene.[21] The question is: to what extent do such elections give the population a significant political experience, i.e., one in which meaningful choices are

[21] See Morris Opler, "Factors of Tradition and Change in a Local Election in Rural India," in Richard L. Park and Irene Tinker, eds., *Leadership and Political Institutions in India*, Princeton, Princeton University Press, 1959, pp. 137–150, for a dramatic case study of the impact of elections on a village community.

made. Insofar as effective control of developmental programs are retained—because financed—by field agents of the central bureaucracy, elected local officials lack significant powers of decision making. Their function becomes primarily ceremonial. Electoral contests then determine relative prestige ratings, not program or policy issues. Insofar as any appointments are made by the locally elected officials, purely personal patronage rather than party or program needs are considered. Electoral victory may depend on who can marshal more of the electorate by mobilizing his kinship alliances, rather than on party commitments to specific policy issues. No doubt in all patronage, personal motives are mixed with policy and program goals—but in significant politics there would have to be at least a minimal concern for issues in the contest and resulting patronage.

For local self-government to be significant as a training ground for national politics, I think it must involve electoral choices between alternative programs for which the voters themselves must pay, at least in part. If one party offers an expanded road and school program at the cost of heavier taxation, and the rival party offers a reduced benefit program with lighter taxation, then the community can make a significant choice. Or, the rival parties may offer different packages of public benefits, undertaking to collect the cost by contrasting tax schedules, in which the burden would fall more heavily upon one group or another in the community. Only in this way can both politician and voter learn the meaning of political choice instead of agitation and demagoguery.

These statements should not leave the impression that in the more developed countries local politics always measure up to this idealized account of effective self-government. However, it is argued here that, relatively speaking, local politics and significant choices by local electorates tend to be more meaningful in the industrialized than in developing countries.[22]

The weakness of local government—at its best—in the more developed countries shows how much room for growth still remains in these societies. It should also be noted that in traditional societies, prior to the impact of industrialization, there often existed a substantial measure of local autonomy, though without the formal machinery and ideology of modern self-government.

The most typical situation in the transitional societies, as I see it, weakens political institutions and strengthens bureaucratic. The more local communities have their appetites whetted by the "demonstration effect" for improvements which can be paid for only by the central government, the more unrealistic local politics becomes, and the more extended the central bureaucratic apparatus.

Even the goals of economic development are not necessarily advanced under these conditions. If local schools are built, for example, the most energetic and intelligent young people to graduate leave for higher schools in market centers and universities in the urban areas, where they seek posts in the expanding bureaucracy. The frailty of local politics and development means there is little to hold the most able. Instead of contributing to the vigorous growth of a locality, centrally based development deprives it of its best potential leadership, leaving a residue of partially educated men and women whose level of aspirations has risen more rapidly than their capabilities. Hence the bitterness and frustration of local politics increases without compensating successes in self-realization and achievement.

No doubt similar phenomena can be found in the more developed countries, but there are significant differences of degree. Since the over-all level of educa-

tion is higher in the developed countries, those who remain in rural areas, while less schooled than the urbanites, nevertheless reach a higher level of training than the village folk of transitional societies. Rural families in developed countries, moreover, are typically closer in terms of communication and transportation to secondary urban centers than are the villagers of non-industrialized countries.

The speed of social transformation also means that the gulf between traditional- and modern-minded people—the unschooled and the schooled—is greater in transitional than in industrial societies. This not only reinforces the motivation for those with schooling to leave their uncongenial, rural homes; it also tends to block the application, by those who remain, of skills and values they acquired in school. The level of effective modern education of rural youth does not equal the level of formal schooling they may have enjoyed, and this differential is probably much greater in the newly developing than in the more developed countries.

It may be that political development, at least toward a democratic type of political action, can be attained only at the cost of slower economic and social development. It is often said that authoritarianism can force economic development at a more rapid rate than democracy. Less familiar is the corollary that efforts to speed the rate of economic development may lead toward bureaucratic authoritarianism.

Bureaucracy and Interest Groups

One of the pillars of political action in advanced countries is the "association," through which functionally specific interests are articulated and communicated to decision-making centers. Although interaction between associations and government takes place through bureaucracy as well as through political institutions, the dominant mode tends to be with political party and legislative organs. The importance of interest groups in politics has only recently been recognized, but research on

[22] See, in this connection, A. B. Lewis, "Local Self-Government: a Key to National Economic Advancement and Political Stability," *Philippine Journal of Public Administration*, **2**, 1 (January 1958), 54–57.

the subject has by now produced a substantial literature.

These same associations also play a key role in policy implementation or rule application. The literature of public administration has made this process a subject of study to some extent. Thereby an unfortunate dichotomy has arisen: interest groups as originators of policy proposals, in the "input" process, are regarded as playing a political role, whereas when these same groups participate in policy execution they are regarded as playing an "output" or administrative role. The activities of the groups are thus viewed from two perspectives, but not as a whole. However arbitrary the dichotomy in the context of advanced societies, in the study of developing countries it has a particularly confusing effect.

If by political development we refer primarily to the process of democratization, the growth of popular control over government, then perhaps this distinction is useful. But in another sense political development refers to the process of politicization; increasing participation or involvement of the citizen in state activities, in power calculations, and consequences. In this sense the regimentation of citizens by the rulers is as much politicization as the initiation by citizens of demands upon the rulers. From this point of view, a modern totalitarian regime, with its total political regimentation, is as much politicized as a fully democratic regime. Both differ from the traditional polity in which, to a great extent, the mass of the subject population is little involved in political decisions, largely ignored by the rulers, and hence predominantly indifferent to their actions.

In the process of development the citizenry becomes progressively involved in matters of state, i.e., politicized. The primary vehicle or "transmission belt"— to use Joseph Stalin's colorful phrase—for such politicization is the interest group. However, in view of its dual role as instrument for popular regimentation as well as

for public control, both should be considered in a full analysis of this process. The politicization of a population by its progressive involvement in groups organized by the state as transmission belts for policy implementation is a political matter, even if we label it an administrative development. But the fact that we do label such developments administrative blinds us to their political significance.

In contemporary developing countries, bureaucratic agencies are set up to implement new programs oriented to the concept of the welfare state, intimately affecting much of the population. Ranging from public health, educational, and agricultural services to community development, these programs necessitate a massive coordination of the population. To carry them out, officials must mobilize those affected in many special-interest groups. Educational programs, for example, may require something like the parent-teachers' association to promote family cooperation for the school attendance of children, and to prepare even more ambitious programs of community or fundamental education. Agricultural programs require the creation of farmers' associations to transmit new techniques, improved seeds, fertilizers, and farm equipment. Women's groups and "4-H clubs" carry innovations into the home. Cooperatives handle credit and marketing problems. Community health units facilitate the dissemination of new drugs, police water supplies, enforce immunization drives, and sponsor clean-up campaigns or the installation of privies. Capping all the special interest groups are community development programs which call for the creation of all-purpose councils to plan and implement, under government supervision, a wide range of activities.

Without questioning the utility of these programs, I wish merely to note their political implications. In almost every case, the creation of these interest groups follows a bureaucratic initiative. They are not a spontaneous product of citizen demand in response to felt needs. The groups extend the reach of the bureaucracy, providing it with transmission belts through which total mobilization can, potentially, be achieved. Hence the growth of state-sponsored interest groups augments bureaucratic control, without necessarily strengthening any centers of autonomous political power capable of bringing bureaucratic machines under popular control. In other words, this process leads to political development in the sense of politicization, but not democratization. Quite the reverse, for here we see how accelerated economic and social development contributes to bureaucratic power, and lays the foundation for totalitarianism, weakening the prospects for democratic control over government.

There are many reasons for the weakness of autonomous interest group formation in the developing countries. One is simply the propensity for bureaucrats to be suspicious of autonomous groups outside their control. It is easier to deal with an orderly, unified system, especially if it has been set up to meet their specifications. Hence groups that start to organize on their own, or with external support—from a foreign government, foundation, or religious body—are viewed with hostility and, if not actually suppressed, are at least given little cooperation as compared with officially sponsored groups.

A second reason is financial. In poor countries the cost of voluntary organization can scarcely be obtained from members who barely get enough to meet their own minimum living needs. After collecting dues and contributions, voluntary groups find their resources still hopelessly inadequate. They must succumb to necessity, and either content themselves with a largely ineffective marginal existence or go, hat in hand, to government, begging financial help. The same dynamism that cripples local government weakens voluntary associations that rely on governmental subventions for existence. Inevitably the government takes control as a condition of granting assistance, and so the would-be

private group becomes another transmission belt.

Thirdly, the leadership 'for modernization comes predominantly from the intelligentsia, an intellectual class schooled in the concepts and aspirations of the "modern" world. This leadership, as I have indicated above, tends to be funneled into the central cities, leaving the hinterland starved of modern leadership. Into this partial vacuum the bureaucracy steps, the local representatives of central government being, by and large, the most modern and best educated persons in their districts. The result, quite naturally, is that in rural areas the bureaucratic leaders of interest groups usually dominate by relative superiority of talent and training the private citizens with whom they deal.[23]

No doubt governmentally sponsored associations sometimes become strong enough to declare their independence of the officials who brought them into being. This might happen in some developing countries. There seems no reason to assume that it would necessarily happen, and under totalitarian conditions mass organizations have remained passive tools of autocracy for a considerable time. Perhaps steps could be taken, as a matter of policy, to offer incentives for the achievement of autonomy by such associations. In any event, the degree of independence of private associations may be determined only by empirical investigation in each case. It is not something which can be assumed a priori.

Urban Interests and Pariah Entrepreneurship

It may be suggested that the situation differs in the urban areas where modern commerce and industry and the non-bureaucratic intelligentsia are concentrated. Here also the example and influence of

[23] For a case study illustrating these and other factors responsible for the weakness of interest groups see my "Interest and Clientele Groups," in Joseph L. Sutton, ed., *Problems of Politics and Administration in Thailand*, Bloomington, Ind., Institute of Training for Public Service, Indiana University, 1962, pp. 153–192.

other countries is strongest. Yet even here powerful factors operate to inhibit the effective political influence of interest groups. Moreover, a new set of factors show up which give a perverse twist to the relation between interest groups, bureaucrats, and politics.

It is at the urban core of government that the processes of development—especially commercial and industrial development—come to focus in the new states. These activities depend for their success upon the enterprise and skill of entrepreneurs who combine the various factors of production and control the process of distribution.

Here is a class which surely has the need, knowledge, and financial capacity to support interest groups—chambers of commerce, trade associations—through which to exercise pressure for the control of government. At least, this has been the history of the democratic developed countries, and an analogy is suggested for the developing areas. However, close inspection suggests risks in this analogy.

All too frequently, the private entrepreneurial class in the new nations suffers from lack of formal access to the political process. Its members are often drawn from a marginal group—racially, ethnically, or religiously—or of alien origin. Discriminatory laws and regulations are imposed against them. In applying these rules, members of the bureaucracy often exploit their power to penalize the entrepreneur unless he rewards them for overlooking infractions of the law.

Hence there develops a symbiotic relationship of "antagonistic cooperation" between government official and private entrepreneur. The official supplements his inadequate official income. In exchange, the businessman is permitted to violate regulations.

Why does such a situation continue? Characteristically in the new nations those who can acquire status, prestige, and power through land or official positions do so in preference to a business career—both because of the low status and

the risks involved. Hence only those who cannot follow the preferred occupations choose entrepreneurship. Thus a self-selecting mechanism restricts the entrepreneurial role to members of marginal or alien communities.

How can the obvious evils of this situation be overcome? Apparently only by imposing the role of law upon bureaucrats, requiring them to enforce the law impartially. At the same time, a legal structure is needed which favors the development of commerce and industry by protecting property and contract rights, imposing non-confiscatory tax rates, opening economic opportunities to all candidates without regard to particularistic criteria, etc. But how can such a regime be established? Clearly a prerequisite is the achievement of sufficient political power by the business community to impose responsibility and favorable laws upon the bureaucrats.

One cannot realistically expect uncontrolled bureaucrats to impose this kind of regime upon themselves when it is clearly against their immediate interests. Moreover, it is in the bureaucratic interest to prevent the creation of any groups in the business community that have a chance of gaining enough power to impose the rule of law upon government. Because entrepreneurs have the greatest potential for group formation, the bureaucrats use their sharpest weapons against them.

A classic bureaucratic weapon designed to meet the threat of entrepreneurial organization is to set up a counter-organization based on would-be entrepreneurs drawn from the dominant community. This counter-organization then seeks policies that discriminate in favor of their members against those of the established entrepreneurial community. Thus political support is mobilized for a continuation of basically anti-entrepreneurial policies, without risking the formation of a strong new entrepreneurial class, since the members of the favored group find it easier to convert their special privileges into cash on the black market than to learn a difficult business and do the hard work required.

Another bureaucratic tactic to counter the threat of growing power in an entrepreneurial community is to establish a public sector, to organize a mixed economy and use public enterprise to set the pace, regulate, or fill the gaps of the private sector. In practice, of course, these governmental undertakings are often run at a loss, requiring subvention from public funds. This enables them to compete with the private entrepreneur, and limit his growth or even force him into bankruptcy. Enterprises which can be readily controlled, especially where the state is the main customer or supplier, are turned into government monopolies, and the private sector eliminated. If a state enterprise is profitable, there may be an irresistible temptation to use official pressure—taxes, regulations, licenses, exchange control— to hamper, perhaps destroy, the competing private enterprises. As a result of these maneuvers, the private entrepreneur is forced to the wall, losing his capacity to organize effective political power. So long as he continues to buy protection from the bureaucracy, he is permitted to survive as a marginal or pariah entrepreneur, but not as a politically influential class.

As to the public sector, it is scarcely possible to expect efficient and honest management of enterprises run by a bureaucracy that is not under political control. Who will prevent officials vested with authority to run public enterprises from dipping into the till, from squeezing the state just as they squeeze the private businessman? If conspicuous peculation is eliminated, more inconspicuous forms abound. Where effective political control over a bureaucracy is lacking, there is no institutional means for preventing bureaucrats from exploiting their power position at the expense of both private entrepreneurs and public enterprise. (Under such conditions, of course, to expect a public sector to remedy the developmental weakness of the private sector is delusory.)

The condition described is scarcely one of equilibrium. Only a relatively passive bureaucracy, drugged by its own self-indulgence, can perpetuate its own regime indefinitely. With the growing pressure of international opinion and example, and the impact of bi-lateral and multi-lateral aid programs, systems of bureaucratic power are energized and thrown on the defensive. They must create more and more mass organizations as instruments for program administration. But the dissemination of organizational skills is the sowing of dragon's teeth. If the entrepreneurial community could organize power effectively, it might impose a middle class revolution on the government, establish the rule of law, create a favorable environment for economic development and administrative efficiency by means of a democratically controlled bureaucracy. This has been the history of the Western democracies, and to a considerable extent also of Japan. The pre-condition, however, was a relatively weak bureaucracy and a socially entrenched burgher class.

The alternative course of events is, unfortunately, more likely. In the inter-organizational struggle reaped from the Cadmean harvest, victory is more likely to go to a mass-movement led by a political fraction under the leadership of an embittered intelligentsia group of the type described above under political parties. Such a group will build a new Thebes. It may embrace the doctrines of international Communism or, perhaps more likely, it will espouse a national-chauvinistic ideology, fascistic and xenophobic. Among the chief targets of its hatred will be the pariah entrepreneurial community, and so its program will almost surely involve destruction of this group and expansion of state power through nationalization and government monopoly of industrial development.[24] It will, of course,

[24] For an extremely suggestive discussion of the emergence of mass-movement, single

bring the bureaucracy under control. But the price of this kind of political development is social disaster—the loss of individual freedom and the risk of international war.

Bureaucracy and the Legislature

With but few exceptions the history of parliamentarism in the new nations is without lustre. In many, as in Egypt, military regimes have suspended representative institutions altogether, after a period of noisy but ineffective experimentation with legislative bodies and ephemeral constitutions. "Guided democracy" is Sukarno's alternative to parliamentary politics after a period of unsuccessful trial and error. Turkey, Pakistan, Burma, the Sudan, many Latin American states fit this pattern. Since the revolution of 1932, Thailand has tried a variety of parliamentary systems and constitutions, but they have uniformly been pliant tools for the group in power. Since the first republic in 1912 the Chinese have followed parliamentarism as a will-o'-the-wisp.

Notable exceptions have been India and the Philippines. In both instances several decades of vigorous parliamentary experience under colonial rule preceded independence,[25] and the political habits established during dependency have stood these nations in good stead since obtaining their freedom. But even in these exceptional cases, closer scrutiny reveals serious weaknesses in parliamentary power.

The case of Japan is instructive for, with all its weaknesses, the Diet has shown itself, despite black periods and long-term deficiencies, a notably effective legislative body. Perhaps the astonishing success of Japan's industrialization drive and the

relative efficiency of its bureaucracy is not unrelated to this fact.

If we ask for an explanation of the miserable record of parliamentary institutions in the new nations, we may look for an answer to the range of parliamentary substructures already examined in this chapter. A parliament or congress is not just an assembly to pass resolutions. As a supreme decision-making body for a polity, it must effectively represent its constituencies and have weapons with which to command the obedience of the governmental apparatus, the bureaucracy.

Among the supports of the legislative body are the electoral system, political parties, and interest groups. Unless the assemblymen have been chosen through an electoral process in which significant choices are registered, they cannot have a meaningful popular mandate. Each or all of the candidates for election may be equally unrepresentative and unresponsive to political demands. If picked up by a ruling clique under plebiscitary conditions, or chosen in a popularity contest or bandwagon-hopping situation where electoral divisions reflect no significant political differences, what and whom do they represent?

As I have suggested above, electoral ineffectiveness largely prevails in the new nations—with some notable exceptions—and the extension of bureaucratic control into local government is one of the reasons for this ineffectiveness. Hence the parliamentary system is undermined at its foundations in most of the new nations, and bureaucratic patterns can be identified as a key element in this weakness.

Unless the political party system is vigorous, assemblies lack an indispensable means of organizing their activities. It is true, I believe, that a strong one-party system can achieve effective control over a bureaucracy. In such a case, however, formally elected parliaments become puppets of the party. If a collegial process does take place in top-level decision making, it is likely to be in a central or political

[footnote 24 continued
party regimes, see Robert C. Tucker, "Towards a Comparative Politics of Movement-Regimes," American Political Science Review, 55 (June 1961), 281–289. Anti-semitism and the myth of racial superiority were the typical signs of such a path in European political development.
[25] Plus, in the Philippine case, the energetic parliamentarism of the Malolos Constitution during the transition period to American rule.

committee of the party rather than in the formal legislature.

One requisite of effective parliamentary life seems to be a vigorous and loyal opposition. But as we have seen, the lack of an effectively organized spoils system in the bureaucracy is one of the reasons why opposition parties are unlikely to be either loyal or unified. Dissident elements take on a sectarian character, and only those driven by fanatical devotion to an alternative political formula are willing, as we have seen, to devote the time and energy needed for the creation of opposition parties or fractions. Such parties undermine the legislative process. They use their positions to disrupt legislation rather than to modify it. Their fanaticism prevents unity as well as loyalty in their opposition. Here again, a fundamental basis of parliamentary vigor is lacking, and one of the contributory factors is the merit and personal patronage system in a bureaucracy oriented to careerism and seniority.

The third pillar of parliamentary vigor is a proliferation of associational interest groups, prepared to speak on behalf of the myriad functional interests of a complex society. Here again, as we have already seen, the weakness of such associations in the new nations, and especially the tendency for bureaucrats to control what associations do exist, deprives legislatures of a major source of independent ideas for policy and for critique of the bureaucracy's performance. In a functioning democracy it is in the bureaucrat's interest to encourage access of interest groups to the legislator—assuming that the bureaucrat's program is already a response, in some degree, to the demands made by the interest groups. In the new nations, by contrast, it is often against the bureaucrat's interest for such a liaison to occur unless the groups are securely under bureaucratic control. Independent interest groups might criticize administrative performance, providing legislators with ammunition for use in establishing legislative supremacy.

But all of these factors are indirect. They involve legislative weaknesses based on non-bureaucratic factors in which bureaucratic factors play an indirect part. In addition, there are reasons for legislative weakness which can be directly attributed to the interaction of bureaucrats with parliamentary bodies. These include matters of *finance* and *policy*.

FINANCE

The traditional basis of parliamentary power in the Western democracies was control over the purse. The need of rulers to seek authorization for new taxes from the representatives of the burghers forced them to limit administrative arbitrariness as a quid pro quo.

In the new nations, under the doctrine that democracy is enhanced by universal suffrage, the vote has been given to a mass public, composed largely of poor peasants and workers who lack any resources for tax purposes. Conversely, those elements of the population which have the most wealth, and hence provide the most promising base for public revenues, are legislatively impotent or disfranchised. The business community in the new states is often composed largely of aliens who, as a matter of constitutional law, are deprived of the vote. Others are drawn from marginal or pariah communities within the state, as we have seen, and lack political power. Even if they can vote, they are swamped in electoral districts where the majority community naturally wins.

Decisions about taxation, therefore, largely involve schedules under which those formally represented in parliament impose taxes upon elements in the population which are not represented.

When those who might pay but are not effectively represented in parliament are called upon to supply the lion's share of the public revenues, it is not surprising that they resist payment—on a principle familiar to all Americans: "no taxation without representation." When revenue officers approach them suggesting that they pay their taxes, they not unexpectedly employ their sharp wits to find ways to evade. One of the most effective ways is to share part of their wealth with the tax collector in order to avoid sharing more of their wealth with the state. Since the bureaucrats are notably underpaid everywhere, and especially in poor countries whose public services expand more rapidly than their national income, they have powerful economic motives for collusion.

To the extent that this situation prevails, bureaucrats even have expedient reasons for encouraging legislatures to impose penalizing taxes and regulations upon the business community. Such measures do not strike at the apparent interests of the majority of the constituents, and they provide a basis for bureaucratic self-enrichment.

A second financial factor has become increasingly important in recent years, namely the extent to which the revenues of many new nations come from external sources. To cite an extreme case, Viet Nam, "more than half of the governmental revenues are directly contributed by American aid, and most of the rest comes from taxes levied on the U.S.-supported commercial import program."[26] While extreme, this situation is typical of many countries, ranging from Korea and Formosa around the Asian rimland to some of the new African countries at the opposite end. The oil-rich lands of the Middle East similarly depend on their royalties.

Insofar as foreign financing prevails, it is apparent that legislatures must again act without effective power. They may adopt budgets expressing a hope for

[26] John D. Montgomery, "Political Dimensions of Foreign Aid," in Ralph Braibanti and J. J. Spengler, eds., *Tradition, Values and Socio-Economic Development*, Durham, N.C., Duke University Press, 1961, p. 266. Montgomery goes on to note that only 15,000 of the total population of 12.3 million paid income taxes, of whom 12,500 were military and civil bureaucrats paying only a nominal amount.

foreign aid, but are scarcely in a position to make the decisive judgment. Even a country like India, which is more nearly self-supporting than most, has adopted development programs which call for substantial foreign subventions. Success in obtaining these funds depends, in large measure, upon bureaucratic rather than political performance. It is the national planners and the diplomatic representatives of the new nations, the bureau chiefs and counterparts who negotiate with their opposite numbers in the USOMs, international banks, and specialized agency headquarters, who influence the extent and type of foreign aid received. Thus external financing serves, effectively, to reinforce bureaucratic control at the expense of legislative authority.

A third major source of revenue in many developing countries consists of income from state monopolies, lotteries, and other income-producing ventures. Here again, elected representatives have only marginal influence. It is perhaps true that these programs rest upon prior legislative authorization—although even this is not always the case—but, once established, such programs become relatively autonomous bureaucratic empires. The scale of revenue depends upon the economics of the operation, and the skill with which they are managed. Even those which lose money have revenues of their own which can be manipulated to political effect.

If the legislatures are deeply handicapped in their efforts to control public revenues as contrasted with bureaucratic influence in these processes, the same is true of budgetary and expenditures controls. Although data are weak, I do not fear refutation of the statement that in very few of the new nations do the budgetary systems actually used offer legislatures an effective instrument for control over the bureaucracy. Generally old-fashioned types of line-item budget, without much distinction between capital and current expense items, are furnished by the administration. Such budgets may enable the legislators to play bureaucratic politics, supporting their friends in the bureaucracy and punishing their enemies, but they give them no effective weapon for influencing the content and conduct of governmental work. Even where a performance budget has been established, as in the Philippines, it remains largely unimplemented while the legislators cling to the particularistic advantages that the old, line-item budget gives them. The bureaucrats are probably also reluctant to implement the performance budget because in the process they would be compelled to reveal crucial defects in their own performance.

An extreme case, but perhaps illustrative, is that of Bolivia, whose budget office and procedures were created in 1928 in accordance with recommendations of the American Kemmerer mission. A more recent American expert writes of the current state of the Bolivian budget, which includes national and local government expenditures, that it:

". . . is prepared by an office that has twelve employees, half of whom have only stenographic and clerical duties. No distinction between capital and current expenses is indicated. Functionally, expenses are broken down by agency into 'Salaries' and 'Other Expenses.' Thus six 'professionals' prepare a budget of better than thirty million dollars . . .

". . . only once in the last thirty-one years has the Congress approved the budget prior to the beginning of the fiscal year. Phrased differently, in thirty of the last thirty-one years, the fiscal year has been at least two-thirds over before the Congress has approved the budget."[27]

In the matter of expenditures control, legislatures in developed systems rely upon some form of auditing which enables them to judge the extent to which funds have been spent in accord with the law. Here again, although the documentation is inadequate, I suggest that in most of

[27] Allan R. Richards, *Administration—Bolivia and the United States*, Albuquerque, University of New Mexico, 1961, pp 11–12.

the new nations legislatures lack effective machinery for auditing administrative spending. Even where, under technical assistance, new tools of accounting and auditing have been provided, they have been largely conceived for management purposes, and hence have perhaps strengthened the internal control system of the bureaucracy, the office of president or prime minister, but not the legislature as a political control center.

No doubt these financial powers of legislative bodies are not highly effective in many of the industrially developed countries themselves. It may also be that such procedures as the line-item budget served a useful purpose in helping legislators achieve effective control over bureaucrats, just as the spoils system did. However, these techniques can also be used for personal patronage and favoritism as well as to strengthen party organization. Thus the crucial test is not so much the particular techniques of financial control used—important as they may be—as the way or the purposes for which they are employed.

The position taken here is that, whatever the weaknesses of parliamentary financial controls in developed countries, they have been strong enough to give legislatures substantial leverage in their struggle to impose the rule of law and political policy upon officials. The same cannot be said of most legislative assemblies in the developing countries. But without such controls, how can these bodies hope to formulate enforceable laws?

POLICY

Needless to say, financial control is only one of the supports of legislative effectiveness. Even a good budgetary system—such as may exist in the Philippines, Viet Nam, or India—does not by itself assure parliamentary control over the bureaucracy. If the political party, electoral and associational base is weak, parliaments will still be weak. An effective legislature must also be able to formulate clear and mutually compatible laws. The strange fruit of legislative necrosis is to be found in the realm of policy making.

According to our conventional model, adoption by congress or parliament of a law gives it legitimacy in the popular mind, enforceability through the courts, and a binding authority upon the bureaucracy charged with its implementation. The source of this legitimacy is a political formula, or constitution, on which substantial consensus prevails throughout the population.

Where bureaucrats exercise considerable power, as in most of the new nations, they may themselves take the initiative in seeking legislative authorization for what they wish to do. When such legislation is adopted it does not represent political control over the bureaucracy so much as bureaucratic manipulation of the symbols of legitimacy.

A major source and symptom of weakness for legislatures is even more potent, namely the phenomenon of formalism. Laws on the statute books of the new nations are often not well enforced by the public bureaucracy. The prevalence of corruption in a country is an index of the extent to which bureaucrats are able and willing to violate laws or permit their violation. Bribes may be given to induce officials to perform their duties—as when granting licenses and permits—as well as to overlook non-performance.

Funds and personnel for the enforcement of a law may not be available, so that laws remain dead letters for lack of resources to implement them.

The lack of adequate information—related to the weakness of interest groups—means that legislation is often inherently unenforceable because of technical defects in draftsmanship and unfounded assumptions as well as mutually contradictory norms.

To the extent that formalism prevails in legislation, laws enacted by legislatures cannot be regarded as real decisions. Rather, we have a process of pseudo rule making. It may, of course, be difficult for legislators to tell whether a particular bill or amendment would or would not be enforceable. Moreover, it must be acutely frustrating for a conscientious legislature to learn that hours of work invested in the preparation of a law were of no avail because of non- or mal-administration. Such frustration leads to a variety of responses, including an apathetic disillusionment with the legislative process and hence diversion of interest to other more rewarding types of activity, including direct intervention in administration processes, appointments, contracts, etc. Another response might be to superimpose new, more drastic laws upon the old, unenforced ones, as though a more severe piece of formalistic legislation could correct failures in a milder rule on the same subject. Other legislators, in disgust, become apathetic and turn to private pleasures. The cynicism and hostility of the political fractions toward the whole legislative process is increased.

Here it ought to be acknowledged that one of the forces which aggravates legislative formalism is foreign pressure, precisely because international agencies and aid programs tend to be preoccupied with technical matters of economic development and administration rather than the crucial problem of political development. For example, pressure is applied to the new nations to live up to international standards in a wide variety of fields—health, labor, statistics, legal standards, civil rights, etc. Indeed, model codes are often drafted and adopted by international bodies to provide a guide for developing countries. The governments concerned find that their international status can be improved at relatively little cost merely by putting such laws on their statute books. The prevalence of legal formalism makes it easy to do this since, if laws are widely disregarded, one can virtually adopt any law that will satisfy the foreign critics without having to worry about enforcement. Thus international standards may weaken legislative vigor without securing the hoped-for substantive effects. Such model legislation, indeed, may contribute to administrative corruption and popular disgust with governmental processes. Examples could be cited from laws setting minimum wage standards and regulating labor relations, providing for the control of drugs and food, for sanitary inspection and quarantine of pests.

At a different level, under the impact of technical assistance programs, reorganization plans may be submitted to institutionalize a distinction between line and staff, to decentralize a government agency, establish a position classification scheme, or organize an "O & M" program. Legislation and even formal bureaucratic reorganization to meet these recommendations—including, especially, expansion of the number of governmental units and positions—often follows. But the advisers responsible are subsequently discouraged to find that the anticipated benefits do not result. Indeed, the costs of government may be increased, but not the output of services. The changes have merely rearranged the formalistic surface structures, but not seriously affected the underlying social and power structure which actually determines bureaucratic action.

It is often thought that a constitution provides the major foundation for effective parliamentary rule. However, we might gain a different perspective on this relationship if we tried reversing it, i.e., suggesting that effective legislative performance validates a constitution. When a legislature is unable to make enforceable decisions, public disillusionment and apathy turns against the constitution as well as the assembly. When the constitution itself rests upon a precarious base of support, reflecting the wishes of a small intelligentsia or aristocratic group, it has to legitimate itself by growing success. Without such success, the system is discredited and easily overthrown. Consensus fails to develop.

It would seem that in the transitional societies, with but few exceptions—the Philippines, India, Meiji Japan—parliamentary structures have proved expensive but largely fruitless. They can be given life only by a middle-class revolution capable of imposing the rule of law on the bureaucracy. If a mass-movement regime is installed, they will be totally crushed as a useless decoration. So long as bureaucratic rule predominates, the assembly may be tolerated as an additional crutch to give some color of legitimacy to the administration, but it will not be permitted to exercise the substance of political power.

Parliamentary and constitutional theory in the advanced countries assumes that legislative action provides an effective lever for the control of bureaucratic behavior. My analysis leads me to conclude that this theory works only under special conditions, and that the formal creation of an elected and voting assembly by no means assures its success.

PART V

THE POLITICS OF SOCIAL STRATIFICATION AND MOBILIZATION

INTRODUCTION

One of the few areas of agreement among students of emerging nations is the observation that the fissures, divergencies, and contradictions in developing polities are more deeply rooted than in the industrialized nations in the West. Class structure, social distance, and enormous economic disparities constitute the basis for a highly stratified social order. At the same time, even more divisive vertical cleavages set people apart on grounds of religion, ethnicity, and commitments to symbols and institutions of the past.

The presence of social stratification by itself is not, of course, the factor which distinguishes the developing nations, for all societies are stratified. It is, rather, the great distance separating strata and the barriers to social mobility which sets them apart from the industrialized nations. In the developing nations, there is simply a greater likelihood that an individual will be born, spend his life, and die as a member of the same social stratum that may be the case in industrialized societies. The two problems of social distance between groups and obstacles to individual mobility, grounded as they are in economic factors, are exacerbated and reinforced by such socio-cultural influences as tradition and ascription.

It is important to recognize, however, the ease with which the differences between industrial and pre-industrial societies tend to become exaggerated when we confine ourselves to a consideration of the latter type of society alone. The contrasts between stratification systems are not as great when we take into account the fact that poverty in the United States tends to affect the same families generation after generation. Similarly, the life style of an Italian industrialist is only remotely related to that of a peasant family in southern Italy. Even today, family background still remains a critical determinant in predicting educational attainment, career routes, and even the life expectancy of a young man in England. In short, the contrast between the social structures of the developing polities and those of the industrialized nations is one of degree rather than of kind.

The importance of social stratification as a factor in society's potential for economic development was explored in the Sjoberg article contained in Part I of this volume. The three articles comprising Chapter 11 offer detailed treatment of some of the political implications of stratification patterns in developing societies.

In the first of these, Arthur L. Stinchcombe provides an analytical typology of stratification patterns in societies where the dominant economic mode is "agricultural enterprise"—that is, a property system in which agricultural production is intended for market. In urban communities occupation is likely to be the significant variable in determining status and position. Rural stratification patterns, on the other hand, are conditioned by property arrangements which affect the legal privileges, life styles, distributions of technical knowledge, and the political behavior and organizations of rural populations. Inasmuch as the economic base of the developing nations is agriculture and the preponderance of the population is rural, Stinchcombe's use of more refined analytical distinctions for understanding class relations and political behavior in rural areas is particularly appropriate for the student of political development. It should also be noted that the analytical distinctions Stinchcombe draws are not presented as empirical descriptions of any particular society. Rather, the article should be valued more for its contribution in raising appropriate theoretical questions about class relations and political behavior among those who derive their living from the soil.

Despite the numerical and economical importance of rural populations in the developing nations, students of development tend to look to other social sectors for sources of dynamic initiative toward modernization. This search derives from the expectation that the impetus toward development will come from groups which are less tradition-bound and more experienced in the organizational skills of national politics than are the rural elements. Although these requisite skills and qualities are more typical of the middle class, the article by Manning Nash points out that the middle class possesses neither the political power nor the numerical strength to achieve political dominance independently. It will be necessary for the middle class to work out an effective political alliance with other social groups who may find, at least for limited purposes, common cause with the modernizing aspirations of the middle class. Drawing primarily from the example of Guatemala, Nash asserts that the modernizing coalition most likely to arise will be one between the urban middle class and the rural-based Indian, a combination identical to that which joined forces in the modernization of Mexico earlier in this century and is described by Eric R. Wolf in Chapter 15.

The article by Martin Kilson highlights the influence of colonial rule on post-independence politics in African states. Kilson notes that, unlike Latin America where colonial rule was terminated during the nineteenth century, African nations acquired independence in relatively recent years. As a consequence, the imprint of colonial rule, which Kilson regards as the source of both modernization and political change in Africa, is still strongly felt in present-day African politics and intergroup relations. With independence, there has been an understandable decline in the influence of the metropolitan state itself, even though, as before, "expatriate interest groups" from the metropolitan state "continue their monopoly of the financial, industrial, technical and strategic ingredients of modernization." While they do, in a sense, represent vestigial holdovers from the colonial context, Kilson nonetheless recognizes that these interest groups have functioned in many ways as "colonial modernizers."

One of the areas most sharply affected by colonial rule in the developing societies of Africa has been that of social stratification patterns. More specifically, Kilson points out that certain regional, ethnic, tribal and religious groups acquired skills, attitudes, and preferred positions vis-à-vis the colonial administration and its expatriate groups which better equipped them to deal with the shape of the social changes taking place in the post-colonial period. The author discusses the factors which explain why particular groups attained favored positions which continue to benefit them to this day. For example, groups which resided in the areas of initial colonization gained a historical advantage over other groups; those groups living closest to the natural resources required for modernization gained similar advantages under colonial rule; and those groups holding positions of political power and authority in the indigeneous system secured favored status as a consequence of their political role in the maintenance of the colonial system.

In the portion of the article reproduced in this volume, the focus of concern is the effect of the indigenous elite, the masses, and the colonial modernizers on African modernization and political change. The author holds that, while there is in some respects an identity of interests between the indigenous elite and the colonial modernizers, the extension of the franchise to the masses is likely to introduce constraints on the way in which African elites will be able to pursue development goals. There is the possibility that the modernizing elites may utilize the power of the state in order to modernize as they see fit, thus raising the question of whether the African elites possess the skills and other qualifications which might warrant action independent of the restraints imposed upon them by the masses.

The political implications of the stratification, cleavage, and mobility patterns found in the developing nations are linked to the way in which these patterns themselves are changed as a result of other modernizing impacts. A case can be made that these are potentially explosive societies which, under the impact of early modernization, will develop deep class antagonisms, a strident and combative style of class politics, and severe discontinuities resulting from an inability to adjust or adapt to change. A different emphasis is presented by Seymour Martin Lipset in Chapter 14 in an article which describes how social classes bent on pursuing their particular economic interests can perform a valuable integrative function. As Lipset has written elsewhere, "The organization of working class groups into trade unions or a labor party, for example, both creates a mechanism for the expression of conflict and, perhaps even more important, integrates the workers into the body politic by giving them a legitimate means of obtaining their wants."[1] Still another view is that voiced by Samuel P. Huntington, who perceives the hierarchical qualities of a highly stratified society as yielding benefits in the form of a deceleration of demands on political systems which have not developed the capacity to meet the problems, challenges, and demands confronting them. This position is explained at greater length in Chapter 14.

To the extent that the process of modernization involves change from one state to another, all developing nations are, in varying degrees, *transitional* societies. They are transitional, of course, not only in the political sphere but also in the psychological sphere, in the sense that individuals are being psychologically and socially uprooted and assaulted by experiences, ideas, and changes over which they have little control or understanding. On the one hand, a very persuasive case has been made that, in the short run at least, the rapid breakdown of traditional and conventional patterns of life may act as a destabilizing force, politically and in other ways as well. Most students of development, however, have taken the position that the assault of modernization on old beliefs, relationships, and values is frequently linked to the emergence of new patterns which are essential to the processes of modernization and development.

Karl Deutsch, in a seminal article in Chapter 12, asserts that governments intent upon achieving the rapid social transformations characteristic of modernization may be required to pursue conscious policies of social mobilization. In the words of Deutsch, social mobilization is defined as "the process in which major clusters of old social, economic, and psychological commitments are eroded or broken and people become available for new patterns of socialization and behavior." Although this process comprises two distinct stages—breaking away from the old, and secondly, inducting mobilized persons into relatively new patterns of group membership, organization, and commitment—Deutsch is more concerned both theoretically and methodologically with the new configurations.

The implications of social mobilization for political development are understandably far-reaching, because a change in the quality of politics occurs by virtue of changes in the range of the human needs which impinge upon the political process. The transformation of social needs on a large scale—particularly in areas such as housing, employment, social security, municipal services, medical care, and so forth—creates impossible demands on governments whose administrative and resource capacities have not adapted or kept pace with growing and divergent needs of a modernizing population.

[1] Seymour Martin Lipset, "Political Sociology," in Robert K. Merton, Leonard Broom, and Leonard S. Cottrell (eds.), *Sociology Today* (New York: Basic Books, Inc., 1959),

More specifically, the processes set in motion by social mobilization generate pressures for increases in the scope of government, expansion of the relative size of the government sector in the economy, and, consequently, an increase in the capabilities of the government. These increments to the functions and roles of government in developing nations create needs for increases in the numbers and qualifications of government personnel, an expansion in governmental offices and institutions, and significant improvements in administrative organization and efficiency.

Similar to its impact on government, social mobilization also tends to exert pressure for a general transformation of political elites. Their numbers are expanded, their functions are broadened and transformed, and their recruitment and communications are changed. The burgeoning numbers of mobilized citizens and the greater scope and urgency of their needs for political decisions and governmental services often result in enhanced political participation, but with a time lag. Likewise, there is a tendency toward a greater voting participation on the part of those already enfranchised and an extension of the franchise itself to additional groups within the population. Finally, Deutsch suggests that rapid social mobilization may be expected to promote the consolidation of the states whose peoples already share the same language, culture, and major social institutions, a process to which we will return in the final chapter of this volume.

In a tightly reasoned and methodologically rigorous article on the relationship between social structure and political participation, Norman H. Nie, G. Bingham Powell, Jr., and Kenneth Prewitt explore some of the critical issues concealed in the social and individual transformations associated with economic development. Although their data is largely drawn from the more economically advanced nations, the analysis has relevance for an understanding of the relative impact of changes in class structure, organizational involvement, and residence patterns on political behavior in the developing nations as well.

The findings of the authors lend support to the contention that economic development leads to a broadening of political participation by expanding the middle class and increasing organizational involvement by individuals. The components of economic development which most markedly affect mass political participation are social class and organizational involvement; yet, at the same time, the authors are careful to stress that the impact of these factors on levels of political participation is not only differentially weighted but achieved by way of different causal paths. The differences in causal linkage patterns identified by the study relate to five basic attitude sets: (1) sense of citizen duty, (2) basic information about politics, (3) perceived stake in political outcomes, (4) sense of political efficacy, and (5) attentiveness to political matters.

Regarding differential impact, the authors maintain that organizational involvement is a much stronger indicator of political participation than is either social status or place of residence. For example, the tendency of a citizen to be politically active is shown to be only marginally influenced by his place of residence. On the other hand, the strength of the correlation between organizational involvement and political participation suggests a basis for speculating that, even before economic development has induced changes in social structure and levels of industrialization and urbanization, it may be possible for a modernizing government to stimulate greater political participation by encouraging and facilitating organizational involvement by its citizens.

Chapter 11

Social Stratification and Group Politics

AGRICULTURAL ENTERPRISE AND RURAL CLASS RELATIONS[1]

Arthur L. Stinchcombe

Marx's fundamental innovation in stratification theory was to base a theory of formation of classes and political development on a theory of the bourgeois enterprise.[2] Even though some of his conceptualization of the enterprise is faulty, and though some of his propositions about the development of capitalist enterprise were in error, the idea was sound: One of the main determinants of class relations in different parts of the American economy is, indeed, the economic and administrative character of the enterprise.[3]

But Marx's primary focus was on class relations in cities. In order to extend his mode of analysis to rural settings, we need an analysis of rural enterprises. The purpose of this paper is to provide such an analysis and to suggest the typical patterns of rural class relations produced in societies where a type of rural enterprise predominates.

Property and Enterprise in Agriculture

Agriculture everywhere is much more organized around the institutions of property than around those of occupation. Unfortunately, our current theory and research on stratification is built to fit an urban environment, being conceptually organized around the idea of occupation. For instance, an important recent monograph on social mobility classifies all farmers together and regards them as an unstratified source of urban workers.[4]

SOURCE. Arthur L. Stinchcombe, "Agricultural Enterprise and Rural Class Relations," *The American Journal of Sociology*, 67, 165–176, September 1961. Reprinted by permission of The University of Chicago Press. Copyright 1961 by The University of Chicago Press.

[1] James S. Coleman, Jan Hajda, and Amitai Etzioni have done me the great service of being intensely unhappy with a previous version of this paper. I have not let them see this version.
[2] This formulation derives from Talcott Parsons' brief treatment in *The Structure of Social Action* (Glencoe, Ill.: Free Press, 1949), pp. 488–495.
[3] Cf. especially Robert Blauner, "Industrial Differences in Work Attitudes and Work Institutions," paper delivered at the 1960 meeting of the American Sociological Association, in which he compares class relations and the alienation of the working class in continuous-process manufacturing with that in mechanical mass-production industries.

[4] S. M. Lipset and R. Bendix, *Social Mobility in Industrial Society* (Berkeley, Calif.: University of California Press, 1959). The exceedingly high rate of property mobility which characterized American rural social structures when the national ideology was being formed apparently escapes their attention. Yet Lipset discusses the kind of mobility characteristic of frontiers and small farm systems very well in his *Agrarian Socialism* (Berkeley, Calif.: University of California Press, 1950), p. 33. In 1825 occupational mobility only concerned a small part of

359

The theory of property systems is very much underdeveloped. Property may be defined as a legally defensible vested right to affect decisions on the use of economically valuable goods. Different decisions (for instance, technical decisions versus decisions on distributions of benefits) typically are affected by different sets of rights held by different sets of people. These legally defensible rights are, of course, important determinants of the actual decision-making structure of any social unit which acts with respect to goods.

But a property system must be conceived as the typical interpenetration of legally vested rights to affect decisions and the factual situation which determines who actually makes what decisions on what grounds. For example, any description of the property system of modern business which ignores the fact that it is economically impossible for a single individual to gain majority stock holdings in a large enterprise, and politically impossible to organize an integrated faction of dispersed stockholders except under unusual conditions, would give a grossly distorted view. A description of a property system, then, has to take into account the internal politics of typical enterprises, the economic forces that typically shape decisions, the political situation in the society at large which is taken into account in economic decisions, the reliability and cost of the judiciary, and so forth. The same property law means different things for economic life if decisions on the distribution of income from agricultural enterprise are strongly affected by urban *rentiers*' interests rather than a smallholding peasantry.

It is obviously impossible to give a complete typology of the legal, economic, and political situations which determine the decision-making structure within agri-

cultural organizations for all societies and for all important decisions. Instead, one must pick certain frequent constellations of economic, technical, legal, and labor recruitment conditions that tend to give rise to a distinct structure of decision-making within agricultural enterprises.

By an "enterprise" I mean a social unit which has and exercises the power to commit a given parcel of land to one or another productive purpose, to achieve which it decides the allocation of chattels and labor on the land.[5] The rights to affect decisions on who shall get the benefit from that production may not be, and quite often are not, confined within the enterprise, as defined here. The relation between the enterprise and power over the distribution of benefit is one of the central variables in the analysis to follow, for instance, distinguishing tenancy systems from smallholding systems.

Besides the relation between productive decisions and decisions on benefits, some of the special economic, political, and technical characteristics which seem most important in factual decision-making structure will be mentioned, such as the value of land, whether the "owner" has police power over or kinship relations with labor, the part of production destined for market, the amount of capital required besides the land, or the degree of technical rationalization. These are, of course, some of the considerations Marx dealt with when describing the capitalist enterprise, particularly in its factory form. Plantations, manors, family-size tenancies, ranches, or family farms tend to occur only in certain congenial economic, technical, and political environments and to be affected in their internal structure by those environments.

[footnote 4 continued
the population of the United States. The orientation of most nineteenth-century Americans to worldly success was that of Tennyson's "Northern Farmer, New Style": "But proputty, proputty sticks, an' proputty graws."

[5] Occasionally, the decisions to commit land to a given crop and to commit labor and chattels to cultivation are made separately, e.g., in cotton plantations in the post bellum American South. The land is committed to cotton by the landowner, but labor and chattels are committed to cultivation by the sharecropper.

A description and analysis of empirical constellations of decision-making structures cannot, by its untheoretical nature, claim to be complete. Moreover, I have deliberately eliminated from consideration all precommercial agriculture, not producing for markets, because economic forces do not operate in the same ways in precommercial societies and because describing the enterprise would involve providing a typology of extended families and peasant communities, which would lead us far afield. I have also not considered the "community-as-enterprise" systems of the Soviet sphere and of Israel because these are as much organizational manifestations of a social movement as they are economic institutions.[6]

Systems of commercialized manors, family-sized tenancies, family smallholdings, plantations, and ranches cover most of the property systems found in commercialized agriculture outside eastern Europe and Israel. And each of these property systems tends to give rise to a distinctive class system, differing in important respects from that which develops with any of the other systems. Presenting argument and evidence for this proposition is the central purpose of this paper.

Variations in Rural Class Relations

Rural class structure in commercialized agriculture varies in two main ways: the criteria which differentiate the upper and lower classes and the quality and quantity of intraclass cultural, political, and organizational life. In turn, the two main criteria which may differentiate classes are legal privileges and style of life. And two main qualities of class culture and organization are the degree of familiarity with technical culture of husbandry and the degree of political activation and organiza-

[6] However, the origin of the *kolkhoz* or collective farm does seem to depend partly on the form of prerevolutionary agriculture. Collectivization seems to occur most rapidly when a revolutionary government deals with an agriculture which was previously organized into large-scale capitalist farms.

tion. This gives four characteristics of rural class structures which vary with the structure of enterprises.

First, rural class systems vary in the extent to which classes are differentiated by legal privileges. Slaves and masters, peons and *hacendados*, serfs and lords, colonial planters and native labor, citizen farmers employing aliens as labor—all are differentiated by legal privileges. In each case the subordinate group is disenfranchised, often bound to the land or to the master, denied the right to organize, denied access to the courts on an equal basis, denied state-supported education, and so on.

Second, rural stratification systems vary in the sharpness of differentiation of style of life among the classes. Chinese gentry used to live in cities, go to school, compete for civil service posts, never work with their hands, and maintain extended families as household units. On each criterion, the peasantry differed radically. In contrast, in the northern United States, rich and poor farmers live in the country, attend public schools, consume the same general kinds of goods, work with their hands, at least during the busy seasons, and live in conjugal family units. There were rwo radically different ways of life in rural China; in the northern United States the main difference between rich and poor farmers is wealth.

Third, rural class systems vary in the distribution of the technical culture of husbandry. In some systems the upper classes would be completely incapable of making the decisions of the agricultural enterprise: they depend on the technical lore of the peasantry. At the other extreme, the Spanish-speaking labor force of the central valley in California would be bewildered by the marketing, horticultural, engineering, and transportation problems of a large-scale irrigated vegetable farm.

Fourth, rural classes vary in their degree of political activity and organization, in their sensitivity or apathy to political issues, in their degree of intraclass communication and organization, and in their degree of political education and competence.

Our problem, then, is to relate types of agricultural enterprises and property systems to the patterns of class relations in rural social life. We restrict our attention to enterprises producing for markets, and of these we exclude the community-as-enterprise systems of eastern Europe and Israel.

Class Relations in Types of Agricultural Enterprise

THE MANORIAL OR HACIENDA SYSTEM

The first type of enterprise to be considered here is actually one form of pre-commercial agriculture, divided into two parts: cultivation of small plots for subsistence by a peasantry, combined with cultivation by customary labor dues of domain land under the lord's supervision. It fairly often happens that the domain land comes to be used for commercial crops, while the peasant land continues to be used for subsistence agriculture. There is no rural labor market but, rather, labor dues or labor rents to the lord, based on customary law or force. There is a very poorly developed market in land; there may be, however, an active market in estates, where the estates include as part of their value the labor due to the lord. But land as such, separate from estates and from manors as going concerns, is very little an article of commerce. Estates also tend to pass as units in inheritance, by various devices of entailment, rather than being divided among heirs.[7]

The manorial system is characterized by the exclusive access of the manor lord (or *hacendado* in Latin America) to legal process in the national courts. A more or less unfree population holding small bits of land in villein or precarious tenure is bound to work on the domain land of the lord, by the conditions of tenure or by personal peonage. Unfree tenures or debts tend to be inheritable, so that in case of need the legal system of the nation will subject villeins or peons to work discipline on the manor.

Some examples of this system are the hacienda system of Mexico up to at least 1920,[8] some areas in the Peruvian highlands at present,[9] medieval England,[10] East Germany before the reconstruction of agriculture into large-scale plantation and ranch agriculture,[11] the Austro-Hungarian Empire, in the main, up to at least 1848,[12] and many other European and South American systems at various times.

The manorial system rests on the assumptions that neither the value of land nor the value of labor is great and that calculation of productive efficiency by the managers of agricultural enterprise is not well developed. When landowners start making cost studies of the efficiency of forced versus wage labor, as they did, for instance, in Austria-Hungary in the first part of the nineteenth century, they find that wage labor is from two to four times as efficient.[13] When landowners' traditional level of income becomes insufficient to compete for prestige with the bourgeoisie, and they set

[7] In some cases, as in what was perhaps the world's most highly developed manorial system, in Chile, an estate often remains undivided as an enterprise but is held "together in the family as an undivided inheritance for some years, and not infrequently for a generation. This multiplies the number of actual owners [but not of haciendas], of rural properties in particular" (George M. McBride, *Chile: Land and Society* [New York: American Geographical Society, 1936,] p. 139).

[8] Frank Tannenbaum, *The Mexican Agrarian Revolution* (New York: Macmillian Co., 1929), pp. 91–133.
[9] Thomas R. Ford, *Man and Land in Peru* (Gainesville: University of Florida Press, 1955), pp. 93–95.
[10] Paul Vinogradoff, *The Growth of the Manor* (London: Swan Sonnenschein, 1905), pp. 212–235, 291–365.
[11] Max Weber, *Gesammelte Aufsätze zur Sozial- und Wirtschaftsgeschichte* (Tübingen: J. C. B. Mohr, 1924), pp. 471–474.
[12] Jerome Blum, *Noble Landowners and Agriculture in Austria, 1815–1848* (Baltimore: Johns Hopkins Press, 1948), pp. 23, 68–87.
[13] *Ibid.*, pp. 192–202.

about trying to raise incomes by increasing productivity, as they did in eastern Germany, the developmental tendency is toward capitalistic plantation or ranch agriculture.[14] When the waste and common become important for cattle- or sheep-raising and labor becomes relatively less important in production, enclosure movements drive precarious tenants off the land. When land becomes an article of commerce and the price and productivity of land goes up, tenancy by family farmers provides the lord with a comfortable income that can be spent in the capital city, without much worry about the management of crops. The farther the market penetrates agriculture, first creating a market for commodities, then for labor and land, the more economically unstable does the manorial economy become, and the more likely is the manor to go over to one of the other types of agricultural enterprise.

In summary, the manorial system combines in the lord and his agents authority over the enterprise and rulership or *Herrschaft* over dependent tenants. Classes are distinct in legal status. In style of life the manor lord moves on the national scene, often little concerned with detailed administration of his estate. He often keeps city residence and generally monopolizes education. Fairly often he even speaks a different language, for example, Latin among Magyar nobility, French in the Russian aristocracy, Spanish, instead of Indian dialects, in parts of Latin America.

The pattern of life of the subject population is very little dependent on market prices of goods. Consequently, they have little interest in political issues. Even less does the peasantry have the tools of political organization, such as education, experienced leadership, freedom of association, or voting power. Quite often, as, for example, in the Magyar areas of the Hapsburg monarchy or among the Indian tribes of Latin America, intraclass communication is hindered by language bar-

riers. A politically active and competent upper class confronts a politically apathetic, backward, and disenfranchised peasantry.

FAMILY-SIZE TENANCY

In family-size tenancy the operative unit of agriculture is the family enterprise, but property rights in the enterprise rest with *rentier* capitalists. The return from the enterprise is divided according to some rental scheme, either in money or in kind. The rent may be fixed, fixed with modification in years of bad harvest, or share.[15] The formal title to the land may not be held by the noncultivator—it is quite common for the "rent" on the land to be, in a legal sense, the interest on a loan secured by the land.

This type of arrangement seems to occur most frequently when the following five conditions are met: (*a*) land has very high productivity and high market price; (*b*) the crop is highly labor-intensive, and mechanization of agriculture is little developed; (*c*) labor is cheap; (*d*) there are no appreciable economies of scale in factors other than labor; and (*e*) the period of production of the crop is one year or less. These conditions are perhaps most fully met with the crops of rice and cotton, especially on irrigated land; yet such a system of tenancy is quite often found where the crops are potatoes or wheat and maize, even though the conditions are not fulfilled. A historical, rather than an economic, explanation is appropriate to these cases.

The correlation of tenancy arrangements with high valuation of land is established by a number of pieces of evidence. In Japan in 1944, most paddy (rice) land was in tenancy, and most upland fields were

[14] Weber, *op. cit.*, pp. 474–477.

[15] But share rents in commercialized agriculture are often indicators of the splitting of the enterprise, as discussed above: it most frequently reflects a situation in which land is committed to certain crops by the landlord and the landlord markets the crops, while the scheduling of work is done by the tenant and part of the risks are borne by him.

owner-operated.[16] The same was true in Korea in 1937.[17] South China, where land values were higher and irrigated culture more practiced,[18] had considerably higher rates of tenancy than did North China.[19] In Thailand tenancy is concentrated in the commercialized farming of the river valleys in central Siam.[20] In Japan, up to World War II, except for the last period (1935–40), every time the price of land went up, the proportion of land held in tenancy went up.[21]

The pattern of family-size tenancy was apparently found in the potato culture of Ireland before the revolution, in the wheat culture of pre-World War I Rumania[22] and also that of Bosnia-Herzegovina (now part of Yugoslavia) at the same period.[23] The sugar-cane regions of central Luzon are also farmed in family-size tenancies, though this is so uneconomical that, without privileged access to the American market, cane culture would disappear.[24] It also characterizes the cotton culture of the highly productive Nile Valley in Egypt[25] and the cotton culture of the Peruvian coast.[26] This pattern of small peasant farms with rents to landlords was also characteristic of prerevolutionary France[27] and southwest England during the Middle Ages.[28] In lowland Burma a large share of the rice land is owned by the Indian banking house of Chettyar,[29] and much of the rest of it is in tenancy to other landlords. The land-tenure system of Taiwan before the recent land reform was typical family-size tenancy.[30]

Perhaps the most remarkable aspect of this list is the degree to which this system has been ended by reform or revolution, becoming transformed, except in a few Communist states, into a system of small-holding farms. And even in Communist states the first transformation after the revolution is ordinarily to give the land to the tiller: only afterward are the peasants gathered into collective farms, generally in the face of vigorous resistance.

The system of *rentier* capitalists owning land let out in family farms (or *rentier* capitalists owning debts whose service requires a large part of farm income) seems extremely politically unstable. The French Revolution, according to De Tocqueville, was most enthusiastically received in areas in which there were small farms paying feudal dues (commuted to rent in money or in kind).[31] The eastern European systems of Rumania and parts of Yugoslavia were swept away after World War I in land reforms. Land reforms were also carried through in northern Greece, the Baltic states, and many of the succession states of the Hapsburg monarchy (the reform was specious in Hungary). A vigorous and long-lasting civil war raged in Ireland up to the time of independence,

[16] Sidney Klein, *The Pattern of Land Tenure Reform in East Asia* (New York: Bookman Associates, 1958), p. 227.

[17] *Ibid.*, p. 246.

[18] See Chan Han-Seng, *Landlord and Peasant in China* (New York: International Publishers, 1936), pp. 100–103.

[19] *Ibid.*, pp. 3–4; and Klein, *op. cit.*, p. 253.

[20] Erich H. Jacoby, *Agrarian Unrest in Southeast Asia* (New York: Columbia University Press, 1949), pp. 232–235.

[21] Ronald P. Dore, *Land Reform in Japan* (London: Oxford University Press, 1959), p. 21.

[22] Henry L. Roberts, *Rumania: The Political Problems of an Agrarian State* (New Haven, Conn.: Yale University Press, 1951), pp. 14–17; Tables IX, X, p. 363.

[23] Jozo Tomasevich, *Peasants, Politics, and Economic Change in Yugoslavia* (Stanford, Calif.: Stanford University Press, 1955), pp. 96–101, 355.

[24] Jacoby, *op. cit.*, pp. 181–191, 203–209.

[25] Doreen Warriner, *Land Reform and Development in the Middle East* (London: Royal Institute of International Affairs, 1957), pp. 25–26.

[26] Ford, *op. cit.*, pp. 84–85.

[27] Alexis de Tocqueville, *The Old Regime and the French Revolution* ("Anchor Books" [Garden City, N.Y.: Doubleday & Co., 1955]), pp. 23–25, 30–32.

[28] George Homans, *English Villagers of the Thirteenth Century* (Cambridge, Mass.: Harvard University Press, 1941), p. 21.

[29] Jacoby, *op. cit.*, pp. 73, 78–88.

[30] Klein, *op. cit.*, pp. 52–54, 235.

[31] De Tocqueville, *op. cit.*, p. 25

and its social base was heavily rural. The high-tenancy areas in central Luzon were the social base of the revolutionary Hukbalahaps during and after World War II. The Communist revolution in China had its first successes in the high-tenancy areas of the south. The number of peasant riots in Japan during the interwar period was closely correlated with the proportion of land held in tenancy.[32] Peasant rebellions were concentrated in Kent and southeast England during the Middle Ages.[33] In short, such systems rarely last through a war or other major political disturbance and constantly produce political tensions.

There are several causes of the political instability of such systems. In the first place, the issue in the conflict is relatively clear: the lower the rent of the *rentier* capitalists, the higher the income of the peasantry. The division of the product at harvest time or at the time of sale is a clear measure of the relative prerogatives of the farmer and the *rentier*.

Second, there is a severe conflict over the distribution of the risks of the enterprise. Agriculture is always the kind of enterprise with which God has a lot to do. With the commercialization of agriculture, the enterprise is further subject to great fluctuation in the gross income from its produce. *Rentiers*, especially if they are capitalists investing in land rather than aristocrats receiving incomes from feudal patrimony, shift as much of the risk of failure as possible to the tenant. Whether the rent is share or cash, the variability of income of the peasantry is almost never less, and is often more, than the variability of *rentiers'* income. This makes the income of the peasantry highly variable, contributing to their political sensitization.[34]

Third, there tends to be little social contact between the *rentier* capitalists living in the cities and the rural population. The *rentiers* and the farmers develop distinct styles of life, out of touch with each other. The *rentier* is not brought into contact with the rural population by having to take care of administrative duties on the farm; nor is he drawn into local government as a leading member of the community or as a generous sharer in the charitable enterprises of the village. The urban *rentier*, with his educated and often foreign speech, his cosmopolitan interests, his arrogant rejection of rustic life is a logical target of the rural community, whose only contact with him is through sending him money or goods.

Fourth, the leaders of the rural community, the rich peasants, are not vulnerable to expulsion by the landowners, as they would be were the landowners also the local government. The rich peasant shares at least some of the hardships and is opposed in his class interests to many of the same people as are the tenants. In fact, in some areas where the population pressure on the land is very great, the rich peasants themselves hold additional land in tenancy, beyond their basic holdings. In this case the leadership of the local community is not only not opposed to the interests of the tenants but has largely identical interests with the poor peasant.

Finally, the landowners do not have the protection of the peasants' ignorance about the enterprise to defend their positions, as do large-scale capitalist farmers. It is perfectly clear to the tenant farmer that he could raise and sell his crops just as well with the landlord gone as with him there. There is no complicated cooperative tillage that seems beyond the view of all but the

[32] Dore, *op. cit.*, p. 72 (cf. this data on tenancy disputes with the data on tenancy, p. 21).
[33] Homans, *op. cit.*, p. 119.
[34] Though they deal with smallholding systems, the connection between economic instability and political activism is argued by Lipset (*op. cit.*, pp. 26–29, 36) and by Rudolf Heberle (*Social Movements* [New York: Appleton-

Century-Crofts Inc., 1951], pp. 240–248; see also Jacoby, *op. cit.*, p. 246; and Daniel Lerner, *The Passing of Traditional Society* [Glencoe, Ill.: Free Press, 1958], p. 227). Aristotle noted the same thing: "it is a bad thing that many from being rich should become poor; for men of ruined fortunes are sure to stir up revolutions" (*Politics* 1266[b]).

landlord and his managers, as there may be in manorial, and generally is in large-scale capitalist, agriculture. The farmer knows as well or better than the landlord where seed and fertilizer is to be bought and where the crop can be sold. He can often see strategic investments unknown to his landlord that would alleviate his work or increase his yield.

At least in its extreme development, then, the landowning class in systems of family-size tenancy appears as alien, superfluous, grasping, and exploitative. Their rights in agricultural enterprise appear as an unjustifiable burden on the rustic classes, both to the peasantry and to urban intellectuals. No marked decrease in agricultural productivity is to be expected when they are dispossessed, because they are not the class that carries the most advanced technical culture of agriculture. Quite often, upon land reform the productivity of agriculture increases.[35]

So family-size tenancy tends to yield a class system with an enfranchised, formally free lower class which has a monopoly of technical culture. The style of life of the upper class is radically different from that of the lower class. The lower class tends to develop a relatively skilled and relatively invulnerable leadership in the richer peasantry and a relatively high degree of political sensitivity in the poorer peasantry. It is of such stuff that many radical populist and nationalist movements are made.

FAMILY SMALLHOLDING

Family smallholding has the same sort of enterprises as does family tenancy, but rights to the returns from the enterprise are more heavily concentrated in the class of farmers. The "normal" property holding is about the size requiring the work of two adults or less. Probably the most frequent historical source of such systems is out of family-tenancy systems by way of land reform or revolution. However, they also arise through colonization of farmlands

carried out under governments in which large landlords do not have predominant political power, for instance, in the United States and Norway. Finally, it seems that such systems tend to be produced by market forces at an advanced stage of industrialization. There is some evidence that farms either larger or smaller than those requiring about two adult laborers tend to disappear in the industrial states of western Europe.[36]

Examples of such systems having a relatively long history are the United States outside the "Black Belt" in the South, the ranch areas of the West, and the central valleys of California, Serbia after some time in the early nineteenth century,[37] France after the great revolution, most of Scandinavia,[38] much of Canada, Bulgaria since 1878,[39] and southern Greece since sometime in the nineteenth century. Other such systems which have lasted long enough to give some idea of their long-term development are those created in eastern Europe after World War I; good studies of at least Rumania[40] and Yugoslavia[41] exist. Finally, the system of family smallholding created in Japan by the American-induced land reform of 1946 has been carefully studied.[42]

Perhaps the best way to begin analysis of this type of agricultural enterprise is to note that virtually all the costs of production are fixed. Labor in the family holding is, in some sense, "free": family members have to be supported whether they work or not,

---

[35] See, e.g., Dore, *op. cit.*, pp. 213–219.

[36] Folke Dovring, *Land and Labor in Europe, 1900–1950* (The Hague: Martinus Nijhoff, 1956), pp. 115–118. The median size of the farm unit, taking into consideration the type of crops grown on different sized farms, ranged from that requiring one man-year in Norway to two man-years in France, among the nations on the Continent.

[37] Tomasevich, *op. cit.*, pp. 38–47.

[38] Dovring, *op. cit.*, p. 143.

[39] Royal Institute of International Affairs, *Nationalism* (London: Oxford University Press, 1939), p. 106.

[40] Roberts, *op. cit.*

[41] Tomasevich, *op. cit.*

[42] Dore, *op. cit.*

so they might as well work. Likewise, the land does not cost rent, and there is no advantage to the enterprise in leaving it out of cultivation. This predominance of fixed costs means that production does not fall with a decrease in prices, as it does in most urban enterprises where labor is a variable cost.[43] Consequently, the income of smallholders varies directly with the market price of the commodities they produce and with variability in production produced by natural catastrophe. Thus, the political movements of smallholders tend to be directed primarily at maintenance of the price of agricultural commodities rather than at unemployment compensation or other "social security" measures.

Second, the variability of return from agricultural enterprise tends to make credit expensive and, at any rate, makes debts highly burdensome in bad years. Smallholders' political movements, therefore, tend to be opposed to creditors, to identify finance capital as a class enemy: Jews, the traditional symbol of finance capital, often come in for an ideological beating. Populist movements are often directed against "the bankers." Further, since cheap money generally aids debtors, and since small farmers are generally debtors, agrarian movements tend to support various kinds of inflationary schemes. Small farmers do not want to be crucified on a cross of gold.

Third, agrarian movements, except in highly advanced societies, tend to enjoy limited intraclass communication, to be poor in politically talented leaders, relatively unable to put together a coherent, disciplined class movement controlled from below.[44] Contributions to the party treasury tend to be small and irregular,

like the incomes of the small farmers. Peasant movements are, therefore, especially prone to penetration by relatively disciplined political interests, sometimes Communist and sometimes industrial capital.[45] Further, such movements tend to be especially liable to corruption,[46] since they are relatively unable to provide satisfactory careers for political leaders out of their own resources.

Moreover, at an early stage of industrial and commercial development in a country without large landowners, the only sources of large amounts of money available to politicians are a few urban industrial and commercial enterprises. Making a policy on the marketing and production of iron and steel is quite often making a policy on the marketing and production of a single firm. Naturally, it pays that firm to try to get legislation and administration tailored to its needs.

Fourth, small-farmer and peasant movements tend to be nationalistic and xenophobic. The explanation of this phenomenon is not clear.

Finally, small-farmer and peasant movements tend to be opposed to middlemen and retailers, who are likely to use their monopolistic or monopsonistic position to milk the farm population. The cooperative movement is, of course, directed at eliminating middlemen as well as at provision of credit without usury.

Under normal conditions (that is, in the absence of totalitarian government, major racial cleavage, and major war) this complex of political forces tends to produce a rural community with a proliferation of as-

---

[43] Wilfried Kahler, *Das Agrarproblem in den Industrieländern* (Göttingen: Vandenhoeck & Ruprecht, 1958), p. 17.

[44] I.e., as compared with polical movements of the urban proletariat or bourgeoisie. They are more coherent and disciplined than are the lower-class movements in other agricultural systems.

[45] An excellent example of the penetration of industrial capital into a peasant party is shown by the development of the party platforms on industry in Rumania, 1921–26 (Roberts, *op. cit.*, pp. 154–156). The penetration of American populists by the "silver interests" is another example.

[46] Cf. *ibid.*, pp. 337–339; and Tomasevich, *op. cit.*, pp. 246–247. The Jacksonian era in the United States, and the persistent irregularities in political finance of agrarian leaders in the South of the United States, are further examples.

sociations and with the voting power and political interest to institute and defend certain elements of democracy, especially universal suffrage and universal education. This tends to produce a political regime loose enough to allow business and labor interest groups to form freely without allowing them to dominate the government completely. Such a system of landholding is a common precursor and support of modern liberal democratic government.

In smallholding systems, then, the upper classes of the rural community are not distinct in legal status and relatively not in style of life. Social mobility in such a system entails mainly a change in the amount of property held, or in the profitability of the farm, but not a change in legal status or a radical change in style of life.[47]

A politically enfranchised rural community is characterized by a high degree of political affect and organization, generally in opposition to urban interests rather than against rural upper classes. But, compared with the complexity of their political goals and the level of political involvement, their competence tends to be low until the "urbanization of the countryside" is virtually complete.

PLANTATION AGRICULTURE

Labor-intensive crops requiring several years for maturation, such as rubber, tree fruit, or coffee, tend to be grown on large-scale capitalistic farms employing either wage labor, or, occasionally, slave labor. Particularly when capital investment is also required for processing equipment to turn the crop into a form in which it can be shipped, as for example in the culture of sugar cane and, at least in earlier times, sugar beets, large-scale capitalist agriculture predominates.

The key economic factor that seems to produce large-scale capitalist culture is the requirement of long-term capital investment in the crop or in machinery, combined with relatively low cost of land. When the crop is also labor-intensive, particularly when labor is highly seasonal, a rather typical plantation system tends to emerge. In some cases it also emerges in the culture of cotton (as in the ante bellum American South and some places in Egypt), wheat (as in Hungary, eastern Germany,[48] and Poland[49]), or rice (as on the Carolina and Georgia coasts in the ante bellum American South).[50]

The enterprise typically combines a small highly skilled and privileged group which administers the capital investment, the labor force, and the marketing of the crops with a large group of unskilled, poorly paid, and legally unprivileged workers. Quite generally, the workers are ethnically distinct from the skilled core of administrators, often being imported from economically more backward areas or recruited from an economically backward native population in colonial and semi-colonial areas. This means that ordinarily they are ineligible for the urban labor market of the nation in which they work, if it has an urban labor market.

Examples of plantation systems are most of the sugar areas in the Caribbean and on the coast of Peru,[51] the rubber culture of the former Federated Malay States in Malaya[52] and on Java,[53] the fruit-growing

---

[47] The best description that I know of the meaning of "property mobility" in such a system is the novel of Knut Hamsun, *Growth of the Soil* (New York: Modern Library, 1921), set in the Norwegian frontier.

[48] Weber, *loc. cit.*

[49] Victor Lesniewski and Waclaw Ponikowski, "Polish Agriculture," in Ora S. Morgan (ed.), *Agricultural Systems of Middle Europe* (New York: Macmillan Co., 1933), pp. 260–263. Capitalist development was greatest in the western regions of Poznan and Pomerania (cf. *ibid.*, p. 264). There seem to have been many remains of a manorial system (*ibid.*, p. 277).

[50] Albert V. House, *Planter Management and Capitalism in Ante-bellum Georgia* (New York: Columbia University Press, 1954), esp. pp. 18–37.

[51] Ford, *op. cit.*, pp. 57–60.

[52] Jacoby, *op. cit.*, pp. 106–108, 113.

[53] *Ibid.*, pp. 43, 45, 56–61.

areas of Central America, the central valleys of California, where the labor force is heavily Latin American, eastern Germany during the early part of this century, where Poles formed an increasing part of the labor force,[54] Hungary up to World War II, the pineapple-growing of the Hawaiian Islands,[55] and, of course, the ante bellum American South. The system tends to induce in the agricultural labor force a poverty of associational life, low participation in local government, lack of education for the labor force, and high vulnerability of labor-union and political leadership to oppression by landlords and landlord-dominated governments. The domination of the government by landlords tends to prevent the colonization of new land by smallholders, and even to wipe out the holdings of such small peasantry as do exist.

In short, the system tends to maintain the culture, legal and political position, and life chances of the agricultural labor force distinct both from the urban labor force and from the planter aristocracy. The bearers of the technical and commercial knowledge are not the agricultural laborers, and, consequently, redistribution of land tends to introduce inefficiency into agriculture. The plantation system, as Edgar T. Thompson has put it, is a "race-making situation"[56] which produces a highly privileged aristocracy, technically and culturally educated, and a legally, culturally, and economically underprivileged labor force. If the latter is politically mobilized, as it may be occasionally

[54] Weber shows that, in the eastern parts of Germany during the latter part of the nineteenth century, the proportionate decrease of the German population (being replaced by Poles) was greater in areas of large-scale cultivation (*op. cit.*, pp. 452–453).

[55] Edward Norbeck, *Pineapple Town: Hawaii* (Berkeley: University of California Press, 1959).

[56] Cf. Edgar T. Thompson, "The Plantation as a Race-making Situation," in Leonard Broom and Philip Selznick, *Sociology* (Evanston, Ill.: Row, Peterson & Co., 1958), pp. 506–507.

by revolutionary governments, it tends to be extremist.

CAPITALIST EXTENSIVE AGRICULTURE WITH WAGE LABOR: THE RANCH

An extensive culture of wool and beef, employing wage labor, grew up in the American West, Australia, England and Scotland during and after the industrial revolution, Patagonia and some other parts of South America, and northern Mexico. In these cases the relative proportion of labor in the cost of production is smaller than it is in plantation agriculture. Such a structure is also characteristic of the wheat culture in northern Syria. In no case was there pressure to recruit and keep down an oppressed labor force. In England a surplus labor force was pushed off the land. A fairly reliable economic indicator of the difference between ranch and plantation systems is that in ranch systems the least valuable land is owned by the largest enterprises. In plantation systems the most valuable land is owned by the largest enterprises, with less valuable land generally used by marginal smallholders. The explanation of this is not clear.

The characteristic social feature of these enterprises is a free-floating, mobile labor force, often with few family ties, living in barracks, and fed in some sort of "company mess hall." They tend to make up a socially undisciplined element, hard-drinking and brawling. Sometimes their alienation from society takes on the form of political radicalism, but rarely of an indigenous disciplined radical movement.

The types of agricultural enterprise outlined here are hardly exhaustive, but perhaps they include most of the agricultural systems which help determine the political dynamics of those countries which act on the world scene today. Nor does this typology pretend to outline all the important differences in the dynamics of agricultural systems. Obviously, the system of family-sized farms run by smallholders in Serbia in the 1840's is very different from the

TABLE 1.

Characteristics of Rural Enterprises and Resulting Class Relations

TYPE OF ENTERPRISE	CHARACTERISTICS OF ENTERPRISE	CHARACTERISTICS OF CLASS STRUCTURE
Manorial:	Division of land into domain land and labor subsistence land, with domain land devoted to production for market. Lord has police power over labor. Technically traditional; low cost of land and little market in land	Classes differ greatly in legal privileges and style of life. Technical culture borne largely by the peasantry. Low political activation and competence of peasantry; high politicalization of the upper classes
Family-size tenancy:	Small parcels of highly valuable land worked by families who do not own the land, with a large share of the production for market. Highly labor- and land-intensive culture, of yearly or more frequent crops	Classes differ little in legal privileges but greatly in style of life. Technical culture generally borne by the lower classes. High political affect and political organization of the lower classes, often producing revolutionary populist movements
Family small-holding:	Same as family tenancy, except benefits remain within the enterprise. Not distinctive of areas with high valuation of land; may become capital-intensive at a late stage of industrialization	Classes differ neither in legal privileges nor in style of life. Technical culture borne by both rich and poor. Generally unified and highly organized political opposition to urban interests, often corrupt and undisciplined
Plantation:	Large-scale enterprises with either slavery or wage labor, producing labor-intensive crops requiring capital investment on relatively cheap land (though generally the best land within the plantation area). No or little subsistence production	Classes differ in both style of life and legal privileges. Technical culture monopolized by upper classes. Politically apathetic and incompetent lower classes, mobilized only in time of revolution by urban radicals
Ranch:	Large-scale production of labor-extensive crops, on land of low value (lowest in large units within ranch areas), with wage labor partly paid in kind in company barracks and mess	Classes may not differ in legal status, as there is no need to recruit and keep down a large labor force. Style of life differentiation unknown. Technical culture generally relatively evenly distributed. Dispersed and unorganized radicalism of lower classes

institutionally similar Danish and American systems of the 1950's.[57] And capitalistic sheep-raisers supported and made up the House of Lords in England but supported populistic currents in the United States.

However, some of the differences among systems outlined here seem to hold in widely varying historical circumstances. The production and maintenance of ethnic differences by plantations, the political fragility of family-size tenancy, the richer associational life, populist ideology, corrupt politics of smallholders, and the political apathy and technical traditionalism of the manor or the old hacienda—these seem to be fairly reliable. Characteristics of rural enterprises and the class relations they typically produce are summarized in Table 1.

This, if it is true, shows the typology to be useful. The question that remains is: Is it capable of being used? Is it possible to find indexes which will reliably differentiate a plantation from a manor or a manor from a large holding farmed by family tenancy?

The answer is that most of these systems have been accurately identified in particular cases. The most elusive is the manor or traditional hacienda; governments based on this sort of agricultural enterprise rarely take accurate censuses, partly because they rarely have an agricultural policy worthy of the name. Often even the boundaries of

landholdings are not officially recorded. Further, the internal economy of the manor or hacienda provides few natural statistical indexes—there is little bookkeeping use of labor, of land, of payment in kind or in customary rights. The statistical description of manorial economies is a largely unsolved problem.

Except for this, systematic comparative studies of the structure and dynamics of land tenure systems are technically feasible. But it has been all too often the case that descriptions of agricultural systems do not permit them to be classified by the type of enterprise.[58] Perhaps calling attention to widespread typical patterns of institutionalizing agricultural production will encourage those who write monographs to provide the information necessary for comparative study.

[57] E.g., in the average size of agricultural villages, in the proportion of the crop marketed, in the level of living, in education, in birth rate, in the size of the household unit, in the intensity of ethnic antagonism, in degree of political organization and participation, in exposure to damage by military action—these are only some of the gross differences.

[58] E.g., the most common measure used for comparative study is the concentration of landholdings. A highly unequal distribution of land may indicate family-tenancy, manorial, plantation, or ranch systems. Similarly, data on size of farm units confuse family smallholding with family tenancy, and lumps together all three kinds of large-scale enterprise. A high ratio of landless peasantry may be involved in family-tenancy, plantation, or manorial systems. Ambiguous references to "tenancy" may mean the labor rents of a hacienda system, or the cash or share rents of family-size tenancy, or even tenancy of sons before fathers' death in smallholding systems. "Capitalistic agriculture" sometimes refers to ranches, sometimes to plantations and sometimes to smallholdings. "Feudalism," though most often applied to manorial systems, is also used to describe family-size tenancy and plantation economies. "Absentee landlordism" describes both certain manorial and family-size-tenancy systems.

THE MULTIPLE SOCIETY IN ECONOMIC DEVELOPMENT: MEXICO AND GUATEMALA

Manning Nash

For the anthropologist the problem of economic development and cultural change is now clearly enough delimited for an investigator to ask crucial questions. An adequate theoretical resolution of that problem area would come through a series of propositions which would give empirically relevant answers to the following questions:

1. What income-raising technology and knowledge will be adopted and how will these be fitted into the social system?
2. What kinds of persons will put into use the production-increasing innovations?
3. What series of social and cultural changes will permit the innovators, together with their new forms of production, to restructure the society and reorient the culture, so that economic development becomes a built-in feature of the ordinary operation of the society?

By detailed analyses of societies and cultures, by invoking what is known of the processes of social and cultural change, and by recourse to the growing theory of the structure and function of social systems, partial answers to these questions have been offered for many of the non-Western peoples now seeking economic betterment or having it thrust upon them.

But in the emerging conceptual apparatus for the study of culture change and economic development, some of the current notions as to the relevant dimensions of the cultural and social entity under observation have proved inadequate. Anthropologists typically analyze non-Western

peoples through a model of interpretation which yields a description of a unified whole called a culture or a society. This procedure is valid and necessary when the interest is in a series of social and cultural types forming the basis of abstraction for scientific generalization. However, it often vitiates anthropological contributions to the study of economic development and cultural change, unless supplemented by concepts and tools facilitating the interpretation of more complex social and cultural situations than the relatively small and culturally autonomous communities for which our theoretical tools have been developed.

The unit of study for economic development is a political one—the nation or, in looser terms, a country. A goodly portion of the so-called underdeveloped countries is composed of more than one cultural tradition and of diverse levels of social organization within the territorial unit over which political jurisdiction is exercised. The anthropologist who studies only one of the cultural traditions, and makes generalizations about the process of culture change and economic development for the whole country, errs conspicuously; even if the generalization is restricted to the segment under observation, the error is great, if not so egregious.[1]

I propose the use of a concept which explicitly takes into account the facts of variant cultural tradition and, at the same time, the scale of social organization as the most useful starting point for an analysis of an underdeveloped country, at least for such countries as the five "Indian" republics of Latin America. The concept suggested is that of a multiple society with plural cultures.

SOURCE. Manning Nash, "The Multiple Society in Economic Development: Mexico and Guatemala," *American Anthropologist*, **59**, 825–833, October 1957.

This concept has had some anthropological currency (Tax 1946; Beals 1953; Nash 1965b) but its employment in the understanding of the process of economic development and culture change has not yet been undertaken.[2] The utility of the concept and its research implications will be shown by reviewing some of the facts of Guatemalan and Mexican economy and society from this perspective.

As a social type, the multiple society with plural cultures is marked by the presence of at least two distinct cultural traditions, each significantly different in breadth of integration. Although the entire population of the national territory is included in a single system of political and economic bonds, only a part of the population is fully aware of the national entity, participates significantly in its cultural and social life, or has control over resources and communications of nationwide scope or impact. That part of the population which carries the national variety of culture is in fact the national society; it is scattered throughout the national territory; it is the link between the nation and other nations in the world and is the segment of the population in whom political control is vested and within which political control is contested. It is also that part of the population whose economic decisions have national repercussions.

This national political and economic segment of the multiple society is within itself divided into classes and marked by rural and urban differences. But as a social segment it is superior to those small-scale societies with different cultural traditions within the same national territory. These subordinate societies are locally organized; economic resources are small compared to the national society; political power is not vested in them; and the cultural cleavage between the national segment and its plural cultures is marked by many symbolic pointers of dress, language, occupation, custom, and perhaps even the physical features of the members.

It is plain that in Guatemala the multiple society refers on the one hand to *Ladinos* and on the other to Indians. In Mexico the chief terms of reference are to *Mexicano* as against *Indio*.[3] The two nations serve as an historical contrast, both as to the degree of persistence of a multiple society and as to different rates of economic progress.

Guatemala is a multiple society *par excellence*, with hundreds of Indian municipios each varying from the other in small and numberless ways and as a cultural tradition distinct from the Ladino society (Tax 1937). The nature of economic development and culture change in Guatemala depends not on the characteristics of the Ladino society nor on the features of the Indian society alone, but on the relations of the segments of the multiple society and the possible and probable roles each segment may or can play in the historical process. The questions which opened this paper are to be asked twice; once for the national segment, and again for the non-national segment. An understanding of economic development will emerge in the relations between these two sets of answers.

The Indian societies of Guatemala are made up of peasants who in economic organization and motivation are, and have been, receptive to changes in technology and knowledge, if such innovations are of comparative economic advantage (Tax 1953). The cultural differences between Ladino and Indian society are not matched by economic differences in type of organization, nor are the Indian economies isolated from the national economy or separate in activity or sphere (Mosk 1954; Tax 1956). Guatemalan Indian receptivity to income-raising innovation is limited then in the same way in which the limits of innovation are set in any society—by the prevailing stock of wealth, by the present command over skill and knowledge, by the estimation of worth of a new item in terms of what it displaces or replaces, by the calculation of how much trouble it is to reorient one's time, energy, and resources to use the new item in light of the rewards it offers, and by the judgment of how one looks to one's fellows by adopting the new way.

Even a cursory acquaintance with the culture of the municipios of the Western Highlands indicates that new items of technology and knowledge are subjected to estimation and calculation in a set of values and preference scales different from that of Ladino society. But the important point is that this set of different values and preference schedules does not preclude the rapid introduction of income-raising innovation or justify the appellation of "resistant to change." On the contrary, change is relatively swift and easy in Guatemalan Indian communities, if the proposed innovation is more productive within the limits of the factors enumerated earlier. The limits are apparently wide and as yet uncharted. They run the gamut from things as relatively undisturbing as a sewing machine or corn mill up to and including Central America's largest textile mill. I have reported earlier on the range and kind of changes made in a traditional Indian community in which a modern textile mill is situated, drawing almost all of its labor from the local Indian community (Nash 1955a, 1955b, 1956b).

If the cultures of the Guatemalan Indians are such as to permit a relatively wide choice among alternatives, why then is the choice not more frequently made? The answer lies, I think, in the social scale of these municipios. The units of production and consumption are households, not firms, and the household's control over resources, its capital stock, and its withholding power, in short its ability to try out something new, is perforce limited.[4] Innovations which it can undertake, almost by definition, cannot materially raise the per-capita income; and those innovations which can materially raise the income, it cannot undertake. The Indian communities, singly or severally, cannot start the self-generating process of

technological improvement and economic reorganization which can in the end lead to abundance.

The major role of taking on a comprehensive new and more productive technology is to lie, then, with some members of the national segment of the multiple society rather than with the Indian communities. But the choice of technology and its spread throughout a large part of the population depends on a proper appreciation of the nature of Indian cultures by the Ladino segment. That is to say, in the process of Guatemala's economic development it falls to the lot of Ladino society to introduce the income-increasing technique and knowledge, but unless that knowledge and technique are acceptable to and used by the Indian communities, little or no economic progress may result. As Tax has pointed out (1956), the Indians' use of the more productive coastal lands instead of the highlands would raise their standards of living and the nation's as a whole, but since in order to use the coastal land under the present system of land redistribution the Indian must move to the coast and occupy the land as a resident, few take advantage of the better land. Indians live in communities, and prefer the highlands for climatic, hygienic, and sentimental reasons. The suggestion is that Indians be allowed to use the land without having to settle there. Some of them normally do this with their own parcels of coast land and presumably would do so as easily, and to everybody's benefit, on government land. The nature of the multiple society is such that only a consideration of all segments and of their relations can lead to economically effective plan or practice, for it is primarily the role of the Indian in Guatemala to provide the bulk of the human material whose choice will decide whether the alternatives presented by Ladino society shall be fruitful.

Ladino society is frequently divided into a series of social classes which correspond rather closely to the various kinds of productive activities each social class manifests (Adams 1956; LeBeau 1956). First of all, there is a social class called upper or cosmopolitan (Wagley and Harris 1955). This class is largely urban in residence, sophisticated in style, education, consumption, and usually well travelled. It is the richest segment of Guatemala, gathering its wealth from the large coffee plantations or other export crop land, and sometimes through a large commercial establishment. Below this social class, in both wealth and status, is a segment often called the local upper class to distinguish it from the metropolitan or cosmopolitan rich and prestigeful. The local upper class is a kind of rural gentry, often with town or city residence. These are the producers of export crops or of cattle and food for internal use, on a lesser scale than the *finquero* of the large export plantation. They are the medium holders who exert political power on the local scene and are important in national politics, but their command of the factors of production is less than that of the cosmopolitans. The third social class usually named is the middle class, more recently denoted as the *masa media* (Gillin 1956). It includes persons on the social and economic scale ranging from school teachers to directors of firms, passing on the way army officers, clerks, minor government officials, and intellectual workers. The fourth social class appears to be the *clase baja*, a lower class composed chiefly in the cities of wage workers, domestics, peddlers, small scale self-employed craftsmen, and the occasional worker; in the countryside this segment includes the agricultural worker on a daily basis, the resident agricultural worker, the small merchant or shopkeeper, the few nonagricultural wage workers, the self-employed petty craftsman, and the occasional worker.

One of the four segments of Ladino society must give impetus to the process of economic development if such a process is indeed to begin and come to fruition. Which segment can and which, given good economic reasons, is likely to do so? Not enough is known in detail about the national culture and social class system to answer this question definitively, but in broad outline the major possibilities are evident. The *clase baja* may be discounted either as the initiators or the carriers-through of the cultural change which will bring about economic development because it does not command sufficient economic means or organization, and it is largely illiterate, unvocal, and unrepresented politically. In a process of economic development this segment is analogous to the Indian societies and cultures in providing the human material whose choice to use the income-raising technology and knowledge is crucial.

At the other extreme, the cosmopolitans have the resources and perhaps the knowledge and political power to make economic development possible but it is unlikely that they will do so, because a major concern of large plantations is the price structure of the export market rather than problems of technological or organizational experiment and advance. Cosmopolitans can get rich and stay rich with their current technology—wasteful or inefficient as it may be—provided the world market offers them sufficient return for their product. Furthermore, it is unlikely that whatever improvements the cosmopolitans make will appeal to the members of Indian societies (whose chief economic role would be that of plantation laborers) or to the clase baja, who will also remain in the role of agricultural laborers with presumably the same levels of skill and knowledge, even if their productivity and income may rise slightly. Despite the need or desire of the cosmopolitans or the upper class for rapid, substantial economic and cultural change, they are unlikely to undertake an extensive program of change even though they command the resources and the political power to beget economic development.

The local upper class is a more promising but still an unlikely choice as a collective candidate for bringing rapid economic change to Guatemala. By and large, the rural gentry aim to expand their economic activities, especially through increasing land holdings and money crops, but the object of such expansion is to move into the social and economic role of the cosmopolitan. That is to say, successful local upper-class persons usually orient economic activity so that they may rise into the cosmopolitan segment, rather than select or implement some program which would lead to general economic change or would enlist or attract in its wake the Indian societies or the clase baja.

By a process of elimination the middle class, the masa media, remains as the only possible segment for economic development and its accompanying cultural and social reformulation. They are, I shall argue, a likely group, but the probability is of uncertain odds. The middle class is literate, politically active, socially mobile, and impoverished (Gillin 1956). Such a combination of characteristics makes them particularly susceptible to the promise of economic betterment and willing to pay the personal costs and run the social risks of rapid social change. The masa media, being poor both in personal incomes in comparison to what their tastes and aspirations consider the decent minimum and in their control over the factors of production, has no special commitment to a going technology or economic organization. They are willing to innovate economically and socially, provided the rewards accrue partly to them in terms of wealth and increased power and prestige.

Since the middle class does not make economic decisions of great scope or impact in view of their current claim on the productive mechanism, their willingness and social susceptibility to economic and cultural change can be translated into social fact and historical process only through political channels. Political power may give them control over sufficient resources to make significant cultural and economic innovation. This political

access to economic means may be achieved only if the masa media can enlist in their cause a sizeable segment of the national population, chiefly from among the clase baja and the Indian societies. Therefore, a condition of the success of the middle class in achieving political power, if indeed they ever do achieve it, is an economic program and policy which appeals to and makes adherents from the Indian society and the lower classes. The middle class, then, is a likely social segment of the multiple society to want and to seek economic development; to consider those innovations in technology and economic organization which the Indians and the clase baja will accept; and to make the necessary social and cultural changes so that economic development, necessary to their political eminence, may become a standard feature of the society.[5]

The brief argument I have here advanced appears to me logically consistent and respectful of the facts of Guatemalan culture and economy, but it has the character of a "just-so story." This may be resolved by bringing into view a neighboring multiple society, Mexico.

Mexico suggests itself for comparative purposes through the common historical experience (albeit differently paced) it shares with Guatemala: the presence of plural cultures in a multiple society and a former similarity in the class structure. It differs through the fact of recent, rapid rises in national income. Mexico of 1910 was much like Guatemala of 1940. The class system was, with some minor variation, of the four-fold variety which Guatemala now exhibits (Iturriaga 1951). A significant part of the population lived in small-scale social units manifesting different cultures, while still part of the larger political and economic national network (Basauri 1940), and of course the Indians of Mexico were culturally so similar to those of Guatemala that propositions are made about the Indians of Mesoamerica (Redfield and Tax 1952). The point need not be labored as to the social, cultural, and economic (Parra 1954) similarity of Mexico of 1910 and Guatemala of 1940, for many of those similarities persist in the two nations today.

But Mexico's economic development has been phenomenal by contrast with Guatemala's, especially in the last decade. Mexico is apparently one of the few nonindustrialized or underdeveloped countries which seems likely to "get over the hump" of transition economically and socially. The national income of Mexico more than doubled in the decade 1940–50 (IBRD 1952); output increased in every branch of production save mining; the network of roads and communication was expanded, overcoming some of the economic atomism and regionalism of the difficult topography. And some of the most isolated Indian groups and technologically backward rural dwellers have come during the past years both to feel themselves Mexicans (cf. Redfield 1930; Lewis 1951) and to use the most modern and industrial of equipment in the economy (Moore 1951).

Although it is still a relatively poor nation Mexico's rapid and substantial economic progress came in the wake of thirty years of revolution in which political control over economic resources was placed in the hands of the middle class, rather than the cosmopolitans or upper class. This segment of the population forms what is sometimes called "the new group of industrialists" (Mosk 1951) on their economic side, and the core of the "institutional" revolutionary party on their political side. This middle class segment appears to have been able to gain political control, and hence economic importance (since without implicit or explicit government blessing nothing prospers for long in Mexico), by adopting a course which appealed both to the clase baja and to the Indian populations. Their experimental attitude toward technology and economic organization was always tempered by the political consideration of not alienating the peasants and Indians upon whom their

economic success was ultimately founded. Consequently, in contemporary Mexico there is a vigorous, government-financed program for Indian betterment which sometimes yields spectacular results and makes of anthropology in Mexico an applied science (Caso et al. 1954; Villa Rojas 1955). At the same time, the government is consciously and continually seeking new technologies and ways of adapting them to Mexico, and plowing back into new investment a significant amount of profit.

I do not mean to imply that Mexican economic development is a fully understood phenomenon, or that the peculiar situation of Mexico during World War II was not of great importance, or even that Mexico will continue at the same rate in the same direction. Many parts of the picture are missing, and problems of population, internal income distribution, terrain and market, still plague Mexico.

However, I think the Mexican experience with economic development is more clearly comprehensible when viewed by means of the concept of multiple society with plural cultures. And Mexico's experience, so understood, prefigures one of the possible courses of Guatemalan development. The notion of a multiple society with plural cultures is a tool which calls attention to the diverse levels of social organization and cultural tradition, so that the anthropologist who looks at a small part of the whole does not make the error of taking the behavior of a member for the behavior of a system. It encourages the selection of strategic variables and the formulation of hypotheses which later history and cross-cultural comparison may confirm or disconfirm, rather than a listing of negative cautions which frequently have been the anthropological hallmark in the study of economic development and cultural change.

NOTES

[1] The volume prepared for the United Nations (Mead 1953) moves between descriptions of a

small segment and generalizations about a larger whole without the apparent intervention of theoretical means of flight. Similarly, a casebook on technological change (Spicer 1952) attempts to make suggestions about improving the economic situation of some 14 different societies without explicit analysis of the larger wholes in which these societies are embedded.

[2] The notion of a multiple society with plural cultures does not derive from formulations aimed at solving the same problem. Boeke's (1953) use of the "dualistic" economy in the Indies does not apply if the country in question is really a multiple society, and Higgins' (1956) strictures on the dualistic theory do much to empty that concept of meaning anywhere. Furnivall's (1950) use of "plural economy" lies closer to the concept of multiple society, but does not conceive of a single political and economic network in the same way.

[3] Not enumerated are all the various cultural traditions to be found in Guatemala or in Mexico. A glance at the census shows that there are foreigners—from the *Chinos* to the *Turcos*—whose culture is different (sometimes) from the national Hispanic-American or the Indian. The number of such persons and their economic and political importance is not large enough to alter my description or the economic development of Mexico and Guatemala.

[4] I use the household as an index to the Indian scale of social organization and command over the factors of production. A complete listing of other social limitations—credit mechanisms, storage facilities, etc.—would serve no purpose here. A detailed exposition of an Indian economy may be found in Tax (1953).

[5] I have in mind those kinds of changes in social structure and value system suggested by Hoselitz (1953).

BIBLIOGRAPHY

ADAMS, R. N.
    1956 Los Ladinos de Guatemala. Guatemala.
ADLER, JOHN H., E. H. SCHLESINGER AND E. C. OLSON
    1952 Public finance and economic development in Guatemala. Stanford.
BASAURI, C.
    1940 La población indígena de México. México.
BEALS, RALPH L.
    1953 Social stratification in Latin America. American Journal of Sociology, **58**, 327–339.

BOEKE, J. H.
    1953 Economics and economic policy of dual societies. New York.
CASO, A., SILVIO ZAVALA, JOSÉ MIRANDA, MOISES N. GONZÁLEZ, GONZALO AGUIRRE BELTRÁN, RICARDO POZAS A.
    1954 Metodos y resultados de la política indigenista. México
FURNIVALL, J. S.
    1950 Co-operation, competition, and isolation in the economic sphere. *In* Phillips Talbot (ed.) South Asia in the world today. Chicago.
GILLIN, JOHN
    1956 Cultura emergenta. *In* Integración Social en Guatemala. Guatemala City.
HIGGINS, BENJAMIN
    1956 The "dualistic theory" of underdeveloped areas. Economic Development and Cultural Change, **4**, 99–115.
HOSELITZ, BERT F.
    1953 Social structure and economic growth. Economia Internazionale, **6**, 1–23.
INTERNATIONAL BANK FOR RECONSTRUCTION AND DEVELOPMENT
    1951 The economic development of Guatemala. Washington.
    1952 The economic development of Mexico. Baltimore.
ITURRIAGA, JOSÉ E.
    1951 La estructura social y cultural de México. México.
LE BEAU, F.
    1956 Económica agricola de Guatemala. *In* Integración Social en Guatemala. Guatemala City.
LEWIS, OSCAR
    1951 Life in a Mexican village: Tepoztlán restudied. Urbana.
MEAD, MARGARET (ed.)
    1953 Cultural patterns and technical change. UNESCO.
MOORE, WILBERT E.
    1951 Industrialization and labor. Ithaca, New York.
MOSK, SANFORD A.
    1951 Industrial revolution in Mexico. Berkeley.
    1954 Indigenous economy in Latin America. Inter-American Economic Affairs, **8**, 3–25.
NASH, MANNING
    1955a Cantel: the industrialization of a Guatemalan Indian Community. Unpublished Ph.D. Thesis, Chicago.
    1955b The reaction of a civil-religious hierarchy to a factory in Guatemala. Human Organization, **13**, 26–28.

1956a The recruitment of wage labor and development of new skills. Annals of the American Academy of Political and Social Science (May), 23–31.

1956b Relaciones políticas entre los indios de Guatemala. *In* Integración Social en Guatemala, Guatemala City.

PARRA, MANUEL GERMÁN
1954 La industrialización de México. México.

REDFIELD, ROBERT
1930 Tepoztlán, a Mexican village. Chicago.

REDFIELD, ROBERT, AND SOL TAX
1952 General characteristics of present-day Mesoamerican Indian society. *In* Sol Tax (ed.) Heritage of conquest. Glencoe, Free Press.

SPICER, E. H. (ed.)
1962 Human problems in technological change. New York.

TAX, SOL
1937 The municipios of the Midwestern

Highlands of Guatemala. American Anthropologist, **39**, 423–444.

1946 The education of underprivileged peoples in dependent and independent territories. Journal of Negro Education, **15**, 336–345.

1953 Penny capitalism: a Guatemalan Indian economy. Institute of Social Anthropology 16. Washington.

1956 Los indios en la economia de Guatemala. *In* Integración Social en Guatemala. Guatemala City.

UNITED NATIONS, Economic Commission for Latin America
1950 Recent trends in the Mexican economy. UNESCO.

VILLA ROJAS, A.
1955 Los Mazatecos y el problema indígena de la cuenca del Papaloapan. Mexico.

WAGLEY, CHARLES and MARVIN HARRIS
1955 A typology of Latin-American subcultures. American Anthropologist, **57**, 428–451.

THE MASSES, THE ELITE, AND POST-COLONIAL POLITICS IN AFRICA

Martin Kilson

Political change among the masses (those Africans relatively untouched by modernization) is an important facet of African political change, for they are inevitably affected by the competition between African and colonial modernizers, especially—but not only—through the medium of nationalism. Unlike the emergent African bourgeoisie, the masses are generally not themselves modernizers, and thus their relationship to colonial modernizers is different. But they do desire to be modernized, or at least to rationalize or clarify the complicated and disturbing situation of partial or peripheral modernization in the midst of traditional life and ways.

When seeking *themselves* to resolve the contradictions arising from this situation, the masses, like the middle class, direct their activity to some facet of the colonial political system, and thus become conscious participants in political change. Their methods and processes, however, normally take a more violent, riotous form, often neo-traditional in' structure, and lacking clear goals. This means, in turn, that political change among the masses is more difficult, more traumatic, than among the middle class.[1] (And within the masses, political change is

SOURCE. Martin Kilson, "African Political Change and the Modernization Process," *Journal of Modern African Studies*, **1**, 425–440, 1963; using only 435–440.

[1] For a detailed analysis of this process, see Martin Kilson, *Political Change in a West African State* (forthcoming).

relatively less difficult in towns or urban centres than in rural areas, since the former provide access to a more intensively modernizing environment and to the African modernizing élite.) This is revealed in the ambivalent attitude of the masses towards indigenous institutions; traditional rulers represent the authoritative unit of colonial political change nearest to the masses, who attack them as a cause of the complex political change they experience, and yet still depend upon them as the only known sources of values capable of providing the stability necessary to any people undergoing relatively rapid socio-political change. Traditional religious forms are also important in this process, being partly rejected and replaced or modified by imported religious forms, and yet simultaneously utilized as instruments for adjustment to socio-political change. Hence the politico-religious cults and messianic movements that have characterized socio-political change in Africa.[2]

As already suggested, political change among the masses becomes less difficult and traumatic only at the point where it fuses with the nationalism of the élite, thereby gaining more articulate leadership, more specific goals, and the psychological transference of aspirations and expectations to others. The nature of this élite-mass nexus, as it may be called, becomes the focal point of political change as the situation shifts from conflict between colonial and African modernizers to competition within the African community. During this shift, tribalism and other traditional or neo-traditional forces become active ingredients of African political change, affecting both the constitutional structure of the state as it moves toward independence, and the processes by which individuals and groups seek power. This occurs, of course, towards the end of the colonial period—during the decolonization of expatriate institutions—and a proper

understanding of it is, I think, crucial to an understanding of post-colonial political change.

Since the emergent African bourgeoisie is not only more deeply involved in the money economy and its social system, but also displays the political and ideological attitudes which may be expected to generate modernization, its members are therefore likely to be the power holders in the new independent state. We can also expect that the apparatus of government will be a major element in their drive for dominance in post-colonial modernization, for at no stage during the colonial era had they even begun to control the necessary elements for dominance: capital, technical skill, managerial capacity, administrative skill, and so on. Indeed, their recognition of this explains their emphasis upon the seizure of the apparatus of government as the primary instrument for competition with expatriate modernizers during the colonial era. The control of the state also becomes their main instrument in the similar competition during the post-colonial period, when the expatriates continue their monopoly of the financial, industrial, technical, and strategic ingredients of modernization, having conceded the structure of political power, but not the totality of what Dahl would call "political resources,"[3] to African modernizers. Yet the emergent African bourgeoisie—fearful of stunting further modernization in the post-colonial national society and of limiting its own progress towards dominance—has little alternative but to treat as indispensable the capital and skills of metropolitan expatriates, and in fact may at points develop a basic identity of interest with them.

It can further be expected, in view of the foregoing, that the main political conflicts during the post-colonial period will arise from competition between different segments or factions of the élite for control over the ingredients of modernization that

[2] Cf. Sylvia Thrupp (ed.), *Millennial Dreams in Action* (The Hague, 1962).

[3] Robert A. Dahl, *Who Governs?* (New Haven, Conn., 1961).

the state and its apparatus possess. Furthermore, this competition raises the problem of the likely identity of interests between expatriate capital, skills, and strategic interests, on the one hand, and at least a part of the African élite on the other hand. How far does this extend? What are its implications for the future development of the new national society? Being so inferior in their modernizing capacity, the masses will be merely peripheral to this conflict, except when middle-class factions manipulate tribalism, religion, and other socio-cultural factors for their own ends; or when the middle class as a whole *appears* incapable, as heirs to the expatriate ruling class, of satisfying the expectations and aspirations developed among the masses during the period of mature anti-colonial nationalism.

The latter problem, however, may be expected to arise only at a relatively late phase of the post-colonial period, due partly to the astute skill of the middle class in manipulating the racial aspect of nationalism to claim the allegiance of the masses and to get the masses to identify the gains of the middle class as being their own. Political parties, of course, assist in reinforcing this allegiance of the masses to their leadership, often with the important aid of the traditional ruling élite, to which most major African parties—save the few radical mass-type parties—are closely linked. They may fail to do so where there is relatively free competition among mainly middle-class-led parties; and then the tendency has been for the dominant party to preempt the political field through an authoritarian use of power, which might lead to a political dictatorship of the middle classes.[4]

What may be called the asymmetrical structure of the middle class—as a social class—also facilitates the maintenance of mass allegiance to it. By asymmetry is meant the fragmented or uneven manner in which persons enter the middle class,

without carrying their own immediate social unit along. Thus a wealthy lawyer or businessman may have a mother, father, and sundry other close kin who remain poor peasants in rural areas or depressed wage-earners in urban slums. Assuming the continuation of some traditional norms governing social relationships,[5] the lawyer or business man retains some measure of responsibility for the welfare of his poorer kin. And in this way the modern affluence of the emergent African bourgeoisie trickles down to the poorer groups, whose allegiance is thereby reinforced and their expectations of a better life in the post-colonial society strengthened.

It should be noted, further, that the gradual extension of the franchise as a filter for political pressures, in the way described above, enabled the masses eventually to secure the respect of the emergent bourgeoisie for their views and interests. Given the heavy dependence of an overwhelming proportion of African professionals, business men, etc., upon government or the political process for their existence and advancement, they have reason to pay some deference to the fact of mass enfranchisement.

There is another feature of mass enfranchisement that is relevant to post-colonial political change. The very existence of the mass franchise constitutes one of the major problems affecting the élite-mass relationship in post-colonial Africa. For, unlike the modernizing period in other countries—for example, Britain or Japan—during which the élite groups were able, for 100 years or more, to determine the nature and course of modernization free from the pressures and restraints of a mass franchise, *in the post-colonial African societies the masses are armed with the*

---

[4] Cf. Frantz Fanon, *Les Damnés de la terre* (Paris, 1961), pp. 118 ff., 124.

[5] This is a valid assumption. For a literary treatment of it, see Chinua Achebe, *No Longer at Ease* (London, 1960). See also Elizabeth Colson, "Native Culture and Social Patterns in Contemporary Africa," in C. Grove Haines (ed.), *Africa Today* (Baltimore, 1955), pp. 69–84.

franchise at the very beginning of the African élite's attempt to direct modernization. In Britain, for instance, only 3 per cent of adults (435,391) had a franchise in 1830—some 100 years after the commencement of the Industrial Revolution and nearly 200 years after the Civil War—and the 1832 Reform Act added only 217,386 voters to the electorate; universal manhood suffrage did not become a reality until the 1880's.[6] At the establishment of the American Republic in 1787—when American élites assumed responsibility for modernization—only 25 per cent of the adult white males were eligible to vote. White women were ineligible, as were Negro slaves and Indians, who constituted 17 out of every 100 of the population. Furthermore, a variety of restrictions on voting continued until the second half of the nineteenth century.[7] By the 1870's the structure of modernization had been laid by American élites, and the process of built-in economic growth was becoming apparent.

This situation becomes of primary concern if one assumes—as I think it valid to do—that the modernizing function is performed by élite groups mainly when their capacity to do so—and to define the direction of modernization and their own stake in it—is relatively free from restrictions and pressures by non-élite groups. Historically, this assumption is demonstrated by both capitalistic and communistic patterns of modernization; in Soviet modernization, for example, the state and its dominant party are explicitly constructed (1) to provide relative freedom for the modernizing (communist) élites from mass claims, or (2) to establish a political framework whereby the modernizing élites can bargain with the masses on terms most favorable to their own conception of modernization.[8]

Africa is unlikely to offer more favorable preconditions of modernization than Britain or Soviet Russia, and therefore one cannot expect African élites to accept the political implications for the modernization process involved in mass enfranchisement. Theoretically, they could discard the mass franchise altogether if they thought it restricted national interest—on their definition—though this would probably cause more political difficulties than it would solve. Alternatively, they could make more authoritarian the framework within which the mass franchise operates, thereby rendering it a more contrived process of mass political participation.[9] This, in fact, has already occurred to some extent in a number of independent African States, and it is likely to be an increasingly important feature of the authoritarian single-party tendencies so apparent in nearly all post-colonial African States.[10]

It is not altogether clear, however, that African modernizing élites are as justified in rejecting mass political pressures upon the modernization process as were their European counterparts. The African élites are not, for one thing, directly comparable *as modernizing elites* to their counterparts during the eighteenth and nineteenth centuries in Europe and Britain, or even in twentieth-century Russia. Having emerged in a colonial situation, the African élites are significantly lacking in capital, and in managerial, technical, scientific, and other modernizing skills. Most of these are still monopolized—as it were, neo-colonially—by expatriates; the African élites have acquired mainly political, administrative, bureaucratic, and intellectual skills, and in some states (e.g. the Congo), not much of these. In fact, for some time the governing function of African élites may not be much more than

[6] Charles Seymour, *Electoral Reform in England and Wales* (New Haven, Conn., 1951), p. 533.
[7] D. O. McGovney, *The American Suffrage Medley* (Chicago, 1959), pp. 16–27.
[8] Cf. Marcuse, *op. cit.*, pp. 26 ff., *passim.*

[9] Cf. Rupert Emerson, *From Empire to Nations* (Cambridge, Mass., 1960), pp. 245–246.
[10] Cf. Martin Kilson, "Authoritarian and Single-Party Tendencies in African Politics," in *World Politics* (Princeton), January 1963, pp. 262–294.

a political holding operation, maintaining a degree of political stability so that expatriate capital and skills can continue the modernization process. Liberia is the purest example, with variations on this model developing in the rest of Africa. On the other hand, the modernizing élites in eighteenth- and nineteenth-century Europe had capital and skills in their own right; even if the most modern-oriented sections of these élites were lacking in administrative or bureaucratic skills, they were able to ally themselves with the traditional or aristocratic élites who possessed them and thereby turn these skills to modern tasks.

Viewed in this context, the African élites certainly have little claim to define the modernization process, *and their stake in it*, free from the restraints of mass enfranchisement. Yet, to make such a definition is fundamentally to have the political power (including police and military power) to do so. And this the new African élites have (or have access to) and show every willingness to use.

Chapter 12

Social Mobilization and Political Participation

SOCIAL MOBILIZATION AND POLITICAL DEVELOPMENT

Karl W. Deutsch[1]

Social mobilization is a name given to an overall process of change, which happens to substantial parts of the population in

SOURCE. Excerpted from Karl W. Deutsch, "Social Mobilization and Political Development," *American Political Science Review*, **55**, 493–514, September 1961; using only pp. 493–511. A draft version of this paper was presented at the meeting of the Committee on Comparative Politics, of the Social Science Research Council, Gould House, Dobbs Ferry, June 10, 1959. An earlier version of this text is appearing in *Zeitschrift für Politik* (Köln, Germany).

[1] Further work on this paper was supported in part by the Carnegie Corporation, and I am indebted for assistance in statistical applications to Charles L. Taylor and Alex Weilenmann.

countries which are moving from traditional to modern ways of life. It denotes a concept which brackets together a number of more specific processes of change, such as changes of residence, of occupation, of social setting, of face-to-face associates, of institutions, roles, and ways of acting, of experiences and expectations, and finally of personal memories, habits and needs, including the need for new patterns of group affiliation and new images of personal identity. Singly, and even more in their cumulative impact, these changes tend to influence and sometimes to transform political behavior.

The concept of social mobilization is not merely a short way of referring to the collection of changes just listed, including any extensions of this list. It implies that these processes tend to go together in certain historical situations and stages of economic development; that these situations are identifiable and recurrent, in their essentials, from one country to another; and that they are relevant for politics. Each of these points will be taken up in the course of this paper.

Social mobilization, let us repeat, is something that happens to large numbers of people in areas which undergo modernization, i.e., where advanced, nontraditional practices in culture, technology and economic life are introduced and accepted on a considerable scale. It is not identical, therefore, with this process of modernization as a whole,[2] but it deals with one of its major aspects, or better, with a recurrent cluster among its consequences. These consequences, once they occur on a substantial scale, influence in turn the further process of modernization. Thus, what can be treated for a short time span as a consequence of the modernization process, appears over a longer period as one of its

continuing aspects and as a significant cause, in the well known pattern of feedback or circular causation.

Viewed over a longer time perspective, such as several decades, the concept of social mobilization suggests that several of the changes subsumed under it will tend to go together in terms of recurrent association, well above anything to be expected from mere chance. Thus, any one of the forms of social mobilization, such as the entry into market relations and a money economy (and hence away from subsistence farming and barter) should be expected to be accompanied or followed by a significant rise in the frequency of impersonal contacts, or in exposure to mass media of communication, or in changes of residence, or in political or quasi-political participation. The implication of the concept is thus to assert an empirical fact—that of significantly frequent association—and this assertion can be empirically tested.

This notion of social mobilization was perceived early in intuitive terms, as a historical recollection or a poetic image. It was based on the historical experiences of the French *levée en masse* in 1793 and of the German "total mobilization" of 1914–18, described dramatically in terms of its social and emotional impact by many German writers, including notably Ernest Jünger. A somewhat related image was that of the long-term and world-wide process of "fundamental democratization," discussed in some of the writings of Karl Mannheim.[3] All these images suggest a breaking away from old commitments to traditional ways of living, and a moving into new situations, where new patterns of behavior are relevant and needed, and where new commitments may have to be made.

Social mobilization can be defined, therefore, as the process in which major clusters of old social, economic and psychological commitments are eroded or broken and

---

[2] For broader discussions of the modernization process, see Rupert Emerson, *From Empire to Nation* (Cambridge, Harvard University Press, 1960); Harold D. Lasswell, *The World Revolution of Our Time* (Stanford University Press, 1951); and Gabriel A. Almond and James S. Coleman, eds., *The Politics of the Developing Areas* (Princeton, Princeton University Press, 1960). Cf. also Daniel Lerner, *The Passing of Traditional Society* (Glencoe, 1958), and Lerner, "Communication Systems and Social Systems: A Statistical Exploration in History and Policy," *Behavioral Science*, 2 (October 1957), 266–275; Fred Riggs, "Bureaucracy in Traditional Societies: Politics, Economic Development and Administration," American Political Science Association Annual Meeting, September 1959, multigraphed; Dankwart Rustow *Politics and Westernization in the Near East* (Center of International Studies, Princeton University, 1956); and Lyle Shannon, "Is Level of Development Related to Capacity for Self-Government?" *The American Journal of Economics and Sociology*, 17 (July 1958), 367–381, and Shannon, "Socio-Economic Development and Political Status," *Social Problems*, 7 (Fall 1959), 157–169.

[3] Karl Mannheim, *Man and Society in an Age of Reconstruction* (New York, 1940).

people become available for new patterns of socialization and behavior. As Edward Shils has rightly pointed out,[4] the original images of "mobilization" and of Mannheim's "fundamental democratization" imply two distinct stages of the process: (1) the stage of uprooting or breaking away from old settings, habits and commitments; and (2) the induction of the mobilized persons into some relatively stable new patterns of group membership, organization and commitment. In this fashion, soldiers are mobilized *from* their homes and families and mobilized *into* the army in which they then serve. Similarly, Mannheim suggests an image of large numbers of people moving away *from* a life of local isolation, traditionalism and political apathy, and moving *into* a different life or broader and deeper involvement in the vast complexities of modern life, including potential and actual involvement in mass politics.

It is a task of political theory to make this image more specific; to bring it into a form in which it can be verified by evidence; and to develop the problem to a point where the question "how?" can be supplemented usefully by the question "how much" In its intuitive form, the concept of social mobilization already carried with it some images of growing numbers and rising curves. In so far as the constituent processes of social mobilization can be measured and described quantitatively in terms of such curves, it may be interesting to learn how fast the curves rise, whether they show any turning points, or whether they cross any thresholds beyond which the processes they depict have different side effects from those that went before. Notable among these side effects are any that bear on the performance of political systems and upon the stability and capabilities of governments.[5]

[4] Edward Shils, at the Social Science Research Council Conference on Comparative Politics.
[5] For a broader discussion of quantitative indicators, bearing on problems of this kind, see Karl W. Deutsch, "Toward an Inventory

An Analytical Formulation

Let M stand for the generalized process of social mobilization, and let us think of it as representing the general propensity or availability of persons for recommitment. In this sense, M could be measured by the average probability that any person, say between fifteen and sixty-five years old, would have undergone, or could be expected to undergo during his lifetime, a substantial change from old ways of living to new ones.

In order to define this change more precisely, it is necessary to make three assumptions: (1) there are different forms of social recommitment relevant for politics; (2) these forms tend to be associated with each other; and (3) these forms tend to reinforce each other in their effects. Two further points may be noted for investigation: (4) each of these forms may have a threshold at which some of its effects may change substantially; and (5) some or all of these thresholds, though not identical in quantitative terms, may be significantly related to each other.

For these constituent processes of social mobilization we may then choose the symbols $m_1, m_2, m_3, \ldots, m_n$. Thus we may call m_1 the exposure to aspects of modern life through demonstrations of machinery, buildings, installations, consumer goods, show windows, rumor, governmental, medical or military practices, as well as through mass media of communication. Then m_2 may stand for a narrower concept, exposure to these mass media alone. And m_3 may stand for change of residence; m_4 for urbanization; m_5 for change from agricultural occupations; m_6 for literacy; m_7 for per-capita income; and so on.

Our m_1 could then stand for the percentage of the population that had been exposed in any substantial way to significant aspects of modern life; m_2 for the

of Basic Trends and Patterns in Comparative and International Politics," *The American Political Science Review*, **54** (March 1960), 34.

percentage of those exposed to mass media, i.e., the mass media audience; m_3 for the percentage of the inhabitants who have changed their locality of residence (or their district, province or state); m_4 for the percentage of the total population living in towns; m_5 for the percentage of those in nonagricultural occupations among the total of those gainfully occupied; m_6 for the percentage of literates; m_7 could be measured simply by net national product, or alternatively by gross national product in dollars per capita. At this stage in the compilation of evidence the exact choice of indicators and definitions must be considerably influenced by the availability of statistical data. In many cases it may be most satisfactory to use the data and definitions published by the United Nations, in such volumes as the *United Nations Demographic Year Book*, the *United Nations World Social Survey*, the *United Nations Statistical Year Book*, and a host of more specialized UN publications.[6]

In a modern, highly developed and fully mobilized country m_7 should be above $600 gross national product per capita; m_1, m_2, and m_6 should all be well above 90 per cent; m_4 and m_5 should be above 50 per cent, even in countries producing large agricultural surpluses beyond their domestic consumption; and even m_3, the change of residence, seems to be higher than 50 per cent in such a country as the United States. In an extremely underdeveloped country, such as Ethiopia, m_7 is well below $100 and the remaining

indicators may be near 5 per cent or even lower.

In the course of economic development, as countries are becoming somewhat less like Ethiopia and somewhat more like the United States, all these indicators tend to change in the same direction, even though they do not change at the same rate. They exhibit therefore to some extent a characteristic which Paul Lazarsfeld has termed the "interchangeability of indicators"; if one (or even several) of these indicators should be missing it could be replaced in many cases by the remaining ones, or by other indicators similarly chosen, and the general level and direction of the underlying social process would still remain clear.[7] This characteristic holds, however, only as a first approximation. The lags and discrepancies between the different indicators can reveal much of interest to the student of politics, and some of these discrepancies will be discussed below.

The first and main thing about social mobilization is, however, that it does assume a single underlying process of which particular indicators represent only particular aspects; that these indicators are correlated and to a limited extent interchangeable; and that this complex of processes of social change is significantly correlated with major changes in politics.

The overall index of social mobilization, M, is a second order index; it measures the correlation between the first order indices $m_1 \ldots m_n$. It should express, furthermore, the probability that the $(n+1)$th index will be similarly correlated with its predecessors, regardless of how large a number n might be provided, only that the index itself was appropriately chosen. Differently put, to assert that social mobilization is a "real" process, at certain times and in certain countries, is to assert that there exists for these cases a large and

[6] Cf. the pamphlets issued by the Statistical Office of the United Nations, Statistical Papers, Series K, No. 1, "Survey of Social Statistics," (Sales No.: 1954. 17, 8), New York, 1954, and Statistical Papers, Series M, No. 11, Rev. 1, "List of Statistical Series collected by International Organizations," (Sales No.: 1955. 17, 6), New York, 1955. For somewhat earlier data, see also W. S. Woytinsky and E. S. Woytinsky, *World Commerce and Governments: Trends and Outlook* (New York, The Twentieth Century Fund, 1955), and *World Population and Production: Trends and Outlook* (New York, The Twentieth Century Fund, 1953).

[7] See Hortense Horwitz and Elias Smith, "The Interchangeability of Socio-Economic Indices," in Paul F. Lazarsfeld and Morris Rosenberg, *The Language of Social Research* (Glencoe, 1955), 73–77.

potentially unlimited number of possible measurements and indicators, all correlated with each other and testifying by their number and by the strength of their correlation to the reality of the underlying phenomenon.

In practice, of course, the range of available measurements and indicators is likely to be limited, and ordinarily there should be no need to compile for any particular time and country even all those data that could be found. On the contrary, one's usual aim will be economy: to get the greatest amount of useful information from the smallest body of data. The seven indicators of social mobilization listed above as m_1 to m_7 should quite suffice, in most cases, to give a fairly good first picture of the situation. They were chosen in part on grounds of availability and convenience, but also because they are less closely correlated, and hence less completely interchangeable, than some other indices might be.

Each of the seven processes chosen could itself be measured by several different indicators, but in each case these sub-indicators are apt to be very closely correlated and almost completely interchangeable. Literacy, for instance, can be measured as a percentage of the population above fifteen or above ten, or above seven years of age; it could be defined as the ability to recognize a few words, or to read consecutively, or to write. Each of these particular definitions would yield a different numerical answer, but so long as the same definition was used for each country, or for each period within the same country, each of these yardsticks would reveal much the same state of affairs. If applied to Morocco between 1920 and 1950, e.g., each of these tests would have shown how the number of literate Moroccans began to outgrow the number of literate Frenchmen in that country, with obvious implications for its political future.

Similarly, urbanization could be measured in terms of the population of all localities of more than 2000 or more than 5000, or more than 20,000 or 50,000 inhabitants; or it could be measured, less satisfactorily, in terms of the population of all those localities that had a charter or a city form of government. Each of these criteria of measurement would have revealed the same process of large-scale urban growth in Finland between 1870 and 1920, for instance, or in India between 1900 and 1940, which had such far-reaching effects on political life in these countries. A recent unpublished study by Frederick E. Tibbetts 3rd suggests once again the close interchangeability of different indicators of urban growth in Canada, as they bear upon the problems of assimilation and differentiation among the French-speaking and English-speaking population of that country. Urbanization, Tibbetts finds, has outstripped in recent decades the learning of English among French-Canadians; he finds among urban residents, and generally in nonagricultural occupations, a growing number of persons who speak no other language but French. The political significance of this development, which was largely concentrated in the province of Quebec, is highlighted by his observation that in 1951 Quebec (omitting Montreal), with 21 per cent of the total population of Canada, had only 4 and 7 per cent, respectively, of the veterans of World Wars I and II.[8]

Among the seven major indicators of social mobilization proposed in this paper, the correlations between economic development and literacy are less complete and the discrepancies more revealing. Ethiopia and Burma both have per-capita gross national products of about $50, but Ethiopia has less than 5 per cent literates and is politically stable; Burma reports

---

[8] Frederick E. Tibbetts 3rd, "The Cycles of Canadian Nationalism," Yale University, typescript, 1959, pp. 24, 26–31. For details of the Finnish and Indian cases referred to above, see K. W. Deutsch, *Nationalism and Social Communication* (New York, 1953), pp. 102–111, 170–182, 197–204.

over 45 per cent literates and is not.[9] Of the states of India, Kerala, with one of the highest rates of literacy, elected a Communist government in the late 1950's.

It may thus be useful to seek answers to two kinds of questions: (1) how good is the correlation between the seven main indicators and (2) how interesting are the variant cases? As regards the first question, it has already been pointed out that the numerical values of the seven main indicators will not be identical. However if we think of each of these indicators as forming a separate scale, on which each country could rank anywhere from, say, the top fifth to the bottom fifth, then we could measure the extent to which the rankings of a country on each of these indicator scales are correlated. From general impressions of the data, I should surmise that these rank order correlations should have coefficients of correlation of about 0.6 to 0.8, accounting on the average for perhaps one-half of the observed variation. As regards the second question, each of the cases showing substantial discrepancies between some of the main indicators will have to be studied separately, but the examples of Burma and Kerala, just mentioned, suggest that such cases may well repay investigation, and that the comparison of indicators may serve political scientists as a crude but perhaps useful research device.

For a somewhat more refined study the notion of two thresholds may be introduced. The first of these is the threshold of significance, S, that is, the numerical value below which no significant departure from the customary workings of a traditional society can be detected and no significant disturbance appears to be created in its unchanged functioning. For each of the particular indicators, m_1 through m_7, we should expect to find a corresponding particular threshold of significance, s_1 through s_7; and our concept of social mobilization should imply that, once several major indicators move to or beyond this threshold of significance, the remaining indicators should also be at or above their respective levels of significance. The probability that this will be in fact the case should indicate once again what degree of reality, if any, may be inherent in the concept of social mobilization as an overall process.

The second threshold would be that of criticality for significant changes in the side effects, actual or apparent, of the process of social mobilization. At what level of each of the indicators we listed above do such changes in social or political side effects appear?

The indicator of literacy may serve as an example. It has often been remarked that even a considerable advance in literacy, say from 10 per cent to 60 per cent of the population above fifteen years of age, does not seem to be correlated with any significant change in the birthrate, if one compares literacy and birthrate levels of a large number of countries in the 1950's. At the level of 80 per cent literacy, however, there appears a conspicuous change: for the same collection of countries, not one with a literacy rate above 80 per cent has a birthrate above 3 per cent a year.[10] As a provisional hypothesis for further testing, one might conjecture that a literacy rate of more than 80 per cent might indicate such an advanced and thoroughgoing stage of social mobilization and modernization as to influence even those intimate patterns of family life that find their expression in the birthrate of a country. Obviously such a' hypothesis would require other evidence for confirmation, but even in its quite tentative stage it may illustrate our point. If it were true, then the 80 per cent level would be a threshold of criticality on the particular

---

[9] Note however, the comment on Burmese literacy, in the Appendix to this article, below.

[10] Rosemary Klineberg, "Correlation of Literacy Rates with 1956 Birth Rates," Fletcher School of Law and Diplomacy, 1959, unpublished.

scale of literacy as an indicator of social mobilization.

Since we called the indicator of literacy m_6, we might write c_6 for the particular threshold of criticality on that scale and put it as equal to 80 per cent. It would then be a matter for further investigation to find out whether other critical changes also occur near the passing of the 80 per cent literacy level. If so, c_6 might turn out to be the main threshold of criticality for this indicator. If important side effects should show critical changes at different literacy levels, we might have to assume several thresholds of criticality, which we might write c_6', c_6'', and so on.

Other indicators might well have their own thresholds of criticality at other percentage points on their particular scales. It might turn out, for instance, that most of the countries with more than 80 per cent literacy were also more than, say, 40 per cent urban, and that the apparent side effects observable above the 80 per cent literacy mark were also observable above the 40 per cent level on the urbanization scale. If such different but correlated thresholds of criticality could be found for all of our seven indicators, then the concept of social mobilization could be expressed as a probability that, if for some country n different indicators should show values equal to or greater than their respective critical levels, then any relevant $(n+1)$th indicator also would turn out to be at or above its own critical threshold.

Much of what has been said thus far may be summarized in concise notation. If we write P as the conventional symbol for probability, M_S as the symbol for the overall process of social mobilization in regard to the thresholds of significance, and M_C as the symbol for the same process in regard to the thresholds of criticality, then we may write the general concept of social mobilization briefly as follows:

1. $M_S = P$ (if $m_n \leqslant s_n$, then $m_{n+1} \leqslant s_{n+1}$)
or briefly,
   $M_S = P\ (m_n \leqslant s_n)$

and

2. $M_C = P$ (if $m_n \leqslant c_n$, then $m_{n+1} \leqslant c_{n+1}$)
or briefly,
   $M_C = (m_n \leqslant c_n)$
and perhaps also
3. $M = P\ (M_S = M_C)$

None of these shorthand formulas should require further comment here. They merely summarize what has been said at greater length in the preceding pages. Readers who find such formulations uncongenial may skip them, therefore, without loss, so long as they have followed the verbal argument.

Some Implications for the Politics of Development

In whatever country it occurs, social mobilization brings with it an expansion of the politically relevant strata of the population. These politically relevant strata are a broader group than the elite: they include all those persons who must be taken into account in politics. Dock workers and trade union members in Ghana, Nigeria, or the United States, for instance, are not necessarily members of the elites of these countries, but they are quite likely to count for something in their political life. In the developing countries of Asia, Africa, and parts of Latin America, the political process usually does not include the mass of isolated, subsistence-farming, tradition-bound and politically apathetic villagers, but it does include increasingly the growing numbers of city dwellers, market farmers, users of money, wage earners, radio listeners and literates in town and country. The growth in the numbers of these people produces mounting pressures for the transformation of political practices and institutions, and since this future growth can be estimated at least to some extent on the basis of trends and data from the recent past, some of the expectable growth in political pressures—we may call it the potential level of political tensions—can likewise be estimated.

Social mobilization also brings about a change in the quality of politics, by changing the range of human needs that impinge upon the political process. As people are uprooted from their physical and intellectual isolation in their immediate localities, from their old habits and traditions, and often from their old patterns of occupation and places of residence, they experience drastic changes in their needs. They may now come to need provisions for housing and employment, for social security against illness and old age, for medical care against the health hazards of their crowded new dwellings and places of work and the risk of accidents with unfamiliar machinery. They may need succor against the risks of cyclical or seasonal unemployment, against oppressive charges of rent or interest, and against sharp fluctuations in the prices of the main commodities which they must sell or buy. They need instruction for themselves and education for their children. They need, in short, a wide range and large amounts of new government services.

These needs ordinarily cannot be met by traditional types of government, inherited from a precommercial and preindustrial age. Maharajahs, sultans, sheikhs, and chieftains all are quite unlikely to cope with these new problems, and traditional rule by land-owning oligarchies or long-established religious bodies most often is apt to prove equally disappointing in the face of the new needs. Most of the attempts to change the characteristics of the traditional ruling families—perhaps by supplying them with foreign advisers or by having their children study in some foreign country—are likely to remain superficial in their effects, overshadowed by mounting pressures for more thoroughgoing changes.

In developing countries of today, however, the increasingly ineffective and unpopular traditional authorities cannot be replaced successfully by their historic successors in the Western world, the classic institutions of eighteenth and nineteenth-century liberalism and *laissez-faire*. For the uprooted, impoverished and disoriented masses produced by social mobilization, it is surely untrue that that government is best that governs least. They are far more likely to need a direct transition from traditional government to the essentials of a modern welfare state. The developing countries of Asia, Africa and parts of Latin America may have to accomplish, therefore, within a few decades a process of political change which in the history of Western Europe and North America took at least as many generations; and they may have to accomplish this accelerated change almost in the manner of a jump, omitting as impractical some of the historic stages of transition through a period of near *laissez-faire* that occurred in the West.

The growing need for new and old government services usually implies persistent political pressures for an increased scope of government and a greater relative size of the government sector in the national economy. In the mid-1950's, the total government budget—national, regional and local—tended to amount to roughly 10 per cent of the gross national product in the very poor and poorly mobilized countries with annual per-capita gross national products at or below $100. For highly developed and highly mobilized countries, such as those with per-capita gross national products at or above $900, the corresponding proportion of the total government sector was about 30 per cent. If one drew only the crudest and most provisional inference from these figures, one might expect something like a 2.5 per cent shift of national income into the government sector for every $100 gain in per-capita gross national product in the course of economic development. It might be more plausible, however, to expect a somewhat more rapid expansion of the government sector during the earlier stages of economic development, but the elucidation of this entire problem—with all its obvious political implications—would require and reward a great deal more research.

The relationship between the total process of social mobilization and the growth of the national income, it should be recalled here, is by no means symmetrical. Sustained income growth is very unlikely without social mobilization, but a good deal of social mobilization may be going on even in the absence of per-capita income growth, such as occurs in countries with poor resources or investment policies, and with rapid population growth. In such cases, social mobilization still would generate pressures for an expansion of government services and hence of the government sector, even in a relatively stagnant or conceivably retrograde economy. Stopping or reversing in such cases the expansion of government or the process of social mobilization behind it—even if this could be done—hardly would make matters much better. The more attractive course for such countries might rather be to use the capabilities of their expanding governments so as to bring about improvements in their resources and investment policies, and an eventual resumption of economic growth. To what extent this has been, or could be, brought about in cases of this kind, would make another fascinating topic for study.

The figures just given apply, of course, only to non-Communist countries; the inclusion of Communist states would make the average in each class of government sectors higher. It would be interesting to investigate, however, whether and to what extent the tendency toward the relative expansion of the government sector in the course of social mobilization applies also, *mutatis mutandis*, to the Communist countries.

A greater scope of governmental services and functions requires ordinarily an increase in the capabilities of government. Usually it requires an increase in the numbers and training of governmental personnel, an increase in governmental offices and institutions, and a significant improvement in administrative organization and efficiency. A rapid process of social mobilization thus tends to generate major pressures for political and administrative reform. Such reforms may include notably both a quantitative expansion of the bureaucracy and its qualitative improvement in the direction of a competent civil service—even though these two objectives at times may clash.

Similar to its impact on this specific area of government, social mobilization tends to generate also pressures for a more general transformation of the political elite. It tends to generate pressures for a broadening and partial transformation of elite functions, of elite recruitment, and of elite communications. On all these counts, the old elites of traditional chiefs, village headmen, and local notables are likely to prove ever more inadequate; and political leadership may tend to shift to the new political elite of party or quasiparty organizations, formal or informal, legal or illegal, but always led by the new "marginal men" who have been exposed more or less thoroughly to the impact of modern education and urban life.

Something similar applies to elite communications. The more broadly recruited elites must communicate among themselves, and they must do so more impersonally and over greater distances. They must resort more often to writing and to paper work. At the same time they must direct a greater part of their communications output at the new political strata; this puts a premium on oratory and journalism, and on skill in the use of all mass media of communication. At the same time rapid social mobilization causes a critical problem in the communications intake of elites. It confronts them with the ever present risk of losing touch with the newly mobilized social strata which until recently still did not count in politics. Prime Minister Nehru's reluctance to take into account the strength and intensity of Mahratti sentiment in the language conflict of Bombay in the 1950's and his general tendency since the mid-1930's to underestimate the strength of communal and linguistic sentiment in India suggest the seriousness of this problem even for major democratic leaders.

The increasing numbers of the mobilized population, and the greater scope and urgency of their needs for political decisions and governmental services, tend to translate themselves, albeit with a time lag, into increased political participation. This may express itself informally through greater numbers of people taking part in crowds and riots, in meetings and demonstrations, in strikes and uprisings, or, less dramatically, as members of a growing audience for political communications, written or by radio, or finally as members of a growing host of organizations. While many of these organizations are ostensibly nonpolitical, such as improvement societies, study circles, singing clubs, gymnastic societies, agricultural and commercial associations, fraternal orders, workmen's benefit societies, and the like, they nevertheless tend to acquire a political tinge, particularly in countries where more open outlets for political activities are not available. But even where there are established political parties and elections, a network of seemingly nonpolitical or marginally political organizations serves an important political function by providing a dependable social setting for the individuals who have been partly or wholly uprooted or alienated from their traditional communities. Such organizations may serve at the same time as marshalling grounds for the entry of these persons into political life.

Where people have the right to vote, the effects of social mobilization are likely to be reflected in the electoral statistics. This process finds its expression both through a tendency towards a higher voting participation of those already enfranchised and through an extension of the franchise itself to additional groups of the population. Often the increase in participation amongst those who already have the right to vote precedes the enfranchisement of new classes of voters, particularly in countries where the broadening of the franchise is occurring

gradually. Thus in Norway between 1830 and 1860, voting participation remained near the level of about 10 per cent of the adult male population; in the 1870's and 1880's this participation rose rapidly among the enfranchised voters, followed by extensions of the franchise, until by the year 1900, 40 per cent of the Norwegian men were actually voting. This process was accompanied by a transformation of Norwegian politics, the rise to power of the radical peasant party *Venstre*, and a shift from the earlier acceptance of the existing Swedish-Norwegian Union to rising demands for full Norwegian independence.[11] These political changes had been preceded or accompanied by a rise in several of the usual indicators of social mobilization among the Norwegian people.

Another aspect of the process of social mobilization is the shift of emphasis away from the parochialism and internationalism of many traditional cultures to a preoccupation with the supralocal but far less than worldwide unit of the territorial, and eventually national, state.

An as yet unpublished study of American communications before the American Revolution, which has been carried on by Richard Merritt, shows how during the years 1735–75 in the colonial newspapers the percentage of American or all-colonial symbols rose from about 10 to about 40 per cent, at the cost, in the main, of a decline in the share of symbols referring to places or events in the world outside the colonies and Britain, while Britain's share in American news attention remained relatively unchanged. Within the group of American symbols, the main increase occurred among those which referred to America or to the colonies as a whole, rather than among those referring to particular colonies or sections.[12]

[11] See Raymond Lindgren, *Norway-Sweden: Union, Disunion, Reunion* (Princeton, Princeton University Press, 1959); and K. W. Deutsch, *et al., Political Community and the North Atlantic Area* (Princeton University Press, 1957).
[12] Richard Merritt's monograph, "Symbols of American Nationalism, 1735–1775," which is

More recent experiences in some of the "development countries" also suggest a more rapid rise of attention devoted to national topics than of that given to world affairs, on the one hand, and to purely local matters, on the other. This, however, is at present largely an impression. The nature and extent of attention shifts in mass media, as well as in popular attitudes, in the course of social mobilization is a matter for research that should be as promising as it is needed.[13]

Some data on the flow of domestic and foreign mails point in a similar direction. Of five development countries for which data are readily available the ratio of domestic to foreign mail rose substantially in four—Egypt, Iran, Nigeria, and Turkey —from 1913 to 1946–51; the fifth, Indonesia, was an exception but was the scene of internal unrest and protracted warfare against the Dutch during much of the latter period. The trend for Egypt, Iran, Nigeria, and Turkey is confirmed in each case by data for the intermediate period 1928–34, which are also intermediate, in each case, between the low domestic-foreign mail ratio for 1913 and the high ratios for 1946–51. Many additional development countries—including the Gold Coast (now Ghana), the Belgian Congo, Malaya, French Morocco, Kenya-Uganda, Tanganyika, Mozambique, and Malaya— for which data were found only for the 1928–34 to 1946–51 comparison, show upward trends in their ratios of domestic to foreign mail.[14] Here again, a relatively moderate investment in the further collec-

tion and study of data might lead to interesting results.

According to some data from another recent study, a further side effect of social mobilization and economic development might possibly be first a substantial expansion, and then a lesser but significant reduction, of the share of the international trade sector in the national economy. Thus, in the course of British development, the proportion of total foreign trade (including trade to British overseas possessions) rose from an average of 20 per cent in 1830– 40 to a peak of 60 per cent in 1870–79, remained close to that level until 1913, but declined subsequently and stood at less than 40 per cent in 1959. Similarly, the proportion of foreign trade to national income rose in Germany from about 28 per cent in 1802–30 to a peak of 45 per cent in 1870–79, declined to 35 per cent in 1900–09, and by 1957 had recovered, for the much smaller German Federal Republic, to only 42 per cent. In Japan, the early proportion of foreign trade to national income was 15 per cent in 1885–89, rising to peaks of 41 per cent in 1915–19 and 40 per cent in 1925–29; but by 1957 it stood at only 31 per cent. Data for Denmark, Norway, France, and Argentina give a similar picture, while the same foreign-trade-to-national-income ratio in the United States fell, with minor fluctuations, from 23 per cent in 1799 to less than 9 per cent in 1958.[15] Here again the evidence is incomplete and partly contradictory, and the tentative interpretation, indicated at the beginning of this paragraph, still stands in need of confirmation and perhaps modification through additional research.

to cover eventually one or more newspapers from Massachusetts, New York, Pennsylvania, and Virginia, respectively, will be published in due course.
[13] For examples of pioneering contributions of this kind, see the series of Hoover Institute Studies by Harold Lasswell, Ithiel Pool, Daniel Lerner, and others, and particularly Pool, *The Prestige Papers* (Stanford, Stanford University Press, 1951).
[14] See charts 1, 3, and 4 in Karl W. Deutsch, "Shifts in the Balance of Communication Flows: A Problem of Measurement in International Relations," *Public Opinion Quarterly*,

20 (Spring 1956), 152–155, based on data of the Universal Postal Union.
[15] See Karl W. Deutsch and Alexander Eckstein, "National Industrialization and the Declining Share of the International Economic Sector, 1890–1957," *World Politics*, 13 (January 1961), 267–299. See also Simon Kuznets, *Six Lectures on Economic Growth* (Glencoe, 1959), esp. the section on "The Problem of Size" and "Trends in Foreign Trade Ratios," 89–107.

The problem of the ratio of the sector of internationally oriented economic activities relative to total national income—and thus indirectly the problem of the political power potential of internationally exposed or involved interest groups vis-à-vis the rest of the community—leads us to the problem of the size of states and of the scale of effective political communities. As we have seen, the process of social mobilization generates strong pressures towards increasing the capabilities of government, by increasing the volume and range of demands made upon the government and administration, and by widening the scope of politics and the membership of the politically relevant strata. The same process increases the frequency and the critical importance of direct communications between government and governed. It thus necessarily increases the importance of the language, the media, and the channels through which these communications are carried on.

Other things assumed equal, the stage of rapid social mobilization may be expected, therefore, to promote the consolidation of states whose peoples already share the same language, culture, and major social institutions; while the same process may tend to strain or destroy the unity of states whose population is already divided into several groups with different languages or cultures or basic ways of life. By the same token, social mobilization may tend to promote the merging of several smaller states, or political units such as cantons, principalities, sultanates, or tribal areas, whose populations already share substantially the same language, culture, and social system; and it may tend to inhibit, or at least to make more difficult, the merging of states or political units whose populations or ruling personnel differ substantially in regard to any of these matters. Social mobilization may thus assist to some extent in the consolidation of the United Arab Republic, but raise increasing problems for the politics and administration of multilingual India—problems which the federal government of India may have to meet or overcome by a series of creative adjustments.[16]

In the last analysis, however, the problem of the scale of states goes beyond the effects of language, culture, or institutions, important as all these are. In the period of rapid social mobilization, the acceptable scale of a political unit will tend to depend eventually upon its performance. If a government fails to meet the increasing burdens put upon it by the process of social mobilization, a growing proportion of the population is likely to become alienated and disaffected from the state, even if the same language, culture, and basic social institutions were shared originally throughout the entire state territory by rulers and ruled alike. The secession of the United States and of Ireland from the British Empire, and of the Netherlands and of Switzerland from the German Empire may serve in part as examples. At bottom, the popular acceptance of a government in a period of social mobilization is most of all a matter of its capabilities and the manner in which they are used—that is, essentially a matter of its responsiveness to the felt needs of its population. If it proves persistently incapable or unresponsive, some or many of its subjects will cease to identify themselves with it psychologically; it will be reduced to ruling by force where it can no longer rule by display, example, and persuasion; and if political alternatives to it appear, it will be replaced eventually by other political units, larger or smaller in extent, which at least promise to respond more effectively to the needs and expectations of their peoples.

[16] For more detailed arguments, see Deutsch, *Nationalism and Social Communication*, and Deutsch, *et al.*, *Political Community and the North Atlantic Area;* see also the discussions in Ernst B. Haas, "Regionalism, Functionalism and Universal Organization," *World Politics*, **8** (January 1956), and "The Challenge of Regionalism," *International Organization*, **12** (1958), 440–458; and in Stanley Hoffmann, *Contemporary Theory in International Relations* (Englewood Cliffs, N.J., Prentice-Hall, 1960), 223–240.

In practice the results of social mobilization often have tended to increase the size of the state, well beyond the old tribal areas, petty principalities, or similar districts of the traditional era, while increasing the direct contact between government and governed far beyond the levels of the sociologically superficial and often half-shadowy empire of the past.

This growth in the size of modern states, capable of coping with the results of social mobilization, is counteracted and eventually inhibited, however, as their size increases, by their tendency to increasing preoccupation with their own internal affairs. There is considerable evidence for this trend toward a self-limitation in the growth of states through a decline in the attention, resources, and responsiveness available for coping with the implicit needs and explicit messages of the next marginal unit of population and territory on the verge of being included in the expanding state.[17]

The remarks in this section may have sufficed to illustrate, though by no means to exhaust, the significance of the process of social mobilization in the economic and political development of countries. The main usefulness of the concept, however, should lie in the possibility of quantitative study which it offers. How much social mobilization, as measured by our seven indicators, has been occurring in some country per year or per decade during some period of its history, or during recent times? And what is the meaning of the differences between the rates at which some of the constituent subprocesses of social mobilization may have been going on? Although specific data will have to be found separately for each country, it should be possible to sketch a general quantitative model to show some of the interrelations and their possible significance.

[17] Cf. Karl W. Deutsch, "The Propensity to International Transactions," *Political Studies*, **8** (June 1960), 147–155.

A Quantitative Model of the Social Mobilization Process

For a quantitative description, it is convenient to express our first six indicators not in terms of the total percentage of the population which is literate, or exposed to modern life, etc., but in terms only of that average annual percentage of the total population which has been added to, or subtracted from, the total share of the population in that category. If for some country our indicator showed, say, 40 per cent exposed to significant aspects of modern life in 1940, and 60 per cent so exposed in 1950, the average annual percentage shift, dm_1 would be 2 per cent. The seventh indicator, per-capita increase, may be broken up into two elements and written as the annual percentage of the total income added, dm_7 and the annual percentage of population growth, p.

Adopting these conventions, we may use in this model, for purposes of illustration, crudely estimated magnitudes from various collections of data. If we add indicators for the increase in voting participation, and in linguistic, cultural or political assimilation, we may write for a case of fairly rapid social mobilization a small table of the sort shown in Table 1. The case represented by this table is an imaginary one, but the different rates of subprocesses of social mobilization are not necessarily unrealistic, and neither are the consequences suggested by this model, for the stability of the government in any country to which these or similar assumptions would apply.

Before discussing these consequences more explicitly, it should be made clear that the annual rates of change are likely to be realistic, at most, only for countries during the rapid middle stages of the process of social mobilization and economic development—say, for a range of between 10 and 80 per cent literacy and for analogous ranges of other indicators of economic development. In the earliest stages, the annual percentages of the population shifting into a more mobilized

TABLE 1. *A Hypothetical Example of a Country Undergoing Rapid Social Mobilization: Rates of Changes*

SYMBOL OF INDICATOR	DESCRIPTION	AVERAGE ANNUAL % OF TOTAL POPULATION OR INCOME ADDED TO CATEGORY	
		RANGE	MEDIAN
Group I: dm_1	Shift into any substantial exposure to modernity, incl. rumors, demonstrations of machinery or merchandise, etc.	2.0 to 4.0	3.0
dm_2	Shift into mass media audience (radio, movies, posters, press)	1.5 to 4.0	2.75
dm_8	Increase in voting participation	0.2 to 4.0	2.1
dm_6	Increase in literacy	1.0 to 1.4	1.2
dm_3	Change of locality of residence	1.0 to 1.5	1.25
p	Population growth	(1.9 to 3.3)	(2.6)
Group II: dm_5	Occupational shift out of agriculture	0.4 to 1.0	0.7
dm_4	Change from rural to urban residence	0.1 to 1.2	0.5
a	Linguistic, cultural or political assimilation	−0.5 to 1.0	0.25
dy	Income growth	(2.0 to 8.0)	(5.0)
dm_7	Income growth per capita	—	(2.3)

Note. Figures in parentheses refer to percentage increases against the previous year, and thus are not strictly comparable to percentage shifts among sub-categories of the total population. A shift of 1.2 per cent of all adults into the category of literates, for instance, would refer to the total adult population, including the part just added by population aging; etc.

state are apt to be much smaller, and in the late stages of the process something like a "ceiling effect" may be expected to appear—once 80 or 90 per cent of the population have become literate, any further annual gains in the percentage of literates in the population are likely to be small.

Within the middle stages of development, however, which are appropriate to the assumptions of the model, a cumulative strain on political stability may be expected. All the rates of change in group I tend to make for increased demands or burdens upon the government, and all of them have median values above 1 per cent per year. The rates of change in group II are related to the capabilities of the

government for coping with these burdens, but the median values of all these rates, with only one exception, are well below 1 per cent. If it were not for this exception—the assumed 5 per cent annual increase in national income—one would have to predict from the model an annual shift of perhaps 1 per cent or more of the population into the category of at least partly socially mobilized but largely unassimilated and dissatisfied people.

If one assumes, in accordance with this model, an annual entry of 2.75 per cent of the population into the mass media audience and a shift of only 0.6 per cent into nonagricultural employment, then the expectable increase in the numbers of not adequately reemployed new members of the mass media audience might be as high as 2.15 per cent of the population per year, or more than one-fifth of the population within a decade. This might be the proportion of people newly participating in their imagination in the new opportunities and attractions of modern life, while still being denied most or all of these new opportunities in fact—something which should be a fairly effective prescription for accumulating political trouble. The spread of more effective methods of production and perhaps of improved patterns of land tenure, rural credit, and other betterments within the agricultural sector could do something to counteract this tendency; but short of major and sustained efforts at such agricultural improvements the dangerous gap between the fast-growing mass media audience and the slow-growing circle of more adequately employed and equipped persons is likely to remain and to increase.

If linguistic, cultural or political assimilation—that is, the more or less permanent change of stable habits of language, culture, legitimacy, and loyalty—is also a relevant problem in the country concerned, then the lag of the slow assimilation rate, put at only 0.25 per cent per year in our model, behind the far more rapid mobilization rates of 0.5 to 3.0 per cent for the various subprocesses in our model, might be even larger for some of them, and potentially more serious.

Table 2 shows some of the implications of our model for a hypothetical country of 10 million population, $100 per-capita income, a principal language spoken by 35 per cent of its inhabitants, and a relatively low degree of social mobilization in 1950. Conditions somewhat similar to these can in fact be found in several countries in Africa and Asia. Table 2 then shows the expectable state of affairs for our imaginary country in 1960 and 1970, if

TABLE 2. *A Hypothetical Example of a Country Undergoing Rapid Social Mobilization: Assumed Levels for 1950 and Expectable Levels for 1960 and 1970*

SYMBOL OF INDICATOR	DESCRIPTION	PER CENT OF TOTAL POPULATION		
		1950	1960	1970
Group I: m_1	Population exposed to modernity	35	65	95
m_2	Mass media audience	20	47.5	75
m_8	Actual voting participation	20	41	62
m_6	Literates	15	27	39
m_3	Persons who changed locality of residence since birth	10	22.5	35
P	Total population (millions)	(10)	(12.9)	(16.7)
Group II: m_5	Population in non-agricultural occupations	18	25	32
m_4	Urban population	15	20	25
A	Linguistically assimilated population	35	35.5	40
Y	Total income (million $)	(1000)	(1629)	(2653)
m_7	Per capita income ($)	(100)	(126)	(159)

Note. Figures in parentheses refer to absolute numbers, not percentages. Because of rounding, calculations are approximate.

we assume the rates of change given in our model, as set forth in Table 1, and their persistence over twenty years. As can be seen from Table 2, the cumulative effects of these changes from 1950 to 1960 will appear still moderate, but by 1970 these effects will have become so great that many of the political institutions and practices of 1950 might be no longer applicable to the new conditions.

As Table 2 shows, a major transformation of the underlying political and social structure of a country could occur—and could pose a potential threat to the stability of any insufficiently reform-minded government there—even during a period of substantially rising per-capita income.

To be sure, many of these political and social difficulties could be assuaged with the help of the benefits potentially available through the 5 per cent increase in total national income, which was assumed for our model. Such a 5 per cent growth rate of total income is not necessarily unrealistic. It is close to the average of 5.3 per cent, found by Paul Studenski in a recent survey of data from a large number of non-Communist countries.[18] Since the rate of population growth, assumed for the model, was 2.6 per cent—which is well above the world average in recent years—the average per-capita income might be expected to rise by slightly more than 2 per cent per year.[19] These additional amounts of available income might well go at least some part of the way to meet the new popular needs and expectations aroused by the mobilization process, if the income can be devoted to consumption and price levels remain stable. But any incre-

[18] Cf. Paul Studenski, *The Income of Nations* (New York, New York University Press, 1958), p. 249; cf. also pp. 244–250.
[19] Cf. United Nations, Department of Social and Economic Affairs, Population Studies No. 28, "The Future Growth of World Population" (New York, 1958), and United Nations, Bureau of Social Affairs, *Report of the World Social Situation* (Sales No.: 1957, **4**, 3) (New York, 1957), p. 5.

ments of income will also be needed for savings (in addition to loans and grants from abroad) to permit a high rate of investment and an adequate rate of expansion of opportunities for education, employment, and consumption for the growing numbers of the mobilized population.

These beneficial consequences could only be expected, however, if we assume that an adequate share of the increase in income would go directly or indirectly to the newly mobilized groups and strata of the population. Unfortunately, no assumption of this kind would be realistic for many of the developing countries of Asia and Africa.

It would be far more realistic to assume that in most of these countries the top 10 per cent of income receivers are getting about 50 per cent of the total national income, if not more. If we assume further, as seems not implausible, that in the absence of specific social reforms the increase in income will be distributed among the various strata of the population roughly in proportion to the present share of each group in the total national income, then we may expect that the richest 10 per cent of the people will get about 50 per cent of the additional income produced by income growth. At the same time, since these richest 10 per cent are not likely to be much more fertile than the rest of the population, they are likely to get only 10 per cent of the population increase; and they will, therefore, on the average not only get richer in absolute terms, but they will also retain the full extent of their relative lead over the rest of the population; and so they will increase in absolute terms the gap in income that separates them from the mass of their countrymen. Under the same assumptions, however, we should expect that the poorest nine-tenths of the population will get only one-tenth of the total income gain, but that they will get up to nine-tenths of the entire population growth; and that on the average these poorest 90 per cent of the people will remain in relative terms as far below the level of the rich one-tenth as ever. The fact that the poorer majority will have become slightly richer in absolute terms may then in the main increase their awareness of the wide gap between their living standards and those of their rulers; and it might at the same time increase their ability to take political action.

Differently put, if for the entire country the *average* per-capita income was assumed to rise, we must now add that under the assumptions stated, the "social gap"— the gap between the incomes of the poorest 90 per cent and those of the top 10 per cent—may well be expected to increase. Political stability, however, may well be more affected by changes in the income gap than by changes in the average which in this respect might be little more than a statistical abstraction. Our model would lead us to expect, therefore, on the whole the danger of a significant deterioration of political stability in any development country to which its assumptions might apply. Since these assumptions were chosen with an eye to making them parallel, as far as possible, to the more rapid among the actual rates found in countries of this type, the expectations of rising political tensions in countries undergoing rapid social mobilization may not be unrealistic.

To rely upon automatic developments in economic and political life in those countries of the Free World to which the assumptions of our model apply, would be to court mounting instability, the overthrow of existing governments and their replacement by no less unstable successors, or else their eventual absorption into the Communist bloc. Deliberate political and economic intervention into the social mobilization process, on the other hand, might open up some more hopeful perspectives. Such intervention should not aim at retarding economic and social development, in the manner of the policies of the regime of Prince Metternich in Austria during much of the first half of the nineteenth century. Those policies of

slowing down social mobilization and economic development in the main only diminished the capabilities of the government, paved the way to domestic failures and international defeats and were followed over the course of three generations by the persistent backwardness and ultimate destruction of the state. A more promising policy might have to be, on the contrary, one of active intervention in favor of more rapid and more balanced growth; a somewhat more even distribution of income, related more closely to rewards for productive contributions rather than for status and inheritance; the more productive investment of available resources; and a sustained growth in the political and administrative capabilities of government and of ever wider strata of the population.

The crude model outlined above may have some modest usefulness in surveying and presenting in quantitative terms some of the magnitudes and rates of change that would be relevant for understanding the basic problems of such a more constructive policy in developing countries.[20] Somewhat as the economic models of the late Lord Keynes drew attention to the need of keeping the national rates of spending and investment in a country in balance with the national propensity to save, so it may become possible some day for political scientists to suggest in what areas, in what respects, and to what extent the efforts of government will have to be kept abreast of the burdens generated by the processes of social mobilization. The first steps toward this distant goal might be taken through

[20] For other highly relevant approaches to these problems, see Almond and Coleman, eds., *The Politics of the Developing Areas*, esp. the discussion by Almond on pp. 58–64. The problem of rates of change and their acceleration is discussed explicitly by Coleman, *ibid.*, pp. 536–558. While this work presented extensive data on levels of development, it did not take the further step of using explicit quantitative rates of change, which would be needed for the type of dynamic and probabilistic models that seem implicit in the long-range predictions of the authors, as set forth on pp. 58–64, 535–544.

research which would replace the hypothetical figures of the model by actual data from specific countries, so that the model could be tested, revised, and advanced nearer toward application.

Any cooperation which social scientists and other students of cultural, political, and economic development and change could extend to this effort—by improving the design of the model or by suggesting more precise or refined definitions of some of its categories, or by furnishing specific data—would be very much appreciated.

APPENDIX

A GLANCE AT ACTUAL CASES: PARTIAL DATA FOR 19 COUNTRIES

(with the assistance of Charles L. Taylor and Alex Weilenmann)

The following data, presented in Tables 3 to 5, have been compiled or computed, respectively, in order to illustrate the possibility, in principle, of the kind of analysis proposed in the main body of this paper, and to demonstrate the availability

TABLE 3-A. *Selected Indices of Social Mobilization for Nineteen Countries: Aggregate Levels*

COUNTRY	(1) GNP PER CAPITA (1955) US $	(2) GNP (1955) MILLION US $	(3) POPULATION (1953, 1958) 1,000	(4) RADIO AUDIENCE %	(5) NEWSPAPER READERS %	(6) LITERATES %	(7) WORK FORCE IN NON-AGRIC. OCCUPATIONS %	(8) URBAN POPULATION %
Venezuela	762	4,400	5,440 / 6,320	12.8 ('48) / 48.9 ('57)	— / 30.6 ('56)	43.5 ('41) / 51.0 ('50)	50 ('41) / 59 ('50)	39 ('41) / 50 ('50)
Argentina	374	7,150	18,400 / 20,248	51.2 ('50) / 65.0 ('59)	— / 54.0 ('58)	69.4 ('14) / 86.7 ('47)	75 ('47) / 77 ('55)	53 ('14) / 63 ('47)
Cuba	361	2,180	5,829 / 6,466	42.7 ('49) / 59.3 ('59)	— / 38.7 ('56)	71.8 ('31) / 76.4 ('53)	59 ('43) / 58 ('53)	50 ('43) / 57 ('53)
Colombia	330	4,180	12,111 / 13,522	17.6 ('50) / 24.7 ('56)	— / 17.7 ('58)	55.8 ('38) / 61.5 ('51)	28 ('38) / 46 ('51)	29 ('38) / 36 ('51)
Turkey	276	6,463	22,850 / 25,932	4.8 ('48) / 17.6 ('59)	— / 9.6 ('52)	20.9 ('35) / 34.3 ('50)	18 ('35) / 23.('55)	24 ('40) / 25 ('50)
Brazil	262	15,315	55,772 / 65,725	19.2 ('50) / 25.5 ('58)	— / 18.9 ('57)	43.3 ('40) / 48.4 ('50)	33 ('40) / 42 ('50)	31 ('40) / 37 ('50)
Philippines	201	4,400	21,211 / 24,010	1.6 ('49) / 5.2 ('57)	— / 5.7 ('56)	48.8 ('39) / 61.3 ('48)	27 ('39) / 43 ('58)	23 ('39) / 24 ('48)
Mexico	187	5,548	28,056 / 32,348	11.4 ('48) / 34.6 ('58)	— / 14.4 ('52)	48.4 ('40)[a] / 56.8 ('50)[a]	35 ('40) / 42 ('58)	35 ('40) / 43 ('50)
Chile	180	1,220	6,437 / 7,298	36.9 ('49) / 38.4 ('58)	— / 22.2 ('52)	71.8 ('40) / 80.6 ('52)	65 ('40) / 70 ('52)	52 ('40)[b] / 60 ('52)[b]
Guatemala	179	580	3,058 / 3,546	2.8 ('50) / 4.6 ('54)	— / 6.6 ('58)	34.6 ('40)[a] / 29.7 ('50)[a]	29 ('40) / 32 ('50)	27 ('21) / 32 ('50)
Honduras	137	228	1,556 / 1,828	5.9 ('48) / 7.2 ('57)	— / 7.5 ('57)	32.6 ('35)[a] / 35.2 ('50)[a]	17 ('50) / 16 ('56)	29 ('45) / 31 ('50)
Ghana	135	624	4,478 / 4,836	0.8 ('48) / 8.9 ('59)	— / 11.4 ('58)	20–25 ('50) / —	— / —	— / —
Egypt	133	3,065	22,003 / 24,781	4.8 ('49) / 13.2 ('57)	— / 7.5 ('52)	14.8 ('37) / 22.1 ('47)	29 ('37) / 36 ('47)	25 ('37) / 30 ('47)
Thailand	100	2,050	19,556 / 21,474	0.5 ('50) / 1.6 ('58)	— / 1.2 ('52)	52.0 ('47) / 64.0 ('56)	11 ('37) / 12 ('54)	— / 10 ('47)
Republic of the Congo (Leopoldville)	98	1,639	12,154 / 13,559	0.2 ('48) / 1.0 ('59)	— / 0.9 ('57)	35–40 ('50) / —	— / 15 ('55)	16 ('47)
India	72	27,400	372,623 / 397,390	0.3 ('48) / 1.6 ('59)	— / 2.7 ('58)	9.1 ('31)[c] / 15.1 ('41)[c] / 19.9 ('51)	29 ('51) / 30 ('55)	11 ('31)[c] / 13 ('41)[c] / 17 ('51)
Nigeria	70	2,250	30,104 / 33,052	0.2 ('48) / 1.0 ('58)	— / 2.4 ('58)	11.5 ('52/3) / —	26 ('31)	4 ('31) / 5 ('52)
Pakistan	56	4,560	80,039 / 85,635	0.3 ('50) / 1.2 ('58)	— / 2.7 ('54)	9.1 ('31)[c] / 15.1 ('41)[c] / 13.5 ('51)[a]	24 ('51) / 35 ('54/6)	11 ('31)[c] / 13 ('41)[c] / 11 ('51)
Burma	52	1,012	19,272 / 20,255	0.2 ('48) / 0.5 ('56)	— / 2.4 ('52)	40.2 ('31) / 57.3 ('54)	32 ('31) / 30 ('55)	10 ('31) / —

[a] Unequal age groups.
[b] Variation of definition of "urban."
[c] Applies to prepartition India, i.e., to India and Pakistan together.

TABLE 3-B.   *Selected Indices of Social Mobilization for Nineteen Countries: Aggregate Levels: Projected for 1945 and 1955*

COUNTRY		(4) RADIO AUDIENCE %	(6) LITERATES %	(7) WORK FORCE IN NON-AGRIC. OCCUPATIONS %	(8) URBAN POPULATION %	(9) EXPOSURE TO MODERNITY %
Venezuela	'45	1	47	54	44	63
	'55	41	55	64	56	75
Argentina	'45	44	85	74	62	> 95
	'55	59	92	77	65	> 95
Cuba	'45	36	75	59	51	83
	'55	52	77	58	58	84
Colombia	'45	12	59	38	33	60
	'55	22	63	52	38	72
Turkey	'45	1	30	21	24	34
	'55	13	39	23	26	40
Brazil	'45	15	46	37	34	52
	'55	23	51	46	40	61
Philippines	'45	0	57	32	24	56
	'55	4	71	41	25	70
Mexico	'45	4	52	37	39	57
	'55	28	61	41	37	64
Chile	'45	36	75	67	56	89
	'55	38	83	71	62	> 95
Guatemala	'45	1	32	31	31	40
	'55	5	27	34	33	42
Honduras	'45	6	35	18	29	40
	'55	7	36	16	33	43
Ghana	'45	0	—	—	—	—
	'55	6	—	—	—	21[b] (1950/58)
Egypt	'45	1	20	35	29	40
	'55	11	28	42	34	47
Thailand	'45	0	49	12	—	38
	'55	1	63	12	—	47
Republic of the Congo (Leopoldville)	'45	0	—	—	—	—
	'55	1	—	—	—	33[b] (1947/50)
India	'45	0	18[a]	27	14[a]	28[c]
	'55	1	24[a]	30	16[a]	34[c]
Nigeria	'45	0	—	—	5	—
	'55	1	—	—	5	23[b] (1931/53)
Pakistan	'45	0	18[a]	7	14[a]	20[c]
	'55	1	24[a]	35	16[a]	37[c]
Burma	'45	0	50	31	—	50
	'55	0	58	30	—	55

Data in Columns 4, 6, 7, 8 based on corresponding data in Tables 3-A and 4-A.

Data in Column 9 are 125 per cent of means of the two highest figures in each of the other columns.

[a] Prepartition India.

[b] Based on the two highest data for country in Table 3-A.

[c] No distinction made between prepartition India and India and Pakistan respectively.

TABLE 4-A. *Selected Indices of Social Mobilization for Nineteen Countries: Shifts and Rates of Growth*

COUNTRY	LEVEL (1) PER-CAPITA GNP (1955) US $	AVERAGE ANNUAL RATES OF GROWTH (2) TOTAL GDP (1954–58) %	(3) POPULA-TION (1953–58) %	(4) PER-CAPITA GDP (1954–58) %	AVERAGE ANNUAL SHIFTS (5) RADIO AUDIENCE %	(6) LITERATE POPULA-TION %	(7) WORK FORCE IN NON-AGRIC. OCCUPA-TIONS %	(8) URBAN POPULA-TION %	(9) * POPULA-TION EXPOSED TO MODERN-ITY %
Venezuela	762	(8.8)	(3.0)	(7.5)	4.0 (1948–57)	0.8 (1941–50)	1.0 (1941–50)	1.2 (1941–50)	1.2 / 3.2 / 2.2
Argentina	374	(2.4)	(1.9)	(0.5)	1.5 (1950–59)	0.7 (1914–47)	0.3 (1947–55)	0.3 (1914–47)	0.0 / 1.4 / 0.7
Cuba	361	(3)[a] (1957–60)	(1.9)	(1.1)[c] (1957–60)	1.7 (1949–59)	0.2 (1931–53)	−0.1 (1943–53)	0.7 (1943–53)	0.1 / 1.5 / 0.8
Colombia	330	(3.1)	(2.2)	(0.8)	1.2 (1950–56)	0.4 (1938–51)	1.4 (1938–51)	0.6 (1938–51)	1.2 / 1.6 / 1.4
Turkey	276	(8.1)	(2.7)	(5.2)	1.2 (1948–59)	0.9 (1935–50)	0.3 (1935–55)	0.1 (1945–50)	0.6 / 1.3 / 1.0
Brazil	262	(6.4)	(2.4)	(4.0)	0.8	0.5 (1950–58)	0.8 (1940–50)	0.5 (1940–50)	0.9 / 1.0 / 1.0
Philippines	201	(4.8)	(2.5)	(2.2)	0.5 (1949–57)	1.4 (1939–48)	0.8 (1939–58)	0.1 (1939–48)	1.4 / 1.4 / 1.4
Mexico	187	(4)[a] (1957–60)	(2.9)	(1.1)[c] (1957–60)	2.3 (1948–58)	0.8[e] (1940–50)	0.4 (1940–58)	0.8 (1940–50)	0.7 / 1.9 / 1.3
Chile	180	(2.0)	(2.5)	(−0.6)	0.2 (1949–58)	0.7 (1940–52)	0.4 (1940–52)	0.7[f] (1940–52)	0.6 / 0.9 / 0.8
Guatemala	179	(8.3)	(3.0)	(5.2)	0.4 (1950–54)	−0.5[e] (1940–50)	0.3 (1940–50)	0.2 (1921–50)	0.2 / 0.4 / 0.3
Honduras	137	(6.6) (1954–57)	(3.3)	(3.2) (1954–57)	0.1 (1954–57)	0.2[c] (1948–57)	−0.2 (1935–50)	0.4 (1945–50)	0.3 / 0.4 / 0.4
Ghana	135	(3)[a] (1957–60)	(1.6)	(1.4)[c] (1957–60)	0.7 (1948–59)	—	—	—	— / 0.9
Egypt	133	(2.1) (1954–56)	(2.4)	(−0.3) (1954–56)	1.0 (1949–57)	0.7 (1937–47)	0.7 (1937–47)	0.5 (1937–47)	0.7 / 1.0 / 0.8
Thailand	100	(3.1)[b] (1950–54)	(1.9)	(1.2)[d] (1950–54)	0.1 (1950–54)	1.3 (1950–58)	0.1 (1947–56)	— (1937–54)	0.9 / 0.9 / 0.9
Rep. of the Congo (Leopoldville)	98	(1.7)	(2.2)	(−0.8)	0.1 (1948–59)	—	—	—	— / 0.1
India	72	(3.3)	(1.3)	(1.9)	0.1 (1948–59)	0.6[g] (1931–41)	0.3 (1951–55)	0.2[g] (1931–41)	0.6[h] / 0.6[h] / 0.6
Nigeria	70	(4)[a] (1957–60)	(1.9)	(2.1)[c] (1957–60)	0.1 (1948–58)	—	—	0.0 (1931–52)	— / 0.1
Pakistan	56	(1.8)[b] (1950–54)	(1.4)	(0.4)[d] (1950–54)	0.1 (1950–54)	0.6[g] (1931–41)	2.8 (1951–54/6)	0.2[g] (1931–41)	1.7[h] / 2.1[h] / 1.9
Burma	52	(3.8)	(1.0)	(2.8)	0.0 (1948–56)	0.7 (1931–54)	−0.1 (1931–55)	—	0.5 / 0.4 / 0.4

* In each box of Column 9, the first figure is based on the levels in Table 3-B, Column 9; the second figure is based on the two largest shifts for country (Columns 5–8, this table), and the third figure is the average of the two preceding figures in the box.
[a] Growth in GNP.
[b] Growth in national income.
[c] Growth in per-capita income.
[e] Based on unequal age groups.
[f] Variation in definition of "urban."
[g] Applied to prepartition India, i.e. to India and Pakistan together.
[h] No distinction made between prepartition India and India and Pakistan respectively.

TABLE 4-B. *Selected Indices of Social Mobilization for Nineteen Countries: Averages in Shifts and Rates of Growth*

	LEVEL	AVERAGE ANNUAL RATES OF GROWTH			AVERAGE ANNUAL SHIFTS				
	(1)	(2)	(3)	(4)	(5)	(6)	(7)	(9)	(9)a
RANGE (ACC'D. TO PER-CAPITA GNP) US $	PER-CAPITA (1955) US $	TOTAL GDPb %	TOTAL POPULATION %	GDP PER CAPITA %	RADIO AUDIENCE %	LITERATE POPULATION %	POPULATION ENGAGED IN NON-AGRICULTURAL OCCUPATIONS %	URBAN POPULATION %	POPULATION EXPOSED TO MODERNITY %
400+ (N = 1)	762	(8.8)	(3.0)	(7.5)	4.0	0.8	1.0	1.2	1.2 / 3.2 / 2.2
300–399 (N = 3)	355	(2.8)	(2.0)	(0.8)	1.5	0.4	0.5	0.5	0.4 / 1.5 / 1.0
200–299 (N = 3)	246	(6.4)	(2.5)	(3.8)	0.8	0.9	0.6	0.2	1.0 / 1.2 / 1.1
100–199 (N = 7)	150	(4.1)	(2.5)	(1.6)	0.7	0.5 (N = 6)	0.3 (N = 6)	0.5 (N = 5)	0.6 (N = 6) / 0.9 / 0 8
50–99 (N = 5)	70	(2.9)	(1.6)	(1.3)	0.1	0.6c (N = 2)	1.0 (N = 3)	0.1c (N = 2)	0.9 (N = 3) / 0.7 / 0.8
Total 50–750 (N = 19)	209	(4.2)	(2.2)	(2.0)	0.8	0.6c (N = 15)	0.6 (N = 16)	0.4 (N = 14)	0.7 (N = 16) / 1.1 / 0.9

These averages are entirely based on data of Table 4-A.

[a] In Column 9, in each box, the first figure is the average of shifts based on highest levels, the second figure is the average of shifts based on largest shifts, and the third figure is the average of the first two.

[b] GDP = gross domestic product.

[c] Data for prepartition India were used only once in calculating the average.

TABLE 5. *Selected Indices of Social Mobilization for Nineteen Countries: Projected Minimum Levels in 1960, 1970*

	(1)		(2)		(3)		(4)		(5)	
	RADIO AUDIENCE %		LITERATES %		PERCENTAGE OF ECONOMICALLY ACTIVE POPULATION IN NON-AGRICULTURAL OCCUPATIONS %		URBAN POPULATION %		EXPOSURE TO MODERNITY %	
COUNTRY	1960	1970	1960	1970	1960	1970	1960	1970	1960	1970
Venezuela	61	> 95	59	67	69	79	62	74	86	95
Argentina	67	82	> 95	> 95	79	82	67	70	95	95
Cuba	61	78	78	80	57	56	60	65	87	93
Colombia	30	42	65	69	59	73	41	47	79	93
Turkey	19	31	43	52	24	27	26	27	45	55
Brazil	27	35	53	58	50	58	42	47	66	76
Philippines	7	12	78	92	45	53	25	26	77	91
Mexico	39	62	65	73	43	47	51	59	70	83
Chile	39	41	86	93	73	77	66	73	95	95
Guatemala	7	11	25	20	35	38	34	36	44	47
Honduras	8	9	37	39	15	13	35	39	45	49
Ghana	10	17	—	—	—	—	—	—	—	—
Egypt	16	26	31	38	45	52	37	42	51	59
Thailand	2	3	69	82	13	14	—	—	52	61
Rep. of the Congo (Leopoldville)	1	2	—	—	—	—	—	—	—	—
India	2	3	26a	32a	32	35	17a	19a	37	43
Nigeria	1	2	—	—	—	—	5	6	—	—
Pakistan	1	2	26a	32a	49	77	17a	19a	46	65
Burma	1	1	62	69	30	29	—	—	57	61

[a] On basis of prepartition India.

of enough actual data to get such work at least started.

For certain categories—such as voting participation, immigration and internal migration, linguistic and cultural assimilation, and the inequality of income distribution—not enough data were readily available to permit even the simple type of tabulation presented here. Even for the data that we have collected, the gaps in such countries as Ghana, Nigeria, and Congo illustrate the need for more research.

Moreover, the data being presented on the basis of the figures that appear in United Nations publications and similar sources make no attempt to estimate the margins of error to which they may be subject, or the differences in significance which a particular indicator of social mobilization may have in the cultural context of certain countries, in contrast with its significance in others. The high literacy rates reported for Burma and Thailand, e.g., include a substantial proportion of literates trained through traditional monastic institutions. These rates show only a weak correlation to other indicators of modernity for those same countries, while the high literacy rates for Chile by contrast, refer to the effect of a more modern type of school system and are far better correlated to other indicators.

We have tried to take some account of these matters by basing estimates of overall exposure to modernity not on the highest single indicator but on the average of the two highest indicators for each country, so as to discount to some extent the effects of any single indicator that seems too far out of line with the rest. Despite these precautions, the figures in projection offered here represent at best a crude beginning intended to stimulate far more thorough and critical statistical work, and its critical evaluation by experts on each of the countries and areas concerned.

[The Notes which discuss the specific data and sources have been deleted.]

SOCIAL STRUCTURE AND POLITICAL PARTICIPATION: DEVELOPMENTAL RELATIONSHIPS

Norman H. Nie, G. Bingham Powell, Jr., and Kenneth Prewitt*

Economic development has consequences for many aspects of social life. Some of these social consequences, in turn, have an impact on a nation's political life. Studies of social mobilization, for example, have demonstrated that economic development is associated with sharp increases in the general level of political participation.[1] These studies report strong relationships between aggregate socio-economic measures such as per capita income, median level of education, and percentage of the population in urban areas, on one hand, and aggregate measures of political participation, such as voting turnout, on the other. Simultaneously, scholars conducting surveys of individual political participation consistently have reported that an individual's social status, education, and organizational memberships strongly affect the likelihood of his engaging in various types of political activities.[2]

In spite of the consistency of both sets of findings across many studies and although the findings appear frequently in analysis of political stability, democracy, and even strategies of political growth,[3] we know little about the connections between social structure and political participation. With few exceptions the literature on individual participation is notable for low level generalizations (the better educated citizen talks about politics more regularly), and the absence of systematic and comprehensive theory. While the literature on the growth of national political participation has been more elaborate theoretically, the dependence on aggregate measures has made it difficult to determine empirically

SOURCE: Excerpted from Norman H. Nie, G. Bingham Powell, Jr., and Kenneth Prewitt, "Social Structure and Political Participation: Developmental Relationships," *American Political Science Review*, **63**, 361–78, June, 1969, and **63**, 808–32, September, 1969, using only pp. 361–70, 372–74, 811–14, 819–20, 824–28. Space limitations have necessitated deleting portions of this two-part article, including extensive methodological comments and explanations. The interested reader will find page references to the omitted material in the text and footnotes. Norman Nie assisted the editing of this article.

* The authors are listed alphabetically to indicate equal co-authorship.

[1] Karl W. Deutsch, "Social Mobilization and Political Development," this REVIEW, 55 (September, 1961), 493–515. Also, particularly, Daniel Lerner, *The Passing of Traditional Society* (New York: Free Press of Glencoe, 1958). For important analysis which in part contradicts the social mobilization hypothesis, see Walter Dean Burham, "The Changing Shape of the American Political Universe," this REVIEW, 59 (March, 1965), 7–28. Burnham indexes political participation with voter turnout; we deliberately exclude voting from our scale of participation (see footnote 7). It is not clear, therefore, whether our general findings are in opposition to Burnham's. There is some reason for presuming that voting and other types of political participation are much more independent than a previous generation of scholarship has assumed.

[2] Gabriel A. Almond and Sidney Verba, *The Civic Culture* (Princeton; Princeton University Press, 1963); Robert A. Dahl, *Who Governs?* (New Haven: Yale University Press, 1961), pp. 282–301; V. O. Key, *Public Opinion and American Democracy* (New York: Alfred A. Knopf, 1961); Lester W. Milbrath, *Political Participation* (Chicago: Rand McNally Co., 1965).

[3] For example, Samuel P. Huntington, "Political Development and Political Decay," *World Politics*, 17 (April, 1965), 386–430.

how these macro social changes structure individuals' life experiences in ways which alter their political behavior.

I. The Problem and the Approach

The task is to identify the significant social experiences which explain the growth of political participation in economically advanced nations. Having identified these social concomitants of economic development, it is also necessary to fill in the *causal* links between macro socio-economic processes and citizen political participation. These links, we hypothesize, are the resources, the attitudes, and the needs of individual citizens.

Multi-level analysis requires data about individuals and about nations. Such data is available in the form of the survey research data from the Almond-Verba five-nation study and aggregate statistics on the level of economic development in these five nations.[4] The theoretical assumptions we explore require a technique showing the relationships between socio-economic attributes, intervening attitudinal characteristics and rates of political participation; such a technique is provided by causal modeling, which is applied to the analysis . . . [below].

II. Social Structure and Economic Development

The process of economic development drastically alters the social structures of a nation, and consequently, the social life of its citizens. The effects of social change on political behavior and on the operation of the political system are numerous and complex. In a given nation the political consequences of economic development cannot easily be separated from such issues as historical social cleavages, existing social patterns, and the timing of the developmental process itself.[5] The complexity and varia-

tions notwithstanding, some changes in social life appear inevitably to be brought about by the process of economic development. It is these persistent changes which, we hypothesize, have a universal and predictable impact on citizen participation in political life.

Economic development and changes in the class structure. As a nation develops economically, the shape of its social stratification structure is substantially altered. There are increased requirements for trained labor, a growth of opportunities for social mobility, and expanded facilities for formal education. As a consequence, the pyramidal class structure associated with peasant and peasant-worker societies changes to a more diamond-shaped structure. The middle stratum expands and eventually becomes the majority class as great numbers of citizens, whose parents were agricultural or unskilled workers, find jobs in the service industry or otherwise become members of the educated white-collar class.

Economic development and changes in organizational structure. As a nation develops economically, its organizational infrastructure becomes increasingly complex. Differentiation and specialization occur. Social life becomes more organized; work groups (such as trade unions and professional societies), leisure groups (such as youth organizations and voluntary associations), and special task groups (such as civic associations) expand in number and take over duties formerly carried out by the extended family or the small, face-to-face social group. Additional organizations become necessary to coordinate activities of an increasingly interdependent social and economic life. There is a corresponding growth of membership in secondary organizations. The group life structure of a society cannot avoid being substantially affected by the development process.

Economic development and changes in residence patterns. As a nation develops economically, it becomes more urban. Youths leave the farms and small towns in search

---

[4] Some of these data were analyzed by Almond and Verba, *op. cit*

[5] See, for example, the introductory chapter in Seymour M. Lipset and Stein Rokkan, *Party Systems and Voter Alignments* (New York: Free Press, 1967).

of education or better paying jobs in the nation's cities. Industry expands where there is population concentration, and availability of jobs attracts yet more people. Larger proportions of the population seek employment and establish homes in urban areas as a consequence of development.

Thus, along with Deutsch and other students of development, we identify three areas of social life known to vary with level of economic development: social stratification, organized economic and secondary associations, and urbanization. The research task is to move from these macro variables to an explanation of whether a given individual citizen will engage in political activity. To carry out this research task, we proceed in three steps:

1. We determine the strength and the cross-national consistency of correlations between the citizen's class position, his organizational involvement, his place of residence (i.e. urban versus rural) and his level of political participation.

2. We integrate the survey data with aggregate information available for the five nations in order to clarify and evaluate the effect that the individual level correlations have on the larger relationship between economic development and national rates of participation.

. . .

3. Finally, with the aid of causal modeling, we examine the role played by several cognitive and attitudinal variables in explaining the persistent relationship between socio-economic attributes on the one hand and political participation on the other. In so doing we attempt to refine further the linkages between national economic development and individual acts of political participation.

III. The Primary Variables: Identification and Correlation

The impact of economic development on class structure, secondary group structure, and residence patterns has been docu-mented.[6] However, in an attempt to assess their impact on levels of participation, we need some means of determining whether they are independent phenomena or a package of relationships which are so tightly intertwined as to be inseparable in terms of their impact on citizens' participation in politics. If, for example, the changes in social class structure take place only in the urban population centers, and if only urban middle and upper class citizens are active in a nation's organizational life, then there would be only one major dimension of social structural change important for this study—urbanization.

In order to answer these questions, we set forth an extensive list of socio-economic items presumed to be related to the social structural changes. We subjected these items to a factor analysis in each nation and then for all five nations grouped together as a single population. In both cases there emerged two relatively independent and very consistent clusters of items. Other items, fewer in number, were consistently unrelated to each other or to either cluster.

The two clusters and two unrelated items are analogs for the individual citizen of the structural variables outlined above. One cluster includes items which measure socio-economic status: education, income, occupation, and an interviewer's rating of social status. The second cluster includes items which measure organizational involve-

[6] For the relationship between economic development indicators and various indices of urbanization and class structure, see the data in Bruce M. Russett, *et al.*, *World Handbook of Political and Social Indicators* (New Haven: Yale University Press, 1964). Also see Donald J. McCrone and Charles F. Cnudde "Toward a Communication Theory of Democratic Political Development," this REVIEW, 61 (March, 1967), 72–79. The literature on general processes of change in the social structure during modernization is, of course, very large. See, among other analyses, S. N. Eisenstadt, "Social Change, Differentiation, and Evolution," *American Sociological Review*, 29 (June, 1964), 375–387; and Talcott Parsons, "Evolutionary Universals in Society," *American Sociological Review*, 29 (June, 1964), 339–357.

ment: number of organizational memberships, amount of organizational activity, involvement in the economic market-place, and involvement in group-related leisure time activities. Thus, there is a cluster which corresponds to the social stratification system and a cluster which corresponds to the organizational infrastructure of the society. Unrelated to these clusters were two items corresponding at the individual level to urbanization; size of present community and length of residence there.

Three summary indexes were constructed: social status, organizational involvement, and size of place of residence. A political participation scale was also constructed, including the following items: talking politics, contacting local authorities, contacting national authorities, involvement in electoral campaigns, and membership in political organizations and political parties. Table 1 presents pertinent correlation coefficients.

The relationships in Table 1 are clear and remarkably consistent from nation to nation. Although problems in the design of the samples are such that significance tests must be used with care, the following inferences are warranted: (1) Organizational involvement is the predictive variable with the most strength. Within each of the five nations the citizen who is an active member of social groups is more likely to be a political participant than the citizen with few or no organizational involvements. The relationships observed in Table 1 are extremely strong for data of the type available.[7] If the correlation coefficients are squared, using the general rule of estimate, organizational involvement alone predicts approximately 25 percent of the variation in participation. The strength of this relationship is consistent across the five nations. (2) in addition, as expected, the citizen's tendency to be politically active is related to his social status; however, and not fully expected, the relationship between social status and political activity is weaker and less consistent cross-nationally than the relationship between organizational involvement and political activity.[8]

On balance, these findings are familiar

[7] For readers unfamiliar with correlation coefficients in assessing the strength of relationships, Table 4 below presents some of the same patterns in terms of differences between percentages. The reader may wish to review that Table before continuing.

[8] It is interesting that social status is a stronger predictor of political participation in the United States than in any of the other nations. However, it still lags behind organizational involvement. For all the nations, of course, the status measure and the involvement measure are moderately correlated, with the U.S. showing the strongest relationship.

Table I. Social Structure and Political Participation: Product-Moment Correlation Coefficients in Five Nations

CORRELATION RELATIONSHIP	NATION				
	U.S.	U.K.	GERMANY	ITALY	MEXICO
Urban Residence with Participation Scale	.068	−.023	−.022	−.002	.073
Social Status with Participation Scale	.431	.303	.181	.283	.238
Organizational Involvement Scale with Participation Scale	.523	.480	.480	.490	.515
Urban Residence with Social Status	.159	.040	.166	.175	.118
Urban Residence with Organizational Involvement Scale	−.010	.043	−.011	−.021	.017
Social Status with Organizational Involvement Scale	.435	.313	.213	.304	.227

ones. The educated, wealthy and occupationally skilled citizen participates in political life at a greater rate than the uneducated, poor and occupationally unskilled.[9] It is well known that social and economic resources provide a citizen with currency he transfers to the political sphere. To turn the statement around, political influence is not randomly distributed across social categories but, rather, tends to concentrate in very disproportionate amounts among the well-to-do and socially involved. Perhaps, however, the difference between social status and organizational involvement as predictive variables is not as familiar. We will have much more to say about this difference.

Urbanization and Political Participation. The least expected pattern in Table 1 is the consistent *absence* of any relationship between urban residence and political participation. Only in two nations (the U.S. and Mexico) is the relationship significant at the .05 level, and even in these nations the relationship is weak, explaining less than one percent of the variance in participation. For nations as developed as the five reported on in Table 1, the tendency for urbanization and mass political activity to co-vary is *not* because city-dwellers are more active than country-dwellers. The absence of a relationship between urban residence and activity rates at the individual level may, thus, help to erase from the

[9] When the individual items composing these summary indices were correlated with political participation, the coefficients obtained were almost always considerably lower than those shown in Table 1. Further, no single item accounts for a disproportionate amount of the correlation between the summary indices and the participation scale. This indicates (1) that the unidimensionality indicated by the factor loadings is justified and (2) that no single variable, such as education, for instance, is the "real" explanation for the strong correlations which appear in Table 1. Social status, in other words, seems to be the common dimension being tapped by the varied findings linking participation to education, income, and the like.

literature on political development an ecological fallacy.[10]

We reason as follows: as nations develop economically, two things increase, the proportion of urban-dwellers and the proportion of active political participants. However, the ecological correlation between urbanization and mass political participation is spurious, as is indicated by the absence of a relationship between urban residence and participation *within* each nation to further investigate the inconsistency between the widely reported ecological correlation and the absence of the correlation at the individual level, we merged the file from the five nations. The correlation between urban residence and activity for the merged file is positive and significant and thus is consistent with the relationship found when aggregated data are used.

It is evident that the ecological correlation is a derivative of the greater levels of urbanization and political participation in more advanced nations. For when the aggregate correlation is decomposed, as in Table 1, political activity is seen to vary hardly at all by urban-rural differences. The fourth and fifth lines in Table 1 suggest part of the reason: while urbanization is somewhat associated with social status, it is not at all related to organizational involvement. As we have seen, in every nation organizational involvement is the strongest predictor of participation.

In making these initial observations we were troubled by the fact that the five nations being studied would be clustered toward the top end of any development continuum on which all nations of the

[10] For a discussion of the general problem of ecological fallacies see W. S. Robinson, "Ecological Correlations and the Behavior of Individuals," *American Sociological Review*, 15 (1950), 351–357. Also see Hayward R. Alker, "A Typology of Ecological Fallacies: Problems of Spurious Associations in Cross-level Inferences," International Social Science Council: Symposium on Quantitative Ecological Analysis in the Social Sciences, Evian, France, September, 1966.

world could be arrayed. Even Mexico, the "low" case, ranks well above the median. What was needed was a nation, with a democratic form of government, much less developed than those studied in the Five-Nation study. Such a nation would provide a "hard test" for the inferences drawn from the patterns in Table 1. As a matter of scientific interest and personal generosity, Professors Sidney Verba, Rajni Kothari, and Bashir Ahmed made available data from a forthcoming study of political participation in India for our purposes. These data, which suit our needs ideally and which have been preliminarily analyzed by Nie, are from the "Cross National Research Program in Social and Political Change."

The India data provide a striking confirmation of the findings presented in Table 1. The correlation between political participation and organizational membership is .420; between participation and social status, .300.[11] These correlations are of the same order of magnitude as those reported in Table 1, although the former is slightly lower.[12] Social status and organizational involvement appear to be similar in their explanatory power even in the much less developed nation of India.

The India data also confirm our inferences about urbanization and political participation. As is to be expected, citizens of

[11] Although the effort was to tap the same basic variables of social status, organizational involvement, and participation as in the 1960 study, different specific questions were believed appropriate to the Indian context. The Indian sample is also particularly useful for testing urbanization hypotheses because interviews were conducted in towns as small as 200 persons.

[12] The slight falling off of the relationship between participation and organization membership might be due to the differences in the measures used in India, on the one hand, and the original five nations, on the other. In India, only information on number of memberships was available and this had to be used in place of a composite involvement scale. The correlations between participation and organizational membership only in the five nations are comparable to the correlation produced by the India data.

high social status and high organizational involvement are more concentrated in urban areas in a nation at India's developmental level than in the more advanced nations. The correlation between urban residence and social status is .339, much higher than in the five more developed nations; the correlation between urban residence and social involvement is .127, again much higher than the other nations. In spite of the greater concentration of persons with social and organizational resources in the cities of India, the correlation between urban residence and political participation is an insignificant .035. Place of residence is no predictor of political activity.

Urbanization and Local vs. National Political Participation. The literature about the effects of urbanization on political participation reveals an interesting anomaly [which should be further explored]. First, stemming largely from Deutsch, there are theoretical notions found in the studies of social mobilization and modernization. Urbanization, it is stressed, creates among citizens new ties to the national scene, increases the amount of political communication, and leads to greater awareness of social and political needs. In short, urbanization is one of the processes of modernization which shifts the political orientations of citizens from parochial to national and participant.[13]

Second, using individual survey data rather than national aggregate data, other investigators have noted that the process of urbanization weakens the ties between individual and community. Presumably one consequence of this has been to decrease citizen participation in local politics. For instance, Dahl writes how living in large political communities can lessen the likelihood of political participation:

> Yet, the larger and more inclusive the unit with a representative government, and the more complex its tasks, the more participation must be reduced for most

[13] See citations under footnote 1 above.

people to the single act of voting in an election

Conversely, the smaller the unit, the greater the opportunity for citizens to participate in the decisions of their government . . .[14]

These seemingly contradictory observations about urbanization and political participation are not actually in direct conflict. The social mobilization literature refers to national participation and mainly uses voter turnout to support the hypothesis. The Dahl thesis refers to local participation and deliberately excludes the act of voting from the consideration.

However, the two observations do present us with difficulties. The operational procedures used in Table 1, which show little to no relationship between urbanization and political participation, combine both national and local items in the participation scale. Thus it is possible that both the Deutsch and Dahl views are correct and that our data manipulation hides two opposing effects, urbanization is increasing national participation and decreasing local participation. To check this possibility, we decomposed the participation scale and separately correlated urban residence, controlling for social status and organizational involvement, with *national* and *local* acts of political activity.[15]

. . .

[14] Robert A. Dahl, "The City in the Future of Democracy," this REVIEW, 61 (December, 1967), p. 960. For a very different perspective on size of city and citizen representation in local matters, see Kenneth Prewitt and Heinz Eulau, "Political Matrix and Political Representation: Prolegomenon to a New Departure from an Old Problem," this REVIEW, 63 (June, 1969) pp. 427–441.

[15] Methodologically it is quite possible and, for that matter, common for items to demonstrate a strong relationship to a principle factor (e.g., participation level) and at the same time contain uncorrelated portions which are strongly related to different orthogonal factors. This may be what is taking place with the local-national distinction.

The results of this analysis[16] tend to confirm the conflicting implications of urbanization for political participation. The citizen living in the city is likely to have the social status and, in less developed nations (if India is a representative case) the organization involvement which leads to political participation. But the city-dweller loses the facilitating effect of small town life on local participation. The general problem sketched out by Dahl appears to be confirmed by these findings: with respect to participation in local matters there is an "optimal" size for cities. However, the effects of city size are not strong, especially when compared with the impact on participation of social status and organizational involvement. In no case does urbanization explain more than two percent of the variance in rates of participation; in most cases it is less than that. This compares to about ten percent of the variance explained by social status and about twenty-five percent explained by organizational involvement. The comparative weakness of urbanization as a predictive variable leads us to pay much less attention to it than to the other two variables in the remainder of the analysis.

IV. Political Participation: Shifting from Individual Correlates to National Patterns.

Analysis presented thus far shows: first, within each of the five nations a citizen's tendency to be politically active strongly varies according to his social status and his organizational involvement; and second, the citizen's tendency to be politically active is but slightly affected by his place of residence, and this weak relationship masks two counter trends. Living in an urban environment depresses the likelihood of local participation while not significantly altering the likelihood of national participation.

We infer from these findings that economic development increases mass political

[16] For the table presenting these results and a more detailed discussion of them, the reader is referred to Table 2 and pp. 367–68 in Part I of the original article.

participation *because* associated with economic development are greater numbers of citizens in the middle and upper social classes and greater numbers involved in organizations. From data presented thus far this can only be an inference. We have yet to examine in a direct manner how economic development affects political participation. It is to this issue that we now turn.

With only five cases it is not possible to devise a single definitive test which would substantiate a hypothesis linking economic development with national rates of political participation. What is possible is to carry out a number of smaller tests, each of which can confirm or reject a part of the more inclusive theory. If each of the independent tests confirms the general theory, the cumulative effect will provide some rationale for considering the theory verified.

If true (a) that economic development is the major determinant of national rates of participation; and (b) that this relationship is largely the result of how development affects society's class structure and organizational infrastructure, then data should demonstrate the following:

1. Strong covariance between a nation's level of economic development and its rate of mass political participation.

2. The disappearance of this relationship when social class and organizational involvement are controlled.

3. The lack of strong relationships between mass political participation and non-development-associated variables.

4. Similar *absolute* rates of participation among citizens of similar social class and organizational involvement irrespective of nation, as well as the same *relative* differences from one nation to the next already indicated by the coefficients in Table 1.

Comparing National Rates of Political Participation. Comparing rates of political participation among the five nations shows that the United States and Great Britain have the highest rate; Germany is slightly lower; Mexico and Italy follow in that order and have considerably lower rates of participation than the three more developed nations.[17] With the exception of the reversal between Italy and Mexico,[18] this ranking corresponds with an economic development ranking constructed from aggregate statistics.

Five cases "prove" nothing, but the predicted pattern is apparent. The correspondence in rankings of economic development and mass political participation, based in the present case on survey and aggregate data from five nations, does conform to the rankings reported in studies using only aggregate data but based on many more than five cases. It is consistent with Deutsch, Lipset, Lerner, and others to conclude that national rates of political participation covary with levels of economic development.

The Component Variables: Social Class and Organizational Life. It comes as no surprise to learn that a nation's level of political participation covaries with its level of economic development. The more difficult task is to identify what components of economic development account for the growing numbers of citizens who become active in political life. The theory which guides our analysis points to two component variables: social class and organizational life. These variables are chosen from a long list of social factors known to be affected by development for two reasons. Findings about individual political behavior indicate that status and organizational membership are strongly related to political activity. Further, at the national level, social

[17] The ranking was achieved by calculating the national means on the participation variable. This is the same variable used in Table 1. Medians were also calculated and in no case did this alter the ranking.

[18] The Mexican sample contains no respondent from communities with populations less than 10,000. The .232 correlation between size of place of residence and social status in Mexico may account for the reversal in rankings between Italy and Mexico. Indeed, the means are so close at present that it is highly probable that they would reverse with a representative Mexican sample.

class composition and organizational life change in highly predictable ways during the process of economic development. It is on the importance of these variables at the individual *and* the national level that our theory depends.

What is needed is some manner of determining whether social class and organizational structure are indeed the components of economic development which predict rates of mass political participation. The theory is strengthened if it can be shown that other components of development are not associated with participation. Although the data available impose constraints on us, and we cannot directly examine the possible impact of additional variables, one simple test can be performed. The relative importance of the two structural variables can be compared to all remaining development-associated variables taken as a residual group.

This can be accomplished by correlating economic development with political participation while controlling for social status and organizational involvement. To accomplish this each respondent was given a score based on his nation's level of economic development. Thus each respondent in the

U.S. was scored 5, each British respondent was scored 4, each German 3, each Italian 2, and each Mexican 1. This variable was added to each respondent's data record and the files from the five nations were merged. Level of economic development, now treated as a property of the individual, was correlated with political participation.

Table 3 presents the results. The now familiar hypothesis derived from social mobilization literature is confirmed. There is a significant relationship between national economic development and individual political participation, as the uncontrolled relationship indicates. The simple correlation between political participation and economic development is .133.

The question we ask, then, is how much of this relationship can be attributed to national patterns of social class and organizational involvement and how much of it can be attributed to other factors associated with economic development. To answer this question we compute the partials, controlling first for social class, then for organizational involvement, and finally simultaneously controlling on both class and organizational involvement. Controlling for social class, the .133 correlation is reduced to .048;

Table 3. *Residence in Nations at Different Levels of Development and Political Participation: Simple and Partial Correlations Controlling for Social Status and Organizational Involvement*

CORRELATION RELATIONSHIP	CONTROL	RESIDENCE ACCORDING TO NATIONAL LEVEL OF ECONOMIC DEVELOPMENT
Residence in nations at different levels of development *with* political participation	NONE	.133 [a]
	SES (only)	.048
	ORG. IN. (only)	.015
	SES and ORG. IN.	− .012

[a] Sample size is about 4000. The zero-order correlation is, of course, significant at better than .001.

controlling for organizational involvement it is reduced to 0.15; controlling for both (the second order partial), it is essentially zero, a nonsignificant −.012.[19]

If other factors associated with economic development were independently affecting levels of citizen political participation, then some significant relationship should have remained when the effects of status and organizational membership were partialed out. However, this clearly is not the case. The partial correlations show that *the two variables alone account for all of the difference between the participation levels of citizens in the more and the less developed nations.*

This finding can be rephrased in terms of the general theory being advanced in this paper. Economic development leads to greater rates of political participation *because* associated with economic development is an expanding middle-class and an expanding organizational infrastructure. Social class and organizational life are the components of economic development which most strongly affect mass political participation.

Since we have only five nations and since there can be nation to nation differences not attributable to economic development, the test we devise is hardly a conclusive one. The test is adequate, however, for us to conclude that the inference about economic development and political participation withstands this particular attempt to falsify

[19] As an additional check stemming from our concern for the accuracy of the rankings among the more developed nations a second dichotomous variable was created giving each respondent in the three developed nations a score of "2" and those in the two less developed nations a "1." The same analysis was then performed on this variable.

The results of this analysis are similar to those reported in Table 3. The simple correlation between the development index and level of participation is .142. The partial for this relationship controlling only for SES is .073. That controlling for only organizational involvement is .030. The second order partial controlling for both SES and ORG. IN. is an insignificant .002.

it. We are unable to show any relationship between development and rates of participation which cannot be explained by reference to the two important social structural variables—social class and organization involvement.

[The analysis so far has left two important questions unanswered. First, do persons of similar social status or organizational involvement differ in their levels of participation from country to country? The theoretical orientation guiding this discussion would suggest that such cross-cultural differences would be minimal. That is, it would predict that a laborer in Mexico would participate at approximately the same level as a laborer in Germany. So too, the level of political activity of a German citizen active in a number of organizations would resemble that of a Mexican citizen similarly involved. The second question is a corollary of the first. Are there historical or cultural factors particular to a nation which, independently of that nation's level of economic development, affect how politically active its citizens are? Again, the theoretical thrust of this paper suggests that the effects of discrete national experiences would be minimal. A comparison of levels of participation of persons of similar social class and organizational involvement in the five countries studied would answer both questions. For if we find that individuals at the same level of social class and organizational involvement are approximately equal in their political participation from one nation to the next, it is unlikely that unique cultural, historical, or political variables are causing different rates of mass political participation. Such a cross-cultural comparison (see Part I of the original article, pp. 370–72, Table 4, p. 371, and footnote #23, p. 373) suggests that important idiosyncratic differences between countries do exist, but they are very small when compared to the extremely strong effects of differences in social status or organizational involvement. With a few significant exceptions individuals with similar social statuses and similar organization involvement display similar absolute levels of political participation no matter in which of the five nations they live.]

Three types of data have now been presented: (a) individual correlations showing the association between social status, organizational involvement, and urban residence, on the one hand, and political participation, on the other; (b) rankings of national levels of economic development and of aggregate measures of political participation; (c) partial correlations showing the effect of economic development on political participation when social class and organizational involvement are controlled. These data, from different perspectives, tend to confirm the general hypothesis that economic development alters the class and organizational structures of societies which

in turn increases the level of mass political participation. No single test is conclusive, but taken together they present a strong case for the theory. Each of the following sections . . . present additional analysis further testing and clarifying these relationships.

. . .

V. The Linking Variables: Political Attitudes and the Developmental Process

Examining general relationships between social structures and political participation can take us only so far. To explicate more fully how economic development relates to political participation it is necessary to complicate the causal model. Up to this point, we have utilized the model suggested by Deutsch and others which looks as follows:

$$\text{Economic Development} \rightarrow \text{Changes in the Social Structures} \rightarrow \text{Increased Political Participation}$$

Discussions involving this model sugest that changes in the social structure affect political participation *because* citizen attitudes about politics are altered. Numerous survey studies in the U.S. and elsewhere show, for example, that persons who feel confident of success in influencing decisions are more likely to be political participants,

and that middle class persons are more likely to feel confident.[20] Hence, increasing the number of middle class citizens increases the number of confident citizens, and this, in turn, increases political participation.

The causal model with the intervening attitude component looks as follows:

$$\text{Economic Development} \rightarrow \text{Changes in the Social Structures} \rightarrow \text{Changes in the Distribution of Certain Political Attitudes} \rightarrow \text{Increased Political Participation}$$

There may be feedback loops in this process. Successful political participation, for instance, promotes greater confidence; successful participation may even alter the political structures of society so that participation itself is facilitated (expanding the franchise, for instance). However, for the moment we set aside the problem of feedback effects and limit attention to testing the basic assumptions of the model.

Questions included in the Five Nation study allow us to explore this causal model in a limited way. We begin by identifying five attitude sets which frequently are cited

as the likely intervening variables explaining why socio-economic attributes predict rates of political activity. The five are: 1) sense of citizen duty, 2) basic information about politics, 3) perceived stake in political outcomes, 4) sense of political efficacy, and 5) attentiveness to political matters.

We examine the relationship of these intervening variables to the general theme of economic development and political participation in two steps. First, at the nation-state level, we examine the relation-

[20] See, for example, Dahl, *Who Governs?*, *op. cit.*

ship between measures of economic development and aggregate scores for the five attitude sets, and between the attitudes and general rates of political participation. Second, using causal modeling techniques, we investigate the importance of these attitude sets in linking socio-economic attributes and political participation.

Table 4 presents data pertinent to the first step. The five nations are ranked by level of economic development. Then, in column B, the nations are ranked in terms of mean level of organizational involvement and social status. The next five columns (C) present the rankings of the various political attitudes (again using mean level). The final coumn shows the mean level of political participation for the five nations.

Although there are various methodological difficulties in such absolute rankings (and we especially must recall the bias in the Mexican sample).[21] Table 4 does confirm the reasoning outlined. Across Table 4, the three more developed nations *always*

[21] See footnote 18 above.

rank above the two less developed. The Kendall coefficient of concordance, or W, which measures the amount of agreement among multiple rankings, is .859 and is statistically significant at the .001 level. (The maximum observable value of Kendall's W is 1.0.)

Economic development alters the social class structure and the organizational infrastructure of a society. One consequence of these alterations is the greater proportion of citizens who have social attributes—education, stable incomes, white-collar jobs, organizational memberships—which, as already shown, relate to political participation. Further, the more developed nations have more citizens holding the views normally associated with political activity. Greater proportions of Americans, British, and Germans than Mexicans or Italians have a sense of civic duty, are politically informed, see the impact of public policies on their lives, feel politically efficacious, are attentive to politics—and, finally, actively participate in political life.

We should emphasize again that there are national differences in political attitude

Table 4. Economic Development, Social Structure, Attitude Structure, and Politica Participation

A		B		C					D
ECONOMIC DEVELOPMENT		SOCIAL STRUCTURE			ATTITUDE STRUCTURE				
RANK ORDER OF COUNTRIES WITH RESPECT TO MEASURES OF ECONOMIC DEVELOPMENT		SOCIAL STATUS	SOCIAL IN- VOLVE- MENT	CITI- ZEN DUTY	POLIT- ICAL INFOR- MA- TION	IM- PACT OF POLI- TICS	POLIT- ICAL EFFI- CACY	POLIT- ICAL ATTEN- TIVE- NESS	POLIT- ICAL PAR- TICIPA- TION
United States	1	(1)	1	1	2	1	1	1	1.5
United Kingdom	2	(2)	2.5	3	3	3	2	3	1.5
Germany	3	(3)	2.5	2	1	2	3	2	3
Italy	4	(4)	5	5	4	5	4.5	5	5
Mexico	5	(5)	4	4	5	4	4.5	4	4

Kendall Coefficient of Concordance W = .859 Sig. > .001.

scores which cannot be explained by differences in developmental levels alone. Obviously cultural heritages and specific national experiences or diverse system arrangements leave their particular impact on national attitude patterns. Germany ranks higher than the United States on mean level of political information, even though its general level of development is lower. An exploration of other attitude patterns, especially those associated with affect towards national institutions and inter-group perceptions and evaluations would reveal further differences.[22] Many of these were pointed out by Almond and Verba in their initial analysis and we shall not explore them here.[23] Nonetheless, we wish to emphasize that insofar as attitudes bearing on individual political involvement and attentiveness and personal political competence are concerned, the development-associated patterns seem to be extremely powerful. Future analyses of cross-national differences should be sensitive to the often overriding power of these relationships.

We can summarize the theoretical argument briefly: economic development alters social structures, particularly the class structure and the secondary group structure. Expanding the middle class and increasing the organizational complexity of society changes political socialization patterns; greater proportions of citizens have those politically relevant life experiences which lead to attitudes such as political efficacy, sense of civic duty, etc. These attitudes motivate the citizen to participate in politics, sensitize him to available opportunities, and provide him with political resources. Thus it is that economic development increases the rate of mass political participation.

The many implicit hypotheses in this causal model cannot be directly examined in a table reporting aggregate measures. To investigate systematically the pathway from development to political participation we must examine the extent to which individual traits associated with position in the class structure and with involvement in organizational life do in fact affect political attitudes and the extent to which political attitudes are intervening variables between socio-economic characteristics and political participation.

. . .

A. The Findings: Differences in the Casual Linkage Patterns of Social Status and Organizational Involvement

We begin with the very general hypothesis that the causal relationship between social status and organizational involvement, on the one hand, and political participation, on the other, can be traced through intervening political attitudes. Figure 1 and Table 5 present data relevant to this hypothesis. . . . [Our discussion will focus on the differences in the causal linkages of the two independent variables, SES and organizational involvement. For discussion of the individual attitudes used as intervening links in the causal chain see Part II of the original article, pp. 814–18.]

Initial examination reveals one pattern of overwhelming strength and consistency:

[22] Further research will have to distinguish, of course, between the different dimensions of the variables here considered. For example, the "information" questions here only cover very basic items like the names of national party leaders. It might be that detailed information would tend to follow, rather than proceed, participation. The various dimensions of political efficacy are also a matter for investigation. At a very abstract level, efficacy seems to become more related to general national affect items. At the more concrete and personalistic level, it follows the pattern here outlined: linked to personal status and involvement, varying little by national pattern. Thus, the only item on which an underdeveloped nation scored higher than a developed one was on an estimate as to whether possible national participation might succeed in influencing outcomes. Here, Mexicans scored higher than Germans, although very few felt they understood local or national events, or could name any potential strategy of influence. Again, the factor analysis justifies the dimension of the scale, but there are obviously additional dimensions to explore.

[23] Almond and Verba, *op. cit.*

Table 5. *Path Components of Relationship Between Two Independent Variables and Political Participation as Percentages of Total Correlations*[a]

| | INDEPENDENT VARIABLES | | | | | | | | | |
| | SOCIAL STATUS | | | | | ORGANIZATIONAL INVOLVEMENT | | | | |
Proportion of Correlation Attributable to:	US	UK	GER	IT	MX	US	UK	GER	IT	MX
(1) Direct link to participation	20%	-8%	-33%	-15%	-1%	57%	62%	61%	51%	68%
(2) Paths thru other independent (1 or 2 variable only)	30	30	35	27	34	7	-2	-3	-2	0
(3) Paths thru other ind var *and* attitude variables	10	12	20	21	13	14	12	6	12	6
(4) Paths thru attitude variables only	40	61	78	67	54	20	25	35	40	26
Total percentage	100	95	100	100	100	98	97	99	101	100
Basic correlation between ind var and participation	.431	.303	.181	.283	.238	.523	.480	.486	.490	.515

[a] The correlations are equal to the sum of all pathways from independent to dependent variable. The pathways are computed by multiplying all path coefficients along the given path. Negative scores arise from negative path linkages. For those percentages, each independent variable is treated as if it were the first, undetermined, variable in the chain. Key: US = United States; UK = United Kingdom; GER = West Germany; IT = Italy; MX = Mexico.

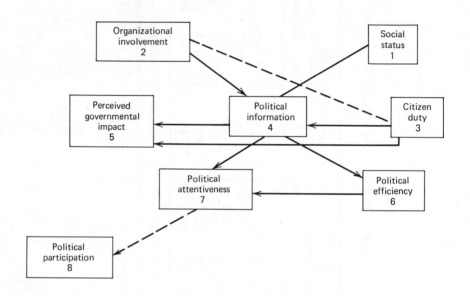

Figure 1.   Eight variable causal model: paths from status and organizational involvement to political participation.

Key to Figure 1:

(1) No arrow between variables indicates that the path coefficients are less than .150 in at least three of the five nations. There are 13 paths *not* shown in the figure.

(2) Heavy arrows between variables indicate path coefficients greater than .250 (about 5 times the average standard error) in at least three of five national samples. Light arrows between variables indicate path coefficients between .150 and .250 in three or more of the five national samples.

(3) Unbroken arrows (both light and heavy) indicate *difference* between largest and smallest of the five coefficients is *less* than .150 (about 3 standard errors). Broken arrows between variables indicate a difference greater than .150.

social status and organizational involvement operate through quite different causal paths in their impact on political participation. This finding holds true in all five countries and remains the case in spite of various manipulations of the data, alteration of the order of the intervening variables, changing the number of the intervening variables, and the like.

The basic finding is both simple and important. Virtually all the relationship between social status and political participation is explained by the intervening linking attitude variables. The high social status citizen does not *just* participate in politics; he does so only when he has the attitudes such as efficacy and attentiveness which are postulated as intervening variables. Social status, then, affects rates of political participation through its effect on political attitudes. This does not mean, it must be emphasized, that the correlation between status and participation is spurious; on the contrary, it means that intervening attitude variables explain *how* a citizen's social status affects his political activity.

On the other hand, a very large part of the relationship between organizational involvement and participation *is unexplained by any variable in this model*. In every case, about 60 percent of the correlation between organizational involvement and political participation is accounted for by the direct link, that line that does not pass through social class or the attitudinal variables. (See link 2 → 8 in Figure 1).

The strength and cross-national consistency of this pattern is shown as well in Table 5. In a causal model of this type, the raw correlation (Pearson Product-Moment) between independent and dependent variable equals the sum of all pathways down the causal chain from independent to dependent variable.[24] The score of a "path-

way" in this sense is the product of all path coefficients along the chain. Table 1 presents the percent of the raw correlation between social status and organizational involvement, on the one hand, and political participation, on the other, accounted for by: (1) the direct relationship only, unaccounted for by other variables in the model; (2) the path through the other independent variable only; (3) the paths going first through the other independent variable and then through the attitude variables; and (4) the paths going directly from each independent variable through the attitude variables to political participation. For example, the correlation between organizational involvement and political participation in the United States is .523. Fifty-eight percent of *this* is accounted for by the direct path between these two variables (that is, the path that passes through no other variable in the model). Seven percent of the correlation between these two variables is accounted for by the path from organizational involvement to social status and then directly to participation; 14% of the correlation is explained by the path from organizational involvement through social status and then through the intervening attitude variables; and the remaining 21% of the correlation is accounted for by the path from organizational involvement through the various attitude variables but by-passing the social status variable.

The structure of the components of the organizational involvement relationship are almost uncannily consistent from nation to nation. The social status to participation relationships are less consistent, with the U.S. having a fairly large porportion accounted for by the direct link (although the path coefficient is less than twice the stand-

---

[24] In the eight variable causal model there are 54 paths from status to participation. No paths moving back along the model at any points are allowed by the constraints imposed. The method employed here has been termed "path analysis" by Otis Dudley Duncan,

"Path Analysis: Sociological Examples," *American Journal of Sociology*, **72** (July, 1966), 6–7. For an explication of the method, the statistical assumptions which it employs and its limitations, see the discussion and references in footnotes 4 and 5 in Part II of the original article.

ard error and would not usually be considered statistically significant). In Germany the direct link between social status and participation has a high negative score, although the percentage is exaggerated by the weakness of the total correlation (and the score is also less than twice the standard error).[25] The basic pattern, nonetheless, is clear, and we suspect inconsistency reflects in part, at least, some of the problems in adequate measures of social status, or its sub-dimensions.

The general pattern for social status finds about 60 percent of the relationship going through the attitude variables, about 30 percent going directly through organizational involvement, and about 10 percent going through the attitude variables by way of involvement. The general pattern for organizational involvement shows about 60 percent accounted for by the direct link, about 30 percent going through the attitude variables only, and about 10 percent going through social status and then the attitude variables.

Thus, a large part of the relationship between organizational involvement and political participation cannot be explained by reference to other variables included in the model. It is clear that those who are organizationally involved participate in politics at rates far greater than citizens who are not

---

[25] At an earlier stage in the analysis, scales were built with consistency checks on the SES dimension. Persons high on one status item and very low on another were deleted. This procedure increased correlations, but decreased the size of the valid sample, and was not, therefore, used in this analysis. It is especially noteworthy that while only about 10% of the original samples in the US, UK, Italy, and Mexico failed to meet the SES dimension consistency check, about *50%* of the German sample failed to meet it. This suggests the disruption of the social stratification system in Germany as a consequence, no doubt, of the historical upheavals. The strong wage position of workers in the post-war boom, following the leveling impact of World War II and the Third Reich, may also be a contributing factor. See the comments by Lewis J. Edinger, *Politics in Germany* (Boston: Little, Brown, 1968), pp. 19–30.

involved. In addition, and of considerable importance, many citizens whose organizational involvement propels them into political life are *not* more politically informed, politically efficacious, or politically attentive than the non-participants. Unlike political participation stemming from high social status, participation stemming from organizational membership does not necessarily imply those attitudes normally thought to be associated with democratic political participation. We return later to the implications of these findings.

There are two alternative, though not mutually exclusive, explanations for why the organizationally involved are politically active even though they lack certain attitudes. First, organizations can mobilize their members toward political goals; and this can occur without an intervening state of changes in attitudes by the members. The organizations might provide inducements and gratifications to their members, such as sociability, which though producing political activity have nothing to do with political information, awareness, and so forth. Further, the organizations can mobilize members for relatively specific, short-term issues, a mobilization which again does not depend upon any facilitating attitudes other than a willingness to follow the lead of the organization leadership. A professional or business group circulating a petition to be signed or a union enjoining their members to vote are examples of such mobilization.

Second, both organizational and political involvement might be strongly affected by an underlying personality attribute or cultural norm. For instance, both types of activity might be related to a general propensity toward social activism which is unrelated to social status. This explanation implies that joining an organization, becoming active in it, and getting involved in politics are subsets of a more general social behavior which, for reasons of personality attributes, is more attractive to some citizens than others. It is an explanation stressing self-selection.

This is not the place to explore the merits of these alternative explanations—and the data available permit no direct test—but we do suggest that the former explanation has more merit than the latter. The self-selection hypothesis is weakened since we would expect a self-selective tendency to correlate with attitudes such as political efficacy and attentiveness. The absence of strong relationships between organizational involvement and these attitudes makes us suspicious of the self-selection explanation. The first explanation, that organizations are mobilizing their members, is intuitively more persuasive and has been supported by additional research. Data collected in the United States show that membership in organizations which have some relationship to public affairs and which have formal or informal discussions of politics at meetings, greatly increases the likelihood of being politically active. In contrast, members who belong to more apolitical organizations are only slightly more likely than non-members to participate in politics.[26]

. . .

B. Social Structure and the Participation of Class Groups[27]

Individuals vary in their political participation according to their social status and according to their organizational involvement, with the latter social characteristic having the stronger impact on political participation. This finding is consistent from one nation to another. Further, and be-cause there is cross-national consistency, both social status and organizational involvement remain strongly related to political participation when we shift from the individual to the nation as a unit of analysis. That is, nations vary in their level of mass political participation according to the proportion of citizens in the middle and upper classes and according to the density and complexity of organizational life.

In addition, organizational involvement may represent an alternative channel for political participation for socially disadvantaged groups. The rural peasant, the industrial laborer, the disadvantaged black may become politically active through his organizational involvement even though he may otherwise lack the status resources for political participation. In these ways the class structure and the organizational structure of societies determine both the overall rate of participation and the relative amount of participation coming from various social groups.

We have argued that economic development changes both the class and organizational structures of a society. This is true, but other factors may also promote such changes. The class structure is, of course, intimately tied to the long-term development of human and capital resources. Governments may establish massive education programs and engage in forceful income redistribution. These efforts may well affect participation patterns. However, obviously major changes in the status structure, involving occupation, education, and income patterns, are extremely difficult to bring about. We suspect that the organizational structure may be susceptible to more direct and short-term manipulation. Assuming that our organizational correlations reflect causal patterns, rather than the operation of self-selection mechanisms (an assumption we feel is tenable), then the great influence of organizational structure on participation suggests important possibilities for political change.

Although there are few systematic and comparative studies of the process of

---

[26] This research, carried out by Sidney Verba and Norman Nie, shows that a great majority of all types of voluntary organizations in the U.S. have an interest in public affairs and members engage in political discussions; this accounts for the strong relationship between organizational involvement and participation even when not controlling for the type of organization. These findings are based on preliminary analysis of the U.S data from the "Cross National Research Program in Social and Political Change "

[27] We are indebted to Mr. Jae-On Kim for help with some of the methodology required for our analysis in this section.

organizational development, there are numerous examples of efforts by governmental and extra-governmental bodies to generate organizational structure. Religious groups, for example, have spawned an enormous variety of organizations. Governments have fostered—and impeded—the development of both political and nonpolitical organizations such as farmers' associations, professional societies, trade unions, and youth groups. The European socialist movements and the accelerating actions of civil rights groups in the United States in the past few years are additional examples of group mobilization only partially related to economic development patterns. We should not underestimate the complexity of the problems. The new African states have discovered the difficulties in penetrating a pre-mobilized economic structure even with a mass political party, as the numerous coups in recent years illustrate. And the history of socialist and labor movements suggest the frequency of middle class leadership in initial generation of working class movements. Nonetheless, the historical examples suggest a potential manipulability of the organizational structure, as well as a potential for mediating the effects of social class, which make it a central variable in the analysis of participant societies.[28]

The shape of the class structure, the extent of organizational involvement, and the relationship between social status and organizational membership are only partially determined by economic development levels. And these three factors have a complicated but identifiable impact on the overall rate of participation as well as on the amount of participation coming from the various social classes. In this section we examine how different mixtures of these factors affect the degree to which class groups will be under- or over-represented in the "stratum" of political participants in a society. An example illustrates what is meant by these terms as we employ them. Suppose that one-fourth of the citizens are active participants (by some explicated criterion) in the political life of their society. Suppose further that lower class peasants and industrial workers numbered half of the total society. Also suppose that a very limited proportion of this group were members of organizations. All of our previous analysis would therefore suggest that while this class group represented 50 per cent of the total society, it would probably represent a *much* smaller porportion of the 25 per cent who are active political participants. We would conclude that the peasants and workers were "under-represented" in the political stratum. . . .

[Table 6 provides some suggestive evidence on this point. For each of the five nations in the study, the table indicates the proportion of persons in the lower, middle, and upper classes, the class-organization correlation, the proportion of those who are politically active who come from each of the social classes, and an index of underrepresentation for the lower class. With one exception, the cutting points for these variables are identical from nation to nation.[29] The patterns in the table suggest

[28] It may also be true that the development of different types of national industries may create differential needs for economic organizations depending upon industry requirements to coordinate production, transportation, marketing and the like. See, for example, Barrington Moore, Jr's. discussion of the differential impact that varying types of national industry have on the social structure, in *Social Origins of Dictatorship and Democracy* (Boston: Beacon Press, 1966).

[29] Since our scales were derived to give intranation distributions of maximum utility, their validity for cross-national absolute comparisons is somewhat limited. Nor is it entirely clear how one should treat an indicator like "years of education" as a social status indicator on a cross-national basis. The meaning of such absolute measures, like the real buying power of formal income equivalents, depends considerably on the distribution of the commodity within the society. Nonetheless, the chosen cutting points fitted four of the societies in fairly plausible fashion. Actual distribution of education in the United States, for example, reported in the 1959 census was about 17% college educated, 48% 9–12 years of education,

Table 6. Social Structure and Class Group Participation: Five Nations

	GIVEN CONDITIONS		PARTICIPATION PATTERNS	
NATION	CLASS STRUCTURE OF SOCIETY: PROPORTION IN LOW, MIDDLE, UPPER CLASSES	CLASS-ORGANI-ZATION CORRE-LATION	CLASS STRUCTURE OF POLITICALLY ACTIVE [a] PORPORTION IN LOW, MIDDLE, UPPER CLASSES	INDEX OF UNDER-REP-RESENTATION FOR LOWER CLASSES [b]
United States	30%—45%—25%	.44	16%—47%—37%	−47
Britain	46 —38 —16	.31	32 —43 —25	−30
Germany	44 —41 —15	.21	41 —36 —23	−7
Italy	54 —32 —14	.30	42 —39 —19	−22
Mexico	77 —16 — 7	.23	64 —25 —10	−17

[a] Being classified as "politically active" is roughly equivalent to discussing politics at least once a week, or more active involvement, as measured by our original scale items.

[b] Computed by (1) subtracting the per cent of lower class among active participants from the total per cent in the lower class, and (2) dividing the difference by the latter.

first that the higher the correlation between status and organizational membership, the more under-represented the lower class becomes. (Compare Germany and Mexico with the other nations. Note especially Germany and Britain which appear quite similar in class structure but which differ sharply in their degree of lower-class under-representation.)

[The most striking though related finding is the extent to which the lower class is under-represented among the politically active citizens in the United States; the lower class is more severely under-represented there than is true in any of the other nations. The severe under-representation in the United States seems to result first from the fact that the lower class is con-

fronted with a basic correlation between class and participation which is higher than average. (Although it is not a powerful part of the phenomenon, the partial correlation between status and participation, controlling for organizational membership, remains higher in the U.S. than in the other nations. We have no explanation for this fact.) Secondly, the high correlation between social class and organizational involvement (.44) eliminates the potential help offered by the organizational structure. (See Column II.)[30]]

It seems likely that the high correlation between social class and organizational in-

and 35% with 8 years or less. (Compare the class distribution in Table 6.) Only in Britain was a slightly different scale cutting point used —the division between lower and middle class was lowered by one level to show 46% in the lower class rather than 60%. This seemed a more plausible distribution in comparable terms, although it does not greatly affect the class analysis.

[30] These findings are both illuminated and somewhat strengthened by their close accord with a series of simulations which sought to reproduce the structure of political activity in "model societies" based on hypothetical values for the shape of the class structure, the proportion of those in the whole society who were members of organizations and the class-organization correlation. For further discussion of the methods employed in constructing the simulations and their implications for the role of organizations in political mobilization, see pp. 820–23, Table 5, and Appendix IX in Part II of the original article.)

volvement in the United States reflects the fact that in the three European countries there existed historical efforts by political parties to mobilize the lower class and, especially in Germany, to create an organizational structure deliberately parallel to that which had traditionally evolved among the established strata. Even where there may have been a considerable subsequent disengagement of the parties from organizational domination, the effects of such mobilization may have continuing consequences. Lipset and Rokkan have suggested the importance of the political organizazational structures initially established during the social mobilization of the society in setting the party alternatives for the society in subsequent years.[31] Their analysis may well apply to the initial formation of organizational infra-structures more generally. In Mexico, the political regime itself has engaged in a protracted attempt to create a lower class infra-structure. For various reasons, such deliberate attempts at group formation in the United States have been more limited, and particular socio-economic features may have also inhibited the development of lower class organizations.[32] Explanation of these historical patterns is beyond the scope of our analysis. But it is at least clear from the American case that the growth of a lower class organizational structure is *not* part of the natural process of economic development. In fact, the con-

[31] Seymour M. Lipset and Stein Rokkan, *Party Systems and Voter Alignments* (New York: Free Press, 1967), pp. 50–56.

[32] A wide range of possible reasons for this failure of group mobilization of the American lower classes has been suggested. These include the presence of the frontier, the general belief in social mobility and economic progress, the tremendous linguistic, ethnic, and religious differences during the period of immigrations, and the lack of traditional social structures such as guilds. Others have suggested more specifically political factors. For example, Walter Dean Burnham, "The Changing Shape of the American Political Universe," this REVIEW, 59 (March, 1965), p. 24. A unified interpretation is obviously beyond the scope of the present discussion.

sistent positive correlation between organizational involvement and social class points just in the opposite direction. As Olsen and other theorists of the costs of organizational development have suggested, the consequent "natural" evolution has limited the formation of mass organizations among groups with low resources.[33]

The evidence presented here, both actual data and the simulation, suggest a basis for analysis of trends in political participation and group representation. If, for instance, it proves to be the case, as recent data suggest, that the American lower class black population is developing a secondary group structure more rapidly than other similarly located groups in society, one should expect an emergent pattern of broader based representation in the political strata. More complete understanding of these processes, *and* of the reliability of the relationships under differing conditions, might enable us to foresee some of the outcomes of patterns of social change in various national settings.

However, although alerting us to conditions which affect the rates of political participation and the relative contribution of different social groups to the participant stratum, the simulation as presented ignores the issue of the "quality of participation." We saw in the previous section that persons mobilized into a politically active role through their organizational involvement need not share the attitudes normally thought conducive to "rational" political involvement. In the conclusion we attempt to sort out some of the issues connected with the costs and benefits of more equitably distributed access to the participant stratum.

[33] Mancur Olson, *The Logic of Collective Action* (Cambridge: Harvard University Press, 1965). The organizational membership cutting points are the same from nation to nation; they correspond closely to the percentage of citizens in each nation reporting membership in one or more organizations (U.S. 57%; U.K. 47%; Germany 44%; Italy 30%; Mexico 24%), although our scale is composed of several items, rather than membership alone.

VI. Summary and Conclusions

Evidence from five nations indicates that the relationship between economic growth and increases in mass political participation is largely explained through two changes in the social structure of society: larger numbers of upper and middle class persons, in both relative and absolute terms; and the emergence of organized economic and social groups. Stating the relationship between economic development and mass political participation in terms of structural changes in society provides strong empirical correlations and leads to inclusive social theory. The frequently cited correlations between such individual traits as years of education or number of organizational memberships and the citizen's specific acts of political involvement can be subsumed into the more general theory advanced in this study.

At the national level economic development is associated with urbanization, with the growth of secondary groups, and with the expansion of the white-collar class. Each of these variables has been cited as producing mass political participation. We find, however, that at the individual level urban residence has little effect on participation. Living in larger cities has some *negative* impact on *local* participation, but the total amount of variance explained is slight. An even weaker relationship between urban residence and national participation seems purely a function of the concentration of status resources in urban areas in these systems.

There is less of a correlation between social status and organizational involvement than is sometimes supposed. In their impact on political participation, these characteristics clearly can operate independently of one another. In addition, social status and organizational involvement are differentially linked to participation by intervening political attitudes.

Social status tends to affect political participation through its impact on political attitudes and cognitions which, in turn, facilitate political activity. Although the findings are tentative, the data do suggest that the most important causal link is the creation of *attitudinal resources* that sensitize an individual to political messages and provide him the sense of competence needed to engage in political behavior. There is also evidence indicating that higher status exposes the citizen to learning situations in which the duty to participate is stressed. Acquiring this normative predisposition leads the citizen to acquire other attitudinal resources, such as information and competence, which further increase his probability of political participation. (There is, however, wide variance from nation to nation in the importance of an attitude of civic duty and we present these remarks very tentatively.) Finally, the data tend to reject the hypothesis that the well-to-do citizens participate more frequently in politics because they perceive a higher stake in the day-to-day conduct of political affairs. Correlations between such views and participation appear to be spurious.

Involvement in organizations can also produce the attitudinal resources which facilitate political participation. In some cases, at least, organizational involvement is a source of the sense of a normative obligation to participate (in Germany, a stronger source than status). However, in the main the extremely strong relationship between organizational involvement and political participation does not operate through the acquisition of attitudes and cognitions which facilitate participation.

The causal links connecting social status with political participation, links which create attitudinal resources enabling the individual to participate when opportunities occur, are a minor part of the causal impact of organizational involvement. There is either some sort of self-selection effect which ushers the same citizens into both political activity and organized group life, or there is a strong role played by organizations in mobilizing group members for political activity. The latter interpretation is the more likely, although the two are not mutually exclusive. But such mobilization, if it occurs, does not necessarily result in or reflect higher levels of general political information or awareness. Apparently mobilization opens direct lines to participation, or provides attitudinal resources relevant to specific problems only. There might be, for instance, group-initiated political discussion, group-organized contacts with political authorities, or group-related political information relevant to a specific issue.

Implications—The findings reported in this research paper have implications more far-reaching than those thus far discussed. The findings are, of course, closely related to an understanding of some of the stresses and strains in mass democracies. A research report of this type is not the most useful vehicle for speculating about issues of democratic theory, but insofar as our data suggest some observations, we would be remiss to ignore them completely. Let us at least consider what the patterns may imply about one particularly critical problem: the paradox of mass involvement in political life.

First, the data confirm one well-known finding: Even in industrialized nations a majority of citizens do not participate very actively in politics and do not have the attitudinal resources which lead to citizen control of public policies.

The data support social theories which suggest that industrialization is a necessary condition for the establishment of mass involvement in democratic politics.[34] A key component in this theory is the observation that the tendency to get involved in politics,

[34] For example, Seymour Martin Lipset, *Political Man* (Garden City: Doubleday and Co., 1960), pp. 27–63. Also see Philip Cutwright, "National Political Development," in Nelson W. Polsby, Robert A. Dentler, and Paul L. Smith (eds.), *Politics and Social Life* (Boston: Houghton Mifflin Co., 1963), pp. 569–582. In his critical analysis of Lipset and Cutwright, Deane Neubauer argues that economic development may be a necessary condition for democracy, at least to some threshold, but that the relationship is not linear, and does not seem to hold within the subset of more developed systems he examines.

and the attitudes associated with involvement are not randomly distributed in society. Rather, these tendencies and attitudes tend to cluster in the middle and upper classes. Political life styles of citizens will not be markedly changed until extensive industrialization alters the status structure of society, and thereby increases the overall level of political information, attentiveness, efficacy, and so forth.

Second, the data suggest the critical role which the structure of organized group life may play in the overall level of mass political participation. It appears that the richness and complexity of organizational life might be altered somewhat independently of economic development. Deliberate governmental policies, for instance, can increase the number of citizens who are politically active. Mobilization parties in the single-party states of Africa are one example of how this might happen. Unionizing the labor force, even if comprised of peasant farmers, is another illustration. That is, although historically the growth of secondary groups has been associated with economic development, mobilization politics need not await industrialization. New stimuli to group organization may provoke new patterns of growth, although we observe that complexities and difficulties (beyond this analysis) have met such efforts in practice.

Organizational membership, then, could be a political resource for the lower classes. Were this resource equitably distributed, the criteria for pluralistic democracy advanced by Dahl, Key and others would be more nearly met.[35] That is, all social strata in the society would participate in those

See Deane Neubauer, "Some Conditions of Democracy," this REVIEW, 61 (December, 1967), pp. 1002–1009.

[35] Robert A. Dahl, *A Preface to Democratic Theory* (Chicago: University of Chicago Press, 1956); Key, *op. cit.*; and see the exchange between Jack Walker, "A Critique of the Elitist Theory of Democracy," and Robert A. Dahl, "Further Reflections on the 'Elitist Theory of Democracy,'" This REVIEW, 60 (June, 1966), 285–305, and Communications to the Editor.

political processes which presumably lead to control of political leadership and through this control to influence over public policy. Group mobilization could attract into political life larger numbers of those persons who presently are political isolates. These citizens need not have the enabling antecedents, such as higher levels of education, now thought to be necessary conditions for political participation. Alterations in the organizational structure, then, can serve to correct the tendency for even the most democratically organized societies to allow a disproportionate amount of political influence to be exercised by the well-to-do.

These observations about the organization-related potential for increasing political participation should be advanced cautiously, however. For one thing, we reemphasize that in every nation examined social status and organizational involvement were somewhat correlated, though the relationship is not determinate. Indeed, it is important for the student of American politics to note that the distribution of organizational resources is more intertwined with the distribution of status resources in the United States than in any of the other four nations in the study. The natural growth of organizations, as Mancur Olson has suggested, seems to be one which places at a disadvantage very large potential groups when the individuals who might make up those groups have limited individual resources.[36] The cost to each individual of organization building is discouragingly great. It is probably no coincidence that those nations in which both political parties and governmental bureaucracies have been most active in encouraging secondary group formation show less upper class domination of the organized life of the society. What must be concluded is that processes of economic development will not automatically help redress class participation imbalances through the growth of secondary groups.

Another note of caution must be voiced

as well. One cannot be certain, particularly on the basis of data presented here, about the quality of organization-based political participation. The individual mobilized by his group membership lacks the attitudes usually associated with political involvement. This may mean that the content of his effort to influence will be largely determined by the mobilizing leaders, a possibility suggesting that organizations are more the base of a "counter-elite" than a source of broader and more democratic patterns of political influence.

Whereas our findings suggest a potential for participatory democracy which is in optimistic contrast to most modern empirical studies of mass participation, these same findings raise again the specter of mass "irrationality" and "ignorant" involvement which has haunted democratic theorists since the Greeks. Organizations mobilizing their members and providing resources for their leaders present the possibility of large numbers of political activists who do not have the attitudes usually assumed to be associated with involvement in political life. Political information, a sense of civic duty, political attentiveness, and a sense of political efficacy are not preconditions for political participation among the organizationally involved.

Just what this implies is not entirely clear from the data at hand. While some modern American theorists have placed great stock in the moderating influence of norms of tolerance and accommodation, and of the gate-keeper role of those thoroughly socialized into recognition of democratic procedures and processes,[37] it is not evident that such norms are necessarily the property of elites rather than masses. If American data showing the informed substratum to be more tolerant and democratically oriented, although also more split on political issues, are correct, then group mobilization in this system is likely to be associated with higher levels of conflict and intolerance.[38] On the

[36] Olson, *op. cit.*

[37] Dahl, *op. cit.*; and Key, *op. cit.*

[38] James W. Prothro and Charles M. Grigg, "Fundamental Principles of Democracy," *Journal of Politics*, 22 (1960), 276–294; Samuel

other hand, there is some evidence that in systems with a more ideological and conflict-ridden history, the better informed and more active citizens may possess belief systems into which deeply rooted hostility and suspicion of the opposition, as well as intransigent issue positions, are firmly integrated.[39] Such would seem to be the case in nations such as France, Austria, and Italy. In these circumstances, group mobilization of a certain type might draw into the system citizens oriented more pragmatically to specific issues and problems, who might press elites to abandon traditional attitudes of rigidity.

The problem is further complicated by the facts that (1) the relationship between basic attitudes, such as information and attentiveness, and the specific affective and normative content of opinions, has not been established; and (2) the possibility that under some conditions group activity itself may structure affective attitudes must be brought into the analysis. In nations where organized groups are linked to partisan camps, and few groups cut across party, class, and religious lines, then involvement itself may reinforce suspicions and hostilities. Thus, in nations such as Italy and Austria, where group members and leaders seem to be more distrustful of the opposition than citizens at large,[40] the mobilization of ever greater numbers of participants through this same group structure may only increase the number of distrustful participants, neither easing our exacerbating the hostility among political elites, but generally intensifying the political interactions in the system.

In short, the place of participation in the nature of democratic processes is a complex one, and the effect of increases in participation, particularly through operation of organized groups, depends on a number of other factors. Even such implications as we have suggested must be advanced only as speculations in no way tested by our data. What we have shown is that the relationship between individual political activity and mass political participation has some properties not heretofore recognized. It is a separate research task to specify how different bases of political participation produce different politics.

Stouffer, *Communism Conformity, and Civil Liberties* (New York: Doubleday and Co., 1955); Herbert McClosky, Paul J. Hoffmann, and Rosemary O'Hara, "Issue Conflict and Consensus among Party Leaders and Followers," this REVIEW, 59 (June, 1960), 406–427.

[39] See, for example, Duncan MacRae, Jr., *Parliament, Parties and Society in France, 1946–1958* (New York: St. Martin's Press, 1967). Also, for suggestive data from a single community, G. Bingham Powell, Jr., *Fragmentation and Hostility in an Austrian Community* (Stanford: Stanford University Press, forthcoming).

[40] See the general discussion of organizational fragmentation; as well as the data on Italy, in Sidney Verba, "Organizational Membership and Democratic Consensus," *Journal of Politics*, 27 (1965), 467–497. Also see the discussion and data of Powell, *ibid.*; Chapters I and IV; Arend Lijphart, *The Politics of Accommodation* (Berkeley: University of California Press, 1968), Chapter I; and Rodney P. Stiefbold, "Elite-Mass Opinion Structure and Communication Flow in a Consociational Democracy (Austria)," paper presented at the 1968 Annual Meeting of the American Political Science Association.

PART VI

POLITICAL DEVELOPMENT: SEQUENCES AND PARTY SYSTEMS

INTRODUCTION

When analyzing political parties in the industrialized nations, political scientists tend to look at them as institutions whose effectiveness can be judged by how well they function as mediating agencies in the realm of politics. Do parties help communicate political demands to critical decision-making areas of government? Do they function effectively in aggregating interests? Do they represent the spectrum of ideas and groups comprising the polity? Ironically, when party systems show a demonstrable inability to cope with problems they are expected to resolve, we then begin to explore the deeper origins of the issues themselves, for it may not be the party system itself which determines its efficacy but the kind, rate, and sequence of the issues which arise.

In the following two chapters comprising Part VI, we introduce a selection of articles which utilizes historical analysis in attempting to identify the kinds of major issues all societies seem to face at some time in their histories. Inasmuch as an important—perhaps the most important—social mechanism for resolving these issues is the political party system, have also included a group of articles concerned with ways by which political parties function in developing polities. If history has been kind to a society and processed its crises slowly over the years, political parties may demonstrate remarkable capacities in meeting new issues. If, however, as is often the case in the developing nations, difficult challenges arise more or less simultaneously, party systems may be overwhelmed and appear helpless as modern organizations having an assumed capability to ease the burdens of other segments of the political system.

Although the term political *development* itself implies a movement through time, most of the literature on political development has lacked a temporal quality in its focus. In contrast to the field of economic development, where the influence of economic historians has been pronounced, the study of political development has leaned more heavily on the concepts, theories, and methodologies of the behavioral sciences rather than history. More recently, however, the search for an understanding of how and why societies behave different politically and show marked contrasts in their capabilities for resolving political problems has led scholars concerned with political development to turn once again to the insights of history. This shift reflects a growing recognition that during the development process Western nations also experienced those very crises which developing political systems currently face. Accordingly, the three analyses in the chapter dealing with sequences of political development attempt to distill the historical experiences of more developed political systems in order to gain a clearer understanding of the present strains in less developed polities. The articles are historical, analytical, and, implicitly if not overtly, prescriptive.

The article by C. E. Black dealing with the phases of modernization constitutes an overview of "the critical problems that all modernizing societies must face." The paramount problems and challenges confronting developing polities, according to Black, include: (1) the challenge of modernity, (2) the consolidation of modernizing leadership, (3) economic and social transformation, and (4) the integration of society. While Black speaks in terms of "phases" and identifies the critical problems inherent in each, he does not conceive of these phases as discrete. Rather, there is a clear recognition on his part that they overlap to a considerable degree, that there are recurrences of particular challenges, and that "traditional ideas and institutions have an extraordinary staying power." Black also calls attention to the advantages that early modernizing nations have had simply because they could afford to respond to the challenges of development at a more leisurely pace. By contrast, those nations entering the phase of economic and social transformation today are deprived of the opportunity for slow, evolutionary change as a result of the increasingly dynamic environment created by the more developed polities.

Eric A. Nordlinger examines a number of the issues inherent in the history and sociology of political development. Nordlinger contends that if problems such as national identity, governmental institutions, and political competition, among others, are confronted and resolved in a certain time sequence, the probability that political system will emerge as democratic, stable, and effective is greatly enhanced. He goes on to say, however, that if a rapid rate of social and economic change takes place as societies deal with these issues, violence and repressive rule rather than an effective and stable democratic system are likely to result.

A concern for the rate and sequence of societal change are also reflected in the analysis of Robert E. Ward, which deals with authoritarianism as a factor in the modernization of Japan. Like the preceding article by Nordlinger, Ward is more broadly concerned with identifying the conditions which can increase the probability that a developing polity will become both modern and democratic. His findings in relation to the Japanese experience lead him to suggest that authoritarianism in the initial stages of modernization may not be destructive of the long-range prospects for democracy; indeed, he views authoritarianism as an extraordinarily effective modernizing force in some instances, depending on what social changes are effected under such rule. He further suggests that a steady and gradual transition from authoritarianism may be essential to the emergence of politics which are both modern and democratic.

Whether the historical and theoretical perspectives of Black, Nordlinger, and Ward offer a basis for hope or despair to students of politics with normative concerns for democratic political development is an unsettled question. Regardless of the time when it is ideally most advantageous for a society to experience social mobilization and mass politics, when political parties may emerge, the process of political development and the diffusion of new institutional forms throughout the developing societies occur in a way which seems to leave little room for choice.

Samuel P. Huntington's influential statement on strategies of institutional development argues for the primacy of parties in the development process, considering them important sources of authority, institutionalization, and legitimacy. Whereas political parties are often valued as institutions with a capacity for articulating and aggregating demands of divergent groups in society, accelerating social mobilization, and increasing the scope of political participation, Huntington takes a different perspective. He sees the political party as a means of slowing these processes, at least until such time as institutional development has occurred and the political system has acquired sufficient acceptance, legitimacy, experience, and capability to deal with the many and complex issues unleashed by rapid social mobilization.

If, as Huntington maintains, political development is institutionalization, then it follows that stability, order, and only moderate rates of change are most conducive to institutionalization. Thus, Huntington boldly carries his argument to its logical conclusion by indicating that political development may be best served by a single-party system rather than a two-party, multiparty, or a no-party system.

The impact of parties on political development is examined by Myron Weiner and Joseph LaPalombara in an article which treats parties and party systems as independent variables affecting some of the major problems facing the developing nations. This conception of parties as "instruments of organized human action" stands in sharp contrast to the view of some observers that parties are divisive forces impeding economic growth and modernization. The authors identify four major areas upon which parties can have a profound impact: (1) national integration, (2) political participation, (3) legitimacy, and (4) the management of conflict. They conclude their analysis by suggesting that the future of political parties in developing nations depends, in large measure, on how successful parties are, in conjunction with governments, in coping with the various challenges of modernization. Their approach suggests further that parties are not simply the trappings of modernity which drain the resources of poor economies; rather, parties can act as vital mechanisms by which governments deal with the societal transformations implicit in the development process.

Political parties are often means for giving expression to the differences between groups in society. The origin, persistence, and contemporary political implications of these differences—or cleavages—is analyzed by Seymour Martin Lipset. While Lipset addresses himself to political parties in the developing nations, he draws upon the historical experiences of Western political development, especially the sociological bases of political parties, for his theoretical appreciation of parties and political groups.

Speaking of the West, he points out that many of the existing differences between parties "reflect the institutionalization of past bases of opinion cleavage; once formalized in political parties, these cleavages have survived the decline or disappearance of the original social conflicts which gave rise to party division." One may reasonably assume that in the developing nations, too, the present as well as the future profile of political parties would reflect the cleavages that generated them. However, as Lipset observes, the developing nations have greater cultural and historical diversity than that which is found in the industrial nations, a factor which makes generalization and prediction even more difficult.

Lipset notes, as have other contributors to this volume, such as Edward A. Shils and Eric R. Wolf, that in the developing nations the better educated and the well-to-do are often aggressively leftist politically, especially to the extent that they are modernization-oriented. Socialism and communism are historically and symbolically associated with the ideology of independence, rapid economic development, social modernization, and equality. Capitalism on the other hand, frequently elicits an image of imperialism, traditionalism, and slow economic growth.

Just as we noted in beginning this Part, Lipset finds that political parties in the West function increasingly as agencies mediating the conflicting demands of diverse groups and strata. The tendency in the developing nations, by contrast, is for political parties—particularly left-wing or nationalist parties—to function not as representatives of particular groups engaged in mediation but as bearers of programs and ideologies intent upon mobilizing society for a massive effort at economic development. There are, however, factors and forces, which Lipset discusses throughout his article, that soften the explosive and authoritarian potential of party politics in the developing nations.

In the following article dealing with peasant society and clientelist politics, John Duncan Powell explores in greater depth some of these influences of parties in many of the developing nations. Although his analysis is not explicitly addressed to political parties, Powell vividly describes the cognitive world of the peasant in developing nations, pointing out that the peasant feels continually harassed or threatened by an environment over which he possesses little control. As a partial consequence of this sense of powerlessness, there evolve in peasant societies basic patterns of social relations—or "anxiety-reduction behaviors"—by which the peasant seeks to make life tolerable within this threatening context. One of these adaptive patterns which the author examines in detail is the "clientele system."

Clientelist politics are delicately balanced reciprocal arrangements in which the government (patron) and the peasantry (client) are involved in a system of payoffs. For its part, the government provides the peasants with small amounts of land, credit services, and technological and marketing assistance. In return, peasant clients seem to provide a government with a measure of protection against destabilizing attacks from both left and right. This relationship between patron and client, according to Powell, is a pragmatic one without rigid policy, doctrine, or dogma. Thus, "a clientelist base of support tends to erode ideological coherence and program content" of the political leaders dependent upon clientelist politics. Powell argues, further, that modern organizational forms such as political parties will inherit many of the characteristics of the patron-client relationship he discusses.

The final article in this chapter on transitional politics and party systems presents Lucian W. Pye's analytical model of transitional politics. Pye has undertaken to identify the distinguishing political characteristics of developing nations which differentiate them from more developed societies. Many of the qualities that Pye imputes to transitional politics, it has been argued, are still to be found in varying degrees within the political systems of more industrialized nations.[1] Yet the degree of difference is sufficiently great that there exists a basis for appproaching the developing nations as a distinct category for study.

[1] Alfred Diamant, "Is There a Non-Western Political Process?" *Journal of Politics*, **21**, 123–27, February 1959.

Chapter 13

Sequences of Political Development

PHASES OF MODERNIZATION

C. E. Black

All aspects of modernization have been fraught with strife, and its politics has been particularly susceptible to crises arising from the struggles of contending leaders to assure the acceptance of their policies. The stakes are high, the pressures are powerful, and the conflict has been intense. The issues have been posed in a great variety of ways in the more than 170 politically organized societies that constitute today the organizational framework of mankind, but it is possible to distinguish certain critical problems that all modernizing societies must face: (1) *the challenge of modernity*—the initial confrontation of a society, within its traditional framework of knowledge, with modern ideas and institutions, and the emergence of advocates of modernity; (2) *the consolidation of modernizing leadership* —the transfer of power from traditional to modernizing leaders in the course of a normally bitter revolutionary struggle often lasting several generations; (3) *economic and social transformation*—the development of economic growth and social change to a point where a society is transformed from a predominantly rural and agrarian way of life to one predominantly urban and industrial; and (4) *the integration of society*

SOURCE: Excerpted from C. E. Black, *The Dynamics of Modernization: A Study in Comparative History* (New York: Harper & Row, Publishers, 1966), Chap. III, using only pp. 67–94.

—the phase in which economic and social transformation produces a fundamental reorganization of the social structure throughout the society.

The central problem faced by modernizing political leaders is that of adapting the particular traditional culture of their own society to a way of life commensurate with the opportunities afforded by modern knowledge, and politics is the struggle for the power to implement the programs that they advocate. The substance of the competing programs nevertheless embraces the aggregate of the problems confronting a society, and the crises of political modernization reflect intellectual, economic, social, and psychological problems, as well as political ones. The discussion of political crises, then, calls for a consideration of the entire process. One could doubtless achieve the same result by discussing the course of modernization in terms of any of its other aspects, but since politics is primarily concerned with public policy and with the organization of society, it provides the most convenient framework for discussing the entire complex development. Although in a sense modernization is accompanied by a continuing crisis, the four phases discussed here mark major problems calling for concentrated effort in the development of nations, and are often designated by national holidays, monuments, constitutions, legislative acts, and treaties. The peaks of these crises are also the periods when domestic or international violence is most likely to occur. Between these crises, on the other hand, there may often be extended periods of relative stability in which the previous gains are digested.

The Challenge of Modernity

When traditional societies are initially confronted by modernity, and when some of their prominent members become the advocates of a new and challenging way of life, the incumbent leaders may adopt one of a variety of courses. They may combat the new ideas and persecute the innovators as heretics; or they may discuss them, accept some, and reject others; or they may find them to be valid and attempt a fundamental reorganization of their institutions accordingly. Usually some combination of these reactions occurs, and the combination is rarely the same in any two cases.

In most respects the societies that were the first to modernize had the easiest time of it, for they were able to digest the new knowledge and technology over a considerable period of time and to absorb the impact gradually. England did this so successfully that despite a revolution and subsequent violence in several forms, the ruling oligarchy—substantially renovated—managed to survive until the second half of the twentieth century. In the westernmost countries of Europe the process was likewise quite prolonged.

The origins of modern knowledge may be traced to the significant new scholarship and technological innovation in the Middle Ages commonly referred to by historians as the renaissance of the twelfth century. Modern ideas and techniques emerged decisively in the fifteenth century, and by the sixteenth and seventeenth centuries a full-fledged scientific revolution was in progress. Rapid economic growth, urbanization, and social mobility were by now well under way, and the need for a more effective organization of human resources led to the development of new methods of communication and business, and especially to political consolidation. Kings began to exert greater authority at the expense both of local lords and of the Church, and practices of administration and taxation were revised to meet the demands of the new situation.

The initial growth of knowledge, as well as the related technology, was largely the work of the traditional elite—a small circle of large landowners, churchmen, merchants, and artisans—and was at first regarded as a useful and acceptable development. As the consequences of early modernization began to become apparent, however, and as the fundamental assumptions of traditional societies were increasingly challenged, the process of transforming the traditional order became increasingly turbulent. The trial of Galileo by the Inquisition in 1632 because of his heretical view that the sun did not rotate around the earth, and his recantation, was only the most dramatic of many confrontations between the new knowledge and the traditional culture.

Despite the wide acceptance by the end of the seventeenth century of the scientific attitude and its many and diverse consequences, the modern way of life had not yet penetrated deeply into society. The rulers now accepted the need for reform, and as "enlightened despots" they generally championed the interests of merchants, manufacturers, and townspeople against those of the provincial and country magnates who had an agrarian base. They kept the reforms within the traditional framework, however, and expected to preserve the privileges and wealth that the oligarchy had always enjoyed. The modernizing reforms of the enlightened despots were defensive or preventative, in the sense that they were calculated to satisfy the demands of a rapidly changing society without destroying the traditional privileges. This policy was not the result of greed so much as of a deeply ingrained belief that the traditional division between leaders and followers was divinely ordained and indispensable to any well-ordered society. Not until the English, American, and French revolutions had run their course was the oligarchic framework of traditional society finally broken.

The relatively small number of European countries where modernity had first emerged had begun in the meantime to exert their worldwide influence from the beginning of the modern era. By the end of the fifteenth century they had discovered America, explored much of the African coastline, and developed much more intensively the ancient contacts with eastern Mediterranean and Asian societies. To this extent, and in this early form, the challenge of modernity was a universal one almost from the start. Yet the modern made contact with the traditional only at its peripheries, and it was not until the eighteenth and nineteenth centuries that the influence of modern ideas and institutions began to penetrate more deeply into political, economic, and social affairs.

The societies immediately adjacent to those that modernized first, the Muscovite and the Turkish, possessed governments that were sufficiently strong to control direct Western influences within their territories and sufficiently farsighted to foresee that they must adopt Western methods if they were to retain their independence. Starting at the end of the fifteenth century in Russia, and somewhat later in Turkey, a systematic policy was adopted of employing Western technicians and specialists to modernize the army and the bureaucracy, to build fortifications and public buildings, to establish factories, and to develop natural resources. This policy reached its most active form in Russia under Peter the Great and in Turkey under Mahmud II. These were classic cases of defensive modernization, in which much of the traditional system was deliberately strengthened—especially the part that involved the strict regulation and taxation of the agrarian sector—against more general modernizing influences exerted directly from without and in-

directly from within, through the reorganization of the administrative system.

The Consolidation of Modernizing Leadership

The most dramatic of the crises of political modernization are those concerned with the transfer of power from traditional to modernizing leaders. "Transfer of power" is perhaps too colorless a phrase to describe these events, for they involved in every country political struggles of the first magnitude. We know now, and many were confident then, that the modernizers would in the end be victorious—but the leaders of the old regimes fought bitterly and often skillfully to maintain their positions.

This struggle may be thought of in terms of three essential features. The first is the assertion on the part of political leaders of the determination to modernize. This assertion may take the form of revolution by disaffected members of the traditional oligarchy or by modernizing leaders representing new political interests. Occasionally the traditional oligarchy itself initiates the process. There is typically a generation or more of political struggle before a program of modernization gains sufficiently wide acceptance to provide a secure basis of support for a modernizing leadership.

The second feature is an effective and decisive break with the institutions associated with a predominantly agrarian way of life, permitting the transition to an industrial way of life. In the case of societies with a relatively closed agrarian economy, this break frequently takes the form of a dramatic emancipation of the bulk of the population from traditional agricultural institutions. In other societies it may come about more gradually as a result of the commercialization of agriculture, changes in the ideology, or other institutional changes.

Finally, the creation of a politically organized society in those cases where one did not exist in the initial phase is also essential. Many societies have encountered difficulties in working out a viable form of political organization, which is so essential to the process of modernization. In other cases whole peoples migrated to new lands, sometimes previously uninhabited, and established offshoots of older societies. In still others the early modernizers extended their political authority over societies in an early stage of modernization and remolded them along modern lines.

The revolutions that bring modernizing political leaders into power vary greatly in their character, but all may be said to have at least two dimensions: they are violent or nonviolent, and they are internal or external. The well-known revolutions—such as the English, the American, the French, the Russian, the Turkish, the Yugoslavian, the Chinese, the Vietnamese, the Cuban, and the Algerian—were all violent and internal. They were internal in the sense that domestic revolutionaries bore the main brunt of the fighting, even though they often received substantial foreign aid. It is also significant that in all of these cases the task of the revolutionaries was not to overthrow firm and vigorous governments but to topple them after their stability had already been undermined. Frequently the traditional government is defeated before the revolution occurs, in the course of a foreign war —as was the case in Russia, Turkey, Yugoslavia, China, and Vietnam; or else it may become so corrupt as to alienate most of its supporters before the onset of the revolutionary crisis—as in the case of England, the American colonies, France, Cuba, and Algeria. Some of the revolutionary movements—such as the American, Vietnamese, and Algerian, and many others in different parts of the world—have had the dual goal of independence and social change. Indeed, these two motives are often so intertwined as to form a single goal.

Revolutions may also be imposed from without, and have at the start little internal support. A foreign army may overrun a country and establish an entirely new set of institutions after destroying the former government. The French did this in many countries of Western and Central Europe in the course of the Napoleonic wars, as did the Soviet Union in Eastern Europe and North Korea after the Second World War. A revolution is no less a revolution for being imposed from without, and many turn out rather well.

Nonviolent revolutions are relatively rare, although some of the most successful have been of this type. The overthrow of the Tokugawa regime in Japan in 1868 was essentially bloodless, and it ushered in a period of fundamental modernizing reforms that have widely been regarded as a model of peaceful change. Similarly the emancipation of the serfs in Russia in 1861 led to widespread reforms and rapid industrialization by the 1890's, and is recognized by both Russian and Western historians as a main turning point in the history of the country.

The second criterion for evaluating the transition to modernizing leadership is the reform of land tenure to permit the most effective use of agriculture in the great economic transformation that was under way. Land ownership has varied greatly in traditional societies, and an equally wide variety of solutions has been applied. The aim of these reforms is to increase the productivity of agriculture in order to feed the growing cities, to provide agricultural goods for manufacturing, and indirectly to furnish further capital for investment in industry.

Agriculture, the principal source of income until modern times, formed the political, economic, and social basis of traditional societies. It was naturally the most conservative sector of society, and efforts to change systems of land tenure and methods of cultivation were bound to be major political issues. In England, where landowners and merchants provided the modernizing leadership, agricultural reform was stimulated by the enclosure of formerly common lands by the landowners so that they could apply modern methods to improve production. The situation in England was the exception rather than the rule, however, for in most parts of the world the large landowners have been opponents of modernization and have not devoted their incomes to economic growth.

In these countries the purpose of agricultural reform was to break up the large estates, either by distributing land to the peasants or by organizing it in some other way so that its surplus could be devoted to industrialization. In places where the landowners opposed modernization, agricultural reform became a crucial issue; because the landlords were the main support of the traditional government, any reform in agriculture involved a thoroughgoing political revolution. This was the case in most countries of Latin America, the Near East, and Asia.

The third criterion for judging whether the transition of modernizing leaders to power has taken place is the creation of a national state with an effective government and a reasonably stable consensus on the part of the inhabitants as to ends and means. It is one of the most striking features of this process that of the 133 independent states in existence today, no more than twenty had approximately their present territory before the accession to power of modernizing leaders. These countries— such as England, France, and Switzerland among the earlier modernizers and Russia, Iran, China, and Japan among those that made the transition somewhat later—already had a distinct national identity before the modern era. They were able to go forward with the work of modernization without having to do more than defend their existing frontiers under conditions in which they generally had an advantage over the aggressors. These countries had many other problems, but at least they did not have this problem.

For all the other countries of the world— as well as for the thirty to forty that are now waiting to be born—the creation of a national state has been a central issue that overshadowed almost all others. The under-

lying ideology of the modernizing leaders maintained that they could not reform, tax, educate, and build until they were free from the foreign lords who discriminated against them and impeded their efforts. This costly process of nation-building took many forms. With Germany and Italy it involved the unification of smaller states, principalities, and other territories into single national states in the course of over half a century of domestic and international wars. In the case of Austria-Hungary and Turkey, it involved the breakup of great multinational empires so that new states could be formed by the component peoples. The countries of the two Americas, Africa, and Asia were with few exceptions formed after long and bitter struggles with the tutelary powers.

In all of these instances nationalism was not an end in itself but a means to an end —modernization. Yet the struggle for independence was in many cases so long and costly, and the emotions aroused were so powerful, that nationalism frequently came to overshadow modernization and to divert it from its main course. The struggle for independence had absorbed so much in lives and effort, and the resources required to defend the frontiers and maintain an independent status were so great, that other matters came to play a secondary role. The powerful appeal of nationalism was, moreover, frequently used by conservative leaders to prevent reforms, and the nationalism that was generally linked with liberalism before independence became more often than not a force for conservatism. Nation-building was essential to modernization, because it was the most effective way to mobilize the efforts of the peoples concerned, but it also caused some of modernization's most difficult problems.

The manner in which these essential categories of change have occurred—political revolutions, agricultural reform, and nation-building—has varied widely in different societies. They have occurred in all possible sequences, and have been combined to form a variety of complex challenges to political leadership. In a few countries other problems may have loomed larger than these three. All were nevertheless essential to the effective mobilization of the efforts of the peoples concerned, and the transfer of power from traditional to modernizing leaders cannot be said to have taken place until solutions to all three sets of problems have been found.

Economic and Social Transformation

The phase of economic and social transformation, as understood in the present context, represents the period between the accession to political power of modernizing leaders and the development of a society to the point at which it is predominantly urban and the focus of mobilization of the great majority of the population is toward the society as a whole rather than toward local communities and specialized groups. Among advanced countries this phase may be considered to have extended from 1832 to 1945 in England, from 1848 to 1945 in France, and from 1865 to 1933 in the United States. Among countries that modernized somewhat later this phase may be thought of as having started in 1917 in Russia, in 1923 in Turkey, in 1930 in Brazil, in 1949 in China, and in 1952 in Egypt, and as still continuing. In many other societies modernizing leadership is still consolidating its position, and the phase of intensive economic and social transformation lies ahead.

If the consolidation of modernizing leadership is a period of dramatic political change—of coups, revolutions, and wars of national liberation and unification—it is nevertheless one of relatively superficial developments that affect the nationality, citizenship, and legal status of the average person more than they affect his daily life. Empires have come and gone for centuries with relatively little effect on the personal affairs of the great majority of their peoples, and the initial impact of the accession

to power of modernizing leaders is in most cases no greater than these earlier changes. Economic and social transformation, on the other hand, is less dramatic but much more profound. The change in values and way of life of the average person in the more advanced countries has been greater between the mid-nineteenth and mid-twentieth centuries than between ancient Mesopotamia, Egypt, or China and the early modern period. This has been a period of transformation in all realms of human activity that is unprecedented in history.

Underlying this rapid transformation has been the dramatic growth of science and technology. In the early nineteenth century the natural sciences were poorly differentiated from philosophy and from one another, and a single individual could specialize in or keep abreast of a considerable variety of fields. Goethe, to take only one example, although obviously an exceptional one, could do original work in law, drama, and the novel, as well as in anatomy, botany, geology, and physics. A century later even scholars within the same disciplines had difficulty understanding one another's work because of the degree of specialization that had been attained. Virtually all of modern science has developed in this period, and at its start technology was just at the beginning of its greatest development. The steam engine was just being harnessed, and the development of electricity, metallurgy, and electronics, not to mention nuclear power, still lay ahead. It is the myriad of applications of science and technology that has led to this great transformation in human affairs.

The concentration of effort required by economic and social transformation is focused primarily at the level of the politically organized society, the national state or polity, rather than at the local or the international level. Typical of this transformation were the German customs union of 1837 and similar movements in other countries designed to eliminate local barriers to trade, to establish national currencies and postal systems, and the like. The implementation of these developments leads to a corresponding concentration of policy-making, both public and private, at the national level. This preoccupation with national affairs tends to weaken the international as well as the local ties of a society. Societies become less cosmopolitan during this phase, and more self-centered. The security and identity of the individual becomes linked to a much greater degree with the national community than with the local or the international.

The political consequences of this concentration of effort at the national level are reflected not only in administrative centralization but also in a significant intensification of nationalism. In the preceding phase nationalism is concerned with independence and unification, and reflects a spirit of freedom from traditional restraints and an anticipation of new opportunities. In the period of economic and social transformation nationalism comes to represent a jealous concern of almost psychotic proportions for the security of one's own society and, at the same time, a systematic attack on loyalties of a local or ideological character that might threaten national cohesion. In France the development of theories of integral nationalism, the long struggle between republicanism and clericalism, and the dramatic confrontation in the Dreyfus case between cosmopolitanism and chauvinism are characteristic of this phase. The French seem to have had a particular capacity for dramatizing these controversies, but they occurred in all societies. Even value systems with a strong international commitment, such as Christianity and socialism, have been overwhelmed by a nationalism that derives its emotional force from the extensive investment of personal security in politically organized societies.

The intellectual and political aspects of this transformation are probably clearer in retrospect than they were at the time, but the economic and social changes were apparent to all. Indeed, their impact was so great that social theorists have been unable to resist the temptation to stress them at the expense of the more profound features of modernization. In the most general sense, the scope of these changes is reflected in the transfer of more than one-half of the work force of a society from agriculture to manufacturing, transportation, commerce, and services, and of an even larger proportion of the population from a rural to an urban environment. The proportions of this transformation have varied a good deal from one country to another. The share of agriculture in national product and in the labor force was already below one-half in the United States and in many countries of Western Europe in the first half of the nineteenth century, but much of the manufacturing was still of a rural character and did not have the profound social impact of the later urban industrialization. In the countries of Asia, Latin America, and Africa the agrarian component has been much higher at the start of this phase and the impact of the transformation is likely to be more profound. There are many statistics that one could cite to describe the economic transformation that occurred, but suffice it to say that in the advanced countries virtually the entire industrial plant and communications system as we know them today were built during this phase.

The social aspects of this transformation brought many benefits, but also heavy burdens. This phase is one of rapid growth in secondary education and medical care, the benefits of which were extended to the great majority of the population. The shift of the work force from agriculture to manufacturing, transportation, communications, and services is accompanied by a significant change in the relationship of social strata to one another and to the exercise of political power. At the start of this phase the individuals directly concerned with political power constitute no more than a fraction of the population, and the great majority are peasants or rural and urban workers who have no political role. In the course of this period there is a rapid growth in the management and service cadres, following upon the development of education. There is also a considerable broadening of the base of the ruling group as the sources of recruitment change from landownership to business, commerce, and areas of activity requiring university-trained specialists. The executive, managerial, and service strata may come to embrace as much as one-half the population of a society.

The burdens of this transformation are borne by the large numbers of peasants who desert the villages that they have inhabited for many generations and move to cities in larger numbers than can be accommodated. While the evidence is not so complete or reliable as one would wish, it appears that in some countries for as much as a generation there may have been an absolute decline in the standard of living for significant segments of the population. In those societies where the labor force was made up largely of immigrants, as in the United States and Canada, such a decline does not seem to have taken place. In others, where the shift of the labor force occurred under great government pressure, the burdens on the labor force have been particularly heavy. Much depends on the circumstances under which a country modernizes and on the policies of its leaders. In the West European countries it took thirty to fifty years to shift as much as one-quarter of the labor force out of agriculture as compared with less than half this time in the Soviet Union, and in general in the countries that developed earlier the tensions of this transformation were more attenuated.

The policies under which this transition from agriculture to industry is made constitute one of the key distinctions between liberal and statist policies. The tightly centralized direction of the Soviet state resulted in a rapid transfer of the labor force, but this dynamism was purchased at a high price in human suffering. It has been estimated that not until the 1950's did the Soviet level of real wages and per capita purchases reach that of 1928. This latter level, in turn, was about the same as that of 1913. The hardships of the peasants and industrial workers, however, were not the result only of Soviet policies. Both the administrative centralization and the pressure on the common man were also characteristic of tsarist methods, and Soviet policy intensified them without altering their essential character. This is only one example of many that one could cite regarding the variations in the policies under which economic and social transformation is implemented. Yet despite these variations, societies in this phase of development share certain fundamental uniformities.

Value systems always seem to lag somewhat behind economic and social developments, and the assumptions and outlook of leaders in this phase remain under the strong influence of the traditional agrarian and rural frame of reference. Indeed, the work force itself, as it moves from the countryside to the cities, retains many of its rural modes of thought and life. Village traditions are carried over into the cities, and the deference of peasant to landlord is transmuted into the respect of the poorly educated for the technically trained. Similarly minority groups retain many of their disabilities throughout this phase despite the actual changes in their status and the cosmopolitan goals of the society. A kind of agrarian cushion protects the bulk of the population from the hardships of urban life, but at the same time delays the fulfillment of their expectations.

The Integration of Society

The stage of development represented by this fourth phase of modernization has been variously referred to as the achieving society, the advanced society, the communist society, the developed society, the free society, the great society, the industrial society, the integrated society, the mass society, the mass-consumption society, the mobilized society, the modern society, the new society, the organic society, the rational society, the reasonable society, the socialist society, the technological society, and the urban society—to list these designations alphabetically. These terms all refer to the same general phenomenon, but reflect a diversity of assumptions, emphases, and expectations. Of these terms, "integrated society" is the most satisfactory. The essence of this phase is that the great movement of peoples from the countryside to the city transforms the structure of society from one of relatively autonomous regional, organizational, and occupational groupings to one that is highly fragmented and in which the individual is relatively isolated.

The concept of integration as used in this connection means in particular that the individual's ties with local, regional, and other intermediate structures are reduced at the same time that his ties with the larger and more diffuse urban and industrial network are strengthened. This shift in relationships gives the individual the advantages of greater opportunities in a more flexible society and a larger share in the distribution of resources in terms of education, consumer goods, and a variety of services. It deprives him, however, not only of the support and consolation offered by membership in a more autonomous community but also of the relative stability of employment and social relations that agrarian life provides in normal times. The urban environment offers the ultimate hope of a greatly enriched way of life, but the agrarian provided the reality of social warmth and personal security.

A society that reaches this stage of integration can make much more efficient use of its human resources—if one may refer to human beings in such an impersonal manner. It has consumer production for a mass market, a high per capita national income, a high level of general and specialized education, widely available provisions for social security, and adequate organization

for leisure. This is the case, however, only if the society is well organized and things are working well. The more highly a society is mechanized, the more susceptible it is to paralyzing forms of disorganization. In times of disorder and economic depression, it is plagued by the possibility of large-scale unemployment and attendant social unrest. In less integrated societies there is also extensive unemployment, or perhaps more accurately underemployment, but it is in considerable measure cushioned and even concealed by the agrarian sector. The urban workers in less developed societies have not usually broken their ties with the rural community and can return to it for support in time of need. In an integrated society the individual is atomized—torn from his traditional community moorings, isolated from all except his immediate family, and left to find his way alone among the large and impersonal public and private organizations that provide him with his employment, medical care, social welfare, and pension. It is under these circumstances that loneliness, insecurity, and the weakening of close human relationships deprive the individual of an environment suited to psychological stability.

There are many indexes by which one can judge the integration of society, although the point at which one sets the beginning of integration is of necessity somewhat arbitrary. If one takes as the central criterion the movement of population from the countryside to the cities, the most satisfactory index of integration is the proportion of population engaged in manufacturing and services as distinct from agriculture and other forms of primary production. It is also often the practice to rank countries by gross national product per capita as a gauge of development. It is readily apparent that other indexes of development—literacy, enrollment in educational institutions, urbanization, health, and availability of means of communication—tend to follow these trends in occupational structure and per capita product.

On the basis of these standards one may identify fourteen countries as having entered the phase of social integration since the First World War: Australia, Belgium, Canada, Denmark, France, Germany, Luxembourg, the Netherlands, New Zealand, Norway, Sweden, Switzerland, the United Kingdom, and the United States. In the course of the next generation another dozen or more will enter this phase, including the Soviet Union and Japan, the countries of southern and eastern Europe, and the more advanced Latin American countries, such as Argentina, Uruguay, and Mexico.

Integrated societies differ from those in the preceding phase of economic and social transformation in their structure of political power. Personal power tends to become institutionalized through bureaucratization, and the exercise of power is divided into many specialties and shared by many people. This corresponds in considerable measure to trends in social stratification, according to which those concerned with the direct exercise of political power are recruited to an increasing extent through university education and are much more numerous than in earlier phases. At the same time that the ruling groups are being enlarged, and come to depend more on merit than on privilege, the number of those at the opposite end of the social scale is reduced.

As societies become more productive, wealth tends to be more evenly distributed and the standard of living of rural and urban workers tends to approximate that of salaried employees. Now four-fifths or more of the relevant age group completes secondary education to age nineteen and as many as one-third may continue to higher education. It also becomes increasingly possible for individuals to rise, and descend, in the social scale without regard to social origins. The result is a great enlargement of the middle ranks of society—salaried employees in a wide range of occupations—recruited from families originally employed as rural and urban workers. This tendency toward the equalization of income and status of the great majority of the members of a society is the inevitable result of economic development. Mass production cannot be maintained without mass consumption. It would be an economic impossibility, even if a ruling group desired to do so, for a society to maintain a high rate of growth of per capita national product without distributing production to the consumer.

The end of this process is not easy to foresee, but as automation reduces the labor force required to sustain economic growth it is not unlikely that a substantial proportion of the work force of an integrated society will be guaranteed an income regardless of whether or not they work. Under these conditions a radical redistribution of employment and leisure becomes normal, and appropriate arrangements are made to adapt societies to it. The wealthy have never been seriously embarrassed by light employment and leisure, and as societies become more affluent the opportunities and problems of a shorter work day will be extended to greater numbers.

When societies reach this phase there is also a much greater consensus than ever before among interest groups regarding the policies of modernization that should be followed. Conservatives, liberals, and socialists can still engage in lively political struggles, but differences in policy regarding major issues are greatly reduced. The degree of integration is such that the pressure for the common welfare predominates over interest groups, and the wide range of theories prevalent in earlier phases regarding policies of modernization tend to be reduced to a substantial agreement as to what is feasible and desirable. In Western Europe socialists and conservatives have more in common today than ever before. If there is not an end to ideological controversies within integrated societies, at least the range of controversy is greatly narrowed.

This type of society has frequently been

referred to as a mass society, and a great deal has been written about it. The central concern of this literature is the fear of "massification"—that the atomized individuals will form an undifferentiated "mass" that can be swayed easily by demagogues and turned to destructive ends; that the gradual weakening of intermediate political structures and social organizations will result in the national government's accumulating all power; that the only culture able to survive will be that which appeals to the instincts and understanding of the lowest common denominator, which is usually calculated to be on a par with that of early adolescence; and that the creative minority that has been responsible for the flowering of modern knowledge will sink into and be suffocated by the popular quicksand.

Much of the writing on totalitarianism has had a similar tendency. The concentration of all political power in the hands of an authoritarian government, at the expense of political power formerly exercised by formal and informal local and associational groups, is sometimes seen as an inevitable consequence of massification. This is not the case. All but one of the totalitarian political systems, in fact, have arisen in societies that were still in a relatively early stage of economic and social transformation. In some cases, as in Soviet Russia and Communist China, totalitarianism has represented in significant degree a modernization of traditionally authoritarian or despotic political systems. This is not to say that these societies necessarily had to evolve into totalitarian systems, but rather that the weight of tradition predisposed them to extreme forms of centralization in the absence of vigorous political movements favoring more liberal policies of modernization. In other societies, such as North Korea and the Communist countries of Eastern Europe apart from Yugoslavia, totalitarian regimes were imposed from outside by military force and were not congruent with local traditions. In a few countries—in Germany in 1933, in Yugoslavia during the Second World War, and in North Vietnam in 1954—totalitarian systems arose for domestic reasons in response to political and economic collapse. Of these countries only Germany of the 1930's represents a society on the threshold of social integration, and it should not be equated with the Soviet Union or with other Communist societies if one is interested in the social origins of totalitarianism. Fascist Italy and Franco Spain are also sometimes considered to be totalitarian, but they in fact resemble traditional authoritarian regimes much more than modern totalitarian systems—and they too were still in a relatively early stage of economic and social transformation when these regimes were established.

Germany is, then, a unique case where a failure to meet problems of social integration led to a sharp decline of public morality of an extreme variety, and its origins should be sought more in local than in general conditions. A dozen countries have moved as far or further along the road to integration without resorting to totalitarianism and mass murder. The way in which a society reacts to the crisis of integration depends a great deal on whether it has had a pluralistic or an authoritarian political tradition, whether representative institutions and the legal protection of individual liberties had deep roots, and whether an oligarchy had normally held untempered power. The character of the leadership is also a vital factor. There are not many Hitlers, and this particular man might well have been struck down by a vehicle or a disease before he achieved power. Chance plays a considerable role in these matters.

The circumstances under which modernizing leaders take power also cast a long shadow over the later development of a society. If the transfer of power from the traditional leaders is achieved with considerable bloodshed, it may lead to the glorification of violence for many generations.

"Massification" is a characteristic problem of the modern integrated society, but it is not its principal characteristic. In the advanced societies that have achieved integration with reasonable stability, a vital role in maintaining social order has been played by religion, ethnic loyalties, and other traditional binding forces that have survived modernization without loss of vigor. The Jewish and Catholic religions and the many Protestant sects have maintained their vitality in most integrated societies and are able to offer solace in life's crises and a framework of social action that helps to counterbalance the dangers of atomization and massification.

The central problem, then, is that individuals in modern integrated societies are torn from their relatively autonomous communities and are brought into contact in the urban context with a wide variety of unfamiliar people. Many problems of human relations that at an earlier stage were avoided or compromised on some local basis now have to be met frontally. The institutions of advanced societies are not yet fully understood, and the means of controlling them in the interest of social stability are still being formulated.

The integration within a single society of peoples of widely differing religious, social, and ethnic backgrounds is also baffling. it is not by chance that the term "integration" is used in the more specialized sense of the desegregation of Negroes in the United States, or that the problem did not become acute until a century after their emancipation from slavery. During most of this period the Negroes lived in the relative autonomy of agrarian life, and were not competitively involved to any great extent with the dominant white majority. Students of this subject have nevertheless noted that during each of the periods of rapid economic growth Negroes have been increasingly drawn into the modern urban centers. The point is finally reached where the inequalities of treatment under which they have lived can no longer be tolerated, and American society has been forced to seek a solution. This is an example, although a particularly acute one, of the crises the integration of society provokes. Those who are discouraged by the slow pace of racial integration in the United States may gain solace from the realization that this is the first time in world history that peoples of such disparate backgrounds have sought to solve the problem of living together in an advanced society.

This description of the course of modernization within societies in terms of four phases is not intended to convey the impression that these are watertight compartments. Indeed, there is a sense in which all of these critical problems continue in some degree throughout the modern period. Modernity represents a recurring challenge long after its underlying principles have been understood and accepted, and traditional ideas and institutions have an extraordinary staying power. Modernizing leaders must struggle to retain their initiative long after their accession to political power. Economic and social transformation is a continuing process, at varying rates, both before and after its period of greatest dynamism. Societies move toward integration gradually over many decades and even centuries.

It is rather a question of successive periods of concentration of effort on individual phases of this complex and interacting process. When a society first becomes cognizant of the challenge of modernity, it must concentrate its efforts on formulating a response to this challenge—whether it comes from within or from without. Modernizing leaders do not gain the ascendancy, in turn, until after the challenge of modernity has engaged a society for a considerable period of time. Similarly economic and social transformation cannot be implemented in a dynamic fashion before leaders who regard this as their primary task come to power. And finally, the integration of society does not become a critical problem until economic and social development has reached a high level.

To distinguish among these four phases is nevertheless not to say that all societies pass through them at the same pace. The countries that were the first to modernize could afford to be more leisurely, and the proportion of their economy devoted to manufacturing, transportation, commerce, and services was much greater in the early nineteenth century than it is in many countries of Asia, Latin America, and Africa today. Nevertheless as each successive society enters the phase of economic and social transformation it does so in an increasingly dynamic environment of more developed societies.

In the European countries where national liberation or unification formed a part of the modernizing leaders' struggle for power, independent statehood was achieved at the end of this phase when these countries were already well on the road to economic and social development. In the later-modernizing societies, on the other hand, modernizing leaders come to power in newly independent states at the beginning of the phase of political consolidation. Their accession to power marks not the end of a long domestic struggle but rather the beginning of one in which they still have to win recognition of their authority on the part of local and regional leaders and a variety of associational groups. At the same time, they are also at an early stage of economic and social development. Indonesia in 1949, for example, or Nigeria in 1960 was nominally at the same stage of political development as Germany in 1871 or Poland in 1919, yet in real terms one would have to go far back in European history to find the type of political organization or the level of economic and social development that the new states of Asia and Africa represent.

The logic of these four successive phases must be seen in the context of wide divergencies of levels of development, and the modernization of each society must be understood in terms of its own traditional heritage, resources, and leadership. A comparison of many societies in terms of these phases is useful as a means of visualizing modernization as a worldwide process, but this does not mean that any given society can gauge its course by the experience of those that have preceded it except in general terms.

Societies in the Process of Political Modernization

An attempt to identify characteristics of political modernization that are intermediate between those that are true of all societies and those that are unique to each will of necessity lead to conclusions that are general and suggestive rather than clearly delimited and precise. They therefore run the risk of being misunderstood by the literal-minded. It is nevertheless desirable at this stage to list the societies of the world in terms of the phases of political modernization discussed in this chapter and the patterns of modernization described in the next.

The phases themselves are only generally defined, and are in fact phases of emphasis on one of a number of concurrent developments rather than distinct stages. Similarly all societies do not fall neatly into the seven patterns—Ethiopia, Israel, Liberia, Nepal, and South Africa, among others, are in significant ways exceptional. Moreover, any periodization based on political events or decisions is open to dispute, and of all the dates that one can cite, perhaps 1789 is the only one that is relatively free from controversy as a milestone in the modernization of a society.

Yet as long as these limitations are understood and taken into account, there is no reason not to suggest specific dates for the various phases of modernization for all the societies in the world. The phase called the challenge of modernity is of necessity more generally defined than the others, and does not need to be detailed on this table. The societies are ranked first by pattern* and

* The nature of each pattern is summarized by the editors in the appendix at the end of this article.

within each pattern chronologically. The chronology is based on the beginning of the consolidation of modernizing leadership (1776 for the United States, 1789 for France, 1803 for Germany, 1861 for Russia, 1868 for Japan, 1964 for Malawi, and so on), with countries that have completed the consolidation of modernizing leadership listed ahead of those that have not.

It will be clear to those who have followed the argument so far that the periodization and typology set forth here are concerned with political modernization rather than with the other aspects of this process. As already noted, intellectual developments are too amorphous to be amenable to comparable categorization. Reasonably accurate information regarding economic and social changes is available only for recent decades, and our understanding of the psychological aspect is still rather rudimentary. At the same time, the available information regarding comparative levels of development of societies tends to show that the other aspects of modernization are reasonably correlated with the political. The bases of resources and skills of traditional societies nevertheless vary so widely that one cannot draw conclusions regarding the general level of development of a society without knowing a great deal more about it than what appears in this table.

Patterns of Modernization

	CONSOLIDATION OF MODERNIZING LEADERSHIP	ECONOMIC AND SOCIAL TRANSFORMATION	INTEGRATION OF SOCIETY
First Pattern			
United Kingdom	1649–1832	1832–1945	1945–
France	1789–1848	1848–1945	1945–
Second Pattern			
United States	1776–1865	1865–1933	1933–
Canada	1791–1867	1867–1947	1947–
Australia	1801–1901	1901–1941	1941–
New Zealand	1826–1907	1907–1947	1947–
Third Pattern [a]			
Belgium	1795–1848	1848–1948	1948–
Luxembourg	1795–1867	1867–1948	1948–
Netherlands	1795–1848	1848–1948	1948–
Switzerland	1798–1848	1848–1932	1932–
Germany	1803–1871	1871–1933	1933–
Italy	1805–1871	1871–	
Denmark	1807–1866	1866–1945	1945–
Norway	1809–1905	1905–1945	1945–
Sweden	1809–1905	1905–1945	1945–
Spain	1812–1909	1909–	
Portugal	1822–1910	1910–	
Austria	1848–1918	1918–	

Third Pattern (cont'd)	CONSOLIDATION OF MODERNIZING LEADERSHIP	ECONOMIC AND SOCIAL TRANSFORMATION	INTEGRATION OF SOCIETY
Czechoslovakia	1848–1918	1918–	
Hungary	1848–1918	1918–	
Greece	1863–1918	1918–	
Poland	1863–1918	1918–	
Finland	1863–1919	1919–	
Ireland	1870–1922	1922–	
Iceland	1874–1918	1918–	
Bulgaria	1878–1918	1918–	
Romania	1878–1918	1918–	
Yugoslavia	1878–1918	1918–	
Albania	1912–1925	1925–	

Fourth Pattern

Uruguay	1828–1911	1911–	
Brazil	1850–1930	1930–	
Argentina	1853–1946	1946–	
Chile	1861–1925	1925–	
Mexico	1867–1910	1910–	
Venezuela	1870–1958	1958–	
Bolivia	1880–1952	1952–	
Costa Rica	1889–1948	1948–	
Puerto Rico	1898–1952	1952–	
Cuba	1898–1959	1959–	
Paraguay	1841–		
Colombia	1863–		
Ecuador	1875–		
Haiti	1879–		
Peru	1879–		
Dominican Republic	1881–		
Guatemala	1881–		
Panama	1903–		
Nicaragua	1909–		
Honduras	1919–		
El Salvador	1939–		
British Honduras (U.K.)	1961–		

Fifth Pattern

Russia	1861–1917	1917–	
Japan	1868–1945	1945–	
China	1905–1949	1949–	
Iran	1906–1925	1925–	
Turkey	1908–1923	1923–	

Fifth Pattern (cont'd)	CONSOLIDATION OF MODERNIZING LEADERSHIP	ECONOMIC AND SOCIAL TRANSFORMATION	INTEGRATION OF SOCIETY
Afghanistan	1923–		
Ethiopia	1924–		
Thailand	1932–		

Sixth Pattern[b]

	CONSOLIDATION OF MODERNIZING LEADERSHIP	ECONOMIC AND SOCIAL TRANSFORMATION	INTEGRATION OF SOCIETY
Algeria	1847–1962	1962–	
Cyprus	1878–1946	1946–	
Taiwan	1895–1945	1945–	
Philippines	1899–1946	1946–	
Korea	1910–1946	1946–	
South Africa	1910–1962	1962–	
India	1919–1947	1947–	
Pakistan	1919–1947	1947–	
Ceylon	1920–1948	1948–	
Israel	1920–1948	1948–	
Lebanon	1920–1941	1941–	
Syria	1920–1941	1941–	
Iraq	1921–1948	1948–	
Malta	1921–1961	1961–	
Mongolia	1921–1950	1950–	
Egypt	1922–1952	1952–	
Indonesia	1922–1949	1949–	
Tunisia	1922–1955	1955–	
Burma	1923–1948	1948–	
Jordan	1923–1946	1946–	
Jamaica	1924–1962	1962–	
Sudan	1924–1956	1956–	
Guyana	1928–1966	1966–	
Morocco	1934–1956	1956–	
Hong Kong (U.K.)	1936–		
Cambodia	1949–		
Laos	1949–		
Vietnam	1949–		
Libya	1952–		
Trinidad and Tobago	1959–		
Malaysia	1963–		
Yemen	1963–		
Saudi Arabia	1964–		
Maldive Islands	1965–		
Singapore	1965–		
Bhutan			
Guadeloupe (Fr.)			
Guiana (Fr.)			

Sixth Pattern (cont'd)	CONSOLIDATION OF MODERNIZING LEADERSHIP	ECONOMIC AND SOCIAL TRANSFORMATION	INTEGRATION OF SOCIETY
Kuwait			
Macao (Port.)			
Martinique (Fr.)			
Masqat and Oman			
Nepal			
Réunion (Fr.)			
Somaliland (Fr.)			
South Arabia Fed. (U.K.)			
Surinam (Neth.)			
Timor (Port.)			
West Indies (U.K.)			

Seventh Pattern [e]

	CONSOLIDATION OF MODERNIZING LEADERSHIP	ECONOMIC AND SOCIAL TRANSFORMATION	INTEGRATION OF SOCIETY
Liberia	1847–		
Ghana	1957–		
Guinea	1958–		
Cameroon	1960–		
Central African Republic	1960–		
Chad	1960–		
Congo (Brazzaville)	1960–		
Congo (Léopoldville)	1960–		
Dahomey	1960–		
Gabon	1960–		
Ivory Coast	1960–		
Malagasy Republic	1960–		
Mali	1960–		
Mauritania	1960–		
Niger	1960–		
Nigeria	1960–		
Senegal	1960–		
Somalia	1960–		
Togo	1960–		
Upper Volta	1960–		
Sierra Leone	1961–		
Tanzania	1961–		
Burundi	1962–		
Rwanda	1962–		
Uganda	1962–		
Western Samoa	1962–		
Kenya	1963–		
Malawi	1964–		
Gambia	1965–		
Rhodesia	1965–		
Zambia	1965–		

Seventh Pattern (cont'd)	CONSOLIDATION OF MODERNIZING LEADERSHIP	ECONOMIC AND SOCIAL TRANSFORMATION	INTEGRATION OF SOCIETY

Angola and Cabinda (Port.)
Basutoland (U.K.)
Bechuanaland (U.K.)
Equatorial Guinea (Sp.)
Mauritius (U.K.)
Mozambique (Port.)
Portuguese Guinea (Port.)
South-West Africa (S. Af.)
Swaziland (U.K.)

ᵃ Also includes Andorra, Liechtenstein, Monaco, San Marino, and the Vatican City State.
ᵇ Also includes the Bahama Islands (U.K.), Bermuda (U.K.), Brunei (U.K.), Comoro Archipelago (Fr.), Ifni (Sp.), Netherlands Antilles (Neth.), Persian Gulf States (U.K.), Protectorate States (U.K.), Seychelles (U.K.), Spanish North Africa (Sp.), Spanish Sahara (Sp.), Virgin Islands (U.S.).
ᶜ Also includes American Samoa (U.S.), Cape Verde Islands (Port.), Fiji (U.K.), French Polynesia (Fr.), Guam (U.S.), New Caledonia (Fr.), São Tomé and Principe Islands (Port.), Tonga (U.K.), Trust Territory of the Pacific Islands (U.S.), and the islands administered by Australia and by the Western Pacific High Commission (U.K.).

Appendix: Seven Patterns of Political Modernization*

FIRST PATTERN

The first pattern of political modernization is formed by Great Britain and France, which were the earliest countries to modernize and which in their different ways set the pattern to a significant degree for all other societies.

SECOND PATTERN

The offshoots of Great Britain and France in the New World may be considered to form a second pattern of political modernization. The term "offshoots," which appears again in connection with the fourth pattern, is employed here to mean countries that are settled by peoples of the Old World who become politically and

*Excerpted by the editors from Black, *ibid.*, Chap. IV.

culturally dominant in the new societies even though they may on occasion form only a minority of the population. These offshoots usually started as dependencies, but they differ from other colonies in that the dominant population was the same as that of the mother country. The United States, Canada, Australia, and New Zealand, with a total population of 225 million, are the societies that form this pattern.

THIRD PATTERN

A third pattern of political modernization comprises the societies of Europe in which the consolidation of modernizing leadership occurred after the French revolution and as a direct or indirect result of its impact. These societies undertook to adapt their political institutions to modern functions somewhat later than Great Britain and France; they also underwent a long and generally violent period of the regrouping of territories and peoples that was one of the most distinctive features of their experience. These societies were predominantly self-governing in the modern era, although the minority peoples of Eastern Europe, and also of Ireland and Iceland, were initially under a form of alien rule that in certain limited respects resembled colonialism. Like the societies in the first two patterns, these countries also had developed institutions in the traditional era that were readily adaptable to modern functions.

FOURTH PATTERN

The offshoots in the New World of the European societies in the third pattern may be considered as forming a fourth pattern of political modernization. The societies in this pattern are the twenty-two independent countries of Latin America, with a combined population of some 230 million. These societies differ from those in the second pattern, also populated predominantly by immigrants from the Old World—apart from differences in their bases of resources and skills—in that modernization came later, was to a much greater degree under foreign influence, and was influenced in particular by those societies of the third pattern that were inclined to place the least emphasis on modernization.

FIFTH PATTERN

Those societies that modernized without direct outside intervention, but under the indirect influence of societies that modernized earlier, represent a fifth pattern of political modernization. The relatively few societies constituting this pattern are Russia, Japan, China, Iran, Turkey, Afghanistan, Ethiopia, and Thailand, inhabited by some 1.2 billion people. What these societies have in common is the fact that their traditional governments were sufficiently effective, because of long experience with centralized bureaucratic government, to enable them to resist direct and comprehensive foreign rule for a prolonged period in modern times. In contrast to most other societies, they modernized essentially at their own initiative and with a significant continuity of territory and population.

SIXTH AND SEVENTH PATTERNS

The more than one hundred independent and dependent societies of Asia, Africa, the Americas, and Oceania that have experienced colonial rule may be divided into two final patterns of political modernization. The sixth pattern is composed of the thirty-four now (p. 123) independent and twenty-nine dependent societies, with a population of about 1 billion, the traditional cultures of which are sufficiently well developed that they could interact with those of the more modern tutelary societies in their adaptation to modern functions. Thus Islam, Hinduism, and Buddhism have faced problems of adaptation to modern knowledge similar to those confronting Christianity and Judaism. Arabic, Hindi, Urdu, and Malayan are being developed and enriched for the purposes of modern communication, as were English, French, and Italian in their day, and Russian, Japanese, Chinese, and Turkish somewhat later. Traditional forms of government in the Near East and Asia are adaptable to modern political needs, as were the feudal institutions of Europe and the bureaucratic systems of Russia, Turkey, Japan, and China earlier. The societies constituting the seventh pattern, however—the thirty-one independent and the approximately twenty dependent societies of sub-Saharan Africa and Oceania, with a population of 200 million—did not have religion, or language, or political institutions sufficiently developed at the time that they faced the challenge of modernity to be readily adaptable to modern conditions. Instead, they have found it more practical to borrow from more modern societies modern ideas and institutions that are more or less unchanged.

Common to these two patterns was the experience of colonialism, which had the effect of stimulating the initial phase of modernization, the challenge of modernity in a traditional society, but of delaying the next phase, the consolidation of political power by modernizing leaders.

POLITICAL DEVELOPMENT: TIME SEQUENCES AND RATES OF CHANGE

Eric A. Nordlinger

Political development is undoubtedly a rich and variegated field of study. We have begun to accumulate first-rate studies of widely divergent cultures and social structures, masses of quantitative data on the socioeconomic variables involved in the modernization process, analyses of political phenomena ranging from the destooling of chiefs to the functioning of complex legislative systems, well-documented surveys of particular political systems, and a smaller number of useful typologies and general hypotheses. It is this burgeoning and many-faceted literature that makes "theory-building" simultaneously most difficult and most desirable—just as the integration problems facing the new states are exceptionally difficult to resolve, while at the same time their resolution is first on the list of political imperatives. We are clearly in need of a set of questions and concepts that are broad enough to encompass the phenomena falling under the rubric of political development, but that are also specific enough to allow for the generation

SOURCE: Eric A. Nordlinger, "Political Development: Time Sequences and Rates of Change," in Nordlinger (ed.), *Politics and Society: Studies in Comparative Political Sociology* (Englewood Cliffs, N.J.: Prentice-Hall, 1970) This essay is a revised version of Nordlinger, "Political Development: Time Sequences and Rates of Change," *World Politics*, **20**, 494–520, April, 1968, and is reprinted by permission of the original publisher.

of testable hypotheses of an explanatory variety.

Two strong candidates for the job are time sequences and rates of change. While these two concepts are not independent variables themselves, when applied to particular variables they are specific enough to facilitate the formulation of explanatory hypotheses, while constituting a broad framework within which the various hypotheses may be integrated. It should be quite apparent that both sequences and rates of change are sufficiently generalizable concepts to allow for the systematic integration of broad slices of the political development field. In dealing with the variables constituting the field, we can analyze all manner of political, social, and economic phenomena in terms of their sequences and rates. Questions involving sequence and rate are also broad enough to allow for comparisons of non-Western countries with comparable phenomena in Europe, thereby remedying the neglect of European countries in the study of political development and encouraging the formulation of hypotheses that may have close to universal applicability after the relevant contextual conditions are included.

Moreover, this focus upon the two dimensions of time may help to fill an important gap in the political science literature. While it is by no means true that history explains everything, it does take us well along the road, especially in the implicitly historically oriented field of political development. Yet until quite recently, political science was practically denuded of any explicit conception of time, thereby eliminating the possibility of constructing generalizations based upon historical patterns of development. Generalizations involving history may be of either a descriptive or an explanatory type, or both simultaneously. The great evolutionary theorists — Condorcet, Comte, Marx, Spencer, Darwin, Spengler, Toynbee, and Sorokin—either restricted themselves to descriptive generalization alone or combined description and explanation. Descriptively, they argued that historical development unfolds according to particular stages; in their explanations, they argued that one stage is unable to emerge until the prior stage has evolved, for each stage is in some way a necessary condition for the emergence of its successor. We are now well aware that history is in no way unilinear—that there are not any "evolutionary universals in society," as Parsons has called them. Yet there is no reason why this major difficulty in the descriptive aspect of evolutionary theories forces political science to ignore various concepts of time.

The point to be made is then this: political scientists could profitably play down the importance of those descriptive generalizations involving time found throughout the development and modernization literature and concentrate upon explanatory ones. Instead of attempting to identify a general pattern according to which political systems develop, we can look at the various developmental patterns and ask questions about their different *consequences*. For instance, rather than suggesting that political systems necessarily become more differentiated and complex over time, we can attempt to construct general explanatory hypotheses of this kind: *if* a political system becomes more differentiated at a particular rate of change, or according to a certain sequence, one part of the system becoming differentiated before another, then certain consequences are likely to follow. The hy-

potheses put forward in this essay are formulated in just this manner.

Besides providing far more extended explanations of political development, this type of emphasis can also contribute to a greater refinement of explanatory generalizations. As one sociologist has put it, "Because few theorists face the relevance of time to their explanations, discussion of social change remains vague, and causal links far from clear."[1] For example, by utilizing the notion of time sequences Giovanni Sartori was able to bring a large breath of fresh air into the perennial debate about the interrelation between electoral arrangements and the party system. Instead of reasserting or refuting the argument that proportional representation leads to the multiplication of parties, Sartori has effectively inserted himself into the debate by developing a number of propositions supporting his contention that PR produces a multiparty system only when it is introduced *prior* to the formation of parties with structured organizations and well-articulated party platforms.[2]

Lastly, a focus upon rates of change implicitly raises questions involving time lag. We may speak of a time lag between two related variables when one of them originates at an earlier time or evolves at a faster rate than the other, so that the two reach similar levels only after a certain time period has elapsed. After having determined such an approximate time lag, it should be possible to offer hypotheses that account for differences in time lag and to suggest the consequences that larger or smaller time lags have for other phenomena. In fact, such hypotheses and suggestions form the centerpiece of Stein Rokkan's study of polarization (or cleavage patterns) in Nor-

[1] Max Hierich, "The Use of Time in the Study of Social Change," *American Sociological Review*, xxix (June 1964), 386.

[2] Giovanni Sartori, "European Political Parties: The Case of Polarized Pluralism," in Joseph LaPalombara and Myron Weiner, eds., *Political Parties and Political Development* (Princeton, Princeton University Press. 1966), pp. 167–69.

way. By bringing together ecological and election data, Rokkan maps out the time lags between rural and urban political mobilization. The fact that it took some fifty-five years for rural voter turnout to match that of the urban population in Norway is accounted for by variations in the social structure and is then related to the country's cleavage patterns. And in his concluding section, Rokkan outlines his reasons for thinking that such time-lag studies in rural and urban political change are one of the most potentially rewarding research strategies in comparative politics generally.[3]

1. Variables and Hypotheses

These then are some of the uses and advantages of an approach to political development that focuses upon sequences and rates of change. Here a preliminary attempt will be made to formulate a number of explanatory hypotheses involving time sequences and rates of change as they help account for certain fundamental aspects of political development. It is hoped that this attempt will serve to illustrate the applications and the explanatory power of sequence and rate-of-change propositions, and that it will concomitantly outline a convenient manner of systematically integrating many of the major conclusions in the political development literature. And it may even turn out that the hypotheses offered here enjoy a respectable measure of validity.

There are four political phenomena whose sequence and rates of change constitute the independent variables:[4] (1) A

[3] "Electoral Mobilization, Party Competition, and National Integration," in *ibid.*, pp. 244–45, 248–49, 258–61.

[4] While the following variables are susceptible to more precise definitions than those offered here, to define them further would be both useless and pretentious. The kinds of hypotheses and illustrative evidence offered below are not refined enough to link up with a set of more closely defined variables, just as certain studies relying upon survey or aggregate data only artifically confirmed the hypotheses when especially sophisticated statistical manipulations are unwarranted by the weak reliability of the data.

national identity may be said to exist when the great majority of the politically relevant actors accord the nation's central symbols and its political elite(s) greater loyalty than that which they maintain toward subnational units, such as tribes, castes, and classes, and toward political elite(s) residing outside the system's territory. (2) A central government that is institutionalized is characterized by a significant differentiation of structures and a specificity of functions, and by regularized decision-making procedures characterized by a hierarchical structure in which the personnel responsible for the execution and enforcement of governmental decisions are subordinate to executive decision-makers. (3) Protoparties, as contrasted with mass parties, are limited in their membership, which is composed of national, regional, and/or local notables, and in their organization, which is minimal. (4) The last independent variable, mass suffrage or near-universal suffrage, is self-explanatory except for the provision that voting is not pro forma, as in single-party states, or inconsequential because the legislators are practically powerless, as in Meiji Japan, or ineffective because votes are weighted, as in Wilhelmine Germany.

The sequence and rate of change of these variables will be analyzed separately in an attempt to account for the three dependent variables defined here: (1) The presence or absence of widespread violence refers to attacks by one group against another (not necessarily against the government itself), commonly centering on tribal, class, ethnic, religious, or territorial hatreds and jealousies. (2) An authoritarian government is one that represses political dissent even when such expressions do not involve the goal of overthrowing the government. This policy involves the punishment of even those dissenters who do not publicly express their disapproval of the form of government and its incumbents or make known their dissatisfaction with governmental outputs. Authoritarianism as repression also refers to the outlawing and destruction of independent intermediary groups, such as farmers' organizations, labor unions, and communal associations, which do not challenge the government's authority, though they may peacefully attempt to persuade the government to alter its policies. It should be heavily underscored that the category of authoritarian rule does not include those dictatorships—colonial regimes, single-party states, military regimes, oligarchies, and monarchies—that are simply concerned with maintaining their position of control and that do not resort to the repression of the rights and liberties of individuals and groups who do not challenge their authority. (3) The last dependent variable is a form of democratic government (i.e., open competition for governmental office, with the population selecting the "winners") which is genuinely representative, durable, and decisionally effective.[5]

Although these three dependent variables refer to certain *forms* of interaction among individuals and between individuals and the government, they also tell us a good deal about the presence or absence of those outcomes that determine the *quality* of life in a society—what Pennock has termed "political goods," constituting an important and much neglected aspect of political development.[6] Some of these "political goods"—such as individual dignity, secur-

ity, justice, liberty, and material welfare— are intimately connected with the presence or absence of widespread violence, repressive rule, and democratic government. Thus in attempting to account for these three dependent variables, the general propositions offered here will presumably also be related to the distribution of "political goods."

Since the secondary arguments supporting the general propositions sometimes become rather involved, it might be helpful to summarize the major propositions at the outset. With respect to time sequences, it is argued that the probabilities of a political system's developing in a nonviolent, non-authoritarian, and eventually democratically viable manner are maximized when a national identity emerges first, followed by the institutionalization of the central government, and then by the emergence of mass parties and a mass electorate.[7] With respect to rates of change, it is argued that a national identity cannot be created in a rapid fashion, and if the attempt is made, it will lead to authoritarian abuses and widespread violence. I shall not offer any hypotheses with regard to the rate at which central governments are institutionalized; although institutionalization cannot be realized quickly, attempts to do so are not likely to have an important bearing upon the three dependent variables. When mass parties are rapidly formed, and when mass electoral participation is ushered in practically overnight, the outcome is likely to be widespread violence and repressive rule, which make it far more difficult to establish a democratic system and, further, assure that if such a system is established, its stability, representativeness, and decisional effectiveness will suffer.

---

[5] Some students of political development would contend that democracy as defined here —in terms of the electroal form that it has taken in Western areas—is inapplicable to the non-Western areas and that governmental responsiveness to the population, if it is achieved, will be achieved through *indigenous* forms of representation. Perhaps—but at this point in history it is a highly dubious proposition since such indigenous forms of representation have not yet been institutionalized in any national political system. Moreover, a number of modernizing systems—such as the Philippines, India, Chile, and Costa Rica— have successfully adopted the Western democratic model, and all but a few of the new states of Asia and Africa have set out to build a political order of the Western type.

[6] J. Roland Pennock, "Political Development, Political Systems, and Political Goods," *World Politics*, XVIII (April 1966), 415–34.

[7] Dankwart Rustow arrives at a broadly similar conclusion (that the most effective sequence for "political modernization" is the one of identity-authority-equality) by a different route than that taken here. See his *A World of Nations* (Washington, 1967), 120–32.

II. National Identity and Governmental Institutions: Sequence

In order to maximize the probabilities of a political system's developing in a nonviolent, nonauthoritarian form and ultimately achieving democratic stability, a sense of national identity should precede the institutionalization of the central government. What then are the secondary hypotheses that support this general argument?

The most fundamental objective of any central government is its own continuation, preferably at the same level of institutionalization and with the same amount of capability in dealing with the nonelite. Going beyond this, many governments are also firmly committed to the realization of change in any number of spheres and directions. Admittedly, governments might achieve their primary goal without the presence of a sense of national identity. However, it would be more difficult for them to do so, and the nonviolent development of the government in any desired direction is highly unlikely to proceed without the prior resolution of the identity question. Sidney Verba makes the point succinctly when he writes that "other problems are likely to be pushed aside until the central problem is met: 'What is my nation?' must be answered before 'What kind of a nation?' "[8] Without a subjective identification with the regime on the part of the political actors, not only will the government have difficulty in applying its decisions, and thus maintaining its authority, but all types of change will remain in abeyance until a national identity is formed.[9]

When a central government is confronted with sharp procedural and substantive conflicts, it can best ensure its survival and the absence of violence if there is already present a set of inclusive attachments that serve as centripetal forces alleviating the divisions produced by the centrifugal ones. Not only might the procedural values be readily challenged if governmental institutions were formed before a sense of national identity had emerged, but the legitimacy of the central government's mere existence might be called into question when parochial groups tried to secede or refused to accept the authority of the governmental incumbents. This point may be taken one step further by noting that the institutionalization of the central government may actually provoke existing parochial groups to resist its authority, for the institutionalization process entails the growth of a firmly structured, decisionally effective and powerful government. In societies where the continuing strength of communal loyalties and hatreds has not allowed a national identity to be formed prior to the institutionalization of the central government, "to permit oneself to be ruled by men of other tribes, other races, or other religions is to submit not merely to oppression but to degradation—to exclusion from the moral community as a lesser order of being whose opinions, attitudes, wishes, and so on, simply do not fully count."[10] And these feelings of oppression and degradation can only be compounded during the process of institutionalization, for the process highlights the presence and increases the power of the incumbents as perceived by the parochial groups.

In Europe the states that have developed most successfully according to the criteria of our three dependent variables are the Scandinavian countries, and in these countries a sense of nationhood developed not only before it did in almost all other European countries (around the eleventh cen-

[8] "Comparative Political Culture," in Lucian Pye and Sidney Verba, eds., *Political Culture and Political Development* (Princeton, 1965), 533.

[9] In a related vein, Carl J. Friedrich has written that "only a firmly established government is capable of being constitutionalized. . . . In the evolution of our Western world this meant that national unification had to precede constitutionalism" (*Constitutional Government and Democracy* [Boston, 1941], 8).

[10] Clifford Geertz, "Primordial Sentiments and Civil Politics in the New States," in Geertz, ed., *Old Societies and New States* (Glencoe, 1963), 127–28.

tury), but before the formation of central governmental institutions. Among these countries, Norway is a particularly illuminating illustration of the hypothesis. Its history is characterized by the absence of revolution and authoritarianism and by a paucity of violence, while its twentieth-century democratic governments have been exceptionally representative, decisionally effective, and stable—and this despite widespread and intensive cleavages (regional, cultural, and religious), together with the strains following in the wake of rapid industrialization. Part of the explanation undoubtedly lies with the prior existence and the continuing strength of exceptionally cohesive bonds (in the form of a sense of national communality) which successfully mitigated the effects of these conflicts upon the central government.[11]

There is also the very real possibility that the absence of a national identity will both warp and weaken governmental institutions. Without a sense of national identity government may easily become detached from society; the government acts by itself and for itself. As in the great majority of Latin American countries, government becomes the "high road" for personal advancement and the furtherance of narrowly conceived group interests, and in this sense, government may be characterized as parasitic. Governmental institutions that grew up before the emergence of a national identity are also likely to be brittle, given the absence of a legitimizing banner decorated with societal goals. Even if political leaders with reformist and modernizing motivations appear in such political systems, the weakness of the governmental institutions will necessarily dictate their failure. There have been instances in which reform minded governments came to power in Latin America, but they were usually forced out of office by the armed forces and/or the economically privileged classes; the governmental institutions were too weak to pro-

tect the incumbents from the opposition of minorities. Only where the army was destroyed, in Mexico, Bolivia, and Cuba, could thoroughgoing land reform take place. And it is patently obvious that viable democratic institutions are not about to flourish—and they have not done so in Latin America—where governmental institutions are parasitic, corrupting and brittle. Even where democratic governments have been instituted in Latin America, the political parties are commonly personalistic, fragmented, and lacking in programmatic goals. These characteristics have partly grown out of the warped and brittle nature of the governmental institutions, and they are hardly conducive to democratic durability, decisional effectiveness or representativeness.

Besides the definitionally universal aspect of a national identity, its substantive content is also relevant. When a sense of national identity precedes the institutionalization of the central government, there is the possibility that the particular values constituting this identity will restrain the government from developing into an authoritarian one. Three examples of this point are found in the United States, Israel, and Japan. The American national identity was formed prior to 1789 around the two interrelated foci of self-government as a British colony and the War of Independence with Britain. Both experiences helped form a national identity based upon a belief in the Americans' superiority in protecting individual and group liberties, a belief that then played an important part in curbing the opposite tendencies (though it did not succeed in eliminating them, as evidenced by the Alien and Sedition Acts) in the first thirty years of independence when the government was being centrally institutionalized. In the case of Israel, the approximately 10,000 immigrants that arrived in Palestine between 1905 and 1914 came with a highly developed and intensely felt group identity. Over and above the political Zionism of Theodore Herzel, with its call for the return of the Jews to their historical home-

[11] Harry Eckstein, *Division and Cohesion in Democracy: A Study of Norway* (Princeton, 1966), esp. 119–20, 181–82.

land, there was a symbiosis of nationalism and egalitarianism which was to define the contours of the Jewish socialist commonwealth. These founding fathers and their followers were deeply imbued with the desirability of establishing an egalitarian, open and mobile society, whose particularistic interests were to be fused with the interests of the collectivity. Clearly such values were important in obviating the possibility of repressive rule, even during the most critical periods in the emergence and maintenance of the Jewish state, simultaneously providing a set of political values that contributed to the development of a highly representative and decisionally effective democracy. In Japan, a strong sense of national identity was exhibited by the political class in the last years of the Tokugawa regime and the first years of the Meiji Restoration, before the Meiji oligarchs turned to the job of centralizing and institutionalizing the government. And it was in part the elite's sense of national identity, expressed in service and responsibility to emperor and nation, that helped keep authoritarian abuses within easily manageable bounds during the period of governmental institutionalization.[12]

III. National Identity: Rate

Having considered some reasons for thinking that national identity ought to precede the establishment of central governmental institutions, we must now note that there are only a handful of political systems that have developed in this manner. The more common sequence is either the emergence of a national identity after central government has been institutionalized (the institutionalized government helping to mold the national identity) or the simultaneous development of the two, as in the postcolonial societies. The exceptional importance of national identity, both for the three dependent variables presented here and for practically all other variables commonly said to constitute "political development," would suggest that a national identity should be formed as rapidly as possible once central government has come into existence, so that it may alleviate the strains and conflicts that hinder the peaceful development of nonauthoritarian and democratic government.[13] However, turning to rates of change, not only is it extremely difficult to form a sense of national identity in a short period of time, but when the attempt is made, the likelihood of repressive rule and widespread violence following in its wake is concomitantly increased.

One reason why it is highly unlikely that a sense of national identity can be rapidly formed is that the process involves a fundamental alteration in the loyalties of those people whose only attachment was previously given to subnational groups, or the massive growth of national consciousness among a politically "unconscious" or indifferent population. (These three prenationalistic situations are primarily applicable to Asia, tropical Africa, and Latin America, respectively.) If the attempt is made to create a national identity in a short space of time, there appear to be only two foci around which it could develop: a set of emotionally charged symbols or a charismatic leader. But in either case the likelihood is that the new, synthetically created national identity will be a fragile one, to be rejected at the onset of the first major crisis, unless of course the improbable happens and such a crisis is so slow in appearing that the new loyalties have time to strike roots

---

[12] Moreover, these particular attachments to the nation allowed for the gradual inclusion of protoparties and limited popular participation into the decision-making process characterized by a bargaining style. See Robert E. Ward, "Japan: The Continuity of Modernization," in Pye and Verba, 55–56. The pre-1868 peasantry and urban lower classes did not manifest a sense of national identity, but their quiescence and acquiescence made them insignificant as political actors.

[13] Frederick W. Frey sets out "four crucial factors leading a group to an early sense of national identity," in *The Turkish Political Elite* (Cambridge, Mass., 1965), 409.

into the culture. Emotional attachments are especially erratic phenomena, particularly when their symbolic centerpiece has faded, as in the case of the colonial nationalist movements ten years or so after independence.[14] And Weber has schooled us in the brittle qualities of charismatic authority.[15] A charismatic leader may help form a basis for unity among contending political factions, legitimate a constitutional form of government, allow protoparties to develop into mass parties, and set a precedent for the peaceful transfer of office. Washington and, to a lesser extent, Atatürk were certainly instrumental in these respects. But in the great majority of new states the charismatic leader has fulfilled only the single task of "acting as a symbol which represents and prolongs the feeling of unity developed prior to the achievement of independence."[16]

In deeply divided societies a rapidly created national identity will not act as an integrative force, at best it will serve as a thin veneer covering over (without bringing together) the cracks in the cultural plaster. Where classes, religious communities, linguistic groups or tribes are mutually mistrustful and hostile, a viable identity cannot be realized by creating common bonds above the particularistic loyalties. In such societies mutual antagonisms will only be assuaged through the emergence of a na-

[14] Emphasis upon "symbol-wielding" and what Shils has termed "demonstrative" and "remonstrative" politics may also lower a government's administrative and economic effectiveness. For an analysis of Indonesia along such lines, see Herbert Feith, "Indonesia's Political Symbols and Their Wielders," *World Politics*, XVI (October 1963), esp. 86, 92–96.

[15] Moreover, Weber's arguments that charisma *may* become routinized contain a number of pitfalls. See W. G. Runciman, "Charismatic Legitimacy and One-Party Rule in Ghana," *Archives européennes de sociologie*, IV, No. 1 (1963), 149–51.

[16] Seymour Martin Lipset, *The First New Nation* (New York, 1963), 22–23. See also Rustow's penetrating discussion of charismatic leaders in the new states, 148–69.

tional identity that builds upon—that takes into account—the particularistic loyalties and traditions. The edifice of a common identity built from the top down will be jerry built; a durable edifice must be built upwards by incorporating the necessarily heterogenous building blocks. If this argument is accepted, then it follows that a common identity cannot be realized in a rapid fashion. Governments cannot legislate minority differences and antagonisms out of existence. In the post-World War I period the democratic governments of Eastern Europe tried to abolish minority languages and educational institutions. Their abysmal failure illustrates the point.

Leaving aside the likelihood of failure, if a charismatic figure or a manipulation of emotion-charged symbols is used in attempting to form a national identity at rapid rate, there remains the distinct danger that authoritarian rule will emerge. In consciously attempting to weld together a positive attachment to the leader or the symbol in a short space of time, the leader or the wielders of the symbol (the party) must necessarily become the embodiment of the nation and thus stand above the nation. Such a claim is often closely bound up with the Rousseauistic notion of the general will, dictating that there not be any partial or independent associations in society. The close relationship between the rapid creation of a national identity, the assertion of the leader's or the party's position as standing above the nation, and the eradication of independent associations is found in post-independence Ghana. In Nkrumah's often reiterated declaration, "The Convention People's Party is Ghana, and Ghana is the Convention People's Party," and in the last five years of Nkrumah's increasingly repressive rule, youth, labor, ex-servicemen's, and farmers' associations were permitted to exist only if they were merged into the CPP, and religious associations could continue only if they were deeply penetrated by the party.

All associations standing outside the party (and there were very few) were saddled with the subversive label.[17] The intimate relationship between the rapid creation of a national identity and the eradication of independent associations is found in even starker form in Guinea, where Sékou Touré has gone further than Nkrumah in directly attacking tribal loyalties in both the society and the ruling party (the Parti Démocratique de Guinée). The society is organized, penetrated, and led by the party so that, as Emerson writes, "all interests and groups . . . [are] closely interlocked with the structure of the ruling party. Touré himself has made it clear that he regards individual and group liberties as having validity only insofar as they promote the realization of the sovereign popular will, again as expressed by the PDG."[18] Thus one danger in attempting to integrate a political system through the rapid creation of a national identity is that individual liberties are repressed and the society is denuded even of its quiescent voluntary associations—associations that would play a singularly important role in the future development and maintenance of democratic government.[19]

Even if these arguments were accepted, it might still be possible to suggest that the use of the past—of a country's traditions— would permit the rapid creation of a na-

[17] Rupert Emerson, "Parties and National Integration in Africa," in LaPalombara and Weiner, pp. 278–81; David E. Apter,"Ghana," in James S. Coleman and Carl G. Rosberg, Jr., eds., *Political Parties and National Integration in Tropical Africa* (Berkeley, 1964), 295–300.

[18] Emerson, in LaPalombara and Weiner, p. 278. See also Charles F. Andrain, "Democracy and Socialism: Ideologies of African Leaders," in David E. Apter, ed., *Ideology and Discontent* (Glencoe, 1964), 157–64.

[19] This argument finds additional support when it is noted that in other single-party African states whose governments and territorial integrity are also endangered by parochial demands—such as the Cameroons, the Ivory Coast and Tanzania—the goal of creating a national identity is being implemented in a relatively gradual fashion, which is related to the maintenance of their intermediary groups.

tional identity. Apter has attributed a good deal of importance to tradition as it helps maximize the chances of averting authoritarianism and establishing democracy. In comparing the new countries of Africa, he finds "that the degree of autocracy which emerges after independence is in virtual proportion to the degree of antagonism the government shows to tradition." He then goes on to state that "respect for the past and cultivation of tradition is a necessary condition of democracy."[20] However, we ought to distinguish between a respect for tradition on the part of the government (which is Apter's concern) and the government's deliberate resurrection of tradition in order to unify the nation around a set of common symbols and values. If the government's resurrection of tradition is to be successful, what is commonly thought of as a calming and unifying factor must necessarily become emotionally supercharged, with the attendant dangers of political excesses and the exacerbation of divisions following in its wake. In addition, one group's glorious tradition may be another group's historical ignominy; a reliance upon tradition might exacerbate rather than mitigate political and social antagonisms.

In the case of Japan, the Meiji oligarchs were exceptionally successful in rapidly developing a national identity in the last two decades of the nineteenth century, utilizing the traditional and semimystical symbols of Imperial Shinto and the imperial institution. Their success in creating this identity among a people who previously had had little knowledge of, and

[20] David E. Apter, *The Political Kingdom in Uganda* (Princeton, 1961), 476–77. Robert E. Ward also places a good deal of emphasis upon tradition as a stabilizing influence that may help to usher in democratic stability, in Pye and Verba, 77–82, and "Political Modernization and Political Culture in Japan," *World Politics*, xv (July 1963), 578–81. For a discussion of Atatürk's successful manipulation of the traditional Sultanate and Caliphate in altering Turkish identity, see Richard D. Robinson, *The First Turkish Republic* (Cambridge, Mass., 1963), 34–92.

even less interest in, what little central government existed was directly related to the institutionalization of the central government and rapid industrialization. But despite these singluar achievements, the necessarily emotional attachments involved in the rapid formation of a popular national identity contributed to the emergence of a xenophobic militarism and authoritarianism in the 1930's. Turning to post-independence Ceylon, we find a telling example of the exacerbation of conflict and violence following the attempt to create a national identity in a short space of time. In its first years of independence the Ceylonese government maintained its legitimacy on the basis of a westernized secularism; the country's two largest ethnic groups (the Tamils and the Sinhalese) were able to accept the government because of its "official disregard for all indigenous cultures.[21] This course was then sharply reversed in the middle fifties. And as Geertz has noted, "the search for a common cultural tradition to serve as the content of the country's identity as a nation . . . led only to the revivification of ancient, and better forgotten, Tamil-Sinhalese treacheries, atrocities, insults and wars."[22] The outcome of this attempt saw the emergence of widespread communal violence. Acting out their slogans of national identity—"Sinhalese only" and "*Apey Aanduwa*" ("the government is ours")—the worst abuses were commited against the Tamils.

In short, despite the desirability of a national identity's preceding the central government's institutionalization with respect to our three dependent variables, this sequence is not a common one, and, at the same time, there does not seem to be a rapid solution for this developmental problem. Not only is it highly unlikely that a

national identity can be created in a space of a few years, but the attempt to do so is likely to usher in the unhappy consequences of repressive rule and exacerbation of potentially violent divisions, with their obviously deleterious consequences for the growth of democratic government.

IV. Governmental Institutions and Political Competition: Sequence

The next general hypothesis suggests that the chances for attaining a nonviolent politics and democratic stability without passing through a phase of authoritarian government are maximized when the institutionalization of central government precedes the formation of mass political parties and a broad based suffrage. However, the consequences for our three dependent variables will not be nearly as detrimental when structures of political competition are established before or along with central governmental institutions as when mass electoral participation precedes or emerges simultaneously with an institutionalized central government.

To begin with, LaPalombara and Weiner stress the point that at any one time a government is capable of handling only a limited "load" of problems, demands, and conflicts if it is to maintain itself at a particular level of institutionalization, stability, and effectiveness.[23] This is to say that whatever loads a government has to deal with ought to be interspersed so that the critical point at which loads exceed capabilities is not reached. Yet a government confronted with the problems of incorporating structures of political competition and mass participation faces a simultaneous increase of loads on three counts: there are the institutional problems of integrating the new structures of competition around entirely new patterns of conflict resolution and decision-making; existing divisions among the voters will be exacerbated and demands heightened as parties attempt to mobilize support in order to

[21] McKim Marriott, "Cultural Policy in the New States," in Geertz, *Old Societies and New States*, 42.

[22] Geertz, *Ibid.*, 123. Also see W. Howard Wriggins, "Impediments to Unity in New Nations: The Case of Ceylon," *American Political Science Review*, LV (June 1961), 316, 319.

[23] Chaps. 1 and 14, *passim*.

win control of the government; and demands for greater participation (in both scope and intensity) will follow once the principle of an extended suffrage has been conceded. Thus if a government is to handle these loads (or crises) without endangering its stability and effectiveness, it would be well if the governmental structures were securely institutionalized beforehand.[24] Otherwise the government's capabilities and legitimacy will be easily impaired, necessitating its use of force in order to maintain itself. In Parsons' words, when loads exceed capabilities, "increasingly severe negative sanctions for noncompliance with collective decisions will be imposed."[25] The Italian political system of the early twentieth century was faced with the simultaneous loads of creating a national identity, institutionalizing and legitimizing governmental structures, and inducting new strata into the electorate. The political elite responded with repression and violence. And once governments rely upon force, they tend to overreact to demands with the application of excessive force; the value of organizations with force at their disposal (the army and the police) is heightened; there is consequently a further loss of legitimacy; and finally the population itself turns to violence, thereby setting up an additional stage prop for authoritarian rule.[26]

On the other hand, when the crises of competition and electoral participation do not appear until the government has had sufficient time to become institutionalized, the governmental structures will actually be able to play a positive role in helping the system to adapt itself to the new situation. As Huntington has persuasively argued, with increasing longevity, institutions become more adaptable to new challenges and more flexible in accommodating change.[27] To this may be added a separate point, which also provides some underpinning for Huntington's: the institutionalization of government before it is faced with the crises of competition and electoral participation might provide the political elite with a sufficient sense of security for it to accommodate itself to these changes in a peaceful manner. And in reverse fashion, where the governmental incumbents are insecure because of the brittleness of governmental structures, claims for wider participation may be seen as threats to their own positions, to be adamantly refused. In such an impasse, the groups seeking entry and access to the political system would adopt an alienated posture, questioning the government's root-and-branch legitimacy and possibly turning to violent means as their demands become increasingly radical. Under these circumstances governmental repression, with its unhappy consequences for the country's future development, could very well follow—especially when the elite is insecure because of the fragile governmental structures.

Another argument relies upon the mitigating effects of institutional arrangements. When governmental structures are stabilized and differentiated before the onset of party competition and mass suffrage, the intensity of partisan conflicts and procedural issues will be dampened as they are channeled through and processed by the

[24] For an analysis of European political parties that supports this proposition and demonstrates how the time factor "merges into and coincides with the load factor," see Otto Kirchheimer, "The Transformation of the Western European Party System," in LaPalombara and Weiner, 177–82. The same type of analysis on a somewhat broader theoretical plane is found in LaPalombara and Weiner's own concluding chapter, 427–33.

[25] Talcott Parsons, "Some Reflections on the Place of Force in Social Process," in Harry Eckstein, ed., *Internal War* (New York, 1964), 64. Also see Geertz, 131.

[26] Aristide R. Zolberg, "The Structure of Political Conflict in the New States of Tropical Africa," *American Political Science Review*, LXII (March 1968), 77.

[27] Samuel P. Huntington, "Political Development and Political Decay," *World Politics*, XVII (April 1965), 394–95. Also see S. N. Eisenstadt, *Modernization: Protest and Change* (New York 1966), 58–61; and Anthony Downs, *Inside Bureaucracy* (Boston, 1967), 18–20.

mediating governmental institutions. On the other hand, when the sequence is reversed, partisan conflicts will tend to escalate as substantive issues evolve into procedural ones in the absence of stable conflict-resolving structures. This point may provide a partial explanation for Pye's observation that "opposition parties and aspiring elites [in transitional systems] tend to appear as revolutionary movements,"[28] for when the government is not sufficiently institutionalized for the effective resolution of conflicts, it is only a small further step for the opposition to challenge the entire spectrum of the government's goals and legitimacy. Zolberg apparently supports this argument when he writes that in West Africa "the incumbent leaders [and] challengers tend to view conflict as an all-or-nothing proposition . . . [since] factors which might make for the limitation of issues are almost nonexistent. Whether it begins by asking for better wages or better prices, whether it is dissatisfied with the delimitation of constituencies or with lack of consideration for generational claims, the opposition almost always ends up challenging the entire order which the regime is dedicated to build."[29]

Especially with reference to highly politicized societies, few political scientists would disagree with the statement that large-scale socioeconomic reform should be instituted as early as possible; such reform would generally have the effect of confronting the regime with far fewer loads. This quite obvious point becomes even more significant when socioeconomic reform has not been effected before the creation of a mass electorate. The conjunction of the two —popular power together with popular dissatisfaction and alienation—has all manner of disabling effects: it raises the specter of widespread violence; the conditions are propitious for the emergence of mass move-

ments or communal politics; the strength of sharply divisive parochial groups is not lessened through the process of "modernization" and the creation of Durkheim's organic solidarity based on value consensus; and the regime suffers from a loss of legitimacy. Taken together, these factors also lead toward repressive rule. This generalization becomes relevant in the present context because a precondition for socioeconomic reform is a central government that has achieved a high level of institutionalization and thus the decisional capacity for adopting and executing, and the bureaucratic capacity for implementing, reformist programs. This is by no means to assert that there is any inherent tendency for an institutionalized government to undertake large-scale reform; but such a government is commonly a necessary precondition *if* such reform is to be instituted.[30] Thus, with respect to sequence, it would be well to see an institutionalized government develop before the expansion of the electorate, with the possibility (and that is all it is) that significant reforms can be achieved before the onset of mass suffrage.

Lastly, there is the problem of limited resources, which makes the simultaneous development of governmental structures and national political parties (under conditions of mass suffrage) a problematic undertaking. As a historical generalization, it may be said that when political systems are in the process of forming central governmental institutions there is usually a paucity of the necessary human resources— i.e., experienced political leaders and administrators. Given this coincidence, the resource scarcity places limitations upon the extent to which the government can be institutionalized while national structures

[28] Lucian W. Pye, *Politics, Personality and Nation Building* (New Haven, 1962), 19–20.
[29] Aristide R. Zolberg, *Creating Political Order: The Party-States of West Africa* (Chicago, 1966), 75.

[30] Three exceptions come readily to mind from the Latin American experience: in both Mexico, Cuba, and Bolivia, prior to governmental institutionalization, land was distributed to the peasants who worked it. However, it is significant that the landholding elites were practically destroyed in the revolutions that preceded the land reforms.

of political competition are being formed, especially if these structures are to perform their functions effectively, a task necessitating both national and local organizational staffing. This problem is, of course, an especially critical one in the postcolonial societies in which scarce resources are simultaneously being devoted to economic modernization and to the development of social services. In the post-independence period, "talents that once were available for the crucial work of party organization may now be preoccupied with running a ministry. . . . This will be particularly true where the conditions under which independence was obtained led to the withdrawal of European advisors and technicians and threw the whole technical and administrative burden on the shoulders of the young indigenous politicans."[31]

Given the scarcity of political and administrative talent there is reason to think that existing resources should be devoted to governmental institutionalization rather than sharing them with political parties. If resources were divided between government and parties there is a good possibility that neither would develop into coherent and effective structures; ineffective parties and governmental incapacity would be the likely outcome.[32] Concentration of human resources within the government may also be the optimum strategy for legitimizing the government. According to Shils, it is the "belief in the effectiveness of authority . . . the fact that it seems 'to mean business' . . . coherence at the center . . . (that) will legitimize the elite and the system within

which it operates."[33] By giving greater priority to the strengthening of governmental institutions it is less likely that governments will have to resort to authoritarian measures in order to maintain themselves, while creating sufficiently coherent and effective governments around which democratic institutions can develop. The importance of governmental institutionalization in this regard, especially the existence of a well-staffed and organized bureaucracy, is highlighted by the fact that among the five new states of Asia that retained Western civil servants after independence we find the only four countries of the larger group whose political systems may be termed democratic —India, Ceylon, the Philippines, and Malaysia (Pakistan is the exception). Moreover, of the dozen or so states in Europe that became democratic overnight after World War I, only two maintained their democratic structures: Finland and Czechoslovakia. Finland enjoyed the advantage of having large numbers of well-trained civil servants with upper-class Swedish backgrounds; Bohemia, while it was part of the Hapsburg Empire, was governed by an able and experienced group of bureaucrats who stayed on to form the core of the new Czechoslovakian civil service.

V. Political Competition: Rate

Having indicated some of the consequences that are likely to follow when a sense of national identity precedes the institutionalization of government and when the latter precedes the emergence of parties and mass suffrage, and having analyzed the consequences of attempts at the rapid formation of a national identity, I should now like to examine the likely consequences of rapid change in the direction of greater competition and wider participation. Rapid change in this instance may occur either when a nonrepresentative system (e.g., a

[31] William J. Foltz, "Building the Newest Nations: Short-Run Strategies and Long-Run Problems," in Karl W. Deutsch and William J. Foltz, eds., *Nation-Building* (New York, 1963) 123–24.

[32] The recent tendency of African states to merge their governmental and party hierarchies is partly necessitated by just this shortage of trained personnel, and it also accounts for the weakening of the parties. See Immanuel Wallerstein, "The Decline of the Party in Single-Party African States," in LaPalombara and Weiner, 201–15.

[33] Edward A. Shils, "Demagogues and Cadres in the Political Development of the New States," in Lucian W. Pye, ed., *Communications and Political Development* (Princeton, 1963), 68.

former colony, monarchy, or dictatorship) is directly transformed into a democratic one, without first taking the form of a semirepresentative oligarchy, or when mass participation through universal suffrage is introduced overnight in the case of a semi-representative oligarchy. To put it differently, when structures of competition are gradually developed (i.e., when protoparties precede full-blown parties and a mass suffrage) and when the rate at which the suffrage is expanded is gradual—under these two closely interrelated conditions, but especially under the latter—our three dependent variables are most likely to be realized. The explanatory power of this hypothesis is presumably increased in those political systems that have not achieved a sense of national identity and a securely institutionalized government and is decreased in those systems that have achieved these ends.

When mass suffrage is instituted before or along with the development of national political parties—or, to put in another way, when protoparties have not preceded mass parties—these national parties will not have sufficient time to form coherent and autonomous organizations before having to meet the participation crisis. They will have neither the experienced leaders nor the firm linkages between the center and local areas required for the effective articulation and aggregation of popular demands, thereby detracting from democratic representativeness and decisional effectiveness while leaving the electorate "available" for mobilization in either extremist mass movements or government-controlled organizations.[34] The national parties' lack of organizational strength and the absence of effective ties with local power centers significantly reduces their role in governmental

decision-making and makes the parties themselves vulnerable to "incorporation" into the (noncompetitive) governmental structure. Thus in the postcolonial African states, the weaknesses of party structures—even in the single-party states they have far more in common with political machines than with mobilized mass parties—have both decreased the amount of popular participation in the political system and left the parties without any influence in preventing, starting, or ending the numerous coups. Political scientists are in general agreement that the chances of achieving viable democratic government are increased when parties perform an integrative function—that is, when they manage to form broad alliances with disparate territorial, communal, and economic groups. Yet if parties are to succeed in this respect, especially under the conditions of a recently extended mass franchise, it would seem desirable that they first be institutionalized to provide the necessary ideological and organizational adaptability.

In the case of Israel, protoparties were formed long before they were transformed into mass parties under conditions of universal suffrage. The United Labor Party was formed in 1919, followed by the Histadrut (The General Confederation of Labor) in 1920, and the growth and consolidation of these political organizations in the Mapai Party in 1929. As highly elitist, self-coopting protoparties, they were able to develop coherent and highly articulated organizational and ideological structures in the three decades preceding independence. As a consequence, even the rapid introduction of universal suffrage (there were not even any residence requirements) in the 1949 national elections could take place in an orderly and non-violent manner. In addition, the Histadrut and Mapai were so highly organized and adaptable that between 1948 and 1955 they were able to integrate 900,000 immigrants (most of whom came from Asia and Africa) into a nation of 600,000 without recourse to authoritarian

[34] Cross-national aggregate data that support this generalization are found in Ted Gurr, with Charles Ruttenberg, *The Conditions of Civil Violence: First Tests of a Causal Model*, Center of International Studies, Princeton University, Research Monograph No. 28 (Princeton, 1967), esp. 12, 86–87.

measures and without detracting from the democratic system's viability.

Besides the organizational dimension of parties, the orientations of the party leaders are also relevant at this point. Leaders of parties that have been rapidly formed or have had to face the participation crisis immediately after their formation tend to respond to this situation with repressive policies toward the electorate and thereby decrease the chances for future democratic stability. Following LaPalombara and Weiner, I can suggest two factors underpinning this hypothesis. By comparing those colonies in which protoparties were repressed and those in which they were able to share some governmental power, it is found that in the former, the "nationalist groups subjected to such repressive measures . . . are not adequately socialized into the art of political compromise and responsible leadership. . . . After independence they are likely to manifest an overly stong identification with the state, view opposition as illegitimate, and be dogmatic, uncompromising, and monolithic in their orientation."[35] The second point is a psychological one: the new wielders of power generally find it difficult to share the power that they themselves have just attained, especially when there is little enough to go around. "In a very rough way, we might say that the probability of resistance [to participatory demands] is associated with the proximity between the creation of a party system and increased demand for participation. Where the new elites are immediately challenged by others who wish to share in the exercise of power the probability of repression is much higher than in those places where the waves of demand are spread over a longer time span."[36] In short, party leaders need time—for organizational consolidation, socialization into the roles of "responsible democratic" leadership, and attainment of psychological security—if they are to allow a democratic politics to emerge.

[35] LaPalombara and Weiner, p. 31.
[36] *Ibid.*, p. 402.

Turning to the rate at which mass suffrage is implemented, when a government undertakes any major change of a procedural variety entailing a wider distribution of power, this change will usually be followed by a multiplication of political demands. When the major change is effected in a short space of time and when it appears that this change will settle the contours and determine the outputs of the regime for the foreseeable future—which is what happens when mass suffrage is introduced overnight—then the government will have to contend with a whole range of intensive demands. This type of situation tends to produce a politicization explosion, in which any group difference—social, linguistic, cultural, economic—may be transformed into political demands.[37] Furthermore, the rapid acquisition of the vote will probably not have afforded the electorate sufficient time to learn to distinguish between partisan opposition and the pressing of demands upon the government, on the one hand, and an attempt to overthrow the regime and secession, on the other.[38] Following the rapid introduction of mass suffrage, there is then likely to be a confluence of many intensely felt and conflicting demands placed upon the government, combined with a resort to direct action—a generalization that is borne out in numerous African and Asian countries whose original democratic systems have consequently "degenerated" into violence, authoritarianism, and, at best, nonrepressive dictatorship.

Nor is the problem only one of the number and intensity of demands facing the government; the rapid realization of electoral power is likely to lead to a greater awareness and exacerbation of just those

[37] For an application of this hypothesis to West Africa, see Zolberg, "The Structure of Political Conflict," 73–76.
[38] The overnight introduction of universal male suffrage in Colombia in 1853, which was followed by two tumultuous civil wars, may serve as a telling Latin American case in which the suffrage was expanded "too far and too fast."

communal differences that have the most deleterious consequences for stable and effective democratic government. The electorate's newly acquired power will magnify its awareness of ethnic, religious, and linguistic divisions since the people now believe themselves to have a good deal of control over such issues. This new awareness is then further heightened by the politicians who utilize communal loyalties and hatreds in accumulating votes. Geertz makes this point about traditionalizing elections in a forceful manner, contending that the exacerbation of "Indonesian regionalism, Malayan racialism, Indian linguism, [and] Nigerian tribalism . . . are part and parcel of the very process of the creation of a new polity and a new citizenship."[39]

Whenever mass suffrage has been rapidly introduced it has been legitimated by an exaggerated populistic rhetoric, engendering high expectations for socioeconomic change, the redress of grievances, and extensive popular influence upon governmental decisions. Yet given the realities of limited resources and the necessarily hierarchical structure of any democratic government, these high expectations are bound to remain unfulfilled. Popular disappointment and frustration are thus likely to follow in the wake of an overnight intro-

[39] Pp. 120–23. Also see Deutsch and others, 61–63, for some European examples that support this generalization; and MacKenzie's conclusion based on close study of five African elections: "If tribalism is the enemy, elections are partly responsible for encouraging it" (W. J. M. MacKenzie and Kenneth E. Robinson, *Five Elections in Africa* [Oxford, 1960], 484). For a detailed account of the way in which the politicians sharpened communal tensions in Ceylon by playing upon communal issues in gaining electoral support, see C. Howard Wriggins, *Ceylon: Dilemmas of a New Nation* (Princeton, 1960), 169–270. Pakistan may be viewed as a case in which the politicians played upon parochial interests and thereby provided the rationale for preserving national unity and governmental effectiveness by doing away with elections. See K. Callard, *Pakistan: A Political Study* (London, 1957).

duction of universal suffrage, producing a greater stress on communal values and interests and an increasing disregard for the claims of other groups and regions.[40] This has even happened where the majority's primary aims were realized. In Rwanda, the Hutu majority had been dominated by the Tutsi minority in a client-patron relationship for four centuries. But even though the Hutu won a decisive majority in the suddenly introduced elections of 1960 and 1961, achieving their intensely felt goals of dominating their former overlords and redistributing the Tutsi wealth, it was their electoral *victory* that triggered a massive bloodbath and the emigration of the Tutsi.

Having considered some of the ways in which rapid extension of the franchise exacerbates communal divisions in some non-Western countries, we can turn to the effects of the franchise expansion rate upon the class divisions in Europe. Although it is by no means one of the most important explanatory factors, there appears to be an inverse relationship between the rate at which the franchise was extended and the bourgeoisie's and the aristocracy's acceptance of democratic government. Where effective universal suffrage was most rapidly extended—in the Second French Republic, the Italian Republic, and Weimar Germany —the bourgeoisie's and the aristocracy's already extensive hostility toward the specter of democracy was intensified and protracted. These groups negated the democratic regimes' legitimacy and actively worked toward the establishment of more or less repressive dictatorships. Even in the case of Weimar Germany, with the upper classes in firm control not only of the bureaucracy and the army, but also of the democratically elected governments in the last half of the Republic's short existence, they maintained their strident opposition to democratic institutions.

In other European countries, such as Britain, Sweden, Norway, Belgium, and

[40] Deutsch and others, 62; Alexis de Tocqueville, *Democracy in America*, I (New York, 1960), 201.

Holland, mass participation was only gradually extended throughout the nineteenth and early twentieth centuries. The effects that this gradual expansion had upon these countries' subsequent development is aptly set out by Daalder: At any one time the new political strata "tended to be given at most only part-power—enough to give them a sense of involvement and political efficacy but not enough to completely overthrow the evolving society. . . . Since at any one time the political stakes were relatively modest, the upper classes were less afraid and the lower classes less threatening. Older and new elites were thus held more easily within the bounds of one constitutional, if changing, political system that neither alienated the one into reactionary nor the other into revolutionary onslaughts on it."[41] In addition, gradual enfranchisement is apparently related to the nonelites' maintenance of respectful and partially acquiescent attitudes toward political authority—a cultural variable that figures prominently in two theories of stable democracy.[42]

[41] Hans Daalder, "Parties, Elites, and Political Developments in Western Europe," in LaPalombara and Weiner, 48–49.

[42] Eckstein, 225–88 and *passim*.; Eric A. Nordlinger, *The Working Class Tories: Authority, Deference and Stable Democracy* (Berkeley 1967), 210–52.

VI. A Final Note

It should be emphasized that the general and secondary hypotheses put forward in this essay are at best of a tentative variety. There are numerous methodological difficulties afflicting hypotheses based upon sequence and rate of change—difficulties that would require a far more extensive treatment than can be carried out here. Moreover, it should be quite clear that a good deal of further work is needed if the hypotheses are to be fully explored rather than simply being illustrated, as has been done here. Nor should the conclusions be taken to mean that the sequences and rates of the four independent variables examined are the most important explanations in accounting for different patterns of political development. If sequence and rate are useful notions, they may just as readily be applied to variables other than the ones examined in this article. However, it is hoped that this essay's primary goal has been at least partially realized—the goal of illustrating the uses and advantages of a focus upon sequence and rate for systematically ordering the field of political development in the form of a series of generalizable explanatory hypotheses.

POLITICAL MODERNIZATION AND POLITICAL CULTURE IN JAPAN

Robert E. Ward

The course of political modernization in Japan raises some interesting questions with respect to the form and organization

SOURCE: Excerpted from Robert E. Ward, "Political Modernization and Political Culture in Japan," *World Politics*, **15**, 569–596, July 1963; using only pp. 588–596.

of authority in modernizing societies. . . . States which have achieved modernity may have democratic, totalitarian, or some intermediate type of political organization. The form of government does not seem to be a defining factor in mature cases of political modernization. The experience of

Japan, however, makes one wonder if the same judgment applies with respect to forms of political organization in all earlier stages of the political modernization process. Is the process neutral in this respect throughout, or can one identify stages which demand authoritarian forms of government and which are antipathetic on grounds of developmental efficiency and potentiality to the introduction of democratic institutions on more than a very restricted basis? The question is of great importance from the standpoint of those who would prefer to see "backward" political systems develop along lines which are both modern and democratic. These are compatible but not necessary consequences of the developmental process. This poses the problem of how one can maximize the probability that developing polities will become both modern and democratic

The experience of Japan alone certainly cannot provide definitive answers to either of the above questions. But neither is it irrelevant, and in circumstances where it represents the sole mature non-Western exemplar of the modernization process in all of Asia, it should be examined with unusual care and attention. The Japanese experience seems to suggest: (1) that authoritarian forms of political organization can be extraordinarily effective in the early stages of the modernization process; (2) that they need not debar the gradual emergence of more democratic forms of political organization; and (3) that some such process of gradual transition from authoritarian to democratic forms may be essential to the emergence of politics that are both modern and durably democratic. It should be emphasized again that these are no more than highly tentative hypotheses based upon the experience of Japan, but they do possess at least this much historical sanction and support. Let us then consider in a general way selected aspects of Japan's experience with the political modernization process which relate to the above three propositions.

First, authoritarian forms of political organization can be extraordinarily effective in the early stages of the modernization process. It is implied—though not demonstrable on the basis of the Japanese experience—that democratic forms are significantly less effective and that their early introduction may in fact result in conditions that will seriously inhibit the prospects of long-term democratic development.

This contention rests primarily on observations with respect to the relationship between the political modernization process and the process of social modernization in a general or total sense. The former is not autonomous, not a goal in itself. It is instrumentally related to the larger process and goal and should serve and expedite its purposes. This larger process of modernization entails for the society concerned, especially in the critical early or "takeoff" stages, a series of shocks and strains of major proportions. It equally creates emancipations and new opportunities for some, but for major segments of the population this is apt to be a lengthy period of adjustment to new economic, social and political situations and demands. Large-scale material and psychological stresses are invariably involved. One of the routine consequences of such a situation—at least in the non-Western world of the late nineteenth and the twentieth centuries—seems to be a greatly expanded role for government. A certain and perhaps very important amount of the modernization process may still take place under private auspices, but in recent times the needs and expectations which set the standards of modernization have been so urgent and expensive that national governments have had to assume a leading and dominant role. Only power organized at this level seemed capable of massing the resources and taking and enforcing the wide-ranging and difficult decisions involved.

This primacy of government in the modernizing process is more or less taken for granted throughout the underdeveloped world today. The situation was doubtless historically different in the case of the modernization of certain Western European societies and their offshoots, but in present-day underdeveloped societies there simply are no plausible and politically viable alternatives to the primacy of government as an agent of modernization. This was also true in the Japanese case at the time of the Restoration.

The overriding problems and goals of the 1870's and 1880's in Japan were well expressed by the popular political slogan of the day—*fukoku kyōhei* (a strong and wealthy nation). This captures the essence of the complex of forces and aspirations which underlay the Restoration movement and motivated its leaders in the difficult days that followed the initial successes of 1868. The greatest and most urgent needs were for national unity and the creation of armed strength sufficient to guarantee the national security against both real and fancied dangers of foreign imperialist aggression and economic exploitation. Instrumental thereto, of course, was the creation of a strong and stable government to lead the nation along suitable paths. Fortunately for Japan, her leaders were wise enough to define these goals in broad and constructive terms. Military strength meant to them far more than a large army and navy well-equipped with Western armaments; it also meant the industrial plant to sustain and expand such a military establishment and appropriate training for the men who must staff it. National wealth came to mean a radical diversification of the predominantly agrarian economy, urbanization, systematic mass and higher education, planned industrialization, new commercial and financial institutions, and a variety of other commitments which were perceived as essential to survival and effective competitive status in a Western-dominated world. Not all of these commitments were either generally perceived or welcomed at the outset by the leadership group, but in their search

for national unity, strength, and security they found themselves embarked upon a species of "modernization spiral" similar in some respects to the "inflationary spiral" of the economists. The most intelligent and able of them adapted to the general course set by the imperatives which these goals entailed; the others were eliminated from leadership circles.

The realization of national goals of this sort did not come easily to a society such as Japan's, even given the forms of covert preparation for modernization which had characterized the later Tokugawa Period. The really critical years between 1868 and 1890 must sometimes have seemed an unending series of crises. Civil war, the threat of international war and the fact of foreign economic exploitation, a series of economic crises, inflation and deflation, the recurrent threat of samurai conspiracies against the government, the embitterment of the peasantry at the failure of the government to improve their lot, the dearth of desperately needed technical knowledge and personnel, and all of the widespread fears and tensions which attend a time of new beginnings—these were merely some of the problems which constantly confronted the new political leadership. Yet, by 1890, policies capable of dealing with all of these problems had been developed and the country was firmly embarked on the path to modernization. The foreign threats had been faced and Japan's international position was secure; the menace of civil war had been permanently liquidated; the structural vestiges of feudalism had been eliminated and the country effectively unified; the position and authority of the government had been confirmed and regularized by constitutional arrangements; the economy had been stabilized and a promising start made upon its diversification and industrialization; a system of mass compulsory education had been inaugurated and mass media of communication established; in every critical category the strength of

Japan showed remarkable and promising improvements.

Under such circumstances it may be that some measure of democratic participation could successfully have been introduced into the political system. There were those who advocated such changes. The *Jiyūminken Undō* (Freedom and Popular Rights Movement), for example, called for the establishment of a national parliament, a limited suffrage, and some dispersion of political authority. Had this been attempted during these years, the results need not have been fatal to the modernization of Japan. But under conditions of more or less constant political or economic crisis, widespread popular disaffection and lack of understanding of the necessity for the sacrifices entailed by many government programs, the unpredictable qualities and perils of the country's foreign relations, and what we have learned in general of the limitations of fledgling democratic institutions in largely unprepared contexts, it is difficult to envisage the feasibility or practicality of any very significant democratic innovations at this time.

These years from 1868 to 1890, or some similar period, would seem to be a time in Japan's modernization when an authoritarian form of political organization offered distinct advantages where rapidity of response, flexibility, planning, and effective action were concerned. This is said with full appreciation of the fumbling and shortcomings of authoritarian leadership groups and irresponsible bureaucracies—including the Japanese of this period—in all of these departments. It thus assumes the availability of some at least minimally competent and unified political leadership. If this is not available—and there are obviously cases where it is not—political modernization is not a practicable proposition for the countries concerned.

In the Japanese case, however, it seems on balance highly improbable that (1) the addition of any significant or effective democratic institutions to the decision-making apparatus at such a stage of national development could have had other than deleterious effects upon the speed and decisiveness with which urgent problems were handled; and that (2) this stage of the modernization process, beset as it inevitably was by so many and such desperate problems, would have been an appropriate time to launch so delicate an experiment as democratization.

Our second hypothesis was that the dominance of authoritarian forms of political organization in the initial stages of the political modernization process need not debar the gradual emergence of democratic forms of organization. This is not intended to imply any quality of inevitability in such a development, although in a secular sense some such tendency may exist.

In the Japanese case, no significant measures of democratization were introduced into the political system until the enactment of the Meiji Constitution in 1890, twenty-two years after the Restoration. Even then it is very doubtful if any of the authors of this document thought of their handiwork as an act of democratic innovation. It is certain that their so-called "liberal" opposition did not. Rather does it seem that the Meiji leadership group conceived of this constitution primarily as a means of regularizing the structure and operations of political authority—the absence of any rationalized or stable structure and the continual innovation and experimentation of the intervening years must have been very trying—and of further unifying and solidifying both the country and their own authority. As a consequence of this and a variety of later developments, there has been a tendency to undervalue both the degree of political change which the Meiji Constitution brought to Japan and the measure of democratic development which took place under it.

It is helpful to look at the Meiji Constitution and its attendant basic laws both in terms of the general political standards and practices of 1890 and in terms of its actual operations as well as its legal and political theory. If this is done, one will note that it makes public, explicit, and authoritative a particular theory of sovereignty and the state, and derives from this a functionally differentiated and rationally organized governmental structure; it establishes the legal status of citizens and specifies their political and civil rights and duties; it distinguishes legislative, executive, and judicial functions and, although establishing a dominant and protected position for the executive, does provide for their separate institutionalization; it specifies legal equality before the law and creates means for the assertion of popular against official rights; it establishes a restricted but expansible franchise and, in terms of this, a popularly elected house in the national legislature; it provides for some measure of decentralization in government, and renders inevitable the introduction of a much greater measure of pluralism into both the Japanese oligarchy and the political system in general.

Against the background of Tokugawa and Restoration political practices, these are notable and democratic innovations. They did not, of course, put an end to the period of authoritarian political rule in Japan. But they certainly launched a process of democratization which has continued to play a major, although usually not dominant, part in Japanese politics ever since. In this sense the history of the democratization of Japan, viewed in the light of present circumstances, is a product of erosive and catalytic agents. Much of the story is told, until 1932 at least, in terms of the erosion of the authoritarian political forms and practices characteristic of the pre-constitutional period. This process never reached the point of establishing what the contemporary West would regard as an authentically democratic political system, but, by the 1920's, the degree of pluralism, responsibility, and popular participation

characterizing Japanese politics would certainly have surprised, and probably appalled, the great leaders of the Restoration Period. Between the 1920's and the 1960's there intervened, of course, the resurgence of military and ultranationalist rule, the war, and the Allied Occupation of Japan. This last acted as a catalytic agent on the submerged but still vital forms of Japanese democracy and gave them institutional and legal advantages, authority, and prestige beyond what they could have hoped for on the basis of their own political position and strength. The consequence has been a great and apparently sudden florescence of Western-style democracy in Japan. In fact, however, the roots of this development lie deep in the political experience of post-1890 Japan.

There are two things about this gradual emergence of democratic politics from the authoritarian system of pre-1890 Japan which might have more general validity and interest. The first is that even the concession of a very carefully restricted and seemingly impotent governmental role to a popularly elected body can, over a period of time, have consequences well nigh fatal to sustained authoritarian rule. It would be hard to be optimistic about the influence or authority of the Japanese House of Representatives in terms of the provisions of the Meiji Constitution or the relevant basic laws. These faithfully reflect and implement the desire of the founders to make of the House an appealing but powerless sop to the demands of the opposition and public opinion. But the lessons to be learned from the subsequent history of the lower house are: (1) that it provides a means of institutionalizing and enlarging the role of political parties; (2) that, in modernizing circumstances, even vested powers of obstructing the smooth and effective flow of governmental decisions and actions can be critical—positive power of initiation and control are not necessary; and (3) that in circumstances where a popularly chosen body can thus blackmail an authoritarian leadership, there is a fair possibility of forcing the latter into piecemeal but cumulative accommodations which are democratic in tendency.

The second generalization suggested by the history of democratic development in Japan relates to the conditions necessary to support an effectively authoritarian system of government. Japanese experience suggests the existence of a close relationship between effective authoritarian rule and the unity and solidarity of the oligarchy involved. The limits involved cannot be described with much precision, but authoritarian government in Japan began to disintegrate as the heretofore fairly solidary oligarchy began to split into competing cliques and factions. The probability of such rifts seems to be very high in modernizing societies. The development of role specialization and professionalization even at high levels is an essential part of the process of modernization, and this makes it hard for an oligarchy to maintain the degree of unity and cohesion feasible in revolutionary or in simpler times. Pluralism in this sense seems to be built into the process. And as an oligarchy breaks down into competing factions in this fashion, the terms of political competition in that society undergo an important change. Extra-oligarchic groups such as emergent political parties acquire new room for maneuver and new political leverages, and the ex-oligarchic cliques themselves acquire new incentives for broadening the basis of their support. Out of these altered political circumstances are apt to come new political alliances involving elements of the former oligarchy with elements of more popularly based bodies—in particular, with political parties. The total process is dilutive from the standpoint of authoritarian government and supportive of the gradual emergence of greater degrees of pluralism and democracy.

It is not intended to depict either of the foregoing generalizations on the basis of

Japanese experience as controlling or inevitable. But they did occur within a fairly authoritarian context in Japan's case and there seem to be some reasons for regarding them as of more general validity. The conclusion would seem to be that an initial or early stage of authoritarian government on the path to modernization (1) does not commit a polity to long-term adherence to authoritarian forms; (2) does not necessarily make an authoritarian course of development probable; and (3) may even contain built-in elements calculated with time and development to break down and liberalize such authoritarian forms.

Our third hypothesis is even more tentatively stated and adds up to a feeling that some such process of gradual transition from authoritarian to democratic forms may be essential to the emergence of a political system which is both modern and durably democratic. In this connection Japan's experience suggests several notions of possible interest.

First, our commonly employed systems of periodization may involve serious distortions where the history of political modernization is concerned. Thus, in Japan's case, while the feudal-modern or Tokugawa-Restoration frameworks have a plausible amount of relevance to the emergence of a modern Japanese political system, they also serve to obscure important aspects of the process. They are calculated, as is the prewar-postwar framework, to produce an overemphasis on the significance of certain dramatic and allegedly "revolutionary" events in a country's history—in this case, the Restoration or the 1945 defeat plus the Occupation. This is conducive to a dichotomous view of the political development process which seriously overstates the enduring importance of alleged discontinuities in a national history at the expense of the less dramatic but fundamentally more important continuities.

Second, if the history of the development of democracy in Japan is weighted for this distorting effect of the commonly employed categories and system of periodization, the differences in preparation, timing, and depth of democratic experience which are often held to distinguish a democratic political system in Japan from its Western analogues would perhaps seem appreciably less valid and important than is usually assumed. The two patterns of development probably have more in common than is generally recognized.

Third, if the foregoing assumptions are valid, one is tempted to conclude that all practicing and at least ostensibly solid and durable democracies today are the products of lengthy and multifaceted evolutionary processes. In the Japanese case, if one looks only to the direct antecedents, seventy-three years intervene between the Meiji Constitution and the present. But far longer periods of preparation are involved if one looks to the less direct consequences of the introduction of mass literacy or a rationalized bureaucratic structure. In this sense it is questionable whether history provides any very encouraging examples of short-cuts to the achievement of a democratic political system.

Finally, such a train of argument suggests the importance of the relationship existing between a "modern" political system and a "democratic" political system. One hesitates to claim that all or a specific proportion of the attributes of a modern polity must be achieved before a society becomes capable of durably democratic performance or achievement, but Japan's experience at least suggests an important correlation between the two. It is hard to specify the proportions involved, but, in a rough and approximate way, one might say that perhaps only modern societies with modern political cultures . . . are practical candidates for democratization.

Chapter 14

Transitional Politics and Party Systems

STRATEGIES OF INSTITUTIONAL DEVELOPMENT*

Samuel P. Huntington

If decay of political institutions is a widespread phenomenon in the "developing" countries and if a major cause of this decay is the high rate of social mobilization, it behooves us, as social scientists, to call a spade a spade and to incorporate these tendencies into any general model of political change which we employ to understand the politics of these areas. If effective political institutions are necessary for stable and eventually democratic government and if they are also a precondition of sustained economic growth, it behooves us, as policy analysts, to suggest strategies of institutional development. In doing this, we should recognize two general considerations affecting probabilities of success in institution-building.

SOURCE: Excerpted from Samuel P. Huntington, "Political Development and Political Decay," *World Politics*, **17**, 386–430, April, 1965, using only pp. 417–27.

---

* *Editors' note:* In the earlier part of the article from which this portion is excerpted, Huntington defines political development as "the institutionalization of political organizations and procedures" (p. 393). He then proceeds to argue, and present substantiating evidence for the conclusion, that social mobilization and political participation "are directly responsible for the deterioration of political institutions" in Asia, Africa, and Latin America (p. 405).

First, the psychological and cultural characteristics of peoples differ markedly and with them their abilities at developing political institutions. Where age-old patterns of thought and behavior have to be changed, quite obviously the creation of political institutions is a far more difficult task than otherwise. "The Tokugawa Japanese could not, as did the Chinese, put family above government," one expert has observed. "The samurai was expected to be loyal to his official superior first, his family second. In mores generally the primacy of the organization over the person was constantly reiterated."[1] This difference in Japanese and Chinese attitudes toward authority undoubtedly accounts in part for their differences in modernization and development. The Japanese peacefully and smoothly created new political institutions and amalgamated them with old ones. The weakness of traditional Chinese political institutions, on the other hand, led to forty years of revolution and civil war before modern political institutions could be developed and extended throughout Chinese society.

[1] John Whitney Hall, "The Nature of Traditional Society: Japan," in Ward and Rustow, eds., *Political Modernization in Japan and Turkey*, 19.

Second, the potentialities for institution-building differ markedly from society to society, but in all societies political organizations can be built. Institutions result from the slow interaction of conscious effort and existing culture. Organizations, however, are the product of conscious, purposeful effort. The forms of this effort may vary from a Meiji Restoration to a Communist Revolution. But in each case a distinct group of identifiable people set about adapting old organizations or building new ones. "Nation-building" has recently become a popular subject, and doubts have been raised about whether nations can be "built."[2] These doubts have a fairly solid basis. Nations are one type of social force, and historically they have emerged over long periods of time. Organization-building, however, differs from nation-building. Political organizations require time for development, but they do not require as much time as national communities. Indeed, most of those who speak of nation-building in such places as tropical Africa see organization-building as the first step in this process. Political parties have to be welded out of tribal groups; the parties create governments; and the governments may, eventually, bring into existence nations. Many of the doubts which people have about the possibilities of nation-building do not apply to organization-building.

Given our hypotheses about the relation of social mobilization to institutionalization, there are two obvious methods of furthering institutional development. First, anything which slows social mobilization presumably creates conditions more favorable to the preservation and strengthening of institutions. Secondly, strategies can be developed and applied directly to the problem of institution-building.

[2] See Karl W. Deutsch and William J. Foltz, eds., *Nation-Building* (New York 1963), *passim*, but especially the contributions of Joseph R. Strayer and Carl J. Friedrich.

Slowing Mobilization

Social mobilization can be moderated in many ways. Three methods are: to increase the complexity of social structure; to limit or reduce communications in society; and to minimize competition among segments of the political elite.[3]

In general, the more highly stratified a society is and the more complicated its social structure, the more gradual is the process of political mobilization. The divisions between class and class, occupation and occupation, rural and urban, constitute a series of breakwaters which divide the society and permit the political mobilization of one group at a time. On the other hand, a highly homogeneous society, or a society which has only a single horizontal line of division between an oligarchy that has everything and a peasantry that has nothing, or a society which is divided not horizontally but vertically into ethnic and communal groups, has more difficulty moderating the process of mobilization. Thus, mobilization should be slower in India than in the new African states where horizontal divisions are weak and tribal divisions strong, or in those Latin American countries where the middle strata are weak and a small oligarchy confronts a peasant mass. A society with many horizontal divisions gains through the slower entry of social groups into politics. It may, however, also lose something in that political organizations, when they do develop, may form along class and stratum lines and thus lack the autonomy of more broadly based political organizations. Political parties in countries like Chile and Sweden have been

[3] These are not, of course, the only ways of slowing mobilization. Myron Weiner, for instance, has suggested that one practical method is "localization": channeling political interests and activity away from the great issues of national politics to the more immediate and concrete problems of the village and community. This is certainly one motive behind both community development programs and "basic democracies."

largely the spokesmen for distinct classes; caste associations seem destined to play a significant role in Indian politics. The disruptive effects of political organizations identified with social strata may be reduced if other political institutions exist which appeal to loyalties across class or caste lines. In Sweden, loyalty to the monarchy and the Riksdag mitigates the effects of class-based parties, and in India the caste associations must, in general, seek their goals within the much more extensive framework of the Congress Party. In most societies, the social structure must be largely accepted as given. Where it is subject to governmental manipulation and influence, mobilization will be slowed by government policies which enhance the complexity of social stratification.

The communications network of a society is undoubtedly much more subject to governmental influence. Rapid gains in some of the most desired areas of modernization—such as mass media exposure, literacy, and education—may have to be purchased at the price of severe losses in political stability. This is not to argue that political institutionalization as a value should take precedence over all others: if this were the case, modernization would never be good. It is simply to argue that governments must balance the values won through rapid increases in communications against the values jeopardized by losses in political stability. Thus, governmental policies may be wisely directed to reducing the number of university graduates, particularly those with skills which are not in demand in the society. Students and unemployed university graduates have been a concern common to the nationalistic military regime in South Korea, the socialist military regime in Burma, and the traditional military regime in Thailand. The efforts by General Ne Win in Burma to cut back the number of university graduates may well be imitated by other governments facing similar challenges. Much has been made of the problems caused by the exten-

sion of the suffrage to large numbers of illiterates. But limited political participation by illiterates may well, as in India, be less dangerous to political institutions than participation by literates. The latter typically have higher aspirations and make more demands on government. Political participation by illiterates, moreover, is more likely to remain limited, whereas participation by literates is much more likely to snowball with potentially disastrous effects on political stability. A governing elite may also affect the intensity of communications and the rate of political mobilization by its policies on economic development. Large, isolated factories, as Kornhauser has shown, are more likely to give rise to extremist movements than smaller plants more closely integrated into the surrounding community.[4] Self-interest in political survival may lead governing elites to decrease the priority of rapid economic change.

The uncontrolled mobilization of people into politics is also slowed by minimizing the competition among political elites. Hence mobilization is likely to have less disturbing effects on political institutions in one-party systems than in two-party or multiparty systems. In many new states and modernizing countries, a vast gap exists between the modernized elite and the tradition-oriented mass. If the elite divides against itself, its factions appeal to the masses for support. This produces rapid mobilization of the masses into politics at the same time that it destroys whatever consensus previously existed among the politically active on the need for modernization. Mobilization frequently means the mobilization of tradition; modern politics become the vehicle of traditional purposes. In Burma during the first part of this century, the "general pattern was one in which the modernizers first fell out among themselves whenever they were confronted with demanding choices of policy, and then

[4] Kornhauser, *Politics of Mass Society*, 150–58.

tended to seek support from among the more traditional elements, which in time gained the ascendency."[5] In Turkey a rough balance between the mobilization of people into politics and the development of political institutions existed so long as the Republican People's Party retained a political monopoly. The conscious decision to permit an opposition party, however, broadened the scope of political competition beyond the urban, Westernized elite. The Democratic Party mobilized the peasants into politics, strengthened the forces of traditionalism, and broke the previous consensus. This led the party leaders to attempt to maintain themselves in power through semilegal means and to induce the army to join them in suppressing the Republican opposition. The army, however, was committed to modernization and seized power in a *coup d'état*, dissolving the Democratic Party and executing many of its top leaders. In due course, the military withdrew from direct conduct of the government, and democratic elections led to a multi-party system in which no party has a clear majority. Thus from a relatively stable one-party system, Turkey passed through a brief two-party era to military rule and a multiparty system: the familiar syndrome of states where mobilization has outrun institutionalization. In the process, not only were political institutions weakened, but the traditional-minded were brought into politics in such a way as to create obstacles to the achievement of many modernizing goals.

Creating Institutions

"Dans la naissance des sociétés ce sont les chefs des républiques qui font l'institution; et c'est ensuite l'institution qui forme les chefs des républiques," said Montesquieu.[6] But in the contemporary world, po-

litical leaders prefer modernization to institution-building, and no matter who leads modernization, the process itself generates conflicting demands and inducements which obstruct the growth of political institutions. Where modernization is undertaken by traditional leaders working through traditional political institutions, the efforts of the traditional leaders to reform can unleash and stimulate social forces which threaten the traditional political institutions. Traditional leaders can modernize and reform their realms, but, where substantial social elements oppose reform, they have yet to demonstrate they can put through reforms without undermining the institutions through which they are working. The problem is: how can the traditional political institutions be adapted to accommodate the social forces unleashed by modernization? Historically, except for Japan, traditional political institutions have been adapted to the modern world only where a high degree of political centralization was not required for modernization and where traditional (i.e., feudal) representative institutions retained their vitality (as in Great Britain and Sweden). If modernization requires the centralization of power in a "reform monarch" or "revolutionary emperor," it means the weakening or destruction of whatever traditional representative institutions may exist and thus complicates still further the assimilation of those social forces created by modernization. The concentration of power also makes the traditional regime (like the eighteenth-century French monarchy) more vulnerable to forcible overthrow. *The vulnerability of a traditional regime to revolution varies directly with the capability of the regime for modernization.* For traditional rulers, the imperatives of modernization conflict with the imperatives of institution-building.

If the traditional political institutions are weak, or if they have been displaced and suppressed during periods of colonial rule, adaptation is impossible. In societies which have undergone colonial rule, incubation

[5] Pye, *Politics, Personality and Nation Building*, 114.

[6] Charles de Secondat, Baron Montesquieu, *Considérations sur les causes de la grandeur des romains et de leur décadence*, in *Oeuvres*, 1 (Paris 1828), 119–20.

can serve as a substitute for adaptation. Unfortunately, the opportunity for incubation was missed in most colonial societies, with a few prominent exceptions such as India and the Philippines. Incubation requires a colonial administration which is willing to permit and *to contend with* a nationalist movement for many years, thus furnishing the time, the struggle, and the slowly increasing responsibility which are the ingredients of institution-building. In general, however, colonial powers tend to postpone incubation for as long as possible and then, when they see independence as inevitable, to bring it about as quickly as possible. Consequently, most of the states which became independent in the 1950's and 1960's had little opportunity to incubate political institutions while still under colonial tutelage.

Where traditional political institutions are weak, or collapse, or are overthrown, authority frequently comes to rest with charismatic leaders who attempt to bridge the gap between tradition and modernity by a highly personal appeal. To the extent that these leaders are able to concentrate power in themselves, it might be supposed that they would be in a position to push institutional development and to perform the role of "Great Legislator" or "Founding Father." The reform of corrupt states or the creation of new ones, Machiavelli argued, must be the work of one man alone. A conflict exists, however, between the interests of the individual and the interests of institutionalization. Institutionalization of power means the limitation of power which might otherwise be wielded personally and arbitrarily. The would-be institution-builder needs personal power to create institutions but he cannot create institutions without relinquishing personal power. Resolving this dilemma is not easy. It can be done only by leaders who combine rare political skill and rare devotion to purpose. It was done by Mustafa Kemal who, for almost two decades, managed to maintain his own personal power, to push through major modernizing reforms, and to create a political institution to carry on the government after his death. Atatürk has been a conscious model for many contemporary modernizing leaders, but few, if any, seem likely to duplicate his achievement.

The military junta or military dictatorship is another type of regime common in modernizing countries. It too confronts a distinct set of problems in the conflict between its own impulses to modernization and the needs of institution-building. The military officers who seize power in a modernizing country frequently do so in reaction to the "chaos," "stalemate," "corruption," and "reactionary" character of the civilian regimes which preceded them. The officers are usually passionately devoted to measures of social reform, particularly those which benefit the peasantry (whose interests have frequently been overlooked by the anterior civilian regime). A rationalistic approach to societal problems often makes the officers modernizers par excellence. At the same time, however, they are frequently indifferent or hostile to the needs of political institution-building. The military typically assert that they have taken over the government only temporarily until conditions can be "cleaned up" and authority restored to a purified civilian regime. The officers thus confront an organizational dilemma. They can eliminate or exclude from politics individual civilian politicians, but they are ill-prepared to make fundamental changes in political processes and institutions. If they turn back power to the civilians, the same conditions to which they originally objected tend to reappear (Burma). If they attempt to restore civilian government and to continue in power as a civilian political group (Turkey, South Korea), they open themselves to these same corrupting influences and may pave the way for a second military takeover by a younger generation of colonels who purge the civilianized generals, just as the generals had earlier purged the civilians. Finally, if the military leaders retain power indefinitely, they need to create authoritative political organizations which legitimize and institutionalize their power. Concern with their own personal authority and unfamiliarity with the needs of political institution-building create problems in the fulfillment of this task. It is still too early to say for certain what sort of authoritative political institutions, if any, will be produced by regimes led by military officers such as Nasser and Ayub Khan.

The Primacy of Party

Charismatic leaders and military chiefs have thus had little success in building modern political institutions. The reason lies in the nature of modern politics. In the absence of traditional political institutions, the only modern organization which can become a source of authority and which can be effectively institutionalized is the political party. *The importance of the political party in providing legitimacy and stability in a modernizing political system varies inversely with the institutional inheritance of the system from traditional society.* Traditional systems do not have political parties. Unlike bureaucracy, the party is a distinctly modern form of political organization. Where traditional political institutions (such as monarchies and feudal parliaments) are carried over into the modern era, parties play secondary, supplementary roles in the political system. The other institutions are the primary source of continuity and legitimacy. Parties typically originate within the legislatures and then gradually extend themselves into society. They adapt themselves to the existing framework of the political system and typically reflect in their own operations the organizational and procedural principles embodied in that system. They broaden participation in the traditional institutions, thus adapting those institutions to the requirements of the modern polity. They help make the traditional institutions legitimate in terms of popular sovereignty, but they are not themselves a source of legitimacy. Their own legitimacy derives from the contributions they make to the political system.

Where traditional political institutions collapse or are weak or nonexistent, the role of the party is entirely different from what it is in those polities with institutional continuity. In such situations, strong party organization is the only long-run alternative to the instability of a corrupt or praetorian or mass society. The party is not just a supplementary organization; it is instead the source of legitimacy and authority. In the absence of traditional sources of legitimacy, legitimacy is sought in ideological, charisma, popular sovereignty. To be lasting, each of these principles of legitimacy must be embodied in a party. Instead of the party reflecting the state, the state becomes the creation of the party and the instrument of the party. The actions of government are legitimate to the extent that they reflect the will of the party. The party is the source of legitimacy because it is the institutional embodiment of national sovereignty, the popular will, or the dictatorship of the proletariat.

Where traditional political institutions are weak or non-existent, the prerequisite of stability is at least one highly institutionalized political party. States with one such party are markedly more stable than states which lack such a party. States with no parties or many weak parties are the least stable. Where traditional political institutions are smashed by revolution, post-revolutionary order depends on the emergence of one strong party: witness the otherwise very different histories of the Chinese, Mexican, Russian, and Turkish revolutions. Where new states emerge from colonialism with one strong party, the problem is to maintain the strength of that party. In many African countries the nationalist party was the single important modern organization to exist before independence. The party "was generally well organized. The conditions of the political struggle and the dedication of the top elite to the party as the prime instrument of political change led the elite to give the major portion of their energies and resources to building a solid, responsive organization capable of disciplined action in response to directives from the top and able to ferret out and exploit feelings of dissatisfaction among the masses for political ends."[7] After independence, however, the dominant political party is often weakened by the many competing demands on organizational resources. A marked dispersion of resources means a decline in the overall level of political institutionalization. "Talents that once were available for the crucial work of party organization," one observer has warned, "may now be preoccupied with running a ministry or government bureau. . . . Unless new sources of loyal organizational and administrative talents can be found immediately, the party's organization—and, therefore, the major link between the regime and the masses—is likely to be weakened."[8]

The need for concentration applies not only to the allocation of resources among types of organizations but also to the scope of organization. In many modernizing countries, the political leaders attempt too much too fast; they try to build mass organizations when they should concentrate on elite organizations. Organizations do not have to be large to be effective and to play a crucial role in the political process: the Bolshevik Party in 1917 is one example; the Indian Civil Service (which numbered only 1,157 men at independence) is another. Overextension of one's resources in organization-building is as dangerous as overextension of one's troops in a military campaign. (The strategic hamlet program in South Vietnam is an example of both.) Concentration is a key principle of politics as well as strategy. The pressures for broad organizational support, however, seem to push towards the all-inclusive organization. In his efforts to create a political structure to bolster his military regime in Egypt, for instance, Nasser first created the Liberation

Rally in 1953, which soon came to have from 5 to 6 million members. The organization was simply too big to be effective and to achieve its purpose. After the adoption of a new constitution in 1956, the Liberation Rally was replaced by the National Union, which was designed to be the school of the nation and also to be universal in membership (except for reactionaries). Again the organization was too broad to be effective. Hence in 1962, after the break with Syria, a new organization, the Arab Socialist Union, was organized with the advice of organizational and ideological experts from Yugoslavia. It was designed to be a more exclusive, more tightly organized body, its membership limited to 10 per cent of the population. Inevitably, however, it also mushroomed in size, and after two years it had 5 million members. In a fourth effort, early in 1964 President Nasser reportedly formed still another group limited to only 4,000 members and called the "Government Party," which would form the core of the Arab Socialist Union. The new organization was to be designed by Nasser "to enforce a peaceful transfer of power and a continuation of his policies if anything happens to him."[9] Whether this organization, unlike its predecessors, becomes an institution remains to be seen. Its likelihood of success depends upon its limitation in size.

American social scientists have devoted much attention to the competitiveness of political systems, devising various ways of measuring that competitiveness and classifying systems according to their degree of competitiveness.[10] The more parties which exist within a system, presumably the more competitive it is. Yet the proliferation of

[7] William J. Foltz, "Building the Newest Nations: Short-Run Strategies and Long-Run Problems," in Deutsch and Foltz, eds., *Nation-Building*, 121.

[8] *Ibid.*, 123–24.

[9] *Washington Post*, February 9, 1964, p. A-17.

[10] See James S. Coleman, in Almond and Coleman, eds., *Politics of the Developing Areas*, Conclusion; Phillips Cutright, "National Political Development: Its Measurement and Social Correlates," in Nelson W. Polsby, Robert A. Dentler, and Paul A. Smith, eds., *Politics and Social Life* (Boston 1963), 569–82; von der Mehden, *Politics of the Developing Nations*, 54–64.

parties usually means the dispersion of organization and leadership talents and the existence of a large number of weak parties. If sufficient resources are available to support more than one well-organized party, this is all to the good. But most modernizing countries will be well off if they can create just one strong party organization. *In modernizing systems, party institutionalization usually varies inversely with party competitiveness.* Modernizing states with multiparty systems are much more unstable and prone to military intervention than modernizing states with one party, with one dominant party, or with two parties. The most unstable systems and those most prone to military intervention are the multiparty systems and the no-party systems. The weak institutionalization of parties in the multiparty system makes that system extremely fragile. The step from many parties to no parties and from no parties to many parties is an easy one. In their institutional weakness, the no-party system and the multiparty system closely resemble each other.

Table 1. Distribution of Coups and Coup Attempts in Modernizing Countries Since Independence

TYPE OF POLITICAL SYSTEM	NUMBER OF COUNTRIES	COUNTRIES WITH COUPS	
		NUMBER	PER CENT
Communist	3	0	0
One-party	18	2	11
One-party dominant	12	3	25
Two-party	11	5	45
Multiparty	22	15	68
No effective parties	17	14	83

SOURCE: Figures are somewhat revised and adapted from the similar table in Fred R. von der Mehden, *Politics of the Developing Nations* (Englewood Cliffs, N.J., 1964), 65.

THE IMPACT OF PARTIES ON POLITICAL DEVELOPMENT

Myron Weiner and Joseph LaPalombara

It is customary to view parties as institutions or organizations for the expression of

SOURCE: Excerpted from Myron Weiner and Joseph LaPalombara, "The Impact of Parties on Political Development," in Joseph LaPalombara and Myron Weiner (eds.), *Political Parties and Political Development* (Princeton, N.J.: Princeton University Press, 1966), pp. 399–435, using only pp. 399–424. This article constitutes the summary and concluding chapter of the volume.

social and economic interests and as mechanisms involved in both the expression and the management of conflict. The literature on parties, especially on American and British parties, assumes that the political system in which parties operate is accepted by most of the population as legitimate, that the public is loyal to the national state, and that there are more or less accepted relationships between political participants and the state and among the participants themselves. These assumptions are not valid in most of the developing areas today. Moreover, there were points in the evolution of modern states at which such assumptions were not valid there either. It is with such considerations in mind that we will explore the impact of parties themselves on the development of the political system in which they operate.

The term "political development" remains elusive, and we have not attempted any systematic definition. We have sought to isolate selected problems of development concerning which political parties appear to be particularly relevant. Four such problems are: national integration, political participation, legitimacy, and the management of conflict. These problems or crises often arise before political parties emerge and may be significant in shaping the types of parties and party systems established. But here our concern is with the impact of existing parties and party systems on the handling of these problems. This concern with parties and party systems as independent variables reflects our understanding that they are not only the product of their environment but also instruments of organized human action for affecting that environment.

I. Political Participation

This independent influence of parties on their environment is clearly revealed in the study of political participation. Movements or demands for political participation are a characteristic feature of political development. Many of the factors which first lead entre-preneurial classes and the urban middle classes to seek power from aristocratic elites and colonial rulers soon affect the rural classes and the urban working class. Even in developed countries the patterns of participation change as technological innovation destroys some occupations and creates new ones, diminishes the economic and political role of some regions and increases that of others.

Authoritarian governments, by achieving large-scale economic growth while preventing any massive political participation, demonstrate that there is nothing inevitable about the expansion of political participation. But increased urbanization, the growth of mass communications, and the spread of education appear to be accompanied by an increased desire for some forms of political participation; and the amount of force needed by an authoritarian regime for maintaining control over its population is often in direct proportion to the development of this desire.

The establishment of the first party government often creates a wide-spread expectation that individuals can now share in the exercise of political power not by birth but through political skill. Individuals who had been denied opportunities for participation during the pre-party era may now attempt to enter party politics. If, as is typical, the first party government is created after an era of violence, governmental repression and pent-up hostilities, then it is likely that popular demands for participation will increase, not diminish. In recent years one need only point to Viet Nam after the overthrow of President Diem or Japan after 1945 for dramatic examples of participation movements at the close of dictatorial eras. A similar pattern is apparent in many of the political participation movements that characterized Continental Europe in the late nineteenth and early twentieth centuries.

The response of party government to the desire for participation is often erratic as a government wavers between repression and accommodation. Some regimes persue the dictum that repression employed early will reduce the need to exercise force later. Other regimes may at first be accommodating and then, as they become concerned with the growth of violence or the threat new groups make toward the regime, turn to a policy of repression. The style of the response, the tone of day-to-day pronouncements, the cohesion or lack of cohesion within the government or among the new groups are all important considerations in the outcome. One can, however, discern four over-all patterns of response by party governments to the demands of groups for greater political participation: repression, mobililization, limited admission, and full admission into the party system.

REPRESSION

The emergence of party systems does not in itself guarantee that governing elites under party systems will welcome expanded political participation. Motivations underlying such resistance undoubtedly vary and it is not easy to isolate what may be the dominant factor. In Europe, for example, it is clear that resistance to participation of the lower classes and religious dissenters was based on motives as wide-ranging as a crass desire to preserve existing economic stratification systems to lofty ideals concerning the "inalienable" right of the religiously elect to control the reins of power. The great debates on representation that date back to Putney and involve momentous intellectual encounters during the Wars of Religion, the advent of Liberalism and several revolutions in the West cannot be explained away by any single-factor formulation such as the mode of production or desires to maintain intact existing stratification systems.

It seems to us, however, that three sets of factors may be associated with tendencies toward repression, whether they occur historically in the West or presently in the developing areas. The first of these may be identified with the system of values held by the dominant elite that exists when the party system materializes. Whatever the economic, religious, social or other nature of these values, if additional participation is viewed as a threat to their maintenance, one can expect to find a heavy incidence of resistance to additional participation.

The second, and related factor would involve the degree of consensus in the society concerning the place in which the maintenance of a representative system itself would have in a hierarchical system of values. Where the idea of representative government is accorded low priority, as compared to other values held by the elite, we might expect considerable reluctance to accept demands for increased participation. Where, indeed, such demands are viewed as actual threats to superior values, repressive measures would seem to be a natural response. Similarly, where representative government is articulated as the highest value held by the dominant elite, we might expect repression to occur regarding participatory demands made by groups that could be defined as anti-system. This is true not merely of the attitudes of developed countries toward parties of the extreme left or right, but also of many developing countries toward "traditional" groups such as tribes, communal aggregates, religious minorities, etc.

A third factor would be purely psychological: it involves the hypothesis that new elites operating under a party system find it difficult to share with new claimants the political powers they themselves have been able to wrest from preexisting systems. This is a classic pattern about which a great deal has been written. It would include the reactions to additional participation by middle-class groups in a number of European countries. It surely must now include the reactions to participatory demands by Western-educated urban elites in Asia and Africa who are manifestly not prepared to act on the very premises that presumably governed their own thrusts against colonial or other indigenous political powers.

In a very rough way, we might say that the probability of resistance is associated with the proximity between the creation of a party system and increased demand for participation. Where the new elites are immediately challenged by others who wish to share in the exercise of power the probability of repression is much higher than in those places where the waves of demand are spread over a longer time span. One of the unfortunate problems of the developing areas is that the first generation of elites operating under party systems are confronted with participatory demands long before they have had a reasonable opportunity to institutionalize party government.

MOBILIZATION

One-party governments typically handle the demand for political participation differently from parties in a competitive system. It would be historically incorrect, however, to assume that all one-party systems simply cope with participatory demands through repression. Quite often the one-party state welcomes, even encourages, political participation but does so under carefully controlled and prescribed limits. Some scholars have suggested that the term "participation" is inappropriate here and that alternatively one should speak of "controlled participation" or "mobilization." The notion, whatever term is used to describe it, is that the one-party leadership is concerned with affecting the political attitudes and behavior of the population as a whole and uses the instrument of the party, along with the state's repressive powers and a controlled mass media, to achieve this goal. It is equally concerned with providing the appearances of participation without at the same time giving up the control of power generally associated with admitting additional actors into the political system.

As we have seen, the party may seek to develop a sense of national identity and loyalty. The party may also be used by government—and here we are speaking of one of the central functions of the dominant party in a one-party state—as an instrument for legitimizing authority. The governing oligarchy may also seek popular support to ensure its own security, to enhance its image abroad, or simply because it has a populist ideology and believes that popular "participation" is good for its own sake.

The one-party government is therefore typically a device for facilitating mass mobilization while preventing—reverting now to the conventional use of the term— mass "participation." To put it another way, the regime may be concerned with developing a subjective sense of participation while actually preventing the populace from affecting public policy, administration, or the selection of those who will in fact govern.

It is important to note that with respect to actual participation the mass single party is generally quite different from the cadre party found in the Soviet Union, Eastern Europe, and China. The cadre party may actually recruit individuals into government, while membership in the mass party of a one-party state may only marginally increase, if at all, a member's political influence and political career opportunities. In short, some one-party governments may use the party as an instrument of political recruitment as well as a device for the management of the public. These two functions are not always compatible. The mobilist party may open its doors to mass membership as a device for increasing popular support and thereby diminish the need for large-scale repression. But the more mass the party becomes the more it risks the possibility of being "taken over," if you will, by the masses and the elite's commitment to sacrifice the present for some future goals is in danger of being subverted. This dilemma—whether to open membership to mass participation and risk ideological subversion or to keep membership small and emphasize ideological purity at the risk of losing popular support—is inherent in the mobilist single party and helps explain why such parties often fluctuate from one position to another. Thus periods of mass recruitment and free discussion are often followed by purges and ideological tightening as the party elite fears—paradoxically—that mass participation threatens to destroy the revolution.

LIMITED ADMISSION

Governments may permit social groups to organize their own parties but deny them access to national power and restrict their participation in the system. Frequently parties are permitted to organize after a period of government repression, but it is clear to all that under no circumstances will the government allow them to assume power even if they win elections. Throughout the nineteenth century several European countries permitted the organization of socialist parties under such restrictive conditions. Similarly, linguistic and regional parties with separatist demands have been allowed to organize with the understanding that government will neither allow them to take office nor accede to their demands. Throughout Western Europe today communist, facist and monarchist parties are aware that, at least at the national level, they will not easily be allowed to exercise power. The degree of limited admission of course varies. In some countries (e.g. West Germany) fascist and communist parties are presumably outlawed and splinter parties impeded by electoral legislation. In others, however, extreme parties are free to hold power at the local level but effectively barred nationally. In view of "popular front" and similar thrusts by the French and Italian Communist parties, it will be of great interest to observe the conditions under which these parties are permitted to share in the formal exercise of national power. It may be that the price extracted for such participation is an abandonment of millennial goals; it may also be that threats to effective participation on the part of other parties will eventuate in a new combination of forces aimed at dislodging existing elites. In such circumstances, limited admission might well be transformed into some form of repression, and, indeed, there are those who, for the very reasons we discussed above (i.e. the preservation of the representative system itself) would counsel such repressive measures.

It is precisely in prolonged situations of limited admission that we find the development of alienated parties. This pattern, typical of several European countries, may be described as permitting the formation of parties without allowing the meaningful participation in government that the formation of the party itself would imply. Thus the alienated political party which integrates the individual into the party rather than into the society at large is a frequent phenomenon in European politics. Such parties of "social integration," to use Sigmund Neumann's felicitous phrase, publish their own newspapers, provide maternity care, medical attention, funerals, and death benefits for party members and their families. Songs, slogans, and literature are directed at cultivating a sense of loyalty to the party, a social class, or religious group rather than to the nation or to the political system under which they are governed. Forged during an era of political repression, the alienated class, ethnic- or regional-based party develops its own myths and legends. It thus alienates its members from the society at large and may institutionalize such alienation.

FULL ADMISSION INTO THE PARTY SYSTEM

The dominant elite may grant individuals and groups demanding political participation the rights of full participation either through existing parties or through newly formed parties. Among well established democracies, this is the typical response. Precisely how new participant groups are absorbed is conditioned very much by whether the governing party, like the Chinese Communist party, is an ideological or, like the Indian Congress party, an electoral instrument. If the governing party is ideologically oriented, that is, if it is concerned with restructuring the values and behavior of its members and its citizens, then it often restricts its membership to those who share a well-defined outlook. Alternatively, when the party's leadership is primarily concerned with winning elections, its program is likely to be pragmatic and it is likely to modify its program to attract the largest number of people. New participation demands are thus more readily handled by electorally oriented rather than ideologically oriented political parties.

Among some democratic parties the desire for electoral victory is so great that ideological commitments will be reduced in order to achieve victory. The toning down of the ideological elements of British Labour party policy in the 1960's in order to win greater support among the middle classes is well known. The willingness with which the Democratic (and in a few instances the Republican) party in America's urban centers eagerly organized and socialized immigrants from Europe during the early part of the twentieth century is also quite familiar. The competition of American political parties for working-class support eliminated opportunities for distinctively ideologically oriented working-class parties. In contrast the reluctance of the Conservative and Liberal parties of the nineteenth century to appeal to the working class—putting, if you will, ideological concerns over electoral calculations—made it possible for the British Labour party to grow.

In all cases where full participation is permitted, we may assume either that additional participation is not perceived as a serious threat to system maintenance or that the commitment to participation itself is so overriding as to supersede any concern for threats to the system or to highly held values of the dominant elite. It is because neither of these conditions is likely to materialize very often that most of the historical and contemporary examples we can point to fall short of achieving this mode of adaptation or response to the crisis of participation.

We have focused at some length on the crisis of participation because the manner of its resolution strongly influences the nature of the parties and of the party systems that emerge. If the impetus to participate comes from a social class, such as the industrial workers or agricultural peasants, and it is opposed or repressed, we can expect class-based parties to emerge; if the demand for participation is geographically based, or reflects a desire for previously denied participation on the part of a religious or ethnic minority, the failure to gradually absorb leaders of such groups into the prevailing system will almost certainly give rise to political parties that reflect these narrow impulses to organization. Moreover, the organization of one party with a relatively narrow base often leads to organizational countermeasures and a proliferation of parties. Socialist parties spur the conservatives and middle class to greater organizational activities; the crystallization of one religiously based party will give rise to others of the same general variety; and workers' parties serve to activate the farmers. As these groups successfully vie for a place in the seats of power and policy they devise electoral systems that facilitate rather than impede this kind of proliferation. Thus, while proportional representation does not *cause* a multi-party system, it most certainly both reflects political fragmentation and helps to maintain it intact. Given the basically unlimited number of ways in which a society can be divided in conflict, it is the two-party system that seems to represent the logical aberration. Whether a two-party arrangement is to have any chance at all of materializing depends in strong measure on the manner in which the participation crisis is handled.

II. Legitimacy

The early phases of party development are almost always accompanied by a problem of legitimizing authority. The first party government in a nation, typically replacing an aristocratic oligarchy, royal authority, a colonial bureaucracy, or a military praetorian rule, must find some basis for legitimizing its new authority in order to win popular support not only for the new government but also for the new *system* of government. While the colonial regime justified its authority on the basis of efficiency and order, royal authority on the basis of religious sanction, longevity, and sheer pomp, and a military government on the basis of its masculine prowess or the charisma of its leader, a party government typically seeks to sanctify popular government and to associate itself with the populace. In fact even the one-party state typically claims the mantle of democracy—that is of popular rule—though a small oligarchy unaccountable for its actions may be in actual control of government.

The early phase of any new system of government, always a period of uncertainty and instability, is especially problematical for party systems if only because the number of participants, and therefore the number of people who must learn the rules, is so much greater than in other kinds of political systems. The instabilities commonly found in the developing areas therefore are not simply a concomitant of rapid social and economic changes but rather the result of establishing new political systems that involve new patterns of political participation. Many new nations experiencing no significant economic or social changes are in the throes of political uncertainty while countries with well established political systems are experiencing rapid socio-economic changes with little political turmoil.

It is for this reason that there is a lack of commitment to newly established governments in most of the developing areas today. There is some evidence to suggest, however, that systems without parties and those with a multiplicity of parties have been among the least successful in establishing a sense of legitimacy.[1] Thus far one-party regimes have been more durable than competitive party systems, but we need a longer period before we can draw any definite conclusions. Multiparty systems have also experienced a substantial number of coups,

but we would suggest that the proliferation of parties in most of the multiparty systems in an indication of the lack of consensus, not a cause. One-party dominant systems (such as the noncompetitive Mexican system and the competitive Indian system) or competitive two-party systems (such as the Philippines and Ceylon) have thus far proved somewhat more durable.

The difficulty which newly established competitive party systems have had in establishing their legitimacy is strongly attested by attempts, successful or otherwise, to overthrow such systems. Instabilities, such as attempted coups, are of course not unknown in the West, as eloquently illustrated by the histories of France and Italy in the nineteenth century, and of Eastern Europe following the breakdown of the Hapsburg and Ottoman Empires. This fragility of party systems, nevertheless, is much more evident in the turbulent histories of Latin American countries in the nineteenth and twentieth centuries and particularly in the more recent evolutions of Asian and African countries that have moved from colonial to independent status.

During the early phases of party development it is common for preexisting political groups—a landed aristocracy or a military elite—to continue to exercise a considerable emotional hold on large sections of the populace. This is especially common in political systems in which parties are largely outgrowths of changes in urban areas, are based primarily on urban support, and are confronted by rual support for the military or landed oligarchy (Japan in the 1920's). But there are also instances in which a rural-based party system, as Bulgaria had in the 1920's and Turkey in the 1950's, is overthrown by an urban supported military. Perhaps the fundamental issue is how widely accepted is the party system throughout the society? To what extent does each major social group view one or more parties as appropriate and adequate vehicles for satisfying their interests? In short, is the party system legitimated?

[1] Some evidence, based upon an analysis of coups among different types of political systems in the developing nations, is suggested by Fred R. von der Mehden, in *Politics of the Developing Nations*, Englewood Cliffs, N.J.: Prentice-Hall, 1964, p. 65.

As we have noted, some parties are themselves not committed to the maintenance of representative government but participate in competitive politics only in order to overthrow the system. Such parties may in fact be associated with the military, the aristocracy, or insurgency groups seeking to destroy the system. Under such circumstances a fundamental issue in many representative governments is whether to admit nondemocratic parties into government (in coalitions, for example) with a high risk that the system may be subverted, or deny them the opportunity for sharing or influencing power, thereby ensuring that such groups will continue to remain alienated and that they will strengthen their efforts to convince supporters that the system does not work precisely because it does not permit them to share power.

The task of establishing a sense of legitimacy for a competitive party system is still further complicated by the general lack of cohesion found in most newly established party governments. While the colonial and aristocratic governments which they displaced may have been unpopular, they often presented to the outsider at least the appearance of cohesiveness. Thus the ideal of united authority that does not publicly bare its disagreements and that masks from the public elements of personal ambitions, corruption, and shabby behavior persists into an era when politics becomes competitive and seems to the public to be disorganized. The shift in public attitudes thus typically lags behind the shift in the nature of the political system. Legitimacy is thus impeded because, in becoming more visible, representative government appears to be a step backward from the image of government associated with colonialism. Thus, since parties often establish themselves through the use of patronage, the opponents of competitive politics can often win popular support for steps to return to oligarchical authority by denouncing unpopular patronage politics.

The problem of legitimacy is further com-plicated by the fact that the early founders of party systems are not themselves necessarily committed to representative government. In many instances parties were created as a device solely for rallying large numbers of people against a foreign government or one dominated by a small social class. The urban middle class that created the parties (or the nationalist movement which precedes parties) was often more concerned with expelling the colonial rulers than in establishing open, competitive, representative government, or in rallying popular support for such a governmental system. The new government may thus take no steps to persuade the public as a whole, or the army, that representative government per se is desirable. Newly formed parties in a newly established party system may be reluctant to test their popular support through free elections; they may take steps to prevent certain social groups from participating in party politics, thereby forcing such groups to find extralegal ways of winning influence or power. Many early party governments are unable to provide leadership which can sustain support within their own party or in the country at large; the qualities which make men effective militant leaders of a nationalist movement are not necessarily the same qualities making for effective leadership of a parliamentary government. Moreover, since there may not be a second-string leadership capable of running ministries and effectively making the governmental machinery work, relations between the new party government and the old bureaucracy—particularly if there is a well-established bureaucracy at work—may be strained, and the bureaucracy itself may undermine efforts to make the system of representative government work.

However, with all of these difficulties, parties have been an important and on the whole successful instrument for establishing legitimate national authority. In general they are more flexible instruments for winning popular support than are armies and bureaucracies—a principal reason why an authoritarian government often organizes a political party. A government-supported party can give government credit for successes while blaming the bureaucracy for its failures. Without responsibility for day-to-day administration, party cadres have more flexibility than bureaucrats for organizing the populace to support government.

The mobilist single party is often as concerned with its image abroad as it is with developing a sense of legitimacy at home. The populist ideologies of Nkrumah and Nasser serve to strengthen the efforts of Ghana and Egypt to extend their influence through Sub-Sahara Africa and the Middle East. Popular demonstrations against foreign "imperialists," attacks against embassies, mass rallies to which the foreign press is invited, and popular plebiscites serve to enhance foreign policy goals as well as to create a sense of popular support at home which intimidates would-be opponents.

But the fundamental issue is not whether government wins popular support, but whether legitimacy with respect to the system is established. After all, an unpopular government may hold power in a system widely accepted by the populace as legitimate (kingship may not be challenged, but a particular king may). Alternatively, a government may be so concerned with its own popularity that it fails to take measures to make the system itself legitimate. A charismatic leader may successfully retain popular support but fail to take steps to institutionalize a new political system.

Perhaps one useful way of observing the legitimacy of a system, in the absence of either full elections or survey data, is to observe the succession process. How is leadership transferred from one man to another, from one generation to another, and most difficult of all, from one party to another? The succession process is a useful checkpoint for looking at the question of legitimacy because when power is transferred, individuals within the system are forced to decide whether their loyalties are confined to those who, up to that point, have exercised authority or to the system of government itself.

The first test of the system often takes place when power is transferred from one leader to another within the same political party—the transference of authority from Washington to Adams, from Lenin to Stalin, from Nehru to Shastri, and from Ataturk to Inonu. The problem of transferring leadership from one individual to another is especially acute in political systems where charisma plays an important role. The attention given by the founding father to the institutionalization of his authority—what Weber referred to as the routinization of charisma—may be a critical factor in how legitimate the party and governmental system becomes. In the Indian case, for example, Nehru chose to work within the framework of parliamentary rule even when it did not suit his immediate needs and however much he dominated the Congress party. The result was that, though his successor could not be predicted with great confidence only months before his death, the procedures for selecting a new Prime Minister were well known and accepted. The problem of tansferring authority from charismatic to non-charismatic leaders, or, to put it another way, the problem of learning how to exercise power without charisma, depends very much upon the establishment of accepted procedures within the governing party. One can find a similar pattern in Turkey when power was transferred from Ataturk to Inonu.

The transference of power from one party to another, especially the first such transfer that occurs within a party system, is often the critical testing point for the legitimacy of the system. In the United States, the election of 1800 provides a striking example of peaceful transition. It was facilitated by an underlying consensus—implying a very high place for the representative system itself in the elite's hierarchy of values.

Similar patterns are very rare in other parts of the world, as Rustow's discussion of Turkey attests. The notion of representation, which underlies the behavior of American parties, appears to be absent through most of the Middle East. In 1945, Ataturk's successor Inonu agreed to transform Turkey's one-party state to a competitive system. In the absence of a near universal commitment to representative government—irrespective of the policies pursued by the winning party—the attempt failed. A victorious rural-based Democratic party (later the Justice party) was overthrown by a military coup as the educated, secular, urban middle classes found unacceptable a party which sought to modify secularism, was rural based, and appeared to lack a commitment to full-scale modernization.

As far as the new nations are concerned only a few have thus far been confronted with the issue of transferring power, and it is not clear yet whether those with parties will be more successful than those without, and whether countries with only one party will be more successful than those with several. The data on coups, however, suggests that new nations totally devoid of parties rarely reach the point where succession is an orderly process. There is moreover a prima facie case for suggesting that countries with at least one effective governing party are more likely to deal successfully with the problem of succession than are countries where parties are not present. Parties, even in totalitarian systems, are experienced in the art of internal elections while bureaucrats and military officers are accustomed to a process of selection and promotion by higher officials. Governing juntas of bureaucrats and military men are thus rarely prepared for the politics of peacefully electing their own leader or of having leadership peacefully pass from one person to another.

How well the new nations can handle the transfer of power from one party to another is even more a matter of conjecture.

There is reason to think that as difficult as the transfer is from one party to another during the early phases of a competitive system, it may prove to be even more difficult if the transfer must be made from a party in an authoritarian state to a party in a competitive system. For in the first instance the transfer of power involves legitimizing an existing system, while in the second, it simultaneously means establishing a new political system. The Turkish case thus raises the fundamental question of how a tutelary system can "prepare" a nation for democratic rule. That a tutelary government can be an instrument for establishing effective central authority there can be little doubt; but whether the attitudes of mind, the tolerance for widely divergent views, and the readiness to see one's opponents in office can be cultivated seems unlikely in the atmosphere of an authoritarian regime.

III. National Integration

. . . For some [the concept of integration] involves primarily the amalgamation of disparate social, economic, religious, ethnic, and geographic elements into a single nation-state. This kind of national integration implies both the capacity of a government to control the territory under its jurisdiction as well as a set of popular attitudes toward the nation generally described as loyalty, allegiance, and a willingness to place national above local or parochial concerns. For other scholars integration means the regularization of structures and processes whereby the discrete elements in a given national territory are brought into meaningful participation in the political system. Whether these processes are regularized and understood by participants to be legitimate can be defined as process integration as opposed to national integration.

Although these forms of integration are closely related, they can and should be analytically separated because empirical cases suggest that one can have one form of integration without the other. Kirchheimer[2] points out, for example, that France achieved national integration several centuries ago, but that process integration still remains imperfectly established. And Rokkan's analysis[3] of Norway shows that long after the nation-state has come to be accepted by a population there may still remain the task of establishing a national political process involving the rural as well as urban population.

The striking thing about several European countries is that the crisis of national integration was reasonably resolved sometime before political parties made their appearance. British political parties of the nineteenth century did not have to confront the issue of nationhood. Nor did the parties of France, Sweden, Norway, and Holland. This was not the case with Germany, Belgium, Switzerland and even less so with Italy where the crises of nationhood and national identity were mismanaged by elites at the time of unification and remained loads the party systems of these nations had to face at the end of the First World War.

An important justification for single-party systems in many new nations, especially in Africa, is that they are essential for the establishment of national integration. There is some historical evidence from Europe to support this position. German unification was achieved largely under the aegis of the Iron Chancellor and the Liberals, often at the cost of dealing rather ruthlessly with religious and social groups, and Italy was "Piedmontized" under Cavour and his successors in the Liberal party. But in both instances a national bureaucracy and army were the major instruments for national unification. One could argue that parties were complementary, perhaps even necessary elements,

but not sufficient conditions for national integration.

In most new nations of Asia and Africa, governing political parties are concerned with two elements of national integration—the issue of control over the nation's territory and the issue of subjective loyalties. In one-party authoritarian states, the government generally justifies the suppression of tribal, religious, and regional parties on the grounds that their very existence constitutes a threat to the nation's territorial integrity. And in competitive as well as in authoritarian party systems, the governing party tends to be concerned with evoking national symbols so as to facilitate the development of a sense of national loyalty. As one leader of Italy's Risorgimento put it after national unification had been achieved, "Fatta l'Italia, bisogna fare gli Italiani"— having made Italy, we must now make Italians. The same refrain can be found in Ghana, Nigeria, Pakistan, and a host of other new nations with heterogeneous cultural and social systems.

It is certainly understandable why single-party patterns grow out of protracted movements for independence and the associated need for a sense of national identity. Where African parties are not narrowly based on tribe, religious, or regional foundations they have helped bring about a sense of national consciousness, if not in the countryside, at least in the urban centers and if not among peasants, at least among large segments of the educated elite. Moreover, one can point out that countries without a single national party reaching geographically into all corners of the territory have often bordered on internal disintegration and violence. Nigeria and Ceylon come readily to mind. Were the Congo, for example, to have a single national party the prospects for national integration would be considerably enhanced. Reflecting on the proliferation of political parties with anti-national loyalties in Africa, Emerson[4] is

[2] Otto Kirchheimer, "The Transformation of the Western European Party System," in LaPalombara and Weiner, *ibid.*

[3] Stein Rokkan, "Electoral Mobilization, Party Competition, and National Integration," in LaPalombara and Weiner, *ibid.*

[4] Rupert Emerson, "Parties and National Integration in Africa," in La Palombara and Weiner, *ibid.*

moved to conclude that while a one-party system is no guarantee of national unity, it is likely in most instances to be better adapted to this mission than would be two or more parties.

There are, however, some shortcomings of one-party systems as an integrating force. In one-party systems the government and party tend to become indistinguishable. As Wallerstein[5] puts it, the party becomes "governmentalized," party work diminishes as leaders assume bureaucratic roles, the party itself loses its effectiveness as an instrument of political participation and recruitment, and party leaders may even become aligned with traditional elites at the price of sacrificing the goals of modernization. Where the party and government are indistinguishable, there tends to be no buffer between the formulation of public policy and its application. The mediating influence of the party is lost, and in the process the party loses much of its ability to interpret government to people and people to power holders. Loyalty to the nation is equated with loyalty to the party and disaffection from the party may mean disaffection both from the national state and from the political process itself. The difficulties of achieving any kind of integration beyond the territorial is enormously complicated by such a pattern.

Which kind of party system exists may affect (and in turn be affected by) the strategy pursued by government in its quest for national integration. Governments may seek to merge the distinctive cultural traits of minority communities into some kind of "national" culture, usually that of the dominant cultural group, or alternatively, may seek a policy of "unity in diversity," politically characterized by "ethnic arithmetic" with the aim of establishing national loyalties without eliminating subordinate cultures. Where this policy of political unity and cultural diversity is pursued,

[5] Immanuel Wallerstein, "The Decline of the Party in Single-Party African States," in LaPalombara and Weiner, *ibid.*

government is more likely to be tolerant of minority parties than when an assimilationist policy is pursued.

The possibilities of the emergence of a single unifying party which reaches into all portions of the country depends too upon the nature and extent of cleavage within the social system. We must look for the scope and intensity of religious differences, ethnic fragmentation, hostility between traditional and modernizing groups, conflict between urban and rural centers, and opposing ideologies. Where a great number of cleavages such as these exist, without the mitigating element of overlapping and cross-cutting cleavages, then it is particularly difficult for any one party to recruit on the basis of appeals that cut across the country. Indeed, frequently political parties associated with such fragmented cultures have no intention of facilitating integration but aim instead at reinforcing the subcultures with which they are identified.

Striking examples of the negative consequences of extreme party pluralism in Europe, based upon religious, regional, class, and ideological cleavages, would be the French Fourth Republic, Weimar Germany, and contemporary Italy. In France neither the Socialists nor the Communists sought to integrate their followers into the existing system. The trauma experienced by the Socialists when a few of their leaders joined a bourgeois government needs no recounting here. It is typical of this hostility toward existing institutions that in Italy it was fully seventy years before Italian Socialists voted to join in the responsibility of government—and only after an emotional appeal by Pietro Nenni, who asked that the madness of 1922 which helped bring the Fascists to power not be repeated.

Whatever integration these mass parties intended was restricted to their own ranks. Their goal was to provide—through auxiliaries—for all of the occupational, social, recreational, professional, associational, and religious needs of their members. Even when such parties have sought to expand their membership to other social or religious groups, the deep cleavages we have nated have proven to be an impediment. Thus, the ability of Italy's Christian Democratic party to expand its base is strongly limited by the party's essentially denominational character. Similarly, Socialist party prospects for expanding in Catholic countries are inhibited by disagreements over such issues as public support for parochial education. Where secular attitudes might appear to be a basis for uniting non-Catholic parties, violent ideological disagreements over economic systems inhibit such a fusion of forces.

Even within some parties organized at a national level there remain manifestations of parochialism that tend to make the party a disintegrative and paralyzing influence in politics. The widespread Latin American pattern is one in which parties impede communications, continuing to serve as instruments of notables who use the parties not to achieve integration but to preserve the status quo. It is significant that the generally most effective parties on that continent are those created and designed to preserve traditional interests and to impede modernization. Thus far cleavage has been relatively contained since parties and government have often been controlled by restricted elites associated with great families, church, military, and bureaucracy. But the increase in political participation now taking place in much of Latin America suggests that further party development will not cut across the existing lines of cleavage but will rather exacerbate and rigidify them, perhaps along patterns typical of southern Europe. We might expect similar fragmentation and proliferation of parties to occur in Africa and Asia where the forces of tribalism, casteism, traditionalism, parochial autonomy, religious variations, and diverse social and economic affiliations are particularly powerful.

It is partly the awareness of the fragility of nationhood and of the centrifugal forces now held in precarious check that leads many leaders of Asian and African countries to advocate single-party rather than competitive-party solutions. When the bureaucratic and military establishment is not well developed or united on a national basis, it is quite common for the nationalist movement to assume what are customarily thought of as governmental functions. But beyond the task of guaranteeing territorial integration—no small matter in many new nations—the single-party pattern, as we have noted, may make attitudinal integration difficult. It may be, as some African leaders claim, that some one-party formulas can be evolved which will facilitate attitudinal integration and a sense of political efficacy. It has been suggested, for example, that factional conflicts within parties may serve the same functions as inter-party competition.

The argument for competition, either within or between parties, has rested largely on the case for democratic values, but competitive-party systems may also facilitate national integration. In competitive systems, political leaders must pay more than lip service to the need for national integration and must do more than seek national symbols, for they must also formulate policies which will amalgamate parochial and national interests. The ruthless adoption of a single language, for example, in a multilingual country may be a successful long-term device for national integration if all dissident elements can be held in check until they, or their descendants, learn the new language. But alternatively, national integration may also be achieved through complicated language formulas arrived at through elaborate negotiations and bargaining. One way of coping with social diversity is to use forceful means to suppress and eradicate it; another is to search out institutional arrangements that will encourage dialogue, unblock communications channels, keep political and governmental leaders on their toes, facilitate the articulation and aggregation of conflicting interests and in these ways create a sense of political efficacy while building national unity out of ethnic diversity.

IV. Conflict Management

Parties as independent factors influencing political participation, legitimacy, and integration direct our attention to problems that are generally viewed in long-range perspective. On a day-to-day basis, however, the essence of politics seems to us to be the management of conflict, that is, the ability of a political system to manage constantly shifting kinds and degrees of demands that are made on it. It seems appropriate, therefore, to examine the role of political parties in handling this vital and universal standard against which any political system should be judged.

How well parties relate to the problems of conflict management will obviously be affected in part by some of the conditioning variables we have already explored. Societal cleavages, for example, may bo so basic and intense as to make open and peaceful conflict by political parties difficult. Since this is particularly the case where cleavages are ideological and translated into competing parties that are fundamentally anti-system, it is reasonable to suggest that ideological parties are less able than pragmatic or "brokerage" parties to handle conflict effectively. Following from this would be the suggestion that in competitive systems the ideological-hegemonic and the ideological-turnover systems are less able to cope (short of repressive measures) with conflicts than either pragmatic-trurnover or pragmatic-hegemonic systems. From the vantage point of political stability, the ideal situation would appear to be one of pragmatic-turnover.

We should not exclude the possibility that parties reflecting ideological or other societal cleavages cannot effectively manage conflict. A federal structure such as in Nigeria, for example, may facilitate national-level bargaining—and even toleration of hegemonic control at that level in

exchange for political power exercised by minority parties over territorial subdivisions. In Austria there is an accommodation between Catholics and Socialists who are divided on both religious and ideological grounds. In Holland religious cleavage dividing Calvinists and Catholics was eventually reflected in political parties that reached a working accommodation at the national level.

Even where the formal structure is unitary, the prospect of sharing in the exercise of power may moderate the rigidity of ideological parties—even anti-system parties—and make them more willing to participate in bargaining relationships at the national level. Note in this regard Sartori's remark[6] that the Italian Communist party has all the power it needs below the level at which power corrupts. The fact is that Italian Communists have not had to face with frustration and despair the prospect of never sharing in the exercise of political power. Below the national level thousands of Communist leaders hold elective and appointive office. While this has not served to make the P.C.I. a willing participant in national conflict resolution it has dulled the cutting edge of the party's anti-systemic drive.

It may be, therefore, that when basic societal cleavages lead to the creation of ideological or sectional parties, one way to cope with this problem (and therefore to facilitate conflict management) is to provide some means whereby power may be shared. One does not have to predicate a decline in ideology in order to see the application here of the familiar observation that there is more in common between two deputies one of whom is a revolutionary than between two revolutionaries one of whom is a deputy.

There are of course alternative ways of coping with the multiplicity of parties that emerge from deeply fragmented societies.

[6] Giovanni Sartori, "European Political Parties: The Case of Polarized Pluralism," in LaPalombara and Weiner, *ibid.*

Government can prevent the appearance of more than one party. When carried to its typical conclusion, this response involves not merely a repression of opposition parties but also establishing tight party control over (or eliminating) secondary associations. In a few pluralistic one-party systems in Africa secondary associations under the aegis of the dominant party are tolerated. But typically, secondary association leaders are under extreme cross-pressure and tend to identify with the unit—in this case the single party—that is more powerful. Evidence also shows that few single-party leaders practice the toleration of dissent that they may preach. Witness on this point Wallerstein's comments[7] about the second thoughts of African leaders regarding the degree of autonomy to be accorded party auxiliary organizations.

The quality of political party leadership or, more precisely, the attitudes and skills of party leadership are an important element in how conflict is managed. As we reflect on the early history of the United States, political leadership skills loom as critically important in the management of conflict; even then it is well to remember that several decades of bargaining and compromise were followed by a civil war. Nonetheless, it is important to note in the developing areas that a handful of men concerned with finding solutions to apparently intractable disputes can maintain a stable system. The success of Malaysia's Alliance party in hammering out a working relationship among the three major ethnic groups must in some measure be attributed to skilled leadership, even if the successful experience proved unfortunately to be temporary. In attempting to assess the probable impact of any party system on the management of conflict, it is essential to know something of leadership style, the degree of tolerance, the measure of trust, and the degree to which leaders are capable of making realistic assessments of the behavior of other people in the system.

[7] *Op. cit.*

The background and experience of party leadership in dealing with conflict is of course important. The memories of past conflicts often condition current behavior. Individuals brought up in a political system in which coups, assassinations, political arrests, and underground movements have existed will not readily move to a political style emphasizing peaceful and rational discussion. Violent nationalist movements —particularly where the violence was directed at competing countrymen as well as against colonial rulers—do not generally produce a bargaining, pragmatic leadership style. With few exceptions the party leaders of the developing states seem ill-prepared to respond in peaceful ways both to pressures from below and to pressures from potential counter-elites.

Broad-based parties which openly recruit are often most likely to be torn by internal conflict, for the more open the party is the more it mirrors the cleavages within the society at large. On the other hand, by penetrating to regional and local levels and by admitting ethnic minorities and dissident elites, the governing party opens the possibility of providing satisfactions to divergent groups and providing opportunities for the settlement of disputes at lower levels within the system. Insofar as disputes are settled at the level of local government or within the local unit of the party, the loads on the national party and national government for the settlement of dispute are thereby reduced. In India for example, the presence of a decentralized broad-based Congress party functioning in a federal system has meant that disputes could be fought out at the local and state level without endangering the stability of the central government. In contrast, the absence of an acceptable procedure for the settlement of inter-island conflict within Indonesia culminated in the eruption of a civil struggle.

The costs of failure are still another factor affecting the capacity of parties to reconcile conflicts. If a defeated politician has no alternate occupation, no alternate source of income, no alternate rewards than politics, there may be an uncompromising desperate style to his politics. In contrast a politician who knows that if he is defeated within the party, or defeated by the opposition, he may move into the House of Lords, become an Ambassador, run for a lesser office, or return to a lucrative law practice, can afford to accept political defeat with some grace. These differences may help account for the violence which characterizes politics in many of the new nations. In this connection it is important to note the function played by honorific positions of status without power as an outlet for defeated politicians. Powerless upper houses in bicameral systems are not without their purpose.

The role of parties and party systems in conflict management will also be affected by their relationship to governmental structures. One will want to know therefore whether a single party—or the governing party or parties of a competitive system— does in fact control other sectors of government such as the bureaucracy, and whether or not such control is balanced. For both too little and too much party control would appear to be a defective situation in so far as conflict management is concerned.

On the lack of control side, the Latin American situation is particularly striking. In some instances the short- and long-range policy processes are hamstrung by the absence of a party system capable of performing certain input functions. Thus the party system may be unavailable either for articulating and aggregating interest or for assisting in the legitimation of public policy output. However, the separation of parties from governmental elites such as the executive, bureaucracy, and military is such that the latter groups can operate pretty much as they choose, unchecked by the need to come to terms with the wishes or demands of parties.

Western political systems, however, provide some strikingly dissimilar examples of the consequences incident to a failure of the party system to achieve adequate control over the bureaucracy. Weimar Germany is often cited as a telling case of the disruptive impact of a bureaucracy opposed to a particular political system and more or less committed to undermining it. Similarly, major crises in the history of the French Third Republic revealed situations in which the threat of political disintegration grew out of the lack of political party attention to the need for taming the military and the civil bureaucracy.

Theoretically, party control of the bureaucracy in competitive systems can also go too far, thus impeding effective conflict management. The typical situation would be a hegemonic system (ideological or pragmatic, although more so when ideological) in which extended control by one or several parties results in a colonization of the bureaucracy. In party coalition situations, the hegemonic group members tend to cut up the national bureaucracy into so many feudal holdings. Recruitment and promotion in each of these feudal sectors then tends to rest on particularistic party criteria. The application of policy in each sector then tends to rest on party rather then national considerations and apparent decisions, and compromises reached among coalition members in the legislative arena are subjected to distortion and fragmentation in the administrative sector.

Where a single party enjoys hegemonic control in competitive systems, the threat of political colonization is even greater. Where it occurs—as in Italy since the Second World War under the Christian Democrats —the ability of the bureaucratic sector to aggregate demands on the basis of a national interest is severely curtailed. Loyalty to, even membership in, the hegemonic party becomes a critical determinant of bureaucratic promotion. Interest groups outside the party's pale will have less opportunity to articulate their views to bureaucratic decision-makers; indeed, outside groups may even be denied access to these latter. Such groups, and the general public, come to view the bureaucracy as indistinguishable from the dominant party and therefore unable or unwilling to act as an impartial implementer of public policy or arbiter among conflicting groups. Rather than serve to reduce tensions (particularly in societies of deep cleavage) this pattern intensifies them. The hobbling effect on parties and conflict management engendered by extreme governmental autonomy is matched by extreme politicization. Needless to say, the problems incident to this second configuration are greatly augmented when single-party alternatives emerge in the more developed systems.

In colonial areas, where the state apparatus was strong, nationalist parties often developed as parallel governments, taking on at the local level certain functions of police, administration, education, and welfare. The party might continue to perform some of these functions following independence but it could not in fact become a substitute for government. If the inherited administrative structures left by colonialism are extremely weak—Guinea is a good example—the line between party and government may be quite blurred and the party will take on almost the whole spectrum of activities that in most societies are considered to be governmental functions. An invariable consequence is that the existing bureaucratic structures become politicized by the dominant party—and possibly that the full force of governmental apparatus can be used to prevent further democratic development.

However, the question of proper balance is not an easy one to deal with. The legacy in many ex-colonial areas is clearly that the strongest unit within the political system turns out to be an entrenched civil and military bureaucracy with its own elite, its own views regarding the new nation's destiny, its own wishes regarding both the priorities and tempo of national development. Where the bureaucracy is strong, while the executive branches are new and not yet deeply entrenched, and the political parties are essentially weak, ideal conditions exist for the domination of the new states by the public bureaucrats. Such bureaucracies are capable of stifling the growth of a democratic infra-structure by making interest groups deeply dependent on the bureaucracy for survival and therefore little more than the bureaucracy's instrumentalities.

Strong bureaucrats, then, can become significant competing elites to the political party leadership. In many of the newly independent areas the bureaucracy has been hostile to the ideology and program of political parties and has often tried to undercut governmental programs or in extreme cases taken steps to destroy the party system. The bureaucracy, as was the case of Japan after the restoration, may see itself as the bearer of economic modernization, national integration, and political order and view political parties as expressions of parochial loyalties, personal ambition, and disorder. Its trenchant opposition to the parties may seriously impede pluralistic political development or actually bring about one variety or another of the one-party systems discussed earlier.

In a sense a strong bureaucracy (including the military) may set standards for the performance of the party system, and if the latter drastically fails to come up to these standards the bureaucrats—military and/or civil—may move to take control of the system. It is this pattern of political development that now characterizes places such as Libya, Egypt, the Sudan, Burma, and Pakistan. If the potential for military takeovers appears greater in the Middle East and Southern Asia than in sub-Sahara Africa, perhaps it is because in the former instances a legacy of strong military establishments was left by the colonial rulers, while in the latter areas the military was very small or almost totally non-African.

Finally, since we are speaking of balance of power among emergent parties and authoritative governmental structures, it is necessary to note that in many developing areas a dominant or single party may well succeed in politicizing the bureaucracy. Whether, where such fusion occurs, the party has absorbed the bureaucracy or vice versa is an open question. The point is that here too party and government are not very distinguishable, and this confusion may work to undermine rather than fortify the party's capacity for handling conflict.

POLITICAL CLEAVAGES IN "DEVELOPED" AND "EMERGING" POLITIES

Seymour Martin Lipset

Although many discussions of the possibilities for democratic politics in the emerging nations of the "third world" are posed in terms of whether or not these nations can successfully absorb political models established in the developed countries, it is not really possible to speak of a "Western" political system. A variety of factors have contributed to the vast array of party systems existing in the developed nations.[1] These include the different ways in which mass suffrage parties first emerged, the various conditions under which lower-class parties formed their basic ideologies,

SOURCE: Excerpted from Seymour Martin Lipset, *Revolution and Counter-revolution: Change and Persistence in Social Science* (New York: Basic Books, Inc., 1968), pp. 179–82, 191–212.

[1] An effort to relate these systematically to theoretical assumptions about basic structures of social systems derived from the concepts of Talcott Parsons may be found in S. M. Lipset and Stein Rokkan, "Cleavage Structures, Party Systems, and Voter Alignments," in Lipset and Rokkan (eds.), *Party Systems and Voter Alignments* (New York: The Free Press of Glencoe, 1967), pp. 1–64. I have also discussed the factors related to varying political systems in various contexts in other books and do not want to repeat them here. See S. M. Lipset, *Political Man: The Social Bases of Politics* (Garden City: Doubleday, 1960), pp. 45–96, and *The First New Nation* (New York: Basic Books, 1963), pp. 207–317.

whether a polity derives its authority from historic legitimacy or from post-revolutionary populism, the extent to which different nations have resolved the tensions flowing from the key power cleavages common in the history of Western industrial societies, such as the place of religion, universal suffrage, the distribution of national income and resources, and the variations in electoral systems. Clearly many of the existing differences reflect the institutionalization of past bases of opinion cleavage; once formalized in political parties these cleavages have survived the decline or disappearance of the original social conflicts which gave rise to party divisions. Parties, like all other institutions, tend to foster self-maintaining mechanisms. They necessarily seek bases of support and new issues to perpetuate themselves. And as Ostrogorski noted, loyalty to parties is often comparable to identification with a religious denomination.[2] Each party retains a body of loyal adherents who see their party allegiance as an important part of their identity.

Variations in national party systems are linked to historical factors but this does not

[2] M. Ostrogorski, *Democracy and Organization of Political Parties* II: *The United States* (Garden City: Anchor Books, 1964), pp. 173, 223–224, 305–306. See my discussion of Ostrogorski's text in Chapter 11 of this book.

prevent the formation of broad generalizations about the development of party systems in democracies of the developed world, for the purpose of comparison with the polities of the "third world." This chapter will deal briefly with some of the varying historical conditions which have affected Western party systems, particularly in their formative periods, in order to point out some major differences in the bases of cleavage in the existing and emerging democracies.

The Development of Western Party Divisions

The modern political party is in large measure the resultant of the democratic electoral system. Before the establishment of the suffrage there were, of course, controversies about the policies of government. In the absolutist state, such disagreements were resolved at the level of the monarchy. As the upper social strata, such as the landed nobility, sought to restrict the powers of the king, parliaments of various kinds emerged and shared some of the state's power. In these parliaments, men with common interests, values, or backgrounds joined together into loose factions which some historians have called parties. These groups, however, had no common program, little or no organization, and little discipline. They did not seek to gain power through elections, but did so by breaking off support from other factions, or by winning the backing of the king. Where an electorate existed, it was usually quite small and under the control of the local nobility, as in Great Britain.

As forms of electoral democracy advanced in nineteenth-century Europe, a contest developed in most countries between two elements, usually labeled liberals and conservatives. The liberals generally supported democratic reforms and some further extension of the initially quite limited suffrage, opposed an established church and religious control of education, and hence attracted to their ranks men who

favored a variety of social and economic reforms. The conservatives tended initially to oppose extension of the suffrage (although they changed to support it in some countries, seeing the possibility of drawing support from "deferential" lower strata who responded to conservative efforts to improve their circumstances on the basis of *noblesse oblige*), to support the privileges of the traditional church, and to have the backing of the more traditionalist elements in society such as the old dominant landed class and the nobility. Given a very restricted electorate, these parties lacked cohesion. Local notables controlled their constituencies regardless of how they voted in Parliament and despite the consequences of government policies. The two parties were subdivided into various factions and new combinations kept re-forming within them.[3]

The introduction of the working class as a political force, however, soon changed this picture. As the workers organized into trade unions and legal or semi-legal political groupings, the upper classes gradually made concessions to the demand for adult suffrage. Sometimes these concessions were a result of the fear of revolution; at other times they were owing to fulfillment of the democratic ideology of a victorious liberal group; and often they resulted from the efforts of one or another party to increase its base of electoral support. Conservatives felt they could rely on the votes of the religious and tradition-minded peasantry in many countries.[4]

The inauguration of manhood suffrage,

[3] Maurice Duverger, *Political Parties* (London: Methuen, 1954), pp. xxiii–xxxvii; Max Weber, *Essays in Sociology* (New York: Oxford University Press, 1946), pp. 100–115.

[4] In 1861, Napoleon III advised the Prussian government to introduce universal suffrage "by means of which the conservative rural population could outvote the Liberals in the cities." F. Meinecke, *Weltbürgertum und Nationalstaat* (Munich: G. R. Oldenbourg, 1922), pp. 517–518; F. Naumann, *Die Politischen Parteien* (Berlin-Schönberg: Buchverlag der Hilfe, 1910), pp. 16–17.

however, whatever the reason for its adoption, changed the nature of politics. The techniques necessary to win votes in a mass electorate required, as Ostrogorski indicated, the creation of the party organization. Thus the first formal party organizations emerged in American cities. Tammany Hall and its brethren were necessary for the mobilization of the voters. Considerable funds were required for campaigning and professional politics developed in response to a felt need.

In Europe, as Max Weber pointed out, the socialist parties were the first to adapt successfully to the new situation and create bureaucratic parties dominated by professional politicians.[5] These parties had an elaborate formal structure, dues-paying members, and branches which held regular meetings. They established party newspapers and created a network of groups tied to the party such as social clubs, women's associations, and youth organizations. They also formulated the concept of rigid party discipline, that the elected representatives were responsible to the party and must act according to party demands.

The emergence of the socialists as a political force within the context of manhood suffrage changed the structure of much of European politics. Mass-based religious and agrarian parties developed in a number of countries, and tended to adopt many of the organizational procedures of the socialists. The conservatives and liberals were also forced to react to the logic of dealing with a mass elecorate by adopting organizational procedures in many ways similar to those of the American or socialist parties. On the whole, however, those parties which are lineal descendants of nineteenth-century liberal and conservative parties, led by notables, have never been so successful in creating large-scale membership parties as parties stemming from mass organizations such as the Marxist and religious ones.

It is impossible to locate the determinants of the varying party systems in the democratic developed nations by a simple analytic framework. The number of parties that exist is a function of the complexity and intensity of the social cleavages which seek political representation, and of the nature of the electoral system. Nations such as France, where the strains derivative from conflicts over the place of the church, the relations among diverse status groups, economic interest struggles, and orientations toward political authority have persisted for more than a century, have a complex cleavage structure difficult to resolve within a two- or three-party system. This issue of the number of parties has been discussed in detail elsewhere and need not be repeated here.[6]

Similarly, the factors which affect the degree of ideological intensity, and the extent to which the democratic rules of the game are accepted by all important actors in the polity, are also too complex to be dealt with in detail in a discussion such as this. To a considerable extent, the intensity of cleavage and the character of attitudes toward the democratic system are associated with the severity of strains experienced by significant strata. Those strata which experience the tensions of rapid industrialization and urbanization tend to be much more radical than those inured to being part of an urban industrial society; nations in which democratic rights (full suffrage and trade unions) for all have been institutionalized prior to the emergence of a mass working class tend to have more moderate and legitimate opposition politics than those in which suffrage or trade-union rights were resisted deep into the present century; those nations which are relatively well to do and which have a high per-capita income reveal less significant strain between the classes and consequently less

[5] Weber, *op. cit.*, pp. 103–104; Guenther Roth, *The Social Democrats in Imperial Germany* (Totowa: The Bedminster Press, 1963), pp. 252–254.

[6] See Lipset, *The First Nation*, pp. 286–317, and Lipset and Rokkan *op. cit.*

ideological politics; those countries which allocated citizenship rights to new classes, the bourgeoisie and later the workers, without requiring revolutionary overthrow of the symbolic source of traditional authority, the monarchy, also tend as a group to have more stable and less virulent politics than others.

If we turn now to an examination of the sources of party cleavage in contemporary democratic countries, it is clear that the role relationships which have proved most likely to generate stable lines of party support are largely aspects of stratification, as between higher and lower orders in status, income and power, or aspects of cultural differences, as between specific groups which vary widely in their views of the nature and values of the good society. The prototype of the first cleavage is class parties, of the second, religious parties. Differences rooted in stratification are likely to be most preponderant in economically developed stable polities in which much domestic political controversy may be described as the "politics of collective bargaining," a fight over the division of the total economic pie, over the extent of the welfare and planning state, and the like. Cultural or deeply rooted value conflicts are much more characteristic of the politics of developing countries with unstable polities. In such nations, in addition to conflicts rooted in class controversy, there is a division based on the differences in outlook related to institutions which originated in the pre-modern era, and to those which foster or are endemic in social and economic development. Examples of cultural conflicts include the confrontation of those who seek to maintain the traditional position of historic religion, the status and privileges of higher social strata such as the nobility, or social relationships within families and other institutions which represent a way of life characteristic of a relatively static rural society, against those who seek to change these patterns of behavior toward a more universalistic social system.

Many of the variables associated with positions in a *Kulturkampf* are not linked to stratification, but to involvement in traditional or modern institutions and to generational experiences, for example, poor religious peasants may be conservatives, while well-to-do young professionals may be radical; the young and better educated may oppose the older and the less educated. Sex, too, may provide a basis for diversity where cultural issues are significant. The woman's role in most societies requires her to be more involved in religious institutions and less in modern economic ones, to be less educated on the average than men, and consequently to be more supportive of traditionalist parties than of modernizing ones.

If we consider the developed countries first, it is clear that in all of them there is a correlation between the generally accepted degree of leftism or conservatism of political parties and their support in terms of stratification variables. The more liberal or left-wing parties are disproportionately supported by those with low income, by workers, by poorer farmers, by the less educated, by members of religious groups defined as low status, and by those invidiously identified in racial or ethnic terms.[7]

This pattern comes out most clearly in the five predominantly English-speaking democracies. In all of these countries the factors of lower-class status, Catholic religion, and recent immigrant background are associated with support for the Democrats or with Labour and Liberal politics. The size of the correlation varies among these nations and other factors enter as well, but it seems clear that stratification as rooted in occupation, income, religion and ethnicity, perceived as status-defining variables, accounts for part of the variation in party support.[8]

[7] These statements are documented in detail in Lipset, *Political Man*, and I will not reiterate the references here.

[8] See Robert R. Alford, *Party and Society. The Anglo-American Democracies* (Chicago: Rand McNally, 1963).

The picture is somewhat more complicated in the various multiparty systems of continental Europe. In some of them, cleavages rooted in the preindustrial society of the late eighteenth and much of the nineteenth centuries continue to influence the nature of party division. Perhaps the most striking example of this is the name of the party which represents the views of the Dutch orthodox Calvinists, the Anti-Revolutionary party. The revolution which this party is against is the French Revolution of 1789.

In spite of the variations among them, these countries do have a number of elements in common. First, the historic cleavage between liberal and conservative, or religious parties, which arose in the nineteenth century before the rise of socialism as a significant force, has been maintained in most of them. In Scandinavia, this cleavage is represented by the continuation of strong Liberal and Conservative parties, in Catholic Europe and Germany by the existence of Christian Democratic parties and liberal or other anti-clerical bourgeois parties. All of these countries have strong working-class oriented parties. Here, however, they differ greatly according to whether there is one dominant Social-Democratic party opposed by a small Communist party, or whether there is a mass Communist party which is larger than the Socialists, as in France, Italy, and Finland. A number of these countries, particularly the Scandinavian, also have agrarian or peasant parties.

In spite of the great diversity in the continental multiparty systems, class and religion would seem to be the preponderant sources of difference among the parties. Lower income and status are associated with voting for the working-class oriented parties. On the whole, where there are large Communist and Socialist parties, the latter derive greater support from the more skilled and better educated workers, although there are important exceptions, particularly in the case of Finland. Communists also tend to draw support among the socially uprooted in rapidly changing areas, and among those who have been unemployed in the past. The religious parties draw their backing from the centers of religious strength, regardless of class, and thus gain support from both rich and poor, although they are disproportionately strong among farm people and among women. The urban religious manual workers seem to have many of the same economic interests and policy orientations as the Social Democratic workers, and they usually adhere to Christian trade unions which work closely with socialist unions. The Liberal parties on the whole, parts of Scandinavia excepted, tend to be relatively small, 7 to 15 per cent, and to be based on the anti-clerical bourgeois and professional groups. Scandinavian Liberalism is somewhat different. It resembles the old English Liberal party and though backed by irreligious bourgeois and professional groups, also draws support from the quite religious Scandinavian equivalents of the English nonconformists, who oppose the Conservatives as supporters of the traditional Lutheran Church Establishment. The Scandinavian Conservatives, in turn, seem to be the party of the more well to do, both rural and urban, and of those involved in the traditional church.

The maintenance of the pluralistic party structure of Scandinavia is facilitated by a system of proportional representation which helps preserve diverse nonsocialist parties. They are under no pressure to unite before elections, though the differences among them have declined. The picture is somewhat different in Catholic and southern Europe. There, a lower level of economic development, failure to develop completely legitimate political institutions, and the superimposition of the various conflicts of the nineteenth century over the status of the old privileged classes, the position of the church, and the economic class struggle, have resulted in a cleavage structure which cannot be readily fitted into a broad two-party coalition structure. Broadly speaking, the "normal" division in these nations is a three-party one consisting of a large multi-class Catholic party, based disproportionately on the rural population, opposed by a large Socialist party rooted in the urban working class, with a much smaller middle-class oriented anti-clerical Liberal party, which holds the balance of power. This pattern is found in Belgium, Luxembourg, Germany, and Austria. In Holland, the problem is complicated further by the presence of three conflicting religions, each of which has its own party, but if the religious parties are considered as one force, the Dutch pattern resembles the above four nations. In France and Italy, however, the strains are clearly more intense, and both the clerical and anti-clerical sectors of the nation have been greatly divided, so that each has a six-party structure.

The Parties of the Third World

In the first flurry of democratic enthusiasm after World War II, many believed that the newly independent states of Africa and Asia, as well as the "old" nations of Latin America, would support democratic polities strongly resembling those of Western Europe and the overseas English-speaking democracies. Currently, with the emergence of military and one-party regimes in many of these nations, an almost total pessimism concerning the democratic potential of these countries has replaced the early hopes. Scholars, journalists, and politicians from the stable democracies now conclude that they erred in anticipating democratic institutions in nations whose economy and culture were not yet ready to sustain the tensions of party conflict. Although it is much too early to make definitive conclusions about the polities of the "third" world, it is clear that neither extreme of optimism or pessimism concerning the future of democracy is justified. In fact, outside of the Communist nations, the

majority of the peoples of Asia and South America lived in democratic polities, in which the press is relatively free and opposition parties operate openly within and outside of parliament. Only in Africa can one say that one-party and military regimes predominate.[9] In Latin America, opposition parties exist in Chile, Uruguay, Brazil, Venezuela, Colombia, Bolivia, Mexico, and Peru. Some of these nations would hardly be considered models of democratic polities, particularly since the military has intervened in the recent past to limit the possible results of elections in Peru, Argentina, and Brazil. But it is clear that the vast majority of South Americans do not live under absolutist dictatorships. The same conclusion holds for non-Communist Asia. There, states containing the bulk of the population are relatively democratic—India, Ceylon, Israel, Lebanon, Turkey, Malaysia, South Korea, the Philippines, and Japan. Unfortunately, the same cannot be said for Burma, and the remaining Moslem states of the Asian continent, but these, while possessing many votes in the United Nations, contain considerably fewer people than the democratic Asian polities.

The considerably greater cultural and historical diversity of the "third" world than that of the developed nations complicates the search for a single set of factors associated with the propensity to sustain competitive party systems among the less developed nations. Evidence for the association between level of economic development, literacy, and the existence of a stable democractic polity is one step in this

[9] The special failing of democracy in Africa clearly deserves some attention. To some considerable extent it would seem to have some relationship to the fact of tribalism. The African states are not societies or nations, they are for the most part heterogeneous collections of linguistically and culturally distinct tribes or smaller nations, without a common language. Before becoming democratic polities they must first *become* polities. See René Servoise, "Whither Black Africa?" *Futuribles*, 1963, esp. pp. 264–267.

search.[10] More fruitful, perhaps, in the long run, are the attempts to locate, and even measure, the consequences for political development of varying rates of social mobilization, of the process by which diverse strata are "integrated" into the larger modernizing sector of society.[11] Such changes, however, may result in a breakdown in national solidarity and early efforts at a democratic polity, since rapid social change, with its consequent high rates of mobility, initially results in considerable social displacement, incongruencies of status, and makes for considerable discontent with existing institutions. Many have pointed out that such processes produce people who are "disposable," available for new, often authoritarian or irresponsible political movements. As European history well demonstrates, modernization involves "a succession of what might be called crises of access . . . [periods involving] a social and political adjustment to new claimants to power, prestige, status."[12] Thus the very tendencies which enhance the conditions necessary to sustain

an integrated and democratic polity may destroy embryonic efforts at such developments. Gino Germani has, in fact, suggested that a condition for increasing the probability that the processes of mobilization and modernization will support rather than undermine the chances for democracy "consists in the possibility of these social processes occurring in successive stages. In other words, a nation requires sufficient time and opportunity between stages of mobilization [incorporation of additional segments of the population] to integrate each given stratum. This is what occurred in the West both with respect to political integration and other forms of participation."[13] The hypotheses which have been proposed concerning variations in extent or rate of economic development, modernization, and mobilization, or integration of populations, and the special characteristics of the polities of the "third" world are yet to be tested by rigorous comparative research.[14] There are few efforts to differ-

[10] Lipset, *Political Man*, pp. 48–67; James S. Coleman, "The Political Systems of the Developing Areas," in Gabriel Almond and J. S. Coleman, (eds.), *The Politics of the Developing Areas* (Princeton: Princeton University Press, 1960), pp. 538–544; Everett Hagen, "A Framework for Analyzing Economic and Political Change," in Robert Asher (ed.), *Development of Emerging Countries* (Washington: Brookings Institution, 1962), pp. 1–8; Charles Wolf, Jr., *The Political Effects of Economic Programs* (Santa Monica, The Rand Corporation, February 1964), RM—3901—ISA, pp. 19–33; P. Cutright, "National Political Development," *American Sociological Review*, 28 (1963), 253–264; and Irma Adelman and Cynthia T. Morris, *Society, Politics, and Economic Development* (Baltimore: Johns Hopkins, 1967).

[11] See Karl Deutsch, "Social Mobilization and Political Development," *American Political Science Review*, 55 (1961), 493–514.

[12] Kalman H. Silvert, "Some Propositions on Chile," *American Universities Field Staff Reports Service*, West Coast South America Series, 11 (1) 1964, 10.

[13] Gino Germani, "Social Change and Intergroup Conflicts," Dittoed, 1963 (translated by I. L. Horowitz), p. 15. See also Gino Germani, *Política y Sociedad en una Epoca de Transición* (Buenos Aires: Editorial Paidos, 1962).

[14] There is an extensive theoretical literature attempting to differentiate the conditions of politics in underdeveloped nations from those in the developed countries. As yet, however, such writings have led to few research studies designed to test out the propositions in them. See, for example, Claude E. Welch, Jr. (ed.), *Political Modernization* (Belmont, Calif.: Wadsworth, 1967); Gabriel Almond and G. B. Powell, Jr., *Comparative Politics* (Boston: Little, Brown, 1966); J. P. Nettl, *Political Mobilization* (New York: Basic Books, 1968); Lucien W. Pye, *Aspects of Political Development* (Boston: Little, Brown, 1966); David Apter, *The Politics of Modernization* (Chicago: University of Chicago Press, 1965); Gabriel Almond, "Introduction: A Functional Approach to Comparative Politics," in Almond and Coleman (eds.), *op. cit.*, pp. 3–64; James S. Coleman, "Conclusion: The Political Systems of the Developing Areas," *ibid.*, pp. 532–576; John H. Kautsky, "An Essay on the Politics of Development," in Kautsky (ed.), *Political*

entiate among the types of party systems which exist within these countries, as has been attempted for the Western democracies. To do so at this early stage of the comparative studies of these nations would be rash, considering the scarcity of intensive studies of their political parties.[15] The following part of this discussion will seek to bring out some additional patterns of political cleavage and of political development in the emerging nations, without attempting to arrive at any definitive statement on the factors involved and their interrelationships.

The political pattern of Latin America is closer to those of Europe than are those in the other areas of the developing world. Nineteenth- and early twentieth-century party conflicts resemble those of Latin Europe, from which Latin America derived much of its culture, religion, and earlier political ideologies.[16] The first cleavages

were largely between pro-clerical, rural upper-class dominated Conservative parties and anti-clerical, bourgeois controlled Liberal parties. Socialist and anarcho-syndicalist movements arose in the working class left before World War I in a number of countries, but secured relatively little strength.[17] During the interwar period, and since World War II, however, political movements have emerged which are comparable to many in Africa and Asia. These movements express various forms of nationalist, anti-imperialist doctrine, oppose foreign domination of the economy, and seek through state control or ownership of the economy to foster rapid economic development. The ideological content of such parties has varied greatly. Between the late 1930's and the end of World War II, some, such as the movements of Perón in Argentina, Vargas in Brazil, and the M.N.R. in Bolivia, took over many of the trappings of Fascism or Nazism. They differed, however, from European fascist movements in being genuinely based on the working class or poor rural population. Since the war each adopted conventional left-wing ideologies, and has cooperated with various Communist movements (Trotskyist in Bolivia, orthodox in the other two). Others have been aligned continually with the Communists, explicitly or in the manner of fellow travelers. Communist parties have been particularly strong in Chile and Brazil. Still other movements such as the Acción Popular of Fernando Belaúnde Terry in Peru, the Acción Democrática of Rómulo Betancourt in Venezuela, and the National Liberation Movement of José Figueres in Costa Rica, may best be described as nationalist Social Democrats, comparable to

Change in Underdeveloped Countries (New York; John Wiley, 1962), pp. 3–119; Edward Shils, "Political Development in the New States," *Comparative Studies in Society and History*, 2 (1960), 265–292, 379–411; Zbigniew Brzezinski, "The Politics of Underdevelopment," *World Politics*, 9 (1956), 55–75; Edward Shils, "On the Comparative Study of New States," in Clifford Geertz (ed.), *Old Societies and New States* (New York: The Free Press of Glencoe, 1963), pp. 1–26; Kalman Silvert and Frank Bonilla, "Definitions, Propositions, and Hypotheses Concerning Modernism, Class and National Integration," in Kalman Silvert (ed.), *Expectant Peoples* (New York: Random House, 1963), pp. 439–450; and S. N. Eisenstadt, *Essays on Sociological Aspects of Political and Economic Development* (The Hague: Mouton, 1961), pp. 9–53.

[15] Although much has been written on these nations, there is little knowledge in depth about them. For example, George Blanksten reported as recently as 1960 that "only one Latin American political party has been the subject of a full-scale monographic study." See "The Politics of Latin America," in Almond and Coleman, *op. cit.*, p. 479.

[16] Donald M. Dozer, *Latin America: An Interpretive History* (New York: McGraw-Hill, 1962), pp. 369–414, and *passim*; George N. Blanksten, *op. cit.*, pp. 481–487; H. Davis (ed.),

Government and Politics in Latin America (New York: Ronald Press, 1958); John J. Johnson, *Political Change in Latin America* (Stanford: (Stanford: Stanford University Press, 1958).

[17] Moisés Poblete Troncoso and Ben G. Burnett, *The Rise of Latin American Labor Movement* (New York: Bookman Associates, 1960).

the Indian Congress party. Most recently, Christian Democratic parties have arisen in many of the Latin American nations, as in Chile and Venezuela, tending on the whole to be relatively leftist supporters of land reform, economic planning, and of state intervention to foster economic development. And the various leftist movements have drawn considerable support from university students and intellectuals, a social category which includes a considerable segment of the university graduates in underdeveloped states.[18] The Castro movement is an example of a successful effort based initially on youthful members of the modernizing elites.[19]

[18] As Shils has pointed out, in the socially less differentiated underdeveloped states the concept of intellectual is broader than in the more advanced countries. It includes "all persons with an *advanced modern education* and the those persons who have become modern not by associated with it. . . . [T]he intellectuals are those persons who have become modern not by immersing themselves in the ways of modern commerce or administration, but by being exposed to the set course of modern intellectual culture in a college or university," *op. cit.*, pp. 198–199; for a discussion of students as intellectuals and their politics see also pp. 203–205, and see the articles on Latin American students and universities in S. M. Lipset and Aldo Solari (eds.), *Elites in Latin America* (New York: Oxford University Press, 1967), pp. 343–453; in S. M. Lipset (ed.), *Student Politics* (New York: Basic Books, 1967), pp. 283–354; and the issue on "Students and Politics" of *Daedalus*, 97 (Winter 1968).

[19] That Castro's initial following was largely based on young, well-educated middle-class Cubans has been documented by Theodore Draper. He points out that of Castro's 18 cabinet members in 1960, everyone was a university graduate, that they were of middle- or upper-class background, and professionals or intellectuals occupationally. Theodore Draper, *Castro's Revolution, Myths and Realities* (New York: Praeger, 1962), pp. 42–43. Draper also points out that the list of Cuban defenders of Castroism who were interviewed by C. Wright Mills in his effort to present the authentic voice of the Cuban Revolution for his book *Listen Yankee* did not include a single worker or peasant. "Without exception, his informants were middleclass intellectuals and professionals" (p. 21).

A special pattern of "elitist" leftism which has appeared in many parts of the "third" world is military support for radical social reforms, i.e., for economic development and modernization. The military in a number of countries such as Turkey, parts of the Arab world, and some in South and Southeast Asia have helped place leftist politicians or officers in power. The basis for military "leftism" would seem to be the concern of many officers to enhance national strength and prestige in a world in which these positions are seemingly a function of the degree of national economic development. While there is no necessary common interest shared by the nationalist leftist elites and the military in underdeveloped areas, governments based on such alliances have operated in many countries such as Burma, Pakistan, Egypt, Mexico, and Indonesia. In countries dominated by traditional-minded oligarchies, the military has often represented the only well-educated, Western-oriented, nationalist group favorable to modernization and capable of taking and holding power.[20] On the other hand, in various parts of Latin America mass-based reformist politicians have been overthrown by military juntas with links to traditional oligarchies. It should be noted,

[20] Harry Benda includes military officers in the category of the "westernized intellectuals" in the emerging nations, pointing out that they "were often the first group to receive Western training," and consequently became a force for modernization, which often brought them "fairly close to the socialism so prevalent among non-western intelligentsias in general." "Non-Western Intelligentsias as Political Elites," in John H. Kautsky, *op. cit.*, pp. 239–244; John J. Johnson (ed.), *The Role of the Military in Underdeveloped Countries* (Princeton: Princeton University Press, 1962); Morroe Berger, *Military Elites and Social Change* (Princeton: Princeton University Center of International Studies, 1960); Sydney N. Fisher (ed.), *The Military in the Middle East* (Columbus: Ohio State University Press, 1963); Edwin Lieuwen, *Arms and Politics in Latin America* (New York: Praeger, 1960); Lucien Pye, "Armies in the Process of Political Modernization," *European Journal of Sociology*, 2 (1961), 82–92.

moreover, that the pessimistic conclusions of Morris Janowitz concerning the inability of the military leaders to engender successfully the processes necessary for economic and social development *when they take power in their own right* would seem to be warranted.[21]

The predominant pattern of political cleavage characteristic of those emerging nations which retain some version of democratic politics is a division between modernizing and traditionalist elements, which overlaps with, and to a considerable extent supersedes, the traditional left-right stratification-based conflict of the older and more stable polities. To an important degree, socialism and communism are strong because they are symbolically associated with the ideology of independence, rapid economic development, social modernization, and ultimate equality. Capitalism is perceived as being linked to foreign influences, traditionalism, and slow growth. Hence leftist movements secure considerable backing from the better educated who favor modernization. In many nations in Asia, Latin America, and Africa the better educated who are also more well to do are often the most significant backers of the more aggressively leftist tendencies.[22] There is ample

evidence for this in the support of conservative parties by both impoverished religious peasants and the landholding elite, while backing for the left is drawn heavily from the better-educated members of the urban white-collar and professional classes, with the urban proletariat and peasants only entering as a force on the left after the modernizing elite groups have turned to them for support.[23] This pattern is brought out clearly in Japan. That nation, although more developed than any other country outside Europe or the English-speaking countries, has resembled the other emerging nations in its politics. In the 1920's, leftist groups were most successful among the students and other sections of the elite.[24] Public-opinion surveys completed in recent years reveal that since World War II, education has been more highly correlated than class position with modernism and

---

[21] Morris Janowitz, *The Military in the Political Development of New States* (Chicago: University of Chicago Press, 1964). For a specification of the sharply different political roles, which may be played by the military in unstable polities, see Gino Germani and Kalman Silvert, "Politics, Social Structure and Military Intervention in Latin America," *European Journal of Sociology*, 2 (1961), 62–81.

[22] The appeal of left-wing ideologies to the intellectuals and other sections of the university-trained intelligentsia in the underdeveloped nations has been analyzed in some detail. See Morris Watnick, "The Appeal of Communism to the Peoples of Underdeveloped Areas," in R. Bendix and S. M. Lipset (eds.), *Class, Status and Power* (Glencoe: The Free Press, 1966), pp. 428–436; Hugh Seton-Watson, "Twentieth Century Revolutions," *The Political Quarterly*, 22 (1951), 251–265; John H. Kautsky, *op. cit.*, pp. 44–49, 106–113; Edward Shils, "The Intellectual between Tradition and Modernity: The Indian Situation," *Comparative Studies in*

Society and History, Supplement I (1961), 94–108. Perhaps the most comprehensive treatment of the subject is Edward Shils, "The Intellectuals in the Political Development of the New States," in John H. Kautsky, *op. cit.*, pp. 195–234.

[23] See Glaucio Ary Dillon Soares, "The Politics of Uneven Development: Brazil," in S. M. Lipset and Stein Rokkan, *op. cit*, pp. 467–496.

[24] "A . . . factor that contributed to the fears of the ruling class was that 'bolshevization' was believed to be penetrating the sons of prominent men, the intelligentsia and the university students who formed the true *elite* of Imperial Japan or who would do so in the future. . . . [A Home Ministry Police Report stated:] 'After the Great Earthquake [1923] graduates from colleges and high schools, the so-called educated class, were most susceptible to the baptism of bolshevist thought. . . .' A situation in which the organization of the workers and farmers was so slight as to present no problem, but in which the *elite* and educated class had become 'bolshevized,' is completely abnormal according to the laws of Marxism. . . . [W]hat gave the rulers of Imperial Japan nightmares until the last was the 'bolshevization' of the State from within rather than revolution from below." Masao Maruyama, *Thought and Behaviour in Modern Japanese Politics* (London: Oxford University Press, 1963), p. 77.

leftism. University students and graduates disproportionately back variants of socialism. On the other hand, less educated poor peasants and workers who are still tied to traditional social structures (e.g., workers in the highly paternalistic, numerous small factories and shops) support the conservative party.[25]

Tendencies similar to those in pre- and post-war Japan are evident in many other less developed emerging nations among university students and occupations requiring higher levels of education.[26] Data from

surveys of student attitudes in various countries reveal a tendency for those taking the more modern fields to be more leftist, while fields which train for the older professions, such as law, tend to be more traditionalistic. The findings from the student surveys are not so clear cut as one might anticipate, in part, perhaps, because of the differential utilization of graduates from different fields. Those studying "modern" subjects are more likely to find lucrative employment after graduation than are those who major in the more classic humanistic disciplines. The discrepancy between the needs of developing societies for technicians and scientists and the preference of students in some of them for the more traditional fields of law and the humanities often means that the latter are found disportionately in the ranks of the "educated unemployed," or underpaid.[27] The inap-

[25] A study based on interviews with a sample of 3,000 Japanese men reports that the most radical segment are "the employed professional specialists. They are more in favor of denuclearized neutrality than laborers or blue-collar workers. They lend as much support to political strikes called by labor unions as do the laborers themselves. Most of the white-collar stratum favors and gives support to the socialist parties." Research Society on Japanese Social Structure, "Special Traits of White-Collar Workers in Large Urban Areas," *Journal of Social and Political Ideas in Japan*, 1 (August 1963), 78. A 1958 national sample reported heavy Socialist support among professionals and managerial groups. See Z. Suetuna, H. Aoyama, C. Hyashi, and K. Matusita, "A Study of Japanese National Character, Part II," *Annals of Institute of Statistical Mathematics* (Tokyo), Supplement II (1961), 54; see also Joji Watanuki, "Patterns of Politics in Present-Day Japan," in S. M. Lipset and Stein Rokkan, *op. cit.*, pp. 448–449, 451–456; Robert A. Scalapino and Junnosuke Masumi, *Parties and Politics in Contemporary Japan* (Berkeley: University of California Press, 1962), p. 177; Douglas Mendel, *The Japanese People and Foreign Policy* (Berkeley: University of California Press, 1961), pp. 44–45, 47. A comprehensive report on many Japanese opinion surveys is Allan Cole and Naomichi Nakanishi, *Japanese Opinion Polls with Socio-Political Significance 1947–1957*, Vol. 1, *Political Support and Preference* (Medford: Fletcher School of Law and Diplomacy, Tufts University, 1960), *passim*.

[26] See S. M. Lipset, "University Students and Politics in Underdeveloped Countries," in Lipset (ed.), *Student Politics*, pp. 3–53; "Student Politics in Comparative Perspective," *Daedalus*, 97 (Winter 1968), 1–20; Kalman Silvert, *The Conflict Society: Reaction and Revolution in Latin America* (New Orleans: The Hauser Press, 1961), p. 166; T. B. Botto-

more, *Elites and Society* (New York: Basic Books, 1965), pp. 86–104. An analysis of data collected from a sample of Indian students in 1951 by the Bureau of Social Science Research indicates that more than 40 per cent backed the Communist or Praha Socialist parties, both of which were quite weak among the general electorate. In some Latin American countries, such as Panama, El Salvador, Peru, Venezuela, and Brazil, Communists and pro-Castro groups are dominant in elections to the student councils. John Scott reports that "a number of important university campuses including those in Caracas, Michoacán, Lima, Santiago are virtually run by Communists." *How Much Progress?* (New York: Time Inc., 1963), pp. 123–125. In North Africa, also, university students are disproportionately to the left of the dominant politics. See Clement Moore and Arlie R. Hochschild, "Student Unions in North African Politics," *Daedalus*, 97 (Winter 1968), 21–50.

[27] The pattern of inappropriate career choice and educated unemployment is discussed in Justin M. van der Kroef, "Asian Education and Unemployment: The Continuing Crisis," *Comparative Education Review*, 7 (1963), 173–180; see also Joseph Fischer, "The University Student in South and Southeast Asia," *Minerva*, 2 (1963), 39–53; on the low economic rewards for Indian university graduates see Edward Shils, "The Intellectual between Tradition and Modernity," pp. 29–41.

propriateness of their university study for a subsequent career may thus contribute to the enhanced leftism of the university educated. In the larger sense, however, it may be argued, as John Kautsky has done, that the university trained, as a class, constitute a socially dislocated group in underdeveloped states:

> The key role of the intellectuals in the politics of underdeveloped countries is largely due to their paradoxical position of being a product of modernization before modernization has reached or become widespread in their own country. In the universities, the intellectuals absorb the professional knowledge and skills needed by an industrial civilization; they become students of the humanities and social sciences qualified to teach in universities, and they become lawyers and doctors, administrators and journalists, and increasingly also scientists and engineers. When they return from the universities, whether abroad or not, the intellectuals find, all too often for their taste, that in their societies their newly acquired skills and knowledge are out of place. . . .
>
> During their studies, the intellectuals are likely to acquire more than new knowledge. They also absorb the values of an industrial civilization. . . . On their return, they find that these values, too, are inappropriate to the old society. . . .
>
> To the extent, then, that a native intellectual has substituted for the values of his traditional society those of an industrial one—a process which need by no means be complete in each case—he becomes an alien, a displaced person, in his own society. What could be more natural for him than to want to change that society to accord with his new needs and values, in short, to industrialize and modernize it?[28]

The politics of developing nations must be seen, then, in the words of the Japanese

[28] Kautsky, *op. cit.*, pp. 46–47.

sociologist Joji Watanuki, as reflecting the cleavages of "cultural politics." By this is meant "the politics where the cleavage caused by differences in value systems have more effect on the nature of political conflict than the cleavages based on economic or status factors." While Watanuki does not deny "the working of economic interest or status interest," he does argue that in countries oriented toward rapid development such as Japan, one finds "the relative dominance of cultural or value factors and the superimposition and effects of these factors on others. . . ."[29] Similarly, two students of comparative Latin American politics, Kalman Silvert and Frank Bonilla, have postulated the hypothesis that in the early phases of modernization or development of the "third" world, one should expect to find "very broad ideological alliances—all those in the innovating camp opposed to all those aligned against it."[30] As Watanuki notes, "cultural politics" are usually presented in *Weltanschauungen*, total ideological terms, in which all issues are "easily universalized as aspects of general principles, and are reacted to in highly emotional terms . . . sometimes suggesting the existence of a more deep-rooted basis for interest conflicts than actually exists."

It should be stressed that none of those who have commented on the politics of developing nations as reflecting value cleavages suggests the absence of class-linked political conflict.[31] They all note that *mass-*

[29] Watanuki, *op. cit.*, p. 457.

[30] "Definitions, Propositions, and Hypotheses Concerning Modernism, Class, and National Integration," Silvert and Bonilla, *op. cit.*, p. 443.

[31] In Japan, it is clear that even if university students, and young professionals, business executives, and the large majority of the intellectuals back the Socialists, Japanese business, both small and large, supports the conservative Liberal-Democrats. Almost all of the vast sums contributed for campaign purposes by Japanese business go to the latter, while the trade unions are the financial backers of the socialist parties. See James A. Soukup, "Comparative Political Finance: Japan," *Journal of Politics*, 25 (1963), 737–756.

based leftist parties necessarily draw support from the workers or impoverished sectors of the rural population. Even the Castro movement, which originated among university graduates and drew much of its support from relatively well-to-do middle- and upper-class advocates of modernization, was able to secure heavy backing from the poor and uneducated after seizing power.[32]

These differences within the emerging nations, of course, have a parallel in the past, and to some extent in the present, in the developed countries in the form of the *Kulturkampf* over the place of religion, discussed earlier. Many of the educated, well-to-do bourgeois groups backed leftist anti-clerical parties in nineteenth-century Europe. The liberal parties stem from this source. The modern scientific professions, such as medicine, tended to back the left, while the professions rooted in tradition, such as the law, were heavily conservative. Teachers and professors in secular schools tended to be on the anti-clerical left. And even today these differences influence political behavior in nations such as France and Italy. Leftist parties, while primarily based on the lower strata, do draw some support from the historically anti-clerical (modernized) sectors of the middle class.[33]

But if the modernizing-traditional division contributes strongly to the support which the radical left draws from privileged elite groups in the emergeing nations, it is also true that the conditions under which democratic politics are attempted in these states produce heavy support for the left from the lower strata as well, thus making it very difficult for conservative parties to find significant bases of support. This is, in

part, because the large mass of the population in such nations live in impoverished conditions. But poverty alone does not breed discontent. In much of nineteenth-century Europe, conservative parties, led by members of the privileged classes, secured heavy backing from the urban and rural poor. They had the weight of traditional legitimacy and identification with the summits of an established status system on their side. Poor persons, like all others, had been reared to accept the old institutional order. Generally speaking, as elaborated in the previous chapter, people are unlikely to change opinions or allegiances which they have held for a long time. Hence leftist groups, modernizing factions, and others favoring large-scale change in the nineteenth century found that significant segments of the lower strata refused to support them. And conservatives, such as Bismarck and Disraeli, consciously sought to keep such support for conservative politics by following a deliberate policy of *noblesse oblige*, of favoring various welfare measures which would enhance the circumstances under which the poorer classes lived. Under such conditions, leftist or innovating parties became serious contenders for political office only after a long and arduous struggle for support.

Those mechanisms inherent in all stratified societies which serve to secure lower-class acceptance of the values of the system thus help to balance the relative strength of conservative and leftist parties. The leftists appeal to the interests of the more numerous lower strata, but the "deference vote" provides the conservatives with a large segment of the votes of the underprivileged. (Japan, Thailand, Iran, and Ethiopia, monarchies which were never colonies, seemingly still retain a large deferential population.)

In many of the new and emerging nations, however, the assumption that the lower classes enter the polity still showing deference to traditional institutions, values,

[32] Maurice Zeitlin, *Revolutionary Politics and the Cuban Working Class* (Princeton: Princeton University Press, 1967).

[33] These continuities are discussed in S. M. Lipset and Mildred Schwartz, "The Politics of Professionals," in H. M. Vollmer and D. L. Mills (eds.), *Professionalization: A Reader in Occupational Change* (Englewood Cliffs: Prentice-Hall, 1966), pp. 299–310.

and privileged classes does not hold.[34] Many high-status positions are associated with hated foreign imperialisms, and with social institutions regarded by large sections of the modernizing elites as contributing to the perpetuation of national inferiority. Thus conservative parties backed by businessmen and/or the rural elite face the difficulty that they do not have the weight of traditional legitimacy or a significant "deference vote" on their side.[35] Leftism and nationalism are often identified with the nation and the modernizing elite. The lower strata, insofar as they are politically conscious, may be won to the side of a radical leftism identified with symbols of national independence.

In such a contest, in which one large section of the elite supports leftist ideological goals, and in which the large majority of the population lives in poverty, the chances are small for the existence of conservative parties representing the traditional elite, or stressing the need for gradual rather than rapid change, as viable electoral alternatives. But as I have noted elsewhere:

> Although conservative groups in most nations are deprived of the link with historic national values which they have in old states, there is at least one traditional institution with which they may identify and whose popular strength they may seek to employ: religion. The leftist national revolutionaries, in their desire to remake their society, often perceive traditional religion as one of the great obstacles; attitudes and values which are dysfunctional to efforts to modernize various institutions are usually associated with ancient religious beliefs and habits. And the efforts by the leaders of new states to challenge these beliefs and habits serve to bring them into conflict with the religious authorities.

> A look at the politics of contemporary new nations indicates that in many of them religion has formed the basis for conservative parties. . . .[36]

In Latin America, for example, religious-linked traditionalism furnishes a large base of support for conservative parties, particularly in relatively unchanging rural areas.[37]

---

[34] Uganda provided an interesting special case of the continuity of traditional mechanisms of authority. Uganda contained a large African monarchy, Buganda, which remained politically autonomous and united under its hereditary monarchy during British rule. Consequently, as Apter has pointed out, Buganda was one of the few large native African states whose population retained that "extraordinary devotion to the king whose hierarchical authority represents what Weber calls hereditary charisma." See David Apter, *The Political Kingdom in Uganda* (Princeton: Princeton University Press, 1961), p. 457.

[35] The weakness of political conservatism in new nations does not mean, of course, that traditional attitudes with respect to other aspects of behavior are also weak. An excellent Indian study points out in detail that the same peasants who vote for modernizing, and even radical, politicians are often strongly attached to the old ways of their village life and resist innovation in agricultural practices. See Kusum Nair, *Blossoms in the Dust* (New York: Praeger, 1962). This distinction between traditional and modern attitudes may be made analytically, but in practice individuals and groups will vary considerably in the extent to which they hold attitudes which are seemingly incongruous. See on this Kalman H. Silvert, "National Values, Development, and Leaders and Followers," *International Social Science Journal*, 15 (1963), 560–570.

[36] S. M. Lipset, *The First New Nation*, pp. 78–79; see also pp. 74–90 for a discussion of factors which weaken potential strength of conservative parties in new states.

[37] See Soares, *op. cit.*, pp. 484–486, 491, for an analysis of the way in which illiteracy, "apathy, religion and traditional values . . . immunize and sterilize the peasants [of impoverished, north-east Brazil] against class organization and the germ of ideological rebellion." Analyses of voting choices in Chile through use of survey data reveal that degree of adherence to Catholicism is the principal correlate of vote decision. See Ruth Ann Pitts, *Political Socialization and Political Change in Santiago de Chile* (M. A. thesis in sociology, University of California, 1963); Brunhilde Velez, *Women's Political Behavior in Chile* (M.A. thesis in sociology, University of California, 1964).

In a number of Moslem countries such as Turkey, Morocco, Pakistan, Malaysia, and Indonesia, religious-linked parties have been able to win considerable support when contesting elections. Similarly, in India, the Hindu religion currently provides a base around which a conservative party, the Jana Sangh, may win support. With very few exceptions, however, religious-linked traditionalism does not appear strong enough to provide conservative opposition parties with a sufficient mass appeal to form a significant alternative to modernizing radical movements.

Conclusions

The differences in the bases of party and ideological cleavage between the developed and underdeveloped world are of more than academic interest to the student of comparative politics. Clearly, the fact that a considerable section of the embryonic (student) and actual elites of the "third world" adhere to seemingly extreme versions of leftist ideologies, while the bulk of the university-educated elites of the developed countries espouse conservative or moderate reform doctrines, makes mutual understanding and communication difficult. In developed Western societies, parties are increasingly agencies of "collective bargaining," representing the conflicting demands of diverse groups and strata. In the emerging nations, parties, particularly left-wing or nationalist ones, and in many of these nations all parties fit this category, see themselves not as representatives of particular groups which seek "more" of the national pie, but rather as the bearers of programs and ideologies most likely successfully to mobilize society for a massive effort at economic development. In the developed nations, Marxism and Socialism are primarily the ideologies of the less well to do, and are naturally opposed by the privileged sectors. In the underdeveloped nations these ideologies serve as slogans to legitimate the efforts of certain elite strata to become or remain the ruling class, and

to exact sacrifice from and impose hardships upon the poor for the sake of achieving the attributes of an economically powerful state.[38]

It should be clear that efforts to generalize about the relation of given statuses and roles to political behavior, seen in terms of the historic left and right categories set in nineteenth- and twentieth-century Europe, prove inadequate when applied to most of the "third" world of Asia, Africa, and Latin America. This chapter has attempted to introduce a discussion of comparative party systems by pointing out some of the historical and other factors which account for diversity in bases of political cleavages. A comprehensive theory of politics which accounts for the behavior of all organizations calling themselves "parties," whether operating in the stable democracies, new states, or totalitarian regimes, is yet to be developed.[39] Meanwhile, we may conclude that exporting models of party systems and

[38] As David Apter has pointed out, the elites of rapidly developing societies require a political myth which will bind to them the masses suffering the dislocations of industrialization and modernization. What religious belief did for the Western countries, he argues, "political religion" must do for the currently emerging nations. See "Political Religion in the New Nations," in Geertz (ed.), *op. cit.*, pp. 57–104. The English sociologist T. B. Bottomore has also suggested that "Marxism . . . is the Calvinism of the twentieth century industrial revolutions," *op. cit.*, p. 94.

[39] This does not mean that I believe that it cannot be developed. I would agree here with the programmatic statement made by Edward Shils for the Committee for the Comparative Study of New Nations in which he asserts, concerning efforts to deal with the politics of all nations: "Our task in this regard is to find the categories within which the unique may be described, and in which its differences with respect to other situations may be presented in a way that raises scientifically significant problems. Orderly comparison is one necessary step in the process of systematic explanation. . . ." "On the Comparative Study of the New States," *op. cit.*, p. 15. This article is an excellent statement of the problems and ambitions of comparative political sociology as derivative from Max Weber.

ideologies which "work" in advanced industrialized areas to less advantaged ones is not only bad social science, but much worse, may result in disastrous politics, as when ideologies of the Western underprivileged serve to justify intensive exploitation by the new ruling classes of the capital-accumulating Communist and "third" worlds. Rather than serving to articulate and justify the demands of the working class, as in the Western industrialized nations, the ideologies of the left as often applied by elites in the developing countries serve to mask a basic cleavage of interest between rulers and ruled, and to legitimate the political myth of a monolithic identity of elites and masses. In nineteenth- and twentieth-century Europe, Marxism and socialism have called to the attention of the workers and the poor generally that there is a basic continuing conflict over economic returns between themselves and those who control the means of production; in the contemporary Communist and the authoritarian states of the underdeveloped world, Marxism and socialism are defined to mean that the interests of both the controllers of the economy and the impoverished workers and peasantry are the same.[40] In nineteenth-century Europe, Marxism justified

a struggle for the creation of free trade unions which exercised the right to strike, and for the rights of free speech, press, assembly, and competitive representative parties; in the contemporary Communist and many "third" world countries, Marxism is used by the ruling strata to supply arguments denying all of these rights.

This use of Marxism as the ideology of the aspiring elites of preindustrial societies was, of course, never anticipated by Marx and Engels. Rather, they conceived of socialist doctrines as helping to fulfill the aspirations of the working class in highly developed capitalist industrial societies. Socialist movements would only come to power in nations which had reached as high a level of industrialization as was possible under capitalism.[41] Socialism was never seen as an approach to rapid industrialization, rather it involved an effort to create a society with a higher state of genuine freedom in which workers and others would be liberated from the authoritarian restrictions inherent in bureaucratic industrial organization. Hense, the very concept of socialism as used by Marx and Engels had no meaning except in a post-capitalist, post-industrial society in which machines liberated humanity from tedious work. Many Marxists, such as Rosa Luxemburg and Julian Martov, consequently, were horrified by the Bolshevik seizure of power in Russia in 1917, because they believed that it was sociologically premature, that it could only result in a severe distortion of socialism and hold back efforts to create the type of society, that is, that of libertarian socialism, envisaged by Marx and Engels. And, in fact, Marxism and socialism in the Soviet Union have served to justify as intensive a form of exploitation of human labor to secure "surplus value" for capital accumulation as the ruling class of any industrializing nation has ever at-

---

[40] Guy Hunter points out that in West Africa, socialism as advocated by the governing elite "includes above all the devotion to central planning of the use of resources, both human and material, for the common good. The West African press, both English and French, and the speeches of leaders hammer home again and again this planning theme, often opposed to the selfishness of the profit motive. . . .
"There is, however, little or no emphasis on the moral aspects of socialism, the gap between rich and poor. In tropical Africa as a whole exactly the reverse process is at present in full swing; the salaries and perquisites of the ruling group and of the whole professional and educated class are at or near the old expatriate level. . . . Despite constant inquiry, we could find little evidence of 'socialist' thinking in this moral sense, save among a few of the younger intellectuals in Lagos and Accra. . . ." *The New Societies of Tropical Africa* (London: Oxford University Press, 1962), pp. 288–289.

[41] A related discussion on the same point may be found in Adam Ulum, *The Unfinished Revolution* (New York: Random House, 1960), *passim.*

tempted since the beginning of the Industrial Revolution.

The possibilities for the establishment and institutionalization of democratic procedures in the nations which now lack them are in large part dependent on the emergence of political cleavages rooted in interest and value differences that do not give any one political force predominant strength. A doctrine which denies sociological validity and political legitimacy to such differences once the party of the "workers" or the "people" is in power is a major obstacle to the formation of democratic polities. In this respect, Marxist doctrines as postulated in the underdeveloped world are profoundly different from those which justified the eighteenth- and nineteenth-century bourgeois revolutions in the West. The latter, although also organized under universalistic ideologies of equality which served to justify the aspirations of the new bourgeois elite to replace the old aristocratic one, nevertheless assumed the validity of interest differences, that the poor and the rich, the landed and the commercial classes, had separate interests. Democracy requires a recognition of the legitimacy of conflict and interest representation among the diverse groups in society, regardless of the form of economic organization. The breakdown of communication between Western and non-Western socialists is a result of the tremendous gap which exists between them given the considerably divergent connotations and social functions which socialism has taken on in different parts of the world. The possibility that socialism may regain in the "third" and Communist worlds its historic role as the ideology sustaining the lower strata's aspirations for more power, status, and income, cannot be ruled out. Endemic in its definition is an anti-elitist, egalitarian view of society. And as recent events in some of the Communist countries suggest, some do use the ideology of socialism to justify efforts to bring the accepted social myth and reality into harmony, much as in the United States men have used the American

Creed to press for social equality.[42] The very concepts around which the members of the "new class" defend their right to exclusive possession of power may yet serve to undermine the autocratic systems which they have erected.

In Europe, at the advent of the modern era, the main sources of political tension revolved around the workers' struggle for citizenship, the right to take part in all decisions of the body politic on an equal level with others, against the dominant conservative aristocratic and business strata who controlled politics. In Latin America, as in Asia, leftist ideologies, usually of a Marxist variety, have been dominant among the modernizing elite and those identifying with nationalism. The polity is committed to giving the lower strata full political and social rights before the development of a stable economy which could support a large, relatively conservative urban middle class.

The left in most of Europe grew gradually in a fight for more democracy, for more

---

[42] Evidence that the economically underprivileged do not share the views of the "socialist elite" concerning income differences comes from Communist Poland. An opinion survey inquiring into the proper level of differences in income for various occupations reported "that there is a strong correlation between the incomes of people and their views concerning a maximum scale of income differences. . . . The poll shows that factory workers, technicians, and certain groups of the intelligentsia with low salaries (teachers, post office workers, social service officials, etc.) are in favor of egalitarianism. On the other hand, an unfavorable attitude prevails among people of whom many have possibilities of high incomes." At the extremes, 54 per cent of the workers favored "relatively equal incomes" as contrasted with 20 per cent of the executives. Fifty-five per cent of the latter were strongly against narrowing the income gap, as compared with 8 per cent of the manual workers. But it should be noted that both the egalitarian-oriented less-privileged respondents and the more well-to-do defenders of inequality justified their opinions by "traditional slogans of the left." See S. M. Lipset, *Political Man*, pp. 224, 228–229, for references.

personal and social freedoms, as well as in the struggle to reduce the discontents inherent in early industrialization. The right retained the support of the traditionalist, aristocratic elements in the society, and the political system eventually developed with economic development into a symbiotic relationship between a modified left and right. The result inevitably, as the next chapter tries to point out, is that political parties in Europe, even those of the left, have ceased being revolutionary—as many still are in most of the "third" world—and have become reformist.

PEASANT SOCIETY AND CLIENTELIST POLITICS*

John Duncan Powell

I. Elements of the Patron-Client Relationship

The basic social relations of peasant life are directly related to an environment characterized by extreme scarcity. The major factor of productive wealth in agriculture is land, to which the peasant has little or no free access. Labor—his own, and that of his family members—is available to the peasant, but this relatively unproductive factor must be applied to land in order to generate wealth. Few other outlets for productive labor employment are available to him. When the peasant is able to combine land and labor in a wealth-generating endeavor, his productivity is likely to be extremely low, due to limiting factors such as technology, capital, marketing information, and credit. All of these life aspects combine to hold down the peasant's income and preclude savings. He is, in a word, poor.

Furthermore, the peasant is powerless against many threats which abound in his environment. There are disease, accident, and death, among the natural threats. There are violence, exploitation, and injustice at the hands of the powerful, among the human threats. The peasant knows that this environmental constellation is dangerous. He also knows that there is relatively little he can do about his situation, and, accordingly, his culture often features themes of vulnerability, calamity, and misfortune.[1] As George Foster has neatly summarized it, the outlook this situation engenders in the peasant is the "Image of the Limited Good." Within this image:

> peasants view their social, economic, and natural universes—their total environment—as one in which all of the desired things in life such as land, wealth, health, friendship and love, manliness and

SOURCE: John Duncan Powell, "Peasant Society and Clientelist Politics," *American Political Science Review*, 64:411–25, June, 1970.

* I am grateful for the support of the Center for International Affairs, Harvard University, during the development of this analysis; and I wish to thank the many individuals who were helpful at various stages of its preparation, including Professors James Kurth, Joan Nelson, Samuel Huntington, and various members of the joint Harvard-MIT faculty Seminar on Political Development to whom the original version was presented in 1968. An intermediate version of this essay was presented at the convention of the American Political Science Association in New York, September, 1969.

[1] Consider the interesting results of Thematic Apperception Tests given to peasant respondents in Southern Italy, reported in Edward Banfield, *The Moral Basis of a Backward Society* (New York: Free Press, 1958), ch. 6.

honor, respect and status, power and influence, security and safety, *exist in finite quantity* and *are always in short supply* as far as the peasant is concerned. Not only do these and all other "good things" exist in finite and limited quantities, but in addition *there is no way directly within peasant power to increase the available quantities*.[2]

But there are basic patterns of social relations which develop in peasant societies in order to cope with these realities. They are, in general, anxiety-reduction behaviors by which the peasant attempts to build some security in the face of his perceived environmental threats, or at least to make life more tolerable within a basically threatening context.[3] These social arrangements are adaptive means for increasing the peasant's access to the "good things" in life, and, as Foster implies, they are, of necessity, indirect. One basic set of such arrangements is found in the various kinship systems—nuclear families, extended families and clan organizations.[4] An extension of such arrangements may be found in the fictive kinship relationships present in many peasant societies.[5] Finally, there are a number of typical peasant social mechanisms which function to "equalize poverty" by means of

individual, group, or even institutional actions—the latter, typically, through rituals of conspicuous consumption.[6]

One of these patterns of cooperative social arrangement I wish to treat in detail: *the extended patron-client relationship, or clientele system*. Such a relationship, involving an interchange of noncomparable goods and services between actors of unequal socio-economic ranks, is of profound importance when extended beyond the confines of the peasant community. An extended patron-client network, or clientele system, is important in two distinct ways: one, in its consequences for the political system in which it concretely manifests itself; and two, as an heuristic device for the understanding of a wide range of political behavior which political scientists, in the main, consider to be either pathological, deviant, or of minor import. I refer to patterns of political behavior such as nepotism, personalism, or favoritism; and political structures such as cliques, factions, machines, and patronage groups, or "followings." A fuller understanding of clientele systems, I believe, will render such phenomena more intelligible and significant.[7]

At the core of the patron-client relationship lie three basic factors which at once define and differentiate it from other power relationships which occur between individuals or groups. First, *the patron-client tie develops between two parties unequal in status, wealth and influence;* hence the most

[2] George Foster, "Peasant Society and the Image of the Limited Good," in *Peasant Society: A Reader* (Boston: Little, Brown, 1967), edited by Potter, Diaz, and Foster, p. 304. This is a very useful collection of materials.

[3] On anxiety-reduction as the most powerful organizer of behavior, see Harry Stack Sullivan's *The Interpersonal Theory of Psychiatry*, as applied by Robert Presthus in *The Organizational Society* (New York: A. Knopf, 1962), esp. ch. 4.

[4] See, among others, C. K. Yang, *A Chinese Village in Early Communist Transition* (Cambridge: MIT Press, 1959), ch. 6.

[5] *Peasant Society, op. cit.,* contains reprints of several good articles dealing with fictive kinship systems and their effects, including Sidney Mintz and Eric Wolf, "An analysis of Ritual Co-Parenthood (*Compadrazgo*)," pp. 174–199, and Mary Hollensteiner, "Social Structure and Power in a Philippine Municipality," pp. 200–212.

[6] Foster, "Image of the Limited Good," *op. cit.,* p. 316. Also, see Eric Wolf, "Closed Corporate Peasant Communities in Mesoamerica and Central Java," pp. 230–246 in the same volume; and Mehmet Bequiraj, *Peasantry in Revolution* (Ithaca: Cornell Center for International Studies, 1966).

[7] Two exceptional treatments of the phenomena in question are found in Alex Weingrod, "Patrons, Patronage and Political Parties," *Comparative Studies in Society and History,* Vol. 10 (July 1968), pp. 376–400; and James C. Scott, "Corruption, Machine Politics, and Political Change," this REVIEW, LXII (December, 1969), 1142–1158.

apt description by Pitt-Rivers, who called the patron-client bond a "lopsided friendship."[8] Second, *the formation and maintenance of the relationship depends on reciprocity in the exchange of goods and services.* Such mutual exchanges involve noncomparable goods and services, however. In a typical transaction, the low-status actor (client) will receive material goods and services intended to reduce or ameliorate his environmental threats; while the high-status actor (patron) receives less tangible rewards, such as personal services, indications of esteem, deference or loyalty, or services of a directly political nature such as voting. Third, *the development and maintenance of a patron-client relationship rests heavily on face-to-face contact between the two parties;* the exchanges encompassed in the relationship, being somewhat intimate and highly particularistic, depend upon such proximity. These three characteristics of the patron-client pattern—unequal status, reciprocity and proximity—hold whether the parties are individuals, which is often the case, or kinship groups, extended kinship groups, informal or formal voluntary groups, or even institutions. *It is important to note that patron-client ties clearly are different from other ties which might bind parties unequal in status and proximate in time and space, but which do not rest on the reciprocal exchange of mutually valued goods and services—such as relationships based on coercion, authority, manipulation, and so forth.* Such elements may be present in the patron-client pattern, but if they come to be dominant, the tie is no longer a patron-client relationship.[9]

Within many rural communities the patron status is highly correlated with land-ownership and the client status with poor cultivators dependent upon the patron's land for their livelihood. Here is how one anthropologist describes such a "traditional" relationship between landlord and sharecropper:

A peasant might approach the landlord to ask a favor, perhaps a loan of money or help in some trouble with the law, or the landlord might offer his aid knowing of a problem. If the favor were granted or accepted, further favors were likely to be asked or offered at some later time. The peasant would reciprocate—at a time and in a context different from that of the acceptance of the favor, in order to de-emphasize the material self-interest of the reciprocative action—by bringing the landlord especially choice offerings from the farm produce, or by sending some member of the peasant family to perform services in the landlord's home, by refraining from cheating the landlord, or merely by speaking well of him in public and professing devotion to him.[10]

Silverman also found, in the same Italian community, that similar patron-client relationships could be established by persons who were not personally linked to a powerful figure through the agricultural system but were merely lower-status persons who lived in the community: "The potential client would approach one of the *signori* with a request, or he might attempt to establish the relationship first by presenting him with some small gift or by making himself available to run errands or help out in various ways."[11] An important aspect of these relationships is that the needs of the client tend to be critical—for example, a peasant may need more land to farm in order to feed his growing family—while the needs of the patron, while important to him, tend to be marginal. Not only can a large landowner get along without the

[8] Julian Pitt-Rivers, *The People of the Sierra* (New York: Criterion Books, 1954), p. 140.

[9] For an elegant and fascinating exploration of the varieties of power relationships, see Frederick W. Frey, "Concepts of Development Administration and Strategy Implications for Behavioral Change," unpublished ms, Department of Political Science, MIT.

[10] Sydel Silverman, "The Community-Nation Mediator in Traditional Central Italy," in *Peasant Society, op. cit.,* p. 284.

[11] *Ibid.,* p. 285.

esteem or loyalty of an individual peasant and his family, but there are many more peasant families with needs than there are patrons with assets. The bargaining power of the patron is by definition greater than that of the client.

Several aspects of the patron-client relationship are fixed—such as unequal status, reciprocity and proximity—and some are variable. We should take note of these variables in the relationship before proceeding to the extension of these relationships beyond the confines of the peasant community. The first variable is the origin of the initiative to establish the relationship. Either patron or client may take the initiative. This is less important in enduring relationships than in *ad hoc* or periodic patron-client ties. Duration or persistence over time, then, is a second variable. Third, the scope of the relationship may vary. A patron-client tie may cover the full range of the client's needs, if he is fortunate—from the cradle to the grave, as it were. Other relationships may be defined by the very narrow range of goods and services which are exchanged. Finally, the patron-client tie may vary in its intensity. Affect, feelings of loyalty, obligation, and satisfaction with the benefits of the relationship may be strong or weak. These variables, furthermore, tend to cluster together in distinct patterns. In a "traditional" village —isolated, with few market-network or governmental ties with the outside— patron-client relationships tend to be enduring, extensive and intense. In a more integrated, differentiated village context, patron-client relationships tend to be periodic, defined by special, narrow interests, and casual.

II. Linkages with the Larger System

This brings us to a most crucial point in the analysis—the linking of the "little community" with the larger socio-economic system in which it exists. Two underlying processes are largely responsible for the establishment of these linkages: state centralization and market expansion.[12] Each involves differentiation and specialization of roles and the elaboration of networks of interdependent parts, or more simply put, transaction systems. At the boundary of the little community stands the "gatekeeper"—the landed patron.[13] As the twin processes of state and market penetration of the peasant village occur, the patron becomes transformed into a broker, mediating the impact of the larger society on peasant society.

As a result of increased attention to the interpenetration of present-day peasant cultures and national cultures over the past twenty years or so, the anthropological community has become increasingly aware of these brokers, "hinge groups," "mediators" or "buffers," as they have been portrayed in the literature. Eric Wolf's original definition of brokers will serve us nicely:

. . . they stand guard over the critical junctures and synapses of relationships which connect the local system to the larger whole. *Their basic function is to relate community-oriented individuals who want to stabilize or improve their life chances, but who lack economic security and political connections, with nation-oriented individuals who operate primarily in terms of complex cultural forms standardized as national institutions, but whose success in these operations depends on the size and strength of their personal following.*[14]

[12] These processes are illuminated and applied with excellent effect by Charles Tilly in *The Vendée* (Cambridge: Harvard University Press, 1964), especially ch. 2.

[13] "Gatekeepers," as described by Kenny, "largely dominate the paths linking the local infrastructure of the village to the superstructure of the outside urban world." See his article "Patterns of Patronage in Spain," in the *Anthropological Quarterly*, 33 (January 1960), pp. 14–23.

[14] Eric Wolf, "Aspects of Group Relations in a Complex Society: Mexico," in *Contemporary Cultures and Societies of Latin America* (New York: Random House, 1965), edited by Dwight Heath and Richard Adams, p. 97. (Italics added).

While they vary in cultural forms, Wolf provides as examples of such brokerage systems, the *compadrazgo* system in Latin America, the Chinese *kan-ch'ing*, and the Japanese *oyabunkobun;* to which I would add *clientela* in Italy and Sicily, the *jajmani* system in India, and the patron-client system in the Philippines.[15] I would hypothesize that such clientele systems might be encountered in any developing country in which kinship systems are unable to perform linkage functions between persons of low and high status, or between the community and the nation. Where kinship systems can perform these linkage functions at all, as in Greece (and under certain conditions in Italy), they are likely to be responsive to only a limited range of needs, leaving low-status clients to rely on non-kinship clientele systems as well.[16]

Of great importance is the manner in which these extended clientele systems change over time. Traditional, land-owning patrons may become brokers, but additional brokers may appear to compete with them for followings on the local level. Power holders on the national level may or may not consolidate and formalize some of these clientele systems, playing off one network of brokers against another in the process. These processes of change, and their significance for political development, will be more understandable if we consider some concrete historic examples.

Sydel Silverman, in "The Community-Nation Mediator in Traditional Central Italy," focusses precisely on such changes over time.[17] According to her, prior to Italian national unification, the patron-client system was almost the exclusive domain of the great landlords, who acted in the main as direct benefactors, but also as links with the larger, Church-dominated society of central Italy. As far as commercial ties were concerned, they too were guarded by the landlords, but extended only to provincial market towns. Following unification in the 1860-1861 period, nation-community contacts grew, and landlords added to their functions as direct benefactors (loans, employment, land-access, dowry gifts, medicines) those of brokerage services. When a peasant client had dealings with bureaucracies—taxes, credits, etc. —or with the police in the area, the patron acted as broker. The role of broker, in fact, became generalized in peasant dealings with "outsiders," and the "letters of recommendation" became more highly valued in many instances than direct patronage benefits. Such letters were considered imperative when undertaking an arrangement with a distant merchant, or in seeking public employment. As outside relationships became more important over time, says Silverman, "the most valuable patron was neither the wealthiest nor the most generous, but the one with the best connections."[18]

In addition to the changes of function of the traditional patrons (the large landowners), which transformed them into brokers, other local people with "outside connections" also began to assume brokerage functions — bourgeois landowners, schoolteachers, physicians and pharmacists, priests, tax collectors and other local officials. Some of these "new" brokers had connections with the marketing system, and some with the political system, but all were intermediate in socio-economic status. They were, in other words, those whom one

---

[15] Latin America, China, and Japan cited by Wolf, *ibid.* A full treatment of *clientela* in Italy is given by Sidney Tarrow, *Peasant Communism in Southern Italy* (New Haven: Yale, 1967). For India, see Lewis and Barnouw, "Castle and the Jajmani System in a North Indian Village," in *Peasant Society, op. cit.*, pp. 110–134. The Philippine materials are presented by Carl Landé in *Leaders, Factions and Parties—The Structure of Philippine Politics* (New Haven: Yale University Southeast Asian Studies, 1965), Monograph No. 6.

[16] Ernestine Friedl, "The Role of Kinship in the Transmission of National Culture to Rural Villages in Mainland Greece," *American Anthropologist*, 61 (Feb. 1959), 30–38; and Joseph Lopreato, *Peasants No More* (San Francisco: Chandler, 1967), Part Two.

[17] In *Peasant Society, op. cit.*, pp. 279–293.
[18] *Ibid.*, p. 289.

writer has recently characterized as the "small intellectuals" of society, whose status and role functions place them in the "strategic middle" of the social structure.[19] The Italian case clearly suggests the impact of state centralization in the little community, transforming traditional patrons into brokers, as well as creating a new pool of potential brokers (i.e., governmental agents) on the periphery of the peasant society. Similarly, the penetration of market networks, with its resultant differentiation and specialization of new roles, further enlarged the pool of potential brokers. These twin forces for change may be seen in another historic case, that of Mexico.

Eric Wolf specifically undertook a diachronic analysis of brokerage groups in rural Mexico in his seminal article, "Aspects of Group Relationships in a Complex Society: Mexico."[20] First, he traced the entry of the Spaniards into the previously autonomous Indian communities, and the establishment of landed power-holding by representatives of the Crown. This was accomplished through the *encomienda* system, and in agriculture as well as mining, enclaves of primary production were established and linked into a rudimentary trade system with the mother country. In addition to the landholdings producing for international trade, landed powerholders, encroaching on the communal lands of the Indians, established autonomous, self-sufficient holdings in the manorial or patrimonial style.[21] Both types of holding provided bases of manpower and wealth for a highly decentralized system of political power. In time, the struggle by Spain for the recapture of its political power and monopoly in the trading system precipitated

the War of Independence by the New World landed elites. During this period of Mexican land history, the same kind of "traditional" patron behavior described for Italy by Silverman, characterized Mexican landlord-peasant relationships, exaggerated by cultural and linguistic differences.

According to Wolf, a byproduct of the trade systems established under the Crown had been a group of "marginals"—small storekeepers, middlemen, casual farmers and specialized workers located in the villages and entrepreneurial communities near mines, *haciendas*, or mills. With the destruction of the ties to Spain, the legal devices which had until that time granted a small measure of protection to the Indian communities were swept aside, and a long period of land-grabbing began. Communal property-holding dissolved into "land as a commodity," and the best remaining Indian lands were taken over by large landlords, or invaded by the upward-striving "marginals." From these processes grew the classic *hacienda* system, the epitome of autonomous, self-sufficient localism.

The Revolution of 1910 had, as one of its major consequences, the recapture of local political power by the central authorities. Violent peasant upheavals eliminated some of the local, landed powerholders, and agents of government were dispatched into the rural areas to foster the business of the "outside" authorities. As in Italy, many of the remaining landowners, more likely to be bourgeois than "aristocratic" in standing, became transformed from direct benefactors (patrons) into brokers. With the greater flow of goods and services into the rural areas which characterized postrevolutionary Mexican governments, not only did local representatives of the national government proliferate and increase in importance as brokers, but the local "small intellectuals" found increasing employment for their specific mediating skills, thereby gaining for themselves a useful channel of socio-economic mobility and influence.

[19] Belden Paulson, "The Role of the Small Intellectual as an Agent of Political Change: Brazil, Italy, and Wisconsin," paper delivered at the American Political Science annual meeting in Chicago, September, 1967.

[20] Originally published in the *American Anthropologist*, 58 (December, 1956), 1065–1078.

[21] See Eric Wolf, *Peasants* (Englewood Cliffs: Prentice-Hall, 1966), especially "Types of Domain," pp. 50–59.

III. The Clientelist State

Small-scale patrons, we have seen, may become transformed into brokers in the course of state and market centralization. This implies that the patron-client pattern is replicated on a higher level of organization; and indeed this is found to be the case. Thus, in discussing the Thai bureaucracy, Shor observed that:

> . . . The personal clique, based on a feudal-like system of personal obligation, provides the principal focus of bureaucratic loyalty and identification. Bonds of reciprocal obligation, reminiscent of earlier patron-client structures in the traditional social system, informally align a number of dependent subordinates with individual political and administrative leaders in more or less cohesive informal structures.[22]

And in commenting on Rustow's study of the Turkish bureaucracy, Guenther Roth points out that there exists "what is imprecisely known as 'corruption': 'connections' count, favoritism prevails, and for the few there is abundant profit in real-estate dealings."[23] There are probably few countries in which such forms of behavior cannot be encountered; the important difference lying in the fact that in some—for example, contemporary South Vietnam—these forms dominate the organization of the polity. What we have then is a variation on Weber's Patrimonial State. As Guenther Roth has said of this variation, "The second type of patrimonialism is personal rulership on the basis of loyalties that do not require any belief in the ruler's unique personal qualifications, but are inextricably linked to material incentives and re-

wards."[24] I propose that we call this model the Clientelist State.

The utility of the clientelist notion is not limited to personalist, primitive polities. As Roth quite rightly points out, "in terms of traditional political theory, some of these new states may not be states at all but merely private governments of those powerful enough to rule" . . . but, on the other hand, ". . . personal rulership . . . is an ineradicable component of the public and private bureaucracies of highly industrialized countries."[25] I should now like to turn to the impact of clientelist politics in the national electoral process of many developing countries. The client-broker-patron network, we shall find, is of key importance as the electoral process reaches the level of the peasant village. I do not intend to digress for the moment to analyze the historic processes by which peasant voters —usually illiterate—become enfranchised, nor the processes by which elections come to play a central role in the distribution and transfer of political authority. Let us simply acknowledge the observable fact that in many countries today, including Italy, Venezuela, India, Turkey, the Philippines, and others, peasants do vote and elections are determinative. Patron-client patterns of behavior become significant for such countries in the periodic mobilization of peasant voters. At the level of the village, we find competition among brokers and potential brokers for peasant votes which can be delivered to a particular political patron or potential patron. Such competition, which

---

[22] Edgar Shor, "The Thai Bureaucracy," *Administrative Science Quarterly*, 5 (June, 1960), pp. 70, 77, 80, as cited in Guenther Roth, Personal Rulership, Patrimonialism, and Empire-Building in the New States," *World Politics* 20 (January, 1968), p. 202.

[23] Roth, *ibid.*, p. 203.

[24] *Ibid.*, p. 196. For vestiges of such behavior in complex societies, see Eric Wolf, "Kinship, Friendship, and Patron-Client Relations in Complex Societies," in *The Social Anthropology of Complex Societies* (New York: Praeger, 1966), edited by Michael Banton, pp. 1–22. An excellent study of clientelist politics in administration is Anthony Leeds, "Brazilian Careers and Social Structures: An Evolutionary Model and Case History," reprinted in Heath & Adams, *Contemporary Cultures, op. cit.*, pp. 379–404.

[25] Roth, *op. cit.*, p. 196.

has been described as "factionalism" in village politics, is an essential ingredient in the process of aggregating clienteles into a widespread network, and linking them to vertical patronage structures in the political system.[26]

National or regional political leaders recruit local political leaders from among the competing patrons and brokers. Local brokers and patrons recruit subleaders, or political workers, in turn; and these workers recruit or assemble small followings from among their kin, caste brothers, occupational colleagues, or voluntary group associates. Mayer calls such a cross-cutting electoral aggregate an "action-set," assembled for a particular action fixed in time and space (i.e., an election). In all essential details, it appears to be an aggregation of clienteles:

> These workers acted as links between the candidate and the electorate. Sometimes they did this for the advantages they calculated would accrue to them if the candidate were elected; sometimes they were acting because of party loyalty and friendships formed over the years without any thoughts of gain from the elec-

tion itself; and at yet other times they were discharging specific obligations contracted at earlier times. *In the same way, there was an attempt to reach voters on the basis of a past or future benefit . . . In consequence, a great deal of the electioneering was carried out by workers, who sought to influence those with whom they had some appropriate relationship.*[27]

The exact nature of the "appropriate" relationship is a significant question. A local political worker may pull together voters on the basis of kinship ties, fictive kinship or caste ties, or through a variety of relationships, including patron-client ties. The worker who pulls such electoral bloclets together assumes the role of broker for that group with a patron group or institution, in this case a political party. Furthermore, there is some evidence which suggests that the "appropriate relationship" for pulling in peasant voters may be distinctly different from one party to another. Table 1 below is a re-arrangement of data presented by Ralph Nicholas from his study of factional politics in Govindapur, West Bengal, in which he analyzed the basis for membership in nine village factions, each with a leader linked to a particular political party.

The data in Table 1 led me to the following tentative hypothesis. The exact nature of the ties to peasant voters which are acti-

---

[26] It would be a mistake, however, to assume that inter-broker competition automatically increases the power of the client in relation to the broker or patron. Individual brokers and/or patrons tend to control different resources, not to have differential control over the same resources. Furthermore, competition may occur in terms of the number of peasant votes, but not necessarily for the votes of the same peasants. Each broker tends to mobilize the votes of the peasants over whom he has some kind of critical leverage. Indeed, inter-broker competition may lead to less bargaining power for the client, rather than more, as for example the case of a peasant who finds himself within the power domain of a landlord, a moneylender, and a storekeeper, all of whom pressure him to vote in accord with their particular preferences. In short, the degree of power asymmetry between patron and client or broker and client is a matter for empirical enquiry; and if there is no asymmetry, the relationship in question is not clientelism.

[27] Adrian Mayer, "The Significance of Quasi-Groups in the Study of Complex Societies," in *The Social Anthropology of Complex Societies, op. cit.*, p. 103 (emphasis added). Note that at this point we might break down brokers into at least three types, or specialists: one, a grassroots mobilizer, or "ward-heeler"; two, a pure broker, of the kind found on the floor of a stock exchange; and three, a high level influence peddler. The mobilizer can turn out the bodies for any particular purpose, the influence peddler locates political patrons who desire mass political services, and the pure broker brings them together in the political market place. Note also the cross-class-cutting nature of this process. In a significant sense, it functions to integrate actors high and low in the social hierarchy, thereby serving as a potential buffer to inter-class conflict.

Table 1. Factional Alignments of all Possible Voters in Govindapur, West Bengal

		BASIS OF MEMBERSHIP SUPPORT (PER CENT)					
FACTIONAL LEADER NO.	PARTY AFFILIATION OF LEADERS	KINSHIP	CASTE	ECO-NOMIC DEPEND-ENCE	NEIGH-BORHOOD HEAD-MAN	MUTUAL ENEMY	TOTAL
1 & 2	Congress	13%	7	44	17	19	100%
3 & 4	Independent	28%	33	14	25	0	100%
5–9	Communist	52%	20	7	20	1	100%

SOURCE: Adapted from Ralph Nicholas, "Factions: A Comparative Analysis," in *Political Systems and the Distribution of Power* (New York: Praeger, 1965), edited by Gluckman and Eggan. Table 1, page 42.

vated in mobilizing an electoral turnout depends on two related factors: the particular needs of the client, and the relationship of the potential patron's political party to the government. In this Indian case, all parties tended to succeed in mobilizing followings based on neighborhood ties—the headman worked well for the Congress, the Independents, and the Communists. But the Independents and Communists were heavily dependent on utilizing kinship and caste ties to assemble their clienteles. This suggests that the brokerage functions which they performed for their clients were essentially defensive in nature—insuring that their relatives and caste brothers received equitable treatment at the hands of governmental representatives such as tax collectors, credit and extension agents, and the police. This is the other side of the coin of the functions most likely performed by the Congress party brokerage system which involved preferential treatment. This might include access to and influence in the making and administration of economic programs and policies which affected rural enterprises (and the people dependent on them); and in addition, knowledge of and influence in the judicial and police systems for the purpose of dealing with mutual enemies.

IV. Clientelist Politics and Political Parties

We need now to examine more broadly the impact of clientele politics on political parties; and further, to project our analysis into the realm of national politics. This can be economically accomplished by comparing two striking cases which have been rather fully documented and analyzed: Italy and Venezuela.[28] While many of the elements of clientelist politics—with a peasant mass base—can be encountered in the recent or current political history of India, Mexico, Bolivia, Chile, Brazil, Peru, and the Philippines, and to a lesser degree in Indonesia, France, Guatemala, Spain, and Turkey, the cases of Venezuela and Italy are not only well-documented, but seem to represent the upper limits, or fullest development, of which such transaction systems are capable.

Both countries are multiparty electoral democracies in which more than one political party has competed for a peasant base of support through the elaboration of clientele systems. The degree to which the various parties depend on the peasant vote

[28] See Sidney Tarrow, *op. cit.*; and John Duncan Powell, *Peasant Mobilization and Agrarian Reform in Venezuela* (Cambridge: Harvard University Press, forthcoming).

varies, of course, but it is very substantial for the Communist Party (PCI) in Italy, and for the Democratic Action (AD) and Social Christian (COPEI) parties in Venezuela. The Italian Christian Democratic Party (PDC) also receives significant support from peasant constituencies in the south. In both cases, peasant clienteles have been organized into a peasant union movement, which interpenetrates the party system at the local, regional, and national levels. In each country, there has been an extensive agrarian reform program which has provided land and a flow of governmental goods and services downward through the same clientele system which

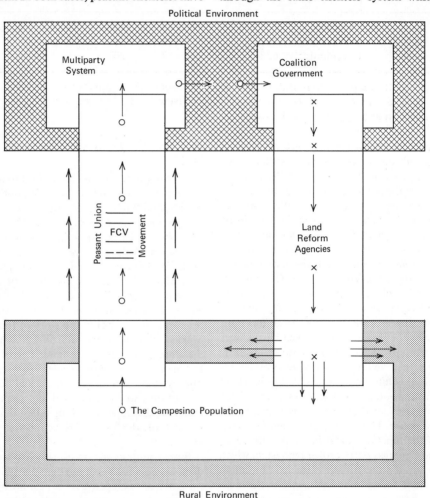

Figure 1.   The rural problem-solving system.

channels votes upward from the peasant base. What we have, in essence, is a transaction system with reciprocal, but unequal, flows of goods and services—votes for agrarian reform benefits. Figure 1 illustrates the Venezuelan system (which I have called the "rural problem-solving system") from the point of view of the peasant. Working through such a network is one of the few instrumental ways in which the peasant can counter his environmental threats.[29] The Italian clientele system, while somewhat more complex, functions in exactly the same manner. An important factor, obviously, is whether or not a particular party is included in a coalition government—and which portfolios or ministries it can influence. In general, the brokerage function is performed by all parties, but those parties outside the government tend to focus on the defense of peasant clients, and the government parties focus on influencing the flow of patronage for their clients. This is a strong tendency, not an absolute distinction.

I wish to emphasize at this point the explicit argument that *peasant clientele systems are built upon, incorporate, and recapitulate the interpersonal patterns of behavior known as clientelism.* Unlike simple patron-client relations, or primitive clientele systems, the Italian and Venezuelan networks have been purposively organized from above, endure in institutionalized form, exchange a wide range of goods and services, and provide quite lengthy chains of linkages—from the peasant to the President or Prime Minister. They are, in a quite specific sense, politically representative. How did such networks come into being, and what effect have they had on national politics in these countries?

In both cases, an urban-based political elite group undertook the organization of the peasantry as a way to mobilize the political capital needed to break into a traditional, elite-dominated inner circle of power in national politics. In Italy, it was the Communist Party which succeeded in organizing the peasantry in the postwar period. In Venezuela, it was the Democratic Action Party (struggling simultaneously to establish a meaningful electoral process and to break the hold of the entrenched, traditional elites on governmental power) which began to organize the peasantry during the 1930's. The responsiveness of the peasantry in both cases rested in part on two factors: a history of bourgeois encroachments on lands formerly available for peasant use; and a recent period of prolonged, serious dislocation of commercial agriculture. In Italy the theme of land *irredenta*, according to Tarrow, originated in the massive takeover of Church and State lands by the bourgeoisie following the national unification in 1861. In Venezuela, there were twin strands of peasant land irredentism: broken promises of land for military service in the armies which fought the War of Independence and the Federal Wars of the nineteenth century; and the encroachment of the bourgeoisie on public lands during the extended, personalistic regime of the dictator, Gómez (1908–1935). The encroachments of the bourgeoisie signalled a "commoditization" of the land, and a subsequent reduction in free land use by the peasantry, often drawing them into a tenancy relationship with the new owners.[30] Dislocations in both commercial and peasant agriculture occurred during the depression in both countries, and were further

[29] See John Duncan Powell, "Venezuela: The Peasant Union Movement," in *Latin American Peasant Movements* (Ithaca: Cornell University Press, 1969), edited by Henry Landsberger, pp. 62–100.

[30] For the proposition that the degree of tenancy correlates positively— and highly— with radical or revolutionary action on the part of the peasantry, see Arthur Stinchcombe, "Agricultural Enterprise and Rural Class Relations," reprinted in *Political Development and Social Change* (New York: Wiley, 1966), edited by Finkle and Gable, pp. 485–497. The same point is made by Bruce Russett in "Inequality and Instability: The Relation of Land Tenure to Politics," in *World Politics*, 16 (April, 1964), p. 452, when tenancy is combined with a high degree of inequality in landholdings.

exacerbated in Italy by World War II. In short, the peasants' status in the prevailing land tenure situation was precarious to begin with, and grew worse prior to their mobilization.

Both AD and the PCI, then, turned to the organization of a discontented peasantry as a way of mobilizing political capital. In the initial stages, before either was in a position to control a government patronage network, their efforts focussed on direct action at the community level, often involving the invasion of farm properties. This was especially true in the case of Italy, where the land invasions of the early 1950's were closely related to the efforts of the PCI to shape and capitalize on peasant discontent. In Venezeuela, AD's opportunity to open up lands to peasant access followed its participation in the *coup d'etat* of October 1945. Dominating the subsequent Revolutionary Government, AD initiated a *de facto* agrarian reform, granting (by decree) access to governmental and private farms to peasant unions organized by the party. The ability to reward followers with land—whether by invasion, as in Italy, or by governmental action, as in Venezuela—quickly expanded the networks of peasanunions, which were actual or aspiring client teles of the parties. Within a period of two or three years, the PCI in the early 1950's and the AD in the mid-1940's, established solid positions in the rural areas.

At this point, the parallels between Italy and Venezuela broke down. AD had established a rudimentary version of its clientele system during the three-year period from 1945–1948, when it was dislodged by a counter-revolutionary coup. When the dictatorship of Pérez Jiménez fell in 1958, and AD was successful in gaining the presidency and dominating a decade of subsequent coalition governments, then the system illustrated in Figure 1 reached fruition, with a well-financed *de jure* agrarian reform program providing a flow of goods and services into the rural areas. In response to AD's successful building of a peasant base

of electoral support, the Social Christian (COPEI) party began its own program of organizing peasant unions. For six years, COPEI was included in the coalition government, providing it some direct access to agrarian reform patronage. After leaving the coalition government, the COPEI peasant unions still maintained indirect access to governmental decision-making (though less effectively than before) through their participation in the multipartisan Federation of Venezuelan Peasants.[31]

In Italy, however, the Christian Democrats, and not the Communists, were in control of the government when the *de jure* agrarian reform program was established. As a result, many of the local leaders and peasant clients organized by the PCI for the purpose of obtaining land (by invasions) were drawn into the Christian Democratic peasant-union-party structure when land and other benefits could be had through the agrarian reform program. As Tarrow describes the resulting dilemma of the Communists:

> . . . the Catholic Confederation of Direct Cultivators is really a corporate arm of the government which dispenses patronage to peasants through a complicated system of interlocking directorates with the provincial agricultural syndicates . . . The chain of causation is revealing. In leading the struggle for the land, the Communists forced the Agrarian Reform; but in the achievements of the Reform, many peasants became dependents of the Christian Democrats and of the state.[32]

With the successful establishment of a state-supported clientele system which provided land, credit, extension services, infra-

[31] In the December 1968 elections COPEI won the presidency and hence control over the formation of a subsequent coalition government from which AD was excluded. As of this date, therefore, access of the two parties is the reverse of the 1964–1968 situation.

[32] Tarrow, *Peasant Communism, op. cit.*, p. 364.

structure and marketing services to peasant clients, the peasantry became "demobilized" in Tarrow's phrase. That is, land invasions and threats of violence subsided. In an important sense, however, the electoral mobilization of the peasantry was not a phenomenon which faded away, but one which was in fact stabilized and institutionalized through the same clientele system which provided the agrarian reform benefits. In short, the notion that peasants will lapse into political inactivity once they obtain a piece of land seems to be a myth. A piece of land is only a necessary, but not sufficient, condition to allow the peasant to escape the world of *la miseria*. He also needs financial, technological, and marketing assistance to significantly improve his standard of living. There is a continuing need for a patron, or patronage system, which can respond to increasingly sophisticated and complex demands, and thus peasant dependency and peasant mobilization become institutionally linked.

Both the Christian Democrats in Italy and Democratic Action in Venezuela have achieved the necessary transactional equilibrium within their peasant clientele systems to stabilize a dependable base of legitimizing electoral support. From the point of view of the party leaders at the national level, a clientele system based on peasants rather than on other societal groups seems to be a sound investment. The peasant is an economical client. His range of needs tends to be narrower and more fixed than that of comparable urban clients. And in meeting the needs of peasants for more land to farm, technological and financial assistance in farm operations, public health and sanitation projects, and finally, marketing assistance, governmental decision-makers are acting in a manner not only compatible with, but prescribed by the logic of economic development. This is not the case in responding to the needs of potential urban client groups, where the costs of improving the quality of the urban environment are high, the gestation periods

long, and the returns on capital investment indirect. But the support of such an electorally-legitimizing clientele system has its disadvantages as well as its advantages in the national political arena.

In analyzing the assets and liabilities of a peasant clientele system for a political party in governmental power, I would like to leave aside the Italian case, in which peasant support is relatively marginal to the position of the Christian Democrats, and consider, in addition to Venezuela, the cases of Bolivia and Mexico.[33] In the latter two cases, peasant clientele support is, or has been, of much more critical import than in the Italian case. In Bolivia and Mexico, as in the other two countries, the peasantry had lost land to an encroaching bourgeoisie. And both countries had experienced a prolonged period of economic dislocation, which was both a contributing cause and a partial effect of the Mexican Revolution of 1910 and the Bolivian Revolution of 1952. In neither of these two cases had a political party seeking to break into the ranks of the traditional elites originally organized a political base among the peasantry as a part of that effort. In Mexico and in Bolivia, governmental parties which grew out of the revolution incorporated embryonic peasant organizations and transformed them into a supportive clientele network as part of their consolidation of political power. As in Venezuela and Italy, an agrarian reform program was the patronage vehicle, partly consolidating and ratifying *de facto* changes brought about by peasant land invasions, and partly distributing land and other goods and services throughout the areas of peasand concentration. While the Bolivian, Mexican, and Venezuelan cases differ in de-

[33] See Peter P. Lord, "The Peasantry as an Emerging Political Factor in Mexico, Bolivia, and Venezuela," (Madison: University of Wisconsin Land Tenure Center, 1965), Research Paper No. 35 (mimeo.); and Charles Erasmus, "Upper Limits of Peasantry and Agrarian Reform: Bolivia, Venezuela, and Mexico Compared," in *Ethnology*, 6 (October, 1967), 349–380.

tail and circumstances, one can state that governmental parties, supported by peasant clientele systems, successfully governed for extended periods of time—in Bolivia from 1952 through 1964; in Mexico, from the mid-1930's to the present; and in Venezuela from 1958 to at least 1968. There is reason to believe that the government which replaced the original sponsor of the Bolivian Revolution (the MNR) in 1964 has continued to rely on the peasant clientele system established by its predecessor.

One of the salient characteristics of governments based on peasant clientele systems has been their capacity to withstand challenges from groups on both extremes of the political spectrum. In Mexico and Bolivia, where the traditional military establishments were eliminated, worker and peasant militias were used to resist the overthrow of the revolutionary governments by right-wing violence. Obregón, with the help of agrarian unions, successfully defended his government in 1923 against the attack by General de la Huerta. In Bolivia miner and peasant militias were instrumental in resisting the overthrow of the Revolutionary government until 1964. In Venezuela, where the professional armed forces were co-opted into the governmental clientele system rather than destroyed, armed peasant and labor militias were never formed, but mass peasant demonstrations were organized in Caracas on several occasions when the threat of a right-wing or dissident military *coup* seemed imminent, as in 1960. We might characterize such a capacity of resistance as stability against the recapture of political power by the traditional elites who were earlier displaced by the parties in government.

A peasant clientele base has been effective in meeting destabilizing challenges from the left, also. In Bolivia and Mexico, one-party states during the period under consideration, this amounted to resistance by the peasant branch, to a left-wing challenge from the labor branch of the party. In Mexico, in 1940, insurrection within the

party by the leader of the left-wing labor sector, Lombardo Toledano, was resisted partly through the intervention of the peasant unions. In Bolivia, Juan Lechín, the leader of the miners' unions, made a similar attempt in 1964 to capture his party's presidential nomination, and was resisted by the peasant branch of the party. In Venezuela, the violent opposition of the Communists and left-wing splinter groups, and guerrilla efforts have been unsuccessful partly because of the disinclination of the peasants—who are clients of the government—to join in an attack on the source of their partronage. The characterization of all of these efforts as "left-wing" probably needs some qualification. In all three of these cases, the longer a peasant-based party has remained in governmental power, the more centrist, pragmatic, and moderate its policies have become. In other words, the drift away from earlier doctrinal positions has been toward the "right." Attacks from the "left," therefore, may also be accurately described in many cases as attacks from party loyalists who are unwilling to make compromises for the sake of maintaining governmental legitimacy among other groups in the political system.

Whatever the ideological implications of these events—and perhaps ideological references are more confusing than helpful in this context—rural-based parties have been able to withstand the destabilizing challenges of a number of urban-based, competing elites. As Samuel P. Huntington sees this phenomenon (which he describes as the result of a "ruralizing election"):

. . . the party which was strong in the countryside normally secured control of the national government and inaugurated a regime characterized by a high degree of political stability. Where no party had a clear base of support in the countryside, some form of instability was the result. In some instances, urban revolts may overturn rural-based governments, but in general governments which are strong in the countryside are able to withstand, if not to reduce or eliminate, the continuing opposition they confront in the cities.[34]

The use of peasant clients for purposes of political combat outside of the electoral realm has its limitations, obviously. But a clientelist base of support is also quite advantageous in political struggle and accommodation short of combat. Since the nature of the "contract" struck between the government (patron) and the peasantry (client) is concerned, really, with the flow of a rather mundane range of pay-offs—small amounts of land, credit, technological and marketing assistance—there is little or no ideological or programmatic content in the "contract" which might entangle a political elite with dissidents within or without its own party. As a result, peasant-based parties enjoy an amazing degree of flexibility in questions of policy, doctrine, and dogma. They are able to accommodate many divergent points of view within their own parties, and to deal pragmatically with opposition points of view without stirring up internal resistances. They are "pragmatic parties" *par excellence.*

But these very advantages of clientelist bases of support suggest the limitations of such systems. First, a clientelist base of support tends to erode the ideological coherence and program content with which the leaders of these parties come to power. This is less true in a revolutionary situation, as in Bolivia and Mexico, where the parties which came to power had no ideological coherence to begin with. But Democratic Action, and to an even greater extent, the Italian Christian Democrats, did attach some importance to doctrine and ideology. The Italian case is especially striking, for both the Communists and the Christian Democrats were frustrated by the manner in which their policy and doctrinal preferences were thwarted by the clientelist

mentality. The power of the peasant culture in this respect was clearly noted by Tarrow:

> . . . social groups remain chaotic, and political organization normally resides latently in the clientele ties between landholder and agricultural worker, lawyer and client, and bureaucrat and favor seeker. Local and parochial loyalties suffuse politics. Politics has very little ideological content, and popular imagery recognizes only two basic social groups: peasants and non-peasants.[35]

The result has been internally traumatic for the Italian Communist Party, which operates in a distinctly different milieu in the north. "Party leaders," notes Tarrow, "complain that southern members cluster around dominant personalities and neglect the day-to-day tasks of organization and proselytism," and "critics maintain that the evidence points to the PCI's being a typical southern party of clienteles."[36]

Ideological erosion in the southern clientelist milieu has equally dismayed the leaders of the Christian Democratic Party, despite the fact that electoral support is derived therefrom:

> Fanfani called for the *political*, and not simply the economic, development of the South. "Above all," he said, "we must create active and efficient party sections and organizations in southern Italy, if we want to create a politics of facts and ideas instead of a politics of agitation and macaroni" . . . terms that epitomized the traditional tools of southern Italian politics: the generic protest, the patronage appointment, the letter of recommendation, the sack of pasta on election day—in other words, the clientele system.[37]

In short, one of the limitations of clientelist politics is the strain it places on coherent ideologies. This may manifest itself

---

[34] Samuel P. Huntington, *Political Order in Changing Societies* (New Haven: Yale University Press, 1968), p. 437.

[35] Tarrow, *Peasant Communism, op. cit.*, p. 261.
[36] *Ibid.*, p. 270.
[37] *Ibid.*, pp. 308–309.

in several important ways. Ideological parties may find it so difficult to reconcile discrepancies in ideas and reality that they will be either unable to build a clientelist base to begin with, or to maintain one if they do. Therefore, other, more pragmatic, parties may outdo them in competition for the peasant vote. Similarly, within parties the stretching of ideology to encompass and legitimate clientelism may work in one of two ways: either the majority of the party leadership accepts the erosion of ideology, in which case the ideological purists among the leadership may leave the party; or the leadership majority may resist the erosion of ideology, in which case the peasant clients may leave or be lured away from the party. In either case, the party is weakened.

A second general limitation of clientelist politics is that it seems to be a transitional phenomenon—or, better put, appropriate and successful only under certain conditions, and then for a limited period of time. As Huntington has analyzed this situation in his book, *Political Order in Changing Societies*, political modernization involves several alternative cycles of change in urban-rural power and stability.[38] The mobilization of a peasant base of support by an urban-based political party is one form of what Huntington calls the "Green Uprising." Eventually, in the course of overall modernization, the growth of the city becomes a destabilizing phenomenon: in some cases, an urban elite group can form an alliance with the peasantry, surrounding, as it were, the unstable city with the stable countryside by bringing the two into an interdependent relationship. The resulting period of governmental stability may then be used to perform many of the necessary modernizing tasks of government in the course of development. Success, however, brings with it a decreasing relevance and effectiveness of the original peasant base of support:

[38] Huntington, *op. cit.*, especially the first and last chapters.

If revolution is avoided, in due course the urban middle class changes significantly; it becomes more conservative as it becomes larger. The urban working class also begins to participate in politics, but it is usually either too weak to challenge the middle class or too conservative to want to do so. Thus, as urbanization proceeds, the city comes to play a more effective role in the politics of the country, and the city itself becomes more conservative. The political system and the government come to depend more upon the support of the city than upon that of the countryside. Indeed, it now becomes the turn of the countryside to react against the prospect of domination by the city.[39]

In terms of a peasant-based clientele system, such as Venezuela's, the end of this cycle is marked by a gradual tapering off of governmental support for the agrarian reform program, as growing urban-based clientele groups exert increasing influence on internal party politics. The budgetary priorities problem may provoke splintering within the party, as brokers in the peasant clientele system find their ability to deliver the goods downward gradually eroded. These party subleaders in many cases demand a "reradicalization" of the agrarian reform—that is, a resumption of larger flows of land and other agrarian reform benefits—and may even try to reinstate the land invasion tactic. In Venezuela and in Mexico, such internal dissension has resulted in brokerage leaders identified with the peasant branch either leaving the party for a more radical alternative, or being purged; and the occasion a establishment of new peasant union splinter movements.

The general pattern, then, seems to be a cyclical one—the rise and fall of peasant-based clientelist politics. Where the political culture is a carrier of patron-client patterns of behavior, the disintegration of peasant clientelist politics does not mark the demise of the generic pattern. To the contrary,

[39] *Ibid.*, p. 77.

urban-based clientelist politics may proliferate. They may be more subtle and complex, but function in essentially the same manner. The agrarian reform, often begun with an initial burst of distributive activities, is slowed down, or consolidated, into a bureaucratic program of gradually receding importance. It may be succeeded by vast programs in worker's housing construction, or public works projects to improve the nature of life for the urban masses. These and other signs may indicate that the cycle described by Huntington is nearing its end.

V. Conclusion

It seems appropriate to conclude this discussion of clientelist politics by placing the concept in perspective: what claims are made for it as an heuristic tool, and what are its limitations? The concept, I believe, helps to illuminate the political behavior of low-status actors, particularly peasants, as they are incorporated, recruited, mobilized, or inducted into the national political process. Inasmuch as the induction of the peasantry into this process has in fact not yet occurred in many of the developing countries, an understanding of clientelist politics may be useful in a predictive sense. And while clientelist behavior may be most visible in the political cultures of Mediterranean extraction, there is much—although scattered—evidence that it can be encountered in political cultures in many parts of the world. This is not a prediction that clientele systems of the type found in Italy or Venezuela are to be anticipated elsewhere, but that clientelist patterns of interpersonal behavior may be a significant factor in the process of peasant politicization everywhere.

Clientele systems clearly differ from other forms of politically representative systems in several ways. In clientelism, there is an almost complete dependency on face-to-face relationships in the building and maintenance of the system. Impersonal communications between persons low and high in the system hierarchy are as ineffective as

they are rare.[40] A low-status participant may, on occasion, personally approach a high-status participant in the same clientele system, but normally he depends on a series of linkages with intermediate brokers. This norm-dependency on personal contact—derives from the nature of the patron-client contract.

The dyadic contract between patron and client—or broker and patron—is a private, unwritten, informal agreement, and highly personalistic in content. There is no public scrutiny of the terms of such agreements. There is no public entity which functions as an enforcement authority concerning such agreements. There is, in short, no process by which either partner of the agreement can go "outside" the dyadic relationship for enforcement of the contract, or to bring sanctions for noncompliance. Enforcement, compliance, and performance are bound up in, and limited to, the face-to-face relationship between the client and broker, or the broker and patron.

This stands in sharp contrast to the relationship between citizen and representative, or even party member and party leader, in modern systems of political transactions. In essence, the patron-client pattern occurs in the realm of private accountability, the modern pattern in the realm of public accountability. In fact, such a distinction is what makes patron-client ties functional in the first place. As Eric Wolf has put it, in a slightly different context:

> The clearest gain from such a relation should therefore appear in situations where public law cannot guarantee adequate protection against breaches of non-kin contracts. This can occur where public law is weak, or where no cultural patterns of cooperation between non-kin

[40] In my study of local peasant union leaders in Venezuela, it was found that 79.9% of all contacts between local and state leaders were in the nature of personal visits. Even contacts with national level peasant union leaders were predominantly in the nature of personal visits (33.1%), rather than through correspondence (11.9%) or other means.

exist to guide the required relationship. It can also occur in dealings which border on the illegal or the extra-processual.[41]

The most obvious difference that the private-public distinction makes is in the degree of power asymmetry between superior and subordinate. Superiors in a clientele system are relatively free to behave in an arbitrary and highly personalistic manner in dealing with their subordinates. Subordinates in a clientele system have relatively little recourse in such a situation. Theoretically, clients could improve their bargaining position relative to patrons through the formation of horizontal organizations, such as peasant unions. In practice, this seems difficult for at least two reasons. First, the power asymmetry between client and broker, or patron, on the local level works against the formation of such independent organizations. Organizers, potential local leaders, and prospective members are all relatively vulnerable to the negative sanctions available to the local broker or patron, who often enjoys the cooperation of other local authorities. Second, clientelist patterns of behavior frequently exist in the relationship between peasant union leader and follower.[42] For both of these reasons, peasant unions tend to be part of a clientele system organized from above, rather than a bargaining organization initiated from below.

The burden of this essay has been to explain the transformation of patron-client ties from a strictly local, landlord-peasant relationship of a traditional kind, into a complex, relatively modernized national transaction system. The main point has been that clientelist patterns of behavior persist in modern organizational form, and that an explanation of interpersonal or institutional behavior will be significantly enhanced by understanding the nature of clientelist politics. The fact that achievement criteria become more important in filling patron and brokerage roles is not inconsistent with the maintenance of traditional values embodied in the ascriptive-oriented traditional forms of clientelism. In fact, just as a relatively high power asymmetry promotes stability within clientele systems, the combination of traditional and modern value orientations in the "new" clientelism may function to perpetuate old forms in a manner quite consistent with modern organizational requirements. Seymour Martin Lipset, in discussing ways in which the Japanese have maintained particularistic and ascriptive traits while at the same time combining universalistic and achievement patterns into the elite recruitment process, illustrates how such a combination can function in a highly successful manner.[43] The example of Japanese industry, in fact, not only suggests that traditional patterns of behavior can be consistent with the requirements of modern organizational life, but may even enhance the performance of such requirements in a highly competitive environment. The implication which might flow from this would be that peasant-based transaction systems successfully perform in a competitive, modernizing political environment because of, not in spite of, the functionality of traditional practices and values.

The argument can be carried one step further. I would submit the proposition that certain traditional elements of the political culture, such as clientelism, become more, not less, important as modernizing changes take place in a peasant-

---

[41] Wolf, "Kinship, Friendship, and Patron-Client Relations in Complex Societies," in *The Social Anthropology of Complex Societies*, *op. cit.*, p. 10.

[42] For a concise picture of such relationships in the Brazilian Peasant Leagues, see Benno Galjart, "Class and 'Following' in Rural Brazil," *América Latina*, 7 (July-September, 1964), 3–23.

[43] Seymour Martin Lipset and Aldo Solari (eds.), *Elites in Latin America* (New York: Oxford University Press, 1967), pp. 42–44. See also Anthony Leeds, "Brazilian Careers . . ." *op. cit.*, and Charles Wagley, "Luso-Brazilian Kinship Patterns: The Persistence of a Cultural Tradition," in *Politics of Change in Latin America* (New York: Praeger, 1964), edited by Maier and Weatherhead, pp. 174–189.

based society. Evidence relevant to this proposition has been turned up repeatedly by social anthropologists studying the adaptation of peasant cultures to the stresses and tensions associated with socioeconomic change. As Mintz and Wolf suggest in their analysis of *compadrazgo* (a fictive kinship tie) in Hispanic America:

> It is extremely noteworthy that the mechanism of *compadrazgo* has maintained itself here in the face of what appears to be progressively accelerating social change. We wonder whether the elaborations of the mechanism's forms may be part of the community's unconscious effort to answer new problems. It must increasingly face the insecurity of growing incorporation into the national structure and increasing local wage-based, cash crop competition. This may call forth an increased emphasis on techniques for maintaining and strengthening face-to-face relationships.[44]

Further evidence that change increases reliance on certain traditional practices was found by Wolf in Mexico. In his study of the changing intergroup relations of Mexican Indian communities, he took note of the "tendency of new group relationships to contribute to the preservation of traditional cultural forms."[45] Myron Weiner's findings in India were also consistent with the proposition advanced above. In *The Politics of Scarcity*, he noted the strong tendency of

post-independence political change to bring about marked increases in the activities of traditional community associations of various kinds. These associations were relied on to link village interests with the emerging structures of a modern nation-state.[46]

In short, modernizing transformations in peasant societies may well make the study and analysis of clientelist politics more relevant than ever before.[47] While scholars generally acknowledge the importance of partimonial type behavior in traditional politics, both at the mass and at the elite levels, there may be insufficient appreciation of the fact that such behavior may survive, quite functionally, very late into the developmental process. Much of the evidence presented here has concerned the nature of such behavior in local politics, but I have also tried to demonstrate the importance of clientelist politics as an organizing principle at all levels of developing polities. Whether or not, and to what degree clientelism exists; whether it functions at the level of the village or throughout the polity; and what impact such behavior has on the course and pace of political development are significant, if not critical, empirical questions in the study of politics in peasant-based societies.

[44] Sidney Mintz and Eric Wolf, "An Analysis of Ritual Co-Parenthood (*Compadrazgo*)," in *Peasant Society, op. cit.*, p. 194.

[45] Eric Wolf, "Aspects of Group Relations in a Complex Society: Mexico," in *Contemporary Cultures and Societies of Latin America, op. cit.*, p. 96.

[46] Myron Weiner, *The Politics of Scarcity* (Chicago: The University of Chicago Press, 1962), especially pp. 36–72.

[47] In fact, such a literature seems about to emerge. For example, Professors René Lemarchand and Keith Legg of the University of Florida presented an excellent comparative study, "Clientelism and Politics: A Preliminary Analysis," to the members of the joint Harvard-MIT faculty Seminar on Political Development in February, 1960. The paper is planned for early publication.

THE NATURE OF TRANSITIONAL POLITICS[1]

Lucian W. Pye

Compared with either traditional or modern industrial societies, the transitional societies represent a far greater diversity, for differences in their traditions are compounded by differences in the degree, intensity, and form with which they have been affected by the diffusion of the world culture. Nevertheless, the political processes of most of them seem to show a striking number of shared characteristics, accounted for, it would seem, by their common experience of breaking down traditional forms and attempting to introduce institutions and practices which originated in the now industrialized areas. As Daniel Lerner has noted, the process of modernization has a distinctive quality of its own, and the elements that make it up "do not occur in haphazard and unrelated fashion" but go together regularly because "in some historical sense they had to go together."[2]

SOURCE. Lucian W. Pye, "The Nature of Transitional Politics: An Analytical Model," *Politics, Personality, and Nation-Building* (New Haven: Yale University Press, 1962), pp. 15–31.

[1] This chapter, in somewhat different form, first appeared as "The Non-Western Political Process," in *Journal of Politics*, **20** (August 1958), 468–486.
[2] Daniel Lerner, *The Passing of Traditional Society* (Glencoe, Ill., Free Press, 1958), p. 438.

It should therefore be possible to outline in gross terms some of the main characteristics of what might be called the transitional or non-Western political process. Since these characteristics not only represent the reactions to profound processes of social change but also define the context and the parameters for all continuing efforts at national development, such an analytical model can serve as an approach in introducing the problems of nation-building.

Our model, thus conceived, follows.[3]

1. *The political sphere is not sharply differentiated from the spheres of social and personal relations.* Among the most powerful influences of the traditional order in any society in transition is the survival of a

[3] The picture of the "transitional" political process contained in this chapter is strongly influenced by George McT. Kahin, Guy J. Pauker, and Lucian W. Pye, "Comparative Politics in Non-Western Countries," *American Political Science Review*, **49** (December 1955), 1022–1041; Gabriel A. Almond, "Comparative Political Systems," *Journal of Politics*, **18** (August 1956), 391–409, reprinted in *Political Behavior: A Reader in Theory and Research*, ed. by Heinz Eulau, Samuel J. Eldersveld, and Morris Janowitz (Glencoe, Ill., Free Press, 1956); Dankwart A. Rustow, "New Horizons for Comparative Politics," *World Politics*, **9** (July 1957), 530–549, and also his *Politics and Westernization in the Near East* (Princeton, Center of International Studies, 1956).

pattern of political relationships largely determined by the pattern of social and personal relations, with the inevitable result that the political struggle tends to revolve around issues of prestige, influence, and even of personalities, and not primarily around questions of alternative courses of policy action.

The elite who dominate the national politics of most non-Western countries generally represent a remarkably homogeneous group in terms of educational experience and social background. Indeed, the path by which individuals are recruited into their political roles, where not dependent upon ascriptive considerations, is essentially an acculturation process. It is those who have become urbanized, have received the appropriate forms of education, and have demonstrated skill in establishing the necessary personal relations who are admitted to the ranks of the elite. Thus there is in most transitional societies a distinctive elite culture which, although its criteria of performance are based largely on nonpolitical considerations, is the test for effectiveness in national politics.

At the village level it is even more difficult to distinguish a distinct political sphere. The social status of the individual and his personal ties largely determine his political behavior and the range of his influence, a condition which places severe limits on the effectiveness of any who come from the outside to perform a political role, be it that of an administrative agent of the national government or of a representative of a national party. Indeed, the success of such agents generally depends more on the manner in which they relate themselves to the social structure of the community than on the substance of their political views.

Thus the fundamental framework of non-Western politics is a communal one, and all political behavior is strongly colored by considerations of communal identification.[4] In the more conspicuous

[4] Even Communist parties reflect this ten-

cases the larger communal groupings follow ethnic or religious lines. But behind these divisions lie the smaller but often more tightly knit social groupings, which range from the powerful community of Westernized leaders to the social structure of each individual village.

This essentially communal framework of politics makes it extremely difficult for ideas to command influence in themselves. The response to any advocate of a particular point of view tends to be attuned more to his social position than to the content of his views. Under these conditions it is inappropriate to conceive of an open market place where political ideas can freely compete for support on their own merits. Political discussion tends rather to assume the form of either intracommunal debate or the attempt of one group to justify its position toward another.

The communal framework also sharply limits freedom in altering political allegiances. Any change in political identification generally requires a change in one's social and personal relationships; conversely, any change in social relations tends to result in a change in political identification. The fortunate village youth who receives a modern education tends to move to the city, establish himself in a new subsociety, and become associated with a political group that may in no way reflect the political views of his original community. Even among the national politicians in the city, shifts in political ties are generally accompanied by changes in social and personal associations.

2. *Political parties tend to take on a world view and represent a way of life.* The lack of a clearly differentiated political sphere means that political parties tend to be clearly oriented not to a distinct political arena but to some aspect of the communal framework of politics. In reflecting the communal base of politics they tend to represent total ways of life; attempts to

dency; see Selig S. Harrison, "Caste and the Andhra Communists," *American Political Science Review*, **1** (June 1956).

organize parties in terms of particular political principles or limited policy objectives generally result either in failure or in the adoption of a broad ethic which soon obscures the initial objective. Usually political parties represent some subsociety or simply the personality of a particularly influential individual.

Even secular parties devoted to achieving national sovereignty have tended to develop their own unique world views: Indeed, successful parties tend to become social movements. The indigenous basis for political parties is usually regional, ethnic, or religious groupings, all of which stress considerations not usually emphasized in Western secular politics. When a party is merely the personal projection of an individual leader, it is usually not just his explicitly political views but all facets of his personality which are significant in determining the character of the movement.

Nationalist movements in particular have tended to represent total ways of life, and even after independence the tendency remains strong, because such parties are inclined to feel they have a mission to change all aspects of life within their society, even conceiving of themselves as a prototype of what their entire country will become in time. Members of such movements frequently believe that their attitudes and views on all subjects will become the commonly shared attitudes and views of the entire population.

3. *There is a prevalence of cliques.* The lack of a distinct political sphere and the tendency for political parties to have world views together provide a framework within which the most structured units of political influence tend to be personal cliques. Thus, although general considerations of social status determine the broad outlines of power and influence, the particular pattern of political relationships at any time is largely determined by decisions made at the personal level. This is the case because the social structure in non-Western societies is characterized by functionally diffuse relationships; individuals and groups do not have sharply defined and highly specific functions and thus do not represent specific interests that distinguish them from other groupings. There is no clearly structured setting that can provide a focus for the more refined pattern of day-to-day political activities. Hence, in arriving at their expectations about the probable behavior of others, those involved in the political process must rely heavily upon judgments about personality and the particular relations of the various actors to each other. It follows that the pattern of personal associations provides one of the firmest guides for understanding and acting within the political process, and that personal cliques are likely to become the key units of political decision making in most non-Western societies.

Western observers often see the phenomenon of cliques as symptomatic of immoral and deviously motivated behavior. This may actually be the case. Considerations of motive alone, however, cannot explain either the prevalence of cliques in non-Western societies or their functions. For the fact that cliques are based on personal relations does not mean that there are no significant differences among them in their values and policy objectives. Since the members of a given clique are likely to have a common orientation toward politics, if their views were fully articulated they might constitute a distinct ideology significantly different from those of other factions.

In order to understand the workings of the political process in most non-Western countries it is necessary to analyze the character of inter-clique reactions. To ignore the importance of cliques would be comparable to ignoring the role of interest groups and elections in analyzing the behavior of American congressmen.

4. *The character of political loyalty gives political leaders a high degree of freedom in determining policies.*[5] The communal

[5] For excellent studies of this characteristic, see Myron Weiner, *Party Politics in India* (Princeton, Princeton University Press, 1957);

framework of politics and the tendency for political parties to have world views inspire a political loyalty which is governed more by a sense of identification with a concrete group than by identification with its professed policy goals. The expectation is that the leaders will seek to maximize all the interests of all the members of the group and not just seek to advance particular policies.

As long as the leaders appear to be working in the interests of the group as a whole, they usually do not have to be concerned that the loyalties of the members will be tested by current decisions. Under such conditions it is possible for leadership to become firmly institutionalized within the group without having to make any strong commitments to a specific set of principles or to a given political strategy.

Problems relating to the loyalty of the membership can generally be handled more effectively by decisions about intragroup relations than by decisions about the goals or external policies of the group. As long as harmonious relations exist within the group, it is generally possible for the leaders to make drastic changes in strategy. Indeed, it is not uncommon for the membership to feel that matters relating to external policy should be left solely to the leadership, and it may not disturb them that such decisions reflect mainly the idiosyncracies of their leaders.

5. *Opposition parties and aspiring elites tend to appear as revolutionary movements.* Since the current leadership in non-Western countries generally conceives of itself as seeking to effect changes in all aspects of life, and since all political associations tend to have world views, any new group aspiring to national leadership seems to present a revolutionary threat. The fact that the ruling party in most non-Western countries identifies itself with an effort to bring about total change in the society makes it difficult to limit the

[*footnote 5 continued*
and Keith Callard, *Pakistan: A Political Study* (New York, Macmillan, 1957).

sphere of political controversy. Isolated and specific questions tend to be transformed into fundamental questions about the destiny of the society.

In addition, the broad and diffuse interests of the ruling elites make it easy for them to maintain that they represent the interest of the entire nation. Those in opposition seeking power are thus often placed in the position of appearing to be, at best, obstructionists of progress or, at worst, enemies of the country. Competition is not between parties that represent different functional interests or between groups that claim greater administrative skills; rather, the struggle takes on some of the qualities of a conflict between differing ways of life.

This situation helps to explain the failure of responsible opposition parties to develop in most non-Western countries. For example, the Congress party in India has been able to identify itself with the destiny of the entire country to such a degree that the opposition parties find it difficult to avoid appearing either as enemies of India's progress or as groups seeking precisely the same objective as the Congress party. Since the frustration of opposition groups encourages them to turn to extremist measures, they may in fact come to be revolutionary movements.

6. *There is little or no integration among the participants due to the lack of a unified communications system.* In most non-Western societies political activities are not part of any single general process; rather there are several distinct and nearly unrelated political processes. The most conspicuous division is that between the dominant national politics of the more urban elements and the more traditional village level of politics. Those who participate in the political life of the village are not an integral part of the national politics, and they can act without regard to developments at the national level. Possibly even more significant, all the various village groups have their own separate and autonomous political processes.

This situation is a product of the communication system common to non-Western societies, where the mass media generally reach only elements of the urban population and those who participate in the national political process, and the vast majority of the people still communicate by traditional word-of-mouth means.[6] Even when the media of mass communication do reach the village through readers of newspapers or owners of radios, there is almost no "feedback" from the village level, and therefore no reflection of the vast majority of the population. Indeed, the Westerner often has less difficulty than the majority of the indigenous population in understanding the intellectual and moral standards reflected in the media of mass communication, for the media are controlled by the more Westernized elements who may be consciously seeking to relate them to the standards of the international systems of communication rather than to the local scene.

The lack of a unified communication system and the fact that there is no common political process limit the types of political issues that can arise. For example, although the non-Western societies are essentially agrarian and their industrial development is just beginning, their peoples have not been concerned with one of the issues basic to the history of Western politics: the clash between industry and agriculture, between town and countryside. The chief reason for this is that the rural elements are without a basis for mobilizing their combined strength and effectively advancing their demands on the government. It is possible that in time the rural masses, discovering that they have much in common, will find ways to mobilize their interests and so exert their full potential influence on the nation's political life. Such a development would drastically alter the national political character. In the meantime, however, the fragmented political process means that in fundamentally agrarian countries politics will continue to be more urbanized than it usually is in the industrial West. In many transitional societies one city alone dominates the politics of an entire country.

7. *New elements are recruited to political roles at a high rate.*[7] Two typical developments have caused a constant increase in the number of participants and the types of organizations involved in the political process. One is the extraordinary rise in the urban population, which has greatly increased the number of people who have some understanding about and interest in politics at the national level. A basic feature of the acculturation process which creates the subsociety of the elite is the development of attitudes common to urban life. The aspiring elites who demand to be heard generally represent a distinct stratum of urban dwellers who have been excluded from direct participation in national politics but whose existence affects the behavior of the current elite.

The other development is the more gradual reaching out of the mass media to the countryside, which stimulates a broadening awareness that, although participation in the nation's political life is formally open to all, the rural elements actually have little access to the means of influence. In some places political parties, in seeking to reach the less urbanized elements, have opened up new channels for communicating with the powerful at the nation's center which may or may not be more effective than the old channels of the civil administration. In any case, the existence of multiple channels of contact with the national government tends to increase the number of people anxious to participate in national decision making.[8]

---

[6] A more detailed elaboration of such a communications system is contained in the author's "Communication Patterns and the Problems of Representative Government in Non-Western Societies," *Public Opinion Quarterly*, **20** (Spring 1956), 249–257.

[7] Kahin, Pauker, and Pye, p. 1024.

[8] For an excellent discussion of this process, see Howard Wriggins, *Ceylon: The Dilemmas of a New Nation* (Princeton, Princeton University Press, 1960).

8. *There are sharp differences in the political orientation of the generations.* The process of social change in most non-Western societies results in a lack of continuity in the circumstances under which people are recruited to politics. Those who took part in the revolutionary movement against a colonial ruler are not necessarily regarded as indispensable leaders by succeeding generations; but their revolutionary role is still put forward as sufficient reason for their continued elite status. As a result, in some countries, as in Indonesia and Burma, and possibly in more acute form in most of Africa,[9] those who were not involved in the revolution feel that they are being arbitrarily excluded from the inner circle of national politics.

This problem is aggravated in societies where the population is rapidly growing because of a high birth rate. In Singapore, Malaya, and Burma, for example, over half the population is under voting age, and the median age in most non-Western countries is in the low twenties. There is thus a constant pressure from the younger generation, whose demands for political influence conflict with the claims of current leaders who consider themselves still young with many more years of active life ahead. In addition, in most of the newly independent countries the initial tendency was for cabinet ministers and high officials to be in their thirties and forties, a condition which has colored the career expectations of the youth of succeeding generations, who now face frustration if they cannot achieve comparable status at the same age.

This telescoping of the generations has sharpened the clash of views so that intellectually there is an abnormal gap in political orientations, creating a potential for extreme changes in policy should the aspiring elites gain power. Ideas and symbols deeply felt by the current leaders

may have little meaning for a generation which has not experienced colonial rule.

9. *Little consensus exists as to the legitimate ends and means of political action.* The fundamental fact that transitional societies are engrossed in a process of discontinuous social change precludes the possibility of a widely shared agreement as to the appropriate ends and means of political activities. At one extreme in such societies are people who have so fully assimilated Western culture that their political attitudes and concepts differ little from those common in the West. At the other extreme are the village peasants who have been little touched by Western influences. Living in different worlds, the two can hardly be expected to display a common approach toward political action.

The profound social changes in the transitional process tend to compound uncertainty, depriving people of that sense of shared expectation which is the first prerequisite of representative government. The possible and the plausible, the likely and the impossible are so readily confused that both elation and resignation are repeatedly hitched to faulty predictions. Thus in the political realm, where conscious choice and rational strategies should vie in promoting alternative human values, it becomes difficult to discern what choices are possible and what are the truly held values of the people. The resulting drift is away from realism and toward either crudely emotional appeals or toward gentle ideals that offer respectability in Western circles but are irrelevant to the domestic scene.

Some people still adhere to traditional views and conceive of politics as primarily providing opportunities for realizing status, prestige, and honor. Such views are sustained by constant demonstrations that the masses in transitional societies still derive a sense of well-being from identifying with the grandeur and glory of their national leaders. There are others, taking their cues from the colonial period, who equate government with the security of office

[9] Cf. James S. Coleman, "The Politics of Sub-Saharan Africa," in *The Politics of the Developing Areas*, ed. by Gabriel A. Almond and James S. Coleman (Princeton, Princeton University Press, 1960).

and the dignity of clerks in the civil service. For them government is above all the ritualization of routine where procedure takes precedence over all other considerations. Still others came to their appreciation of politics out of the excitement of independence movements; they continue to expect politics to be the drama of group emotions and to despise those who would give in to the humdrum calculation of relative costs and risks. For them the politician should remain the free and unfettered soul who can stand above tedious consideration of public policies. There are also those who look to politics and government to change their society and who feel that their dreams of a new world are shared by all. Some so grossly underestimate what must be done before the fruits of modernization can be realized that their ambitions incite little sustained effort and they are quick to declare themselves frustrated. Others who accept the need to deal first with the prerequisites of development may learn that all their energies can be absorbed in distasteful enterprises without visibly advancing the ends they seek. Thus the lack of a common, elementary orientation to the goals and the means of political action reduces the effectiveness of all.

Since such diversity in orientations makes it almost impossible to identify genuine social interests, the basic function of representative politics of sensitively aggregating the diverse values of a people and translating them into public policies cannot be readily realized. Without stable groups having limited interests, the processes by which power is accumulated and directed tend to be less responsive to social needs and more responsive to personal, individual desires.

This situation has direct effects on leadership. It reinforces the tendency for the personalities of the leaders to figure more prominently and for the idiosyncrasies of their followers to be more crucial in shaping developments than the functional needs of social and economic group-

ings throughout society. Moreover, although the national leadership may appear to represent a widely shared consensus about politics, more often than not this apparent national agreement reflects only the distinct qualities of the elite subsociety. The mass of the population cannot fully appreciate the values and concepts that underlie the judgments of the elite and guide its behavior.

Lastly, since most of the groupings within the political process represent total ways of life, few are concerned with limited and specific interests. Their functionally diffuse character tends to force each group to develop its own ends and means of political action, and the relationship of means to ends tends to be more organic than rational and functional. Indeed, in the gross behavior of the groups it is difficult to distinguish their primary goals from their operational measures. Consequently, the political actors in non-Western societies tend to demonstrate quite conspicuously the often forgotten fact that people generally show greater imagination and ingenuity in discovering goals to match existing means than in expanding their capabilities in order to reach distant goals; and it is difficult to distinguish within the general political discourse of the society a distinction between discussions of desired objectives and analyses of appropriate means of political action.

10. *The intensity and prevalence of political discussion bear little relationship to political decision making.* Western observers are impressed with what they feel is a paradoxical situation in most non-Western countries. The masses seem to be apathetic toward political action, and yet, considering the crude systems of communication, they are remarkably well informed about political events. Peasants and villagers often engage in prolonged discussions on matters related to the political world outside their immediate lives, but they rarely seem prepared to translate the information they receive into action that

might influence the course of national politics.

This is a survival of the traditional pattern of behavior. In most traditional societies an important function of the elite was to provide entertainment and material for discussion for the common people, but the people did not discuss the activities of the elite in any expectation that discussion should lead to action. Now the contemporary world of elite politics has simply replaced the drama of court life and royal officialdom.

A second explanation is that one of the important factors in determining social status and prestige within the village or local community is often a command of information about the wider world; knowledge of developments in the sphere of national and even international politics has a value in itself. But skill in discussing political matters again does not raise any expectation of actual participation in the world of politics.

There is also the fact that the common people of non-Western societies often seek to keep informed about political developments only in order to be able to adapt their lives to any major changes. The experience of former drastic changes has led them to seek advance warning of any developments which might again affect their lives; but it has not necessarily encouraged them to believe that their actions might influence such developments.

11. *Roles are highly interchangeable.*[10] It seems that in non-Western societies most politically relevant roles are not clearly differentiated but have a functionally diffuse rather than a functionally specific character. For example, the civil bureaucracy is not usually limited to the role of a politically neutral instrument of public administration but may assume some of the functions of a political party or act as an interest group. Sometimes armies act as governments.[11] Even within bureaucracies

and governments individuals may be formally called upon to perform several roles. A shortage of competent personnel encourages such behavior either because one group may feel that the other is not performing its role in an effective manner or because the few skilled administrators are forced to take on concurrent assignments. However, the more fundamental reason for this phenomenon is that in societies just emerging from traditional status it is not generally expected that any particular group or organization will limit itself to performing a clearly specified function. Under these conditions there usually are not sharply defined divisions of labor in any sphere of life. All groups tend to have considerable freedom in trying to maximize their influence.

12. *There are relatively few explicitly organized interest groups with functionally specific roles.*[12] Although there are often large numbers of informal associations in non-Western countries, such groups tend to adopt diffuse orientations that cover all phases of life in much the same manner as the political parties and cliques. It is the rare association that represents a limited and functionally specific interest. Organizations which in name and formal structure are modeled after Western interest groups, such as trade unions and chambers of commerce, generally do not have a clearly defined focus.

Groups such as trade unions and peasant associations which in form would appear to represent a specific interest are often in fact agents of the government or of a dominant party or movement. Their function is primarily to mobilize the sup-

[10] See Almond, "Comparative Political Systems," p. 402.
[11] On the role of armies in transitional socie-

ties, see the forthcoming study sponsored by the RAND Corporation; Dankwart A. Rustow, "The Army and the Founding of the Turkish Republic," *World Politics*, 11 (July 1959), 513–552; and Daniel Lerner and Richard D. Robinson, "Swords and Ploughshares: The Turkish Army as a Modernizing Force," *World Politics*, 13 (October 1960), 19–44.
[12] For discussions of the problems of interest articulation throughout the non-Western world, see Almond and Coleman.

port of a segment of the population for the purposes of the dominant group, and not primarily to represent the interests of their constituency. Where the associations are autonomous, the tendency is for them not to apply pressure openly on the government in order to influence the formation of public policy but to act as protective associations, shielding their members from the consequences of governmental decisions and the political power of others.

The role of the protective association was generally a well-developed one in traditional societies and in countries under colonial rule. Under such authoritarian conditions, since informal associations could have little hope of affecting the formal lawmaking process, they focused on the law-enforcing process. Since they were likely to be more successful if they worked quietly and informally to establish preferential relations with the enforcing agents of the government, each association generally preferred to operate separately in order to gain special favors. The strategy of uniting in coalitions and alliances to present the appearance of making a popular demand on the government, as is common in an open democratic political process composed of pressure groups, would have only weakened the position of all as it would have represented a direct challenge to the existing governmental elite.

The fact that this approach to political activity was a common characteristic of traditional societies and still so widely survives as a feature of the politics of societies in transition suggests the following general hypothesis:

Whenever the formally constituted lawmakers are more distant from and more inaccessible to the general public than the law-enforcing agencies, the political process of the society will be characterized by a high degree of latency, and interests will be represented by informally organized groups seeking diffuse but particularistically defined goals which will neither be broadly articulated nor claimed to be in the general interest.

The corollary of this hypothesis would, of course, read:

Whenever the formally constituted lawmakers are less distant from and more accessible to the general public than the law-enforcing agencies, the political process of the society will be open and manifest, and interests will be represented by explicitly organized groups seeking functionally specific but universalistically defined goals which will be broadly articulated and claimed to be in the general interest.

13. *The national leadership must appeal to an undifferentiated public.* The lack of explicitly organized interest groups and the fact that not all participants are continuously represented in the political process deprive the national leadership of any readily available means for calculating the distribution of attitudes and values throughout the society. The national politician cannot easily determine the relative power of those in favor of a particular measure and those opposed; he cannot readily estimate the amount of effort needed to gain the support of the doubtful elements.

It is usually only within the circle of the elite or within the administrative structure that the national leaders can distinguish specific points of view and the relative backing that each commands. They have few guides as to how the public may be divided over particular issues. Thus, in seeking popular support, they cannot direct their appeal to the interests of particular groups. Unable to identify or intelligently discriminate among the various interests latent in the public, they are inclined to resort to broad generalized statements rather than to adopt specific positions on concrete issues; and whether the question is one of national or of merely local import, they must appear to be striving to mobilize the entire population.

The inability to speak to a differentiated public encourages a strong propensity toward skillful and highly emotional forms of political articulation. Forced to reach for the broadest possible appeals, the individual leader tends to concentrate heavily on nationalistic sentiments and to present himself as a representative of the nation as a whole rather than of particular interests within the society. This is one of the reasons why some leaders of non-Western countries are often seen paradoxically both as extreme nationalists and as men out of touch with the masses.

14. *Leaders are encouraged to adopt more clearly defined positions on international issues than on domestic issues.* Confronted with an undifferentiated public, leaders often find the international political process more clearly structured than the domestic political scene. Consequently, they can make more refined calculations as to the advantages in taking a definite position in world politics than they can in domestic politics. This situation not only encourages the leaders of some non-Western countries to seek a role in world politics that is out of proportion to their nation's power, but it also allows them to concentrate more on international than on domestic affairs. It should also be noted that in adopting a supranational role, the current leaders of non-Western countries can heighten the impression that their domestic opposition is an enemy of the national interest.

15. *The affective or expressive aspect of politics tends to override the problem-solving or public-policy aspect.* Traditional societies generally develop to a very high order the affective and expressive aspect of politics. Pomp and ceremony are basic features of their politics, and the ruling elite are generally expected to lead more interesting and exciting lives than those not involved in politics. In contrast, traditional societies do not usually emphasize politics as a means for solving social problems, questions of policy being largely limited to providing certain minimum social and economic functions and maintaining the way of life of the elite.

Although in transitional societies there is generally a somewhat greater awareness of the potentialities of politics as a means of rationally solving social problems than there is in traditional systems, the expressive aspects of politics usually continue to occupy a central place in determining the character of political behavior. The peculiar Western assumption that issues of public policy are the most important aspect of politics, and practically the only legitimate concern of those with power, is not fully accepted in non-Western politics. Indeed, in most non-Western societies the general assumption is not that those with power are committed to searching out and solving problems, but rather that they are the fortunate participants in an exciting and emotionally satisfying drama.

In part, the stress on the affective or expressive aspect of politics is related to the fact that, as we have already noted, questions of personal loyalties and identification are recognized as providing the basic issues of politics and the bond between leader and follower is generally an emotional one. In fact, in many non-Western societies it is considered highly improper and even immoral for people to make loyalty contingent upon their leaders' ability to solve problems of public policy.

There is also the fact that where the problem of national integration is of central importance, the national leaders often feel that they must emphasize the symbols and sentiments of national unity since substantive problems of policy may divide the people. It should be noted that the governmental power base of many non-Western leaders encourages them to employ symbols and slogans customarily associated with administrative policy in their efforts to strengthen national unity. The Western observer may assume that statements employing such symbols represent policy intentions when in fact their function is to create national loyalty and to condition the public to think more in policy terms.

16. *Charismatic leaders tend to prevail.*[13] Max Weber, in highlighting the characteristics of charismatic authority, specifically related the emergence of charismatic personalities to situations in which the hold of tradition has been weakened. By implication, he suggested that societies experiencing cultural change provide an ideal setting for such leaders, since a society in which there is confusion over values is more susceptible to a leader who conveys a sense of mission and appears to be God-sent.

The problem of political communication further reinforces the position of the charismatic leader. Since the population does not share the leaderships' modes of reason or standards of judgment, it is difficult to communicate subtle points of view. Communication of emotions is not confronted with such barriers, especially if it is related to considerations of human character and personality. All groups within the population can feel confident of their ability to judge the worth of a man for what he is even though they cannot understand his mode of reasoning.

As long as a society has difficulties in communication, the charismatic leader possesses great advantage over his opponents, even though they may have greater ability in rational planning. However, the very lack of precision in the image that a charismatic leader casts, especially in relation to policy, does make it possible for opposition to develop as long as it does not directly challenge the leader's charisma. Various groups with different programs can claim that they are in fact seeking the same objectives as those of the leader. For example, in both Indonesia and Burma the Communists have been able to make headway by simply claiming that they are not directly opposed to the goals of Sukarno and U Nu.

Charisma is likely to wear thin. A critical question in most non-Western societies that now have charismatic leaders is whether such leadership will become

[13] Kahin, Pauker, and Pye, p. 1025.

institutionalized in the form of rational-legal practices before this happens. This was the pattern in Turkey under Kemal Ataturk. Or will the passing of the charismatic leader be followed by confusion and chaos and possibly the rise of new charismatic leaders? The critical factor seems to be whether or not the leader encourages the development of functionally specific groups within the society that can genuinely represent particular interests.

17. *The political process operates largely without benefit of political "brokers."* In most non-Western societies there seems to be no institutionalized role for, first, clarifying and delimiting the distribution of demands and interests within the population, and, next, engaging in the bargaining operation necessary to accommodate and maximize the satisfaction of those demands and interests in a fashion consistent with the requirements of public policy and administration. In other words, there are no political "brokers."

In the Western view, the political broker is a prerequisite for a smoothly operating system of representative government. It is through his activities that, on the one hand, the problems of public policy and administration can be best explained to the masses in a way that is clearly related to their various specific interests and, on the other hand, that the diverse demands of the population can be articulated to the national leaders. This role in the West is performed by the influential members of the competing political parties and interest groups.

What is needed in most non-Western countries in order to have stable representative institutions are people who can perform the role that local party leaders performed in introducing the various immigrant communities into American public life. Those party leaders, in their fashion, were able to provide channels through which the immigrant communities felt they could learn where their interests lay in national politics and through which the national leaders could discover the social concerns of the new citizens.

In most non-Western societies, the role of the political broker has been partially filled by those who perform a mediator's role, which consists largely of transmitting views of the elite to the masses. Such mediators are people sufficiently acculturated to the elite society to understand its views but who still have contacts with the more traditional masses. In performing their role, they engage essentially in a public relations operation for the elite, and only to a marginal degree do they communicate to the elite the views of the public. They do not find it essential to identify and articulate the values of their public. Since their influence depends upon their relations with the national leadership, they have not generally sought to develop an autonomous basis of power or to identify themselves with particular segments of the population as must the political broker. As a consequence, they have not acted in a fashion that would stimulate the emergence of functionally specific interest groups.

PART VII

THE POLITICS OF

NATION-BUILDING

INTRODUCTION

With the exception of Latin America, most of the transitional societies that we have treated as developing nations have achieved independence in the twentieth century—many in the years since World War II. An unreal optimism and faith accompanied this attainment of independence which found expression in the belief that the cure for "underdevelopment" was national autonomy and economic growth. Although Western society had relinquished the belief in progress as an inherent quality of life, largely as a result of its own twentieth-century disillusionments, the idea of progress was embraced by the leaders of the developing nations. In spite of the fact that imperialism did appear to contain the "seeds of its own destruction," it did obscure or silence many of the tensions and sources of conflict in colonial nations. Colonialism impeded or limited the expression of deeply felt demands that were welling up within the social systems of Asia, Africa, and the Middle East. Thus, the end of imperialism saw the simultaneous release of social pressures which had been pent up under colonialism and the beginnings of the drive for economic growth, launched by newly independent peoples with far-reaching social and political expectations.

Neither East nor West was prepared for the extraordinary and complex problems which have accompanied independence or for the painful "rites of passage" to nationhood. This state of intellectual, psychological, and even emotional unpreparedness had its origins in an oversimplified understanding of nationalism in the developing nations and of the social, economic, and political changes which accompanied independence. It was usually assumed that a single revolution was in progress, whereas in reality nationalism was an embracing label for multiple revolutions which were occurring in most new and developing nations. In addition to the anti-imperialist revolution that culminated in national independence, other forces were operative that may be designated "revolutionary." While acknowledging that nationalism for many was an expressive value, there were powerful groups in the new nations who saw nationalism as an instrumental means to diminish rapidly the discrepancies between the industrial nations and their own societies. This approach, of course, assumed accelerated economic growth and industrialization.

Another often latent, sentiment of revolutionary proportions was the belief that national independence would also give birth to an internal social revolution eliminating social imbalances and benefiting all elements of society. While only a restricted group of the intelligentsia was committed to egalitarianism, various ethnic, tribal, and religious elements were more interested in eliminating specific inequalities, specifically those which were to their disadvantage.

Admittedly, these considerations were not present in all of the developing nations; nevertheless, we feel that it is more realistic to conceive of what has transpired and what is still in progress in the developing world as part of a multiple revolution rather than a single movement for independence. What is most unfortunate is that these multiple revolutions converged in the time of their appearance rather than having occurred at staggered intervals over a span of decades or even centuries. In the terminology of systems analysis, these multiple revolutions created demand overloads on the system.

One may readily grasp the overwhelming character of this problem in developing nations—one which converted the optimism of nationalism into a cynical pessimism among many people—by comparing it with a number of critical events in American history. In a sense, the developing nations are confronted at a single point in history with the types of social problems and conflicts inherent in the American Revolution, the framing of the Constitution, the age of Jackson, the Civil War, the Industrial Revolution, the extension of the franchise, the depression of the 1930's, and the "Negro Revolt" of today. The issues underlying these historical movements appeared over a period of almost two hundred years and have not yet been resolved to the satisfaction of significant segments of American society.

In facing up to these issues—which have increasingly become political issues—the political system of the United States was slowly able to acquire new system capacities and capabilities. At an earlier time in history, for example, the present Negro revolt might have taken place somewhat outside the political system *per se*. Political development, as Gabriel Almond pointed out in his essay in Part I of this book, implies that more and more issues will be resolved by the political system. The political system in the United States is attacking an increasing number of problems and is acquiring increased capabilities for dealing effectively with them. Hopefully, the American political system will demonstrate a capacity to resolve more or less successfully the issues implicit in the Negro revolt. In the developing nations, comparable issues are being confronted prior to the appearance of political or social mechanisms with the capabilities of resolving them. Even when the political and social mechanisms do exist, they have been unable to cope with the rapid changes occurring in transitional societies which lead to recurring political instability and often violence, rebellion, and revolution.

Not only the developing nations but the more industrialized nations as well have learned through painful experience that the political system may not acquire the capabilities to deal with the issues confronting it or that it may actually decline in its capacity to deal with complex political issues. In other words, the process of development is, to say the least, not an even one. A nation at any stage may encounter political breakdowns, for the mere existence of modern political, administrative, and economic structures does not imply that they are sufficiently viable to absorb and sustain the growth and social change taking place in other institutional spheres. As S. N. Eisenstadt has reminded us elsewhere,[1] a "breakdown" does not simply constitute a reversion to traditional social institutions; it is, more precisely, a reversion to a lower level of system capabilities.

At this point attention should be drawn to the all-too-frequent tendency by students of political development to regard political instability and revolution as the ultimate form of political breakdown. That this equation is far too facile will become evident in the final two chapters of this volume, which deal with political instability and revolution and, lastly, the issue of what may be the overriding problem confronting the developing nations—creating and maintaining sufficient internal unity and cohesion and unity for purposes of modernization and political development.

Political leaders and observers of the development scene have usually assumed that economic growth leads toward political stability. Mancur Olson, Jr., takes issue with this view, maintaining that rapid economic growth is actually a major force leading toward revolution and instability. Both those who gain and those who lose from economic growth can act as destabilizing forces. The gainers may be a destabilizing influence because their position in the social order is changing; a status inconsistency may be created between the new distribution of economic power and the old distribution of social prestige and political power, so that the new economic elites are in a socially ambiguous situation which may leave them alienated from society. They also have the resources with which to ultimately alter the social and political order in their own interests.

Those who experience relative disadvantage from economic growth find that their position in the social order is changing as well, and they are apt to be much more resentful of poverty and aware of the possibilities of a better life than those who have known nothing but privation. Olson does not conclude, however, that rapid economic growth is undesirable, despite the fact that it may be accompanied by political instability. Rather, his purpose is to warn that societies seeking to promote economic growth should at the same time brace themselves to meet political instability.

The article by Ivo K. Feierabend, Rosalind L. Feierabend, and Betty Nesvold lends support to the analysis of Olson. Their extensive study examines selected aspects of social change and their effect upon political violence and the internal political stability of nations. The inquiry is pre-

[1] "Breakdowns in Modernization," *in* Jason L. Finkle and Richard W. Gable, eds., *Political Development and Social Change*, New York: John Wiley and Sons, Inc., 1966.

dominantly empirical rather than speculative, but the empirical analysis is conducted within a carefully designed theoretical frame of reference. Moreover, the study compares nations for their relative levels of political stability or instability, modernization, and rates of socioeconomic change.

The theoretical assumption linking change to violence begins with the commonsense notion that political turmoil is the consequence of social discontent; that is, revolution begins in the minds of men. Changes in the environmental and structural circumstances of political systems create the revolutionary state of mind.

The frustration-aggression hypothesis, which is used to analyze individual behavior, is adapted by the authors to the investigation of aggregate violent political behavior within the social system. They formulate the concept of systemic frustration which, according to their hypothesis, instigates violent behavior. Systemic frustration is presumed to stem from socioeconomic and political changes in society.

The authors empirically test the relationship between political violence and various quantitative measures of change and development. They find that neither lower nor higher levels of development will be as prone to violence as are the middle levels. This finding has been reported by other researchers. If valid, it corroborates the authors' theoretical insights. In brief, the transitional stage of development is the most frustration-ridden and, therefore, the most prone to political instability.

The articles by Eric R. Wolf and Aristide R. Zolberg examine specific cases of political instability, violence, and revolution. Wolf's article was written as the conclusion for his book-length study of peasant rebellions and revolutions in Mexico, Russia, China, Vietnam, Algeria, and Cuba, *Peasant Wars of the Twentieth Century*.[2] He finds that the peasant wars which he studied have all resulted from tensions which had their roots in the past. The world-wide spread and diffusion of capitalism was a revolution which produced revolutions of its own. Capitalism liberated man as an economic agent, but the process of liberation itself caused human suffering, separated men from accustomed social ties, and created a profound alienation. Capitalism, further, cut through the web of custom, severing people from their habitual social matrix in order to transform them into economic actors, independent of prior social commitments to kin and neighbors.

As traditional groups were weakened and new social groups emerged, a crisis of power and authority occurred. In all six countries, some of the "rootless" new groups joined with the peasants to bring about revolution. Many peasants, especially the poor peasants and landless laborers, are often passive spectators of political struggles. The fusion leading to rebellion was with either the landowning "middle peasantry" or the peasantry located in a peripheral area outside the domains of landlord control. The middle peasantry have some internal leverage because they are a population which has secure access to land of its own and cultivates it with family labor.

[2] (New York: Harper & Row, Publishers, 1969.)

This fusion was not effected easily, but, as Wolf illustrates, it did eventually occur.

Throughout the presentation Wolf develops the argument that the peasant is an agent of forces larger than himself, forces produced by a disordered past as much as by a disordered present. There is no evidence for the view that if it were not for outside agitators the peasant would be at rest. On the contrary, although peasants rise to redress wrong, the inequities against which they rebel are but parochial manifestations of great social dislocations. Thus, rebellion leads easily into revolution and massive movements to transform the social structure as a whole.

Zolberg notes that almost every new African state has experienced military or civilian coups, insurrections, mutinies, severe riots, and political assassinations. He maintains that these violent events should be viewed as characteristic processes which themselves constitute an important aspect of certain political systems. Zolberg then proceeds to analyze African political systems and their environment, the shift from power to force (including the politicization of primordial ties and the inflation of demands), the use of the coup as a political institution, and the use of force as an instrument of major political change.

Zolberg does not regard conflict in a society as wholly negative: "Integration into a free society does not entail the total elimination of conflict from political life, but rather its containment within acceptable limits as indicated by a shift from force to power and authority . . . Progress in this direction requires an acceptance of the premise itself—the institutionalization at the cultural level of a belief that conflict is a potentially manageable aspect of society . . ."

The concluding chapter of this volume addresses the integration problems which all nations confront in the course of political development. The term "integration" is often used to cover an extraordinarily broad range of political phenomena. Myron Weiner's article analyzes the various uses of this term and shows how they are related. The concept of "integration" may refer to creating a territorial unit, establishing a national authority over subordinate units, linking the government with the governed, achieving a value consensus, or creating the capacity of people in a society to organize for some common purpose.

In the process of identifying the major integrative problems and underscoring the significance of each in holding the society and the political system together, Weiner examines various paths which might be taken to deal with these problems. He emphasizes that outcomes are not ineluctable; rather, political leaders do have certain strategy options and policy choices open to them which may facilitate the resolution of basic integration problems.

Clifford Geertz sees primordial attachments on the part of individuals as the basis for serious disaffection in the new states. A primordial attachment is one that derives from the "givens" of social existence—kin connection, mainly, but also the "givens" which stem from being born into a particular religious community, living in a certain village, speaking a particular language (or even a dialect of language), and following particular social practices. For centuries in the West, with a few notable exceptions, a complex network of allegiances to a civil state has replaced calls to blood and land as the important basis for national unity. In modernizing societies, on the other hand where the tradition of civil politics is weak, primordial ties tend to be adhered to and preferred as bases for building nations. The ensuing conflict between primordial and civil sentiments gives rise to one of the most serious and intractable problems faced by the new states—tribalism, parochialism, and communalism. Civil discontent finds its natural outlet in the seizure, legally or illegally, of the state apparatus, a phenomenon discussed in the previous chapter. Primordial discontent, by contrast, tears more deeply into the social fabric and is mended less easily.

Geertz constructs a typology of the concrete patterns of primordial diversity and explains why political modernization tends initially not to stifle such sentiments but to quicken them. The effective operation of developed national political institutions is not simply a matter of replacing primordial ties and identifications with civil ones. Such a replacement is a sheer impossibility. What the situation requires, Geertz maintains, is an adjustment between civil and primordial attachments so that the processes of government can proceed freely without serious threat to the cultural framework of personal identity.

The concluding article of this volume offers a hopeful interpretation of the effects of tribalism and ethnicity. Wallerstein suggests that, although they may be in many respects impediments to national integration, tribalism and ethnicity can in other respects be highly functional. Ethnicity serves to aid national integration in four ways: (1) Ethnic groups tend to assume some of the functions of the extended family and to diminish the importance of kinship roles. (2) Ethnic groups serve as a mechanism for resocialization. (3) Ethnic groups keep the class structure fluid and so prevent the emergence of classes, an explanation which contrasts with that of Lipset in Chapter 14. And, (4) Ethnic groups serve as an outlet for political tensions.

Notwithstanding the positive contributions of ethnicity to national integration, there are lingering dysfunctional aspects to ethnic ties which permeate the characteristics of developing polities in the form of particularistic orientations, nepotism, corruption, and even separatism. This conflict between ethnicity and national integration has sometimes been reduced, as it has been in many African states, by the emergence of a dominant single party.

Chapter 15

Political Instability, Violence, and Revolution

RAPID GROWTH AS A DESTABILIZING FORCE*

Mancur Olson, Jr.

I

Many writers—some of them reputable scholars, others important public officials—have implicitly assumed or explicitly argued that economic growth leads toward political stability and perhaps even to peaceful democracy. They have argued that "economic development is one of the keys to stability

SOURCE: Excerpted from Mancur Olson, Jr., "Rapid Growth as a Destabilizing Force," *Journal of Economic History*, 23:529–52, December, 1963, using only pp. 529–44, 550–52.

* I am thankful to the Center of International Studies of Princeton University and to the Institute for Defense Analysis of Washington, D.C., for the support they have given my research, and particularly to Dr. Stephan Enke of the latter organization, from whose writings I have drawn several of the examples used to support the argument of this paper. Professors Kenneth Curran and William Hochman of Colorado College, Lt. Gerald Garvey of the Air Force Academy, Mr. Richard Zeckhauser of Harvard University, and my wife, Alison G. Olson, have also offered very helpful criticisms. But I am alone responsible for the errors.

and peace in the world";[1] that it is "conditions of want and instability on which communism breeds";[2] and that economic progress "serves as a bulwark against international communism."[3] A recent and justly famous book on revolution by Hannah Arendt ascribes the most violent forms of revolutionary extremism mainly to poverty.[4]

This view has had an influence on American foreign aid policy and more often than not foreign economic aid is regarded as "an investment in peace and orderly political

[1] Grant S. McClellan, ed., *U.S. Foreign Aid* (The Reference Shelf, Vol. XXIX, No. 5 [New York: The H. W. Wilson Company, 1957]), 90, taken from a speech by Eugene R. Black, made when he was President of the World Bank.

[2] *Ibid.*, p. 205, taken from a report by Richard Nixon to President Eisenhower.

[3] *Ibid.*, p. 140, taken from "Final Report of Eleventh American Assembly."

[4] Hannah Arendt, *On Revolution* (New York: The Viking Press, 1963), pp. 15, 54–57, 61–63, 66–69, 74–76, 80–85, 87, 105–8, 135, 181, 224, 249.

evolution toward a democratic world."[5] In one of his presidential messages to Congress, for example, Eisenhower justified a request for foreign aid funds by saying that unless the underdeveloped nations "can hope for reasonable economic advance, the danger will be acute that their governments will be subverted by communism."[6] A committee of scholars, so distinguished that they nearly make up a *Who's Who* of American students of economic development, has prepared for the guidance of the Senate Foreign Relations Committee a report which later was published as a book on *The Emerging Nations*,[7] and which argues that the United States should offer most of its economic aid to the countries in the "take-off" stage of economic development. The countries that are not yet ready for this stage of rapid development should get only modest amounts of aid, mainly in the form of technical assistance. This favoritism in the allocation of aid is justified on the grounds that a given amount of aid will bring about more growth if it is concentrated in the nations that are, in any case, in a stage of rapid development. This prescription for policy is justified, not on straightforward humanitarian grounds, but rather in the long term political interest of the United States, particularly in view of the cold war with the Soviet Union. While at least some of these students of economic development have denied that they accept a "crude materialist" explanation of the

causes of political stability,[8] the obvious premise of their policy is that the rapid economic growth of selected underdeveloped countries is the "key to an effective foreign policy" for the United States in its cold war with the Soviet Union. Many communists have also shared the faith that poverty was the prelude to revolution: the poor, they argue, "have nothing to lose but their chains."

Several scholars, however, have suggested that the assumed connection between economic growth and political stability was much too simple, or that there was no such connection. But their denials of any positive relationship between economic growth and political stability have too often been mere *obiter dicta*. They have at least failed to convince many people. It is not, therefore, enough simply to deny that economic growth necessarily brings political stability. What is needed instead is a bold and sustained argument in the opposite direction. What is needed now is, not a cautious qualification of the argument that economic growth leads toward political stability, but rather a clear and decisive argument stating that rapid economic growth is a major force leading toward revolution and instability. Many of the reasons why rapid economic growth should lead to political instability have apparently never been discussed, at least in print; it is thus time that these reasons were stated and put together in an attempt to show that rapid economic growth is a profoundly destabilizing force.

II

Any adequate analysis of the relationship between economic growth and revolutionary political changes must consider the problem in terms of the individuals who

[5] McClellan, *Foreign Aid*, p. 122, taken from an article by Max F. Millikan.

[6] *Ibid.*, pp. 53–54, taken from a message to Congress of May 22, 1957. It is significant that all five of the quotations cited so far to illustrate the view that economic growth leads to political stability could be found in one anthology. The number of writers who have accepted this argument must be very large indeed.

[7] Max Millikan and Donald Blackmer, eds., *The Emerging Nations* (Boston: Little, Brown, & Co., 1962), pp. 142–45; and Andrew Shonfield, *The Attack on World Poverty* (New York: Random House, 1960), pp. 3–14.

[8] Max Millikan and W. W. Rostow, *A Proposal Key to an Effective Foreign Policy* (New York: Harper & Brothers, 1957), pp. 19–23. See the criticism of this book in Edward C. Banfield's *American Foreign Aid Doctrines* (Washington, D.C.: American Enterprise Institute, 1963), especially p. 6.

bring revolutions about. Students of the sociology of revolution often argue that those people who participate in "mass movements" of the radical left or radical right—movements designed to bring about revolutionary rather than evolutionary change—tend to be distinguished by the relative absence of bonds that tie them to the established order. They tend to lack close attachments to any of the social sub-groups that comprise a society—to extended families, for example, or to voluntary associations, professional groups, or social classes.

Thus some of these scholars have argued, not without evidence, that labor unions, which are often regarded as particularly likely sources of strength for communist revolutionaries, are in fact a force tending to reduce the chances for communist revolutions, mainly because they provide one more group connection that can hold the worker to the prevailing system. The social class, which Marx thought was the engine of revolutionary change, some sociologists regard instead as a stabilizing institution. Those who are *déclassé*, whose class ties are weakest, are most apt to support revolutionary changes, while those who are firmly caught up in a class are least likely to do so. Even those who are firmly caught up even in the lowest and least fortunate class are not normally in the revolutionary vanguard, for they are secure in their modest place in the social hierarchy. Those who are very poor, after meeting the exigencies of life, have in any case very little energy left for agitation for a better political system, even if they had much hope that real improvement was possible. "There is thus a conservatism of the destitute," says Eric Hoffer, "as profound as the conservatism of the privileged."[9] It is not those who are

[9] Eric Hoffer, *The True Believer: Thoughts on the Nature of Mass Movements* (New York: The New American Library, 1951), p. 17 and *passim*. See also William Kornhauser, *The Politics of Mass Society* (Glencoe, Ill.: The Free Press, 1959), especially pp. 14–15; Seymour

accustomed to poverty, but those whose place in the social order is changing, who resort to revolution.

III

The next thing is to ask how rapid economic growth might affect the number of individuals who are *déclassé*, or who have lost their identification with other social groups, and who are thus in circumstances conducive to revolutionary protest.

It is now generally understood that economic growth proceeds not so much through simple capital accumulation—through continuing the old methods of production with more capital—as it does through innovation and technical change. Economic growth—especially rapid economic growth—therefore involves vast changes in the methods of production. It involves vast changes in the importance of different industries, in the types of labor demanded, in the geographical configuration of production. It means vast changes in the ways and places in which people live and work. Above all, economic growth means vast changes in the distribution of income.

The fact that some gain a lot and others lose a lot, in a rapidly growing economy, means that the bonds of class and caste are weakened. Some rise above the circumstances of their birth and others fall behind. Both groups are normally *déclassé*. Their economic status keeps them from belonging wholly to the class or caste into which they were born, and their social situation keeps them from belonging to the caste or class into which their income bracket should put them. Rapid economic growth therefore loosens the class and caste ties that help bind men to the social order.

But castes and social classes are not the only social groupings which rapid economic growth breaks down. Even the family

Martin Lipset, *Political Man, The Social Bases of Politics* (Garden City, N.Y.: Doubleday and Co., 1960).

group, and especially the clan or extended family, can be destroyed by the occupational and geographic mobility associated with economic growth. The replacement of subsistence agriculture and cottage industry, normally organized around the family, with factory production by workers hired individually, can weaken family ties. Similarly, modern business institutions are bound to weaken or even to destroy the tribe, the manor, the guild, and the rural village. The uprooted souls torn or enticed out of these groups by economic growth are naturally susceptible to the temptations of revolutionary agitation.

IV

When the focus is on the fact that rapid economic growth means rapid economic change, and that economic change entails social dislocation, it becomes clear that *both the gainers and the losers from economic growth can be destabilizing forces.* Both will be imperfectly adjusted to the existing order. This paper will argue, first, that economic growth increases the number of *nouveaux riches*, who may use their economic power to change the social and political order in their interest; and second, that economic growth may paradoxically also create a surprisingly large number of "*nouveaux pauvres*," who will be much more resentful of their poverty than those who have known nothing else.

The fact that there will be some who gain disproportionately from economic growth means that there will be a new distribution of economic power. But there will be an (almost Marxian) "contradiction" between this new distribution of economic power and the old distribution of social prestige and political power. Certain individuals are left in places in the economic order that are incompatible with their positions in the old social and political hierarchy. This means, not only that these people are in socially ambiguous situations that may leave them "alienated" from society; it means also that they have the resources with which they can ultimately

change the social and political order in their own interest. The economic system, the social system, and the political system are obviously interdependent parts of a single society, and if one part changes quickly, there must also be instability in other parts of the society. The fact that the distribution of wealth will have both social and political effects is beyond dispute. In time, those groups who have gained the fruits of economic growth (or their children) will probably have built a new social and political order that is suited to the new distribution of economic power. But, especially if the economic growth is very rapid, the path to any new equilibrium may be highly unstable.

Something very like this seems to have happened in Europe as a result of the commercial and industrial revolutions. The growth of commerce and industry in early modern Europe created a larger and wealthier middle class; and as this middle class gained in numbers and in wealth, expecially in relation to the landed aristocracy, it demanded, and it got, extra political power to match that wealth. These demands were obviously behind the middle class participation in the French Revolution, and were also fundamental to many of the other instances of political instability in the history of modern Europe. Liberalism and laissez-faire economic doctrine were also related to the newly achieved gains that the industrial revolution brought to Europe, and these ideas in turn tended further to destabilize the political environment.

The middle class in early modern and modern Europe was not the only group of gainers from economic growth that destabilized its environment. There are other types of gainers from economic growth who have also attempted to change the prevailing order. Urban areas, for example, normally grow disproportionately during periods of economic growth, and those who move from farm to city in pursuit of the more remunerative opportunities there are often also discontented gainers. The man who has been tempted away from his village, his manor, his tribe, or his extended family, by the higher wages of burgeoning urban industry may well be a disaffected gainer from economic growth. He has been, albeit voluntarily, uprooted and is not apt soon to acquire comparable social connections in the city. He is, therefore, prone to join destabilizing mass movements. Those who leave rural areas for the higher wages or other gains that economic growth brings to the cities often display a nostalgia for the economically poorer, but socially more secure, life they left. The Chartists, for example, at one time proposed schemes that would give factory workers small agricultural estates.[10] But after British workers had had some time to adjust to the urban, industrial order, this sort of scheme lost its popularity to programs designed to improve the conditions of urban industrial life. The degree of extremism of the different labor movements in the Scandinavian countries has also been related to the varying proportions of migrants from rural areas in the industrial work force, which in turn resulted from different rates of economic growth. The first and most gradual industrialization took place in Denmark, and there the rate at which migrants from rural areas were recruited into the urban work force was slow. In Sweden, and still more in Norway, industrialization and the absorption of rural migrants was later and faster, and the labor movements in turn revealed, expecially in Norway, more disaffection and political extremism.[11] The fact that the concentration of population in cities can sometimes make agitation

cheaper and the spread of new ideas faster is also important, as is the fact that riots and revolts are often technically easier to organize in cities. Whenever an ideology, like Marxism, designed explicitly for the urban proletariat, is in the air, the growth of cities induced by economic expansion will be particularly conducive to revolt.

The movement from farm to city is moreover only one of the types of geographic mobility brought about by economic growth. Some industries and localities will expand rapidly with economic growth, and others, urban as well as rural, will decline. Individuals may move from city to city or from rural area to rural area in search of the gains from economic growth. These sorts of mobility can also lead to a frustrating severance of social ties. The radical elements in Jacksonian democracy, in Populism, in the unusually strong Socialist parties of some of the frontier states of the Great Plains, in the violent western mining unions, and in the Non-Partisan League, cannot be adequately explained by any hypothesis of economic decline or stagnation. The western areas near the frontier were growing rapidly when these destabilizing movements began, and they were often filled with people who had gained from this expansion. Perhaps in frontier areas, or in areas that have only recently been on the frontier, the social groupings that bind people to the social order have not had time to develop, and as a result there is a susceptibility to protests against established governments and inherited conventions. This factor may explain Turner's alleged "quasi-revolutionary" or rebellious frontier democracy, which has sometimes been ascribed to "self-reliant pioneer" and "labor safety valve" theories.

V

Just as the gainers can be a destabilizing force, so, of course, can the losers. Their position in the social order is changing too, and they are also imperfectly adjusted to the existing society.

[10] M. Beer, *A History of British Socialism* (London: George Allen and Unwin, Ltd., 1940), pp. 153–54.

[11] See Walter Galenson, *The Danish System of Labor Relations* (Cambridge: Harvard University Press, 1952); and "Scandinavia" in *Comparative Labor Movements*, Galenson, ed. (New York: Prentice-Hall, 1952), especially pp. 105–20. See also Lipset, *Political Man*, pp. 68–72.

Moreover, contrary to what is usually assumed, economic growth can significantly increase the number of losers. It can be associated with a decided increase in the number whose standard of living is falling. This may seem absurd at first glance, since economic growth by definition leads to an increase in average income—to a situation such that the gains of the gainers are more than sufficient to compensate for the losses of the losers. But when average income increases, the number who are getting poorer may nonetheless increase. The gains of a small percentage of large gainers may be so large that they may exceed the combined losses of a larger percentage of losers; median income might fall while average income rises. In other words, while average income is increasing, the income of the average man may be falling.

It is not only a logical possibility, but also at times a practical probability, that the number getting poorer will increase with rapid economic growth.[12] This is because in periods of rapid economic growth there are often several forces that work toward a concentration of most of the gains in a relatively small number of hands and to a widespread diffusion of the losses. One of the forces that can work in this direction is the tendency for wages to be more sticky

[12] Simon Kuznets, while pointing out that in recent times the *long-run* trend in the advanced economies is toward greater equality of incomes, has suggested that in the early phases of economic growth (which are the main concern of this paper) there is a tendency toward increasing inequality. Kuznets' focus is on the inequality of the *overall* income distribution, while this paper is concerned with the distribution of the gains and losses only; thus it would be logically possible that even when the distribution of gains and losses from economic growth was extremely unequal, the overall distribution of income could become less unequal, since the poorer people could get the gains and the richer the losses. Nonetheless, Kuznets' conclusions about changes in income distribution in the early phases of economic growth would appear to support the argument offered here. See "Economic Growth and Income Inequality," *American Economic Review*, XLV (Mar. 1955), 1–28.

than prices. Thus, as demand increases with economic growth, businessmen may raise prices *pari-passu* with the increase in demand, but wages may rise much more slowly. The particular importance of this phenomenon during periods of inflation, which also seem to be correlated somewhat with economic growth, is of course familiar to every economic historian, because this same argument has been used to contend that inflation leads to a redistribution of income from wage earners to entrepreneurs.[13]

Another force that leads toward inequality in the distribution of the fruits of rapid economic growth is the change of technology involved in economic growth. When one firm, or some group of firms, begins to use a new technique, a technique sufficiently superior to the old techniques to lead to rapid increases in productivity and efficiency, those firms with the old technology are apt to fail or at least to suffer falling profits. Unless the new technology is adopted by all firms in an industry at the same time, one would expect that the introduction or the arrival of this technology would increase the differences in profits or lead to the failure of some of the firms. When the factors of production—especially the labor—that the declining firms employ are considered, the problem becomes more important in human, and political, terms. The unskilled laborers or skilled craftsmen replaced by machines are apt to be a destabilizing force.

The increased productivity of the modern machinery and new techniques introduced in periods of rapid economic growth will no doubt in the long run increase the income of all classes. But those who suffer in the short run know that in the long run they will be dead and are all too apt to be

[13] R. A. Kessel and A. A. Alchian have in an interesting article denied the usual contention that wages rise more slowly than prices and profits during inflations, but I do not find their conclusion persuasive. See "The Meaning and Validity of the Inflation Induced Lag of Wages Behind Prices," *American Economic Review*, L (Mar., 1960), 43–67.

susceptible to disruptive agitation. The British weavers who were left unemployed in the advance of the industrial revolution certainly lost a great deal in a period when the nation's total wealth and per capita income doubtless increased. The Luddite-type movements against new machinery that increased productivity illustrate the reactions against the unevenness of the short-run benefits of growth.

The fact that some groups in the population may in the short run lose from rapid economic growth is made all the worse by the fact that societies in the early stages of industrialization rarely have suitable institutions for mitigating the adversities that the losers in the process suffer. While traditional social institutions, like the tribe, the extended family, and the manor will often have appropriate ways of helping those among them who suffer adversities, and while mature industrial societies have developed welfare institutions, the society in an early stage of rapid industrialization will probably not have adequate institutions to care for those who suffer from the economic advance. Unemployment is not normally a serious problem for the preindustrial society. It could hardly have meaning in, say, a tribal society. The word "unemployment" is indeed a rather recent coinage. The unemployment, frictional or otherwise, that may result when a traditional society begins to industrialize and grow will therefore lead to serious losses for some parts of the society. And, since the problem is new, the society is not apt to deal with it successfully. The United States and Great Britain certainly had not yet developed systems for dealing with the unemployment that was becoming increasingly serious in their societies in the nineteenth century.

In short, rapid economic growth will bring about a situation where some lose part of their incomes, and others, because of the new problem of unemployment, lose *all* of their incomes. Thus a sense of grievance and insecurity may be a destabilizing force resulting from the fact that with economic growth, as with so many other things, there are both winners and losers.

In those cases where the number of gainers from economic growth exceeds the number of losers, there is apt to be a number of those who, while they have gained in absolute terms, have lost in relative terms; that is, they have come to have a lower position relative to the rest of the income earners in that society. Some of those whose gains from economic growth are rather modest may find that they have fallen in the economic scale because of the larger advances of some of the other gainers. There have been some studies that provide interesting indirect evidence about the reactions of people who are experiencing an absolute increase in income and a relative decline in their economic position. These studies, arising out of the controversies over the Keynesian consumption function, have suggested that families with a given level of income tend to spend a smaller percentage of that income when the others in that society have low incomes than they do when the others in that society have high incomes. A family's consumption, in short, is affected, not only by that family's level of income, but also by the level of incomes of the other people in that society. The evidence on this point Professor James S. Duesenberry has explained in terms of the "demonstration effect." The demonstration or evidence of higher consumption patterns in one's neighbors will increase one's desire for additional consumption, in the sense that it leads to saving a smaller proportion of income. From this in turn one can perhaps infer that, when a group's position in the economic hierarchy falls, there may be some dissatisfaction—dissatisfaction that would not necessarily be counteracted by an absolute increase in that group's level of income.

Therefore, quite apart from the fact that even the relative gainers may, as earlier parts of this paper argued, be destabilizing, and quite apart from the possibility that economic growth may increase the number of losers, there is still the further fact that, when the number of gainers from economic growth exceeds the number of losers, some of the gainers may have lost ground relative to the society in general and may display some degree of disaffection.[14]

VI

But the most important error involved in the all-too-common assumption, "when the economy grows, the standard of living improves," is that it neglects the very important possibility that the level of consumption will decline when the rate of economic growth increases greatly. This can best be explained by using an elementary Domar-type model. Let the marginal propensity to save be equal to the average propensity to save, and let it be symbolized by the letter S. Let the marginal capital-output ratio be symbolized by the letter R, and income by the letter Y. Then the increase in income with economic growth will be given by the equation $dY = dS/dR$. Assume a rather typical capital-output ratio of, say, 3 to 1. The shortcomings of the capital-output ratio as a tool of prediction, or planning, or rigorous analysis, are obvious enough, but they are not relevant to the merely illustrative use of the concept here. Whether capital accumulation is as fundamental a force in economic growth as some have assumed is doubtful, but there can be

[14] Is this factor offset by those who have lost in absolute terms but gained in relative terms? It is not, because in any society in which there has been economic growth, from which more have gained than have lost, all those who have lost in absolute terms will also have lost in relative terms, so there will be in this case no class of absolute losers and relative gainers to offset the class mentioned above. The only case in which there could be a class of absolute losers and relative gainers would be that in which the number of losers exceeded the number of gainers. But the Duesenberry investigations also tell us that those whose incomes are falling absolutely have a higher propensity to consume than those people who have the same level of income but whose incomes have not been falling. Those who are absolute losers and relative gainers may therefore also feel that they are suffering from the economic advance.

no question that capital accumulation is associated with growth. Let us therefore accept the usual assumption that a stagnant underdeveloped nation will normally be saving only about 5 per cent of its income, and growing at less than 2 per cent per year —that is, at a rate barely sufficient to compensate for normal population growth. Now, suppose such a nation is, through its own efforts, going to increase its rate of growth to 5 per cent per year. Then it must, as long as the capital-output ratio remains constant, increase its rate of savings until it saves 15 per cent of its total income: it must *reduce* its standard of living by 10 per cent, in order to triple its rate of savings. So when growth is financed primarily out of domestic sources, as it normally is, a rapid increase in the rate of growth will tend to be associated with a decline in the standard of living.[15] To be sure, the increased rate of growth will after a time put a nation in a position such that it can reduce its rate of savings again and enjoy a higher standard of living than before (provided that population growth doesn't then catch up with this increase in income). It can even, if it waits long enough, get a higher standard of living than it had before without reducing the rate of its savings, for in time it will have grown so much that the smaller fraction of this larger income will still mean more consumption that it had before. Yet the fact remains that a nation that greatly increases the rate at which it grows through its own efforts must normally sustain a reduction in its standard of living for a significant period.

The all-too-common argument that hunger and deprivation breed discontent and disaffection and that economic growth therefore reduces the chances for revolt is, apart from its other shortcomings, ruined by the simple fact that there is in the short run no necessary, or even likely, connection between economic growth and amelioration

[15] The importance of this factor will be limited by the likelihood that most of the saving will come from the rich.

of hunger and the other deprivations of poverty. There may, instead, very well be a general decrease in living standards with rapid economic growth.

It may be only a remarkable coincidence that Marx, writing during a period of rapid economic growth and tremendous capital accumulation in Europe, emphasized the "rising organic composition of capital" (the increased importance of capital invested in things other than labor) as the fundamental reason why the *advance* of capitalism would lead to the immiseration of the workers. But it is an interesting coincidence: perhaps Marx's insight was better than his logic.

The upshot of the foregoing arguments, then, is that the gainers from economic growth may themselves be a destabilizing influence because their position in the social order is changing. Those who lose from economic growth will also find that their position in the social order is changing, and they are apt to be much more resentful of poverty, and aware of the possibilities of a better life, than those who have known nothing but privation. The assumption that economic growth ameliorates social discontents is, in addition to its other shortcomings, weakened by the fact that there is no necessary connection between rapid economic growth and short-run increases in the incomes of the mass of the people. And even when the incomes of the mass of the people are increasing, it does not follow that their standards of living are increasing, for the increased rate of saving concomitant with economic growth may reduce the level of consumption.

VII

Since economic growth is associated, not only with capital accumulation, but also with the advance of education, skill, and technology, it will be connected in underdeveloped countries with an increasing knowledge of the possibilities of a better life, of new ideologies, and of new systems of government. It will be associated with a "revolution of rising expectations" that is apt to involve, above all, rising expectations about what the government should do. Economic growth, since it leads to higher incomes for some people who were previously at a lower standard, will itself stimulate and exacerbate these rising expectations. Thus it is possible that there may be something in the economic sphere corresponding to the tendency for the demands for reform to increase as soon as reform is begun. Alexis de Tocqueville made this point particularly clearly.

It is not always by going from bad to worse that a society falls into revolution. It happens most often that a people, which has supported without complaint, as if they were not felt, the most oppressive laws, violently throws them off as soon as their weight is lightened. The social order destroyed by a revolution is almost always better than that which immediately preceded it, and experience shows that the most dangerous moment for a bad government is generally that in which it sets about reform. Only great genius can save a prince who undertakes to relieve his subjects after a long oppression. The evil, which was suffered patiently as inevitable, seems unendurable as soon as the idea of escaping from it is conceived. All the abuses then removed seem to throw into greater relief those which remain, so that their feeling is more painful. The evil, it is true, has become less, but sensibility to it has become more acute. Feudalism at the height of its power had not inspired Frenchmen with so much hatred as it did on the eve of its disappearing. The slightest acts of arbitrary power under Louis XVI seemed less easy to endure than all the despotism of Louis XIV.[16]

The awareness of racial injustice and the willingness to do something about it seem to be higher among American Negroes now

[16] Alexis de Tocqueville, *L'Ancien Regime*, trans. M. W. Patterson (Oxford: Basil Blackwell, 1947), p. 186.

then they have been for a long time. The discont seems to have increased *after* the historic Supreme Court decision outlawing segregated schools and *after* a series of other steps in the direction of racial justice. (This discontent also appears to have been correlated with an economic improvement in the position of American Negroes.) Many other cases could be cited where reform nourishes revolt; but the relevant point here is that economic growth, like political reform, can awaken a people to the possibilities of further improvement and thereby generate additional discontent.

There is, however, at least one situation where economic growth need *not* be correlated with increased knowledge of new ideologies, new systems of government, and the like, or perhaps even with the possibilities of a better material life. That is in a modern totalitarian country, where the media of communication are controlled in such a way that they glorify the existing situation and keep out any ideas that would threaten the existing system. Modern totalitarian regimes of the Stalinist and Hitlerian kinds will also have other techniques for guaranteeing their own stability, most notably the practice of liquidating anyone who shows any lack of enthusiasm for the prevailing regime. There was rapid growth in the Soviet Union under Stalin's five-year plans; yet the nation was relatively stable, and for obvious reasons.[17] Some other despotic regimes have been less thoroughgoing in their repression than Stalin or Hitler yet have nonetheless managed to control dis-

sent fairly effectively. Japan before World War II would provide an example of this sort of situation.

Repression is not, of course, the only thing besides economic growth that can affect the degree of political instability. Clearly, charismatic leadership, religious controversy, ideological change, and probably other things as well, also have an independent influence on the degree of instability in any country. It would be absurd to attempt to explain political instability through economic growth alone. Indeed, a severe depression, or a sudden *decrease* in the level of income, could of course also be destabilizing—and for many of the same reasons that rapid economic growth itself can be destabilizing. A rapid economic decline, like rapid economic growth, will bring about important movements in the *relative* economic positions of people and will therefore set up contradictions between the structure of economic power and the distribution of social and political power. (Severe inflation of the German and Chinese types will have the same effect.) There is, accordingly, nothing inconsistent in saying that both rapid economic growth and rapid economic decline would tend toward political instability.[18] It is economic stability —the absence of rapid economic growth or rapid economic decline—that should be regarded as conducive to social and political tranquility. But it would be absurd to suppose that economic stagnation would guarantee political stability. Since there are many factors in addition to rapid economic change that cause political insta-

[17] E. A. J. Johnson, after hearing this paper presented at the Economic History Association meeting, objected that totalitarian nations fit the author's hypothesis better than other nations do, in part because the subject people naturally blame the ubiquitous state for all difficult economic adjustments. He seemed to relate the opposition leading to Stalin's purges, after a period of rapid Soviet growth, and the apparent liberalization in some current communist regimes (especially Tito's), to the rapid economic development. I feel that his criticism, if I have understood it correctly, is very much worth investigating.

[18] For models in which a variety of economic conditions can lead to instability, see Ronald G. Ridker, "Discontent and Economic Growth," *Economic Development and Cultural Change*, XI (Oct. 1962), 1–15, and James C. Davis, "Toward a Theory of Revolution," *American Sociological Review*, XXVII (Feb. 1962), 5–19. Davis contends that it is when a period of growth is interrupted by a depression that revolution is most likely. Davis' conclusion is not necessarily inconsistent with this paper's, which deals with growth as a cause of instability rather than with the precise timing of revolutions.

bility, there can be political instability in a wide range of economic conditions.

This makes it extremely difficult to test the hypothesis that rapid economic growth is conducive to political instability. The hypothesis would not be proven even if every period of rapid economic growth were shown to be politically destabilizing, for the instability in these periods of rapid economic growth could be due to other factors that were operating at the same time. Similarly, the hypothesis that rapid economic growth is destabilizing would not be disproven if there were a negative relationship between rapid economic growth and political instability, for the extent of totalitarian repression or the presence of other stabilizing forces might keep the destabilizing tendencies of rapid economic growth from being manifest. If rapid economic change and political instability are positively or negatively correlated, all this will do is establish some tentative *presumption* that rapid economic growth is, or is not, destabilizing. A final judgment, if one could ever be made, would have to rest on detailed historical studies of a vast variety of cases. These historical studies would have to be so careful and so detailed that they looked, not only at the connection over time between economic and political change, but also at the complex of detailed economic, social, and political changes. They would have to identify both the gainers and the losers from rapid economic growth and all of the other factors affecting political stability, and then attempt to come to a judgment about the role of the economic changes. A massive set of historical studies of the kind needed, covering all historical periods and countries in which there has been rapid economic growth or political instability, is obviously out of the question in a brief paper, even if it were within my competence, which it is not. But it is nonetheless important that historians should start studying at least parts of the problem, however difficult, as soon as possible.

VIII

If there is indeed a connection between rapid economic growth and political instability, then those Western scholars who criticize the underdeveloped countries for attempting to provide some of the services of the modern welfare state may be a bit off the mark. It is no doubt true that the underdeveloped countries cannot afford modern welfare measures as well as the advanced nations can. But it is perhaps also true that they need these modern welfare institutions more than the advanced countries do. These welfare measures, though they might retard growth, could nonetheless be a profitable investment in social peace. They could ease the plight and alleviate the discontents of those who lose from economic growth.

Those who assume that, because certain welfare measures in underdeveloped countries might decrease the rate of growth, they are therefore undesirable, make the mistake that Karl Polanyi discussed in *The Great Transformation*. Polanyi was, in my opinion, quite correct in emphasizing that the relative merits of alternative economic policies had not been decided when it was shown that one led to a faster rate of growth than the others. The differing impacts of capitalistic and socialistic economic systems on the political and social life of a society also had to be considered. Polanyi felt that, while laissez-faire capitalism led to a high rate of growth, it imposed too great a burden of adjustment on society. His argument is indeed interesting; but to me he is quite wrong in identifying the social disorganization resulting from economic change with capitalism alone. Whatever the organization and control of the means of production, rapid economic growth must require painful adjustments. In few places has economic growth involved such painful adjustments as in the Soviet Union in Stalin's first five-year plan. And in the underdeveloped countries today, nationalized industries are often playing a major role in the struggle for economic growth.

It would be hard to see how the nationalization of industry itself would reduce the disruption that economic growth causes. The person who leaves the tribe, the manor, the peasant village, or the extended family for the modern factory in the growing city will find that he is in an alien environment, no matter who runs the factory. If the factory is to be run in the interest of maximum production, under socialist or private management, it cannot fail to impose a new and burdensome discipline and a new style of life upon the recently recruited work force.

Thus the point is that rapid economic growth, whatever the nature of the economic system, must involve fast and deep changes in the ways that things are done, in the places that things are done, and in the distribution of power and prestige. Most people spend such a large proportion of their time working for a living and draw such a large part of their social status and political influence from their economic position that changes in the economic order must have great effects on other facets of life. This is especially true in underdeveloped societies, where the institutions that exist were developed in relatively static conditions and are not suited to making rapid adjustments.[19] Therefore, until fur-

ther research is done, the presumption must be that rapid economic growth, far from being the source of domestic tranquility it is sometimes supposed to be, is rather a disruptive and destabilizing force that leads to political instability. This does not mean that rapid economic growth is undesirable or that political instability is undesirable. It means, rather, that no one should promote the first without bracing to meet the second.

---

[19] The relatively brittle character of most institutions in traditional, underdeveloped societies is illustrated by Max Weber's analysis of the origins of castes and classes. He argued that a caste system would thrive only in a relatively static society, for it makes virtually no provision for the changes in individual rankings that changing societies require. A modern class system, by contrast, allows for some changes in the positions of individuals. See Max Weber, *From Max Weber: Essays in Sociology*, H. H. Gerth and C. Wright Mills, ed. and trans. (New York: Oxford University Press, 1946), especially pp. 193–94. Presumably most institutions of traditional societies have not had to develop a great deal of flexibility, while those that have evolved in dynamic industrial societies have acquired some capacity to adjust to rapid change. Accordingly, the thesis of this article would explain the social and political effects of rapid growth much better in underdeveloped societies than in economically advanced societies. The thesis here would fit countries like the United States, Canada, Australia, and New Zealand least of all, for these countries of relatively recent settlement have inherited fewer feudal institutions than other nations, and their institutions have had to evolve in rather rapidly changing conditions from the beginning.

SOCIAL CHANGE AND POLITICAL VIOLENCE: CROSS-NATIONAL PATTERNS

*Ivo K. Feierabend, Rosalind L. Feierabend, and Betty A. Nesvold**

This study examines selected aspects of social change and their effect upon political violence and the internal political stability of nations.[1] The inquiry is predominantly empirical rather than speculative in nature. It is also extensive in scope, scrutinizing 84 nations in an attempt to discern broad global patterns of both change and violence.

In general, the study compares nations for their relative levels of political stability or instability, modernization, and rates of socioeconomic change. By means of these comparisons, the study approaches the question: In what ways are social change and development related to political violence within the sample of 84 nations at mid-20th century?

SOURCE: Ivo K. Feierabend, Rosalind L. Feierabend, and Betty A. Nesvold, "Social Change and Political Violence: Cross-National Patterns," in Hugh Davis Graham and Ted Robert Gurr (eds.), *Violence in America: Historical and Comparative Perspectives,* A Report to the National Commission on the Causes and Prevention of Violence, June 1969 (New York: The New American Library, 1969), Chap. XVIII.

* Ivo Feierabend is professor of political science; his wife Rosalind, associate professor of psychology at San Diego State College. Dr. Nesvold is assistant professor of political science at the College. The Feireabends have written a number of articles and papers based on their comparative studies of political instability, including "Aggressive Behaviors Within Polities, 1948–1962: A Cross-National Study," *Journal of Conflict Resolution,* vol. X (Sept. 1966), pp. 249–271. Their work received the American Association for the Advancement of Science's 1966 Socio-Psychological Prize for research in the behavioral sciences. Dr. Nesvold is the author of "A Scalogram Analysis of Political Violence," *Comparative Political Studies,* vol. II (July 1969).

This broadly comparative, cross-national approach has its shortcomings. Important depth and detail are lost in the panoramic overview that would be more thoroughly preserved in intensive exploration of a single country. On the other hand, the advantage of the broader method lies in its scope. The examination of many cases can reveal patterns that may go unnoticed, or that may be obscured, in the unique circumstances of a specific case.[2]

Theoretical Considerations

The notion of social change is complex. It refers to movement through time of a variety of ecological, socioeconomic, political, structural, cultural, and ideational aspects and conditions of social existence. The problem is not only to clarify those aspects of social reality that are changing but also to specify the nature of the change. Is the social universe changing slowly or swiftly; is change continuous or discontinuous, or perhaps accelerating in some aspects and lagging in others? Elusive notions such as progress, growth, decline, and decay all entail some particularized view of change. Assumptions as to the direction of change are implicit in the concept of development, which suggests that change proceeds from one stage to another, or perhaps through several developmental phases. Withdrawal from one stage and movement toward another is referred to as "transition." The entire notion of change is sometimes identified with such periods of transition.[3]

SOCIAL CHANGE AND VIOLENCE

The assumption of a relationship between change and violence is based on arguments that are intuitively persuasive. Change, especially extensive, rapid, and abrupt change, is an unsettling and bewildering human experience. It is likely to create strain in the psyche of the individual and crisis in the social order. Old ways, familiar environments, deep-seated habits, and social roles become obsolescent, while a new way of life and a new routine are not yet clearly established. Social change is perhaps analogous to the experience of the individual who moves suddenly from one community to another. He lives in a new dwelling, interacts with a new set of individuals, faces new and strange situations that require an inordinate amount of difficult adjustment.

To project this example to a broader social base, one might argue that massive change that moves people physically into new environments, exposes their minds to new ideas, and casts them in new and unfamiliar roles is very likely to create collective bewilderment. This bewilderment may find its expression in turmoil and social violence. However, there are other, conflicting theoretical speculations that are equally persuasive. These suggest that change has beneficial and pacifying social consequences. If social change is perceived as bringing gratification, if it fulfills aspirations, there is no reason to expect social crisis in its wake. On the contrary, obstructing such change, or slowing its pace, should result in social discontent registered in protest movements and violence.[4]

Given these contradictory insights, the idea of change alone is not sufficient to explain the occurrence of violent political behavior. It is only when change brings with it social circumstances that breed discontent and strain, that it may be assumed to be responsible for social turmoil. Other modes of change will not so qualify. On the contrary, they may have a stabilizing effect on the political order. The blanket assertion that change breeds violence is too simplistic.

Our theoretical assumption linking change to violence begins with the notion that political turmoil is the consequence of social discontent. This commonsense assumption is predicated on a motivational rather than a structural orientation. And it reaffirms the often-repeated insight that political protest and revolution begin in the minds of men. Nevertheless, structural and processual variables are intimately a part of the wider view, since men's experience of change in the ecological, social or political universe may create the revolutionary state of mind. In other words, although our assumptions are based on psychological, motivational factors, we are nevertheless interested in analyzing change in environmental, structural circumstances of political systems. What is required is some refinement of the idea of discontent and strain. Also needed is an effort to identify those modes of change and development that can be presumed to lead to the discontent that is the necessary precondition of political instability and violence.

CHANGE, SYSTEMIC FRUSTRATION, AND AGGRESSION

While the concept of aggression has received extensive elaboration within psychology, the frustration-aggression hypothesis seems the most useful for our purposes.[5] In its most basic and fundamental formulation, this hyphothesis maintains that aggression (as well as some other specified behaviors) is the result of frustration. Frustration itself is defined as the thwarting or interference with the attainment of goals, aspirations, or expectations. On the basis of frustration-aggression theory, it is postulated that frustration induced by the social system creates the social strain and discontent that in turn are the indispensable preconditions of violence. The commonsense assertion that revolutionary behavior has its root in discontent, and the more technical postulate that frustration precedes aggression, are parallel statements indicating a common insight.

The concept of frustration is often thought more appropriate to individual than to social circumstances. We believe, however, that the notion of *systemic frustration* makes the concept applicable to the analysis of aggregate, violent political behavior within social systems.[6] We define systemic frustration in reference to three criteria: (1) As frustration interfering with the attainment and maintenance of social goals, aspirations, and values; (2) as frustration simultaneously experienced by members of social aggregates and hence also complex social systems; and (3) as frustration of strain that is produced within the structures and processes of social systems. Systemic frustration is thus frustration that is experienced simultaneously and collectively within societies.

Guided by this definition, we may adopt two basic propositions from the frustration-aggression hypothesis and restate them with reference to social systems: (1) Violent political behavior is instigated by systemic frustration; and (2) systemic frustration may stem among other circumstances of the social system, from specific characteristics of social change.

Four general hypotheses further qualify the notion of systemic frustration: (1) Systemic frustration at any given time is a function of the discrepancy between present social aspirations and expectations, on the one hand, and social achievements, on the other. (2) In addition, present estimates or expectations of future frustrations (or satisfactions) are also responsible for level of present frustration (or satisfaction). (3) Uncertainties in social expectations in themselves increase the sense of systemic frustration. (4) Conflicting aspirations and conflicting expectations provide yet another source of systemic frustration.

The first hypothesis focuses on the discrepancy between aspirations, expectations, and attainments within the present situation. This discrepancy is a result of the interplay between these factors in the present, and level of frustration is postulated to be a function of the number of aspirations involved, their level of valua-

tion, their frequency of occurrence within various population strata, their expected level of attainment, and the degree of certainty with which these expectations are held. Similar criteria apply to the notion of social attainment. It should also be pointed out that is is perceived rather than actual social attainment that is important.

The distinction between aspirations and expectations needs clarification. In simplest definition, aspirations are the goals that people wish to attain. Also included in the definition are presently valued possessions that people desire to maintain. Expectations, on the other hand, include only the portion of aspirations which we expect to achieve. Strictly speaking, expectations refer always to the future. Yet expectations are disappointed (or fulfilled) in the context of the present. And this is the measure of systemic frustration as formulated in the first hypothesis.

The expectation of future frustration or satisfaction may also intensify or counteract present predicaments. The second hypothesis recognizes this possibility, hence uses the term "expectation" in a somewhat different sense. It does not refer to expectations regarding the present situation, but present expectations of future occurrences. The third hypothesis singles out uncertainty as yet another source of frustration. Uncertainty is a special quality of expectations. Ambiguity as to whether the future will bring disaster or salvation should be considered a distressful experience, adding to the present sense of frustration. Only in the case of disaster is certainty likely to be judged as more frustrating than uncertainty. Finally, the fourth hypothesis sees conflict as a systematically frustrating circumstance. Conflict is considered a specific case of frustration in which an individual's alternative motives, aspirations, and expectations work at cross-purposes, blocking one another.[7] The notions of intensity, scope, and distribution of aspirations are as relevant in this context as in the previous one.

PATTERNS OF SOCIAL CHANGE AND DISCONTENT

These theoretical propositions refine the general notion of systemic frustration and social discontent, but the important question still remains: What modes of change and development may we assume to lead toward systemic frustration? Let us point to a few studies in the recent literature of political violence, in order to identify objective social situations that are presumed to create a sense of systemic frustration.

Davies, in his analysis of several revolutions, concludes that, contrary to Marxian expectations, revolutions do not occur during periods of prolonged abject or worsening situations of social deprivation.[8] Neither does the evidence sustain the insight of de Tocqueville and others, that revolutions are perpetrated during periods of relative prosperity and improvement. Instead, Davies postulates a J-curve of socioeconomic development, whereby revolution occurs in social systems in which social well-being has been continually raised for an extended period of time, followed by an abrupt and sharp setback. His explanation is in accord with our notion of discontent and systemic frustration. We may suggest that certainty of social expectations was reinforced during the period of continued socioeconomic development. The sharp reversal in social fortunes creates an intolerable discrepancy between achievement and expectation. It is also possible that the unexpected reversal in attainment creates an alarmist expectation of continued severe decreases in levels of achievement. Such a fear for the future, possibly an exaggerated fear, motivates present actions as much as do actual present conditions.

Figure 1 graphically portrays Davies' hypothesis of the J-curve pattern of change. Furthermore it takes into account not only the sense of frustration that is created by disappointed expectations in the present, but also depicts estimates of the future. If men still anticipate future gratifications (depicted by line *A* in Fig. 1), political violence is less likely to occur in the present. If, on the other hand, they anticipate intensified frustration (depicted by line *B*), the likelihood of violence is strengthened. In the latter case, the sense of frustration resulting from disappointed expectations in the present is intensified by the gap between present level of achievement and an even more pessimistic estimate of the future.

Another type of J-curve may be equally productive of social discontent. A sudden

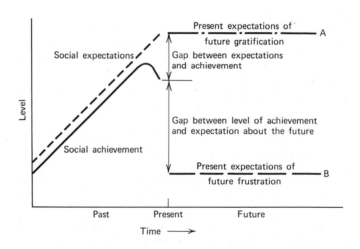

Figure 1. J-curve change model—deterioration pattern.

and unexpected improvement in social circumstances may give rise to hopes of better things to come. If actual improvement is not sufficiently high to meet the newly aroused expectations, an intolerable gap between expectation and attainment will ensue, constituting systemic frustration. Again the argument is based on a contrast effect, one that gives impetus to expectations. The novelty of gratification following a long history of deprivation may give the aspect of reality to long-suppressed aspirations. It is exaggerated hope for the future, in this case, which inevitably breeds disappointment.[9]

Figure 2 illustrates this situation. As shown, the social achievement line intersects the line of expectations at time t_1, or shortly after achievement exceeds expectations. Hence this is the point of social satisfaction. Yet at t_2, where achievement does not keep pace with soaring, newly awakened expectations, a gap occurs comparable to that in Davies' J-curve model. Expectations regarding the future in this model also may either detract or add to the present sense of systemic frustration.

These models of social change indicate the dynamics of motivational factors stipulated in the first two hypotheses. There are also social circumstances that can be judged as unlikely to stimulate social discontent. Examples in the social process are situations in which objective achievement remains constant, no matter what that level may be, or situations in which acceleration and deceleration of change are either consistent or slight. Situations in which a minimal, gradual, or constant amount of change is experienced are the least likely to introduce striking discrepancies between present social expectations and present levels of achievement. Also, by avoiding contrast effects in achievement, expectations about the future are held fairly realistically in line with attainments. These social situations are represented in Figure 3.

With reference to Figure 3c, it should be noted that even deteriorating social circumstances may not in themselves be stimulants to violent behavior, provided the deterioration is gradual and constant. On the other hand, very rapid social deterioration should have the consequences postulated in the J-curve of Davies: a discrepancy between expectations and achievements is created by rapid decline in social attainments. It is also conceivable that a rapidly improving situation could follow the pattern of the J-curve in Figure 2.

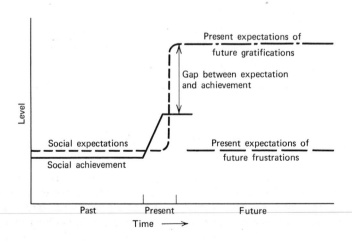

Figure 2. J-curve change model—improvement pattern.

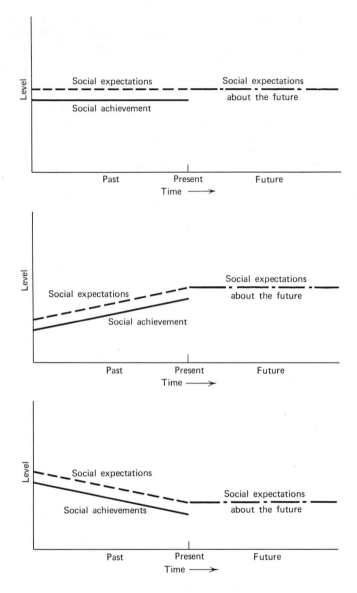

Figure 3. Minimal changes model.

This impact of rapid and consistent change is illustrated in Figures 4 and 5. The model in Figure 4 assumes that a rapidly deteriorating level of attainment creates not only an increasing gap between presently disappointed expectations and achievement but also that the speed of deterioration is almost certain to create a very pessimistic outlook for the future. In the case illustrated in Figure 5, which may seem less persuasive as a model for the outburst of civil violence, the rise in social achievement is outstripped by an even steeper curve of rising expectations. Another point to be made

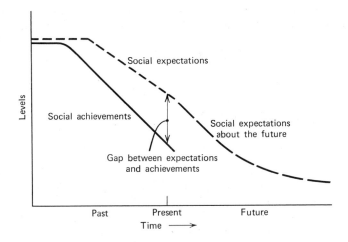

Figure 4.   Rapid-change model—deterioration pattern.

regarding the rapid-change model is that, if social achievement were growing as a power function rather than as a straight line, the gap between expectations and achievement could be eliminated.

The dynamics of the systemic frustration situations sketched in the figures reflect the sudden onset of improvement or deterioration, as well as rapid rates of growth or decline. The point to be stressed is that levels of social expectation depend very much on past performance of the social system. Men who experience a constant history of either frustration or satisfaction will develop learned expectations consistent with their experience. Abrupt change in objective cir-

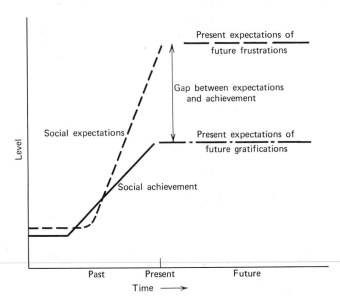

Figure 5.   Rapid-change model—improvement pattern.

cumstance, especially a reversal of direction but also, at least at the outset, a very rapid rise or decline, will have a sharp and sometimes unrealistic impact on expectations. The consequent lack of alignment between expectations and attainments creates the intolerable discrepancy which is postulated as the motivational antecedent to political violence.

Unrealistic expectations regarding the future may also be pinned to a major change in circumstance that is clearly certain to occur at a particular point in time. The irreality of such expectations is that a variety of other changes are also anticipated concomitant with the single, clearly stated event:

There are situations in the present century in which exaggerated expectations regarding some future event are likely to bring an immediate sense of sharp systemic frustration. Speaking of the trauma of independence in West Africa, Victor LeVine points out that the advent of independence is often counted upon to provide a panacea for all the social ills besetting a country.[10] When independence does occur, however, it falls far short of providing a perfect solution to all problems. This experience proves a shattering frustration if, in fact, such high

expectations were held (Fig. 6). It is indisputable that the extent of revolutionary behavior in Africa increased sharply after independence was granted. It was the expectation of momentous change that proved illusory.

In Figure 7, flux in social and economic performance or policy is postulated as creating social discontent and political violence. Flux is likely to create ambiguity and uncertainty of expectations, as suggested in the third hypothesis. Discontinuous economic growth, that is, alternating periods of relative prosperity and economic slump in short succession, or conflicting policies simultaneously pursued or sequently administered, as well as other inconsistencies within the domain of social change, exemplify another set of circumstances that ripen the impulse toward political violence.[11]

CONFLICT BETWEEN THE TRADITIONAL
AND MODERN

All of these change models—and more could be generated[12]—suggest situations that give rise to a sense of systemic frustration, as postulated in the first three propositions. The fourth proposition introduces the idea of systemic conflict and may best be traced to the process of transition. Here,

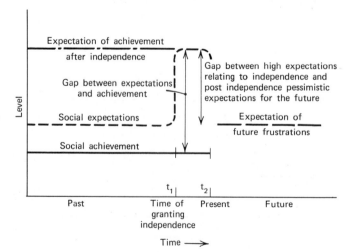

Figure 6.   Disappointed expectations tied to future events.

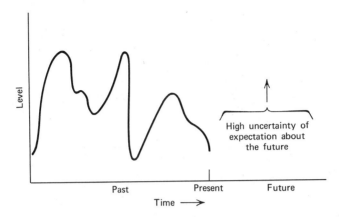

Figure 7. Fluctuation change model.

social change is of the kind that transforms the social order from one form, or stage of development, to another. Since these forms may differ radically in social structure, economic achievement, culture, or other respects, and since one form is receding and another only slowly gaining ground, a large area of struggle and conflict between the new and the old is likely to occur. Indeed, conflict may be seen as indispensable to the very notion of transition and transformation. If the new and the old were similar and harmonious, if little or no change were required, it would be superfluous to speak of transition.

The notions of development, stages, and transition are familiar themes, as is the idea that political violence is associated with the transitional process. In different periods of history, the process of transition has been conceptualized in different ways; for example, as a change from religious to secular society or from small principalities to nation-states. The dominant contemporary view stresses the process of modernization, which is seen as engulfing the less-developed nations of today's world. In this view, nations may be classified into three groups: modern societies, traditional societies, and modernizing societies. The latter are pass-

ing through the transitional stage from traditional society to modernity. Generally, this period of transition is regarded as one that entails an inordinate amount of strain, tension, and crisis.[13]

On the evidence, members of transitional societies aspire to the benefits of modernity, yet modern goals may be blocked by the values inherent in traditional society.[14] Any modicum of modernity introduced into traditional society will conflict with its traditions. The farther the process of transition progresses, the more likely and the more intense the conflicts between modern and established patterns. The situation may be depicted as a massive conflict, reflected in myriad individual psyches of different strata of the population and infecting different domains of the social process. It may lead to intergroup conflict between more traditional and more modern strata with conflicting social roles, structures, and expectations.

Figure 8 attempts to schematize the pattern. If we assume that many traditional patterns are in fact incompatible with modernity, then the midpoint of the transitional process is the point of highest intensity of conflict and hence the point of highest systematic frustration. The stage of transi-

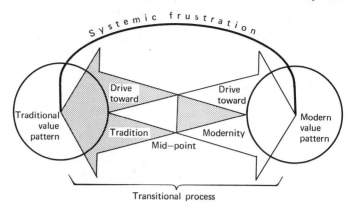

Figure 8.   Systemic-conflict model of transition.

tion is also the one most likely to be characterized by a high incidence of violent
activity. It is at this midpoint that the accomplishments of modernity equal those of
tradition, and the drive toward modernity
is offset by the contradictory and equal
attraction of traditional ways. This should
be the stage of the most intense struggle between the traditional and the modern.
Figure 8 symbolizes this systemic conflict
situation with two intersecting arrows representing traditional and modern drives. The
closer the transitional process to the stage
of modernity (tradition), the stronger the
modern (traditional) drive, and the weaker
the traditional (modern) drive. (This
strengthening and weakening of drives is
depicted by the varying width of the two
arrows.) The forces determining the strength
and weakness of the two drives are specified
by the psychological hypothesis that postulates a strengthening of drive with proximity
to the goal.[15] Hence the closer the transitional country to either modernity or tradition, the less the systemic conflict. As a
country approaches either end of the transition continuum, the attraction toward the
closest value pattern overcomes the drive in
the opposite direction.

THE PROCESSES OF MODERNIZATION

It can be argued that all of the conditions
conducive to systemic frustration are pro-

duced by the modernization process, in
addition to the occurrence of systemic conflict. Modernization, especially since World
War II, affects an uneven array of nations
at different levels of development. The less-
developed nations, even those very close to
the image of traditional society, are exposed
to the modern ways of the more advanced
nations. This exposure alone may create
new aspirations and expectations and leave
them unmatched by social achievements.

Modernity itself denotes a very specific
mode of culture and social organization.
It includes the aspiration and capacity in
a society to produce and consume a wide
range and quantity of goods and services.
It includes high development in science,
technology, and education, and high attainment in scores of specialized skills. It includes, moreover, a secular culture, new
structures of social organization and more
specialized and differentiated participation,
new sets of aspirations, attitudes, and
ideologies. Modern affluent nations with
their complex economic, political, and social systems serve best as models of modernity to nations emerging from traditional society.

The adoption of modern goals, although
an integral aspect of modernity, is hardly
synonymous with their attainment. The
arousal of an underdeveloped society to
awareness of complex modern patterns of

behavior and organization brings with it a desire to emulate and achieve the same high level of satisfaction. But there is an inevitable lag between aspiration and achievement. The more a country is exposed to modernity and the lower its level of development, the greater the discrepancy between achievement and social aspirations. It is postulated that the peak discrepancy between systemic goals and their satisfaction, and hence maximum systemic frustration, is likely to occur during the transitional phase. Highly modern and truly traditional nations should experience less systemic frustration—in the modern nations, because of their ability to provide a high level of attainment commensurate with modern aspirations; in the traditional nations, unexposed to modernity, because modern aspirations are still lacking. Figure 9 depicts the increasing and decreasing gap between modern aspirations and modern achievements.

A similar logic is applicable not only to social aspirations but also to social expectations. Furthermore, there may also be a feedback effect stemming from modern social attainment. It could be argued that

the satisfaction of modern wants and aspirations reinforces the expectation of further satisfaction. As modern aspirations are formed through the process of exposure to modernity, if even a few aspirations are satisfied, these few satisfactions may create the drive and expectation for more, thus adding to the sense of systemic frustration. If so, it could be assumed that the faster the rate of modern achievement, the greater the feedback effect and the more thorough the "revolution of rising expectations." It is in this sense that rapid rates of change, as opposed to gradual change toward modernity, could lead to more rather than less frustration, the situation postulated in the model in Figure 5. At the same time, rapid achievement could reduce the gap between aspirations and attainment and hence reduce the sense of frustration. Rapid rate of change in the establishment of modernity in this estimation then could have contradictory effects.

The aura of uncertainty also hangs over the entire process of social change, a consequence of its conflicts and confusions. There is ambivalence of attitudes to old ways now on the wane, as well as toward

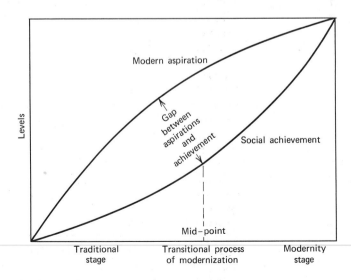

Figure 9.   Model of uneven growth of modern aspirations and achievement during transition.

the modern future. Ambiguity epitomizes the transitional process, and ambiguity is postulated to increase frustration.

Measurement of Political Instability

The complexity of the theoretical propositions elaborated in the previous section make them difficult to test precisely through the use of cross-national aggregate data. We may, however, assess empirically the relationship between levels or stages of development and political violence, as well as between violence and some selected measures of rate of socioeconomic change.[16]

To do so, the first task is to measure the level of political violence or political instability in a large sample of nations of the world. The study includes 84 nations which are examined for an 18-year period, 1948–65. Every reported event relevant to political instability that occurred in these countries during the time period is recorded to form a cross-national data bank of political instability events. (See the appendix for a detailed description of the data.)

Events are scaled in terms of an intensity weighting that assigns values on a seven-point scale. The scale ranges from 0, extreme stability, to 6, extreme instability. In assigning scale values to events, the criteria used are the amount of violence accompanying the event, the number of persons involved in the event, its duration, the political significance of persons involved in the event, and an estimate of the political repercussions of the event upon the society as a whole. Typical scale positions assigned to events are the following: regularly scheduled election, 0; dismissal or resignation of cabinet official, 1; peaceful demonstration or arrest, 2; assassination (except of chief of state) or sabotage, 3; assassination (of chief of state) or terrorism, 4; coup d'etat or guerrilla warfare, 5; civil war or mass execution, 6.

Countries are profiled in a number of different ways. One basic technique is to assign countries to groups on the basis of the event with the highest scale value experienced during the time period under investigation. Within these intensity groupings, countries are ranked according to both frequency and intensity scores. The types of profiles yielded by this grouped intensity and frequency technique are illustrated in Table 1. Table 1A shows country instability profiles for the entire 18-year period, 1948–65, grouped according to the single most violent event experienced. It will be noted that the distribution is highly skewed, with most countries falling at scale position 5 and quite a few at scale position 6. This profiling tells us that, within this relatively long time period, a large number of countries experienced a high level of instability, although perhaps only temporarily. It also shows that there is a smaller number of countries that did not experience a single severely unstable event in the entire 18 years. If instability scores are averaged for three six-year subperiods within the 18 years, as in Table 1B, a more normal distribution is obtained. In this profiling, countries that have experienced severe internal turmoil, but only briefly, have their scores tempered by the periods of relative quiescence. Only Indonesia remains in scale position 6, indicating that it has experienced civil war during each of the three subperiods.

Another method of profiling nations on political instability is to sum the scaled events for the entire time period without grouping the nations. The profiles yielded by this method rank countries somewhat differently than previously. Frequency of events, though weighted for intensity, is a more dominant factor than in the grouped scoring method. A final scaling method uses only violent events. The profiling of nations with these violent events (scored by the Guttman technique, see appendix) is presented in Table 2.

It should be pointed out that all of these scaling methods show a high level of agreement, while at the same time shifting the position of specific countries in response to different emphases in the scaling criteria.

Table 1A. National Political Instability Profiles, 1948-65 [Group scores, n = 84]

1	2	3	4	5	6
Stability					Instability
Luxembourg 1:012					
	Finland 2:056				
	Australia 2:026				
	Netherlands 2:021				
	Sweden 2:020				
	New Zealand 2:015				
		U.K. 3:112			
		W. Germany 3:087			
		Canada 3:084			
		Libya 3:069			
		Romania 3:060			
		Switzerland 3:042			
		China (Tiawan) 3:039			
		Norway 3:034			
		Ireland 3:031			
		Iceland 3:026			
		Saudi Arabia 3:018			
			United States 4:318		
			Spain 4:284		
			Iran 4:237		
			Pakistan 4:231		
			Italy 4:192		
			U.S.S.R. 4:165		
			Belgium 4:162		
			Chile 4:156		
			Ceylon 4:152		
			Japan 4:123		
			Mexico 4:111		
			Ghana 4:106		
			Uruguay 4:100		
			Yugoslavia 4:077		
			Bulgaria 4:071		
			Albania 4:067		
			Israel 4:064		
			Austria 4:057		
			Liberia 4:036		
			Denmark 4:030		
			Afghanistan 4:029		
				France 5:435	
				Venezuela 5:429	
				So. Africa 5:422	
				India 5:360	
				Syria 5:329	
				Guatemala 5:234	
				Lebanon 5:212	
				Brazil 5:209	
				Haiti 5:205	
				Peru 5:196	
				Morocco 5:194	
				Portugal 5:190	
				Turkey 5:189	
				Poland 5:179	
				Egypt 5:152	
				Thailand 5:152	
				Jordan 5:145	
				Ecuador 5:117	
				Malaya 5:108	
				Philippines 5:105	
				Nicaragua 5:096	
				El Salvador 5:079	
				Cambodia 5:071	
				Ethiopia 5:034	
					Argentina 6:445
					Indonesia 6:416
					Bolivia 6:318
					Korea 6:291
					Cuba 6:283
					Iraq 6:274
					Colombia 6:244
					Greece 6:236
					Burma 6:213
					Dom. Rep. 6:195
					Sudan 6:189
					Paraguay 6:141
					E. Germany 6:138
					Laos 6:129
					Tunisia 6:126
					Cyprus 6:123
					Hungary 6:113
					Honduras 6:105
					Panama 6:101
					Czech. 6:100
					China (mainland) 6:086
					Costa Rica 6:058

Table 1B. Political Instability Profiles of 84 Countries (1948-65) [Stability Score Shown for Each Country is Grouped Score, Averaged]

Country	Score	Country	Score	Country	Score
U.K.	07112	France	13435	Argentina	16445
Belgium	10162	Union of S. Africa	13422	Bolivia	16318
Chile	10156	Brazil	13209	Cuba	16283
		Morocco	13194	Iraq	16274
		Portugal	13190	Colombia	16244
		Turkey	13189	Burma	16213
		Poland	13179	Venezuela	15429
		Thailand	13152	Syria	15329
		Jordan	13145	Korea	15291
		Cyprus	13123		
		Hungary	13113		
		Philippines	13105		
		Czecho-slovakia	13100		
		China (mainland)	13086		
		Cambodia	13071		
		India	12360		
		Iran	12237		
		Pakistan	12231		

1	2	3	4	5	6
Stability					Instability
Netherlands 04021	Ghana 07106	Mexico 10111	Sudan 12189	Haiti 15205	Indonesia 18416
Luxembourg 03012	Austria 07057	Uruguay 10100	U.S.S.R. 12165	Peru 15196	
	Denmark 07030	Israel 10064	Ecuador 12117	Greece 14236	
	Iceland 07026	Liberia 10036	Nicaragua 12096	Guatemala 14234	
	W. Germany 06087	Ethiopia 10034	United States 11318	Lebanon 14212	
	Finland 06056	Italy 09192	Spain 11284	Egypt 14152	
	China (Taiwan) 06039	Libya 09069	Dom. Rep. 11195	Paraguay 14141	
	Australia 06026	Romania 09060	Ceylon 11152	E. Germany 14138	
	Sweden 06020	Costa Rica 09058	Japan 11123	Laos 14129	
	Ireland 05031	Afghanistan 09029	Malaya 11108	Tunisia 14126	
	Saudi Arabia 05018	Canada 08084	Yugoslavia 11077	Honduras 14105	
	New Zealand 05015	Switzerland 08042	Bulgaria 11071	Panama 14101	
		Norway 08034	Albania 11067	El Salvador 14079	

The United States, for example, is at the midpoint of the 84 countries in Tables 1A and 1B, but among the most unstable 25 percent of countries in Table 2.

In subsequent sections of the study in which we analyze the relationships among measures of development, rates of change, and political instability and violence, we use these several techniques of quantifying the notion of instability and violence. In all of the studies, a consistent patterning of relationships is found, no matter which measure of instability is used. In most of the analyses, data are used from the entire time period, 1948–65. In some cases, however, a particular subperiod of time is selected because of its relationship to measures of the ecology of the system.

Level of Development and Political Violence

The hypotheses stated in the theoretical portion of this paper are that modern and traditional nations tend toward stability,

Table 2. Political Violence Profiles of 84 Countries (1948-65) [Sources Derived from Guttman Sealogram]

COUNTRY	SCORE	COUNTRY	SCORE	COUNTRY	SCORE
Finland	0	Yugoslavia	27	Dominican	
Luxembourg	0	China		Republic	70
Denmark	1	(mainland)	28	Sudan	71
Iceland	1	El Salvador	28	Laos	72
New Zealand	1	Belgium	31	Greece	73
Saudi Arabia	1	Albania	32	Paraguay	74
Netherlands	2	Japan	32	Haiti	77
Norway	3	Czecho-		Pakistan	77
Sweden	3	slovakia	33	Portugal	77
Australia	4	Mexico	33	Morocco	79
Afghanistan	7	Ghana	35	U.S.S.R.	81
Austria	7	Malaya	36	Lebanon	83
Ireland	7	Chile	38	Burma	87
Switzerland	7	East Germany	39	France	95
Israel	8	Cyprus	41	Colombia	96
China		Ecuador	41	United States	97
(Taiwan)	9	Jordan	41	Guatemala	109
Canada	10	Honduras	42	Syria	111
Liberia	15	Panama	42	Iran	114
Uruguay	16	Hungary	45	Bolivia	120
United		Nicaragua	48	Iraq	120
Kingdom	17	Ceylon	51	Spain	121
Ethiopia	19	Philippines	51	Cuba	123
Italy	19	Poland	54	India	124
Romania	20	Tunisia	54	Korea	125
West Germany	20	Egypt	56	Argentina	134
Costa Rica	21	Brazil	57	Venezuela	153
Cambodia	24	Peru	64	Union of South	
Bulgaria	25	Thailand	65	Africa	158
Libya	25	Turkey	65	Indonesia	190

while transition leads to political turmoil and violence. Also, the closer a country to some theoretical midpoint between tradition and modernity, the stronger the impulse to political instability. This is the logic of the conflict model of the transitional process, as well as of the exposure-to-modernity model.

In order to test these hypotheses, some cross-national measure of modernity is necessary, to compare levels of political violence. Given the complexities of the notion of modernity and the process of modernization, the measurement task is an exceedingly difficult one. Our measurement cannot embrace all aspects of modernity. It is confined to a specific set of indicators which, in combination, yield a rough indication of developmental level.

ECONOMIC DEVELOPMENT

Let us turn first to a rather narrow definition of modernity, assuming that the difference between a modern and a traditional country lies in their relative wealth. Highly affluent modern nations are those capable of producing great quantities of goods and services and of providing their citizens with high standards of living, high incomes, adequate education, health, and other socioeconomic benefits. With this approach, modernity may be measured in terms of the degree to which a nation enjoys some very specific commodity such as per capita gross national product (GNP), caloric intake, telephones, physicians, etc. These indices of modernity may be used singly, to indicate that particular aspect of modernity, or they may be combined, indicating a more comprehensive and summary view of modern development. In this study, a set of separate indicators is employed, as well as a composite modernity index. The modernity index combines GNP per capita, caloric intake, telephones, physicians, newspapers, radios, literacy, and urbanization.[17]

Level of modernity is thus assessed quantitatively: those countries scoring high on the selected indicators are judged modern,

while the median range denotes the transitional group of nations. It should be pointed out that a country which is low on these indicators may be a traditional country, but not necessarily. A further criterion for distinguishing a traditional society is that it is static and unchanging. By this definition, a traditional country must not only be low in its level of development, but it must maintain this low level over time. A tendency toward improvement in economic conditions places it in the transitional group. In terms of this criterion, we have very few if any traditional countries in our sample. This lack is inevitable since a traditional country in this sense will not collect statistical data and so not be amenable to study in terms of our empirical approach. This is not to say that there are no extremely underdeveloped countries among our sample of 84. On the contrary, there are a number that are characterized by minimal industrialization, almost total dependence on agriculture or extractive industry, and a very thin stratum of educated persons within the population.

While we have predicted that very little political unrest will occur in the most traditional nations, with violence increasing with modernization to reach a peak among nations at midpoints of development, and then subsiding again among modern, industrial states, this complete pattern may not be evident in our cross-national sample. If, in the present analysis, most of the nations are either caught in the midst of transition to modernity or have achieved a high level of industrialization, we would expect the prevailing relationship to show a consistent trend of decreasing political unrest with increasing development.

Let us look first at the relationship between the composite index of modernity and political unrest. In Table 3, countries are classified into three groups: modern, transitional, and so-called traditional states, and further subdivided into stable and unstable categories.[18] We see that the modern countries are predominantly stable (20

Table 3. Relationship Between Modernity and Political Instability, 1948-1965 [Grouped Scores]

	I. TRADITIONAL	II. TRADITIONAL	III. MODERN	
Stable (1:012–5:096)	Bolivia Burma China (mainland) Haiti India Indonesia Iraq Jordan Laos Malaya Morocco Philippines Sudan 13	Brazil · Lebanon Colombia · Panama Costa Rica · Paraguay Cuba · Peru Cyprus · Poland Dom. Rep. · Portugal Ecuador · Syria Egypt · Thailand Greece · Tunisia Guatemala · Turkey Honduras · Union of South Africa Hungary · Venezuela Korea 25	Argentina Czechoslovakia East Germany France 4	42
Unstable (5:105–6:445)	Afghanistan Cambodia China (Taiwan) Ethiopia Ghana Iran Liberia Libya Pakistan Saudi Arabia 10	Albania Bulgaria Ceylon Chile El Salvador Italy Japan Mexico Nicaragua Romania Spain Yugoslavia 12	Australia · Netherlands Austria · New Zealand Belgium · Norway Canada · Sweden Denmark · Switzerland Finland · United Kingdom Iceland · United States Ireland · Uruguay Israel · U.S.S.R. Luxembourg · West Germany 20	42
	23	37	24	84

stable and 4 unstable). Transitional countries, on the other hand, are unstable by a ratio of 2:1. And among so-called traditional countries (which are those lowest in developmental level), instability also predominates but by a less striking ratio of 13:10. Very similar results are obtained using Russett's five-level classificatory scheme of economic development, shown in Table 4.[19]

We may also determine socioeconomic conditions that represent critical threshold levels of political stability and instability. The possibility of finding such threshold values is illustrated in Table 5, which presents eight tables based on environmental indicators (literacy, GNP per capita, radios, newspapers, telephones, physicians, calories, and urbanization).[20] From these empirical tables, a composite picture of the stable country emerges: it is a society which is 90 percent or more literate; with 65 or more radios and 120 or more newspapers per 1,000 population; with 2 percent or more of the population having telephones; with 2,525 or more calories per day per person; with not more than 1,900 persons per physician; with a GNP of $300 or more per person per year; and with 45 percent or more of the population living in urban centers. If all of these threshold values are attained by a society, there is an extremely high probability that the country will achieve relative political stability. Conversely, to the extent that gratifications are less than these threshold values, the greater the likelihood of political instability.

To complete this picture of the relationship between economic modernization and political instability, we may look at a further set of economic, social, and political indicators of development and their relationship to the level of political violence within society.[21] The emphasis in this case is on violence, with the scoring of political unrest based solely on violent events (as illustrated in Table 2).

The following were selected as broad indices of industrialization and development in the economy: (1) percent of the population living in urban centers; (2) percent of the gross domestic product (GNP) that comes from agriculture; (3) percent of the labor force engaged in agriculture; and (4) GNP/capita. To supplement these data, other attributes of society were also examined, such as the spread of modern communications (newspapers, radios, and mail); the distribution of social benefits (education, literacy, life expectancy); and the level of participation in politics (voting, executive stability). We find that these indicators of economic, social, and political modernization are a clue to the level of political violence within a society. Economic modernity, modern communications, health, education, and political participation are all associated with lower levels of political violence, although the relationships are not equally strong in all cases. (The correlation values for these relationships are given in the appendix.)

In combination, these analyses demonstrate some of the hypothesized relationships between level of socioeconomic development and political unrest and violence: modern countries show a lower level of political unrest, less-developed countries a higher level.

POLITICAL DEVELOPMENT

To supplement the findings relating economic development to political instability, we sought an assessment of developmental level that would depend more on political than on socioeconomic factors. A broad framework was provided by judgments regarding democracy-authoritarianism made by Almond and Coleman for 45 nations. These authors classified nations into several groupings. Table 6 presents these groupings arranged to indicate increasingly concentrated authority structures.[22] If these groupings can be considered indicative of political development, as well as indicative of increasingly democratic political structures, one can see among them a pronounced re-

Table 4. Relationship Between Economic Development and Political Instability, 1948-1965*

	I. TRADITIONAL PRIMITIVE	II. TRADITIONAL CIVILIZATION	III. TRANSITIONAL	IV. INDUSTRIAL REVOLUTION	V. HIGH MASS CONSUMPTION	
Unstable (5:105–6:445)	Burma Laos Sudan	Bolivia China (mainland) Haiti India Thailand	Dominican Republic Ecuador Egypt Guatemala Honduras Indonesia Iraq Jordan Korea Morocco Paraguay Peru Philippines Portugal Syria Tunisia Turkey	Argentina Brazil Colombia Costa Rica Cuba Cyprus Czechoslovakia East Germany Greece Hungary Lebanon Malaya Panama Poland Union of South Africa Venezuela	France	
	3	5	17	16	1	42

					Totals
Afghanistan	Cambodia	Albania	Austria	Australia	
Ethiopia	Liberia	Ceylon	Bulgaria	Belgium	
Libya	Pakistan	China (Taiwan)	Chile	Canada	
		El Salvador	Finland	Denmark	
		Ghana	Iceland	Luxembourg	
		Iran	Ireland	Netherlands	
		Nicaragua	Israel	New Zealand	
		Saudi Arabia	Italy	Norway	
			Japan	Sudan	
			Mexico	Switzerland	
			Romania	United Kingdom	
			Spain	United States	
			Uruguay	West Germany	
			U.S.S.R.		
			Yugoslavia		
Stable (1:012–5:096) 3	3	8	15	13	42
6	8	25	31	14	84

* These categories of economic development are from Russett et al., *op. cit.*

Table 5. Relationships Between the Eight Indicatiors of Level of Development, 1948-55, and Degree of Political Stability, 1955-61

A. PERCENT LITERACY	LOW (BELOW 90%)	HIGH (ABOVE 90%)	TOTAL
Unstable	48	5	53
Stable	10	19	29
Total	58	24	82

Chi square = 25.93, $p < 0.001$
Yule's $Q = 0.90$

B. RADIOS PER 1,000 POPULATION	LOW (BELOW 65)	HIGH (ABOVE 65)	TOTAL
Unstable	45	6	51
Stable	9	20	29
Total	54	26	80

Chi square = 25.02, $p < 0.001$
Yule's $Q = 0.887$

C. NEWSPAPERS PER 1,000 POPULATION	LOW (BELOW 120)	HIGH (ABOVE 120)	TOTAL
Unstable	48	5	53
Stable	6	10	16
Total	54	15	69

Chi square = 17.34, $p < 0.001$
Yule's $Q = 0.88$

D. PERCENT OF POPULATION OWNING TELEPHONES	LOW (BELOW 2%)	HIGH (ABOVE 2%)	TOTAL
Unstable	35	6	41
Stable	7	18	25
Total	42	24	66

Chi square = 19.68, $p < 0.001$
Yule's $Q = 0.875$

E. CALORIES PER CAPITA PER DAY	LOW (BELOW 2525)	HIGH (ABOVE 2525)	TOTAL
Unstable	39	10	49
Stable	8	20	28
Total	47	30	77

Chi square = 17.43, $p < 0.001$
Yule's $Q = 0.81$

F. PEOPLE PER PHYSICIAN	LOW (BELOW 1900)	HIGH (ABOVE 1900)	TOTAL
Unstable	40	13	53
Stable	6	19	25
Total	46	32	78

Chi square = 11.41, $p < 0.001$
Yule's $Q = 0.81$

Table 5. Relationships Between the Eight Indicators of Level of Development, 1948-55, and Degree of Political Stability, 1955-61—Continued

	G. GNP PER CAPITA IN U.S. DOLLARS)				H. PERCENT OF POPULATION LIVING IN URBAN CENTERS		
	LOW (BELOW 300)	HIGH (ABOVE 300)	TOTAL		LOW (BELOW 45%)	HIGH (ABOVE 45%)	TOTAL
Unstable	36	8	44	Unstable	38	6	44
Stable	9	18	27	Stable	11	15	26
Total	45	26	71	Total	49	21	70

Chi square $= 14.92$, $p < 0.001$ Chi square $= 13.08$, $p < 0.001$
Yule's $Q = 0.80$ Yule's $Q = 0.79$

lationship to economic and social development. Calculating the average scores on GNP per capita and on percentage of the population literate within each level of political development, a clear pattern emerges. The higher the level of political development of a society, the higher the level of the population of both income and literacy.

On the other hand, a different tendency is apparent when average scores for political violence are calculated. In Table 6 it may be seen that conservative and traditional oligarchies are relatively stable, while significant increases in political violence are noticeable in the modernizing oligarchy, the tutelary democracy, and the Latin American authoritarian groups. Declining instability appears in the political democracy group, followed by the Latin American semicompetitive and competitive groupings. A return to relative political stability is apparent in the developed nations.

From these data one can infer that with growth in the economic and social sectors of society, the political system also undergoes change. Concomitant with these changes, there is an increasing amount of manifest conflict within society. On the other hand, once the system approaches full modernization (as indicated by almost uni-

versal adult literacy) and its economy approaches the high mass-consumption level (as indicated by a GNP per capita well above the subsistence level), political stability tends to reemerge.

COERCIVENESS OF REGIME

A second technique for evaluating the structure of authority in the political system is to develop a typology of the coerciveness-permissiveness patterns of the regime. A six-point classification scheme was applied to the nations in this sample, rating each for level of coerciveness of regime.[23] The resultant groups are arrayed in Table 7. As may be seen, the most coercive group of nations comprises primarily the Communist bloc and the most permissive group the Western democracies.

On the composite modernity index, the Western democracies are the most modern nations in the world. Some of the Communist nations also score relatively high in modernity, but others are closer to the midpoint on the index. If one tests for patterning of modernity within levels of coerciveness, the pattern demonstrated in Table 8 emerges. The highly coercive nations are not as modern as the permissive or highly permissive nations, but clearly tend to be

*Table 6. Economic and Social Development, Political Violence, and the Political Systems**

POLITICAL SYSTEM	GNP CAPITA	PER-CENT LITER-ATE	POLIT-ICAL VIO-LENCE	IN-STABILITY GROUPED AVERAGED	IN-STABILITY GROUPED
Developed and/or European (n = 23)	$943	98.5	6	07116	3087
Latin American competitive (n = 5)	379	80.1	28	10156	5203
Latin American semicompetitive (n = 5)	262	55.7	37	14101	5196
Asia and Africa political democracy (n = 7)	220	47.5	43	12360	5108
Latin American authoritarian (n = 9)	189	39.4	57	14141	5429
Asia and Africa tutelary democracy (n = 4)	136	17.5	55	15169	6169
Asia and Africa modernizing oligarchy (n = 6)	119	16.4	56	13650	5241
Asia and Africa conservative oligarchy (n = 6)	99	16.2	22	12654	4604
Asia and Africa traditional oligarchy (n = 3)	92	2.5	5	09029	4029

* Median scores, 1948–65.

more modern that those nations at mid-levels of coerciveness. The least modern nations are those that are coercive, but not at the extreme of coerciveness. The same patterning occurs between coerciveness and political violence. Violence is lowest among permissive states. It increases with increasing coerciveness of regime, but subsides to some degree with extreme coerciveness. When one compares this patterning to that in Table 6, it is apparent that the coerciveness dimension is not identical to Almond and Coleman's typology of political development. On the latter, economic and political development go hand in hand. On the former, economic development is high among nations at both extremes of coerciveness-permissiveness. Political violence, however, shows the same relationship to both coerciveness and political development.

In summary of the relationship between development and political violence, we find that with increased levels of economic modernity there is a tendency toward lower levels of political unrest. Countries in the transitional stage of economic modernization are the most beset by political turmoil. Among the very few countries that might be characterized as yet untouched by the process of economic change, there is a tendency toward political quiescence. Regarding political development, we find in these results and others that permissive, democratic regimes, by and large, experience low levels of political unrest. This is also true of repressive, totalitarian governments that are capable of effectively suppressing the overt political expression of popular dissatisfaction. It is governments at midlevels of coerciveness and political development that experience the most political turmoil. And these governments also tend to be at a midpoint of economic modernization.

Table 7. *Level of Coerciveness*

1. HIGHLY PERMISSIVE	2. PERMISSIVE	3. MILDLY COERCIVE	4. MODERATELY COERCIVE	5. COERCIVE	6. HIGHLY COERCIVE
Australia	Belgium	Austria	Bolivia	Afghanistan	Albania
Canada	Costa Rica	Brazil	Colombia	Argentina	Bulgaria
Denmark	Finland	Burma	Ecuador	Cuba	China (mainland)
Netherlands	Iceland	Cambodia	El Salvador	Egypt	China (Taiwan)
Norway	Ireland	France	Ghana	Ethiopia	Czechoslovakia
Sweden	Israel	Greece	Honduras	Haiti	Dominican Republic
Switzerland	Italy	India	Guatemala	Korea	East Germany
United Kingdom	Luxembourg	Japan	Indonesia	Morocco	Hungary
United States	Mexico	Malaya	Iran	Nicaragua	Poland
	New Zealand	Pakistan	Iraq	Paraguay	Romania
	Uruguay	Panama	Jordan	Portugal	U.S.S.R.
	West Germany	Philippines	Laos	Saudi Arabia	Yugoslavia
		Turkey	Lebanon	Spain	
			Liberia	Union of South Africa	
			Libya	Venezuela	
			Peru		
			Syria		
			Sudan		
			Thailand		
			Tunisia		

Table 8. Modernity, Political Violence, and Coerciveness of Political Systems*

LEVELS OF COERCIVENESS-PERMISSIVENESS	MO-DERNITY	POLITICAL VIOLENCE	IN-STABILITY GROUPED AVERAGED	IN-STABILITY GROUPED
1. Highly permissive (*n* = 9)	1.54	4.0	07030	3083
2. Permissive (*n* = 12)	.70	12.0	08042	3574
3. Mildly coercive (*n* = 15)	− .36	51.0	13071	5108
4. Moderately coercive (*n* = 21)	− .49	65.0	14105	5209
5. Coercive (*n* = 15)	− .40	77.0	13427	5194
6. Highly coercive (*n* = 12)	.55	32.5	11680	4672

* Median scores.

Societal Change and Political Violence

The final question, which was raised at the outset of this paper, is whether empirical relationships can be discovered between patterns of socioeconomic change within society and levels of political unrest. We now seek to go beyond an assessment of attained levels of socioeconomic development, to examine the rates at which these levels were achieved. Are countries that modernize gradually less susceptible to political violence than those in which change is rapid? Some of our hypotheses suggest this relationship, although others do not.

In order to measure rate of change, we confined ourselves to the same types of socioeconomic indicators adopted for measuring levels of development.[24] Data were gathered on these indicators for the time period 1935–62, for all of the 84 countries. An average annual percentage rate of change for each country was calculated on each indicator and a combined rate-of-change index was developed by pooling the country's separate change scores.[25] Differences in percentage change rates among countries were then compared to political instability profiles. To the procedures for measuring political violence discussed above, we added another which seemed particularly applicable to assessment of rate of change. This is a dynamic, rather than a static, scoring of political unrest, yielding a measure of change in instability level over time.[26] (See appendix.)

The results obtained from interrelating percentage rates of change on the environmental indicators and levels of political instability indicate, in general, that the faster the rate of socioeconomic change within a society, the higher the level of political unrest. The combined rate-of-change index shows a strong relationship to political instability, as do change rates on many of the indicators taken singly.[27] Looking at the dynamic instability measures, we find a similar set of relationships (see Table 9). Countries with the lowest socioeconomic rate of change show a trend toward political stability; countries with the highest rate of socioeconomic change are beset by increasing instability; and countries experiencing intermediate rates of change toward modernization are also intermediate in instability pattern.

These general findings point to the fact that we cannot assume that modernization will bring political stability in its wake. While highly modern countries tend to be politically stable, the process of attaining modernity is one that is rife with political unrest. Furthermore, the more rapid the modernization, the greater the impact in increasing political violence. Only after cer-

Table 9. Relationship Between Mean Rate of Change on Ecological Variables, 1935-62, and Change in Stability as Measured by Variance and Slope, 1948-62

MEAN RATE OF CHANGE ON ECOLOGICAL VARIABLES	STABLE — LOW VARIANCE AND EITHER- NEGATIVE SLOPE	ZERO SLOPE		INDETERMINATE — LOW VARIANCE/POSITIVE SLOPE OR HIGH VARIANCE/NEGATIVE SLOPE		UNSTABLE — HIGH VARIANCE AND EITHER- POSITIVE SLOPE	ZERO SLOPE		TOTAL
Low change	Norway, New Zealand, West Germany, Australia, Denmark, Iceland	United States, Canada, Sweden, Switzerland, Netherlands, Luxembourg, Israel	13	Great Britain, Austria	2		Belgium	1	16
Moderately low change	Ireland, Guatemala, Bulgaria, China (Taiwan)	Finland, Italy, Chile, Philippines	8	France, Union of South Africa, Mexico, Pakistan, Greece / Argentina, Uruguay, Spain, Ecuador	9	Cuba, Paraguay, Hungary		3	20
Moderately high change			0	Thailand, Colombia, Egypt, Ceylon, Poland / Costa Rica, Ghana, Turkey, India	9	Peru, Portugal, Panama, Brazil, Haiti, Iraq	Japan, Yugoslavia, Tunisia, Burma, U.S.S.R.	11	20
High change	Syria		1	Korea, Malaya	2	El Salvador, Bolivia, Venezuela, Dom. Rep.	Cambodia, Morocco, Honduras, Indonesia	8	11
Total			22		22			23	67

tain threshold socioeconomic values have been attained may the stabilizing political benefits of modernity be experienced.

The rationale for those findings may be found in the models presented in the theoretical section of this paper, particularly in Figures 2, 5, 8, and 9. There it was hypothesized that rapid change will serve to increase the gap between expectations and achievements. The feedback effect of a few satisfactions will increase the demand for more accomplishments, beyond the level that can possibly be attained within the society. Also, the conflict between traditional and modern ways of life will be intensified by rapid transition between the two patterns, allowing less time for adjustment.

If we look at the socioeconomic indicators individually, however, we find that they do not all have the same impact upon society. For example, while a rapid increase in percent of the population being educated does entail a higher level of political instability, a rapid increase in percent of the population owning telephones is accompanied by more stability within the society. Similarly, rapid increase in national income brings a lessening of political unrest.[28]

Furthermore, for theoretical reasons, we are particularly interested in examining the relationships between rates of change on these various socioeconomic indicators and level of political unrest among the transitional group of countries. It was postulated at the outset of this paper that this group of countries suffers the most deleterious effects of change. Change occurring at a higher level of development presumably does not mean change in the sense of developing new patterns and new ways of life; it may simply be an intensification or logical extension of existing patterns. Moving from a low to a high level of development, however, entails conflict and discrepancies between aspirations, expectations, and attainments.

Some of the findings at this midlevel of development confirm expectations based on the wider analysis. Among transitional countries, those experiencing a faster rate of change in proportion of population receiving primary education, 1935–62, also experience a higher level of political instability at some time during 1948–65, and show a trend toward greater instability over time during this period.[29] Furthermore, if we control for the maximum value attained on ratio of population receiving primary education, we find that the relationship between an increase in this ratio and political instability is still high.[30] This is significant, since it tells us that it is actually the rate of increase in education as well as the maximum number of educated persons in the society that is important for political unrest. Using the dynamic measure of political unrest, we corroborate the tendency for change in proportion of the population receiving primary education to be positively associated with an increase in political instability over time.[31] Again, change, per se, emerges as important.

We also find that, within this group of countries, percentage change in income (gross domestic product (GDP) per capita), 1951–59, shows the opposite relationship to political unrest: the faster the increase in income, the less the political instability. This indicates that a percentage increase in GDP per capita is associated with a decrease in level of political unrest. If we control for attained level of GNP per capita within the society, we again find that rapid change in increasing incomes is important in reducing instability, apart from the impact of the absolute level of income achieved.[32]

The most detrimental combination of factors appears to be a rapid increase in proportion of the population receiving primary education, but a slow rate of percentage change in GDP per capita. This set of circumstances is most conducive to political unrest among the transitional group of countries.[33]

The relationship between these two change indicators and political instability fits a number of the models proposed at the outset of his paper. Education, like literacy, is a means of arousing awareness of modern goals and hence of raising aspirations within a society. It is also likely that education raises expectations regarding the fulfillment of these aspirations. GDP per capita, on the other hand, is an achievement indicator; it provides gratification of aroused aspirators. A society in which the trend is toward increasing numbers of educated persons within the population, without an increase in their level of income, is a society in which rates of change are widening the gap between aspirations/expectations and their satisfaction. This would appear to be particularly explosive for the transitional society.

The challenge in these findings is whether it is possible to avoid an imbalance between number of educated in the population and opportunity for increased income. Unfortunately, it would seem that the process of modernization makes this imbalance highly probable. Education is a necessary first step to infusing the society with the skills appropriate to industrialization. But the lag between this first step and the second—that of developing the industrial society—is hazardous indeed. Huntington speaks of the dangers of education in the underdeveloped society, a danger that many leaders of non-industrialized states themselves recognize.[34] He particularly stresses the pitfalls of an increasingly educated population for a society in which political opportunity is lacking. While the political and economic aspects of society are clearly interrelated, our findings suggest that if economic opportunities were immediately available to the newly educated, the lack of political opportunities might not be so disruptive.

A second challenge in these findings relates to a proposition advanced by some economists, that widespread psychological discontent is a precondition for economic growth within society.[35] This view stresses, as a psychological antecedent for modernization, the type of discontent that certainly is fostered by increased education. Again, in this view it seems that a lag between aspiration and achievement is inevitable within societies in transition, a period of hiatus that is particularly violence prone.

The question is whether, in fact, an optimal combination of all relevant conditions is feasible: a sufficient level of psychological discontent to foster change, a sufficient level of education to supply the society with a skilled population, a sufficient level of development to provide jobs and income to match popular skill levels, and a political system sufficiently open to offer access to an educated people. To maintain an optimum balance among these factors, especially during a period of rapid change, may be difficult indeed. Typically, it is education that is expanded most rapidly in response to expressions of popular discontent, an expansion that creates the discrepancy between skill and opportunity.

Conclusions

To interpret the relationships that we have uncovered between levels of development, rates of socioeconomic change, and political violence, we must return to some of the initial questions raised in this study. The first of these concerns the meaning of social change. As has been pointed out, change is a complex concept that cannot simply be identified with increases, decreases, or fluctuations in the economic characteristics of a society. If these quantifiable ecological traits do have bearing on the question, it must be because they reflect a wide variety of other, unmeasured, qualitative societal factors. The validity of this assumption, that quantifiable economic change is a clue to other types of change, may depend upon the historical era under investigation. As discussed earlier, the prevailing insight of contemporary social science is that the process of modernization provides the pathway of change in the postwar world. This process is generally regarded as socioeconomic and amenable to quantification.

This, however, is not the only interpretation. For example, quite a different view is presented by Sorokin, from the perspective of a major portion of human history. In this light, our 20-year span of analysis is but a wave in a much larger cycle.[36] Sorokin's view of change is essentially ideological or attitudinal, not economic. Civilizations vary between an emphasis on material ("sensate") culture and an absorption in ideological ("ideational") concerns. Sensate culture is accompanied by a rise in economic conditions, which is only to be expected since such a culture deems these economic factors of importance. Ideational culture, however, is generally accompanied by a low level of material success, since material welfare is not a valued commodity and material concerns are considered of secondary importance. Sorokin traces the rates of change in the general economic situations of the ancient world of Greece and Rome from 600 B.C. to A.D. 400, of France from 800 to 1926, and of Germany from 700 to 1932. These curves show considerable fluctuation, tending to be low during eras which Sorokin identifies as ideational and high during periods of sensate culture. In this long-range view, the 20th century is the epitome of sensate culture. From this we may deduce that change is inevitable, since Sorokin's model is a cyclical one in which the penultimate realization of the goals of either type of culture inevitably breeds the conditions of its own decline. Transition then sets in, a period of social disruption and violence in which the dominant cultural theme begins to move in the opposite direction.

If this Hegelian, "poison-fruit" approach is correct, we would be led to a different investigation of change than we have pursued in this study. In the Sorokin view, disruptive change will occur at the highest levels of modernity, when sensate culture is at its peak. Some intuitive and empirical support might be found for this view in the apparently restless dissatisfaction of intelligentsia and student elements within American society, a phenomenon that Sorokin identifies as typical of the last stages of sensate culture. On the other hand, our examination of the economic situation of the postwar world certainly indicates that the economic decline of modern countries is not yet in sight. Also, it shows that the highest levels of turbulence occur at lesser levels of development.

Thus, while Sorokin's broader vision may prove to be correct in the long run, the crisis of transition in our era still seems to be tied to the effort at achieving the higher levels of economic well-being sought by members of a materially oriented culture. And it is a particular attribute of the modernization process that its quality can be indexed not only in quantitative, but specifically in socioeconomic terms. With sufficient ingenuity, other attributes of society, even ideational, could conceivably be reduced to observable, quantifiable indicators.[37] With the process of modernization, however, this effort at ingenuity is superfluous since economic levels and stages of development are well nigh synonymous.

Interest in the relationship between economic development and political violence has characterized a number of recent investigations. All begin with the common insight that the more advanced countries are less subject to political disturbances. This finding is corroborated by those who define development in political terms, as well as by those who define it in economic terms.[38] The kernel of agreement among these investigators is that the highest level of development is accompanied by a decrease in violence, while levels that fall short of modernity are more prone to political unrest. The consistency of this general relationship has been corroborated using quite different measures of violence and different samples of nations. Its stability as a finding may be due to the fact that there is a sufficient sample of identifiable modern and transitional nations in the present-day world.

It is not equally clear whether, in the relationship between development and violence, the least-developed countries show less of a tendency to violence than states at midlevels or transitional stages of development. The problem of discovering the direction of the relationship between violence and development at the low end of the modernity continuum is largely due to the fact that extremely few countries now qualify as traditional, in the sense that they are unaware of modernity. We have suggested earlier in this report, and elsewhere,[39] that such countries do not report data to the United Nations, which makes it difficult to include them in this type of empirical study. Nevertheless, if we are willing to base our assessments on a very few cases, we find that countries at the lowest levels of development are less prone to political instability than are countries at the next higher stages of modernity. Political development, in combination with economic development, shows this pattern (Tables 6 and 8), as does economic development alone, but to a lesser degree (Tables 3 and 4). Again, this slight tendency has been found by other researchers.[40] If it is an actual trend, it corroborates theoretical insights regarding the gap between aspirations/expectations and their achievement, the effects of uncertainty of expectations, and the occurrence of motivational conflict elaborated in the theoretical section of this study. All of these hypotheses point to the transitional stage of development as the most frustration ridden. Neither lower nor higher levels of development will be as prone to violence.

Since this study is specifically concerned with rates of change, it may be asked why so much attention has been paid to attained levels of development. The answer is twofold. On the one hand, an assessment of level of development gives a cross-sectional view of the same process that, in longitudinal perspective, is indexed by rates of change. It is true that knowledge of the present level of development of a nation cannot tell us how rapid or slow, how continuous or discontinuous was the process of attainment. But we may infer from the relationship between development and violence that as countries become more mod-

ern, they will also become more politically stable. This inference may be correct in broadest perspective, but it may also be misleading regarding the impact of change on a society that is still far removed from the threshold economic values accompanying political stability (Table 5).

Therefore, the second point regarding the importance of attained modernity lies in the interrelationships between the static levels and rates of socioeconomic change. It is suggested that rates of change have different implications for societies that differ in modernity level. Furthermore, different indicators, and rates of change on these indicators, have varying impacts on society. There are thus three factors that must be taken into account in assessing the relationship between change and political instability: attained level of development, the nature of the specific socioeconomic indicator, and the rate of change.

This more detailed approach may help to explain some of the conflicting claims of researchers who have explored this problem. For example, in our own first investigation of the question, we found that the faster the rate of socioeconomic change, the higher the level of political unrest.[41] We also noted that rate of change, measured in percentage terms, was strongly related to attained level of development. Modern countries showed smaller percentage change rates; less-developed countries showed higher percentage change rates. At the same time, we discovered that on one indicator, national income, the relationship was reversed: the vaster the rate of increase on this variable, the lower the level of political unrest. Furthermore, rate of change in national income, unlike change rates on the other indicators, was related to modernity level in such a way that modern countries showed the highest percentage change rates while underdeveloped countries showed the lowest.

A similarly complex set of findings regarding the relationship between rate of economic change and political violence occurs in the work of other researchers. Alker and Russett find that the highest annual growth rates occur at midlevels of per capita income.[42] Furthermore the higher the level of income within a society and the greater the growth in income levels, the lower the level of political unrest. Gurr, on the other hand, finds no relationship between measures of civil violence for 119 countries, 1961–63, and growth rate in per capita income, 1953–62.[43] Using only Latin American countries, Bwy finds that the higher the rate of annual growth of GNP per capita, 1950–59, the lower the levels of both organized and anomic violence.[44] Since his study is limited to countries beyond a suggested threshold level of attained development Bwy speculates that for countries at lower levels of modernity, the relationship may operate in the reverse direction. Finally, Tanter and Midlarsky assess the relationship between rate of increase in GNP per capita in the 7 years immediately prior to the outbreak of revolution, and the number of deaths from domestic group violence in all successful revolutions occurring between 1955 and 1960.[45] They find more revolutionary violence with higher economic growth rates in 10 revolutions occurring in the Middle East and Asia, but the opposite relationship in 4 Latin American revolutions. For all 14 cases combined, there is some indication of greater numbers of persons killed in revolutions preceded by higher annual growth rates in GNP per capita.

It is suggested that the resolution of these contradictions will be found in an approach that differentiates between rates of change on different types of indicators and among nations at different levels of development. A beginning in this direction has been made in this study and further work is intended. Our preliminary efforts have been directed toward distinguishing indicators in terms of their implications for the members of a society. This categorization is based upon the distinction between social aspirations/ expectations and social achievement.

Change on one type of indicator may imply greater gratification for society; change on another indicator may simply broaden aspirations and expectations.

Evidence in support of this interpretation comes from the finding that a rapid increase in primary school enrollment is positively related to political violence, while a rapid increase in GNP per capita is negatively related. One change increases the level of political unrest; the other tends to decrease it. Furthermore, the impact of both change rates was separately analyzed among countries at the transitional stage of development. We find that for these nations, the combination of factors most closely associated with political violence is a rapid spread in society of an awakened population, combined with a slow rise in income.

As a final application of this study, we may ask whether our findings have any bearing on the occurrence of violence within our own society. In socioeconomic terms, the United States is the most modern nation in the world, showing the highest attained level on almost all indicators. On the other hand, it is not among the most politically stable societies, although neither is it among the most violent. Using various methods of measurement for the 18-year period, 1948–65, the United States falls generally at the median position of world violence: half of the nations exceed our violence level; half do not attain it. There is thus some discrepancy between our economic level and our level of political unrest, given the expected form of relationship.

It should also be pointed out that the occurrence of violence in the United States has increased during the 1960's. In the previous two decades, the internal aggression profile of the United States was lower and generally more in line with the majority of Western democratic political systems. During 1955–61, for example, the United States was among the group of nations at position 3 on the seven-point instability scale. It ranked 24th among 84 states, falling within the more stable third of the sample. In the subsequent period, however, it moved into the 4th scale position, joining nations experiencing more severe internal turmoil. From 1961 to 1965, 12 percent of this country's events were at scale position 4.

· · ·

REFERENCES

1. We are grateful for the support of the National Science Foundation (Grant No. GS-1781), which made it possible to collect and analyze the data on internal political aggression as well as the underlying conditions of political instability.

   We wish to thank Rosemary J. Roth and Antonia E. Williams for their help in constructing tables for this manuscript, and Franz Jaggar for the computer analyses.

2. Cross-national quantitative analysis of political and social variables is a relatively recent development. For an overview, see Richard L. Merritt and Stein Rokkan, eds., *Comparing Nations: The Uses of Quantitative Data in Cross-National Research* (New Haven: Yale University Press, 1966). Two impressive cross-national data collections and analyses should also be mentioned: Arthur S. Banks and Robert B. Textor, *A Cross-Policy Survey* (Cambridge: MIT Press, 1963), and Bruce M. Russett, Hayward R. Alker, Jr., Karl W. Deutsch, and Harold D. Lasswell, *World Handbook of Political and Social Indicators* (New Haven: Yale University Press, 1964). Among the few cross-national analyses of internal political violence we may mention: Harry Eckstein, *Internal War: The Problem of Anticipation* (a report submitted to the Research Groups in Psychology and the Social Sciences, Smithsonian Institution, Washington, D.C., Jan. 15, 1962); Ted Gurr with Charles Ruttenberg, *The Conditions of Civil Violence: First Tests of a Causal Model*, Research Monograph No. 28 (Princeton: Center of International Studies, Princeton, University, Apr. 1967); Rudolph J. Rummel, "Dimensions of Conflict Behavior Within and Between Nations," *General Systems Yearbook*, vol. VIII (1963), pp. 1–50; Raymond Tanter, "Dimensions of Conflict Behavior Within and Between Nations, 1958–60," *Journal of Conflict Resolution*, vol. X (Mar. 1966), pp. 41–65; Ivo K. and Rosalind L. Feiera-

bend, "Aggresive Behaviors Within Polities, 1948–1962: A Cross-National Study," *Journal of Conflict Resolution*, vol. X (Sept. 1966), pp. 249–271; and Betty A. Nesvold, "A Scalogram Analysis of Political Violence," *Comparative Political Studies*, forthcoming, July 1969.

3. For a sample of contemporary literature using these notions, see Gabriel A. Almond and James S. Coleman, eds., *The Politics of the Developing Areas* (Princeton: Princeton University Press, 1960); David E. Apter, *The Politics of Modernization* (Chicago: University of Chicago Press, 1965); H. R. Barringer et al., *Social Change in Developing Areas* (Cambridge: Schenkman, 1965); Karl W. Deutsch, "Social Mobilization and Political Development," *American Political Science Review*, vol. LV (Sept. 1961), pp. 493–514; Samuel P. Huntington, "Political Development and Political Decay," *World Politics*, vol. XVII (Apr. 1965), pp. 386–430; Everett E. Hagen, *On the Theory of Social Change* (Homewood: Dorsey Press, 1962); Daniel Lerner, *The Passing of Traditional Society* (Glencoe: Free Press, 1958); W. W. Rostow, *The Stages of Economic Growth* (Cambridge: Cambridge University Press, 1960); Pitirim A. Sorokin, *Social and Cultural Dynamics*, vol. III: *Fluctuation of Social Relationships, War, and Revolution* (New York: The Bedminster Press, 1937, 1962); and George K. Zollschan and Walter Hirsch, eds., *Explorations in Social Change* (Boston: Houghton Mifflin, 1964).

4. The theme that social change carries with it political crisis and turmoil is commonly acknowledged in the literature, as is the contradictory insight. See the literature cited in footnote 2.

5. For the classic theoretical statement of the frustration-aggression hypothesis, see John Dollard et al., *Frustration and Aggression* (New Haven: Yale University Press, 1939). Also, there are several more recent general restatements, among them Leonard Berkowitz, *Aggression: A Social Psychological Analysis* (New York: McGraw Hill, 1962), and Arnold H. Buss, *The Psychology of Aggression* (New York: Wiley, 1961).

6. In the literature of political science, Ted Gurr systematically applies the frustration hypothesis and modifies its terms to develop a coherent empirical and multivariate theory of political violence. His use of the concept of relative deprivation comes very close to our use of systemic frustration. Also, we believe that the broad insights,

hypotheses, and models presented in this section would generally be sustained by his theoretical constructs, although they might be couched in different terminology. See Ted Robert Gurr, *Why Men Rebel* (Princeton: Princeton University Press, 1969, in press), and "Psychological Factors in Civil Violence," *World Politics*, vol. XX (Jan. 1968), pp. 245–278.

7. In the most recent literature on revolution, David Schwartz uses the notion of conflict, as well as of cognitive dissonance, to build a processual model of revolution; see his "Political Alienation: A Preliminary Experiment on the Psychology of Revolution's First Stage," paper presented at the annual meeting of the American Psychological Association, Washington, D.C., 1967. The psychological literature on which these applications are based may be found in F. Heider, "Social Perception and Phenomenal Causality," *Psychological Review*, vol. LI (1944), pp. 358–374; Theodore Newcomb, "An Approach to the Study of Communicative Acts," *Psychological Review*, vol. LX (1953), pp. 393–5; and Leon Festinger, *The Theory of Cognitive Dissonance* (New York: Harper & Row, 1957).

8. See James C. Davies, "Toward a Theory of Revolution," *American Sociological Review*, vol. XXVII (Jan. 1962), pp. 5–19.

9. The notion of a marked contrast among sets of ecological conditions having a greater effect on expectations and behavior than would a continuous series can be viewed as an application of adaptation level theory. See Harry Helson, *Adaptation-Level Theory: An Experimental and Systematic Approach to Behavior* (New York: Harper & Row, 1964). According to this view, a cohesive set or series of stimulus conditions creates adaptation; a contrast within the stimulus conditions triggers response.

10. Victor LeVine, "The Trauma of Independence in French Speaking Africa," paper presented at the Midwest Conference of Political Scientists, 1967.

11. Robert LeVine observes that, in sub-Saharian Africa, those colonial powers that over the decades consistently denied self-rule to the indigenous populace, or those which consistently fostered such a goal, experienced the lowest incidence of anti-European violence. Those regimes that vacillated between the two policies of permissiveness and coerciveness were often subject to intense outbreaks of violence. See his article, "Anti-European Violence in Africa: A Comparative Analysis," *Journal of Conflict Resolution*, vol. III (Dec. 1959), pp. 420–429.

12. These models are given fuller elaboration in I. K. Feierabend, R. L. Feierabend, and B. A. Nesvold, "Political Violence and Social Discontent," in David C. Schwartz, ed., *Revolution Studies*, forthcoming.

13. For example, Lucian W. Pye, in *Aspects of Political Development* (Boston, Little, Brown, 1966), identifies six such crises that hamper smooth political processes: the identity crisis, the legitimacy crisis, the penetration crisis, the participation crisis, the integration crisis, and the distribution crisis.

14. Apter, *op. cit.*, among other authors, describes these more or less intense conflicts, especially in the African context and on the Gold Coast. Destruction of the traditional culture may ensue if the indigenous culture is entirely hostile to innovation and the acceptance of modernity. On the other hand, if the traditional culture is more instrumentally oriented, the conflict may be less intense. Apter also speaks of the appropriate political systems that may follow from these situations.

15. This is the goal-gradient hypothesis, which derives from psychological learning theory and has wide applicability to both animal and human behavior. It maintains that the impulse to action, or the strength of attraction, varies as a function of the distance (spatial or temporal) between the organism and the goal. The closer the individual comes to attaining a desired goal, the stronger the level of attraction and the greater the impulse to action. The further the individual is from a goal, the less the attraction and the weaker the impulse to action. See N. E. Miller, "Experimental Studies of Conflict Behavior," in J. McV. Hunt, ed., *Personality and the Behavior Disorders* (New York: Ronald Press, 1944), and C. L. Hull, *Principles of Behavior* (New York: Appleton-Century-Crofts, 1943).

16. Other researchers have also attempted to measure stages of development and rates of change for the purposes of cross-national study of political violence. For example, see Seymour M. Lipset, *Political Man: The Social Basis of Politics* (Garden City: Doubleday, 1960); Russett et al., *op. cit.*; Gurr with Ruttenberg, *op. cit.*; Raymond Tanter and Manus Midlarsky, "A Theory of Revolution," *Journal of Conflict Resolution*, vol. XI (Sept. 1968), pp. 264–280;

Douglas Bwy. "Political Instability in Latin America: The Cross-Cultural Test of a Causal Model," *Latin American Research Review*, vol. III (Spring 1968), pp. 17–66.

17. Betty A. Nesvold, "Modernity, Social Frustration, and the Stability of Political Systems: A Cross-National Study" (San Diego: San Diego State College, Master's thesis, June 1964). Data on these indicators were collected for the 84 nations from United Nations sources. The country raw scores were converted into standard scores and a mean standard score was calculated for each country as a measure of level of development.

18. The cutting points for these three groups are to some extent arbitrary. The 24 countries that are highest on the modernity index are selected as the modern group. The traditional group is set equal in size to the modern group, while ranking at the opposite end of the modernity continuum. The remaining countries, falling between the modern and traditional groups, are designated transitional. As already pointed out, the countries designated "traditional" are simply less modern than those classed as "transitional," but they have nonetheless been exposed to modernity.

19. Russett et al., *op. cit.* The correlation coefficient between our Modernity Index and Russett's level of development, which is based on GNP per capita, is $r = 0.90$.

20. The cutting points on these modernity indicators were chosen in such a way as to maximize the loading of countries in one set of diagonal cells and minimize it in the other. In this way, threshold values may be determined.

21. Data for these measures of development were taken from the compilations in Russett et al., *op. cit.*

22. Nations were rated according to characteristics of participation in governmental and political groups and the existence of a viable legislative body and freedom of the press. The underlying assumption of the classificatory scheme was that when an agency such as the military or a political party fills a specialized role in the polity, the conditions for a democracy, or pluralism, are present. If, on the other hand, a few such agencies monopolize policymaking, the conditions for elite authority structures are generated. Within this classification scheme, Latin American nations are trichotomized into competitive, semicompetitive, and

authoritarian political systems. The Asian and African classifications contain seven such groupings: political democracy, tutelary democracy, modernizing oligarchy, conservative oligarchy, and traditional oligarchy. Of the remaining nations in our study that were not rated by Almond and Coleman, 23 qualify as Western European, developed nations. One can assume that these latter nations served as a model for Almond and Coleman's original typology and that it would be reasonable to classify them as highly competitive political systems. See Almond and Coleman, *op. cit.*

23. Information regarding such matters as the competitiveness of the political system, the protection of free speech, and the degree to which police actions inhibit the freedoms of the citizenry were used to assign nations to one of the six categories. Case studies were examined for 84 nations for the time period 1948–60. See Jennifer G. Walton, "Correlates of Coerciveness and Permissiveness of Nation Political Systems: A Cross-National Study" (San Diego: San Diego State College, Master's thesis, 1965). Also I. K. Feierabend and R. L. Feierabend, "The Relationship of Systemic Frustration, Political Coercion, International Tension and Political Instability: A Cross-National Study," paper presented at the annual meeting of the American Psychological Association, Sept. 1966.

24. The initial analyses using these data concentrated on nine indicators: urbanization (percent of the population living in localities of 100,000 or more inhabitants); percent of the population literate; primary education (ratio of total school enrollment to total population age 5–14); postprimary education (percentage of total population enrolled in all educational institutions beyond the primary schools); national income in local currencies; cost-of-living index; calories per capita per day; infant mortality rate; and total number of radios per 1,000 population. See Wallace W. Conroe, "A Cross-National Analysis of the Impact of Modernization Upon Political Stability" (San Diego: San Diego State College, Master's thesis, 1965), and Feierabend and Feierabend, "Aggressive Behaviors Within Politics."

25. The yearly percent rate of change on the ecological variables was calculated by subtracting the lowest value of the variable in the 28-year period from the highest value attained, dividing by the lowest value to convert to a percentage change, and then

dividing by the number of years spanned to obtain the yearly percentage change. The advantage of the combined rate of change index, assuming substitute-ability of indicators, is that it makes it possible to compensate for missing data. The index is based on data for six or more indicators per country.

26. Stability scores for the 84 nations were calculated on a year-by-year basis and plotted as a function of time. To characterize the time function, two measures were used: the slope of a best fit-in line, indicating the average instability trend over the time period; and amplitude of change from year to year, as estimated by variance.

27. The correlation with the combined rate of change index is Pearson $r = 0.66$, using the seven-point scaling of political instability for the 1948–65 time period.

28. The correlation between rate of change in primary education and scaled level of political instability is $r = 0.49$. The corresponding correlation for rate of increase in percent of the population owning telephones is $r = 0.44$, for increase in national income, $rho = -0.34$ with the static measure of stability, and -0.45 with the dynamic measure.

29. The correlation is $r = 0.50$ with the static level of instability and $r = 0.31$ with the dynamic measure.

30. The partial correlation technique makes it possible to assess the degree of relationship between two variables, with the influence of a third variable statistically controlled or removed. The partial correlation in this case is 0.49.

31. The partial correlation is 0.29.

32. The correlation with political instability level, 1948–65, is $r = 0.34$ and with trend in instability over time it is -0.37. Controlling for GNP per capita in 1957, the partial correlation is -0.40 with scaled instability and -0.37 with trend in instability. Growth rate in GDP per capita, 1951–59, is taken from "World Tables of Economic Growth," Economics Department, MIT, mimeographed.

33. The multiple correlation is $r = 0.56$ using the static measure of instability and $r = 0.44$ using trend in instability over time.

34. Samuel P. Huntington, *Political Order in Changing Societies* (New Haven: Yale University Press, 1968), especially pp. 47–49.

35. See, for example, Ronald G. Ridker, "Discontent and Economic Growth," *Economic Development and Cultural Change*, vol. XI (October 1962), pp 1–15.

36. Sorokin, *op. cit.* Cyclical and historicist conceptions of history are, of course, not peculiar to Sorokin. They are especially current in 19th-century literature, but also span earlier and later times. Marx and Engels' conceptions are the best known and certainly the most influential Other names that come immediately to mind are Gobineau, Hegel, Spengler, and Toynbee.

37. Efforts in this direction today are associated with the tremendous increase in awareness of the possibilities of social data. See, for example, Eugene Webb et al., *Unobtrusive Measures* (New York: Wiley, 1967).

38. See, for example, Lipset, *op. cit.*; Philip Cutright, "National Political Development: Measurement and Analysis," *American Sociological Review*, vol. XXVIII (Apr. 1963), pp. 253-264; Grr with Ruttenburg, *op. cit.*, Hayward A. Alker, Jr., and Bruce M. Russett, "The Analyses of Trends and Patterns," in Russett et al., *op. cit.;* Feierabend and Feierabend, "Aggressive Behaviors Within Polities"; and Bwy, *op. cit.*

39. Feierabend and Feierabend, "Aggressive Behaviors Within Polities."

40. Alker and Russett, *op. cit.*; Gurr, *op. cit.*; Bwy, *op. cit.*

41. Feierabend and Feierabend, "Aggressive Behaviors Within Polities," and Conroe, *op. cit.*

42. Alker and Russett, *op. cit.*

43. Gurr with Ruttenburg, *op. cit.*

44. Bwy, *op. cit.*

45. Tanter and Midlarsky, *op. cit.*

PEASANT WARS OF THE TWENTIETH CENTURY

Eric Robert Wolf

[Six major social and political upheavals, fought with peasant support, have shaken the world of the twentieth century: the Mexican revolution of 1910, the Russian revolutions of 1905 and 1917, the Chinese revolution which metamorphosed through various phases from 1921 onwards, the Vietnamese revolution which has its roots in the Second World War, the Algerian rebellion of 1954 and the Cuban revolution of 1958. All of these were to some extent based on the participation of rural populations. The tensions which gave rise to these revolutions and rebellions all had their roots in the past. We have tried to present, in each case, an outline of that past.] We have striven to do so not in terms of abstract categories—such as the retention of "tradition" or the advent of "modernity"— but in terms of a concrete historical experience which lives on in the present and continues to determine its shape and meaning. Everywhere, this historical experience bears the stigmata of trauma and strife, of interference and rupture with the past, as well as the boon of continuity, of successful adaptation and adjustment—engrams of events not easily erased and often only latent in the cultural memory until some greater event serves to draw them forth again. In all our six cases this historical experience constitutes, in turn, the precipitate in the present of a great overriding cultural phenomenon, the world-wide spread and diffusion of a particular cultural system, that of North Atlantic capitalism. This cultural system—with its distinctive economics— possesses its own distinctive history of development within a distinctive geographical area. Not only were its characteristic features different from those of other cultural systems both before it and after; it was profoundly alien to many of the areas which it engulfed in its spread.

Its hallmark is its possession of a social organization "in which labor is sold, land is rented, capital is freely invested" (Heilbroner, 1962, 63). These

> do not exist as eternal categories of social organization. Admittedly, they are categories of *nature*, but these eternal aspects of the productive process—the soil, human effort, and the artifacts which can be applied to production—do not take on, in every society, the specific separation which distinguishes them in a market society. . . . Modern economics thus describes the manner in which a certain kind of society, with a specific history of acculturation and institutional evolution, solves its economic problems. It may well be that in another era there will no longer be "land," "labor," and capital (1962, 63).

The guiding fiction of this kind of society— one of the key tenets of its ideology—is that land, labor, and wealth are commodities, that is, goods produced not for use, but for sale. Land, labor, and money could,

> of course, not be really transformed into commodities as actually they were not produced for sale on the market. But the fiction of their being so produced became the organizing principle of society. Of the three, one stands out: labor is the technical term used for human beings, in so far as they are not employers but employed; it follows that henceforth the organiza-

SOURCE: Eric Robert Wolf, *Peasant Wars of the Twentieth Century* (New York: Harper & Row, Publishers, 1968), pp. 276–302.

tion of labor would change concurrently with the organization of the market system. But as the organization of labor is only another word for the forms of life of the common people, this means that the development of the market system would be accompanied by a change in the organization of society itself. All along the line, human society had become an accessory of the economic system (Polanyi, 1957, 75).

Land, also, is not a commodity in nature; it only becomes such when defined as such by a new cultural system intent on creating a new kind of economics. Land is part of the natural landscape not created to be bought and sold, and it is not regarded as a commodity in most other kinds of societies where rights to land are aspects of specific social groups and its utilization the ingredient of specific social relationships. To the Mexican Indian, to the Russian or Vietnamese peasant, land was an attribute of his community. Before the advent of the French, the Algerian peasant had access to land by virtue of his specific membership in a tribe or through political relationships with the *bey* as head of state. Even the Chinese peasant, long used to buying and selling land, regards land as more of a family heirloom than as a commodity. Possession of land guaranteed family continuity, selling it offended "the ethical sense" (Fei, 1939, 182). Only in Cuba, already established as a plantation colony under capitalist auspices, was land relatively unencumbered by social ties and requirements. In all of the other cases, if land was to become a commodity in a capitalist market, it had first to be stripped of these social obligations. This was accomplished either by force which deprived the original inhabitants of their resources in land—as happened notably in Mexico and Algeria; or through the colonization of new land, unencumbered by customary social ties, as in Cochin China; or it could be accomplished indirectly by furthering the rise of "the strong and sober" entrepreneurs within the peasant communities, who could abandon their ties to neighbors and kin and use their surpluses in culturally novel ways to further their own standing in the market. Thus capitalism necessarily produces a revolution of its own.

This revolution from the beginning, however, takes the form of an unequal encounter between the societies which first incubated it and societies which were engulfed by it in the course of its spread. The contact between the capitalist center, the metropolis, and the pre-capitalist or non-capitalist periphery is a large-scale cultural encounter, not merely an economic one. It is not often realized to what extent European capitalism owes its growth to special historical and geographical circumstances in which the barbarians of northwest Europe took over the technological repertoire of Rome without its constraining organizational framework.

> The actual experience of the European peoples was that of a frontier community endowed with a full complement of tools and materials derived from a parent culture and then almost completely severed from the institutional power system of its parent. The result was unique. It is doubtful if history affords another instance of any comparable area and population so richly endowed and so completely severed (Ayres, 1944, 137).

Europe emerged as an area technologically well endowed for overseas commerce and raiding, yet relatively unrestrained by entrenched institutions and their "ceremonial" overhead. Oriented toward overseas conquest, it could benefit both from the plunder of archaic states located along its transoceanic paths of exploration, and from the slave trade, prerequisites for "primary accumulation," unique opportunities, unlikely to repeat themselves after the nineteenth century. Finally, success in plundering the world offset the internal dislocations occasioned by conversion of men, land, and money into commodities within the homeland and gave citizens a stake in overseas expansion. Although this development was essentially predatory in character, it is not so much its use of force and its penchant for exploitation which is at stake in this discussion, but the character of its specific mode of operation. Capitalism surely did not invent exploitation. Everywhere it spread in the world, it encountered social and cultural systems already long dependent upon the fruits of peasant labor. Nor can it be supposed that the peasantry did not revolt repeatedly against the transfer of its surpluses to superior power holders; the historical record is replete with peasant rebellions. It is significant, however, that before the advent of capitalism and the new economic order based on it, social equilibrium depended in both the long and short run on a balance of transfers of peasant surpluses to the rulers and the provision of a minimal security for the cultivator. Sharing of resources within communal organizations and reliance on ties with powerful patrons were recurrent ways in which peasants strove to reduce risks and to improve their stability, and both were condoned and frequently supported by the state. Indeed, "many superficially odd village practices make sense as disguised forms of insurance" (Lipton, 1968, 341). What is significant is that capitalism cut through the integument of custom, severing people from their accustomed social matrix in order to transform them into economic actors, independent of prior social commitments to kin and neighbors. They had to learn how to maximize returns and how to minimize expenditures, to buy cheap and to sell dear, regardless of social obligations and social costs.

The market society had not, of course, invented this drive. Perhaps it did not even intensify it. But it did make it a *ubiquitous* and *necessitous* aspect of social behavior. . . . With the monetization of labor, land, and capital, transactions became *universal* and *critical* activities (Heilbroner, 1962, 64).

Where previously market behavior had been subsidiary to the existential problems of subsistence, now existence and its problems became subsidiary to marketing behavior. Yet this could only function if labor, land, and wealth were turned into commodities, and this, in turn, is only a shorthand formula for the liquidation of encumbering social and cultural institutions. Capitalism "liberated" man as an economic agent, but the concrete process of liberation entailed the accumulation of human suffering against which anticapitalist critics, conservatives *and* radicals alike, would direct their social and moral criticism. This liberation from accustomed social ties and the separation which it entailed constituted the historical experience which Karl Marx would describe in terms of "alienation." The alienation of men from the process of production which had previously guaranteed their existence; their alienation from the product of their work which disappeared into the market only to return to them in the form of money; their alienation from themselves to the extent to which they now had to look upon their own capabilities as marketable commodities; their alienation from their fellow men who had become actual or potential competitors in the market: these are not only philosophical concepts; they depict real tendencies in the growth and spread of capitalism. At work everywhere, they were most starkly in evidence in the new colonies, regarded by the colonists as outright supply depots for the metropolitan market. There the racial and cultural prejudices of the new conquerors allowed them a latitude in treating the native population as "pure" labor which they had not enjoyed in the home country.

Everywhere the dance of commodities brought on an ecological crisis. Where in the past the peasant had worked out a stable combination of resources to underwrite a minimal livelihood, the separate and differential mobilization of these resources as objects to be bought and sold endangered that minimal nexus. Thus in

Russia land reform and commercialization together threatened the peasant's continued access to pasture, forest, and plowland. In Mexico, Algeria, and Viet Nam commercialization menaced peasant access to communal land; in Mexico and Cuba it barred the peasant from claiming unclaimed public land. In Algeria and China, it liquidated the institution of public granaries. In Algeria, it ruptured the balance between pastoral and settled populations. In Mexico, Viet Nam, Algeria, and Cuba, finally, outright seizures of land by foreign colonists and enterprises drove the peasants back upon a land area no longer sufficient for their needs.

Paradoxically, these processes of containment, subversion, and forced withdrawal of the peasantry coincided with a rapid acceleration of population growth. This acceleration was in large part a side effect of the very process of commercial expansion which threatened the stability of the peasant equilibrium. American food crops hitherto confined to the New World —like maize, manioc, beans, peanuts, and sweet potatoes—began a world-wide diffusion in the wake of the transoceanic conquests, and took root in many parts of the world where they furnished an expanded existential minimum for growing populations. Improved communication permitted the transport and sale of food surpluses into deficit areas. Colonization frequently opened up new areas, providing hitherto unavailable niches for developing populations. Somewhat later, incipient industrialization began to offer new alternatives for support, and improved health care cut into mortality rates. Yet, the new generations often found themselves in situations where many resources, and especially land, were already spoken for and where existing social structures often failed to absorb the added burden of supernumerary claimants. Some of the magnitude of the pressures generated can be guaged from figures showing total population increases. At the beginning of

the nineteenth century, Mexico had a population of 5.8 million; in 1910—at the time of the outbreak of the revolution—it had 16.5 million. European Russia had a population of 36 million in 1796; at the beginning of the present century it had 129 million. China numbered 265 million in 1775, 430 million in 1850, and close to 600 million at the time of the Revolution. Viet Nam is estimated to have sustained a population between 6 million and 14 million in 1820; it counted 30.5 million inhabitants in 1962. Algeria had an indigenous population of 3 million in 1830, of 10.5 million in 1963. Cuba's population rose from 550,000 inhabitants in 1800 to 5.8 million in 1953. The peasant thus confronted a growing imbalance between population and resources. In such a situation the peasant's risks multiplied, and the mechanisms for the alleviation of these risks grew ever more unreliable. Such an imbalance could not, in the long run, endure; the fiction that men, land, and wealth were *nothing but* commodities entailed its own ruin. For the complete application of this ideology could not but

> result in the demolition of society. For the alleged commodity "labor power" cannot be shoved about, used indiscriminately, or even left unused, without affecting also the human individual who happens to be the bearer of this particular commodity. In disposing of a man's labor power the system would, incidentally, dispose of the physical, psychological, and moral entity "man" attached to that tag. Robbed of the protective covering of cultural institutions, human beings would perish from the effects of social exposure (Polanyi, 1957, 73).

Thus, paradoxically, the very spread of the capitalist market-principle also forced men to seek defenses against it. They could meet this end either by cleaving to their traditional institutions, increasingly subverted by the forces which they were trying to neutralize; or they could commit themselves to the search for new social forms which would grant them shelter. In a sense all our six cases can be seen as the outcome of such defensive reactions, coupled with a search for a new and more humane social order.

Yet the advent of capitalism produced still another—and equally serious—repercussion. It initiated a crisis in the exercise of power.

Tribal chief, mandarin, landed nobleman —the beneficiaries and agents of an older social order—yield to the entrepreneur, the credit merchant, the political broker, the intellectual, the professional. The social weight of peasantry and artisans decreases, as other groups—miners, railroad workers, industrial workers, agricultural laborers, commercial agricultural producers—gain in relative importance. The managers of fixed social resources yield to the managers of "free-floating" resources. Groups oriented toward subsistence production diminish, and groups committed to commodity production or to the sale of labor power grow in size and social density. Such a circulation of elites and social groups is characteristic of all culture change in a complex society: the new processes at work evoke positive responses in some groups, defensive reactions in others. Yet capitalism is unusual both in the speed and intensity of its operation, as it creates "free-floating" resources previously held fast by a tissue of social and political connections. It mobilizes economic resources and renders them amenable to new forms of allocation and use; yet in so doing it also cuts the tie between these resources and any connection they may have had with traditional social prerogatives and political privileges. It proves a powerful solvent of the integument of power, exacerbating tension not only through its own action, but freeing also tensions and contradictions previously contained by the traditional system of power. As the economic resources of chiefs, mandarins, and landed nobles become subject to the movement of the market, their claims to social and political command are in-

creasingly called into question. Many of their inherited titles end up on the auction block.

These processes do not, of course, proceed at an even pace in all realms of society and in all of its regions. For some time, the power holders of the older order coexist with the power holders of the new; social groups which once controlled the foundation of the society retreat only slowly before groups harnessed to novel processes. Some regions of the country involved remain anchored in tradition, while others are caught up completely in the grip of change. This coexistence of old and new strata, of regions dominated by the past and regions in the grip of the future, spells trouble for the society as a whole.

Commitments and goals point in different directions: the old is not yet overcome and remains to challenge the new; the new is not yet victorious. The dislocations caused by rapid change are still visible to all; the wounds caused by them, raw and open. New wealth does not yet have legitimacy, and old power no longer commands respect. Traditional groups have been weakened, but not yet defeated, and new groups are not yet strong enough to wield decisive power. This is especially marked in colonial situations, where capitalism has been imported from abroad by force of arms. The conquerors drive a wide wedge into the body of the conquered society, but only rarely can they be certain of the ramifications of their actions, of the ways in which cultural shock waves propagate themselves through the traditional strata of society, of the ultimate repercussions in the hinterland and in the nether regions of the social order. Moreover, both cultural barriers and the logistic difficulties of sustained dominance tend to leave uncontrolled wide areas of society which become sanctuaries for groups that seek refuge in time of stress. Finally, abdication of ultimate decisions to the "invisible hand" of the market affects both the willingness and the capacity to take responsibility for local consequences.

Inherited control mechanisms fail, but the new mechanisms engage only rarely, with considerable slippage.

Such a situation of weak contenders, unable to neutralize each other's power, seems to invite the rise or perpetuation of a dominant central executive, attempting to stand "above" the contending parties and interest groups, and to consolidate the state by playing off one group against the other. All our cases show such a phenomenon before the revolution: Díaz ruled over Mexico; tsarist autocracy held Russia in its grip; Chiang Kai-shek strove to install such a dictatorship in China; France exercised autocratic rule in Viet Nam and Algiers through her governor general, vastly more authoritative than the head of the government at home; and Cuba was dominated by Batista. Yet because the dictatorship is predicated on the relative debility of the class groups and political forces which constitute society, its seeming strength derives from weakness, and its weakness ultimately becomes evident in its impotent struggle against challengers from within, unless it can find allies strong enough to sustain it against the challenge.

Two examples show that this is possible, but that the conditions for such consolidation are apt to be unique. In both Germany and Japan the executive allied itself not with new groups, but with a section of the traditional feudal aristocracy which provided the backbone of an efficient centralized bureaucracy. The commercial and professional groups, rather than striving for independent ends, accepted the feudal values as their own, thus consenting to guidance by the aristocrats. The peasantry was similarly held fast to the inherited cultural ceremonial of obligations between social superiors and inferiors, and by the development of a national ideology of kinship or kinship-based *Gemeinschaft*. The entire structure received further cohesion through its integration with a military machine, and projection of tension within the society outward against real and putative enemies. Such an effective mobilization of feudal relationships and values served as a check on the social dislocations produced by the widening market, but did so at the cost of increased militarism and final military defeat (see Moore, 1966, 313).

Where the social dislocations produced by the market go unchecked, however, the crisis of power also deranges the networks which link the peasant population to the larger society, the all-important structure of mediation intervening between center and hinterland. Increased commercialization and capitalization of rent produce dislocations and tensions which often weaken the agents of the process themselves. A good example is furnished by the condition of Ch'uhsien, a market town in Anhwei, studied by anthropologist Morton Fried shortly before the Communist take-over in 1949. The landlords of Ch'ushien relied largely on a system in which tenants paid in rent 40 percent of the staple crops at harvest time. This allowed for some flexibility in determining the amount to be paid, and arguments between landlord and tenant over the disputed margin were mediated by a culturally standardized form of "good will," called *kan-ch'ing*. By extending "good will" to his tenant, the landlord essentially granted a discount on the rent in return for the tenant's reliable performance in paying rent; the tenant traded the promise of his reliability for the protection by the landlord in case of some untoward event, like a poor harvest or sickness in the family. In the unsettled conditions of Chinese Anhwei, the landlord was thus passing on to the tenant the margin of gain which he would otherwise have had to pay out to agents or to political power holders in order to attach the rent by force. Yet even this flexible system soon encountered limitations. Not all tenants can have good *kan-ch'ing* with their landlords; when landlords are hard-pressed, *kan-ch'ing* was abrogated; and tenants in some rural areas

away from the police power of the county seat, defied the landlords and paid no rent. In such instances the rents were frequently collected by an armed squad of the local militia, or even, on special occasion, by a unit of the Nationalist Army, which accompanied the agent or landlord (Fried, 1953, 196).

The best the gentry can do under these circumstances "is to establish good *kan-ch'ing* with a few persons while relationships with others deteriorate" (Fried, 1953, 224). In response to this situation, the landlords of Ch'uhsien had, over the last fifty years, begun to move away to town. Elsewhere in China the process had already run its course. In much of Southeast China, landlords had interposed between themselves and the dependent peasantry a corps of agents who collect rent or interest, and hire or remunerate labor on an impersonal basis. They were thus able to respond to the promptings of the market, but at the cost of insulating themselves completely from the populace and from any noneconomic cues regarding its condition.

The Chinese case is but a paradigm for a general process, at work in all six cases we have encountered. The economic mediators are bearers of the process of monetization and the agents of social dissolution; at the same time their obedience to the market demands that they maximize returns, regardless of the immediate consequences of their actions. By rendering the process of commodity-formation bureaucratic and impersonal, they remove themselves physically from these consequences; at the same time they lose their ability to respond to social cues from the affected population. Instead, they couple economic callousness with a particular kind of structurally induced stupidity, the kind of stupidity which ascribes to the people themselves responsibility for the evils to which they are subject. Defensive stereotypes take the place of analytical intelligence, in one of those classical cases of blindness with which the gods strike those whom they wish to destroy.

At the very same time, the political mediators who man the relays of power connecting state and village also face increased un-

certainty. The traditional power holders—be they mandarins or aristocrats—have had their power curtailed, unless they enter into collusion with economic agents to their mutual advantage and to the disadvantage of the state. In either case, however, they can no longer shield the local populations against encroachment from outside, a role which in the past often redounded to their own interests. The new power holders, on the other hand, find their exercise of power already shorn of effectiveness by the axiom that economic transformation takes precedence over social order. If they are aware of social dislocations caused by the spread of the market, they may be able to raise their voice in protest, but they cannot—at the cost of losing their position—stop them of their own accord. They thus lack control over the decisive processes which affect society; this would involve the mobilization of dissatisfied populations against a state of which they are the primary beneficiaries. They are thus caught up in the characteristic conflict between "formal" and "substantive" bureaucracy, between the operations of a bureaucracy which merely administers rules, and operations which answer to the strategic issues of social coordination and conflict. Like the economic power holders they retreat from participation in the existential problems of the population into the protective carapace provided by the administrative machinery. At best they can keep their ear "to the ground" through the use of police spies and informants, not to cope with the causes of unrest, but to curtail its symptoms. In a situation in which they have abdicated the power to formulate new goals and to marshal resources as means to these goals, they retreat into administration. Their social hallmark becomes *attentisme*, their slogan, as in the Vietnamese, to withdraw, "to wrap themselves in their blankets" (*trum men*).

Yet they are soon faced with competition from new social groups which begin to emphasize substantive problems against purely administrative ones. Some of these are geared to the service of the new economic arrangements: comprador merchants, "financial experts," labor bosses, foremen. But in addition to these junior executives of the capitalist market in the dependent country, there also appear other groups, similarly sponsored by culture contact and answering to its new requirements: the petty officials of the state bureaucracy, the professionals, the schoolteachers. These share certain characteristics. For one thing, they are not involved in the transmission and sale of goods; they are purveyors of skills. These skills are only in the rarest of cases traditional within the society; they are much more likely to have been learned from the West or from Western-type educational institutions established within the dependency. Moreover, these skills are based on literacy, of specialized acquaintance with a corpus of literature which departs from the traditions of the country and suggests new alternatives. Within the traditional society literacy was in most cases a hallmark of high status. The new literati partake of the reflected glory of this traditional evaluation of literacy, but at the same time their acquaintance with nontraditional sources makes them participants in a communication process which far outstrips the inherited canons of knowledge. They operate in a communication field vastly larger than that of the past, and full of new learning which suggests powerful visions not dreamed of in the inherited ideology.

At the same time, they are caught up in professional predicaments. Many of them do not find employment, or must supplement their professional work with other sources of endeavor. Yet if they do they find themselves in direct communication with clients whose problems they must to some extent make their own; they are caught up in the strain between the demands placed upon them and their limited ability "to do anything" about them. The petty official is limited in his freedom of action by bureaucratic restraints; the professional, the teacher, and the lawyer soon become aware that they are limited to coping with symptoms, but do not have a handle on the conditions which produce these symptoms. Moreover, their clients are drawn from society at large, rather than being confined to any particular group to which they might be tied by heredity or tradition. They thus confront a situation in which they answer to a much larger social field and communication network than the traditional power holder, and yet experience every day the very real limitations on their power. Finally, they suffer directly from the crisis of power and authority. A member of such a group is apt to evince

> a deep preoccupation with authority. Even though he seeks and seems actually to break away from the authority of the powerful traditions in which he was brought up, the intellectual of underdeveloped countries, still more than his confrere in more advanced countries, retains the need for incorporation into some self-transcending, authoritative entity. Indeed, the greater his struggle for emancipation from the traditional collectivity, the greater his need for incorporation into a new, alternative collectivity. Intense politicization meets this need (Shils, 1962, 205).

For such "marginal men" political movements often provide a "home," of which they are otherwise deprived by their own skill, their social positions, and their divorce from traditional sources of power. Increasingly, these "intellectuals" of the new order press their claims against both economic and political power holders. What they need is a constituency; and that constituency is ultimately provided by the industrial workers and dissatisfied peasants whom the market created, but for whom society made no adequate social provision. In all of our six cases we witness such a fusion between the "rootless" intellectuals and their rural supporters.

Yet this fusion is not effected easily (see Hindley, 1965). The peasant is especially handicapped in passing from passive recognition of wrongs to political participation as a means for setting them right. First, a peasant's work is most often done alone, on his own land, than in conjunction with his fellows. Moreover, all peasants are to some extent competitors, for available resources within the community as well as for sources of credit from without. Second, the tyranny of work weighs heavily upon a peasant: his life is geared to an annual routine and to planning for the year to come. Momentary alterations of routine threaten his ability to take up the routine later. Third, control of land enables him, more often than not, to retreat into subsistence production should adverse conditions affect his market crop. Fourth, ties of extended kinship and mutual aid within the community may cushion the shocks of dislocation. Fifth, peasant interests—especially among poor peasants— often crosscut class alignments. Rich and poor peasants may be kinfolk, or a peasant may be at one and the same time owner, renter, sharecropper, laborer for his neighbors and seasonal hand on a nearby plantation. Each different involvement aligns him differently with his fellows and with the outside world. Finally, past exclusion of the peasant from participation in decision-making beyond the bamboo hedge of his village deprives him all too often of the knowledge needed to articulate his interests with appropriate forms of action. Hence, peasants are often merely passive spectators of political struggles or long for the sudden advent of a millennium, without specifying for themselves and their neighbors the many rungs on the staircase to heaven. But, ultimately, the decisive factor in making a peasant rebellion possible lies in the relation of the peasantry to the field of power which surrounds it. A rebellion cannot start from a situation of complete impotence; the powerless are easy victims. Power, as Richard Adams has said (1966, 3–4),

refers to the control that one party holds over the environment of another party . . . power ultimately refers to an actual physical control that one party may have

with respect to another. The reason that most relationships are not reduced to physical struggles is that parties to them can make rational decisions based on their estimates of tactical power and other factors. Power is usually exercised, therefore, through the common recognition by two parties of the tactical control each has, and through rational decision by one to do what the other wants. Each estimates his own tactical control, compares it to the other, and decides he may or may not be superior.

The poor peasant or the landless laborer who depends on a landlord for the largest part of his livelihood, or the totality of it, has no tactical power: he is completely within the power domain of his employer, without sufficient resources of his own to serve him as resources in the power struggle. Poor peasants and landless laborers, therefore, are unlikely to pursue the course of rebellion, *unless* they are able to rely on some external power to challenge the power which constrains them. Such external power is represented in the Mexican case by the Constitutionalist army in Yucatán which liberated the peons from debt bondage by action "from above"; by the collapse of the Russian Army in 1917 and the reflux of the peasant soldiery, weapons in hand, into the villages; by the creation of the Chinese Red Army as an instrument designed to break up landlord power in the villages. Where such external power is present, the poor peasant and landless laborer have latitude of movement; where it is absent, they are under near-complete constraint. The rich peasant, in turn, is unlikely to embark on the course of rebellion. As employer of the labor of others, as money lender, as notable co-opted by the state machine, he exercises local power in alliance with external power holders. His power domain within the village is derivative: it depends on the maintenance of their domains outside the village. Only when an external force, such as the Chinese Red Army, proves capable of destroying these other superior power domains, will the rich peasant lend his support to an uprising. The only component of the peasantry which does have some internal leverage is either landowning "middle peasantry" or a peasantry located in a peripheral area outside the domains of landlord control. Middle peasantry refers to a peasant population which has secure access to land of its own and cultivates it with family labor. Where these middle peasant holdings lie within the power domain of a superior, possession of their own resources provides their holders with the minimal tactical freedom required to challenge their overload (see Alavi, 1965). The same, however, holds for a peasantry, poor or "middle," whose settlements are only under marginal control from the outside. Here landholdings may be insufficient for the support of the peasant household; but subsidiary activities such as casual labor, smuggling, livestock raising—not under the direct constraint of an external power domain—supplement land in sufficient quantity to grant the peasantry some latitude of movement. We have marked the existence of such a tactically mobile peasantry in the villages of Morelos, in the communes of the Central Agricultural Region of Russia; in the northern bastion established by the Chinese Communists after the Long March; as a basis for rebellion in Viet Nam; among the fellahin of Algeria; and among the squatters of Oriente in Cuba.

Yet this recruitment of a "tactically mobile peasantry" among the middle peasants and the "free" peasants of peripheral areas poses a curious paradox. This is also the peasantry in whom anthropologists and rural sociologists have tended to see the main bearers of peasant tradition. If our account is correct, then—strange to say—it is precisely this culturally conservative stratum which is the most instrumental in dynamiting the peasant social order. This paradox dissolves, however, when we consider that it is also the middle peasant who is relatively the most vulnerable to economic changes wrought by commercialism, while his social relations remain encased within the traditional design. His is a balancing act in which his balance is continuously threatened by population growth; by the encroachment of rival landlords; by the loss of rights to grazing, forest, and water; by falling prices and unfavorable conditions of the market; by interest payments and foreclosures. Moreover, it is precisely this stratum which most depends on traditional social relations of kin and mutual aid between neighbors; middle peasants suffer most when these are abrogated, just as they are least able to withstand the depredations of tax collectors or landlords.

Finally—and this is again paradoxical—middle peasants are also the most exposed to influences from the developing proletariat. The poor peasant or landless laborer, in going to the city or factory, also usually cuts his tie with the land. The middle peasant, however, stays on the land and sends his children to work in town; he is caught in a situation in which one part of the family retains a footing in agriculture, while the other undergoes "the training of the cities" (Germaine Tillion). This makes the middle peasant a transmitter also of urban unrest and political ideas. The point bears elaboration. It is probably not so much the growth of an industrial proletariat as such which produces revolutionary activity, as the development of an industrial work force still closely geared to life in the villages.

Thus it is the very attempt of the middle and free peasant to remain traditional which makes him revolutionary.

If we now follow out the hypothesis that it is middle peasants and poor but "free" peasants, not constrained by any power domain, which constitute the pivotal groupings for peasant uprisings, then it follows that any factor which serves to increase the latitude granted by that tactical mobility reinforces their revolutionary potential. One of these factors is peripheral location with regard to the center of state control. In fact, frontier areas quite often show a tendency to rebel against the central authorities, regardless of whether they are inhabited by peasants or not. South China has constituted a hearth of rebellion within the Chinese state, partly because it was first a frontier area in the southward march of the Han people, and later because it provided the main zone of contact between Western and Chinese civilization. The Mexican north has similarly been a zone of dissidence from the center in Mexico City, partly because its economy was based on mining and cattle raising rather than maize agriculture, partly because it was open to influences from the United States to the north. In the Chinese south it was dissident gentry with a peasant following which frequently made trouble for the center; in the Mexican north it was incipient businessmen, ranchers, and cowboys. Yet where you have a poor peasantry located in such a peripheral area beyond the normal control of the central power, the tactical mobility of such a peasantry is added to by its location. This has been the case with Morelos, in Mexico; Nghe An Province in Viet Nam; Kabylia in Algeria; and Oriente in Cuba. The tactical effectiveness of such areas is strengthened still further if they contain defensible mountainous redoubts: this has been true of Morelos, Kabylia, and Oriente. The effect is reinforced where the population of these redoubts differs ethnically or linguistically from the surrounding population. Thus we find that the villagers of Morelos were Nahuatl-speakers, the inhabitants of Kabylia, Berber-speakers. Oriente Province showed no linguistic differences from the Spanish spoken in Cuba, but it did contain a significant Afro-Cuban element. Ethnic distinctions enhance the solidarity of the rebels; possession of a special linguistic code provides for an autonomous system of communication.

It is important, however, to recognize that separation from the state or the surrounding populace need not be only physical or cultural. The Russian and the Mexican cases both demonstrate that it is possible to develop a solid enclave population of peasantry through state reliance on a combination of communal autonomy with the provision of community services to the state. The organization of the peasantry into self-administering communes with stipulated responsibilities to state and landlords created in both cases veritable fortresses of peasant tradition within the body of the country itself. Held fast by the surrounding structure, they acted as sizzling pressure cookers of unrest which, at the moment of explosion, vented their force outward to secure more living space for their customary corporate way of life. Thus we can add an additional multiplier effect to the others just cited. The presence of any one of these will raise the peasant potential for rebellion.

But what of the transition from peasant rebellion to revolution, from a movement aimed at the redress of wrongs, to the attempted overthrow of society itself? Marxists have long argued that peasants without outside leadership cannot make a revolution; and our case material would bear them out. Where the peasantry has successfully rebelled against the established order—under its own banner and with its own leaders—it was sometimes able to reshape the social structure of the countryside closer to its heart's desires; but it did not lay hold of the state, of the cities which house the centers of control, of the strategic nonagricultural resources of the society. Zapata stayed in his Morelos; the "folk migration" of Pancho Villa receded after the defeat at Torreón; Nestor Makhno stopped short of the cities; and the Russian peasants of the Central Agricultural Region simply burrowed more deeply into their local communes. Thus a peasant rebellion which takes place in a complex society already caught up in commercialization and industrialization tends to be self-limiting, and, hence, anachronistic.

The peasant utopia is the free village, untrammeled by tax collectors, labor recruiters, large landowners, officials. Ruled over, but never ruling, they also lack acquaintance with the operation of the state as a complex machinery, experiencing it only as a "cold monster." Against this hostile force, they had learned, even their traditional power holders provided but a weak shield, even though they were on occasion willing to defend them if it proved to their own interest. Thus, for the peasant, the state is a negative quantity, an evil, to be replaced in short shrift by their own "homemade" social order. That order, they believe, can run without the state; hence, peasants in rebellion are natural anarchists.

Often this political perspective is reinforced still further by a wider ideological vision. The peasant experience tends to be dualistic, in that he is caught between his understanding of how the world ought to be properly ordered and the realities of a mundane existence, beset by disorder. Against this disorder, the peasant has always set his dreams of deliverance, the vision of a Mahdi who would deliver the world from tyranny, of a Son of Heaven who would truly embody the mandate of heaven, of a "white tsar" as against the "black tsar" of the disordered present (Sarkisyanz, 1955). Under conditions of modern dislocation, the disordered present is all too frequently experienced as world order reversed, and hence evil. The dualism of the past easily fuses with the dualism of the present. The true order is yet to come, whether through miraculous intervention, through rebellion, or both. Peasant anarchism and an apocalyptic vision of the world, together, provide the ideological fuel that drives the rebellious peasantry.

But the peasant rebellions of the twentieth century are no longer simple responses to local problems, if indeed they ever were. They are but the parochial reactions to major social dislocations, set in motion by overwhelming societal change. The spread of the market has torn men up by their roots, and shaken them loose from the social relationships into which they were born. Industrialization and expanded communication have given rise to new social clusters, as yet unsure of their own social positions and interests, but forced by the imbalance of their lives to seek a new adjustment. Traditional political authority has eroded or collapsed; new contenders for power are seeking new constituencies for entry into the vacant political arena. Thus when the peasant protagonist lights the torch of rebellion, the edifice of society is already smoldering and ready to take fire. When the battle is over, the structure will not be the same.

No cultural system—no complex of economy, society, polity, and ideology—is ever static; all of its component parts are in constant change. Yet as long as these changes remain within tolerable limits, the over-all system persists. If they begin to exceed these limits, however, or if other components are suddenly introduced from outside, the system is thrown out of kilter. The parts of the system are rendered inconsistent with each other; the system grows incoherent. Men in such a situation are caught painfully between various old solutions to problems which have suddenly shifted shape and meaning, and new solutions to problems they often cannot comprehend. Since incoherence rarely appears all at once, in all parts of the system, they may for some time follow now one alternative, now another and contradictory one; but in the end a breach, a major disjuncture will make its appearance somewhere in the system (Wilson and Wilson, 1945, 125–129). A peasant uprising under such circumstances, for any of the reasons we have sketched, can, without conscious intent, bring the entire society to the state of collapse.

But in the cases which we have analyzed, we have encountered not only the peasant rebels, rising for "land and liberty." On the battlefield, the peasants also encounter other groups, most often the intelligentsia-in-arms, ready to benefit from the prevailing disorder in order to impose on it a new order of their own. Two organizational phenomena, over and above the armed peasant band, make their appearance in our case histories; one is the military organization; the other is the para-military party organized around a certain vision of what the new society is to be. Yet our cases also show marked differences in the way these two organizational forms are conjugated with each other.

In the Mexican case, final victory was won neither by Zapata's guerrillas nor by Villa's cowboy *dorados*. The palm of success went to a civilian-military leadership in control of a specialized army—separate and distinct from any *levée en masse* of the peasantry; equipped with a rudimentary experience in bureaucratic management; and in possession of the strategic resources of Mexico's export trade. As a result this "revolutionary family" of civilians-turned-generals proved able to construct a new apparatus of central control which transformed itself over time from a coalition of military commanders into a unitary official party. This party, in turn, used the state to give support to rising clusters of entrepreneurs and professionals, while at the same time allocating a share of the proceeds from capitalist development to previously unrepresented agricultural and industrial groups in the interest of "social justice." A somewhat similar course was followed in Algeria. Although the Algerian nationalists began the war as a guerrilla operation closely linked to the villages of the hinterland, French success in reducing the guerrilla threat within the country finally placed the external army in Tunis and Morocco in command of the country, as the only remaining organized body in the new independent polity. Efforts to organize the wartime coalition of nationalists against the French into a monolithic party "after the fact" met with failure. Thus it fell to the army to stabilize the society. While a socialist rhetoric was used to promise a measure of reward to peasants and workers, as in Mexico, the state has placed its reliance

on a guided maximization of private enterprise. In both these cases, then, the peasant rebellions of the hinterland set fire to the pre-existing structure; but it fell to the army and its leadership to forge the organizational balance wheel which would enable the post-revolutionary society to continue on its course.

In Russia, China, and Viet Nam, however, we must note that the roles of army and party were reversed. In these three cases, it was the political parties of middle-class revolutionaries who engineered the seizure of power and created the social and military instruments which conquered the state, and ensured transition to a new social order. It is probably not an accident that these are also three countries which were characterized by patterns of conspiratorial and secret societies before the advent of revolution. Furthermore, a common Marxist ideology—and especially the Leninist concept of the revolutionary leadership, leading the masses in the interest of the masses—furnished a ready-made idiom in which to cast their own experience of fusion between rebel soldiery and revolutionary leadership. Such common denominators also facilitated rapid learning and transfer of successful patterns from one situation to another. It is here—and only here—that the party as a separate body comes to dominate the other organizations thrown up by the revolution.

Yet there are also important distinctions between the Russian experience on the one hand, and the Chinese and Vietnamese experience on the other. In Russia the Communist party seized power on the crest of worker uprisings in the cities and organized the state for a war in defense of the revolution. The peasantry, in the meantime, staged its own uprisings in the countryside, parallel with the industrial insurrection in the cities, but in essential independence of them. Linking their village councils as village soviets to the soviet structure in name, they in fact simply expanded their living space and traditional organizations over the countryside. The war in defense of the revolution then followed the seizure of power, it did not accompany it. In marked contrast to China and Viet Nam, the Red Army—by putting a military shield around the central peasant regions, in defense against the periphery—reinforced still further the "settling-in" process of the rebellious peasants.

In China and Viet Nam, however, we not only find warfare directed by the party, but a kind of warfare which organizes the peasant population as it proceeds. Again special cultural predispositions appear to have been at work: these are areas in which manifold village associations have always been traditional in the villages. Under Communist control these came to serve as a template for welding army and peasantry into a common body. This common organizational grid—connecting the centralized army mainly recruited from the peasantry, the part-time guerrilla forces stationed in the villages, and the village population— both obviated the development of uncoordinated peasant revolts and the autonomous entrenchment of the peasantry which had occurred in Russia. It proved to be a system capable not only of withstanding prolonged warfare, but of even thriving upon it. It can be argued that this organizational grid gains in strength as it is engaged in combat, as evidenced both by Chinese Communist resistance to the Japanese invasion and by the Vietnamese experience over the last twenty years.

Finally, in the Cuban case, we find an island not populated primarily by peasants, but by a wage-working sugar proletariat. Organized into trade-unions by Communists—and under their continuing influence —the sugar proletariat, however, did little to assist the rebellion. The Communist party and allied organizations were, together with other groups, caught in a political deadlock in which no one group possessed sufficient independent leverage to break out of the governmental spoils system. This leverage was provided instead by a small group of armed rebels who, very

much by accident, had established themselves in the one part of the island inhabited by a tactically mobile peasantry. Once in power, this rebel group could make use of the Communist party apparatus to provide a new organizational grid for the country and to carry through a social revolution in an unusual symbiosis of rebel army and party organization.

The question of why in some cases it is the army which generates the new political controls, while in other situations this task falls to the party, has no easy answer. We found army controls to have been important in Mexico and Algeria. Perhaps it is no coincidence that these two societies continue to operate on the basis of the market: controls must fall upon society rather than upon the economy. The army furnishes the organizational pivot for the social order, but the economy is left unencumbered to develop according to the dictates of the market. Where both society and economy rest upon command, however, as in Russia, China, Viet Nam, and Cuba, the market is abrogated, and ideological considerations and appeals take the place of the "invisible hand" in moving men to action. For a long time Russia remained the model case of party dominance over the means and ends of command; yet recently China has moved in a quite different direction. In Russia, the party remained clearly dominant over the army; it even proved successful in checking the growth of a new quasi-army within its own ranks, when it curtailed the powers of the secret police. In China, after a period of initial fusion of party and army during the years of protracted war and in the initial years of consolidation after the revolution, party and army appear to have come into conflict during the Great Cultural Revolution, and party dominance has been curtailed. We may hazard a guess that this divergence is a function of the different development of the two revolutions, including their very different bases of social support (see Lowenthal, 1967, 387–388; Schram, 1967, 325, 341–342).

The Russian Revolution drew its main

support from industrial workers in key industrial regions, and not from the peasantry. To the Russian Communists, control of the strategic heights of the economy remained a primary goal; and the rapid expansion of the scale and scope of these strategic heights through rapid industrialization, the main guarantee of Soviet continuity. To the extent that industrialization also aided effectiveness in warfare, the ends of party and army clearly coincided. Industry and school were seen as the two templates upon which Soviet Man was to be forged, and ideology was used primarily to fan the flames of forced-draft industrial progress. Industrialization went hand in hand with the growth of an effective managerial class and a population of skilled industrial workers. Emphasis was on differential reward for skill and labor. The outcome was a strongly hierarchical society, operated by technocrats, "experts and Red," but above all experts. China, too, embarked on a program of rapid industrialization, but from the beginning there seem to have been tensions between groups in the party which favored the Russian model of development, and those who, during the years of protracted war, had learned to put their faith in a peasant army with an egalitarian ideology. The experience of war in the hinterland had taken them far from cities and industrial areas; it had taught them the advantages of dispersal, of a wide distribution of basic skills rather than a dense concentration of advanced skills. The citizen-soldiers of the guerrilla army had, in fact, lived lives in which the roles of peasant, worker, soldier, and intellectual intermingled to the point of fusion. Moreover, army experience—rather than industry and school—had provided the inspiration to discipline and initiative, sacrifice and commitment. Where in Russia the peasant could become an effective member of the new order only by passing through the fiery ovens of industrialization, in China the relation of the peasant to the citizen-army was immediate and concrete. Perhaps it is for this reason that it was the People's Liberation Army which increasingly emerged as an effective counterforce to the ever more managerial and bureaucratic party. While any interpretations of the Great Cultural Revolution from the outside remain guesswork, it is at least clear that the role of the party in China has been greatly reduced in favor of a coalition of armed forces with local nonparty committees. Nor is this trend confined to China. A similar trend is evident in Cuba where Castro has studiously avoided the installation of a permanent managerial apparatus, pivoted upon the Communist party, and relied instead on the ongoing mobilization of a citizenry-in-arms. As in China, it is the rural area which furnishes the energy for this army-as-party, while the traditional urban center, Havana, loses in organizational importance. In both cases, it is too early to know whether this represents a relapse into rural romanticism, or whether such politicized militarization of the populace can lead—with the aid of modern means of communication—to new and viable forms of popular organization.

These considerations have taken us a long way from the parochial rebellions of the peasantry with which we began our study. Yet it has been the argument of these chapters that the peasant is an agent of forces larger than himself, forces produced by a disordered past as much as by a disordered present. There is no evidence for the view that if it were not for "outside agitators," the peasant would be at rest. On the contrary, the peasants rise to redress wrong; but the inequities against which they rebel are but, in turn, parochial manifestations of great social dislocations. Thus rebellion issues easily into revolution, massive movements to transform the social structure as a whole. The battlefield becomes society itself, and when the war is over, society will have changed and the peasantry with it. The peasant's role is thus essentially tragic: his efforts to undo a grievous present only usher in a vaster, more uncertain future. Yet if it is tragic, it is also full of hope. For the first time in millennia, human kind is moving toward a solution of the age-old problem of hunger and disease, and everywhere ancient monopolies of power and received wisdom are yielding to human effort to widen participation and knowledge. In such efforts—however uncertain, however beset with difficulties, however illunderstood—there lies the prospect for increased life, for increased humanity. If the peasant rebels partake of tragedy, they also partake of hope, and to that extent theirs is the party of humanity. Arrayed against them, however, are now not merely the defenders of ancient privileges, but the Holy Alliance of those who—with superior technology and superior organization—would bury that hope under an avalanche of power. These new engineers of power call themselves realists, but it is a hallmark of their realism that it admits no evidence and interpretation other than that which serves their purposes. The peasantry confronts tragedy, but hope is on its side; doubly tragic are their adversaries who would deny that hope to both peasantry and to themselves. This also is America's dilemma in the world today: to act in aid of human hope or to crush it, not only for the world's sake but for her own.

BIBLIOGRAPHY

Adams, Richard N., 1966, "Power and Power Domains," *América Latina*, year 9, pp. 3–21.

Alavi, Hamza, 1965, "Peasants and Revolution," in Ralph Miliband and John Saville, eds., *The Socialist Register*, Merlin Press, London, pp. 241–277.

Ayres, C. E., 1944, *The Theory of Economic Progress*, University of North Carolina Press, Chapel Hill.

Fei, Hsiao-Tung, 1939, *Peasant Life in China: A Field Study of Country Life in the Yangtze Valley*, Kegan Paul, Trench, Trubner and Co., London.

Fried, Morton H., 1953, *Fabric of Chinese Society: A Study of the Social Life of a Chinese County Seat*, Praeger, New York.

Heilbroner, Robert L., 1962, *The Making of Economic Society*, Prentice-Hall, Englewood Cliffs, N.J.

Hindley, Donald, 1965, "Political Conflict Potential, Politicization, and the Peasantry in Underdeveloped Countries," *Asian Studies*, Vol. 3, pp. 470–489.

Lipton, Michael, 1968, "The Theory of the Optimising Peasant," *Journal of Development Studies*, Vol. 4, pp. 327–351.

Lowenthal, Richard, 1967, "Soviet and Chinese Communist World Views," in Donald W. Treadgold, ed., *Soviet and Chinese Communism*, University of Washington Press, Seattle, pp. 374–404.

Moore, Barrington, Jr., 1966, *Social Origins of Dictatorship and Democracy: Lord and Peasant in the Making of the Modern World*, Beacon Press, Boston.

Polanyi, Karl, 1957, *The Great Transformation: The Political and Economic Origins of Our Time*, Beacon Press, Boston.

Sarkisyanz, Emanuel, 1955, *Russland und der Messianismus des Orients*, J. C. B. Mohr, Tübingen.

Schram, Stuart, 1967, *Mao Tse-tung*, Penguin Books, Baltimore.

Shils, Edward, 1962, "The Intellectuals in the Political Development of the New States," in John H. Kautsky, ed., *Political Change in Underdeveloped Countries*, Wiley & Sons, New York, pp. 195–234.

Wilson, Godfrey, and Monica Wilson, 1945, *The Analysis of Social Change*, Cambridge University Press, Cambridge.

THE STRUCTURE OF POLITICAL CONFLICT
IN THE NEW STATES OF TROPICAL AFRICA

Aristide R. Zolberg, The University of Chicago

I. Introduction[1]

Having assumed the burden of understanding political life in two-and-a-half dozen unruly countries, political scientists who study the new states of tropical Africa must leap with assurance where angels fear to tread. We have borrowed, adapted, or invented an array of frameworks designed to guide perceptions of disparate events, and Africa is now uniformly viewed through the best lenses of contemporary comparative politics with a focus on political modernization, development and integration. Unfortunately, it appears that when we rely exclusively on these tools in order to accomplish our task, the aspects of political life which we, as well as non-specialists, see most clearly with the naked eye of informed common sense, remain beyond the range of our scientific vision. In our pursuit of scientific progress, we have learned to discern such forms as regular patterns of behavior which constitute structures and institutions; but the most salient characteristic of political life in Africa is that it constitutes an almost institutionless arena with conflict and disorder as its most prominent features.

In recent years, almost every new African state has experienced more or less success-

SOURCE: Aristide R. Zolberg, "The Structure of Political Conflict in the New States of Tropical Africa," *American Political Science Review*, 63:70–87, March, 1968.

[1] Earlier versions of this paper were presented at the September 1966, meeting of the American Political Science Association (New York City) and at the Seventh World Congress of the International Political Science Association (Brussels, September, 1967). The category "new states of Tropical Africa" excludes Liberia and Ethiopia.

ful military or civilian coups, insurrections, mutinies, severe riots, and significant political assassinations. Some of them appear to be permanently on the brink of disintegration into several new political units. With little regard for the comfort of social scientists, the incidence of conflict and disorder appears unrelated to such variables as type of colonial experience, size, number of parties, absolute level or rate of economic and social development, as well as to the overall characteristics of regimes. The downfall of what was widely regarded as the continent's most promising democracy in January, 1966, was followed in February by the demise of what many thought to be the continent's harshest authoritarian regime. Furthermore, recent events in Nigeria, Ghana, and elsewhere indicate that military regimes are as fragile as their civilian predecessors. Given the presence of almost every "gap" ever imagined by scholars concerned with development and modernization, and in the absence of the requisites most commonly posited for the maintenance of a political system, there is little place for countries such as these in the conceptual universe of political science. Yet, more often than not, these countries do persist. Hence, we have little choice but either to play an academic ostrich game or come to grips with their reality.

In order to deal in an orderly manner with such disorderly countries, we must alter our vision. Our normal focus on institutions and their concomitant processes resembles the focus of the untrained eye on the enclosed surface, or figure, of an image. The naive observer sees interstices as "shapeless parts of the underlying ground. He pays no attention to them, and finds it difficult and unnatural to do so."[2] Like trained painters, however, we must force ourselves to reverse the spontaneous figure-ground effect in order to perceive "interstices," shapes which initially do not appear worthy of our attention, but are in fact fundamental to our perception of the surface under observation. To understand political life in Africa, instead of viewing political disturbances as the shapeless ground surrounding institutions and processes which define the regimes of the new states, we must try to view them as characteristic processes which themselves constitute an important aspect of the regime in certain types of political systems.[3]

II. African Political Systems and Their Environment

On the whole, African countries are distinguished from other Third World clusters by extremely weak national centers, a periphery which consists of societies until recently self-contained, and levels of economic and social development approaching the lowest limits of international statistical distributions.[4] They continue to reflect the fact that their origins stem from a recent European scramble for portions of an international system or subsystem constituted by interacting tribal societies. Although the French, British, Belgian, Portuguese or German nets were sometimes cast over an area dominated by a single society or by a group of societies with similar characteristics, this was usually not the case at all. Within the administrative nets which later

[2] Rudolf Arnheim, *Art and Visual Perception: A Psychology of the Creative Eye* (Berkeley and Los Angeles: University of California Press, 1965), p. 230.

[3] Notions concerning the political system apparent in this paper are inspired by the works of David Easton, but clearly lack the intellectual rigor of *A Systems Analysis of Political Life* (New York: John Wiley and Sons, 1965).

[4] For the concepts used see Edward Shils, "Centre and Periphery," in *The Logic of Personal Knowledge—Essays in Honor of Michael Polanyi* (London: Routledge & Kegan Paul, 1961), pp. 117–130. See also note 42, below.

became states there were only a few decades ago a varying number of more or less disparate societies, each with a distinct political system, and with widely different intersocial relationships.

Although the new political units provided a territorial mold within which social, economic, political, and cultural changes that accompanied colonization occurred, we are becoming increasingly aware that these processes, although related, did not necessarily vary "rhythmically," i.e., at the same rate;[5] and that the rates of change varied not only between countries but also between regions of the same country. If we conceive the original African societies as sets of values, norms, and structures, it is evident that they survived to a significant extent everywhere, even where their existence was not legally recognized as in the most extreme cases of direct rule. Furthermore, the new set of values, norms, and structure, which constituted an incipient national center did not necessarily grow at the expense of the older ones, as if it were a constant-sum game in which the more a country becomes "modern" the less it remains "traditional." Although many individuals left the country for the new towns, they did not necessarily leave one society to enter a new one; instead, the behavior of a given individual tended to be governed by norms from both sets which defined his multiple roles and even mixed to define a particular role. Because the new center had nowhere expanded sufficiently at the time of independence, we cannot characterize what is contained within these countries today as a single society in the normally accepted sociological sense of the word, with its connotation of a relatively integrated system of values, norms, and structures. But since the new African states in reality do provide territorial containers for two sets of values, norms, and structures, the "new" and the "residual," with the latter itself usually subdivided into dis-

[5] See the discussion in C. S. Whitaker, Jr., "A Dysrhythmic Process of Political Change," *World Politics*, 19 (January, 1967), 190–217.

tinct sub-sets, it is useful to think of these sets as forming a particular type of *unintegrated* society which can be called "syncretic."[6]

The syncretic character of contemporary African societies tends to be reflected in every sphere of social activity, including the political. If we seek to identify their political systems by asking how values are authoritatively allocated within these societies, it is evident that in every case the most visible structures and institutions with which political scientists normally deal, such as executive and legislative bodies, political parties and groups, the apparatus of territorial administration, the judiciary, and even the institutions of local government provided by law, deal with only a portion of the total allocative activity, and that the remainder must therefore be allocated by other means, by other structures. This is fairly obvious where some functional division of labor between "modern" and "traditional" institutions was provided for initially as part of the constitutional settlement at the time of independence, but it is equally the case where traditional political structures have no recognized legal or political standing, or even where they have been formally abolished, as in Guinea or Mali.[7]

Without denying important variations in

[6] The problem with which I am dealing here is akin to that of the "plural society" conceptualized by M. G. Smith in *The Plural Society in the British West Indies* (Berkeley and Los Angeles: University of California Press, 1965). The word "syncretic" distinguishes the present societies from the "plural," which is a particular type involving super-ordination between components. I prefer it to the more passive "heterogeneous," because "syncretic" connotes that a process of amalgamation and integration is being attempted.

[7] For a further development of this point, see my book *Creating Political Order: The Party-States of West Africa* (Chicago: Rand McNally, 1966), Chapter V. My reasoning here is deductive; but empirical evidence from micro-political studies of Ghana by David Brokensha and Ernst Benjamin, of Mali by Nicholas Hopkins and of Tanzania by Henry Bienen, confirm the validity of the assumption.

the degree of institutionalization of national centers in different countries, it is suggested that from the present vantage point, even the most prominent variations in political arrangements at the time of independence must be viewed as superficial features of the political system since they were never firmly institutionalized. An examination of political parties, the best studied feature of the African scene, reveals such a wide gap between the organizational model from which the leaders derived their inspiration and their capacity to implement such schemes, that the very use by observers of the word "party" to characterize such structures involves a dangerous reification.

These comments may be extended to include constitutional arrangements, which in the absence of anchorage in supporting norms and institutions had little reality beyond their physical existence as a set of written symbols deposited in a government archive; about the civil service, in which the usual bureaucratic norms are so rare that it is perhaps better to speak of "government employees" as a categoric group; of "trade unions," which are more by way of congeries of urban employed and unemployed intermittently mobilized for a temporary purpose, such as a street demonstration; and even of "the Army," which far from being a model of hierarchical organization, tends to be an assemblage of armed men who may or may not obey their officers. It is generally evident that the operations of even the most "modern" institutions in Africa are governed by values and norms that stem from both the "new" and the "residual" sets.

The societal environment shared by all the new African states thus imposes severe limits upon the range within which significant variations of regimes can take place. Whether we define political integration in terms of the existence of a political formula which bridges the gap between the elite and the masses, or in terms of linkages between the values, norms, and structures that constitute the political system, it is clear that the level of political integration was, at the time of the founding, very low throughout Africa. Hence, although we can refer to the existence of "states" and "regimes" in Africa, we must be careful not to infer from these labels that their governments necessarily have authority over the entire country, any more than we can safely infer from the persistence of these countries as sovereign entities proof of the operations of endogenous factors such as a sense of community and the ability of authorities to enforce cohesion against people's will. Persistence may only reflect the initial inertia which keeps instruments of government inherited from the colonial period going, as well as the inertia of claimants which assures in most cases that all the problems will not reach the center simultaneously; it may reflect also the absence of effective external challenges and even to a certain extent the protection provided by the contemporary international system which more often than not guarantees the existence of even the weakest of sovereign states born out of the decolonization of tropical Africa.

Under these generally shared circumstances, it is not surprising that the founding fathers of most African states behaved very much in the same way in order to achieve the dual goal of modernizing as rapidly as possible while maintaining themselves in office. Like any other government, they had to cope with the problem of managing the flow of demands while at the same time eliciting sufficient support. They could obtain support in exchange for the satisfaction of demands (distribution); they could enhance support on the basis of the internalization by a sufficiently large proportion of the population of a belief in their right to rule (socialization, legitimacy); they could suppress demands by negative reinforcement, while at the same time punishing non-support (coercion and force). In the face of overwhelming problems stemming from the syncretic character of the society they relied increasingly on the latter techniques, thus contributing substantially to the escalation of political conflict.

Initially, the founding fathers of African states benefited from the sudden creation of a multitude of new political offices, from the departure of a number of colonial officials, from the expansion of administrative and state-directed economic activity which had begun during the latter years of welfare-state colonialism, as well as from a prevalent sense that they had earned the right to rule through their leadership of protest movements and that they were the legitimate successors of colonial officials. On these foundations, many were able to construct adequate political machines based primarily on the distribution of benefits to individual and group claimants, in the form of shifting coalitions appearing either as a "multiparty system," or more commonly, as a "unified" party. In the light of the politicians' inability to maintain themselves in office for very long (except in a very few cases) and of the lurid revelations of their corruption and ineptitude which made headlines after their downfall, it is easy to forget that many of them were initially quite successful in developing symbols and organizations which could be used to channel support and to establish the legitimacy of their claim to rule in the eyes of their countrymen. Beyond this, they also benefited from the sort of inertia already referred to, whereby those individuals who were aware of the existence of country-wide political institutions simply accepted them as a continuation of what they were already used to, the colonial order, but with a welcome populist flavor. The inheritance of instruments of force (police, gendarmerie, small armies), usually among the more professionalized bodies and often under the continued supervision of European officers, provided a certain backing in case the political process failed.

III. The Shift from Power to Force

The shift to a new phase of political activity is related to two sets of mutually reinforcing factors, stemming from the interaction of the rulers with the syncretic society in which they operated. First, there was a growing gap between the leaders' ideological aspirations and their capacity to implement the policies these aspirations entailed. Whether or not it is appropriate to speak of a "revolution of rising expectations" throughout the continent, there is little doubt that such a revolution has occurred among those responsible for government, in the form of a commitment to rapid modernization. The most obvious examples here are the "mobilizing" states, such as Ghana (until 1966), Mali, or Guinea, in which this commitment was defined in a very specific manner to include the transformation of the syncretic society into a homogeneous society by eliminating the "residual" set of values, norms, and structures and institutionalizing the new set according to ideological directives; the creation of an all-pervasive state apparatus, including both an all-encompassing mass party which could function as a controlling organization in the Leninist sense and as an aggregative organization, and an effective Africanized bureaucracy; and a planned economy geared to the achievement of very high increase in the rate of total output, as well as economic self-sufficiency in which the State plays the dominant role. Whether or not they espoused "socialism" in this form, most other African leaders shared these aspirations, albeit in some modified form. Since African countries are farther behind with respect to most of these goals than any other set of countries in the world, however, the result is that governments with the lowest load capability have assumed the heaviest burdens. But in the process of trying to raise the capability of their governments to achieve these goals, African rulers frittered away their small initial political capital of legitimacy, distributive capacity, inertia and coercion by investing it in non-essential undertakings, much as many of them did in the economic sector. A major source of the vulnerability of African regimes thus stems from adherence to self-imposed ideological directives.

Secondly, even if properly allocated this capital was seldom adequate to deal with political difficulties stemming from the very character of the syncretic society, the circumstances of decolonization, and the characteristics of the new institutions themselves. This was most obvious in the case of the Congo, where challenges stemming from every direction occurred simultaneously and most dramatically within a few weeks after independence. Although elsewhere the challenges have been less extreme and have usually been spaced over a few years, while the countervailing power and force at the disposal of the government was somewhat greater, their cumulative impact has not necessarily been much less severe. Everywhere, African governments have been faced with some or all of the consequences of the politicization of residual cleavages which occurred in the course of the rapid extension of political participation prior to independence; and of an inflationary spiral of demands stemming from the very groups whose support is most crucial for the operations of government. Since these processes are often discussed in the literature, only their major features will be noted here.

1. *The Politicization of Primordial Ties:*[8] Pre-existing distinctions between groups in Africa were usually supplemented by others stemming from the uneven impact of European-generated change. Often, by the time of independence, one tribe or group of tribes had become more urban, more educated, more Christian and richer than

[8] For a general treatment of this topic, see Clifford Geertz, "The Integrative Revolution," in Clifford Geertz (ed.), *Old Societies and New States* (New York: The Free Press of Glencoe, 1963) pp. 105–157. Although every serious monograph on African politics has also dealt with the subject, it is unfortunate that no effort has been made to refine for Africa the comparative analysis of the phenomenon along the lines suggested by Geertz.

others in the country. Hence, at the mass level, old and new cleavages tend to be consistent rather than cross-cutting; camps are clear-cut and individuals can engage wholeheartedly in the disputes that occur; almost any issue can precipitate a severe conflict; the history of conflict itself tends to make the next occurrence more severe; with few intervening layers of community organization, even localized conflicts rapidly reach the center. They tend to be particularly severe where there is an asymmetry between the old and the new stratification system within a single society or between complementary societies, as when for some reason serfs become more educated than their masters or when their greater number becomes a source of political power at the time universal suffrage is introduced.

At the level of the modernizing leadership, recruitment is usually uneven, but nevertheless open to a certain extent to the various groups in the country; common life-experiences insure a certain degree of solidarity which provides off-setting cross-cutting affiliations; and ethnic ties make an important contribution to national integration by preventing the formation of the sharp elite-mass gap that is common in peasant societies. But there is always a very great strain on the solidarity of the modernizing leadership because, regardless of their ideological orientation, political entrepreneurs who seek to establish or maintain a following must necessarily rely on primordial ties to distinguish between "us" and "them." When it appeared that the shape of the polity was being settled rapidly, perhaps once and for all, a multitude of groups began to press their legitimate claims for the protection of their way of life, for a redefinition of the relationship between their own peripheral society and the center, and for a more satisfactory distribution of benefits. Many latent disputes were revived and flowed into the new arena provided by central institutions. Hence it is not surprising that even in countries where one party seemed to be solidly established the leadership felt that their country was less integrated than ever before. Where several ethnic-regional movements vied for power, and especially where participation was extended very suddenly, the consequences of these cleavages and ensuing conflicts upon the center were even more disturbing.[9]

In general, almost any difference between two groups can become politically significant, even if from the point of view of the ethnographer the two groups belong to the same cultural classification. Although each of the oppositions tends to involve but a small proportion of the total population, because of the very nature of the groups involved, many permutations are possible and contagion can set in. Suitable institutional arrangements, such as various forms of territorial federalism, proportional or communal representation, and institutional quotas, are not easily designed in situations where primordial identities are as numerous and fluid as they are in most of the countries under consideration.

2. *The Inflation of Demands:* The second major source of challenge involves three crucial categories of individuals: civilian employees of government, men in uniform, and youths. Government employees, who include not only professional civil servants but also a large number of low-level, unskilled clerical personnel and manual workers employed in the operation of the governmental infrastructure (railways, harbors, road maintenance, and public works generally) usually constitute a very large proportion of those gainfully employed outside of agriculture. Promotions were initially rapid because of Africanization and the vast expansion of government agencies; many programs of economic development have had as their major consequence a reallocation of national revenue to the benefit of the managers, including both govern-

[9] I have attempted to deal with this question in *One-Party Government in the Ivory Coast* (Princeton: Princeton University Press, 1964), pp. 47, 77, 128–134.

ment employees and politicians; and government employees often constitute in terms of income and prestige the most privileged group in the society, after the politicians themselves. Yet, these same factors have contributed to a process of acute relative deprivation. Because of their very occupation and training, government employees have internalized to a greater extent than most others the style of life of their European predecessors; they feel that on the grounds of native ability and training they are qualified to rule rather than merely to execute policies; rapid promotions only lead to higher aspirations among those who have already been promoted and among those left behind, while the rate of governmental expansion tapers off soon after independence. During the colonial period, government employees who vented their grievances against their employer were "good nationalists"; as they continue to do so after independence, they are a "selfish privileged class." The deterioration in the relationship between government employees and the politicians is relatively independent of the ideological orientation of the regime itself: in most of French-speaking Africa, government employees are "leftists" in relation to whatever the government's orientation happens to be at a given time; but in Ghana, under Nkrumah, civil servants constituted a sort of "rightist" opposition to the regime. Since personnel expenditures constitute as much as two-thirds or more of the government's annual expenditures, any demands that require translation into resource allocation tend to create a major financial crisis.

The grievance orientation toward government extends also to those employed in the private sector, since even in countries that are not nominally "socialist," *étatisme* prevails; the private industrial or commercial sector is closely regulated since major firms usually operate on the basis of government guarantees concerning manpower costs. So much of the workers' real income takes the form of benefits rather than money wages

(family allocations, housing, etc.) that any sort of collective bargaining usually involves a modification of rules governing labor and leads to a showdown between the government and the unions. Finally, a similar process prevails among cash-crop farmers, for example, since marketing operations are managed or at least closely regulated by government. Demands in this sector are therefore necessarily and automatically "political," and governments are even viewed as responsible for controlling the fluctuations of world markets for tropical commodities, over which most of them have but a very limited leverage.

Men in uniform tend to act very much like other government employees. In the absence of institutionalized values and norms which transform men in uniform into a military establishment and a police force, officers and men are ruled by the norms that prevail among other groups; hence what has been said above applies to them as well. Furthermore, they rapidly find out that by virtue of their organizational characteristics and their control of certain instruments of force, they are indeed the best organized trade union in the country. As I shall point out below, this is not the only factor which has led the military to intervene in African politics; but it has helped set the mood for certain types of interventions and for the general relationship between the military and civilian politicians.[10]

As Lucian Pye has noted, "The non-Western political process is characterized

[10] The most useful recent surveys of African military establishments are presented in the publications of the Institute of Strategic Studies, London. See in particular, M. J. V. Bell, "Army and Nation in Sub-Saharan Africa," *Adelphi Papers*, No. 21 (August, 1965); and David Wood, "The Armed Forces of African States," *Adelphi Papers*, No. 27 (April, 1966). For an earlier essay, see James S. Coleman and Belmont Bryce, Jr., "The Role of the Military in Sub-Saharan Africa," in John J. Johnson (ed.), *The Role of the Military in Underdeveloped Countries* (Princeton: Princeton University Press, 1962), pp. 359–405.

by sharp differences in the political orientation of the generations," primarily because of a "lack of continuity in the circumstances under which people are recruited to politics."[11] In most African countries, it was easy for a particular age-cohort to move from relatively modest positions in the occupational structure to the highest positions in both the polity and the economy. Within a single decade, clerks and elementary school teachers became Presidents, cabinet ministers, members of party executives, directors of large trading establishments, etc. But for the next generations, whose expectations are based on the experience of their predecessors, conditions have fundamentally changed. First of all, the uppermost positions have already been filled by relatively young men who see no precise time limit to their tenure. Secondly, men with some education and occupational qualifications have rapidly become much less scarce because of the huge growth of secondary and higher education during the post-World War II decade. Thus, there has been a manifold increase in supply while the demand has abruptly decreased. The result is that newer generations face an insurmountable glut which frustrates their aspirations, with very few opportunities for movement into alternative spheres of activity.[12] Hence, the intergenerational gap within the political sphere can be noticed in almost every other institutional sphere, including especially the civil service and the military. It is exacerbated by the fact that the newer generations are usually in fact better trained and more highly qualified than their predecessors and hence have a very legitimate claim to take their place. To these discrepancies in recruitment must be added gaps in political socialization. In syncretic societies, the regime has very

little control over the major mechanisms of socialization, the family and the primary group, and only partially over the educational structure. There is little likelihood that new generations will have a set of attitudes compatible with the requirements of the new order. This is particularly important given two factors: the rapid growth of a large body of slightly educated, unemployed young urbanites; and the general shape of the demographic pyramid in which adolescents and young adults constitute a very large proportion of the total population. Intergenerational conflict is exacerbated by the fact that youthful discontent tends to be manifested not only by individual deviance from established norms, but also in the appearance of age-homogeneous movements and organizations, functional equivalents of the familiar youth gangs of industrialized societies, which tend to maintain a distinctive sub-culture and to act autonomously in the political sphere.[13] "Youth" is thus transformed from a mere categoric group into a movement.

In concluding this brief review of the consequences of the politicization of residual cleavages and of the inflationary spiral of demands voiced by crucial groups in the society it is important to note that the two processes are seldom insulated from each other. Government employees, soldiers, or young men in the towns are *also* members of ethnic groups; yet, these several affiliations do not constitute the sort of web of group affiliation characteristic of "pluralist" societies. Hence, the two processes reinforce each other to produce recurrent, serious, and complex conflicts, which easily penetrate into the political arena because of the weakness of aggregative structures. But even if they do not immediately result in an increase in demands or in a withdrawal of support, they constitute serious disturbances from the point of view of governments engaged in building a nation since by

[11] Lucian Pye, "The Non-Western Political Process," in H. Eckstein and D. Apter (eds.), *Comparative Politics* (New York: The Free Press of Glencoe, 1963), p. 660.

[12] On patterns of recruitment of new elites and their consequences see Rémi Clignet and Philip Foster, *The Fortunate Few* (Evanston: Northwestern University Press, 1966).

[13] Conditions under which the phenomenon occurs are specified by S. N. Eisenstadt, *From Generation to Generation* (Glencoe: The Free Press, 1956).

their very existence they provide evidence that this goal has not been achieved.

The added weight contributed by these processes to the burdens of government is relatively independent of the wisdom or devotion of particular political leaders, factors which will not be considered here. The difficulties of government in syncretic societies are so great, however, that the marginal consequences of human error, of weakness, and of sheer roguery—whose incidence among African politicians may be assumed to be about the same as among equivalent men elsewhere—are vastly magnified. For example, corruption among government officials, which probably did not interfere with the industrial take-off of European countries or the United States (and perhaps even facilitated it), can have very damaging consequences where it diverts a large proportion of very scarce, nonexpanding resources, away from the public domain into the pockets of a non-productive bureaucratic bourgeoisie. Impatience and arbitrary actions, which elsewhere may only lead to the discrediting of a public figure and to personal tragedy, can become sparks which ignite a major conflict.

Within a few years the two types of challenges discussed above strained the restricted distributive potential of the new governments and rapidly undermined the limited legitimacy of the founders. The center's weakness, hitherto hidden from sight, was unmercifully exposed, as when the value of the currency issued by a national banking system is drastically reduced when the credit pyramid, itself based on the productivity of the economy, collapses.[14]

[14] The analogy is drawn from Talcott Parsons, "Some Reflections on the Place of Force in Social Process," in Harry Eckstein (ed.), *Internal War* (New York: The Free Press of Glencoe, 1964), p. 59–64. A similar analysis is provided by Martin Kilson in *Political Change in a West African State: A Study of the Modernization Process in Sierra Leone* (Cambridge: Harvard University Press, 1966), with emphasis on the initial growth of "reciprocity" and the eventual inadequacy of this political technique.

In the new situation, demands are expressed more vociferously; depositors knock down the gatekeepers and seek to invade the vault. Parsons has suggested that the system's response can be twofold: "First, an increasingly stringent scale of priorities of what can and cannot be done will be set up; second, increasingly severe negative sanctions for non-compliance with collective decisions will be imposed."[15] Political power, normally based on the overall social structure, gives way to force.

Although no African rulers ever abandoned completely their reliance on the techniques of machine politics to maintain themselves in office, illustrations of a trend toward the use of force abound and constitute by now a monotonous recitation of unpleasant but familiar facts of African political life: intimidation, exile, detention, or assassination of political opponents; modification of the electoral system to make competition either impossible or at least very costly to those who attempt to engage in it; reduction of the independence of the judiciary or creation side-by-side with it of dependable political courts; redefinition of loyalty into unquestioning obedience and sycophancy; use of the military, of the police, and of political thugs to bulldoze dissidents into passivity, and passives into demonstrative supporters; creation of additional quasi-military or quasi-police bodies to offset the questionable loyalty of the existing ones. Although coups which result in changes of government have attracted the most attention, the most frequent coups in Africa have probably been those initiated by an incumbent government against threatening individuals or groups (real or alleged), and those launched by rulers or dominant factions against their associates.

Beyond its immediate unfortunate consequences for the individuals affected, the shift from power to force as a technique of government has serious long-term consequences for political life more generally in that it serves as the prelude to anti-govern-

[15] Parsons, *op. cit.*, p. 64.

ment coups and revolutions, in the following manner:

a. In the process of shifting from power to force, governments tend to become overconfident in their ability to reduce the disturbing flow of demands by dealing harshly with their source. They become afraid that any concession might be interpreted as weakness and open up a Pandora's box of claims. Hence, less change occurs altogether. Governments become less adept at discriminating among danger signals and tend to deal with even the smallest disturbances by expending a great deal of force.[16] But since the capital of force is small it becomes rapidly used up in relatively unnecessary undertakings, thus increasing the government's vulnerability to more serious threats.

b. When a shift from power to force occurs, it is accompanied by a change in the relative market value of existing structures. In the case of the new African states, the relative value of political parties and of civilian administrative agencies has undergone a sort of deflation, while the value of the police, of the military, and of *any* organization capable of exercising force, even by the sheer manipulation of large numbers of people in demonstrations and civil disobedience actions, has been vastly increased.

c. Although the shift to force represents an attempt to overcome deteriorating legitimacy and inadequate power, paradoxically it enhances the problem of the legitimacy of the rulers in the eyes of those to whom the implementation of force must necessarily be entrusted. As Parsons has indicated: "Most important, whatever the physical technology involved, a critical factor in socially effective force is always the social organization through which it is implemented. There is always some degree of

dependence on the loyalties of the relevant personnel to the elements of the social structure ostensibly controlling them."[17] Attempts to balance one instrument of force which is thought to be unreliable by creating another merely modifies the problem of control of force by political means, but does not eliminate it. In fact, resort to this technique may exacerbate the very problem it seeks to overcome by antagonizing individuals identified with the relevant institution.

d. When individuals and groups are deprived of the right and opportunity of exercising power to express their demands, they have no choice but to submit to force or use it themselves to express their demands. But when the government's capital of force is discovered to be limited, the latter alternative tends to be frequently chosen. Furthermore, since authority is personalized and the government is committed to a rigid course, specific demands tend to be translated into demands for a general change of rulers.

It is within the context of this interrelationship between governments who rely on force and the remainder of the society that the growing frequency of military and civilian coups, successful or unsuccessful; of mutinies, large-scale and prolonged urban strikes or rural disturbances; of near-civil wars, insurrections, and revolutionary-minded movements, must be understood.

IV. The Coup as a Political Institution[18]

The coup can be viewed as an institutionalized pattern of African politics on statisti-

---

[16] This proposition is related to Apter's suggestion that there is "an inverse relationship between information and coercion in a system." (David E. Apter, *The Politics of Modernization* [Chicago: University of Chicago Press, 1965], p. 40.)

[17] Parsons, *op. cit.*, p. 66.

[18] It is difficult to analyze the patterns of coups because it is impossible to identify the components of the universe with which one must deal. If incumbent rulers are to be believed, attempted coups against the government are extremely frequent in almost every African country; but what appear to be anti-government plots may in fact be only government-initiated purges. The present analysis is based exclusively on secondary sources. Unless otherwise specified, data are drawn from reports in *West Africa* (London), *Afrique Nouvelle* (Dakar), *Le*

cal grounds since in recent years it has become the modal form of governmental and regime change. More significantly, however, the coup is a normal consequence of the showdown between a government and its opponents who use force against each other in a situation where the force at the disposal of the government is very limited. This condition, which is met in most African countries, is most important because it distinguishes the conflict situation that tends to lead to a coup from others which tend to develop into some form of internal war as the result of extensive mobilization of support by both sides. In Africa, the government usually falls too soon for this to occur; there is some evidence that governments even prefer dissolving themselves to fighting. Coups determine who will rule, at least temporarily, but do not in themselves affect the fundamental character of the society or of its political system. The scope of the conflict is limited in relation to the society as a whole. Coups may be accompanied by some brutality but seldom entail more strategic forms of violence.

As of mid-1967, the set of new states of tropical Africa could be divided into two subsets of almost equal numbers: those which had experienced at least one change of central government personnel as the result of a coup, and those which had not. But almost all the units in the second subset had experienced some serious challenge; some had withstood it only through external intervention on behalf of the incumbents; and it appeared probable that the next coup, or the one after that, would be successful. As I suggested in the introduction, the incidence of coups appears to be independent of the quantitative or qualitative variables normally used to differenti-

ate among African states. Attempted or successful coups are always justified by the initiators, and often explained by observers, with reference to the corruption, ineffectiveness, and arbitrariness of the incumbents; but it is impossible to distinguish any significant threshold beyond which these faults and weaknesses become intolerable and it would probably be impossible to demonstrate that the regimes of countries in which successful coups have occurred were, as a group, more vulnerable to these criticisms than others. Whether or not a coup occurs in a given African country at a particular time is related to specific and circumstantial features of that country's current political and economic situation, rather than to any fundamental and lasting characteristics which differentiate that country from others on the continent. The most significant variable may well be the passing of time, a factor often neglected in studies of regime stability in the developing countries.[19] Except in the most extreme situations, coups are more likely to occur after a few years of independence than initially because it takes some time for a government to use up its initial political capital and for opponents to test the government's strength.

If the *incidence* of coups appears random, this is not true of the manner in wh'ch they develop. The atmosphere within which a coup is likely to occur can be created by almost any type of conflict situation, originating almost anywhere in the social structure, within the ruling elite or outside of it. But not every kind of showdown between the government and its opponents is equally likely to lead to the government's downfall. The government has to be physically threatened, which means that the initiators of the coup must be able to deploy force in the capital. Hence, successful coups usually

---

Monde, *Sélection Hebdomadaire* (Paris), *The Times* (London), *The New York Times*, *Jeune Afrique* (Tunis), *Africa Report* (Washington), and *Africa Digest* (London). A more detailed analysis of military interventions will appear in my contribution to Henry Bienen (ed.), *The Military Intervenes* (New York: Russell Sage, 1968).

[19] As for example in the hypothesis discussed by Samuel P. Huntington, "Political Development and Political Decay," *World Politics*, 17 (April, 1965), p. 427. His data are based on Fred R. von der Mehden, *Politics of the Developing Nations* (Englewood Cliffs, N.J.; Prentice-Hall, Inc , 1964), p. 65.

involve two bodies of manpower: trade unions and the formal bearers of force, the Army and the police (including of course such bodies as the gendarmerie, where one exists). But these two bodies are related in an asymmetrical fashion: the unions cannot bring about the downfall of the government without the support of the Army (active or passive), while the Army can carry out a successful coup without securing any alliances. In the final analysis, then, the role of the Army is determinative. As one African journalist has put it, "the Army has established itself as a no man's land between the elite and the masses."[20]

Given the small size and organizational weakness of the military establishments inherited by most countries from the colonial era, few students of African politics devoted much attention to its potential political role until it became manifest. Yet, James Coleman and Belmont Bryce, Jr. indicated in one of the first essays on the subject that the Congo crisis of 1960, in which an Army which had recently shown every sign of disaggregation was able to act as the arbiter between the President and the Prime Minister, demonstrated "the determinative influence which a small military force could exercise in a situation in which countervailing institutions of power groups are absent."[21] How small "small" can be is now clear in the light of the successful interventions by the Togolese Army of 250 men in 1963 and by the Central African Republic's Army of 600 men in 1966, each of which was the smallest military establishment on the continent at the time of its coup. Perhaps the only reason for the slight delay in the army's prominence was the fact that in some countries the uppermost levels of the army were not Africanized until several years after independence, while in others the presence of European garrisons or bilateral defense agreements provided some protection against the Afri-

can government's own military.[22] Even under these conditions, however, the determinative role of the military in political conflict should have been apparent to us much earlier: for example, the breakup of the Federation of Mali in 1960 involved initially a dispute between Senegal and Soudan over the appointment of the chief of the general staff, while the eventual showdown involved a clash between the pro-Senegalese gendarmerie (with the help of French Community officers) and troops under the command of the Soudanese Chief of Staff; the gendarmerie's action turned the tide in favor of Senegal.[23] In Senegal two and a half years later, President Senghor's control over a single batallion of airborne troops insured his victory over Prime Minister Mamadou Dia, who had initially deployed the gendarmerie (with some Army support) against the President's partisans.[24]

Relationships between civilian governments and the military have steadily deteriorated, in keeping with the processes discussed in the preceding section. In addition, the government's very reliance on the military as an instrument of force brought about a transformation of the military outlook as officers became intimately acquainted with the seamy side of political life and were able to form an accurate estimate of the government's authority. Initially, the military tended to intervene against obviously weak governments such as the Congo-Kinshasa, Togo, the Congo-Brassaville, or Dahomey; but later, even the strongest governments appeared to be much less formidable. Hence, there has been a steady escalation of the character of

---

[20] Justin Vieyra in *Jeune Afrique*, December 12, 1965.

[21] Coleman and Bryce, *op. cit.*, p. 399.

[22] The Congo crisis of 1960 reminds us, however, that African troops can launch mutinies against their European officers.

[23] William J. Foltz, *From French West Africa to the Mali Federation* (New Haven: Yale University Press, 1965), pp. 176–183.

[24] Victor Du Bois, "The Trial of Mamadou Dia," *American Universities Field Staff Report Service*, West Africa Series, VI, No. 6 (June, 1963), pp. 4–8.

military interventions. Initially they took the form of strike-mutinies (to secure better pay, the removal of unpopular officers, better pensions for veterans, or an expansion of the army) and referee actions (in the face of prolonged stalemate between contending politicians, or urban disorder resulting from strikes and demonstration). These early interventions usually led to the establishment of a compromise civilian government satisfactory to the military and to a return of the military to its barracks.[25] More recently, however, the military has tended to engage in comprehensive takeovers. Several of these have occurred after earlier referee actions failed to bring about the desired changes; in others, a coup which appeared to be initially intended as a referee action was gradually transformed into a full-scale takeover when attempts to bring about a reconciliation among civilian politicians failed; in the light of these experiences, military leaders have become even less hesitant to establish military rule from the very beginning.

The institutionalization of the coup as an important means of government change in Africa stems not only from the internal characteristics of each country but also from the phenomenon of contagion. When African states first became independent, they were still isolated from one another, except when they formed colonial groupings, such as British East or French West Africa; international physical, social, and political communications were almost nonexistent. Hence, during an initial period, disturbances in one country (Sudan, 1958; Congo-Kinshasa, 1960; Ethiopia, 1960) do not seem to have had any significant consequences for others, except when they occurred within one of the colonial groups

(as in former French-speaking Africa from mid-1962 to early 1964, and in former British East Africa in January, 1964). More recently, however, the countries of the continent have become much more of an interacting international sub-system as denoted not only by the formation of the Organization of African Unity and other formal groupings that cut across former colonial boundaries, but also by the growth of informal political ties among leaders and of intervention by one country in another country's politics. Within this new context, waves of coups are more likely to occur. Although it is very difficult to show direct connections between events in Algeria (June, 1965), the Congo-Kinshasa (October), and the other countries in which military interventions occurred during the four months that followed, the first two did set the precedent for an escalation from referee actions to takeovers. For West Africa as a region, the links are much more specific. The military leaders of the Central African Republic, of Upper Volta, and of Dahomey have known one another since they served their apprenticeship together in Indo-china; and although there is no evidence of concerted action, it is likely that for each of them the promotion of the group as a whole created new political aspirations. Beyond this, General Soglo has explained that his takeover in Dahomey was prompted by the fear that the elections scheduled for early 1966 might crystallize the North-South cleavage and result in disorder similar to that which prevailed among the Yoruba of neighboring Western Nigeria during recent elections, and about which Dahomeyans, many of whom are also Yoruba, were well informed.[26] Conversely, Soglo's success probably affirmed the resolution of Nigerian officers next door; their success in turn may have inspired their Ghanaian counterparts, with whom they share not only British professional traditions but also

[25] See, for example, the analysis of Dahomey and the Congo-Brazzaville in Emmanuel Terray, "Les révolutions congolaise et dahoméene de 1963: essai d'interpretation," *Revue Française de Science Politique*, 14 (October, 1964), 917–942. A more detailed account of the process of escalation is presented in my paper cited in note 18.

[26] Reported by Philippe Decraene in *Le Monde, Sélection Hebdomadaïre*, June 30–July 6, 1966.

exposure to the disastrous consequences of political disorder gained while serving in the Congo with ONUC.

Within one country also coups engender other coups. The success of one set of claimants encourages others to try. Even the establishment of military regimes does not lessen the probability of future civilian or military coups, since the very characteristics of African armies insure that the solidarity of their leadership, the control they have over their own organization, and their authority over the society at large, are not likely to be much greater than what they were in the government they replaced.[27]

V. Force as an Instrument of Major Political Change

Both the ins and the outs in Africa have also attempted to use force in order to achieve more fundamental changes including the modification of political communities, the alteration of important aspects of the stratification system, and the transformation of regimes (in Easton's sense of "regularized method for ordering political relationships"). These attempts may be initiated by the original founders, by new governments resulting from successful coups, or by alternative elites who seek to construct a competing system of authority while the government they oppose is still in place. Since these attempts usually involve the mobilization of extensive support, they tend to lead to an enlargement of the scope of conflict and may entail more strategic forms of violence. Except in a few specific situations discussed below, however, force fails to bring about major political change in Africa. In particular, political revolutions are unlikely to succeed because they entail prerequisites which are absent from the syncretic societies of contemporary Africa.

1. *The Modification of Political Communities:* Force is often invoked in Africa to bring about a redefinition of the territorial extent of the political community or of the internal relationship between some of its major components. Many countries contain regions that wish to secede, either to constitute an autonomous state or to join a neighbor. Such situations usually arise when one or more of the following features are present: an ethnic group which straddles two countries, one segment of which comes to believe that it is in the wrong country; territorially contiguous societies with asymmetrical status cultures, particularly in countries which straddle the borderline between Arabized Muslim and "Black" Africa; rich areas (with income based on mineral deposits or on an important export crop) which resent having their revenue reallocated on a national basis and are geographically in an eccentric position from the point of view of the larger unit.

The most prominent case is of course that of Katanga, where secession did occur and was accompanied by a clash of organized military bodies in the form of a small-scale war, because of the availability of non-Congolese instruments of force on both sides. By contrast, the breakup of the Federation of Mali did not involve strategic violence, but only a show of limited force by the two sides. Many other countries have experienced small-scale versions of this phenomenon: border tensions, involving armed incursions or attempted subversion, are common. Because of the nature of African armies and of the terrain (especially the absence of land communications suitable to military movement between countries with different colonial experiences), however, it is unlikely that these conflicts will lead to international wars; attempts to alter the territorial definition of political communities will either succeed without much violence, or will result in recurrent but minor irritations.[28]

[27] For a further discussion, see my paper, "Military Rule and Political Development in Tropical Africa," presented at the Conference on Armed Forces and Society sponsored by the World Association of Sociologists (London, September, 1967).

[28] Intra-national and international conflicts involving Ethiopia and the Sudan are major exceptions; they are not considered here because these two countries are peripheral to the universe of post-colonial tropical Africa with which I am particularly concerned.

Conflict over the relationship of one or more relatively integrated and distinct parts of the political community to the remainder stems most commonly from the sequels of indirect rule, as in Nigeria and in Uganda. The constitutional settlement achieved under British leadership and supervision as a condition of the grant of independence, which provided for a loose form of federation approaching confederacy for all Nigerian regions, and between Buganda and the rest of Uganda, represented merely a truce in a protracted conflict because it could not be anchored in congruent political norms and structures. Although there are many other unsettled issues in both countries, conflict over the role of the North in Nigeria and of Buganda in Uganda have dominated political life since independence, with power rapidly giving way to force as a means of settlement. In Nigeria, the North attempted to preserve its identity by controlling policy-making at the federal level as the indispensable major partner in successive coalitions. Force came to be used by all sides to insure favorable results in critical elections. The new situation led to a first military coup in January, 1966. When the new military government announced its intention of transforming the country into a unitary state—a decision which was interpreted in the Nigerian context as a fundamental change in the character of the political community—the North resorted to force (attacks upon southern residents of northern towns) to obtain concessions. In August, 1966, a new military coup put an end to unitary government before it had even begun to function. The sequels have involved an extension of inter-regional conflict, including the breakup of the Army into regional factions, and the sucession of the Eastern region in May, 1967, and subsequently a protracted civil war.

In Uganda, Buganda long resisted all attempts by the national government to obtain control of the police on Buganda territory, organized a para-military body of veterans to occupy contested territory (in the "Lost Counties" dispute), and used force to intimidate Baganda whose political loyalty was not assured. Whatever the reasons which led to the strange government-initiated coup of February, 1966, in the course of which Prime Minister Obote assumed full executive powers, his decision to eliminate the offices of President and Vice-President (held by the traditional rulers of Buganda and Busoga respectively), the purge of pro-Baganda elements from the national army, and the eventual proclamation of an entirely new constitution without consulting the federal units, clearly constituted the prelude to an attempt to alter the most important features of the political community by force. Force gave way to the strategic use of violence in the next phase of conflict; and although the Obote government successfully repressed the Buganda uprising of May 1963, it is unlikely that this constitutes the end of the affair.[29]

Although such clear-cut cases are relatively rare, there are numerous instances which involve similar sequels of quasi-indirect rule, as with the Mossi of Upper Volta or the Agni of the Ivory Coast. Related situations occur in countries that contain pastoral and/or nomadic societies which the colonial powers had been satisfied to contain rather than to rule, and for which the end of European presence represents an opportunity to return to a traditional way of life that includes internal feuding and raiding upon neighbors. These patterns of behavior not only involve violence in and of themselves, but often lead to violent clashes with the military and the police.[30] The conflict may be exacerbated by specific factors, as in Mali where the nomads are "white" while the new African government is "black," or by the nationalist ideology of the rulers of new states from whose vantage point successful containment alone is not a satisfactory solution.

[29] This account is based on the excellent analysis by M. Crawford Young, "The Obote Revolution," *Africa Report*, June 1966, 8–14.

[30] Manifestations of this process in Uganda are discussed by Colin Leys, "Violence in Africa," *Transition*, 5 (Fourth Quarter, 1965), 17–20.

2. *Stratification Change:* A few African countries deviate from the general pattern discussed in section (1) in that the territorial boundaries established by European colonizers coincided with the domain of a single unit whose stratification system included a clear-cut hierarchical organization of ethnic strata defined in relation to each other with a socially, economically, and politically dominant minority and a subordinate majority approaching the "plural society" discussed by M. G. Smith.[31] The introduction of the principle of legitimacy based on popular sovereignty and of opportunities to implement this principle by means of elections based on universal suffrage in such societies can have genuinely revolutionary consequences, as was the case in Rwanda and in Zanzibar.

In Rwanda, the pastoral Tutsi, who constituted approximately 15 percent of the population, ruled for four centuries over the agricultural Hutu linked to them by an inheritable client-patron "contract" through a highly centralized administration headed by their Mwami, backed by their specialized warrior caste, and based on a monopoly of all cattle and land.[32] Although both the Germans and the Belgians ruled indirectly, reserving educational opportunities and administrative posts almost exclusively for the Tutsi elite, changes began to occur after World War II when the Hutu engaged in the cultivation of a new major cash crop (Arabica coffee) and were encouraged to attend Catholic mission schools. Although political participation was slowly extended

[31] See Note 6, above.
[32] For background on Rwanda, see in particular Jacques Maquet and Marcel d'Hertefelt, "Elections en Société Feodale," *Académie royale des Sciences coloniales, Classe des Sciences Morales et Politiques*, XXI, Fasc. 2 (1959); and Jacques Maquet, *The Premise of Inequality in Ruanda* (London: Oxford University Press, 1961). For more recent events, I have relied on Aaron Segal, "Rwanda: The Underlying Causes," *Africa Report*, 9 (April, 1964), 3–8; and on an unpublished paper by Donald Attwood, graduate student in anthropology at the University of Chicago.

by means of indirect elections in 1953 and 1956, its effects were initially mediated by fears of Tutsi retaliation; nevertheless, Hutu-led political organizations began to emerge by the end of the period. In 1959, following the death of the ruling Mwami, Hutu leaders organized a popular uprising against the coming to power of an extremist Tutsi faction which advocated immediate independence in order to forestall further political and social reforms. Many Tutsi fled the country at this time, and again in the midst of the serious violence that accompanied the 1960 and 1961 elections in which the Hutu party won a decisive victory. The new government went beyond earlier reforms and destroyed the basis of the stratification system by abolishing the old contract relationship and redistributing cattle. A large number of Tutsi still in the country were slain when Tutsi exiles forcibly attempted to reenter Rwanda in 1963; there have been repeated cycles of violence since then.

As a political unit, Zanzibar is composed of the island of that name and of Pemba. On the island of Zanzibar, the stratification system involved consistent cleavages between an Arab minority, who owned most of the land and the revenue-bearing trees on it, and the Shirazi majority, island Africans who lived on the land on a squatter basis; there were also some mainland Africans with ties to Kenya and Tanganyika. Cleavages were less consistent on Pemba, where the Shirazi were economically less differentiated from the Arabs. The British governed the island indirectly through the traditional Arab rulers but extended participation in the usual manner toward the end of the colonial period. The growth of political organizations entailed a mobilization of the various communities accompanied by the expected exacerbation of cleavages and ensuing disturbances. In the elections preparatory to independence of June, 1963, the Afro-Shirazi party (with support among Zanzibar Shirazi and mainland Africans on both islands) won 63 percent of the votes on Zanzibar alone, and a 54 percent majority on both islands together; because of the system of single-member constituencies, however, it failed to obtain a majority of seats, and the government was organized by the ZNP (with support among the Pemba Shirazi and Arabs on both islands), together with the smaller ZPP. One month after independence, on January 21, 1964, insurgents broke into the police arsenal and armed themselves; the police offered minimal resistance, and the insurgents rapidly gained control of the island of Zanzibar. In the course of this coup and after a new Shirazi-dominant government was installed, large numbers of Arabs were slain, fled, or left under duress. Permanent change in the stratification system was thus brought about.[33]

In Zanzibar and in Rwanda, genuine revolutions were possible, with or without a coup, because the stratification system was defined by some central features which could be modified by force. But this is a rare situation in the new African states, found at the national level only in Burundi and sometimes in a particular ethnic group within a country (as in Nigeria and others that contain Fulani societies with serf-like clients or captives). The potential for drastic modifications of the stratification systems involving violence is thus present, but is unlikely to have the spectacular effects it had in Zanzibar or in Rwanda.[34]

3. *The Second Revolution:* Aside from the cases just discussed, there have been few attempts in tropical Africa to bring about rapid and profound changes in established political arrangements and in the underlying social structure by drastic means. The

few radical-minded regimes established at independence have tended to choose survival over revolutionary purity and have bowed to necessity by curtailing their goals. Most coups have resulted in military rule, and the main concerns of general-presidents are rule of law, honesty, efficiency, and financial responsibility. Their institutional models resemble those of dedicated European officials during the last phase of colonialism. Yet, many members of newer political generations and older radicals who were by-passed by machine politicians during the first go-around have begun to view the original founding and more recent changes as abortive beginnings. Like the thinkers who launched a wave of political messianism in mid-nineteenth century Europe, they believe that the true revolution is yet to come. The shape it might take has been analyzed by Frantz Fanon, who believed that it would be based upon the total mobilization of the youthful sub-proletariat of the growing cities and of the neglected rural masses.[35] Two situations so far seem to approximate what African revolutions might entail, the aftermath of the Congo-Brazzaville coup of 1963 and the Congo-Kinshasa (ex-Leopoldville) rebellions that began in 1964.

With 65 percent of the school-age population in schools at the time of independence and with one-fifth of its population in three cities, but without much economic development, the Congo-Brazzaville experienced very early and in an unusually acute form the consequences of growing cities peopled by semi-permanently unemployed youths. Opportunities for employment probably even declined absolutely when Brazzaville ceased to be the administrative capital of French Equatorial Africa. Political life had long reflected a sharp antagonism between the Mbochi of the North

[33] This account is based on Keith Kyle, "Coup in Zanzibar," *Africa Report,* 9 (February 1964), 18–20. See also Michael F. Lofchie, *Zanzibar: Background to Revolution* (Princeton: Princeton University Press, 1966).

[34] The political emancipation of Fulani "captives" probably contributed to the rise of the nationalist movements of Mali and Guinea in 1956–58.

[35] See *The Wretched of the Earth* (New York: Grove Press, 1965). For a more general discussion of Fanon's thought in the context of his life, see my article "Frantz Fanon: A Gospel for the Damned," *Encounter,* November, 1966.

and several related Bakongo groups, including the Lari (Balali), who had been a focal point for the activities of numerous religio-political protest movements such as Matswanism during the colonial era and provided basic support for the rise to power of a Catholic priest, Fulbert Youlou.[36] Having emerged as a strong man around 1960 after a period of coalition government, Youlou stepped up the construction of a one-party state in mid-1963 in the face of growing unrest stemming from unemployment, open corruption, ruthless elimination of opposition leaders, and his unabashed espousal of causes usually defined as "neo-colonialist." In the course of a confrontation between the government and trade unions in August, the Army, which only a few months earlier had been involved in a near-mutiny put down by the gendarmerie with the aid of French troops, shifted from support of the government to neutrality and eventually demanded Youlou's resignation. This time, French troops did not intervene and the government fell. A moderate provisional government, without direct Army or trade union participation, was immediately installed.

Except for the provision of a dual executive (President and Prime Minister), the other steps in constitutional reform and policy reorientation in the economic and international fields since 1963 have merely brought the country in line with African "radicals" such as Guinea or Mali; on the ethnic side, the Balali (Lari) have been replaced as the leading political group by other Bakongo tribes. The more significant feature of political change is the apparent accountability of the new authorities to the "street," represented by the *Jeunesse*. The lowering of the voting age from 21 to 18 immediately after the coup suggests that it

was among young adults, who probably constitute the bulk of the urban population, that the new leaders hoped to find much of their support or, alternatively, that they were already dependent upon them. Although the youth was formed into an ancillary wing of the *Mouvement National pour la Révolution*, it appears that it is the youth branch which is the most powerful part of the organization. The major manifestation of its political role are the activities of the "revolutionary militia" whose major weapon seems to be terror, including a political protection racket backed by the threat of violence and occasional assassinations. The *Jeunesse* as a whole was characterized in 1965 as a "curious mixture of revolutionary idealism and juvenile delinquency," which the government could barely control.[37] Although in the absence of additional information it is impossible to analyze the sociology of this movement, it seems that much of the ire of the *Jeunesse* and of the new regime more generally has been directed at Catholic trade union leaders (including those who had participated in the initial coup), youth leaders, schools, and at the Church more generally. This would suggest that a rejection mood, akin to that which activated earlier messianic movements, underlies contemporary political life. The regime's future remains uncertain. Discontent among the Balali followers of Youlou, the inability of the regime to solve fundamental problems of development and unemployment, factionalism among trade union leaders, have been reflected in sporadic antigovernment riots, plots, and changes of leadership at the top. In June, 1966, the Army reacted to the growing importance of quasi-military political organizations by staging a coup; although this one failed, the next one might well succeed.

The loosely connected movements usually referred to as the Congolese rebellion which originated in Kwilu, (near Leopold-

---

[36] For background on Brazzaville, see the several works of Georges Balandier and also Jean-Michel Wagret, *Histoire et Sociologie Politiques de la République de Congo (Brazzaville)* (Paris: Librarie Générale de Droit et de Jurisprudence, 1963). For an analysis of the 1963 coup, see Terray (note 25 above).

[37] *Jeune Afrique*, August 8, 1965. There is some evidence that similar youth groups helped bring Youlou to prominence in 1956 (Wagret, *op. cit.*, p. 65).

ville) and in Maniema (Eastern Congo) in 1964 can all be attributed to general factors which are not unique to the Congo, but are exacerbated by the special Congolese situation.[38] They must be distinguished from dissidence elsewhere in Africa, however, not only by their scope and the massive violence engendered, or by their international implications and long-term consequences for the areas involved, but also by their clearly rural rather than urban character. The case of Kwilu is particularly interesting in the present context because of the special ideological meaning it was given by its leaders and the basis on which it was organized. As one study puts it, the Kwilu rebellion emerges as "a revolutionary attempt to correct some of the abuses and injustices by which large segments of the population of the region felt oppressed four years after official Independence and an effort to try once again to express and to concretely realize the goals and dreams promised by the 'First Independence of 1960'."[39]

Kwilu, a densely populated area inhabited by several different ethnic groups whose traditional political organization does not extend much beyond the village level, and whose adult males work mostly as palm cutters on European-owned plantations, had a history of rebellion against

the *Force Publique* (1931) and of religio-political protest movements throughout the colonial period. When political participation was extended in 1959, A. Gizenga, P. Mulele, and C. Kamitatu, representing different tribes, organized the *Parti Socialiste Africain* (PSA) whose socialism took the form of a "village paradise-on-earth." It was allied at the national level with the Lumumba coalition. After the Congo crisis of 1960, the *PSA* itself splintered; Gizenga, connected with the Stanleyville government of 1960–61, became the "imprisoned martyr"; Mulele left the country and spent some time in Communist China; while the more "moderate" Kamitatu faction obtained control of the regional government when Kwilu became a province in 1962.

The growing discontent throughout the region in 1962–63, manifested by palm-cutter strikes and a resurgence of messianic cults, was channeled into an organized movement by Mulele upon his return in mid-1963. He established forest camps in which *équipes*, led by a President and a *Commissaire Politique*, and accompanied by a *soigneur* (healer—usually a practitioner of traditional magic and medicine), were trained in guerilla warfare. The *équipes* formed the *maquis;* above them were the *directions* ultimately responsible to the *centrale*. Mulele also provided the movement with a rudimentary ideology which defined what was wrong, diagnosed causes, and indicated remedies. Within this framework, the culprits are the "Congolese colonialists" or *retardataires* who presently man government at all levels. The remainder of the society is divided into *avancés* (Mulele partisans) and *réactionnaires* (moderates, fence-sitters). The goal is to achieve a new society "conceived as a gigantic village made up of thousands of small villages in which the people find their own authenticity; all that they need materially; justice, creativity, and happiness in working the soil together."[40] In order to achieve it, the *avancés* must destroy the *retardataires* and

---

[38] Succinct and well-balanced analyses of the Congolese Rebellion can be found in Marvin D. Markowitz and Herbert F. Weiss, "Rebellion in the Congo," *Current History*, April 1965, 213–218; and M. Crawford Young, "The Congo Rebellion," *Africa Report*, 9 (April 1965), 6–11. The present discussion of the Kwilu case is based on Renée C. Fox, Will de Craemer, and Jean-Marie Ribeaucourt, " 'The Second Independence'; a Case Study of the Kwilu Rebellion in the Congo," *Comparative Studies in Society and History*, 8 (October 1965), 78–105. The most comprehensive source of information on these rebellions is Benoit Verhaegen, *Rébellions au Congo*, Vol. I ("Les Etudes du C.R.I.S.P." Leopoldville and Brussels, 1966). This work, as well as Herbert Weiss, *Political Protest in the Congo* (Princeton: Princeton University Press, 1967), became available too late to be fully consulted.

[39] Fox *et al*, p. 78.

[40] *Ibid.*, p. 97.

persuade the *réactionnaires*. They are bound to triumph if they obey their leaders and adhere to prescribed norms, including certain taboos, such as the prohibition against speaking French, which guarantee their invulnerability.

Support for the movement was generally drawn from Mulele's and Gizenga's own ethnic groups, the BaMbunda and the BaPende; it attracted much of the *jeunesse*, especially teachers and clerks who hoped to be rapidly promoted in the bureaucracy of the new state; ex-policemen dismissed because of a pay mutiny; and a variety of chiefs and lineage and age segments involved in local conflicts. The initial attacks of January, 1964, were planned, systematic, and well-controlled; they were aimed at religious, industrial, governmental, and educational establishments, but spared those considered friendly to the rebels (such as the mission schools which the leaders had attended). In the absence of outside communications, Mulele was able to persuade much of the local population that the revolution had already been victorious elsewhere; hence, in much of the area, after the initial uprising life tended to go back to normal within the framework of the "new society." Only later, after Europeans had been evacuated and the undisciplined Congolese Army advanced into the region did full-scale, indiscriminate *terre brulée* violence occur. Although the Congolese Army was able to contain the Kwilu area as early as April, 1964, they still clashed with rebels at the beginning of 1966, and their present control over the area remains tenuous.

It is likely that growing tensions and the availability of dissident leaders will contribute to the emergence of similar movements elsewhere, that the activities of these movements will generate large-scale violence, and that participation in them will genuinely lift the spirits of those involved. But even if we combine Brazzaville and Kwilu, it is unlikely that movements such as these will be able to translate their revolutionary aspirations into the institutionali-zation of a new regime and of new social structures. African society does not have a center; its syncretic character insures that it cannot be turned upside down, or that if an attempt is made to do so, some groups will shift their relative positions but the society as a whole will remain very much as it was before. If the revolutionaries succeed in obtaining control of the government, they will resemble at best the radical-minded regimes created in the course of the "first revolution." If they do not succeed, however, they might give rise to a "vendetta morality" or become full-scale withdrawal movements which consume themselves in senseless violence.[41] In the final analysis, it is unlikely that even the most glorious dedication to force can broaden the limits of the range of variation imposed on political arrangements by contemporary African society.

VI. Conclusions

Seeking to overcome the parochialism of area studies and the intellectual irrelevance of raw empiricism, many scholars dealing with the politics of new states have hit upon the device of bringing the foreground of the contemporary scene into sharp focus, extracting it from context, and blowing up the recorded image for leisurely contemplation. The background tends to be reduced to an indistinct blur called "tradition," which is discarded because it yields little interesting information. But vastly blown-up stills of political development, modernization, or integration obtained in this manner tend to make these processes appear similar regardless of what is being developed, modernized, or integrated. One wonders, however, whether the similarities genuinely stem from the phenomena observed or whether they are artifacts arising from the manipulation of the recorded images; whether the information on which many current generalizations are based pertains to the reality

[41] For similar outcomes elsewhere see, for example, E. J. Hobsbawn, *Primitive Rebels* (New York: W. W. Norton & Co., Inc., 1965).

the image sought to capture, or whether it pertains mainly to the characteristics of the lens and of the film used to record it.

Surely, as we begin to explore an unknown world, we must master the techniques of *cinéma-vérité*, using hand-held cameras that are a more direct extension of the observer's eye, suitable for obtaining intimate moving pictures of the varying patterns subsumed under the terms political development, modernization or integration. Understanding of these processes will be achieved, not by reducing them prematurely to a common denominator, but by seeking to preserve their singularity and then comparing their manifestations in different settings. The characteristics of political life in all the new states can easily be subsumed under relatively few general headings. However useful such efforts may be in clearing the ground, however, we must remember that the same headings will refer to very different things where, for example, national communities are being carved out of a more universal one and the stratification system is defined by an opposition between urban elites that control land and peasant masses, as against situations where many small societies devoid of this sharp differentiation are being amalgamated into arbitrarily defined larger wholes under the aegis of an open stratum of recently educated men drawn more or less evenly from the component societies that constitute the country.

The situation in most of tropical Africa is so extreme that studies focused primarily on incipient central institutions almost necessarily exaggerate their importance in relation to the society as a whole.[42] Hence, I have tried in this essay to provide some balance by considering politics in the more general context of African societies and by focusing on conflict as a major element of political life. This is not to say that no institutionalization is taking place, but rather that until such processes reach a certain level—as yet unspecified—force and violence are likely to remain salient features of political action.[43] Since various factors insure the persistence of most of the new territorial units even if political institutionalization does not occur at a very high rate, we must make a place for conflict in our conceptual apparatus. Although the incidence of certain manifestations of conflict may be relatively random, political conflict is not a random process but derives a discernible structure from the characteristics of the society itself, as do other patterns of political life. Much more precision can be achieved than in this essay by operationalizing independent and dependent variables in a manner to obtain elements from which a comparative typology can be constructed.

From this point of view, it is clear that a small number of countries, e.g., the Ivory Coast and Ghana, stand out from the rest of the pack and are on the verge of reaching a threshold of societal development which may be labeled "incipient modernity." These are exceptional in the contemporary African scene, and are likely to become even more exceptional in the predictable future as the spillover effects of incipient modernization become infused into every sphere of social life, including the political. At the other extreme, there is a fairly large group of countries, such as the Central African Republic or Upper Volta, which are among

---

[42] For example, the most recently compiled *Selected Economic Data for Less Developed Countries*, published by the Agency for International Development in June, 1967 (data for 1965 and 1966), shows that Africa (not including the United Arab Republic and the Union of South Africa) is the lowest ranking of four areas (Africa, East Asia, Latin America, Near East–South Asia) on total GNP, Annual Growth of GNP, electric power per capita, life expectancy,

people per physician, literacy, pupils as percent of population. It was tied with one other area for bottom place on several other indicators, and ranked relatively high only on acres of agricultural land available per capita.

[43] An approach to the study of institutionalization and integration is suggested in my paper, "Patterns of Integrations," in *The Journal of Modern African Studies* (forthcoming, 1968).

the least developed countries in the entire world. Unfortunately, they are likely to remain at the bottom for a long time, since it has become increasingly evident that the die was cast several decades ago in the sense that wherever there was *some* potential for relatively rapid modernization, it was brought out during the colonial period. In between are countries with some potential but with a complex of problems which has so far prevented it from emerging. Some of these will join the first group, while the others will, unfortunately, join the second. It is not necessary to view politics as merely epiphenomenal to suggest that the general characteristics of the social structure, and especially the nature of primordial solidarities combined with gross differences in degree of modernization, impose limits within which variations of regime can occur.

Although the relationship between political conflict and political development has not been explicitly examined in this essay, this does not imply that I view the functions of conflict in a society as wholly negative. Integration into a free society does not entail the total elimination of conflict from political life, but rather its containment within acceptable limits as indicated by a shift from force to power and authority.[44] How that is achieved remains a central problem of the social sciences which far transcends the parochial concerns of particular disciplines or of sub-fields within each. One thing is clear, however: Progress in this direction requires an acceptance of the premise itself—the institutionalization at the cultural level of a belief that conflict is a potentially manageable aspect of society, rather than the persistence of wishful thinking about its permanent disappearance expressed in the form of ideologies or scientific theories.

[44] This view is inspired by Ralf Dahrendorf, *Class and Class Conflict in Industrial Society* (Stanford: Stanford University Press, 1959), especially p. 318. See also my general argument in *Creating Political Order: The Party-State of West Africa* (Chicago: Rand McNally, 1966).

Chapter 16

The Politics of Integration

POLITICAL INTEGRATION AND POLITICAL DEVELOPMENT*

Myron Weiner

It is often said of the developing nations that they are "unintegrated" and that their central problem, often more pressing than that of economic development, is the achievement of "integration." The term "integration" is now widely used to cover an extraordinarily large range of political phenomena. It is the purpose of this article to analyze the various uses of this

SOURCE. Myron Weiner, "Political Integration and Political Development," *The Annals of the American Academy of Political and Social Science*, **358**, 52–64, March 1965.

* This article is a preliminary version of a portion of a study I am preparing for the Social Science Research Council Committee on Comparative Politics. The final and full version will be published in a volume entitled *The Political System and Political Development*. I want to take this opportunity to express my appreciation to the Committee for granting me permission to publish this version at this time, and to express my intellectual appreciation to my four collaborators in this study—Lucian Pye, Leonard Binder, Joseph LaPalombara and James S. Coleman, not only for their comments on this manuscript and for the many ideas of theirs which found their way into these pages, but for the intellectual excitement of the entire venture. Needless to say, I alone am responsible for any errors and follies which this essay contains.

term, to show how they are related, then to suggest some of the alternative strategies pursued by governments to cope with each of these "integration" problems.

Definitions

1. Integration may refer to the process of bringing together culturally and socially discrete groups into a single territorial unit and the establishment of a national identity. When used in this sense "integration" generally presumes the existence of an ethnically plural society in which each group is characterized by its own language or other self-conscious cultural qualities, but the problem may also exist in a political system which is made up of once distinct independent political units with which people identified. National integration thus refers specifically to the problem of creating a sense of territorial nationality which overshadows—or eliminates—subordinate parochial loyalties.[1]

[1] This is perhaps the most common use of the term. For a precise view of the many attempts to define "nationality," see Rupert Emerson, *From Empire to Empire* (Boston: Beacon Press, 1960), especially Part 2: "The Anatomy of the Nation." K. H. Silvert, the editor of a collection of studies of nation-

643

2. Integration is often used in the related sense to refer to the problem of establishing national central authority over subordinate political units or regions which may or may not coincide with distinct cultural or social groups. While the term "national integration" is concerned with the subjective feelings which individuals belonging to different social groups or historically distinct political units have toward the nation, "territorial integration" refers to the objective control which central authority has over the entire territory under its claimed jurisdiction.[2]

3. The term "integration" is often used to refer to the problem of linking government with the governed. Implied in this usage is the familiar notion of a "gap" between the elite and the mass, characterized by marked differences in aspirations and values.[3] The "gap" may

[*footnote 1 continued*
alism prepared by the American Universities Field Staff, *Expectant Peoples: Nationalism and Development* (New York: Random House, 1963), suggests as a working definition of nationalism "the acceptance of the state as the impersonal and ultimate arbiter of human affairs" (p. 19). See also Karl W. Deutsch, *Nationalism and Social Communication* (New York: John Wiley and Sons, 1953) and Karl W. Deutsch and William J. Foltz (eds.), *Nation-Building* (New York: Atherton Press, 1963).
[2] For a discussion of some of the problems of territorial control in Africa see James S. Coleman, "Problems of Political Integration in Emergent Africa," *Western Political Quarterly* (March 1955), pp. 844–857.
[3] For an explanation of this use of the term integration in the literature see Leonard Binder, "National Integration and Political Development," *American Political Science Review* (September 1964), pp. 622–631. Elite-mass integration is also one of the usages in James S. Coleman and Carl G. Rosberg (eds.), *Political Parties and National Integration in Africa* (Berkeley: University of California, 1964). They use integration in two senses: "(1) political integration, which refers to the progressive bridging of the elite-mass gap on the vertical plane in the course of developing an integrated political process and a participant political community, and (2) territorial integration, which refers to the progressive reduction of cultural and regional tensions

be widest in society with a passive population and modernizing elite, but a relatively stable if frustrating relationship may exist. More often the masses are beginning to become organized and concerned with exercising influence, while the elite responds with attempts to coerce, persuade, or control the masses. It is under these conditions of conflict and often internal war that we customarily speak of "disintegration."

4. Integration is sometimes used to refer to the minimum value consensus necessary to maintain a social order. These may be end values concerning justice and equity, the desirability of economic development as a goal, the sharing of a common history, heroes, and symbols, and, in general, an agreement as to what constitutes desirable and undesirable social ends. Or the values may center on means, that is, on the instrumentalities and procedures for the achievement of goals and for resolving conflicts. Here the concern is with legal norms, with the legitimacy of the constitutional framework and the procedures by which it should operate—in short, on desirable and undesirable conduct.

5. Finally, we may speak of "integrative behavior," referring to the capacity of people in a society to organize for some common purposes. At the most elementary level all societies have the capacity to create some kind of kinship organization—a device whereby societies propagate themselves and care for and socialize their young. As other needs and desires arise within a society we may ask whether the capacity grows to create new organizations to carry out new purposes. In some societies the capacity to organize is limited to a small elite and is only associated with those

and discontinuities on the horizontal plane in the process of creating a homogeneous territorial political community" (p. 9). These two definitions correspond with our first and third definitions.

who have authority.[4] Only the state, therefore, has a capacity to expand for the carrying out of new functions. In still other societies organizational capacities are more evenly spread throughout the population, and individuals without coercive authority have the readiness to organize with others. Societies differ, therefore, in the extent to which organizational proclivities are pervasive or not, and whether organizations are simply expressive in character—that is, confined to kinship and status—or purposive.

The term "integration" thus covers a vast range of human relationships and attitudes—the integration of diverse and discrete cultural loyalties and the development of a sense of nationality; the integration of political units into a common territorial framework with a government which can exercise authority; the integration of the rulers and the ruled; the integration of the citizen into a common political process; and, finally, the integration of individuals into organizations for purposive activities. As diverse as these definitions are, they are united by a common thread. These are all attempts to define what it is *which holds a society and a political system together*. Scholars of the developing areas have groped for some such notions of integration, for they recognize that in one or more of these senses the political systems they are studying do not appear to hold together *at a level commensurate with what their political leadership needs to carry out their goals*. If each scholar has in his mind a different notion of "integration," it is often because he is generalizing from one or more specific societies with which he is familiar and which is facing some kind of "integration" problem.

[4] For an analysis of the attitudes which inhibit organized activity see Edward Banfield, *The Moral Basis of a Backward Society* (Glencoe, Ill.: Free Press, 1958). Though Banfield's study is confined to a single village in Italy, he raises the general problem of analyzing the capacities of a people to organize for common purposes.

Since there are many ways in which systems may fall apart, there are as many ways of defining "integration."

To avoid further confusion we shall use a qualifying adjective hereafter when we speak of one kind of integration problem. We shall thus speak of national integration, territorial integration, value integration, elite-mass integration, and integrative behavior and use the term integration alone when we are referring to the generalized problem of holding a system together.

Forms and Strategies

Transitional or developing political systems are generally less integrated than either traditional or modern systems. This is because these systems cannot readily perform the functions which the national leadership—or in some instances, the populace too—expects them to perform. In other words, as the functions of a system expand—or the political leadership aspires to expand the functions of the system—a new level of integration is required. When we speak of political development, therefore, we are concerned first with the expanding functions of the political system, secondly with the new level of integration thereby required to carry out these functions, and, finally, with the capacity of the political system to cope with these new problems of integration. It is necessary, therefore, that we now take a more concrete look at the kinds of expanding functions which occur in the course of political development, the specific integrative problems which these pose, and the public policy choices available to governmental elites for coping with each of these integrative problems.

NATIONAL INTEGRATION

It is useful to ask why it is that new nations with pluralistic social orders require more national integration than did the colonial regimes which preceded them. The obvious answer is that colonial governments were not concerned with national loyalties but with creating classes who would be loyal to them as a colonial power. Colonial governments, therefore, paid little or no attention to the teaching of a "national" language or culture, but stressed instead the teaching of the colonial language and culture. We are all familiar with the fact that educated Vietnamese, Indonesians, Nigerians, Indians, and Algerians were educated in French, English, and Dutch rather than in their own languages and traditions. Although the colonialist viewed the development of national loyalties as a threat to his political authority, the new leadership views it as essential to its own maintenance. Moreover, since the colonial rulers permitted only limited participation, the parochial sentiments of local people rarely entered into the making of any significant decisions of essential interest to policy makers. Once the new nations permit a greater measure of public participation, then the integration requirements of the system are higher. Moreover, the new elite in the new nations have higher standards of national integration than those of their former colonial rulers and this, too, creates new integration problems.

So long, for example, as export-import duties were imposed by a colonial ruler whose primary concern was with the impact of commercial policies upon their trade and commerce, then no questions of national integration were involved. Once these areas of policy are in the hands of a national regime, then issues immediately arise as to which sections of the country—and therefore which communities—are to be affected adversely or in a beneficial fashion by trade policies. Once educational policy is determined by national rather than colonial needs, the issues of language policy, location of educational facilities, the levels of educational investment, and the question of who bears the costs of education all affect the relations of culturally discrete groups. Finally, once the state takes on new invest-

ment responsibilities—whether for roads and post offices or for steel mills and power dams—questions of equity are posed by the regions, tribes, and linguistic groups which make up plural societies. Even if the assent of constituent groups is not necessary for the making of such decisions—that is, if an authoritarian framework is maintained —at least acquiescence is called for.

How nations have handled the problems of national integration is a matter of historical record. Clifford Geertz[5] has pointed out that public policy in the first instance is effected by patterns of social organization in plural societies. These patterns include (1) countries in which a single group is dominant in numbers and authority and there are one or more minority groups; (2) countries in which a single group is dominant in authority but not numbers; (3) countries in which no single group by itself commands a majority nor is a single group politically dominant; and (4) countries of any combination in which one or more minorities cut across international boundaries. Examples of the first group are prewar Poland (68 per cent Polish), contemporary Ceylon (70 per cent Sinhalese), and Indonesia (53 per cent Javanese). The dominant minority case is best exemplified by South Africa (21 per cent "white"). The best examples of complete pluralism with no majorities are India, Nigeria, and Malaya and, in Europe, Yugoslavia and Czechoslovakia. And finally, among the minorities which cross international boundaries, the most troublesome politically have been the Kurds, the Macedonians, the Basques, the Armenians, and the Pathans. In contemporary Africa, there are dozens of tribes which are cut by international boundaries, and in Southeast Asia there are substantial Chinese and Indian minorities.

[5] See Clifford Geertz, "The Integrative Revolution: Primordial Sentiment and Civil Politics in the New States," *Old Societies and New Nations*, ed., Clifford Geertz (New York: Free Press of Glencoe, 1963).

In general there are two public policy strategies for the achievement of national integration: (1) the elimination of the distinctive cultural traits of minority communities into some kind of "national" culture, usually that of the dominant cultural group—a policy generally referred to as assimilationist: "Americanization," "Burmanization," "detribalization;" (2) the establishment of national loyalties without eliminating subordinate cultures—the policy of "unity in diversity," politically characterized by "ethnic arithmetic." In practice, of course, political systems rarely follow either policy in an unqualified manner but pursue policies on a spectrum somewhere in between, often simultaneously pursuing elements from both strategies.

The history of ethnic minorities in national states is full of tragedy. If today the future of the Watusi in East Africa, the Hindus in East Pakistan, the Turks in Cyprus and the Greeks in Turkey, and Indians in Burma and Ceylon is uncertain, let us recall the fate of minorities in the heterogeneous areas of East Europe. Poland in 1921 had minorities totalling 32 per cent of the population. Since then 2.5 million Polish Jews have been killed or left the country and over 9 million Germans have been repatriated. Border shifts and population exchanges have also removed Ruthenian, white Russian, and Lithuanian minorities, so that today only 2 per cent of the population of Poland belongs to ethnic minorities. Similarly, the Turkish minority in Bulgaria was considerably reduced at the end of the Second World War when 250,000 Turks were forced to emigrate to Turkey in 1950, and three million Germans and 200,000 Hungarians have been repatriated from Czechoslovakia since the war. Killings, the transfers of populations, and territorial changes have made most Eastern European countries more homogeneous today than they were at the beginning of the Second World War. Yugoslavia and Czechoslovakia are the only remaining East European countries which lack a single numerically dominant ethnic group.[6]

It is sad to recount an unpleasant historical fact—that few countries have successfully separated political loyalties from cultural loyalties. The dominant social groups have looked with suspicion upon the loyalty of those who are culturally different—generally, though not always (but here, too, we have self-fulfilling prophecies at work) with good reason. Where killings, population transfers, or territorial changes have not occurred, the typical pattern has been to absorb the ethnic minority into the dominant culture or to create a new amalgam culture. Where cultural and racial differences continue in Europe or the United States, they are generally accompanied by political tensions. No wonder that so many leaders of the new nations look upon assimilation and homogenization as desirable and that strong political movements press for population transfers in Cyprus, India, and Pakistan, and are likely to grow in importance in sub-Sahara Africa. It remains to be seen whether the ideal of unity and diversity, that is, *political* unity and *cultural* diversity, can be the foundation for modern states. Perhaps the most promising prospects are those in which no single ethnic group dominates—Nigeria, India, and Malaysia. The factors at work in prewar Eastern Europe seem tragically in the process of being duplicated in many of the developing nations: the drive by minorities for ethnic determination, the unsuccessful effort by newly established states to establish their own economic and political viability, the inability of states to establish integration without obliterating cultures—and often peoples— through assimilation, population transfers or genocide, and, finally, the efforts of larger more powerful states to establish control or absorb unintegrated, fragile political systems.

[6] These figures are taken from Lewis M. Alexander, *World Political Patterns* (Chicago: Rand McNally), pp. 277–325.

TERRITORIAL INTEGRATION

The associations of states with fixed territories is a relatively modern phenomenon. The fluctuating "boundaries" of historic empires, and the fuzziness at the peripheries where kinship ties and tributary arrangements marked the end of a state are no longer acceptable arrangements in a world where sovereignty is characterized by an exclusive control over territory. In time the control over territory may be accompanied by a feeling of common nationality—our "national integration," but there must first of all be territorial integration. For most new states —and historic ones as well—the establishment of a territory precedes the establishment of subjective loyalties. A Congo nation cannot be achieved, obviously, without there being a Congo state, and the first order of business in the Congo has been the establishment by the central government of its authority over constituent territorial units. Some scholars have distinguished between the state and the nation, the former referring to the existence of central authority with the capacity to control a given territory and the latter to the extent of subjective loyalty on the part of the population within that territory to the state. There are, of course, instances where the "nation" in this sense precedes the "state"—as in the case of Israel and, according to some, Pakistan—but more typically the "state" precedes the "nation." "Nation-building," to use the increasingly popular phrase, thus presumes the prior existence of a state in control of a specified —and, in most instances, internationally recognized—territory. Territorial integration is thus related to the problem of *state-building* as distinct from *nation-building*.

Colonial rulers did not always establish central authority over the entire territory under their *de jure* control. The filling of the gap between *de jure* and *de facto* control has, in most instances, been left to the new regimes which took power after independence.

Thus, the areas under *indirect* control by colonial authorities have been placed under the *direct* control of the new governments—in India, Pakistan, Malaya, and in many areas of Africa. This process has been accomplished with relatively little bloodshed and international disturbance— although the dispute over Kashmir is an important exception—largely because the colonial regimes denied these quasi-independent pockets of authority the right to create their own armies.

The more serious problem of territorial integration has been the efforts of the new regimes to take control over border areas which were, in effect, unadministered by the colonial governments. Since both sides of a boundary were often governed by the same colonial power—as in French West Africa—or by a weak independent power—as in the Indian-Tibetan and Indian-Chinese borders—the colonial government often made no effort to establish *de facto* authority. Moreover, some of these areas are often occupied by recalcitrant tribes who forcefully resisted efforts toward their incorporation in a larger nation-state.

Some of the new governments have wisely not sought to demonstrate that they can exercise control over all subordinate authorities—wisely, because their capacity to do so is often exceedingly limited. But no modern government can tolerate for long a situation in which its laws are not obeyed in portions of its territory. As the new regimes begin to expand their functions, their need to exercise control grows. As an internal market is established, there is a need for a uniform legal code enforceable in courts of law; as state expenditures grow, no area can be exempt from the tax collectors; with the growth in transportation and communication there is a need for postal officers and personnel for the regulation in the public interest of communication and transport facilities. Finally, there is pride, for no government claiming international recognition will willingly admit that it cannot exercise authority in areas under its recognized jurisdiction, for to do so is to invite the strong to penetrate into the territory of the weak.

VALUE INTEGRATION

The integration of values—whatever else it encompasses—at a minimum means that there are acceptable procedures for the resolution of conflict. All societies—including traditional societies—have conflicts, and all societies have procedures for their resolution. But as societies begin to modernize, conflicts multiply rapidly, and the procedures for the settlement of conflict are not always satisfactory. There are societies where the right of traditional authority to resolve conflict remained intact during the early phases of modernization—Japan comes readily to mind—and were thereby able to avoid large-scale violence. But these are the exceptions. Why does the system require a new level of value integration?

First of all, the scale and volume of conflict increases in societies experiencing modernization. The status of social groups is frequently changed, even reversed, as education opens new occupational opportunities, as the suffrage increases the political importance of numbers, and as industrial expansion provides new opportunities for employment and wealth. A caste or tribe, once low in status and wealth, may now rise or at least see the opportunity for mobility. And social groups once high in power, status, and wealth may now feel threatened. Traditional rivalries are aggravated, and new conflicts are created as social relationships change.

The modernization process also creates new occupational roles and these new roles often conflict with the old. The new local government officer may be opposed by the tribal and caste leader. The textile manufacturer may be opposed by producers of hand-loomed cloth. The doctor may be opposed by a traditional healer. To these, one could add an enormous list

of conflicts associated with modernization: the conflicts between management and labor characteristic of the early stages of industrial development, the hostility of landlords to government land-reform legislation, the hostility of regions, tribes, and religious groups with one another as they find it necessary to compete—often for the first time—in a common political system where public policies have important consequences for their social and economic positions. Finally, we should note the importance of ideological conflicts so often found in developing societies as individuals try to find an intellectually and emotionally satisfying framework for re-creating order out of a world of change and conflict.

There are two modal strategies for integrating values in a developing society. One stresses the importance of consensus and is concerned with maximizing uniformity. This view of consensus, in its extreme, emphasizes as a goal the avoidance of both conflict and competition through either coercion or exhortation. A second view of the way integrative values may be maximized emphasizes the interplay of individual and group interests. Public policy is thus not the consequence of a "right" policy upon which all agree, but the best policy possible in a situation in which there are differences of interests and sentiments.

Since most developing societies lack integrative values, political leaders in new nations are often self-conscious of their strategies. In practice, of course, neither of these two strategies is pursued in a "pure" fashion, for a leadership which believes in consensus without conflict may be willing to permit the interplay of some competitive interests while, on the other hand, regimes committed to open competition often set limits as to which viewpoints can be publicly expressed.

Though movements often develop aimed at the elimination of conflict—Communists, for example, see class harmony as the culmination of a period of struggle—such movements in practice simply add another element of conflict. The problem has been one of finding acceptable procedures and institutions for the management of conflict. It is striking to note the growth of dispute-settling institutions in modern societies. When these bodies are successful, it is often possible to prevent conflicts from entering a country's political life. Here we have in mind the social work agencies, churches and other religious bodies, lawyers and the courts, labor-management conciliation bodies and employee councils, and interracial and interreligious bodies. The psychiatrist, the lawyer, the social worker, and the labor mediator all perform integrating roles in the modern society. In the absence of these or equivalent roles and institutions in rapidly changing societies in which conflict is growing, it is no wonder that conflicts move quickly from the factory, the university, and the village into political life.

A modern political system has no single mechanism, no single procedure, no single institution for the resolution of conflict; indeed, it is precisely the multiplicity of individuals, institutions, and procedures for dispute settlement that characterizes the modern political system—both democratic and totalitarian. In contrast, developing societies with an increasing range of internal conflict, typically lack such individuals, institutions, and procedures. It is as if mankind's capacity to generate conflict is greater than his capacity to find methods for resolving conflict; the lag is clearly greatest in societies in which fundamental economic and social relationships are rapidly changing.

ELITE-MASS INTEGRATION

The mere existence of differences in goals and values between the governing elite and the governed mass hardly constitutes disintegration so long as those who are governed accept the right of the governors to govern. British political culture stresses the obligations of citizens toward their government; the American

political culture stresses the importance of political participation. In both, a high degree of elite-mass integration exists. At the other extreme are societies faced with the problem of internal war, and in between are many countries whose governments are so cut off from the masses whom they govern that they can neither mobilize the masses nor be influenced by them. The integration of elite and mass, between governors and the governed, occurs not when differences among the two disappear, but when a pattern of authority and consent is established. In no society is consent so great that authority can be dispensed with, and in no society is government so powerful and so internally cohesive that it can survive for long only through the exercise of cohesive authority. We need to stress here that both totalitarian and democratic regimes are capable of establishing elite-mass integration and that the establishment of a new pattern of relations between government and populace is particularly important during the early phase of development when political participation on a large scale is beginning to take place.

It is commonplace to speak of the "gap" between governors and the governed in the new nations, implying that some fundamental cultural and attitudinal gaps exist between the "elite" and the "mass," the former being secular-minded, English- or French-speaking, and Western-educated, if not Western-oriented, while the latter remain oriented toward traditional values, are fundamentally religious, and are vernacular-speaking.[7] In more concrete political terms, the government may be concerned with increasing savings and investment and, in general, the postponement of immediate economic gratification in order to maximize long-range growth, while the public may be more concerned with immediate gains in

[7] For a critique of "gap" theories of political development, see Ann Ruth Willner, "The Underdeveloped Study of Political Development," *World Politics* (April 1964), pp. 468–482.

income and, more fundamentally, equitable distribution or social justice irrespective of its developmental consequences. Often the governmental elite itself may be split with one section concerned with satisfying public demands in order to win popular support while the other is more concerned with maximizing growth rates, eliminating parochial sentiments, establishing a secular society, or achieving international recognition. The elite-mass gap also implies that communications are inadequate, that is, that the elite is oriented toward persuading the mass to change their orientation, but the feedback of political demands is not heard or, if heard, not responded to.

Perhaps too much is made of the attitudinal "gap" between governors and governed; what is more important perhaps is the attitude of government toward its citizens. Nationalist leaders out of power are typically populist. They generally identify with the mass and see in the "simple peasant" and the "working class" qualities which will make a good society possible. But once the nationalist leadership takes power and satisfies its desire for social status it tends to view the mass as an impediment to its goals of establishing a "modern," "unified," and "powerful" state. From being the champion of the masses the elite often becomes their detractor.

In all political systems, those of developing as well as developed societies, there are differences in outlook between those who govern and those who are governed. In a developed system, however, those who govern are accessible to influence by those who are governed—even in a totalitarian system—and those who are governed are readily available for mobilization by the government. In modern societies governments are so engaged in effecting the economy, social welfare, and defense that there must be a closer interaction between government and the governed.[8]

[8] Karl Deutsch has pointed out that governments of industrial societies, whether totali-

Governments must mobilize individuals to save, invest, pay taxes, serve in the army, obey laws. Modern governments must also know what the public will tolerate and must be able to anticipate, before policies are pursued, what the public reaction to a given policy might be. Moreover, the modern government is increasingly armed with sophisticated tools of economic analysis and public opinion surveys to increase its capacity to predict both the economic and political consequences of its actions. In contrast, the elites of new nations are constantly talking to the masses; it is not that they do not hear the masses, but what they hear is often so inappropriate to what they wish to do. To ban opposition parties, muzzle the press, and restrict freedom of speech and assembly does indeed close two-way channels of communication, but often this is precisely what is intended.

But whatever their fear of the masses, governmental elites in new nations cannot do without them. While the elite may be unsympathetic to mass efforts to exercise influence, the elite does want to mobilize the masses for its goals. In some developing societies an organizational revolution is already under way as men join together for increasingly complex tasks to create political parties, newspapers, corporations, trade unions, and caste and tribal associations. Governmental elites are confronted with a choice during the early stages of this development. Should they seek to make these new organizations instruments of the authoritative structures or should these organizations be permitted to become autonomous bodies, either politically neutral or concerned with influencing government? When the state is strong and the organizational structures of society weak— a condition often found in the early phases of postcolonial societies with a strong

tarian or democratic, spend a larger proportion of their GNP than do governments in underdeveloped economies, irrespective of their ideologies.

bureaucratic legacy—then government leadership clearly has such an option.[9] It is at this point that the classic issue of the relationship of liberty and authority arises, and the elite may choose to move in one direction rather than the other.

The choices made are often shaped by dramatic domestic or international crises of the moment. But they are also affected by the society's tradition of elite-mass relations. The traditional aloofness, for example, of the mandarin bureaucracy toward the Vietnamese populace and the traditional disdain of the Buddhist and Catholic Vietnamese toward the *montegnards* or "pagan" hill peoples have probably been more important factors affecting elite-mass relations in contemporary Vietnam than any strategic or ideological considerations on the part of the Vietnamese government. Similarly, the behavior of many African leaders can often be understood better by exploring the customary patterns of authority in traditional tribal society than by reference to any compulsions inherent in the development process.

In the analysis of elite-masses relations much attention is rightly given to the development of "infra-structures"— that is, political parties, newspapers, universities, and the like—which can provide a two-way communication channel between government and populace.[10] Much attention is also given to the development of a "middle strata" of individuals who can serve as links—newspapermen, lobbyists, party bosses, and precinct workers. While in the long run these developments are of great import-

ance, in the short run so much depends upon the attitude of the governmental elites, whether the elites fundamentally feel—and behave—as if they were alienated from and even antagonistic to the masses as they are, or whether the elites perceive the values of the masses as essentially being congruent to their own aims.

INTEGRATIVE BEHAVIOR

The readiness of individuals to work together in an organized fashion for common purposes and to behave in a fashion conducive to the achievement of these common purposes is an essential behavioral pattern of complex modern societies. Modern societies have all encountered organizational revolutions— in some respects as essential and as revolutionary as the technological revolution which has made the modern world. To send a missile into outer space, to produce millions of automobiles a year, to conduct research and development, to manage complex mass media all require new organizational skills. During the last few decades we have begun to understand the nature of managerial skills and the complexity of organizations— how they carry out their many purposes, how they adapt themselves to a changing environment, and how they change that environment. We know less about why some societies are more successful than others in creating men and women capable of establishing, maintaining, and adapting complex organizations for the achievement of common purposes.

The consequences of an organizational lag as an impediment to development are, however, quite apparent. The inability of many political leaders to maintain internal party and government unity in many new nations has resulted in the collapse of parliamentary government and the establishment of military dictatorships. The much vaunted organizational skill of the military has also often failed in many new nations. In Ceylon a planned military coup

---

[9] This theme is amplified by Fred W. Riggs, "Bureaucrats and Political Development: A Paradoxical View," *Bureaucracy and Political Development*, ed., Joseph LaPalombara (Princeton, N.J.: Princeton University Press, 1963).

[10] For a discussion of the role of infra-structures in political development, see Edward Shils, *Political Development in the New States* (The Hague: Mouton, 1962).

collapsed when several of the conspirators spoke of their plans so openly that even a disorganized civilian government had time to take action, and in many Latin American countries, and now in Vietnam, the military has proven to be as incapable of maintaining cohesive authority as their civilian predecessors.

The capacity—or lack of capacity—to organize with one's fellow men may be a general quality of societies. A society with a high organizational capacity appears to be organizationally competent at creating industrial organizations, bureaucracies, political parties, universities, and the like. Germany, Japan, the United States, the Soviet Union, Great Britain come quickly to mind. In contrast, one is struck by a generalized incompetence in many new nations where organizational breakdowns seem to be greater bottlenecks to economic growth than breakdowns in machinery. In some new countries technological innovations—such as industrial plants, railways, telegraph and postal systems—have expanded more rapidly than the human capacities to make the technologies work, with the result that mail is lost, the transport system does not function with any regularity, industrial managers cannot implement their decisions, and government administrative regulations impede rather than facilitate the management of public sector plants. Though some scholars have argued that the skill to create complex institutions will accompany or follow technological innovation, there is good reason to think that organizational skills are a prerequisite for much political and economic development. In fact, the pattern of interpersonal relations appears to be more conducive to organization-building in some traditional societies than in others. Just as the presence of entrepreneurial talents in the traditional society is a key element in whether or not economic growth occurs, so may the presence of organizational talents be an important element in whether there emerges a leadership with the capacity to run a political party, an interest association, or a government.[11]

Surprisingly little is known about the conditions for the development of effectual political organizations. If the modernization process does produce political organizations, why is it that in some societies these organizations are effectual and in others they are not? By effectual, we mean the capacity of an organization to establish sufficient internal cohesion and external support to play some significant role in the decision-making or decision-implementing process. The multiplication of ineffectual political organizations tends to result either in a highly fragmented unintegrated political process in which government is unable to make or implement public policy, or in a political system in which the authoritative structures make all decisions completely independently of the political process outside of government. In the latter case we may have a dual political process, one inside of government which is meaningful and one outside of government which, in policy terms, is meaningless.

Some scholars have suggested that political organization is a consequence of increased occupational differentiation which in turn results from economic growth and technological change—an assumption, incidentally, of much foreign economic assistance. The difficulty with viewing political change as a consequence of social changes which in turn are the consequence of economic development is that, however logical this sequence may appear to be, in the history of change no such sequence can be uniformly found. Indeed, political organization often precedes large-scale economic change and

[11] For an attempt to relate traditional patterns of social and political relations to modern party-building, see Myron Weiner, "Traditional Role Performance and the Development of Modern Political Parties: The Indian Case," *Journal of Politics* (November 1964). The problems of party-building in a new nation are treated in my *Party-Building in a New Nation: The Indian National Congress* (in preparation).

may be an important factor in whether or not there is large-scale economic change.

In recent years greater attention has been given to the psychocultural components of political organization. Attention is given to the existence of trust and distrust and the capacity of individuals to relate personal ambition with some notion of the public good and of moral behavior. For explanations, psychologists focus on the process of primary socialization.

While psychologists focus on the working of the mind, sociologists and social anthropologists have been concerned with the working of society, and focus on the rules that effect the relationship among men—why they are kept and why they are broken. Sociologists have given attention to the complex of rules that organize social relationships, the patterns of superordination and subordination as among and between groups and individuals, how these change, and what effects they have on political and social relationships. While psychologists give attention to the primary process of socialization, sociologists and social anthropologists are concerned with the way in which the individual, during his entire life, comes to learn the rules and, under certain circumstances, to break them. It is from these two complementary views of man that we may expect the more systematic study of politically integrative and disintegrative behavior.

Conclusion

We have tried to suggest in this essay that there are many different kinds of integration problems faced by developing nations, for there are innumerable ways in which societies and political systems can fall apart. A high rate of social and economic change creates new demands and new tasks for government which are often malintegrative. The desire of the governing elite or the governed masses, for whatever reasons, to increase the functions of government are often causes of integration problems. Since modern states as well as modernizing states are often taking on new functions, it would be quite inappropriate to view integration as some terminal state. Moreover, the problems of integration in the developing areas are particularly acute because so many fundamentally new tasks or major enlargements of old tasks are now being taken on. Once the state actively becomes concerned with the mobilization and allocation of resources, new patterns of integration between elite and mass are called for. Once the state takes on the responsibilities of public education and invokes sentiments of "national" solidarity, then the integration of social groups to one another becomes an issue. And once men endeavor to create corporations, newspapers, political parties, and professional associations because they perceive their individual interests served by common actions, a new set of values is called for which provides for the integration of new structures into the political process. The challenges of integration thus arise out of the new tasks which men create for themselves.

THE INTEGRATIVE REVOLUTION: PRIMORDIAL SENTIMENTS AND CIVIL POLITICS IN THE NEW STATES

Clifford Geertz

The peoples of the new states are simultaneously animated by two powerful, thoroughly interdependent, yet distinct and often actually opposed motives—the desire to be recognized as responsible agents whose wishes, acts, hopes, and opinions "matter," and the desire to build an efficient, dynamic modern state. The one aim is to be noticed: it is a search for an identity, and a demand that that identity be publicly acknowledged as having import, a social assertion of the self as "being somebody in the world."[1] The other aim is practical: it is a demand for progress, for a rising standard of living, more effective political order, greater social justice, and beyond that of "playing a part in the larger arena of world politics," of "exercising influence among the nations."[2] The two motives are, again, most intimately related, because citizenship in a truly modern state has more and more become the most broadly negotiable claim to personal significance, and because what Mazzini called the demand to exist and have a name is to such a great extent fired by a humiliating sense of exclusion from the important centers of power in world society. But they are not the same thing. They stem from different sources

and respond to different pressures. It is, in fact, the tension between them that is one of the central driving forces in the national evolution of the new states; as it is, at the same time, one of the greatest obstacles to such evolution.

This tension takes a peculiarly severe and chronic form in the new states, both because of the great extent to which their peoples' sense of self remains bound up in the gross actualities of blood, race, language, locality, religion, or tradition, and because of the steadily accelerating importance in this century of the sovereign state as a positive instrument for the realization of collective aims. Multiethnic, usually multilinguistic, and sometimes multiracial, the populations of the new states tend to regard the immediate, concrete, and to them inherently meaningful sorting implicit in such "natural" diversity as the substantial content of their individuality. To subordinate these specific and familiar identifications in favor of a generalized commitment to an overarching and somewhat alien civil order is to risk a loss of definition as an autonomous person, either through absorption into a culturally undifferentiated mass or, what is even worse, through domination by some other rival ethnic, racial, or linguistic community that is able to imbue that order with the temper of its own personality. But at the same time, all but the most unenlightened members of such societies are at least dimly aware—and their leaders are acutely aware—that the possibilities for social reform and material progress they so intensely desire and are so determined to achieve rest with increasing weight on their being enclosed in a reasonably large, independent, powerful, well-

SOURCE: Excerpted from Clifford Geertz, "The Integrative Revolution: Primordial Sentiments and Civil Politics in the New States," in Clifford Geertz (ed.), *Old Societies and New States: The Quest for Modernity in Asia and Africa* (New York: The Free Press of Glencoe, 1963), pp. 105–57, using only pp. 108–28, 153–57.

[1] I. Berlin, *Two Concepts of Liberty*, New York, Oxford University Press, 1958, p. 42.

[2] E. Shils, "Political Development in the New States," *Comparative Studies in Society and History*, 2:265–292; 379–411, 1960.

ordered polity. The insistence on recognition as someone who is visible and matters and the will to be modern and dynamic thus tend to diverge, and much of the political process in the new states pivots around an heroic effort to keep them aligned.

II

A more exact phrasing of the nature of the problem involved here is that, considered as societies, the new states are abnormally susceptible to serious disaffection based on primordial attachments.[3] By a primordial attachment is meant one that stems from the "givens"—or, more precisely, as culture is inevitably involved in such matters, the assumed "givens"—of social existence: immediate contiguity and kin connection mainly, but beyond them the givenness that stems from being born into a particular religious community, speaking a particular language, or even a dialect of a language, and following particular social practices. These congruities of blood, speech, custom, and so on, are seen to have an ineffable, and at times overpowering, coerciveness in and of themselves. One is bound to one's kinsman, one's neighbor, one's fellow believer, *ipso facto* as the result not merely of personal affection, practical necessity, common interest, or incurred obligation, but at least in great part by virtue of some unaccountable absolute import attributed to the very tie itself. The general strength of such primordial bonds, and the types of them that are important, differ from person to person, from society to society, and from time to time. But for virtually every person, in every society, at almost all times, some attachments seem to flow more from a sense of natural —some would say spiritual—affinity than from social interaction.

In modern societies the lifting of such ties to the level of political supremacy—though it has, of course, occurred and may again occur—has more and more come to be deplored as pathological. To an increasing

degree national unity is maintained not by calls to blood and land but by a vague, intermittent, and routine allegiance to a civil state, supplemented to a greater or lesser extent by governmental use of police powers and ideological exhortation. The havoc wreaked, both upon themselves and others, by those modern (or semimodern) states that did passionately seek to become primordial rather than civil political communities, as well as a growing realization of the practical advantages of a wider-ranging pattern of social integration than primordial ties can usually produce or even permit, have only strengthened the reluctance publicly to advance race, language, religion, and the like as bases for the definition of a terminal community. But in modernizing societies, where the tradition of civil politics is weak and where the technical requirements for an effective welfare government are poorly understood, primordial attachments tend, as Nehru discovered, to be repeatedly, in some cases almost continually, proposed and widely acclaimed as preferred bases for the demarcation of autonomous political units. And the thesis that truly legitimate authority flows only from the inherent coerciveness such attachments are conceived somehow to possess is frankly, energetically, and artlessly defended:

> The reasons why a unilingual state is stable and a multilingual state unstable are quite obvious. A state is built on fellow feeling. What is this fellow feeling? To state briefly it is a feeling of a corporate sentiment of oneness which makes those who are charged with it feel that they are kith and kin. This feeling is a double-edged feeling. It is at once a feeling of "consciousness of kind" which, on the one hand, binds together those who have it so strongly that it overrides all differences arising out of economic conflicts or social gradations and, on the other, severs them from those who are not of their kind. It is a longing not to belong to any other group. The existence of this fellow feeling is the foundation of a stable and democratic state.[4]

[3] E. Shils, "Primordial, Personal, Sacred and Civil Ties," *British Journal of Sociology*, June, 1957.

It is this crystallization of a direct conflict between primordial and civil sentiments—this "longing not to belong to any other group"—that gives to the problem variously called tribalism, parochialism, communalism, and so on, a more ominous and deeply threatening quality than most of the other, also very serious and intractable problems the new states face. Here we have not just competing loyalties, but competing loyalties of the same general order, on the same level of integration. There are many other competing loyalties in the new states as in any state—ties to class, party, business, union, profession, or whatever. But groups formed of such ties are virtually never considered as possible self-standing, maximal social units, as candidates for nationhood. Conflicts among them occur only within a more or less fully accepted terminal community whose political integrity they do not, as a rule, put into question. No matter how severe they become they do not threaten, at least not intentionally, its existence as such. They threaten governments, or even forms of government, but they rarely at best—and then usually when they have become infused with primordial sentiments—threaten to undermine the nation itself, because they do not involve alternative definitions of what the nation is, of what its scope of reference is. Economic or class or intellectual disaffection threatens revolution, but disaffection based on race, language, or culture threatens partition, irredentism, or merger, a redrawing of the very limits of the state, a new definition of its domain. Civil discontent finds its natural outlet in the seizing, legally or illegally, of the state apparatus. Primordial discontent strives

⁴ B. R. Ambedkar, *Thoughts on Linguistic States*, Delhi, B. R. Ambedkar, ca. 1955, p.11. Noting that the modern bilingual states of Canada, Switzerland, and (white) South Africa might be quoted against him, Ambedkar adds: "It must not be forgotten that the genius of India is quite different than the genius of Canada, Switzerland, and South Africa. The genius of India is to divide—the genius of Switzerland, South Africa and Canada to unite."

more deeply and is satisfied less easily. If severe enough, it wants not just Sukarno's or Nehru's or Moulay Hasan's head, it wants Indonesia's or India's or Morocco's.

The actual foci around which such discontent tends to crystallize are various, and in any given case several are usually involved concurrently, sometimes at cross-purposes with one another. On a merely descriptive level they are, nevertheless, fairly readily enumerable:⁵

1. Assumed Blood Ties. Here the defining element in quasi-kinship. "Quasi" because kin units formed around known biological relationship (extended families, lineages, and so on) are too small for even the most tradition-bound to regard them as having more than limited significance, and the referent is, consequently, to a notion of untraceable but yet sociologically real kinship, as in a tribe. Nigeria, the Congo, and the greater part of sub-Saharan Africa are characterized by a prominence of this sort of primordialism. But so also are the nomads or seminomads of the Middle East —the Kurds, Baluchis, Pathans, and so on; the Nagas, Mundas, Santals, and so on, of India; and most of the so-called "hill tribes" of Southeast Asia.

2. Race. Clearly, race is similar to assumed kinship, in that it involves an ethnobiological theory. But it is not quite the same thing. Here, the reference is to phenotypical physical features—especially, of course, skin color, but also facial form, stature, hair type, and so on—rather than any very definite sense of common descent as such. The communal problems of Malaya in large part focus around these sorts of differences, between, in fact, two phenotypically very similar Mongoloid peoples. "Negritude" clearly draws much, though perhaps not all, of its force from the notion of race as a significant primordial property, and the pariah commercial minorities— like the Chinese in Southeast Asia or the Indians and Lebanese in Africa—are similarly demarcated.

⁵ For a similar but differently conceived and organized listing, see Emerson, *op. cit.*, Chapters 6, 7, and 8.

3. *Language.* Linguism—for some yet to be adequately explained reasons—is particularly intense in the Indian subcontinent, has been something of an issue in Malaya, and has appeared sporadically elsewhere. But as language has sometimes been held to be the altogether essential axis of nationality conflicts, it is worth stressing that linguism is not an inevitable outcome of linguistic diversity. As indeed kinship, race, and the other factors to be listed below, language differences need not in themselves be particularly divisive: they have not been so for the most part in Tanganyika, Iran (not a new state in the strict sense, perhaps), the Philippines, or even in Indonesia, where despite a great confusion of tongues linguistic conflict seems to be the one social problem the country has somehow omitted to demonstrate in extreme form. Furthermore, primordial conflicts can occur where no marked linguistic differences are involved, as in Lebanon, among the various sorts of Batak-speakers in Indonesia, and to a lesser extent perhaps between the Fulani and Hausa in northern Nigeria.

4. *Region.* Although a factor nearly everywhere, regionalism naturally tends to be especially troublesome in geographically heterogeneous areas. Tonkin, Annam, and Cochin in prepartitioned Vietnam, the two baskets on the long pole, were opposed almost purely in regional terms, sharing language, culture, race, etc. The tension between East and West Pakistan involves differences in language and culture too, but the geographic element is of great prominence owing to the territorial discontinuity of the country. Java versus the Outer Islands in archipelagic Indonesia; the Northeast versus the West Coast in mountain-bisected Malaya, are perhaps other examples in which regionalism has been an important primordial factor in national politics.

5. *Religion.* Indian partition is the outstanding case of the operation of this type of attachment. But Lebanon, the Karens and the Moslem Arakenese in Burma, the Toba Bataks, Ambonese, and Minahassans in Indonesia, the Moros in the Philippines, the Sikhs in Indian Punjab and the Ahmadiyas in Pakistani, and the Hausa in Nigeria are other well-known examples of its force in undermining or inhibiting a comprehensive civil sense.

6. *Custom.* Again, differences in custom form a basis for a certain amount of national disunity almost everywhere, and are of especial prominence in those cases in which an intellectually and/or artistically rather sophisticated group sees itself as the bearer of a "civilization" amid a largely barbarian population that would be well advised to model itself upon it: the Bengalis in India, the Javanese in Indonesia, the Arabs (as against the Berbers) in Morocco, the Amhara in—another "old" new state—Ethiopia, etc. But it is important also to point out that even vitally opposed groups may differ rather little in their general style of life: Hindu Gujeratis and Maharashtrians in India; Baganda and Bunyoro in Uganda; Javanese and Sundanese in Indonesia. And the reverse holds also: the Balinese have far and away the most divergent pattern of customs in Indonesia, but they have been, so far, notable for the absence of any sense of primordial discontent at all.

But beyond such a mere listing of the sorts of primordial ties that tend, in one place or another, to become politicized it is necessary to go further and attempt also to classify, or somehow order, the concrete patterns of primordial diversity and conflict that in fact exist in the various new states and of which these ties are the components.

Initially, a useful analytic distinction can be made with respect to this matter of classification between those allegiances that operate more or less wholly within the confines of a single civil state and those that do not but which run across them. Or, put somewhat differently, one can contrast those cases in which the racial, tribal, linguistic, and so on, reference group that is charged with a "corporate sentiment of oneness" is smaller than the existing civil state, and those where it is larger, or at least transgresses its borders in some fashion. In the first instance primordial discontent arises from a sense of political suffocation; in the second, from a sense of political dismemberment. Karen separatism in Burma, Ashanti in Ghana, or Baganda in Uganda are examples of the former; pan-Arabism, greater Somaliism, pan-Africanism, of the latter.

Many of the new states are plagued by both these sorts of problems at once. In the first place, most interstate primordial movements do not involve entire separate countries, as the pan-movements at least tend to do, but rather minorities scattered through several, for example: the Kurdistan movement to unite Kurds in Iran, Syria, Turkey, and the Soviet Union, perhaps the most unlikely-to-succeed political movement of all time; the Abako movement of Kasuvubu and his Republic of The Congo and Angola allies; the Dravidistan movement, in so far as it comes to see itself as extending across Palk Strait from South India into Ceylon; the movement—or perhaps it is so far only a formless sentiment—for a unified and sovereign Bengal independent of both India and Pakistan. And there are even a few classical irredentist-type problems scattered among the new states—the Malays in South Thailand, the Pushtu speakers along the Afghan border of Pakistan, and so on; and when political boundaries become more firmly established in sub-Saharan Africa there will be a great many more of them. In all these cases, there is—or there may develop—both a desire to escape the established civil state and a longing to reunite a politically divided primordial community.[6]

In the second place, interstate and intrastate primordial attachments often cross-

cut one another in a complex network of balanced—if most precariously balanced—commitments. In Malaya one of the more effective binding forces that has, so far at least, held Chinese and Malays together in a single state despite the tremendous centrifugal tendencies the racial and cultural difference generates is the fear on the part of either group that should the Federation dissolve they may become a clearly submerged minority in some other political framework: the Malays through the turn of the Chinese to Singapore and China; the Chinese through the turn of the Malays to Indonesia. In a similar way, in Ceylon both the Tamils and Sinhalese manage to see themselves as minorities: the Tamils because 70 per cent of the Ceylonese are Sinhalese; the Sinhalese because the eight million of them in Ceylon are all there are, while in addition to the two million Tamils on the island there are 28 million more in South India. In Morocco, there has tended to be both a within-state split between Arab and Berber, and an extra-state split between partisans of Nasser's pan-Arabism and of Bourguiba's and Balafrej's *regroupement maghrebin*. And Nasser himself, until the Syrian debacle perhaps the new States' most accomplished virtuoso in the primordial arts, is absorbed in juggling pan-Arabist, pan-Islamic, and pan-African sentiments in the interests of Egyptian hegemony among the Bandung powers.

But whether the relevant attachments outrun state boundaries or not, most of the major primordial battles are for the moment being fought within them. A certain amount of international conflict focusing around, or at least animated by, primordial issues does exist among the new states. The hostility between Israel and her Arab neighbors and the quarrel of India and Pakistan over Kashmir are the most prominent cases, of course. But the embroilment of two older states, Greece and Turkey, over Cyprus is another; the impending clash between Somalia and Ethiopia concerning an essentially irredentist problem a third; the Indonesian difficulties vis-à-vis

[6] The intensity, prevalence, or even the reality of such desires in each case is another matter, about which nothing is being asserted here. How much, if any, feeling in favor of assimilation to Malaya exists among the South Thailand Malays, the actual strength of the Abako idea, or the attitudes of Tamils in Ceylon toward the Dravidian separatists of Madras are matters for empirical research.

Peking with respect to the issue of "dual citizenship" for Chinese residents of Indonesia a mild fourth, and so on. As the new states solidify politically, such disputes may well grow both more frequent and more intense. But as of now they have not yet become—with the exception of the Israeli-Arab conflict and, sporadically, the Kashmir problem—paramount political issues, and the immediate significance of primordial differences is almost everywhere primarily domestic, though this is not to say that they are therefore without important international implications.[7]

The construction of a typology of the concrete patterns of primordial diversity that are found within the various new states is severely hampered, however, by the simple lack of detailed and reliable information in the overwhelming majority of the cases. But, again, a gross and merely empirical classification can nonetheless fairly easily be devised, and should prove useful as a rough-and-ready guide to a wilderness otherwise uncharted, and facilitate a more incisive analysis of the role of primordial sentiments in civil politics than is possible in terms of "pluralism," "tribalism," "parochialism," "communalism," and the other clichés of commonsense sociology:

1. One common and, relatively speaking, simple pattern seems to be that of a single dominant and usually, though not inevi-

[7] Nor does the interstate significance of primordial sentiments lie wholly in their divisive power. Pan-American attitudes, weak and ill-defined as they may be, have provided a useful context of mild solidarity for the confrontation of leaders of major African countries —Arab and Negro alike—as at Casablanca in January, 1961. Burma's strenuous (and expensive) efforts to strengthen and revitalize international Buddhism, as in the Sixth Great Council and Yegu in 1954, have served to link her more effectively with the other Theravada countries—Ceylon, Thailand, Laos, and Cambodia. And a vague, mainly racial, feeling of common "Malayness" has played a positive role in the relations between Malaya and Indonesia and Malaya and the Philippines (though not, as yet, between Indonesia and the Philippines).

tably, larger group set over against a single strong and chronically troublesome minority: Cyprus with Greeks and Turks; Ceylon with Sinhalese and Tamils; Jordan with Jordanians and Palestinians, though in this last case the dominant group is the smaller.

2. Similar in some ways to this first pattern, but more complex, is that of one central—often enough in a geographic sense as well as a political—group and several mediumly large and at least somewhat opposed peripheral groups: the Javanese versus the Outer Island peoples in Indonesia; the Irrawaddy Valley Burmese versus the various hill tribes and upland valley peoples in Burma; the central plateau Persians and the various tribes in Iran (though, again, this is not strictly a new state); the Atlantic Plain Arabs encircled by the diverse Berber tribes of the Rif, the Atlas, and the Sous; the Mekong Lao and the tribal peoples in Laos; and so on. How far such a pattern is to be found in black Africa is unclear. The one case where it might have crystallized, with the Ashanti in Ghana, the power of the central group seems to have, at least temporarily, been broken. And whether in a new state the Baganda will be able to maintain their dominant position vis-à-vis the other Uganda groups through their greater education, political sophistication, and so on, and despite their comprising but about a fifth of the population, remains to be seen.

3. Another pattern that forms an internally even less homogeneous type is a bipolar one of two nearly evenly balanced major groups: Malays and Chinese in Malaya (though there is also a smaller Indian group); or Christians and Moslems in Lebanon (though here both groups are actually aggregates of smaller sects); or Sunnis and Shiis in Iraq. Perhaps the two regions of Pakistan, although the Western region is far from wholly homogeneous within itself, gives that state a somewhat bipolar primordial pattern. Vietnam before partition tended to take this form—Tonkin versus Cochin—this problem now having been solved with the assistance of the great powers. Even Libya, which has scarcely enough people to develop decent group conflicts, has something of this pattern with the Cyrenecia-Tripolitania contrast.

4. Next, there is the pattern of a relatively even gradation of groups in importance, from several large ones through several medium-sized ones to a number of small ones, with no clearly dominant ones and no sharp cut-off points. India, the Philippines, Nigeria, Kenya are perhaps examples.

5. Finally, there is simple ethnic fragmentation, as Wallenstein has called it, with multiple small groups, into which somewhat residual category it is necessary to toss much of Africa, at least until more is known about it.[8] One proposal, issuing from the nothing if not experimental Leopoldville Government, suggesting a grouping of the Congo Republic's estimated 250 or so separate tribal-linguistic groups into eighty autonomous tribal regions, which would then be organized into twelve federated states, gives something of an indication of the extent to which such fragmentation can go, and the complexity of primordial allegiances it may involve.

III

The reduction of primordial sentiments to civil order is rendered more difficult, however, by the fact that political modernization tends initially not to quiet such sentiments but to quicken them. The transfer of sovereignty from a colonial regime to an independent one is more than a mere shift of power from foreign hands to native ones; it is a transformation of the whole pattern of political life, a metamorphosis of subjects into citizens. Colonial governments, like the aristocratic governments of premodern Europe in whose image they were fashioned, are aloof and unresponsive; they stand outside the societies they rule, and

act upon them arbitrarily, unevenly, and unsystematically. But the governments of the new states, though oligarchic, are popular and attentive; they are located in the midst of the societies they rule, and as they develop act upon them in progressively more continuous, comprehensive, and purposeful manner. For the Ashanti cocoa farmer, the Gujerati shopkeeper, or the Malayan Chinese tin miner, his country's attainment of political independence is also his own attainment, willy-nilly, of modern political status, no matter how culturally traditional he may remain nor how ineffectively and anachronistically the new state may in practice function. He now becomes an integral part of an autonomous and differentiated polity that begins to touch his life at every point except the most strictly private. "The same people which has hitherto been kept as far as possible from government affairs must now be drawn into them," the Indonesian nationalist Sjahrir wrote on the eve of World War II, defining exactly the character of the "revolution" that was in fact to follow in the Indies over the next decade—"That people must be made politically conscious. Its political interest must be stimulated and maintained."[9]

This thrusting of a modern political consciousness upon the mass of a still largely unmodernized population does indeed tend to lead to the stimulation and maintenance of a very intense popular interest in the affairs of government. But, as a primordially based "corporate feeling of oneness," remains for many the *fons et origo* of legitimate authority—the meaning of the term "self" in "self-rule"—much of this interest takes the form of an obsessive concern with the relation of one's tribe, region, sect, or whatever to a center of power that, while growing rapidly more active, is not easily either insulated from the web of primordial attachments, as was the remote colonial regime, or assimilated to them as are the workaday authority systems of the "little

[8] I. Wallerstein, "The Emergence of Two West African Nations: Ghana and the Ivory Coast," unpublished Ph.D. thesis, Columbia University, 1959.

[9] S. Sjahrir, *Out of Exile*, New York, John Day, 1949, p. 215.

community." Thus, it is the very process of the formation of a sovereign civil state that, among other things, stimulates sentiments of parochialism, communalism, racialism, and so on, because it introduces into society a valuable new prize over which to fight and a frightening new force with which to contend.[10] The doctrines of the nationalist propagandists to the contrary notwithstanding, Indonesian regionalism, Malayan racialism, Indian linguism, or Nigerian tribalism are, in their political dimensions, not so much the heritage of colonial divide-and-rule policies as they are products of the replacement of a colonial regime by an independent, domestically anchored, purposeful unitary state. Though they rest on historically developed distinctions, some of which colonial rule helped to accentuate (and others of which it helped to moderate), they are part and parcel of the very process of the creation of a new polity and a new citizenship.

For a telling example in this connection one may look to Ceylon, which, having made one of the quietest of entries into the family of new states is now the scene of one of its noisiest communal uproars. Ceylonese independence was won largely without struggle; in fact, without even very much effort. There was no embittered nationalist

mass movement, as in most of the other new states, no loudly passionate hero-leader, no diehard colonial opposition, no violence, no arrests—no revolution really, for the 1947 transfer of sovereignty consisted of the replacement of conservative, moderate, aloof British civil servants by conservative, moderate, aloof British-educated Ceylonese notables who, to more nativistic eyes at least, "resembled the former colonial rulers in everything but the color of their skin."[11] The revolution was to come later, nearly a decade after formal independence, and the British governor's valedictory expression of "profound satisfaction that Ceylon has reached its goal of freedom without strife or bloodshed along the path of peaceful negotiation,"[12] proved to be somewhat premature: in 1956 wild Tamil-Sinhalese riots claimed more than a hundred lives, in 1958, perhaps as many as two thousand.

The country, 70 per cent Sinhalese, 23 per cent Tamil, has been marked by a certain amount of group tension for centuries.[13] But such tension has taken the distinctively modern form of an implacable, comprehensive, and ideologically instigated mass hatred mainly since the late S. W. R. D. Bandaranaike was swept into the premiership on a sudden wave of Sinhalese cultural, religious and linguistic revivalism in 1956. Himself Oxford-educated, vaguely Marxist and essentially secularist in civil matters Bandaranaike undermined the authority of the English-speaking (and bi-

---

[10] As Talcott Parsons has pointed out, power, defined as the capacity to mobilize social resources for social goals, is not a "zero-sum" quantity within a social system, but, like wealth, is generated by the working of particular, in this case political rather than economic, institutions. "The Distribution of Power in American Society," *World Politics*, 10:123–143, 1957. The growth of a modern state within a traditional social context represents, therefore, not merely the shifting or transfer of a fixed quantity of power between groups in such a manner that aggregatively the gains of certain groups or individuals match the losses of others, but rather the creation of a new and more efficient machine for the production of power itself, and thus an increase in the general political capacity of the society. This is a much more genuinely "revolutionary" phenomena than a mere redistribution, however radical, of power within a given system.

[11] D. K. Rangenekar, "The Nationalist Revolution in Ceylon," *Pacific Affairs*, 33: 361–374, 1960.

[12] Quoted in M. Weiner, "The Politics of South Asia," in G. Almond and J. Coleman, *The Politics of the Developing Areas*, Princeton, N.J., Princeton University Press, 1960, pp. 153–246.

[13] About half the Tamils are stateless "Indian Tamils"—that is, individuals transported to Ceylon in the nineteeth century to work on British tea estates, and now rejected as citizens by India on the ground that they live in Ceylon, and by Ceylon on the ground that they are but sojourners from India.

ethnic Colombo) patriciate by appealing openly and one suspects somewhat cynically to the primordial sentiments of the Sinhalese promising a "Sinhala-only" linguistic policy, a place of pride for Buddhism and the Buddhist clergy, and a radical reversal of the supposed policy of "pampering" the Tamils, as well as rejecting Western dress for the traditional "cloth and banian" of the Sinhalese countryman.[14] And if, as one of his more uncritical apologists claims, his "supreme ambition" was not "to set up an outmoded, parochial, racialist government," but to "stabilize democracy and convert his country into a modern welfare state based on Nehru-style socialism,"[15] he soon found himself the helpless victim of a rising tide of primordial fervor, and his death, after thirty hectic and frustrating months in power, at the hands of an obscurely motivated Buddhist monk was merely that much more ironic.

The first definite move toward a resolute, popularly based, social reform government led, therefore, not to heightened national unity, but to the reverse—increased linguistic, racial, regional, and religious parochialism, a strange dialectic whose actual workings have been well described by Wriggins.[16] The institution of universal suffrage made the temptation to court the masses by appealing to traditional loyalties virtually irresistible, and led Bandaranaike and his followers to gamble, unsuccessfully as it turned out, on being able to tune primordial sentiments up before elections and

down after them. The modernizing efforts of his government in the fields of health, education, administration, and so on, threatened the status of consequential rural personages—monks, ayurvedic doctors, village schoolteachers, local officials—who were thereby rendered that much more nativistic and insistent upon communal tokens of reassurance in exchange for their political support. The search for a common cultural tradition to serve as the content of the country's identity as a nation now that it had become, somehow, a state, led only to the revivification of ancient, and better forgotten, Tamil-Sinhalese treacheries, atrocities, insults, and wars. The eclipse of the Western-educated urban elite, within which class loyalties and old-school ties tended to override primordial differences, removed one of the few important points of amicable contact between the two communities. The first stirrings of fundamental economic change aroused fears that the position of the industrious, frugal, aggressive Tamils would be strengthened at the expense of the less methodical Sinhalese. The intensified competition for government jobs, the increasing importance of the vernacular press, and even government-instituted land-reclamation programs—because they threatened to alter population distribution and so communal representation in the parliament— all acted in a similarly provocative manner. Ceylon's aggravated primordial problem is not a mere legacy, an inherited impediment to her political, social, and economic modernization; it is a direct and immediate reflex of her first serious—if still rather ineffective—attempt to achieve such modernization.

And this dialectic, variously expressed, is a generic characteristic of new state politics. In Indonesia, the establishment of an indigenous unitary state made the fact that the thinly populated but mineral-rich Outer Islands produced the bulk of the country's foreign-exchange earnings, while densely populated, resource-poor Java consumed the bulk of its income, painfully apparent

---

[14] Commenting on the spectacular failure of Sir Ivor Jennings's 1954 prediction that Bandaranaike was unlikely to win the leadership of the nationalist movement because he was a "political Buddhist," having been educated as a Christian, Rangenekar shrewdly remarks, "In an Asian setting a Western-educated politician who renounces his Westernization and upholds indigenous culture and civilization wields a much greater influence than the most dynamic local thoroughbred can ever hope to do." Rangenekar, *op. cit.*

[15] *Ibid.*

[16] H. Wriggins, "Impediments to Unity in New Nations—the Case of Ceylon," unpublished MS.

in a way it could never become in the colonial era, and a pattern of regional jealousy developed and hardened to the point of armed revolt.[17] In Ghana, hurt Ashanti pride burst into open separatism when, in order to accumulate development funds, Nkrumah's new national government fixed the cocoa price lower than what Ashanti cocoa growers wished it to be.[18] In Morocco, Riffian Berbers, offended when their substantial military contribution to the struggle for independence was not followed by greater governmental assistance in the form of schools, jobs, improved communications facilities, and so on, revived a classic pattern of tribal insolence—refusal to pay taxes, boycott of market places, retreat to a predatory mountain life—in order to gain Rabat's regard.[19] In Jordan, Abdullah's desperate attempt to strengthen his newly sovereign civil state through the annexation of Cis-Jordan, negotiation with Israel, and modernization of the army provoked his assassination by an ethnically humiliated pan-Arab Palestinian.[20] Even in those new states where such discontent has not progressed to the point of open dissidence,

[17] H. Fieth, "Indonesia," in G. McT. Kahin (ed.), *Government and Politics of Southeast Asia*, Ithaca, N.Y., Cornell University Press, 1959, pp. 155–238; and G. McT. Kahin (ed)., *Major Governments of Asia*, Ithaca, N.Y., Cornell University Press, 1958, pp. 471–592. This is not to say that the crystallization of regional enmities was the sole motivating force in the Padang rebellion, nor that the Java-Outer Islands contrast was the only axis of opposition. In all the quoted examples in this essay, the the desire to be recognized as a responsible agent whose wishes, acts, hopes, and opinions matter is intertwined with the more familiar desires for wealth, power, prestige, and so on. Simple primordial determinism is no more defensible a position than economic determinism.

[18] D. Apter, *The Gold Coast in Transition*, Princeton, N. J., Princeton University Press, 1955, p. 68.

[19] W. Lewis, "Feuding and Social Change in Morocco," *Journal of Conflict Resolution*, 5:43–54, 1961.

[20] R. Nolte, "The Arab Solidarity Agreement," American University Field Staff Letter, Southwest Asia Series, 1957.

there has almost universally arisen around the developing struggle for governmental power as such a broad penumbra of primordial strife. Alongside of, and interacting with, the usual politics of party and parliament, cabinet and bureaucracy, or monarch and army, there exists, nearly everywhere, a sort of parapolitics of clashing public identities and quickening ethnocratic aspirations.

What is more, this parapolitical warfare seems to have its own characteristic battlegrounds; there are certain specific institutional contexts outside the customary arenas of political combat into which it has a strong inclination to settle. Though primordial issues do, of course, turn up from time to time in parliamentary debates, cabinet deliberations, judicial decisions and, more often, in electoral campaigns, they show a persistent tendency to emerge in purer, more explicit, and more virulent form in some places where other sorts of social issues do not ordinarily, or at least so often or so acutely, appear.

One of the most obvious of these is the school system. Linguistic conflicts, in particular, tend to emerge in the form of school crises—witness the fierce dispute between Malay and Chinese teachers' unions over the degree to which Malay should replace Chinese in Chinese schools in Malaya, the three-way guerrilla war between partisans of English, Hindi, and various local vernaculars as instruction media in India, or the bloody riots staged by Bengali-speaking university students to block the imposition of Urdu by West on East Pakistan. But religious issues, too, tend to penetrate educational contexts quite readily. In Moslem countries there is the enduring question of the reform of traditional Koranic schools toward Western forms; in the Philippines there is the clash between the American-introduced tradition of the secular public school and the intensified clerical effort to increase the teaching of religion in such schools; and in Madras there are the Dravidian separatists announcing sanctimoniously that "education must be free from political, religious or communal bias," by which they in fact mean that it "must not stress Hindu writings such as the epic Ramayana."[21] Even largely regional struggles tend to engulf the school system: in Indonesia the rise of provincial discontent was accompanied by a competitive multiplication of local institutions of higher learning to the point where, despite the extreme shortage of qualified instructors, there is now a faculty in nearly every major region of the country, monuments to past resentments and perhaps cradles for future ones; and a similar pattern may now be developing in Nigeria. If the general strike is the classical political expression of class warfare, and the *coup d'état* of the struggle between militarism and parliamentarianism, then the school crisis is perhaps becoming the classical political—or parapolitical—expression of the clash of primordial loyalties.

There are a number of other poles around which parapolitical vortices tend to form, but so far as the literature is concerned they have been more noted in passing than analyzed in detail. Social statistics, for example. In Lebanon there has not been a census since 1932, for fear that taking one would reveal such changes in the religious composition of the population as to make the marvelously intricate political arrangements designed to balance sectarian interests unviable. In India, with its national language problem, just what constitutes a Hindi speaker has been a matter of some rather acrimonious dispute, because it depends upon the rules of counting: Hindi enthusiasts use census figures to prove that as many as a half of India's people speak "Hindi" (including Urdu and Punjabi), while anti-Hindiists force the figure down as low as 30 per cent by considering such matters as script differences, and evidently even religious affiliation of the speaker, as

linguistically significant. Then, too, there is the closely related problem of what, in connection with the strange fact that according to the 1941 census of India there were 25 million tribal peoples but in the 1951 one only 1.7 million, Weiner has aptly called "genocide by census redefinition."[22] In Morocco, published figures for the percentage of the population that is Berber run all the way from 35 to 60 per cent, and some nationalist leaders would like to believe, or have others believe, that the Berbers are a French invention altogether.[23] Statistics, real or fancied, concerning the ethnic composition of the civil service are a favorite weapon of primordial demagogues virtually everywhere, being particularly effective where a number of local officials are members of a group other than the one they administer. And in Indonesia a leading newspaper was banned, at the height of the regionalist crisis, for printing, in mock innocence, a simple bar graph depicting export earnings and government expenditure by province.

Dress (in Burma hundreds of frontier tribesmen brought to Rangoon for Union day to improve their patriotism are cannily sent home with gifts of Burmese clothing), historiography (in Nigeria a sudden proliferation of tendentious tribal histories threatens to strengthen the already very

[21] P. Talbot, "Raising a Cry for Secession," American University Field Staff Letter, South Asia Series, 1957.

[22] M. Weiner, "Community Associations in Indian Politics," unpublished M.S. The reverse process, "ethnogenesis by census redefinition," also occurs, as when in Libreville, the Gabon capital, Togolese and Dahomeans are lumped statistically into a new category, "the Popo," or in Northern Rhodesia copperbelt towns Henga, Tonga, Tambuka, and so on, are "by common consent" grouped together as Nyasalanders, these manufactured groupings then taking on a real "ethnic" existence. I. Wallerstein, "Ethnicity and National Integration in West Africa," *Cahiers d'etudes africaines*, 3: 120–139 October, 1960.

[23] The 35 per cent figure can be found in N. Barbour (ed.), *A Survey of North West Africa*, New York, Oxford University Press, 1959, p. 79; the 60 per cent figure in D. Rustow, "The Politics of the Near East," in Almond and Coleman, *op. cit.*, pp. 369–453.

powerful centrifugal tendencies plaguing the country), and the official insignia of public authority (in Ceylon, Tamils have refused to use automobile license plates marked with Sinhala characters, and in South India they have painted over Hindi railroad signs) are other as yet but impressionistically observed spheres of parapolitical controversy.[24] So, also, is the rapidly expanding complex of tribal unions, caste organizations, ethnic fraternities, regional associations, and religious sodalities that seems to be accompanying urbanization in virtually all the new states, and has made the major cities in some of them—Lagos, Beirut, Bombay, Medan—caldrons of communal tension.[25] But, details aside, the point is that there swirls around the emerging governmental institutions of the new states, and the specialized politics they tend to support, a whole host of self-reinforcing whirlpools of primordial discontent, and that this parapolitical maelstrom is in great part an outcome—to continue the metaphor, a backwash—of that process of political development itself. The growing capacity of the state to mobilize social resources for public ends, its expanding power, roils primordial sentiments because, given the doctrine that legitimate authority is but an extension of the inherent moral coerciveness such sentiments possess, to permit oneself to be ruled by men of other tribes, other races, or other religions is to submit not merely to oppression but to degradation—to exclusion from the moral community as a lesser order of being whose opinions, attitudes, wishes, and so on,

simply do not fully count, as those of children, the simple-minded and the insane do not fully count in the eyes of those who regard themselves as mature, intelligent, and sane.

Though it can be moderated, this tension between primordial sentiments and civil politics probably cannot be entirely dissolved. The power of the "givens" of place, tongue, blood, looks, and way-of-life to shape an individual's notion of who, at bottom, he is and with whom, indissolubly, he belongs is rooted in the nonrational foundations of personality. And, once established, some degree of involvement of this unreflective sense of collective selfhood in the steadily broadening political process of the national state is certain, because that process seems to touch on such an extraordinarily wide range of matters. Thus, what the new states—or their leaders— must somehow contrive to do as far as primordial attachments are concerned is not, as they have so often tried to do, wish them out of existence by belittling them or even denying their reality, but domesticate them. They must reconcile them with the unfolding civil order by divesting them of their legitimizing force with respect to governmental authority, by neutralizing the apparatus of the state in relationship to them, and by channeling discontent arising out of their dislocation into properly political rather than parapolitical forms of expression. This goal, too, is not fully achievable or at least has never yet been achieved— even in Mr. Ambedkar's Canada and Switzerland (the less said of South Africa in this connection, the better) with their admitted "genius to unite." But it is relatively so, and it is upon the possibility of such relative achievement that the hope of the new states to turn the attack upon their integrity and their legitimacy by unfettered primordial enthusiasms rests. As with industrialization, urbanization, restratification, and the various other social and cultural "revolutions" these states seem feted to undergo, the containment of diverse primordial communities under a single sovereignty promises to tax

[24] On Burmese dress, see H. Tinker, *The Union of Burma*, New York, Oxford University Press, 1957, p. 184. On Nigerian tribal histories, see Coleman, *op. cit.*, pp. 327–328. On Ceylonese license plates, see Wiggins, "Ceylon's Time of Troubles, 1956–8," *Far Eastern Survey*, 28: 33–38 (1959). On Hindi railroad signs, see Weiner, "Community Associations . . . ," *op. cit.*

[25] For a general discussion of the role of voluntary associations in the urbanization process in modernizing societies, see Wallerstein, "The Emergence of Two West African Nations," *op. cit.*, pp. 144–230.

the political capacity of their peoples to its utmost limits—in some cases, no doubt, beyond them. . . .

V

Over the cases reviewed here, at least, one common developmental tendency does stand out: the aggregation of independently defined, specifically outlined traditional primordial groups into larger, more diffuse units whose implicit frame of reference is not the local scene but the "nation"—in the sense of the whole society encompassed by the new civil state. The leading principle in terms of which this lumping is mainly carried out varies—region in Indonesia, race in Malaya, language in India, religion in Lebanon, custom in Morocco, and quasi-kinship in Nigeria. Whether it involves becoming an Outer Islander in addition to a Minangkabau, a Kachin over and above a Duleng, a Christian as well as a Maronite, or a Yoruba rather than only an Egba, the process, though variously advanced, both as between countries and within them, is general. It is a progressive extension of the sense of primordial similarity and difference generated from the direct and protracted encounter of culturally diverse groups in local contexts to more broadly defined groups of a similar sort interacting within the framework of the entire national society, an extension Freedman has described particularly well for Malaya:

Malaya was and remains a culturally plural society. Paradoxically, from a purely structural point of view, its plural nature is more marked today than ever before. Nationalism and political independence in their early phases have tended to define, on a pan-Malayan basis, ethnic blocs which in former times were merely categories. Then the social map of Malaya was, so to speak, made up of a kaleidoscope of small culturally defined units rearranging themselves in accordance with local conditions. "The Malays" did not interact with "the Chinese" and "the Indians." Some Malays interacted with some Chinese and some

Indians. But as "Malays," "Chinese" and "Indians" come to be realized as structural entities on a nation-wide scale, they can begin to have total relations with one another.[26]

The emergence of a nation-wide system of "ethnic-blocs" engaged in "total relations with one another" sets the stage for a direct clash between personal identity and political integrity in the new states. By generalizing and extending tribal, racial, linguistic, or other principles of primordial solidarity, such a system permits the maintenance of a profoundly rooted "consciousness of kind," and relates that consciousness to the developing civil order. It allows one to continue to claim public acknowledgment of one's existence and import in terms of the familiar symbols of group uniqueness, while at the same time becoming more and more drawn into a political society cast in a wholly different mold than the "natural" community those symbols define. But, on the other hand, it also simplifies and concentrates group antagonisms, raises the specter of separatism by superimposing a comprehensive political significance upon those antagonisms, and, particularly, when the crystallizing ethnic blocs outrun state boundaries, stirs international controversies. The integrative revolution does not do away with ethnocentrism; it merely modernizes it.

Yet modernizing ethnocentrism does render it more easily reconciled to the presence of developed national political institutions. The effective operation of such institutions does not require the simple replacement of primordial ties and identifications by civil ones. In all probability, such a replacement is a sheer impossibility. What it does demand is an adjustment between them, an adjustment such that the processes of government can proceed freely without seriously threatening the cultural framework of personal identity, and such

[26] M. Freedman, "The Growth of a Plural Society in Malaya," *Pacific Affairs*, 33: 158–167, 1960.

The Politics of Nation-Building

that whatever discontinuities in "consciousness of kind" happen to exist in the general society do not radically distort political functioning. At least as they have been conceived here, primordial and civil sentiments are not ranged in direct and implicitly evolutionary opposition to one another in the manner of so many of the theoretical dichotomies of classical sociology—*Gemeinschaft* and *Gesellschaft*, mechanical and organic solidarity, folk and urban society; the history of their development does not consist simply of the expansion of the one at the expense of the other. Their marked tendency to interfere with one another in the new states stems not from any natural and irremovable antipathy between them but rather from dislocations arising from the differing patterns of change intrinsic to each of them as they respond to the disequilibrating forces of the mid-twentieth century. Their clash is an outcome of the contrasting sorts of transformation that traditional political institutions and traditional modes of self-perception undergo as they move along their separate paths toward modernity.

On the self-perception side, the nature of the modernizing process is virtually uninvestigated; it is not usually even recognized that such a process exists. The already mentioned aggregation of narrowly circumscribed tribal, linguistic, religious, and so on, groups into larger more generalized ethnic blocs set within the context of a common social frame is certainly a crucial part of it. A simple, coherent, broadly defined ethnic structure, such as is found in most industrial societies, is not an undissolved residue of traditionalism but an earmark of modernity. But how this reconstruction of the system of primordial affiliation takes place, the stages through which it passes, the forces that advance or retard it, the transformations in personality structure it involves, all are largely unknown. The comparative sociology (or social psychology) of ethnic change remains to be written.

With respect to the political side, it can hardly be said that the problem is unrecog-

nized, for the notion of a civil society, of the nature of citizenship and the diffuse social sentiments on which it rests, has been a central concern of political science since Aristotle. But it remains none the less vague; much easier to point to than describe; much easier to sense than to analyze. What the civic sense more than anything else seems to involve is a definite concept of the public as a separate and distinct body and an attendant notion of a genuine public interest, which though not necessarily superior to, is independent of and at times even in conflict with, both private and other sorts of collective interest. When we talk about the changing forms of civil politics in the new states or elsewhere, it is the vicissitudes of just this sense of the public and the public interest, its waxings and wanings, its alterations in mode of expression, to which we refer. Again, however, though we have at least a general idea of the nature of civility and the range of forms through which it is materialized in industrial states, very little is known about the processes by which the present patterns have come to be what they are. A genuine civil sense is often even denied—incorrectly in my opinion— to traditional states at all. In any case, the stages through which a modern sense of political community arises out of a traditional one has been at best but impressionistically traced, and thus both the roots and the character of civility remain obscure.

A satisfactory understanding of the reasons for the chronic tension in the new states between the need to maintain a socially ratified personal identity and the desire to construct a powerful national community demands, therefore, a more circumstantial tracing of the stages through which their relationship to one another passes as each proceeds along the special lines of its own development. And it is in the histories of those states as they unfold before our eyes that such a tracing is most readily to be accomplished. The diverse constitutional, quasi-constitutional, or simply *ad hoc* experiments in government that characterize at least those new states described here represent, among other things, an attempt to establish a pattern of politics in which the looming headlong clash of primordial and civil loyalties can be averted. Whether ethnic differentiation is given its political expression in terms of territorial subunits, political parties, government posts, executive leadership, or, as is most common, one or another combination of these, the effort is everywhere to find a formula that will keep the pace of modernization of the nation's sense of selfhood in step with the parallel modernization not only of its political, but of its economic, stratificatory, domestic, and so on, institutions as well. It is by watching the integrative revolution happen that we shall understand it. This may seem like a mere wait-and-see policy, inappropriate to the predictive ambitions of science. But such a policy is at least preferable, and more scientific, to waiting and not seeing, which has been largely the case to date.

In any case, the success of the efforts to find a formula for balance in the midst of change now taking place in the new states is nowhere assured. A high degree of governmental immobilism resulting from the attempt to reconcile divergent primordial groups is everywhere apparent. The mere prejudices that must be tolerated in order to effect such reconciliations are often repugnant. But as the alternatives to such attempts as these to construct a civil politics of primordial compromise would seem to be either Balkanization, *Herrenvolk* fanaticism, or the forcible suppression of ethnic assertion by a leviathan state, can they be viewed, especially by members of a society that has notably failed to resolve its own most troublesome primordial problem, with either indifference or contempt?

ETHNICITY AND NATIONAL INTEGRATION IN WEST AFRICA[1]

Immanuel Wallerstein

Many writers on West Africa, whether academic or popular, assert that there is currently a conflict between tribalism and nationalism which threatens the stability of the new West African nations. In fact, the relationship between tribalism and nationalism is complex. Although ethnicity (tribalism) is in some respects dysfunctional for national integration (a prime objective of nationalist movements), it is also in

SOURCE: Immanuel Wallerstein, "Ethnicity and National Integration in West Africa," *Cahiers d'Etudes Africaines*, No. 3 (October, 1960), pp. 129–39.

some respects functional. Discussion of the presumed conflict might be clarified by discussing this hypothesis in some detail. Before doing so, it should be noted that we deliberately use the term ethnicity in preference to tribalism, and we shall preface our remarks by carefully defining our use of the term ethnicity.

In a traditional, rural setting, an individual is a member first of all of a family and then of a tribe.[2] The demands the tribe makes on him vary with the complexity of

[1] Revised version of a paper delivered at the Annual Meeting of the American Sociological Society, 1959.

[2] A tribe is what Murdock calls a community, and he notes: "The community and the nuclear family are the only social groups that are genuinely universal. They occur in every known human society . . ." (G. Murdock, *Social Structure*, New York, Macmillan, 1949, p. 79.)

the tribal system of government,[3] as does the degree to which family and tribal loyalties are distinct. To a large extent, however, family and tribal loyalties support each other harmoniously.

Under colonial rule, the social change brought about by European administrators and the process of urbanization has led to widespread shifts of loyalty. This process has been called "detribalization." Writers speaking of tribal loyalty often confuse three separate phenomena which it would be useful to distinguish: loyalty to the family; loyalty to the tribal community; and loyalty to the tribal government, or chief.[4] Often what a writer means by detribalization is simply a decline in chiefly authority. It does not necessarily follow that an individual who is no longer loyal to his chief has rejected as well the tribe as a community to which he owes certain duties and from which he expects a certain security.[5]

[3] Statements on the typologies of tribal organizations in Africa are to be found in: M. Fortes and E. Evans-Pritchard, ed., *African Political Systems*, Oxford, 1940;— J. Middleton and D. Tait, *Tribes without Rulers*, London, 1958;—D. Forde, "The Conditions of Social Development in West Africa," in *Civilisations*, III, No. 4, 1953, pp. 472–476.

[4] We shall not discuss further the role of the family in West Africa today. We note here that it would be an oversimplification to suggest that family ties have drastically declined in the urban areas. In any case, the strength of family ties can vary independently of the strength of tribal ties.

[5] There are, to be sure, cases where the two loyalties decline together, and there is consequently severe anomy. Failure to distinguish this case from one in which primarily loyalty to the chief alone diminishes can result in much confusion. See this comment by Mercer in which he tries to clarify this confusion: "C'est dans cette minorité [la population saisonniére] que l'on peut parler réellement de faits de *détribalisation* au sens de pure dégradation du role des anciens cadres sociaux. Au contraire, nous avons vu que, dans la population permanente, *les structures de parenté et l'appartenance ethnique* jouaient un role considérable." (P. Mercier, "Aspects de la société africaine dans l'agglomération dakaroise:

It may be objected that West Africans do not make a distinction between the tribal government and the tribal community. This is perhaps true in the rural areas but they do when they reach the city. For in the city they find that there are new sources of power and prestige which, for many persons, are more rewarding than the tribal government. Hence they tend to lose some of their respect for the authority of the chief. The tribe, however, still can play a useful, if partially new, function as an ethnic group. The *Gemeinschaft*-like community to which the individual belongs may no longer be exactly the same group as before; the methods of government are different; the role in the national social structure is different. This community, however, bears sufficient resemblance to the rural, traditional "tribe" that often the same term is used. In this discussion, however, we shall use "tribe" for the group in the rural areas, and ethnic group for the one in the towns.

Some writers have challenged the very existence of detribalization. Rouch, for example, says he finds instead "supertribalization" among the Zabrama and other immigrants to Ghana.[6] For as Mitchell has commented of another part of Africa: "People in rural areas are apt to take their tribe for granted, but when they come to the town their tribal membership assumes new importance."[7] This is, however, a false debate. We shall see that quite often the group from which the individual is "detribalized" (that is, the tribe to whose chief he no longer pays the same fealty) is not necessarily the same group into which he is "supertribalized" (that is, the ethnic group to which he feels strong bonds of attachment in the urban context).

Membership in an ethnic group is a matter of social definition, an interplay of the

groupes familiaux et unités de voisinage," p. 39, in P. Mercier et al., "L'Agglomération Dakaroise," in *Etudes sénégalaises*, No. 5, 1954.)

[6] J. Rouch, "Migrations au Ghana," in *Journal de la Société des Africanistes* XXVI, No. 1/2, 1956, pp. 163–164.

self-definition of members and the definition of other groups. The ethnic group seems to need a minimum size to function effectively, and hence to achieve social definition.[8] Now it may be that an individual who defined himself as being of a certain tribe in a rural area can find no others from his village in the city. He may simply redefine himself as a member of a new and larger group.[9] This group would normally correspond to some logical geographical or linguistic unit, but it may never have existed as a social entity before this act.

Indeed, this kind of redefinition is quite common. Two actions give such redefinition permanence and status. One is official government sanction, in the form of census categories,[10] or the recognition of "town chiefs"; the other is the formation of ethnic (tribal) associations which are described more accurately by the French term, *association d'originaires*. These associations are

the principal form of ethnic (tribal) "government"[11] in West African towns today.

Some of these ethnic associations use clearly territorial bases of defining membership, despite the fact that they may consider their relationship with traditional chiefs as their *raison d'etre*. For example, in the Ivory Coast, Amon d'Aby has described the process as follows:

"L'un des phénomènes les plus curieux enregistrés en Côte d'Ivoire au lendemain de la Libération est la tendance très marquée des élites autochtones vers la création d'associations régionales . . .

"Ces associations groupent tous les habitants d'un cercle ou de plusieurs cercles réunis. Leur objet est non plus le sport et les récréations de toutes sortes comme les groupements anodins d'avant-guerre, mais le progrès du territoire de leur ressort. Elles ont le but d'apporter la collaboration des jeunes générations instruites aux vieilles générations représentées par les chefs coutumiers accrochés aux conceptions périmés, à une politique surannée."[12]

It should be observed that the administrative units in question (les cercles) are the creation of the colonial government, and have no necessary relationship to traditional groupings. Such ethnic associations, formed around non-traditional administrative units, are found throughout West Africa.[13] A presumably classic example of

---

[7] J. C. Mitchell, "Africans in Industrial Towns in Northern Rhodesia," in *H.R.H. The Duke of Edinburgh's Study Conference*, No. 1, p. 5.

[8] Mercier observes: "Il faut noter également que, moins un groupe ethnique est numériquement important dans la ville, plus la simple parenté tend a jouer le role de liens de parenté plus proches." (*Op. cit.*, p. 22.)

[9] In Dakar, Mercier notes: "Un certain nombre de personnes qui étaient manifestement d'origine Lébou . . . se déclaraient cependant Wolof, preuve de la crise de l'ancien particularisme Lébou." (*Op. cit.*, p. 17.)

[10] For example, G. Lasserre writes: "L'habitude est prise a Libreville de recenser ensemble Togolais et Dahoméens sous l'appellation de 'Popo'." (*Libreville*, Paris, Armand Colin, 1958, p. 207.)

Epstein notes a similar phenomenon in the Northern Rhodesian Copperbelt towns, where one of the major ethnic groups, sanctioned by custom and by census, is the Nyasalanders. Nyasaland is a British-created territorial unit, but people from the Henga, Tonga, Tumbuka, and other tribes are by common consent grouped together as Nyasalanders. (A.L. Epstein, *Politics in an Urban African Community*, Manchester, Manchester University Press, 1958, p. 236.)

[11] By government we mean here the mechanism whereby the norms and goals of the group are defined. There may or may not be an effective, formal structure to enforce these norms.

[12] F. Amon d'Aby, *La Cote d'Ivoire dans la cité africiane*, Paris, Larose, 1952, p. 36.

[13] Similar phenomena were reported in other areas undergoing rapid social change. Lewis reports the growth in Somalia of a "tribalism founded on territorial ties [in] place of clanship," at least among the southern groups (I. M. Lewis, "Modern Political Movements in Somaliland, I", in *Africa*, XXVIII, July 1958, p. 259). In the South Pacific, Mead observes: "Commentators on native life shook their heads, remarking that these natives were quite

the significance of tribalism in West African affairs is the role which traditional Yoruba-Ibo rivalry has played in Nigeria politics. Yet, Dr. S. O. Biobaku has pointed out that the very use of the term "Yoruba" to refer to various peoples in Western Nigeria resulted largely from the influence of the Anglican mission in Abeokuta in the 19th century. The standard "Yoruba" language evolved by the mission was the new unifying factor. Hodgkin remarks:

> "Everyone recognizes that the notion of 'being a Nigerian' is a new kind of conception. But it would seem that the notion of 'being a Yoruba' is not very much older."[14]

Sometimes, the definition of the ethnic group may even be said to derive from a common occupation—indeed, even dress—rather than from a common language or traditional polity. For example, an Accra man often tends to designate all men (or at least all merchants) coming from savannah areas as "Hausamen," although many are not Hausa, as defined in traditional Hausa areas.[15] Similarly, the Abidjan resident may designate these same men as Dioula.[16] Such designations may originate in error, but many individuals from savannah areas take advantage of this confusion to merge themselves into this grouping. They go, for example to live in the *Sabon Zongo* (the Hausa residential area), and even often adopt Is-

lam, to aid the assimilation.[17] They do so because, scorned by the dominant ethnic group of the town, they find security within a relatively stronger group (Hausa in Accra, Dioula in Abidjan, Bambara in Thiès), with whom they feel some broad cultural affinity. Indeed, assimilation to this stronger group may represent considerable advance in the prestige-scale for the individual.[18]

Thus we see that ethnic groups are defined in terms that are not necessarily traditional but are rather a function of the urban social situation. By ethnicity, we mean the feeling of loyalty to this new ethnic group of the towns. Epstein has urged us to distinguish between two senses of what he calls "tribalism": the intratribal, which is the "persistence of, or continued attachment to, tribal custom," and tribalism within the social structure, which is the "persistence of loyalties and values, which stem from a particular form of social organization."[19] This corresponds to the distinction we made above between loyalty to tribal government and loyalty to the tribal community. In using the term ethnicity, we are referring to this latter kind of loyalty. This distinction cannot be rigid. Individuals in West Africa move back and forth between city and rural area. Different

---

incapable of ever organizing beyond the narrowest tribal borders, overlooking the fact that terms like 'Solomons,' 'Sepiks' or 'Manus,' when applied in Rabaul, blanketed many tribal differences." (M. Mead, *New Lives for Old*, New York, Morrow, 1956, p. 79.)

The article by Max Gluckman, which appeared since this paper was delivered, makes the same point for British Central Africa. *Cf.* "Tribalism in British Central Africa", in *Cahiers d'Etudes Africaines*, I, janv. 1960, pp. 55–70.

[14] T. Hodgkin, "Letter to Dr. Biobaku," in *Odu*, No. 4, 1957, p 42.

[15] Rouch, *op. cit.*, p. 59.

[16] A. Kobben, "Le planteur noir," in *Etudes éburnéennes*, V, 1956, p. 154.

[17] The religious conversion is often very temporary. N'Goma observes: "L'Islam résiste mal à la transplantation des familles musulmanes de la ville à la campagne. On a remarqué que le citadin qui retourne à son groupement d'origine revient souvent au culte de la terre et des Esprits ancestraux." (A. N'Goma, "L'Islam noir," in T. Monod, ed., *Le Monde noir*, Présence africaine, No. 8–9, p. 342.) The motive for the original conversion may in part explain this rapid reconversion.

[18] G. Savonnet observes in Thiès, Sénégal: "Le nom de Bambara est employé généralement pour désigner le Soudanais (qu'il soit Khassonké, Sarakollé, ou meme Mossi). Ils acceptent d'autant plus volontiers cette dénomination que la Bambara (comme tout a l'heure le Wolof) fait figure de race évoluée par rapport à leur propre." ("La Ville de Thiès," in *Etudes sénégalaises*, No. 6, 1955, p. 149.)

[19] Epstein, *op. cit.*, p. 231.

loyalties may be activated in different contexts. But more and more, with increasing urbanization, loyalty to the ethnic community is coming to supersede loyalty to the tribal community and government. It is the relationship of this new ethnic loyalty to the emergent nation-state that we intend to explore here.

There are four principal ways in which ethnicity serves to aid national integration. First, ethnic groups tend to assume some of the functions of the extended family and hence they diminish the importance of kinship roles; two, ethnic groups serve as a mechanism of resocialization; three, ethnic groups help keep the class structure fluid, and so prevent the emergence of castes; fourth, ethnic groups serve as an outlet for political tensions.

First, in a modern nation-state, loyalties to ethnic groups interfere less with national integration than loyalties to the extended family. It is obvious that particularistic loyalties run counter to the most efficient allocation of occupational and political roles in a state. Such particularistic loyalties cannot be entirely eliminated. Medium-sized groups based on such loyalties perform certain functions—of furnishing social and psychological security—which cannot yet in West Africa be performed either by the government or by the nuclear family. In the towns, the ethnic group is to some extent replacing the extended family in performing these functions.

The role of the ethnic group in providing food and shelter to the unemployed, marriage and burial expenses, assistance in locating a job has been widely noted.[20] West African governments are not yet in a position to offer a really effective network of such services, because of lack of resources and personnel. Yet if these services would not be provided, widespread social unrest could be expected.

It is perhaps even more important that ethnic associations counter the isolation and anomy that uprooted rural immigrants feel in the city. Thus Balandier has noted in Brazzaville the early emergence of ethnic associations tends to indicate a high degree of uprootedness among the ethnic group, which tends to be found particularly in small minorities.[21]

But from the point of view of national integration is the ethnic group really more functional than the extended family? In the sense that the ethnic group, by extending the extended family, dilutes it, the answer is yes. The ties are particularistic and diffuse, but less so and less strong than in the case of kinship groups. Furthermore, such a development provides a precedent for the principle of association on a non-kinship basis. It can be seen perhaps as a self-liquidating phase on the road to the emergence of the nuclear family.[22] Thus, it can be said with Parsons, that ethnic groups "constitute a focus of security beyond the family unit which is in some respects less dysfunctional for the society than community solidarity would be."[23]

The second function suggested was that of resocialization. The problem of instruct-

---

[20] Mercier notes: "Nombreux sont ceux qui, dans l'actuelle crise de chomage, ne peuvent se maintenir en ville que grace à l'aide de leurs parents. Cela aboutit à une forme spontanée d'assurance contre le chomage." (*Op. cit.*, p. 26.)

See also *passim*, K. A. Busia, *Report on a Social Survey of Sekondi-Takoradi*, Accra, Government Printer, 1950; I. Acquah, *Accra Survey*, London, University of London Press,

1958; O. Dollfus, "Conakry en 1951–1952. Etude humaine et économique," in *Etudes guinéennes*, X–XI, 1952, pp. 3–111; J. Lombard, "Cotonou, ville africaine," in *Etudes dahoméennes*, X, 1953.

[21] G. Balandier, *Sociologie des Brazzavilles noires*, Paris, Armand Colin, 1955, p. 122.

[22] Forde suggests that "This multiplicity of association, which is characteristic of the Westernisation procedure, is likely to preclude the functional persistence of tribal organisations as autonomous units in the economic or political sphere." (*Op. cit.*, p. 485.)

[23] T. Parsons, *The Social System*, Glencoe, Free Press, 1951, p. 188.

ing large numbers of persons in new normative patterns is a key one for nations undergoing rapid social change. There are few institutions which can perform this task. The formal educational system is limited in that it is a long-range process with small impact on the contemporary adult population. In addition, universal free education, though the objective of all West African governments at the present time, is not yet a reality in any of these countries. The occupational system only touches a small proportion of the population, and a certain amount of resocialization is a prerequisite to entry into it. The government is limited in services as well as in access to the individuals involved (short of totalitarian measures). The family is in many ways a bulwark of resistance to change.

The ethnic groups, touching almost all the urban population, can then be said to be a major means of resocialization. They aid this process in three ways. The ethnic group offers the individual a wide network of persons, often of very varying skills and positions, who are under some obligation to retrain him and guide him in the ways of urban life.

By means of ethnic contacts, the individual is recruited into many non-ethnic nationslist groupings. Apter found evidence of this in Ghana, where he observed a remarkable number of classificatory brothers and other relatives working together in the same party, kinship thus providing a "reliable organizational core in the nationalist movement."[24] Birmingham and Jahoda similarly suggest the hypothesis that kinship (read, ethnic) links mediated Ghana political affiliation.[25]

And lastly, members of the ethnic group seek to raise the status of the whole group,

which in turn makes it more possible for the individual members to have the mobility and social contact which will speed the process of resocialization.[26]

The third function is the maintenance of a fluid class system. There is in West Africa, as there has been historically in the United States, some correlation between ethnic groups and social class, particularly at the lower rungs of the social ladder. Certain occupations are often reserved for certain ethnic groups.[27] This occurs very obviously because of the use of ethnic ties to obtain jobs and learn skills.

It would seem then that ethnicity contributes to rigid stratification. But this view neglects the normative context. One of the major values of contemporary West African nations is that of equality. Individuals may feel helpless to try to achieve this goal by their own efforts. Groups are less reticent, and as we mentioned before, its members usually seek to raise the status of the group. The continued expansion of the exchange economy means continued possibility of social mobility. As long as social mobility continues, this combination of belief in equality and the existence of ethnic groups striving to achieve it for themselves works to minimize any tendency towards caste-formation. This is crucial to obtain the allocation of roles within the occupational system on the basis of achievement, which is necessary for a modern economy. Thus, this is a self-reinforcing system wherein occupational mobility contributes to economic expansion, which contributes to urban migration, which contributes to the formation of ethnic associations and then

[24] D. Apter, *The Gold Coast in Transition*, Princeton, Princeton University Press, 1955, p. 127

[25] W. B. Birmingham and G. Jahoda, "A Pre-Election Survey in a Semi-Literate Society," in *Public Opinion Quarterly*, XIX, Summer, 1955, p. 152.

[26] Glick explains the role of Chinese ethnic groups in Chinese assimilation into Hawaiian society in just these terms. (C. Glick, "The Relationship between Position and Status in the Assimilation of Chinese in Hawaii," in *American Journal of Sociology*, XLVII, September, 1952, pp. 667–679.)

[27] P. Mercier, "Aspects des problemes de stratification sociale dans l'Ouest Africain," in *Cahiers internationaux de sociologie*, XVII, 1954, pp. 47–55; Lombard, *op. cit,*, pp, 57–59.

to group upward mobility, which makes possible individual occupational mobility.

The fourth function we suggested was the ethnic groups serve as an outlet for political tensions. The process of creating a nation and legitimating new institutions gives rise to many tensions, especially when leaders cannot fulfill promises made. Gluckman's phrase, the "frailty in authority"[28] is particularly applicable for new nations not yet secure in the loyalty of their citizens. We observed before that ethnic groups offered social security because the government could not. Perhaps we might add that this arrangement would be desirable during a transitional period, even were it not necessary. If the state is involved in too large a proportion of the social action of the individual, it will be burdened by concentrated pressure and demands which it may not be able to meet. It may not yet have the underlying diffuse confidence of the population it would need to survive the non-fulfilment of these demands.[29] It may therefore be of some benefit to divert expectations from the state to other social groups.

The existence of ethnic groups performing "an important scapegoat function as targets for displaced aggression"[30] may permit individuals to challenge persons rather than the authority of the office these persons occupy. Complaints about the nationalist party in power are transformed into complaints about the ethnic group or groups presumably in power. This is a common phenomenon of West African politics, and as Gluckman suggests:

"These rebellions, so far from destroying the established social order [read, new national governments] work so that they even support this order. They re-

solve the conflicts which the frailty in authority creates."[31]

Thus, in rejecting the men, they implicitly accept the system. Ethnic rivalries become rivalries for political power in a non-tribal setting.

The dysfunctional aspects of ethnicity for national integration are obvious. They are basically two. The first is that ethnic groups are still particularistic in their orientation and diffuse in their obligations, even if they are less so than the extended family. The ethnic roles are insufficiently segregated from the occupational and political roles because of the extensiveness of the ethnic group. Hence we have the resulting familiar problems of nepotism and corruption.

The second problem, and one which worries African political leaders more, is separatism, which in various guises is a pervasive tendency in West Africa today.[32] Separatist moves may arise out of a dispute between élite elements over the direction of change. Or they may result from the scarcity of resources which causes the "richer" region to wish to contract out of the nation (e.g., Ashanti in Ghana, the Western Region in Nigeria, the Ivory Coast in the ex-federation of French West Africa). In either case, but especially the latter, appeals to ethnic sentiment can be made the primary weapon of the separatists.

In assessing the seriousness of ethnicity as dysfunctional, we must remember that ethnic roles are not the only ones West Africans play. They are increasingly bound up in other institutional networks which cut across ethnic lines. Furthermore, the situation may vary according to the number and size of ethnic groupings. A multiplicity of small groups is less worrisome, as Coleman reminds us, than those situations

---

[28] M. Gluckman, *Custom and Conflict in Africa*, Oxford, Basil Blackwell, 1955, ch 2.

[29] Unless, of course, it compensates for lack of legitimation by increase of force as a mechanism of social control, which is the method used in Communist countries.

[30] Parsons, *op. cit.*, p. 188.

[31] Gluckman, *op. cit.*, p. 28.

[32] Separatism, of course, arises as a problem only after a concept of a nation is created and at least partially internalized by a large number of the citizens.

where there is one large, culturally strong group.[33]

The most important mechanism to reduce the conflict between ethnicity and national integration is the nationalist party. Almost all of the West African countries have seen the emergence of a single party which has led the nationalist struggle, is now in power, and dominates the local political scene.[34]

In the struggle against colonial rule, these parties forged a unity of Africans as Africans. To the extent that the party structure is well articulated (as, say, in Guinea) and is effective, both in terms of large-scale program and patronage, the party does much to contain separatist tendencies.

Linguistic integration can also contribute, and here European languages are important. It is significant that one of the Ghana government's first steps after inde-

pendence was to reduce the number of years in which primary schooling would be in the vernacular. Instruction in English now begins in the second year. We might mention, too, that Islam and Christianity both play a role in reducing centrifugal tendencies.

Lastly, there is the current attempt to endow pan-Africanism with the emotional aura of anti-colonialism, the attempt to make Unity as much a slogan as Independence. Even if the objective of unity is not realized, it serves as a counterweight to ethnic separatism that may be very effective.

Thus we see that ethnicity plays a complex role in the contemporary West African scene. It illustrates the more general function of intermediate groups intercalated between the individual and the state, long ago discussed by Durkheim.[35] It points at the same time to the difficulties of maintaining both consensus and unity if these intermediate groups exist.[36]

[33] J. S. Coleman, "The Character and Viability of African Political Systems," in W. Goldschmidt, ed., *The United States and Africa*, New York, The American Assembly, 1958, pp. 44–46.

[34] There is normally room for only one truly nationalist party in a new nation. Other parties in West African countries, when they exist, tend to be formed on more particularistic (ethnic, religious, regional) bases.

[35] E. Durkheim, *The Division of Labor in Society*, Glencoe, Free Press, 1947, p. 28.

[36] See the discussion of this problem in S. M. Lipset, "Political Sociology," in R. K. Merton, L. Broom, L. S. Cottrell, Jr., eds., *Sociology Today*, New York, Basic Books, 1959.

Index